£75·00

D0321904

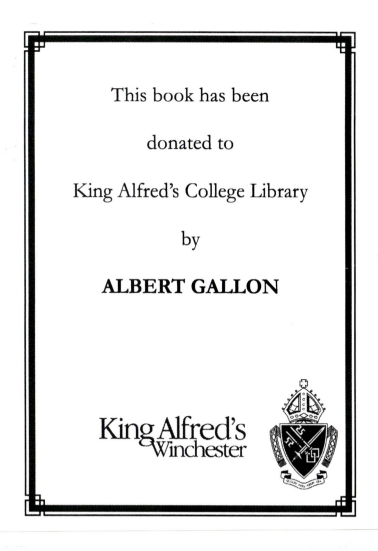

This book has been

donated to

King Alfred's College Library

by

ALBERT GALLON

King Alfred's
Winchester

The Christian's ABC

Catechisms and Catechizing in England c.1530–1740

IAN GREEN

'The Christian's hornbook or ABC. In forty questions and answers, containing principles necessary to be known for holy hearing, blessed believing, powerful praying, right receiving, well doing and dying, and life everlasting'.

(Title of John Boyes's catechism, used at Halifax in the early seventeenth century: BL Addit. MS 4928, fo. 2ᵛ.)

CLARENDON PRESS · OXFORD

1996

Oxford University Press, Walton Street, Oxford OX2 6DP

Oxford New York

Athens Auckland Bangkok Bombay
Calcutta Cape Town Dar es Salaam Delhi
Florence Hong Kong Istanbul Karachi
Kuala Lumpur Madras Madrid Melbourne
Mexico City Nairobi Paris Singapore
Taipei Tokyo Toronto
and associated companies in
Berlin Ibadan

Oxford is a trade mark of Oxford University Press

Published in the United States
by Oxford University Press Inc., New York

British Library Cataloguing in Publication Data
Data available

Library of Congress Cataloging in Publication Data
Data applied for
ISBN 0–19–820617–8

1 3 5 7 9 10 8 6 4 2

Typeset by Jayvee, Trivandrum, India
Printed in Great Britain
on acid-free paper by
Biddles Ltd., Guildford & King's Lynn

Q. *To whom is this book dedicated, with love and gratitude?*

A. *Judith. (Prov. 18: 22)*

PREFACE

WHILE collecting material on the careers of the parish clergy of the Stuart church, I became curious about what they were teaching their flocks. The large number of catechisms they published seemed to offer a potentially valuable vein of ore to mine, and from catechisms I moved on to other instructional works which, though not necessarily the work of the lower clergy, were, like catechisms, printed in large quantities and scattered widely among the clergy and laity of early modern England: collections of sermons, aids to Bible study, psalters, devotional works, religious verse, and a variety of other works containing explicit or implicit religious instruction. Then there were the new forms of music provided by metrical psalms and change–ringing, and the new visual aids inside and outside the parish churches, such as Commandment boards and scripture texts on the church walls, symbols and inscriptions on the gravestones in the churchyard, and engravings and woodcuts in books, pamphlets, and broadsheets. Unfortunately, by this stage the materials amassed were threatening to topple over and smother any author—or publisher— unwise enough to come too close to them. Since there had proved to be many more catechisms than had been expected, and a study of them offered the unusual prospect of examining a whole genre both as medium and message, and over a longer period of time than is usually attempted, the decision was taken to publish a separate monograph on catechisms, which is in front of you, and then two further volumes. The first of these (provisionally entitled *Print and Protestantism in Early Modern England*) will focus on the production of Bibles, aids to Bible study, psalters, prayer books, and other works widely disseminated through the medium of print, while the second (*Religious Instruction in Early Modern England*) will try to cover the complete gamut of commonly used methods of religious instruction, with references back to the previous volumes where necessary. Readers of this study should bear in mind, therefore, that the aims and impact of catechizing have to be seen in the broader context of a whole range of techniques of imparting religious ideas.

This study would not have been possible without the enormous efforts and great skills shown by the compilers of the two Short-Title Catalogues referred to below as STC[2] and Wing[2], and to the as yet incomplete Eighteenth-Century STC. The first of these in particular has set standards which it will be hard for others to match, and I am very grateful for additional help from Ms Katherine Pantzer in tracking down catechisms. I am also grateful to Michael Smallman of Queen's University Library for helping me conduct several computer searches in the files of the embryonic Eighteenth-Century Short-Title Catalogue; and to all the librarians in that Library for their help and co-operation with more conventional forms of enquiry and publication over the years. I have also accumulated debts to a number of scholars and librarians, among whom I must name Marvin Anderson, Margaret Aston, Melanie Barber, John Bidwell, Patrick Collinson, Claire Cross, Barbara Donagan, Ken Fincham, Jane Freeman, Paul Griffiths, Susan Hardman-Moore, Arnold Hunt, Andrew Johnston, Bernard Keane, Neil Keeble, Tony Lane, Judith Maltby, Anthony Milton, Denise Monbarren, Geoffrey Nuttall, Charles Parry, Margaret Spufford, Irene Turner, Nicholas Tyacke, and Helen Weinstein. I have also benefited greatly from exchanging ideas with Dennis Danielson who is currently engaged in a study of catechisms which begins from a very different angle from this one. I am also much indebted to the Huntington Library in California for awarding me a Fellowship in 1985 during which I was able to read a number of new catechisms, and to the British Academy for financial help in visiting a number of American repositories in the same year, and for the award of a Research Readership in the Humanities. Until recently my own university has also been in a position to offer generous help with the costs of visiting mainland libraries, microfilming, xeroxing, and interlibrary loans, for which I am very grateful; without it this book would have taken even longer to finish. My debt to the support and patience of my wife is indicated in the dedication.

Part of the material used in Chapter 2 first appeared in an article entitled ' "For Children in Yeeres and Children in Understanding": The Emergence of the English Catechism under Elizabeth and the Early Stuarts', which was published in vol. 37 of the *Journal of Ecclesiastical History*, printed by Cambridge University Press.

The rationale and main sources for this study are described in the introduction which follows, but a couple of technical points may be raised here. Spelling in quotations has been modernized. Not every one today will immediately recognize the meaning of 'geue', 'iust', 'couet', 'slaundring', and 'sobrenes' which occur in two consecutive answers of the original 1549 catechism (congratulations to those who immediately identified the words 'give', 'just', 'covet', 'slandering', and 'soberness'). Punctuation in quotations has also been modernized, and the use of upper-case and lower-case has been standardized to modern norms: no case of interpretation rests upon the original spelling, punctuation, or use of capitals, and in the case of printed texts such usages regularly varied from one early modern edition to another. The only exception to these general rules is in the titles of published works, where the original spelling has been retained, and the punctuation and capitalization used in the Short-Title Catalogues followed. In Part I, works not in the list of abbreviations have, after an initial citation in full in each chapter, been referred to by a shortened title; where such a reference in a later footnote is not likely to be sufficient to distinguish between similar sounding works by the same author or anonymous authors, additional information has been provided. In Part II, however, all citations to the catechisms in the sample which forms the basis of the survey of teaching in Chapters 7 to 12 are to the works listed in Appendix 2. Unless stated otherwise, the place of publication is London. Where a modern edition of a contemporary work has been cited, the text has been compared with an original. All quotations from the Bible are from the Authorized Version of 1611 unless otherwise stated.

As I approach the end of this particular study, I am increasingly conscious of its shortcomings. Had there been world enough and time, more could have been attempted in the assessment of technique and the group dynamics of catechizing, the interaction between orality and literacy and between catechizing and popular religious cultures, and the relationship between catechizing and other methods of instruction, and between Protestant and Catholic catechetics. I am also aware that more catechisms are likely to be known or found than appear in Appendix 1, and that a number of my tentative attributions or comments about individual works or editions will soon need revising. All that I can say is that my first priority was to try to see catechisms as contemporary Protestants did, as vehicles of instruction in Christian doctrine, and that the advantages of following one particular genre right through the early modern period seemed to me to outweigh the disadvantages of having to make hasty conclusions on particular works or periods. In short, at this stage it seemed wiser not to attempt the last word on what will be seen to have been a complex phenomenon, but simply to draw to other scholars' attention the richness and the potential significance of the materials available.

I.M.G.

Belfast
May 1995

CONTENTS

Abbreviations   xii

Introduction   1

Part I. The Medium   11

1. 'What is catechizing?'   13
2. The Emergence of the English Catechetical Tradition   45
3. Catechizing in Theory and Practice: In Church   93
4. Catechizing in Theory and Practice: In School and at Home   170
5. Changes in Catechetical Technique   230

Part II. The Message   277

6. Catechetical Structures   279
7. The Apostles' Creed   300
8. Predestination   350
9. Assurance, Justification, and the Covenant of Grace   387
10. The Ten Commandments   422
11. The Lord's Prayer   479
12. Sacraments   508

Conclusion   557

Part III. A Finding List of English Catechisms   571

Appendix 1. Catechisms and Catechetical Material Produced, Used, or
            Recommended for Use in England *c*.1530–1740   573
Appendix 2. The Sample of Catechisms Used in Chapters 7–12   752

Index   759

ABBREVIATIONS

Unless stated otherwise, all the books listed here were published in London.

Andrewes, *Works*	*The Works of Lancelot Andrewes*, ed. J. P. Wilson and J. Bliss (11 vols.; Oxford, 1841–54)
Aston, *England's Iconoclasts*	M. Aston, *England's Iconoclasts*, i. *Laws against Images* (Oxford, 1988)
BL	British Library
Brachlow, *Communion of Saints*	S. Brachlow, *The Communion of Saints: Radical Puritan and Separatist Ecclesiology 1570–1625* (Oxford, 1988)
Brightman, *English Rite*	F. E. Brightman, *The English Rite* (2 vols.; 1921)
Calvin, *Institutes*	John Calvin, *The Institutes of the Christian Religion*, ed. J. T. McNeill (2 vols.; Philadelphia, 1970)
Cardwell, *Documentary Annals*	E. Cardwell, *Documentary Annals of the Reformed Church of England ... from ... 1546 to ... 1716* (2 vols.; Oxford, 1844)
Cardwell, *Synodalia*	E. Cardwell, *Synodalia: A Collection of Articles of Religion, Canons and Proceedings of Convocations* (2 vols.; Oxford, 1852)
Carruthers, *Three Centuries*	S. W. Carruthers, *Three Centuries of the Westminster Shorter Catechism* (Fredericton, New Brunswick, 1957)
Clarke, *Lives of sundry eminent persons*	S. Clarke, *The lives of sundry eminent persons in this later age* (1683)
Clarke, *Lives of ten eminent divines*	S. Clarke, *A collection of the lives of ten eminent divines* (1662)
Clarke, *Lives of two and twenty divines*	S. Clarke, *The lives of two and twenty English divines*, published as part 2 of *A generall martyrologie* (1660)
Clifford, *Atonement and Justification*	A. C. Clifford, *Atonement and Justification: English Evangelical Theology 1640–1790—An Evaluation* (Oxford, 1990)
DNB	*The Dictionary of National Biography*, ed. L. Stephens and S. Lee (63 vols.; 1885–1900)
ESTC	Eighteenth-Century Short-Title Catalogue—database in progress
Fincham, *Prelate as Pastor*	K. Fincham, *Prelate as Pastor: The Episcopate of James I* (Oxford, 1990)
Frere, *Visitation Articles*, i–iii	W. H. Frere and W. M. Kennedy, *Visitation Articles and Injunctions of the Period of the Reformation 1536–1558* (Alcuin Club Collections, xiv–xvi; 1910)
Gibson 13–15	Bishop Gibson's queries to the clergy of the archdeaconry of Lincoln in 1721, and their replies: Lincolnshire Record Office, Gibson 13–15

Grant, 'Cure of Souls'	L. T. Grant, 'The Practice of the Cure of Souls in Seventeenth-Century English Puritanism', Ph.D. thesis (Edinburgh, 1961)
Green, 'Emergence of the English Catechism'	I. M. Green, ' "For Children in Yeeres and Children in Understanding": The Emergence of the English Catechism under Elizabeth and the Early Stuarts', *JEH* 37 (1986), 397–425
Herring, *York*, i–v	*Archbishop Herring's Visitation Returns, 1743*, ed. S. L. Ollard and P. C. Walker (Yorkshire Archaeological Society Record Series, lxxi–lxxii, lxxv, lxxvii, lxxix; 1928–31)
Jaggard, *Catalogue*	W. Jaggard, *A catalogue of such English books* (1618)
Janz, *Three Reformation Catechisms*	D. Janz (ed.), *Three Reformation Catechisms: Catholic, Anabaptist, Lutheran* (Lewiston, NY, 1982)
JEH	*Journal of Ecclesiastical History*
Kendall, *English Calvinism*	R. T. Kendall, *Calvin and English Calvinism to 1649* (Oxford, 1979)
Kennedy, *Episcopal Administration*, i–iii	W. M. Kennedy, *Elizabethan Episcopal Administration* (Alcuin Club Collections, xxvi–xxvii; 1924)
Lake, *Anglicans and Puritans?*	P. Lake, *Anglicans and Puritans? Presbyterianism and English Conformist Thought from Whitgift to Hooker* (1988)
Lake, *Moderate Puritans*	P. Lake, *Moderate Puritans and the Elizabethan Church* (Cambridge, 1982)
London, *Catalogue*	W. London, *A catalogue of the most vendible books* (1658)
McGrath, *Iustitia Dei*	A. E. McGrath, *Iustitia Dei: A History of the Christian Doctrine of Justification* (2 vols.; Cambridge, 1986)
Maunsell, *Catalogue*	A. Maunsell, *The first part of the catalogue of English printed bookes* (1595)
Milton, *Catholic and Reformed*	A. Milton, *Catholic and Reformed: The Roman and Protestant Churches in English Protestant Thought, 1600–1640* (Cambridge, 1995)
Mitchell, *Catechisms of the Second Reformation*	A. F. Mitchell, *Catechisms of the Second Reformation* (1886)
Schaff, *Creeds*	P. A. Schaff, *The Creeds of the Evangelical Protestant Churches* (1877)
Secker, *Oxford*	H. A. Lloyd Jukes (ed.), 'Articles of Enquiry Addressed to the Clergy of the Diocese of Oxford at the Primary Visitation of Dr Thomas Secker, 1738', *Oxfordshire Record Society*, 39 (1957)
Second Report on Ritual	*Second Report of the Royal Commission on Ritual*, Appendix E (published in Parliamentary Papers 1867–8, xxviii)
STC²	*A Short-Title Catalogue of Books Printed in England, Scotland and Ireland and of English Books Printed Abroad 1475–1620*, first compiled by A. W. Pollard and G. R. Redgrave; second edn. revised and enlarged, begun by

	W. A. Jackson and F. S. Ferguson, completed by K. F. Pantzer (2 vols., 1976–86)
Strauss, *Luther's House of Learning*	G. Strauss, *Luther's House of Learning: Indoctrination of the Young in the German Reformation* (Baltimore/London, 1978)
TC	E. Arber (ed.), *The Term Catalogues 1668–1709 A.D.* (3 vols.; 1903–1906)
Torrance, *School of Faith*	T. F. Torrance, *The School of Faith: The Catechists of the Reformed Church* (1959)
TSR	E. Arber (ed.), *A Transcript of the Registers of the Company of Stationers of London 1554–1640 A.D.* (5 vols.; 1875–94)
Tudor, 'Religious Instruction'	P. Tudor, 'Religious Instruction for Children and Adolescents in the Early English Reformation', *JEH* 35 (1984), 391–413
Tyacke, *Anti-Calvinists*	N. Tyacke, *Anti-Calvinists: The Rise of English Arminianism c.1590–1640* (Oxford, 1987)
von Rohr, *Covenant of Grace*	J. von Rohr, *The Covenant of Grace in Puritan Thought* (Atlanta, 1986)
Weir, *Federal Theology*	D. A. Weir, *The Origins of the Federal Theology in Sixteenth-Century Reformation Thought* (Oxford, 1990)
White, *Predestination*	P. White, *Predestination, Policy and Polemic: Conflict and Consensus in the English Church from the Reformation to the Civil War* (Cambridge, 1992)
Wing[2]	*Short-Title Catalogue of Books Printed in England, Scotland, Ireland, Wales and British North America and of English Books Printed in Other Countries 1641–1700*, compiled by D. Wing, second edn. revised and enlarged by the Index Committee of the Modern Language Association of America (3 vols.; New York, i (1972; newly revised and enlarged 1994); ii (1982); iii (1988))

Introduction

In 1578 Lancelot Andrewes initiated a series of catechetical lectures at Pembroke College, Cambridge. On Saturday and Sunday afternoons at three o'clock he lectured the undergraduates on a staple item of catechetics, and so popular did these lectures prove that they were said to have attracted students from other colleges and lay people from the surrounding area. It was also later claimed that notes of his lectures on one of those staples, the Ten Commandments, had 'ever since passed from hand to hand in manuscripts, and been accounted one of the greatest treasures of private libraries'. Certainly when these notes were published, in three slightly different versions, they quickly passed through several editions in the 1630s, 1640s, and 1650s.[1] Andrewes's purpose was not merely to impart to the undergraduates in his care his own understanding of the full implications of the Decalogue, but also to prepare them for the day when they too would be catechizing the young; and among his preliminary observations on the necessity and best methods of instructing children was the claim that 'By our catechizing the papists have lost ground of us, and can never recover it again unless by a more exact course of catechizing than ours'.[2]

This bold claim was probably an echo of the admission in the preface of the catechism of the Council of Trent that the Protestants had done great 'mischief' to the church 'especially by those writings called catechisms',[3] and it was in turn echoed by the 'godly' Richard Greenham late in Elizabeth's reign, by Thomas Fuller in the early 1640s, and half a century later by a future archbishop of Canterbury, John Tillotson, when he said that 'catechizing and the history of the martyrs'—John Foxe's *Actes and monuments*—'have been the two great pillars of the Protestant religion'.[4] Many other contemporary testimonies to the benefits of catechizing could be cited, for example that of John Syme in his rural parish in Essex in 1617 who wrote that the question-and-answer form of instruction was 'without question' (probably no pun was intended) 'the most profitable way for the simpler sort of people' to learn the basics of the faith.[5] There were also, it is true, a number of contemporary

[1] H. Isaacson, 'An exact narration of the life and death of ... Lancelot Andrewes', in Andrewes, *Works*, vol. xi, p. vi; P. A. Welsby, *Lancelot Andrewes, 1555–1626* (1958), 22–3; see also Appendix 1, s.v. L. Andrewes.

[2] Andrewes, *Works*, vi. 10.

[3] The Tridentine preface is cited in A. J. Stephens, *The Book of Common Prayer* (3 vols.; 1849–54), 1475.

[4] R. Greenham, *Second part of the workes* (1600), 75; Fuller's claim, in *The holy and profane state* (1642), is cited in T. Wood (ed.), *Five Pastorals* (1961), 158–9; J. Tillotson, *Six sermons ... preached in the church of St Lawrence Jewry* (1694), 162; and cf. Samuel Bourn II, *Lectures to children and young people* (1738), p. vi, and C. Ellis, *The scripture catechist* (1738), p. vii.

[5] J. Syme, *The sweet milke of Christian doctrine* (1617), sig. A3ʳ; and cf. R. Cawdrey, *A short and*

allegations that catechizing was frequently neglected by the clergy and generally spurned by the laity. However, on closer inspection some of these contemporary allegations appear to be self-contradictory or exaggerated, and the evidence for moderately frequent, moderately conscientious catechizing in early modern England turns out to be rather better than we had been led to believe, suggesting that we should pay at least as much attention to the enthusiasts as to the cavillers.[6]

Perhaps because of the criticisms made at the time, the history of catechizing in early modern England has been neglected until recently. This is the more surprising in that the catechisms of mainland Europe have attracted much attention. Those produced in Germany and Switzerland in the late Middle Ages and sixteenth century were closely scrutinized in the late nineteenth and early twentieth centuries by German scholars approaching the material (sometimes perhaps rather obviously) from either a Protestant or Catholic standpoint.[7] Again, from the 1960s, these forms were put under the microscope, this time from scholars based in America as well as Germany and often asking rather different questions of the material.[8] The last few decades have also seen the publication of important studies of catechisms and catechizing in pre-revolutionary France and of the impact of catechizing in seventeenth- and eighteenth-century Scandinavia.[9] In the case of British catechisms, it is true, there were some pioneering studies in the late nineteenth and early twentieth centuries, mainly by those interested in presbyterianism or in the type of education provided by English grammar schools.[10] But then with some honourable exceptions

---

fruitefull treatise (1604), sigs. A1ᵛ, A5ᵛ; W. Crashaw, *Milke for babes* (1618), sigs. A2ᵛ–3ʳ; also see below, p. 21 nn. 32–3.

[6] See below, Ch. 3.

[7] J. Geffcken, *Der Bildercatechismus des Fünfzehnten Jahrhunderts und die Catechetischen Haupstücke in dieser Zeit bis auf Luther* (Leipzig, 1855); C. A. G. von Zezschwitz, *System der Christlich Kirchlichen Katechetik* (2 vols.; Leipzig, 1863–74); C. Moufang (ed.), *Katholische Katechismen des 16 Jahrhunderts in Deutscher Sprache* (Hildesheim, 1880); F. Cohrs, *Die Evangelischen Katechismusversuche vor Luthers Enchiridion* (Monumenta Germaniae Paedogogica, ed. K. Kehrbach, vols. 20–3 and 29; Berlin, 1900–7).

[8] E. Weidenhiller, *Untersuchungen zur Deutschsprachigen Katechetischen Literatur das Späten Mittelalters* (München, 1965); Ernst-Wilhelm Kohls, *Evangelische Bewegung und Kirchenordnung: Studien und Quellen zur Reformationsgeschichte der Reichstadt Gengenbach* (Karlsruhe, 1966), 4; id., *Evangelische Katechismen der Reformationszeit vor und neben Luthers Kleinem Katechismus* (Texte zur Kirchen- und Theologiegeschichte, no. 16; Gütersloh, 1971); Manfred Müller *et al.*, *Der Katechismus von dem Anfängen bis zur Gegenwart* (Munich/Zurich, 1987); S. Ozment, *The Reformation in the Cities* (New Haven/London, 1975), 23–32, 67–74, 152–64; id., *Protestants: The Birth of a Revolution* (1993), 104–17; Strauss, *Luther's House of Learning*, ch. 8; Janz, *Three Reformation Catechisms*.

[9] J.-C. Dhotel, *Les Origines du catéchisme moderne* (Paris, 1967); E. Germain, *Langages de la foi à travers l'histoire* (Paris, 1972); see also some of the contributions in *Transmettre la foi: XVIᵉ–XXᵉ siècles* (Actes du 109ᵉ Congrès National des Sociétés Savantes; Dijon, 1984), Section d'Histoire Moderne et Contemporaine, tome 1 (Paris 1984); H. Pleijel, *Katekesen som Svensk Folkbok* (Lund, 1942), and *Husandakt, Husaga, Husförhor* (Stockholm, 1965); E. Johansson, 'The History of Literacy in Sweden', in H. J. Graff (ed.), *Literacy and Social Development in the West: A Reader* (Cambridge, 1981), 151–82.

[10] A. F. Mitchell, *Catechisms of the Second Reformation* (1886); W. Carruthers, *The Shorter Catechism of the Westminster Assembly of Divines* (1897); F. Watson, *The English Grammar Schools to 1660* (Cambridge, 1908), esp. ch. 4.

(again from those working in the presbyterian tradition),[11] relatively little interest was shown by scholars until the 1970s. Since then there has been a steady growth of interest from a number of different directions: political scientists, students of literature, and bibliographers, as well as leading religious historians and theologians.[12] That yardstick of intellectual fashion—the doctoral thesis—also suggests a growing awareness among both supervisors and postgraduates of the value of studying the nature of early modern catechetics or the role of catechizing in the dissemination of Protestantism in England.[13] The subject is huge and the room for further enquiry on many fronts abundant but perhaps restricted by the absence of a finding list of English catechisms and a general introduction to their content and use. The following study is an attempt to supply these needs.

What did contemporaries think was the purpose or the chief benefit of catechizing? How far did English catechists borrow from Continental practice and how far develop their own ideas and techniques? In what ways and how often was the act of catechizing performed, and how much impact did it have? What message did the catechisms of the period convey, and how far did that message change? The questions may be straightforward, but the available evidence has a number of built-in biases for which the historian has to make some allowance. A certain amount of impartial information about intentions can be gleaned from brief official statements on the duty to catechize or be catechized—in Prayer Book rubrics, royal injunctions, canons, visitation articles, and episcopal circulars.[14] This can be supplemented by comments in a score of sermons, pamphlets, and treatises published between the 1570s and the

[11]   The work by Carruthers mentioned in the previous note was revised by S. W. Carruthers, as *Three Centuries of the Westminster Shorter Catechism* (Fredericton, New Brunswick, 1957); see also T. F. Torrance, *The School of Faith: The Catechisms of the Reformed Church* (1959); and L. T. Grant, 'The Practice of the Cure of Souls in Seventeenth-Century English Puritanism', Ph.D. thesis (Edinburgh, 1961), ch. 3 and appendices.

[12]   G. J. Schochet, *Patriarchalism in Political Thought* (Oxford, 1975), 75–80; S. Fish, *The Living Temple: George Herbert and Catechizing* (Berkeley, 1978); a new study of catechisms from a literary standpoint is being prepared by Dennis R. Danielson; B. Ritter Dailey, 'Youth and the New Jerusalem: The English Catechistical Tradition and Henry Jessey's *Catechisme for Babes*', *Harvard Library Bulletin*, xxx (1982), 25–54; P. Collinson, *The Religion of Protestants* (Oxford, 1982), 232–4, 264–6; C. Haigh, 'The Church of England, the Catholics and the People', in Haigh (ed.), *The Reign of Elizabeth I* (1984), 209–13; Aston, *England's Iconoclasts*, esp. 344–70; P. Demers, *Heaven upon Earth: The Form of Moral and Religious Children's Literature, to 1850* (Knoxville, Tenn., 1993), ch. 4; J. H. Westerhof III and O. C. Edwards, Jr. (eds.), *A Faithful Church: Issues in the History of Catechesis* (Wilton, Conn., 1981). See also the bibliographies in ibid., and in Durbin's thesis, cited in the next note.

[13]   P. F. Jensen, 'The Life of Faith in the Teaching of English Protestants', D.Phil. thesis (Oxford, 1979), ch. 5; R. M. E. Paterson, 'A Study in Catechisms of the Reformation and Post-Reformation Period', MA thesis (Durham, 1981); P. Hutchison, 'Religious Change: The Case of the English Catechism 1560–1640', Ph.D. thesis (Stanford, 1984); L. D. Durbin, 'Education by Catechism: The Development of the Sixteenth-Century English Catechism', Ph.D. thesis (Northwestern, 1987); C. H. Lettinga, 'Covenant Theology and the Transformation of Anglicanism', Ph.D. thesis (Johns Hopkins, 1987); D. B. Lowry, 'Alexander Nowell, his Catechism and the Elizabethan Settlement of Religion', Ph.D. thesis (Indiana, 1989).

[14]   These are discussed in Ch. 3 below.

1730s which were at least in part devoted to exhorting the clergy, teachers, and house-holders to catechize their charges, or to encouraging the young and ignorant to submit to the instruction of their elders and betters.[15] Furthermore, some idea of how often and in what ways catechizing was performed can be gained from a variety of other sources: answers to visitation enquiries and church court proceedings, the (usually flattering) references in biographies to catechists who took this task very seriously, the handbooks on how to catechize, and the sections on how to be a good catechist in the growing number of pastoral handbooks published in this period.[16] But as can be imagined a number of these materials tell us more about the ideal than the reality; while those which do indicate what took place tend to leave us with either a very general impression or a highly localized one.[17]

Fortunately, there is another major source of information: the several hundred different catechisms composed between the Reformation and the early eighteenth century. In many ways, these are invaluable: they were composed in all corners of the country at a variety of dates to meet a wide range of educational needs, and in the prefaces or epistles dedicatory many authors were candid about the problems and the benefits of catechizing which they had encountered at first hand. On the other hand, these works also complicate the issue considerably. An initial problem is posed by labels. In the early modern period the term 'catechism' was applied by authors to a bewildering variety of works: statements of principles in continuous prose as well as in (what to us today may be the more familiar) question-and-answer form; very short forms, abridged down to a few dozen words or designed to elicit single-word answers, right up to a thousand-page or multi-volume exposition of catechetical material clearly intended to be studied rather than memorized; works designed for use in church or school and works intended for domestic catechizing; forms for 3-year-old children, and for ignorant adults or even old people on their deathbed; works in Latin, Greek, Hebrew, Arabic, Dutch, French, and German as well as English; works with a political message or a point to make about church government as well as works which, more conventionally, were focused on the Apostles' Creed, the Ten Commandments, and the Lord's Prayer.[18] The term 'catechism' was also used

---

[15] See the works in Appendix I by J. Stockwood (1578); R. Cawdrey (1580, 1604); anon., *A catechisme, or short kind of instruction*, ed. T. Sparke and J. Seddon (1588); T. Watts (1589); R. Bernard (1613); C.P. (1616); I.F. (1617); E.B. (1617); anon., 'Of catechisinge' (in Emmanuel College Cambridge Library MS III. 1. 13[8]); I. Bourne (1622); E[dward] A[lport] (1623); T. Downing (1623); anon., *An exhortation to catechising* (1655); Z. Crofton (1656); anon., *The address of some ministers of Christ ... in the Isle of Wight* (1658); L. Addison (1674); O. Stockton (1672); T. Doolittle (1692); anon., *An earnest call to family-catechising* (1693); T. Bray, *A pastoral discourse to young persons* (1704); J. Gaynam (1709); S. Harris (1712); and E. Creffeild (1713); and n. 4 above; other examples will be found in succeeding paragraphs.

[16] e.g. in R. Bernard, *The faithfull shepheard* (1607); R. Baxter, *Gildas Salvianus. The reformed pastor* (1656); T. Lye, *A plain and familiar method of instructing the younger sort* (1662); G. Burnet, *A discourse of the pastoral care* (1692); and T. Doolittle, *A complete body of practical divinity* (1723), the note opposite the title-page signed by twenty fellow-clergy.

[17] See Chs. 3–4 below.   [18] See below Chs. 2–4 and Appendix 1, *passim*.

to describe a form of preparation, either for confirmation or holy communion, while in other cases, such as the Heidelberg Catechism and the Westminster Larger and Shorter Catechisms, the term was almost synonymous with a statement or confession of faith for both clergy and laity.[19]

The method of deploying these catechisms also meant that a single text might be called upon to fulfil different functions. A 'catechism' could be a manuscript or printed copy possessed by the catechist alone, from which catechumens were taught orally, rather like a copy of the Koran which is read out to and repeated collectively by the faithful. Alternatively, the same text could be reproduced in multiple copies which literate catechumens possessed and studied, sometimes privately by themselves and sometimes with a catechist; in this case the catechism was a working tool of instruction and examination much like any other schoolbook. It could also be something in between: when benefactors gave away copies of catechisms or catechetical expositions to large numbers of potential catechumens, regardless of whether they could or would read them, the catechism was more like an icon, a semi-sacred object which would secure some kind of reward to the giver for his concern for others' spiritual welfare, and might be treasured by the receiver rather like a family Bible—not used very often perhaps, but kept in a safe place in the parlour.

The existence of hundreds of different 'catechisms' and different methods of deployment also make it very evident that what we are examining was never a uniform national pattern of catechizing, imposed from above and remaining uniform thereafter, but a technique that spread and evolved over many decades, resulting in great local variation. There were officially prescribed catechisms which were very widely used, as we shall see in the next few chapters, but the authors of the many alternative forms clearly wished to have theirs available to supplement the existing ones in church, school, or home. By the late sixteenth or early seventeenth centuries, 'catechizing' was not a single operation but a whole range of overlapping and interlocking activities; and in a given parish it might well involve the use of more than one form, either simultaneously (for different groups of catechumens) or in sequence.

Some rather less obvious problems with our prime source stem from the fact that all but a handful of the hundreds of supplementary catechisms that survive have done so in a printed form.[20] There is an irony here in that, like the great majority of early modern sermons known to us today, if they had not been reproduced hundreds or thousands of times through the press they might not have survived at all: manuscripts can fall to pieces if used a great deal, or if neglected can moulder away.[21] But the fact that they were converted into print means they may have undergone a sea change. When the author of a catechism first put pen to paper, he may have been

[19] Torrance, *School of Faith*, 67, 183–4; and next two chapters below.

[20] For surviving handwritten copies of catechisms, see below, pp. 46–7.

[21] Unless copies were preserved in official archives, as in Germany: Strauss, *Luther's House of Learning*, 164.

driven primarily by a sense of pressing pastoral need or by spiritual or pedagogical zeal. Moreover, the reason sometimes given for printing a catechism was to save the drudgery of making enough hand-written copies for all those who wanted or needed them.[22] But there is the possibility, to put it no stronger, that in the case of those forms which were printed the desire to impress was as important as the sense of pastoral need, especially where the text is preceded by a dedication to a powerful layman or bishop or the leading members of a corporation. Scores of examples of such dedications, often fulsome in tone, could be given, but as examples the curious reader should look at the dedications or prefaces of the works listed below in Appendix 1 by Richard Saintbarb (to Sir Francis Walsingham), Gervase Babington (to the earl of Pembroke), Robert Cawdrey (to Lord and Lady Russell), Thomas Pearston and Edmund Reeve (to their respective bishops), Richard Webbe (to a local knight and to the bishop of Gloucester's chancellor), James Balmford and William Hinde (to the Carpenters' and Haberdashers' Companies of London, respectively), and Thomas Becon and William Crompton (to the mayor and aldermen of Sandwich and Barnstaple, respectively).[23] In such cases, and they can be found in both 'godly' and ultra-conformist circles, it is quite possible that either from the outset or by the time it had been sent to the publisher the text of the catechism was at least partly phrased in terms that the prospective dedicatee was expected to welcome or admire.

A collection of printed catechisms may contain another kind of bias in that the author of an unconventional or controversial work was unlikely to get it past the official censor. The anonymous publication of some catechetical works and the occasional printing abroad of a catechism written by an author who had run into trouble with the authorities in England remind us that there were considered to be limits as to who could publish what.[24] However, it would appear that the system of censorship was marked by either moderate tolerance or simple ineffectiveness. How else can we explain the appearance and sale of many episcopalian catechisms in the 1640s and 1650s, or the relative ease with which nonconformist works were published between 1662 and 1689?[25] That there were limits to such tolerance, even in the 1650s, is suggested by the fact that editions of what were widely regarded as outrageous works like

---

[22] For example, M[ordechai] A[ldem], *A short, plaine and profitable catechisme* (1592), sigs. A2ʳ⁻ᵛ; R. Horne, *Points of instruction for the ignorant* (1617), sig. A3ʳ; W. Crompton, *An explication of those principles* (1633), sig. ¶6ᵛ; J[ohn] S[talham], *A catechisme for children* (1644), sig. A2ʳ; S. Austin, *A practical catechisme* (1647), sig. A5ᵛ; and cf. *Historical Manuscripts Commission: Gawdy MSS.* (1885), 23.

[23] The Babington dedications are in the first two works listed in Appendix 1; the Cawdrey is in the 1604 edition. Many other examples of dedications, especially to patrons, are extant.

[24] The first edition of John Geree's catechism was published anonymously in 1629 when he was still under a cloud with the authorities, the second openly under his own name in 1647 after he had returned to his post: see Appendix 1. For works published abroad, see below, pp. 48–50.

[25] See Appendix 1, s.v. J. Taylor; anon., *A catechisme to be learned* (1653); W. Nicholson; and R. Sherlock; and after 1662, s.v. J. Alleine; T. Lye; R. Baxter; T. Doolittle; and T. Vincent; see also London, *Catalogue* for the offering for sale in the late 1650s of many episcopalian works, including a controversial one like that of Edmund Reeve.

the Racovian Catechism and John Biddle's *Twofold catechism* soon ran into difficulties; equally Catholic catechisms were not allowed to be published openly in early modern England, except in the reigns of Mary and James II.[26] But although there were limits, these do not appear to have inhibited the great majority of authors who were anxious to publish a catechism. It also seems clear that reprints of older works were not subjected to severe control by the authorities, to judge from the numerical preponderance in the anti-Calvinist 1630s of catechisms published by Calvinists like Alexander Nowell, William Perkins, and John Ball.[27]

A printed catechism raises other questions. If the text, and in particular the catechumen's share, was printed in black letter (the sort of 'gothic' type-face that one nowadays encounters only in some German publications and 'olde worlde' signboards), was this a conscious attempt by the author and the publisher or printer to reach the kind of inexperienced or slow reader most familiar with that type of typeface? If it was printed in roman and italic type, as were most of the academic and other works aimed at a more sophisticated reader from the 1580s and 1590s, was this also a deliberate decision, or due merely to changing fashions in publishing or even a shortage of black-letter fount?[28] The role of the publisher might have been felt in another way: his anxiety to sell as many copies as possible may have led to a work being described on the title-page as being suited to a much wider readership or as having a larger number of uses than the author had intended. One wonders, for example, if the subtitle of a work by John Boughton, *God and man*, published in 1623, was composed by this zealous, Calvinistic 'preacher of the Word', or by his publisher, Samuel Man, whose family had done very well indeed out of religious publications in the previous half century. The full subtitle is as follows:

A treatise catechistical, wherein the saving knowledge of God and man is plainly, and briefly declared, whereby such as are ignorant may be helped, to hear sermons with profit, to read the Bible or other books with judgement, to receive the Lord's Supper with comfort, to discern between truth and error with understanding, and to give an answer to their minister, or any other that shall ask them a reason of their faith, with readiness. Collected out of sacred scriptures, and the most orthodox and best approved divines ancient and modern, for the good of such as desire to be made wise to salvation and heirs of eternal life.[29]

Who could resist such an offer?

---

[26] See Appendix 1, s.v. *Catechesis ecclesiarum quae in regno Poloniae*, and Biddle; and s.v. E. Bonner; P. Canisius (1687); anon., *The catechism for the curats* (1687); anon., *Catechismus* (1687); J. Roucourt; and anon., *A summe of Christian doctrine* (1686).

[27] See below, pp. 78–9, and for the terms anti-Calvinist and 'Calvinist', Ch. 8.

[28] For the use of black-letter as opposed to roman typeface, see below, pp. 255–6.

[29] For further details, see Appendix 1; for another good example, see the title-page of T. Watts, *The entrie to Christianitie* (1589).

There is a further paradox about the printing of catechisms which Boughton's subtitle also serves to illustrate. In its most elementary form, catechizing was an essentially oral exercise, but to expedite the exercise, catechumens who were literate might be given copies to help them memorize the answers that their illiterate fellow-pupils could only grasp aurally. It was not a large step from this to composing other 'catechisms' which were less a simple aid to memorizing than a help to comprehend-ing what had already been learnt or a means of introducing fresh material to the more advanced students. This situation did not develop fully, at least not in catechizing in church where a mixture of orality and use of print was probably the norm for both instruction in the basics and examination of what had been learnt. But historians have to remind themselves that in using printed catechisms they are reliant on a medium—print—that in some ways was at odds with the skills needed in oral com-munication, even if in other ways it reinforced them.[30] The fixed nature of a printed text may also conceal from us the extent to which a catechist was prepared to be flex-ible, either by adding some off-the-cuff remarks to what appeared on the page to help catechumens understand a difficult point, or by encouraging them to answer in their own words, as in 1646 when Isaac Bourne stressed that the catechumen was 'not to answer verbatim or by rote ... but each according to his own sense and understand-ing of the question'.[31] How common was this?

One further problem with a reliance on surviving catechisms may be mentioned. A historian is on familiar ground when dealing with administrative sources such as visitation returns, or biographical sources with a predictable bias in favour of or against the person concerned. But if he or she has to rely on a close analysis of the lit-erary conventions, the different 'personae' and voices in a text, the structure, syntax, and vocabulary used in a text, as well as the doctrinal opinions of a large number of different authors, then he is entering territory which is more familiar to the student of language and literature or the theologian. The number of caveats entered in the last few paragraphs should not create the impression that we cannot get reasonably close to our subject. It is true that there are questions, especially about the frequency and effects of catechizing, to which we are never likely to obtain a full answer. But a combination of institutional and biographical materials, handbooks, and catechisms should enable us to offer a picture of the theory, practice, and content of English cat-echizing that is at least moderately sharp in focus.

One final comment may be made by way of preliminary. Some recent studies have used categories such as 'puritan' or 'household' to help make sense of certain forms

---

[30] See below, Ch. 5.

[31] I. Bourne, *A light from Christ ... or, the rich jewel* (1646), title-page; and e.g. J. Nichols, *An order of household instruction* (1596), sigs. C4v–5r; R. Webb, *A key of knowledge* (1622), sig. A4v; J. Mayer, *Mayers catechisme abridged* (1632), sig. A2r; G. Towerson, *An explication of the catechism ... Part I* (1685), p. xiv; [W. Beveridge], *The church-catechism explained* (1704), pp. xii–xiv; anon., *A new method of catechizing* (1712), p. iii.

of catechizing, especially those that may have been employed outside the parish church. The author of one thesis on the 'cure of souls' in the seventeenth century assumed that most catechisms other than official ones *must* have been written by puritans, and the authors of two more recent theses on catechizing also tend to distinguish between 'puritan' and 'Anglican' forms and between catechizing in church and in the household.[32] These categories have some value, but for reasons that will become clear I am reluctant to use them without qualification. There were tensions in the minds of many catechists, but arguably these were due more to the gulf between the ideal they hoped to achieve and the reality for which they had to settle than to feelings of hostility towards the existing church or its catechetical forms. Equally there is no convincing evidence that a form nominally published for domestic use, such as the *Briefe and necessarie catechisme* by Edward Dering and John More was used solely or primarily in households, as opposed to in school or church; if anything, the reverse may have been the case.[33]

This study is divided into three parts. In the first, Chapters 1 to 5, we deal with the medium. Thus in Chapter 1, the theory of catechizing is examined: how the act was defined by contemporaries, and what they thought were the main aims of catechizing. In the next chapter the different phases and the underlying continuities of English catechizing from about 1530 to about 1740 will be outlined through an analysis of the new catechisms and repeat editions produced during that period. Next, in Chapters 3 to 5 we will try to establish how far the official view on the practice of catechizing matched the reality, and an attempt will also be made to elucidate some of the different techniques adopted by catechists. Part II consists of seven chapters on the message, in so far as it is possible to separate that from the medium. In Chapter 6 the typical catechetical structures of the period will be outlined, and then in Chapters 7 to 12 we will examine a sample of just under 60 best-selling or influential catechisms to try to determine the characteristic catechetical teaching on the four staples of such instruction—Apostles' Creed, Decalogue, Lord's Prayer, and sacraments—and on some other contemporary preoccupations, notably double predestination and covenant theology. Part III consists of a provisional finding list of English catechisms composed between the 1530s and the 1730s, together with some comments on their possible value to scholars with differing interests. The author would welcome details of additional titles or editions, and corrections or different assessments of the works listed, and it is envisaged that when enough are to hand a supplement to this list will be made available. In this way the neglect of early modern English catechizing could soon be ended.

---

[32] Grant, 'Cure of Souls', ch. 3; Hutchison, 'English Catechism', p. 5, and chs. 6–8; and Durbin, 'Education by Catechism', chs. 4 and 5 and conclusion; and cf. R. L. Greaves, 'Introduction' to *Miscellaneous Works of John Bunyan* (general editor, R. Sharrock), viii (Oxford, 1979), pp. xxx–xxxv, and C. J. Sommerville, *The Discovery of Childhood in Puritan England* (Athens, Ga./London, 1992), 135–45.

[33] See below, p. 210.

PART I

The Medium

1

'What is Catechizing?'

IF one looks up the terms 'catechism' or 'catechesis' in an encyclopaedia of religious history, one finds an account of elementary instruction from the first centuries of the Christian church to the present day.[1] In the early modern period, however, most Protestants, including the English, did not use these terms in the same way as their medieval predecessors. Indeed, many Protestant clergy denied that the medieval church had catechized at all. 'Among us', claimed Luther, 'the catechism has come back into use, as it were by right of recovery.' What we set before you, wrote Calvin in the preface of his catechism, is what was used among Christians in ancient times before the devil ruined the church.[2] Catechizing, it was said in an English translation of a work by a French Protestant (in 1580), had in 'the last ages come again' after being abandoned by the papists in the Middle Ages.[3] A few years later Richard Greenham put the point even more forcefully: catechizing had been 'put down' between the time of the Fathers and that of Luther.[4] Some Protestants, including Luther and Calvin, did not deny that there had been attempts at religious instruction before the Reformation, but they tended to view it as both misleading and ineffective: the 'remnants' of instruction in the medieval period could only 'beget superstition, without any edification', said Calvin.[5]

If we are to get to the heart of English catechetics in the early modern period, we must first try to see how and why the usages of that era differed from those of the previous thousand years. The leaders of neither the established church nor the major alternatives to it in England ever issued a clear definition or rationale of the practice, such as Luther provided in the preface to his catechisms, but from the few indications that English church leaders did provide, together with the views of the scores of catechetical authors who served in that church and have left us evidence, it is possible to reconstruct what was probably a majority view. 'Q[uestion]. What is catechizing?

---

[1] *Oxford Dictionary of the Christian Church*[2], ed. F. L. Cross (Oxford, 1974), 248–50; *New Catholic Encyclopedia* (New York, 1967), iii. 208–40; *The New International Dictionary of the Christian Church*, ed. J. D. Douglas (Exeter, 1974), 199–201; there is also a wide definition in J. H. Westerhof III and O. C. Edwards, Jr. (eds.), *A Faithful Church: Issues in the History of Catechesis* (Wilton, Conn., 1981), 2–6.

[2] Strauss, *Luther's House of Learning*, 155; Torrance, *School of Faith*, 5.

[3] W. Charke, 'Of the use of catechising', sig. D2ᵛ, in R. Cawdrey, *A short and fruitefull treatise* (1580).

[4] R. Greenham, *Second part of the workes* (1600), 75.

[5] Janz, *Three Reformation Catechisms*, 181–3; Torrance, loc. cit.; and see below, pp. 21–5.

A[nswer]. An instruction especially for the ignorant in the grounds of religion', was the opening exchange in Thomas Cartwright's short catechism, which probably dates from the closing decades of Elizabeth's reign.[6] Catechizing, said Richard Bernard in 1613, is 'a divine ordinance, from old times used in God's church, as a necessary means, to inform the ruder sort, summarily, by questions and answers in the principles of religion'.[7] In 1707 an episcopalian, Matthew Hole, put it even more briefly: catechizing is a general instruction in the fundamental principles of the Christian religion by way of question and answer.[8]

Most of the elements common to these and other definitions then on offer from English Protestants[9] would have been acceptable to medieval churchmen. In the early Church, adult converts preparing for baptism were referred to as *katechumenoi* and given oral instruction in the rudiments of the faith, such as the Creed, Lord's Prayer, and sacraments. The abstract noun for this exercise was *katechesis*, this word like *katechumenoi* deriving from the Greek verb *katechizo*, which means literally to make hear, hence to instruct. At this stage, however, there does not seem to have been a noun to refer to the manual containing catechetical material.[10] In subsequent centuries the task of the instructors changed from preparing converted adults for baptism to ensuring that those baptized at birth understood the faith of the church of which they were a member, and from the thirteenth century this was often linked to preparing the faithful for confession. By the late Middle Ages, a number of English versions of the earlier Greek terms, mediated through Latin or French equivalents, can be found being used to describe basic oral instruction, not just 'catechumynys' (those who were being catechized) and 'cathezized' (the act of catechizing), but also 'cathecysme' or 'catechyzon' (the form containing the catechetical material).[11] Indeed, in the later Middle Ages, religious instruction was being rapidly expanded, and covered part of the same ground that Protestant catechetics would do, in that

---

[6] A. Peel and L. Carlson (eds.), *Cartwrightiana* (1951), 159.

[7] R. Bernard, *Two twinnes* (1613), 5. [8] M. Hole, *A practical exposition* (1707), 1.

[9] Other definitions can be found on the title-pages or in the prefaces or texts of the works listed in Appendix 1 under [T. Cranmer] (1548); Edmond Allen (1548); J. Ponet (1553); J. Calvin (1556/60); J.F. [c.1585]; R. Allen (1600); T. Wilson (1609); I.F. (1617); J. Frewen (1621); J. Boughton (1623); T. Downing (1623); G. Scarbrough (1623); D. Featley (1626); R. Bernard (1630); W. Crompton (1633); W. Jones (1633); H. Peters (1641); 'J. Ussher' (1645); anon., *Some gospel truths* (1647); R. Mather (1650); G. Masterson (1654); W. Gay (1655); R. Ram (1655); S. Ford (1655); anon., *A door opening* (1662); L. Addison (1674); G. Towerson (1678); T. Jekyll (1690); anon., *Earnest call* (1690); T. Doolittle (1692); G. Keith (1698); W. Wake (1699); E. Wetenhall (1698); E. Wells (1707); S. Harris (1712); and anon., *Catechumenorum* (1714).

[10] See works cited in n. 1 above, esp. *New Catholic Encyclopedia*, iii. 208–11, 220–1; see also Westerhof and Edwards (eds.), *Faithful Church*, ch. 3.

[11] Ibid. 79; *Oxford English Dictionary*, s.v. 'catechumen', 'catechize', and 'catechism'; and E. Germain, *Langages de la foi à travers l'histoire* (Paris, 1972), 32 n. 14. The title of the fourteenth-century work published as *The Lay Folks' Catechism*, ed. T. F. Simmons and H. E. Nolloth (Early English Text Society, o.s., 118; 1901) is a later insertion. See also, L. D. Durbin, 'Education by Catechism: The Development of the Sixteenth-Century English Catechism', Ph.D. thesis (Northwestern, 1987), ch. 1.

adults and children were taught by rote to memorize the Paternoster and at least some would have mastered the Credo too. In addition the more zealous or better educated clergy probably offered vernacular expositions of Creed, Lord's Prayer, and Ten Commandments, either of their own devising or drawn from approved works. The Decalogue received particular attention in the manuals prepared for the late medieval clergy and laity because it was hoped it would lead to an increased awareness of the sins which had to be confessed by the committed Christian.[12]

Where Catholic and Protestant differed was partly over language and content, and partly over function and technique. Protestants insisted that the Lord's Prayer and other formulae were taught in English, whereas Catholics had usually used Latin and continued to do so in services and primers, though this was changing in a number of printed works aimed at the laity; and Catholics taught the Ave Maria, the seven works of mercy, the seven deadly sins, the seven cardinal virtues, the seven sacraments, and other material which the Protestants rejected.[13] There was also a difference of interpretation or emphasis over the main function of catechizing. For Protestants a catechism was essentially a manual of belief, and catechizing was a means of leading young Christians towards knowledge and understanding of the faith and towards confirmation or admission to holy communion, though it could also tell them (and usually did) how to lead a better life. For Catholics a catechism was as much a manual of practice as of belief: catechizing was often seen as a means of preparing an adult or an adolescent for confession (and then participation in the mass) by helping him to identify his sins. For children below the age of confession, therefore, oral training in the memorizing of the basics was probably irregular.[14] A further contrast stemmed from this stress on confession in that a number of Catholic catechetical works used visual aids—wall-paintings, carvings on fonts, woodcuts—and other techniques such as rhymed couplets and religious plays to help the faithful learn the names of the different sins to be confessed, works of mercy, and sacraments. Protestants, on the other hand, though at first permitting the use of pictures, images, and drama, became increasingly suspicious of them and stressed the importance of

[12] B. L. Manning, *The People's Faith in the Time of Wyclif* (Cambridge, 1919), 42–6 and *passim*; M. Reu, *Catechetics or Theory and Practice of Religious Instruction* (Chicago, 1927), esp. 61–79; W. A. Pantin, *The English Church in the Fourteenth Century* (Cambridge, 1955), chs. 9–10; J. A. Jungman, 'Religious Education in Late Medieval Times', in G. Sloyan (ed.), *Shaping the Christian Message* (New York, 1958), 38–62; Westerhof and Edwards (eds.), *Faithful Church*, ch. 4; J.-C. Dhotel, *Les Origines du catéchisme moderne* (Paris, 1967), 27–38; E. Duffy, *The Stripping of the Altars: Traditional Religion in England c.1400–c.1580* (New Haven/London, 1992), ch. 2; Tudor, 'Religious Instruction', 392–3; J. A. Bossy, 'Moral Arithmetic: Seven Sins into Ten Commandments', in *Conscience and Casuistry in Early Modern Europe*, ed. E. Leites (Cambridge, 1988), 214–34; id., *Christianity in the West 1400–1700* (Oxford, 1985), 118–21; Aston, *England's Iconoclasts*, 344–6.

[13] As last note.

[14] T. N. Tentler, *Sin and Confession on the Eve of the Reformation* (Princeton, 1977), chs. 2, 4; Bossy, *Christianity in the West*, 48–9, 116. For a distinction between the material needed for confession (e.g. seven deadly sins, Decalogue) and catechetical material (e.g. Lord's Prayer), see D. W. Robertson, 'The *manuel des péches* and an English Episcopal Decree', *Modern Language Notes*, 40 (1945), 441.

the plain, unvarnished word, in both the scriptural and the pedagogical sense.[15] But the most striking outward difference was that from the 1520s in Germany, and later elsewhere, most Protestants replaced the older pattern of a series of statements of belief by a system of questions and answers designed not only to test catechumens' knowledge but also to keep their attention and enhance their comprehension. Where the typical pre-Reformation form for beginners was declaratory, its post-Reformation equivalent was interrogatory.[16]

This last difference between the two can be seen by comparing the 'catechyzon' written by Dean Colet about 1510 for boys who were to be admitted to St Paul's School and the catechism in the first Edwardian Prayer Book of 1549, probably the first occasion on which the word 'catechism' received official sanction in England. Colet's form began with the Apostles' Creed in English ('I believe in God the father almighty, creator of heaven and earth') moved on to the seven sacraments ('I believe also that by the seven sacraments of the church cometh great grace to all that taketh them accordingly'), and then on to further statements of belief followed by precepts ('Fear god ... Subdue thy sensual appetites ... Flee foul language') and some Latin prayers. At no stage were any questions asked.[17] The 1549 catechism, however, began by asking 'What is your name? ... Who gave you this name? ... What did your godfathers and godmothers then for you?', and the catechumen had to memorize the answers, which explained how he or she had been given their Christian name in baptism and what that entailed: therein 'I was made a member of Christ, the child of God, and an inheritor of the kingdom of heaven'. Having been asked to repeat the Apostles' Creed, the child was then requested to explain what he understood by it; similarly having recited the Commandments, he was asked 'What dost thou chiefly learn by these?'; and finally he was requested not only to repeat the Lord's Prayer but also to explain what he desired of God in that prayer.[18]

What had happened between 1510 and 1549? The answer is far from straightforward, since it has to be set against changes in teaching methods over a longer period of time and in methods of secular instruction as well as religious, as in the use of questions and answers to teach the elementary parts of Latin speech in the often reprinted treatises based on Donatus's *Ars grammatica*. But to risk a rather crude simplification, one may focus attention on a number of developments taking place on the

---

[15] J. Geffcken, *Der Bildercatechismus des Fünfzehnten Jahrhunderts und die Catechetischen Haupstücke in dieser Zeit bis auf Luther* (Leipzig, 1855), *passim*; Reu, *Catechetics*, 97; S. Ozment, *The Reformation in the Cities* (New Haven/London, 1975), 27–8; M. Aston, *Lollards and Reformers* (London, 1984), ch. 4; for an English edition of Bellarmine's shorter catechism illustrated with woodcuts but published abroad in 1614, see Appendix 1. For the Protestants' growing distrust of visual images, see C. M. N. Eire, *War against the Idols* (Cambridge, 1986); Aston, *Lollards*, chs. 5–6, and ead., *England's Iconoclasts, passim*; and for English catechists' scriptural emphasis, see below, pp. 32–3, 92.

[16] These terms seem to me more readily understood than the technical ones such as acromatic and erotematic used by Reu, *Catechetics*, 450.

[17] J. H. Lupton, *A Life of John Colet*[2] (1909), appendix B, 286–90.

[18] Brightman, *English Rite*, ii. 779–87.

Continent from the late fifteenth century, and in particular the fusion of three related but distinct methods of instruction by the second quarter of the sixteenth century. The first of these methods was the rote repetition of statements which, as we have just seen, had become the norm by the later Middle Ages. The second method—the bare question-and-answer technique—is nowadays often associated with Luther, though he was not the first to use it. From the early 1520s Luther had been anxious that the laity should be able not only to memorize the Decalogue, the Lord's Prayer, and the Apostles' Creed in the vernacular, but also to understand them. So in his small catechism of 1529 these three formulae were broken up into much shorter sections, each of which was followed by the question 'What does this mean?' and by an answer of Luther's own devising. To modern eyes the result may appear stilted and impersonal: the form of the questions was repetitious, the questioner offered no words of encouragement or praise, and the answers were all put in the first-person plural rather than singular. Moreover, some of the answers were so long that those country-bred children who were less used to rote learning than their school-attending urban cousins probably found them hard to memorize.[19]

A third approach that had already found support among a variety of early reformers was the use of a dialogue. This technique had been used by the ancient Hindus and Greeks, and in some parts of the Bible; and although in essence a literary rather than an oral genre, it had been used in the Middle Ages to provide informal means of religious instruction, such as the dialogues of Gregory the Great, 'The owl and the nightingale', and 'Dives and pauper', as well as more advanced teaching such as the 'Questiones by-tweene the maister of Oxenford and his clerke'.[20] In the sense of providing confessors with a long list of questions to put to their charges, and some useful comments to make about their replies, a form of dialogue had also been used to help train some late medieval confessors.[21] Christian humanists like Erasmus, Châteillon, and Cordier also regularly used dialogues or 'colloquies' as educational tools to teach Christian behaviour or scriptural knowledge; indeed, in the Renaissance period dialogues were being used in many parts of Europe to perform a wide variety of functions. Recently, Peter Burke has suggested that there were then four main types of dialogue. At one end was the catechetical (which he sees as little better than a monologue, with the student asking the odd question or making an occasional interjection while the master expatiated at great length); in the middle was the disputation (in which two points of view were expressed but one speaker was allowed to win), and the conversation (as the last, but open-ended and not loaded in one speaker's favour); finally, at the other extreme came the dramatic type (where the

[19] Schaff, *Creeds*, 74–92; Strauss, *Luther's House of Learning*, chs. 8, 12, 13.

[20] P. Burke, 'The Renaissance Dialogue', *Renaissance Studies*, 3 (1989), 2; *The Owl and the Nightingale, Cleanness and St Erkenwald*, tr. B. Stone (1988), 155–244; *Dives and Pauper*, ed. P. H. Barnum (Early English Text Society, os, 275, 280; 1976–80); J. Burke Severs and A. E. Hartung, *Manual of the Writings in Middle English 1050–1500*, iii (Hamden, Conn., 1972), 669–745.

[21] Ozment, *Reformation*, 23–5; and Pantin, *English Church*, 197.

situation was as important as what was said, for example Erasmus's portrayal of Julius II arguing with St Peter at the gates of heaven).[22] The first two are the types which concern us in this chapter and the next, though as will be seen not even the first corresponds exactly with what emerged as the typical catechism of the later sixteenth century, since in the latter it was usually the senior who asked and the junior who replied, and in many but not all cases the balance between question and answer was not too one-sided. Perhaps 'educational' or 'instructive' would be a better term for Burke's first type of dialogue.

Looked at from the point of view of a religious instructor in the early sixteenth century, an instructive dialogue of the type used by Erasmus had two clear advantages. First, unlike most late medieval instruction which involved simple rote repetition, a dialogue had two *dramatis personae*, usually a teacher and a student, sometimes two siblings or neighbours, though there could be three or more characters involved. It was hoped that the dramatic situation posed by a meeting of two acquaintances, together with the cut and thrust of questioning and answering, would keep students on their toes better than rote repetition. (In some cases apparently the 'colloquies' of Erasmus and others were acted out in class.) Secondly, by disguising and interspersing the didactic elements with conversational ones or with comments or praise put into the teacher's mouth, an author could try not only to keep the student's attention, but also give regular encouragement, so that the material might be absorbed more readily than by rote repetition of the Colet type or the bare inquisition of the Luther type. Before Luther had polished and published his catechisms, a number of dialogue-type instructions had begun to circulate, such as the *Christian catechism* of the Anabaptist Balthasar Hubmaier who referred to it as a 'dialogue or conversation' between two brothers, and the dialogue entitled *De pueris instituendis* by another early reformer, Wolfgang Capito.[23] The main limitation of a dialogue was, ironically, that it was not well suited to oral instruction if by that we mean a method of helping poorly educated people to memorize a small corpus of information. A typical dialogue contained extraneous material such as greetings, exhortation, and praise which, compared to the bare essentials in Luther's catechism, did not require committing to memory. Moreover, the authors of dialogues often gave way to the temptation to write long, complex answers to relatively simple questions or to insert the cut and thrust of a disputation. Most authors of dialogues seem, in fact, to have had in mind a literate, moderately well-informed audience who would gain knowledge and understanding through regular *reading* of the text, either privately or in class. Even if a dialogue was acted out in class, the emphasis would still have been on the ability to read in a meaningful way rather than memorization. As we shall see, dialogues would continue to have a part to play in intermediate or advanced works of religious instruc-

---

[22] Burke, 'Renaissance Dialogue', 1–12.
[23] Janz, *Three Reformation Catechisms*, 12–14, 131–78 (the quotation is on p. 139); Capito's work was also published in German and English: Westerhof and Edwards (eds.), *Faithful Church*, 120.

tion and in works of controversy, but probably only a limited role at elementary level.[24]

By the second quarter of the sixteenth century what we find is the fusion of these three different methods: the rote repetition of statements that had become the norm in the late Middle Ages; Luther's attempt to convey meaning as well as material; and the dialogue tricks of capturing and holding the pupil's attention. If we look, for example, at Calvin's second attempt at drawing up a catechism, that of 1541, what we find is a catechism, in French, which has the same aims and handles the same material as Luther's, but in which the catechist is portrayed as a real person who occasionally summarizes what has been said or offers extra help at a difficult point, as in the following exchange about God:

The minister: What meanest thou by that, thou callest him almighty?
The child: ... He hath a power which he does not exercise, but ... disposeth all things by his unsearchable wisdom and providence: that he ruleth the world as it pleaseth him ...
The minister: So then by thy saying, the power of God is not idle ... [you mean] that nothing is done, but by him, or by his leave and ordinance ...
The child: It is even as you say.[25]

Not only was the phrasing of Calvin's questions much more varied than Luther's, but also most of the questions and some of the answers were moderately short; and the text could be divided up into subsections so that children could master a new segment of the whole each week. Calvin also left out some of the more perplexing topics included in the 1537 form, such as predestination. On the other hand, the 1541 catechism was prepared in a great hurry and was far from perfect. As the example cited indicates, the concepts and terminology used made few concessions to the capacities of those 10 to 15-year-olds for whom it had been designed, and its tone was businesslike rather than the more relaxed one found in a conventional dialogue. Also in many of the answers Calvin still manœuvred students into using the first-person plural. As a result many contemporaries who were admirers of Calvin borrowed from it or tried to improve its technique rather than using it in its original form.[26]

English experience mirrored that of the Continent. As we shall see in the next chapter, a number of the first question-and-answer forms to appear in England were clearly influenced by the older tradition of the dialogue; indeed, some of them were

[24] Burke, 'Renaissance Dialogue', 8; and see below, pp. 54–6, 60–1, 63–4. For the use of dialogues in Catholic catechetics, see Joannes Petrus (Luccensis), *A dialogue of dying well* (1603); W. Warford, *A briefe instruction by way of dialogue* (1604); anon., *A select manuel of godly prayers* (1716); and [R. Challoner], *The young gentleman instructed ... in three dialogues* (1735).

[25] J. Calvin, *The catechisme* (Geneva, 1556), 9; this catechism will be referred to as Calvin's 1541 catechism, since it was perhaps prepared late in that year, even if it was not issued until 1542 and not printed until 1545: F. Wendel, *Calvin: The Origins and Development of his Religious Thought*, trans. P. Mairet (1965), 70, 78–80; Torrance, *School of Faith*, 3.

[26] Dhotel, *Origines*, 23–7, 38–50; P. Y. de Jong, 'Calvin's Contributions to Christian Education', *Calvin Theological Journal*, 2 (1967), 174–86; Torrance, *School of Faith*, pp. xli–xlii, 4, 8.

translations of such works from abroad.[27] But increasingly the elementary forms adopted in England, not least the official short catechism of 1549, came to resemble the hybrid style of work being tried out abroad. The genesis of the catechism of 1549, which will be referred to here as the Prayer Book catechism from its inclusion in successive versions of the Book of Common Prayer, is unclear. We do know that Thomas Cranmer, to whom it has been attributed, was well aware of what was happening in the Lutheran churches of Germany, partly through a period spent as ambassador at Ratisbon and the family contacts then made, and partly through his extensive correspondence. By 1548–9 it was also clear that like Luther he was anxious there should be both a short catechism and a more advanced form of instruction in the shape of a series of catechetical sermons.[28] The relative shortness of the 1549 form is similar to Luther's shorter catechism, as is the stress on simple explanations of Decalogue, Creed, and Lord's Prayer. The Prayer Book catechism also bears some resemblance to Calvin's 1541 form, which might have been known to English churchmen in a French or Latin edition: the greater fluidity and more personal tone of the exchanges between catechist and catechumen, and the sequence in which the material is treated, are more like Calvin's than Luther's.[29] (The resemblance stops there: Calvin's work was a much longer and more difficult work.)

However, there was also an insular element in the development of question-and-answer forms in England. The short catechism in the 1549 Prayer Book, for example, was designed to bridge a gap in the liturgy between the charge to godparents in the baptism service (to ensure their godchild learnt the basics of the faith) and the presentation of the child at the ceremony of confirmation. As a result, its content was somewhat different from Continental works in that it did not have a section on the sacraments until one was added unofficially in the early 1570s, and officially (in a modified form) in 1604. Also unlike both Luther's and Calvin's forms and long before the Heidelberg Catechism (which is often given the credit for this innovation), the English Prayer Book form used the first-person singular throughout, both for catechist and catechumen. Moreover, where a possible derivation of a particular phrase in the Prayer Book catechism can be offered, it is likely to be a biblical text or an English source, such as Colet, the 'dialogue' used in the modified primers of the 1530s, or the baptism service of the Prayer Book itself, rather than a Continental model.[30] On a wider front, as we shall see in the next chapter, from the 1550s to the 1580s a number of reformers were busily translating into English a variety of hybrid

[27] See below, pp. 54, 60–1.

[28] J. Ridley, *Thomas Cranmer* (Oxford, 1962), 40–7, 85–90, 159–64, 177, 193–4, 215–16, 281–3, 327–30; Appendix 1, s.v. Book of Common Prayer and Cranmer; Strauss, *Luther's House of Learning*, 159, 209.

[29] On the sequence of the contents, see below, pp. 280–2.

[30] Brightman, *English Rite*, ii. 776–90; G. J. Cuming, *A History of Anglican Liturgy²* (1982), 62, 104–5; see also above, n. 17, and E. Burton (ed.), *Three Primers Put Forth in the Reign of Henry VIII* (Oxford, 1834), 216–21; and below, pp. 529–32.

interrogatory forms then in use in Germany, Switzerland, France, and the Netherlands, and responding to any criticisms of the new-style catechizing by pointing to the strong support it had already been given by Protestant churches abroad.[31] It will be suggested, however, that both in the first generation of English catechists and in succeeding generations there were a number of creative native talents, and that the more catechizing was pursued in England the more these would come to the fore. During this period it also seems to have become widely accepted in England, by authors of both official and alternative catechisms, that the interrogatory rather than the declaratory was the most natural and effective form of oral elementary religious instruction, especially for teaching the 'simpler' or the 'ruder sort'.[32] Questions and answers, wrote a chaplain of Charles II in 1674, were an easy means of instilling the rudiments of *any* art, science, or faculty into those of limited understanding, but they were particularly useful in teaching them the basics of Christianity.[33]

Sincere though these authors were in praising the technique, however, they do not seem to have regarded it as an innovation, but as a long overdue revival. They were highly critical of what they saw as the man-made fictions and senseless repetition which had passed for instruction in the Middle Ages, and claimed that their catechisms, like their doctrine, church organization, and worship, were a more accurate reflection of the practice of biblical times and of the early church.[34] Protestants of a later generation who felt less threatened by Catholicism might take a different view, but until the seventeenth century it was a basic tenet among Protestant catechists that their role was not to innovate but to renovate.

Given Protestant concern for scriptural warrant for all their actions, it is not surprising that so many authors argued that catechizing had biblical origins. In England a lead was given by Cranmer in 1548 when he told Edward VI that ever since the time of Christ knowledge of the Commandments, the Creed, and the Lord's Prayer had

[31] See below, pp. 61–2, 64–5; also J. Stockwood's preface to R. Cawdrey, *A short and fruitefull treatise* (1580), sigs. A1^r–2^r, and C6^v–7^r; W. Wood, *A fourme of catechising* (1581), sig. *2^r; anon., *A catechisme, or short kind of instruction*, ed. T. Sparke and J. Seddon (1588), sigs. A4^v–5^r, and p. 4; T. Watts, *The entrie to Christianitie* (1589), sigs. A3^v, B1^r–3^r, B4^v; Greenham, *Second part*, 75; T[hos.] W[ilson], *An exposition of the two first verses* (1609), 7–8.

[32] See e.g. J. Syme, *The sweet milke of Christian doctrine* (1617), sig. A3^r; R. Bernard, *The faithfull shepheard* (1607), 9; T. Fuller, *A History of the Worthies of England*, ed. P. A. Nuttall (3 vols.; 1840), ii. 516; W. Perkins/R. Hill, *A golden chaine ... now drawn into familiar questions and answers* (1621), sigs. ¶6^v–7^r; I. Bourne, *A light from Christ ... or, the rich jewel* (1646), sigs. a2$^{r–v}$; Z. Crofton, *Catechizing Gods ordinance* (1656), sig. A5^v; S[amuel] L[angley], *A catechisme shorter than the short catechisme* (1649), sig. A2^v; T. Doolittle, *Catechizing necessary for the ignorant* (1692), 23; and see below, Chs. 3–5 for other endorsements.

[33] L. Addison, *The primitive institution* (1674), 10, 13.

[34] See e.g. John Bale, *The image of both churches* [1548?]; id., *The first two partes of the actes ... of the Englyshe votaryes* (1560); and id., *A dialogue ... gathered out of the holy scriptures* (1549); R. Bernard, *Looke beyond Luther* (1623), 3 and *passim*.

been required of all, both young and old.[35] In 1564 there was published Thomas Becon's long list of Old Testament patriarchs who had insisted on the virtuous education of youth, and another list of parents in both Old and New Testaments who had taken care to rear their children according to God's doctrine and commands—unlike those of his own day, grumbled Becon.[36] In succeeding decades, other authors created a fund of scriptural citations to justify catechizing—a fund that may well have been in part borrowed from Continental sources, and was almost certainly in turn plundered by later authors anxious to impress on their catechumens the biblical precedents for their actions.[37]

This anxiety does, however, seem to have tested their powers of ingenuity. Thus one author stated that God catechized Adam, while others said that Adam catechized his sons when teaching them to sacrifice to the Lord. These assertions either equate the idea of catechizing with one party telling another what to believe and do, or, if these authors were suggesting that some form of question-and-answer instruction was used, stretch the text of the opening chapters of Genesis beyond its natural limit.[38] Other authors suggested that Abraham and Joshua in the Old Testament and Cornelius in the New must have used 'some fit catechism' when they taught their households, though this was pure conjecture.[39] A couple of authors admitted that they had had to use their reason to deduce that the act of catechizing had taken place,[40] but most authors referred to these acts of 'catechizing' as if they were scriptural facts, and thus beyond dispute. Similarly, various authors stated categorically that the Old Testament required fathers to teach their children, though some of the texts they cited are far from precise about what (apart perhaps from the Jewish law) was to be taught or by what means, for instance Genesis 18: 19, Deuteronomy 6: 7, Psalm 34: 11, Proverbs 22: 6, and Ecclesiastes 12: 1.[41] The ministers who translated Proverbs 22: 6 ('Train up a child in the way he should go') as 'Catechize a child …' were sincere but perhaps rather naïve in imagining that the training referred to by the

---

[35] [T. Cranmer], *Catechismus, that is to say a shorte instruction* (1548), sig. v^r.

[36] T. Becon, *Workes*, i (1564), fos. cclxxxvii^v–cclxxxviii^v.

[37] J. Stockwood, *A sermon preached at Paules Crosse* [24. Aug. 1578] (1578), 131–2, 141, and Stockwood's preface to Cawdrey, *Short treatise* (1580), sigs. 3^r–6^v; T. Sparke, 'Treatise', in [Sparke and Seddon], *A catechisme, or short kind of instruction*, 3, 6–13, 18–20, 28–40, and *passim*; Greenham, *Second part*, 73–6; Bernard, *Two twinnes*, 2–4, 6–7.

[38] G. Babington, 'Exposition of the Catholike Faith' in *Workes* (1615), 205; I.F., *The necessitie and antiquitie of catechising* (1617), sigs. A2^v, A3^v–6^v; Greenham, *Second part*, 74; R. Cawdrey *A short and fruitefull treatise* (1604), sig. *vi^r; J. Bristow, *An exposition of the Creede* (1627), sig. A3^r; [George Day], *The communicant's instructor* (1692), sig. a4^r cited early modern scholars who had written on the matter.

[39] J. Leech, *A plaine and profitable catechisme* (1605), sig. A3^v.

[40] Babington, *Workes*, loc. cit.; I.F., *Necessitie of catechising*, sigs. A3^r, B1^r.

[41] Ibid., title-page and sigs. A6^v–8^v; Babington, *Workes*, loc. cit.; Greenham, *Second part*, 74; [W. White], *A paraphrase with annotations* (1674), sig. A2^v; anon., *An earnest call to family-catechising* (1693), 5–8; E[dward] A[lport], *David's catechisme* (1623), 2; T. Comber, *A companion to the temple* (1684), 209; Doolittle, *Catechizing necessary*, 10–15; J. Tillotson, *Six sermons … preached in the church of St Lawrence Jewry* (1694), 114–16.

wisdom literature of the sixth to tenth century BC bore much resemblance to the methods they were using in their parishes in Lincolnshire or Berkshire in the 1650s.[42]

Similarly with the New Testament, there was a certain amount of creative glossing. Different forms of the Greek verb *katechizo* do occur in the New Testament and were sometimes translated into English as 'to catechize' rather than the more accurate 'to impart information', an action which could have been performed in any one of a number of different ways. Thus Galatians 6: 6 ('Let him who is taught the word share all good things with him who teaches') was on one occasion paraphrased as 'taught or catechized', and Paul (in 1 Corinthians 14: 19) was quoted as saying 'I had rather speak five words with mine understanding that I might catechize others in the church, than ten thousand words in a strange tongue'.[43] Philip was described by one author as having catechized the eunuch of Ethiopia (Acts 8: 37), and Timothy was held up as an example of someone who not only had been catechized by his relations (his grandmother and mother in this case) but also in turn catechized others (2 Timothy 1: 5 and 3: 15).[44] Moreover, a number of those who were held to have been 'catechized' in the New Testament were adults, not surprisingly, since there is relatively little in the New Testament about teaching the young.[45]

A number of authors, perhaps following Melanchthon's lead, suggested that the second syllable of the Greek verb referred to an echo, and so defined catechizing as a 'resounding or answering again' or as 'repetition of words as by the reflection of an echo'. This was another example of enthusiasm triumphing over accuracy.[46] The young Christ, it is true, asked questions of the elders in the Temple, and later sometimes asked his disciples an open-ended question; but his more common use of the question was rhetorical, for example, 'What went ye out into the wilderness to see?',

[42] R. Ram, *The countrymans catechisme* (1655), 116; S. Ford, *A sermon of catechizing* (1655), 1; and cf. T. Lye's sermon in [S. Annesley], *A supplement to the morning exercise* (1674), 154.

[43] Anon., *Earnest call*, 5; and T. Downing, *The catechisers holy encouragement* (1623), 2; and see I.F., *Necessitie of catechising*, sig. B2ᵛ; Crofton, *Catechizing Gods ordinance*, title-page and 12; W. Wake, *The principles of the Christian religion* (1700), 1; Bernard. *Two twinnes*, 3. A number of authors equated 'instructed' with 'catechized' in Luke 1: 4; see works by Babington, Crofton, and Wake cited above, and [E. Wetenhall], *A tried method of catachising* (1698), 1.

[44] For these and similar suggestions, see Alport, *David's catechisme*, 17; [White], *Paraphrase*, sig. A2ᵛ; Comber, *Companion*, 209–10; Stockwood, *Sermon*, 131–2; Becon, *Workes*, fo. cclxxxviiiᵛ; Greenham, *Second part*, 75; Cawdrey, *Short and fruitefull treatise* (1604), sig. viᵛ; I.F., *Necessitie of catechising*, sigs. B3ʳ⁻ᵛ; anon., *Earnest call*, 7; R. Wensley, *The form of sound words* (1679), 3, 5, argued that the 'form of sound words' in 2 Tim. 1: 13 was a catechism.

[45] It is not clear from Mark 10: 14–16, John 21: 15, or Eph. 6: 4 if Christ taught the little children he took in his arms, or how or what Simon Peter was supposed to have taught his 'lambs'. See also e.g. 'J. Ussher', *A body of divinitie* (1645), 4; E. Reeve, *The communion booke catechisme* (1635), title-page; and loc. cit. in the works by Becon, Greenham, Cawdrey, I.F., White, Comber, and Wetenhall cited in previous notes.

[46] Reu, *Catechetics*, 3; Strauss, *Luther's House of Learning*, 172; Greenham, *Second part*, 73; Downing, *Catechisers holy encouragement*, 2; W. Gay, *XI choice sermons* (1655), 1; Crofton, *Catechizing Gods ordinance*, 12; W. Nicholson, *A plain, but full exposition* (1661), 1; Addison, *Primitive institution*, 10; anon., *Catechumenorum ductor* (1714), p. ii.

and his more characteristic form of instruction was the parable.[47] In the epistles there were similes onto which many English authors pounced, for example that babes should be given spiritual milk to help nurture them in the faith.[48] But these similes do not offer much guidance as to the method or content of instruction, or they refer not to children so much as to grown men who are said to be *like* babes in their understanding of religion and so not yet ready for meatier fare.[49] In short, in the Bible there were only fairly general grounds for elementary instruction, mainly of adults, and nothing to justify a strong insistence that one particular type of catechizing was quintessentially scriptural.

When Protestant catechists appealed to the practice of the early Church, they were on much firmer ground. There undoubtedly had been catechetical schools at Alexandria and elsewhere which had used simple, oral methods to teach the unlearned, mainly adults at the outset, the rudiments of the faith; Augustine had written a work called *De catechizandis rudibus* and other catechetical works; and the actions or recommendations of other eminent churchmen and the canons of a number of councils were all listed with some justification as evidence for the lively state of the art in the early Church.[50] Not only conservative figures like Lancelot Andrewes but also a number of the 'godly' were among those who deployed precedents from the early Church or the early Middle Ages.[51] What English authors of all standpoints do not seem to have realized or at least did not spell out (until the late seventeenth century) was that these early examples of catechetical instruction were not of the question-and-answer type. A little-known interrogatory form does seem to have existed in Germany by the early ninth century, a 'Disputatio puerorum per interrogationes et responsiones', and there were, as we have seen, dialogues for the literate few; but the typical late medieval form of elementary teaching, like that of the first centuries, was almost

---

[47] Luke 2: 46; Matt. 16: 15, and 11: 7–9 (and ch. 13); and Luke 12: 25.

[48] 1 Cor. 3: 1–2; Heb. 5: 12–14; 1 Pet. 2: 2; and cf. Cawdrey, *Short and fruitefull treatise* (1580), sigs. A6^{r-v}, D4^r; Allen, *Treasurie*, 1; Bernard, *Two twinnes*, 4; W. Crashaw, *Milke for babes* (1618), title-page and sig. A2^v; anon., 'Of catechisinge', Emmanuel College Cambridge Library MS III. 1. 13^8 [fo. 30^v]; W. Attersoll, *The principles of Christian religion* (1623), sig. a2^r; Reeve, *Communion book catechisme*, sig. C3^v; Doolittle, *Catechizing necessary*, title-page.

[49] Green, 'Emergence of the English Catechism', 409; and on the dearth of explicit evidence for the nature of Christian education in the first centuries of the Christian era, see Westerhof and Edwards (eds.), *Faithful Church*, ch. 2.

[50] Ibid., ch. 3; *New Catholic Encyclopedia*, iii. 209, 220–1, 225–7; A. Gerardus ('Hyperius'), *The foundation of Christian religion* (1583), title-page; Cawdrey, *Short and fruitefull treatise* (1580), sigs. ☞6^{r-v}, D2^v; Watts, *Entrie*, sigs. A8^r, B2^r; I. Bourne, *The true way of a Christian* (1622), 29–33; Alport, *David's catechisme*, 3, 9; Ford, *Sermon of catechizing*, 4, 31; Crofton, *Catechizing Gods ordinance*, 27; Comber, *Companion*, 209–11; G. Towerson, *An explication of the catechism ... Part I* (1685), pp. ii, v; [W. Beveridge], *The church-catechism explained* (1704), 220–22.

[51] Andrewes, *Works*, vi. 9–10; Greenham, *Second part*, 73, 75; Ford, *Sermon of catechizing*, 4; Bernard, *Two twinnes*, 7, 10; see also the citations of early Church practice by Stockwood, Charke, Sparke, Greenham, Bourne, and Crofton in previous notes; Wensley, *Form of sound words*, 14–46, cited not only the Fathers but also Calvin, Beza, and the Westminster divines on what a catechism should be and what should be in it.

certainly declaratory.[52] This did not deter the enthusiasts. 'Is every instruction a catechism?', ran a question in a 1633 form; 'No', came the reply, a catechism was 'an instruction in the grounds of religion, by word of mouth by way of question and answer'.[53] Nor did it deter the late seventeenth-century commentator who cited Acts 8: 38 and 1 Peter 3: 21 to prove that the English church's catechism had been drawn up 'according to the primitive forms, by way of question and answer'.[54]

One or two authors had already shown caution about the use of scripture to justify a particular type of catechizing,[55] but it was not until the later seventeenth century that this caution became more common, and a correspondingly greater stress was placed on tradition or the consistent usage of the church over centuries or at least over decades.[56] In a sermon published in 1694, John Tillotson not only conceded that the question-and-answer method was *not* enjoined in scripture, but also admitted that the Greek term simply meant teaching in general, and had been appropriated by ecclesiastical writers to describe a method long in use in the Christian church.[57] Gabriel Towerson, writing shortly before this, pointed out that Augustine's chief catechetical work had been a discourse, not a question-and-answer form, and that it had taken so long to deliver that the catechumens had been allowed to sit down while they listened to it. He also made it quite clear that in his opinion it was only in 'the latter ages', since the Henrician Reformation, that the question-and-answer form had been developed.[58]

There had, in fact, been an element of wishful thinking on the Protestants' side. When they traced the practice of question-and-answer catechizing back to the Bible or to the works of Pantaenus, Clement, or Origen, either they were not aware of or conveniently overlooked the fact that such instruction had been not of the interrogatory type and was mainly directed at adults. The readiness with which they condemned medieval Catholicism blinded them to the similarities between the old church's efforts at instruction and their own, and the pride with which they lauded their own success in 'reviving' supposedly suppressed forms obscured the fact that they were developing a technique which if not brand new was for purposes of religious instruction relatively novel and at the outset untried.

For most Protestant enthusiasts, then, catechizing was God's wish, as proved by

[52] *New Catholic Encyclopedia*, iii. 225: the 9th-century work has been attributed to Alcuin, but this is doubtful.

[53] W. Jones, *An exposition of the whole catechisme* (1633), sig. A1ᵛ.

[54] Comber, *Companion*, 210; and cf. W. Cradock, *A discourse of due catechising* (1718), 5.

[55] Babington, *Workes*, 205; W. Crompton, *An explication of those principles* (1633), 1.

[56] Addison, *Primitive institution*, 8–10, and cf. his use of 'probably' and 'no doubt' on 29 and 42; Nicholson, *Plain exposition*, 1–2.

[57] Tillotson, *Six sermons*, 159–60; and cf. Wake, *Principles*, 1; and for a dissenter's view: S. Harris, *Scripture-knowledge promot'd by catechizing* (1712), 13.

[58] Towerson, *Explication*, pp. ii–xiv.

scripture, and it was the practice of the church, as shown by the early Church and other Protestant churches since the Reformation. But it was also held to be a highly profitable exercise, and its English advocates were always ready to enlarge on what those benefits were.[59] The five most commonly found in the catechisms listed in Appendix 1 are the following: catechizing laid the necessary basis of religious knowledge without which an individual could not hope for salvation; it enabled members of the church to achieve a deeper understanding of the scriptures and of what took place during church services; it also prepared them for a fuller part in church life by helping them to frame a profession of faith and to participate in the Lord's Supper; it enabled them to distinguish true doctrine from false; and it promoted Christian virtue and dissuaded from vice. It may be useful to examine each of these five reasons at greater length.

Without the knowledge of the fundamental doctrines of the Christian religion, wrote Perkins, a man cannot have faith, and without faith he could not be saved. 'Justifying faith presupposeth the knowledge of God and Christ, of the precepts of the Word, and promises of the Gospel', wrote another Calvinist, John Ball, a few years later. 'What is true religion?' asked William Attersoll at the start of his catechism; 'It is the knowledge of God's will', which consisted of repentance from dead works, and faith in Christ.[60] The idea of an essential core of religious knowledge was spelt out by those authors who offered a clear definition of catechizing, as we saw earlier in this chapter. In the case of many other authors, however, it was implicit in the way in which they described their works, either on the title-page or in a preface: 'the sum of Christian religion', 'the main and fundamental points' or the 'grounds of divinity', the 'several heads' or the 'first principles' of religion, 'the ABC of Christianity', 'milk for babes', and so on. When explaining the difference between a catechism and a sermon, authors told their charges that the former compressed the whole of Christianity into a short sum, whereas the latter took a single element of Christian teaching and enlarged it into a treatise.[61] In the 1570s and 1580s, and again in the early seventeenth century, a number of different catechisms were referred to by such titles as 'the sum of the principles of Christianity', the 'sum of saving knowledge', and 'the sum of the gospels'.[62] Another label often used in the late Elizabethan period was 'points', as in 'chief' or 'principal points', the stress here being

[59] e.g. E.B., *A catechisme or briefe instruction* (1617), sigs. A3ʳ–5ᵛ; the title-page of John Boughton's 'treatise catechistical': I[ohn] B[oughton], *God and man* (1623); and cf. anon., *An explicatory catechism* (1675), sigs. A2ᵛ–5ʳ.

[60] *The Work of William Perkins*, ed. I. Breward (Abingdon, 1970), 139; J. Ball, *A treatise of faith* (1631), 16; Attersoll, *Principles*, sig. A2ʳ; and cf. also below nn. 75–6; L. Bayly, *The practise of pietie* (1619), 3; and James Nayler's *Love to the lost*, which offered the 'simple' an account of what is 'needful to be known by all who profess godliness'.

[61] Andrewes, *Works*, vi. 6; Greenham, *Second part*, 73; Wilson, *Exposition of the two first verses*, 6; C.P., *Two briefe treatises* (1616), 6; R. Abbot, *Milk for babes* (1646), sig. aa2ʳ; Crofton, *Catechizing Gods ordinance*, 53–7 (in part citing Greenham).

[62] See the title-pages (or prefaces) of the works in Appendix 1 by J. Ponet (1553); C. Shutte (1579 and

less on the totality implied by sum than on the most important or distinctive elements of Protestant–Christian teaching.[63]

In catechisms produced in the first half of the seventeenth century, the term 'grounds', qualified by such adjectives as 'true', 'principal', 'main', 'chief', or 'whole', is commonly found, as in the subtitle of the printed version of Thomas Cartwright's catechism.[64] 'Grounds' could be taken to mean valid reasons or something that provided the basis of an argument—an interpretation that would have had some appeal to the many authors who had undergone some training in formal logic; but in this context it probably meant also base or foundation. 'The principles of religion' wrote one catechist in 1617 'are called grounds' which was a very fit term, since anyone not skilled in these principles is 'as a building which stands upon no firm ground'; another catechist, writing in the 1650s, glossed the verb 'to catechize' as to 'build or edify'.[65] The idea that catechizing provided the foundation without which any attempt to build a superstructure was bound to fail is one that was also often explored when catechists were trying to explain the relationship between catechisms and sermons.[66] Another title, used in some Stuart catechisms was 'heads', in the sense of headings such as sin, faith, and salvation which would help a catechumen to recognize the significance of a particular point and to organize his thoughts about religion.[67] As we shall see shortly, some catechists thought the members of a congregation would be able to understand a sermon better if they could relate what they had heard to the 'heads' of the catechism that they had learnt.[68]

later editions); E. Paget and R. Openshaw (both shorter and larger forms); J. Craig (1581); G. Gifford (1583); J. Davidson (c.1588, sig. A2ʳ); H. Graie (1588); anon., *A short catechisme* (1590); T. Ratcliffe (–1619); J. Sprint (1613); E. Littleton (1616); J. Yates (1621); G. Scarbrough (1623); R. Sedgwick (1624); J. Hall (1625); D. Featley (1625); S. Browne (1630); W. Whitaker (1630); H. Burton (1631, sig. A2ʳ); F. Peck (1644); 'J. Ussher' (1645); V. Powell (1646); H. Isaacson (1647); T. Greaves (1656); and N. Vincent (1691).

[63] See the title-pages of the works in Appendix 1 by T. Beza (1572); anon., *A booke of Christian questions and answers* (1578); J. Gibson (1579); A. Gee (1582); R. Harrison (1583); W. Horne (1585); O.R. [c.1585]; R. Saintbarb (1589); M. Aldem (1592); S. Egerton (1615); J. Nichols (1595); J. Balmford (1597); and R.C. (1599). The word 'points' also appears on the title-pages or in the prefaces of at least half a dozen catechisms of the reign of James I and of another half dozen of the second half of the seventeenth century.

[64] See e.g. the title-pages of the works in Appendix 1 by F. Davis (1612); J. Ball (1615); E. Elton (1616); anon., *The elements of the beginning* (1619); T. Cartwright (1623); J. Carter (1628); anon., *The main grounds of religion* (1630); E. Rogers (1642). At least twenty other examples could be given, mostly from the first half of the century.

[65] E.B., *Catechisme or briefe instruction*, sigs. A5ᵛ–6ᵛ; Nicholson, *Plain exposition*, 1.

[66] Andrewes, *Works*, vi. 13; Bourne, *True way*, 28–9; Boughton, *God and man*, 4; C. Blackwood, *A soul-searching catechism* (1658), sig. A2ʳ; T. Lamplugh, *[A pastoral letter to the clergy of the diocese of Exeter]* [167?], 1–2; G. Burnet, *An exposition of the church catechism* (1710), sig. [A2ᵛ]. See also below, pp. 31–2.

[67] G. Scarbrough, *The summe of all godly and profitable catechismes* (1623), sigs. A5ᵛ–6ʳ; G. Walker, *The key of saving knowledge* (1641), sig. A3ʳ; and see the title-pages or prefaces of works in Appendix 1 by W. Ames (1612); J. Ussher (1644); D. Burch (1646); R. Ram (1655); J. Arrowsmith (1659); and J. Davenport and W. Hooke (1659).

[68] See below, p. 31; for an English author's awareness of Continental authors' stress on 'heads', see Wilson, *Exposition of the two first verses*, 7–8.

Another common label from the 1580s but especially after 1640 when it became much the most frequently used term both with presbyterians and episcopalians, was 'principles', either by itself or in harness with the term 'grounds'.[69] Today, the term 'principles' is usually equated with a code of belief or conduct, but in the seventeenth century it probably also retained much of its older meanings, from the Latin *principium* or *principia*: the primary elements or sources, the foundations, or the fundamental truths which could be used as a basis for reasoning. Thus in his popular and influential set of catechetical lectures, Lancelot Andrewes compared catechizing to erecting a building: 'the principles of religion are called a foundation, that must be digged deep till we come to the rock, that our building may not be shallow upon the earth without foundation'.[70] There was possibly a certain amount of unconscious plagiarism or publishing fashion in the choice of title, and even the occasional pun: *A stock of divine knowledge* printed in 1641 was the posthumously published work of a London minister, Richard Stock.[71] On the other hand, it is perhaps not surprising that many of those who had received a classical education, as most catechetical authors probably had done, were attracted to 'principles'—the most Latinate of the descriptions, as well as the one which embodied many of the nuances suggested by the other labels discussed in the last few paragraphs.

What the authors who used any one or combination of these labels were doing was to suggest that the complex teachings of Christianity could be reduced to an essential and manageable minimum, a set of signposts that even an uneducated person could decipher and follow. 'Why should you learn?' asks the catechist in one of Thomas Doolittle's catechisms: 'Because the knowledge will lead me at the end of my travelling to eternity', was the reply he wished to hear.[72] Some catechists felt that the first principles were also the hardest to teach, since they contained the deepest mysteries, and more than one author warned that catechizing was harder to perform successfully than preaching.[73] Opinions on the exact amount of knowledge that constituted the essential minimum seem to have varied, as the abundance of alternative catechisms we will examine in the next few chapters clearly shows. But what all catechists would probably have agreed was that 'the greatest stones

[69]   See e.g. the title-pages of the works in Appendix 1 by R. Cawdrey (1580); W. Horne (1585); H. Graie (1588); W. Perkins (1590); G. Webbe (1612); W. Gouge (1615); W. Hill (1616); E.B. (1617); H.S. (1628); I.G. (1630); H. Palmer (1640). The authors of at least two dozen catechetical works published prior to 1640 and over fifty thereafter refer to the content of their works as the 'principles' of religion.

[70]   Andrewes, *Works*, vi. 13–14; and cf. E. Wells, *The common Christian rightly and plainly instructed* (1707), 1.

[71]   See Appendix 1.

[72]   Doolittle, *Catechizing necessary*, 4, 15–16; and cf. C.P., *Two briefe treatises*, 5–6; the title-page of D. Featley, *The summe of saving knowledge* (1626); J. Boyes, 'The Christian's horne booke or ABC', BL Addit. MS 4928, fo. 2ᵛ.

[73]   T. Greaves, *A brief summe of Christian religion* (1656), title-page and sig. a2ʳ; and cf. anon., *The art of catechizing* (1691), sigs. A3ʳ⁻ᵛ; Cradock, *Discourse of due catechising*, 7; and next note.

are laid in the foundation': the principles learned first had to support a lifetime of edification.[74]

However, as most catechists, whether 'godly' or conformist, hastened to add at this point, they were not suggesting that mastery of the basics was sufficient to ensure salvation. It was a fine line that catechists had to tread between, on the one hand, saying that without a certain minimum knowledge a Christian could not expect to become a full member of the church or have a healthy soul, and on the other implying that once that minimum had been acquired the individual was ready to meet his maker. Knowledge, wrote John Ball, is an antecedent of faith, and faith is 'not only a knowledge or assent in the mind, but a godly affection in the will'.[75] Those who had begun to turn to God must have a care to increase in knowledge *and* practice, said Perkins. 'Conscience ... bindeth by virtue of known conclusions in the mind', he wrote on another occasion, and without information and understanding the conscience could not bind. Or as George Herbert put it:

The country parson values catechizing highly; for there [are] three points of his duty, the one, to infuse a competent knowledge of salvation in every one of his flock, the other to multiply and build up this knowledge to a spiritual temple; the third to inflame this knowledge, to press and direct it to practice, turning it to reformation of life by pithy and lively exhortations.[76]

For the authors whose works have been cited in the last few paragraphs, then, a beginner's catechism not only had to contain the quintessence of Christianity, but also could and should serve as a springboard to higher things: greater knowledge and understanding, and a stronger degree of commitment.

———

The second chief benefit of catechizing was held to be that it enabled those who had learnt the basics to understand more of the scriptures and of what they heard, saw, and did in church. This link was made explicit by Daniel Featley in his catechism of 1625 when he stated that the proper end of catechizing was not only to instruct the ignorant and confirm the learned in the principles of religion, but also to prepare both for the profitable use of the special means of their salvation, namely, hearing the

[74] Anon., *An exhortation to catechising* (1655), 8; and cf. J. Ussher, 'A brief declaration of the universality of the church', in *Workes* (1631), 34–5; Tillotson, *Six sermons*, 60, 171–2, 213–17, 224–6; and [Beveridge], *Church-catechism explained*, p. xii.

[75] Ball, *Treatise*, 16, 142; and cf. Wensley, *Form of sound words*, 3, 5; J. Lewis, *The church catechism explain'd* (1712), sig. A4ʳ, perhaps following [T. Ken], *An exposition on the church catechism* (1686), sig. A2ʳ. Cf. also Durbin, 'Education by Catechism', 2, and Strauss, *Luther's House of Learning*, 159; and anon., *The true beliefe in Christ* (1550), sig. A2ᵛ.

[76] W. Perkins, *A graine of musterd seede* (1621), 44–5; Breward, *Perkins*, 139–40; G. Herbert, *A priest to the temple*, ch. 21 (*The Works of George Herbert*, ed. F. E. Hutchinson (Oxford, 1967), 255–7), and cf. S. Fish, *The Living Temple: George Herbert and Catechizing* (Berkeley, 1978), 55–77 for an extended discussion of the 'building a temple' simile; cf. also Nicholson, *Plain exposition*, 25–6; Wake, *Principles*, 2; and see below, Ch. 5.

Word preached, receiving the sacraments, and public and private prayer.[77] The link between learning a catechism and understanding what was said in church was commonly made in the Elizabethan and early Stuart periods both by those who might be thought of as pillars of the established church and by those who might not.[78] Ministers who published catechisms in the unsettled atmosphere of the mid-1640s continued to express the hope that their works would enable their parishioners to understand more of what they heard in church; and similar statements emanated from conformist and nonconformist works under the later Stuarts.[79] One of the particular benefits of domestic catechizing (and one of the reasons not to separate it too sharply from catechizing in church) was held to be that it reinforced what the minister did in church on Sundays; the same point was also made negatively, that lack of catechizing at home undermined the value of church instruction and worship.[80]

Of the three special means mentioned by Featley, the first two—sermons and sacraments—attracted most attention from catechists, as we shall see. But a few catechetical authors did show particular concern that the liturgy should also be more fully understood, for example the Laudian cleric Edmund Reeve in 1635, a pious layman John Clutterbuck in 1694, and Edward Creffeild in 1713.[81] The relative lack of concern in other catechisms about comprehension of the liturgy was probably due to some authors' dislike of parts of the Book of Common Prayer, or the fact that integral parts of that liturgy, such as the Lord's Prayer, Apostles' Creed, Decalogue, and the sacraments of baptism and communion, were automatically discussed in most catechisms. It should be added, however, that catechists as a body did hold prayer, both public and private, in high esteem. Throughout the early modern period, a small but steady stream of catechisms were printed with prayers for everyday use, including a number of best-sellers: *The ABC with the catechisme*, *The primer and catechisme*, some versions of the Nowell and the Dering–More catechisms, both of which were first published in the 1570s, and Sherlock's catechism, first published in 1656. At least three dozen of the catechisms listed in Appendix 1 below had prayers for general use printed at the end.[82] Surprisingly few authors offered specific prayers for the catechist

[77] Featley, *Summe of saving knowledge*, 2–3.

[78] Babington, *Workes*, 206; J. Hall, *Works* (1625), 799–800; Reeve, *Communion booke catechisme*, sigs. C3ᵛ–4ʳ; Leech, *Plaine and profitable catechisme*, sig. A3ᵛ; R. Bernard, *The common catechisme* (1640), sig. A4ʳ; R[ichard] S[edgwick], *A short summe of the principall things* (1624), sig. A2ᵛ; J. Ball, *A short treatise contayning all the principall grounds* (1650), sigs. A5ʳ⁻ᵛ.

[79] J.H., *The principles of Christian religion* (1645), sigs. A2ʳ⁻ᵛ; [W. Bridges], *A catechisme for communicants* (1645), sig. A7ᵛ; J. Clutterbuck, *A plain and rational vindication* (1694), *passim*; E. Creffeild, *The great duty of catechising* (1713), 77–8; Cradock, *Discourse of due catechising*, 5, 7.

[80] S. Denison, *A compendious catechisme* (1621), sigs. A3ʳ⁻ᵛ; Lewis, *Church catechism explain'd*, sigs. A5ʳ⁻ᵛ; [Bridges], *Catechisme for communicants*, sig. A7ᵛ; J. Mayer, *A short catechisme* (1646), sig. A4ʳ; and see below, Ch. 4.

[81] See Appendix 1 under names indicated; cf. also [R. Nelson], *Mr Nelson's Companion … abridged* (1739).

[82] These works and those named in the text are all marked 'prayers at end' in Appendix 1.

or catechumen to use before and after catechizing, to ask for guidance or to offer thanks for it;[83] but some authors did turn the catechetical material they had just been expounding into the form of a prayer which could be used to round off a session.[84] A connection between learning a catechism and praying was thus frequently drawn in this more general sense, as well as in the more specific stress on the importance of prayer in the discussion on the Lord's Prayer incorporated into most catechisms.

For many catechists, however, one of the greatest potential benefits of catechizing was as a means of helping their flocks to understand their sermons. In the first decades after the Reformation, preaching was held in high esteem, and in many quarters was regarded as the chief means by which the Word, through the intervention of the Holy Spirit, was made profitable to fallen man.[85] The value of catechizing, said Thomas Sparke in 1580, was that if the simple and ignorant were taught the basics they could benefit much more from communion and spiritual exercises, but 'to their far greater profit', he added (revealing his own priorities), they would be able to understand the Word, both read and preached, and to apply it to their lives.[86] In 1581 William Wood cited the opinion of 'the godly learned father' Heinrich Bullinger to support his case that unless the people were properly catechized they would not understood the minister when he spoke of the covenant, the Commandments, the Law, grace, faith, prayer, and sacraments.[87] It was 'the ignorance of the heads of catechism' that prevented so many from understanding the points of religion preached to them, wrote Immanuel Bourne in 1622.[88] In 1624 James Ussher, in a sermon before the king (often quoted by both conformists and nonconformists in the later seventeenth century), praised James's care for catechizing in England and opined that 'the laying of the foundation skilfully, as it is a matter of greatest importance in the whole building, so it is the very master-piece of the wisest builders'. Upon such a foundation preachers could build; but no matter how many sermons they preached, warned Ussher, if ministers neglected to catechize they would frustrate the whole work of the ministry.[89] In the sixteenth and seventeenth centuries literally scores of catechists of

[83] [E. Paget], *Short questions and answeares* (1580), sigs. A7r–8r, C3r–4v; J. Harrison, *A scriptural exposition of the church-catechism* (1735), 230–5. In his popular collection of prayers for all occasions, *The crumms of comfort* (1622–), Michael Sparke included prayers for before and after catechizing.

[84] B.A., *A treatise of the way to life* (1580?), sigs. C1r–2r; E. Coote, *The English school-maister* (1596), 46–7; R. Bernard, *A large catechisme* (1602), 53–61; N[ich.] A[llsopp], *Certaine briefe questions and answeres* [c.1620], sigs. A6r–7r; W. Gouge, *A short catechisme* (1635), sigs. C2v–4r; T. Bray, *The church catechism* (1704), lessons 7–13; see also [T. Ken], *The church-catechism, with directions for prayer* (1685) (also published as part two of Ken's *Exposition on the church catechism*); and R. Harris, *Peter's enlargement upon the prayers of the church* (1624).

[85] B.A., *Treatise of the way to life*, sigs. A6r, B4v.

[86] [Sparke and Seddon], *A catechisme, or short kind of instruction*, 32.

[87] Wood, *Fourme of catechising*, sigs. *2r–v; and cf. E.B., *Catechisme or briefe instruction*, sigs. A5r–6r; and Scarbrough, *Summe of all ... catechismes*, sigs. A5v–6v, and p. 53.

[88] Bourne, *True Way*, 28–9, 34–5; and cf. id., *Light from Christ ... or, the rich jewel*, sigs. A6r–v, A7r, A8r, a4r, a8r.

[89] Ussher, 'Brief declaration', 34 (the quotation is from 2 Cor. 3: 10), and for later citations of this

widely differing standpoints drew a similar connection between catechetical knowledge and an ability to understand sermons.[90]

But increasingly the benefits of catechizing were held to be not just when the
Word was expounded by a minister, but also when passages of the Bible were heard
or studied by the laity themselves. The Word could be heard through the regular
Bible readings in church, grammar schools, and devout households, and it could be
studied by those fortunate enough to be literate and to have the use of a copy of the
Bible (the latter at least being much more common after the early Stuart boom in
Bible production).[91] Some catechists seemed to envisage independent Bible study
for their students on the model of early Christian practice.[92] But in other cases it was
clear that at least part of what the catechist had in mind was that catechumens
should read the Bible to confirm what they had already heard in the sermon or in the
catechism itself.[93] The many authors, drawn from all quarters of the church, who in
the printed version of their catechism provided references or gave full citations to
support their points, were trying to guide their students along routes which the
authors, with their greatly superior knowledge of scriptural topography, had chosen
for them.[94] That these scriptural citations were more than window-dressing is suggested by John Stockwood's remark in the preface to the third edition of his version
of the Dering–More catechism that he had reduced the number of proofs, since he
himself had noted (and others had told him) that there were too many for those of
weak capacity, and that rather than helping they were confusing the 'ignorant and
simple soul'.[95]

A small but significant number of authors went one step further and tried to devise
catechisms in which all the answers were in the actual words of the scripture. Despite
the best endeavours of Luther, Calvin, and the rest to reproduce in their catechisms

sermon, see below, p. 130, n. 163; see also R. Bernard, *The common catechisme* (1640), sigs. A4ʳ⁻ᵛ; R. Sherlock, *The principles of holy Christian religion* (1663), sigs. A3ʳ⁻ᵛ; anon., *No popery or a catechism* (1683), sigs.
A2ʳ⁻ᵛ; J. Gaynam, *The use and excellency of the church catechism* (1709), 6–9; G. Bull, *A companion for the
candidates of holy orders* (1714), 46. See also below, Ch. 3, on catechetical sermons.

[90]   The relationship between these will be discussed in my forthcoming volume on *Religious Instruction
in Early Modern England*.

[91]   This boom will be discussed in my volume on *Print and Protestantism in Early Modern England*.

[92]   Watts, *Entrie*, sig. A8ᵛ; Cawdrey, *Short and fruitefull treatise* (1604), sig. *viᵛ; and cf. anon., *Some
forms of catecheticall doctrines* (1647), sigs. A4ʳ⁻ᵛ; and Bernard, *Common catechisme*, sig. A4ʳ.

[93]   Explicitly in Ball, *Short treatise*, sig. A5ʳ; implicitly in the Westminster Shorter Catechism and other
forms.

[94]   As a random sample, the following works listed in Appendix 1 all include scriptural references:
Perkins, *Foundation*; J. Ball, *A short catechisme*; anon., *Main grounds of religion*; E. Rogers, *Chief grounds*;
H. Palmer, *An endeavour of making the principles*; O. Sedgwick, *A short catechisme*; Nicholson, *Plain exposition*; and Wake, *Principles of Christian religion*. As a general rule the larger format in which a catechism
was printed, the more likely there were to be references in the margin or text, or even full citations; cf. also
the growing number of references in the increasingly advanced lessons in Josias Nichols's *Order of household instruction*.

[95]   E. Dering, J. More, and J. Stockwood, *A short catechisme for householders. With prayers [and] the
prooves of the scripture* (1583), sigs. A2ᵛ–3ᵛ.

what they had read in the Bible, there was inevitably in the phrasing of their questions and answers an element of human invention; and in England, as in some Protestant countries abroad, a few people grew uneasy at the thought that catechumens might come to attach undue weight to man-made answers rather than the very words of the Bible.[96] By using nothing but scripture texts for answers, some authors hoped that growth in knowledge of the rudiments of the faith and of the scriptures would proceed hand in hand. Such an approach tended to encounter technical problems, for example rather stilted questions phrased in such a way as to lead to a scriptural reply, and a disjointed sequence of ideas as the author moved from one selected text to the next. But by the late seventeenth and early eighteenth centuries, there was a not insignificant number not only of 'scripture catechisms' but also a significant proportion of conventional catechisms with supporting scripture references printed in full as part of the text.[97]

––––––––––

Catechizing was also seen as a means of preparing catechumens for fuller participation in the life of the church in other ways, and in early modern England the first step towards this was confirmation. In the later Middle Ages confirmation had often been administered soon after birth, especially for royal or noble infants, but in the Protestant Church of England confirmation was deferred until childhood or adolescence.[98] The official short catechism of 1549 was 'to be learned of every child before he be brought to be confirmed by the bishop', and none were to be confirmed who could not say in their mother tongue the articles of the faith (the Apostles' Creed), the Lord's Prayer, and the Ten Commandments, and could also answer such questions in the short catechism as the bishop (or his appointee) should pose them. This last provision was later altered to a system whereby the incumbent of the parish was supposed to send a certificate to the bishop listing the names of those who from his own experience he knew could answer the questions in the catechism.[99]

Confirmation services were probably not very common in the early Elizabethan period, since there were practical problems in establishing the procedures required, and there were some doubts among returning exiles and others over the provenance and nature of the ceremony. But the doubts were never universal: in the 1570s the Calvinist Alexander Nowell defended the practice, and in the early seventeenth century, Richard Bernard, who had been a critic of a number of aspects of English

[96] For caution in England, see below, Ch. 3 nn. 320–1; A. Peel and L. Carlson (eds.), *Cartwrightiana* (1951), 158; and [P. Nye], *Beames of former light* (1660), 10, 12, 111; and in the United Provinces, J. Hales, *Golden Remains* (1688), 385.

[97] For later Stuart scriptural catechisms, see Ch. 2; also a high proportion of the later Stuart expositions discussed in Chs. 3–4 contained scripture references.

[98] Tudor, 'Religious Instruction', 395.

[99] S. L. Ollard, 'Confirmation in the Anglican Communion', in *Confirmation or the Laying On of Hands* (2 vols.; 1926), i. 81–2, 92–3, 111, 124–5, 128.

ceremonial, also defended confirmation in his widely used catechism.[100] Moreover, the administrative problems were gradually overcome, and by the turn of the sixteenth century there were a growing number of confirmations, and in the later Stuart and early Hanoverian period the system of confirmation was approaching its heyday.[101] This latter period was also characterized by growing efforts on the part of many episcopalian clergymen to help both children and adults understand the ceremony, which was described by one schoolmasterly advocate as conferring entry into 'a higher form in the school of Christ'.[102]

One of the main purposes of confirmation in the eyes of the church was to enable a child who had reached the age of discretion to confirm those promises which his or her godparents had made on his behalf at baptism: to renounce the devil and all his works, to believe all the articles of the Christian faith, and to keep God's commandments. But the ceremony was also a solemn recognition of church membership: confirmands renewed their vows 'in the presence of God and of this congregation', and the bishop prayed to God that, having vouchsafed to regenerate them and forgive them their sins, he would daily increase in them his manifold gifts of grace, that they might continue his for ever.[103] Flawed as the ceremony often was in execution, it seems to have struck a chord, and if most of those who participated were in fact able to say the Creed, they were at least in a position to make a bare profession of their faith, as the catechists who had taught them had intended.[104]

The other main purpose of confirmation, also very evident in the minds of many catechists using the official catechism or their own versions, was to prepare catechumens for admission to the Lord's Supper. The official line in the first decades after the Reformation was that no one should be admitted to holy communion until he or she had been confirmed, or, if they were already adults, could say the Creed and knew

---

[100] Ollard, 'Confirmation', 92, 103; Bernard, *Common catechisme*, sig. A4ᵛ; W. Kaye, *The reformed protestant's catechism* (1658), 4. In general, see R. L. DeMolen, 'Childhood and the Sacraments in the Sixteenth Century', *Archiv für Reformationgeschichte*, 66 (1975), 49–70. For English presbyterian practice in the later seventeenth century, see below, pp. 167–9.

[101] Ollard, 'Confirmation', 86–200; Fincham, *Prelate as Pastor*, 123–9; S. J. Wright, 'Catechism, Confirmation and Communion: The Role of the Young in the Post-Reformation Church', in Wright (ed.), *Parish, Church and People: Local Studies in Lay Religion 1350–1750* (London, 1988), 209–16.

[102] The phrase by B. Camfield, in *Of episcopal confirmation in two discourses* (1682), is cited in Ollard, 'Confirmation', 164. See also the sections on confirmation at the end of the exposition of the Prayer Book catechism by E. Boughen (1668), N. Blithe (1674), E. Wetenhall (1678), W. Wake (1700), T. Wilson (1707), and J. Lewis (later editions); see also Ollard, 'Confirmation', 154–68, 178–95; [H. Colman], *An essay by way of catechism* (1709, 1716); anon., *Short instructions for them that are preparing for confirmation* (1736); and the following commentaries on the Book of Common Prayer: A. Sparrow, *A rationale upon the Book of Common Prayer* (1657), 303–16; Comber, *Companion*, 216–28; and Clutterbuck, *Plain and rational vindication*, 62–5.

[103] Brightman, *English Rite*, ii. 793–5.

[104] C. Barksdale, *Memorials of worthy persons: two decades* (1661), i. 97–8; Ollard, 'Confirmation', 118–22, 167, 175–6, 188–9, 198–201; and cf. J. Obelkevich, *Religion and Rural Society: South Lindsey 1825–1875* (Oxford, 1976), 131–5.

the Lord's Prayer and Decalogue in English.[105] After the addition of a section on the sacraments to the official shorter catechism in 1604, adolescents who had been confirmed had in theory not only renewed their baptismal vows, but also learnt the last answer of that catechism, which stated that before communicating they had 'to examine themselves, whether they repent them truly of their former sins, steadfastly purposing to lead a new life; have a lively faith in God's mercy through Christ, with a thankful remembrance of his death; and be in charity with all men'.[106] Some children mastered the catechism so quickly that they were eligible for confirmation long before they were of an age which was considered suitable for taking communion. As a result, some senior churchmen recommended that children should not be confirmed until they were 12 or 13 and not admitted to communion until they were two or three years older still; in practice, a great deal probably depended on the individual child and the local minister.[107] A supplementary solution that was broached as early as the reign of Edward, and adopted increasingly both by conformist churchmen and others thereafter,[108] was to have a sequence of two or more catechisms ready for different age-groups, so that the brighter child would always have a new form to learn, regardless of whether he or she was old enough to be confirmed or admitted to communion in the near future, and the forgetful adolescent or one who had not fully understood from the first catechism how to examine himself before communion, could have a refresher course on this very point. The titles of some of these catechisms make the point: *An helpe for young people, preparing them for the worthy receiving of the Lords Supper*; *The pastors passport to the younger sort of Christians, from the font to the communion table*; *A short catechisme to prepare young ignorant people for the sacrament*; and *The communicant's instructor ... recommended to the ... younger and more ignorant sort.*[109]

Indeed, if we turn our attention for a moment from the preparation of young people for the Lord's Supper to that of adults, we find that a large number of catechists had strong views on this as well. 'It is impossible for any man, without the knowledge

---

[105] See below, p. 94 n. 2.   [106] Brightman, *English Rite*, ii. 791.

[107] See Ch. 3 for examples of early mastery of the catechism; on ages for confirmation and communion, see Ollard, 'Confirmation', 52–4, 62–3, 87, 108–9, 118, 134, 145, 176, 185, 189; Wright, 'Catechism', 213–17.

[108] For Cranmer's desire for two levels of catechism and the three levels of Nowell catechism, see above, p. 20 and below, pp. 42, 142–3, 189–90.

[109] These are respectively by William Lyford in 1640, 'Philo Probaton' (or B.S. who signed the epistle) in 1642, 'anon.' in 1657 (ascribed to John Ball by Wing), and George Day in 1692 and 1700: see Appendix 1 for further details. See also e.g. G. Wither, *Certaine necessarie instructions meet to be taught the younger sorte before they come to be partakers of the holy Communion* (1579); S. Denison, *A compendious catechisme ... for children and servants to learne, before they go to the Holy Communion* (1621); W. Gouge, *A short catechisme* (1635) sigs. C1ʳ–2ᵛ (the abstract of his larger catechism, intended for the 'younger and ignoranter sort'); G. Dochant, *A new catechism, short and plain, and very necessary to be learned of the younger sort, before they come to be partakers of the Holy Communion* (1654); and L. Addison, *The Christian's manual* (six editions between 1691 and 1719).

of the first and necessary principles of religion, to make due examination of himself'
before the Lord's Supper (wrote Thomas Sparke in his preface to a translation of the
Heidelberg Catechism published in 1588), and it was the minister's duty to prepare
his people for the sacrament. His own practice, to judge from an earlier publication,
was to use a thirty-six page catechism of his own devising in public, and then in private to put to would-be communicants a short four-page form of 'Questions to be
proposed even to the simplest, and thus to be answered of them'.[110] Indeed, it is probably true that the single most important impulse for drafting catechisms for *adults* to
learn was a concern to ensure that they did not run the risk of being unworthy
receivers, or a fear that they would not receive the full benefits of the sacrament,
either through ignorance or through a failure to examine their consciences before
communicating.[111]

Given that in this instance they were dealing with adults, many of the parish clergy
would probably have preferred their charges to have displayed a higher level of
knowledge and to have been capable of making a fuller or more personal statement of
faith than that envisaged by the authorities. A few stated in the preface that they were
issuing their catechisms to counter the ignorance they had encountered among their
parishioners, or that until the answers were learned no one could expect admission to
communion (though the fact that such works were clearly designed for use by liter-
ates and were sometimes quite long tells us how high such clergy were aiming).[112] In
the early 1640s, William Lyford envisaged three years of catechizing for those of his
'people' who had not yet convinced him (and those of the congregation who had
already been admitted to communion) of their readiness for the sacrament; at the end
of that period, he hoped, even those of meanest capacity would be able to make a profession of their faith and undertake the covenant of faith and obedience which all had
entered at baptism.[113] But among the hundreds of catechists whose works survive,
relatively few seem to have set their sights so high, or if they did their forms of catechizing or of examination of potential communicants are not extant.[114] It would seem

---

[110] [Sparke and Seddon], *A catechisme, or short kind of instruction*, 16–17, and T. Sparke, *A short treatise*
(1580), sigs. E2ʳ⁻ᵛ; and cf. J. Frewen, *Certain choise grounds* (1621), title-page; and Crofton, *Catechizing
Gods ordinance*, 44–5, and cf. 42–3; and see below, n. 117.

[111] This comment is based on analysis of all the catechisms in Appendix 1, not just those which devoted
a large proportion of text to preparation for communion or were avowedly pre-communion, and which are
marked as such in Appendix 1. See also below, Ch. 12.

[112] R. Gawton, *A short instruction* (1612), sigs. A2ʳ⁻ᵛ; J. Baker, *A short preparation* (1645), sigs. A2ʳ⁻ᵛ,
A4ʳ–5ʳ, and *passim*; and cf. J. Parker, *A true patterne of pietie* (1599), 50–3; T. Gataker, *The Christian mans
care* (1624), sig. I2ᵛ; Crompton, *Explication*, 302–4, 342–69; anon., *An instruction for all those that intend to
goe to the sacrament of the Lords Supper* (1634) (a broadsheet); J. Owen, *The principles of the doctrine of Christ*
(1645), 7; S. Austin, *A practical catechisme* (1647), 8–10; W. Cotton, *A new catechisme* (1648), 9–10; T.
Gouge, *The principles of Christian religion* (1679), 172.

[113] W. Lyford, *Principles of faith* (1642), sigs. A2ᵛ–3ʳ.

[114] It is interesting to note, for example, that in the preface to his 1645 catechism, John Owen wrote that
he had said little of the sacraments in it because 'I have already been so frequent in examinations about
them': *Principles of the doctrine*, sig. A3ᵛ.

from some authors' comments that if a communicant showed signs of faith, no matter how weak, together with a desire for communion, an intention to amend, and a modicum of knowledge, this was enough; complete assurance of salvation was not necessary.[115] Other authors perhaps feared that if they fulminated too much against unworthy receivers they would not just put off a few truly unworthy individuals, but also deter some genuinely worthy individuals—'simple men … able to yield small reason of their faith' or unsure if their faith was sufficient—from attending as often as they should; the latter tended to be given the benefit of the doubt.[116] For many catechumens the minimum knowledge required before admission to communion was not great: the impulse behind a work like the anonymous *Breefe catechisme so necessarie and easie to be learned even of the symple sort, that whosoever can not or will not attaine to the same, is not be counted a good Christian, much less to be admitted to the Supper of the Lorde* (1576) was shared by other authors such as Samuel Hieron, whose 'Brief direction for the comers to the Lord's table' consisted of just thirteen questions and answers, and J.F., who in 1645 wrote that anyone who could not learn the sixteen answers in his catechism should be ashamed to participate in the sacrament.[117]

It is also revealing that when in the mid-1640s the strongest critics of the established church had abolished confirmation and tried to find an alternative yardstick for admission to communion, they came out with one very similar to the old. The ordinance of 20 October 1645 'concerning suspension from the sacrament of the Lord's Supper' laid down not a personal profession of faith, but merely a minimum amount of knowledge, much of it the same as that contained in the Prayer Book catechism of 1549, and a competent level of understanding of what those heads contained. In some ways it demanded less than the episcopalian church had done, in that although a communicant had to know that 'a godly life is consciionably ordered according to the word of God', he did not have to prove that he could repeat the Ten Commandments verbatim. It also provided less help, stating merely that 'every one is to examine himself' before communion but not explaining how to perform that examination or on what basis.[118] To be fair, it should be added that several authors stepped into the breach and devised short catechisms based on this ordinance,[119] and even after the Westminster Larger and Shorter Catechisms had been published,

---

[115] e.g. A. Hildersham, 'The doctrine of communicating worthily', in W. Bradshaw, *A direction for the weaker sort* (1634), 123–7; Jones, *Exposition*, sig. I8ᵛ; question and answer no. 172 of the Westminster Larger Catechism; and W. Lyford, *Lyford's legacie* (1656), 17, 31 (though in general Lyford demanded much from communicants); and see next note.

[116] A. Dent, *A pastime for parents* (1629), sigs. G8ʳ⁻ᵛ; and see Frewen, *Certain choise grounds*, 382–3; and G. Day, *A persuasive to full communion* (1698), *passim*.

[117] See Appendix 1, s.v. *Breefe catechisme*; S. Hieron, *The workes* [1620?], [501–2]; and J.F., *A compendious chatechisme* (1645), sig. A3ʳ; and cf. J. Downe, 'Instructions for preparation', in *A treatise* (Oxford, 1635), 313–15.

[118] *Acts and Ordinances of the Interregnum*, ed. C. H. Firth and R. S. Rait (2 vols.; 1911), i. 789–91.

[119] For a list of these, see below, pp. 79–80.

forms based on the 1645 ordinance continued to appear until 1660 as a means of ensuring that candidates for communion had the required minimum of knowledge.[120]

What young and old were also expected to be able to do before communicating was to examine their consciences. In fact, it was considered to be a mark of the maturity needed by a communicant to be able to do this; children were often grouped with idiots, madmen, and fools as being incapable of rational analysis.[121] But once they had reached the years of discretion they were, like their elders, deemed to be able to perform the introspective analysis required. Once again, the link with catechizing is strong. None can receive, said William Jones in 1633, until they can examine themselves, and they cannot do that until they have learnt the grounds of the Christian religion in a catechism.[122] What a high proportion of catechists that touched on the sacraments also did was to provide a checklist of what the worthy communicant should expect to find. One did this in the form of a 'card for communicants to look upon before they presume to come to the Lord's Table'; others did it in a broadsheet to be stuck on the wall.[123] Equally some catechists issued quite long lists of *desiderata*, but the great majority indicated just four or five (in addition to the minimum knowledge mentioned in previous paragraphs): a strong desire to partake of the sacrament; faith; repentance (or hatred of sin) and an intention to lead a new life; love for one's brethren (or reconciliation, or charity); and thankfulness.[124] A number of authors, especially those who were writing a catechetical form specifically for use before communion, also offered communicants a step-by-step guide to what to think, do, and say in the days and hours before, during, and after the service, including prayers to help the individual put himself in the right frame of mind beforehand and to express his thanks to God afterwards.[125] Few aspects of the worthy communicant's needs were neglected by the conscientious catechist.

The fourth benefit that was thought to derive from catechizing was that it enabled the individual to tell false doctrine from true, and thus to avoid error. When authors

[120] See below, pp. 79–80.
[121] G. Whiting, *Short questions and answeres* (1629), 8; J. Balmford, *A short catechisme* (1597), 8; Dent, *Pastime for parents* (1612), sig. G7^r.
[122] Jones, *Exposition*, sig. A2^r.
[123] J. Parker, *A true patterne of pietie* (1599), 50–3; anon., *An instruction for all* (1634); anon., *A shorte catechisme to prepare young ignorant people* (1657); and *Rules for self-examination* (1685).
[124] As previous notes.
[125] e.g. M[ordechai] A[ldem], *A short, plaine and profitable catechisme* (1592), 63–73; and R. Jenison, *Directions for the worthy receiving of the Lords supper* (1624); [W. Fleetwood], *The reasonable communicant* (1704); and T. Green, *The sacrament of the lord's supper* (1744), *passim*. I hope to discuss those pre-communion handbooks written in continuous prose rather than question and answer in my forthcoming study of *Print and Protestantism in Early Modern England*.

were talking about catechizing *in theory*—in exhortations to catechize or be catechized, or in the prefaces of their catechisms—they often stressed the value of the insights gained in helping catechumens to distinguish between truth and error. In his preface to the English translation of Alexander Nowell's catechism, Thomas Norton suggested that there was no better way to advance true religion and root out errors than catechizing; one of the aims listed by E.B. in the preface of his catechism in 1617 was to keep the people safe against such seducers as the Jesuits and seminarists; and Alexander Grosse's *Fiery pillar*, first published in 1641, was also said on the title-page to be for the 'preservation of God's people from the spreading evils and pernicious enchantments of papism', though by then a rather wider definition of popery was current in the circles in which he moved.[126] However, when it came to the practice of composing the questions and answers of the main part of their texts, most authors took great pains to ensure that their criticism of erroneous views was stated implicitly rather than explicitly. Thus the four catechisms most commonly used in early modern England, either in their original form or in a modified version—the Prayer Book catechism, Calvin's catechism, Nowell's original catechism, and the Westminster Shorter Catechism—contained either nothing or very little in the way of overt criticism of Catholicism or radical Protestantism.[127] Instead, catechists encouraged catechumens to see the 'truth' by ensuring that all catechetical teaching was soundly based on or consonant with the scriptures, and that catechetical material such as the Creed, Decalogue, Lord's Prayer, and doctrine of the sacraments was presented to them in a strongly Protestant light. As a result, it was hoped, catechumens would be able to distinguish between, on the one hand, middle-of-the-road Protestantism and, on the other, Catholic or sectarian error, such as papal supremacy, veneration of saints, transubstantiation, and believers' baptism. For example, rather than attack Catholic teaching explicitly on the seven sacraments or the use of saints as intercessors, authors would stress that there were only two sacraments authorized in scripture, and that we are also told there to pray to God alone and that the only acceptable intermediary was Christ. As we shall see in Part II of this study, most English authors, like Luther and Calvin before them, appear to have taken a self-denying ordinance when it came to catechetical instruction: the armoury of polemical weapons that the same author might be prepared to use in a sermon or a treatise he would generally refrain from using in a catechism, at least before the 1640s. If we continue with the preface by Norton cited at the start of this paragraph, we find him saying that 'I

---

[126] A. Nowell, *A catechisme, or first instruction*, ed. G. E. Corrie (Parker Society, Cambridge, 1853), 109; E.B., *Catechisme*, sig. A4ʳ; A. Grosse, *A fiery pillar of heavenly truth* (1644), title-page; and cf. Watts, *Entrie*, title-page; Ball, *Short treatise*, sig. A3ʳ; J. Bristow, *An exposition of the Creede* (1627), sig. A2ᵛ; and T. Hodges, *A scripture-catechism* (1658), 233–80.

[127] These four works form part of the sample of catechisms the content of which is discussed in Part II of this study; for works derived from these four, see the next three chapters.

have long thought it a much better way towards removing of heresies and superstitions (whereof Rome hath brought us and left us plenty) to deal first with plain setting out of truth as not in controversy, without dealing at the beginning with the strife of confutation'.[128]

There were always a few authors who, especially in a time of crisis, were prepared to make explicit the difference between Protestant truth and popish error by means of a question-and-answer form. The text of Beza's *Booke of Christian questions and answers* (1572) contained some strongly anti-Catholic material, and a similarly entitled work of 1578 by an unidentified author consisted almost entirely of denunciations of a wide range of Catholic teaching; a number of works described as 'catechisms' were published to help the laity reject the overtures of Rome, detect and condemn idolatry, and denounce the mass and prayers to the Virgin or saints.[129] But such works were not typical of the genre as a whole, in that they either had a much higher proportion of controversial material than usual, or reverted to the format of a disputatious dialogue rather than a typical catechism.

It is also true that from the 1640s, many catechists evinced a growing concern that their charges should also be able to tell true Protestant doctrine from false. Before that decade, there had been occasional barbed comments by 'godly' authors, sometimes in the text but more usually in the preface, about the recalcitrance or lacklustre formality of many laymen, the poor example set by some clergy, and the excesses of the sectaries; and there were a few complaints in works by conformable clergy about the posturings of the precisians.[130] But these had been rare, at least in works of English origin, due either to censorship, or a feeling that, given their function as a means of teaching the ignorant, catechisms were not the place in which to engage in controversies against fellow-Protestants. One of the first catechisms to be published in England to offer a serious warning against the doctrines of fellow-Protestants was that of Hugh Peters, in 1641 (it was originally published abroad in 1629). In *Milke for babes, and meat for men*, he warned against both Romish and Pelagian adversaries, and a few pages later bracketed the views of the Pelagians with those of the hated 'Arminians'. In 1645 Lewis Hughes published a frontal attack on the theology of the Prayer Book catechism, though Hughes's work must be classed as a tract rather than an alternative catechism.[131] In succeeding years some catechists

---

[128] Nowell, *Catechisme*, 110.

[129] See Appendix 1, s.v. Beza; *Book*; *Protestant catechisme* (1673 and 1681); *No popery*; Rawlet, *Dialogue*; and J. Williams, *Catechisme truly representing*; cf. also Lamplugh, *Pastoral letter*, 1–3; and T. Jekyll, *A brief and plain exposition* (1690), sig. A6[r].

[130] G[eorge] W[ebbe], *A briefe exposition of the principles* (1612), sig. A2[v]; T. Ratcliffe, *A short summe of the whole catechisme* (1620), sig. A2[v]; A4[r]; anon., 'Of catechisinge', fos. 29[r], 30[r]; Bourne, *A light from Christ ... or, the rich jewel*, sigs. A6[r]–7[r], and a6[r]; James Martin's preface to W. Whitaker, *A short summe* (1630), sig. A3[r]; Reeve, *Communion booke catechisme*, sigs. C2[r–v], pp. 92–5, 206–7.

[131] H. Peters, *Milke for Babes* (1641), 21–31; L. Hughes, *The errors of the common catechisme* (1645).

began to criticize opponents more openly, including growing numbers of presbyterians nervous of the impact on their flocks of the of 'fearful inundation of pestilent heresies' emanating from the sects.[132] Then, after the re-establishment of the old church in the early 1660s, episcopalians began to warn their catechumens against the false doctrines of the nonconformists, while presbyterians tried to arm their supporters against the siren call of the sects, and Baptists and Quakers replied in kind or attacked each other.[133] Those of a more conservative disposition tended to blame a lack of catechizing for the 'large spreading of heresies in the late licentious times', and then from the 1670s to warn against new enemies: profanity, libertinism, infidelity, atheism, and deism.[134] By the early eighteenth century, a few catechisms had also been written (though perhaps fewer than might have been expected from the scale of polemical activity on the subject) to stress the rationality of revealed religion and to persuade deists of the errors of their ways.[135] It must be stressed again, however, that the great majority of authors of catechisms, even at the end of our period, either did not include much potentially divisive material, or if they did presented it in an orthodox but uncontroversial manner. Like Norton, they still saw their prime role as 'setting out [the] truth not in controversy' rather than beginning with 'the strife of confutation'.

A fifth benefit to be derived from catechizing, according to many authors, was that it taught the catechumen how to lead a Christian life. The full title of one of the earliest English question-and-answer forms, Edmond Allen's in 1548, was *A catechisme, that is to saie a familiar introduction and training of the simple in the commaundements of God*. We have already touched upon the Protestants' insistence that all catechumens should be able to repeat the Ten Commandments, which in their ethics played the pivotal role that the seven deadly sins had played in Catholic moral teaching until the fifteenth century.[136] We have also encountered it in the confirmation service, with its restatement of the baptismal vow to reject sin and lead a new

---

[132] Anon., *An exhortation to catechizing* (1655), 14; Hodges, *A scripture-catechism*, 208–32.

[133] Nicholson, *Plain exposition*, pp. vii–viii, 61–3; Sherlock, *Principles*, 51–61, 165–74; Lamplugh, *Pastoral letter*, 5–6; W. Assheton, *A short exposition* (1694), *passim*; R. Baxter, *The Quakers catechism* (1651), *passim*; T. Doolittle, *A plain method of catechizing* (1698), sig. A5ʳ; J. Tombes, *A short catechism about baptism* (1659); R. Barclay, *A catechism and confession of faith* (1673); T. Grantham, *St Paul's catechism* (1687). See also below, pp. 83–6.

[134] Towerson, *Explication*, sig. b2ʳ; Sherlock, *Principles*, sig. A2ʳ; Lamplugh, *Pastoral letter*, 1–2, 7; Harris, *Scripture-knowledge promot'd*, 13; J. Wright, *The most material difficulties* (1713), p. iv; T. Bishop, *A plain and practical exposition* (1736), 5. For the general situation, see J. Spurr, *The Restoration Church of England, 1646–1689* (New Haven/London, 1991), *passim*.

[135] e.g. J. Mears, *A catechism* (1731); anon., *A catechism: or an instruction* (1733); 'Philander', *A catechism for the use of deists* (1739). For a recent survey of the debate between the church and its critics, see J. A. I. Champion, *The Pillars of Priestcraft Shaken* (Cambridge, 1992).

[136] Bossy, *Christianity in the West*, 38, 116; Durbin, 'Education by Catechism', 72–3.

life. But English catechists took the matter a stage further by stressing the particular value of catechizing in training the young to walk in the paths of righteousness. Clergymen as varied as Thomas Cranmer, Richard Rogers, Archbishop
Whitgift, Richard Baxter, and Jeremy Taylor, were agreed on this.[137] Thus in the
preface to the *Catechismus* of 1548, Cranmer told the young Edward VI that as the
young were nourished by early instruction, so they would grow up in godly knowledge and virtue. By this 'little treatise' (in fact, a series of sermons for young people) youth would learn to know God, to learn their duty to God, the king and all his
ministers, their parents and others.[138] The rules governing children's behaviour
were derived from the Decalogue in particular and were the same as those for
adults, with certain adjustments for different responsibilities such as work, marriage, and parenthood. Parents could be reminded of these directly or indirectly: in
1548 Cranmer hoped that many of the 'older sort' who had been brought up in
ignorance would learn their duty through being present while their children listened to the *Catechismus*.[139] Alternatively, sections on the Decalogue could be and
were inserted into many of the catechisms aimed at older catechumens or at scholars who were likely to become teachers or clergy. Most English authors who had
the time and space discussed each Commandment in turn, often in both a negative
and a positive sense of sins prohibited and duties commanded; and they might do
so in very general, theoretical terms (all theft is wrong) or in quite specific terms
(how far driving a hard bargain in business might constitute a breach of the eighth
commandment).[140]

English catechists were not alone in the stress they placed on catechizing as a guide
to godly living. In his shorter catechism, Luther may have had only a brief section on
the Decalogue at the start, but he added a section on the duties owed by various sections of society at the end. Calvin's catechism and the Heidelberg Catechism also
devoted generous space to the treatment of the duties implicit in the Decalogue.[141]
The balance between doctrinal and ethical content may have altered since the days

---

[137] R. Rogers, *The house-holders helpe* (1615), sigs. A2ʳ–8ʳ; J. Whitgift, *The Works*, ed. J. Ayre (3 vols.;
Parker Society; Cambridge, 1851–3), iii. 610–11; R. Baxter, *The catechizing of families* (1683), esp. preface
and ch. 1; J. Taylor, *The Whole Works*, ed. R. Heber (15 vols.; 1822), xi. 293; cf. also N. Taylor, *A practical and short exposition* (1684), sig. [A3ʳ] (citing Hammond's *Practical catechisme*), and the various attempts
to turn *The whole duty of man* into question and answer, listed in Appendix 1, s.v. [R.E.]; *Art*; and
[Nelson].

[138] [Cranmer], *Catechismus*, sigs. iiiᵛ–ivᵛ, and cf. Fiʳ–Gviʳ.

[139] Ibid. sig. viʳ; and see below, Ch. 3.

[140] e.g. T[hos.] C[artwright], *A treatise of Christian religion* (1616), 148–52; W. Dyke, *A treasure of
knowledge* (1620), 49–50; J. Mayer, *The English catechisme* (1621), 372–93; Attersoll, *Principles of Christian
religion* (1635), sigs. B1ᵛ–2ʳ; R[ichard] S[edgwick], *A short summe* (1624), 108–20; M[artin] N[icholes], *A
catechisme* (1631), 37–41; Jones, *Exposition*, sigs. F7ᵛ–8ʳ; T. Vincent, *An explicatory catechism* (1673),
252–68; anon., *Rules for self-examination* (1685) (broadsheet). See also Durbin, 'Education by Catechism',
216–17.

[141] See Ch. 10 below.

when the late medieval confessor had been particularly anxious for his flock to be able to identify their sins, but we are looking at a shift in content between the late fifteenth and sixteenth centuries rather than a transformation.[142] Similarly, although English catechists may have evinced greater concern than their Continental counterparts at some sins, such as the dangers of idolatry perhaps,[143] their vision of a Christian society shared a good deal with that of their Catholic counterparts and their fellow-Protestants abroad, because of a common scriptural basis, and also because of the common impact of humanism on their own education and their attitudes towards the education of others.[144] A good catechism was a guide to piety as well as knowledge and understanding.

What we have seen in this chapter is the way in which the idea of a new form of basic instruction, which contemporaries thought was a revival of an old one, caught on. The question-and-answer catechism was a most timely addition to the Protestant armoury of education and exhortation at a point when many older forms of instruction, such as wall-paintings, carvings, elaborate priestly gestures and vestments, confession, and religious drama, were all being cast aside as unscriptural or denounced as idolatrous. But the catechism was seen as being much more than a simple method of imparting and acquiring information, important as that was as a starting-point for the laity. Through the firm grasp of the basic principles of the faith which the catechumen (in theory) obtained from being catechized, he or she would be better able to understand the teaching of the Bible, the arguments of the preacher, the significance of the sacraments, and the role of the individual in church life. Catechizing would arm the laity against error and show them the paths in which they should walk to please God. In this light it is not surprising that the idea caught on and spread so quickly, in England as in Protestant countries aborad, and subsequently in many Catholic ones as well, and that so many new forms were produced.[145]

This chapter has tried to take a cross-section through the theory of catechizing over two centuries, but we have already seen that catechizing did not remain static. If catechists saw a gap, whether it was for a question-and-answer form for young people to learn before or after confirmation, for adults to use before communion, or to warn against dangerous new ideas, they would try to plug it. This element of flexibility in responding to catechetical need is another reason for the increasing number of catechisms produced in early modern England. There is another reason for this increase, though we have not yet encountered it properly: the need to improve

---

[142] See above, pp. 15, 17; and Durbin, 'Education by Catechism', ch. 1.
[143] Ibid. 123; Aston, *England's Iconoclasts*, ch. 7.
[144] On this, see the start of Chs. 4 and 5 below.
[145] See the recent studies cited above, pp. 2–3 nn. 7–13; many new Catholic catechisms were still declaratory rather than interrogatory, e.g. that of the Council of Trent.

catechetical technique. Much hope was invested in catechizing, and while disappointment at initially limited results may in some cases have led to disillusion and reliance on other methods of instruction, in many cases it led to a reappraisal of existing methods and yet more catechisms and expositions being produced as catechists sought to produce just the right form for their particular needs. It is to the dynamics of change in catechizing as well as the attempt to turn theory into practice that we turn in the next four chapters.

2

The Emergence of the English Catechetical Tradition

In 1589 a Somerset minister, Thomas Watts, ended his *Entrie to Christianitie* with a carefully chosen and graded list of works 'extant in our English tongue' suitable for use by English catechists. The list began with the Prayer Book catechism, then listed eight other forms by English authors before finishing with general expositions like Bullinger's *Decades*, the *Commonplaces* of Musculus and Peter Martyr, Calvin's *Institutes*, and Jewel's defence of his *Apology*—the origin of most of these larger works reminds us that England may have started to produce catechists but had not yet produced many systematic theologians.[1] When Immanuel Bourne published his larger catechism in 1646, he prefaced it with an account of catechizing through the ages in which 'Our English, Mr Nowell, Mr Perkins, Mr Egerton ... Mr Baal [*recte* Ball] ... and many other laborious workmen in the Lord's vineyard' were proudly paraded in the same company as a number of famous teachers of the early Church and the Continental Reformation.[2] In the reign of Charles II, the anonymous author of *Eniautos: or a course of catechizing* was able to recommend by name over three dozen English writers, mostly authors of printed catechisms which he had found useful and hoped other catechists would too; similarly, when John Lewis was asked to write a catechism for use in Charity Schools, he tells us in his autobiography that he looked through the thirty expositions of the Prayer Book catechism which he had by him before venturing to compose his own.[3] Many others prefaced their works with modest disclaimers as to the simplicity, meagre value, or lack of originality of their own composition compared to that of the 'many excellent and profitable catechisms set forth' or 'the almost infinite number of models' from which catechists could already choose.[4] In 1660 Philip Nye expressed the belief that there were then 'no less than five hundred several catechisms extant', a figure which was echoed the same year by Richard Baxter (himself a very conscientious catechist and composer of instructional works as well as a voracious reader of other men's writings), and again in 1693 by an

---

[1] T. Watts, *The entrie to Christianitie* (1589), sig. B4ᵛ; for more details of the works cited, see below, pp. 266–7.

[2] I. Bourne, *A light from Christ ... or, the rich jewel* (1646), sigs. A8ᵛ–a2ʳ, and p. 3.

[3] Anon., *Eniautos: or a course of catechizing* (1674), sigs. B10ʳ–11ᵛ.

[4] J. Leech, *A plain and profitable catechisme* (1605), sig. A2ʳ; J. Syme, *The sweet milke of Christian doctrine* (1617), sig. A3ᵛ.

anonymous divine making an *Earnest call* for parents to catechize.[5] This estimate might be dismissed as hyperbole but for the fact that it can be confirmed today, as we shall see shortly. Nor should this come as a surprise, since we now know that there were possibly thousands rather than just hundreds of different catechisms circulating in sixteenth-century Germany, and scores of different ones in other parts of Europe, including some Catholic states.[6] In this chapter we will look first at the grand totals of catechisms produced for use in early modern England, and then try to show the different phases through which catechizing passed and the different types of catechism that emerged at different stages.

The main obstacles to reaching an exact figure for the number of catechisms in use during the early modern period are only in part problems of definition. In the first place, there is the problem of uneven survival. It seems likely that many forms which existed only in manuscript have disappeared without trace. There are cases where manuscript forms or notes are known to have passed from hand to hand for some time before they were printed, for example those of Lancelot Andrewes and Thomas Cartwright; there are also many references to manuscript catechisms being copied by hand for distribution in a parish, though these are very hard to find today.[7] A copy of 'Mr Morehouse catechisme' survives in the commonplace book of a layman living in County Durham in the late Elizabethan period, and a copy of 'Mr Boyes catechism wherein he catechized the congregation at Halifax', probably in the early seventeenth century, is extant due (in part) to the interest shown by an eighteenth-century antiquary. Similarly a 'scripture catechism' of unknown origin has survived mainly because it was written (in a seventeenth-century hand) onto the blank leaves of a copy of the 1626 edition of the Heidelberg Catechism.[8] The chance survival in a Cambridge college library of a substantial manuscript volume, perhaps dating from the late 1620s and containing a number of catechisms and catechetical expositions of the early Stuart period, most of which are otherwise unknown, serves to indicate how many forms may have been lost as well as preserved.[9] There are also occasional examples of authors claiming that they intended to publish a catechism, such as John Thaxter who asked his patron to obtain some printed copies of his two

[5] [P. Nye], *Beames of former light* (1660), 85; R. Baxter, *Universal concord* (1660), sig. A3ᵛ; anon., *An earnest call to family-catechising* (1693), p. vii.

[6] Strauss, *Luther's House of Learning*, 164; and see works cited in the Introduction above, pp. 2–3, and J. Delumeau, *Catholicism between Luther and Voltaire* (1977), 200.

[7] See above, p. 1 n. 1; A. Peel and L. H. Carlson (eds.), *Cartwrightiana* (1951), 158–9; and see W. Gouge, *A short catechisme* (1621), sig. A3ʳ; G[eorge] W[ebbe], *A brief exposition of the principles* (1612), sig. A3ʳ; and J[ohn] S[talham], *A catechisme for children* (1644), sig. A2ʳ.

[8] BL, Egerton MS 2877, fo. 83 (I am most grateful to Dr Jane Freeman for this reference); BL Addit. MS 4928, fos. 2ᵛ–34ᵛ; BL, Huth 81 (1); and cf. Cambridge University Library, Syn. 7.68.91¹, for another handwritten text (with thanks to Helen Weinstein for the reference).

[9] Emmanuel College Cambridge Library MS III. 1. 13⁸; and for a longer, manuscript version of the often-printed *Exposition* by William Nicholson, see Magdalen College, Oxford, Archives MS 546.

short catechisms for use in his parish; there is now no trace of the originals (or any copies).[10]

Secondly, as far as printed catechisms are concerned, it is equally obvious that a number of different forms were printed of which not a single copy survives. We know, for example, that in the mid-1540s copies of early catechisms by Thomas Becon and Miles Coverdale were ordered to be destroyed.[11] We also know that in 1590 a short catechism was published by a minister called Miles Mosse, because its preface was attacked by Thomas Rogers (a chaplain of Archbishop Whitgift) in a book published the same year, and because it was listed by the bookseller Andrew Maunsell in his catalogue of books for sale in 1595. However, not a single copy survives: all that we have today are those sections of Mosse's preface which were cited in Roger's intemperate attack.[12] In Maunsell's list of catechisms, there are a number of other works which cannot now be identified or traced: a *Catechisme for housholders* by a Thomas Michelthwait published in 1589, a work by 'R. Bird' entitled *Communication dialogue wise, to bee learned of the ignorant*, a work entitled *Instructions for Christians*, an abridgement of Ursinus's catechism by John Morecroft, and a translation of a catechism by Olevian.[13]

In addition to these, there are a number of Elizabethan and early Stuart forms which are known to us solely through an entry in the register of the Stationers' Company, in which—in theory—all works to be printed were recorded. Some of these sound quite interesting, for example the anonymous catechism for 'all those professors who may be reckoned for true Christians to receive the Lord's Supper worthily' entered in 1589, R.B.'s 'brief and learned catechism' of 1608, T.A.'s 'catechism for young children' and Robert Hutchins's 'short catechism', both entered in 1619.[14] Other examples could be given from the Stationers' Register, or later in the seventeenth century from the Term Catalogues which carried advertisements of books recently published or about to be published.[15] Entry in the Register or Term Catalogue does not necessarily mean the work was printed. Entering the title of a work in the Register and paying the Stationers' Company a fee was done as much to guard copyright from piracy as to secure official sanction for publication, and not all copyrights were utilized; equally publishers might have a number of reasons for changing their minds about publishing a title they had already advertised in the Term

---

[10] *Historical Manuscripts Commission: Gawdy MSS.* (1885), 23.

[11] Tudor, 'Religious Instruction', 407.

[12] T. Rogers, *Miles Christianus* (1590), title-page (the BL has an annotated copy of this work: C124.c.7; I am grateful to Professor Patrick Collinson for drawing this copy to my attention); and Maunsell, *Catalogue*, 32. It is possible that Mosse's work was published in Middelburg in 1590—see Appendix 1, s.v. *Short catechisme*—though this does not have a preface, and the text is not inflammatory.

[13] Maunsell, *Catalogue*, 31–3; and Appendix 1. Maunsell also lists 'catechisms' by W.C., I.R., and T.W. which cannot now be identified.

[14] These are listed in Appendix 1, s.v. *Catechism to be learned*, R.B., T.A., and Hutchins.

[15] e.g. anon., *A brief and plain exposition of the church catechism, The church catechism resolved into scripture proofs*, and *A new sacramental catechism*: see Appendix 1.

Catalogue. However, the fact that these titles existed at all reinforces the point that there were more catechisms in circulation than can be judged from surviving printed copies. In all there are over seventy titles listed in Appendix 1 of which no copy survives.[16]

A third reason for regarding any estimate as on the low side is author error. The present author has taken advantage of existing lists of religious publications by contemporary booksellers such as Andrew Maunsell, William Jaggard, and William London,[17] and lists of catechisms by historians such as Mitchell and Carruthers,[18] but has had to track down other forms by going through the Short-Title Catalogues for the early modern period item by item, looking for authors of religious works in general and for titles which might prove to be catechetical in particular. Apart from the more obvious labels such as 'short questions and answers', there are the kind of labels or phrases which we saw in the last chapter often indicated a catechetical work: 'introduction', 'main points', 'grounds and principles', 'sum', and so on. But this system is fallible, especially where a work is anonymous or the author otherwise unknown, or where the title is elliptical, or all three, as in T.T.'s *A handfull of goateshaire* (1616).[19] Equally where a catechism was placed in the middle of a text such as a handbook on godly living or dying, or a primer on learning to read, or was tucked in at the end of a larger work such as a treatise or set of sermons without being mentioned in the short title, it may easily be overlooked.[20] New forms of this type will probably continue to be found in years to come.

Even if one could be precise about the number of catechisms published in early modern England, this would still not represent the full total of different forms that might have been used in England at that time, since a number of catechisms in English were printed abroad, and a number of more specialized works, such as editions of Calvin's catechism in Greek which were strongly recommended by some English schoolteachers, were not published in England, or not for some time.[21] The catechisms in English which were printed abroad mostly fall into one of three categories. The first includes a number of translations into English which were published

---

[16] See Table 1, col. 3. In a few cases it is possible that the work does exist under a similar title: some possible connections are suggested in Appendix 1.

[17] See the list of abbreviations above, p. xiii.

[18] Mitchell, *Catechisms of the Second Reformation*, pp. lxxv–xci; F. Watson, *The English Grammar Schools to 1660* (Cambridge, 1908), 83–4 (based on Maunsell's *Catalogue*); Carruthers, *Three Centuries*; Grant, 'Cure of Souls', appendix B; my list was nearly complete by the time that I was able to consult P. F. Jensen, 'The Life of Faith in the Teaching of English Protestants', D.Phil. thesis (Oxford, 1970), ch. 5, *passim*, and P. Hutchison, 'Religious Change: The Case of the English Catechism, 1560–1640', Ph.D. thesis (Stanford, 1984), appendices B and C, and *passim*. I am very grateful to Ms K. Pantzer for generously sharing with me the slips she had kept on catechisms while preparing STC².

[19] See Appendix 1 for three possible authors of this work.

[20] See the works in Appendix 1 by Heasse and Cotton; Coote and Thomas; the anonymous author of *Christian directorie*, and James Peirce (1728).

[21] For the latter, see Appendix 1, s.v. Calvin, *Katechesis*.

abroad because at the time the English authorities were still hostile to Protestant forms, for example, Capito's dialogue printed at Strasburg in 1527, the *Breife catechisme* published at Antwerp in 1545, and the *Short catechisme* of Leo Jud published in English at Zurich in 1550; how many copies of these different works actually reached England is unclear.[22] A second group of works in English published abroad were by authors who had fallen foul of the new Protestant authorities at home. Robert Harrison's *Three forms of catechismes* had to be published in Middelburg in Holland 1583 because the author was in hot water for having said in that work that ungodly rulers could be disobeyed; Dudley Fenner and William Ames also published their forms in Holland, though Ames's *Chiefe heads of divinitie ... in forme of catechising* was dedicated to the sons of Lady Vere whom he had taught back in England before he had been driven into exile.[23] Like many other Dutch imprints of the day, these forms may have established a limited circulation in England. Certainly the fact that booksellers like Andrew Maunsell in the 1590s and William London in the 1650s could offer works published in Scotland or abroad alongside those produced by English presses, and the fact that a parish priest working in Derbyshire knew of various catechetical texts by Continental authors, some of which are not known to have been published in England, confirms the existence of a flourishing international book trade.[24] For the purposes of this study, it has been assumed that catechisms published in English in Scotland (from the late sixteenth century), New England (from the late 1640s), and Ireland (from the end of the seventeenth century) were for the most part intended for use by the natives of those countries;[25] but it cannot be denied that at least some copies of such works probably found their way to England.

For to mobility of books can be added mobility of men. In 1588 a Scots minister, Patrick Galloway, published in London a catechism which he said he had used in the family of a 'Scottish nobleman then resident at Newcastle'.[26] His was not the only work of Scots origin to be carried south of the border: the *Maner and forme of examination before the admission to the table of the lorde* printed in London in 1581 had, according to the title-page, been 'used by the ministry of Edinburgh', and John Craig's *Short summe of the whole catechisme* passed through more editions in England than in its country of origin.[27] (The printer who produced two editions of this work in England, Robert Waldegrave, is another example of cross-border movement;

---

[22]   These are all listed in Appendix 1 under author or, where anonymous, the first word of the title. See also the *Dialogue or communication* published at Rouen in 1554 and Calvin's *Catechism* at Geneva in 1556.

[23]   See Appendix 1 for the works by Harrison and Ames, and Dudley Fenner's *The groundes of religion*.

[24]   Maunsell, *Catalogue, passim*; and London, *Catalogue* (1657–60), *passim*; and see Immanuel Bourne's reference to works by 'Alstedius' and 'Danaeus', which are not known to have been published in England: *A light from Christ ... or, the rich jewel* (1646), sig. a2^r.

[25]   For some basic guidance on catechisms published in Scotland, New England, and Ireland, see the Introduction to Appendix 1, p. 574; see also below, nn. 30–1.

[26]   See Appendix 1.   [27]   Ibid.

trained in London, Waldegrave moved north, became printer to James VI, and returned south with him when he became James I as well.[28]) The first edition of Hugh Peters's catechism, *Milke for babes and meat for men*, was published in 1630 in the United Provinces, to which he had been driven from his post as lecturer of St Sepulchre's in London for nonconformity; the second was published in 1641 after his return to England, though by then Peters had also spent a few years in North America.[29] A few of the catechetical forms published in England in the 1640s and 1650s had either definitely or most probably been devised in New England, such as those by John Cotton printed in England in 1642 and 1646, Richard Mather in 1650, Christoper Blackwood in 1653, and John Davenport and William Hooke in 1659.[30] (Conversely, when the *Chief grounds of Christian religion* which Ezekiel Rogers had written for an 'honourable family' in England was published in London in 1642, the author was said to be 'now in New England'.[31]) Not all the forms in English that were published abroad were the product of men who by English standards were dissenters: the *Catechisme of the Church of England explain'd* was published in Rotterdam by Luke Milbourne because in 1700 he was pastor of the English church there at the time, but by the time of the fourth edition it was being published in London.[32] The third category of work published abroad may be mentioned briefly. With short exceptions during the reigns of Mary and James II, most catechisms for English Catholics were published abroad, mainly in the Southern Netherlands; and the fact that many copies were successfully smuggled in demonstrates that a group could get copies into England from abroad if they set their mind to it. The four dozen Catholic forms which have been traced during work for this study are listed in Appendix 1 to help distinguish Protestant from Catholic catechisms, especially the anonymous ones with similar sounding titles.[33] The Catholic ones deserve a study on their own, or a carefully planned comparison of Protestant and Catholic catechizing, but that is not possible in the limited space available here.

In view of what has been said in the last few paragraphs about lost manuscripts, ghostly titles, foreign publications, and peripatetic publishers and catechists, it is obvious that any figures given for the number of catechisms used in England must be regarded as a minimum rather than a maximum. If we confine our attention to forms published by Protestants in England, we can find good evidence for the production

---

[28] R. B. McKerrow, *A Dictionary of Printers and Booksellers ... 1557–1640* (1910), 277–9.

[29] Appendix 1 and *DNB*.

[30] See Appendix 1; I am very grateful to Dr Susan Hardman-Moore for help with these Anglo-American forms. For some forms published in Cambridge, Mass., about the same time, see E. Norris/Norice, *A short catechisme* (1649); T. Shephard, *A short catechisme* (1654); J. Fisk, *The watering of the olive plant* (1657); and A. Peirson, *Some helps for the Indians* (1658).

[31] See the title-page of Rogers's *Chief grounds* and *DNB*.   [32] See Appendix 1.

[33] As explained in the Introduction to Appendix 1, these works can be identified by the description 'Catholic' in col. 6, and by the insertion of square brackets round the number of editions in col. 3. See also J. A. Bossy, *The English Catholic Community 1570–1850* (1975), 272–7.

of nearly six hundred and eighty different question-and-answer forms between 1530 and 1740, or over eight hundred if we count catechisms published in England but in languages other than English, and those titles of which no copy can now be traced. The appearance of new catechisms in English of which a printed or manuscript copy survives is indicated decade by decade in the first column of Table 1, while the publication of forms in languages other than English is represented in column 2 and the

TABLE 1. *New catechisms or catechetical works, or new translations of the same, published in England c.1530–1740*

Decade	1[a]	2[b]		3[c]	4[d]	5[e]	6[f]	Total
1530–9	4	—		1	—	3	—	8
1540–9	4	—		1	2	5	—	12
1550–9	3	6	(4)	1	1	1	—	12
1560–9	3	6	(5)	—	3	8	—	20
1570–9	20	9	(6)	1	1	4	2	37
1580–9	41	2	(2)	7	4	12	2	68
1590–9	26	1		7	—	5	1	40
1600–9	29	1		3	9	5	2	49
1610–19	53	—		3	10	5	3	74
1620–9	52	1	(1)	9	3	4	4	73
1630–9	33	4	(4)	4	—	3	—	44
1640–9	83	3	(3)	1	3	4	1	95
1650–9	43	2	(2)	4	6	10	5	70
1660–9	28	3	(1)	1	3	5	2	42
1670–9	39	4	(4)	3	2	8	4	60
1680–9	35	1	(1)	5	7	11	1	60
1690–9	49	3	(3)	8	3	5	5	73
1700–9	47	2	(2)	12	4	8	6	79
1710–19	31	2	(2)	1	5	10	3	52
1720–9	21	2	(2)	—	5	6	—	34
1730–40	31	—		—	1	2	1	35
undated	3	—		3	—	—	—	6
TOTAL	678	52 (42)		75	72	124	42	1043

[a] Catechisms in English of which a copy survives.
[b] Catechisms in languages other than English of which a copy survives.
[c] Catechisms of which no copy survives.
[d] Improving or instructive dialogues.
[e] Catechetical material not predominantly in question and answer.
[f] Works containing exhortations to and advice on catechizing.

probable date of origin of 'missing' works is indicated in column 3. The 678 catechisms in column 1 varied a good deal in length, but are all forms which by their purpose, content, and technique can be firmly labelled catechisms in the sense normally used at the time, as described in the previous chapter. The content of these forms poses a slight problem for us today in trying to decide what constituted a catechism then, in that with the passage of time more and more topics were covered in catechisms. Authors such as Eusebius Paget, Richard Baxter, Clement Ellis, and Isaac Watts seem to have felt that the question-and-answer method could also be used profitably to teach knowledge of the Bible, while other authors evidently thought it could be used to good effect to help explain matters of church practice, such as the use of a set liturgy, confirmation, or the nature of a visible church, or to teach more difficult points of doctrine such as the Calvinist *ordo salutis*, or how to help the old and sick prepare for death.[34] It seems arbitrary for a historian to accept some forms and reject others on the grounds of content alone, and so in this exercise I have accepted as a catechism any form which was in question and answer and in which the basic intention of the author seemed to be to provide instruction on a religious topic, broadly defined.

Variation in length presents another dilemma. A question-and-answer form filling several hundred pages was unlikely to be used in the same way as one of eight pages: the longer one was likely to be read and reread until it was understood, the shorter could be taught orally to those who could not read. But again it would be high-handed for us to say the shorter was a 'proper' catechism and the longer not. Since the great majority of forms listed in column 1 were what has been classified in Appendix 1 as very short (ten pages or less), short (twenty-five pages or less), or intermediate (twenty-six to sixty pages long), and there are indications that catechumens at the time learnt even longer works, the problem is not a major one. Moreover, as we shall see in Chapter 5, the borderline between orality and literacy was very fluid, so that some short or intermediate forms may have been taught and tested by a mixture of methods, so that we should be not too anxious to draw a line between forms taught by oral methods alone and those which required reading skills. Finally, a number of longer catechisms were aimed at helping the current or the next generation of catechists, whose ignorance was obviously not as great as that of young children, but who still needed help with content and technique. Once again, it is probably best to regard these longer forms as part of an expanding and diversifying genre rather than a discrete type of work.

The total of 678 in column 1 incorporates 41 composite works which contained two or three or occasionally more question-and-answer forms inside the one publication, adding up to a total of 105 forms in all. Whether in any grand total these are counted as 41 or 105 items is a matter of choice; in so far as the authors of these multiple works seem to have felt that different members of their flocks needed different types or levels of instruction or needed different forms at different times, I have opted for the higher figure and counted 105 towards the total.[35] The total of 678 also

---

[34] In addition to the works by the named authors, which are listed in Appendix 1, see also the works there by J. Clutterbuck; H. Colman; J. Cotton (1643); A. Grosse; C. Cotton; and T. Draxe (1609).

[35] These titles can be identified by the description in col. 6 of Appendix 1.

includes 68 cases in which the catechism was not published separately or as the main item in a publication but as an appendage to a work in another, non-catechetical genre.[36] Catechisms are sometimes to be found in the middle of educational works whose main function was to provide instruction on how to read and write, together with improving thoughts, psalms, verses, and prayers, for example Edmund Coote's best-selling *English schoolmaster*.[37] Other catechisms were published as part of a devotional work, such as the Edwardian primers, and, later on, John Parker's *True patterne of pietie* (1599) and William Brough's *Sacred principles* (1650); or they formed a part of works designed to give advice on running a godly household, such as William Chub's *Christian exercise for private householders* [1585?] and Richard Baxter's *The poor man's family book* (1674).[38] Others were printed as a supplement to a treatise, collection of sermons, or an even larger work: Thomas Cartwright's 'methodical short catechism' was appended to later editions of Dod and Cleaver's exposition of the Ten Commandments, and the anonymous *Certaine questions and answers* was inserted into the preface of some editions of the Geneva Bible.[39] Yet others first appeared in a volume of the collected works of an author, for example Gervase Babington, Richard Greenham, and Joseph Hall, though in most of these cases, as in Cartwright's, the catechism was also published separately on at least one occasion.[40] In a headcount of catechisms, all of these should undoubtedly be included as distinct forms, but with a mental note that the people who purchased the volumes in which they appeared were not necessarily buying them for the catechism. By the same token, the total of 678 (or 805) is an underestimate in that I have not included in that total more than two dozen cases where an existing form in English (or another language) was published unchanged in a new and different publication, as happened for example with the Prayer Book catechism which was published first in the Book of Common Prayer, then in *The ABC with the catechisme*, *The primer and catechisme*, and other locations, or the catechisms of Isaac Watts which were published in various combinations in the 1730s and later.[41] If we were counting the different publications in which catechisms appeared, these would warrant separate treatment, but since we are counting only new or discrete forms they have been counted only once.

In column 2 are listed just over fifty catechisms published in England but in languages other than English, mainly Latin, but with a sprinkling of Greek or Greek and Latin forms, some Hebrew ones, and a small number printed in Welsh, Irish, Dutch, French, German, and Arabic. The figures in brackets in column 2 indicate where a catechism in Latin, Greek, or whatever existed also in an English version listed in column 1, and as can be seen there is a good deal of overlap between forms in these

---

[36] As last note; however, in col. 4 brackets have been placed round the numbers of editions of such catechisms: see Introduction to Appendix 1.

[37] See Appendix 1, and also the reading primers listed there by John Owen, Lambrocke Thomas, George Fox, Benjamin Keach, and William Scoffin.

[38] See Appendix 1. [39] Ibid. [40] Ibid. [41] Ibid.

two columns. In some cases, the catechism was written in Latin and then translated into English, as was the case with the catechisms of Ponet in 1553 and Nowell in 1570; in others, it was the reverse, with the Prayer Book catechism and later the Westminster Shorter Catechism being translated into Latin, Greek, and Hebrew, and in the case of the former into Arabic as well; in yet others, it was a matter of producing an English version from a French original such as Calvin's, or from a German such as the Heidelberg, though possibly by way of a Latin translation.[42] It might be thought strange to include the items in column 2 in our grand total, either the full 52 titles or the 10 that are left if we knock out the 42 which overlap with items in column 1. But the fact is that learning a catechism in a foreign tongue was deemed a very good idea, as we shall see in Chapter 4; and that this was actually done is shown by the number of repeat editions of these forms which had to be printed.[43] Although the function of these works was to improve students' linguistic skills as much as to deepen their religious knowledge and understanding, I am inclined to include the great majority of them in the grand total by the thought that extra insights into the meaning of words used in a catechism may have been gained by a catechumen translating a form from English into Latin or Latin into Greek. Only forms published (in London) in French and Dutch, and probably intended for the use of the 'stranger' churches of émigré communities based in England, can reasonably be discounted.[44] Even then some copies of a French edition of the Prayer Book catechism might have been destined for use in the Channel Islands, and there are a couple of works which look as though they may have been designed to help teach French to English-speakers by using a bi-lingual edition of the Prayer Book catechism.[45]

One of the most difficult decisions when trying to decide what should be counted as a catechism concerns dialogues. As will be seen in the next section of this chapter, there is no sense in trying to impose a rigid distinction between a dialogue and a catechism in the mid-sixteenth century, since there was still a great deal of fluidity in question-and-answer techniques at that stage. By the 1570s, however, there is a case for suggesting a measure of separation, with the term 'dialogue' being reserved for those instructive or disputatious works of the type which had been used in the Middle Ages and were still being used by the Christian humanists to impart information or ideas in an engaging or entertaining manner to those who could read. In the works of Continental authors like Pierre Viret, and the longer works penned by English authors such as George Gifford and Arthur Dent, and by

---

[42] See Appendix 1, s.v. Westminster Assembly of Divines; Calvin; and Heidelberg Catechism.

[43] See below, pp. 188–92.

[44] e.g. the works by Joannes a Lasco listed in Appendix 1, and anon. *Le catéchisme* (1664) and anon., *Les psaumes de David* (1701); on the stranger churches, see Tudor, 'Religious Instruction', nn. 12, 72; and A. Pettegree, *Foreign Protestant Communities in Sixteenth-Century London* (Oxford, 1986), 48, 50, 54, 59–65, 88, 91, 306.

[45] See the works in Appendix 1 by Pierre du Ploiche, and Jean de Grave; and anon., *A, B, C, des Chrétiens*.

a variety of later Stuart authors such as William Blake, John Rawlet, and Daniel Defoe, we find works in which the typical features of a dialogue extended well beyond the characteristic opening greetings and pervaded the whole work. This meant a complete plot of meeting, disagreement, argument, resolution, and parting; in some cases the author used fictitious characters such as the Nathaniel and Philip, Timothy and Daniel, or Simon and Zachary used by Viret, and often a third or fourth party was introduced into the discussion. The material covered was also often contentious, with the wise man or the virtuous man being given the opportunity to speak at much greater length than the fool or the knave, and always being guaranteed victory in the end. In all there are over seventy of these dialogues in Appendix 1, which seem to me to have some of the features of both the instructive and the disputatious types suggested by Peter Burke; I have not counted these in the total of catechisms in column 1 but placed them in column 4 as a category of works closely related to but distinct from those in column 1.[46] What has been treated here as a standard catechism, by contrast, had just two *dramatis personae*, usually minister and child, but sometimes teacher and pupil, or parent and child; it might contain, but did not need, the opening and closing exchanges of greeting and farewell, and although it had a shape it certainly had no plot; it kept conversational ploys such as encouragement to a minimum; and it tended to avoid controversy and aggressive language.

However, even after the 1570s, there are a few works to which neither the label 'catechism' nor 'dialogue' can be neatly applied, and which have been designated in Appendix 1 as 'dialogue-catechisms'. These are basically those catechisms, as defined in the last paragraph, which retained a more than usual amount of the trappings of a dialogue. They were in most cases larger works, designed for regular reading rather than memorizing, and were likely to have just two characters, which were liable to be master and scholar or father and child, rather than minister and child or 'Timothy' and 'Daniel'. They include such conventions of the dialogue as polite opening remarks and conversational interjections to ease the flow, but lack a plot or simulated quarrels. While most of the questions in these works are relatively brief, a number are much longer than those in a typical short catechism, the extra length being due to the fact that these questions are either more probing than a bare request for information and might even require a denial from the respondent, or like the passage of Calvin cited near the start of the last chapter they might contain a restatement of the last answer in slightly different words to which the catechumen might then agree. Works like Nowell's original *Catechisme* and Hammond's *Practical catechisme* and over twenty others seem to me to be neither completely catechism (as defined above) nor dialogue, though in their technique and focus on the staple formulae associated

---

[46] All the works mentioned in this paragraph are listed in Appendix 1; see also Introduction to Appendix 1.

with catechizing they are more a catechism than a conventional dialogue. As such these dialogue-catechisms have been included in the grand total of catechisms in column 1.[47]

In the later Stuart period, a related but different problem emerges. From the 1640s we regularly find works which were referred to as catechisms and which used question-and-answer technique, but which had a different function from the kind of catechisms we have been looking at in the last few paragraphs; they are, in fact, much closer to Burke's disputatious dialogue than anything discussed so far. *The Quakers catechism* published by Richard Baxter four times in the mid-1650s was not a form to teach the basics of the faith to Quakers, but a controversial piece trying to persuade them to stop believing what they had already learnt and sincerely believed. It was a catechism in the sense that it offered a series of questions to the Quakers, but it was a disputation in that the questions were loaded, and the tone of the answers was often hostile, very unlike those in the simple, educational catechisms which Baxter himself wrote for the less well-informed parishioners of Kidderminster and elsewhere.[48] *The Cavaliers catechisme* published in 1643 was a satirical, anti-Royalist piece which parodied the Prayer Book catechism in places; the *Protestant catechisme: or a dialogue* of 1673 was a largely controversial anti-Catholic form; the *True-protestant catechism* published in 1683 was a political attack on dissenters; the three catechisms published in 1709 under the names of leading political figures of the day were all political tracts; while the catechisms published in Anne's reign for 'town-misses', 'country-gentlewomen', 'widows', and 'beaux' satirized the mores of fashionable society.[49] In addition we find a growing number of works in which ideas or phrases used in catechisms were held up to detailed and hostile scrutiny in a pamphlet or larger work. This was not totally new, as the case of Miles Mosse and Thomas Rogers shows, but it was certainly much more common in the later Stuart period than in the preceding century.[50]

The political and satirical catechisms can be rejected fairly easily from our count, in that the techniques of propaganda were to the fore, and the ecclesiastical or doctrinal content was limited or subordinated to political or other purposes. Forty-five of these works, mainly dating from the 1640s and the reign of Queen Anne, are listed in Appendix 1 for the sake of completeness, but they have been excluded from the calculations for Table 1. The existence and indeed the number of such works is worthy of note, suggesting as it does that 'normal' catechizing was sufficiently prevalent by then for such propagandists to judge that the use of a question-and-answer technique would be familiar to and might even attract the attention of potential readers.

[47] As last note.   [48] For Baxter's other works, see below, Ch. 4 and Appendix 1.

[49] See Appendix 1, s.v. Duke, and Duchess, of Marlborough, and Prince Eugene, and cf. Palatine; and also s.v. Ladies, Beaux, Town-misses, Widows, and Country-gentlewomen, and s.v. U. Price.

[50] For some examples from the second half of the seventeenth and early eighteenth centuries, see next paragraph below.

In the case of catechisms which tackled ecclesiastical and doctrinal matters but in a controversial fashion, the two criteria I have used are balance and tone: was a work predominantly negative, that is attacking a rival set of ideas, or positive in the sense of pushing the author's own beliefs; and was the tone used in the questions and answers strident, seeking to score points, or firm but fairly neutral? If the former in both cases, the 'catechism' has been included in the finding list in Appendix 1 but not counted in the total for column 1 in Table 1; if the latter, it has been included in both. To keep Appendix 1 within bounds, the decision was taken that for the sake of completeness a work like *The Quakers catechism* would be included where the term 'catechism' appears in the title, but the line was drawn at the hundreds of polemical 'dialogues', 'discourses', 'disputes', and 'questions and answers' between two or more characters, such as *A dialogue between a Brownist and a schismatick* (1643), *A dialogue between a papist and a quaker* (1680), *A dialogue between a new Catholic convert and a Protestant* (1686), and *A dialogue between the Arch-B[ishop] of C[anterbury] and the bishop of Heref[ord]* (1688), which have all been omitted.[51] A similar guideline was adopted when confronted by works of controversy about catechisms, such as Joseph Hacon's *Review of Mr. Horn's catechisme* (1660) and Benjamin Camfield's *A serious examination of the Independent's catechism* (1668), and the controversies sparked off by Samuel Clarke's exposition of the Prayer Book catechism in 1729 and by James Strong's revision of the Westminster Shorter Catechism in the mid-1730s.[52] If the word 'catechism' appears or is implied in the title, it has been included in the Appendix as part of the story of English catechesis, but not in the count of items in Table 1. In all, 86 catechetical works of a controversial nature are listed in Appendix 1; they date mainly from the 1640s to the 1660s, the 1680s, and the 1730s. Like the political and satirical forms mentioned earlier, these works can be identified in Appendix 1 by the description in column six, and the insertion of square brackets round the number of published editions in column four.[53]

A final comment may be offered about two other marginal categories of works. The first includes declaratory forms described at the time as 'catechisms', catechetical sermons or lectures, expositions of or commentaries on existing catechisms in continuous prose, works recommended for use by catechists or catechumens, confessions of faith, and other expositions of avowedly catechetical material that did not employ question-and-answer technique at any point or did so only intermittently, including a few in verse. There is perhaps only a difference of degree between, on the one hand, a lecture or exposition on a catechetical topic in which the author threw in

[51] See Wing² for further details of these and other similarly entitled works.

[52] See Appendix 1 under the authors named.

[53] Also in the list but not the headcount are oddities like Anthony Nixon's *Dignitie of man*; *Daniel Ben Alexander the converted Jew of Prague*; Abraham Jagel's *Jews catechism*; and the Russian catechism of Feofan, Archbishop of Novgorod. The last three of these may have had curiosity rather than practical value.

the occasional rhetorical question or raised a series of objections to break the monotony, and, on the other, a 'catechism' in which the author certainly asked questions
from start to finish, but then allowed his enthusiasm to tempt him into writing
exceedingly long answers. Over a hundred and twenty examples of the former—predominantly declaratory forms handling the usual catechetical material—have been
traced and included in Appendix 1, since they may well have been used by catechists
preparing for the task of catechizing, and perhaps even read by more advanced catechumens; on the other hand, they clearly do not count as catechisms which could be
taught or learnt orally, and so have been included as a related genre in column 5 of
Table 1.[54] Secondly, there are works containing exhortations to catechize or be catechized, or offering detailed advice on how to set about it, which number over forty.
These often provide a great deal of insight into the attitudes of catechists to catechizing, and, at one remove, of the catechumens whom they were trying to persuade to
co-operate, as well as about the techniques of instruction which catechists thought
practical and desirable. They too have been recorded in the list, though not counted
as catechisms proper, and are indicated in column 6 of Table 1.[55] As can be seen,
together with the instructive or improving dialogues listed in column 4, these two
last categories of work in columns 5 and 6 add 238 items to the 805 catechisms listed
in columns 1, 2, and 3.[56]

In the rest of this chapter we shall seek some of the reasons for the production of so
many new forms, and the changing character of those forms. This can perhaps best
be done by dividing our period into three phases. The first lasted from the late 1520s
to the 1560s: a period when the question-and-answer form was still in its infancy and
when English catechists came under strong Continental influence, but also witnessed the drafting of two native catechisms which were to have considerable impact
in the future. The second phase lasted from the 1570s to the early 1640s: in these
years greater sophistication of technique and a greater degree of independence of
Continental models was shown by English catechists; this was a period of growing
diversity of forms, but of relative homogeneity of doctrine. The third phase was from
the late 1640s to the mid-eighteenth century (a point midway between the storms
of Queen Anne's reign and the full impact of the Evangelical Revival): in this period
the catechetical world was dominated by two forms—the Prayer Book catechism and
the Westminster Shorter Catechism—and the scores of explanations or variations
on these works, but there were also continuing experiments with technique, and

---

[54] These are usually described in col. 6 of Appendix 1 as 'not q + a' (not question and answer), and
where applicable 'exposition'; and in col. 4 round brackets have been placed round the numbers of editions
of such works: see Introduction to Appendix 1.

[55] Usually described as exhortation or advice in col. 6 of Appendix 1.

[56] The total would be much higher if *all* the scores of treatises and sermons on such catechetical staples as the Ten Commandments and the Lord's Supper were included, instead of just those with some
stated connection to catechizing or recommended for use by catechists. A study of some of these in tandem with the more popular catechisms would be most instructive.

catechetical forms were also characterized by a wider range of doctrine and a higher proportion of polemic than before.

In the years between 1536 and 1553, as Philippa Tudor has ably demonstrated, 'an ambitious programme of religious instruction for children and adolescents was planned on a nation-wide basis in England'. While it was clearly hoped that parents might also benefit from this programme, the main thrust was at teaching the young.[57] As Dr Tudor's account makes clear, however, much of the instruction from the 1530s to the early 1550s was conceived and executed in fairly conventional terms. The insistence that all priests and teachers instruct their charges in *English* was relatively new, as was the trend towards the exclusion of material like the Ave Maria and the seven deadly sins; but in other respects, such as the stress on learning the Lord's Prayer, Creed, and to a lesser extent the Decalogue, the content was similar to that of the preceding period. Moreover, the technique of delivery was still for the most part declaratory rather than question and answer: the clergy were to repeat part or all of the basic formulae, in the presence of both children and adults until they had learnt them; and a number of the works referred to at the time or by Dr Tudor as 'catechisms' were in fact not interrogatory, like Colet's 'Catechyzon' which we looked at briefly above, and Richard Taverner's *Catechisme or institution of the Christen religion* of 1539, which was an adaptation of Calvin's first attempt at a catechism in 1537 and contained a series of statements on the Decalogue, Creed, Lord's Prayer, and sacraments for the young to learn by rote.[58] Similarly the work entitled *Catechismus* put out by Archbishop Cranmer in 1548, a translation of a work by the Lutheran Osiander and based on Luther's smaller catechism, was in reality a series of short sermons for children and young people, who were meant to listen and understand rather than memorize or repeat them.[59] At this stage, other published works of religious instruction still owed more to the medieval traditions of the primer (a devotional work with some educational material and function), of Mirk's *Festial* (a handbook in common use among the clergy), or *The lantern of light* (a Lollard manual of basic instruction) than to anything new.[60] Even relative innovations like Richard Whitford's *Werke for housholders*—a very popular Catholic manual of the 1530s which provided short household sermons and encouraged the reading out loud at mealtimes of Whitford's own exposition of the Paternoster, Ave Maria, and Creed—were relatively conservative in

---

[57] Tudor, 'Religious Instruction', 391–413.

[58] See above, p. 16; and below, Appendix 1, s.v. Taverner. There were exceptions: the Prayer Book catechism of 1549 and the form by Ponet in 1553 were both in question and answer; but it is indicative of the target and function of the latter that four editions of it were published in Latin but only one in English: see Appendix 1.

[59] See Appendix 1, s.v. Cranmer; Cranmer had been in Germany for some time, and Osiander was a relation of his: J. Ridley, *Thomas Cranmer* (Oxford, 1962), ch. 3.

[60] Tudor, 'Religious Instruction', 392–3, 398; Aston, *England's Iconoclasts*, 112–15.

their technique of instruction.[61] Under Henry and Edward the final parting of the ways between the use of questions and answers for teaching the basics, and reliance on a series of statements (as in a sermon, treatise, or handbook) for more advanced instruction, was still some distance away.

At this stage there was also no clear distinction between a dialogue and a catechism. In England, most of the earliest interrogatory forms known to us were at one time or another called 'dialogues', for example, the translation into English of Capito's *De pueris instituendis* published at Strasburg in 1527, immediately banned in England but cropping up again with a new title in 1550; the short 'dialogue' in George Joye's translation of *Hortulus anime* which, with slight modifications, was used in some primers in the early 1530s; *The ABC with the pater noster* of 1545; and the *Fruteful and a very Christen instruction* of 1547.[62] While these and other such forms contained some of the marks of a conventional dialogue, they were relatively few. Thus in the short 'dialogue' between a child and his father in George Joye's *Hortulus anime*, only the opening exchange is personal: 'Speak, my dear child, what art thou?'. Thereafter there are only occasional superfluities of expression to ease the flow: 'I pray thee tell me again', or the 'Why' in 'Why, is thought then sin?'.[63] Also while some of these works, like Bale's 'dialogue ... between two children', were quite demanding in their terminology, others, like Joye's, were as short and straightforward as many later catechisms. In short, some of these forms of the 1530s and 1540s which were referred to as a dialogue were more like a typical short catechism of the later sixteenth century.

Conversely, some of the early question-and-answer works referred to as a catechism were more like a dialogue, at least in the characteristic opening exchanges which explained who the main characters were and why they were discussing this particular subject. A good example is the opening exchange of Edmund Allen's *Catechisme* of 1548. The 'master' begins: 'My dear child, for as much as I have taken much pain and labour to instruct thee in those principles all Christians ought to learn', and goes on to explain that to test the child's knowledge he is going to ask him some questions, of which the first is 'What art thou?'. The 'scholar' begins by apologizing for the fact that his 'wit and understanding be very base, and simple', and that he has not been as diligent in his studies as he should, so his answers will not be perfect; he engages to try, and only then launches into a reply to the first question: 'by my first birth, I am a creature of God endued with understanding and reason, but

---

[61]   Aston, *England's Iconoclasts*, 409–10; Tudor, 'Religious Instruction', 398–9.

[62]   See Appendix 1, s.v. Capito, *Primer*, *ABC*, and *Fruteful*; and cf. Aston, *England's Iconoclasts*, 414 n. 98, 416–17. Other examples of works of this period called 'dialogues' include John Bale's *Dialoge betwene two chyldren*; the anonymous *Dialogue or communication* (Rouen, 1554); and even Calvin's catechism: see anon., *The forme of common praiers used in the churches of Geneva ... and the catechisme, made by maister Iohn Calvyne* (1550).

[63]   C. C. Butterworth, *The English Primers (1529–45)* (Philadelphia, 1953); E. Burton (ed.), *Three Primers Put Forth in the Reign of Henry VIII* (Oxford, 1834), 216–21.

conceived in sin, and therefore miserable and of no value'.[64] Other authors also seem to have regarded catechisms and dialogues as being almost synonymous, for example the English translation of Leo Jud's short catechism, published in Zurich in 1550 as *A short catechisme ... in maner of a dialogue*, and Thomas Becon's *New catechisme sette forthe dialogue wise in familiare talke betwene the father and the son*.[65]

The relative novelty of catechizing in the Edwardian and early Elizabethan periods, whether using a declaratory or an interrogatory technique, is also indicated by the number of occasions on which it was felt necessary to explain the term 'catechism' to the public. The full title of the work issued by Cranmer in 1548 was *Catechismus, that is to say a shorte instruction into Christian religion for the synguler commoditie and profyte of children and yong people*, and the English translation of Calvin's catechism which was published in Geneva in 1556 and in London in 1560 was entitled *The catechisme or manner to teach children the Christian religion*.[66] The full title of the catechism in the first Edwardian Prayer Book not only offered a definition but also helped explain its role in the individual's progress towards full church membership: 'A catechism, that is to say, an instruction to be learned of every child, before he be brought to be confirmed by the bishop'.[67]

To distinguish the new technique that was evolving from older approaches, authors and publishers often adopted other labels for those works consisting purely of statements. One of these was 'confession' or 'declaration', as in Zwingli's series of articles of belief, translated into English twice, in the 1540s and 1550s, and Jean Garnier's 'brief confession', which was translated three times, once by Bishop Hooper and then in the 1560s and 1570s.[68] Another label used was 'instructions', as in the works by Wither and Capelin published in 1579 and 1582; another was 'sum' as in Beza's *Brief and piththie summe* (1563), John Rogers's *Summe of Christianitie reduced unto eight propositions* [1578?], and the anonymous *Short summe of the trueth* (1592) (though as we have seen, 'sum' is often found applied to question-and-answer forms too).[69] The publication of these works suggests that there was still a place for this kind of instruction, but as we shall see shortly such works were soon overshadowed by the rising demand for interrogatory forms.

The other most striking feature of the first catechisms in English is the extent to which they were influenced by Continental models. To those works by Capito, Jud, Osiander, and others already mentioned, we can add translations of question-

---

[64] [E. Allen], *A catechisme* (1550/1), sig. Aii[r].

[65] See Appendix 1. Erasmus's *Playne and godly exposytion*, which is a dialogue, was often referred to as his *catechismus*: *Opera Omnia Desiderii Erasmi Roterodami*, V: 1 (Amsterdam/Oxford, 1977), 179–83; Aston, *England's Iconoclasts*, 201–2, 418–20. Cf. also the *Briefe catechisme and dialogue* published in the Netherlands in 1545.

[66] See Appendix 1; and also the title-pages of the works by Edmond Allen, John Ponet, and Theodore Béza published in 1548, 1553, and 1578, respectively.

[67] Brightman, *English Rite*, ii. 778–9.   [68] See Appendix 1 under the relevant names.

[69] Ibid.

and-answer forms by a German Lutheran, Johann Spangenberg, whose *Sum of divini-tie* was published five times between 1548 and 1567, and a Dutchman, Marten Micron, whose *Short and faythful instruction ... for ... symple christianes, which intende worthely to receyve the holy supper of the Lorde* was published first in Emden *c*.1556 and then in London in 1560.[70] There were also various works translated from French originals, though apart from Calvin's these were relatively specialized rather than wide-ranging works.[71] The full extent of Continental influence went beyond these translations, for even the catechisms of English origin were in varying degrees influenced by European models. That of Edmund Allen in 1548 is said to have been influenced by Zwinglian ideas;[72] it was been suggested that there are echoes of Lutheran models at a couple of points in the Prayer Book catechism of 1549;[73] the section of Ponet's catechism of 1553 on the sacraments was influenced by Swiss thought;[74] while Nowell's catechism of 1570, drawn up in the 1560s at the request of Convocation for the use of more advanced catechumens, adopted a Lutheran framework but borrowed extensively from Calvin's catechism.[75] That having been said, it should be added that the Prayer Book catechism of 1549 was perhaps the least affected by specific foreign models or ideas,[76] and Nowell, despite his debt to Geneva, found space to pursue some characteristically English concerns on the role of the Law, the dangers of idolatry, the role of worship, and the need for confirmation;[77] and it was these two forms which, as we shall see, were to have by far the greatest impact in the longer term.

In the 1570s a second phase began which would last to the mid-1640s, and in which a number of the trends begun in the first phase would reach their culmination. Thus, one distinguishing feature of this phase was the final victory of question-and-answer over declaratory forms. As late as the 1580s and 1590s and very occasionally in the early seventeenth century, there were a few cases of Protestant authors using the term 'catechism' to describe a declaratory form, probably because the material they handled was in many cases the staple items of question-and-answer catechisms:

---

[70] See Appendix 1 s.v. Spangenberg and Micron; the *Ordinarye for all faythfull Chrystians* by Cornelis van der Heyden was not in question and answer.

[71] Ibid., s.v. Calvin, Heasse, Caussé, and Rouspeau.

[72] An impression based on some parallels with the short catechism of Leo Jud, published in Zurich in 1541.

[73] Brightman, *English Rite*, ii. 776, 780, and cf. 790.

[74] W. P. Haugaard, *Elizabeth and the English Reformation: The Struggle for a Stable Settlement of Religion* (Cambridge, 1970), 17.

[75] W. P. Haugaard, 'John Calvin and the Catechism of Alexander Nowell', *Archiv für Reformationgeschichte*, 61 (1970), 50–66.

[76] See above, p. 20 n. 30; Brightman, *English Rite*, ii. 776–90; G. J. Cuming, *A History of Anglican Liturgy*[2] (1982), 62.

[77] Haugaard, *Elizabeth and the English Reformation*, 258–72, 289; L. D. Durbin, 'Education by Catechism', Ph.D. thesis (Northwestern, 1987), 122–4.

Creed, Decalogue, Lord's Prayer, and sacraments.[78] Publishers and booksellers like Andrew Maunsell were also inclined to conflate declaratory and interrogatory forms, since from their point of view they were closely related genres, and a minister or teacher might be interested in buying either or both types of work. Nevertheless, despite a measure of continuing ambiguity, it is clear from the usage very widely adopted by Elizabethan authors, and from the forms listed in Appendix 1 below and represented numerically in Table 1 above, that a catechism was seen as an interrogatory form of religious instruction.

The distinction between a catechism and a religious dialogue also became much clearer. Dialogues continued to be regarded as means of imparting information in an entertaining or conversational way, and were meant to be read and reread rather than memorized, as in the case of works like George Gifford's *Brief discourse* and Arthur Dent's *Plain man's pathway* (part one), *A pastime for parents*, and *The opening of heaven gates*. The colloquial language and dramatic character of much of Dent's work, for example, is in many ways closer to the allegorical narratives in Richard Bernard's *Isle of Man* and John Bunyan's *The pilgrim's progress* than to the stern approach of the theologians of Heidelberg or the Westminster Assembly. Compare Asunetus's blustering at the start of *The plain man's pathway*—'Tush, tush, what needs all this ado'—with the grim opening of the Heidelberg Catechism—'What is thy only comfort in life and in death?'[79] A clear distinction can also be drawn between an ordinary, elementary catechism and the controversial 'dialogues' or 'discourses' on religious topics occasionally deployed by 'godly' opponents of the new church in the reign of Elizabeth, as in Anthony Gilby's *A pleasaunt dialogue betweene a souldior of Barwicke, and an English chaplaine* (published abroad in 1581),[80] or as a vehicle for anti-Catholic propaganda, as in the two violently anti-Catholic dialogues by Alexander Cooke published in 1610 and 1624—*Pope Joan* and *The abatement of popish braggs*—and George Jenney's *Catholike conference, between a protestant and papist* (1626).[81] These can readily be distinguished from an ordinary catechism by the much greater polemical content or intent and the abrasive language used.

The only complicating factor is the existence of a few longer catechisms which retained some of the features of a dialogue, and which it was suggested above could

---

[78] e.g. R. Some, *A godly and short treatise upon the lordes prayer* (1583), sig. A1ᵛ (Maunsell also referred to it as a catechism in his *Catalogue*, 33); J. Nichols, in his *An order of household instruction* (1596) referred to seven 'catechisms' in chs. 3–9, but they were mostly not interrogatory; see also 'Mr Mayden his catechisme' in Emmanuel College Cambridge Library MS III. 1. 13⁸; and F. Inman, *A light unto the unlearned* (1622), title-page, and sig. A2ʳ.

[79] A. Dent, *The plaine mans pathway to heaven* (1601), 27; Schaff, *Creeds*, 307; the other works listed in this paragraph are all listed in Appendix 1.

[80] STC² 11888, and cf. the anonymous *Dialogue concerning the strife of our church* (1584) and the *Dialogue where is plainly laide open* (the 'tyrannical dealings' of the bishops) [1589]: STC² 6801, 6805.

[81] See Appendix 1, and cf. the *Dialogue agaynst the tyrannye of the papists* (1562), STC² 19176, which was translated from a Latin original.

be termed dialogue-catechisms. These were designed mainly aimed for use in either the school or the home. Schoolboys would have been accustomed to the conventions of an instructive dialogue from their enforced reading of some grammars and improving works by humanists such as Erasmus, Châteillon, Viret, Cordier, and others, and to have had similar works of a predominantly doctrinal character put in front of them, as in the case of Alexander Nowell's *Catechisme*, Alexander Gee's *Ground of Christianitie*, Matthieu Virel's *Treatise*, and much later Henry Hammond's *Practical catechisme*, would probably not have struck them as odd.[82] The inordinately long dialogue-catechisms composed by Thomas Becon, William Cotes, John Lyster, John Carpenter, and William Herbert, on the other hand, were apparently all written for domestic use, usually by father and son, sometimes daughter; and the extra time available for catechizing in such a context, and the closer bond between catechist and catechumen, perhaps facilitated the use of these long and often quite difficult forms.[83] If we take Nowell's catechism, the most widely used of this hybrid type of form in the phase we are currently examining, we can see that it contains features common to both catechisms and dialogues. On the one hand, there is a high proportion of simple factual questions and answers, for example on the Decalogue, but at the end of this as of other sections the master summarizes, and the student acknowledges this summary. The catechist also breaks up the exposition but keeps the flow going by occasional interjections such as 'Thou sayest true. Go forward therefore' or 'Say on', accompanied by a fresh question or request for further information, or he asks the occasional leading or trick question; and both at the start and end of the complete work, the teacher exhorts, sets matters in context, and summarizes.[84] Such ploys are not found in the majority of early modern English catechisms, especially shorter ones, but while the overall design of Nowell's work is clearly catechetical it retains just enough of the old dialogue to mark it out from those forms.

Another of the features of the second phase was the rapid growth of home-produced catechisms. The relatively fast decline of the publication in England of Continental catechisms can probably be explained in large part by the passing of those first- and second-generation reformers who had spent some time in exile or had known Continental leaders personally, and to a lesser degree by the fact that the leaders of the English church were by then pursuing a more independent path. Continental works were still being translated in the 1570s, 1580s, and 1590s, as editions of Beza's *Little catechisme*, Robert le Maçon's *Catechisme*, Gerardus's *Foundations of Christian religion*, and Virel's *Learned and excellent treatise* bear witness.[85] Moreover,

---

[82] All these works are listed in Appendix 1, and some are discussed further in Ch. 4 below.

[83] See Appendix 1 for further details of these works.

[84] A. Nowell, *A catechisme, or first instruction*, ed. G. E. Corrie (Parker Society, Cambridge, 1853), 120; 141; 145, 194–5, 201; 115, 140, 152, 182, 217; 113–14, 219–20.

[85] See Appendix 1.

in the 1570s and 1580s appeared the first of a number of translations of the Heidelberg Catechism, while in 1585 and 1587 the immense commentaries of Ursinus on the Heidelberg Catechism were published in England, first in Latin, then in English, and in 1589 appeared Bastingius's lengthy but more manageable exposition of the same form.[86] In the early seventeenth century, however, apart from new versions of the Heidelberg Catechism,[87] few works were based on foreign originals. Even works already established in the first phase, such as Calvin's catechism, became less popular: after more than a dozen separate editions between 1556 and 1598, and a few more tacked on at the back of *The form of common prayers used in the churches of Geneva*, an English version of Calvin's work was not published again until 1645, and not at all thereafter.[88] The sort of Continental work which retained an audience after the 1590s was usually of a more specialized variety, such as Virel's long dialogue (for those who were literate and had the opportunity to read it) and the several hundred pages of Ursinus's lectures on the Heidelberg Catechism (for undergraduates, ordinands, and the well-educated or highly motivated laity).[89]

Increasingly foreign works were ousted by the two official forms of 1549 and 1570 and by a number of other forms written by clergymen familiar with conditions in the Elizabethan and early Stuart church. A few of these works rapidly established themselves as runaway best-sellers. The short form of 1549 appeared not only in hundreds of editions of the Elizabethan and Stuart Prayer Books, but also in two other frequently reprinted works: *The ABC with the catechisme*, designed to teach children first the alphabet and then the catechism; and *The primer and catechisme*, an officially approved collection of instruction and devotions. By these means, as we shall see in Chapter 4, the Edwardian catechism soon became the most frequently reproduced form of the early modern period. A limited range of titles which had official approval were allowed to be printed in longer runs than the official limit of 1,250–1,500 laid down in 1587, which in 1635 was raised to 2,000 and upon petition 3,000.[90] The *Book of Common Prayer*, the *ABC*, and the *Primer* were among those officially sponsored works exempted from these limits, often being printed in runs of up to twice the normal limits; and for reasons that will be made clear later it is possible that in the case of the *ABC* alone anything between 20,000 and 100,000 copies were published every decade from the 1560s to the 1630s, depending on whether one allows for only one edition per year or, more realistically, for two, three, or even four, of about 2,500–3,000 copies per edition. An estimate of one-quarter of a million copies having been printed by the early 1640s would probably be on the

---

[86] Anon., *The catechisme or maner to teach* (1572), tr. W. Turner; anon., *A catechisme or short kind of instruction* (1588), ed. T. Sparke and J. Seddon; Z. Ursinus, *Doctrinae Christianae compendium* (1585), and *The summe of Christian religion* (1587); J. Bastingius, *An exposition or commentarie* (1589); for further details, see Appendix 1.

[87] R.B., *A breife catechisme* (1601); E.B., *A catechisme or briefe instruction* (1617); and *Catechesis religionis Chistianae* (1623); see Appendix 1, s.v. Heidelberg Catechism, for details of other related works.

[88] See Appendix 1, s.v. Calvin.   [89] Ibid. and Ch. 4 below.   [90] *TSR* ii. 43; iv. 21–2.

conservative side; one of a half to three-quarters of a million is not beyond possibility.[91] Then there are copies of the *Primer* and the copies of the catechism available in copies of the Prayer Book itself, which were probably printed in comparable quantities. It is not being suggested that all these copies were acquired for the use of the catechism alone, but as we shall see, it is likely that the first text on which the majority of people who learnt to read practised their new skills was the catechism of 1549.[92]

Nowell's form also soon took root, and between 1570 and 1645 passed through at least fifty-six editions in six different versions: full-length in English, Latin, and both Greek and Latin, and condensed in the same three modes (there were other versions too which we will come to in due course). Of these much the most frequently reprinted was the condensed version, often referred to as Nowell's 'middle catechism': at least twenty-three editions of the 'middle' form would eventually be published in Latin, and about eighteen in English. This work retained much of the character of the original, Nowell having chosen to compress the original form not by simplifying the language or shortening individual answers but by omitting whole questions and answers at various points.[93] The comments in the preface, the names given to the catechist and catechumen—'master' and 'scholar'—and the prayers for 'scholars' printed at the end, the woodcut of a schoolroom scene added to many editions, and the popularity of the intermediate Latin version all point to the fact that the main aim and function of this catechism was as a pedagogical tool in the grammar schools of the day. The Nowell form was, together with Calvin's catechism which was also recommended in some school statutes, of particular significance in spreading moderate Calvinist ideas in schools and other places of formal instruction,[94] though in terms of numbers printed and exposure to the general public it was never more than a gallant second to the 1549 form.

In addition to these two forms, there were others which, to judge from their sales, proved very popular and in so far as they were licensed and frequently reprinted may be regarded as having official approval. In 1572 there appeared the first edition of John More's catechism, later often associated with the man who signed the preface on its first appearance in print—Edward Dering. Dering's preface makes it absolutely clear that most of the work of composition was by another 'faithful labourer', but he seems to have collaborated in the first edition, and by 1573 the work had been extensively revised, though by whom is not clear. By 1634 this revised version had been published over forty times, in two forms, one the revised text of 1573, the other the same but with the addition of full scriptural quotations,

---

[91] See below, pp. 175–6, for the pirating of ten thousand copies of the *ABC* at a time.

[92] See below, pp. 172–8.

[93] Bibliographical details of the different editions are given in Appendix 1.

[94] For a discussion of the possible dissemination of Calvin's and Nowell's catechisms, see below, pp. 188–92.

this last being the work of the 'godly' schoolmaster and preacher John Stockwood.[95] The catechism of Eusebius Paget or Pagit, also often ascribed to a co-worker, in this case Robert Openshaw, survives in thirty-one known editions between 1579 and 1641, again in the original shorter form, and in a longer with the scripture references in full (Openshaw's contribution).[96] William Perkins's unusual form, *The foundation of Christian religion*, survives in over thirty editions between 1592 and 1642; the enterprising little work by Stephen Egerton, *A brief methode of catechising*, apparently reached its forty-third edition by 1638; and John Ball's best-known catechism had probably been reprinted at least thirty-three times by 1645, in two forms, one with and one without an exposition of each answer.[97] If we take these five works (slightly more allowing for different versions) and multiply the total number of repeat editions by a figure of 1,250–1,500 for the late Elizabethan and Jacobean periods, and 2,000 for the late 1630s, we have something like 250,000 copies in circulation between the 1570s and the early 1640s.

But these were not the end of the story, for to these could be added over two dozen titles which passed through several editions, and scores which passed through merely one or two. As can be seen from column 1 of Table 1 another characteristic of this phase was, in fact, the sharp rise in the numbers of new catechisms being published. The total number of new forms published each decade rose from a handful in the 1560s to twenty in the 1570s and over forty in the 1580s. This level was not sustained throughout the rest of phase two, but an average of about five new forms a year was reached again in the 1610s and the 1620s, and the average rarely dropped below three new forms a year in the rest of the late Elizabethan and early Stuart periods. In all, well over two hundred and fifty new catechisms in English were published in our second phase of catechetical development from the 1570s to the early 1640s, representing perhaps another 300,000 copies in circulation on top of those already discussed. These totals would, of course, be even higher if we included catechisms in other languages, and the cognate categories given in columns 3 to 6 of Table 1.

Producing an estimate of repeat editions of these works is even harder than producing one for new catechisms, due mainly to the problem of missing editions. There are no surviving copies of most editions of *The ABC with the catechisme* and *The primer and catechisme* which we know from other sources to have been printed, probably because they were worn to pieces. Similarly a copy or copies of only seventeen of more than fifty editions of John Ball's original catechism have survived.[98] But taking *all* those represented in Table 1 except for the official forms and the five unofficial best-sellers discussed in previous paragraphs, we are probably looking at a total of something between four and five hundred repeat editions, and so around another half

---

[95] See Appendix 1, s.v. Dering; and P. Collinson, *A Mirror of Elizabethan Puritanism: the life and letters of 'Godly Master Dering'* (Friends of Dr Williams's Library, 17th lecture), London, 1964, 9–10, 33–4.
[96] Appendix 1, s.v. Paget. [97] Ibid., s.v. Perkins, Egerton, and Ball.
[98] See cols. 4–6 of the relevant entries in Appendix 1, and on *ABCs* and *Primers* below, pp. 174–7.

a million copies of catechisms or catechetical works being printed between the 1570s and the early 1640s. As might be expected, the upward curve of repeat editions starts later than that of new forms, and it also appears to have been less subject to fluctuation. In an admittedly crude exercise based on trying to allocate missing editions to an appropriate decade, there seems to have been only one dip—in the 1590s—in the steadily rising number of repeat editions from the 1580s to the 1640s; and from the 1610s there were probably in the region of a hundred repeat editions every decade, well over a hundred if we count in repeat editions of the best-sellers by Dering and More, Paget, Perkins, Egerton, and Ball. The 1630s was a decade in which there were relatively few new forms, only thirty-three straightforward catechisms in English, or forty-four if we include cognate works; but to compensate for that is the fact that there were nearly a hundred and fifty repeat editions of existing unofficial catechisms and catechetical works, as well as a peak of production of the official short catechism in copies of the Book of Common Prayer, and quite possibly of copies of the *ABC* and *Primer* too.[99]

The scale of the estimates offered in the last few pages is admittedly high. If added together, the totals might even exceed the known population of England at a given moment. This is not in itself a reason for disbelieving them. The estimates are for a period of over seventy years during which several generations of English catechumens came and went. Moreover, those who were catechized in school, for example, may well have been made to learn more than one catechism, moving from the short form in the *ABC* and/or the *Primer* to the middling and/or larger version of Nowell's catechism; and in the process enough copies of these works were probably worn to pieces to require frequent purchase of replacements. To judge from what happened to Bibles published in England, we may also surmise that a proportion of the catechisms produced there were sent to Ireland and New England, and perhaps Scotland as well.[100] Certainly, we should not imagine that all of the copies produced in England were actually sold there, or that those sold there were necessarily used; the estimates of production in the last few pages must be weighed against the evidence of use to be offered later in Chapters 3 to 5. But whichever way you look at it, it seems safe to say that publishing catechisms had very rapidly become big business in the late Elizabethan and early Stuart period.

Why was there such a surge of new works from the 1570s to the early 1640s? There is no sign of an official plan to further elementary religious instruction comparable to that outlined by Dr Tudor for the period 1536–53. The reiteration of the Edwardian injunctions and the renewed publication of the Book of Common Prayer, *The ABC*

---

[99]   See Table 1 above, and for the massive production of Prayer Books, Bibles, and editions of the metrical psalms in the 1630s, see my forthcoming study of *Print and Protestantism in Early Modern England*.
[100]   Ibid.

with the catechisme, and *The primer and catechisme*, together with the first editions of Nowell's catechism in the 1570s, were apparently seen by the Elizabethan authorities as all that was needed for young Christians as they proceeded from elementary to more advanced stages. There was, of course, a sustained increase in the provision of secondary education and to a lesser extent primary schooling and tertiary education in this period, though this owed much more to private philanthropy or to the leading officials of church and state acting individually rather than in concert.[101] However, there was an element of religious instruction in all these new schools and colleges, and the needs of this growing body of schoolchildren and undergraduates were probably a stimulus to the production of new forms.[102] It is also possible that political pressures may have played a part in the production of new forms. Growing fears of Catholic powers abroad and dissident Catholics at home led to tougher government action against recusancy in the 1570s and 1580s, which may have galvanized some authors or translators and publishers into action.[103] Another period of rising anti-Catholic sentiment, the closing years of the reign of James I, saw a second peak of publication of new catechisms, though in this case there may be another reason: pressure from bishops trying to ensure the regular performance of catechizing.[104]

It is possible that another reason for the appearance of many new forms at that time was the desire of many puritans to provide alternative forms to those of the established church. It cannot be denied that many of those who composed a new form during phase two were called 'puritans' by contemporaries or have been labelled that since by historians; nor can it be gainsaid that, either by their actions or in their other publications, some of these men indicated a desire for further reform of church structure and discipline.[105] It was also the case that many clergy were not happy with the short catechism of 1549. It was, by the standards of beginners' catechisms deployed on the Continent, an unusually short form, and from the standpoint of those Calvinists who came to the fore in academic circles in Elizabeth's later years, it was also unsatisfactory in two other respects: in what it said at the start, and what it did not say later on. At the start, it seemed to say that through baptism all children

---

[101]   On this, see the works cited at the start of Ch. 4 below.

[102]   See Appendix 1, and Ch. 4, pp. 174–7, 185–201 below.

[103]   See e.g. T. Beza, *A brief and piththie summe* (seven editions between 1563 and 1589), and anon., *A booke of Christian questions and answers* (perhaps three editions between 1578 and 1592). On anti-Catholic sentiment, see P. McGrath, *Papists and Puritans under Elizabeth I* (1967), ch. 8; R. Clifton, 'Fear of Popery', in C. Russell (ed.), *Origins of the English Civil War* (1973), 152–4, 157–8; J. P. Kenyon, *The Stuart Constitution* (Cambridge, 1969), 29, 43–6, 449; P. Lake, 'Anti-Popery: The Structure of a Prejudice', in R. Cust and A. Hughes (eds.), *Conflict in Early Stuart England* (1989); and P. Collinson, *The Birthpangs of Protestant England* (1988), ch. 1.

[104]   A point made by Dr Christopher Haigh in an unpublished paper on 'The Church of England and its people, 1604–40'; but now see also Fincham, *Prelate as Pastor*, 134–6.

[105]   For a list of 'puritan' authors of catechisms, see Grant, 'Cure of Souls', appendix A; for puritan and presbyterian objections to official catechisms, see E. Cardwell, *A History of Conferences and Other Proceedings* (Oxford, 1849), 186–7, and F. Procter and W. H. Frere, *A New History of the Book of Common Prayer* (1925), 183, 600–2.

were called to a state of salvation, which made strict Calvinists unhappy; they would have preferred a clearer statement that the benefits of baptism were felt only by the elect, and only at the moment of their effectual calling by the Holy Ghost which was usually much later in life.[106] Also the 1549 catechism said nothing about the divine decree of election and reprobation, and hardly anything about the classic reformed *ordo salutis* of effectual calling, justification, and sanctification. Indeed, it contained phrases which some later Calvinists felt were positively dangerous, such as a reference to 'God the Son who hath redeemed me and all mankind', which could be read as implying universal redemption rather than the Calvinist idea that Christ had atoned in effect for the sins of the elect alone.[107]

But caution should be exercised before reaching the conclusion that the main purpose of the men who produced their own catechisms was to avoid using the 1549 form or to propound an alternative doctrine or strategy to those of the church leadership. When one examines the texts of the new catechisms one finds remarkably little criticism of the established church's structure or forms of worship, certainly not enough to justify separating 'puritan' from non-'puritan' authors on this score alone. Though some authors, such as Thomas Cartwright, were perfectly capable of engaging in acrimonious debate over church government on other occasions, when it came to writing catechisms they appear to have taken a self-denying ordinance to avoid contentious issues, or to avoid using polemical techniques to justify their views on these matters.[108] Perhaps the fear of Protestants appearing divided in the face of the Catholic threat made this self-denial easier. There was also, as we shall see in the second part of this study, a large amount of common ground in the doctrinal content of the great mass of new catechetical writing, and, even when they had the opportunity, relatively few authors of alternative catechisms took the opportunity to spell out contentious matters such as limited atonement or the fate of the reprobate in any detail, which makes it equally difficult to separate forms into distinct theological categories.[109] Moreover, the 1549 catechism was capable of sustaining a Calvinistic interpretation or was used with few alterations by Calvinists or alleged 'puritans' such as Richard Bernard, Martin Nicholes, and John Ball.[110] Indeed, the more advanced of the official catechisms, that of Alexander Nowell, did raise the subjects of predestination and election (though not reprobation) and treated part of the *ordo salutis*, a fact which may also help to explain why relatively few authors of new forms felt it necessary to press on their younger catechumens those features of reformed theology not covered fully in the Prayer Book catechism.[111]

---

[106] See below, pp. 528–39.   [107] See below, pp. 354–5, 367–70.

[108] See Cartwright's subdued reference to presbyterian organization in his short catechism: Peel and Carlson, *Cartwrightiana*, 171; and Nowell's passing reference to Geneva-style discipline: Nowell, *Catechisme*, 96, 218.

[109] See Part II below, esp. chs. 8–9, 12.   [110] See below, pp. 78, 292.

[111] Ibid. pp. 325, 362, 398–9.

Another possible motive for writing new forms at this stage was to provide cate-chisms for household use, but again this should not necessarily be seen as bringing about a sharp divide on the basis of party loyalties. The authors of some of the cate-chisms which were said to have been designed for use in the home made it clear that either they expected the Prayer Book form to have been learnt before their own cate-chism was attempted, or they anticipated that their own form would be used in both home and church; other 'household' forms were apparently used in schools. In fact, both 'godly' and ultra-conformist clergy were anxious to use domestic catechizing as a support system to the minister's catechizing in church, rather than to let it develop into an independent activity.[112] In catechetical terms the main difference between 'puritans' and non-'puritans' may well have been that one had a more optimistic and the other a less optimistic estimate of what a typical householder was capable of teaching and an average child could learn. 'Godly' authors, who were themselves for the most part highly educated and zealous men, actively targeted households of the type with which they were most familiar: firmly Protestant, moderately leisured or prosperous, often urban and above all literate. The leaders of the church, on the other hand, expressed the hope that parents would teach their children at home but did not hold their breath until it happened, and in the mean time put most of their trust in the clergy and to a lesser extent schoolmasters as the chief agents of catechizing.[113]

One of the main reasons for the composition of many new forms between 1570 and 1640 was almost certainly a desire to supplement rather than replace the two official catechisms. As Reynolds, one of the puritan spokesmen at the Hampton Court con-ference, complained, the Prayer Book catechism was too short and Nowell's too long for use by the average catechumen.[114] In its original form the Edwardian catechism contained only twelve questions and answers, later raised to twenty-four when a sec-tion on the sacraments was added in 1604.[115] The 1549 form covered only six or seven pages, in the revised version of 1604 it covered eight to ten, and at that length stood a reasonable chance of being memorized, even if some of its individual answers were unduly long.[116] But compared to Luther's smaller catechism or to those of Geneva or Heidelberg, it was unusually brief, with relatively little in the way of additional mate-rial to explain difficult terms or phrases, or to enlarge on the duties required of a good Christian—lacunae which a number of authors set about filling. Owing to Cranmer's desire for a form that would bridge the gap between baptism and confirmation rather than pave the way for communion, the 1549 form also did not have a section

---

[112]   These points will also be developed in Ch. 4 below.   [113]   See below, Chs. 3–4.
[114]   Cardwell, *History of Conferences*, 186–7; and for a request in 1641 that the Prayer Book catechism 'receive a little more enlargement', see anon., *A copy of the proceedings of some worthy and learned divines* (1641), 8.
[115]   There is a complication in that in the interim period a revision was prepared in which two sections were added, but this was perhaps printed only in the version which appeared in *The ABC with the cate-chisme*; this will be treated in Ch. 4.
[116]   Brightman, *English Rite*, ii. 776–91; see also below, pp. 94–5, 246.

explaining what the sacrament of communion was and how to prepare for it, until one was added officially in 1604. For those catechists preparing communicants using the form printed in the Book of Common Prayer, this was a major omission, and, as was indicated in Chapter 1, a number of the first alternative catechisms had the preparation of parishioners for communion as one of their main objectives.[117] Although the authorities made good the omission, the tide of new forms or commentaries was by then too well advanced to be halted by that change alone.

Nowell's catechism, on the other hand, avoided most of the pitfalls into which the shorter official catechism fell. It contained a full treatment of the sacraments as well as an abundant supply of supplementary explanations and applications. What is more, it was strongly indebted to the catechism which Calvin wrote for use in Geneva. The main problem with Nowell's catechism, however, was its length. In its original form, it ran to 176 pages of quarto, was sufficiently long to require an eight-page index, and required literacy, time, and probably a personal copy for methodical study— conditions which few catechumens outside a grammar school could meet. As early as 1581 William Wood, who had tried it on his parishioners, complained that Nowell's answers were 'somewhat burdensome for the unlettered, and many words to them over scholastical'; and at Hampton Court in 1604 Reynolds confirmed that it was 'too long for young novices to learn by heart'.[118] A condensed version of Nowell's work had soon been produced, aimed (it said in the preface) at catechumens who had mastered the Prayer Book catechism but found the full-length version too difficult; and it is instructive that three times more copies of the condensed version were published than of the original. But even the condensed form was not a soft option: it ran to 94 pages of octavo and used similar phrases and terms to those in the longer version. Though suited to the middle forms of a school or perhaps a better-educated urban congregation, it must have been a daunting prospect for the inhabitants of a typical rural parish, and catechists continued to voice criticism of the difficulty of existing forms.[119]

The strongest evidence to support the suggestion that many of the new forms written in phase two were designed to supplement rather than replace the official catechisms is derived from their size.[120] The great majority of these forms, approximately three out of four, were longer than the 1549 catechism but shorter than Nowell's condensed form. Of the remaining quarter, many are not strictly comparable, being either specialized works—short forms for the very young or long works for more advanced catechumens—or specially abbreviated versions of larger

---

[117] See above, pp. 35–8.

[118] Haugaard, 'The Catechism of Nowell', 76; W. Wood, *A fourme of catechising* (1581), sig.*3ʳ; Cardwell, *History of Conferences*, 187.

[119] It is just possible that Wood and Reynolds were talking of the condensed Nowell form, but more likely they were attacking the full-length version. For Nowell's estimate of the potential readership of the condensed form, see the letter of 1572 printed at the start of the work.

[120] This calculation is based on an analysis of the forms listed in Appendix 1 for the period 1570–1645. For an explanation of the categories of size used in col. 6, see the Introduction to Appendix 1.

catechisms. Length alone was not, of course, the only consideration. When we compare official and alternative catechisms, what we find is that where the Prayer Book catechism had depicted the Christian faith with broad strokes and Nowell with a fine brush, the authors of many alternative forms used a medium-sized brush: they provided a brief explanation of each article in the Creed and each petition of the Lord's Prayer (the 1549 form had paraphrased these in a couple of sentences each, while Nowell took several paragraphs on each article and petition), they offered a brief exposition of each Commandment in turn (the 1549 form had tackled the Decalogue in one long answer, while Nowell devoted many pages to each Commandment), together with an account of the nature and purpose of the sacraments (omitted in 1549 but treated at great length by Nowell). The typical alternative catechism was between thirty and forty octavo pages in length, and the whole did not demand the memorizing of more than a few answers each week.[121] Even those forms which were not built around the four staples of catechizing, for example that of Perkins, were often of this same middling length, and although in some cases their authors used concepts and terms which were harder than those in the 1549 form, their forms were in general less demanding than Nowell's.[122]

In a number of cases, it was either assumed that alternative forms would be learnt after the Prayer Book form, as was the case with the graded list of catechisms offered by Thomas Watts with which we began this chapter, or it was stated explicitly that a new form was designed to build upon knowledge derived from the Prayer Book form. This was the case with William Hill's *First principles*, which sold fourteen editions between 1616 and 1639, John Mayer's *English catechisme*, which passed through six editions in the 1620s and 1630s in a full-length form and a further seven editions in a condensed form, and Richard Bernard's *Common catechisme* which had sold eleven editions by 1640.[123] In yet others the intention of building on knowledge derived from the Prayer Book form was made clear in the preface, as when William Crashaw said that his 'short and easy catechism' was intended 'to help to understand that good catechism given us already in the Common Prayer Book', or was implicit in the fact that the Creed, Commandments, and Lord's Prayer were not given in full but assumed to have been learnt already.[124] In all these cases, authors were not rejecting the official forms but intercalating an additional level between them.

There was, however, at least one other important motive for the construction of many alternative forms in phase two: to attempt to provide instruction for older catechumens as well as for younger. What stands out from many of the titles and

---

[121] As last note, plus Brightman, *English Rite*, ii. 776–91, and Nowell, *Catechisme, passim*.

[122] Perkins's *Foundation* is listed in Appendix 1, and discussed on pp. 286–7 below.

[123] For further details of these works, see Appendix 1.

[124] W. Crashaw, *Milke for babes* (1618), sigs. A2ᵛ–3ʳ; and e.g. E. Fenton, *So shorte a catechisme* [*c*.1582]; M[artin] F[ist], *A briefe catechisme* (1624); and J. Downe, 'A short catechisme', in *A treatise* (Oxford, 1635), 310–13.

prefaces of these works is the extent to which adults were thought to be in as much need of instruction as the 'children' and 'youth' for whom the Prayer Book form had been produced and the 'scholars' for whom Nowell's work had been designed. A large number of authors said that their catechisms were for 'all Christians', 'all sorts of people', 'all those that seek to enter the path-way of salvation', or all the members of a family.[125] Sometimes it was pointed out that a work had already been used by a whole congregation or a complete household, to the benefit of young and old, masters and servants.[126] A number of forms were aimed at combinations such as 'children and ... all poor ignorant souls', 'youth and ignorant persons', or 'youth, and simpler sort of people'.[127] Other authors talked of adults as 'babes in Christ' or 'babes in knowledge' who needed to be suckled on milk before they moved on to stronger meat, or paired them with their juniors in phrases such as 'children in years and children in understanding', 'children in years or in knowledge', 'children in Christ', or 'novices in the school of Christ'.[128] A number of adjectives or phrases would also seem from their context or internal logic to have been aimed less at children and adolescents than at adults with little formal education or limited ability to retain religious formulae: the 'ignorant', the 'unlearned', the 'weak' or 'weaker sort', the 'simple' or 'simpler sort', those of 'meanest capacity' or with 'weak or crazed memories', 'country people', or those lacking the money to buy or the time to read a larger catechism.[129] Concern with adults is also evident in the preoccupation of many forms with the Lord's Supper, for in theory if not always in practice children were not admitted to communion, as they were considered to be incapable of the sort of reasoning and self-analysis that preparation for communion required.[130]

If one tries to divide the new forms produced between the 1570s and the early

---

[125] The following paragraphs are based on Green, 'Emergence of the English Catechism', 408–12, where fuller references to the material discussed here can be found. For examples of catechisms pitched at a wide audience, see the title-pages of W. Horne, *A Christian exercise* (1585); J. Ball, *A short catechisme*; and G[eorge] G[ifford], *A catechisme containing the sum of Christian religion* (1583).

[126] See I[ohn] D[avidson], *A short Christian instruction* [1588], sig. A4ʳ; John Owen, *The principles of the doctrine of Christ* (1645), sig. A3ʳ; anon., *A short catechisme collected by a Christian* [1575?], preface; Bourne, *Light from Christ ... or, the rich jewel*, sigs. a2ʳ⁻ᵛ, a8ᵛ; and [Paget], *Short questions and answeares* (1580), sigs. A3ʳ⁻ᵛ.

[127] See the title-pages of G. Scarbrough, *The summe of all godly and profitable catechismes* (1623); E. Reeve, *The communion book catechisme* (1635); and C. Watson, *Briefe principles of religion* (1578).

[128] R. Bernard, *Two twinnes* (1613), 8–10; I[ohn] B[oughton], *God and man* (1623), 3; J[ohn] S[talham], *A catechisme for children* (1644), title-page; I[ohn] G[ibson], *An easie entrance into the principall points of Christian religion* (1579), sig. A1ᵛ; I[ohn] P[aget], *A primer of Christian religion* (1601), title-page; D.V., *An enlargment of a former catechisme* (1637), title-page.

[129] See the title-pages of R.B., *A breife catechisme* (1601); E. Parr, *The grounds of divinitie* (1614); R. Bernard, *A double catechisme* (1607); W. Bradshaw, *A direction for the weaker sort of Christians* (1609); C[hristopher] S[hutte], *The testimonie of a true fayth* (1581), sigs. E5ʳ–7ᵛ; T. Gataker, *The Christian mans care* (1624); J.H., *The principles of Christian religion* (1645); R[obert] H[arrison], *Three formes of catechismes* (Middelburg, 1583), sig. A2ᵛ; I[ohn] B[rinsley], *A breviate of saving knowledge* (1643); Crashaw, *Milke for babes* (2nd edn.); anon., *The main grounds of religion* [1624?].

[130] R. Hill, *Christs prayer expounded* (1606), 3; S. Crooke, *The guide unto true blessedness* (1613), 56; G. Whiting, *Short questions and answers* (1629), 9.

1640s according to the target group stated by the author, one is soon defeated by the vagueness of some writers, and the wide variety or combinations of categories used by others (or perhaps by their publishers). But what is, I think, beyond reasonable doubt is that, compared to the preoccupation in the first phase with teaching children and schoolboys, there is in the second phase a much greater concern with instructing youth and ignorant adults as well, and perhaps the single most frequently stated reason for designing a new form was to prepare would-be communicants for the Lord's Supper. By the 1570s and 1580s many ministers were finding that, despite the growing numbers of sermons and vernacular services, their older parishioners were simply not responding to Protestant stimuli in the way that had been anticipated, or that many would-be communicants were falling below an adequate standard of knowledge, faith, or penitence for sin. As in Germany in not dissimilar circumstances in the late 1520s and 1530s, the idea of catechizing adults as well as children began to take hold among the clergy.[131] Those who tried to use the two official catechisms to this end may have found them unsuitable. Neither had been designed for teaching adults, and the older members of a congregation may have resisted instruction in the children's catechism of 1549 as beneath their dignity, even though many of them were probably not capable of digesting the meatier Nowell version.[132] Conscientious pastors began the search for a form that would be more suitable or acceptable to older catechumens—or even better a form that could be used with both young and old in the limited time available for instruction. The search was prolonged well into the next century, due partly to resistance or apathy from adults and partly to the difficulty of finding just the right form for a particular congregation or a particular combination of ignorant catechumens.[133]

Other reasons for the composition of new catechisms in the late sixteenth and early seventeenth centuries should be considered, in particular the hope of providing more skilful or effective instruction through improved techniques of catechizing. As a result of failure with an old form, many authors experimented with other ways of getting the essential message across—perhaps shorter answers or simpler words, or getting the students to ask the questions and the catechist to reply, or inserting short revision tests from time to time. Having refined their form through trial and error, they then published it in the hope that other catechists might find it of value.[134]

---

[131] Strauss, *Luther's House of Learning*, 158.

[132] Ibid. 167, 164–75 and ch. 13; and Green, 'Emergence of the English Catechism', 417–19. See also the puritans' demand at the Hampton Court conference for a standard new form: *Historical Manuscripts Commission: Montagu of Beaulieu MSS.* (1900), 33 (clause 9).

[133] Ibid. 37–40; R. Gawton, *A short instruction* (1621), sigs. A2^{r-v}; J. Frewen, *Certain choise grounds* (1621), sigs. A4^r–6^r; H. Vesey, *The scope of the scripture* (1633), sigs. A2^r–4^r. The ecclesiastical authorities do not seem to have placed any obstacles in the path of those parish clergy who were trying to find or design a form for adults or communicants—Green, 'Emergence of the English Catechism', 412. n. 65—at least not until the 1630s perhaps: see n. 146 below.

[134] See Ch. 5 below.

Although in one sense the target for catechizing was widening as adults were increasingly tackled as well as children, in another sense it was also narrowing, in that some of the new catechisms of this period were specialized ones aimed at a relatively narrow group such as the very young, like the *Catechisme, or short kind of instruction*, which was said to be capable of being learnt by 2- to 3-year-olds (presumably before they embarked on the Prayer Book catechism), or those who were seriously ill, like *The sicke mans ABC*—a short form which Clement Cotton added to later editions of his popular treatise called *None but Christ*.[135] A growing minority of authors also evidently decided that what they needed was a variety or a carefully graded sequence of catechisms, and like Stephen Egerton, John Mico, and others set about providing two, three, or more different forms for their catechumens to tackle in turn; some even specified the age range for each level of catechism. A concern with technique and with levels of difficulty are subjects to which we shall return in more detail in Chapter 5, but they are worth noting here as another explanation of the continuing flow of new forms throughout phase two and well into phase three.

There is one further motive to be considered, less altruistic but perhaps not uncommon at the time. A number of the catechisms published in phase two were dedicated to a bishop, a peer, a gentleman, or a corporation, which may suggest that the author hoped to impress those in power by his catechism.[136] Of course, such a motive could coexist with one or more of the other reasons already mentioned. Indeed, it goes without saying that different authors were probably inspired by different combinations of the motives mentioned in the last few pages.

Against this background of rapid growth of new forms, the fall in the numbers of *new* catechisms being published in the later 1620s and 1630s deserves a moment's consideration before we move on to phase three. It has already been pointed out that the number of *repeat* editions probably reached a new peak in the 1630s, so that we are certainly not looking at a diminution in overall production. But why the fall in new forms? Three explanations spring to mind. The first is that the very success of earlier efforts to plug the gaps in the market may have meant that by the early 1620s there was less need to write one's own. A number of the popular catechisms mentioned above must have been widely known and widely available by then, and with the appearance of a number of works designed to provide better technique or a sequence of forms for different catechumens, some of the more obvious reasons for composing your own form were evaporating.

Secondly, it is possible that a reaction against the multiplication of new forms was gaining ground in the early Stuart period. The attitude of 'the more the merrier' expressed by some authors in the later sixteenth century and to a lesser degree in the

---

[135] See Appendix 1, s.v. *Catechisme* and Cotton.

[136] See above, p. 6; and the epistles dedicatory of T. Pearston, *A short instruction unto Christian religion* (1590); J. Foorthe, *The apostles catechisme* (1623); E. Reeve, *The communion booke catechisme expanded* (1635); J. Balmford, *A short catechisme* (1597); and R. Abbot, *Milk for babes* (1646).

seventeenth was giving way, at least temporarily, to 'the fewer the better'. The older attitude can be found in those catechists who admitted there was little new in their work, but expressed the hope that their form might reinforce another catechist's efforts by restating the same message in a different way; what a catechumen found hard in one form, he might understand better in another.[137] Allied to this in the late sixteenth century had been the feeling that the times were so bad that there could not be enough catechisms available.[138] As late as 1629 when a John Hart was hesitating whether to publish a catechism, an exposition on the Lord's Prayer, and a treatise on repentance by his 'dear friend', John Smith, who until his death had been preacher at Clavering in Essex, he tells us he remembered the words of a bishop (unnamed but still alive) to the effect that ' "If a thousand several men had all written on these several subjects: yet he could wish them all printed" '; they might vary in presentation but they would agree in the main.[139]

Not all clergymen saw matters that way by then, even among the 'godly'. In 1604 Robert Cawdrey noted the inconvenience of having so many different catechisms in use when some families and servants were frequently moving from one parish to another, and wondered if the king (advised by some 'godly learned ministers') should not authorize just two—for those with weaker and those with better memories. At the start of the next reign, Richard Bernard, although he had been a vocal critic of the church on many points, can be found arguing in favour of using nothing but the official catechism at elementary level. Bernard argued that the official short catechism differed 'not in substance, nor in manner of delivery' from other catechisms, but only in being approved by authority, and like Cawdrey pointed out that if people moved from one parish to another their children and servants would find it easier to follow the catechism if it was the same one they had already started to learn.[140] By the 1620s and 1630s we find various clergymen arguing in favour of using just one form, but while most opted for the church's short form,[141] one or two opted for a form that they just happened to have about their person. John Yates, for example, complained in

---

[137] e.g. W. Charke, 'Of the use of catechising', sigs. D5^{r-v}, printed at the end of the 1580 edition of Robert Cawdrey's *Short and fruitefull treatise*; T. Sparke, *A short treatise* (1580), sig. Ei^v; Davidson, *Short Christian instruction*, sigs. A2^v–3^r; R. Horne, *Points of instruction for the ignorant* (1617), sigs. A2^{r-v}; J. Syme, *The sweet milke of Christian doctrine* (1617), sig. A3^v.

[138] T. Watts, *The entrie to Christianitie* (1589), sig. B4^r; J. Leech, *A plaine and profitable catechisme* (1605), sigs. A2^{r-v}; and R. Linaker, *A short catechisme* (1610), sigs. A3^r–4^r.

[139] Hart's comments come in the epistle to the reader at the start of J. Smith, *Essex dove* (1629). For earlier recognition by one of the 'godly' that some people thought there could be too many catechisms, even though he himself had decided to go ahead and publish anyway, see G. Gifford, *A cathechisme* (1583), sig. *2^r.

[140] R. Cawdrey, *A short and fruitefull treatise* (1604), sigs. B7^v–8^r; R. Bernard, *The common catechisme* (1630), sig. A3^v.

[141] J. Mayer, *The English catechisme* (1623), sig. A4^r; W. Crompton, *An explication of those principles* (1633), sig. q4^v; *The Works of George Herbert*, ed. F. E. Hutchinson (Oxford, 1967), 255; Reeve, *Communion book catechisme*, sigs. B4^v–C1^r, C3^r; and on the mobility of young catechumens, see below, pp. 123–5.

1622 that the people were being catechized 'by as many forms as there are teachers', but if catechists were to use his *Modell of divinitie* they would find it suitable both for babes in Christ and grown men.[142]

There was also the argument that diversity could lead to heterodoxy, and that there was safety in using just one or two forms. This was the view that came to be adopted by many Lutherans and Calvinists abroad and by Cranmer in the 1540s as well as some English clergy in the early Stuart period.[143] It would also be a view which gained ground in the later seventeenth century, among both conformist episco-palians and nonconformist ministers, especially after the appearance of many hereti-cal, sectarian, or polemical catechisms in the 1640s and 1650s.[144] This brings us to our third possible explanation for the somewhat reduced level of publication of new forms: Laudian censorship, which has been held to be very severe, especially against Calvinist authors.[145] Certainly, one or two of the new forms published in the 1630s were written by Laudians, such as Edmund Reeve, whose *Communion book cate-chisme* of 1635 was one of the few catechisms of the Elizabethan and early Stuart peri-ods to contain offensive remarks about fellow English Protestants. It is also of interest that, looking back from the late 1650s, Philip Nye thought there had been considerable liberty in the choice of catechisms from the Reformation to the 'latter end' of the bishops' reign, at which point, he said, the use of the Prayer Book cate-chism alone had been insisted on.[146] However, if one looks closely at the list of authors whose catechisms were published between 1629 and 1640, one finds a number of men who from their other works were clearly far from being 'Arminians' or Laudians, and might well be described as prominent Calvinist divines, such as William Whitaker, John Geree, Daniel Rogers, and John Ball (who published an exposition of the Prayer Book catechism in 1639). The list also includes some who went on to be nominated to the Westminster Assembly of Divines in the early 1640s, such as William Twisse and Herbert Palmer.[147] If to the publication of new forms one adds the repeat editions of older works by 'godly' authors such as Nowell, Dering and More, Paget, Ursinus, Perkins, Cartwright, Egerton, Ball (his original two forms), Edward Elton, Elnathan Parr, William Gouge and Nicholas Byfield, one might rapidly reach the conclusion that the 1630s were a heyday for 'godly' or Calvinist catechisms, or to put it more accurately Calvinists' catechisms, since their Calvinism did not necessarily dominate their catechetical writing.[148] Viewed in this light, Laudian censorship of catechisms

---

[142]   J. Yates, *A modell of divinitie* (1622), sig. 2ᵛ.

[143]   Cranmer's apparent preference, like Luther's, was for a two-pronged programme of official instruc-tion comprising the 1549 Prayer Book catechism and the *Catechismus* (see Appendix 1, s.v. Cranmer).

[144]   For the views of a number of later Stuart clergy on this subject, see below, p. 88.

[145]   Tyacke, *Anti-Calvinists*, 81–2, 101, 184–5.

[146]   Reeve, *Communion book catechisme*, sigs. C1ᵛ–2ᵛ, and pp. 65–7, 76–8, 102–3, 206–7; [P. Nye], *Beames of former light* (1660), 100, and cf. p. 239 for a parallel remark about the removal of latitude in visitation articles.

[147]   The catechetical works of these authors are all listed in Appendix 1 under their authors' names.

[148]   Ibid.

must be deemed to have been either very mild or ineffective.[149] By the same token, the rise in production of new forms in the 1640s and 1650s was perhaps a temporary phenomenon due as much to the exceptional conditions of those decades as to the removal of censorship. Certainly in the years *after* 1660, the philosophy of 'the fewer the better' would again prevail in that many of the new forms then published were devoted to explaining the meaning of one or other of the two most widely used forms—the Prayer Book catechism inside the established church, and the Westminster Shorter Catechism outside it—while some of the other new forms were for minority groups whose interests were not served by the range of catechisms then available.

There was no sharp dividing line between the end of the second and the start of the third phase of English catechizing. The 1640s witnessed a number of developments, some of which were short-lived, others of which did not reach completion until the 1650s or later; but the combined effect was a distinct shift away from the pattern of the 1620s and 1630s. One short-term development was the appearance of an unusually large number of short catechisms in the 1640s. Prior to that decade, shorter forms of twenty-five pages or less had been published in relatively small numbers, perhaps no more than five new forms a decade. But in that decade the proportion of smaller catechisms was much higher; fairly typical examples are John Brinsley's *Breviate of saving knowledge* (1643), Francis Peck's *Kernell of Christianity* (1644), and John Stalham's *Catechisme for children in yeeres and children in understanding* (1644).[150] One explanation for the unusual number of short forms may lie in the attack on the liturgy and rubrics of the Book of Common Prayer and to a lesser extent on the catechism it contained; if the standard short form was no longer acceptable, another had to be found to put in its place. In at least one case a temporary easing of censorship allowed the second edition of Hugh Peters's short catechism to be published in England.[151] But the group of pre-communion questionnaires of 1645–8 offers another, much more specific explanation. In October 1645 an ordinance was passed by the presbyterian majority in both houses empowering ministers and elders to suspend 'all ignorant and scandalous persons' from the sacrament, but in the absence (until 1648) of a new official catechism to breathe life into these 'rules and directions', at least eight authors stepped in, including two, John Ball and John Mayer, who between them had already composed five different forms between the 1610s and the

---

[149] For a sceptical view on censorship, see S. Lambert, 'Richard Montagu, Arminianism and Censorship', *Past and Present*, 124 (1989), 36–68.

[150] See Appendix 1. For the temporary decline in production of *ABCs* and *Primers*, see below, pp. 176–7, 186.

[151] See above, p. 50 nn. 29, 31 and p. 6 n. 24, for the case of Peters and the partly comparable cases of Geree and Ezekiel Rogers.

1630s.[152] The techniques of presenting and testing the knowledge required by the ordinance, and the closeness with which its words were followed, varied from form to form. In his *Rules and directions of the ordinance of parliament ... resolved into a short catechisme* which appeared in 1646, Jeremy Cateline stuck close to the original by dividing his text into four columns: on the left there was a phrase from the ordinance, in the second and third columns were a question and an answer based on that phrase, and in the right-hand column was a scripture text to prove the point.[153] A form prepared for his Northamptonshire parishioners by a leading divine, Edward Reynolds, and published in 1648, was clearly based on the same source, but this work consisted of no more than a series of bare questions linked to the statements in the ordinance followed not by a full answer but a couple of biblical references in each case. Those of his parishioners who desired admission to communion were clearly expected to be able to look up the texts they did not immediately recognize.[154]

The clutch of catechisms based on the ordinance of October 1645 were in their turn overtaken by another development, one with much greater significance in the long term: the drafting of the Westminster catechisms. In 1643 the members of the Long Parliament had summoned a large number of divines to Westminster to help the MPs devise a doctrinal and liturgical settlement to replace the episcopal one, and at an early stage it was decided to draft a completely new form. However, due to a variety of problems only slow progress was made, and then in January 1647 there was yet another twist when it was decided to prepare not one but two catechisms, both of which were to reflect the contents of the newly agreed Confession of Faith. Of the two, one was to be 'more exact and comprehensive', and the other 'more easy and short for beginners', or as it was later put 'for the more rude and ignorant'. A large number of previously published catechisms had been examined in an attempt to find the correct content and the clearest formulations, but the main sources for the final two forms seem to have been the original draft begun in 1645 and the phrases of the Confession of Faith. Disagreements still arose, for example over the inclusion of the Apostles' Creed, which was not to be found in the scriptures. As a result it was not until 25 November 1647 that the Assembly was ready to present its 'humble advice' to parliament 'concerning a larger and a shorter catechism', and even then, there was a further delay while scripture proofs were added to both forms and parliament scrutinized the confession and the two catechisms and made some amendments. It was September 1648 before parliamentary approval for the publication of the Shorter

---

[152] *Acts and Ordinances of the Interregnum*, ed. C. H. Firth and R. S. Rait (2 vols.; 1911), i. 789–91; and Appendix 1 for details of all the catechisms by Ball and Mayer.

[153] Ibid.

[154] Reynolds's work, *Questions extracted out of the ordinance* (1648), was also unusual in being printed on a single sheet of folio paper, so that it could be hung up on a wall. The other four authors who to a greater or lesser degree built round the 1645 ordinance were Robert Austin, Edward Bury, Thomas Mockett, and the anonymous author of *The short catechisme or the examination* (1646–7) (and cf. J. Owen and O. Sedgwick): see Appendix 1.

Catechism was given. The Larger was approved by the Commons but not accepted by the Lords, probably due to the pressure of political developments at that time. Despite this lack of approval for the Larger, both forms were printed regularly throughout the 1650s.[155]

The Larger was quite a substantial work, containing a hundred and ninety-six questions and answers; the Shorter had only a hundred and seven, and in size—thirty to forty pages of octavo including the proofs—was much closer to those alternative catechisms of phase two described above.[156] Of the two, however, the Shorter was to prove much the most important. Like the Prayer Book catechism its sales (as measured by repeat editions) soon outstripped those of the larger official form, and remained well ahead thereafter.[157] Its many excellent qualities won it praise not only from contemporary and succeeding generations of presbyterians, whose leaders had come to dominate the Assembly, but also from churchmen as diverse as Archbishop Ussher, Richard Baxter, Peter du Moulin, and John Wesley.[158] Large parts of it were adopted or expounded by Independents like Isaac Chauncy and Isaac Watts, and it was still being used by some congregationalists in the late nineteenth century.[159] Some of the early Baptists also adopted it, after they had modified the section on infant baptism;[160] and after the Restoration, a Yorkshire clergyman and future dean of Durham, Thomas Comber, quoted extensively from the Shorter Catechism in the preface to his exposition of the Prayer Book catechism, and John Worthington, a friend of the Cambridge Platonists and preacher in Restoration London, prepared a catechism which owed much to the same Shorter Catechism and sold steadily for a century.[161]

While it is fair to say that the face of English catechizing was changed permanently by the appearance of the Westminster Shorter Catechism, it would be going too far

---

[155] This account is based on Carruthers, *Three Centuries*, 3–6, 15; but see also H. Palmer, *An endeavour of making* (1640), preface and *passim*; Mitchell, *Catechisms of the Second Reformation, passim*; *Lords' Journal*, x. 511 and *Commons' Journals*, vi. 27 (and *pace* John Morrill, 'The Church in England, 1642–9', in Morrill (ed.), *Reactions to the English Civil War, 1642–1649* (1982), 94, 96); and W. A. Shaw, *A History of the English Church … 1640–1660* (2 vols.; 1900), i. 375; for versions of the two catechisms, see Appendix 1, s.v. Westminster Assembly of Divines.

[156] There was some variation according to the format and typeface used by the printer, and according to what the catechism was published with: the Westminster Confession, the other catechism, an *ABC*, etc.: see Carruthers, *Three Centuries*, 19–94.

[157] An attempt at assessing production, using Carruthers, *Three Centuries*; Wing[2]; and the Eighteenth-Century Short-Title Catalogue has been made in Appendix 1; while absolute precision is not possible, the greater popularity of the shorter is manifest.

[158] T. Doolittle, *A complete body of practical divinity* (1723), sig. **[r]; I. Watts, *Catechisms* (1730), 117; Carruthers, *Three Centuries*, 6.

[159] Ibid., and see Appendix 1 for the catechisms of Chauncy and Watts.

[160] The work which came to be known as 'The Baptist Catechism' apparently dates from the early 1690s when it was entitled *Brief instruction in the principles of the Christian religion*: see Appendix 1. The text was largely the same as the Westminster Shorter Catechism, perhaps as an irenic gesture.

[161] T. Comber, *The church-catechism with a brief and easie explanation* (1686), 5; J. Worthington, *Hupotuposis … A form of sound words* (1673).

to say that it ended the quest for a perfect form. It was the product of a committee of men working in a tense atmosphere and with limited time, who may also have been conscious of the historic nature of their task: producing an English confession and catechism to stand for ever in the pantheon of European Protestantism alongside those of the Swiss churches, Heidelberg, and the United Provinces.[162] The debt of the Shorter Catechism to the phrases of the Confession of Faith gave it authority but often at the expense of simplicity or clarity. Those catechists who used it found that its answers needed explaining or subdividing to make them digestible to the young or ignorant, and soon a growing number of expositions, explanations, paraphrases, and modified versions of the original began to appear.[163] The first of these appeared almost instantly: John Wallis's *Brief and easie explanation of the shorter catechism*, 'wherein the meanest capacities may in a speedy and easy ... way be brought to understand the principles of religion'. Using the 'Yes' or 'No' technique pioneered by Herbert Palmer in the 1630s but rejected by the Assembly in 1645, Wallis's work proved an instant success and between 1648 and 1662 passed through eight editions.[164] In 1650 part of the Shorter Catechism was turned into verse by someone calling himself T.D., M.A., in a work entitled *Zions song for yong children*; and perhaps as early as 1658 Joseph Alleine published his *Most familiar explanation of the assemblies shorter catechism* in which the 'longer answers are broken into lesser parcels, thereby to let in the light, by degrees, into the minds of the hearers'; by 1702 this had been printed five times in England alone.[165] In the 1660s and 1670s, Thomas Lye devised no less than three different versions of the Shorter Catechism and a handbook on how to catechize using the Assembly's 'lesser catechism' which also sold well.[166] Thomas Doolittle was another minister who during a ministry of fifty years made various attempts to promote understanding of the Shorter Catechism: by reducing its contents to a 'scheme' capable of being printed on a single sheet; by a catechetical exercise to help explain it to young and old; by modifying it in his *Plain method of catechizing*; and by using it as the basis for a set of lectures and then turning these into a series of questions or comments to be posed to the individual soul—a curious work in some ways more akin to a meditation than a catechism.[167] In all, at

---

[162] The pastor of the French church at Canterbury, Philip Delmé, was a member of the Assembly and on the committee to prepare the catechism; at an early stage he advised his fellow-members to learn from the experience of Reformed churches abroad: Carruthers, *Three Centuries*, 4.

[163] For contemporary criticisms, see those of Watts, below, p. 243, and [J. Strong], *The Assembly's shorter catechism revised, and render'd fitter for general use* (1735) (copy in Liverpool University Library), pp. v–vii.

[164] See below, pp. 260–2 and Appendix 1; the clause cited in the text comes from the title-page of Wallis's work.

[165] For the first, see Appendix 1, s.v. the letter D; the 1658 edition of the second cannot now be traced, though Grant, 'Cure of Souls', listed it, and given what we know of Alleine's activities at the time (see below, p. 222) this is not impossible; for surviving editions, see Appendix 1, s.v. J. Alleine.

[166] T. Lye, *An abridgement of the assemblies shorter catechism*; *The assemblies shorter catechism*; and *An explanation of the shorter catechism*; and cf. *A plain and familiar method*; for further details, see Appendix 1.

[167] Doolittle's single-sheet 'scheme' is referred to in anon., *An earnest call to family-catechising* (1693),

least thirty supplements to or modified versions of the Shorter Catechism had appeared in England by the end of our period, reaching (with reprints) a total of over seventy editions in England alone.[168] The authors of another dozen catechisms had clearly been influenced by its structure or content.[169] It cannot be doubted that the Westminster Shorter Catechism was widely read and widely used, and that after 1660 it became the biggest single rival to the standard form used by the restored episcopal church. But its impact owed a good deal to the many ministers who helped to translate it into terms which the weaker members of their congregations could understand, and the publishers who made copies of these explanations widely available.

———————

Two other features of the third phase that can be traced back to the 1640s were the growing variety of doctrines in the catechisms of the period and the increased element of polemics which accompanied that growth. It was during that decade that the element of controversy directed against fellow-Protestants changed from being most unusual to not uncommon. This was true of some of the more conventional, broadly-based catechisms, especially those written by sectaries, but it was perhaps more true of the growing number of forms which tackled nothing but a single contentious issue, such as church government, infant baptism, admission to communion, or the nature of the Trinity, as we shall see shortly.

From the early 1650s the increased diversification of doctrine is clearly visible in a spate of Baptist and Quaker catechisms. Henry Jessey's *A catechisme for babes* of 1652 contained three short forms of a relatively uncontentious nature, but the *Soul-searching catechism* published a year later by his fellow-Baptist, Christopher Blackwood, did not shirk from tackling many 'questions of the highest concernment in Christian religion', and John Tombes's *Short catechism about baptism* made a firm case against infant baptism and for believers' baptism.[170] Half a dozen more catechisms with Baptist features can be found in the period from the 1650s to the 1720s,

---

4; for further details of his *The young mans instructor*, *Plain method*, and *A complete body of practical divinity*, and also his exhortation—*Catechizing necessary for the ignorant young and old*—see Appendix 1.

[168]   These works are indicated in Appendix 1 by the initials WSC ('Westminster Shorter Catechism') in col. 6; repeat editions have been calculated from the information in cols. 3–5 (approximately 45 editions of the Westminster Shorter Catechism in English are suggested by adding up the relevant entries under 'Westminster Assembly of Divines' in Appendix 1). Historians owe a great debt to Carruthers for his survey of works related to the Westminster Shorter Catechism: *Three Centuries*, 95–128, but his survey should not be used uncritically. More than once he detects the influence of the Shorter Catechism on a work that was actually produced before 1647, e.g. R. Jones, *A briefe and necessarie catechisme* (first published in 1583), the anonymous *Short treatise* of 1647 and the anonymous *Short catechisme* of 1671 (which were actually repeat editions of the best-selling works of John Ball—see Appendix 1). He also missed some anonymous works which are listed in the Term Catalogues or which the ESTC database has helped to uncover, e.g. anon., *The second book for children* (1704).

[169]   These are indicated in Appendix 1 as owing a debt to the WSC, e.g. Thomas Gouge's *Principles of Christian religion*, John Worthington's *Hupotuposis*, and the irenic forms mentioned below, pp. 91–2.

[170]   See Appendix 1 for further details.

one of which was a modest best-seller: Benjamin Keach's *Instructions for children*, which contained catechisms for children of three ages. By 1723 this had reached its fifteenth edition in the space of about sixty years.[171]

Given the sharp differences between the Friends' views and those of other Protestants on a number of issues, it was always likely that the Quakers would produce their own catechisms. The first known is Fox's *Catechisme for children* of 1657, which was translated into Latin and enlarged in the 1660 edition.[172] Five more catechisms were printed between 1663 and 1673: two by William Smith, one by Thomas Richardson, a reading primer and catechism by Fox and Ellis Hookes, and one by Robert Barclay, whose book also contained a confession of faith. In the 1660s and 1670s another Quaker, Isaac Penington the younger, also issued a number of works entitled *Some queries* or *Some questions and answers* which were mainly rhetorical or polemical defences of the Quaker position, but which overlapped at some points with more conventional catechisms.[173] Thereafter the number of new Quaker forms seems to have declined, though in fairness it should be added that Barclay's work sold consistently under the later Stuarts, and by the early eighteenth century was also available in Latin.[174]

Other authors used the format of a catechism to make a narrower case. In 1641, for example, a work by the separatist John Robinson was republished in England with the title *An appendix to Mr Perkins his six principles* (it was also published in 1642 as *A briefe catechisme concerning church-government*); its tone was studiedly moderate, but many of the comments about the nature of the church would have been much too radical for Perkins.[175] About the same time was published John Cotton's *Doctrine of the church*; his manner was also mild, though both episcopalians and sectaries would have found much of what he said about the visible church not to their liking.[176] Two works published in 1645—Thomas Colyer's *Certaine queries: or points now in controvercy [sic] examined and answered by scripture*, and John Bernard's *The Independents catechisme*—used question-and-answer form to tackle similar subjects, as did *The main points of church-government and discipline*, attributed to Christopher Love and published in January 1649. Love tackled the subject of church-government 'plainly and modestly ... by way of question and answer'; the work would, it was claimed, be very useful for those who lacked either money to buy or leisure to read larger tracts. In twenty-three questions and answers it made a very specific case for the presbyterian form of church government which the Long Parliament had tried to set up in the

---

[171] For other works by Keach and by other Baptists, see Appendix 1, s.v. Keach, W. Saller, M. King, E. Hall, and 'Brief instruction'.

[172] Ibid., s.v. Fox. [173] Ibid., under the respective authors' names.

[174] Ibid., s.v. Barclay; this was still selling well enough to warrant several more editions in the later eighteenth century. The *Christian catechisme* of George Keith should also be noted, but had a chequered history: see Appendix 1.

[175] This work had a chequered publication history: see Appendix 1.

[176] J. Cotton, *The doctrine of the church* (1643), title-page and *passim*.

late 1640s.[177] John Tombes's *Short catechism about baptism* of 1659, mentioned above, is another example of the trend towards an element of controversy in catechetics, in this case on infant baptism; Tombes's work might have been a riposte to any one of a number of sermons or tracts attacking the Baptists' position, though there is a possibility that it was a reply to a work put out by Daniel Evance in 1655: *A baptismal catechisme*.[178] Similarly when Richard Baxter and James Nayler clashed in the 1650s, Baxter posed questions to the Quakers, many of them rhetorical, and Nayler used a mixture of ordinary prose and question-and-answer in reply.[179]

Other contests flared up in the 1650s and 1660s, for example, over the Socinianism of the Racovian catechism, published in Latin in 1651 and in English in 1652 (both were ostensibly published abroad, but may actually have been published in London); over the *Twofold catechism* published by a Unitarian, John Biddle, in 1654; and over the alleged Arminianism in John Horne's *Brief instructions for children* published in the same year.[180] Later in the century, John Field followed in Nayler's footsteps by publishing an answer to a work called *An answer to a catechism against Quakerism*, the offending work being written by someone calling himself N.N.; the latter has not survived, though to some extent it can be reconstructed from the quotations Field made from it in order to clarify and defend the Quaker position.[181] The Church of England was not immune as is shown by the controversy provoked by an exposition of the church catechism by Samuel Clarke, published posthumously in 1729; the disagreement involved at least three authors and rumbled on into the early 1730s.[182] But perhaps the noisiest of these debates was provoked by James Strong's revision of the Westminster Shorter Catechism in the mid-1730s, which left out the reference to the decrees of election and reprobation in question seven and the reference to election in the answer to question twenty; the assertion that Christ was the 'redeemer of God's elect' in question twenty-one was altered to 'redeemer of mankind'.[183] Strong should have known better. Conservative presbyterians denounced the revision in chorus, and even a Baptist minister, David Rees, wrote in defence of the original Shorter Catechism. The revision was quashed, though the whole affair is of further interest in that it straddled the border with Scotland.[184] From the mid-seventeenth century, different religious groups had a good deal of

---

[177] See Appendix 1 for these works; and cf. [W. Prynne], *Diotrephes catechised* (1646), title-page and *passim*.

[178] See Appendix 1 for further details of these works.

[179] R. Baxter, *The Quakers catechism* (1655); and J. Nayler, *An answer to a book called the Quakers catechism* (1655), *passim*.

[180] See Appendix 1, s.v. *Catechesis ecclesiarum*; *Racovian catechism*; J. Owen; M. Wren; *Votes of Parliament*; J. Biddle; and J. Horne and J. Hacon.

[181] See Appendix 1 for further details.

[182] See Appendix 1, s.v. S. Clarke, T. Emlyn, A. A. Sykes, and D. Waterland; Clarke's brother John also became involved in the debate which drifted further and further away from its starting-point.

[183] [Strong], *The assembly's shorter catechism revised*, preface and *passim*.

[184] See Appendix 1, s.v. Strong for his vindication of the revision, the attacks by J. Guyse, D. Millar,

capital tied up in their catechisms, both as a public statement of where they stood doctrinally and as a standard form of instruction and examination for meeting-place or home—of particular value where members were widely scattered. So it is perhaps not surprising that these forms were stoutly defended when they came under attack.

In the mid-seventeenth century, an element of political calculation also crept into catechetics. An early example of this was *The covenanters catechisme* of 1644 which was 'first delivered in sundry sermons to a congregation and now resolved by questions and answers for the more public good'. This work explained that there were various types of covenant: civil, spiritual, and mixed; the Solemn League and Covenant (recently drawn up to bind the English Parliament and the Scots army together) was a mixed one, it said, and could be taken with a clear conscience.[185] Other excellent examples are furnished by the rival catechisms prepared for the two armies fighting in the English civil war: *The souldiers catechisme* by Robert Ram, printed for the parliamentary forces in 1644, and *The souldiers catechisme composed for the kings armie* by Thomas Swadlin, published in 1645.[186] Both works reassured soldiers that if they died fighting they would win a martyr's crown, but whereas the parliamentarian form said that the war was being fought to save the king from a 'popish malignant company' and to save the laws and liberties of England and the true Protestant religion, the royalist one said that the war was being fought to defend the rightful authority of the king against rebels and to recover what had been unjustly taken from him. Rebellion was a great sin, and only Jesuits and puritans taught subjects to resist their king. Thus both authors stressed that the cause for which the soldier was fighting had a religious as well as a political dimension.[187]

In a number of other works given the title of catechism, the intention was satire or attack rather than reassurance, for example *The cavaliers catechisme* and *The round-heads catechisme*, both published in 1643. A brief example from the former, which parodied the 1549 Prayer Book catechism while striking a propaganda blow for the parliamentary cause, will have to suffice: 'What is your name? Cavalier. Who gave you that name? My seducers and deceivers, in my innocency, wherein I was made a member of the Church of Rome, and consequently a limb of anti-Christ.'[188] The intrusion of politics continued after the Restoration, as in *A short*

---

and D. Rees, and support from S. Bourn and P. Gibbs; cf. also the charge that in Scotland the clergy were putting too much emphasis on the Shorter Catechism, in anon., *The usefulness of catechisms* and *The use of catechisms further considered* published in Edinburgh in 1736 and 1737 (both are listed in the BL Catalogue, s.v. 'Usefulness').

[185] Anon., *The covenanters catechisme* (1644), title-page and *passim*.

[186] See Appendix 1: in the revised version of the Wing STC, the several later editions of Ram's work in 1644–5 that appeared in Wing¹ have been deleted.

[187] R. Ram, *The souldiers catechisme: composed for the parliaments army* (1644), 1–2, 23–4; T[homas] S[wadlin], *The souldiers catechisme composed for the kings armie* (Oxford, 1645), 1–3, 9–11. There are a number of other works hovering on the borders between the military, the political, and the religious which I hope to describe and analyse at a future date.

[188] Anon., *The cavaliers catechisme* (1643), sig. A2ʳ; for similar works, see Appendix 1, s.v. *Round-heads*

catechisme for all the kings ... subjects of 1660, which used religious precepts to urge obedience to the crown, and in a series of question-and-answer works produced during the renewed period of anti-Catholic hysteria in the late 1670s and the 1680s.[189] In the early 1690s we find works entitled *The Jacobites catechism* and *The Williamites catechism* (both by Benjamin Bird who had earlier written a 'normal' catechism), and in the reign of Queen Anne, there was a whole series of 'catechisms' attributed facetiously to leading figures such as the duke and duchess of Marlborough, Louis XIV, and Prince Eugene, while *The ladies catechism*, *The beaus catechism*, *The town-misses catechism*, *The country-gentlewoman's catechism*, and Uvedale Price's *New catechism for the fine ladies* contained attacks on the foppishness and hypocrisy of the upper ranks of contemporary society.[190] But since all these depended for at least part of their effect on the contrast between a real catechism and a fake, they too are indicative of the familiarity which the man and woman in the street—or the bookshop—was expected to have had with such forms by the later Stuart period.

The largest element of continuity between the first two phases and the third was provided, almost inevitably, by the Prayer Book catechism. Although the Book of Common Prayer was officially replaced by the presbyterian Directory early in 1645, it seems clear that the older liturgy was still being used in many parishes during the later 1640s and the 1650s.[191] So too may have been the 1549 catechism: the fact that it was out of official favour did not prevent at least five works being published in the next fifteen years which owed a great deal to it. In 1646 a sequestered rector from Kent, Edward Boughen, published in royalist Oxford a work entitled *Principles of religion* which was in fact an enlargement of the Prayer Book catechism; and two other expositions of the same work appeared in 1655 and 1656: William Nicholson's was quite long and clearly aimed at a more advanced readership than Richard Sherlock's. In addition, there were two anonymous works: *A catechisme to be learned for the training up of youth* published in 1653, which was largely the same as the 1549 form— only the opening questions and answers and a few phrases later on had been changed;

(1643), H. Parker (1643), E. Gilbert (1645), another *Cavaliers catechisme* (1647), *Parliaments new and perfect catechism* (1647), and *Satyrical catechisme* (1648); and for a piece of revenge in 1660, see anon., *The redcoats catechisme*.

[189] e.g. anon., *A protestant catechisme for little children* (editions in 1673 and 1687); anon., *A protestant catechisme shewing the principal errors of the church of Rome* (1681); anon., *No popery, or a catechism against popery* (1682); anon., *A true-protestant-catechism* (1683); anon., *A popish political catechism* [168–?]; and *A catechism truly representing the doctrines and practices of the church of Rome* (1686); and see the dialogues by Matthew Poole and John Rawlet, and Thomas Comber's *Plausible arguments*, which are also listed in Appendix 1. Wing[2] lists literally hundreds of works under 'Dialogue', 'Dispute', or 'Disputation', where STC[2] has only a few.

[190] See Appendix 1, s.v. Bird and the relevant titles; and above, p. 56.

[191] Morrill, 'The Church in England', 103–14.

and the *Short catechisme to prepare young ignorant people for the sacrament* of 1657, which had clear echoes of the same original.[192]

At the Restoration, the Book of Common Prayer was revived, modified slightly, and once again printed in dozens of editions every decade, and as always these volumes contained the 1549 catechism, as modified in 1604 and with a few additional alterations.[193] The old faithfuls, *The ABC with the catechisme* and *The primer and catechisme*, were once again published in large quantities, and continued to earn good money for the Stationers' Company, who held the copyright, for many decades to come.[194] In the second half of the seventeenth century, as noted above, we again hear the idea that it was best for all beginners to learn one and the same catechism being commonly expressed, and in most people's mind that catechism was the Edwardian catechism of 1549, now increasingly often referred to simply as 'the church catechism'.[195]

Like the Westminster Shorter Catechism, however, the Prayer Book catechism was the focus for a large number of authors who sought to enhance the value of the original by adding their own explanations or additions. This trend had begun before the civil wars and continued in the 1640s and 1650s, but at the Restoration gathered pace fast, so that from the 1660s to the 1730s nearly a hundred different works were produced to help teach and explain the meaning of the church catechism. The peak decades were from the 1680s to the 1710s when, with the extra stimuli of fear that the church was in danger and on the more positive side demand from the newly created Charity Schools, there was on average more than one new exposition published each year (as can be seen from Table 1 these decades also witness a peak of production of works containing exhortations to catechize and advice on catechizing).[196] Moreover, since a number of these works sold well, for example those of Edward Boughen, Richard Sherlock, Thomas Marshall, Thomas Comber, John Williams, William Wake, Zachary Isham, and John Lewis, these expositions of the church catechism account for well over two hundred repeat editions, or perhaps half a million copies on top of the sales of hundreds of thousands of copies of Prayer Books, *ABC*s, and *Primer*s.[197] Together with the similar expositions from the early Stuart period, these

---

[192] For further details of Boughen's work, Nicholson's *Ekthesis pisteios or A plain but full exposition* (1655–89), Sherlock's *Principles of holy Christian religion* (1656–99), and the two anonymous works, see Appendix 1. Cf. also *The ancient church catechisme, with some small additional explanations*, published *c.*1680 but said to have been 'printed in the time of the church's dissettlement'.

[193] See Brightman, *English Rite*, ii. 778–9, 789.   [194] See below, pp. 176–7.

[195] e.g. L. Addison, *The primitive institution* (1674), ch. 14; [W. Beveridge], *The church-catechism explained* (1704), 1.

[196] These expositions mentioned are indicated in col. 6 of Appendix 1 by the initials PBC (Prayer Book catechism). The total given does include translations into Welsh, Irish, German, as well as classical or Near Eastern languages, the first three of which were presumably used outside England or for training older schoolboys and ministers who might subsequently become catechists outside England. But the great majority of works, as we shall see in Ch. 3, were in English and designed to help explain the Prayer Book catechism to English catechumens. On the teaching of the church catechism in Charity Schools, see below, pp. 177–82.

[197] These calculations are based on repeat editions of the items marked PBC in Appendix 1, and using

works will form a significant part of the story of catechizing that will be described in the next two chapters; and they will also figure prominently in the sample of best-selling catechisms upon which our survey of catechetical doctrine will be based in Part II of this study. But here we may note that nearly all were written by serving clergy, including a number who were soon to be or were already bishops,[198] while at a humbler level there were anonymous works drawn up for the schools or country parishes with which their authors were associated.[199] Not only the leading lights of the day, such as Thomas Bray—a key figure in the early days of the Society for Promoting Christian Knowledge—but also a number of less well-known but equally conscientious pastors took time to ensure that the official catechism was fully understood, and the sales of their works suggest their efforts were appreciated by other clergy as well.

There are some obvious parallels between the history of the episcopalians' short catechism and that of the presbyterians during this third phase. Both achieved dominance in their own spheres of influence—the Prayer Book form among the conformist majority, the Westminster Shorter among more conservative nonconformists. Both forms were widely used and stimulated the creation of a large number of ancillary works to help give them greater impact. And both survived the successive political and religious crises of the period to march into the age of the Evangelical Revival. Indeed, both forms were reprinted regularly throughout the upheavals of the Industrial Revolution and two World Wars, and, despite the existence of rivals, are still in use in some English-speaking areas today (or were so until very recently). The existence of many translations into the native languages of four continents, products of the great age of missionary activity, bears witness to the fact that the two forms, though very much the product of their own time, left a mark not only on early modern England but also on succeeding centuries and on many other countries as well.[200]

On the other hand, there are a number of contrasts between the two works as well. It was not just that, owing to the contrast in size of their clientele, there was a huge imbalance between the numbers of copies of each form and the numbers of expositions of each form published.[201] It was rather that for the most part the Prayer Book

a multiplier of anything between 2,000 and 3,000, for which, see above, p. 65 n. 90. The work of Helen Weinstein on *ABC*s and *Primer*s in the later Stuart period has produced some startling results on the scale at which these officially approved works were produced.

[198] e.g. William Nicholson, John Williams, William Wake, and Richard Kidder; Thomas Ken, William Beveridge, and Gilbert Burnet; the careers of most of these men are described in *DNB*, and their catechetical works are listed in Appendix 1.

[199] e.g. anon., *The church catechism broke into short questions* (1709) (with prayers for use in Charity Schools); anon., *A short exposition of the church-catechism* (Norwich, [17—]) (recommended for use in Charity Schools); anon., *The country-parson to the country people* (1712); 'A country parson', *A short and plain exposition of the church catechism* (1715); other examples may be found in Chs. 3–4 below.

[200] See BL Catalogue, s.v. 'Liturgies. Church of England. Common Prayer. Separate Parts. Catechism. Adaptations' and 'England. Religious Bodies. Assembly of Divines, Shorter Catechism. Translations'.

[201] A provisional estimate would be that hundreds of copies of the Prayer Book catechism were

catechism remained an essentially simple form which had to be supplemented by extra information and ideas if a catechumen was to extract full value from it; whereas the Shorter Catechism was not only a longer but also a much more difficult work which had to be made *easier* if catechumens were to learn and understand it. Another major difference between the two forms was in their structure and content, not least their doctrine of salvation and their ecclesiology, as we shall see in Chapters 6 to 8 below. This contrast was the more stark after 1660 due to the fact that the longer catechism adopted by the Elizabethan and Jacobean churches, the catechism of the moderate Calvinist Alexander Nowell, was effectively dropped by the later Stuart church—only one edition of it appeared in English (in 1663)[202]—which left the non-Calvinist 1549 catechism in sole possession of the field against the hard-line Calvinism of the Westminster catechisms. Thus another undoubted reason for the appearance of so many commentaries on the Prayer Book form was the desire to provide the fuller statement of the established church's position which to some extent the Nowell catechism had provided in earlier days.

Through these supplements, however, the 1549 catechism lost its relative immunity to controversy and became involved in that trend towards greater polemic that became marked in the 1640s and 1650s, since a number of the expositions mentioned above tackled key areas of dispute with fellow-Protestants openly and firmly.[203] A very revealing example of this can be seen in the section on Boughen's exposition where he was tackling the question of whether Christ died for all men or only for those whom God had already decreed should be saved. Not content with quoting key passages from the scriptures, the Book of Common Prayer, and the Thirty-nine Articles in defence of a general atonement, he decided to reinforce the point by a free use of capitals: God so loved the world 'that he gave his only begotten son, to the end that ALL THAT BELIEVE IN HIM should not perish, but have life everlasting' (John 3: 16); 'If ANY MAN sin, WE have an advocate with the Father'; Christ died 'for the sins of the WHOLE WORLD' (1 John 2: 1–2); St Paul assures us that 'Christ tasted death for EVERY MAN' (Hebrews 2: 9); and so on.[204] The tone of these expositors towards Protestants who deviated from the church's path was for the most part one of mild rebuff rather than sharp condemnation,[205] but it was no longer possible to conceal disagreement between Protestants from the young or simple members of their flocks. Indeed, in

---

published for every one of the Westminster Shorter Catechism, and that perhaps three times as many expositions of the Prayer Book catechism, and three times as many repeat editions of those expositions, were produced compared to those of the Westminster Shorter: see sources cited in last few pages.

[202] See Appendix 1, s.v. Nowell; a limited number of Latin or Greek and Latin versions were also printed after 1660: ibid.

[203] See e.g. the prefaces of B. Bird, *The catechism of the Church* (1674) and [William Assheton], *A short exposition of the preliminary questions and answers* (1694).

[204] Boughen, *Principles* (1668), 12.

[205] Bird, *Catechism*, sigs. A2r–v; N. Taylor, *A practical and short exposition* (1684), title-page and *passim*; and cf. J. Gaynam, *The use and excellency of the church catechism* (1709), 39–47.

the eyes of many churchmen it would have been foolhardy and an abnegation of their duty to refrain from criticism of dissenters when the dissenters were so free with their criticisms of the church.

———————

As in the previous phases, however, there was a great deal of common ground on a number of basic issues in the catechisms produced and reprinted from the mid-1640s to the late 1730s and aimed at those of 'weakest' or 'meanest' capacity.[206] There was even the occasional coming together, as in the stress on the covenant which, as we shall see in later chapters, was common to many episcopalian and presbyterian forms of the later seventeenth century, and in the increasingly common practice of supporting answers with scripture proofs printed in full.[207] As an example of moderation we may take Richard Baxter. Throughout his ministry Baxter was a great advocate of catechizing, but the different catechisms and dialogues that he published are notable for their evangelical zeal rather than their acerbity.[208] Baxter could be an obstinate foe, as the episcopalians found at the Worcester House Conference in 1660 and the Savoy Conference in 1661, and as Quakers and others with whom he clashed could bear witness.[209] But when it came to religious instruction, either in England or elsewhere, for example converting the Indians of North America, he sought to avoid the excesses of what he once called 'a contentious, dividing age'.[210] Other irenic gestures were made. According to Isaac Watts, many children were taught the Prayer Book catechism before they learnt the Westminster Shorter; and there were some episcopalians who appear to have been prepared to praise the good qualities of the Westminster Shorter Catechism and even to use it or a modified version of it.[211] Although the form taught in most Charity Schools was the church catechism, it seems that the Westminster Shorter was taught in some of them.[212] At least one attempt was made

---

[206] e.g. anon., *A plain and easie way of catechising such as are of weakest memories and of the meanest capacities* (1680); and anon., *The art of catechizing* (1691) ('fitted for the meanest capacities, the weakest memories, the plainest teachers, and the most uninstructed learners').

[207] See below, Chs. 9 and 12 on convenant teaching; examples of conventional works citing scripture texts in full are Z. Isham, *The catechism of the church: with proofs* (1694); J. Lewis, *The church catechism explain'd* (1701); M. Henry, *A scripture catechism in the method of the Assembly's* (1703); [W. Bunbury], *The church catechism; with single proofs* (1710).

[208] R. Baxter, *Universal concord* (1660), *Poor man's family book* (1674), *The catechizing of families* (1683), and *The grand question resolved* (1692), and others listed in Appendix 1 below; and see G. F. Nuttall, *Richard Baxter* (1965), ch. 4, and below, pp. 222–7.

[209] Nuttall, *Baxter*, 87–90, and above, p. 56 for his brushes with the Quakers.

[210] Baxter, *Universal concord*, title-page.

[211] I. Watts, *Catechisms* (1730), 39; anon., *An earnest call to family-catechising* (1693), p. vii; J. Clifford, *A catechism containing the principles* (1694) (a work by a conformist which owed a heavy debt to the Westminster Shorter Catechism at the start, and to a lesser degree later).

[212] Anon., *A short catechism containing the principles* (1718) was approved for use in a London charity school, though question and answer 95 (in favour of infant baptism) was omitted, presumably to make it acceptable to an even wider range of dissenters.

by a nonconformist, Thomas Adams in 1675, to demonstrate that the Shorter Catechism contained nothing contrary to the official formularies of the Church of England, and as late as 1716 a 'British Protestant Divine' tried to compose a catechism which was based on the common principles of religion shared by those who used the church catechism and those who used the Westminster Shorter Catechism.[213] There was also a small cluster of 'scriptural catechisms' in the 1670s, and a steady stream of similar works from the 1680s to the 1720s,[214] some of whose authors were trying to get back to the roots of Protestantism by using nothing but biblical texts for the answers to their catechisms. Most of them may have soon betrayed a bias, but the intention if not the result provides another indication that catechizing was far from having degenerated totally into polemics. At this point we might also cite the case of the Woodwards: the father, Joseph, a nonconformist, much concerned with catechizing the poor, and the son, Josiah, a pillar of the various societies for the reformation of society and the spreading of the Gospel in the 1690s and 1700s.[215]

1740 is an arbitrary date at which to stop this brief survey of the emergence of an English catechetical tradition, since many of the features of what we have called the third phase of English catechisms can be found in the late eighteenth century, or later. But a line has to be drawn somewhere, and a point after the storms of Queen Anne's reign, but before the waves caused by the Evangelical Revival will do as well as any. To judge from the figures in Table 1, it is also possible that by 1740 the production of new forms was beginning to wane after reaching a second peak in the 1690s and 1700s. In some ways the third phase was less productive than the second, and, owing to the sharp divisions that had surfaced from the 1640s to the early 1660s, some of its products may have reached a smaller audience than comparable works during the second phase. On the other hand, the third phase was arguably characterized by greater innovation in technique, as we shall see in Chapter 5. Moreover, even in the dynamic second phase there was not necessarily a close correlation between the production of new forms and success in getting catechumens to attend and learn a form: success in catechizing may well have lagged a few years or even decades behind success in creating a body of catechetical writing suited to English conditions. It is to the success or failure of catechists in using the new forms described in this chapter that we now turn in Chapters 3 and 4.

---

[213] T. Adams, *The main principles* (1675), preface and *passim*, and cf. S. Harris, *Scripture-knowledge promot'd by catechizing* (1712)—a dissenter referring to Adams's work and hoping those in the Church of England would still have a friendly opinion of the Westminster Shorter; [Ferdinando Shaw], *A catholic catechism* (1717), title-page, pp. iii–iv (where he mentions earlier irenic efforts by Clement Ellis and Matthew Henry), and *passim*; cf. also the popularity of the conformist John Worthington's *Hupotuposis* with presbyterians.

[214] e.g. O. Stockton, *A scriptural catechism* (1672); S. Petto, *A large scriptural catechism*, and id., *A short scriptural catechism* (both 1672); anon., *A catechism containing the substance* (1676); and R. E., *A scriptural catechism* (1676); also cf. anon., *A scriptural catechism in opposition to the popish catechism* (1686); C. Ellis, *The lambs of Christ* (1692); [F. Shaw], *A catholic catechism* (–1717); J. Peirce, *A scripture-catechism* (1722); and B. Stinton, *A short catechism* (–1730).

[215] E. Calamy, *An account of the ministers … ejected or silenced* (1713), ii. 324–7.

3

Catechizing in Theory and Practice: In Church

IN this chapter and the next, we will turn to different questions: who was catechized and by whom; how often and in what way; and where and when did this catechizing take place? The verb 'to catechize' was regularly used to cover at least five operations: teaching catechumens to remember the set answers to set questions; testing their memory of those answers by oral examination; explaining to catechumens what the answers meant; testing how much they had understood of what they had learnt; and encouraging catechumens to put their new knowledge and insights into practice. For more advanced catechumens, in the higher forms of a grammar school and at university, catechizing also regularly took on other functions, such as helping them to acquire and understand extra information about the faith and to master classical languages. Moreover, catechizing could take place in church, in the home, or in school, or any combination of these, and it could take place in large groups of mixed age, ability, and origin, or in small cohesive ones, or even on a one-to-one basis. In this chapter and the next, it will be suggested that the best way to get to grips with catechizing is by sorting these different operations and venues into three types or levels of activity. These three levels were not totally separate, and techniques were never static. Nevertheless, some kind of division seems advisable, and so in the next few paragraphs the three levels will be described in broad terms, and then in the rest of this chapter and the next they will be examined in more detail in each of the three main locations of catechizing: church, school, and home.

At its simplest level, catechizing was a means of ensuring that all members of the church could 'say by heart' a number of formulaic answers, usually including the Apostles' Creed, the Lord's Prayer, and the Ten Commandments. Elementary catechizing thus embraced the first two of the five operations mentioned above: teaching a set of answers, and checking on catechumens' capacity to remember those answers. Comprehension of what had been memorized and application of the same, for example by trying to keep the Commandments or examining oneself for faith and repentance before participating in the Lord's Supper, were greatly desired by catechists; but practical considerations and (as we shall see in Chapter 5) the educational theory of the day both suggested that the indispensable first step towards understanding and commitment was the rote learning and regular testing of a certain number of answers. Because catechizing at this level was targeted at the largest numbers of people, regardless of whether they were literate or not, it was characterized by a strong reliance on oral instruction, though copies of the catechism being used might be circulated among those who possessed or were acquiring basic reading skills. It will be suggested below that by the early seventeenth century such elementary catechizing, especially of children from about the age of 6, 7, or 8 years to 12 or 13, was taking place moderately frequently in the majority of churches and in a great many elementary schools; and that by the early eighteenth century it was an established—if sometimes short-lived—feature of the religious life of the young. In the longer term, this kind of catechizing came to be seen as a mechanical exercise, a mere parroting of set answers with little or no understanding or application of what had been learnt—a situation which conformists and nonconformists alike were anxious to remedy, either by better techniques of elementary instruction or by moving on to more advanced methods of catechizing. But of its widespread adoption by the Stuart period and its moderately successful application to large numbers of children (though probably many fewer adolescents or ignorant adults) there can be little doubt.[1]

The most commonly used form at this level in churches and schools by the early seventeenth century and, after a hiatus in mid-century, again in the late seventeenth and early eighteenth centuries, was undoubtedly the Prayer Book catechism of 1549. This form was by no means ideal for the purpose, in that some of the answers in the central section were very long and a number of technical terms were not explained. But besides being the officially approved form for this level, the 1549 form had certain advantages. Even after the addition of some short questions and answers on the sacraments in 1604, it was still a relatively short form, which could easily be tested by the minister or his assistant, the dame or usher in a school, or even by a parent or master in the home; and it was built squarely around the three formulae—Creed, Commandments, and Lord's Prayer—which figured large in the liturgy (and wall decorations) of the established church, and which the authorities regarded as the minimum knowledge for those who were going to receive the Lord's Supper, get married, or act as godparents.[2] There were a large number of other simple forms which were probably used at elementary level, but most of these fall into one of three groups: either they were for the very young—in well-disposed and well-regulated households—to learn *before* the standard beginner's catechism;[3] or they were part of a package of instructional material designed to teach the young how to read and write, and so were more likely to have been used in school or home

---

[1] These points will be developed in the rest of this chapter and the next.

[2] Brightman, *English Rite*, ii. 778–91; 798–9; and Frere, *Visitation Articles*, iii. 3, 10, 98, 100, 156, 161, 220; Kennedy, *Episcopal Administration*, ii. 71, 113–14, 119; iii. 144, 147–8, 179, 212; and *Second Report on Ritual*, 401, 408, 412, 422, 425, etc.

[3] See B. Ritter Dailey, 'Youth and the New Jerusalem: The English Catechistical Tradition and Henry Jessey's *Catechisme for Babes* (1652)', *Harvard Library Bulletin*, 30 (1982), 25–54.

than in church;[4] or they were aimed at would-be communicants, and to have been designed to be learnt through being *read* rather than heard read,[5] and so are nearer to the second, intermediate level of catechizing.

This second level was by far the most complex. At its lower limit it shaded regularly into the one beneath, often being the product of a conscious attempt to improve on what had been achieved at the elementary level, either by adding more knowledge through a new and more demanding catechism or an upgraded version of the one already mastered, or by ensuring a greater measure of understanding or application of what that knowledge involved (the third, fourth, and fifth operations listed above), by means of an exposition of what had been learnt already or by an exhortation to apply it. At its upper limit this level shaded with no very clear line of demarcation into the top one, that of advanced catechetical instruction given to more able schoolboys, undergraduates, and ordinands.[6] However, catechizing at the intermediate level *was* different from the other two levels in the wide range of catechumens at which it was targeted, and in the increased reliance on written or printed forms, which was more than at elementary level but less than at the advanced. Thus, while intermediate catechizing was aimed as usual at the young, it was in this case targeted also and sometimes especially at two other groups: those older children and adolescents who had mastered the basic catechism, either in church or in the first years of schooling; and those adults who were deemed capable of understanding more, either by teaching themselves a form to advance their knowledge and help them prepare for communion, or by listening to what was said by way of exposition to the young. The first group—older children—might have to memorize a number of scripture texts to prove the truth of the statements in the catechism they had just learnt or move on to an explanation of that form, or on to a brand new form such as that of Calvin or Nowell. In the case of the second group—adults—the catechist's concern was not simply to remind them of what they should already have known or fill in the gaps in their knowledge, but also to ensure that they understood as much of the faith they professed as their ability and circumstances permitted, and that they acted upon it in their everyday life through hearing sermons, praying, praising God, and preparing themselves for communion on Sundays, or that at the least they showed signs of a readiness to act or to accept criticism of their conduct.

This stress on comprehension brings us to another characteristic of intermediate catechizing, at least compared to elementary catechizing: the greater amount of time devoted to explaining matters, to both young and old. In some cases this meant time being given to a short oral explanation of one of the more difficult terms or doctrines raised in an elementary form. This exposition might take the form of a few fairly

---

[4] See below, Ch. 4. [5] See above, pp. 36–8, and below, pp. 143–5.
[6] Again the points made in this and the following four paragraphs will be developed in the rest of this chapter and the next.

informal or extempore remarks, or might consist of a more formal prepared homily
or lecture or even a full sermon; and it might be delivered in the presence of catechumens alone, but often and increasingly it was given in the presence of older non-
catechumens, during service time. In other cases the explanation might take the form
of hand-written or printed copies designed to enable literate catechumens, whether
children or adults, to follow what was being taught in church or to study privately. A
reliance on such copies was not surprising, given the catechists' own great familiarity
with and strong dependence upon written texts, and the growing rates of literacy in
Tudor and early Stuart Engand. But it also created problems for those groups among
whom standards of illiteracy remained high, especially the poor, those living in rural
areas, and women. There are differing views of the extent of literacy, but the extent
to which English clergy, like their counterparts in Lutheran Germany, *assumed* a
level of basic literacy would tend to support the more optimistic interpretations of
the available evidence. However, outside London and the leading provincial towns
they could probably not *guarantee* that the majority were able to learn from printed
copies.[7]

This may also help to explain two other differences between intermediate and
other levels of catechizing: the greater amount of resistance, and the patchy pattern
of performance. Among adults this resistance may have been provoked by one or
more of a number of factors: in the first generation or two, there was probably a sense
of disquiet at the novelty of the exercise or at being bracketed with their children and
servants as catechumens; in later generations there was perhaps resentment at the
extra demands being imposed on adults compared to those of the elementary level
that they had experienced themselves as children; there may have been a sense of
embarrassment at being given copies of works they could not read; or being questioned closely about their understanding of doctrine, their sins, or their commitment
to leading a new life. Resistance may also have been offered to the attitudes or actions
of the 'godly' ministers who at this intermediate level led the way in the late sixteenth
century and again in the 1640s and 1650s in trying to ensure higher standards of
knowledge and commitment among inhabitants of communicable age, but who also
proved divisive in some communities.[8] By the early seventeenth century, mainstream catechists had come to share the same concern as the 'godly' about raising

---

[7] D. Cressy, *Literacy and the Social Order: Reading and Writing in Tudor and Stuart England* (Cambridge, 1980); M. Spufford, *Small Books and Pleasant Histories* (London, 1981), ch. 2; T. Watt, *Cheap
Print and Popular Piety, 1550–1640* (Cambridge, 1991), 1–8; K. Thomas, 'The Meaning of Literacy in
Early Modern England', in G. Baumann (ed.), *The Written Word: Literacy in Transition* (Oxford, 1986),
101–3; Strauss, *Luther's House of Learning*, 127–9, 193–202; and see below, pp. 174–84, 241–3.

[8] K. Wrightson and D. Levine, *Poverty and Piety in an English Village: Terling, 1525–1700* (London,
1979); K. Wrightson, *English Society 1580–1680* (London, 1982), ch. 7; C. Haigh, 'Puritan Evangelism in
the Reign of Elizabeth I', *English Historical Review*, 92 (1977), 30–58; W. Hunt, *The Puritan Moment*
(Cambridge, Mass., 1983); D. Underdown, *Revel, Riot and Rebellion* (Oxford, 1985), and id., *Fire from
Heaven: Life in an English Town in the Seventeenth Century* (1992); but see also M. J. Ingram, *Church
Courts, Sex and Marriage in England, 1570–1640* (Cambridge, 1987), 121 and ch. 3.

standards of understanding and soul-searching before communion; but they too faced resistance as adults for the most part made clear their continued disinclination to go back to what they saw as the status of a beginner.[9] Thus the performance of catechizing at this intermediate level was probably patchy compared to the more widespread performance at elementary level. But catechizing at this level was apparently not uncommon and moderately successful in some smaller groups: in the households of the 'godly' and the more zealous conformists, at least until the mid-seventeenth century; in the grammar schools where study of Calvin's or Nowell's catechism was part of the curriculum and the students formed a captive market; in some less populous parishes where an energetic minister and a well-disposed laity found common cause for a period of time; and in the compact and in many ways more consistently amenable communities which Protestant dissenters formed in the wake of the Restoration and Revolution settlements.

The third level of catechizing was the narrowest of all: it was the level of the higher forms of grammar schools and the first years at university, during which students were exposed to longer and more difficult forms. Catechizing here had much the same aims as at intermediate level: greater knowledge, understanding, and application, but was conducted at a more advanced intellectual level and by more advanced methods. It was predominantly performed through the medium of the printed book, and private study probably loomed larger than oral instruction or examination, though there were catechetical lectures at certain leading schools and in many colleges at the universities. Many of the printed works were so large or complex that there simply would not have been time for them to be mastered properly in half an hour or so each Sunday, especially not if the group of catechumens was large or of mixed ability. Indeed, in many cases these catechisms were studied in parallel texts of English and Latin, Latin and Greek or even Hebrew, with which only a very small minority of the population was familiar. Moreover, the aim here was comprehension rather than memorization: catechumens were told to read the form through again and again until they understood it all, and some catechists were prepared for answers to be made in students' own words rather than the exact words of the text, as long as the student demonstrated that they clearly understood what was meant. Resistance was probably limited here: some of the catechumens at this level may have seen mastering yet another catechism as just another academic hurdle to jump as a means of reaching some academic goal, but others may well have been intent on joining the ministry or becoming teachers or attaining some personal target of religious understanding. Catechizing in such cases was a means of training the next generation of catechists in church, school, and home. As such we are talking about a much narrower band of catechumens but one subject to strong external and in some cases internal pressures to co-operate in being catechized.

---

[9] Green, 'Emergence of the English Catechism', 418–19.

Having indicated the different levels of catechetical activity with broad strokes, we can now turn to depict each in more detail. But instead of looking at elementary cat-echizing in church, school, and home, then at the intermediate and then advanced levels in the same three venues in turn, which might be repetitious and disjointed, we will see how the different levels operated in each of the three main locations, begin-ning with the church.

The attitude of the English church to basic catechizing was not very different from that of the mature Luther or Calvin in the stress that was put on the role of the min-ister. Luther did not abandon his earlier belief that parents had a duty to teach their children the basics at home, but by the time he published his shorter catechism, it was on the shoulders of the 'faithful, godly pastors and preachers' that he put the main responsibility for teaching it.[10] As the number of schools increased in Germany, so the minister's role was supposed to turn more to testing and explaining the answers that the schoolteacher had instilled; but even then in some poorer areas an element of instruction as well as exposition may have fallen to the clergy's lot.[11] Calvin too thought that householders and schoolteachers had a role to play, but in the text of his 1541 catechism the exchanges were between 'minister' and 'child', and in the *ordonnances ecclésiastiques* of the same year it was to the minister in church at mid-day on Sundays that parents were told to bring their children to be catechized.[12] In England, too, while many bishops and enthusiasts envisaged a role for parents in instructing their charges (as we shall see), there is no sign of great confidence that they would play it, or of any official attempt to make domestic instruction compul-sory. Instead, in England from an early stage the brunt of the burden of ensuring the basic catechism was mastered and understood, especially by those who never attended a school, fell on the parish clergy. They were not expected to be completely alone in this: they were to receive support from a wide variety of schoolteachers, who were mostly kept up to the mark in their duty of catechizing; indeed, in many cases the posts of schoolteacher and clergyman were combined.[13] But in the absence of a national system of primary education such as was set up in some Lutheran and Calvinist states, it was a matter of chance who received such education, and so was

[10]   Janz, *Three Reformations Catechisms*, 181–8; S. C. Karant-Nunn, 'Luther's Pastors: The Reforma-tion in the Ernestine Countryside', in *Transactions of the American Philosophical Society*, 69 (1979), 27–30; Strauss, *Luther's House of Learning*, chs. 1–3, 6, 8–10.

[11]   Ibid., ch. 13; B. Vogler, 'Catéchisme et catéchèse dans l'orthodoxie Luthérienne à Strasbourg (1560–1750)', in *Transmettre la foi: XVIe–XXe siècles* (Actes du 109e Congrès National des Sociétés Savantes, Dijon, 1984), Section d'Histoire Moderne et Contemporaine, tome 1 (Paris, 1984), 9–16.

[12]   J.-C. Dhotel, *Les Origines du Catéchisme Moderne* (Paris, 1967), 40–1; while at the Synod of Dort, John Hales noted that some were in favour of a threefold catechizing, by parents, schoolteachers, and min-isters: *Golden Remains* (1688), 385–7, but it did not always work out that way. For Catholic catechizing in church at midday on Sundays, see J. Delumeau, *Catholicism between Luther and Voltaire* (1977), 200.

[13]   See below, pp. 182–3.

exposed to elementary catechizing through this channel as well. In England, therefore, the role of the minister as drill sergeant as well as chief examiner and exponent
persisted longer than in comparable churches abroad.

The official reliance on the clergy for basic catechizing was laid down in the
rubrics of the Edwardian, Elizabethan, and Caroline Prayer Books and the canons of
1571 and 1604.[14] Catechizing was to be performed by what the rubric in the original
Book of Common Prayer called 'the curate of every parish'. In the absence of assistant clergy in the majority of parishes at this time, 'curate' referred literally to the
man with the cure of souls: the 'parson', rector, vicar, or perpetual curate, or 'minister' as he was often referred to in later episcopal injunctions and visitation articles.[15]
This responsibility was communicated to the parish clergy in various ways: through
the questions put by archbishops, bishops, archdeacons, and rural deans (or their
deputies) during their regular visitations of the churches in their jurisdiction;[16] by
intermittent pastoral letters or 'charges' given by bishops to their clergy;[17] by sermons delivered at visitations, such as that given by Richard Bernard on a text chosen
by the archbishop of York, to exhort the clergy of Nottinghamshire to perform their
duty of catechizing;[18] and increasingly by pastoral handbooks written or approved by
senior clergymen.[19] That the clergy were aware of their duty to catechize can be
demonstrated by the number who in their publications insisted that catechizing was
enjoined by public authority, or cited the appropriate rubric or injunction for their
action, or praised the authorities for their care in insisting on the regular performance
of catechizing in church.[20] In an exposition of the Prayer Book form designed for use
by his parishioners in Devon in 1633, William Crompton referred not only to the

---

[14]　Brightman, *English Rite*, ii. 796–9; Cardwell, *Synodalia*, i. 121–2, 198–9, 280–1.

[15]　The 1552 rubric added to the 'curate of every parish' of 1549 the phrase 'or some other at his
appointment': Brightman, *English Rite*, ii. 796–7; for examples of the other appellations, see Frere, *Visitation Articles*, iii. 22; Kennedy, *Episcopal Administration*, ii. 42–3, 71, 75, 95, 114; and *Second Report on
Ritual*, 401, 405, 406, 617, 627, etc.

[16]　Frere, *Visitation Articles*; Kennedy, *Episcopal Administration*; and *Second Report on Ritual*, 401–685
passim; in some sets of articles the relevant canon was cited or placed alongside the article, e.g. *Second
Report on Ritual*, 453–6, 463–5, 471–2, 488–9, 588–94, 624–30, 634–6, 638–42, 646–52, 658–61, etc.

[17]　R. B[addiley], *The life of Dr Thomas Morton, late Bishop of Duresme* (York, 1669), 89–90; R. Skinner,
The speech ... at the visitation at Dorchester September 18 1637 (1744), 19–20; Thomas Lamplugh, *[A pastoral letter to the clergy of the diocese of Exeter]* [167?]; W. Bassett, *A discourse on my Lord Arch-bishop of Canterbury's ... letters* (1684); [W. Beveridge], *The church-catechism explained* (1704), sig. a3ʳ; J. R. H.
Moorman (ed.), *The Curate of Souls* (London, 1958), 20–2, 72, 109, 160–1, and cf. 88–9; *Diary of Francis
Evans, Secretary to Bishop Lloyd, 1699–1706*, ed. D. Robertson (Worcestershire Historical Society, 45;
1903), 15–19.

[18]　R. Bernard, *Two twinnes* (1613), 2; cf. R. Wensley, *The form of sound words* (1679); and W. Cradock,
A discourse of due catechising (1718).

[19]　R. Bernard, *The faithfull shepheard* (1607), 8–9; T. Downing, *The catechisers holy encouragement*
(1623); G. Herbert, *A priest to the temple* (1632), ch. 21; R. Baxter, *Gildas Salvianus. The reformed pastor*
(1656), *passim*; G. Burnet, *A discourse of the pastoral care* (1692), ch. 8.

[20]　See John Stockwood's preface to R. Cawdrey, *A short and fruitefull treatise* (1580), sigs. C3ᵛ–6ʳ;
Downing, *Catechisers holy encouragement*, sig. [2]ᵛ; Bernard, *Two twinnes*, 6, 14; W. Crashaw, *Milke for
babes* (1618), sigs. A2ᵛ–3ʳ; J. Phillips, *The Christians A. B. C.* (1629), sigs. A4ᵛ–5ᵛ; E. Reeve, *The communion*

king's 'late pious directions for the renewing and continuing of the ordinance of catechesis', but also to orders by Henry VIII, Edward VI, Elizabeth, and James; and the author of *Eniautos* in 1664 was even better informed in this respect, citing not only the injunctions of Edward VI and Elizabeth, canon 59 of 1604, and royal directions by James I, Charles I, and Charles II, but also the revised rubric in the revived Prayer Book of 1662.[21] To these royal directions we may add the exhortations to the clergy issued by Archbishop Whitgift in 1591, and by Archbishops Sheldon and Sancroft in 1672 and 1688, and the royal injunction of 1694 mentioned by various clergy in their publications.[22] Even clergy who knew that they were not meeting the official ideal still referred to its existence.[23]

As means of seeing how far the official ideal on elementary catechizing by the clergy was put into practice, we have a variety of sources, such as references in biographies, autobiographies, diaries, and the prefaces of supplementary catechisms.[24] But the two most important are the churchwardens' presentments in reply to bishops' and archdeacons' queries, and the clergy's replies to parallel queries addressed to them by some bishops in the early eighteenth century. The former are problematic in that experience has shown historians that like-minded clergy and laity could conceal a certain amount of nonconformity or dereliction of duty from the gaze of the authorities,[25] but the latter are less open to this objection. What happened in the early eighteenth century was that large numbers of clergy were faced by a list of questions, probably designed in 1712 by William Wake when he was bishop of Lincoln, and printed on four sides of quarto with large gaps for the clergy's answers. As Wake explained in the introduction to that questionnaire when he used it in his new diocese of Canterbury in 1716, 'it was my constant practice, when I visited my late diocese, together with the Book of Articles to the churchwardens, to send a paper of such questions to my clergy'.[26] The same questionnaire or a slightly modified one was deployed by other bishops, including Edmund Gibson in Lincoln diocese in 1718 and 1721 and Thomas

---

book catechisme (1635), sigs. B4ᵛ–C1ʳ, and p. 89; [T. Marshall], *The catechism set forth* (1683), sigs. a2ᵛ–3ʳ; Z. Isham, *The catechism of the church* (1695), sig. A4ᵛ.

[21] W. Crompton, *An explication of those principles* (1633), title-page; anon., *Eniautos: or a course of catechizing* (1674), sigs. A5ʳ–B1ʳ.

[22] J. Whitgift, *The Works*, ed. J. Ayre (3 vols.; Parker Society; Cambridge, 1851–3), iii. 610; Cardwell, *Documentary Annals*, ii. 337–8; D. Wilkins, *Concilia magnae Britanniae et Hiberniae* (4 vols.; 1737), iv. 618; *The Rector's Book, Clayworth, Nottinghamshire*, ed. H. Gill and E. L. Guilford (Nottingham, 1910), 112; C. Ellis, *The scripture catechist* (1738, but probably written in the 1690s); [John Morrice], *A defence of lecturers* (1733), 6.

[23] Secker, *Oxford*, 173; Wake MS 284, Christ Church, Oxford, fo. 427ᵛ; Herring, *York*, ii. 164.

[24] e.g. I. Walton, *The Lives of Dr John Donne, Sir Henry Wotton, Mr Richard Hooker, Mr George Herbert* (1670), 100; John Fell, 'The Life of ... Henry Hammond', published in *A Practical Catechism by Henry Hammond* (Library of Anglo-Catholic Theology; Oxford, 1847), pp. xxiv–xv; 'Some account of the life of ... John Lewis', BL Addit. MS 28,651, 30–4, 74; Downing, *Catechisers holy encouragement*, sig. [2]ᵛ; J. Mayer, *The English catechisme* (1623), sigs. A3ʳ⁻ᵛ; L. Addison, *The primitive institution*, (1674), sig. A6ʳ; Cradock, *Discourse of due catechising*, 7; and see the diaries of Evans and Sampson in nn. 17, 22 above.

[25] See below, pp. 137–8.   [26] Wake MS 284, fo. 1ʳ.

Herring in the diocese of York in 1743; the questions asked by Thomas Secker in the diocese of Oxford in 1738 were a considerably modified version, but the question on catechizing was basically the same as Wake's. Many of the clergy's replies to these questionnaires are extant, 219 for Canterbury in 1716, 176 for Oxford in 1738, and 644 for York in 1743; in the case of Lincoln I have chosen the returns for the archdeaconry of Lincoln in 1721 which number 452.[27] Together these replies furnish a very rich and under-used vein of material on ecclesiastical conditions in the early eighteenth century. Certainly they provide a much fuller picture of catechizing than the churchwardens' more formulaic returns for that period, and indeed for the previous century and a half.

Wake and Herring were at pains to stress to their clergy that they did not intend to take disciplinary steps on the basis of the replies they received. In 1712 Wake told the Lincoln clergy that he wanted to know only if duties were being done as they should be done *or* if the minister was resolved to do them properly thereafter, and when he moved to Canterbury he told his new clergy that he had found the replies he received in the past 'clear and satisfactory'.[28] Wake and Herring therefore invited the clergy to deal freely and plainly with them, and some like John Lewis in Kent clearly did so. Lewis not only described conditions in his own livings in detail, but covered a dozen large sheets of paper with a description of the difficulties that the clergy faced in the discharge of their duties and proposals for remedying that situation.[29] Not all of the clergy were as forthcoming, or perhaps as frank: the answers of some clergy seem evasive, as we shall see later. The ninth of Wake's questions was the one that concerned catechizing; Gibson used almost exactly the same question in Lincoln, while for Oxford and York dioceses Secker and Herring either modified or omitted the last two sentences, which dealt with explanation and exposition rather than basic instruction:

How often, and at what times do you catechize in your church? Do your parishioners duly send their children and servants who have not learned their catechism, to be instructed by you? Do they learn any other catechism, for the better understanding of that of the church? What catechism do they learn for that purpose?[30]

The extant replies will be referred to regularly in the next few pages as a means of testing how far practice matched theory.

It has to be recognized that the sources described in the last few paragraphs are not going to provide as full a picture of catechizing in church as we would like: while

---

[27] Gibson 13–15; Herring, *York*, vols. i–iii, *passim*; Secker, *Oxford*, 4–5 and *passim*.

[28] Lincolnshire Archives, V/vii/1/4, 1 (for an earlier version see/3); Wake MS 284, fo. 1ʳ.

[29] Ibid. and fos. 420–36; and Herring, *York*, i. 2.

[30] Wake MS 284, fo. 1ʳ; Gibson 13–15, *passim*; in 1721 Gibson left out the phrase 'who have not yet learned their catechism', inserted 'and catechized' after 'instructed', and substituted 'larger' for 'other': Gibson's 1718 questions are printed in *Speculum dioeceseos Lincolniensis sub episcopus Gul. Wake et Edm. Gibson A. D. 1705–1723*, ed. R. E. G. Cole (Lincoln Record Society, 4; 1913) [hereafter *Speculum Lincolniensis*], pp. iii–iv; Secker, *Oxford*, 4–5 and *passim*; Herring, *York*, i. 2–3 and *passim*.

some features, mainly on the theory and the organizational side, are moderately well covered, others, especially the frequency and the actual methods of handling face-to-face catechizing, are frustratingly hard to recapture. However, there is enough to offer the basis for a provisional framework into which further research, in court records, diaries, and anecdotal sources, may be able to insert more detail. Let us take the theory and practice of elementary catechizing in church under seven headings: the day or days of the week when such catechizing was supposed to take place; the place where it should have taken place; the time of day at which it was supposed to occur; the length of time it should have lasted; the frequency of catechizing; the composition of the catechumenate at this level; and the credibility of allegations of clerical neglect and lay resistance. What we will find under most of these headings is a large measure of continuity, but also a degree of change or shift, so that elementary catechizing by 1740 was not exactly the same as it had been in 1640 or in 1580. We will also find lacunae in official thinking and grey areas in the legal position: exactly where in church should catechizing take place, and how be conducted? what should be done with children who had learnt the first form and been confirmed but were not yet old enough to take communion? If we come to terms with the fact that the official programme for basic catechizing was not fully thought through at the outset, and if we try to identify not only the continuities but also the shifts, and try to explain these shifts, we may be in a position to make a more realistic assessment of elementary catechizing in England than has sometimes been the case.

———————

The first two aspects are fairly straightforward and can be dealt with fairly quickly. Basic catechizing was to take place on those days when all the faithful were supposed to attend church: Sundays and those holy days retained by the Protestant church. The most common formulae used in visitation articles of the Elizabethan and early Stuart period were either the one used in the rubric of 1552—'Sundays and holy days'—or the rather more precise 'every Sunday and holy day'. In some cases after 1660 the authors of visitation articles did not mention catechizing on holy days, or at least not in the enquiry about clerical behaviour; but the older ideal of Sundays and holy days can still be found in a number of later Stuart articles.[31] However, it is worth noting that regular catechizing on a weekday was not unheard of in Elizabethan and early Stuart times. According to Samuel Clarke, the puritan hagiographer, a number of 'godly' clergy not only preached twice on Sundays but also catechized or gave a catechetical lecture on weekdays as well: Richard Greenham catechized the youth in his rural parish in Cambridgeshire on Thursdays as well as Sundays; Thomas Gataker delivered a catechetical lecture in his Surrey parish on Friday evenings; Ezekiel Culverwell had 'weekly meetings in his church for all sorts,

---

[31] *Second Report on Ritual*, 408, 411, 414, 416, 419, etc., and 601–2, 604, 609, 611, 614, 616–7, etc.

distinctly on several days, to catechize them'; Thomas Wilson took up public cate-chizing on weekdays later in his ministry in Maidstone; while in their London parishes Richard Stock and Thomas Gouge both catechized regularly on weekdays, Stock teaching the boys and girls separately on different days.[32] It is also worth not-ing that in at least a third of those early eighteenth-century replies sent to Wake, Gib-son, and Herring in which the days of catechizing were specified, there was mention of a weekday, most commonly Wednesdays and Fridays, less often Thursdays or Saturdays, and very occasionally a Monday.[33]

One reason for this development was probably pressure of work on Sundays. When weekly catechizing became the official norm in the early 1550s, Bishop Hooper had warned that only those clergy 'that be not weekly occupied with preaching' should be responsible for catechizing the young members of their parish: it was ask-ing too much of the better educated clergy to expect them both to preach and cate-chize on a Sunday.[34] Equally, men like Greenham and Stock who were preaching regularly twice every Sunday (as had been the 'godly' practice for a while and became the official ideal in 1604), and some of the Lincolnshire clergy who replied to Gibson in 1721 had concluded that preaching twice on Sundays was not compatible with cat-echizing as well on that day, hence their catechizing on a weekday instead.[35] In other cases weekday catechizing was probably part of that shift towards more intensive cat-echizing for part of the year only to which we shall come in due course. In these cases catechizing on a Sunday was often supplemented for a short period of time by cate-chizing on one or more weekdays as well to maximize effect.[36] Another reason men-tioned by some clergy in the early eighteenth century arose from the situation where a minister had two poor livings or a mother church and a chapel that he was expected to serve every Sunday. Owing to time lost in travelling between churches, he felt he did not have enough time on a Sunday to conduct the required services, preach, and catechize; and, as one of them pointed out to Herring, catechizing was the one item that he felt could be moved to a weekday without too much damage to divine service.[37] Indeed, some incumbents, usually serving in urban areas where rival

[32] Clarke, *Lives of two and twenty divines*, 14, 79; id., *Lives of ten eminent divines*, 138; id., *Lives of sundry eminent persons*, 33, 203; William Gouge's preface to E. Culverwell, *A treatise of faith* (1648), sig. A11ʳ; W. R. Parker, *Milton: A Biography* (2 vols.; Oxford, 1968), i. 9; Stock apparently moved on past the Prayer Book catechism: see his *Stock of divine knowledge* (1641); and Gataker's lectures were probably of inter-mediate level.

[33] Wake MS 284, fos. 4ʳ, 71ʳ, 79ʳ, 93ʳ, 99ʳ, 179ʳ, 306ʳ, 350ʳ, 408ʳ, 423ʳ; Gibson 13, pp. 75, 147, 167, 255, 295, 319, 403, 563, Gibson 14, pp. 73, 77, 209, 241, 301, 415, 523, 563, 579, 603, and Gibson 15, pp. 31, 151, 257, 397, 401, 449, 461, 489; Secker, *Oxford*, 35–6, 66, 171; Herring, *York*, vols. i–iii, *passim*.

[34] Frere, *Visitation Articles*, ii. 306; for similar feelings from the clergy, see *Diocese of Norwich: Bishop Redman's Visitation 1597*, ed. J. F. Williams (Norfolk Record Society, xviii; 1946), 18.

[35] Gibson 13, p. 75, and 14, p. 241.

[36] Wake MS 284, fos. 266ʳ, 404ʳ, 406ʳ, 425ʳ; Secker, *Oxford*, 31; Herring, *York*, i. 17, ii. 47, 51, 60, 64, 127, etc.; and for an example in the 1650s, anon., *The agreement of the … ministers in … Norfolk* (1659), sig. C1ʳ.

[37] Wake MS 284, fos. 350ʳ, 438ʳ; Herring, *York*, i. 118, ii. 137, iii. 198, and cf. i. 99, 118.

dissenting establishments existed close by, were quite firm that if they dropped a Sunday sermon in favour of catechizing they would lose older members of their congregation to the lure of nonconformist preaching.[38] Thus while Sunday was the normal day for elementary catechizing in church, this was by no means always the case.

A not dissimilar but less pronounced change can be seen in the location of catechizing. This was to be 'openly in the church'—though quite where in church was not specified by the Prayer Book rubric or subsequent visitation articles[39]—and in 95 per cent or more cases the parish church was almost certainly the location adopted. When children and servants were expected to attend for catechizing by themselves before the service, it would have been natural for them to have been grouped together near the minister for instruction; but where they attended with their parents or masters, for catechizing either before or during the service, they may have sat initially with their mentors. Certainly one early eighteenth-century author wrote of children 'standing forth' to be catechized, and some respondents to episcopal questionnaires spoke of 'calling out' children to say their catechism 'before the face of the congregation', which suggests that English catechumens were brought out of their respective pews to stand at the front of the nave facing the congregation or to cluster round the minister's reading-desk.[40] Wordsworth remembers how as a young boy he and others were made to stand in a carefully arranged group round the minister, and the system adopted in one church in the Wirral in the eighteenth century was later described as follows: 'After the second lesson on Sunday afternoons in Lent the children of the parish left their seats and were ranged round the reading desk to say the catechism to the minister.' Equally, we know that in eight London churches on the second Sunday of each month in the reign of Queen Anne, local Charity School children were publicly tested before a congregation of well-wishers on what they had learnt, and a similar physical arrangement probably applied on those occasions.[41]

There is, however, some anecdotal and other evidence for the clergy having sometimes catechized elsewhere than the nave or chancel. Occasionally we hear of catechizing in the vestry; more frequently we hear of it taking place in the incumbent's house, as in Hertfordshire where in the 1630s Herbert Palmer was said to catechize

---

[38] Wake MS 284, fo. 126ʳ; Herring, *York*, ii. 42; in general, cf. J. Briggs, *Catechetical exercises* (Cambridge, 1696), sig. A2ᵛ.

[39] Brightman, *English Rite*, ii. 796–7, 791.

[40] Cradock, *Discourse of due catechising*, 11; Wake MS 284, fos. 14ʳ, 171ʳ; Gibson 13, p. 223; and Herring, *York*, i. 133; and cf. P. Hewit, *A brief and plain explication* (1704), sig. A2ᵛ; and ['A country parson'], *A short and plain exposition* (1715), p. v. See also the illustration of 'catechizing' opposite the title-page of anon., *Eniautos* (1674), though the position of the pulpit and desk seems rather odd.

[41] *The Poetical Works of William Wordsworth*, ed. E. de Selincourt and H. Darbishire (Oxford, 1963), iii. 395; J. Brownbill, *West Kirby and Hilbre* (Liverpool, 1928), 123; anon., *An account of Charity-Schools lately erected in England, Wales and Ireland* (1707), 32; for catechumens in the Genevan area and Netherlands being seated on benches, and in one case the minister sitting with them, see A. Duke, G. Lewis, and A. Pettegree (eds.), *Calvinism in Europe 1540–1610: A Collection of Documents* (Manchester/New York, 1992), 54–5, 153.

both in public and at his own house, and in Lincolnshire in 1721 where a minister told Gibson that he catechized openly in the church every Sunday in Lent and at other times in his own house.[42] There was not an exact correlation between catechizing on weekdays and at the minister's home: mid-week catechizing often took place in church, especially where large numbers were involved, as we know they sometimes were;[43] and we find some ministers inviting catechumens back to their house on a Sunday after evening prayer for further instruction. In his less well-known role as vicar of Sutton on the Forest in Yorkshire, Laurence Sterne reported that he taught children and servants 'in my own house every Sunday night during Lent' from six o'clock till nine, rather than in church; and a Leicestershire parson tried to sweeten the pill by disguising his intention: on Sundays 'I prevailed upon the young people to come to my house under the notion of teaching them to sing', though what he really wanted was to slip in some teaching as well.[44] But there was some overlap between these two deviations from the norm, as at Rucking in Kent in 1718 where the minister reported 'I have them to my house in the weekdays, to explain it [the Prayer Book catechism] to them', though with the idea of explanation we are moving from our elementary level to the intermediate level of exposition.[45]

When we reach the third and fourth headings—the time of day on Sunday at which catechizing should have occurred, and the length of time supposed to be taken—we begin to enter more difficult terrain. Most Elizabethan and early Stuart bishops and archdeacons followed the 1552 rubric and canon 59 of 1604 in saying that the curate should catechize before evening prayer: parents and masters were to send their children, servants, and apprentices along on Sunday afternoons before the service was due to start, at an hour specified by the incumbent, usually half an hour or an hour before evening prayer began. This was almost certainly the norm for the period 1558–1640. In her diary for 1599–1600 the pious Lady Margaret Hoby regularly records the catechizing and sermon that took place on Sunday afternoons; and the fact that on one occasion she walked with her husband until the catechizing was over, and then went into church for the sermon, suggests she had a clear idea of when one gave way to the other.[46] As we shall see, the rubric of 1552 was altered in the revised Prayer Book of 1662 which stipulated that catechizing should take place after the second lesson in the middle of the evening service. However, even before the Restoration

---

[42] Clarke, *Lives of two and twenty divines*, 224; Gibson 14, p. 93; and cf. Wake MS 284, fos. 203[r], 213[r]; Herring, *York*, i. 35; and see below, p. 183.

[43] See above n. 32, and Wake MS 284, fo. 453[r].

[44] Herring, *York*, iii. 93; J. H. Pruett, *The Parish Clergy under the Later Stuarts: The Leicestershire Experience* (Urbana, Ill., 1978), 117.

[45] Wake MS 284, fos. 224[r], 252[v], and 267[v].

[46] Brightman, *English Rite*, ii. 799, 791; Cardwell, *Synodalia*, i. 280; *Diary of Lady Margaret Hoby 1599–1605*, ed. D. M. Meads (1930), 66, 72, 75, 79–80, 82–4, 87–8, 139, and cf. 170.

some catechizing may have taken place during rather than before the second service on Sundays. Grindal's articles for York in 1571, Sandys's for London in the same year, and Aylmer's for London in 1577 all referred to catechizing 'before *or at*' evening prayer, and Parker's articles for Canterbury in 1575 enquired about catechizing '*at* evening prayer' on Sundays and holy days; and in his circular letter to the bishops of the Southern province in 1591, Whitgift urged the clergy to catechize the young '(if it may be conveniently) before their parents and others ... who thereby may take comfort and instruction also'—a situation which could have been most easily arranged if the young were catechized when both old and young were present at a service.[47] Richard Hooker and his curate were said (by Izaak Walton) to have catechized during evening prayer after the second lesson, decades before that became the official position in the revised rubric of 1662; Richard Greenham was said to have catechized the young people of his parish constantly before the evening sermon on Sunday, and Herbert Palmer to have catechized some at home and others 'publicly' in church before the afternoon sermon on Sundays: in both cases if the sermon was given during the service rather than before, then the catechizing may also have taken place 'at' service time.[48]

We also have King James's Directions on Preaching of 1622. Angered by controversial and contentious sermons, James told Archbishop Abbot that on Sunday afternoons and holidays preachers should preach on some part of the catechism, and that those preachers were to be most encouraged who spent their afternoon's exercise testing children's knowledge of the catechism and 'in expounding of the several parts and heads of the catechism, which is the most ancient and laudable custom of teaching in the Church of England'. James's direction (perhaps penned by Andrewes) may indicate that he intended all afternoon sermons to be converted into catechizing classes consisting of testing and exposition, but his primate, Abbot, while agreeing with the damage caused by contentious sermons and the need for more catechizing, put a rather different slant on the royal orders. In an open letter to his fellow-archbishop at York, he wrote that the king did not expect the number of sermons to be reduced but rather increased by renewing in all parish churches the primitive and profitable *exposition* of the catechism, so that thereby the people and even young children might be 'timely seasoned and instructed in all the heads of Christian religion'. In other words, the catechizing should take the form of a sermon which built on the phrases or doctrines of the catechism which, according to the canon of 1604

---

[47] *Second Report on Ritual*, 408, 418; Frere, *Visitation Articles*, iii. 305; Whitgift, *Works*, iii. 610. Sandys at York and Bancroft at London in 1601 asked about catechizing 'before or after evening prayer': *Second Report on Ritual*, 422, 437 (and cf. Frere, *Visitation Articles*, ii. 265). For hints that parents should be present for the catechizing (before or at the service), see *Visitation Articles and Injunctions of the Early Stuart Church*, i, ed. K. Fincham (Church of England Record Society, 1994), 77–8, 167, 183.

[48] Walton, *Lives*, 100; Clarke, *Lives of two and twenty divines*, 14, 224: on the other hand, 'afternoon sermon' may have been a 'godly' euphemism for evening prayer, and so before the sermon meant before the service.

still in force, the clergy should have been teaching the young *before* the service began.[49] How far James's direction or Abbot's gloss led to a change in the pattern of elementary catechizing in the later 1620s is not yet clear. But since most visitation articles continued to ask if there was catechizing before the afternoon service, we should perhaps assume that the normal time for the actual drilling and testing of catechumens remained the period immediately before evening prayer and that such changes as there were involved an increase in the catechetical content of the sermon given during that service. In this context we may note that John Frewen claimed to have been spending part of 'the evening exercise' handling one of the catechetical points he was teaching his flock even before James's directions had been circulated; that in the preface to a catechism published in 1644 John Rowlandson implied that during his thirty-year ministry in a Northern parish he had regularly catechized the young between morning and evening prayer, and expounded the catechism during evening prayer; and that in the late 1620s James Ussher was reported to have told his assistant, Nicholas Bernard, to catechize the young before evening prayer, and then spend half an hour after the first and second lessons of that service explaining the principles in 'the public catechism'.[50]

In the 1630s elementary catechizing was pushed briefly into the spotlight of ecclesiastical politics. The old and rather simplistic view, restated until very recently, was that the enforcement of the royal orders of 1629 against nonconforming lecturers led to a deliberate restraint on all preaching. Not only lecturers but regular beneficed clergy (it was said) were told to replace their afternoon sermons with a catechizing class, as part of a wider 'Arminian' campaign to downgrade the significance of preaching in relation to that of the sacraments. This view receives support from the wording of a few sets of visitation articles in the 1630s in which it was asked if afternoon sermons were 'turned into catechizing by question and answer' (and which became the basis for one of the charges at Laud's trial in 1645), and also from the actions of some bishops, who gave the impression, even to a supporter of episcopacy such as Viscount Falkland, that the Laudian authorities had 'cried down lectures by the name of factions' and 'brought in catechizing only to thrust out preaching'.[51] As Julian Davies has recently demonstrated, this version of what happened is much too simple, though the perception of MPs like Falkland was not without some foundation. On the one hand, long before Laud reached Canterbury, some senior churchmen such as

---

[49] Cardwell, *Documentary Annals*, ii. 146–54; Fincham, *Visitation Articles*, 212–14; Abbot's reply was cited by Thomas Marshall in *The catechism set forth* (1683), sigs. a4r–v.

[50] J. Frewen, *Certaine choise grounds* (1621), title page, sig. A7r, and p. 7; Clarke, *Lives of ten eminent divines*, 223; and cf. Fincham, *Prelate as Pastor*, 245–6. There is also a suggestion that the catechetical exercises of Thomas Taylor (who died in 1633 and had been ill for some time before that) were delivered 'sermon-wise' on Sunday afternoons: *TSR* iv. 518; see also below, nn. 229–30.

[51] *Second Report on Ritual*, 539, 560, 577, 590; Fincham, *Visitation Articles*, 112; id., *Prelate as Pastor*, 257, and cf. 231–47; [Viscount Falkland], *A speech made to the House of Commons concerning episcopacy* (1641), 3 (I am most grateful to Dr Judith Maltby for this reference).

Whitgift and Andrewes had begun to feel that preaching had its limitations as a tool of instruction and edification, especially where the foundation for understanding sermons had not been properly laid by catechizing.[52] Moreover both Charles and Laud, like some monarchs and bishops before them, were concerned at the number of sermons which they saw as theologically or politically divisive, and which were often blamed on those semi-independent lecturers without cure of souls supported by the zealous in many towns and cities.[53] On the other hand, the enforcement of the order against lecturers in the early 1630s did lead to a fair amount of confusion as to whether just lecturers' afternoon sermons or all afternoon sermons were to be transformed into catechizing; and during this confusion Charles and Laud, at least in the mid-1630s, either went along with or did little to rein back those hard-liners in the episcopate who went beyond the original intention of the orders of 1629 and attacked *all* afternoon sermons. By the end of the 1630s the confusion had to some extent been sorted out: beneficed clergy could preach on a Sunday afternoon on two conditions: that they had already had a session of question-and-answer catechizing; and that any sermon was upon the 'heads' of the catechism, for the people's 'better understanding' of the questions just handled. But by then the damage had been done.[54] In so far as the matter affected catechizing in the 1630s, we may make one or two further points.

First of all, it seems clear, as Dr Davies has argued, that the authorities' initial concern was with those afternoon sermons which were being given by lecturers in the period immediately before evening prayer, that is at the very time when regular clergy were supposed to be catechizing the young.[55] Secondly, it is evident that catechizing—in the sense of teaching set answers to set questions, and testing that they had been learnt—was still expected to be performed by the minister of the parish before the afternoon service. The visitation articles of the 1630s, even in the second half of that decade, continued to ask whether catechizing took place for half an hour or more before evening prayer, and in some cases asked separate questions about the fate of afternoon sermons. The authors of these articles included 'Laudians' such as the primate himself (in 1635), Wren (in 1636), Montagu (in 1638), and Juxon (in

---

[52] J. Davies, *The Caroline Captivity of the Church* (Oxford, 1992), 126–61; Whitgift, *Works*, i. 337; Fincham, *Prelate as Pastor*, 240–7.

[53] For the difference between full-time and part-time lecturers and their activities, see P. L. Seaver, *The Puritan Lectureships* (Stanford, Calif., 1970); P. Collinson, 'Lectures by Combination: Structures and Characteristics of Church Life in 17th-Century England', *Bulletin of the Institute of Historical Research*, 48 (1975), 182–213; and for a threefold distinction, see *Second Report on Ritual*, 581.

[54] *The Works of William Laud*, ed. J. Bliss and W. Scott (7 vols.; Oxford, 1847–60), v. 368; iv. 301, and for the differing messages being emitted by bishops like Neile and Laud in 1633–4, see Fincham, *Visitation Articles*, 88, 112. The bald summary offered in this paragraph is much the same as that in Davies, *Caroline Captivity*, 136–46, though I tend to the view that there was more confusion at the centre as well as regionally than he implies, and that Laud may have shifted his ground in response to conflicting pressures from, first, hard-liners, and then confused moderates, than to have been a relative moderate throughout, as Davies argues.

[55] Ibid. 139; for separate questions about lecturers compared to regular clergy, see *Second Report on Ritual*, 581–2, 590.

1640, using a set of articles drawn up by Convocation for use throughout England), as well as a semi–detached bishop like Williams.[56] Thirdly, although the ideal laid down in the canons of 1604 was two sermons every Sunday in every parish church, one at morning prayer and one at evening prayer, this was far from being the norm in practice, especially in areas where a thinly scattered population or meagre resources led to one minister holding two or more cures simultaneously. In other words, it is far from clear that most parishes by the 1630s were in a position to *lose* their afternoon sermon—a state of affairs that was acknowledged in the questions of Wren and Juxon about afternoon sermons ('if there were wont to be any', 'if you had any formerly').[57] Fourthly, even where the minister was accustomed to give an afternoon sermon during evening prayer, it was not necessarily subject to being converted to question-and-answer catechizing. If he catechized by question and answer before the service, and then during the following service preached on some aspect of catechetical teaching (as Abbot had said was James's wish for preachers in 1622, and Laud indicated was acceptable in 1639 and at his trial), then he was acting well within the law.[58]

The exact effect of the royal orders of 1629 on elementary catechizing in the 1630s is hard to establish, since owing to the confusion both at the centre and in the dioceses there were various possible outcomes, and most previous historical thinking on the subject has been guided by the either/or terms in which the matter was presented in the 1640s. One possible result was little or no change: elementary instruction and examination in the catechism took place before the service, and where a parish was fortunate enough to have two sermons a day, the afternoon sermon was either unaffected or became more catechetical in content.[59] In some parishes, but probably a minority, basic instruction and testing may have been transferred from a point before the service to the point inside it where the sermon had previously been given, or where there would have been a sermon if the incumbent had had time to give one. This was the assumption implicit in the actions of Piers and Wren and some visitation articles of the period; it may also have been what George Herbert, who was just about to enter the ministry, meant when he said that on Sundays the country parson 'read divine service twice fully, and preached in the morning and catechized in the afternoon', in the presence of parents as well as children (though even then the afternoon catechizing could have taken place before the service rather than during).[60]

[56] Ibid. 548, 560, 581–2, 590.

[57] For a continuing dearth of preaching in some areas, see D. M. Barratt, 'The Condition of the Parish Clergy between the Reformation and 1660', D.Phil. thesis (Oxford, 1949), ch. 3; Fincham, *Prelate as Pastor*, 134–7, 181–3, 193–5, 199–206, 280; and R. L. Arundale, *Richard Neile, Bishop of Lincoln 1614–17* (Lincoln, 1987), 16; *Second Report on Ritual*, 560, 590.

[58] See above, nn. 49, 54; and for the dean and chapter of Winchester's comparable decision not to move their lecture because it did not clash with the time of catechizing, see *The Diary of John Young S. T. P. Dean of Winchester*, ed. F. R. Goodman (1928), 88.

[59] See above, n. 50.

[60] Davies, *Caroline Captivity*, 136–45; *Second Report on Ritual*, 577, 600; *The Works of George Herbert*, ed. F. E. Hutchinson (Oxford, 1967), 236, 255.

Another possibility not inconsistent with Laud's and Charles's comments in 1639 and Laud's remarks at his trial was that both question-and-answer catechizing *and* a short catechetical exposition took place during the service, which could have anticipated what may have happened in a number of parish churches in later Stuart England. Yet another is that the catechetical *instruction* took place before the service and catechetical *examination* during the service instead of or in addition to a sermon. Until or unless we know more about the balance between these different possible patterns, we should perhaps not be dogmatic about radical change having taken place in the pattern of catechizing in the late 1630s.

The revised rubric of 1662, as already noted, differed in that it specified that catechizing should take place after the second lesson at evening prayer.[61] The reason for this is not clear, but at least two lines of argument may have been advanced. One was that such a move was the logical culmination of the royal orders of 1622 and 1629: the former had stressed the importance of catechizing and, at least in Abbot's gloss, the value of a preacher delivering a catechetical sermon in the presence of older as well as younger parishioners during a service; the latter again reinforced the value of catechizing, and in some dioceses perhaps led to the insertion of catechizing into the middle of the service where the sermon would have been. The second line may well have been that catechizing had been badly neglected during the troubles of the 1640s and 1650s, for which there is some evidence, and that catechizing during the service rather than before would serve to instruct both those born when the troubles were coming to an end, and those of their parents who had not been catechized in previous decades.[62] A third possibility, related to the second, is that the instruction to catechize during the service was a tacit admission that it had proved impossible to get parents to attend catechizing before the service, either as witnesses or participants. These lines of argument receive some support from the text of Charles II's 'Directions concerning preachers', issued in 1662 but modelled on those of James I in 1622, and presumably the initiative of someone like Gilbert Sheldon, then bishop of London and the effective leader of the church due to the advanced years of Archbishop Juxon.[63] They also receive support from the comments of other churchmen active in the later Stuart church which we shall examine when we turn to the second level of catechizing in church, namely the exposition of the church catechism. Here what we should note are the perceived pastoral advantages that accrued from having some question-and-answer catechizing immediately followed by a short catechetical

---

[61] Brightman, *English Rite*, i. 791.

[62] Addison, *Primitive institution*, 74–5; [Beveridge], *Church-catechism explained* (1704) sig. a3^r; M. Hole, *A practical exposition* (1707), sigs. A3^{r-v}; and see p. 106–7 above and pp. 131, 139, 226 below. The slight alteration from 'child' to 'person' in the title of the Prayer Book catechism is also consistent with this argument: Brightman, *English Rite*, ii. 778–9.

[63] Wilkins, *Concilia*, iv. 577; Sheldon had been urged by one of the surviving pre-war clergy to take steps to encourage frequent catechizing and catechetical sermons: W. Nicholson, *An exposition of the catechism* (Library of Anglo-Catholic Theology; Oxford, 1842), p. viii.

homily, and the regularity with which catechetical exposition and preaching during a service was encouraged as a means of instructing both children in years and children in knowledge, as Bishop Lamplugh put it in the 1670s.

Unfortunately, it is no easier to establish the impact of the revised rubric of 1662 than that of the royal instructions of 1622 and 1629. If we look at a selection of the official sources of the period, we find that the new ideal was barely mentioned in the visitation articles and episcopal charges of the later Stuart and Hanoverian periods.[64] Quite a few of the authors of these articles, especially older clergy operating in the early 1660s, followed the older practice of asking if there was catechizing before evening prayer, while others did not specify a time at all, or used a rather general phrase such as 'Sunday afternoon'.[65] The replies to the early eighteenth-century episcopal questionnaires for once do not throw much light on the practice either. Half a dozen Kentish clergy said that they catechized after the second lesson, usually at evening prayer, occasionally in the morning if they had two cures; nearly a dozen Lincolnshire clergy and a dozen Yorkshire clergy stated that they catechized after the second lesson or during evening service.[66] But the great majority of respondents in these dioceses and in others merely stated that they catechized 'on Sunday' or on 'Sunday afternoon', with no indication whether this was before or during the service.[67] The verb used in the second question of Wake's questionnaire—'Do your parishioners duly *send* their children and servants to be instructed and catechized?'—may indicate that the young were to be sent ahead, that is for catechizing before the service. But it would be unwise to read too much into this: the same verb was used in the sentence of the 1662 rubric which referred to catechizing after the second lesson.[68] This is another area where we need to do much more work to find out what was the usual practice, though it will not be surprising if what is found is not a little confusion, as in the 1630s, and a considerable variety of practice according to local conditions and traditions. Perhaps the most that can be asserted safely is that whereas the norm in the first century after the Reformation was for elementary catechizing to take place before the service, in the period after 1660 there were two patterns—either before, or during evening prayer. Which option an individual minister chose might depend on local conventions, or on whether he wished to get the catechizing out of the way before the service in order to concentrate on

---

[64] *Second Report on Ritual*, 648 (further instruction after the second lesson); 666–70 (catechizing in presence of older parishioners at evening prayer); [Beveridge], *Church-catechism explained*, p. v.

[65] *Second Report on Ritual*, 606, 608, 623–4, 627, 631, 645; 616, 631, 637, 639, 642; 604, 620, 629, 634, 654–5, 682.

[66] Wake MS 284, fos. 20ʳ, 26ʳ, 93ʳ, 171ʳ, 220ᵛ, 362ʳ; Gibson 13, pp. 79, 179, 183, Gibson 14, pp. 301, 395, 451, and Gibson 15, pp. 11, 95, 111, 405, 511; Herring, *York*, i. 36, 42, 149, 191, 201, 206, 220; ii. 44, 76, 101, 176; iii. 44, 47, 89, 182.

[67] Wake MS 284, and Herring, *York*, vols. i–iii, *passim*.

[68] Wake MS 284, fo. 1ʳ; Brightman, *English Rite*, ii. 791. The sense of 'send' might even have included parents propelling their unwilling charges up to the front of the church when the time for catechizing came.

other matters—and perhaps enjoy greater freedom in choosing a text for a sermon than if he was tied to expounding the section of the catechism he had just taught.

Our fourth heading was the ideal length of the period of instruction. At the outset, in 1552, and in some early Elizabethan articles, this was given as half an hour,[69] but in the wave of enthusiasm for catechizing that swept along many leading churchmen in the later sixteenth century a longer period was often indicated. Thus the relevant canon of 1571, drafted at a time when ignorance of Protestant teaching was still considerable, specified two hours,[70] and some Elizabethan bishops suggested either an hour or one hour 'at the least'.[71] Others, however, were content with 'half an hour at the least', and in visitation articles produced in the reigns of James I and Charles I this became the norm (as, incidentally, it was in seventeenth-century France).[72] Half an hour was the duration indicated by that enthusiastic Laudian catechist, Edmund Reeve, though the equally zealous Henry Hammond was said to have catechized regularly for a whole hour in the 1630s (perhaps at a more advanced level given the nature of his published catechism).[73]

The effect of the 1662 rubric in placing the period of instruction in the middle of evensong is unclear: the revised rubric gave no indication of how long this catechizing should last. Evening prayer without a sermon would have been a relatively short service which could have accommodated half an hour or more of questions and answers without too much difficulty. But evensong with a half-hour session of basic catechizing *and* a sermon, whether a full-length one or perhaps a short explanation of a phrase or concept in the church catechism for the benefit of parents as well as children, would have been quite a long service, which could have created pressure to keep the number of questions and answers within bounds. We are infuriatingly short of systematic evidence of what actually took place at this period, but there are occasional clues. In the 1690s Isham prepared his explanation of the church catechism, he tells us, to help fit catechizing into the 'public service of God in a large congregation' in London. His work, divided into twelve short weekly sections, served to test not only knowledge of the answers but also comprehension of their meaning, and was thus an attempt to condense these two operations into a time-span which enabled him during a normal service to check the progress of a large number of catechumens

---

[69] Brightman, *English Rite*, ii. 797; and cf. *Second Report on Ritual*, 406, 408, 425.

[70] Cardwell, *Synodalia*, i. 121.

[71] *Second Report on Ritual*, 419, 422, 430, 435, 437; Kennedy, *Episcopal Administration*, ii. 43, 71; iii. 211, 338.

[72] Ibid. ii. 127; iii. 224, 289; *Second Report on Ritual*, 454, 459–60, 463–4, 475–6, 494–5, 504–5; Delumeau, *Catholicism between Luther and Voltaire*, 200.

[73] Reeve, *Communion booke catechisme*, 89; Fell, 'Life of Hammond', p. xxiv. The difference was perhaps limited: as bishop of St David's in 1622, Laud specified an hour or half an hour at the least, but in his metropolitical articles for Norwich in 1635, he said half an hour or more: *Second Report on Ritual*, 489, 548.

without losing the attention of their elders.[74] A few years later, in 1704, Bishop Beveridge implied that the whole half hour specified in the 59th canon had been transferred to the period after the second lesson at evening prayer, 'that those also of riper years' who were not taught the catechism when young (the majority of most congregations in England, he opined) might learn by hearing the younger sort both examined and instructed.[75] In both these cases, the move to the middle of the service involved a measure of (first-level) teaching and testing being combined with one of (second-level) exposition.

Other senior clerics seem to have thought half an hour too long, and talked instead of 'instruction' at evening prayer lasting about a quarter of an hour (though again elementary and intermediate elements may have been combined). In an address to the clergy of his diocese of Ely, in 1692, Simon Patrick distinguished between the two parts of catechizing: examining children in the catechism, 'that is, to ask them the questions, and receive their answers', and instructing them in the meaning thereof. From the context it seems to have been on the latter 'exercise' that he thought the clergy should spend 'a quarter of an hour ... all summer long ... at evening prayer, after the second lesson, as the rubric appoints', though it is just possible he may have been referring to both.[76] Similarly in his *Discourse of the pastoral care*, published in the same year as Patrick's letter, Gilbert Burnet also distinguished between rote repetition and understanding, and spoke of the need for catechetical discourses of no more than a quarter of an hour. A few years later, in his own catechism, published for use in the diocese of Sarum in 1710, Burnet spoke of the quarter of an hour spent catechizing the youth and explaining the catechism on a regular weekly basis as the most useful of all pastoral exercises.[77]

Some indirect light is thrown on the situation by those replies to the early eighteenth-century episcopal questionnaires which indicated that many catechumens had already learnt the catechism at school or home, or in church during the week, so that during the Sunday service less time was needed for basic instruction and more was available for testing and exposition.[78] If, as we shall see later, there had been a move towards a short catechetical sermon or exposition during evening prayer for at least part of the year in the later Stuart and early Hanoverian period, then we should perhaps expect that by that period there was a two-stage exercise: a few minutes were directed specifically towards teaching and testing catechumens' knowledge of the answers in the Prayer Book catechism, either before the service or after the second lesson (or indeed separately, with drilling beforehand and examination during the service), and a few minutes of more general explanation or exhortation were directed

---

[74] Isham, *Catechism of the church*, sig. A2ʳ.

[75] [Beveridge], *Church-catechism explained*, sigs. a3ʳ⁻ᵛ.   [76] Moorman, *Curate of Souls*, 72.

[77] Ibid. 89; G. Burnet, *An exposition of the church catechism* (1710), 1.

[78] e.g. in Lincolnshire, Gibson 13, pp. 7, 11, 55, 58, 375, 395, 407; Gibson 14, pp. 133, 165, 256, 280–1, 375, 483; Gibson 15, pp. 249, 253, 397.

towards the congregation at large, either immediately after the questions and answers, or later after the Creed and collects where the sermon would normally have been given. In short, some clergy may have considered the advantages of catechizing little and often, either before and during the service or just during the service, to have outweighed the advantages of a single, longer session of separate instruction of children beforehand.

This brings us to our fifth heading: the frequency with which elementary catechizing took place. The rubric in the confirmation service of the first Edwardian Prayer Book and early Edwardian articles had indicated that catechizing should take place at least every six weeks, or about once every eight weeks.[79] But the man who was then acting as liaison between English and Continental reformations (and was himself the author of at least two catechisms), Martin Bucer, pointed out that catechizing took place much more frequently abroad, often on as many as three days in the week of which Sunday was one. He recommended catechizing on Sundays and holy days, and in the 1552 Prayer Book this was adopted.[80] The authors of the royal injunctions of 1559, perhaps mindful of the likely dearth of suitable clergy, suggested a compromise of catechizing on every second Sunday plus holy days,[81] a pattern also enjoined by a number of senior Elizabethan churchmen such as Sandys (in Worcester and York dioceses), Cox (Ely), and Cooper (Lincoln). At St Paul's in London the period suggested for catechizing children and cathedral choristers was weekly 'or at least monthly'.[82] In the great majority of late Elizabethan and early Stuart visitation articles, however, it was the ideal of 1552 that was incorporated, using either the formula 'Sundays and holy days' (which could be interpreted as meaning on a Sunday or holy day rather than a normal weekday, but not necessarily on every such day) or the more precise wording 'every Sunday and holy day'. In fact, a number of bishops used both formulae, the latter when asking about the actions of the clergy and the former when enquiring about lay co-operation with them.[83]

In urban areas where the children could more easily attend the parish church throughout the year, and in parishes with zealous clergy and laity, weekly catechizing may well have been the norm. But there are fairly good reasons for thinking that in rural areas, where the parishioners were often scattered over several hamlets or the

[79]   Brightman, *English Rite*, ii. 796; Frere, *Visitation Articles*, ii. 239, 244, 265.

[80]   A. J. Stephens, *The Book of Common Prayer* (3 vols.; 1849–54), iii. 1474; E. -W. Kohls, *Evangelische Katechismen der Reformationszeit vor und neben Martin Luthers Kleinem Katechismus* (Gütersloh, 1971), 35–75.

[81]   Frere, *Visitation Articles*, iii. 22, 87–8.

[82]   Ibid. iii. 223–4, 296–7, 299, 371; Kennedy, *Episcopal Administration*, ii. 93; iii. 306 and cf. iii. 289.

[83]   For the former, see Kennedy, *Episcopal Administration*, ii. 127–8, 183, 240, 243–4, 320; and *Second Report on Ritual*, 445, 501, 529, 544–5; for the latter Kennedy, *Episcopal Administration*, ii. 119; iii. 211, 256, 338; and *Second Report on Ritual*, 459–60, 463–4, 489–90, 548–9, 552, 560.

value of livings was low and pluralism necessary, weekly catechizing throughout the year remained an ideal rather than a reality. In 1597 Bishop Redman found over a dozen parishes where catechizing was irregular, in some cases being performed during Lent only or in the weeks preceding one of the three celebrations of communion each year. In the early 1620s, John Mayer claimed to have catechized throughout the year for a number of years and complained of those catechists who taught 'for outward formality only in Lent'; and in 1635 the bishop of Winchester reported to Laud some negligent ministers who were also catechizing in Lent alone.[84] The practice of catechizing in the six weeks of Lent in particular may have had a lot to commend it to hard-pressed parish clergy: it was a period when other duties such as performing weddings were in temporary abeyance; it was the time of year when the days were getting longer and the weather would have been improving, so that children could get to church with less difficulty than in the depth of winter; it preceded one of the three standard celebrations of the Lord's Supper, at Easter, and some bishops suggested that clergy should check the religious knowledge of would-be communicants in Lent; and it preceded also the months of the year when most episcopal and other visitation procedures ground into action, and when there was the possibility of a confirmation if the bishop conducted the visitation in person. Dr Fincham has found a number of cases in the counties of Leicestershire, Somerset, and Ely in the early Stuart period which would seem to indicate that many clergy took catechizing seriously in Lent, even if as one warden replied 'we have seldom any catechism but in Lent'.[85] The summer months were a viable alternative to Lent: the 'godly' John Ball was said to have spent much time catechizing on Sunday afternoons 'especially in the summer season'; and the equally conscientious Henry Hammond, who catechized for an hour before service in the 1630s, did so according to his biographer 'during the warmer seasons of the year'.[86]

To judge from some of the visitation articles, exhortatory literature, and expositions of the Prayer Book catechism divided into fifty-two parts, and from a bill put before Parliament in 1657 to force ministers to catechize for at least forty-two Sundays a year, the ideal in the later seventeenth century probably remained that catechizing should take place all year round, even if the reality was very different.[87] A

[84] *Bishop Redman's Visitation*, 18; Mayer, *English catechisme*, sigs. A3ʳ⁻ᵛ; *Works of William Laud*, v. 339.

[85] Frere, *Visitation Articles*, iii. 85–6, 142, 275, 287, 307, 337; Kennedy, *Episcopal Administration*, ii. 75; *Second Report on Ritual*, 412; for the points about weather, visitations, and confirmations, see below, pp. 117–19, 126–8; Leicestershire RO, ID41/13/63, fo. 27ʳ; Cambridgeshire Univ. Lib., Ely Diocesan Records, D/2/35, fos. 46ʳ, 71ᵛ, 73ᵛ, 132ᵛ; Somerset RO, D/D/Vc 77 fos. 35ᵛ, 58ᵛ (and D/D/Ca 173 and 204 for catechizing in Lent *and* at Christmas, and before a visitation); I am most grateful to Dr Fincham for these references.

[86] Clarke, *Lives of two and twenty divines*, 173; Fell, 'Life of Hammond', p. xxiv. Lady Margaret Hoby's *Diary* mentions catechizing from August to December in 1599 and in May 1601, but not in other months: 66–88, 139, 170.

[87] J. Ball, *Short questions and answers* (1639); anon., *Eniautos: or a course of catechizing* (1664); [Beveridge], *Church-catechism explained*, pp. xix–xx; J. Talbot, *The church-catechism explained* (1705);

minority of post-Restoration bishops and archdeacons continued to ask if there was catechizing every Sunday and holy day (or every Sunday), and in 1674 Lancelot Addison was obviously displeased when he reported that too often catechizing took place only in Lent.[88] A few years later Thomas Comber tried to keep a foot in both camps by glossing the Prayer Book rubric as saying that catechizing was required 'every Sunday, and especially in Lent' (some Sundays appear to have been more equal than others), and in 1696 an Irish bishop with experience of English conditions told his clergy that catechizing was not for Lent alone, but every Sunday: only in 'the dark quarter of dead winter [do] we forbear catechizing'.[89] Other, equally zealous clergy do, however, seem to have come to terms with a shorter period of instruction. In 1692 Simon Patrick suggested that catechizing should take place all through the summer, 'when the days are long', and exactly the same phrase was used by another conscientious pastor, Gilbert Burnet, in his *Discourse of the pastoral care*, when he recommended catechizing for the six summer months.[90] In 1716 John Lewis (a great supporter of catechizing and author of one best-selling form) told his diocesan, William Wake (author of another), that catechizing every week 'neither is done nor can be done in abundance of churches'.[91] It is also noticeable that in many of the visitation articles sent out after the 1660s, there was no reference to frequency, merely a question whether the minister diligently instructed the youth of the parish in the church catechism, this often being linked to a query whether the minister was presenting those so instructed for episcopal confirmation.[92]

There is plenty of evidence from various sources that in the early eighteenth century catechizing for only part of the year was the norm. Of the replies to Wake's questionnaire which specify the time of year, the great majority indicated that catechizing took place either in Lent or in the summer. In Canterbury diocese in 1716, 154 replies gave some indication of the time of year or number of weeks each year during which catechizing took place; of these 72 referred to Lent alone, 30 to part or all of the summer, and 41 to Lent or summer and some other part of the year. The balance gave a more general indication, such as 'frequently' or before a confirmation.[93] In the archdeaconry of Lincoln in 1721, 377 replies gave some indication of the season during which catechizing took place in church: in 129 cases it was Lent alone, in 65 part

J. Harrison, *A scriptural exposition* (1735); and cf. P. Newcome, *A catechetical course of sermons* (1700). The 1657 bill can be traced in W. A. Shaw, *A History of the English Church … 1640–1660* (2 vols.; 1900), ii. 92–3, 152–3; *The Diary of Thomas Burton, Esquire*, ed. J. T. Rutt (4 vols.; 1828), i. 376, ii. 202–3, 205–6; and [P. Nye], *Beames of former light* (1660), 101–7. For a recommendation of catechizing six months a year, in 1659, see anon., *The agreement of the … ministers in … Norfolk*, sig. B4ᵛ.

[88]   *Second Report on Ritual*, 631, 634, 645, 648, 682; Addison, *Primitive institution*, 76–7.

[89]   T. Comber, *Discourses upon the Common Prayer*, cited in Stephens, *Book of Common Prayer*, iii. 1450; [E. Wetenhall], *The catechism of the Church of England* (Dublin, 1696), sig. iiiʳ; Sampson began on 30 April 1676: *Rector's Book, Clayworth*, 19.

[90]   Moorman, *Curate of Souls*, 72, 89; cf. also J. Harrison, *An exposition of the church-catechism* (1708), 6.

[91]   Wake MS 284, fo. 427ᵛ.   [92]   *Second Report on Ritual*, 637, 639, 642, 644, 655, 657, 678, 680.

[93]   Wake MS 284, *passim*.

or all of the summer, in 81 some combination of Lent and summer, and in 31 some other combination of Lent or summer and another time of year, for example alternate Sundays in Lent and Advent, or during Lent and then monthly or quarterly for the rest of the year. The balance gave a more general indication such as 'at all seasons', 'several convenient seasons', 'most Sundays', or 'one month in the year'.[94] In the diocese of Oxford in 1738, 133 replies provided some indication of the time of year; of these 87 mentioned Lent, 13 the summer, and 16 Lent and some other time.[95] In the diocese of York in 1743 (excluding livings in Nottinghamshire), 531 replies mentioned a time, of which 262 specified Lent alone, 93 part or all of the summer, and 112 referred to Lent and some other part of the year; the balance referred to a different combination of seasons or offered a less precise answer, such as several Sundays each year.[96]

The reasons given in the early eighteenth century for this situation were basically threefold. The first was that it was the custom, which is of interest as indicating that catechizing for part of the year had perhaps been the norm for more than a generation or two. As we have seen in previous paragraphs, as early as the 1590s, and again in the 1620s, 1630s, and 1670s, there had been complaints that some clergy were catechizing in Lent alone. Certainly clergy in Kent, Lincoln, Oxford, and York thought they could plead custom for their actions, and in some cases such as the deanery of Ospring in Kent we find that these clergy are clustered close together, suggesting either collusion in their replies to the bishop, or a strong feeling of local tradition.[97]

The second reason was the most commonly stated of all. The summer was 'a season when I find children in the country can most conveniently be brought to church', one minister told Wake, 'the days then being longest' added others, echoing the phrase used by Patrick and Burnet in the early 1690s and regularly found in the records of other dioceses.[98] Other ministers reflected the pressures of rural life on household labour: one Kentish minister said that he catechized from May until the harvest in August, another 'at such times as the season and country business will allow them to attend', while a Lincolnshire incumbent pointed out that he catechized in Lent and on all holy days 'except in hay and harvest'.[99] Others made the point that

---

[94] Gibson 13–15, *passim*.   [95] Secker, *Oxford, passim.*

[96] Herring, *York*, vols. i–iii, *passim*; and see the similar pattern in Warwickshire and in Holsworthy deanery in Exeter diocese: J. L. Salter, 'Warwickshire Clergy, 1660–1714', Ph.D. thesis (Birmingham, 1975), 96; A. Warne, *Church and Society in Eighteenth-Century Devon* (New York, 1969), 48. For the French clergy's habit of catechizing in Advent and Lent, see Delumeau, *Catholicism between Luther and Voltaire*, 200.

[97] Wake MS 284, fos. 228ʳ, 241ʳ, 258ʳ, 280ʳ; Gibson 14, pp. 479, 547; Secker, *Oxford*, 130; Herring, *York*, i. 209; iii. 22, 194, 240.

[98] Wake MS 284, fos. 26ʳ, 319ʳ, 326ʳ, 346ʳ; Gibson 13, pp. 83, 315, Gibson 14, pp. 97, 109, 253, and Gibson 15, pp. 373, 429, etc.; Herring, *York*, i. 130, 213, 214; iii. 63, 195.

[99] Wake MS 284, fo. 338ʳ; Gibson 13, p. 503 and Gibson 14, p. 77, and cf. 73. For a French diocese where the clergy were told to catechize every Sunday except during harvest and grape-gathering, see Delumeau, *Catholicism between Luther and Voltaire*, 200.

travelling was not easy in winter months,[100] or indicated that they began catechizing in the spring and continued for as long as it took the children to learn the catechism, or as long as any children were sent.[101] In quite a few cases, it was reported that catechizing took place also or only for a few weeks or months before a confirmation ceremony was due, which was nearly always in the spring or summer months.[102]

Another reason for catechizing only part of the year was the one offered to Wake by Lewis: pressure of other work. Weekly catechizing was not possible in many churches, 'especially those where the congregation is large, there is but one minister, and preaching twice a day'. The extra effort of catechizing could be sustained for only part of the year, and from Lent to the beginning of harvest was from both catechists' and catechumens' point of view the best time for that effort to be made.[103] Conversely, where an incumbent held two or more small livings close together, or a mother church with dependent chapels which also had to be served on Sundays, he may have spent a lot of time on a Sunday simply travelling between churches and not had the time or energy for catechizing every week in every church.[104] Other, perhaps more cynical reasons could be suggested for the practice of catechizing in Lent or summer only, such as idleness, a reluctance to offend parishioners or catechumens by trying to insist on longer bouts of catechizing, or keeping a weather eye on the next set of visitation enquiries due in the spring or midsummer. But the generally frank tone of the hundreds of replies examined here may suggest that the local clergy had come to terms with the fact that catechizing for part of the year was possible but for all year unlikely, and that they hoped the authorities would also become reconciled to this.

The replies to the episcopal questionnaires of the early eighteenth century also suggest that in some dioceses catechists considered six weeks to be adequate or the norm for elementary catechizing in church. Many who said that they catechized in Lent, referred to 'all Lent', 'every Sunday' or 'several Sundays' in Lent, or 'during the time of' or 'in the season (or whole season) of' Lent, or 'throughout' or 'constantly' in Lent, which has six weeks if we include the Sunday before Easter.[105] Similarly the interval from Easter to Whitsun which was often mentioned by other respondents contains six weeks, and among the more general indications of length of catechizing we also have a number of references to five, six, or seven weeks, or to

---

[100] Gibson 14, pp. 127, 257; Wake MS 284, fo. 224^r; and cf. Herring, *York*, ii. 5, 61 (and cf. 149: before the archdeacon's visitation); iii. 150.

[101] Ibid. i. 61, 63, 80, 92; ii. 26, 76, 141; iii. 57, 66, 95, 148.

[102] Wake MS 284, fos. 56^r, 85^r, 95^r, 109^v, 132^r; Secker, *Oxford*, 53, 129, 155; Herring, *York*, i. 38, 109, 120, 145; ii. 45, 82; S. L. Ollard, 'Confirmation in the Anglican Communion', in *Confirmation or the Laying On of Hands* (2 vols.; 1926), i. 86–208; Fincham, *Prelate as Pastor*, 114–16, 123–9; *Rector's Book, Clayworth*, 72, 93, 103, 124; *Diary of Francis Evans*, 17–19; *Speculum Lincolniensis*, pp. ii–iv.

[103] Wake MS 284, fos. 427^v, 423^r.

[104] Ibid. fos. 71^r, 173^r, 288^r, 319^r and 326^r, 438^r, 445^r; Herring, *York*, i. 219, and vols. i–iii, *passim*; Secker, *Oxford*, 23, 155; and Gibson 13–15, *passim*.

[105] Wake MS 284; Secker, *Oxford*; and York, *Herring, passim*.

'several' Sundays.[106] However, it is worth noting that in a number of cases clergy did indicate that they catechized for more than this period, or on more than six occasions. At least some early Hanoverian catechists said that they catechized on two weekdays during Lent, or on weekdays and Sundays in Lent, or on even more occasions. Thus one Kentish minister told Wake that he catechized every Wednesday and Friday in Lent, and on Sundays and holy days at other times of year 'if the day's length permit'; and another said that he catechized in his East Sutton living on Sundays in Lent, and in his Sutton Valence living on Wednesdays, Fridays, and Saturdays. Similar examples can be cited from other dioceses, indicating that a dozen or even more sessions may have taken place in these livings during Lent.[107] Many others claimed that they had catechized in Lent and for some other part of the year. To cite examples from Yorkshire alone, we find the following: Sundays in Lent and the greater part of the summer season; Sundays in Lent and six or seven Sundays, sometimes more, in the summer; Lent and for a period before a confirmation—the usual practice, said the rector of West-Heslerton, and a number of similar replies from other Yorkshire livings and in other dioceses shows that he was not alone in that view.[108] Some Yorkshire ministers, though admittedly a small minority, claimed to have catechized for at least half the year or longer: Wednesdays in Lent and Sunday afternoons 'during the summer half year'; Lent to Michaelmas; all year except a little in winter; Wednesdays and Fridays for much of the year; the first Sunday in every month and every Saturday in the school run by the respondent: the permutations were endless.[109]

If we try to represent these claims in fairly broad statistical terms, we find that 62 of the 154 Kentish ministers whose replies to Archbishop Wake provided details of the length of time for which they catechized, indicated that they catechized for more than six weeks or on more than six occasions. This proportion was 40 per cent, and the equivalent proportions for the Oxfordshire replies in 1738 was 32 out of 133 (or 24 per cent), and for the Yorkshire ones in 1743, 189 out of 531 (or 36 per cent).[110] The exception to these figures was Lincoln where the mean was much higher. An admittedly crude exercise of transforming phrases such as 'from Lady Day to Michaelmas' or 'the greater part of the year' into numerical equivalents suggests that of the 377 replies which gave some impression of how often catechizing took place, 139 indicated up to six weeks (or occasions) a year, another 139 implied six to twelve weeks, 26 implied thirteen to eighteen weeks, 42 implied nineteen to

---

[106] Wake MS 284, fo. 207[r] (and cf. 187[r] and 232[r]: Easter to mid-summer); Secker, *Oxford*, 83, 162–3; Herring, *York*, i. 5, 73, 76, 81, 105, 123, 136, 183, 204; ii. 40, 128.

[107] Wake MS 284, fos. 169[r], 403[r] and 408[r], 130[r]; Herring, *York*, i. 17, 28, 29, 100, 140, 150, 153, 161, 166, 1941; and cf. n. 43 above.

[108] Herring, *York*, i. 44, 86, 93, 120, 145; ii. 66, 82; iii. 28; Wake MS 284, fos. 56[r], 71[r]; Secker, *Oxford*, 53, 155.

[109] Herring, *York*, 41, 42, 61, 171; ii. 89; and volumes i–iii, *passim*.

[110] Ibid.; Wake MS 284 and Secker, *Oxford*, *passim*.

twenty-four weeks, and 31 implied over 24 weeks or occasions per annum.[111] The explanation for the much higher proportion of clergy catechizing for six weeks or more in Lincolnshire, about three-fifths compared to one-quarter or one-third elsewhere, may lie in the relatively stable nature of the population and clergy in that county, or in the pressure brought to bear by a succession of conscientious bishops such as William Fuller, Thomas Barlow, Thomas Tenison, James Gardiner, William Wake, and Edmund Gibson.[112] The cumulative effect of such pressure might have been to raise expectations among the clergy and overcome resistance among the laity to the point where catechizing for up to a quarter or half the year was expected and accepted.

If, for the moment, we assume that there *had* been a reduction from catechizing for much or all of the year in the late sixteenth and early seventeenth centuries to catechizing for only part of the year by the early eighteenth century, then one reason for this situation was changing demographic patterns. In the second half of the sixteenth century it was evidently expected that there would be so many catechumens that they might have to attend in rotation rather than all together, as was sometimes the case abroad, for example in Strasburg.[113] The English authorities seem to have recognized that in the time available it would be possible to test the knowledge of only a proportion of catechumens effectively: the incumbent was therefore to call only as many 'as the time will serve, and as he shall think convenient', in the words of the 1549 rubric. Visitation articles of the Elizabethan period referred to as many catechumens attending 'as he can hear in half an hour', or 'as [the] time will suffer', or to their attending 'in their course' or 'by order of households'.[114] This required a measure of organization and a number of Elizabethan visitors, like Grindal in the province of York, Cox in Ely, Sandys in London, and lesser fry such as the bishop of Chichester in 1586 and the archdeacon of Nottingham in 1599, all expected ministers and churchwardens to prepare a list of children's names or of households, or at the least to warn the older members of their congregation in what order the young people of their households should attend.[115] Church court records also show some Elizabethan clergy being reprimanded for not keeping a proper list of names.[116] After 1604, however, phrases like 'as many as time allows' appear less often in visitation articles, probably because of the absence of such a phrase in canon 59 of that year; and although the rubric in the 1662 Prayer Book restated the principle of teaching conveniently sized groups (as it had to for the larger concentrations of population), there are hardly any references to

[111] Gibson 13–15, *passim.*   [112] See relevant articles in *DNB.*

[113] Vogler, 'Catéchisme à Strasbourg', 13.

[114] Brightman, *English Rite*, ii. 798–9; Kennedy, *Episcopal Administration*, ii. 43; iii. 154, 224, 244, 320, 338; *Second Report on Ritual*, 445, 448.

[115] Frere, *Visitation Articles*, iii. 220, 258, 275–6, 287, 297, 305; Kennedy, *Episcopal Administration*, iii. 211, 320; Fincham, *Visitation Articles*, 54, 74, 189; and cf. I. W. Archer, *The Pursuit of Stability: Social Relations in Elizabethan London* (Cambridge, 1991), 88.

[116] e.g. F. G. Emmison, *Elizabethan Life: Morals and the Church Courts* (Essex Record Office Publications, 63; Chelmsford, 1973), 143.

catechizing in rotation in the visitation articles of the period, nor in the replies from the rural parts of Yorkshire and from Lincolnshire in the eighteenth century.[117] Outside the more populous or extended parishes rotations were probably no longer needed or expected.

The population of England had increased rapidly until the early or mid-seventeenth century, but this increase was not distributed evenly across the existing parishes. Uneven distribution took two forms. On the one hand, some parishes were overpopulated. In his combined livings at Minster in Kent in 1716, for example, John Lewis had a total of six hundred families which, he complained, was too large a number for him to be able to get to know them all personally. At Folkestone with three hundred families, the incumbent said it was impractical to instruct all potential catechumens in the church to the level he would wish; and in St Peter's Sandwich, up to a hundred children were catechized together in church, boys one Friday, girls the next.[118] In these cases and similar ones elsewhere, recourse was had either to rotation of catechumens based on surname or district, to catechizing in dame schools and Charity Schools to compensate for the lack of time on Sundays (some children being supported in these schools at the minister's expense), or even to exhorting parents to teach the catechism at home[119] On the other hand, perhaps a much more common case in some parts of the country, many parishes were left with a reduced population: a surprisingly large number of incumbents in the early eighteenth century made it clear that in their parishes there were not enough or barely enough young people of an appropriate age to constitute a catechism class. This was especially the case in parishes in which, due to migration or other changes in circumstances since their medieval heyday, there were only a few families left. At Stodmersh in Kent in 1716 there were but eight families and, it was reported, there had only lately been any young children in the parish; at nearby Newenden with only twelve families 'there are hardly any young persons in the parish to be catechized'; at Fairfield, with only six houses, there were but three or four children whom the minister said 'I design to catechize in time'.[120] In Kent, Lincolnshire, Yorkshire, and elsewhere, many incumbents indicated that where there was a very small number of children in the parish, they did not catechize at set times but when the few children there had reached an appropriate age; alternatively, they encouraged the children to go to a nearby church where there was a class of catechumens. In Lincolnshire one report was even bleaker: the church was in ruins, there was only one family in the parish, and they were

---

[117] Brightman, *English Rite*, ii. 791; lists mentioned in later visitation articles were of potential confirmands, e.g. *Second Report on Ritual*, 639; Herring, *York*, vols. i–iii and Gibson 13–15, *passim*.

[118] Wake MS 284, fos. 420ʳ, 424ʳ–6ʳ; 310ʳ; 142ʳ.

[119] Herring, *York*, i. 169 (200 families in the parish); ii. 44 (350 families), 48 (105 families), 104 (156 families), 141 (20,000 people); iii. 63 (350 families); for Charity Schools and parental instruction, see below, pp. 181–3, 228–9.

[120] Wake MS 284, fos. 40ʳ, 119ᵛ, '197' [*recte* 198]ʳ; cf. Secker, *Oxford*, 41, 57, 62, 68, 119, 125, 172, 176; Herring, *York*, i. 45, 69, 157, 177; ii. 70, 85.

Quakers![121] It also seems fairly clear that from a relatively early stage older children and servants proved reluctant to attend or co-operate with the elementary catechizing that took place in church, thus reducing the number of potential catechumens, and perhaps the number of weeks in the year needed to instil the Prayer Book catechism into those who did turn up. But here we are entering the sixth area of elementary catechizing: the composition of the catechumenate.

Potential catechumens had been identified at the outset in various ways. One was by age: some episcopal articles suggested 6 as the proper starting age, but from the 1570s the most frequently stated figures in the visitation articles of the Elizabeth period were 7 or 8 years for starting and 19 for finishing.[122] These figures were almost certainly intended as general guidelines rather than rigid rules: as we shall see, some children below the age of 7 mastered the catechism, and adults of 20 or more were not considered immune from catechizing if they wished to take a full part in church life. But in the pioneering days of English catechizing, it may have been thought helpful to supply catechists with some indication of age, both for their own guidance and as a weapon against defaulters. Two other ways of describing catechumens were also adopted: the specific but wide-ranging formula found in the Edwardian Prayer Book and many Elizabethan visitation articles—'children, apprentices, and servants' of both sexes, sometimes with a qualifying phrase such as 'of convenient age' or 'who have not yet learned their catechism';[123] and the less precise 'youth', again of both sexes and sometimes with the rider 'of convenient age'.[124]

The description used by Bancroft in his metropolitical articles of 1605, however, was to become very common in the early seventeenth century: 'youth and ignorant persons'—a translation of 'juventutem et plebem rudiorem' in canon 59 of 1604.[125] This phrase might be thought to mark a shift in emphasis towards older children and towards adults. As far as the latter are concerned this may have been the case, though if so it was temporary in that later Stuart visitation articles and catechisms evinced much more concern about younger catechumens than older ones.[126] Another possible explanation of the reference to adults is that the canons of 1604 did not contain a

---

[121] Wake MS 284, fos. 195[r] (13 families), 218[r] (18 families), 331[r] (20 families); Herring, *York*, i. 19, 110, 112; ii. 21, 57, 137; Gibson 13, p. 633, and Gibson 15, pp. 34–5, 333.

[122] Kennedy, *Episcopal Administration*, ii. 43, 127–8; iii. 211, 320; *Second Report on Ritual*, 414, 419, 422, 425, 435, 445, 489–90, etc. For the limits of 9 and 16 years in a French diocese *c*.1610, see Delumeau, *Catholicism between Luther and Voltaire*, 200.

[123] Kennedy, *Episcopal Administration*, ii. 93–4; iii. 154, 289, 338; *Second Report on Ritual*, 451, 454, 504–5.

[124] Ibid. 416, 427, 428; Kennedy, *Episcopal Administration*, iii. 183, 224, 240, 244, 256.

[125] *Second Report on Ritual*, 451, 459–60, 489–90, 544–5, 548–9, 552, 577–8, and cf. 497.

[126] Ibid. 601, 602, 604, 606, 611, 616, 620, 627, 631, 637, 639, 640, 642, 644, etc., though cf. 608 ('parishioners').

clause insisting on adults' knowledge of the Creed, Decalogue, and Lord's Prayer in English as the canons of 1571 had done, and 'ignorant persons' was meant to cover those who either had slipped through the catechetical net or were thought to retain insufficient knowledge of the faith to be admitted to holy communion. The term 'youth' was probably also not used in a very precise, carefully considered way, to describe those in their teens and early twenties who were no longer children but not yet married or financially independent; it was probably deployed more in the sense of all young people, including children, as opposed to parents and masters of households. Thus, while many bishops incorporated the phrase 'youth and ignorant persons' into their enquiry about clerical activity, they also often retained the older formula of 'children, servants, and apprentices' when asking about parental co-operation in sending their charges to be catechized; or they used 'youth' or 'younger sort' in the same sentence or article as they used 'children' or 'children and servants', suggesting the two were interchangeable in their minds.[127]

What is clear from a number of recent studies not only in religious but also social history, however, is that in England as on the Continent youth and servants often had a mind of their own.[128] The three 'youths' at Coggeshall in 1586 who would not rehearse the Ten Commandments as their minister asked were reported not simply because of their disobedience but also because of the evil example they were setting the other, probably younger catechumens; and many other examples of reports that 'youths' were not attending or proving disruptive have been found in church court records.[129] A century later, Thomas Bray divided catechumens into three classes, up to 9 years, 9 to 13, and 14 to 20-year olds, and complained how hard it was to get this third class to submit to catechizing. He hoped the 'more manly method' of teaching them after Sunday service, rather than before or during the service, when the younger catechumens were instructed, would help to overcome this opposition.[130] Again in the replies to the questionnaires sent out by Wake and other bishops, there are many reports which stated quite specifically that few or no servants were being sent by their masters.[131]

[127] Ibid. 471–2, 485, 489–90, 494–5, 504–5, 510–11, 513 and 515, 531, 534, 548, 552; and Fincham, *Visitation Articles*, 9, 24, 163, 180, 183.

[128] S. Brigden, 'Youth and the English Reformation', *Past and Present*, 95 (1982), 37–67; P. Collinson, *The Religion of Protestants* (Oxford, 1982), 224–30; Ingram, *Church Courts* (see index, s.v. adolescents, apprentices, and servants); I. K. Ben-Adams, *Adolescence and Youth in Early Modern England* (New Haven/London, 1994), ch. 1; and see the important forthcoming study by Paul Griffiths. For the Continent, see e.g. Vogler, 'Catéchisme à Strasbourg', 15, and Strauss, *Luther's House of Learning*, 169–70.

[129] Emmison, *Elizabethan Life*, 118; and cf. *Chetham Miscellanies V*, os, 96 (1875), 2; the frequency with which 'youths' were reported may either mean that older catechumens *were* more problematic than younger, or that respondents were following the wording of an article which asked specifically about 'youth'.

[130] T. Bray, *An introductory discourse to catechetical instruction* (1704), sig. A2ᵛ. For other examples of catechizing after Sunday service, though not necessarily of older catechumens, see above, nn. 44–5, and Herring, *York*, i. 40, 59, 116, 168; iii. 142.

[131] Wake MS 284, fos. 2ʳ, 26ʳ, 66ʳ, 69ʳ, 77ʳ, 81ʳ; Secker, *Oxford*, 77, 90, 94, 107, 112, 140, 147; Herring, *York*, i. 21, 71, 72, 81, 124, 149, etc.; and following notes.

As far as servants are concerned, there are various possible reasons for their being hard to pin down. By their terms of employment they were likely to shift from place to place after a year's service, as was pointed out by clergy in Lincolnshire and Oxfordshire: the servants are from out of town (wrote one minister) and do not stay long but are 'frequently shifting', and when challenged over their non-attendance at catechizing reply that clergy in other parishes had not been as fussy.[132] Not only were church court procedures too clumsy to be effective against such mobile defaulters, but also it must have been hard for the clergy in larger or less stable parishes to keep track of all the changes in domestic arrangements. Another factor may have been employers' reluctance to dispense with the labour of their servants. The servants of the farmers, wrote John Lewis, are 'so constantly employed in their master's business that a minister can have no opportunity to apply himself personally to them but in the field or stable'; there are few servants in this town, wrote a Lincolnshire colleague, and they are seldom to be spared for attending catechizing.[133] 'Godly' clergy were praised by Samuel Clarke for going without proper meals on a Sunday so that their own servants could attend the services and hear the master preach; while a satirist in the reign of Queen Anne described a 'country-gentlewoman' who made her servants go to church with her—or at least such of them as could be spared from the really important business of everyday life.[134]

But the more common reason given was that 'servants will not submit to public catechizing', as the incumbent of Tunstal in Kent put it bluntly in 1716. As other incumbents pointed out to Wake, many servants were 'commonly men and women grown, and they think themselves too great to appear among children'. Like attempts in Lutheran Germany to lump together 'hired men' and 'hired women' with boys and girls in the same catechism class, the blow to the older servants' pride led to stubborn resistance.[135] Servants were 'always … the most disorderly and ungovernable part of a clergyman's charge', one minister complained to Secker in 1738; too much pressure on them to attend catechizing in church might induce servants to go to a meeting-house instead, an East Riding rector suggested in 1743.[136]

In fairness, it should be pointed out that a number of ministers reported that servants did attend alongside children. The second sentence of Wake's ninth question had been 'Do your parishioners duly send their children and servants to be instructed and catechized?', and if we divide up the replies from Canterbury, Lincoln, and York dioceses into those which referred specifically to children and

[132] Gibson 13, p. 223; Secker, *Oxford*, pp. 39, 63.   [133] Wake MS 284, fo. 426[r]; Gibson 13, p. 563.

[134] Clarke, *Lives of two and twenty divines*, 169; id., *Lives of ten eminent divines*, 15; id., *Lives of sundry eminent persons*, 203–4; anon., *The country-gentlewoman's catechism* [1710?], 4.

[135] Wake MS 284, fos. 356[r], 270[r], 298[r–v], 144[r]; and cf. Secker, *Oxford*, 39; Herring, *York*, iii. 34; Strauss, *Luther's House of Learning*, 169–70. Though complaining of masters' demands on servants, Lewis admitted that it did not lie in their power to persuade the latter to attend catechizing: Wake MS 284, fo. 425[r], and cf. 134[r].

[136] Secker, *Oxford*, 39, and cf. 63; Herring, *York*, iii. 34.

servants duly attending and to those which, deliberately or accidentally, referred to children only attending, we find that in Canterbury 36 replies mentioned both children and servants attending as opposed to 62 which mentioned children alone; in the archdeaconry of Lincoln 74 mentioned both children and servants attending as opposed to 68 which mentioned children only attending, and in Yorkshire, 206 mentioned children and servants, as opposed to 215 which mentioned children only attending. The equivalent ratio in Oxfordshire in 1738 was 11 to 79, indicating either a higher level of resistance or perhaps fewer young domestic servants of catechizable age and more of the older and predominantly male servants in husbandry.[137] Where difficulty was experienced in securing servants' attendance, some ministers delivered catechetical sermons aimed at those members of their flock who were no longer being catechized. One Oxfordshire incumbent reported that children were duly sent to be catechized before the service, and servants attended with their masters to hear him explain the catechism during the service; and as a Yorkshire vicar told Herring a few years later, he did not catechize the servants because they were nearly all communicants.[138]

As for youth, one is probably faced with a similar set of circumstances: mobility due to apprenticeships, or parental demands on their labour at certain times of the year, together with growing independence of mind. One should also note here the significance of a parallel development to catechizing, namely that of more regular confirmation ceremonies. One purpose of learning the official catechism was, as we have seen, that the young should be enabled to proceed to confirmation, and then at the appropriate age to participate in the Lord's Supper.[139] The link between mastering the catechism and being confirmed by the bishops was made explicit not only in the Prayer Book rubric and on the title-page of the *ABC with the catechisme*, but also in a minority of visitation articles in the late sixteenth and a larger number in the early seventeenth centuries. The connection was actually made twice in Bishop Morley's visitation articles of 1662 which became the norm for visitors in the next twenty years.[140] It is also moderately clear that in the seventeenth century, and especially the later seventeenth and early eighteenth centuries, episcopal confirmation was being performed more frequently and to some extent more carefully than before.[141]

---

[137] Wake MS 284; Gibson 13–15; Herring, *York*, vols. i–iii; and Secker, *Oxford, passim*; and A. Kussmaul, *Servants in Husbandry in Early Modern England* (Cambridge, 1981), 3–4, 70–1; note also the reference to 'children and *younger* servants' in anon., *The church catechism with scripture proofs* (1705), sig. A2r.

[138] Secker, *Oxford*, 159 (and for a parallel case in Canterbury diocese, Wake MS 284, fo. 374r); Herring, *York*, iii. 34.

[139] S. J. Wright, 'Catechism, Confirmation and Communion: The Role of the Young in the Post-Reformation Church', in Wright (ed.), *Parish, Church and People: Local Studies in Lay Religion 1350–1750* (London, 1988), 214, 217.

[140] Brightman, *English Rite*, ii. 776–99; Ollard, 'Confirmation', 97–102, 115–17, 125–8, 168–74; Fincham, *Visitation Articles*, 29, 40.

[141] Ollard, 'Confirmation', 86–200; Fincham, *Prelate as Pastor*, 123–9; Wright, 'Catechism', 214–15;

Up to a point confirmation may have given a boost to catechizing. As early as 1598 and 1630 we have two examples of a phenomenon which would become more common in later centuries: the desire of curious youths to be 'bishoped'. On the first occasion, the 5-year-old Nicholas Ferrar managed to get himself confirmed twice because at the time he thought 'it was a good thing to have the bishop's prayers and blessing twice'; on the second, the 15-year-old Richard Baxter, who had wandered along idly to see a bishop passing by, tagged onto a group of thirty to forty boys of similar age who had been assembled to be confirmed, and so received the episcopal blessing.[142] Some incumbents even offered cash inducements to those who would attend catechizing, an anticipation of the treats associated with confirmation in the late eighteenth and nineteenth centuries, and looking back from middle age to his own confirmation Wordsworth described the 'holiday delight on every brow' of the young ones gathered in from hill and dale for the big occasion.[143]

But this is where the boost could also become a handicap. In Protestant ideology, confirmation was a rite of puberty which preceded admission to the Lord's Supper, and it was supposed 'to be administered only to those children who had reached the "perfect age of adolescence" '.[144] In early visitation articles, various ages were given as the appropriate point for admission to the Lord's Supper: 12 or 13, 13 or 14; 14 was specified by the canons of 1571, by 1604 it had become 16.[145] Less detail was given as to the appropriate age for confirmation, but it also seems to have been raised from a relatively young age—in 1565 Bishop Bentham of Coventry and Lichfield and in 1640 John Cosin both stated that many were confirmed as young as 7 years old—to the point at which those who had mastered the catechism were nearer to the years of discretion required for communicating.[146] Some bishops, like Strafford of Chester in 1701 and Gibson of Lincoln in 1718, were careful to warn their clergy that they would confirm none below a certain age, in their case 14; shortly afterwards Archbishop Wake set minima of 14 for boys and 12 for girls.[147] But many other bishops, either because they confirmed so rarely that large numbers were confirmed at a time without proper supervision, or because they were responding to what was widely recognized as a great demand for confirmation, confirmed all who sought it, even

---

W. M. Marshall, 'Episcopal Activity in the Hereford and Oxford Dioceses, 1660–1760', *Midland History*, 8 (1983), 114–16; and see references in n. 102 above.

[142] Ollard, 'Confirmation', 118, 124.

[143] Wake MS 284, fo. (315)ʳ; J. Obelkevich, *Religion and Rural Society: South Lindsey 1825–75* (Oxford, 1976), 131, 134.

[144] R. L. DeMolen, 'Childhood and the Sacraments in the Sixteenth Century', *Archiv für Reformationsgeschichte*, 66 (1975), 59–63.

[145] Frere, *Visitation Articles*, iii. 62, 161, 259, 276, 287, 297, 306, etc.; Ollard, 'Confirmation', 87, 98–9; Cardwell, *Synodalia*, i. 120, 309.

[146] Ollard, 'Confirmation', 87, 134, and cf. 145 and *passim*.

[147] *Second Report on Ritual*, 662; *Speculum Lincolniensis*, p. iii; and N. Sykes, *Church and State in England in the Eighteenth Century* (Cambridge, 1934), 121. For Lloyd's minimum of above 10 years in 1700, see *Diary of Francis Evans*, 17.

though many of these same confirmands might then have had to wait some years before they became communicants.[148] Despite attempts to curb the practice, another of John Lewis's complaints to Wake in 1716 was that too many were being confirmed while they were still 'very children' who were not mature enough to ratify their baptismal vows in person, and yet once they had been confirmed thought that they could put such childish things as catechizing behind them. He went on to warn that unless the practice of confirming the very young was stopped, thus allowing the catechist to continue to teach them until they reached the point where, as adolescents, they knew what they were doing at confirmation, then catechizing would continue to be 'dismissed as an exercise fit only for children'.[149] A Yorkshire incumbent made a similar complaint in 1743: 'as infants are become the catechumens, the adults think it below 'em'.[150] It would also seem that in some cases clergy could get children of 6, 7, or 8 to attend catechizing, but if they were not confirmed at once they tended to drift away until the time for confirmation came, when they might again attend briefly prior to that ceremony.[151]

Again we may note that other incumbents do seem to have managed to secure the attendance of older children, and given them more advanced material to learn than the younger ones, as we shall see shortly. During the seventeenth and early eighteenth centuries, as noted in an earlier chapter, we can see more and more provision being made for catechumens at this stage: extra sections on confirmation being added at the end of expositions of the Prayer Book catechism; separate question-and-answer works explaining the nature and importance of confirmation, to be learnt after the Prayer Book catechism but before confirmation; and works to be mastered by adolescents before they took communion.[152] The beginning and end of childhood in a small town in the Lake District are captured in two sonnets later written by Wordsworth.[153] The small size and tender years of the catechumens are captured in 'Catechising', as also is the sense of occasion, the tension induced, the fact that the season was probably Lent, and that at least one adult (Wordsworth's mother) was present. The poem begins:

> From little down to least, in due degree,
> Around the pastor, each in new-wrought vest,

---

[148] Ollard, 'Confirmation', 122–3, and cf. 119–24, and Fincham, *Prelate as Pastor*, 128–9; Wright, 'Catechism', 214–15; I. M. Green, *The Re-establishment of the Church of England 1660–1663* (Oxford, 1978), 141–2; and T[homas] B[ray], *A course of lectures upon the church catechism* (1696), sig. b1ʳ.

[149] Wake MS 284, fo. 426ʳ; and cf. Gibson 14, p. 117 and Gibson 15, p. 31 (and for a parallel case involving servants, Gibson 13, p. 495).

[150] Herring, *York*, ii. 114.

[151] Ibid, iii. 216, and cf. i. 92; ii. 4, 78, 114, 178; iii. 31, 104, 125; and [Beveridge], *Church-catechism explained*, p. x.

[152] See above, pp. 33–5. For occasional episcopal indications that those who had been confirmed should continue to be catechized before they communicated, see Fincham, *Visitation Articles*, 40, 189.

[153] *Poetical Works of William Wordsworth*, iii. 395.

> Each with a vernal posy at his breast,
> We stood, a trembling, earnest company!
> With low soft murmur, like a distant bee,
> Some spake, by thought-perplexing fears betrayed;
> And some a bold unerring answer made:
> How fluttered then thy anxious heart for me,
> Beloved mother!

'Confirmation', on the other hand, refers to 'young-ones' who were nervous about 'taking the baptismal vow / Upon their conscious selves'. Those described are adolescents rather than 6-year-olds:

> … Strongest sinews fail,
> And many a blooming, many a lovely, cheek
> Under the holy fear of God turns pale.

But nor are they adults, and the poet also imagines the regret of 'the Omnipotent'

> Who, looking round the fair assemblage, feels,
> That ere the sun goes down their childhood sets.

We cannot make too much of this, since we are not sure how often Wordsworth was catechized between the two events he describes here. But his memories are worth setting alongside those more hostile remarks about a laity who had come to the conclusion that, as Lewis put it, elementary catechizing in church was 'an exercise fit only for children'.

Before we go any further, we should in fairness point out that another explanation of the diminution of elementary catechetical activity in the early modern period recorded under our fourth, fifth, and sixth headings—from a temporary peak of an hour (in theory) in the late sixteenth century to half an hour or less in practice in the seventeenth century, from all year (in theory) to a few weeks or months only (in most cases) in the early eighteenth, and from all 7- to 19-year-olds (in theory) at the outset to mainly the younger end of this spectrum later on—is that in each instance the church was unable to insist on the higher standard and settled for a lower. Protestantism is still seen in some quarters as having failed to penetrate popular consciousness in the way that medieval Catholicism had clearly done. It was a religion of the book, of a powerful social minority, a well-educated and zealous élite opposed to the culture of the ale-house or the part-magical, part-Christian synthesis of popular religion.[154] A more balanced view that has emerged in recent years, for example in the writing of Martin Ingram, is that popular religion in England was an integral element in 'a range of overlapping and interacting religious cultures, not related in any

---

[154] e.g. E. Duffy, *The Stripping of the Altars: Traditional Religion in England c.1400–c.1580* (New Haven/London, 1992); Wrightson, *English Society*, ch. 7.

clear-cut way to the divisions of the social hierarchy, and in complex interaction with official doctrines and precepts which were themselves by no means unitary or unchanging'. Even here, however, catechizing has been cited as an example of the limitations of popular participation rather than an instance of integration or appropriation: the clergy did what they could but were apt to give up in the face of apathy.[155] Set in either of these contexts, the history of catechizing can be seen as that of a failure, and certainly there are enough contemporary complaints of clerical defeatism or neglect and of lay opposition to catechizing to make us take such a view seriously.

The first thing one notes about the complaints of clerical neglect, however, is their very general nature: chapter and verse are rarely if ever given. In 1588 Thomas Sparke did suggest that not one minister in twenty in England was catechizing (and not one householder in a hundred), but he did not indicate how he came to these particular and suspiciously round figures.[156] A Welsh bishop in 1583 berated his clergy for the fact that the catechizing of youth was 'altogether neglected' in his diocese; more commonly the complaints were of 'general' or 'much' neglect, or of 'long' or 'sad neglect'.[157] However, we have no way of telling whether this was supposed to mean that the great majority or merely a large minority of ministers were not catechizing regularly, or that they were perhaps catechizing only alternate weeks or for only part of the year when (it was felt by the complainant) they should have been catechizing all year. Also we have no way of knowing whether comments emanating from Devon in the 1630s, London in the 1650s, and Yorkshire in the 1690s were based on anything wider than local impressions.[158] A second point to note is that the context in which the great majority of these complaints were voiced is usually a call for higher standards of performance as a solution to the problems caused by ignorance. The number of such calls also tended to rise at times of crisis, such as the threat of Catholic invasion from abroad in the 1580s and early 1590s, the revived fear of militant Catholicism on the Continent in the 1620s, the world turned upside down of the late 1640s and 1650s, and the renewed fear of Catholicism in the 1680s and early 1690s.[159] This does not mean there was no basis of fact in the

---

[155] Martin Ingram, 'From Reformation to Toleration: Popular Religious Cultures in England, 1530–1690', in T. Harris (ed.), *Popular Culture in England, 1500–1850* (1995), 100, 116; see also T. Watt, *Cheap Print and Popular Piety, 1550–1640* (Cambridge, 1991), *passim*.

[156] T. Sparke, 'A treatise', in *A catechisme, or short kind of instruction*, ed. Sparke and J. Seddon (1588), 1.

[157] *Second Report on Ritual*, 427; Crompton, *Explication*, title-page and sig. ¶6ʳ; R. Bernard, *The common catechisme* (1640), sig. A2ʳ; E. Bury, *A short catechisme* (1660), sig. A2ʳ; T. Lamplugh, [*A pastoral letter to the clergy of the diocese of Exeter*] [167?], 7; [Beveridge], *Church-catechism explained*, p. ii; G. Bull, *A companion for the candidates of holy orders* (1714), 46; Cradock, *Discourse of due catechising*, 6; and see following notes.

[158] Crompton, loc. cit.; Z. Crofton, *Catechizing Gods ordinance* (1656), sigs. A8ʳ⁻ᵛ; Briggs, *Catechetical exercises*, sigs. A2ʳ⁻ᵛ.

[159] e.g. W. Wood, *A fourme of catechising* (1581), sig. *2ᵛ; J.F., *A most breefe manner of instruction* [c.1585], sig. Aiiᵛ; Sparke, loc. cit.; W. Perkins, *The foundation of Christian religion* (1591), sigs. A2ʳ–3ᵛ; Mayer,

complaints, but it does indicate a clear predisposition to state the case for neglect as strongly as possible.[160]

A third point is that a number of the complaints were directed against clergy who preferred preaching to catechizing. Thus in a work republished in 1604, a 'godly' minister, Robert Cawdrey, complained not only of the idle or ignorant shepherds who neglected to catechize, and of catechists who simply ensured their charges could recite the catechism without ensuring that they understood it, but also of those clergy who were zealous preachers but who neglected to catechize.[161] This allegation was echoed a dozen years later by C.P., when he said that some of his fellow-clergy were so 'dazzled' by preaching that they were 'slumbering' over catechizing, and by two authors writing in the 1620s.[162] Moreover, in a sermon given before King James in 1624, James Ussher observed that 'great scholars may think it stands not so well with their credit to stoop thus low in teaching' the rudiments of the faith through catechizing, but their neglect would frustrate the whole work of the ministry.[163] Was it possible that *less* learned clergy were more disposed to catechize regularly, if perhaps less knowledgeably, than their more learned brethren? Dr Thomas Jackson recalled that in the 1580s he was

first instructed in the church's catechism, by the curate of the parish, from whose lips (though but a mere grammar scholar, and one that knew better how to read an homily ... than to make a sermon, in English) I learned more good lessons, than I did from many popular sermons: and to this day remember more than men of this time of greater years shall find in many late applauded catechisms.[164]

One thinks also of the more bashful parishioners in Kidderminster in the 1650s who seem to have been readier to be catechized by Baxter's assistant, Richard Sargeant, because they could be 'bolder' with him than with the great man himself.[165]

English catechisme, sig. A3ʳ; Phillips, *Christians A. B. C.*, sig. A4ᵛ; [W. Bridges], *A catechisme for communicants* (1645), sigs. A3ʳ, A7ᵛ; anon., *No popery* (1683), sig. A2ʳ; [T. Ken], *An exposition on the church catechism* (1686), sig. A2ʳ; [T. Comber], *The plausible arguments of a Romish priest answered* (1686); [J. Williams], *A catechism truly representing the doctrines* (1686); anon., *The art of catechizing* (1691), sig. A3ʳ.

[160] See examples in the preceding and following notes.

[161] R. Cawdrey, *A Short and fruitefull treatise* (1604), sig. A1ʳ; for examples of neglect of catechizing by 'godly' clergy in Lancashire, see C. Haigh, *Reformation and Resistance in Tudor Lancashire* (Cambridge, 1975), 305–6.

[162] C.P., *Two briefe treatises* (1616), sig. A3ᵛ; anon., 'Of catechisinge', in Emmanuel College Cambridge MS III. 1. 13⁸, fo. [30]ʳ; I. Bourne, *The true way of a Christian* (1622), 28.

[163] T. Greaves, *A brief summe of Christian religion* (1656), sigs. a2ʳ⁻ᵛ; [Marshall], *Catechism set forth*, sig. a4ᵛ; Cradock, *Discourse of due catechising*, 6; the sermon was also cited for a different purpose in Richard Baxter in *Gildas Salvianus: The Reformed Pastor* (London 1860), 477–8.

[164] C. Wordsworth, *Ecclesiastical Biography* (6 vols.; 1818), v. 349 n. It is possible that the curate who taught Jackson did so in the capacity of schoolteacher.

[165] N. H. Keeble and G. F. Nuttall (eds.), *Calender of the Correspondence of Richard Baxter* (2 vols.; Oxford, 1991), no. 348; and cf. R. Baxter, *Reliquiae Baxterianae*, ed. M. Sylvester (1696), pt. iii, 91–2. See also L. Fogg, *Two treatises* (1712), sig. A3ʳ, for an assistant minister in Cheshire who was 'singularly beloved' by the people there; and below, nn. 233–5.

By the late 1640s and 1650s we find another vein of complaint which sits rather uncomfortably with the complaints made during the previous fifty years of neglect by idle clergy and proud preachers. In 1645 Walter Bridges said that many catechisms which like candles had been 'lighted and burning bright' were now burning out; a year later John Mayer, the author of two best-selling catechetical forms in the 1620s and 1630s, wrote that catechizing had lately 'grown obsolete'; and four years later the author of *The summe of Christian religion* opined that catechizing was now much out of favour in these 'times of distraction', and called upon the experience of former times to prove that catechizing was the only way to build up a church.[166] Concern was strong among not only former conformists like Mayer and John Evelyn, who in the 1650s catechized his own family because it was 'universally ceasing in the parish churches',[167] but also the newly powerful presbyterians who shared the episcopalians' worry at the rapid development and spread of new sects. The *Exhortation to catechising* issued by the Provincial Assembly at London in 1655 equated current ignorance and apostasy with the neglect of catechizing, partly by ministers who thought it 'beneath the dignity of their station'; it also called for the speedy 'reviving' of 'that most necessary, though neglected exercise of catechizing'.[168] Similar complaints were voiced in 1655 and 1656 by other concerned ministers, such as Simon Ford, Zachary Crofton, and Richard Baxter.[169]

Another feature of the literature of complaint—allegations of insufficient care being taken—actually indicates that clerical catechizing was taking place, albeit at a lower standard of performance than the complainants desired—'very slenderly only, to meet legal obligations' as the zealous William Wood put it in 1581.[170] Both 'godly' clergy like William Perkins and John Mico and conformists like William Crompton conceded that adults had been taught the Apostles' Creed and Decalogue (as well as the Lord's Prayer) when they were young, presumably through some form of catechizing, but complained that they were so ignorant of their significance that they used them as if they were prayers.[171] Similar charges can be found throughout the seventeenth century, and in different parts of the country.[172] In 1704 Bishop

---

[166] Bridges, *Catechisme for communicants*, sig. A3^r; J. Mayer, *A short catechisme necessary to be learned* (1646), sig. A3^v; anon. *The summe of Christian religion* (1649), sig. A2^r.

[167] *The Diary of John Evelyn*, ed. E. S. de Beer (6 vols.; Oxford, 1955), iii. 160.

[168] Anon., *An exhortation to catechising* (1655), 6, 14; and cf. T. Hodges's statement in *A scripture-catechisme* (Oxford, 1658), sig. B2^v, that he was not ashamed to catechize in person in his own congregation.

[169] S. Ford, *A sermon of catechizing* (1655), sig. G5^r; Crofton, loc. cit.; Baxter, *Reformed Pastor*, 1, 392, and *passim*; see also the 'neglect' cited in D. Hirst, 'The Failure of Godly Rule in the English Republic', *Past and Present*, 132 (1991), 43–4; and below, n. 206.

[170] Wood, *Fourme of catechising*, sig.*2^v.

[171] Perkins, *Foundation*, sigs. A3^{r-v}; J. Mico, *Spirituall food, and physicke* (1631), sig. A2^v; Crompton, *Explication*, sig. ¶7^r; cf. the comment in [Bridges], *Catechisme for communicants*, sigs. A4^{r-v}, that in religious terms few today were deaf and dumb but many had palsied limbs.

[172] Above p. 115 n. 84 and p. 130 n. 161; R. Baxter, *Confirmation and restauration* (1658), 157–65; Moorman, *Curate of Souls*, 88; Addison, *Primitive institution* (1674), 74–7; Briggs, *Catechetical exercises*, sigs. A2^{r-v}.

Beveridge told his clergy in St Asaph that catechizing had been generally neglected or slightly performed for 'many years together'; like Burnet he pointed out that getting children to repeat the catechism by rote 'signifies very little, unless they understand what they say', and that to achieve this was 'one of the hardest duties belonging to the ministerial office'.[173] The wealth of new expositions of the Westminster Shorter Catechism and the Prayer Book catechism offered by zealous catechists to the general public and fellow-clergy was also sometimes accompanied by implied criticism of the way that fellow-catechists were setting about instruction based on those forms.[174] What all these complaints bear testimony to is the desire of some clergy to raise standards from the most basic rote repetition of the first level to the point where catechumens understood and applied what they learnt, which it was suggested earlier was one of the characteristic aims of the intermediate level of catechizing.

One other charge made against the clergy was that they failed to overcome the resistance of parents and masters to sending their children and servants to church. It must be said at once that in the literature of complaint much the most common charge made against adults was that they were reluctant either to be catechized themselves, in public or private, or that they refused to conduct catechizing in their own households—an allegation to which we shall return at the appropriate point. But there are still plenty of complaints of parental neglect to send their children and servants to be catechized in the Elizabethan and early Stuart periods, together with peremptory commands and sharp reproofs from the authorities and the 'godly' to those clergy who allowed parents to get away with this offence.[175] In the later Stuart period, there are similar complaints. A Leicestershire rector in 1673 said that he had repeatedly tried and failed to persuade parishioners to send their children to church, and could not 'bring them to church on his back'; and in the early eighteenth century there were still a number of quite specific reports of parents refusing flatly to cooperate with the clergy in the catechizing of their young, despite repeated requests to do so.[176]

Certainly, it would be foolish to doubt that lay opposition was severe enough in many parishes to deter all but the most determined minister from trying to insist on catechizing according to the letter of the law. It is also likely that in many cases clergy were reluctant to bring in the authorities to coerce unco-operative parents, for fear of

---

[173] [Beveridge], *Church-catechism explained*, pp. ii, xii.

[174] e.g. Cradock, *Discourse of due catechising*, 7–8 and *passim*.

[175] *Bishop Redman's Visitation*, 18; Emmison, *Elizabethan Life*, 143; Haigh, *Reformation and Resistance*, 247; S. D. Amussen, *An Ordered Society: Gender and Class in Early Modern England* (New York/Oxford, 1988), 35, 149; and e.g. *Second Report on Ritual*, 406, 408, 412, 444, 448.

[176] Pruett, *Parish Clergy*, 116 (and for a parallel complaint from a parent, see Ingram, 'From Reformation to Toleration', 116); *Rector's Book, Clayworth*, 38; and Wake MS 284, fos. 18ʳ, 217ʳ, 278ʳ, 280ʳ, 300ʳ, 386ʳ; Gibson 13, p. 55, Gibson 14, pp. 177, 335, 347, and Gibson 15, p. 143; Herring, *York*, i, 51, iii. 90, 125.

making relations worse. But there was another side to this coin. One of the complaints of the insurgents in Kett's rebellion in 1549 was that their children were not being catechized, and there are periodic echoes of this grievance in the next century and a half (and parallel complaints in France that local clergy were neglecting to catechize the young).[177] Equally, as we have seen already there are a remarkably large number of positive answers to the question put by Wake and others as to whether parents sent their children or children and servants to be catechized on Sundays in the early eighteenth century. Moreover, when describing parents' attitudes towards sending their charges, some respondents added a phrase such as 'very diligent', 'particularly careful', and 'with great willingness and cheerfulness', or noted that young people attended 'very well', 'very regularly', or were sent 'in considerable numbers'.[178] The range of clerical comments on lay attitudes in Lincolnshire varied from disgust at flat refusal, through grudging approval (parents sent their charges 'tolerably' well) and a degree of warmth (the young are sent 'pretty well'), to the positively grateful (every Sunday afternoon parishioners send their children and servants and there is a considerable number of young persons to catechize).[179] Nor did the clergy necessarily follow the wording of the questionnaires in their replies: one Lincolnshire minister with two cures reported that in one of them parishioners sent children and servants 'duly', but in the other were 'very careful' to send them; another said parishioners in his curacy sent children 'pretty well', but in his main living they sent children and servants 'very well'.[180]

There is also the striking case reported by the rector and curate of a heavily populated parish in the West Riding in 1743, of the number of parents who were 'proud to have their children catechized as young as possible and vie with one another in the forwardness of their babes'.[181] And we can cite other cases where a distinct impression was conveyed that older people actually enjoyed watching and hearing the young being catechized, or were certainly prepared to go along and watch, just as in more recent times older members of a family can be inveigled into church if their offspring are performing some part in a concert or pageant there. Writing of the

[177] J. F. C. Harrison, *The Common People: A History from the Norman Conquest to the Present* (1984), 123; C. Haigh, 'The Church of England, the Catholics and the People', in Haigh (ed.), *The Reign of Elizabeth* (1984), 210; Wright, 'Catechism', 205–6; I. M. Green, 'The Persecution of "Scandalous" and "Malignant" Parish Clergy during the English Civil War', *English Historical Review*, 94 (1979), 520 and n. 4; Hirst, 'Failure of Godly Rule', 42 n. 48 (Salisbury city council); D. A. Spaeth, 'Parsons and Parishioners: Lay–Clerical Conflict and Popular Piety in Wiltshire Villages, 1660–1740', Ph.D. thesis (Brown University, 1985), 73; Delumeau, *Catholicism between Luther and Voltaire*, 200; and for an earlier lay initiative, see J. A. Bossy, 'The Counter-Reformation and the People of Catholic Europe', *Past and Present*, 47 (1970), 64–5.

[178] Wake MS 284, fos. 146ʳ, 179ʳ, 197ʳ, 222ʳ, 398ʳ; Gibson 13, pp. 35, 43, 51, 115, 191, 523, 531, 535, 603, etc.; Herring, *York*, i. 37, 89, 164, 182, 215, etc.

[179] For the range of reactions, see Gibson 13, pp. 523, 603; Gibson 14, pp. 177, 201, 295, 431; and Gibson 15, p. 111.

[180] Ibid., pp. 131, 123; Gibson 13, pp. 451, 459.   [181] Herring, *York*, ii. 114.

practice of catechizing the young in the presence of adults, one bishop confidently asserted that he 'never yet heard catechizing in a church, where I did not see the oldest and the gravest people attend as seriously as any else, and I dare say they were as much edified, and more pleased to be so, than the younger'; another clergyman told his parishioners in a country parish in East Anglia of the great pleasure given him by the attendance of 'you and your little ones at the public examination upon the church-catechism'; and in 1722 an elderly widow in Gloucestershire left money to the local parish church for the continuation of catechizing after a method developed by the current incumbent of which she evidently approved.[182] We may also anticipate a point to be made later, that a number of clergy reported that parents had either taught their children the church catechism at home or ensured they had learnt it at school before sending them to church to be tested and further instructed there.[183] Finally, one may raise again the apparent popularity of confirmation: there are even reports that parents would not send children or servants unless there was a confirmation in the offing.[184]

These hints of popular support for or acceptance of catechizing need to be taken into account and explained as much as the allegations of hostility and neglect. There was the perhaps natural feeling, as in the case of the Kett rebels, that they did not want their children to miss what was on offer in other parts of the country. Equally, as in the West Riding case, there may occasionally have been pressure from the peer group impelling parents to ensure that their offspring did not fall behind others of their age group. What psychologists refer to as social roles, social norms, and reference groups could work as much in favour of co-operation in catechizing in one set of circumstances as in a different set they could work against.[185] Being catechized in church was part of a process of growing up in a village or town in which community and congregation regularly overlapped, and was, at least in theory, a means to the end of further participation in the rites of passage which (as parents knew full well) only the church could provide. And from the point of view of a highly perceptive child like William Wordsworth, there may have been a frisson of excitement about being catechized and an element of anticipation about being 'bishoped', as an initiation rite into adulthood. By the eighteenth century (and sometimes earlier) there was also the prospect of a reward or treat for those who were confirmed.[186] Such thinking may

---

[182] *Second Report on Ritual*, 666; anon., *First principles of the oracles of God* (Norwich, 1712), sig. A2ʳ; [J. Harrison], *A scriptural exposition of the church-catechism* (1735), 228–9; and Wordsworth's mother—see above, p. 127 n. 153.

[183] See below, pp. 228–9.

[184] See above, nn. 142, 148; Gibson 13, p. 495; Herring, *York*, ii. 78, iii. 125. One must enter the caveats that the attitudes of clergy and confirmands to confirmation were often not the same, and that not all who were confirmed had been properly catechized.

[185] C. D. Batson, P. Schoenrade, and W. L. Ventis, *Religion and the Individual: A Social-Psychological Perspective* (Oxford, 1993), ch. 2.

[186] There are three cases where inducements were offered to adults, with some success it was

have made children accept, if not necessarily welcome, their parents' insistence that they attend church for catechizing for a period of time.

Historians should perhaps approach relations between laity and clergy over the catechizing of the young without too many stereotypes in mind, and be alert to a possibly wide variety of experience, from a fair degree of co-operation to absolutely none at all, from a measure of appropriation by the laity to complete indifference. One can suggest a number of questions to be asked in future studies of parish religion. Was there a tradition of catechizing in the area, and had the parents themselves been catechized when young? or had it been a parish where for one reason or another—size, dissent, poor clergy—it had never been successfully established? Was the size of the congregation such that a single clergyman could get to know them all, or impossibly large; and did the minister get on well with parishioners in general on matters of common interest, or was he seen as aloof or alien?[187] Was there a powerful lay person resident in the parish who set an example, such as the Barnardistons in Suffolk, the 'worthy and religious family of the Filmers' and the earl of Thanet in Kent, and the earl of Malton and the duke of Leeds in Yorkshire, or not?[188] Was there catechizing in surrounding parishes, which might lead parents to think their children were missing out if their minister did not catechize, or a dearth of catechizing nearby, which might provoke resistance on the grounds of unfair treatment? Were there religious dissenters in the parish, or a conventicle or meeting-house to which parishioners could turn if pressurized by the incumbent of the parish church to attend catechizing?

Where relations between minister and parishioners (or even between parents and children) were not good for one reason or another, where the need for child labour was urgent or the parish church some distance away, one can well believe that parents were reluctant or unable to send their children to be catechized. But where some or all of these conditions did not apply to a serious degree, there were incentives for parents to co-operate, and co-operation may have been the norm for at least a few years at a time. This was the experience of Michael Hutchinson in Leicestershire. By preaching catechetical lectures which attracted the parents, he managed to turn round a situation from irregular attendance at catechizing to great numbers of children and servants being sent to be catechized and a good attendance by parents as well. But 'this good humour spent itself by degrees', and as attendance dropped again

---

felt: anon., *A short catechism collected by a Christian* [1575?], preface; Clarke, *Lives of sundry eminent persons*, 203; *Second Report on Ritual*, 666.

[187] For clergy having some success in catechizing in middle-sized parishes, see e.g. *Speculum Lincolniensis*, pp. xii, xiv, 133, 158, and Gibson 13, pp. 19, 51, 54.

[188] Clarke, *Lives of sundry eminent persons*, 110–13; Wake MS 284, fos. 404ʳ, 117ᵛ–118ʳ, and cf. fo. 343ʳ; Herring, *York*, ii. 147–8; note also the example set by Lady Margaret Hoby (*Diary*, 66, 75, 79, 80, 82–4, 87–8, etc.), and the bishop of St Asaph's confident assurance to his clergy that persons of worth and quality would set an example to tenants and neighbours by sending their children and servants to be catechized in church: [Beveridge], *Church-catechism explained*, p. vi.

Hutchinson decided to let his campaign drop for a while too.[189] In short, complaints of lay hostility are well attested and perfectly credible, but we should perhaps not regard them as universally true or consistently valid.

———————

The point has been reached at which we may offer a provisional answer to the larger question implicit in a number of the questions raised in preceding paragraphs: just how much elementary catechizing was there in the churches of early modern England? The start was certainly slow. The first two generations of clerical catechists were less well educated and fewer in number than they should have been, and they faced a daunting struggle to impart a set of formulae and ideas which were in a different language and in some ways very different from those normally taught in previous centuries, and to do so by a question-and-answer technique that was relatively new to both teachers and taught. Early complaints of neglect and resistance were almost certainly true, though not necessarily as true as Sparke's complaint that only 5 per cent of the clergy were catechizing by the 1580s; as in later sixteenth-century Italy, the Low Countries, and France, catechizing took some time to take hold.[190] By the close of the sixteenth century, however, this situation was probably starting to change as the number of better educated clergy and aids to catechizing rose rapidly and the laity began to turn its back on the old religion. In the archdeaconry of Nottingham, a few defaulters were reported each year in the 1590s and 1600s, but in general the churchwardens reported that the clergy were discharging their obligation to catechize satisfactorily. In the county of Lancashire, in a part of the world in which the Reformation had taken a long time to overcome the old religion, there were an average of six or seven parishes (out of about sixty-four) where it was reported that there was no catechizing between 1578 and 1604, though the fact that at most of the half dozen visitations of which records survive only half the county was covered means the situation was probably worse. In the diocese of Norwich in 1597 there were reported to be 78 (out of over 800) parishes with no catechizing and a further 15 with only irregular catechizing.[191] The other way of looking at this is that in nearly 80 per cent of the parishes in Lancashire and in well over 80 per cent of those in Norwich diocese there was, at least in theory, some catechizing taking place.

[189] Pruett, *Parish Clergy*, 117.

[190] R. Houlbrooke, *Church Courts and the People during the English Reformation 1520–1570* (1979), 200–1, 248; and cf. Emmison, *Elizabethan Life*, 89, 118, 129, 142–3, 185–6; and Haigh, 'Church of England', 209–11; also Delumeau, *Catholicism between Luther and Voltaire*, 199–200.

[191] R. G. Riley, 'The Ecclesiastical Control of Parochial Life in the Nottingham Archdeaconry 1590–1610', MA thesis (Nottingham University, 1954), 56–7; Haigh, *Reformation and Resistance*, 246–7; *Bishop Redman's Visitation*, 17–18; and for London and Yorkshire, see also Archer, *Pursuit of Stability*, 88, and the Hoby diary (above n. 188); cf. also the years of catechizing put in by John Thaxter in the early 1580s: *Historical Manuscripts Commission: Gawdy MSS.* (1885), 23.

The interpretation of statistics derived from the disciplinary procedures of the church, and especially from presentments made by churchwardens, is of course subject to a large margin of error. If in most dioceses and for most parishes there was no presentment by churchwardens of a failure to catechize, this could mean one of two quite different things: either the minister was catechizing as he was supposed to be; or the people did not want to be catechized, and the minister did not want to admit that he was not catechizing, and so there was a conspiracy of silence between wardens and minister to conceal the fact.[192] The pessimistic view would be that presentments for neglect of catechizing were the tip of the iceberg, that catechizing was infrequent and confined either to a minority of parishes with zealous clergy and amenable laity, or to a somewhat larger number of parishes but on an erratic basis rather than every week. As one commentator has recently implied, the pattern of prosecution suggests that there was a stand-off in many parishes.[193]

A more optimistic view would be that the church's corrective procedures were far from perfect, but that not a great deal escaped the attention of an archdeacon or bishop who was putting some effort into his enquiries: either the laity or the clergy would soon reveal what the situation was.[194] One reason for the clergy to blow the whistle on lay resistance was that the penalties for ministers who neglected to catechize were stiff: a sharp reprimand for the first offence, suspension for a second, and excommunication for a third. Dr Stieg has commented on the fact that while a number of clergy in the early Stuart diocese of Bath and Wells were presented again and again for not reading prayers or preaching as often as they should, not one minister was presented a second time for failure to catechize, a fact she attributes to the severity of the penalties laid down in canon 59.[195] Moreover, there is reasonably good ground for believing that at least periodically a number of bishops *were* concerned to ensure regular catechizing throughout their dioceses.[196] Dr Fincham has suggested that the result of one such campaign at the start of James's reign was to reveal a much higher number of clergy failing to hold weekly catechizing classes, and that failure to catechize was the second most common fault reported of clergy in the episcopal visitations in the diocese of Bath and Wells in the early seventeenth century.[197] Again

---

[192] For examples of churchwardens' selectivity in presenting offences, see Ingram, *Church Courts*, 325–9; Fincham, *Prelate as Pastor*, 133; and id., *Visitation Articles*, pp. xxii–iii.

[193] Ingram, 'From Reformation to Toleration', 116.

[194] For the laity's attitude to the church courts, see Houlbrooke, *Church Courts*, and Ingram, *Church Courts*.

[195] M. Stieg, *Laud's Laboratory: The Diocese of Bath and Wells in the Early Seventeenth Century* (London/Toronto, 1982), 189; and cf. the archdeacon of Gloucester's remark to Laud in 1638 that those opposed to catechizing did not take their opposition too far for fear of losing their livings: *Works of William Laud*, v. 359.

[196] Barratt, 'Condition of the Parish Clergy', 118–19; Fincham, *Prelate as Pastor*, 134–5, 245–6, 256–7.

[197] K. Fincham, 'Ramifications of the Hampton Court Conference in the Dioceses 1603–1609', *JEH* 36 (1985), 212; and id., 'Personalities and Politics in Early Stuart England', review article in *Historical Journal*, 27 (1985), 1005 and n. 13.

one can take this either way: catechizing was still being neglected in too many cases, *or* the bishops were anxious to ensure that as near a 100 per cent performance of catechizing as possible (presumably on a weekly basis) was achieved. It is not inconceivable that clerical catechizing for part of the year allowed churchwardens to report that the minister catechized the young 'duly', or 'on Sundays', or even 'weekly' (for example throughout Lent) without too much evasion; only tougher and more literal enquiries might throw up the fact that in some parishes catechizing was an occasional rather than a regular event. The stand-off between clergy and laity may thus in some cases not have been over whether there should be any catechizing at all, but over how much there should be and whether adolescents and servants (or even adults) had to attend as well as children.[198]

It should be added that where elementary catechizing was practised in church at this stage, not all catechists may have been using the Prayer Book catechism. However, such evidence as there is of the use of alternative forms tends to work in favour of a moderately optimistic view of the scale of catechizing. In 1653 the 'godly' Simeon Ash claimed that Perkins's *Foundation* had been for fifty years 'much approved, and improved in the Church of England and elsewhere, for the instruction of many thousands in matters necessary to salvation'.[199] Writing in the late 1640s Samuel Langley said John Ball's form (first published in the 1610s) had been used in many congregations and families—the implication was for some time—and a few years later Zachary Crofton suggested that the value of Ball's form had been proved by the many editions of it which had been printed; he preferred to carry on using it in his own parish even after the Westminster Shorter Catechism had been approved in 1647.[200] That having been said, in the great majority of cases where official pressure was being applied,[201] it was almost certainly the Prayer Book form which was being used, since this is what was required by the rubric and canons being enforced by the bishops and archdeacons. It was clearly the Prayer Book catechism that was circulated by Thomas Morton, successively bishop of Chester (1616–19), Coventry and Lichfield (1619–32), and Durham (1632–59), of whom his biographer wrote:

for the fuller instructing of children in the grounds of religion, he caused many thousands of catechisms (according to that form which is prescribed in the Book of Common Prayer) to be printed at his own charge, and to be dispersed in the several deaneries and archdeaconries of the dioceses where he had been bishop, which he commanded his (respective) chancellors,

---

[198]   These suggestions are in part based on reading the early eighteenth-century pattern back into the early seventeenth century, which is admittedly a far from satisfactory method.

[199]   R. G. Usher, *The Reconstruction of the English Church* (2 vols.; New York/London, 1910), i. 263; C. Broxolme, *The good old way* (1653), sig. A7ʳ; Davies, *Caroline Captivity*, 145.

[200]   S[amuel] L[angley], *A catechisme shorter than the short catechisme* (1649), sig. A2ᵛ; Crofton, *Catechizing Gods ordinance*, sig. A5ᵛ; it was also said to be fellow-clergy who persuaded Ball to publish his larger catechism with its useful expositions: Mitchell, *Catechisms of the Second Reformation*, p. lxxv.

[201]   For bishops' efforts to find out if other catechisms were being used, see R. C. Richardson, *Puritanism in North-West England* (Manchester, 1972), 38–9; *Second Report on Ritual*, 419, 432, 437, 454, 463, 475, etc.; and Stieg, *Laud's Laboratory*, 208.

registrars, and other ecclesiastical officers, in their places to distribute in every parish; and likewise admonished the several ministers to be diligent and careful in the due catechizing of their youth, according to that form.[202]

Perhaps a reasonable compromise between optimism and pessimism might be to think in terms of moderate success—that the elementary catechizing of children took place for at least part of every year—in those areas where episcopal pressure and/or favourable circumstances prevailed, but only limited success in other areas where neither operated as well as they might. In some dioceses such as some of the Welsh ones, with problems of limited personnel, poor finance, and a language barrier to boot, catechizing was perhaps the exception rather than the rule. But where bishops did choose to be forceful, they could get results in the short term, and the impression given by some of the bishops' replies to Archbishop Laud's queries in the 1630s is often quite positive, for example from Winchester, Gloucester, Norwich, and Peterborough.[203] The level of catechizing in Winchester in particular was reported to be very high, though this was a diocese which had richer livings, better clergy, and probably a more stable population than many other dioceses.[204] Another differential might have been between urban and rural, with clergy in small or moderate-sized towns, backed up by zealous magistrates, parents, and schoolteachers, achieving a higher level of catechizing than their counterparts in the countryside. This was what the 'godly' Robert Cawdrey implies was the case in the latter part of Elizabeth's reign, and we may also note the praise and thanks given to the civic authorities and inhabitants of Barnstaple in 1633 by the more conformable William Crompton in the preface of the catechism he wrote and used there.[205] Commentators looking back from the troubled years of the mid-seventeenth century might well have been thinking of conditions in these better endowed areas or towns when they talked of a rapid decline in catechizing in the 1640s and 1650s. With the rapid growth of separatism, the removal of the old church courts and a reluctance to replace them by alternative methods of discipline, and a severe shortage of clergy in many areas by the 1650s, the prospects of ensuring regular catechizing in church were not good. A recent study of the 'godly' experiment of the 1650s and the publication of a calendar of Richard Baxter's correspondence both show an increased awareness of the need for more catechizing, but, with some exceptions, such as Baxter's success in Kidderminster, only limited success.[206]

---

[202] Baddiley, *Life of Dr Thomas Morton*, 89–90.

[203] Fincham, *Prelate as Pastor*, 182; Davies, *Caroline Captivity*, 144–5; *Works of William Laud*, v. 327, 334, 339, 348, 350, 368 (most of these reports concerned the extent of obedience to the royal instructions about lecturers, but some seem to have been describing catechizing by regular clergy as well).

[204] Ibid. 339, 348.

[205] Cawdrey, *Short and fruitefull treatise* (1604), sig. A1ᵛ; and Crompton, *Explication*, sigs. ¶2ʳ–3ᵛ, and cf. 11ʳ–12ʳ.

[206] Hirst, 'Failure of Godly Rule', *passim*; Keeble and Nuttall, *Baxter Correspondence*, nos. 262, 285, 290, 293, 301, 320, 324, 345, 348, 403, 405, 407, 408, 410, 459, 462; and cf. anon., *The agreement of the …*

In the later Stuart period, catechists again faced an uphill struggle. Not only did they have to re-establish, or even in some cases perhaps establish, catechizing on a regular basis in a period of not inconsiderable religious tension, but after 1689 they had to do so in the context of a measure of religious toleration which not only allowed dissenters to stay away from church but also encouraged the idle and the luke-warm to do the same.[207] However, a lead was given by some bishops, including one who was reported in the 1670s to have been catechizing the young in his own cathedral; and analyses of the records for Nottinghamshire and Warwickshire in the period between Restoration and Revolution have suggested relatively few prosecutions for outright neglect of catechizing.[208] Moreover, when we reach the point in the early eighteenth century where we have the replies to the episcopal questionnaires, the situation looks moderately good. The replies to the enquiry about catechizing can be broken down into three categories: a firm or reasonably convincing 'yes', a rather evasive 'yes', and a flat 'no'. Into the second category I have placed answers that indicated a willingness to catechize rather than the actual performance of that task, or suggested catechizing was not a regular annual event but either erratic (due to inadequate numbers attending in some years), only occasional (for example when warning of a confirmation had been given), had not taken place recently (due to lack of lay co-operation or the temporary indisposition of the minister), or had taken place only a couple of times recently because the incumbent had only just been appointed to the cure.[209] The reasons given for a flat 'no' were varied but often much the same as for those in the second category: complete absence or non-attendance of candidates of suitable age, or the minister's ill-health or recent arrival, but in some cases the absence of catechizing was attributed to the fact that there was no church or that all children of appropriate age were being catechized in the local school.[210]

For Canterbury diocese in 1716, there were 219 replies in all, and the figures are 151 for a positive 'yes', 28 for an ambiguous 'yes', and 40 for a definite 'no', due mainly to lack of catechumens in small parishes. The equivalent breakdown for the 452 replies for the archdeaconry of Lincoln in 1721 was 364 'yes' replies, 40 ambiguous, and 48 'no' (due mainly to derelict churches and lack of catechumens in small parishes). For the 176 replies for the diocese of Oxford in 1738 the breakdown is 130 'yes', 23

---

ministers in ... *Norfolk* (1659), *passim*; and I[ohn] B[atchiler], *A tast of a catechisticall-preaching-exercise* (1668), sig. A2^r.

[207] G. V. Bennett, 'Conflict in the Church', in G. Holmes (ed.), *Britain after the Glorious Revolution, 1689–1714* (1969), 163.

[208] Addison, *Primitive institution*, 219; W. A. Pemberton, 'Studies in the Ecclesiastical Court and Archdeaconry of Nottingham 1660–89', Ph.D. thesis (Nottingham, 1952), 49, but cf. ch. 4, pt. 1, appendix 1; Salter, 'Warwickshire Clergy', 96. For occasional complaints of neglect in the 1670s and 1680s, see Cardwell, *Documentary Annals*, ii. 337–8, and N. Taylor, *A practical and short exposition* (1684), sig. [A3^r].

[209] e.g. Wake MS 284, fos. 28^r, 50^r, 85^r, 97^r, 109^r; Gibson 13, pp. 39, 55, 63, 79, 111; Herring, *York*, i. 23, 94, 190, 192; ii. 38, 94.

[210] e.g. Wake MS 284, fos. 117^v, 282^r, 329^r, 348^r; Gibson 13, pp. 23, 247; Gibson 14, pp. 567, 587, 595; Herring, *York*, i. 39, 69, 101; iii. 198.

ambiguous, and 23 'no'; and for the 644 replies in Yorkshire in 1743, it is 498 'yes', 113 ambiguous, and 33 'no'.[211] Taking the reasonably convincing 'yes' replies we have 69 per cent in east Kent, 81 per cent in Lincolnshire, 74 per cent in Oxfordshire, and 77 per cent in Yorkshire. Taking the first and the second categories together, to find how many livings had had *some* catechizing in recent years, we have 82 per cent in Kent, 89 per cent in Lincolnshire, 87 per cent Oxfordshire, and 95 per cent in Yorkshire. The differences between the four dioceses are not large, and probably reflect a variety of factors: population distribution, prevalence of dissent, alternative sources of catechizing such as schools, and the attitudes of both senior and parish clergy as well as the laity. These totals are not unimpressive, and those scholars who have looked at these early eighteenth-century episcopal questionnaires have commented on the bishops' concern to ensure regular catechizing. Indeed, one historian seems to have been mildly shocked that bishops seem to have put greater priority on catechizing than increasing the frequency of Sunday services or of celebrations of holy communion, though this surprise reflects a later and rather different set of pastoral priorities.[212]

These totals should not be taken too literally. In Canterbury diocese over a dozen clergy, in Lincolnshire nearly a score, and in Yorkshire over three dozen reported both that they had been catechizing (which in this last exercise has been counted as a 'yes' reply) and that attendance was not nearly as good or lasted as long as they would have liked. Such a reply can be counted either as evidence of the difficulties facing catechists, or of the persistence of the practice at a low level in spite of these problems.[213] But there are other indicators of moderately regular and conscientious performance, in biographies and autobiographies, prefaces to catechetical works, the scores of different expositions on the Prayer Book catechism, and the large number of repeat editions of some of these works that we saw in the previous chapter, editions which would have been superfluous if children had not already learnt or were currently learning the church catechism.[214] Together with the evidence of the church's disciplinary procedures, episcopal reports to Laud, and the early eighteenth-century clerical questionnaires, these would seem to suggest that by the 1630s and again by the 1740s the church was ensuring a modicum of catechizing in many, perhaps even most parishes for at least part of the year.

The apparent reduction in the frequency, length of performance, and target audience for elementary catechizing noted above can certainly be made out to be a defeat. But it can equally be presented as a realistic adjustment to changing circumstances. By the early seventeenth century the political as well as the ecclesiastical pressures to

[211] Wake MS 284; Gibson 13–15; Secker, *Oxford*; and Herring, *York*, vols. iii–v, *passim*.
[212] *Speculum Lincolniensis*, p. xx.
[213] Wake MS 284, fos. 6ʳ, 97ʳ, 134ʳ, 164ʳ, 187ʳ, etc.; Gibson 13, pp. 55, 179, 183, 231, 511, 579, etc.; Herring, *York*, i. 5, 10, 36, 206, etc.
[214] See above, n. 24, and previous chapters.

ensure that the next generation were raised as good Protestants were still keen, but arguably not as keen as under Edward and Elizabeth, so that some older children and servants were allowed to get away with not being catechized on Sundays. Once episcopal confirmation ceremonies became more regular features of diocesan life, the case for insisting on youth and servants over the age of about 12 to 14 being catechized was further weakened. The reduction of the number of catechumens from the initial flood of the 1560s to a more consistent and less demanding surge later on, the increase in the number of resident clergy, and the fact that a growing proportion of children were receiving a school education on weekdays which included learning the church catechism—all meant that the time needed to teach the young the basic Prayer Book catechism was less than before, especially in parishes from which many of the younger adults had drifted away, leaving mainly old people behind. By adjusting in this way to changing circumstances and a measure of lay resistance, perhaps strong in many cases, the catechists of the Stuart and early Hanoverian church probably ensured that many of the children who did not attend a school or were not catechized at home were exposed to the church catechism at some stage of their young lives, at least for a few weeks in Lent, often more. Some apparently mastered the catechism fairly well, others may soon have forgotten the little they had learnt. The experience may not have transformed their lives, but it perhaps touched them at a receptive age, as in the case of Wordsworth, and enriched the stock of ideas and words with which, later in life, they could try to come to terms with and explain their situation in the world. The partial shift towards catechizing in service time and towards explaining at the same time as teaching and testing (about which we shall say more shortly) also had the distinct advantage from a wider pastoral perspective that older parishioners were drawn into the act as well as the young.

So far in this chapter we have been trying to isolate the most basic type of catechizing—teaching the young to memorize the set answers to some set questions and testing their knowledge of those answers—as it was practised in church, though at certain points we have shaded into the intermediate level of catechizing which, it was suggested, was targeted not just at children but also at adolescents and adults, and tried to produce a higher level of comprehension and a greater degree of commitment. Before we turn in the next chapter to catechizing in school and the home, we must first look at other types of catechizing in church. Here the opportunities for technical experiments in teaching methods were limited, and so what we are looking at here is essentially the use of rather more advanced catechisms than the Prayer Book form of 1549 or the adoption of more frequent or more sophisticated forms of catechetical exposition of the 1549 form.

As early as 1553, the need for an additional catechism to be learnt after that of 1549 was appreciated, but the ones provided by the authorities were either, like John

Ponet's *Short catechisme*, for schoolboys and not intended for use in church,[215] or, like Nowell's 'larger' and 'middle' catechisms, proved to be unsuitable.[216] In this situation, in the period from the 1570s to the 1630s there were various alternatives open to those catechists who wished to find something more advanced (and until 1604 more comprehensive) than the Prayer Book form, but not as demanding as the Nowell forms, for use in church: compose your own; look outside the officially approved forms to one of the many semi-official alternatives that the authorities had allowed to be published; or make better use of the Prayer Book form by making it the basis for a more advanced exposition of the principles of Christian religion. At the outset the lead in the first and second directions was taken by the 'godly', but increasingly from the reign of James I the third solution was adopted by zealous authors drawn from a variety of backgrounds and opinions, such as William Hill, John Mayer, Richard Bernard, and Edmund Reeve, and it was this solution which came to dominate the landscape of the intermediate catechizing that took place in church in the later Stuart period.

The type of alternative catechism that might have been used in church as a supplement or alternative to the Prayer Book and Nowell forms in the later sixteenth century were described in the previous chapter: works like Perkins's *Foundation of Christian religion*, and the forms by Dering–More, Paget–Openshaw, and John Ball, all of which were fuller than the Prayer Book form but relatively simple in design and content. There is, however, only limited evidence to show that these were used much in church, and given the hardening of official attitudes by the early Stuart period, with even 'godly' bishops like Abbot insisting on the use of the official catechisms, we may perhaps more safely assume that their popularity derived more from their deployment in school and home than church.[217] Another group of alternative forms were clearly designed to help adults and older children prepare for communion—a need which not all copies of the Prayer Book catechism met before 1604.[218] However, it is again hard to know how far such pre-communion forms were used in church as opposed to the home. Occasionally a minister made it clear that his charges had already heard what was in the printed copy that he was giving them as a reinforcement;[219] but where a form

---

[215] See Appendix 1.

[216] Only occasionally did visitation articles ask if Nowell's catechism was used in church, as opposed to school: e.g. *Second Report on Ritual*, 431; see also above, pp. 66, 72, and below, pp. 188–9.

[217] See above, pp. 66–8, and below, pp. 185–6, 210–11; for Abbot, see Fincham, *Visitation Articles*, 214, and cf. 103.

[218] Green, 'Emergence of the English Catechism', 410–12; and the title-pages of anon., *A breefe catechisme so necessarie* (1576); E. Fenton, *So shorte a catechisme* [*c*.1582]; H. Graie, *A short and easie introduction* (1588); [E. Dering and J. More], *A brief and necessarie catechisme* (1590); [J. Dod and R. Cleaver], *A brief dialogue, concerning preparation* (1614); [W. Gouge], *A short catechisme* (1635), sigs. C1ʳ–2ᵛ; anon., *The maine grounds of religion* [1624?]; Joseph Hall, 'A brief summe', in *Works* (1625), 799–800; [J. Geree], *A catechisme in brief questions and answeres* (1629); and T. Sanderson, *A brief summe of Christian religion* (1640). Many other examples could be given from works over thirty pages long or published after 1640.

[219] e.g. R. Jenison, *Directions for the worthy receiving of the Lords Supper* (1624), sigs, A2ᵛ, C8ʳ–D3ᵛ.

was said to have been for parents and masters to use to prepare themselves and their older children and servants for the Lord's Supper, it may well have been meant to have been used primarily within a household.[220] In these and other cases the emphasis was definitely on self-instruction and self-examination, which demanded more of the catechumen in the way of skills than the typical elementary catechism taught orally in church.[221] At this point it may also be pointed out that although there were many occasions in the Elizabethan and early Stuart period when adults were told that they should not be ashamed to be catechized, these comments were on the whole not made in the context of adults being instructed by a minister *in church*, either alone or alongside their children and servants. They were usually made in one or more of the following contexts: allegations by the clergy that the adult laity were ignorant of the essentials of the faith and must cure that ignorance; allegations that adults were unwilling to make a statement of their faith in church; suggestions that if adults would not learn a catechism in church, they might be prepared to learn one at home; and assertions that householders should back up the minister's efforts by catechizing in the home, where no one should be exempt—young or old, male or female.[222]

We do find the occasional reference in the Elizabethan and early Stuart period to a minister announcing his intention of examining his parishioners on the basis of a form that he is circulating, but even then it is often not clear whether this testing was to be in public, or it was stated quite specifically to have taken place in private. Thomas Sparke used one catechetical form in public, but the shorter set of 'questions to be propounded even to the simplest' that he gave to those who wished to take communion in his parish were, he tells us in the preface to the published edition of 1580, to be answered in private.[223] Similarly, when Richard Gawton issued his Hertfordshire parishioners with a revised version of his catechism in 1612, so that 'when I shall examine you before you come to the Lord's Table, I may not find you so ignorant, as formerly I found you, and your families', his reference to families suggests that the examination took place in a household unit rather than the church.[224] William Gouge published his *Short catechisme ... needfull to be knowne of all such as come [to] the Lords Table* in 1615, and we are told by the biographer Samuel Clarke

---

[220]   e.g. B. Andrewes, *A very short and pithie catechisme* (1586), title-page and sigs. A2^r, B1^r; B. Robertson, *The heavenly advocate* (1617), sigs. C2^r–5^r.

[221]   Fenton, *So shorte a catechisme*, sigs. A3^v–4^r; J. Parker, *A true patterne of pietie* (1599), 50–3; R. Hill, 'A communicant prepared' in *Christs prayer expounded* (1606), 3–16; W. Bradshaw, *A briefe form of triall* (1609), title-page; anon., *Motives to godly knowledge* (1613), 10–13; R. Cox, *A short catechisme* (1620), sigs. B5^r–6^r; Gouge, *Short catechisme*, sigs. B8^v–C1^r; J. White, *A plain and familiar exposition* (1632), title-page; and [W. Lyford], *An helpe for young people* (1649), sigs . A3^v–4^v.

[222]   M[ordechai] A[ldem], *A short, plaine, and profitable catechisme* (1592), sigs. A3^v–4^r; Cawdrey, *Short and fruitefull treatise* (1604), sigs. viii^v–Aiv^r; J. Leech, *A plaine and profitable catechisme* (1605), sigs. A3^r–4^r; Bernard, *Two twinnes*, 22–5; C. P., *Two briefe treatises*, 10–11 (though the author clearly had seen older catechumens laughed at: ibid. 16–17); J. Frewen, *Certain choise grounds* (1621), sigs. A4^v–6^v.

[223]   T. Sparke, *A short treatise* (1580), sigs. E2^{r-v}.

[224]   R. Gawton, *A short instruction* (1612), sig. A2^v.

that his practice was to visit the houses of the better sort separately and those of 'sundry small families' together, to test their inhabitants' fitness for the sacrament. By the mid-1630s, Gouge had also prepared 'a brief abstract of the former catechism' to help 'the younger and ignoranter sort'.[225] The most that might be expected of adults in church (and this was probably the exception rather than the rule) was that they would show themselves able to repeat the answers of a catechism which they had once learnt or of which they had just been given a copy by the minister; and even then, if the testing took place in public, the learning part of the process was expected to have taken place at an earlier date, in youth, or recently but privately. In other words, many of these pre-communion forms may have been intended for use as much in the home as in church, if not rather more the former than the latter. However, in a contest of wills between minister and congregation over the testing of adults' knowledge of the faith before communion, it would take a stout-hearted cleric like Baxter to overcome lay resistance, as events in the 1650s made clear.[226]

There is one other vein of material we may look at before returning to the third alternative. In the prefaces to a number of catechetical works published between the 1590s and the 1630s, usually either longer or more specialized works, we can find references to the material in the text having been already deployed in church. Readers were told that the printed work was intended to present to their eye what had already been presented to their ear; it was to act as a reminder of what they had already heard and (it was hoped) learnt.[227] In a number of cases it would appear that the material had been presented originally in the form of a sermon or some other mode of instruction, and that it had been turned into question and answer only at a later stage. The 'plain', 'short' exposition of the Creed 'gathered' by Arthur Dent for the use of 'the simple' in Essex contained material that he said he had taught his flock, but in the printed form Dent turned this teaching into something that contained an element of entertainment as well as edification, like some of his later and better known works.[228] Similarly William Burton's exposition of the Lord's Prayer, published in 1594 'at the request of divers godly and well disposed' persons, consisted of 'divers lectures ... now drawn into questions and answers for the greater benefit of the simpler sort'.[229] At least eight other catechetical works published in the early seventeenth century, mostly before the royal orders of 1622 and 1629, were also based on sermons or expositions that had been given in church.[230] These works give

---

[225] Gouge, *Short catechisme*, and Clarke, *Lives of ten eminent divines*, 107; cf. also W. Gouge, *Briefe answers to the chiefe articles of religion* (1642).

[226] See below, pp. 221–6; and Hirst, 'Failure of Godly Rule', 38–42.

[227] T[homas] W[ilson], *An exposition of the two first verses* (1609), sig. A3ᵛ; Henry Vesey, *The scope of the scriptures* (1633), sig. A3ʳ; W. Jones, *An exposition of the whole catechisme* (1633), 2.

[228] A Dent, *A plain exposition of the articles* (1589), title-page and *passim*.

[229] W. Burton, *Certaine questions and answers* (1591), and id., *An exposition of the Lordes Prayer* (1594), title-pages and prefaces.

[230] R. Allen, *A treasurie of catechisme* (1600), and id., *The doctrine of the gospel* (1606), title-pages and

us both proof of the existence of catechetical sermons in the early Stuart period, and a clear picture of their content if not their original form.

This brings us to the third alternative: making better use of the Prayer Book catechism by building up a catechumen's comprehension of and commitment to their faith on the foundation provided by their knowledge of that form.[231] This could be attempted orally, either by taking time at the teaching or testing stage to explain a word or concept in the question and answer just handled, or by a short sermon or homily delivered separately, usually afterwards, but sometimes (especially later on) beforehand; it could also be attempted by issuing copies of a printed exposition or paraphrase which served much the same purpose; or it could be done by a measure of both oral and written instruction. If we take oral exposition first, we may note that in his visitation articles of 1584 for the diocese of Coventry and Lichfield, William Overton asked whether the clergy 'catechize every Sunday with exposition of the same for the better instruction of the youth of the parish and Christian reformation of other the hearers'; in 1586 Aylmer asked whether the clergy of London diocese taught the church catechism, or Nowell's, 'with the understanding thereof'; and Whitgift's circular letter to bishops on catechizing and confirmation in 1591 urged them to give their clergy a 'strait charge' to 'expound' the Prayer Book catechism to children as well as test their knowledge of it.[232] The diocesan records at Worcester also suggest that in 1585 some clergy were giving a type of instruction which was something in between catechizing and preaching: 'expounding' or 'exhorting' as some called it.[233] This seems to have been seen as an approved alternative to reading out the official homilies, and may not have been done from the pulpit. Whitgift's 'Orders for the better increase of learning in the inferior ministers, and for more diligent preaching and catechising', submitted to Convocation in 1586, envisaged ministers of 'reasonable ability' but limited education being encouraged to expound the Prayer Book catechism 'standing in their stalls' (from where the service was read) rather than the pulpit (the traditional location for the sermon); if they did well in this half-way house, they might then be licensed as preachers.[234] A national list of preachers in 1603 said that in addition to licensed

---

prefaces; S. Crooke, *The guide unto true blessednesse* (1613), and id., *A brief direction to true happinesse* (1613); Clarke, *Lives of ten eminent divines*, 36; Wilson, *Exposition of the two first verses*, sigs. A3^{r-v}, and p. '151' [*recte* 51]; Vesey, *Scope*, sigs. A2^v–3^r; W. Tye, *A matter of moment* (1608), sig. A3^r and passim; G[eorge] W[ebbe], *A briefe exposition of the principles* (1617), sig. A3^r; H[enry] B[urton], *Grounds of Christian religion* (1636), sigs. A2^{r-v}; J. Owen, *The principles of the doctrine of Christ* (1645), sig. A3^r.

[231] For some clergy who said quite explicitly that the Prayer Book catechism was the best basis on which to build, see e.g. W. Hill, *The first principles of a Christian* (1616), sig. A2^r; Mayer, *English catechisme*, sig. A3^r; W. Ward, *Short grounds of catechisme* (Cambridge, 1627), sig. A3^r; R. Alleine, *A brief explanation of the common catechisme* (1631), sig. A2^v.

[232] Kennedy, *Episcopal Administration*, iii. 162; *Second Report on Ritual*, 431.

[233] Barratt, 'Condition of the Parish Clergy', 119–20.

[234] Cardwell, *Synodalia*, ii. 563; and cf. *The Registrum Vagum of Anthony Harison*, ed. T. F. Barton (Norfolk Record Society, 32; 1963), 46.

preachers, there were 'many honest ministers well able to catechize and privately to exhort', but who lacked the gifts or the courage to preach in the pulpit, presumably like the grammar-school educated curate who 'knew better how to read a homily ... than make a sermon', but was able to teach the young Thomas Jackson such good lessons from the church catechism in the 1580s.[235]

From the late 1570s, those clergy who had attended one of the best schools of the day, such as Winchester or Harrow, or been to a university were increasingly likely to have come into contact with catechetical lectures such as the famous ones given by Lancelot Andrewes at Pembroke College, Cambridge,[236] so that the idea of expounding not a specially selected text of scripture as in the typical sermon of the day, but the meaning of a particular article of the Apostles' Creed, or a particular Commandment or petition of the Lord's Prayer, was probably becoming fairly widespread among the better educated clergy who became licensed preachers in the late Elizabethan and early Stuart periods. The publication of English translations of works like Osiander's catechetical homilies on Luther's shorter catechism (the *Catechismus* of 1548) and Olevian's *Exposition of the symbole of the Apostles* (a set of catechetical lectures translated from Latin to English by John Field and printed twice in the early 1580s) and of sets of catechetical lectures or sermons given by English clergy probably helped the dissemination of the idea too, as perhaps did the fact that in the Netherlands from an early date catechetical sermons or exhortations based on a phrase of an officially approved catechism became the norm for the parish clergy.[237]

At this point, we may also note that in the early seventeenth century visitation articles often reflected the wording of the 59th canon of 1604 which had ordered the clergy to 'examine and instruct the young and ignorant persons' in the Decalogue, Creed, and Lord's Prayer and 'diligently hear, instruct, and teach them the catechism set forth in the Book of Common Prayer': both these clauses suggest that more than mere drilling and testing was expected.[238] We may also recall Archbishop Abbot's gloss on James's 'directions on preaching' of 1622: what James wanted was not a reduction in preaching but rather the primitive and profitable exposition of the official catechisms, so that young and old alike might be instructed in the heads of the Christian faith, which had been performed less diligently in England than in all the reformed churches abroad, he added.[239] Then in the 1630s, Charles and Laud

---

[235] Cited Barratt, 'Condition of the Parish Clergy', 121; and see above, p. 130.

[236] See below, pp. 202–3.

[237] See Appendix 1 below, s.v. T. Cranmer and C. Olevian; Elton, Randall, and Broxolme (I intend to return to the theme of catechetical sermons in my forthcoming survey of *Religious Instruction in Early Modern England*). For the Netherlands, see Duke, Lewis, and Pettegree, *Calvinism in Europe*, 170–1, 192, 196, and 198–9; and J. Hales, *Golden remains* (1688), 386–7; and for a curate in Ipswich in 1598 who claimed he did not catechize because in his sermons he 'delivereth exhortations in principal parts of religion', see *Bishop Redman's Visitation*, 18.

[238] Cardwell, *Synodalia*, 280; *Second Report on Ritual*, 451, 454, 460, 463, 472, etc. (for Patrick's gloss on 'examine and instruct', see below).

[239] See above, p. 107 n. 49; Abbot slipped in a reference to the 'greater catechism', that is Nowell's,

allowed preaching on Sunday afternoons if it was on the same heads of the catechism that the clergy had just been teaching the children, and in 1662 Charles II issued further 'directions concerning preachers', modelled on those of James I but with some variations which again worked to the benefit of those who put a high premium on catechizing. The fourth clause of the 1662 directions exhorted all preachers to catechize the younger sort diligently, and in their ordinary sermons—presumably on Sunday mornings as well as afternoons—to 'insist chiefly upon catechetical doctrines' rather than handle controversial matters. Also if there was an 'afternoon exercise', it should 'be especially spent either in explaining some part of the church catechism' (in the later Stuart period the Prayer Book catechism of 1549 was regularly referred to as 'the church catechism'), or in preaching on a text designed to explain some aspect of the catechism or the official liturgy.[240] These orders were picked up a few years later in a pastoral letter sent by Thomas Lamplugh to his clergy in the diocese of Exeter. It was important to give 'catechistical instructions' to children in years as well as understanding; this should be done not through controversial discourses which were welcome only to 'itching ears', but in simple grounding in the basics on a Sunday afternoon. 'Think not therefore that your preaching is restrained, or abridged', he added, echoing Abbot's gloss of 1622; 'The manner of your preaching is only altered, and that for the better' in that people would understand the church catechism and thus the basics of the faith better.[241] In 1695 a Yorkshire vicar, Joseph Briggs, published a set of 'catechetical exercises' in the preface of which he recalled the 'excellent advice' he had been given many years before by an aged divine, to concentrate his first sermon-writing on the Creed, Lord's Prayer, and Decalogue, since these would furnish useful discourses for Sunday afternoon catechizing.[242]

These oral explanations of the church catechism did not have to be very long, as we can see from the advice offered by two senior clergymen on oral exposition of the church catechism. In a pastoral letter to the clergy of Ely diocese in 1692, Simon Patrick reminded them of the duty laid down in the 59th canon of 1604:

not only to examine the children in the catechism (that is, to ask them the questions, and receive their answers) but 'to instruct them therein', that is, teach them the meaning, and make them understand the weight of every word. If you would spend a quarter of an hour in this exercise all the summer long ... it would be of wonderful use both to yourselves and to your people ... because it would put you upon considering, collating, and digesting such proper places of scripture as relate to every article of the Creed ... the Commandments and ... all

which had not been there in James's original directions. Also cf. Ussher's instructions to his assistant in Ireland: Clarke, *Lives of ten eminent divines*, 223–4.

[240]   See above, pp. 110–11; Wilkins, *Concilia*, iv. 577.

[241]   T. Lamplugh, *[A pastoral letter to the clergy of the diocese of Exeter]* [167?], 2–4; cf. Addison, *Primitive institution*, 74–5, 136–8, 142–5.

[242]   Briggs, *Catechetical exercises*, sigs. A3ʳ⁻ᵛ; also cf. the advice of Archbishop Tenison to preach in the afternoon on catechetical heads: Morrice, *Defence of lecturers*, 6; and the practice of William Whiston after moving from a Cambridge fellowship to a living in Suffolk: *DNB*.

other parts of the catechism; and upon studying also and framing the plainest and clearest explications and illustrations of every point, couched in so few words that they might easily be carried away and remembered.[243]

In the same year, in his *Discourse of the pastoral care*, Gilbert Burnet wrote in a very similar vein (indeed, he may simply have been elaborating on Patrick), and urged the conscientious minister 'once every year to go through the whole church catechism, word by word, and make his people understand the importance of every tittle in it'. Burnet argued that such 'catechetical discourses' would be 'generally of much greater edification than an afternoon sermon', though he warned that if the catechist handled more than one point or went on for more than fifteen minutes 'it will grow tedious and be too little remembered'. Burnet also believed such discourses would 'draw an assembly to evening prayers', which he thought were much neglected if there was no accompanying sermon or discourse.[244]

So much for the theory: the clergy must not just teach the catechism; they must explain it as well. What about the practice? While clues may be gained from other quarters on a circumstantial basis, there are two sources from which it is possible to construct a more systematic answer: over a hundred different expositions of the Prayer Book catechism published between the 1610s and the 1730s, and the many repeat editions through which a number of these expositions passed; and the replies to the episcopal questionnaires of 1716–43. Together these present a moderately convincing picture of catechizing at the secondary level having taken place in many parish churches by the later Stuart and early Hanoverian periods (and also in many schools and some homes as we shall see in Chapter 4).[245] Let us take the printed expositions first. These may in turn be divided three ways: into a dozen which in their published form consisted of sermons, lectures, or discourses in connected prose on the Prayer Book catechism; just under thirty which used one or more of a variety of techniques—including marginal notes, definitions, explanations, paraphrases, extra questions and answers, scripture proofs, prayers, and exhortations—to try to render the church catechism more comprehensible and applicable to catechumens; and about sixty-five which relied primarily on extra questions and (usually but not always) extra answers to throw light on the content of that catechism. (As always, these categories are not water-tight: some forms began life in one category, but had been transferred into another by the time they were published.) Not all of these printed expositions were designed for use in church or in church alone; some were meant to be used in school or home as well. Nor is it being suggested here that all of these forms were necessarily *used* in church, though a great many were as will appear. What is pertinent and valuable about these expositions is that they reveal what many conformist ministers claimed to have said in church, or what they hoped

---

[243] Moorman, *Curate of Souls*, 72.   [244] Ibid. 88–9.

[245] For some comments on the situation in presbyterian churches and separatist chapels from the 1650s, see below, pp. 166–9.

their congregations would come to understand, about the meaning of the Prayer Book form.

Of the dozen expositions of the Prayer Book catechism which are in continuous prose, some are reported to have been delivered in church prior to publication, while others clearly reflect the kind of preparatory collections of material which Patrick and Burnet advised, or were designed to act as a quarry from which other instructors could—and evidently did—extract material for their own 'catechetical discourses'. An early example of this genre was the product of special circumstances. The *Plain, but full exposition of the catechisme of the Church of England* was published in 1655 by William Nicholson after he had been sequestered from his Welsh living for his support for the old church. 'For those many years I was permitted to be your pastor', he then wrote to his former parishioners, '[I was] all that time your catechist', and what he had then opened at large to them, he was now here putting into their hands in a short summary, 'to inform your understanding and rectify your will'. His exposition of the banned church catechism struck a sufficient chord to require eight reprintings after the Restoration.[246] Gabriel Towerson's monumental *Explication of the catechism of the Church of England*, which was published in four parts and six instalments between 1676 and 1688 and eventually covered nearly fifteen hundred folio pages, was, he said, the result of having to supply his own charges (in Welwyn, Hertfordshire) with the knowledge of the principles of Christianity, and we may guess at his own practice from the stress he put on the profitability of preaching from the desk as much as from the pulpit. Repeat editions of the different instalments, in later cases in both folio and octavo sizes, suggest his efforts were appreciated by other catechists seeking for ready comments on different parts of the church catechism.[247]

In the 1690s Thomas Bray's 'course of lectures upon the church catechism' did not get past the first of a projected four-volume series. This first volume, consisting of thirty lectures on the opening questions and answers alone, covered over three hundred and forty folio pages, though it sold moderately well after its first appearance in 1696, again presumably among catechists. However, it sold much faster when a year later he decided to condense it down to a 'short discourse upon the doctrine of our baptismal covenant', covering a mere hundred and seventy octavo pages, and designed to be read by 'youth[s]' aged 12 to 15 who had got past the elementary level of memorizing the Prayer Book form and were preparing for confirmation. This work was apparently intended to be studied in private, since he urged these using it to see the minister after the service on Sunday to go over what they had read the

---

[246] Nicholson, *Plain exposition*, pp. xiii–xv, and below, Appendix 1; for praise or use of this form by other authors, see S. Ford, *A plain and profitable exposition* (1684), sig. A5ʳ; anon., *Eniautos: or a course of catechizing*, sig. B10ʳ; N. Taylor, *A practical and short exposition* (1684), 16, 187.

[247] G. Towerson, *An explication of the catechism of the Church of England Part I* (1685), sig. A2ʳ and p. xv; id., *Of the sacrament of baptism* (1687) sig. A3ʳ, and Appendix 1.

previous week, though one can imagine it being used by catechists as well.[248] Another large work was the 'catechetical course of sermons' on the church catechism published in two volumes in 1700: the fifty-two discourses ran to nearly twelve hundred pages. Its author, Peter Newcome, a Hertfordshire vicar, cited the moderate episcopalian Robert Sanderson's opinion that the way to restore the nation to meek and Christian temper was to have a body of common divinity, or as much as was needful to be known by the common people, in fifty-two homilies or sermons to be read, one each Sunday, every year, like the circulation of the blood. But Newcome seems to have realized that the work was too long for some needs, since he indicated that he was designing an abridgement for the young and the most ignorant. Nevertheless, the fact that he was able to publish the volumes by subscription at 12s. unbound, and that there were three editions in twelve years, again suggests there was a sizeable demand for catechetical sermons at the time.[249] The twenty-four lectures on the church catechism 'read in the parish church of St. Augustine' (in London) and published in 1727 were on average twenty-six octavo pages long, and the 'course of [seven] catechetical lectures' given by another minister a few years later were on average twenty-two quarto pages—a length not far short of the topical sermons of the day.[250] One might also mention here that John Morrice, the London lecturer who took exception to some remarks by William Wake about lectureships being a new-fangled institution which got in the way of catechizing on a Sunday afternoon, pointed out that for the last seven years his discourses had 'chiefly turned upon the Creed, the Lord's Prayer, the commandments, the sacraments, and the other fundamental points laid down in the church-catechism', adding for good measure, 'and sure I am, that many other gentlemen in my station pursue the same course'.[251]

While many full-length sermons or lectures given in church by men like Morrice were therefore catechetical (in the sense of enlarging on and applying the standard catechetical formulae) and catechizing in church by men like Bray and Newcome might often take the form of a full-length sermon, the catechetical sermons that survive in print were on the whole rather shorter than this, or consisted of a mixture of exegesis and interrogation. The hundred separate 'catechetical exercises' delivered in a rural parish in Somerset by Matthew Hole and described when published in 1707–8 as 'useful for all families' were on average only six or seven quarto pages long; the thirty lectures published by Benjamin Farrow in 1708 as a practical exposition of the church catechism were on average only eight octavo-sized pages (and from his

---

[248] Bray, *Course of lectures*, title-page, sigs. cl^{r-v} and *passim*; id., *A short discourse upon the baptismal covenant* (1697), sigs. al^v–2^r and *passim*.

[249] P. Newcome, *A catechetical course of sermons* (2 vols.; 1700), i. sig. A4^r; *TC* iii. 148, 180, 192, 224, 314; and Appendix 1.

[250] R. Newton, *A practical exposition of the church catechism* (1727), 1–392; R. Bundy, *Sermons on several occasions* (1740), ii. 307–461.

[251] Morrice, *Defence of lecturers*, 27, and cf. 42.

reply to Gibson's questionnaire we know that he was still reading them to his Lincolnshire parishioners in 1721); and the twenty-six short discourses on the same catechism published by Roger Davies in 1726 varied between two to three and seven to eight duodecimo pages.[252]

In other cases authors indicated that their publications had started life as sermons or lectures but been changed into something more like an ordinary catechism either before or at publication. Joseph Briggs, who had followed the aged divine's advice about writing his first sermons on the catechetical staples, devised a series of catechetical exercises which he tells us he used wherever he taught. These consisted of a mixture of introductory comments to each section of the church catechism, supplementary questions and answers, some enlargement on these extra questions and answers, and the occasional piece of information, lamentation, or exhortation.[253] The 'several lectures' on the church catechism given by Edward Wells in his Leicestershire parish were turned into supplementary questions and answers when they were published in 1707; the parishioners to whom the *Short and plain exposition of the church catechism. By way of question and answer* published by an anonymous country parson in 1715 was dedicated were told that they should recognize its content, since they had already heard it expounded at much greater length from the desk, and preached to them in better words from the pulpit, to the extent of a whole year's preaching; the course of lectures on the same subject given in an Oxfordshire parish by Samuel Adams were condensed and likewise turned into question and answer for publication in 1718, as were some of the catechetical lectures given by John Shaw in East Knoyle in Wiltshire about 1715, published in three volumes in 1720–2; and the anonymous *Christian knowledge and practice* (1737) apparently began life as six catechetical lectures before being turned into questions and answers, meditations, and thanksgivings.[254]

We have already moved into our second category of printed expositions: the works of authors who combined a variety of techniques to get their point across. Again there is evidence that some of these works had been used in church prior to publication, while in other cases they were certainly intended for use in the author's parish or to help reinforce what was being done there. Moreover, a number of the works in this category passed through many more repeat editions than the larger expositions or

---

[252] Hole, *Practical exposition*; B. Farrow, *A practical exposition of the catechism* (1708) (and Gibson 14, p. 249); R. Davies, *An explanation of the principles* (1726), *passim*.

[253] Briggs, *Catechetical exercises*, *passim*; for a revised version, see id., *The church-catechism explain'd* (1722).

[254] E. Wells, *The common Christian rightly and plainly instructed* (1707), preface (not paginated); ['A country parson'], *A short and plain exposition of the church catechism* (1715), p. iii; S. Adams, *A plain and full instruction* (Oxford, 1718), title-page; J. Shaw, *The fundamental doctrines of the Church of England* (3 vols.; 1720–2), vol. i, p. iii; anon., *Christian knowledge and practice* (Hamburg, 1737), title-page and text. Note also that the 'General view' of Lawrence Fogg (*Two treatises*, 1712) was said to be an abbreviation of material in which his parishioners had been 'frequently and copiously instructed' already (sig. A2ᵛ).

lectures in continuous prose described in previous paragraphs. Noting the absence of a printed exposition of the Prayer Book catechism in the late 1610s, John Mayer made two attempts to provide one in the early 1620s. The first he described as both a catechism and a commentary: the catechism was the Prayer Book form with some extra questions and answers of his own inserted, and the commentary was a series of long and detailed discourses on each of the answers thus provided. The result was a fat quarto volume of five hundred and sixty pages which sold moderately well, presumably among catechists wanting a ready exposition. But Mayer also saw the need for a shortened form, and *Mayers catechisme abridged* passed through seven editions between 1623 and 1639. The latter was said to have been published 'at the request of … many', and while providing the substance of the larger commentary was cleverly constructed in two interwoven sets of questions and answers, the one in black letter providing milk for babes which was to be learnt first, and the other in roman type providing meat to be learnt later by those who had 'attained more growth in knowledge'.[255] An even more popular work was Richard Sherlock's *Principles of holy Christian religion*, first published in 1656 but into its eighteenth edition by the end of the century. This was described as a paraphrase, to assist the understanding of the church catechism by spelling out its meaning more clearly, but it also used extra questions and answers and marginal notes, some quite long, to get the message across. It was intended to lay a sound foundation in the young, but the prayers printed at the end included prayers to be said by wives and husbands as well as by children, scholars, and servants. We must therefore conclude that it was intended, at least in part and especially in the late 1650s, for use in the home as well as the church, though we will find parish clergy referring to their use of it in church in later decades.[256]

Eniautos: or a course of catechizing, first published in 1664, was, according to the title-page, 'useful for ministers and their people, schoolmasters and scholars, parents and children, masters and servants', but the fact that it was divided into fifty-two parts labelled 'Sunday 1', 'Sunday 2', etc., suggests that the minister was thought to be likely to come into play either at the teaching or the testing stage. The anonymous author claimed to have produced 'the marrow of all orthodox and practical expositions upon the church-catechism', though the authors he cited and recommended included 'godly' authors like Perkins, Dod, Ball, and Gouge as well as more predictable figures such as Andrewes, Hammond, and Nicholson. His technique was to mix into the original Prayer Book form extra questions and answers, scripture references, occasional interjections by the catechist to explain a particular point further, exhortations, and prayers; the second edition was also (most unusually) illustrated with eighty-four engravings 'fitted to the several occasions'.[257] But perhaps the most

---

[255] Mayer, *English catechisme*, sigs. A3^{r-v} and *passim*, id., *Mayers catechisme abridged* (1632), sig. A2^r and *passim*, and Appendix 1.

[256] R. Sherlock, *The principles of holy Christian religion* (1656), title-page and *passim*, and Appendix 1.

[257] Anon., *Eniautos: or a course of catechizing*, sigs. B10^r–12^v and *passim*.

popular of the works in what might be called the mixed media category of expositions was Thomas Marshall's *The catechism set forth in the Book of Common Prayer briefly explained by short notes*. In the first instance this consisted simply of notes, but by the fifth edition in 1683 it was supplemented by 'an essay of questions and answers' in which the material in the notes became the basis of supplementary questions and answers to those in the church catechism. The preface to the original work indicated that Marshall was aiming at brevity and plainness, and hoped that through the care of instructors, parents, or governors it would gradually be learnt by young Christians who could then return more understanding answers to any questions on the church catechism put to them by their regular catechist. He stressed that his 'short expository notes' were not intended to forestall the use of larger or more learned expositions of that catechism, or the 'seasonable enlargements' of the industrious catechist, but rather as a preparative to both. The ready sales of the work (especially with its extra 'essay') and the regular references to its use by parish clergy suggest that he had got it about right.[258] Lack of space prevents detailed discussion of all the other forms in this mixed media category, but perhaps space can be found for mention of William Beveridge's *The church-catechism explained: for the use of the diocese of St. Asaph* (1704), in which a series of brief expositions of part of the catechism were followed by questions and answers designed to test the level of understanding achieved. If a catechumen failed to understand the exposition by this means, said Beveridge, the catechist should explain all over again in new words. Again the regular repeat editions and reports of the use of his work by parish clergy suggests that his technique rang a chord with other catechists.[259]

Of the different types of exposition of the church catechism, however, much the most numerous was the type which relied solely on adding extra questions and answers to those in the Prayer Book form in order to aid comprehension. Rather than provide definitions, explanations, new material, and exhortations in prose, the authors of these works did so by slipping in extra questions and answers between the two dozen in the church catechism (as modified in 1604). This group of over sixty different forms was quite varied in difficulty and length. At one end were a few simple forms which were designed to make it easier to learn the longer answers in the church catechism by breaking them up into shorter questions and answers,[260] while at the other were quite long and complex forms designed to enhance both under-

---

[258] [Marshall], *Catechism set forth* sigs. A2r–v, and Appendix 1. See also Ford, *Plain and profitable exposition*, sig. A5r.

[259] [Beveridge], *Church-catechism explained*, pp xii–xiii, and see below, Appendix 1; for other works in this group, see anon., *The art of catechizing* (5 editions, 1691–1718); J. Fowler, *The catechism of the Church of England, poetically paraphrased* (1678), preface and *passim*; [Ken], *Exposition on the church catechism*, 14, 35, and *passim*; id., *The church-catechism, with directions for prayer* (1685); Burnet, *Exposition of the church catechism, passim*; anon., *First principles of the oracles of God* (Norwich, 1712), sigs. A2r–v and *passim*; anon., *An easy method of instructing youth* (1728), sigs. A2r–v and *passim*.

[260] e.g. [Simon Ford], *The catechism of the Church of England* (1694); anon., *The church catechism,*

standing and knowledge.[261] But most of the group were between thirty and ninety pages long in the printed version, and as we shall see many of the shorter and middling ones were apparently considered to be capable of being remembered in their entirety. Again it is not being suggested that all were used in church, but in many cases there is either a specific reference to the form having already been used in church or there is an implication that a catechumen's memory or understanding of the answers would be tested by the minister in church or in some other forum. A few of the landmarks and more frequently used examples from the early and later Stuart periods may be cited here as demonstration of this.

William Hill justified the publication of his *First principles of a Christian: or, questions and answers ... for the further opening of the ordinarie catechisme* in 1616 on the grounds, first, that although there were 'so many and so excellent catechisms' already put forth and being used profitably 'none as yet have expounded the ordinary catechism that ever I did see', and, secondly, that he had found the following work most profitable for 'the people of mine own charge'. Parents were expected to help teach their children his form, as well as making sure they attended church for further instruction in it by the minister; in another preface children were urged to learn the 'principles', and so grow daily in grace. His form was less than forty octavo pages long, and by the late 1630s had reached its fourteenth edition.[262] William Jones did not publish his *Exposition of the whole catechisme of the Church of England* until 1633, but wrote in the preface that he had laboured for seventeen years to imprint the contents of the form in the hearts of his parishioners on the Isle of Wight. But having found that children and servants had forgotten so much, he was now having his words printed and offering it to the eyes as well as the hearts of his parishioners, in the hope that children would be taught first by parents and masters, and then by ministers. Its limited sales compared to Hill's form may be explained by its much greater length or the availability of several other question-and-answer expositions by 1633. The same may be true of another work published in that year: William Crompton's *Explication of those principles ... in the catechisme of our church*, which was based on his notes—the sum of all he had delivered to his parishioners in Barnstaple, he told them.[263]

In the 1630s and 1640s the Prayer Book catechism was used as a basis for enlarged

analysed, explained, and improved ... For beginners (1683, and Norwich, 1703); R. Kidder, *An help to the smallest children's more easie understanding of the church-catechism* (1709); see also R. Bernard, *The common catechisme expressed* (1630); I.B., *The catechism of the Church of England* (1669); anon., *The church catechism resolved into short questions and answers* (1681) (not traced and possibly the same as the 1683 work cited above); and anon., *A plain and profitable scheme of the catechism* (1711).

[261] e.g. S. Ford, *A plain and profitable exposition* (1684); and W. Wake, *The principles of the Christian religion* (1699).

[262] Hill, *Principles*, sigs. A2^r, A3^r, A4^r and *passim*, and Appendix 1.

[263] Jones, *Exposition*, 2–4, sig. A2^r; Crompton, *Explication*, title-page and sigs. ¶8^r–10^v; and cf. Ward, *Short grounds of catechisme*, sigs. A3^{r-v}, and *passim*; W[illiam] D[ickenson], *Milke for babes* (1628), title-page and sigs. ¶2^r–3^r; and R. Alleine, *A briefe explantion of the common catechisme* (1631), sigs. A2^r–3^v, and Appendix 1.

question-and-answer forms by clergy of quite differing views, such as, on the one hand, Richard Bernard, Martin Nicholes, and John Ball, and, on the other, Edmund Reeve and Edward Boughen who were anti-Calvinist and strong supporters of the policies of Charles I and Laud. Bernard's *The common catechisme ... with a commentary thereupon by questions and answers* was reprinted ten times in as many years after its first publication in 1630. The author had a background of trouble with the authorities, but in the 1630s he argued for the use of the official catechism alone on the ground that the children and servants of parents who moved from one parish to another would then be able to understand the catechist in the new parish.[264] Nicholes leant towards double predestinarianism, and Ball in his non-catechetical writings was clearly Calvinist, but Nicholes's medium-length work sold better than Reeve's long-winded and often tendentious work, as also, after 1639, did Ball's studiedly neutral and practical form, which was divided into fifty-two sections of between three and six questions to be learnt each Sunday.[265] After the Restoration, however, it was Boughen's question-and-answer form which, together with Nicholson's and Sherlock's prose expositions from the 1650s, became the most frequently reprinted of Prayer Book expositions.[266] Dozens of new question-and-answer expositions continued to appear, some quite long, but others only thirty pages or so, such as Thomas Comber's *Church catechism with an easie explanation* (1681), the anonymous *The catechism of the Church of England briefly paraphrased and explained by way of question and answer* (1688) (for children and servants who 'have not the capacity or leisure to learn the larger expositions'), and *An exposition on the church-catechism by way of question and answer* (1689) (to help 'young persons ... retain and recollect the substance ... of those larger expositions on the church-catechism which have been delivered in this method'). Comber's form is of special interest in that he borrowed ideas and material from the presbyterians. He had the Prayer Book questions and answers printed on the left-hand page, and on the right (imitating Palmer and Wallis) put matching, open-ended questions which catechumens had to answer 'Yes' or 'No'. The purpose of this, he said, was to make catechumens exercise their judgement rather than be a fresh burden to their memories; and he claimed to have had great success when using it with children and country people in Yorkshire, and recommended its use in families and rural congregations elsewhere. The form proved popular in the 1680s, passing through half a dozen editions in the 1680s and 1690s.[267]

---

[264] Bernard, *Common catechisme* (1640), sigs. A2ʳ–4ʳ, B4ʳ; the 1630 edition of this work was cited above (n. 260) as a work which for its technique could be classed as elementary, but there is perhaps just enough additional material, especially in the 1640 edition with the scripture proofs added, to tilt the balance towards regarding this work as intermediate.

[265] M. Nicholes, *A catechisme* (1631); J[ohn] B[all], *Short questions and answers explaining the catechisme* (1639); Reeve, *Communion booke catechisme* (1635); E. Boughen, *Principles of religion or a short exposition of the catechism* (1646); for the views of the first two and last, see below, Ch. 8.

[266] See Appendix 1.

[267] T. Comber, *The church-catechism with a brief and easie explanation* (1686), sigs. A2ʳ⁻ᵛ, and Appendix

But the question-and-answer category was transformed in the reign of William III by the first appearance of three forms which between them would dominate the next fifty years and more: John Williams's *Brief exposition of the church-catechism*; Zacheus Isham's *Catechism of the church*; and John Lewis's *The church catechism explain'd by way of question and answer*. All were medium-sized, between forty and ninety pages according to the format used by the printer; Williams's was sold at 6*d.* in 1690, Isham's at 4*d.* or 4*s.* a dozen in 1703, and Lewis's 4*d.* or 25*s.* a hundred in 1705. Williams's had sold 23 editions by 1731 and 28 by 1804, and Isham's over a dozen by 1735, while Lewis's had passed through 15 editions by 1732 and 58 by 1820. It was perhaps their use in Charity Schools that led to the extra sales of Williams's and Lewis's forms, but there is plenty of evidence for their being used in church as well.[268]

Williams made adept use of typefaces: the 'young reader' was told to note that the original Prayer Book catechism was published in 'the old English or black letter', Williams's additional questions and answers were interspersed in 'Roman letter, the largest white letter', while the supporting scripture quotations were printed in italic. But the form was sufficiently manageable to be taught orally in church as well.[269] Isham's form we have already encountered as an example of a minister trying to squeeze as much catechizing into the middle of a service as possible. As he wrote in his preface, the other enlargements of the church catechism that he had seen were too copious or elaborate, or did not fit his needs. He designed instead a three-month cycle of twelve parts, and each time the cycle was repeated the catechist was to teach an extra one of the four scripture proofs which Isham had provided under each heading for that purpose. In a year therefore catechumens would not only master Isham's exposition , but also learn all four proofs, and both they 'and the whole congregation' (who would witness all this) 'may be thus edified'. The same method, he added, could be used in private families as he was using in public, but we have clear evidence of its being taught by the clergy in church.[270] Lewis drew up his form in response to a request from the Society for Promoting Christian Knowledge, though it is clear from his manuscript autobiography that he had already read a large number of other catechetical works and had a draft for use in his own living. The final product was almost entirely derivative, but was carefully divided into relatively short questions and answers collected together into twelve sections which could be tackled realistically and methodically either in church or school.[271]

1; anon., *The catechism of the Church of England briefly paraphrased* (1688), title-page; anon., *An exposition on the church-catechism* (1689), sig. A3ʳ.

[268] See following pages and Appendix 1 under the relevant authors.

[269] J. Williams, *A brief exposition of the church-catechism* (1707), sigs. E8ʳ⁻ᵛ, and see next section of this chapter.

[270] Ibid., and Isham, *Catechism of the church* (1695), sigs. A2ʳ–4ʳ.

[271] 'Some account of the life of the Reverend Mr. John Lewis', BL Addit. MS 28,651, pp. 30–4, and the preface to Lewis's *The church catechism explain'd*.

The popularity of a number of the different expositions of the church catechism examined in the last few pages tells us something about the probable scale of intermediate catechizing. Many of their authors clearly hoped that parents, masters, and schoolteachers would co-operate in moving beyond mere rote repetition on to a further level of achievement—a point to which we shall return in the next chapter. But we can gain some further insight into how far these works were used in church and what other efforts were made to advance the cause of catechizing there if we return again to the episcopal questionnaires of the reigns of George I and II.

In the questionnaire Wake circulated among his clergy were the following two queries about catechumens: 'Do they learn any other catechism, for the better understanding of that of the church? What catechism do they learn for that purpose?' Gibson made the same enquiries, though in 1721, probably finding the adjective 'other' causing some confusion, substituted 'larger' for it. Secker modified the last two sentences to ask 'And do you either expound it to them yourself, or make use of some printed exposition, and what is it?', while Herring omitted these sentences altogether from his query about catechizing, though some evidence of efforts to ensure better understanding of the church catechism can be found in the replies sent to him as well.[272] As with the opening sentences of Wake's question (on elementary catechizing), some clergy were prepared to be forthcoming while others were terse or evasive. But what the fuller replies indicate, especially in Kent, Lincolnshire, and Oxfordshire where there was episcopal pressure to be specific, is the moderately widespread practice of offering some kind of exposition or explanation, either by catechetical sermons or some other kind of oral explanation, or by the deployment of printed expositions in some way or other, or by a combination of these methods.

In Kent over thirty respondents—about one in seven of those who replied to Wake's questionnaire in 1716—indicated that they offered some type of oral exposition of the Prayer Book catechism that was more or less of their own devising. At the top end, this might take the form of a full catechetical sermon or lecture, usually as a supplement to elementary instruction, though sometimes as a substitute. Thus one incumbent reported that he taught the catechism in Lent and before a confirmation, but at other times of the year 'I preach upon some part of our catechism'; and another wrote that (two years before) he had catechized in Lent, including weekdays, and had a catechism lecture in the church 'at the time of prayers'.[273] A Canterbury minister tried to excuse his failure to catechize the young by saying that 'I preach often in a catechetical way on Sundays', while another said that in the absence of a suitably

---

[272] Wake MS 284, 1; Gibson 13, p. 1; Secker, *Oxford*, 5; Herring, *York*, i. 3.
[273] Wake MS 284, fos. 56ʳ, 350ʳ.

prepared group of catechumens he made good the defect by dwelling on the catechism during his sermons in Lent; a third reported that though parents were remiss in sending children and servants, 'I constantly explain the church-catechism to the congregation'.[274] At a less exalted level, exposition might take the form of a short, informal explanation: 'I constantly expound it to them in the most familiar manner I can', said one; 'after examination' (of the catechumens' knowledge of the church catechism answers), wrote others, 'I expound some part of it', or 'I explain at large every question and answer'.[275] The verb 'to catechize' was often used here in the sense of imparting and testing knowledge of the church catechism as distinct from explaining the meaning of that form, as in 'we not only catechize, but expound upon the same'.[276] Occasionally this exposition might take the form of asking extra questions of the minister's own devising: one said he endeavoured to fix the sense of the catechism in the minds of children and servants 'by as easy questions and as familiar way of expounding it, as I can possibly use'; another said he explained the church catechism by asking them questions 'and so inform myself how much they understand of it'.[277] In many cases the clergy admitted that in offering an exposition they relied on one or more of the printed forms we have examined in the previous section, such as those of Mayer, Sherlock, Williams, Beveridge, and Hole.[278]

In all, four dozen Kentish incumbents, or nearly a quarter of those who replied to Wake, reported the deployment of a printed exposition in one way or another in their parishes (there is some overlap between this four dozen and the thirty mentioned in the previous paragraph). Much the most frequently mentioned exposition was Isham's form (19 references), followed by those of Williams (12), Beveridge (7), Lewis and Wake (6 each), and Marshall (3); over a dozen other works were mentioned.[279] In some cases, as just seen, the deployment of these works took the form of a minister periodically reading out or perhaps paraphrasing a section of a published exposition.[280] In several other cases, ministers tried to get their catechumens to memorize a complete printed exposition, usually of moderate size. Those who can repeat the church catechism perfectly (reported one minister) learn Isham's exposition, and 'repeat one of the twelve sections of it every Sunday'; since 'the young persons generally say their catechism well' (wrote another), they were being instructed by the curate from Bishop Williams's exposition, while the incumbent himself had got as far as the Lord's Prayer in his own exposition of the catechism, 'and intend to proceed

---

[274] Ibid., fos. 60ʳ, 298ʳ, 321ʳ. [275] Ibid., fos. 2ʳ, 6ʳ, 62ʳ, etc.
[276] Ibid., fo. 114ʳ, and cf. fos. 213ʳ, 356ʳ, 382ʳ, 388ʳ, and 398ʳ. [277] Ibid., fos. 179ʳ, 443ʳ.
[278] Ibid., fos. 106ʳ, 109ᵛ, 123ᵛ (the *Explanation ... for a private parish* could have been either anon., *The church catechism, with explanations and scripture-proofs. For the use of a private parish* (1705) which was in use in a nearby parish—see fo. 118ʳ—or anon., *An exposition on the church catechism ... for the use of a private parish* (1688)); 408ʳ.
[279] Wake MS 284, *passim*; this calculation leaves out references to the use of printed expositions in schools in Kent, for which, see Ch. 4 below.
[280] See above n. 278, and cf. Wake MS 284, fo. 54ʳ.

having taken the advantage of your grace's exposition' (Wake's *Principles of the Christian religion*, first published in 1699).[281]

Another method of deployment was for ministers to give or recommend copies of a printed exposition to parents or children: this was perhaps the most common of all methods of using printed forms. It might be done as a follow-up to the use of such a form in church: thus a member of the famous Dering family, Edward, vicar of Charing, said that he used Isham's form with his catechumens, and 'as I see occasion' gave out copies of the work, 'having always a dozen or two of them by me for that purpose'.[282] In this and other cases care was taken in deciding who should receive copies, as in the case of a minister who wrote that 'to such as will make use of it I give Isham's exposition', or the minister in Canterbury who said that he had given *some* parishioners copies of Isham's and Wake's expositions, as well as giving *many* of them copies of two works, one of which he had penned himself.[283] Gifts were limited by clerical poverty: one incumbent said that he had not provided expositions yet, but 'I have proposed that some part of the offertory [the money collected at certain services] be disposed for that purpose'.[284] Occasionally one suspects that a clergyman's gift may have been an attempt to cover his back in the case of episcopal enquiries, or as a sop to conscience for having given into lay resistance to catechizing.[285] In other cases, the minister got no further than recommending a work without actually giving or lending a copy.[286] In general, however, the picture in East Kent is of a good deal of activity or at least well-meaning intention by the clergy in their attempts to ensure the better understanding of the church catechism, perhaps helped by the proximity of booksellers in London and the larger Kentish cities. This picture also does not yet take into account the considerable use of expositions in the many Charity Schools and other primary schools in the same area at the same time, which we will come to in the next chapter.

The broad pattern revealed by the answers to Gibson's enquiry in Lincolnshire in 1721 was much the same as that in Kent, though the details are different. A rather smaller proportion of about one in nine referred to providing some oral explanation of the church catechism based entirely or largely on their own efforts. Several replied that they gave catechetical lectures of their own composing, though one admitted that his were grounded in some measure on Wake's and Beveridge's expositions.[287] Others spoke of having prepared their own expositions or notes on the church catechism, though again one or two admitted a debt to existing expositions.[288] Over thirty more

---

[281]　Wake MS 284, fos. 26ʳ, and 400ʳ; and cf. 54ʳ, 213ʳ, 237ʳ, 253ʳ, 260ʳ, 264ʳ, 268ʳ, and 362ʳ.

[282]　Ibid., fo. 99ʳ.

[283]　Ibid., fos. 390ʳ, 60ʳ (my italics): for T. Wise's *Knowledg and practice*, see Appendix 1; the other work was a *Sacramental catechism*—a pre-communion form with prayers annexed. For unselective distribution of copies leading to mixed results, see Wake MS. 284, fos. 319ʳ, 327ʳ.

[284]　Ibid., fo. 258ʳ.　　　[285]　Ibid., fos. 333ʳ, 390ʳ.　　　[286]　Ibid., fo. 183ʳ.

[287]　Gibson 13, pp. 47, 147, 539; Gibson 14, pp. 149, 249, 269; Gibson 15, pp. 143, 467, 489.

[288]　Gibson 13, pp. 87, 95, 135, 423, 427, 431, 463; Gibson 14, pp. 395, 451, 467, 555, 583; Gibson 15, p. 221.

said that they 'explained' or 'expounded' the church catechism to the best of their ability: 'in the most familiar and instructive way as I am able', as one put it.[289] Some clergy were very sensitive to the needs of their particular catechumens: breaking the larger sentences of the Prayer Book catechism into shorter ones to help their understanding, and explaining only as much of it at a time as the capacity of those present warranted.[290] A number pointed out that since their charges were young, they were not yet fit to be taught larger forms, 'they being above their understanding', but efforts were clearly made to ensure that the church catechism itself was explained to them orally.[291]

In the Lincolnshire replies there are over a hundred and twenty replies (just over a quarter of the total) which mention the use or possession of printed expositions of the church catechism. In all, since some respondents mentioned two or more works, these replies contain over a hundred and forty references to specific titles, and a few more to unspecified publications. The breakdown of these references is dominated by 83 to Wake's catechism (for reasons we shall come to in a moment), but there were also 18 references to Lewis's catechism and 18 to Beveridge's exposition, 7 to Williams's, and one or two references to at least seventeen other works.[292] The reason for the very large number of references to Wake's exposition of the church catechism is that while he had been bishop of Lincoln (from 1705 to 1716) he had had an edition printed especially for distribution in that diocese, perhaps in 1708; as a result, about a quarter of the references to printed expositions were to copies of Wake's form that were already in the possession of families in the respondent's parish.[293] However, we can see from the replies to Gibson's enquiries in 1721 that Wake's exposition was still being used in a variety of ways in Lincoln diocese some years after Wake been elevated to Canterbury: as the basis for lecture or exposition notes or more informal or impromptu explanations of the church catechism; as a form to be taught to and memorized by more advanced catechumens; or as something to be lent, or of which new copies were to be given to those who could make good use of them.[294]

Given the greater length of Wake's form compared to that of Williams or Lewis, it is perhaps surprising to find so many ministers instructing their catechumens in that form. But in some cases, all that was said was that in explaining the church catechism the incumbent used Wake, which may have meant little more than a short reading or paraphrase of the relevant section of that work.[295] In other cases, there are clues to the

---

[289]   Ibid. 95; and cf. Gibson 13, pp. 35, 43, 109, 151, 165, 169, 263, 491, 547, 551, 555, 603; Gibson 14, pp. 41, 293, 463; Gibson 15, pp. 27, 47, 59, 91, 179, 195, 217, 345, 353, 357, 417, 507, and see next notes.

[290]   Gibson 13, p. 475; Gibson 14, p. 241.

[291]   Gibson 13, pp. 503, 625; Gibson 14, pp. 269, 471; Gibson 15, p. 405.

[292]   Including those of Sherlock, Comber, Ken, Ford, and Burnet, and *The art of catechizing* (all mentioned in the text or notes above, and in Appendix 1): Gibson 13–15, *passim*.

[293]   See Appendix 1, s.v. 'Lincoln', and Gibson 13, pp. 59, 67, 207, 239, 407; Gibson 14, pp. 281, 487, 539, 603, etc.

[294]   Gibson 13, pp. 323, 391, 539; Gibson 14, pp. 9, 29; Gibson 15, pp. 309, 429.

[295]   Gibson 13, pp. 351, 355 (and cf. 319); Gibson 14, p. 387 (and cf. 355).

way in which that form was deployed which suggest that not all catechumens were expected to master it in full. One incumbent mentioned that catechumens 'read' Wake's catechism, suggesting a degree of literacy and presumably possession of a copy to facilitate getting to grips with it; another said that he catechized every week, and to those that were capable he lent copies of Wake, 'one book amongst four to read and peruse for their better understanding that of the church'; a third replied that 'our reading families' all have a copy of Wake's explanation for their better understanding 'and generally make good use of it'.[296] We find a similar degree of selectivity and a close link to literacy in some of the comments about the use of Lewis's catechism in Lincoln diocese.[297] These efforts to get children to learn a second form did not always meet with success. One minister said he had tried using a small exposition until he grew weary of the children neglecting the tasks he had set them; another who catechized for half a year had wanted to catechize for the other half as well, but meeting resistance had to give up teaching Lewis's catechism.[298] To balance these defeats, we may point to some successes, even in difficult circumstances: a minister who complained that parents were very backward in sending children and servants, nevertheless could report that some of those that did come gave a good account of the church catechism and 'are tolerably perfect' in Bishop Williams's exposition.[299] Again what we seem to be finding is a fair amount of effort and a modicum of success as well as some failures in trying to ensure that young catechumens could do more than simply repeat the Prayer Book catechism by rote.

When we turn to the replies to the questions sent round Oxford diocese at the primary visitation of Thomas Secker in 1738, we get a quite different pattern in a number of respects: a much higher reported level of exposition of the Prayer Book catechism in church, a larger number of catechetical sermons or lectures being delivered, and a relatively smaller number of reports of the use or distribution of printed expositions. The main reason for these differences was probably the wording of the question. Where Wake and Gibson had focused on the use of other catechisms as a means of enhancing understanding of the church catechism, Secker asked 'do you either expound it to them yourself, or make use of some printed exposition, and what is it?'[300] In over half of the replies—93 out of 176—we find a positive statement about exposition by the minister himself, the balance being made up of replies that avoided a direct answer to this part of the questionnaire or said that the pressure of serving two or more cures prevented an exposition being given.[301] There are various possible explanations for the disparity between the level of clerical exposition in Oxfordshire and that in Kent and Lincolnshire. Perhaps the Oxfordshire clergy were simply

---

[296] Gibson 14, pp. 165, 169; Gibson 13, pp. 123, 395, 375 and 407; Gibson 14, p. 281.
[297] Gibson 13, p. 637; Gibson 14, pp. 93, 253.
[298] Gibson 14, pp. 459, 265; and cf. Gibson 13, p. 499.   [299] Gibson 14, p. 205.
[300] Wake MS 284, 1; Gibson 13, p. 1; Secker, *Oxford*, 5.
[301] Ibid., *passim*; as examples of pressure, see 12, 45, 130.

better pastors: with its proximity to the university, the county of Oxford tradition-
ally enjoyed a higher proportion of graduate clergy, and the compact unit of which
the diocese consisted was easier to supervise from an administrative and pastoral
point of view. Equally there may have been more schools in the area, nearly all teaching the church catechism and so preparing the young for more advanced catechizing
in church. Alternatively there may have been an element of bluff in some of the positive replies about exposition: a quarter of them consisted of a bare statement that 'I
expound the catechism myself', or 'I expound sometimes' or 'in Lent', and incumbents may have hoped that an occasional word of explanation would stand for formal
exposition if the bishop made closer enquiries.[302] Thirdly, it may have been the case
that in the *other* dioceses that we have been examining, where the wording of the episcopal question seemed to suggest that use of a more advanced catechism was the
norm, clergy may have thought that the bishop did not want to know about their
more modest attempts at oral explanation and so forbore to mention it.

That having been said, the attempted standard of exposition in some parishes in
Oxford diocese does seem to have been quite high. What sticks out straight away is
the higher proportion of replies—almost two dozen, or one in eight over-all—which
stated that ministers gave catechetical lectures either of their own composition or
derived in part or in full from existing works, for example 'I use an exposition chiefly
of my own composition, which in eight lectures of about half an hour each, runs
through the whole catechism'.[303] In addition, several claimed to have made 'collections' of suitable material partly from their own thoughts and partly from well-known
catechetical authors such as Nowell, Hammond, Nicholson, Wake, Lewis, Beveridge, and others.[304] It was not only the children but their parents who reaped the
benefit: the minister at Bladon said that because an above average number of catechumens 'could make their responses [to the church catechism] well', he expounded
the catechism to the congregation at the same time, since the adults needed instruction as much as the young.[305] Even the more extempore expositions could be moderately impressive,[306] and we can see the sensitivity of some clerical catechists to the
needs and abilities of their pupils. 'I make use of a method of my own in expounding,
adapting myself to the respective ages and capacities of my catechumens', wrote one;
another said that reading the collection of points he had culled from various expositions seemed too like a sermon and not sufficiently edifying for an unlearned congregation, so he had adopted a simpler method of asking the children 'questions all
along the catechism' and enlarging on the answers 'in a familiar way', which he felt
was more instructive both for the children and the rest of the congregation 'who cannot so well attend to, or comprehend the reasonings of a set speech'.[307] Relatively few

---

[302]   Ibid. 8, 37, 42, 43, 54, 58, 60, 65, 84, 89, 90, 94, 95, 111, 113, 121, 122, 129, 159, 160, 161, 166–7, 172, 179, 181.
[303]   Ibid. 80, and cf. 8, 24–5.   [304]   Ibid. 18, 20, 31, 51, 140.   [305]   Ibid. 19.
[306]   Ibid. 69.   [307]   Ibid. 63, 140, and cf. 112, 144.

references to printed expositions were made in Oxford, the most commonly mentioned being Lewis (eight mentions) and Wake (five),[308] and there are even fewer references to copies of printed expositions being given away or handed out.[309]

Archbishop Herring's enquiry in York diocese in 1743 contained no question specifically about expounding, or the use of other catechisms or printed expositions, and a number of respondents clearly thought that the question about the 'instruction' of children and servants referred to teaching and testing basic knowledge of the church catechism, as in the reply that 'parishioners are careful to send their children and servants to church, who have not learned their catechism, to be instructed therein'.[310] As a result perhaps, the great majority of the more than six hundred replies say nothing about exposition. However, a number of other clergy thought the verb 'instruct' might have been used to indicate something more than this, and in addition to a number of replies which appear to have drawn a distinction between catechizing, on the one hand, and (further) instruction on the other,[311] there are over fifty replies which contain more specific references to some form of exposition having taken place in church. Some of these replies are similar to those we have encountered in Kent, Lincolnshire, and Oxfordshire, while others are rather different and of no little interest. The similarities are evident in the number of respondents who made a distinction between catechizing and expounding, for example the curate at Bradfield chapel near Doncaster, who reported that he 'catechized' both in Lent and again from Easter to Whit, and 'in going a second time over, after catechizing I publicly explained some part of the catechism', the curate of Chapel Allerton in Leeds parish who catechized every week in Lent 'with expositions on Sundays', and the vicar of Fishlake who instructed the young every Sunday after the second lesson at evening prayer and then 'shew[ed] them the meaning thereof'.[312]

Where there are shades of difference are in the replies which suggested that many children had already been 'instructed' in the church catechism at home or school, and were being sent to church for further instruction by the minister. There were similar cases in the other three counties we have been examining, but there do seem to be a proportionally significant number of such cases, almost certainly linked to the large number of primary schools in Yorkshire teaching the church catechism, as we shall see in the next chapter. 'I find the children very well instructed in the church catechism by their parents and have not been wanting in doing my duty to explain it', wrote the vicar of Acomb, while his counterpart at Burton Agnes said that in addition to teaching the catechism to those who did not know it and expounding the catechism

---

[308] Secker, *Oxford, passim*; I have counted forty-five references to printed expositions (some of the vaguer referring to more than one work used, e.g. 'authors', 'others', and 'several').

[309] Ibid. 37, 49, 155, 173, 179; in one case (p. 155) the minister admitted he had given copies of expositions because the pressure of work in serving two chapels prevented him from explaining the church catechism himself.

[310] Herring, *York*, i. 30.   [311] e.g. ibid. i. 29, 48; ii. 15, 86, 117, 128; ii. 205.

[312] Ibid. i. 74, 125, 201; and cf. i. 80.

in his church he also visited the local school where thirty children were taught the church catechism once a week, and 'frequently hear them repeat, and do expound the catechism to them'.[313]

Another difference is the references to large numbers, especially in urban areas, attending catechetical lectures in Yorkshire. Gilbert Burnet, it may be recalled, had suggested in the early 1690s that short 'discourses' explaining the church catechism would 'draw an assembly to evening prayers', and in succeeding decades a number of clergy, like the vicar of Packington in Leicestershire noted above and a few in Yorkshire, found this to be the case.[314] The vicar of Bradford's answer to Herring's ninth question was:

I catechize in the church every year betwixt Easter and Midsummer, and during that interval, I frequently expound the catechism after evening service on Sundays to great numbers of persons who have and have not learned their catechism.[315]

The vicars of Beverley and Wakefield wrote in a similar vein, as did the vicar of Leeds who was probably talking of something more than impromptu explanations when he replied that:

we begin to catechize the first Sunday in Lent in the evening and continue it till the whole town is called over and during the time of Lent I explain some part of the catechism to a numerous congregation the same evening.[316]

There are reports of catechetical lectures or expositions being attended by adults in less heavily populated parishes, as at Kirk Deighton where 'many of the parishioners have usually come along with their children to hear them in the church say their catechism and my exposition thereon', and Holme upon the Wolds where the children were catechized on Sunday afternoons in Lent, 'and my parishioners give due attendance and attention to the explanations and lectures that I then read to them upon the catechism'.[317] All this does not constitute a religious revival, but nor is it the usual picture that we are given of the Church of England in the first half of the eighteenth century.[318]

What we may safely assume from the replies to episcopal questionnaires to the clergy in the period 1716–43 is that, first of all, many clergy drew a distinction between, on the one hand, mere rote repetition, and, on the other, a measure of understanding being shown by catechumens, and, secondly, in a substantial minority of churches there were attempts for at least part of the year to go beyond repetition and to explain the church catechism to young catechumens, often in the presence of their elders. There was possibly a good deal of variation between dioceses in the

---

[313] Ibid. i. 26, 37–8.   [314] See above, nn. 244, 188.   [315] Herring, *York*, i. 59.
[316] Ibid. i. 102; iii. 186–7; ii. 141.   [317] Ibid. ii. 103, 80; and cf. iii. 53, 87, 169.
[318] But now see the important collection of essays, and esp. the introduction in J. Walsh, C. Haydon, and S. Taylor (eds.), *The Church of England c.1689–c.1833: From Toleration to Tractarianism* (Cambridge, 1993).

quantity and quality of such attempts, and even within one diocese or deanery there were probably considerable differences in practice owing to the varying expectations of clergy, varying age and educational level of the catechumens sent, the different amounts of time and money available, and so on. But in some parishes there was apparently not only a good deal of activity but also a fair measure of response.[319]

By way of conclusion and comparison, a word may be said about catechizing in presbyterian churches and separatist congregations from the 1650s. In the 1650s the exercise was certainly comparable to what had taken place in the established church before the 1640s, and after 1662 catechizing in chapel or meeting-house may reasonably be regarded as comparable to that in 'church', though it is not susceptible to quite the same kind of assessment as has been offered here of catechizing in the established church. This is a subject which deserves more attention than the author is equipped to provide or has the appropriate space to give it here. However, those who are interested in this might like to search through the catechisms listed in Appendix 1 for those marked presbyterian, Independent or Congregational, Baptist, or Quaker, and examine not only their texts but also their prefaces. What they will find is on the whole a comparable commitment at the elementary level to inculcating a body of basic information by question-and-answer catechizing, and a growing effort to move from that elementary standard to more advanced levels of catechizing.

The phrase 'on the whole' is used because there is a suspicion that some of the 'godly' were not quite as keen on catechizing as others. As early as the 1580s, there had been a debate in the Dedham classis on the legitimacy of using catechisms. A majority were in favour, but a hard core felt that there was a risk of private men's judgements intruding into the text of a catechism, and that in church it was better to use the word of God alone, rather than 'the word of God and man ... confounded'.[320] In subsequent decades there were, as we have seen, periodic complaints about the neglect of catechizing in favour of preaching by some of the 'godly'; and at the end of the 1650s we find Philip Nye implying that question-and-answer catechizing was better suited to a former age when the blind led the blind, and that nowadays it was best to teach the young 'according to scripture direction in the fundamentals of religion', which did not necessarily involve the use of a set form.[321] In 'godly' and later in

---

[319] To the type of evidence adduced in previous pages can be added anecdotal evidence such as William Sampson's note (in *Rector's Book*, *Clayworth*, 19) that in April 1676 he 'began to catechize the children on Sundays afternoon, and to expound the same to them'; and the claim in [W. Fleetwood], *The reasonable communicant* (1704) that the author never failed to explain the latter part of the church catechism to his parishioners before administering the sacrament (sig. A2^r).

[320] R. G. Usher, 'The Presbyterian Movement in the Reign of Queen Elizabeth as Illustrated by the Minute Book of Dedham Classis 1582–1589', *Camden Society*, 3rd ser., viii (1905), 89–91, and cf. 28, 32, 53, 99.

[321] See above, p. 130 nn. 161–3; and cf. Philip Henry's comment that by the late 1650s preaching was 'jostling out' catechizing: M. Henry, *The Life of the Rev. Philip Henry*, ed. J. B. Williams (1825), 29 n; [P. Nye], *Beames of former light* (1660), 10, 78, 111–12.

nonconformist households, as we shall see, catechizing was only one of a number of techniques of instruction and edification, such as reading the Bible, repeating the contents of sermons heard recently, or preparing answers to specific questions circulated in advance; catechizing of the type described above had its place in these circles, but perhaps not always as central a place.[322] Finally, when we look at biographies of clergy ejected in 1662 and compare their subsequent careers with those of earlier 'godly' ministers we seem to find less mention of public catechizing, though given the legal and physical restrictions under which they worked until 1688 this is perhaps not altogether surprising.[323] In this context we should note the significance of the subtitle of John Flavell's *Exposition of the Assemblies catechism* published in 1692: 'as it was carried out in the Lord's Days' exercises in Dartmouth, in the first year of liberty, 1688'. Oliver Heywood's diaries also seem to show him catechizing much more in chapel after 1688 than before.[324]

For there were always many presbyterians and other nonconformists who *were* anxious to catechize in public if they could. Hence the elementary catechisms prepared by men like John Owen, John Wallis, Richard Baxter, George Fox, Benjamin Keach, Isaac Watts, and others for their particular groups of catechumens.[325] There was also a comparable commitment to securing understanding as well as instilling knowledge, a growing variety of catechetical forms and methods, and some extremely zealous catechists, such as Richard Baxter, Henry Stubbs, Thomas Wadsworth, Thomas Lye, Thomas Doolittle, Thomas Vincent, Philip Henry and his son Matthew, Samuel Bourn the younger, and many others.[326] Baxter's achievements at Kidderminster in the 1650s were remarkable by any standards, but since they took place largely outside the church will be reserved for the next chapter.[327] Thomas Lye's thirty-year ministry, mainly in London, was marked by his zeal for catechizing, and his unflagging attempts to find new ways to make the Westminster Shorter catechism easier to master and understand, especially by those with 'weakest capacities and memories' (his experience as a schoolmaster may also have encouraged him to experiment). He taught catechism publicly on Saturday afternoons at Dyers' Hall in the mid-1670s, and among

---

[322] See below, pp. 209–12, 220.

[323] It may also be that the relative brevity of the entries in the *Nonconformists' Memorial*, ed. S. Palmer (3 vols., 1802), compared to those in Samuel Clarke's biographies, and A. G. Matthews's concern with details of career and persecution rather than pastoral activity in *Calamy Revised* (Oxford, 1934), has hidden from us much of what public catechising there was. For some examples, see next paragraph below.

[324] J. Flavell, *An exposition of the assemblies catechism* (1692), title-page; *The Rev. Oliver Heywood, B.A., 1630–1702: His Autobiography, Diaries, Anecdote and Event Books*, ed. J. Horsfall Turner (4 vols.; Brighouse and Bingley, 1882–5), i. 223–304; ii. 38–123; iv. 184–305.

[325] See Appendix 1, s.v. the authors named.

[326] For Stubbs and Wadsworth, see E. Duffy, 'The Godly and the Multitude in Stuart England', *Seventeenth Century Journal*, 1 (1986), 48. For the last three of these, see Henry, *Life of Philip Henry*, 29, 41, 79, 195; J. B. Williams, *Memoirs of the Life ... of the Rev. Matthew Henry* (1828), 130–1, 156–7 394; Samuel Bourn II, *Lectures to children and young people* (1738), pp. vii, xxxi. For the others, see preceding and succeeding notes.

[327] See below, pp. 222–6.

those he instructed was a very young Edmund Calamy.[328] Of Thomas Doolittle it was said that 'catechizing was his special excellency and delight, wherein he took much pains himself, and which he earnestly recommended to his brethren in the ministry, as greatly tending to their people's profit, and their own comfort'. By his own account, his normal catechumens ranged from 6 to 28 years in age, though he also tells us he had helped some in their thirties and forties, and up to their seventies. Like Lye he was both a schoolteacher and a preacher for a while, and regularly experimented with new techniques, producing in the end works for everyone from children to *A complete body of practical divinity; being a new improvement of the Assembly's catechism* for educated adults, which had first seen the light of day as mid-week lectures in London. In the preface of an early venture, which turned the Shorter Catechism into a series of questions requiring 'Yes' or 'No' answers, Doolittle recorded the delight that children found in this exercise: they 'would with great willingness for an hour or two together, answer Yes or No to the questions herein propounded, and so may yours', he added to the householders to whom the published work was dedicated.[329] Thomas Vincent's *Explanatory catechism* was said to have been composed 'at first for his own particular congregation', again in London, and committed entirely to memory by some catechumens who then had to 'answer this explicatory catechism in our public assembly'. (Later editions were prefaced by an epistle signed by forty clergymen commending its contents and recommending its use in families as well, and the wide sales enjoyed by the work suggests that it may have been used privately, in families and schools, as well as publicly.[330]) Indeed, in one respect nonconformists set the pace in the early eighteenth century by setting up catechetical societies in which youthful catechumens banded together to learn and to hear special sermons by leading ministers; a number of these sermons were printed subsequently.[331]

But for the most part it is the similarities between conformist and nonconformist which are striking. Parallel to the many full-blown catechetical sermons on the contents of the church catechism, there were regular catechetical lectures on the Westminster Larger and Shorter catechisms and other catechetical topics by men like Doolittle, Philip and Matthew Henry, and others.[332] Parallel to the many

---

[328] T. Lye, *A plain and familiar method of instructing the younger sort according to the lesser catechism* (1662); *An abridgement of the late reverend Assemblies shorter catechism* [1662?], title-page; *The assemblies shorter catechism drawn out into distinct propositions* (1672); and *An explanation of the shorter catechism* (1675); Matthews, *Calamy Revised*, 331–2.

[329] T. Doolittle, *A complete body of practical divinity* (1723), a note signed by twenty ministers placed opposite title-page; id., *The young man's instructer* (1673), sigs. A3ʳ–5ʳ; id., *Catechizing necessary for the ignorant* (1692), 23; see also Appendix 1, and Matthews, *Calamy Revised*, 167–8.

[330] Ibid. 502–3; T. Vincent, *An explicatory catechism* (1701), sigs. A3ʳ–4ʳ.

[331] M. Henry, *A sermon concerning the catechizing of youth* (1713); and the catechetical sermons by B. Grosvenor, W. Harris, E. Calamy, D. Mayo, and J. Wood listed in Appendix 1.

[332] See above, pp. 82–3 and below, pp. 227–8, and Appendix 1, s.v. H. Binning, T. Doolittle (1723), and T. Watson, and cf. S. Willard, *A compleat body of divinity in two hundred and fifty expository lectures on the Assembly's Shorter Catechism* (Boston, New England, 1725).

publications designed to explain the Prayer Book catechism were a number of explanations and expositions of the Westminster Shorter Catechism, by non-presbyterians such as Keach and Watts as well as presbyterians.[333] And parallel to the hopes expressed by conformist clergy that parents and schoolteachers would help them to teach a basic catechism and take catechizing a stage further were similar expressions by many authors of works for dissenters.[334] We even find a measure of mutual understanding or respect with some conformists borrowing from forms used by nonconformists, and some of the latter acknowledging the existence and value of the church catechism and some of the expositions based on it.[335] Historians have tended to denigrate 'Anglican' catechizing as conservative and hide-bound compared to the zeal and flair shown by 'puritans'.[336] A more balanced picture would be that both conformists and nonconformists had their zealous catechists and their half-hearted ones, and as far as public catechizing was concerned, in church or chapel, both had some success as well as many failures.

[333] See above, Ch. 3, and Appendix 1, for details of these expositions.

[334] Z. Cawdrey, *A brief and methodical catechism* (1664), title-page; anon. *An explicatory catechism* (1675), sigs. A2ᵛ–5ʳ; T. Doolittle, *Catechizing necessary for the ignorant young and old* (1692), 5–32; id., *A plain method of catechizing* (1698) title-page; anon., *The doctrines of the Christian religion* (1708), 122; W[illiam] N[otcutt], *A short explanation of the Assembly's shorter catechism* (1726), p. iii.

[335] T. Comber, *The church-catechism resolved* (1686), sig. A3ʳ; J. Worthington, *Hupotuposis ... A form of sound words* (1673); T. Adams, *The main principles of Christian religion* (1675); Flavell, *Exposition*, sig. A2ʳ; anon., *An earnest call to family-catechising* (1693), p. vii; M. Henry, *A scripture catechism* (1703), sig. A2ʳ; S. Harris, *Scripture-knowledge promot'd* (1712), 15; I. Watts, *Catechisms* (1730), 39. For other forms with some irenic intent, see B. Bird, *The catechism of the Church of England* (1674); anon., *A short catechisme according to the doctrine* (1688) (also in anon., *Catechism made practical*); and [B. Keach?], *A brief instruction in the principles of the Christian religion* [*c*.1693].

[336] For a recent example, see C. J. Sommerville, *The Discovery of Childhood in Puritan England* (Athens, Ga./London, 1992), 135–45.

4

Catechizing in Theory and Practice:
In School and at Home

WHEN Hamlet protests to Guildenstern that he still loves him, he holds out his hands and swears by 'these pickers and stealers'—an odd phrase unless one realizes that in the Prayer Book catechism the child is taught to say that the eighth Commandment means that he or she must 'keep my hands from picking and stealing'. There is good evidence from a number of other references in the plays of Shakespeare that he became thoroughly familiar with that catechism and attendant material in the form in which it was taught in Elizabethan schools: *The ABC with the catechisme*.[1] Although the main thrust of early modern English catechizing was undoubtedly made in church, the English authorities were all in favour of catechizing in school and home, especially the former, if it could be relied on to assist the minister's catechizing in church.[2] Catechizing in school was much the more common of the two in practice, and took various forms. In the first stages of formal education in dame or ABC schools or the first form of a grammar school, an elementary catechism such as the Prayer Book form was usually taught. In the lower or middle forms of a grammar school or perhaps the upper forms of a Charity School, either a larger catechism or an exposition of the Prayer Book catechism might be learnt, or a Latin translation of a shorter catechism studied. Finally, in the middle or upper forms of a grammar school or the first years at university, there was the study of yet more advanced catechetical forms, or of a middling or larger catechism in Latin, Greek, and sometimes Hebrew as well.

A number of exceptions to this general picture must be entered. First, there was regular overlap between students at different stages of achievement, for example, between those entrants to a grammar school who had not yet learnt the Prayer Book catechism properly and those who had mastered it years before, and between undergraduates fresh from provincial schools who might still be learning a catechism that

---

[1] T. W. Baldwin, *William Shakespere's Petty School* (Urbana, Ill., 1943), 173 and ch. 10, *passim*.

[2] For royal injunctions, canons, visitations articles, and school statutes drawn up or approved by leading figures in church and state, see Frere, *Visitation Articles*, ii. 48–9; iii. 21, 71, 91, 96, 105, 114, 132, 153, 160, 214, 270, 291, 312, 333, 342, 371; D. Cressy, *Education in Tudor and Stuart England* (1975), 28–35; T. W. Baldwin, *Shakespere's Small Latine and Lesse Greeke* (2 vols.; Urbana, Ill., 1944), i. 296–7, 302–3, 345, 432–3; J. Simon, *Education and Society in Tudor England* (Cambridge, 1966), 323–4.

fellow-students from more prestigious schools had finished some time before. This brings us to the second caveat: there was much variation between well-established or well-endowed schools such as St Paul's, Westminster, Winchester, or Harrow and other schools which could not attract the same quality of teacher or afford the same range of books.[3] Even the schools below grammar-school level are now portrayed as having been more varied in type than was once thought; and the so-called Charity School movement it now appears did not so much produce a large number of identical new schools as briefly take under its wing a wide range of existing and new schools.[4] Thirdly, the more advanced the educational institution, the fewer the number of girls who would be admitted. In dame schools, free schools, and Charity Schools as much attention was paid to the catechizing of girls as boys, and to judge from the number of satirical catechisms about 'young ladies' and 'pretty misses' it seems likely that the girls who were sent to finishing schools in the seventeenth and eighteenth centuries were thought to have learnt a catechism there. But it is not clear how many, if any, girls attended grammar schools, and certainly women were barred from the universities.[5] Fourthly, we cannot always be certain that teachers always catechized when they were supposed to do by their school statutes, or that they used the forms prescribed there or in the church's regulations.

Nevertheless, there are grounds for cautious optimism in surveying catechizing in early modern schools. The authorities may not have tried to set up a complete system of elementary education such as was set up in Germany and other Protestant countries, but in the statutes of the schools that were set up they did insist on certain standards of morality and conduct among teachers, and laid down patterns of instruction, religious observance, and church attendance by both masters and scholars which were regularly investigated by the local bishop and archdeacon during their visitations.[6] It was obviously easier to check on the performance of teachers in permanently endowed schools than that of part-time instructors or freelance teachers who moved around. However, there is evidence that by the early eighteenth century if not sooner, teachers in even the poorest or most short-lived schools came under some sort of official scrutiny, or were checked out by a local clergyman who would either

---

[3] Baldwin, *Shakespere's Small Latine, passim*; K. Charlton, *Education in Renaissance England* (1965) and Simon, *Education and Society* both stress the variable quality of grammar school education.

[4] R. O'Day, *Education and Society 1500–1800* (London, 1982), 26–34; J. Simon, 'Was there a Charity School Movement? The Leicestershire Evidence', in B. Simon (ed.), *Education in Leicestershire 1540–1940: A Regional Study* (Leicester, 1968), 55–100.

[5] N. McMullen, 'The Education of English Gentlewomen 1540–1640', *History of Education*, 6 (1977), 87–101; O'Day, *Education and Society*, ch. 10; W. Lempriere, *A History of the Girls' School of Christ's Hospital, London, Hoddesdon and Hertford* (Cambridge, 1924), 6 (£5 left in 1638 for a man to catechize the girls); and on Charity Schools, see below, pp. 172–3, 177–82; for the satirical forms, see Appendix 1, s.v. *The ladies catechism, The town-misses catechism, The country-gentlewoman's catechism*, and U. Price, *A new catechism for the fine ladies*.

[6] Cardwell, *Synodalia*, i. 128–9, 291–2; Frere, *Visitation Articles*, Kennedy, *Episcopal Administration*, and *Second Report on Ritual, passim*.

visit the school himself or see if the scholars who came to church had learnt their cat-echism.[7] Moreover, those children who were sent to such a school by their parents formed a much more captive audience than their older siblings and servants who had passed into the world of work; and, at the elementary level of catechizing in particu-lar, the story is often one of apparently fruitful co-operation between incumbent and schoolteacher.

Children who received an elementary education in early modern England did so in various settings. The most informal was instruction by parents or older siblings, as in the well-known case of Adam Martindale in the late 1620s. Given an 'ABC' by his godmother, young Adam was taught to read it by 'my brethren and sisters that could read, and a young man that came to court my sister'. Having then mastered the 'primer', he 'fell to reading the Bible' and any other book in English he could lay his hands on.[8] Beyond family teaching, there was part-time instruction by a literate farmer, spinner, or parish clerk who earned a few extra pence by teaching some local children their letters, or by peripatetic freelance teachers who persuaded a few par-ents in one area to pay them for a few weeks' or months' instruction before moving on to another.[9] Such education was not primarily religious, but the 'ABC' and 'primer' used by Martindale and taught by a parish clerk almost certainly contained the Prayer Book catechism as we shall see shortly.

Perhaps the more common and certainly the more formal settings for elementary instruction, however, were either a local 'small' school, or the lower forms of the nearest grammar school which might be some distance away from the child's home. The former was referred to by various names: 'dame school', 'ABC school', 'petty' or 'small school', 'free school' (where some local benefactor had left a sum to ensure for free education for any local child), 'private school' (where parents had banded together to keep a school going for as long as they could afford), 'English school' (as opposed to the grammar school where the focus on learning Latin led it in some areas to be known as a 'Latin school'), or, later on, 'Charity School'. At their most basic these schools might teach no more than the ability to read and write, but in many of them a simple skill such as casting accounts or sewing might also be taught. In either case, catechizing was likely to play a part, for reasons that will become clear. More-over, the statutes of most Charity Schools made it crystal clear that their purpose was to provide 'a Christian' as well as 'a useful education' for the children of the poor, and catechizing was high on that agenda.[10]

---

[7] O'Day, *Education and Society*, 26–7; and e.g. Wake MS 284, Christ Church, Oxford, fos. 14ʳ, 59ᵛ, 67ᵛ, 178ᵛ, 210ᵛ, 322ᵛ, 328ᵛ, 332ᵛ, 336ʳ, 349ᵛ, 387ᵛ.

[8] *The Life of Adam Martindale Written by Himself*, ed. R. Parkinson (Chetham Society, 4; 1845), 5, 24–5; see also M. Spufford, 'First Steps in Literacy', *Social History*, 4 (1979), 435.

[9] O'Day, *Education and Society*, 27–8, 168; and for parish clerks, see below, p. 182.

[10] Baldwin, *Shakespere's Petty School*, ch. 1; O'Day, *Education and Society* 26–31, 168; anon., *An account of Charity-Schools lately erected in England, Wales and Ireland* (1707), 3–6; M. G. Jones, *The*

Admission to a grammar school depended more on the child's ability or his parents' ability to pay the fees.[11] The prime function of the lower forms in a grammar school was to prepare pupils for the more demanding work ahead of them, in particular by grounding them in Latin grammar; and, ideally, this work was to be kept distinct from that done in elementary schools. Grammar-school teachers made it clear that they did not want the time-consuming chore of teaching absolute beginners their letters if they could possibly help it.[12] That this view was moderately widespread is suggested by a petition for the renewal of the licence of a petty master or 'abecedarius' at Stratford-upon-Avon in 1604 who argued that the continued existence of his school would save the local grammar-school teacher the 'tedious trouble' of teaching reading, and by statements made elsewhere to the effect that running an elementary school was fair employment for a literate man who had fallen on hard times or a widow who was unable to earn a living by other means.[13] In smaller towns or more isolated parishes, however, children might well be taught their letters and their catechism in the lowest form of the nearest grammar school, either by the usher who assisted the master or by some pupils from the higher forms. When Bishop Pilkington was helping to set up a grammar school at Rivington on the edge of the Pennines in Lancashire in the early 1570s, he conceded that 'in great need' the usher would have to teach reading and mastery of the Prayer Book catechism to those who had not managed to learn them prior to admission.[14] Indeed, from an early stage most schools of any size found it easier or wiser to have an usher whose duties would include the training up of 'young beginners in the ABC, Primer, Catechism, and such other English books whereby they may attain to the perfect reading of the English tongue'.[15] Children might enter a petty school as early as the age of 4 or 5 in a town, or 6 or 7 in the country, while entry to a Charity School was supposed to be no earlier than 6 or 7; admission to the lower forms of a grammar school was occasionally as early as 5 or 6, but more commonly 7 or 8. Pupils would then spend two, three, or four years at this level according to the nature of the school and their ability, though again we should not expect these matters to have been absolutely standard across the country.[16]

Charity School Movement (Cambridge, 1938), 81–2; Simon, 'Was there a Charity School Movement?', 63–4; see also the variety of teachers cited in Spufford, 'First Steps', 410–30; and below, pp. 181–3.

[11] For grammar school education in general, see Baldwin, *Shakespere's Small Latine, passim*, and Simon, *Education and Society*, chs. 13–14.

[12] J. Brinsley, *Ludus Literarius or The Grammar Schoole*, ed. E. T. Campagnac (1917), 12, and cf. 13 (the first edition of this work appeared in 1612, but Campagnac reproduces the edition of 1627).

[13] Baldwin, *Shakespere's Petty School*, 137–9, and below, p. 181.

[14] J. Whitaker, *The Statutes and Charter of Rivington School* (Wigan, 1837), 207; Baldwin, *Shakespere's Little Latine*, i. 345–7.

[15] Ibid. 38, 432–3, 388; R. L. DeMolen, 'Age of Admission to Educational Institutions in Tudor and Stuart England', *History of Education*, 5 (1975), 209–10.

[16] Ibid. 207–15; Simon, 'Was there a Charity School Movement?', 63; for a stress on flexibility in admission practice, see also D. Cressy, 'School and College Admission Ages in Seventeenth-century

Whatever the school, the first texts they would probably have encountered were twofold: *The ABC with the catechisme* and *The primer and catechisme*, two works which served the double function of helping children to learn to read English and to learn the catechism. Both Elizabethan theorists like Richard Mulcaster and William Kempe and early Stuart ones like John Brinsley and Charles Hoole accepted this. In 1582 Mulcaster wrote of the religious and civil functions of education, adding that:

> to lay the first ground of learning, which is to learn to read, in religion towards God, and in religion itself to observe the law and ordinances of my country, I will after the ABC set down the ordinary catechism set forth by my prince.[17]

Six years later Kempe stated that children, having learnt their letters, vowels, consonants, and syllables, 'shall proceed to practise the same in spelling and reading other men's works, as the Catechism and Primer';[18] Brinsley expected children to 'go through their Abcie and Primer' as part of the process of learning to read and spell,[19] and writing nearly half a century after that, and basing his comments on over twenty years' teaching experience, Charles Hoole confirmed that

> the ordinary way to teach children to read is, after they have got some knowledge of their letters, and a smattering of some syllables and words in the horn-book, to turn them into the ABC or Primer, and there to make them name the letters and spell the words, till by often use they can pronounce (at least) the shortest words at the first sight.[20]

There were other ways of learning one's ABC, for example through the hornbook mentioned by Hoole,[21] and periodic attempts were made to attach an ABC to other catechisms than the official short catechism of 1549, which were soon rebuffed. But in most cases, as the sources just cited and the bibliographical evidence suggest, it was the officially approved *ABC* or *Primer* which provided children's first reading-matter and their introduction to knowledge of the Christian faith.

The idea of pairing an ABC with a dialogue or catechism seems in England to date from the mid-1540s,[22] and in the version most commonly found thereafter, which varied relatively little between its first appearance in 1551 and its early eighteenth-century manifestation, there were six sets of alphabets (in black letter, roman, and italic type-faces, all in upper and lower case), syllables, numbers from one to three hundred, the Prayer Book catechism, and at the end a series of 'graces' to be said before and after meals. The whole was contained in a flimsy little pamphlet of sixteen

England', in *History of Education*, 8 (1973), 167–77, and O'Day, *Education and Society*, 56, 62; and for variety of time spent in school, see Spufford, 'First Steps', 415, 417–18, 421, 425.

[17] R. Mulcaster, *The First Part of the Elementarie*, ed. E. T. Campagnac (1925), 61.

[18] Baldwin, *Shakespere's Petty School*, 9.   [19] Brinsley, *Ludus literarius*, 15–17.

[20] C. Hoole, *A new discovery of the old art of teaching schoole*, ed. E. T. Campagnac (London, 1913), 20 (the epistle is dated December 1659 and the original edition appeared in 1660).

[21] A. W. Tuer, *The History of the Horn Book* (2 vols.; 1896); F. Davies, *Teaching Reading in Early England* (1973), chs. 5–6.

[22] STC² 20–20.2; for the dialogue in this 1545 *ABC*, see C. C. Butterworth, *The English Primers (1529–1545)* (Philadelphia, 1953), 32, 65, 76, 111, 122, 213, 253–4.

octavo or duodecimo pages, which was so easily worn out that few copies now survive.[23] Indeed, so few complete copies survive from the Elizabethan period that we are not perfectly sure of one part of its content from the 1570s to the late 1590s. There are good grounds for thinking that in the early 1570s two short sections were added to the original Prayer Book catechism of 1549, one amplifying the duties implicit in the Commandments, and the other describing the sacraments of baptism and the Lord's Supper; in 1604 the former was discarded but the latter became the basis for the section on the sacraments officially added in 1604.[24] However, this slightly enlarged Elizabethan form survives in full only in copies of the Latin and Greek versions, and attempts to reconstruct the English equivalent from the fragments that remain are not without their problems.[25] It was also the case that the catechism in the many repeat editions of the Book of Common Prayer published under Elizabeth (and required to be used in church by the canons of 1571 and most visitation articles) remained the same as that of 1549, even after that in *The ABC with the catechisme* had acquired some additions. The situation between *c.*1570 and 1604 may have been that those acquiring literacy and mastering the catechism at the same time learnt the enlarged form of the early 1570s, while in church the minister or curate taught or tested from the original 1549 version in his Book of Common Prayer.[26]

Whatever its exact content, *The ABC with the catechisme* was a huge best-seller, as can be seen in a series of incidents in the 1580s. In 1582 John Day, who held the patent for *The ABC with the catechisme*, alleged that Roger Ward, a leading figure among the smaller printers who resented the privileges of the larger ones, had arranged for his apprentice to print about 10,000 pirate copies of that work.[27] This was an enormous figure, equivalent to about six or eight editions of a normal work such as a sermon or treatise or at least four editions of the handful of the religious and educational titles which were permitted print runs of up to 2,500 or 3,000 copies at most. Three years later, Day's son, Richard, who had inherited his father's privileges, together with five of his assigns, charged several printers and publishers with selling another 10,000 illegal copies of the same work, and three other men, including two senior members of the trade with printing yet another 15,000 pirate copies.[28] Perhaps the pirates thought they could dispose of thousands of copies so quickly as to evade detection by the authorities; perhaps they simply hoped to flood the market and so ruin the patentees' sales: either way they must have expected a ready sale for

---

[23] STC² 20.6–21.3, Wing² A36A–38B, and BL Catalogue, s.v. ABC.

[24] Baldwin, *Shakespere's Petty School*, 89–90, 94, 123–5.

[25] STC² 18711–11.5, 18711a–c; the fragments are in Worcester College Library (id. 20.6, and H. Anders, 'The Elizabethan ABC with the Catechism', *The Library*, 4th ser., 16 (1936), 32–4); in the Bodleian, according to Baldwin (*Shakespere's Petty School*, 124); and in the Library of Peterhouse College, Cambridge (I.8.54), which is the most complete but still lacks title-page and sig. Aii.

[26] For editions of the Book of Common Prayer, see Appendix 1, s.v. Book.   [27] *TSR* ii. 753–69.

[28] Ibid. i. 791; H. R. Hoppe, 'John Wolfe, Printer and Publisher, 1579–1601', *The Library*, 4th ser., 14 (1933–4), 261; on print runs, see above pp. 65, 67.

their copies. Equally, the determination of the patentees to see off these challenges, and similar trespasses in the 1590s, early 1600s, and 1620s,[29] suggest they were making a steady profit from its production. Similarly large quantities were being produced at the Restoration: research in progress by Helen Weinstein into the records of the English Stock of the Stationers' Company suggests that batches of five or ten thousand copies of the *ABC* were delivered to the Company's warehouse two, three, or even four times a year in the first dozen years of the reign of Charles II. Immediately after the Great Fire, for example, twenty reams (equivalent to 10,000 copies) of *ABC*, were printed to replenish the stocks then destroyed, and as late as the reigns of George II and George III sales of around 20,000 copies a year were still common.[30] If one posits only one edition a year, then something like 25,000 copies of *The ABC with the catechisme* were published every decade from the 1560s to the 1630s, and probably even more from the 1660s to the early eighteenth century as print runs were gradually increased. Two or even more editions a year might be nearer the mark if we compare it with works such as the Prayer Book and the Psalter, or the official grammar book of the day which often passed through two, three, or four editions a year during those decades.[31]

The partnership with *The primer and catechisme* is summarized in a jingle at the end of *The ABC with the catechisme*: 'This little catechism learned / by heart (for so it ought) / The PRIMER next commanded is / for children to be taught'.[32] The *Primer* in question had its origins in the late medieval idea of a short book containing a number of psalms and prayers to enable the literate laity to perform private devotions, though it had often doubled as an ABC too, and the idea of a reading 'primer'—a book on which to practise one's newly acquired reading skills—can still be found in the late seventeenth century. The Elizabethan *Primer and catechisme* was an abridged version of an Edwardian primer of 1553, which itself was the product of a series of hybrid works produced in the 1530s and 1540s. The *Primer* contained everything that the *ABC* did: alphabets, Prayer Book catechism and graces; but in addition it had a calendar and an almanac at the start, and at the end the services of morning and evening prayer and a number of prayers, psalms, and sentences of scripture.[33] Like its junior partner, the

---

[29] *TSR* ii. 824, and see below, n. 91; for a complaint by the Stationers' Company against the university press at Cambridge for infringement of their patent to print the *ABC*, see *TSR* iv. 527.

[30] The numbers of ABCs per ream is subject to different possible interpretations: I have taken the higher one (which seems defensible to me), but even the lower one provides striking totals. See H. Weinstein, 'Learning the ABC: Rudimentary Religion and National Identity in Seventeenth-Century England' (Ph.D. thesis in progress, Cambridge); Robin Myers, *The Records of the Stationers' Company 1554–1920*, 115 reels of microfilm (Chadwyck-Healey, Cambridge, 1989): *Books in the Treasurer's Warehouse 1663 to 1723*, reel 84 (no foliation); see also C. Blagden, *The Stationers' Company: A History 1403–1959* (London, 1960), 186, 242; and R. Myers, *The Stationers' Company Archive: An Account of the Records 1554–1984* (1990), 68.

[31] For the scale of production of the Book of Common Prayer, Sternhold and Hopkins's metrical psalms, and Lily's grammar, see STC² and Wing².

[32] Baldwin, *Shakespere's Petty School*, 124–5.

[33] H. C. White, *The Tudor Books of Private Devotion* (Wisconsin, 1951), chs. 4–6; C. C. Butterworth,

Primer was officially authorized, was mentioned in some school statutes, and recommended by some theorists of the day for use with young children.[34] It was reprinted sufficiently often in the early Stuart period for a deputation of binders to complain to the republican government, which suspended publication of the work in 1651, that they had been deprived of their livelihood; and after the Restoration it was soon being reprinted in large quantities, apparently even larger than those of the *ABC*.[35] Thus the accounts of the 'English school' (i.e. the lower forms) at Colfe's grammar school in 1660 record 'Paid for 12 primers' two shillings; and the register of the Great Yarmouth Children's Hospital shows that between 1698 and 1715 many boys and girls from poorer homes were taught to read the primer once they had learnt their letters on the hornbook.[36] Although the use of the *Primer* was supposed to follow that of the *ABC*, it may well have been used as an alternative to it: there seems little reason otherwise for the inclusion of the alphabets, unless perhaps to remind slow learners of the shape of different letters or the appearance of different type-faces. For slightly older students, however, it also had the advantage of containing not only the catechism they had to keep in their memory, but also the church services they were likely to have to attend on a Sunday or holy day, and the disadvantage of having psalms and verses of the sort that contemporary pedagogues loved to make their students memorize. The latest editions of which I have found copies date from 1775 and 1785.[37]

The association of literacy with mastery of a catechism is evident in the statutes and records of grammar schools of the late sixteenth and seventeenth centuries and in the Charity School regulations of the early eighteenth century. At the start of Elizabeth's reign, admission to the Merchant Taylors' school in London was open to those who had mastered the catechism in English or Latin, and could read perfectly and write competently.[38] At Burford in Oxfordshire in 1571, the school was to consist of 'petties' and 'grammarians', and when one of the former had mastered 'his ABC, catechism, primer, and to read and write' he would be transferred to the seniors.[39] A century later the founder of Hampton school indicated that the schoolmaster was to

---

'Early Primers for the Use of Children', *Papers of the Bibliog. Soc. of America*, 43 (1949), 374–8; E. Birchenough, 'The Prymer in English', *The Library*, 4th ser., 18 (1938), 177–94; Butterworth, *English Primers, passim*; Baldwin, *Shakespere's Petty School*, 64–7; STC² 16053–4, 16057, 16090–2, 20373–7, 20377.3–77.7.

[34] Baldwin, *Shakespere's Petty School*, chs. 1–4.

[35] Birchenough, 'Prymer', 194; *Books in the Treasurer's Warehouse* (as n. 30 above); and Weinstein, 'Learning the ABC'.

[36] L. L. Duncan, *The History of Colfe's Grammar School 1652–1952* (1952), 47; D. Cressy, *Literacy and the Social Order: Reading and Writing in Tudor and Stuart England* (Cambridge, 1980), 30–3. For an older person who learnt to read from the *Primer* rather than the *ABC*, see the case of Thomas Tryon: Spufford, 'First Steps', 416.

[37] See BL Catalogue, s.v. Primer.

[38] Baldwin, *Shakespere's Little Latine*, i. 398; and cf. Norwich and Almondbury: ibid., i. 415, and G. Hinchliffe, *A History of King James's Grammar School in Almondbury* (Huddersfield, 1931), 26–7.

[39] A. M. Stowe, *English Grammar Schools in the Reign of Queen Elizabeth* (New York, 1908), 105–6; and cf. St Bees in Cumberland: Baldwin, *Shakespere's Little Latine*, i. 432.

teach his pupils 'to write and read and to instruct them in their catechism, that they may know their duties both to God and man', and the regulations drawn up by the founders of the Charity School movement said that poor children were to be taught the church catechism, spelling, syllables, punctuation, and writing, and some other useful skill.[40]

These same sources and related ones also tell us a little of how this catechism was used with younger students. There is the occasional reference to the catechism being written out in English in the usher's forms, as an exercise both of writing and memory.[41] But the more common pattern was probably instruction through constant reading and oral repetition until all the pupils were word-perfect, as at the earl of Huntingdon's free school at Leicester where the youngest students were to be taught during the week to 'answer without book' that part of the catechism which they would have to 'answer in church on Sundays'.[42] In many grammar schools catechizing seems to have taken place on a Saturday, with the younger students in turn repeating the Prayer Book catechism to the usher or a senior student, while their elders tackled a larger form. Thus at Rivington on Saturdays and the eves of holy days, the usher was to 'exercise his younger sort in learning their short catechism in English' in the Prayer Book; they may also have had to sit in with their elders while the master read part of Nowell's or Calvin's catechism to 'all sorts', though they were excused from having to memorize it at that stage.[43] At Bosworth school in Leicestershire in the 1630s, the usher was to spend an hour once a fortnight teaching his charges the 'ordinary catechism' in the Prayer Book, while the master took matters a stage further with *his* pupils.[44] After the Restoration, other examples can be given of catechizing on Saturdays for an hour or more, for instance at Wigan, Bury St Edmunds, Lymm, Bristol, and Almondbury,[45] while in the original regulations for the Charity Schools, teachers were told to teach the church catechism twice a week, first teaching them 'to pronounce distinctly and plainly', and then at a later stage explaining it with the help of an exposition approved by the local minister. Parents of Charity School children were also 'frequently to call on them at home to repeat their

---

[40] B. Garside, *A Brief History of Hampton School 1557–1957* (Richmond, 1957), 11–12; anon., *An account of Charity-Schools lately erected* (1707), 3–6; Jones, *Charity School Movement*, 79–80.

[41] Stowe, *Grammar Schools*, 186–7; Baldwin, *Shakespere's Little Latin*, i. 388.

[42] M. C. Cross, *The Free Grammar School of Leicester* (Dept. of English Local History Occasional Papers, 4; Leicester, 1953), 15–18, 26–7.

[43] Baldwin, *Shakespere's Petty School*, 99–103; and cf. Brinsley, *Ludus literarius*, 254–5.

[44] S. Hopewell, *The Book of Bosworth School, 1320–1950* (Leicester, 1950), 138; and cf. N. Carlisle, *A Concise Description of the Endowed Grammar Schools in England and Wales* (2 vols.; 1818), i. 415, 419; and H. M. Luft, *A History of Merchant Taylors' School, Crosby* (Liverpool, 1970), 34; and on the 1650s, cf. *Dorchester-on-Thames Grammar School* (Dorchester-on-Thames Archaeology and Local History Group, 1976), 3; and F. Watson, *The English Grammar Schools to 1660* (Cambridge, 1908), 82.

[45] Ibid. 82; R. W. Elliott, *The Story of King Edward VI School Bury St. Edmunds* (Bury St Edmunds, 1963), 175; D. M. Kay, *The History of Lymm Grammar School* (Altrincham, 1960), 47; and Hinchliffe, *History of King James's Grammar School*, 68.

catechism', to read the Holy Scriptures, and to say their prayers twice a day; if parents neglected to do this, their children would be dismissed and their school clothes forfeit.[46]

The close connection between this elementary catechizing in school and the minister's efforts in church on Sunday is suggested not only by the fact that Saturday was the preferred day for the teachers' contribution, but also by the occasions on which the minister used the Sunday session either to test knowledge of the church catechism, or to instruct catechumens in the meaning of the catechism. Most Elizabethan and Stuart school statutes prescribed attendance at church on Sundays and holy days which would have put such pupils within the orbit of ministerial catechizing on that day.[47] There is also the occasional strong injunction for pupils to be catechized on Sundays as well as weekdays, as at Chigwell in Essex, where the founder wished the scholars of his free schools to be taught the Prayer Book catechism on Saturday afternoons,

that they may by this means be seasoned and prepared to receive public instruction, by way of catechizing from the vicar in the church, which I more desire than the seasoning them with learning.[48]

At Wigan in 1664 it was laid down that scholars were to submit 'to be publicly catechized as the rector of Wigan or his curate shall from time to time appoint'; and in the early 1700s there is evidence of a twice-yearly examination of the grammar-school students at Christ's Hospital, London, who had all been called upon 'several times … every week … to repeat their catechism and have it expounded to them'.[49] In Charity Schools the master or mistress was to wait until a number of children could say the catechism, and then give notice to the minister of the parish in which the school was set up 'in order to their being catechized in the church'. In the reign of Queen Anne, large-scale public examinations of these pupils in their spelling and reading skills and religious knowledge were held on the second Sunday of each month in eight London churches, beginning at five in the evening; these were said (rather cynically) to have proved to be a good way of raising subscriptions from the adults who attended.[50]

Outside London with a more scattered distribution of schools, such examinations as there were were probably usually on a smaller scale and less frequent. The replies

---

[46] Anon., *Orders read and given to the parents on the admittance of children into the Charity-Schools* (1708)—a single sheet 'to be set up in their houses' (copy in Bodleian); the orders stressed that the school would in this way serve to instruct also parents who could not read.

[47] Stowe, *Grammar Schools*, 147–52; Baldwin, *Shakespere's Petty School*, ch. 4; Simon, *Education and Society*, 240–1, 308, 326; W. A. L. Vincent, *The Grammar Schools: Their Continuing Tradition* (London, 1969), 88–9.

[48] Carlisle, *Endowed Grammar Schools*, i. 519; the founder was an archbishop and an alleged 'Arminian' to boot: Fincham, *Prelate as Pastor*, 243–6, 279–88.

[49] Watson, *Grammar Schools*, 82; T. Cooke, *A brief but plain explication of the church-catechism* (1706), sig. a3ʳ.

[50] Anon., *An account of Charity-Schools lately erected* (1707), 6, 32.

to the questionnaires sent out by Wake and other bishops in the early eighteenth century nevertheless show not only a large number of schools in which the church catechism was being taught, but also in a number of cases a degree of interaction between catechizing in school and in church. The third question that Wake, Gibson, and Herring asked their clergy was as follows:

Is there any public or Charity School, endowed, or otherwise maintained in your parish? What numbers of children are taught in it? And what care is taken to instruct them in the principles of the Christian religion, according to the doctrine of the Church of England; and to bring them duly to church, as the canon requires?[51]

The wording of this question led to some confusion. The reference to 'public or Charity School' and to endowment or other form of maintenance seems to have persuaded many clergy that the bishops were enquiring about only well-established grammar schools or newly established Charity Schools. As a result there were many negative returns, even where the answer to question nine (on catechizing) then went on to say that the children were taught the catechism by 'the schoolmaster', who was presumably operating a private school without a permanent endowment or outside the Charity School movement's umbrella.[52] Other clergy replied that they had 'only' an old widow or the parish clerk to teach children their letters and the church catechism, as at Moor Monkton in Yorkshire in 1743, where 'a poor woman teaches a few small children to read, and say the catechism', and at nearby Barwick in Elmet whence it was reported 'we have no Charity School or other school endowed but one taught in the English tongue by the clerk of the parish who is careful to instruct children in the principles of the Christian religion and brings them duly to church'.[53] Other clergy took 'otherwise maintained' to include any form of schooling, even by parents, and so readily provided details of even the most elementary or informal kinds of teaching.[54] But in general there is probably some under-representation in the reporting of schooling at the lowest levels. The reference in the second sentence of Wake's question to instruction in 'the principles of the Christian religion, according to the doctrine of the Church of England' was also ambiguous. It seems to have persuaded some respondents to use exactly the same words in their replies (like the rector of Barwick in Elmet above), whereas others assumed quite rightly from the reference to the canon (number 79 of 1604) that these phrases were a synonym for the use of an approved catechism.[55] Hence the rector of Adel in Yorkshire said that

---

[51] Wake MS 284, 1; Gibson 13, p. 1 (Gibson omitted the word 'duly'); Herring, *York*, i. 2; Secker's questions on schools were placed later than the one on catechizing, and concentrated on funding and other arrangements rather than religious content of the instruction provided: *Oxford*, 4–5.

[52] Herring, *York*, i. 189–90; ii. 83; Gibson 13, p. 579.

[53] Herring, *York*, i. 44; ii. 474; and cf. Wake MS 284, fo. 332ᵛ, and Gibson 13, p. 347.

[54] See following paragraphs, and for parental instruction the section on domestic catechizing at the end of this chapter.

[55] *The order and rules of the charity-school* [1701?] also referred to the principles of the Church of England 'as they are laid down in the church catechism' (p. 5).

the twenty-five poor children in the school in his parish 'are instructed and catechized as the canon requires'; and the curate of Horbury chapel near Doncaster replied that forty to fifty children were 'taught to read and write and to give an account of their faith, according to the church-catechism'.[56] Given the status of most of the teachers (to which we will come shortly) and the regular references to the catechumens being brought to church, we may safely assume that in most of those replies in which it was stated that there was instruction in 'Christian principles' or 'according to the doctrine of the Church of England', this instruction took the form of catechizing using the church catechism. Where a teacher was a dissenter, it was usually pointed out in the clergy's reply, though there is the occasional case of such a teacher instructing his pupils in the official catechism while declining to attend church with them.[57]

The fullest replies to question three were made by the clergy in Canterbury and York dioceses. Among the 219 replies from East Kent, there were reports of at least 68 schools or teachers using the church catechism or teaching Christian principles according to the church's doctrine; in Yorkshire, the equivalent figures are just over 250 out of 644.[58] Given that there was probably some under-representation, these proportions of about one-third and two-fifths are not unimpressive. The types of teachers mentioned in these replies were quite varied. There is an isolated scathing reference to 'vagabond fellows who stay briefly',[59] but most teachers appear to have been very respectable, if poor. In St Dunstan's parish in Canterbury, a poor widow and regular church attender, Mrs Brown, taught children the church catechism; and at nearby Fordwich a dame taught a few children the catechism and brought them to church to be 'catechized' by the minister.[60] In other dioceses, too, we hear of 'dames', a 'poor woman', a widow not able to get a teacher's licence but able to teach 'Christian principles according to the catechism of the Church of England', and of 'poor, honest, sober, and well-meaning persons' able to teach reading and the church catechism.[61] Where these teachers were deemed insufficiently equipped to teach the catechism, the minister might step in, as at Doddington and Newnham in Kent where the minister taught the pupils himself on Sundays and after school in the vicarage.[62]

Another commonly mentioned category of teacher was the Charity School teacher. Not only the regulations of the Charity School movement as a whole, but the statutes or regulations of individual schools put a stress on the piety and conformability of the teachers and the importance of religious instruction in school and attendance at church.[63] Many of these schools were supported by donations from parishioners, often including the incumbent, and there are regular reports of

[56]   Herring, *York*, i. 6; ii, 41, and cf. ii. 159, and Gibson 15, p. 42.
[57]   Herring, *York*, i. 74; ii. 210.   [58]   Wake MS 284, and Herring, *York*, vols. i–iii, *passim*.
[59]   Gibson 14, p. 177.   [60]   Wake MS 284, fos. 64ᵛ, 66ᵛ, and cf. 265ᵛ.
[61]   Lincoln 13, pp. 222, 374, 406; Lincoln 15, p. 42; Secker, *Oxford*, 29; Herring, *York*, i. 77.
[62]   Wake MS 284, fos. 252ᵛ and 267ᵛ.
[63]   Vincent, *Grammar Schools*, 86–90, 112; Jones, *Charity School Movement*, 96–102, 104–9; and e.g. Wake MS 284, fo. 178ᵛ; Lincoln 13, p. 26.

the children being taught to read and write and 'get by heart' the church catechism, and being brought to church, as at Maidstone in 1716, where three Charity Schools, maintained by subscription, clothed and educated eighty children in all, taught them the church catechism, and ensured they went to church every day.[64] In some cases the teacher of the Charity School might also be the parish clerk, as at Skipwith in Yorkshire, who was 'very capable of it', according to the incumbent.[65] In many other cases, however, the parish clerk operated independently of the Charity School scheme, but in partnership with the incumbent of the parish. At Littlebourne in Kent, where the incumbent had been ill for some time, the parish clerk kept a school and catechized the older children himself, while his wife catechized the younger children at their house every Thursday; both were supplied with advice and catechetical literature by the minister.[66] At Sittingbourne, the incumbent paid the clerk and his wife, 'both very sober persons', to teach in the vestry, while at Eastchurch the incumbent paid the parish clerk to teach a few poor children in one of the side chancels of the church which had a separate entrance; in both cases the clergy checked that the clerk was teaching the catechism properly.[67] At Wyberton in Lincolnshire, the parish clerk taught twenty boys to read, write, cast accounts, sing psalms, and say the church catechism, while the minister catechized them sometimes upon Fridays, 'to prepare the scholars for more public examination' in church on Sundays after the second lesson at evening prayer; and from Thornton in Yorkshire it was reported that the parish clerk taught the children 'the principles of the Christian religion, and brings 'em regularly to church on Wednesdays and Fridays in Lent to be catechized'.[68] One is reminded strongly of the reliance on the sexton in those German villages in the early stages of the Lutheran reformation where the minister and teacher were unable or unwilling to undertake basic instruction in the catechism themselves.[69]

Where the teacher was reported to be a clergyman, this did not necessarily mean that he had a cure of souls: despite some moves towards the professionalization of the teaching profession, it was still a not uncommon situation for ordained men to act as full-time teachers.[70] As might be expected, these teachers took care to ensure that their charges were taught the church catechism and brought to church, as at the

---

[64] Wake MS 284, fos. 314[v], 424[r], 395[v]; and cf. Gibson 13, pp. 26, 358; Gibson 15, p. 312; Herring, *York*, iii. 96.

[65] Ibid. iii. 105.

[66] Wake MS 284, fo. 30[r]: the minister gave them copies of expositions by Williams, Beveridge, Newcome, and others.

[67] Ibid., fos. 349[v]–350[r], 322[v]–323[r].

[68] Gibson 14, pp. 300–1, and cf. Gibson 15, pp. 38–9; Herring, *York*, iii. 174, and cf. 197. 'Catechized' here, as in some other examples cited in these paragraphs, probably refers to the *testing* of knowledge of the catechism.

[69] Strauss, *Luther's House of Learning*, 167, 194, 198, 277, 281.

[70] Vincent, *Grammar Schools*, 112–16, 119–22; O'Day, *Education and Society*, ch. 9; and e.g. Wake MS 284, fos. 307[v], 405[r]; Gibson 15, pp. 400–1; Herring, *York*, i. 55.

grammar school at Beverley in Yorkshire where a hundred boys were instructed on Saturdays by their long-serving teacher, John Clark, prior to their being catechized in church by the incumbent on Sunday afternoons in Lent.[71] In other cases, the teacher might be the curate of the parish, or even the incumbent, on either a regular or irregular basis. In one East Riding parish, where the curate received £20 per annum to teach fifteen to sixteen children, his duties included teaching and explaining the church catechism to them and bringing them to church; while in two Lincolnshire parishes we find examples of clergy teaching the poor children of the parish without charge.[72] There are also several examples of a minister paying for the basic education of the children of the poorer members of his congregation out of his own pocket, or ensuring that funds were diverted from the communion collection to the same end. Thus at Boxley in Kent there was no endowed school, but the incumbent reported that 'I put the children of poor people to be taught reading and the church-catechism from the surplus of oblations that remain in my hands'; and at Cornwell in Oxfordshire the school was supported by 'sacrament-money', which paid for a widow to teach children to read and to learn the church catechism.[73] There are also many examples of clergy dropping into the local school, either to watch the teacher as he catechized the children, or to do some teaching or testing himself, or to explain the meaning of part of the catechism; and as we have seen there are isolated cases of a minister inviting the schoolchildren to his house to be taught there after school or service hours.[74] A Lincolnshire incumbent told Wake that since parents were very remiss in sending children and servants to church to be catechized, 'I sometimes go to the school and catechize them there'.[75]

These last examples form but a few of the many threads in the web which linked catechizing in school to catechizing in church by the first half of the eighteenth century. On Sundays the minister could choose to play one or more roles. He might choose merely to test the schoolchildrens' knowledge of the church catechism by the routine question–and–answer technique (and perhaps as a model to those catechumens who were not at school or had not yet learnt it).[76] To quote but two examples from Yorkshire, 'we have a small school, wherein fourteen or fifteen children learn to read, and to say their catechism, whereof they frequently give a very good account in the church'; and 'the master takes so great care to teach his scholars their catechism

---

[71] Ibid. i. 104; and cf. Gibson 15, pp. 400–1.

[72] Herring, *York*, ii. 85, and cf. i. 58, 93–4; Gibson 13, pp. 394–5; Gibson 14, p. 164.

[73] Wake MS 284, fos. 369ᵛ, and cf. 50ᵛ, 69ʳ, 123ᵛ, 252ᵛ, 369ʳ, 395ᵛ; Gibson 13, p. 502; Secker, *Oxford*, 8, 33, 35, 47, 117, 144, 170–1; and for a bishop urging his clergy to help in the education of poor children in their parishes, see *Diary of Francis Evans, Secretary to Bishop Lloyd, 1699–1706*, ed. D. Robertson, (Worcestershire Historical Society, 45; 1903), 16.

[74] Herring, *York*, i. 35, 98–9; ii. 83; iii. 93; Gibson 14, p. 93; Gibson 15, p. 155; and above, nn. 62, 67.

[75] Gibson 13, p. 479.

[76] e.g. Gibson 13, pp. 74–5, 106–7, 402–3, 498, 554–5, 571, 602–3; Gibson 14, pp. 502–3, 588; Gibson 15, pp. 30–1, 38–9, 110–11, 312–13.

that I never meet with any that say it so well'.[77] Alternatively, the minister might decide to spend part of his time on a Sunday going a step further and explaining the meaning of part of the catechism which the scholars had just learnt or recited; again there are a number of examples of this too.[78] It is interesting to see the incumbent of two Lincolnshire parishes using 'a short exposition which I have made for that purpose' after the second lesson on Sunday afternoons in summer, since we know from his replies to Gibson that there were schools in those parishes.[79] Finally, a minister might move on to teaching them a further catechism, such as Lewis's or Wake's exposition of the church catechism, of which again there are a number of examples.[80] Indeed, from some replies it is clear that some children had already started to master an exposition of the Prayer Book catechism in school before they were tested on it in church. At Milton-next-Sittingbourne in Kent the schoolchildren were taught first the church catechism then Lewis's exposition, 'which is short and plain and easily to be understood', and were then tested on both on Sunday afternoons in summer.[81]

So strong had the equation between primary education and catechizing become by the early eighteenth century, if not earlier, that some clergymen sought to excuse their failure to catechize on a Sunday by saying there was no school in the parish. The excuse offered in some cases was that the young people in the parish could not read, as if mastering the catechism required literacy.[82] In other cases incumbents implied that their task was merely to test knowledge already acquired by catechumens elsewhere, at school or home.[83] But such clergy were a small minority, and most of the clergy who replied to the episcopal questionnaires do not seem to have regarded illiteracy or the absence of local schools as barriers to teaching or learning the catechism. Conversely, many clergy clearly realized the value of education as a support to catechizing, and would rather have had this support than not. As the vicar of Digby in Lincolnshire wrote in 1721, the fact that the children were so well trained in the church catechism by the two teachers in the parish made the duty of catechizing so much easier for him.[84]

So far in this chapter we have concentrated on the use of the church catechism in schools, but before we move on to tackle school catechizing at a more advanced level,

---

[77] Herring, *York*, i. 58; iii. 14–15, and cf. 119; and Gibson 15, p. 348.

[78] Gibson 13, pp. 34–5; Gibson 14, pp. 209, 462–3, 554–5, 582–3; Gibson 15, pp. 94–5, 506–7.

[79] Gibson 14, pp. 394–5, 450–1; and cf. Gibson 15, pp. 94–5.

[80] Gibson 13, pp. 6–7, 10–11, 18–19, 102–3; Gibson 14, pp. 196–7, 232–3, 300–1, 304–5; and Gibson 15, pp. 2–3, 237, 248–9, 252–3, 396–7.

[81] Wake MS fo. 336^r, and cf. fos. 220^r, 309^r, 394^r; and cf. Gibson 14, pp. 256–7, and Secker, *Oxford*, 13.

[82] Cf. Herring, *York*, i. 213, 220; ii. 131, 195, etc.; Wake MS 284, fo. 348^r; Secker, *Oxford*, 98, 158; and cf. N. Sykes, *Edmund Gibson Bishop of London 1669–1748* (Oxford, 1926), 227–8.

[83] Wake MS 284, fo. 298^r; Gibson 13, p. 223; Gibson 15, p. 237; Herring, *York*, ii. 180; iii. 188.

[84] Gibson 14, pp. 44–5; and cf. Gibson 13, p. 617. See also Ch. 5 below.

we should perhaps consider one of the caveats mentioned above: that not all teachers used the elementary forms they were supposed to use. On this point, such evidence as there is does seem to support the conclusion reached by Dr John Morgan, in his recent study of puritan attitudes towards education in Elizabethan and early Stuart England, that 'most schools seem to have confined themselves to the approved catechism, protestant colloquies, and the mandatory primer'.[85] But there were a few schools where forms other than the officially approved ones were used, either as alternatives or supplements. Some authors of school statutes were less than precise on which catechism was to be used, while others, at least at the very outset before the official pattern was clearly established, specified alternative forms.[86] Thus Calvin's catechism was prescribed in the statutes for the schools at Leicester in 1574 and Ashby-de-la-Zouch in 1575; we also know that the first book bought for Philip Sidney when he entered Shrewsbury school in 1564 was Calvin's catechism.[87] It is possible that the long catechism written by Thomas Becon and recommended for use in the school at Sandwich in Kent in 1577—*The demaundes of holy scripture*—was used there.[88] 'Besides our ordinary catechisms by law established', the 'godly' schoolmaster John Brinsley recommended Perkins's *Foundation* 'for the further unfolding and demonstrating of the principles' of religion; and looking back from the 1650s, Charles Hoole described the school week of a Mr Bonner, an experienced schoolmaster at Rotherham, which included spending part of Thursday afternoons teaching the church catechism and Perkins's *Foundation*.[89] Perkins's catechism continued to be published after the Restoration, and in a copy of the 1677 edition in the Bodleian there is an inscription on the back: 'This book was given me per [by the] Company of Haberdashers the 9th day of December 1681. J. Crompton his book'; perhaps young Crompton was receiving a bursary from the Merchant Haberdashers Company or had just become one of their apprentices.[90]

It also seems more than likely that the catechisms prepared by schoolteachers like John Stockwood and Richard Jones in the 1580s, Edmund Coote in the 1590s, and Herbert Palmer in the 1630s were used by them in their own schools. Stockwood was schoolmaster at Tonbridge in Kent from 1578 to 1585, and prepared a revised form

---

[85] J. Morgan, *Godly Learning: Puritan Attitudes towards Reason, Learning, and Education, 1560–1640* (Cambridge, 1986), 184; the colloquies mentioned were works by Châteillon and Cordier much beloved by educational theorists with a humanist background: cf. Baldwin, *Shakespere's Little Latine*, i. 343, 444, 503, and Appendix 1.

[86] M. Cox, *A History of Sir John Deane's Grammar School Northwich* (Manchester, 1975), 39–40; Baldwin, *Shakespere's Little Latine*, i. 425; R. Watts and M. Hunt, *The History of King James's Grammar School Knaresborough* (n.p., 1966), 3; and Morgan, *Godly Learning*, 186–7.

[87] Cross, *Free Grammar School*, 16–18; L. Fox, *A Country Grammar School: A History of Ashby-de-la-Zouch School* (Oxford, 1967), 10–12; Simon, *Education and Society*, 326.

[88] See Appendix 1: its unusual structure—commonplaces culled from Becon's other works—may have appealed to teachers accustomed to studying and producing commonplace books.

[89] J. Brinsley, *A consolation for our grammar schooles* (1622), 79; Hoole, *New discovery*, 298–304.

[90] Bodleian Library, Douce A.385(3).

of the Dering and More catechism; the presence of an ABC on the reverse of the title-page of editions of this work published between 1590 and 1603 gives an indication of his intended target.[91] Jones was a teacher in South Wales, and his catechism was a modified version of the form by Paget and Openshaw, with the addition at the end of four quotations showing Christ examining his pupils.[92] Edmund Coote's best-selling *English schoolmaster* contained not only graded exercises to teach children how to read, but also included a very short catechism covering all the usual staples, a prayer formed around that catechism, more prayers, improving verses from the Bible to learn, and religious texts to copy. However, Coote was also aiming at tradesmen and craftsmen who were responsible for teaching apprentices; one advantage of his little work, he said was that 'it could be propped up on a counting-house desk and used to hear lessons without undue interruption of work'.[93] Herbert Palmer's intended target, by contrast, was those of 'the meanest capacities ... and weakest memories', including perhaps those in the school he taught in a remote part of rural Hertfordshire. He was also concerned to test comprehension as well as memory, as we shall see later.[94]

A clutch of works produced in the late 1640s and early 1650s may reflect both the temporary fall from official favour of the catechism in the *ABC* and *Primer*, and a growing demand for an alternative catechism for use in schools. The *Summe of Christian religion* composed for private use in a country parish, school, and family and published in 1649, had some parallels with the Westminster Shorter Catechism.[95] In 1652 John Owen, the leading Independent of the day, took time off from writing advanced theological and polemical works to produce *The primer: or, an easie way to teach children*—a reading primer, but with a short 'necessary catechism' to teach the young the grounds of Christian religion, and suitable scripture readings and prayers.[96] In the same year, the episcopalian Jeremy Taylor published a short catechism for use in schools in South Wales, including the school at Golden Grove in which he himself was then teaching,[97] and in 1654 Lambrocke Thomas, a vicar in Sussex and doctor in divinity, produced a reading primer entitled *Milke for children* which contained a short catechism, a dialogue enlarging on the same, and exposition of the Creed, Ten Commandments, and Lord's Prayer in prose; this was said to be for ministers, teachers, and parents to use with the 'ruder sort' and the young.[98] In

---

[91] A 1577 edition of Dering and More, *Briefe and necessary instruction* and the 1590, 1595, 1597, and 1603 editions of Dering, More, and Stockwood, *A short catechisme for housholders*, all had an ABC on the title-page verso, but this was prohibited in 1606; and see above n. 29.

[92] R. Jones, *A briefe and necessarie catechisme* [1609], sigs. C7ʳ–8ᵛ; the short pre-communion form added by Jones also made his form suitable for older students and adults.

[93] See Appendix 1, s.v. Coote; Simon, *Education and Society*, 383.

[94] See Appendix 1, s.v. Palmer; see also below, pp. 260–1.   [95] See Appendix 1.

[96] Ibid.; Helen Weinstein has suggested that the fact that Owen's work was 'approved and allowed by a committee of Parliament' may mean that it was designed as an official alternative to the old *Primer*.

[97] See Appendix 1.   [98] Ibid.

the same year, George Dochant, a minister and teacher at a private school, produced a very short catechism to help prepare the younger sort, and especially those at 'Shaffham School' in Norfolk, for communion.[99]

After the return of the old ways in 1660 and the onset of further persecution in 1662, different nonconformist groups also decided to produce their own reading primers, presumably for use in schools and homes rather than congregations. Such was the *Primer and catechism* which the Quakers George Fox and Ellis Hookes published first in 1670 and in a revised version in 1673; eight editions may have been published by 1700.[100] The Baptist Benjamin Keach produced two reading primers entitled *Instructions for children* and *The child's delight* which passed through various manifestations and many editions between the 1660s and the mid-eighteenth century. The *Instructions* contained an ABC and syllables, suitable reading material and precepts, and no less than three catechisms, for a little child, a child, and a youth; *The child's delight* contained an ABC, a small dictionary, lessons on how to tell the time, count coins, and make simple calculations, a catechism, a confession of faith, godly verses, prayers, and woodcuts of a number of scriptural characters.[101] Various other examples of reading primers with catechisms (and much else) in them appeared in the 1690s and 1700s, again probably nonconformist in provenance.[102] But by then the commercial potential of such works had become clear. A number of works with *School* in the title were probably part of that speculative but apparently very successful market in cheap religious pamphlets that had developed by the later seventeenth century: *The school of grace* by 'John Hart' (perhaps nineteen editions by 1688); *The school of learning* (57 editions by 1687); *The school of holiness ... together with a short catechism* (14 editions by 1686); *The school of piety*; and so on.[103] These either contained short catechisms, lists of moral precepts, scripture passages to learn or questions and answers on the Bible; they may have been aimed at children or those with limited reading skills, but were probably used more for self-education than formal education in school. For most pupils, the norm almost certainly remained the equally cheap *ABC* and *Primer*.

Having acquired the ability to read and to memorize a catechism, schoolchildren were then expected to move on to another plane, either by demonstrating the ability to understand the contents of that catechism and the will to put it into practice, or by

---

[99] Ibid.; cf. also the arrangements made by Hoole in the 1650s: *New discovery*, p. xvii, 53, 59.
[100] See Appendix 1.   [101] Ibid.
[102] Ibid., s.v. W. Scoffin, *A help to true spelling* (1690? and 1705); *The second book for children* (1704), which was probably a partner of *The first book*, which also had a catechism; and the *Spelling-book for children* (1707); Joseph Jacob's *The scripture instructor* (1701) cannot now be traced, but for his surviving catechism, see Appendix 1.
[103] See Appendix 1, s.v. Hart, and *School*.

mastering a more advanced catechism or exposition, or the same catechism in a new language. At first the church seems to have favoured the former tactic—learning a new form, but by the later seventeenth century or even earlier had come round to the latter. The idea of students progressing from one form to another was not completely new: Colet's students at St Pauls had been expected to move on from his own 'cate-chyzon' to a work prepared for him by his friend Erasmus— the *Institutum Christiani hominis*, a collection of precepts in verse.[104] And as early as 1553, a form had been issued with the king's consent for schoolboys to learn after the Prayer Book form of 1549: this was John Ponet's *Catechismus brevis*—a long and demanding form in Latin, in which the author tackled the sacraments as well as the other three staples. Four editions were published in rapid succession, though a version in English was soon prepared for those not yet proficient enough in Latin to use the original. However, since this version was published with the most recent set of doctrinal articles approved in Convocation, it was also at the eye of the storm that broke at the young Edward's death, so that only one edition of it had appeared by the time that Mary came to the throne.[105]

By the 1560s and 1570s opinion seems to have moved in favour of two alternatives to Ponet: the catechisms of John Calvin and Alexander Nowell. An English translation of Calvin's catechism for 10- to 15-year-olds had been published in London in 1550, and again in Geneva in 1556, and after the accession of Elizabeth it was reprinted in England a dozen times between 1560 and 1598 and several times in Scotland as well.[106] Although it was recommended for use by petties in some English schools in the 1560s and 1570s, it was several times longer than the Prayer Book catechism and much more suited to middle or upper forms than beginners. At Harrow in the 1580s, for example, the master was supposed to read a lecture from Calvin's or Nowell's catechism every Sunday and holy day to those of his scholars whom he thought would benefit, and in 1579 Calvin's form was recommended for use by undergraduates at Oxford.[107] The simple fact was that in the early 1560s Calvin's catechism had a head start over poten-tial rivals. It had been used in that most perfect school of Christ—Geneva—which gave the form cachet in many exiles' minds; it was available in multiple copies in print (whereas Nowell's remained in manuscript until 1570); and for those teachers who liked to move from a catechism in one language to the same form in another, from 1562 there was a Latin version available in print in England too; there was also a version in Greek, by Estienne and later revised by Berchet, though at this stage copies of this probably had to be obtained from abroad.[108] The fact that after 1574–5 (the years in

---

[104] Watson, *Grammar Schools*, 72–3, 79–80; and for Erasmus's *Dilucida et pia explanatio symboli* (often called his 'catechismus'), see *Opera Omnia Desiderii Erasmi Roterodami* 5.3 (Amsterdam/Oxford, 1977), 179–81, and Appendix 1, s.v. Erasmus.

[105] See below, Appendix 1.   [106] Ibid.

[107] See above, n. 87; Baldwin, *Shakespere's Little Latine*, i. 311; and below, p. 197.

[108] See Appendix 1, s.v. Calvin; no editions of the Greek translation seem to have been published in

which the Leicester and Ashby-de-la-Zouch statutes stipulated the use of Calvin's catechism) it is hard to find examples of Calvin's form being prescribed for beginners or even intermediate students, probably has something to do with the fact that it was in 1575 that the complete set of Nowell forms in English, Latin, and Greek was available in print.

From the early 1570s, the author whose work was mentioned most often in school statutes and in visitation articles enquiring about religious instruction in schools was Alexander Nowell, whose two main contributions to the welfare of mankind were as the author of a famous catechism and the inventor of bottled beer.[109] The historian's problem when trying to come to terms with the deployment of Nowell's work is that there was not one but six versions of Nowell's original text in print by 1575, and two (or three) more works which both then and since have been attributed to Nowell though only a small part of them were his work. Of this tribe of 'Nowells', the patriarch was the original full-length catechism in Latin which he had composed by the early 1560s. Nowell had been appointed master of Westminster School in 1543 and, after his return from exile under Mary, it was to him that Convocation had turned for a catechism to follow the 1549 form. This was ready to be viewed by Convocation in 1562 and, like Ponet's, was composed in Latin, to help less educated clergy and 'studious youth' perfect their knowledge of that language and of sound religion. Publication was delayed until 1570, but then it was translated into English, by Thomas Norton, and in 1573 a version in Greek and Latin appeared, the Greek translation being the work of Nowell's nephew, William Whitaker.[110] Moreover, as he had promised in the preface of his *Catechismus*, Nowell soon prepared a condensed version of his original work, again in Latin, and this was also translated into English by Norton and into Greek by Whitaker. The boiled-down version in English was said to be for those who had mastered the 1549 catechism and were 'desirous of further instruction' but found Nowell's full-length original 'too long and tedious either for their capacity or leisure'. In 1572 Nowell proudly claimed that all ages and capacities were now catered for: as the 1549 form was 'most meet for the first entering of children', so the condensed version would provide a 'middle catechism' in English for those who had profited from the 1549 form but were 'yet desirous of further instruction'; and if those who had studied the middle catechism wanted to know more of the reasons and proofs of the main points of Christian religion, they could move on to his original form, in English.[111] The Latin and Greek versions of the full-length and

England before the 1640s; and on the same form being studied in different languages, see A. F. Leach, *History of Winchester College*, 273 (cited by Stowe, *Grammar Schools*, 185, though the date must be later than that given); and Hoole, *New discovery*, xvii–xix.

[109] See article on Nowell in *DNB*.

[110] Ibid.; Cardwell, *Synodalia*, ii. 496; below Appendix 1, s.v. Nowell, and A. Nowell, *A catechisme, or first instruction*, ed. G. E. Corrie (Parker Society; Cambridge, 1853), 108.

[111] Appendix 1, and A. Nowell, *A catechisme, or institution* (1572), sigs. A1ᵛ–2ʳ. STC² seems to imply

condensed versions of Nowell's form were clearly designed for those studying classical languages, especially in school, as the prefaces make clear.

Compared to the three versions of the full-length original form and the three of the condensed version (in Latin, Greek and Latin, and English in each case), the other three members of the tribe of Nowell were more in the nature of foster children. There were almost certainly three, but only two survive in complete copies: the *Catechismus parvus pueris primus Latine* of 1573, and the *Catechismus parvus ... Latine et Graece* of 1574, with Whitaker once again doing the honours. Although often referred to as Nowell's 'shorter' form as opposed to his 'larger' original and 'middle' condensed, this is more than a trifle misleading, since the 'shorter' is basically the Prayer Book form of 1549 with a much enlarged section on duties after the answers on the Decalogue, and a new section on the sacraments added at the end. For Nowell's authorship of the new sections there is moderately good evidence: in the initials A.N. in the preface of surviving editions of the 'shorter'; in Whitaker's statement in the Greek-Latin 'middle' version that Nowell had composed three catechisms; and the fact that the new questions and answers on the sacraments in the 'shorter', derive in part from Nowell's 'larger' or 'middle' form.[112] Some bishops appear to have seen a version of this 'shorter' form in English in 1571 to judge from their subsequent commendation in visitation articles of 'the little English catechism with the right use of the sacraments lately set forth' or the catechism 'lately set out with certain additions' by Dean Nowell.[113] But, as mentioned above, the English version of this enlargement of the 1549 form appears to have been published only in new editions of the *ABC with the catechisme*, not in repeat editions of the Book of Common Prayer; and apart from a nearly complete copy of a late edition dated 1601, only fragments remain of this Nowell foster-child in English, so that we have to take it on trust that the English version was exactly the same as the 'shorter' catechism in Latin and Greek, of which copies do survive.[114] There are only a few copies still extant of these last two of Nowell's foster children: the 'shorter' in Latin and in Latin and Greek, due perhaps to limited demand or rough handling; but their existence suggests that schoolmasters thought there was a need in the lower or middle forms of a grammar school for works that were simpler and shorter than Ponet's catechism and Nowell's full-length and 'middle' versions.

that Thomas Norton made the abridgement of the 'larger' into the 'middle' version, and lists a first English edition of the 'middle' dated 1572 and the first surviving Latin edition of the 'middle' dated 1574. But in the preface of the 1572 'middle' version in English 'A.N.' says *he* abridged the original, and in the preface of the first surviving edition of the Latin 'middle' version, Nowell refers to one friend translating it into English and another into Greek. Either way, it does not make much difference to the situation after 1574.

[112] See article on Nowell in *DNB*; H. Anders, 'The Elizabethan ABC with the Catechism', *The Library*, 4th ser., 16 (1936), 33–4; and Baldwin, *Shakespere's Petty School*, 89–90, 123–3; neither the *DNB* article nor the Baldwin sections can be relied on in every detail.

[113] Baldwin, loc. cit.; Frere, *Visitation Articles*, iii. 328, 376; Kennedy, *Episcopal Administration*, ii. 43.

[114] See above, p. 175; the 1601 copy of *The ABC with the catechism* is in the Library of Peterhouse, Cambridge: I.8.54; for Latin and Greek versions, see Appendix 1, s.v. Nowell.

Our problem is trying to determine which of the tribe of Nowells were actually used in the schools of the period.[115] The relevant canon of 1571 ran as follows:

Schoolmasters shall teach no ... other Latin catechism than that which was set forth in the year 1570. The which also, that is translated into English, we will have taught unto children that are ignorant of the Latin tongue.[116]

This clearly refers to the original 'larger' Nowell version of 1570, in Latin and English, but left the status of the other six or seven forms, apparently first published after the convocation of 1571 had finished sitting, in limbo. Nor was this picked up in canon 79 of the 1604 canons which read: 'All schoolmasters shall teach in English or Latin, as the children are able to bear, the longer or shorter catechism, heretofore by public authority set forth',[117] presumably the original Nowell and the Prayer Book form of 1549. Only occasionally do we find references to the existence of more than one form by Nowell, as in the school statutes at Leicester in 1574, and the licence to teach in London given to a William Swetnam in 1599 which ordered him to teach 'the catechisms made and set forth by Mr Alexander Nowell'.[118] Equally the school statutes at Oundle specified the use of 'Mr Nowell's little catechism' in the second form and his 'large catechism' in the third, though in which language is not clear.[119]

To help us cut through this web, we can try a mixture of common sense and bibliographical evidence. For the students in the lower to middling forms of a grammar school which are our current interest, one may hazard a guess that if they were required to read and memorize a form in English after they had learnt the Prayer Book form, as at Oundle and Winchester, it would have been the 'middle' version of Nowell that they tried to master. This conclusion is based mainly on the absence of editions of the full-length Nowell catechism in English after 1577 and the much higher number of editions of the 'middle' version in English that were printed between the 1570s and the 1630s. As was pointed out above, the woodcut of a school interior on the cover, the use of 'master' and 'scholar' for the characters involved, and the inclusion of prayers for 'scholars' at the end all point to this form being used primarily in schools.[120] If, on the other hand, the younger students were using a catechism to improve their Latin, then it was probably the *Catechismus parvus pueris*

---

[115] For rather vague references in visitation articles to the use in schools of 'the catechism in English', 'the Latin catechism lately set forth', or 'the official catechism in English and Latin', see e.g. *Second Report on Ritual*, 410, 415, 423, 425, 438.

[116] A contemporary translation of the 1571 canons, cited in Baldwin, *Shakespere's Petty School*, 86.

[117] Cardwell, *Synodalia*, i. 290.

[118] Cross, *Free Grammar School*, 16–17 (assuming the 'catechismus parvus', 'middle catechism', and the 'great Latin catechism' are the three levels); Cressy, *Education in Tudor and Stuart England*, 33–4.

[119] Baldwin, *Shakespere's Petty School*, 96; and cf. the reference to 'the catechism ... set forth ... with the additions' in the St Bees regulations for 1583: ibid. 94.

[120] See above, Ch. 2, p. 66, and Appendix 1; and Baldwin, *Shakespere's Little Latine*, i. 311; of course, where 'Nowell' was read out *to* students, as at Harrow, a single copy of the full-length version could have been used for many years.

primus Latine ('first little catechism for boys in Latin') of 1573, or given the much higher number of repeat editions, the *Christianae pietatis prima institutio* ('first instruction in Christian piety')—Nowell's 'middle' form in Latin.[121] The 'middle' form in Latin and in Greek and Latin were still being reprinted after the Restoration; a couple of copies of the latter survive in Eton College Library.[122] But it is interesting to note that from the 1670s a number of schools seem to have replaced the *Catechismus parvus* with small publications tailor-made for their own institutions but all including translations of the revised Prayer Book catechism of 1604 rather than Nowell's 'shorter' form. In 1673 and 1691 the masters of King Edward's School in Bury St Edmunds and Whitgift School in Croydon had printed the 1604 form in Greek and Latin with morning prayers in Latin and evening prayers in English (a copy of the Whitgift form with the name of its student owner, Scrope Egerton, inscribed on the cover survives in the school library). A similar form but with the addition of hymns and the Lord's Prayer, Creed, and Decalogue in English at the end was published for the pupils of St Paul's School in London in 1705 and 1718.[123] In the 1680s and 1690s Merchant Taylors' School, Eton College, and Ipswich School had printed not only the church catechism but also the official confirmation service in Greek and Latin, together with Latin prayers which differed from school to school.[124] The presence of the confirmation service indicates that the students using these forms were perhaps aged no more than 12 to 14, which by that stage was emerging as the favoured age for confirmation.[125] Hoole's ideal sequence in the late 1650s tells us what teachers in nonconformist schools in the later Stuart period may have aimed at at these lower and intermediate levels: the Westminster Shorter Catechism in English in the second form, in English and Latin in the third, and in Latin and Greek in the fourth.[126]

---

[121] See Appendix 1, s.v. Nowell, and Watson, *Grammar Schools*, 80. For a catechetical form in Latin blank verse by the High Master of St Paul's in London which was built round the 1549 form but was much more detailed, see Appendix 1, s.v. Mulcaster; it should also be noted that the standard Latin grammar of the period (ibid., s.v. Lily) contained the Creed, Decalogue, and Lord's Prayer in Latin verse.

[122] Eton's possession of the Nowell editions (and of a Heidelberg Catechism in Latin and Greek published in Amsterdam in 1623) is derived from the *Catalogue of An Exhibition of Manuscripts and Printed Books* held at Eton College Library in 1984, pp. 29–30.

[123] See Appendix 1, s.v. *Catechesis ecclesiae anglicanae, una cum precibus* (1673–1702), and *Preces, catechismus, et hymni* (1705–18); F. H. G. Percy, *Whitgift School: A History* (1991), 72–3. For a similar form in Latin only, produced for Ipswich School by the son of a former Master of Bury, see *Catechesis ecclesiae anglicanae … in usum scholae … Gippovicensi* (Ipswich, 1722); and the Latin church catechism in the *Liber precum ecclesiae cathedralis Christi Oxon.* of 1726 may have been for the use of the choristers there.

[124] See Appendix 1, s.v. *Catechismus cum ordine … Katechesis kai taxis* (1683–97); Robert Coningsby had been Under-Master at Merchant Taylors' and moved to Ipswich as Master in 1690 bringing the former's school form with him. I am most grateful to Mr Percy and through him Dr J. M. Blatchly for their help in sorting out these school catechisms.

[125] On the appropriate age for confirmation, see above pp. 126–7.

[126] For the full sequence, see Hoole, *New discovery*, pp. xvii–xxiv, 53, 59, 165, 189, 201, and below p. 197.

The alternative strategy to introducing students in the lower or middle forms to a new form in English or Latin, such as Calvin's or Nowell's 'middle' form, or to the Prayer Book form they had already learnt but this time in Latin or Greek, was to spend more time on the Prayer Book form, concentrating this time on its meaning and relevance. We have already touched on this when discussing exposition of the Prayer Book catechism in church and drawing attention to school statutes which stipulated that students should learn the catechism on Saturdays so that they could be instructed in it by the minister on Sundays in church.[127] However, we may review some of the evidence briefly, drawing attention this time to the extent to which expositions of the Prayer Book catechism were aimed partly or wholly at intermediate-level students. An early example was the condensed version of John Mayer's *The English catechisme*, published in the early 1620s. This was only a tenth as long as his original effort (for 'young students in theology'), and contained both a simple text printed in black letter for 'babes', and a more advanced one in roman type for more advanced catechumens or teachers, to help expand and explain the simpler.[128] The fact that at least five of the seven editions of Edward Boughen's *Short exposition of the catechism of the Church of England* published after 1662 were in parallel English and Latin texts, and the fact that the prefatory material included the confirmation service, indicate a potential audience of older children or young teenagers in school, and since copies cost only a shilling bound, they were affordable by teachers and some students in grammar schools.[129] It seems likely that the editions of Boughen in English and Latin were intended to act as an alternative to the tribe of Nowell, of which as we have seen only a few copies were printed after 1660.[130]

How great a public blessing would it be [wrote Bishop Lloyd of Worcester to his clergy in 1700] if there were in every parish … discreet masters and dames, maintained with public salaries for the teaching of … children … to read and to say their catechism, and as many of them as were capable to learn an exposition thereof.[131]

The expositions of the church catechism which were recommended for use in schools by 1700 and in succeeding decades varied in size and probable target-group. At the simpler, cheaper end of the scale were anonymous works like *The church catechism broke into short questions*, *The church catechism, analysed, explained, and improved*, and *A short exposition of the church-catechism*. The first of these was published in 1709, and

---

[127] See above, pp. 153, 178–9; and cf. the school at Dronfield in 1579: Watson, *Grammar Schools*, 80.

[128] See Appendix 1, s.v. Mayer; and for a university student reading Mayer, see Thomas Dugard, below, pp. 199–200.

[129] See Appendix 1, s.v. Boughen. For use of Nicholson's exposition in a school on the Isle of Wight in the 1680s, see P. F. W. Erith, *Brief History of Newport Grammar School, Isle of Wight* (1950) (cited in F. H. G. Percy, *History of Whitgift School* (1976), 50–2, 340–1).

[130] Though according to C. Wase, *Considerations concerning free-schools* (1678), 92, 'Nowell' was still being used at St Paul's in the 1670s as its statutes dictated.

[131] *Diary of Francis Evans*, 16; Lloyd's letter had been prompted by a letter from Archbishop Tenison urging clergy to look after the 'religious education of children (which indeed is a principal part of your duty)'.

is of interest in that its aim was 'to try whether children repeat their catechism by rote, to engage their attention, and to imprint a sense of it in their minds'. A price of 2*d*. or 12*s*. for a hundred, and the fact that it contained prayers for use in Charity Schools, indicates its intended market, though it was also being used in churches in Kent in 1716.[132] The second appeared in 1683, but another edition was published in Norwich in 1703 for use in the city's grammar school.[133] The third was also published in Norwich, and consisted of a drastic abridgement of the forms of John Williams and William Wake, which the author thought were too hard for children. The work was recommended to Charity Schools and parents for use with children ('and inspection by the minister'), and the author claimed to know from experience that it could easily be learnt by a 10-year-old child of 'the most ordinary capacity' in the space of a few months.[134]

In the middle of the range were works like Thomas Jekyll's *Brief and plain exposition* (1690) which was 'composed for the use of a private school' recently erected and maintained by charitably-minded persons in the parish of Westminster, and Thomas Cooke's *Brief but plain explication* (1706), which was designed for use by students at Merchant Taylors' (where he had himself been educated) and at Christ's Hospital school (where he examined the catechumens).[135] *The faith and practice of the Church of England explain'd* 'for the use and benefit of the Charity Schools' (2nd edn., 1719), was also intermediate, being forty-six pages long and priced at 3*d*. or 20*s*. a hundred 'to those who give them away'. It was said to be suitable as an introduction to Wake's exposition, and the author thought it could be mastered by a 5-year-old in fifty-two weekly instalments.[136] Also in the middle were John Williams's *Brief exposition of the church-catechism* (1689) and John Lewis's *The church catechism explain'd ... and confirm'd* (1701), both of which were recommended for use in Charity Schools, even though we have again seen their being used for catechizing in parish churches as well.[137]

In the autobiographical sketch he wrote later in life, Lewis recalls that when the SPCK was set up he was proposed as a corresponding member—one of those who sent in reports and received advice. A Bedfordshire rector had complained of the 'want of a short and plain exposition of the church catechism to be put into the hands of the children taught in the Charity Schools to be learnt by them, that could be afforded cheaper than any of those that were already in being'. Lewis was requested to fill the gap, and he tells us that he looked through the thirty expositions of the church catechism he had by him, and concluded that Williams's form was the fullest

---

[132] Appendix 1, s.v. *Church catechism broke*, and Wake MS 284, fos. 60ᵛ, 237ʳ.

[133] See Appendix 1, s.v. *Church catechism analysed*.   [134] Ibid., s.v. *Short exposition*.

[135] Ibid., s.v. Jekyll and Cooke.   [136] Ibid., s.v. *Faith*.

[137] Ibid., s.v. Williams and Lewis; Carlisle, *Endowed Grammar Schools*, ii. 112; and above, pp. 157, 159–64. For a list of titles (not always accurately recorded) which were recommended to teachers and children of Charity Schools and which was constructed from SPCK reports and school accounts in the eighteenth century, see Jones, *Charity School Movement*, 373–5.

and clearest, but Isham's method was the plainest and 'best suited to the capacities of children'. Lewis soon had a draft ready[138] which relied heavily on Williams and Isham, but borrowed some material from other expositions and a preface from Comber's catechism. Two thousand copies were printed initially, but soon other editions were being called for and produced. Lewis gave the copyright to the printer, reserving only 200 out of the 2,000 copies of each new edition for himself or the SPCK, and fixed the price of each copy at 4*d*. each or 3*s*. a dozen. Being 'so much cheaper than any other exposition' (Boughen's, it may be recalled, cost a shilling bound), they were widely used in the new Charity Schools, and the printer's successors apparently took advantage of the fact that the maximum of 2,000 was not specified, and printed any number they chose, up to 6,000 per edition.[139] Not all of these copies seem to have ended up in the hands of Charity School children, but it is useful to have such clear confirmation of what kind of exposition of the Prayer Book catechism such children were expected to move on to once they had mastered the original.

Continuing up the scale, at the top we find a work like William Wake's *Principles of the christian religion*, nearly two hundred pages long but recommended for use in Charity Schools, perhaps out of deference to Wake's rising importance in the church.[140] Also of above-average length was the *Catechumenorum ductor* of 1714 by an anonymous 'divine of the Church of England', a work which he freely admitted was 'collected from the writings of the best catechists and most approved divines of the Church of England', but hoped would be useful for 'all persons, and children in general, especially those of the Charity-Schools'. At nearly a hundred and fifty pages with quite long, detailed answers, it was not an easy option, and was probably intended to be studied rather than memorized in toto.[141]

There was a considerable variety of other question-and-answer works which were composed and published for use in schools at this time which went beyond the church catechism and offered explanations of such matters as the church's liturgy, its festivals, the technical terms used in sermons and religious books, and the nature and importance of confirmation, as in Henry Colman's *Essay by way of catechism on confirmation*, which was sold at 4*d*. or 28*s*. per 100.[142] The number of items offered at reduced prices for large orders suggests large orders were anticipated, and the repeat

---

[138] From a later remark, it seems Lewis had already devised a catechism for use in his 'own little parish', though how far this was the same as that he designed for the Charity Schools is not clear.

[139] BL Addit. MS 28,651, pp. 30–4.

[140] See Appendix 1, s.v. Wake, and above, pp. 100, 159–64; it is listed twice in Jones, *Charity School Movement*, 374–5, s.v. Lincoln, Bishop of, and Wake; and for a recommendation to undergraduates to read Wake's work, see C. Wordsworth, *Scholae Academicae* (Cambridge, 1910), 336.

[141] See Appendix 1, s.v. *Catechumenorum.*

[142] See Appendix 1, s.v. J. Clutterbuck; E. Creffeild; R. Nelson (second and third titles); the anonymous *A farther instruction to those who have learnt the church catechism* (priced at 1*d*. or 6*s*. a 100 according to the advertisement in anon., *The order and rules of the charity-school for girls/boys* [1701?]); and see above n. 102.

editions through which some of these works passed suggest that authors and publishers were correct in thinking that they had spotted a niche in the market.

A certain number of catechetical forms prepared by nonconformists in the later Stuart period were also intended for catechumens who had already mastered a simpler form, and at least some of whom would have been attending a school. Richard Baxter's *The catechizing of families* (1683) was meant 'for those that are past the common small catechisms, and would grow to a more rooted faith, and to a fuller understanding'; it was intended primarily for householders, but was said to be 'useful also to schoolmasters and tutors of youth'.[143] Benjamin Keach and Isaac Watts also prepared a succession of catechisms for different age groups up to their mid-teens, Keach's being for a 'little child', a 'child', and 'youth', Watts's for those aged from 3 to 4 up to 6 or 7, from 8 to 12, from 12 to 14, and so on. These may have been used in schools: Watts certainly indicated that one of his forms could be used for lessons in school as well as the home.[144] But many obstacles were placed in the path of dissenters' efforts to set up schools, and this, together with the fact that dissenting catechetical activity tended to focus round the Westminster Shorter and Larger Catechisms,[145] means that we find relatively few original catechisms for older schoolchildren composed, or at least published, by dissenters in the later seventeenth and early eighteenth centuries.

Finally, in this section on the catechizing of students we can turn to the third and highest level: the upper forms of grammar schools and at university. The characteristics here were probably threefold: study of the forms already encountered in English and perhaps Latin too (such as the Prayer Book, Nowell's, or Calvin's) but this time in Greek or Hebrew; study of more advanced work, often Continental in origin at the start of our period (such as the writings of Spangenberg, Bullinger, and Ursinus), but more likely to be of domestic origin later (such as the larger catechism of John Ball or the *Practical catechisme* of Henry Hammond); and attendance at catechetical lectures given by the headmaster or college catechist. Of the first two of these it may be said that they probably entailed a larger proportion of time being spent in private preparation than at lower levels and were probably conducted in smaller groups and perhaps at less frequent intervals than before. But there would appear to have been some public catechizing for sixth-formers and undergraduates, either in question and answer or through catechetical lectures.

At this level the strategy of learning catechisms not only in Latin but also in Greek or Hebrew, at least in those schools where tuition in those languages was available,

---

[143] See Appendix 1, s.v. Baxter.

[144] As last, and I. Watts, *Catechisms: or, instructions in the principles of the Christian religion* (1730), 194.

[145] On expositions of the Westminster Shorter Catechism, see above, pp. 82–3, and for Latin and Greek versions the following paragraphs below.

reached its zenith. At Leicester in the early 1570s, Calvin's catechism was to be studied in English by the petties, but in Greek by the upper forms; on Sundays at Westminster School in the 1620s, the king's scholars had to construe 'some part of the Gospel in Greek or repeat part of the Greek catechism', presumably one of the Nowell–Whitaker versions; and at Winchester College in 1647, while the fourth form studied Nowell's catechism in Latin (which version was not specified), forms five and six studied the same work in Greek.[146] Hoole's ideal sequence of the late 1650s for the upper forms may also be cited: after the Westminster Shorter Catechism had been mastered in three languages in forms two to four, students were to study Nowell's 'middle' in Latin and Greek or the Heidelberg Catechism in form five, and Calvin's catechism in Greek and the church catechism in Hebrew in the top form.[147]

The strategy was continued at university. In Oxford a statute was passed in 1579 with the aim of extirpating heresy and encouraging undergraduate piety, but the works recommended were all in Latin, Greek, or Hebrew. In the first group were the larger Nowell catechism ('majorem') in Latin or Greek, Calvin's catechism in Greek or Hebrew, and Hyperius's *Elementa Christianae religionis* and the Heidelberg Catechism in a language not stated, but the titles like the rest of the statute were in Latin. These works were said to be 'pro captu auditorium et arbitrio legentium', which may be translated as 'in accordance with the capacity of hearers and the judgement of readers' (that is the 'catechism reader'—the fellow appointed to act as catechist); this seems to indicate that the works in question were to be read out loud and chosen to suit the linguistic skills of the listening catechumens. To these four, the statute went on, may be added, if desired, Bullinger's *Catechesis pro adultoribus*, Calvin's *Institutes*, Jewel's *Apologia*, or the Thirty-nine Articles (again the titles were all in Latin).[148] The range of these works indicates the continued breadth of the notion of what constituted catechesis, while the inclusion of Gerardus ('Hyperius'), Bullinger, and indeed the Heidelberg Catechism alongside Calvin and Nowell shows a university which still, as Dr Dent has put it, 'looked to a wider tradition than that of Geneva alone'.[149] Although English translations of most of the works listed were available or soon would be,[150] what is relevant to us here is the specification that a catechumen should study the first two items in the first group in Latin, Greek, or Hebrew, and the rest (implicitly) in Latin.

How far was this practice intended as a means of improving linguistic skills, and how far as a means of increasing religious knowledge and understanding? Perhaps contemporaries would have seen no clash between what today would be separate

---

[146] Cross, *Free Grammar School*, 16; Watson, *Grammar Schools*, 81; J. D'E. Firth, *Winchester College* (London, 1949), 296.

[147] Hoole, *New discovery*, pp. xvii–xxiv, 53, 59, 165, 189, 201.

[148] A. Clark (ed.), *Register of the University of Oxford, 1571–1622*, vol. ii, part i (Oxford Historical Society, 10; 1887), 155–6.

[149] C. M. Dent, *Protestant Reformers in Elizabethan Oxford* (Oxford, 1983), 92.   [150] Ibid. 88–92.

lessons. By learning the rudiments of the Christian religion along with the elements of Latin speech, said Nowell, catechumens were growing in piety and literacy at the same time.[151] Latin was still the *lingua franca* of Europe, and anyone who wished to delve into the wisdom of the past or contemporary works of biblical scholarship or reformed theology needed to be fluent in Latin. The fact that it was Thomas Norton who translated two of Nowell's forms into English, and that he arranged the text of the larger English version to mirror the Latin text to help those learning Latin, should come as no surprise, since Norton had been active for some time in securing or producing large numbers of translations of Reformed works for use in England, notably Calvin's *Institutes*.[152] Greek, on the other hand, was the language of the New Testament, and the fact that William Whitaker translated three catechisms into Greek in the early 1570s should again be no surprise, since in addition to being Nowell's nephew and protégé, Whitaker was one of the leading Greek scholars of his day, had already translated the Book of Common Prayer into Greek in 1569, and in his other writings made it very clear that any self-respecting student of the Bible should acquire facility in Hebrew and Greek (and preferably other relevant languages as well).[153] When he gave reasons for using the New Testament in Greek as a means of teaching Greek construction, Brinsley wrote as follows (in 1612):

First, for that this book together with the Hebrew of the Old Testament, were written by the Lord himself. ... Secondly, for that eternal life is only in these books, being truly understood and believed ... every one who can have opportunity, should labour to see with his own eyes, for the fullness of his assurance, rather than to rest on others.[154]

Brinsley's comments also provided a justification for studying the Old Testament in Hebrew. Nowell's forms were not translated into Hebrew, but the Prayer Book catechism was, by Thomas Ingmethorpe, who published it at a time—the early 1630s—when efforts were being made to improve the standards of language teaching at university. In 1638 the same catechism was produced in a version containing parallel columns of English, Latin, Greek, and Hebrew text.[155] In 1689 the Westminster Shorter Catechism of 1647, which had been published in a Latin version as early as 1656 and a Greek in 1659, was also published in Hebrew.[156] By providing catechetical forms in these languages, translators and publishers were providing avenues

---

[151] Nowell, *Catechism Written in Latin*, p. i*; note the alternative for fifth-form students at Leicester on Monday afternoons: study of the Latin catechism or Cicero's epistles: Cross, *Free Grammar School*, 26.

[152] See *DNB* and *STC²*, s.v. Thomas Norton.

[153] See article on Whitaker in *DNB*; Lake, *Moderate Puritans*, 58; and P. E. Hughes, *Theology of the English Reformers* (London, 1965), 40–2.

[154] Brinsley, *Ludus literarius*, 226.

[155] See Appendix 1, s.v. *Short catechisme, by law authorized*, and *Catecheticae versiones variae*. The Prayer Book catechism was also translated into Welsh, Irish, Arabic, French, and German in the early modern period, but these were probably not intended for use in schools in England but for proselytising purposes overseas.

[156] See Appendix 1, s.v. 'Westminster'.

along which the abler students who would make up the next generation of scholars, ministers, and teachers—and indeed monarchs[157]—could be shepherded towards the ultimate goal of being as well equipped as their mentors to read the Bible in the original language and to recognize sound doctrine.

The works mentioned in previous paragraphs would not have been the only ones available to students honing their skills in ancient languages. English publishers produced editions in Latin of shorter works which could be tackled in schools, such as Eusebius Paget's catechism and the Heidelberg Catechism, and in the later seventeenth century in addition to a Latin version of Boughen's catechism, there were also Latin versions of two Quaker catechisms, by George Fox and Robert Barclay, showing that not all sectaries were opposed to academic learning.[158] English publishers also produced Latin editions of larger catechetical works more suited to undergraduates or graduates, such as Johann Spangenberg's *Margarita theologia*, two long question-and-answer works by Beza, catechetical lectures by Ursinus, an exposition by Piscator, and Grotius's *Baptizatorum puerorum institutio*.[159] Searches in the libraries of universities and colleges, the lists of books owned by individuals, and the diaries kept by undergraduates would certainly produce more information on these and other forms.[160] However, except in the case of the diaries, in most cases there is a dearth of hard evidence as to how many of these works were used, and how often, and even the entries in diaries can be so abbreviated or laconic as to make it very hard for us to know what was going on.

We know, for example, that in the mid-1590s Samuel Ward reprimanded himself for his drowsiness in reading Ursinus; in view of the sleepiness induced this was almost certainly the enormous commentary on the Heidelberg Catechism rather than the catechism itself.[161] We also know that Thomas Goodwin used 'Ursinus' catechism' in the 1610s to see if he had grace or not, presumably again the larger commentary rather than the shorter original;[162] and in Thomas Dugard's careful record of his studies at Cambridge in 1632–3, we also find a student regularly reading sections of Ursinus's work.[163] In this diary Dugard also recorded the sermons he heard on Sundays, and whether he had attended a session of catechizing on that day. He

---

[157] An edition of Nowell in Latin and Greek was among the books used by the young James VI: Baldwin, *Shakespere's Little Latine*, i. 533.

[158] References to editions of these works published in England can be found in Appendix 1 under the relevant author's name or heading.

[159] Ibid.

[160] See e.g. E. S. Leedham-Green (ed.), *Books in Cambridge Inventories* (2 vols.; Cambridge, 1986), ii. 68, 92, 137, 160, 172–3, 183, 192–3, 268–9, 413, 574–5; and the diaries and other materials listed in H. Kearney, *Scholars and Gentlemen: Universities and Society in Pre-Industrial Britain 1500–1700* (1970), 193–9.

[161] M. M. Knappen (ed.), *Two Elizabethan Puritan Diaries* (Chicago/London, 1933), 113; and Appendix 1, s.v. Ursinus for editions of his lectures in Latin, and from 1587 in English too.

[162] H. C. Porter. *Reformation and Reaction in Tudor Cambridge* (Cambridge, 1958), 272.

[163] BL Addit. MS 23,146, fos. 3ʳ–46ʳ.

was at this stage aged about 24, completing his MA, and destined very soon after-wards for a career first in teaching and then the ministry, but, even after nearly two decades of being a student he clearly saw the need or the advantage of regular attendance at catechizing sessions. On occasion, the roles were reversed: 'pupillos in Ursino institui' (I taught pupils Ursinus), he noted on 21 July 1633, just after a note of his attending another catechizing session by 'Mr Naylor' (perhaps James Naylor, fellow of Sidney at the time).[164] Dugard's reading was very catholic: he read the poetry of Sidney, Quarles, and Herbert, and seems to have studied the expositions of the Prayer Book catechism by the conformists John Mayer and William Crompton, and had a look at Ingmethorpe's Hebrew translation of the same form, as well as studying the Heidelberg Catechism and the larger catechism of the orthodox Calvin-ist John Ball.[165] His diary is of particular interest to us here because it shows how the catechetical student of one generation could move on almost without a break to being the catechist of the next.

From the 1640s, there was a non-Calvinist alternative to Nowell and Ball for undergraduates to read: Henry Hammond's large *Practical catechisme*. When he reached Oxford in 1643, Hammond had already been deprived of the living in Kent where he had catechized the youth for an hour on Sunday afternoons in summer. He showed the draft of his catechism to Christopher Potter, the Provost of Queen's, who was so impressed that he offered to pay for its publication himself, though in the end the two divided the cost.[166] Hammond's work soon established a niche, passing through five editions in as many years. It was one of the two books sent from Caris-brooke by Charles I to his youngest son, the duke of Gloucester; it was used by Simon Patrick with his students in the 1650s, and recommended to a wider and more mature readership in a later work of his; and it was praised by Gilbert Burnet in his *Discourse of the pastoral care* as 'a rare book', though he warned that 'too many' tried to *begin* with Hammond, whereas 'it does require a good deal of previous study, before the force of his reasonings is understood'.[167] William Whiston remembered his father saying that after the Restoration all seriousness in religion would have been laughed out of court had it not been for 'two very excellent and serious books': Allestree's *The whole duty of man* and Hammond's *Practical catechisme*. In the 1690s Whiston himself became a tutor and later recounted how he read Hammond's work to his pupils in the evenings.[168] The *Practical catechisme* was also mentioned in advice drawn up by Daniel Waterland for his pupils at Magdalene College, Cambridge, in

---

[164] BL Addit. MS 23,146 fos. 3ʳ–7ʳ.

[165] Ibid., fos. 3ʳ–46ʳ; Ball's catechism—again probably the larger in view of the level of the students concerned—was also recommended to John Oxenbridge's students at Magdalen College, Oxford at much the same time: Morgan, *Godly Learning*, 289.

[166] J. W. Packer, *The Transformation of Anglicanism 1643–1660* (Manchester, 1969), 19, 26–7.

[167] Ibid. 28; S. Patrick, *The Works*, ed. A. Taylor (9 vols.; Oxford, 1858), ix. 425; i. 628; and Appendix 1, s.v. H. Hammond.

[168] Packer, *Transformation*, 27.

1707; in the 'scheme of study' for students drawn up by Robert Green, fellow of Clare, in the same year; and in a list of works recommended by Thomas Hearne to a young divine in 1711.[169] As an alternative to Hammond, there were the multivolume expositions of the church catechism prepared and published by scholars like Gabriel Towerson in the 1670s and 1680s, John Ollyffe in the reign of Queen Anne, and John Shaw in the early 1720s, or the catechetical lectures on the Prayer Book catechism published by Newcome, Hole, Farrow, Newton, and Bundy between 1700 and 1740 that we have encountered in the last chapter.[170] These works were so weighty that they could not possibly have been used for question-and-answer catechizing, but were presumably aimed at budding ordinands as well as clergy, teachers, and zealous laity.

In the deployment of the more advanced Latin forms and the Greek and Hebrew forms described above, and also with the more advanced forms in English just described, the emphasis would probably have been on studying the text in private or in small groups. To the examples of small group work involving Dugard, Patrick, and Whiston mentioned above one might add the example of Samuel Ward, while still a student at Christ Church, Oxford, 'instructing' his younger brother Henry on Sundays, though whether this was catechetical instruction or not is not clear.[171] Catechizing in the upper reaches of school and at university could, however, still be a public event as well. Headmasters of grammar schools could give a catechetical reading or lecture to the whole school, and from the 1570s we have details of the catechists appointed by colleges at Oxford and Cambridge to perform some kind of public catechizing of their junior members. Some of those appointed were either quite senior members or destined for greater fame in later years. The *lector catechismi* at St Edmund Hall in Oxford in 1579 was the Principal; at Cambridge, Roger Goad, Provost of King's from 1570 to 1610, also claimed to have catechized the whole college.[172] Others appointed catechist included Lancelot Andrewes at Pembroke College, perhaps William Perkins at Christ's, and Richard Crashaw at Peterhouse, Cambridge, and John Day at Oriel and William Twisse at New College, Oxford. James Ussher's first post after graduating from the newly created Trinity College, Dublin was as catechist there.[173] The potential influence of the post can be seen in an incident in the 1570s at Merton College, Oxford, when a suspected papist was barred from catechizing the postmasters.[174]

[169] Wordsworth, *Scholae Academicae*, 335 (2), 340; other expositions recommended were those of Wake and Beveridge: 336, 340, and see Appendix 1 for those works.

[170] See above, pp. 150–2, and Appendix 1, s.v. authors' names.

[171] Knappen, *Two Puritan Diaries*, 111.

[172] See next paragraph; Clark, *Register*, 156; and Morgan, *Godly Learning*, 288.

[173] For Andrewes and Day, see below; S. Clarke, *The marrow of ecclesiastical history* (1650), 851; Clarke, *Lives of sundry eminent persons*, 14; A. Warren, *Richard Crashaw: A Study in Baroque Sensibility* (London, 1939), 41.

[174] C. Russell, *The Causes of the English Civil War* (Oxford, 1990), 77 n. 58.

This more public form of catechizing for advanced pupils probably consisted for the most part of one-way traffic, with the catechist reading out a text and making occasional comments of his own and perhaps asking a limited number of questions to test that students had understood or were paying attention. Thus at Harrow school from the 1580s, the master was to 'read a lecture to all, or the most part of his scholars, which he shall think meet to hear thereof, out of Calvin or Nowell's catechism, or some such other book, at his discretion';[175] and at Winchester College, catechism lectures were given every Sunday throughout the early modern period: college accounts show forty-three were given in the school year 1644–5, and thirty-nine in 1645–6.[176] At university too it would appear from the references to *lectors* and *auditores* noted above that public catechizing could take the form of expounding a set text, often in Latin or Greek, rather than oral testing: there was little point in removing a suspected papist if he was doing no more than hear set answers to set questions.[177] At Christ's College, Cambridge, an order was passed in the late 1570s saying that not only was a catechist to be appointed to teach from three to four in the chapel the day before a holiday, but also all undergraduates and BAs were to attend to listen, and there were fines for non-attendance. However, the fact that it was laid down that undergraduates had to answer when questioned, that admission to communion was dependent on receiving a certificate from the catechist, and that anyone found to be unfit after six months might be expelled, indicates that in this case there was a question-and-answer element, and that the individual student's progress was to be monitored.[178]

The catechetical lectures which survive are also for the most part not in question-and-answer form. Moreover, while most might be described as covering the basic principles of the faith, they did so in ways which reflected the difference between lecturers' interests and styles. Lancelot Andrewes's lectures at Pembroke College, Cambridge, appear from the surviving notes to have included prose expositions of the Ten Commandments, though they also exhibit his extensive patristic learning.[179] The lectures given monthly in Oriel College, Oxford in 1612–13 by John Day, acting as 'catechism reader' for a year, were published rather sooner, in 1614, as *Day's dyall, or ... twelve severall lectures by way of catechisme*. In the preface, Day said that he presupposed his hearers or readers were grounded in Nowell's catechism, and in his elaborate text, he covered a number of predictable aspects such as the nature of God and the Trinity, the Creed, Commandments, and Lord's Prayer, but some less predictable ones as well, such as the Thirty-nine Articles (part of an attack on the Church of Rome), fasting, and alms.[180] When it came to John Preston's turn to be dean and catechist at Queens', Cambridge, he resolved to provide 'a body of divinity

[175] Watson, *Grammar Schools*, 80.
[176] Frere, *Visitation Articles*, iii. 327; Firth, *Winchester College*, 67, 251–2, 254: that the lectures were fairly meaty is indicated by the fact that the warden or fellow who gave them received 6s. 8d. for his pains.
[177] Clarke, *Register*, 156; and above, p. 197.   [178] J. Peile, *Christ's College* (1900), 90.
[179] See above, p. 1 n. 1.   [180] See Appendix 1, s.v. Day.

that might be a guide unto the scholars in their studies in divinity', and like Andrewes's these were soon so well attended that an order had to be issued saying that only students from his own college could attend.[181] What Anthony Tuckney did at Emmanuel College Cambridge in 1628 is not altogether clear. His 'brief and pithy catechism as it was delivered in Emmanuel College chappel' survives in four sides of closely-written folio in a volume of miscellaneous works dating from the 1620s. It is scholarly in tone, complete with Latin tags, and tackled topics such as the covenants of works and grace and the *ordo salutis* which had not been covered in most question-and-answer forms published by that date. Whether Tuckney simply read out his catechism in such a way that the undergraduates could copy it down verbatim, or whether they learnt to repeat each answer in turn is not known.[182]

In the late 1640s and 1650s the practice of public catechizing was still alive. When John Arrowsmith returned as Master to his old college of St John's, Cambridge, he gave a set of catechetical lectures, published a few years later as *Armilla catechetica. A chain of principles* (1659). He had been a parish priest for some time, and in the preface of the printed version he admitted that the catechetical lectures were based on thirty aphorisms which were the sum of his labours in the ministry.[183] On the other hand, when Owen Stockton was chosen catechist at Gonville and Caius at Cambridge in 1654, he undertook 'a constant course of preaching' which was in fact his first experience of such an enterprise.[184] Looking at the works of Day, Preston, Arrowsmith, and Stockton, we may conclude that the longer the practice of catechetical lectures went on, the more the lecturer might feel free to move away from a set text and what had been seen as the basics at the outset—Decalogue, Creed, and Lord's Prayer—and deliver instead a set of sermons on what he saw as the necessary basis of faith. Here was yet another way then in which catechizing at university could help to prepare the next generation of catechists.

We have looked at catechizing at school and university at three levels, and should remember that the greater number of students, especially girls, may not have passed beyond the level of petty school or Charity School; equally, many of those who went to grammar school did not necessarily reach the top forms or pass on to university, even if, like Richard Baxter, they were well equipped to do so. We are probably faced with the usual pyramid: a very wide base of children aged from 4, 5, or 6 to 10 or 11 studying the Prayer Book catechism; a narrower band studying that same form in other languages or the forms of Calvin and Nowell instead; and a much narrower tip of students completing a university course and well exercised in the more advanced catechetical works of the day, including the larger catechisms of Mayer or Ball and

---

[181] Clarke, *Lives of two and twenty divines*, 105–6.

[182] See Appendix 1, s.v. Tuckney. Although Dugard records hearing three men catechizing undergraduates—Messrs Naylor, Garbut, and Hall—he unfortunately gives no clue to the technique of instruction used: BL Addit. MS 23,146, fos. 4ʳ–15ʳ.

[183] See Appendix 1, s.v. Arrowsmith.   [184] Clarke, *Lives of sundry eminent persons*, 190–1.

the works of Ursinus or Hammond. But the evidence presented in the first half of this chapter may justify the conclusion that the not insignificant proportion of 5 to 16-year-olds who received some formal education were exposed to catechizing for part or all of that period of education. And the fact that they formed a captive market (compared to their peers in the parish who did not go to school) may have meant that the imprint of that catechizing was quite strong. Certainly, it is hard to see how their elder brethren who stayed at school and went to university could have escaped the impress of repeated catechizing in a variety of forms and languages.

Another forum for catechizing was the home, usually in a household unit of parents and children or masters and servants, but occasionally with a minister or chaplain present or with a number of like-minded families gathered for some kind of 'conference'.[185] There has been a temptation to see 'household' catechisms as somehow different from other catechisms, and domestic catechizing as a 'godly' alternative to the ministry of a clergyman who was judged by the puritans to be less than fully reformed.[186] While there is probably some mileage in these ideas, at least for certain types of household in the Elizabethan and Jacobean periods, they should not be taken too far. As we shall see, relatively few works were designated as being for use in households only, and many bishops and conformable clergy were as anxious as their godly or dissenting counterparts to encourage catechizing in the home, if it was as a support to catechizing in church or chapel. It was widely hoped that in the more intimate atmosphere of the home—in which the parents knew their children's capacities much better than a minister or teacher—catechizing could take place every day rather than once a week, and moral pressure rather than ecclesiastical authority could be exerted to get results and so help the minister to catechize more effectively on Sundays. Certainly the converse was often stated: that a lack of household catechizing was undermining the efforts of the minister to instruct the young and overcome the ignorance of the old.[187] However, because the duty of parents and masters to catechize their households was a spiritual or moral one—at bottom it was a voluntary act rather than a legal requirement—we have no institutional records to help us decide how far or in what ways the duty was actually performed. The types of source which throw some light on domestic catechizing have a sameness about them: exhortations in improving literature, the prefaces of catechisms written by strong believers in the value of catechizing, and accounts of the 'godly' by the 'godly', especially in lauda-

---

[185] For the last of these, see below pp. 218, 220.

[186] P. Hutchison, 'Religious Change: The Case of the English Catechism 1560–1640', Ph.D. thesis (Stanford, 1984), chs. 7–8; Morgan, *Godly Learning*, 154. See also T. Sparke, 'Treatise', in *A catechisme, or short kind of instruction*, ed. Sparke and Seddon (1588), 52–3; and J. Nichols, *An order of household instruction* (1596), sigs. B4ᵛ–5ʳ.

[187] e.g. Sparke, 'Treatise', 36–7; Nichols, *Household instruction*, sig. B5ʳ; [W. Bridges], *A catechisme for communicants* (1645), sig. A7ᵛ; Morgan, *Godly Learning*, 154.

tory funeral sermons or biographies, though a more detached view can occasionally be gleaned from other sources, such as autobiographies, diaries, and letters.[188] As a result, while bearing in mind the possibility of catechizing being performed at different levels and in different ways, we will discuss domestic catechizing as a single phenomenon, and approach it by looking at what we know first of the theory and then of the practice.

The attitude of the English episcopate to domestic catechizing was occasionally hopeful but collectively sceptical, perhaps because like the older Luther many bishops doubted the capacity or willingness of most householders to teach those in their charge.[189] In the baptism service of 1549 the godparents of every child undertook to ensure that their godchild would master the basics of the faith,[190] but there was no machinery for ensuring that godparents themselves did this teaching. Equally the rubric at the end of the catechism in 1552 and the canons of 1571 and 1604 did no more than insist that parents and masters should send their charges to church to learn the catechism there. Most visitation articles followed this line, warning churchwardens to present any householders who refused to send to church those in their care who did not know the catechism or any 'young folks' who refused to attend.[191] In 1562 a proposal was put before Convocation (but not passed) suggesting that a fine of ten shillings be imposed on any parent or master whose charge could not 'say by heart the short catechism in English set forth', but even this seems to have been based on the assumption that the curate would do the teaching.[192] It is possible that the authorities did not do more to encourage domestic catechizing out of fear, in the first instance of the continuation behind closed doors of the kind of household instruction that the late medieval church had been actively encouraging, and, later, fear of Protestant zealots using catechizing as a cover for fostering ideas critical of the church and state.[193] But if so, the obvious course would have been to ban domestic catechizing and to refuse to license any catechism but the official ones. Since neither step was taken, one must assume the authorities took the view that more good than harm was likely to come of such domestic catechizing as did take place,[194] and that they would not intervene unless there were signs of its getting out of hand, for example by moving beyond rote instruction into controversial exposition.

Some bishops actively encouraged adults to teach the catechism to the young. In

---

[188] Examples of these different sources will be found in the notes on the next few pages.
[189] Strauss, *Luther's House of Learning*, chs. 1–3, 6, 8–10.   [190] Brightman, *English Rite*, ii. 744.
[191] Ibid. ii. 799; Cardwell, *Synodalia*, i. 120, 198–9, 280–1; and e.g. *Second Report on Ritual*, 405, 406, 408, 414, 419, etc.
[192] Cardwell, *Synodalia*, ii. 510–11.
[193] Tudor, 'Religious Instruction', 398–9; S. Brigden, *London and the Reformation* (Oxford, 1989), 78; E. Duffy, *The Stripping of the Altars: Traditional Religion in England c.1400–c.1580* (New Haven/London, 1992), ch. 2; Morgan, *Godly Learning*, 153 n. 71, 154 n. 80.
[194] While a few bishops asked if schoolteachers (with their better education) gave lectures, readings, or expositions under pretence of catechizing, they did not ask the same about parents: *Second Report on Ritual*, 433, 438, 466.

his visitation articles for Norwich in 1561, John Parkhurst told the clergy to 'warn the parents and masters to cause their children and youth to learn the catechism, either in schools or else at home so as they may be examined by the minister every Sunday and holy day', and in a sermon Edwin Sandys also urged householders to catechize.[195] In his capacity as visitor of the diocese of Chester, Sandys also ordered each parish to buy copies of the official 'little catechism' to be sold to the people, and in the early 1580s the local bishop tried to force parishioners to buy them, with only limited success.[196] Thomas Morton must have had a similar venture in mind in distributing copies of the Prayer Book catechism among the children and servants who could read in the parishes of his different dioceses, but at least in his case he met the cost of the copies himself.[197] All of these Elizabethan and early Stuart bishops were perhaps rather optimistic, however, in assuming that most people could read, though a growing proportion certainly could.[198] A clutch of bishops in the 1660s and 1670s, perhaps following the lead of the demanding John Cosin, also enquired: 'Doth every householder ... cause their children and servants duly to learn their catechism, and to give an account thereof unto your minister ... upon Sundays and holy days?'[199] 'Cause ... to learn' could mean that the parents were supposed to do the teaching, but it could also mean that it might be done by a third party such as a schoolteacher. Reynolds of Norwich, however, left no doubt on this point: 'Do all governors of families instruct their children and servants in the catechism?'[200] Archbishop Sancroft gave his approval to the 'cause to learn' formula in articles for his own diocese of Canterbury in 1682 and in metropolitical articles for Lincoln diocese in 1686,[201] but the legal position remained as before, that only failure to send to church those who did not know the catechism was a breach of the canons.

Further support for domestic catechizing from senior clergy and conformable parish clergy can be demonstrated from the catechetical works which some of them published. Not all of these were based on the Prayer Book catechism, for example, Joseph Hall's pre-communion form *A brief summe of the principles of religion* aimed at those who 'would address themselves to God's table', and Clement Ellis's *Summe of Christianity*, said at the time to have been 'reckoned one of the best of its kind' and 'distributed in great numbers among the poorer sort of people' in Nottinghamshire and other counties in the later Stuart period.[202] But the majority *were* based on the Prayer Book catechism. William Dickenson thought that his Berkshire

[195] *Second Report on Ritual*, 401; R. L. Greaves, *Society and Religion in Elizabethan England* (Minnesota, 1981), 294.

[196] C. Haigh, *Reformation and Resistance in Tudor Lancashire* (Cambridge, 1975), 311.

[197] See above, p. 139 n. 202; and Fincham, *Visitation Articles*, 116.

[198] For literacy rates, see above, p. 96 n. 7.

[199] *Second Report on Ritual*, 603, 605, 617, and the twenty other examples listed on 615.

[200] Ibid. 620.   [201] Ibid. 653, 655.

[202] J. Hall, *A brief summe* (1624), title-page; C. Ellis, *The summe of Christianity* (1696); id., *The scripture catechist* (1738), p. xxxvii.

parishioners would rather die than admit they could not digest the doctrinal 'meat' he offered them at first, so in 1628 he switched tactics and published an exposition of the Prayer Book form for 'the private use of the younger and more unlearned sort of his parishioners'. Through *Milke for babes* he hoped to be a domestic chaplain to them all, a teacher always in the house. 'Fix and fasten me to some convenient place in your houses', he urged (echoing the contemporary practice of fixing broadsheets to the walls of homes and inns), and do not be content merely with memorizing, but try to understand what you learn.[203] Another of Clement Ellis's forms, *The scripture catechist*, was intended as a body of practical divinity on the church catechism for those families in his Nottinghamshire parish who were not able to consult larger volumes.[204] In the preface to his *Paraphrase with annotations*, William White wrote that 'perpetual catechizing ... is the plain will and word of God', and that the Christian faith 'cannot ordinarily be had without being instructed in it, either by father, or mother, or nurse, or teacher, man or woman, or master or dame, or some catechist ordained'.[205] Dozens of other examples could be given of expositions of the church catechism published between the 1620s and the 1710s in which their authors either expressed the hope that their forms would be taught or learnt at home,[206] or said on the cover or in the preface that their form could be used in the home as well as in church or school,[207] or suggested that their form was 'fitted for the meanest capacities, the weakest memories, the plainest teachers, and the most uninstructed learners'.[208]

That parents were increasingly being asked to do more than simply ensure their offspring knew the church catechism is also evident, in various ways. Parents may think they had done enough when they have taught their children to repeat the Prayer Book catechism by rote and to answer readily in the face of the congregation, wrote Peter Hewit in 1704; once they had achieved this they sat back and left the rest

---

[203] W[illiam] D[ickenson], *Milke for babes* (1628), title-page and sigs. [¶] 2ʳ–3ʳ. The idea of fixing printed items to a wall is described in T. Watt, *Cheap Print and Popular Piety, 1550–1640* (Cambridge, 1991), ch. 6.

[204] Ellis, *Scripture catechist*, p. vi.

[205] W. White, *A paraphrase with annotations* (1674), sigs. A2ʳ⁻ᵛ.

[206] W. Hill, *The first principles of a Christian* (1629), sigs. A2ʳ–4ʳ; W. Ward, *Short grounds of catechisme* (Cambridge, 1627), sigs. A3ʳ⁻ᵛ; R. Bernard, *Common catechisme* (1640), sigs. A2ʳ–4ʳ, B4ʳ; W. Jones, *An exposition of the whole catechisme* (1633), 2–4, sig. A2ʳ; W. Nicholson, *A plain but full exposition of the catechism* (Oxford, 1842), pp. xiii–xv; B. Bird, *The catechism of the Church of England* (1674), sig. A2ᵛ; S. Lowth, *Catechetical questions* (1674), sig. A2ʳ; T. Comber, *The church catechisme with a brief and easie explanation thereof* (1686), sigs. A2ʳ⁻ᵛ; T. Ken, *An exposition on the church catechism* (1685), and id., *The church-catechism, with directions for prayer* (1685), *passim*; J. Briggs, *Catechetical exercises* (Cambridge, 1696), sig. A4ʳ; B. Love, *The catechism of the Church* (1699), pp. i–v; A. Seller, *An exposition of the church-catechism* (1695), sig. A7ᵛ; J. Harrison, *An exposition of the church-catechism* (1708), 9.

[207] J. Mayer, *English catechisme* (1623), title-page and sigs. A3ʳ⁻ᵛ; id., *Mayers catechisme abridged* (1632), sig. A2ʳ and *passim*; [T. Marshall], *The catechism set forth* (1683), title-page and sigs. 2ʳ⁻ᵛ; title-page and *passim*; anon., *Eniautos: or a course of catechizing* (1674), title-page and 11–12.

[208] Anon., *Art of catechizing* (1691), title-page; and cf. Lowth, *Catechetical questions*, sigs. A2ʳ⁻ᵛ, and Comber, *Church catechisme*, title-page.

to the minister. But this was not enough: 'you may teach a parrot to speak'. Parents should also teach their children to understand as well as to memorize the church catechism, and his form would show them how to do this.[209] Such optimism was obviously shared by William Wake, who a few years later had a special edition of his own exposition published and distributed round the households of Lincoln diocese, and by those parish clergy in other dioceses who distributed copies of Wake's or similar works among the families in their parish.[210] To balance this, it should be added that even those who encouraged domestic catechizing were often sceptical about the likely standard of performance. Parents, wrote James Talbot in the exposition he was circulating amongst them in 1705, should send their youth to church as well instructed in his form 'as their private capacity and opportunities permit'; ideally, suggested William Beveridge in the preface to his *The church-catechism explain'd* in 1704, parents should teach children at home 'as well as they can'.[211] By the end of our period, the official attitude towards domestic catechizing in general perhaps remained what it had been at the outset—a mixture of cautious hope and pragmatism, but in the later Stuart period many clergymen were clearly expecting parents to achieve more with their children than the simple repetition of a couple of dozen answers in the church catechism.

If we compare the attitudes of 'godly' and non-'godly' clergy in the Elizabethan and early Stuart period or of conformists and nonconformists in the later Stuart period, we find many parallels and some differences. Both sides were anxious to use private catechizing in the home as a support system to public catechizing in church or chapel; and both hoped that it would benefit 'children in understanding' among the elders in the household as well as 'children in years' among the younger, and would lead to a greater degree of self-awareness and proper preparation for the Lord's Supper. Perhaps the main difference (apart from the conformists' preference for the church catechism and the dissenters' for the Westminster Shorter) was that the 'godly' and the dissenters had a more optimistic estimate of what a typical householder was capable of doing, and (to judge from the length of many of their works) of what his or her children were capable of absorbing. What this may in turn reflect is that the 'godly' clergy, who were themselves for the most part highly educated and zealous men, were at the time actively targeting households of the type with which they were most familiar or which they felt would set the best example—firmly Protestant and above all literate. Indeed, some forms published for domestic use had actually been drawn up for a minister's own family.[212]

---

[209] P. Hewit, *A brief and plain explication of the catechism* (1704), sigs. A2ʳ⁻ᵛ.

[210] See above, pp. 160–2.

[211] J. Talbot, *The church-catechism explained by a paraphrase* (1705), sig. A4ᵛ; [W. Beveridge], *The church-catechism explained* (1704), pp. vii–x.

[212] See below, pp. 212, 219–21.

Perhaps optimism is not quite the right term: for the 'godly', catechizing in the home was not just advisable but essential, in two ways. First of all, it was vital because it was part of what Patrick Collinson has called the 'stereotyped, programmed corporateness' which kept the 'godly' together and helped them to survive in the face of the reprobate and the Antichrist.[213] James Leech's diatribe against the growing number of 'wicked atheists, superstitious papists, profane worldlings, carnal gospellers, vain and idle professors, and great multitudes of ignorant people' was made in the preface to his *Plaine and profitable catechisme … meete for parents and householders to teach their children and servants* which he published in 1605 to try to remedy the situation. Long experience had taught him that this form, a heavily modified version of the Dering–More catechism, was 'of very fit and profitable use for the instruction of a family'.[214] Such catechizing in the home was part of a package of 'godly' instruction and worship which also included Bible-reading, prayers, questions about the content of sermons recently heard, singing psalms, mutual counsel, and other forms of edification which conformists might approve of, but in most cases did little more than recommend to their flocks.[215] There is also the obvious but important point that after 1660 or 1662 catechizing in the parish church was no longer an option for nonconformists, and catechizing in schools made very difficult. Not until 1689 would dissenters have a limited freedom to catechize in a public congregation, and not until even later did they have the freedom to set up schools in which the young could be catechized in the way that they would have wished. For a few decades after 1660 the potential importance of the household was thus greatly reinforced.[216]

The other way in which catechizing was essential for the 'godly', especially in the home, was a result of a combination of contemporary views on child psychology and Calvinist theology. Both regarded children as proud and wilful creatures, totally corrupted by sin. It was the duty of parents to break this will, by discipline and by force if necessary, and to instil some civilized habits and piety into them. The child might be among the elect, but the sooner he or she began to put off the old and put on the new, the better. The rote learning involved in catechizing was a means of both enforcing proper discipline on a child and providing the knowledge of God's will which was a prerequisite of salvation.[217] Indeed, the 'godly' position on education, as

<hr />

[213] Morgan, *Godly Learning*, 308.

[214] J. Leech, *A plaine and profitable catechisme* (1605), title-page and sigs. A2^r, A3^v.

[215] R. Cawdrey, *A short and fruitefull treatise* (1604), sigs. A6^r–8^v; Greaves, *Society and Religion*, chs. 6–7; Morgan, *Godly Learning*, ch. 8; J. T. Cliffe, *The Puritan Gentry: The Great Puritan Families of Early Stuart England* (London, 1984), ch. 2; for a parallel programme recommended for adoption in schools, see J. Dury, *The reformed school* (1651), 24–5.

[216] See above, pp. 167, 187, and below, pp. 227–8; M. Watts, *The Dissenters*, i. *From the Reformation to the French Revolution* (Oxford, 1978), chs. 3–4.

[217] Morgan, *Godly Learning*, 46–7, 129–30, 146, 148. Such views were not confined to the 'godly'; see e.g. L. Addison, *The primitive institution* (1674), 159–60, and E. Creffeild, *The great duty of catechising* (1713), 13–24, 49.

John Morgan has pointed out, was suffused with 'optimistic preparationist notions',[218] of preparing a child for conversion, which did not sit altogether easily with their strong predestinarian beliefs, as we shall see in a later chapter. It remains the case, however, that in the Elizabethan and early Stuart periods, and indeed later, it was the 'godly' who articulated most clearly the need for discipline and knowledge and for regular catechizing in the home.

We can to some extent see these attitudes in the catechisms the 'godly' wrote for the 'household'. The first of these was Dering and More's *Brief and necessary instruction, verye needefull to bee knowen of all housholders* (1572). Driven to despair by the shortage of good preachers in England in the 1560s, the two seem to have seen domestic catechizing in the first instance as an emergency measure until the pulpits could be filled with proper preachers.[219] It was not, however, a subversive work: no form would have been reprinted so often, including three editions in the 1630s, if the church authorities had not seen it as an acceptable supplement to official forms. Its doctrine was decidedly Protestant, but contained nothing that had not been stated already in the official formularies of the day; and it also gave due weight under the fifth Commandment to the authority of 'princes, rulers, magistrates, pastors, teachers and masters' as well as that of natural parents.[220] It clearly filled a need, and is said to have been widely used among the congregations of More's Norfolk, though we should not be too ready to confine that need to 'godly' *households*. In the early Stuart period we find the occasional presentation in the church courts for use of 'Mr More's' catechism in church instead of the official one.[221] The version prepared by John Stockwood, as noted above, also seems to have been intended for use in schools and churches rather than just the home.[222]

Another standard-bearer for 'godly' instruction in the home was Eusebius Paget's *Short questions and answeares* (1579), which contains the famous preface in which Paget described how in four months of domestic catechizing in a 'godly' household, presumably that of his uncle and patron, John Isham, in Northamptonshire, 'I have seen these principles learned by gentlemen, yeomen, horsekeepers, shepherds, carters, milkmaids, kitchen-boys' and all in the household, except three or four 'whose capacity was but mean and simple'; even the simplest had derived some benefit from the experience, he felt. The 'godly' nature of the household is made clear by the reference to the need for daily meetings for confession of sins, prayers and

[218] Morgan, *Godly Learning*, 146; and on preparation, see also below, Ch. 8.

[219] P. Collinson, *A Mirror of Elizabethan Puritanism: The Life and Letters of 'Godly Master Dering'* (Friends of Dr Williams's Library Seventeenth Lecture, London, 1964), 8–11.

[220] See Appendix 1, s.v. Dering–More; [E. Dering and J. More], *A brief and necessary catechisme* (1590), sigs. A7ᵛ–8ʳ.

[221] Collinson, *Mirror*, 10; R. G. Usher, *The Reconstruction of the English Church* (2 vols.; New York/London, 1910), i. 263.

[222] See above, pp. 185–6, and E. Dering, J. More, and J. Stockwood, *A short catechisme for householders. With prayers [and] the prooves of the scripture* (1583), sig. A3ᵛ.

meditations, and Bible-reading as well as catechizing.[223] Paget was convinced that similar results could be obtained in other households, and the fact that the form itself was not very much longer than the Prayer Book catechism and was carefully divided up into short answers for ease of learning makes this seem reasonable. However, not all households would have had the advantage of the Isham one, that the co-operation of catechumens could be ensured through the presence of the gentleman house-holder and a minister (whether the latter was present as catechist or eye-witness is not clear); and not all families would have had the time or the inclination to spend as much time on the various exercises prescribed by Paget. One may also note that Paget published a Latin version of his catechism in 1585, and another question-and-answer work on the contents of the Bible in 1603 which also became a best-seller, both of which may well have been designed for use in school rather than the home.[224]

An awareness of the advantages of domestic catechizing but also of the need to meet the needs of different levels of ability is evident in two other works by 'godly' authors: Stephen Egerton's *Briefe method of catechizing*, and Josias Nichols's *Order of household instruction*, both of which first appeared in print in the mid-1590s. Egerton did not say his work was aimed particularly at families—only one form is described as 'familiar' (in the sense of 'for use in the family', rather than 'well-known')—and the initial long form could have been used in any context. However, the rest of the work was innovative and designed to provide a wide variety of catechetical forms for those who were literate and catechized regularly, which would certainly have included 'godly' householders. The work included successive reductions of the long opening form, first to forty questions and then to four; a form of examination before the Lord's Supper in two short sections; the 'familiar' form, 'the most plain and easy of all the rest', for parents and masters to propound to their families, especially before communion; rules for a Christian life presented first in continuous prose, then in metre with each new verse starting with the next letter of the alphabet; and finally prayers before and after a meal. It may have been the variety of forms which appealed, for the work was reprinted almost every year in the early Stuart period, including about ten editions in the 1630s.[225] But as with the previous works, it is not impossible that it was used also in schools or even churches.

Josias Nichols's work is often cited today, but does not seem to have had the same impact at the time compared to the works described in previous paragraphs. In a preface to 'all governors of families', he explained that he was aiming for 'the lowest place of the church, which is the family', especially 'the meaner sort'. How-ever, the four groups he then urged to take special care to catechize were hardly of the

---

[223] For different editions and the Isham connection, see Appendix 1, s.v. Paget–Openshaw, and P. Collinson, *The Religion of Protestants* (Oxford, 1982), 234; [E. Paget], *Short questions and answeares* (1580), sigs. A3^{r-v}, A5^{v}–7^{r}.

[224] See Appendix 1, s.v. Paget for *Eusebii Pagetti catechismus*, and *The history of the Bible*.

[225] S. Egerton, *A briefe methode of catechising* (1615), *passim*, and Appendix 1.

'meaner sort': nobles, gentlemen, and the masters of other 'great households'; tutors; schoolmasters; and women (who were often marked out in 'godly' literature for a leading role in domestic instruction).[226] On top of the catechizing, he insisted that householders made sure that their children and servants engaged in sermon repetition, listened to the reading of a chapter from both Old and New Testaments every day, and were taught to read—fifteen minutes a day should be enough to get them reading, he confidently asserted.[227] This demanding work-load was made more onerous by the nature of the 'catechisms' in the text, most of which were not in question-and-answer format, but slabs of scriptural material with supporting interpretations or elaboration of points of doctrine which the 'catechist' had to repeat endlessly until the material was memorized by the students. The stress on rote learning was eased or alleviated to some extent by the sorting of the material into five grades of increasing difficulty, by the suggestion that teachers vary any questions and answers to ensure comprehension as well as memorization, and by the permission given to sing metrical psalms during occasional breaks.[228] The value of the form in practice is hard to assess. Nichols himself made no great claims for success with this work in his prefaces, and the fact that there was only one repeat edition presumably indicates a limited take-up.

Perhaps more practical (and more acceptable to judge from its sales) was the technique of Samuel Crooke, who in 1613 published two separate catechisms: a larger— *The guide unto true blessednesse*—which was a by-product of his sermons and the form which he seems to have intended to use in church but which he wanted members of the congregation to have copies at home; and a shorter—*A briefe direction to true happinesse*—which was an abridgement of the former but which he seems to have envisaged being taught by 'private families' to 'the younger' and the 'weaker sort' at home.[229] Robert Linaker did something similar in publishing catechisms for those who were old enough to be 'careful to know the way to everlasting life' and who wished to receive the Lord's Supper, and then a few years later two much shorter forms as a 'cordial preservative for little children, against the infection of popery and atheism'. It seems from the preface that these had been drawn up to teach his own children, but he had been persuaded to publish them for 'parents in private families' to use.[230] In each case the larger forms indicate the extent to which instruction in church and home was intended to go hand in hand, while the shorter forms tempered the wind to the shorn lambs.[231]

---

[226] See below, pp. 214–15, 217–19.

[227] Nichols, *Order of household instruction*, sigs. B3^v–4^r, B7^r–C2^r.   [228] Ibid., sig. C6^r and *passim*.

[229] S. Crooke, *The guide unto true blessednesse* (1613), sigs. A6^{r-v}; id., *A briefe direction to true happinesse* (1613), title-page; Clarke, *Lives of ten eminent divines*, 36.

[230] R. Linaker, *A short and plaine instruction* (1591), title-page and *passim*; id., *A short catechisme* (1610), title-page, and sig. A3^r.

[231] See also the title-pages and texts of the 1645 and 1647 editions of I. Bourne, *A light from Christ ... or a divine directory* for his aim of producing a shorter version of his own work which would be 'profitable also

Other forms written by 'godly' authors but more clearly designed for use in the home were those in which the speakers were designated 'father' or 'mother' and 'child'. The *New catechisme sette forth dialogue wise in familiare talk betwene the father and the son* by Thomas Becon was dedicated to his children, Theodore, Basil, and Rachel; but at over five hundred and forty folio sides, and covering the duties of all degrees and estates, it comprised a forbidding introduction to the Christian life, and presumably demanded both literacy and time to negotiate.[232] John Lyster dedicated his *A rule how to bring up children* to the 'Puritan Earl', Henry Hastings, and his fellow-clergy. The work was subtitled 'a treatise wherein is declared, how the father opposeth his son in the Holy Scripture, whereby all parents may be taught a rule how to bring up their children', and was very similar to Becon's: more dialogue than catechism, heavily scriptural, often anti-Catholic, and covering the duty of all estates and degrees of people. How its two hundred and seventy pages of text were to be used, as an early form of Dr Spock, or with a parent reading the questions and a child the answers, is again not clear.[233] With William Herbert's *Careful father and pious child* we are left in no doubt: it was to be learnt, all twelve hundred questions and answers, six hundred confutations of errors and heresies, and four hundred pages of it. The work, which was begun on his daughter's birth in 1640, is not devoid of human touches, but one is not surprised to learn that it took five years to complete, even with a civil war intervening.[234]

By comparison works by R.R. (possibly Richard Rogers) and William Blake were a good deal shorter. *The house-holders helpe for domesticall discipline* by R.R., published in 1615 and dedicated to 'all religious householders', consisted of three much shorter 'familiar conferences' between 'a gracious gentleman' and 'his eldest son'—an adult who had failed to catechize in his own household, but was left in no doubt as to its necessity.[235] As the title suggests, the author of *The farmers catechize, or a religious parly between the father and the son*, William Blake, was a layman; he was also an anticlerical and a republican, and the work, published in 1657, was dedicated to 'all those honest families that desires Christ may dwell in their hearts'. The text was only seventy-five pages long, combined simple factual questions and homely anecdotes with some practical and some decidedly quirky comments. It was probably meant to be learnt and perhaps acted out, since the father begins by saying 'Come sirrah, if you will be a good boy, learn your catechize [*sic*], and then teach your brothers and sisters, I will give you a farthing', and the son replies 'Well sir, do you ask and I will answer'.[236]

for parents ... or masters', or 'persons and families in private'.

[232] T. Becon, *A new catechisme*, in *Workes* (1564), fo. cclxxxvii[v] and *passim*.
[233] J. Lyster, *A rule how to bring up children* (1588), sig. A2[v] and *passim*.
[234] W. Herbert, *Herberts careful father and pious child* (1648), title-page, sig. B4[r] and *passim*.
[235] R.R., *The house-holders helpe* (1615), sig. A2[r] and *passim*.
[236] W. Blake, *The farmers catechize* (1657), title-page, p. 1, and *passim*. In Sir William Popple's *Rational catechism* (1687)—an 'instructive conference between a father and a son'—there is also an axe being audibly ground.

Catechisms featuring mother and child were on the whole more indulgent or realistic. *The mother and the child*, a summary of a longer catechism by a Scot, John Craig, was published in 1611 'for the fitting of little children for the public ministry' (that is, attendance at church services). The questions and answers were very short, mostly one or two lines in length, and the whole form filled only twenty-six pages.[237] Robert Abbot's *Milk for babes; or, a mother's catechism for her children* (1646) contained a very short form 'to be opened at first', a slightly longer one 'for children', and then a much longer one which incorporated long expositions of the same questions and answers, extra questions and answers, 'uses' of the doctrinal points raised, and short revision exercises. It is interesting to see in the epistle that the form had already been used in both the family and the congregation of Lady Honoria Newton of Southwick in Hampshire, and by the author in 'private exercises' with others in his flock.[238] In the same year Dorothy Burch went one better by publishing her own form. Having been told by her minister that she and others were 'poor ignorant simple people' who knew nothing of God (I hope God pardons him, she wrote in her preface), she decided to 'set pen to paper', and by 'asking myself questions, and answering of them' produced the eighteen-page *Catechism of the severall heads of Christian religion*. Signing herself 'Thy friend in Christ, Dorothy Burch', she published the work to vindicate God's honour, to explain her beliefs, and for the use of her children.[239]

The first surviving edition of *The mother's catechism for the young child* by the presbyterian John Willison was published in London in 1735, though there were many other editions printed in Scotland and North America. It consisted of a short form of seventeen pages to prepare children to learn the Westminster Shorter Catechism, an even shorter form with 'historical questions' about the Bible, the Decalogue in verse, a paraphrase of the Lord's Prayer, and a 'spiritual song for young children'.[240] Given the variety of material in this work, its popularity is perhaps not surprising. By comparison, Richard Baxter's *A familiar way of catechising* (1701) between 'mother' and 'child', and Mrs J.C.'s *The mother's catechism* (1734) were much longer. Baxter's form was less a catechism than a means of showing how a child could ask questions about the Bible and a mother answer; but the answers got longer and longer, and after a hundred and thirty pages, he had still not got past the Old Testament and seems to have aborted the project.[241] Mrs J.C. was trying to provide 'an explication of some

---

[237] [John Cragge/Craig], *The mother and the child* (1611), title-page and *passim*; and see Appendix 1, s.v. H.S.

[238] R. Abbot, *Milk for babes; or, a mother's catechism* (1646), sigs. aa1ʳ–ᵛ and *passim*.

[239] D. Burch, *A catechism of the severall heads of Christian religion* (1646), sigs. A2ʳ–3ʳ and *passim*.

[240] J. Willison, *The mother's catechism for the young child* (1735)—said to be the 15th edn.: see Appendix 1. For the influence of Willison outside England, see L. E. Schmidt, *Holy Fairs: Scottish Communions and American Revivals in the Early Modern Period* (Princeton, 1989).

[241] R. Baxter, *A familiar way of catechising* (1701) and [A reverend divine], *The mother's catechism* (Nottingham, 1717) are the same work: see Appendix 1.

questions of the Assembly's shorter catechism … for the use of her children and ser-vants'; after eighty pages she had covered only 40 of the 107 questions, and also appears to have given up.[242] On the other hand, the series of moralistic dialogues between father, mother, and children in Daniel Defoe's *Family instructor* and *New family instructor*, although very long, proved very popular, perhaps because of the story-line he provided to link the points he was making about the gulf between Chris-tian profession and practice.[243]

The work of Mrs J.C. and Willison remind us of another genre that had developed since the late 1640s: explanations and expositions of the Westminster Shorter Cate-chism, designed in part or totally for use in the home, especially after 1662. In his *Plain and familiar method of instructing the younger sort according to the lesser catechism*, Thomas Lye provided seven rules to help householders go through the whole cate-chism in a month on a daily basis; his *Assemblies shorter catechism drawn out … and proved* divided the whole into thirty sections for daily use, and again gave very clear guidelines to 'masters of families, how to use this book to the best advantage'; and he also published another *Explanation of the shorter catechism* 'specially intended for governors of families', in particular near the Somerset town where he had been born and first been a minister.[244] Thomas Gouge's *Principles of Christian religion explained to the capacity of the meanest* was only partly based on the Westminster Shorter Cate-chism, but also offered simple rules on how the 'great and necessary duty of family-catechizing' could be accomplished in a family unit.[245] The preface to Thomas Vincent's *Explicatory catechism* reveals a rather different approach and the fact that the work had taken him years to complete, catechumens having had to make do at first with manuscript copies of each new instalment. Vincent gave priority to the learning and repetition of the catechism in church, but saw printed copies as hav-ing value both for literate young catechumens, and for 'private families' who were encouraged to read copies at home, in the following manner. After a question and answer of the Shorter Catechism had been rehearsed, a member of the circle should 'be called upon to read (if not to rehearse) the explanation of it' offered by Vincent, 'the rest reading along with him in several books, by which means their thoughts (which are apt to wander) will be the more intent on what they are about'.[246] Where other authors had written forms for use in the home to prepare the very young or the educationally disadvantaged for the task of learning the Westminster Shorter Cate-chism, Vincent was using the home as a support system in the task of explaining its meaning to all members of a family who could read.

---

[242] Mrs J.C., *The mother's catechism* (1734), title-page and *passim*.

[243] D. Defoe, *The family instructor* (1715–18) and *A new family instructor* (1727), *passim*.

[244] See Appendix 1 for the complex publication history of these works by Lye. See also Z. Cawdrey, *A brief and methodical catechism* (1664), title-page; and J. Alleine, *A most familiar explanation* (1672).

[245] T. Gouge, *The principles of Christian religion* (1684), sigs. A2^r–3^r and *passim*; for similar calls, see Appendix 1, s.v. Z. Cawdrey; *Explicatory catechism*; *Doctrines*; and W. Notcutt.

[246] T. Vincent, *An explicatory catechisme* (1701), sigs. A2^r–5^r.

No one wrote more about the theory of catechizing than Isaac Watts, whose ill-health prevented him from taking up a full-time ministry but who more than made up for this in his writing of hymns, children's verse catechisms, and other improving works. Not only did he write a seventy-five page 'Discourse on the way of instruction by catechisms: and of the best manner of composing them', but he also prefaced at least five of his catechisms with precise details of how each was to be taught, to whom and why—remarks which he seems to have been addressing primarily to parents (though they would have been of value to schoolteachers and ministers who catechized).[247] Watts was another strong believer in graded teaching, enabling catechumens of different ages or capacities to proceed from basic forms to intermediate and then to more difficult forms, though he put more stress on the individual pupil proceeding at his or her own pace, which was easier to arrange in smaller family units than in larger classes in school or chapel. Watts also assumed that not only the householder who was called on to act as catechist would be literate, but also children would be able to read by an early age, certainly by the age of 5.[248] It is perhaps fair to say that dissenting authors of catechisms demanded higher standards of literacy than their conformist counterparts, and that after the Restoration while the latter made more experiments in catechetical works aimed at use in school or church, the former (perforce) showed more interest and inventiveness in domestic catechizing.

Let us now turn to the practice of domestic catechizing and examine it in two stages: until the 1640s, and from the 1650s. It must be confessed that many of the pointers for the first period are negative. In a sermon preached at Paul's Cross in August 1578, John Stockwood (the Tonbridge schoolmaster who played a part in popularizing the Dering–More catechism) delivered a jeremiad on the condition of England, and amongst the many crimes of the 'common people' was that few were like Cornelius, the centurion who with all his household feared God (Acts 10: 2). Not only was it necessary for those in positions of domestic authority to be well versed in the scriptures and to teach the fear of the Lord to those in their charge, he said, but they should be punished for neglecting to instruct them.[249] Ten years later, Thomas Sparke complained that scarce one householder in a hundred was performing their duty to catechize, and in the 1590s Josias Nichols warned that the backwardness of householders was undoing the good achieved by the minister's efforts; he urged them to put aside all the vain excuses which the devil and their own corrupt natures

---

[247] Watts, *Catechisms*, 1–75, 77–8, 84–7, 117–19, 192–4, 203–6; and see above, p. 196.
[248] Watts, *Catechisms*, 77–8, 80, 193.
[249] J. Stockwood, *A sermon preached at Paules Crosse [24.8.1578]* (1578), 23, 48–51, 77–93, 131–2. In addition to the references in this and following footnotes, see T. Becon, *A new catechisme*, in *Workes* (1564), fo. cclxxxvii^v; E.B., *A catechisme or briefe instruction* (1617), sig. A2^v; and anon, 'Of catechisinge', sig. [29^r].

provided for their failure to catechize at home.[250] In 1604 Robert Cawdrey also told 'fond parents' that they were culpable for the disobedience of their children; and in 1645 Walter Bridges urged householders in London not to let all the catechisms that were currently available 'rise up in judgement against you', while they and theirs remained uninstructed.[251] 'Too many use catechisms as they do almanacs', wrote William Crompton in 1633, 'for a year and then their date is out'—a remark which cuts two ways, on the one hand suggesting lack of consistent application, but on the other a frequent distribution of new forms as far south-west as the Devonshire town where he was minister.[252] We may also note the energy with which a number of authors responded to complaints by adults that they were either not capable of teaching or learning a catechism, or were not willing to do so, though there is also the ambiguous remark by Perkins in the mid-1590s that it was 'very common in this age' for those who had been regular church-goers but were very sick and possibly dying to be 'catechized in the doctrine of faith and repentance'—presumably at home— when they should have learnt this many years before.[253] Other authors were equally pessimistic, arguing that many parents were themselves so ignorant that they needed to learn a catechism every bit as much as their children and servants, though as Christopher Haigh has pointed out only small numbers of adults appear to have been rejected from communion on grounds of ignorance of the simple Prayer Book catechism, as opposed to a more advanced form.[254]

Perhaps the only exceptions to this gloomy picture were provided by the 'godly'. The evidence for this comes in part from funeral sermons, hagiographical biographies, and autobiographical accounts by the 'godly'. From these we learn that Lady Anne Waller catechized her children and servants once a week and made them give an account of the sermons they had heard; that Lady Margaret Hoby provided catechetical instruction for servants as well as the 'poor and ignorant' in her Yorkshire household; and that Sir John Holland would punish his daughter if she failed to learn her catechism by making her go without food.[255] If we take references to parents teaching children 'the most useful things for the benefit of their souls and bodies' or 'the first grounds and principles of religion' or some other kind of 'religious' or 'sweet instruction' as referring to some kind of catechizing, then we can add to these examples the cases cited by Samuel Clarke: the households of Sir Nathaniel

[250] [Sparke and Seddon], *Catechisme, or short kind of instruction*, 1, 5–6; Nichols, *Household instruction*, sigs. B5ʳ, B7ʳ; and cf. [Bridges], *Catechisme for communicants*, sig. A7ᵛ.

[251] R. Cawdrey, *A short and fruitefull treatise* (1604), sigs. Aiiʳ–iiiʳ; [Bridges], *Catechisme*, sig. A5ʳ.

[252] W. Crompton, *An explication of those principles* (1633), sig. ¶4ᵛ.

[253] Green, 'Emergence of the English Catechism', 418–19; W. Perkins, *A salve for a sick man* (1595), 57–8.

[254] Ibid. 408–9; C. Haigh, 'The Church of England, the Catholics and the People', in Haigh (ed.), *The Reign of Elizabeth I* (London, 1984), 210–11; M. Ingram, 'From Reformation to Toleration', in T. Harris (ed.), *Popular Culture in England, 1500–1850* (1995), 117.

[255] Haigh, loc. cit; Cliffe, *Puritan Gentry*, 33, 73; *Diary of Lady Margaret Hoby 1599–1605*, ed. D. M. Meads (1930), 65–6, 68, 74.

Barnardiston, Mrs Katherine Clark, Lady Elizabeth Langham, and Lady Alice Lucy.[256] We also know of catechisms used by noble or gentry households, such as those of Paget and Abbot already mentioned and others to which we shall come shortly.[257] And the church courts provide examples of families being accused of conventicling when their defence was that they were catechizing or discussing a catechism class they had attended recently. William Walker of Cold Norton in Essex said he used to catechize 'in his own house and with his own family only'; in 1584 in the same county about ten 'kindred and neighbours' came to the house of one Davies for supper, at which they 'conferred together of such profitable lessons as they had learned that day at a public catechizing' (though in at least one of these cases a suspended clergyman was present).[258]

Examples of domestic catechizing using the Prayer Book form or an exposition of that form or one of the tribe of Nowell are harder to pin down. One East Anglian curate in the late 1590s was catechizing parishioners in their homes in 'the catechism newly set forth', perhaps because they were reluctant to be taught or examined in groups or in public.[259] The royal households also probably set an example to the aristocracy: Princes Henry and Charles and Princess Elizabeth were confirmed between 1607 and 1613, and we may assume that they were put through their catechetical paces beforehand. Also in 1634 a work entitled *The Christian directorie* was published with a short catechism at the end, the whole being dedicated to the governess of the young prince of Wales.[260] At a less exalted level, Richard Bernard tells us that copies of his exposition of the Prayer Book catechism had been sought by various people for use in their own households, and he also praised Sir Walter Earle for his great care in catechizing his family despite his many other tasks. From the context it seems that Earle had been using this form too, and Bernard, an experienced catechist, said he had never seen the like.[261] However, such examples are relatively few compared to those in 'godly' households of which we know, and Nicholas Ferrar actually rejected the idea of catechizing his household in favour of teaching them psalms.[262] As a result one's estimate of the prevalence of domestic catechizing between the 1570s and the 1640s depends on one's estimate of the strength of the 'godly'.

That having been said, there are indications that catechizing was more likely to take place in some types of 'godly' household than others, or in some situations more often than others. Readers of the last few paragraphs may have noted, on the one

[256] Clarke, *Lives of sundry eminent persons*, 111, 155, 201, 141; and cf. Sir Francis Pile in Cliffe, *Puritan Gentry*, 71.

[257] Ibid., and E. Rogers, *The chiefe grounds of Christian religion* (1642); and see above, p. 51 n. 31.

[258] P. Collinson, *The Elizabethan Puritan Movement* (London, 1967), 376, 379.

[259] *Diocese of Norwich: Bishop Redman's Visitation 1597*, ed. J. F. Williams (Norfolk Record Society, 18; 1946), 18.

[260] Fincham, *Prelate as Pastor*, 124; and Appendix 1: the publisher of the *Christian directorie* was the future Royalist and publisher of Jeremy Taylor's works, Richard Royston.

[261] R. Bernard, *The common catechisme* (1640), sigs. A2ʳ⁻ᵛ.

[262] A. L. Maycock, *Nicholas Ferrar of Little Gidding* (Grand Rapids, 1980), 202–3.

hand, Stockwood's reference to the absence of catechizing among the 'common people', and on the other the references or appeals to the nobility and gentry made by Paget, Nichols, Rogers, and Lyster. Other examples of catechisms written for use in a noble or gentry household include Patrick Galloway's ('used in the family of the Scottish noblemen then resident at Newcastle'); William Ames's *Chief heads of divinitie* (based on the teaching he had given to the two 'hopeful young gentlemen', the sons of Lady Vere, when he had been their tutor); Ezekiel Rogers's *Chief grounds of Christian religion* ('gathered long since for the use of an honourable family'—the Barringtons); and Robert Abbot's (used in the family of his patroness, Lady Honoria Norton in Hampshire).[263] Works which were dedicated to members of the nobility, as gestures of thanks or with the hope that they would protect it or actually use it, include Seddon and Sparke's edition of the Heidelberg Catechism in 1588 (dedicated to Lord Grey of Wilton), Robert Cawdrey's treatise on catechizing in 1604 (Lord and Lady Russell), Gervase Scarbrough's catechism of 1623 (Ann, Countess of Dorset and her mother, the countess of Cumberland); and John Rowlandson's of 1644 (the earl of Rutland).[264]

Another hallmark of domestic catechizing among the 'godly' was the presence of a minister. As we have seen, Paget was an eyewitness to the success of his catechism with the grooms, shepherds, carters, milkmaids, and kitchen-boys of the Isham household, and Abbot used his catechism in 'private exercises' in his Hampshire parish; we also know that Lady Margaret Hoby's chaplain helped her to catechize the servants in her Yorkshire household, and that a nonconforming clergyman was present at one of the occasions of household catechizing which led to prosecutions in Elizabethan Essex.[265] Arthur Hildersham, who was regularly harried by the authorities in the 1590s, 'sojourned in many families', and during his stay in each household he would pray, expound, and 'by private conference … instruct the ignorant'.[266] A variant on the situation in which the clergyman was a domestic chaplain, a relative, or a guest, was where ministers with responsibility for a whole parish visited each household in turn, to instruct or to test the inhabitants' fitness for the Lord's Supper, as William Gouge did in London from the 1610s and Edmund Staunton in Kingston-on-Thames before 1635.[267] In 1645 John Owen wrote that for the last two

---

[263] P. Galloway, *A catechisme: conteyning summarely the chief points* (1588), title-page; [W. Ames], *The chiefe heads of divinitie* (Dordrecht, 1612), sigs. A2^{r-v}; E. Rogers, *Chiefe grounds*, title-page; Abbot, *Milke for babes*, sigs. aal^{r-v}.

[264] Anon., *A catechisme, or short kind of instruction* (1588), sigs. A2^r–3^v; Nichols, *Household instruction*, sig. A2^r; Cawdrey, *Short and fruitefull treatise* (1604), sigs. ii^{r-v}; G. Scarbrough, *The summe of all godly and profitable catechismes* (1623), sig. A3^v; J. Rowlandson, *A brief and plain catechisme* (1644), sigs. A2^r–3^v. Appeal to a powerful patron was not confined to 'godly' authors, but among conformable clergy was as likely to be to a bishop as a lay peer or corporation; see above, p. 6.

[265] See above, pp. 210–11, 217–18.

[266] Collinson, *Puritan Movement*, 405; Clarke, *Lives of two and twenty divines*, 153; for a later example, see J. T. Cliffe, *The Puritan Gentry Besieged, 1650–1700* (1993), 138.

[267] Clarke, *Lives of ten eminent divines*, 107; id., *Lives of sundry eminent persons*, 162.

years he had been teaching his flock both publicly and house to house, and Samuel Winter appointed to a living near Hull in the 1640s is also said to have gone from house to house instructing the ignorant.[268]

There are also records of rather larger meetings, of something between a family unit and a whole congregation, often held in the house of one of the 'godly' but with a minister present. In the Wirral in the 1620s the 'godly' from all over the peninsula, including the later puritan hagiographer Samuel Clarke, met every three weeks in 'all the richer men's houses' for 'days of conference' which included prayer, discussion, and a form of catechizing in which the questions were apparently set in advance, the younger had to hand in their answers first, and then the more experienced.[269] It was recorded of Thomas Taylor (again by Clarke) that he kept fasts among the 'godly' of his area, 'which in those days was something of a dangerous exercise':

and, to make them solid professors indeed, he put them upon a weekly way of handling cate-chetical points of divinity; that is, every week to confer of one of the heads of religion accord-ing to the catechism subjoined to Master Dod's treatise on the Commandments [by Thomas Cartwright], still proving the doctrines by testimonies of scripture.[270]

When he published his *Principles of Christian doctrine* for the householders of Hat-field Broad Oak in Essex in 1654, their minister, John Warren, let it be known that it was an abstract of the principles which had been discussed in 'your constant meet-ings for conference' in recent years, and at which from the sound of it Warren him-self had been present.[271]

In other cases the household in which a catechism had been used or was about to be used was that of the minister himself. Robert Linaker's shorter form had been drawn up for 'some younglings ... near and dear unto me' before it was offered to other 'private families'; William Hinde had an edition of his *Path to pietie* published in 1613 'for more private use', that is with his own family and flock; Gervase Scar-brough published his form 'for the common good of God's church' and all children and poor ignorant souls, but 'more especially ... for the instruction and building up of mine own family and the people' of his London parish.[272] In the pages of Samuel Clarke we find many other clergymen who catechized their own children.[273] Again this was not a phenomenon confined to the 'godly': Henry Isaacson, the protégé and biographer of Lancelot Andrewes, had his 'orthodox' catechism published in 1647 for use in his own family and some private friends.[274] But it was a practice that we are

---

[268] J. Owen, *The principles of the doctrine of Christ* (1645), sig. A2ᵛ; Clarke, *Lives of sundry eminent persons*, 96.

[269] Ibid. 4.   [270] Clarke, *Lives of two and twenty divines*, 158.

[271] J. Warren, *Principles of Christian doctrine* (1654), sigs. A3ʳ⁻ᵛ.

[272] R. Linaker, *A short catechisme* (1610), sig. A3ʳ; W. Hinde, *A path to pietie* (1626), sigs. A6ʳ⁻ᵛ; Scar-brough, *Summe of catechismes*, title-page.

[273] Clarke, *Lives of ten eminent divines*, 69, 145; id., *Lives of two and twenty divines*, 158, 173, 227 and cf. 236; id., *Lives of sundry eminent persons*, 34, '178', 196.

[274] H[enry] I[saacson], *The summe and substance of Christian religion* (1647), sig. A1ᵛ.

more likely to pick up among the 'godly' owing to their energy in producing catechisms for their own household and others like it, and their penchant for edifying
biographies. In this context, we might also mention that although Richard Rogers
was content to leave the *academic* teaching in his home-cum-school to others, he
always insisted on performing the catechizing himself; and other 'godly' clergy or
teachers who had pupils living in as part of their households also made sure that they
were catechized along with or parallel to their own families.[275] Asking their children
and servants questions on the last sermon they had heard was another regular practice of the 'godly', but perhaps took place with particular regularity and rigour in the
home of the preacher himself.[276]

In short, catechizing among the 'godly'—as also among Catholic recusants in gentry households with resident priests or 'tutors'—may have taken place more often in
the homes of those who had the time, the resources, the literacy, and the support of a
minister. Catechizing, as John Morgan has put it, was a venture which 'bound household and ministerial office together' but in which the minister took the lead.[277] We
may also recall Robert Cawdrey's observation in 1604 that God's religion had taken
effect only in those towns 'where catechizing is diligently practised both by ministers
publicly, and by householders privately'.[278] Where the mutually reinforcing corporateness of the 'godly' was incomplete or temporary, their programme was probably
much harder to implement.

This was partly the case in the 1650s, when the 'godly' fell out among themselves,
and rapidly ran into even greater difficulties than before. The picture presented of
the situation in the 1650s by the presbyterians, the strongest of the new groups, is of
considerable gloom, relieved by only sporadic shafts of light. The 'fearful inundation
of pestilent heresies' of the early 1650s was blamed in part on the fact that catechizing in church had sunk to a low level, with the clergy failing to catechize because they
regarded it as beneath their dignity, and adults refusing to attend catechizing in
church and not requiring the attendance of those in their care; while catechizing in
the home was said by three different authors to have been either almost completely
abandoned or everywhere neglected.[279] In his *Catechizing Gods ordinance*, Zachary
Crofton urged the case for more catechizing by ministers and schoolmasters as well
as heads of households, but took most space to reprove the neglect of householders
and the resistance of catechumens, to dismiss any excuses they might offer, and to

[275] Morgan, *Godly Learning*, 154; Clarke, *Lives of two and twenty divines*, 173–4, 227; id., *Lives of sundry eminent persons*, 112.

[276] e.g. Clarke, *Lives of sundry eminent persons*, '181'.

[277] Morgan, *Godly Learning*, 86–7, and cf. 153 n. 76; and for the Catholic practice, J. A. Bossy, *The English Catholic Community 1570–1850* (1975), 272–7 on priests taking the lead, but see also Greaves, *Society and Religion*, 276, 294–5, 315 for lay involvement being encouraged.

[278] Cawdrey, *Short and fruitefull treatise* (1604), sig. A1ᵛ; and cf. I. W. Archer, *The Pursuit of Stability: Social Relations in Elizabethan London* (Cambridge, 1991), 88.

[279] Anon., *An exhortation to catechising* (1665), 3–6, 8, 10–13; S. Ford, *A sermon of catechizing* (1655), sig. G5ʳ; D. Cawdrey, *Family-reformation promoted* (1656), sigs. A3ᵛ–5ᵛ, and pp. 37–8; and next note.

offer incentives to the 'restoring' of family catechizing.[280] In 1653 a chaplain to a peer in London told Richard Baxter that 'our family' had never been catechized since he had arrived there, and with the peer's approval he was writing to Baxter for advice on how to begin, since some in the family were high and proud, others profane, some illiterate, some young, others old, and so on.[281]

There were occasional gleams of light in the 1650s, for example in Somerset and Worcestershire. When appointed to a post in Taunton in the late 1650s, and perhaps in response to pressure of the type described in the previous paragraph, the young Joseph Alleine went from house to house instructing his parishioners, having given them notice the day before of his intention to call. According to Clarke, when Alleine visited he instructed the young by asking questions out of 'the catechism' (presumably the Westminster Shorter of which Alleine produced a 'familiar explanation'); he then enlarged upon and explained their answers, and enquired about their spiritual estate. Visiting three or four families a day between one or two and seven in the afternoon for five afternoons a week, Alleine went through the whole town and then began again, blessing God for the great success he had in these exercises. He was ejected by the Act of Uniformity in 1662, but carried on promoting the education of the young, giving catechisms to many poor families and urging the elder to teach the younger, and himself catechizing once a week in public.[282]

Richard Baxter's route to the idea of catechizing households and his technique of performing it in Kidderminster were similar but not quite the same. In 1653 he had been a leading light in the creation of the Worcester Association, a body of moderate clergy of differing doctrinal and ecclesiastical opinions but united by a common concern to exercise some kind of discipline over their flocks, and in particular to prevent unworthy or ignorant adults profaning the sacrament of the Lord's Supper. To this end they agreed a profession of faith, based on the Apostles' Creed but published with a long explication by Baxter.[283] Two years later, the same clergy were still worried about the ignorance of both old and young and the continued spread of heresy, and decided to try to counter it by 'familiar instruction of families in their order'.[284] In August 1655 Baxter was paving the way for this when he wrote to a parallel Association in Ireland that 'we are now upon a joint agreement to bring all the ancient persons in our parishes (who will not do it in the congregation) to our houses on certain

---

[280] Z. Crofton, *Catechizing Gods ordinance* (1656), sigs. A8^{r-v}, a2^v–4^r, a7^r, pp. 60–4, 78–86, 93–110, and *passim*.

[281] N. H. Keeble and G. F. Nuttall, *Calendar of the Correspondence of Richard Baxter* (2 vols.; Oxford, 1991), no. 146.

[282] Clarke, *Lives of sundry eminent persons*, 143–4, 148, 157 (much of Clarke's information came from T. Alleine, *The life and death of … Mr. Joseph Alleine* (1672), 39–47); J. Alleine, *A most familiar explanation of the Assemblies shorter catechism* (1672).

[283] [R. Baxter], *Christian concord: or the agreement of the associated pastors and churches of Worcestershire* (1653); G. F. Nuttall, 'The Worcestershire Association: its membership', *JEH* 1 (1950), 197–206.

[284] For this phrase, see Keeble and Nuttall, *Baxter Correspondence*, no. 408.

days every week, by turns, to be catechized or instructed'.[285] In December 1655 the members of the Association entered into a public agreement to carry through their plan, turned their brief confession of faith into a very short catechism of twelve questions and answers 'comprehending as much as is necessary to be believed, consented and practised', and exhorted their people to submit to the task of learning this simple catechism, either publicly or privately. They fixed a day of fasting and prayer to seek God's blessing on their scheme, but unfortunately Baxter was unable to attend and preach because of ill-health. Instead in April 1656 he published some of the material he had assembled for that occasion, under the title *Gildas Salvianus*—two authors of the fifth and sixth centuries who had been outspoken in their condemnation of sin. The dedication to fellow-clergy all over Britain and Ireland alerted others to this local agreement to step up 'the work of catechizing, and private instruction of all in their parishes who would not obstinately refuse their help', and invited them to do the same.[286] As we have already seen, Baxter was not the first to think of 'private instruction' of each household in turn, but there is good evidence that Baxter's publication, better known today by its subtitle *The reformed pastor*, proved timely and was not only widely read but also well received.[287]

Meanwhile, Baxter had read out the agreement, exhortation, and catechism to his own flock in Kidderminster, and preached two or three times on the necessity of everybody learning the catechism, even the old 'loiterers'. The Worcestershire Association had published their agreement, confession, and catechism in a little pamphlet entitled *The agreement of divers ministers of Christ in the county of Worcester ... for catechizing or personal instruction*, and the next step was for Baxter's assistant and one of the deacons to deliver a copy of the *Agreement* to every one of the more than eight hundred families in the parish; only five or six were reported to have refused to accept it. Having allowed six weeks for each family to master its contents, Baxter then made arrangements through the parish clerk for the different families to come to his house in sequence on a Monday or Tuesday. At the start, his assistant, Richard Sargeant, sat in while Baxter heard each family repeat the words and gave a discourse on what had been rehearsed, but then the two men divided the rest of the families in the town equally between them. At first many parishioners gibbed at being allocated to the assistant until good reports reached them, and then, Baxter found, the more bashful often went to Sargeant 'because they are bolder with him'.[288]

Whether we count this as domestic catechizing or not is a moot point. In the sense that the initiative was taken by the clergy in distributing the copies, and the clergy did the testing and explaining, this can be classed as ministerial catechizing. But Baxter's

---

[285] Ibid., no. 262.

[286] R. Baxter, *Gildas Salvianus. The Reformed Pastor* (1860), 1–2 and preface, *passim*.

[287] See below, pp. 225–7.

[288] Keeble and Nuttall, *Baxter Correspondence*, nos. 290, 348; on Sargeant, see also R. Baxter, *Reliquiae Baxterianae* (1696), lib. I, pt. II, p. 179, and pt. III, pp. 91–2.

intention seems to have been that the form in the *Agreement* should be learnt by the members of each household before they came to see him; and the testing of the results took place either in the householders' own homes or in the home of Baxter or one of his assistants. Baxter later gave three reasons for his insistence that most families should come to him and Sargeant, rather than the ministers going to them: because of the size of the parish (twenty miles in circumference by his calculation); because parishioners were 'unwilling for us to come to their houses'; and because it was 'fitter' for them to show some respect to the minister by coming to his house or to another, or even the church, at a fixed hour.[289] There is a slight discrepancy in the strictly contemporary accounts here about the minority of families which were visited in their own homes,[290] but the resolution is found in the autobiography which Baxter wrote later, where he says 'those in the town [of Kidderminster] came to our houses', while those living outside the town but within the parish received visits in their own homes from the mobile Sargeant. In both cases, the essence of the matter was that the catechizing was 'private' and not public, that it was 'familiar', that is conducted in a family unit, and that it took place in a home rather than a church. As Baxter put it in a letter of advice to a minister in Surrey, be sure that you take all your parish personally, man by man, in private 'as we do'.[291] So although there was a strong ministerial role, the operation was in essence a household one.

What Baxter wanted to do was not simply to hear each family recite the short catechism agreed by the Association, but also help them to understand it, enquire 'modestly' into the state of their souls, and then try 'to set all home to convince, awaken and resolve their hearts according to their several conditions'.[292] Bestowing an hour on each family, Baxter found that it took him and Sargeant (and sometimes another assistant from a chapel) a whole year to get through four thousand souls.[293] At the outset he, Sargeant, and the other assistant used to 'spend Monday and Tuesday, from morning to almost night, in the work ... taking about fifteen or sixteen families in a week'. But at some stage he seems to have decided to drop the rate to three families each, every Monday and Tuesday, with appointments set at one, two, and three o'clock in the afternoon. Even this he found very taxing; it was as demanding as giving two sermons on a Sunday, he said.[294] However, when one crusty old minister in 1657 complained that two days a week would take young ministers away from their studies and so hamper their preparation of sermons, Baxter replied that he and his assistant had catechized only two half days each a week, and that one day in six, which

---

[289] Keeble and Nuttall, *Baxter Correspondence*, no. 462.

[290] Ibid., nos. 462, 1064; *Reliquiae Baxterianae*, lib. I, pt. I, p. 88 (para. 137 (11)); and cf. Baxter, *Reformed Pastor*, 27.

[291] *Reliquiae Baxterianae*, lib. I, pt. II, pp. 179–80 (para. 41); Keeble and Nuttall, *Baxter Correspondence*, no. 290.

[292] *Reliquiae Baxterianae*, lib. I, pt. II, pp. 179–80 (para. 41).

[293] Keeble and Nuttall, *Baxter Correspondence*, no. 768; Baxter, *Reformed Pastor*, 360–1.

[294] Ibid. 27, 360–1; Keeble and Nuttall, *Baxter Correspondence*, no. 290.

had been the minimum agreed by the Association, did not represent an excessive amount of time, especially given the benefits of the time thus spent.[295]

For, despite his gloomy prediction of the 'world of work' and the 'pitiful life' that this project would involve, Baxter was soon convinced that it was well worth it for the many insights it provided into the spiritual state of his flock.[296] By April 1656 not one family had refused to come to see him, 'and but few persons excused themselves'; later he wrote that only half a dozen of the 'most ignorant and senseless' of the town refused to come to him.[297] Some 'not noted for any extraordinary profession' were found to be 'solid godly people'; others who were 'noted professors' were found to be ignorant of the essentials of Christian teaching; many who were found at first to be ignorant 'seemed in a little time instructed and resolved for a holy life'—all of which, it should be noted, confirms that what Baxter was up to was not simply testing knowledge of the catechism but comprehension of what that form contained and a commitment to put its lessons into practice.[298] Baxter was able to compile a list of those who were 'tolerable in knowledge and life' who could be admitted to the sacrament, and to suggest that any who were 'intolerably ignorant' but wished to claim church membership should 'learn awhile as catechumens and then come again'.[299] His only complaint seems to have been that owing to pressure of numbers he was forced to deal with a whole family at once, whereas on some occasions he would have preferred to deal with individuals within that unit.[300] 'We never hit the way of pulling down the kingdom of the devil till now', Baxter wrote in triumph to one correspondent at the time; 'Of all the works that ever I attempted, this yielded me most comfort in the practice of it', he later wrote in his autobiography.[301]

Baxter's pleasure was increased by the interest his scheme attracted. From various sources, not least his own enormous correspondence, we can see that *The reformed pastor* did, as he had hoped, rouse clergy in other areas, even from abroad, to try to bring their people to submit to 'this course of private instruction'; and we can also see that Baxter did his best to offer them further advice on how to reproduce his scheme in their parishes.[302] One minister wrote from Wiltshire reporting earnest efforts to catechize by members of the local Association; another from Sussex told Baxter that

---

[295] Ibid., nos. 405, 410, but cf. *Reformed Pastor*, 359–61, 413–29.

[296] Ibid. 23–7, 114–18, 288, 413–29.

[297] Ibid. 27; *Reliquiae Baxterianae*, lib. I, pt. II, pp. 179–80 (para. 41).

[298] Keeble and Nuttall, *Baxter Correspondence*, no. 768. For a recent examination of Baxter's typology of his parishioners, see E. Duffy, 'The godly and the multitude in Stuart England', *Seventeenth Century Journal*, 1 (1986), 38–40.

[299] Keeble and Nuttall, *Baxter Correspondence*, no. 403, and cf. *Reformed Pastor*, 349–52.

[300] Baxter, *Reformed Pastor*, 27.

[301] Keeble and Nuttall, *Baxter Correspondence*, no. 290 (but cf. similar phrases in *Reformed Pastor*, 26, 347); and *Reliquiae Baxterianae*, lib. I, pt. II, p. 179 (para. 41).

[302] Baxter, *Reformed Pastor*, 436, and chs. 7–8, *passim*; Keeble and Nuttall, *Baxter Correspondence*, nos. 242, 262, 285, 290, 293, 320, 333, 345, 348, 403, 459, 462, 712; *Reliquiae Baxterianae*, lib. I, pt. I, p. 115 (para. 177: 22), and pt. II, p. 180 (para. 42).

he had prevailed with many other ministers in the county to promote 'that most excellent work of catechizing and personal instruction of whole families'.[303] As we noted above, Clarke's account of the ministry of Joseph Alleine in Taunton from 1655 to 1662 has many parallels with that of Baxter for Kidderminster.[304] However, we do know that associations were set up in at least eight or nine counties, and looking back from the late 1660s Baxter saw a movement which was 'just set, and beginning to spread all over England ... at 1659' when 'confusion buried all'—a guarded way of saying that the fall of Richard Cromwell led to the return of the old church and the dissolution of the Association Movement.[305]

There was more than a hint of rose-tinted glass colouring Baxter's view of the wider success of the movement by 1659, since as his own correspondence makes clear, other ministers experienced difficulties in getting families to co-operate, or were frankly amazed at the success Baxter was reporting. One minister reported from Wiltshire that, despite their earnest endeavours, some members 'could not get a family' to co-operate, though they were not giving up yet.[306] Another wrote from Surrey: '800 families submit! I should hardly have credited it'. He anticipated considerable resistance in his own parish, and later on reported that even those willing to come for instruction were not willing to submit to the assistant whom he had appointed to 'explain' the little catechism to them.[307] Baxter also had to admit that in Kidderminster 'God gave me a tractable willing parish', while in 'my neighbours' congregations' catechizing was scorned by the ungodly and unruly, who used any pretence, such as the Worcester Association's omission of the article in the Creed about Christ's descent into hell, to kick up a fuss.[308] A fellow-member of the Worcester Association, admittedly elderly and somewhat remote from the other members, reported sadly to Baxter in December 1657 that 'I find that old Adam is too strong for young Melanchthon', and that he was planning to suspend the Lord's Supper to prevent its being sullied by ignorant or unworthy recipients.[309] Meanwhile in the Manchester area a younger Adam—Martindale—and his presbyterian colleagues also soon gave up the unequal struggle against lay resistance and the logistics of trying to visit every household.[310] What may have coincided in Worcestershire were two things: the enormous drive and vision of Baxter himself; and—in so far as there was success in other parishes than Kidderminster—the effect of social conformity which we raised in the last chapter: that what people in one parish were doing or receiving was likely soon to be copied or coveted by those in others nearby.[311] The further from the epicentre of Kidderminster, the weaker the vibrations became.

---

[303] Keeble and Nuttall, *Baxter Correspondence*, nos. 285, 320.
[304] Clarke, *Lives of sundry eminent persons*, 143–4: Clarke did not mention Baxter's lead.
[305] Keeble and Nuttall, *Baxter Correspondence*, no. 768; and cf. Hirst, 'Failure of Godly Rule', 43–4.
[306] Keeble and Nuttall, *Baxter Correspondence*, no. 285.   [307] Ibid., nos. 293, 345.
[308] *Reliquiae Baxterianae*, lib. I, pt. II, p. 179 (para. 41); Keeble and Nuttall, *Baxter Correspondence*, no. 407.
[309] Ibid., no. 408.   [310] Hirst, 'Failure of Godly Rule', 44–5.   [311] See above, pp. 133–5.

At the Restoration the system of pastors conferring with parishioners house by house and man by man was abandoned in Kidderminster and in most of the other parishes where it had been adopted.[312] But not all was lost. Baxter could still publish, and as a 'pen in God's hand' he produced works for household instruction such as *The poor man's family book* (1674) and *The catechizing of families* (1683), as well as the apparently unfinished *Mother's catechism* mentioned above.[313] The inspirational qualities of Baxter's work in Kidderminster also survived in the pages of *The reformed pastor* and later the *Reliquiae Baxterianae*, and were still being felt by Philip Doddridge and the Wesleys in the eighteenth century and by Anglicans, Congregationals, and Baptists in the nineteenth century.[314] Even in the shorter term, it left its mark. Oliver Heywood recorded in his diary how he read *The reformed pastor* during a period of sickness and 'resolved, if I recovered, to set upon the work of personal instruction', which he duly did, starting 'June 23, 1661, going from house to house'. Even in Heywood's last years there are regular references in his diary to catechizing, though more often in his own house than in chapel by then, due to his infirmities.[315] The fact that he was visiting individual members of his flock rather than expecting them to come to him is nearer to Owen's and Alleine's approach than to Baxter's, but in the changed circumstances of the 1660s to the 1680s this was perhaps a natural move for ejected clergy, constantly under the eyes of informers and JPs.

We may also note the practice of domestic catechizing in these years by clergy such as Heywood, Owen Stockton, and Philip Henry. Stockton is said to have catechized his own children and servants weekly, and in addition every fortnight explained some principle of religion in a catechetical way,[316] while on Thursday evenings Henry 'catechized his children and servants in the Assembly's catechism, with the proofs, or sometimes in a little catechism, concerning the matter of prayer'. By the 1680s, however, if not sooner he was also catechizing those outside his household: those in his congregation who had grown to years of discretion were ordered 'to come to him severally' for discussion and exhortation, and then 'for several Lord's-days he catechized them, particularly in public, touching the Lord's Supper, and the duty of preparation for it, and their baptismal covenant, which in that ordinance they were to take upon themselves'.[317] After 1689 nonconformist clergy like Henry's son Matthew were able to catechize more freely in public, though, as in his father's case,

---

[312] Keeble and Nuttall, *Baxter Correspondence*, no. 768, and cf. 674.

[313] These works are listed in Appendix 1. For some examples of gentry concern for domestic catechizing at this period, see Cliffe, *Puritan Gentry Besieged*, 140, 144, and W. Lamont, 'The Two "National Churches" of 1691 and 1829', in A. Fletcher and P. Roberts (eds.), *Religion, Culture and Society in Early Modern Britain: Essays in Honour of Patrick Collinson* (Cambridge, 1994), 343.

[314] See the preface by J. I. Packer to the edition of the *Reformed Pastor* published by the Banner of Truth Trust (Edinburgh/Pennsylvania, 1974), 15–16.

[315] Ibid. 14; *The Rev. Oliver Heywood, B.A. 1630–1702: His Autobiography, Diaries, Anecdote and Event Books*, ed. J. Horsfall Turner (4 vols.; Brighouse and Bingley, 1882–5), iv. 185, 188, 192, 198, 201, 206–7.

[316] Ibid. i. 234; Clarke, *Lives of sundry eminent persons*, 196–7.

[317] M. Henry, *The Life of the Rev. Philip Henry*, ed. J. B. Williams (1825), 79, 195.

when he had a group of catechumens ready to receive the Lord's Supper, Matthew 'conversed with them, severally and apart, upon their everlasting interests'.[318] Indeed, in general, after 1689 we seem to hear rather less than before about catechizing in the home, with or without a minister present.[319] Perhaps the dissenters' success in securing limited toleration for public worship and schooling tended to reduce the need for and possibly the scale of domestic catechizing.

The situation on the episcopalian side of the fence in the period from the 1650s was, allowing for the obvious contrasts, in many ways not very different. There was a certain irony in the fact that John Evelyn seems to have begun to catechize his family at home in the 1650s because it had ceased to take place in church in that decade.[320] One may also guess that sequestered clergy in their own homes or in the houses of the royalist gentry where they took shelter may have performed some catechizing, as their 'godly' counterparts had done in the previous decades when roles were reversed.[321] As for the practice of domestic catechizing after the Restoration, we have to fall back on the indications of moral pressure which Restoration bishops tried to exert on parents, together with the comments of Peter Hewit in 1704 (cited above) that parents seemed to think they had done their part when they had taught their children to repeat the words of the church catechism by rote.[322] For the early eighteenth century, however, there are the clergy's replies to the episcopal questionnaires. Parents are slow to send their children and servants to church, wrote the incumbent of Cranbrook to Wake in 1716, but 'they commonly teach them the church catechism in private'; in two other Kentish parishes it was said 'they use the church catechism at home'; in three other cases it was reported that children were taught by their parents or the local schoolmaster; two incumbents also referred to their going to the homes of catechumens to catechize them there.[323] In Lincolnshire five years later, there are again references to parents teaching their own children the church catechism or taking care that they were instructed in it, perhaps by a local teacher.[324] In Yorkshire in 1743, we find the same story: 'I find the children very well instructed in the church catechism by their parents and have not been wanting in my duty to explain it'; 'my parish takes good care to instruct their families, and to send them to

[318] J. B. Williams, *Memoirs of the Life ... of the Rev. Matthew Henry* (1828), 131: the location is not clear, but as with his father it would seem that the catechumens came to him rather than he to them.

[319] This is only an impression and may be due to the nature of the surviving sources for the post-revolutionary period.

[320] *The Diary of John Evelyn*, ed. E. S. De Beer (6 vols.; Oxford, 1955), iii. 160; two weeks before he began, Evelyn had heard some catechizing taking place in the Huguenot church in London: ibid.

[321] R. S. Bosher, *The Making of the Restoration Settlement: The Influence of the Laudians 1649–1662* (London, 1951), 39–40; R. Beddard, 'The Restoration Church', in J. R. Jones (ed.), *The Restored Monarchy 1660–1688* (1979), 156–9.

[322] Hewit, *Brief and plain explication*, sigs. A2ʳ⁻ᵛ.

[323] Wake MS 284, fos. 21ᵛ, 56ʳ, 104ᵛ, 133ᵛ, 142ʳ, 212ᵛ, 236ʳ, 250ʳ, 419ʳ.

[324] Gibson 14, p. 144; Gibson 15, pp. 277, 449. Here and in Kent some clergy also reported parents for negligence in teaching their children, as if this was the norm: Wake MS 284, fo. 298ʳ; Gibson, 14, p. 177.

church to be farther instructed by me'; others reported that parents were careful that all had learnt the catechism before they were sent to church for instruction, and this was the case even in parishes where there was no record of an endowed school.[325] There is also the occasional complimentary remark about the use of catechetical expositions in the household, and we find in the diary of a Sussex shopkeeper, Thomas Turner, that he voluntarily read Wake's exposition of the church catechism in the evenings, and concluded that it was 'a very good book, and proper for all families'.[326] We should not make too much of all this, but it does suggest, first, that the idea and the practice of religious instruction in the household was not completely dead in the conformist community, even if it was not as lively as it may have been on the nonconformist side in the late seventeenth century, and, secondly, that further enquiry might fruitfully be made into this aspect of religious life in the early modern period.

The material examined in the second half of this chapter does little, it may be suggested, to alter the conclusions reached at the end of the first half and of the previous chapter. Younger children were likely to be exposed to catechizing for at least a few months in one location or another—church, school, or home; but protracted exposure to catechizing or to a more advanced level of catechizing was more likely to have been the lot of those who were sent to school or (we might add, after the evidence in the last few pages) who lived in a parish or household where a zealous minister found a co-operative laity. Catechizing in the household was as open to changes in local circumstance as that in church or school, perhaps more so, since the authorities were more likely to try to secure some continuity in the public fora. As a result, domestic catechizing may have contributed to supporting church and school catechizing in certain areas for limited periods, but was unlikely to have done so on a large scale for a long period. On a broad front, it is probably fair to conclude that in all three locations, catechizing took place less often than the idealists of the time wished, but more often than contemporary opponents and later sceptics were prepared to admit, especially at the elementary level. Moreover, the catechists themselves tried to increase the impact of such opportunities as they did have for catechizing by taking steps to improve their techniques of instruction; and it is to these changes we now turn.

[325] Herring, *York*, i. 26, 52, 123, 137, and cf. i. 34, 188, 202, and iii. 221.
[326] Gibson 14, p. 281; and *The Diary of Thomas Turner 1754–65*, ed. D. Vaisey (Oxford, 1984), 149.

5

Changes in Catechetical Technique

FOR more than two thousand years, advice on the best way to educate children was more a matter for philosophers and theologians than teachers or scientists.[1] It was only in the late nineteenth century that scientific study of the processes involved in learning began, and in succeeding decades that a new breed of educational theorist began to apply to the classroom what was being discovered in the laboratory about the memory and the development of intelligence. One result of this by the mid-twentieth century was an almost universal condemnation of rote memorization and parrot-like recitation as an archaic remnant of a discredited tradition. Children, it was argued, learnt more through 'discovery learning', in which the material to be learnt must be solved or discovered, than by 'reception learning', in which the material is presented in its final form and which in a purely verbal form implies quite a high level of ability to handle abstract concepts. Even religious education was affected: Bible-based teaching was discounted in favour of 'problem-oriented' and 'child-centred' approaches.[2]

In the second half of the twentieth century, however, a reaction set in, with some educational psychologists arguing that rote learning can be meaningful if it incorporates material into students' cognitive structure in a way that relates it to what they already know, as was the case in some early modern catechizing where the catechist took the trouble to explain as well as instil information, or to relate what was said in one part of a catechism to what was said in another. Six- or seven-year olds (we now know) may find it easier to understand abstract concepts through concrete examples, but in the absence of such exemplars much can be achieved through a careful choice of words.[3] Studies of the operation of the memory have also shown that a better way

---

[1] Strauss, *Luther's House of Learning*, chs. 3–4; K. Charlton, *Education in Renaissance England* (1965), chs. 3–4 and *passim*; J. Simon, *Education and Society in Tudor England*, (Cambridge, 1966), ch. 3 and *passim*; see also T. W. Baldwin, *William Shakspere's Small Latine and Lesse Greeke* (2 vols.; Urbana, Ill., 1944), *passim*; C. Webster, *The Great Instauration: Science, Medicine and Reform 1626–1660* (1975); and id., 'The Curriculum of the Grammar School and Universities 1500–1660: A Critical Review of the Literature', *History of Education*, 4 (1975), 51–67.

[2] D. P. Ausubel, J. P. Novak, and H. Hanesian, *Educational Psychology: A Cognitive View*[2] (New York, 1978), 117–20; E. B. Turner, 'Intellectual Ability and the Comprehension of Religious Language', *Irish Journal of Psychology*, 4 (1980), 182; I am most grateful to Dr Irene Turner of the Department of Psychology of the Queen's University of Belfast for her valuable advice and help in introducing me to some of the works cited in this and subsequent footnotes.

[3] Ausubel, Novak, and Hanesian, *Educational Psychology*, ch. 6; E. B. Turner, 'Towards a Standardized

to learn than trying to absorb a whole block of information at one time is 'little and often', such as every day or twice a week and once on Sundays, as was the case with catechizing in the first form of Leicester's grammar school in the 1570s and the Charity Schools of the early eighteenth century.[4] Repetition, it is now said, not only consolidates recently learned material and helps to isolate possible confusions or difficulties, but also helps in the mastering of new material thereafter; and where a child is literate, a combination of reading and recitation out loud leads to more being retained, and retained for longer (even if the material is not all meaningful) than if it is merely read silently. As for recitation in a group, which is what some early modern catechumens were probably encouraged to practice in the first instance, this has been found to be not without value in facilitating learning and retention, especially with the help of prompting from a sympathetic teacher.[5] It is also worth stating the obvious that until the late modern period communication was predominantly oral, so that people were accustomed to keeping in their memory large quantities of information pertinent to their trade. The ability to compose and recite epic poems and sagas may have been a skill confined to certain men and women in ancient and early medieval times, but even today in some parts of the world children without special skills manage to memorize the whole of the Talmud or the Koran.

Early modern theorists were also aware that there were stages of development in children's capacity to assimilate concepts, and that a carefully graded set of materials is one of the best ways to match the way that that capacity develops between infancy and adolescence.[6] A catechist preparing for a catechism class today certainly has access to more information about these stages and about the wide number of variables that can affect learning, both within the learner and in the learning situation.[7] But among the growing body of publications on the psychology of religion, and the extent to which schoolchildren and others can come to terms with and retain specifically religious concepts,[8] there is again some material which might persuade us to hesitate before making unfavourable comments about early modern practice. Thus one study in Northern Ireland (described by one sociologist in 1977 as a 'partially modernized

Test of Religious Language Comprehension', *British Journal of Religious Education*, 1 (1978), 14; id., 'Intellectual Ability', 183.

[4] M. C. Cross, *The Free Grammar School of Leicester* (Dept. of English Local History Occasional Papers, no. 4; Leicester, 1953), 18, 26–7; anon., *The order and rules of the charity-school* [1701?], 5; M. G. Jones, *The Charity School Movement* (Cambridge, 1938), 77, 83–4; and for other examples of regular repetition, see below, nn. 33–7.

[5] Ausubel, Novak, and Hanesian, *Educational Psychology*, 23–7, 309–12, 329–31; I. M. L. Hunter, *Memory* (1957), 97–9, 104–6, 120, 133; A. Baddeley, *Your Memory: A User's Guide* (1983), 27–8.

[6] Ausubel, Novak, and Hanesian, *Educational Psychology*, ch. 3; E. B. Turner, 'Intellectual Ability', 186.

[7] Ausubel, Novak, and Hanesian, *Educational Psychology*, 29–31, and chs. 5–14.

[8] E. B. Turner, 'Towards a Standardized Test', 14–21; E. B. Turner, I. F. Turner, and A. Reid, 'Religious Attitudes in Two Types of Urban Secondary School: A Decade of Change?', *Irish Journal of Education*, 1 (1980), 43–52; E. B. Turner, 'Intellectual Ability', 182–90; and C. D. Batson, P. Schoenrade, and W. L. Ventis, *Religion and the Individual: A Social-Psychological Perspective* (New York/Oxford, 1993).

society') has suggested that where there is a close connection between school and church life, and where instruction was 'specific, authoritative, and clearly related to an active church membership', it is likely 'to promote a feeling of purposeful progress' among students; understanding will develop faster and further than in schools where the place and aims of religious education are less clearly defined.[9] Not only were early modern catechists (especially schoolteachers) usually working in a much more hierarchical and paternalistic society than ours, but also the potentially close relationship between home or school and church life was evident in the importance attached to the rites of passage and other church rituals in village life, and to the connections between attendance at school and attendance at church laid down in the canons of 1571 and 1604 and many school statutes and curricula.[10]

One further point may be made by way of introduction: while there was undoubtedly a great deal of continuity in the ways in which catechizing was performed in the early modern period, especially in the stress on rote repetition, there is also clear evidence of efforts to improve methods: by trying to ensure swifter learning, longer retention, and greater understanding. At the outset, for example, there was a tendency to assume that the more something was repeated the more it would be understood, and an equation of the ability merely to recite three formulae and a few catechetical answers with a conscious statement of faith—a 'giving an account' or 'making an open confession of … faith'.[11] As late as 1710 a bishop in Wales was still treating regular repetition of the basic formulae as the best means of 'keep[ing] religion alive in people's hearts', and putting them in mind of 'many useful truths and important duties'.[12] By the turn of the sixteenth century and increasingly from the mid-seventeenth century, however, we find distinctions being drawn between, on the one hand, the mechanical parroting of words and, on the other, a real understanding of their meaning and commitment to their implementation; and we also find a growing insistence that catechists should try to ensure comprehension at the same time as memorization. 'Teaching is not thrusting a set of ideas into the memory', but helping the learner to understand what is said, wrote an anonymous catechist in the early eighteenth century[13]—a comment cited approvingly in the late 1720s by Isaac Watts in his 'Discourse on the way of instruction by catechisms', in which he listed six 'inconveniences' of the idea that children should learn first and understand afterwards. He argued forcefully that it was much easier for children to remember words that were plain and easily understood, and that the youngest children should be

---

[9] E. B. Turner, 'Intellectual Ability', 187–8; Turner, Turner, and Reid, 'Religious Attitudes', 45, 49–50; I. F. Turner and J. Davies, 'Religious Attitudes in an Integrated Primary School: A Northern Ireland Case-Study', *British Journal of Religious Education*, 5 (1982), 28–32.

[10] See above, pp. 126–8, 177–9.

[11] *Second Report on Ritual*, 424, 427; Cardwell, *Synodalia*, i. 281 (and cf. Strauss, *Luther's House of Learning*, 154).

[12] *Second Report on Ritual*, 669; and for a similar statement by Andrewes in the 1620s, see ibid. 494.

[13] Anon., *The beginner's catechism* (1707), sig. A1[v].

taught concrete examples taken from 'the greater and more remarkable names and actions' recorded in the Bible. Authors should choose material which showed religion in practice, rather than 'mere notions', he said, and frame their questions and answers in such a way that the children felt involved all the time, for example by the use of the first and second rather than the third person.[14] Watts may not have been typical of early Hanoverian catechists, but he was part of a growing movement for improvement of techniques which we will examine in this chapter alongside the basic continuities.

In the early modern period a number of catechists were also teachers, and vice-versa,[15] so many of them may have encountered the view commonly found among educationalists ancient and modern that there were three phases in the development of the young: infancy (from birth to about 6 years old), childhood (from about 7 to about 13), and adolescence (from the age of 14 to the early or late twenties). Of these, childhood was considered to be the crucial one: not much could be achieved with an infant, while if a child had not been properly trained by the age of 14, it was thought to be probably too late to try. Between 7 and 14, therefore, children had to be broken into submission and sound habits ingrained, or else they would become like wild animals. The older Christian belief in the need to restrain the natural vice with which the young, since the fall of Adam, had been born and to instil at least outwardly virtuous behaviour was reinforced by the humanists' stress on the formation of character in the young rather than the mere acquisition of knowledge, and by the Reformed stress on the complete depravity of fallen mankind. There were degrees of pessimism about the essential nature of children, with some influential humanists like Erasmus leaning towards the more optimistic view of Quintilian that they had some goodness in them, while most reformers (in theory, if not always in practice) leant more towards the pessimistic view of Augustine, that children were potentially wicked and depraved from the moment they were born. English education was an interesting blend of the humanist thrust to encourage civic virtue and the evangelical, proselytizing impulse of Protestantism, but although the latter tended to come to the fore under Edward and Elizabeth the former retained a very powerful hold on the attitudes and curricula of many English educators throughout the early modern period.[16]

According to contemporary theory, largely derived from the ancients but modified somewhat by the time of the early Reformation, knowledge was supposed to

---

[14] I. Watts, *Catechisms: or instructions in the principles of the Christian religion* (1730), 25–75, 77–8, 84–7, 117–19, 192–4, 203–6; and for Watts's own catechisms, see below, pp. 271–3.

[15] See above, pp. 182–3.

[16] This paragraph and the next are based on the surveys in Strauss, *Luther's House of Learning*, pt. 1, and Simon, *Education and Society*, ch. 3 and *passim*.

reach the brain through messages or copies of images transmitted to the brain by the five senses. The 'common sense', the one which was common to all five, sorted, combined, and classified the messages it received, and prepared them for memory and judgement of which the end-product was knowledge. While the senses were inborn, memory, judgement, and knowledge could be developed through special care and training, as indeed also could the will and the conscience. For in addition to the sensible part of the soul, that which involved the senses and the brain, there was also the vegetable part, which controlled the basic processes of life, and there was the rational part, which was composed of the powers of wit or reason and will or desire. The will tended to strive for what the intellect saw as desirable and to shun what it saw as abhorrent; but the power of reason when applied to divine (as opposed to human) matters was weak in the unregenerate, and so human will tended to oppose God's, to be vainglorious and inconstant, and to be in need of restraint. Since most of the raw material on which the intellect and will relied for their operation was not innate but received as signals from outside, if the educator was in a position to regulate the data received through the senses he could control the ideas and the power to act on those ideas. Finally, conscience, the point at which the different faculties of knowing, judging, and feeling were held to converge, should have warned man that he was for ever falling into sin, but this was also a broken reed in the unregenerate, neither restraining them from evil nor moving them to the good, and it too needed to be trained to function properly.[17]

The importance of all this for our purpose here is that childhood, instead of being idealized or, as today, seen as a period of great potential development, was seen as a period when what was needed above all was discipline and the avoiding of all occasions of wilfulness or sin. Effective learning among the young was generally seen by theorists such as Erasmus as being dependent on three factors: the natural endowment of each child, good instruction, and practice. Careful instruction could ensure that the right impulses reached the child's senses, while endless, repetitive practice would not only ensure that good habits of self-discipline and thought were formed while the child was still malleable, but also keep the child so busy that he or she would not have the time to give way to his or her naturally corrupt instincts. Repetition in particular would help to train and stretch the memory, inform the intellect, and restrain the will. Whether the matter to be mastered was the rules of grammar or the rules of holy living and dying, drill and repetition were considered to provide the best means of teaching and learning.[18] The religious components of such instruction and practice took many forms: attending church, paying close attention to the Bible readings and memorizing verses selected by teachers, listening to and summarizing

---

[17] As previous note, and esp. Strauss, *Luther's House of Learning*, 74–80.

[18] Ibid. 82; Simon, *Education and Society*, 115; Charlton, *Education in Renaissance England*, 106; and on educational practice in general, T. W. Baldwin, *William Shakespere's Petty School* (Urbana, Ill., 1943), and id. *Shakspere's Small Latine and Lesse Greeke, passim.*

sermons, memorizing and saying prayers, singing psalms, reading good books, and so on. But the component which offered the highest measure of doctrinal input and the greatest scope for regular practice was the catechism. The catechism in Luther's Germany has been described as 'perfectly suited to the pedagogical model transmitted from the past and adopted by the reformers as an answer to their special needs'—the rapid conversion of whole populations at a time. The typical catechism contained a safe, short summary of a complex set of principles, in a format simple enough for all to learn; it delivered a government approved health warning—that all without exception were guilty under the Law and had to turn to Christ to be saved; if taught orally, it was cheap to operate, and the voice was then widely thought to impress itself on the mind better than the printed word, whether the voice of the catechist or of the catechumen 'echoing' back; catechizing involved the self-discipline of memorizing, and the social discipline of saying it in front of others.[19] Much the same could be said of the English attitude to catechizing, at least at the outset, with two additional comments: first, that many English catechists soon came to realize the limitations of the one-way technique of instruction embodied in preaching, compared to the advantages of the two-way processes involved in persuading students first to mimic them and then to answer their questions from memory; and, secondly, that in England catechizing was often reinforced by closely related routines or visual aids such as we have already seen or will see later.[20]

In the advice to catechists in the preface to his shorter catechism, Luther had treated repetition and memorization as the essential first steps. The catechist should begin by teaching the young and unlearned to repeat and retain the exact words of the catechism 'in such a way that we do not alter a single syllable'; only then should the catechist go on to 'teach them what it means'.[21] The equivalent English catechism had no detailed advice in the preceding rubric, but in the relevant canon of 1571 it was laid down that clergy were to 'read and teach the catechism' which implies a twofold technique: reading the text out loud, and teaching it to the assembled catechumens until they had mastered it.[22] Beyond this we have to rely on what the authorities anticipated would be the results of catechizing. A measure of skill in saying the catechism was hinted at in another canon of 1571, where it was stated that none could be admitted to communion, get married, or act as a godparent who could not reply 'fitly and accurately [*convenienter et dextre*] to all parts of the catechism'.[23] But other official statements insisted on no more than people's ability to say the Creed, Lord's Prayer, and Decalogue 'in their mother tongue', or 'say' the catechism

---

[19] Strauss, *Luther's House of Learning*, 146–7, 151–75.
[20] See above, pp. 1–2, 21, 31–2, 167, and below, pp. 253–4.
[21] Janz, *Three Reformation Catechisms*, 182–4. [22] Cardwell, *Synodalia*, i. 121.
[23] Ibid. i. 121–2: the reference to accuracy may have referred not only to the correct words, but also to the appropriate answer being given to the relevant question, which was not always the case: see below, p. 245.

'by heart'.[24] Although this stress on a bare knowledge of the catechism was stated most strongly and regularly in episcopalian sources, we may note that the alternatives put forward by the presbyterians in Parliament in 1645 and the Worcestershire Association in the mid-1650s were not all that different. The ordinance of October 1645 stated that all who wished to be admitted to the Lord's Supper 'ought to *know* that there is a God ... maker of heaven and earth and governor of all things', and so on for ten paragraphs, at least half of which consisted of phrases taken from the Creed or were worded in very similar terms to comparable material in the Prayer Book catechism. Only at the very end was there a mention almost in passing of this material being understood as well as known.[25] The 'profession' of faith agreed by the members of the Worcestershire Association consisted of a paraphrase of the Apostles' Creed in a series of statements of belief: 'I believe that there is only one God, the father, infinite in being', and so on; and although members of the Association like Richard Baxter were looking for signs of regeneration as well as mere knowledge in their parishioners, they were prepared to accept a willingness to learn and repeat the 'profession' or the catechism, and to accept criticism, as possible indications of a new beginning.[26]

From other informed sources there is no shortage of evidence for the importance attached to constant repetition and simple memorization. It was the duty of the catechist, said Andrewes in the late 1570s, to go over and over the same material 'as the knife doth the whetstone' until the children know it perfectly; and a few years later J.F. sounded like a typical Elizabethan schoolmaster when he spoke of catechists having to 'beat' a right understanding of the principles of religion into the heads and hearts of youth (the beating may have been metaphorical, though we find occasional references to catechumens' ears being boxed and catechists resorting to scare tactics).[27] William Lyford admitted in 1642 that he had repeated some material in the text of his catechism, but this was deliberate, he said, because repetition helped to root the most important points in those of weak understanding. Constant repetition

[24] See above, p. 94 n. 2.

[25] *Acts and Ordinances of the Interregnum*, ed. C. H. Firth and R. S. Rait (2 vols.; 1911), i. 789–91 (my italics); and for the catechisms based on it, see above, pp. 79–80.

[26] [R. Baxter], *Christian concord: or the agreement of the associated pastors* (1653), sigs. C2ᵛ–3ᵛ; [id.], *The agreement of divers ministers of Christ* (1656), 39–42; and cf. R. Baxter, *Universal concord* (1660), 5–10; id., *Gildas Salvianus. The Reformed Pastor* (1860), 493–4; N. H. Keeble and G. F. Nuttall, *Calendar of the Correspondence of Richard Baxter* (2 vols.; Oxford, 1991), no. 348.

[27] Andrewes, *Works*, vi. 7; J.F., *A most breefe manner of instruction* [c.1585], sig. Aiiʳ. One mother explained that she had not sent her son to be catechized lest he get his ears boxed, as had happened to widow Warner's son (F. G. Emmison, *Elizabethan Life: Morals and the Church Courts* (Essex Record Office Publications, 63; Chelmsford, 1973), 143); another boy was told 'the devil was upon his shoulder' and ran screaming from the church 'to the terror of all that were present' (*Diocese of Norwich: Bishop Redman's Visitation 1597*, ed. J. F. Williams, (Norfolk Record Society, 18; 1946), 148). For a similar case, see J. S. Craig, 'Reformation, Politics and Polemics in Sixteenth-Century Anglian Market Towns', Ph.D. thesis (Cambridge, 1992), 27.

is beneficial if skilfully done, wrote Lancelot Addison in the mid-1670s, probably aware of growing unease in some quarters about the mechanical nature of rote learning; to catechize, wrote Edward Wetenhall in the 1690s, restating the older view, is to instruct by often repeating the first, certain, and most necessary points of religion.[28] From Nichols's awareness of the need for recreational psalm-singing to break up the monotony of frequent repetitions of his forms, to Isaac Watts's rueful admission that many adults in the 1720s had had the words of the Shorter Catechism 'thrust' into their memory 'as if it was so much Greek or Latin', the pattern was the same as in Luther's Germany: the more a catechism was repeated, the better was thought the chance of its staying in the memory.[29] Whether we look at more negative comments—such as warnings to ministers not to be deterred by the tedium involved in teaching a catechism, and complaints of replies being 'parroted' with no sense of the meaning involved—or at more positive remarks—such as the successes recorded in the Charity Schools' public examinations, or the early eighteenth-century clergy's descriptions of the facility with which some of their parishioners could repeat the answers of the catechism—we are left in no doubt as to the priority placed on memorization and rote repetition as the basic elements of catechizing.[30] 'Remembrance is the mother of the muses in our schools, and more in the house of God', wrote Thomas Downing in 1623; memory is the faculty first used by children and remains predominant in children and 'childish professors', wrote the anonymous author of *Some forms of catecheticall doctrines* (1647): only later did their faculty of judgement and conscience develop. Hence the importance of feeding their memories with information, so that later they would be able to understand its meaning and their consciences would be able to act accordingly.[31]

From the educational theory, the official requirements, and the practitioners' comments summarized in the last few paragraphs, we can gain some impression of what elementary catechizing was intended to achieve and likely to involve. But exactly how the teaching and testing of a simple form was performed is unclear, since detailed accounts of catechizing at this level are very hard to find. Did the master read out one answer or just one sentence at a time, and then get the whole group

---

[28] W. Lyford, *Principles of faith and good conscience* (1642), sig. A4ʳ; L. Addison, *The primitive institution* (1674), 170–3; [E. Wetenhall], *A tried method of catachising* (1698), preface, 1. For a defence of repetition in a related case (that of Nicholson's exposition of the church catechism), see Magdalen College, Oxford, Archives MS 546, fo. 2ᵛ.

[29] J. Nichols, *An order of household government* (1596), sig. C6ʳ; Watts, *Catechisms*, 33; and Strauss, *Luther's House of Learning*, 154.

[30] R. Bernard, *The faithfull shepheard* (1607), 9; Baxter, *Reformed Pastor*, 288–90, 422–6; and L. Addison, *The primitive institution* (1674), 219–20; and for a Catholic complaint about how boring catechizing could be, C. Fleury, *An historical catechism* (1726), p. x; and see below, p. 245, and above, pp. 179, 183–4.

[31] T. Downing, *The catechisers holy encouragement* (1623), 14; anon. *Some forms of catecheticall doctrines* (1647), sigs. A5ʳ–6ᵛ; and cf. B. Stinton, *A short catechism* (1730), sig. A2ʳ: experience showed that what was fixed soonest in the minds of the young left the deepest impressions.

of catechumens to chant it back? If so, how many times was this done before the cat-echumens were asked, collectively or individually, to repeat it without a preliminary prompting? If some catechumens could read, were they encouraged to memorize the answers by themselves beforehand, and then come to the catechist for testing? Indeed, when students learnt to read through the *ABC with the catechisme* or the *Primer and catechisme*, did they learn the letters first and then move on to learn the answers in the catechism, or had they already memorized those answers through oral instruction and then used their memory of those answers to help them identify the different words of the printed text?[32]

One surviving account is that of Richard Bernard in the first edition of his pastoral handbook, *The faithful shepheard*, published in 1607. Much of his section on cate-chizing was concerned with what we have treated above as a characteristic of the intermediate level of catechizing—ensuring that a catechism already learnt was properly understood; but some of his material seems to refer to the basic teaching and testing of a form. Teach catechumens (he wrote) as schoolmasters do their pupils—probably a reference to the importance of drill in contemporary schools—rather than 'after a discoursing manner' which he had found of little or no benefit in country con-gregations. Like Luther, he insisted that catechists should begin by getting the peo-ple to learn the catechism word for word, and answer to every question. Do not interrupt beginners with interpretations, he said, nor go further at a time than an individual can manage—a hint that individuals were taken through the form to see how far they had succeeded in memorizing it. Again like Luther, he thought that only when catechumens had learnt a catechism should they be taught the meaning. Ask how they understand this or that answer, but 'note the variety of wits, and as they be so deal with them'. If there is a delay in answering from one catechumen, pass on to the next—an indication that at some stage Bernard was going round the class one by one; 'if any but stammer at it, help him', and encourage his efforts; if none can give an answer, give one yourself plainly, and ask again, and praise a respondent who shows understanding. Do not allow laughter at anyone's expense; rebuke only the wilfully obstinate. Experience, he wrote, had taught him to teach with a cheerful countenance, 'familiarly' and 'lovingly'; if the catechist is disdainful or impatient, few will come willingly to be taught by him.[33]

A few years later Bernard gave a visitation sermon on catechizing, which he later turned into a 'tractate'. This referred to catechizing as 'a necessary means to inform the ruder sort, summarily, by questions and answers in the principles of

---

[32] *The order and rules of the charity-school* [1701?], 5, mentioned repetition of the catechism before it mentioned the teaching of reading, but this was possibly a statement of priorities rather than a detailed curriculum; on the other hand, other sources speak of teaching children 'to read and to say their catechism' in that order: *Diary of Francis Evans, Secretary to Bishop Lloyd, 1699–1706*, ed. D. Robertson, (Worces-tershire Historical Society, 45; 1903), 16; and see above, p. 177 n. 36. For another possible solution, see below, pp. 240–1.

[33] Bernard, *Faithfull shepheard*, 9–10.

religion'—again note the stress on information as the first stage of the process. It was the best means of enabling a minister to see an increase in knowledge in his congregation, which Bernard paired with an increase in their ability to judge their faith aright. Bernard also used other common metaphors to stress the basicness of the instruction—as babes in Christ, we need milk before meat; the catechism is 'the ABC of our religion'. He then went on to divide catechizers into three types: diligent, negligent, and diligent but not as effective as they might be. What he seems to have seen as ineffective was testing the knowledge of one particular answer by asking the same question to half a dozen in turn—again we have the impression of him going round a group—when all but the first respondent were merely copying that first answer (using their short-term memory) rather than trying to commit it permanently to memory. He also condemned asking an individual only two or three questions; it was better to carry on and see how far that student could go, and then start at that point with him or her the next time, until he or she could get to the end (did he keep a record of how far each student had got each week?). When all have committed the catechism to memory, their understanding of it should be tested through more questions and answers rather than discourses, though the catechist could end with a few minutes' 'dilation' if he wanted.[34] Much of this is of more interest on the *testing* of knowledge and comprehension, but perhaps confirms the hints in the *Faithful shepheard* on how the catechism was taught in the first place.

Two accounts published at almost the same time as Bernard—the 'method' for ministers suggested by Robert Cawdrey in his treatise on catechizing in 1604, and the account provided by a 'godly' schoolteacher, John Brinsley, in 1612—reflect the way catechizing was meant to be performed in a context where many or all of the pupils were assumed to be literate and there were copies of the catechism available for private study. Half an hour on Saturdays should be spent on learning and answering the catechism, said Brinsley, who as a teacher was in the fortunate position of being able to guarantee catechumens' attendance on a weekday. Both said that each pupil should learn half a page at a time—a rare indication of the kind of unit thought practicable to learn in a session—till he could say it all. The more the student went over it, Brinsley suggested, 'the sooner ... will come ... understanding'—a good example not only of the importance attached to regular repetition but also of the tendency to equate repetition and comprehension. When it came to testing the student's memory, the two authors' paths diverged a little. Cawdrey was prepared to start off by allowing one or two boys to recite the catechism as far as they could, before turning to testing the others. Then, unlike Bernard, he was quite happy to recommend the same question being asked over and over again, so that 'by often hearing' the answer the 'ignorant and unlearnedner sort may the easily conceive it by heart'.

---

[34] R. Bernard, *Two twinnes* (1613), 5, 8–9, 12, 15–18. The reference to this work as a 'tractate' is in the 1621 edition of *Faithfull shepheard*, 104–5.

Brinsley suggested that in schools the usher or the senior boy in each form should hear each pupil recite in turn; and then the senior master should himself test them, and help them to understand the difficult words. (The prospect of one boy testing another reminds us that in one Lutheran state children were ranged in ranks with one side intoning the questions and the others the answers.)[35] The fact that students had to repeat the same material twice orally, once before the usher or senior and once before the master, may again have helped to fix it in their memories. Both Cawdrey and Brinsley were also in favour of testing those who showed some skill in reciting the catechism by asking them questions 'back and forth', that is putting questions 'suddenly out of order' such as what is the sixth Commandment, or the fourth, and jumping about between the different articles of the Creed or petitions of the Lord's Prayer. Brinsley also recommended using subdivided questions and explaining the harder words, as means of aiding pupils to understand and remember better. Some of these suggestions were perhaps fairly advanced for their time, but in other cases they typified the 'godly' approach to instruction in the early modern period. Cawdrey said that explanations of the standard formulae should be made by the minister through some suitable scriptural text, and that catechumens' understanding of the points raised in this way, as well as their memory of the scripture text used, should then be tested. Brinsley concluded by urging catechists to 'apply every piece unto them', to work holy affections in them, so that they might fear the Lord and walk in his commandments.[36]

The only other account of catechetical method is much later but is by an author whom we know had already had some experience of elementary catechizing and produced an innovative form of his own. James Talbot, vicar of Spofforth in Yorkshire, was asked to write *The Christian schoolmaster* by the SPCK, and from its appearance in 1707 it was used as a handbook by Charity School and other teachers. Talbot stated that children can memorize as soon as they can speak, and so all those admitted to school, even those who could not yet read, were 'to be taught to say the Creed and the Lord's Prayer, with the explanatory answer [in the church catechism] belonging to each, by frequent repetition, either from the mouth of the master, or (which perhaps may be as well) of some of the older scholars'. Once they had mastered their letters, their 'first lessons' were to be in those parts of the church catechism which they had *not* already learnt by heart before they could read, so that 'by frequent repetition of the words, while they are thus practising to read them, they may become familiar both to their eye and memory'. When mastery of the catechism was complete, they should be ready to give an audible account of it in church, and to be taught an exposition of the catechism such as Lewis's, again by a combination of repeating out loud, reading, and testing. They should also be ready to switch from the church catechism

---

[35] Strauss, *Luther's House of Learning*, 169.

[36] R. Cawdrey, *A short and fruitfull treatise* (1604), sigs. A6ᵛ–7ᵛ; J. Brinsley, *Ludus Literarius or the Grammar Schoole*, ed. E. T. Campagnac (1917), 254–5.

as their reading book to the Book of Common Prayer, then the psalter, and then New and Old Testaments.[37]

Although not quite what we need, the accounts of these four authors offer some clues. The text of a catechism was probably taught in short stages, either by repeated oral repetition where most of the catechumens were illiterate, or by giving literate catechumens copies to master, or by a mixture of oral repetition and reading. Testing of what had been learnt was done orally and individually with the catechist moving from one catechumen to the next. Those who were quicker to learn were encouraged to recite as many answers as possible in succession to help those who were slower or less able. At the outset accurate recitation of the 'correct' replies was encouraged more than comprehension, but as soon as memorizing was going well, the focus was shifted to comprehension. And the catechist had always to be patient and supportive. We may pause a moment to consider a little further the role of literacy at this stage of ensuring memorization, since in recent decades some cultural historians have argued that the early modern period witnessed a turning-point in the relationship between orality and literacy or at the least a speeding up of the process whereby literacy replaced orality. Others have thrown doubt on the speed or completeness of such changes: rather than seeing orality and literacy at opposite poles, they say, we should allow for ' "mixed" and interacting modes', or for one form of communication borrowing or appropriating ideas from another.[38] The case of catechizing provides reinforcement for both points of view: the former especially at advanced and to some extent at intermediate levels of catechizing, but the latter more at elementary level.

As we can see from many of the definitions of catechizing and the comments of catechists cited above,[39] the stress at the outset was on oral instruction of illiterate catechumens by a literate catechist (which can be treated as a primarily oral exercise, or as a mixed mode involving a literate catechist reading from a printed text to illiterate catechumens). But the further we proceed in the early modern period, and the greater the number of people who could read (and especially read print rather than handwriting),[40] the more we find catechetical authors either associating literacy with learning a catechism (as in the *ABC* and various reading primers we looked at in the last chapter, and the entry requirements laid down in some school statutes), or

[37] J. Talbot, *The Christian school-master* (1707), 25–6, 79–82 (though cf. also 27, 95, 132–3); and see below, Appendix 1, s.v. Talbot.

[38] B. V. Street, *Literacy in Theory and Practice* (Cambridge, 1984), 5, and cf. 11, 133, 142; R. Chartier, *The Cultural Uses of Print in Early Modern France* (Princeton, 1987), 5–7; id., *Cultural History: Between Practices and Representations* (Oxford, 1988), 11–14; for a recent discussion of some of the issues involved, see T. Watt, *Cheap Print and Popular Piety 1550–1640* (Cambridge, 1991), 1–8, 136, 242, 244, 257–8, 328–31.

[39] See above, pp. 13–14, 25, 235.

[40] See M. Spufford, 'First Steps in Literacy', *Social History*, 4 (1979), 408–13; K. Thomas, 'The Meaning of Literacy in Early Modern England', in G. Baumann (ed.), *The Written Word: Literacy in Transition* (Oxford, 1986), 101–3; and Watt, *Cheap Print and Popular Piety*, 1–8; and below, p. 255 n. 111.

assuming that those using a form would already be literate, as was the case with those householders who from the 1570s to the 1710s and beyond were urged to catechize those in their charge.[41] As early as 1590 William Perkins seems to have envisaged most of the catechumens who used his catechism being literate, since in the preface he advised them when reading his form to go over the six principles repeatedly until they could repeat them 'without book'. And three years earlier, on the title-page of Thomas Settle's catechism on the 'mystery of our redemption in Christ', it was said that it was designed for the 'ruder sort of people', who, if they used a little diligence to commit it to memory or read it regularly, 'or if they cannot read' would hear it read by others, would be much furthered 'unto knowledge, and godliness'.[42] A similar line was taken by Thomas Ken in the 1680s and William Beveridge in the 1700s. Ken evidently anticipated his work falling into the hands of literate readers, but did not omit to add a note at the end that 'they that are ignorant, or that cannot read, should go to their parish priest' or some other minister 'and desire him to teach them their duty in private'.[43] Beveridge showed he was aware that in the rural parts of his Welsh diocese there might be 'few or none of the parishioners that can read or say the catechism themselves, much less teach others to read or say it', and raised the question of whether the minister should teach parishioners to read. He thought not, and commented that it was harder to teach the catechism if children could not read, but not impossible. His solution in the short term was to encourage adults to attend catechizing held during evening service so that they might learn by hearing the younger sort being examined and instructed. But in the middle to long term he favoured the setting up of 'catechetical schools', a proposal which in some ways anticipated by several decades the setting up of Sunday Schools, which in many cases taught not only children but also adolescents and quite a few adults how to read as well as some basic religious knowledge.[44]

But this growing reliance on literacy and print should not be exaggerated: it was a great convenience to catechists in that it held out the prospect of avoiding the boring job of drilling a form into students' heads, but it was not an absolute necessity. As was pointed out in an earlier chapter, even in the early Hanoverian period, most clergy were still prepared to cope with a situation in which catechumens were illiterate or had only poor reading skills. Although the growth of literacy had probably had a significant impact on elementary catechizing by then, it would perhaps be wiser at this stage to conclude that if necessary, and it was frequently necessary, catechists

---

[41] See Ch. 4 above.

[42] W. Perkins, *The foundation of Christian religion* (1591), sig. A3ᵛ; T. Settle, *A catechisme briefly opening the misterie* (1587), title-page; and for Watts's expectation that the very young would be taught to read, see his *Catechisms*, 19, 77–8, 80.

[43] [T. Ken], *An exposition on the church catechism* (1686), 82.

[44] [W. Beveridge], *The church-catechism explained* (1704), 219–25, sigs. a3ʳ⁻ᵛ; cf. also *Diary of Francis Evans*, 16; and T. W. Laqueur, *Religion and Respectability: Sunday Schools and Working Class Culture 1780–1850* (New Haven/London, 1976), 38, 90–1, 108.

throughout the early modern period buckled down to teaching their charges by end-less oral repetition of the set answers.[45] In fact, at elementary level, many catechu-mens probably learnt through a mixture of hearing *and* reading, even within one parish, family, or school class: the illiterates learnt from oral instruction alone, by hearing the work read in church or home, while those who could read probably learnt through a mixture of hearing others read or recite and reading the same text for themselves, with the latter reinforcing the former. As one experienced catechist put it in the reign of Queen Anne, he was confident that his form would make a greater impression on catechumens than mere oral instruction because it gave them some-thing to see and read as well as hear.[46] Equally, where mastery of a simple or even an intermediate catechism was tested, this was as far as we know always done orally rather than through a written examination, even where the memorizing had been achieved as much through reading as hearing. In short, what we have here is another 'mixed mode'.

From an early stage, catechists were aware of the problems that many forms posed for catechumens, and of the limitations of existing techniques of instruction that were revealed by regular catechizing. The most commonly voiced complaints about the most frequently used forms were that they were either too long or too hard or both. In 1585 John Tomkys told his Shrewsbury parishioners that most of the catechisms he had come across had brief questions but long answers, which children with short memories and weak capacities had difficulty remembering and great difficulty in understanding; and others at that date complained of forms that were too long for the 'ignorant' to absorb, or not suited for 'tender wits'.[47] Fifty years later, Daniel Rogers felt that the sections on God, creation, and predestination in most catechisms were above the understanding of 'most hear-ers', while the sections on the Commandments, Creed, sacraments, and Lord's Prayer were beyond the capacity of their memory. Another forty years later Anthony Palmer still felt that some of the catechisms written by learned men were 'too hard and the answers too long for the youngest', while Richard Baxter made a slightly different point: if a catechism consisted of too few words, 'the vulgar cannot understand it', but if it was 'too long and in many words, they cannot learn and remember it'.[48]

---

[45] See above, pp. 183–4; and for the persistence into the nineteenth century of the view that the cate-chism could be effectively taught verbally, see Laqueur, *Religion and Respectability*, 102.

[46] T. Cooke, *A brief but plain explication of the church-catechism* (1706), sig. A3ʳ.

[47] J. Tomkys, *A briefe exposition of the Lordes prayer* (1585), sigs. 2ᵛ–3ʳ; and cf. [E. Dering and J. More], *A briefe and necessarie catechisme* (1590), sigs. A2ᵛ–3ʳ; [E. Paget and R. Openshaw], *Short questions and answeres ... newly enlarged* (1617), sig. A2ᵛ.

[48] D[aniel] R[ogers], *A practicall catechisme* (1640), sig. A7ʳ; A. Palmer, *Childrens bread* (1671), sig. A3ʳ; R. Baxter, *The catechizing of families* (1683), sig. A3ʳ.

Reservations were felt about the length of some of the individual answers and the difficulty of some of the terms used in the Prayer Book form, to judge from the revisions made in a number of forms in the seventeenth century which we shall look at shortly.[49] There were also implicit or explicit criticisms of other works which were quite widely used in the Elizabethan and early Stuart period, such as the Dering–More, Perkins, and Ball forms, all of which were reduced in size or simplified by later authors.[50] Although the divines at the Westminster Assembly had the opportunity to learn from previous mistakes and took the trouble to look at a number of existing forms, the Shorter of the two forms they produced was also felt to be far from ideal for beginners. In 1660 Edward Bury said that he had used the Shorter Catechism for several years, but 'many (especially of the elder sort)' complained that it was too hard and long, and that they had neither the time to learn it, nor the memories to retain it.[51] Thomas Lye thought it had some 'hard and difficult words and phrases'; in 1691 another presbyterian Nathaniel Vincent published a form which was briefer than the Assembly's catechism and which (he claimed) had words that those of 'meanest capacities' should find easier to understand; the author of *The beginner's catechism* (1707) was convinced that the divines at the Westminster Assembly had never intended the Shorter Catechism to be suitable for 'babes', 'some answers being so long, and so full of great sense' that though the catechumens might recite the words they did not apprehend the meaning; while in 1718 a hostile source suggested that two or three abler catechumens out of twenty might get the answers to the Westminster Shorter right, but the rest would stand speechless.[52] Isaac Watts was prepared to use the form, but was also critical of it: it did not 'condescend' enough to the weak understanding of children, for example in its use of Latinized words and theological terms; at more than a hundred questions it was too long, and at the start it was too theoretical: almost one-third of it had to be mastered, covering the highest mysteries and more speculative doctrines of the Gospel, before 'any thing practical' was learnt.[53]

In the case of older catechumens especially, allied to the problems of inserting material into their memory was the difficulty of ensuring that it was retained there for more than a few weeks or months. Adults complained that being old they could not learn or retain large numbers of (unusual) words, that they were not book-learned, and that it was not 'comely' for them to sit and learn with children.[54] Certainly the number of catechetical authors who insisted that their works were for those with

[49] R.M., *The church-catechism enlarg'd and explain'd* (1697), sig. A2ʳ, and see below, pp. 246–7.

[50] See below, pp. 247–8.

[51] E. Bury, *A short catechisme* (1660), sig. A2ʳ; and cf. [P. Nye], *Beames of former light*, 11.

[52] Watts, *Catechisms*, 21; N. Vincent, *The principles of the doctrine of Christ* (1691), sigs. a2ʳ⁻ᵛ; anon., *Beginner's catechism*, sig. A1ᵛ; W. Cradock, *A discourse of due catechising* (1718), 12.

[53] Watts, *Catechisms*, 21–5, 57–8.

[54] I[ohn] G[ibson], *An easie entrance into the principall points* (1579), sig. A1ʳ; M[ordechai] A[ldem], *A short, plaine and profitable catechisme* (1592), sigs. A3ᵛ–4ʳ; Cawdrey, *Short and fruitfull treatise* (1604), sigs.

'short', 'weak', 'frail', or 'crazed memories', or for those of 'meanest' or 'weakest capacity' or 'simple understanding', implies that these were the problems that as catechists they had encountered most frequently among older catechumens.[55] The regular pairing of references to 'short memories and dull wits', 'weakest capacity and frailest memory', 'meanest capacities and weakest memories', and 'meanest capacity and shortest memory'[56] also suggests that the difficulties some had in comprehending a particular answer or technical term were seen as contributing to their difficulty in committing it to memory. (To show that this was not a local problem we may note that at the Synod of Dort, John Hales heard complaints that the catechism commonly used in the United Provinces, the Heidelberg, was 'too obscure for the simple, and too long for the memory').[57]

Indeed, even when catechists had some success in storing a form in catechumens' memories, they then faced allegations that their students did not understand what they had been taught. One complaint often heard in England (as abroad) was of catechumens 'parroting' a form—gabbling or mumbling it through without any sense of the meaning, suggesting that their memory might have been engaged but not all of their minds.[58] Herbert Palmer also complained that it was a 'common error' of catechumens who had learnt a catechism by rote to give the correct answer to one question in response to a completely different question.[59] Another criticism, already encountered, was of the misuse of elements within a catechism—students declaiming the Creed or the Decalogue as if it was a prayer, or the Lord's Prayer as some kind of spell against evil—which also indicated a lack of proper understanding of what had been learnt.[60] A third complaint was that catechumens were slow to put the lessons

---

F3ᵛ–4ʳ; C.P., *Two briefe treatises* (1616), 10–11, 21–4; 'James Ussher', *A body of divinitie* (1645), 4; Z. Crofton, *Catechizing Gods ordinance* (1656), 116–21; Bury, *Short catechisme*, sig. A2ʳ; T. Doolittle, *A plain method of catechizing* (1698), 92; C. Ellis, *A catechism wherein the learner* (1674), sigs. A3ᵛ–5ᵛ.

[55] R[obert] H[arrison], *Three formes of catechismes* (Middelburg, 1583), sig. A2ᵛ; I[ohn] D[avidson], *A short Christian instruction* [1588], sig. A3ᵛ; S. Hieron, *The doctrine of the beginning of Christ* (1606), title-page; J. Brinsley, *A breviate of saving knowledge* (1643), title-page; J.F., *A compendious chatechisme* (1645), sig. A3ʳ; J.H., *The principles of Christian religion* (1645), title-page; S[amuel] L[angley], *A catechisme shorter than the short catechisme* (1649), sig. A2ʳ; anon., *A plaine and easy way of catechizing such as are of weakest memories and of the meanest capacities* (1680).

[56] J.F., *A most breefe manner of instruction* (c.1585), sig. Aiiʳ; W. Whitaker, *A short summe of Christianity* (1630), sig. A4ᵛ; [Herbert Palmer], *An endeavour of making the principles* (1644), title-page; T. Mockett, *A new catechisme* (1647), title-page; and see previous note.

[57] John Hales, *Golden Remains* (1688), 385.

[58] [Dering and More], *Briefe and necessarie catechisme*, sig. A2ᵛ; R[obert] S[herard], *The countryman with his houshold* (1620), sig. A6ᵛ; anon., *Some formes of catecheticall doctrines*, sig. A6ʳ; E. Creffeild, *The great duty of catechising* (1713), 86–90; Cradock, *Discourse of due catechising*, 12; anon., *An exposition of the preliminary questions and answers* [1730?], sig. A2ᵛ; Clarke, *Lives of two and twenty divines*, 226; id., *Lives of sundry eminent persons*, 178.

[59] Palmer, *Endeavour*, sig. A2ᵛ; Beveridge was worried that the act of subdividing questions and answers—of which more shortly—would lead not to greater understanding but only an extension of rote-learning: *Church-catechism explained*, pp. xii–xiii.

[60] See above, p. 131; on mindless repetition of the Lord's Prayer, see W. Cotes, *A dialogue of diverse*

learnt into practice, for example by examining their hearts for sin, praying devoutly, and regularly attending sermons and the Lord's Supper.[61] Too few were acting on the pithy advice of George Masterson to those who used his catechism: after you have learned it, live it.[62] Catechists who felt that the revelations provided by the typical catechism were of tremendous significance were liable to think that any catechumen who did not respond to them in some way must have failed to grasp their real meaning.

Undeterred, the more innovative catechists suggested various solutions to the problems which many catechumens seemed to be experiencing with remembering and with understanding, and in the next few paragraphs we will look at these in turn, though it will soon become apparent that solutions to problems of memorizing often overlapped with solutions to problems of comprehension. One obvious solution has been hinted at already, namely dividing the longer answers in an original form into a larger number of much shorter questions and answers, a move which was probably designed primarily to help the memory but might also help understanding too. An obvious candidate for this subdivision was the original Prayer Book catechism of 1549. The thirteen answers in this form ranged from a few words to over a hundred (on the Creed and the meaning of the second table of the Law and the Lord's Prayer) and in one case over three hundred (the answer containing the Decalogue in full). We may assume that by the time the extra section on sacraments was added in 1604, a lesson had been learnt from the problems these excessively long answers caused, since the twelve answers in the new section averaged only twenty words, compared to nearly eighty in the original part.[63] But the original opening section remained the official norm, and a number of catechists decided that the best way to deal with this was to subdivide the questions in that section, and where necessary in the new section too. Richard Bernard was an early exponent of this idea, in the 1630s, but rather took it to extremes, as in the case of the fourth Commandment: 'What is here commanded? To remember. What? The sabbath day. Wherefore? To keep it holy', and so on.[64] A better balanced effort was *The church catechism, analysed, explained, and improved*, first published in 1683, which was intended for 'beginners' who had yet to learn the Prayer Book form and consisted almost entirely of the same material as the church catechism but broken up into shorter questions and answers.[65] Similarly Simon Ford's second venture into publishing a catechism was entitled *The catechism*

---

quections [sic] [1585], sig. C2^v; and W. Attersoll, *The principles of Christian religion* (1635); and for a parallel complaint from the Continent, see B. Vogler, 'Catéchisme et catéchèse dans l'orthodoxie Lutherienne à Strasbourg (1560–1750)', in *Transmettre la foi: XVIe–XXe siècles* (Paris, 1984), 16.

[61] Perkins, *Foundation*, sigs. A2^r–3^v; G[eorge] W[ebbe], *A brief exposition of the principles* (1617), sig. A3^v; T. Ratcliffe, *A short summe of the whole catechisme* (1620), sig. A4^r; [W. Bridges], *A catechisme for communicants* (1645), sigs. A4^{r-v}; A. Palmer, *Childrens bread* (1671), sigs. A3^{r-v}; [Ken], *Exposition on the church catechism*, sigs. A2^r–3^r and *passim*; T. Doolittle, *Catechizing necessary for the ignorant* (1692), 24–32.

[62] G. Masterson, *Milk for babes* (1654), sig. A3^r.   [63] Brightman, *English Rite*, ii. 778–91.

[64] R. Bernard, *The common catechisme* (1640), sig. B4^r.

[65] Anon., *The church catechism, analysed, explained, and improved* (1703), title-page and *passim*.

of the Church of England wherein each answer is broken into several questions and answers, most of which are taken out of the very words thereof (1694); this was intended 'for the greater benefit of the younger learner' and for householders, especially those in his own parish in Worcestershire, to use 'to instruct their children and servants (and … it may be sometimes themselves too) thereby in private'.[66] In Richard Kidder's *An help to the smallest children's more easie understanding of the church-catechism by way of question and answer*, none of the answers was longer than four or five lines, and most were only one or two lines long; and *A plain and profitable scheme* for breaking each answer of the church catechism into 'several questions and answers' was also designed for 'the younger sort of catechumens'.[67] All of these forms probably helped increase comprehension as well; indeed, in some cases, like Bernard's version and that of I.B. in 1669, the aim of increasing understanding was perhaps as important to the author as facilitating memorization.[68]

Similar action was taken with other popular forms. The final version of the Dering–More catechism consisted of seventy questions with very long answers, averaging a hundred words each; the whole was five times longer than the Prayer Book catechism. The anonymous author of the *Short catechisme. Brieflie contayning the whole summe of Christian religion* (1590) was heavily reliant on the Dering–More form for a number of its answers, but was in all only seven pages long.[69] Eusebius Paget's form was in part a simplification of the Dering–More catechism and in part contained material of his own: the end-product had half as many questions again as the Dering–More but the individual answers were much shorter, averaging little more than twenty words, so that the total wordage was less than half that of its predecessor. Indeed, Paget (or Openshaw) subsequently revised the length of the questions and answers in the original Paget form, in such a way as to double the number of questions but halve the length of the non-scriptural answers.[70] At least two authors felt the need to abbreviate Perkins's form, and one to offer a shortened form of Stephen Egerton's main form which (the anonymous author said) he was publishing especially for those 'poor souls as want either money to buy, or time to learn, or memories to retain' a larger treatise.[71] Another author abbreviated John Ball's best-selling short

---

[66] [Simon Ford], *The catechism of the Church of England* (1694), title-page and sig. A3ᵛ.

[67] R. Kidder, *An help to the smallest children's more easie understanding the church-catechism* (1709), *passim*; anon., *A plain and profitable scheme of the catechism* (1711), title-page and *passim*.

[68] See Bernard, *Common catechisme*, and I.B., *The catechism of the Church of England with some questions and answers tending to the explanation thereof added* (1669).

[69] See Appendix 1, s.v. 'Short'; Stockwood also saw the need to reduce the number of scripture proofs he added to the Dering–More catechism because he and others had noted the burden of them was handicapping those of weaker capacity: E. Dering, J. More, and J. Stockwood, *A short catechisme for householders. With prayers [and] prooves of the scripture* (1583), sig. A2ᵛ.

[70] The editions used for this comparison were [E. Dering and J. More], *Briefe and necessarie catechisme* (1590); E. Paget, *Short questions and answeares* (1580); and Paget and Openshaw, *Short questions and answeres* (1627).

[71] R. Marshall, *Fifteen considerations stirring us up* (1645), 1–8; anon., *A short catechisme: holding forth*

catechism. Ball's answers were commendably brief: on average they were less than twenty words each, but the number of questions was even higher than in Paget's form: three hundred and fifty. Samuel Langley explained that he had reduced the number of questions in Ball's form to forty-one (grouped in twelve short sections), so that 'weak memories' might retain the contents better; the ones he omitted were what he saw as the more difficult and less necessary questions. Langley also moved in the opposite direction to Ball by making every answer a complete proposition in itself. Ball's brevity had meant that the answer to be memorized might consist of a phrase or clause which by itself was incomplete and potentially meaningless, for example, the three-word answer 'By faith alone' to the question: 'How are we made partakers of Christ with all his benefits?' Experience had shown Langley that this separation of one part of a sentence from the main part of the sentence of which it formed an integral part hindered young, weak, or less careful students from learning the answers they repeated, so in his work each answer was made complete: 'We are made partakers of Christ with all his benefits by faith alone.'[72]

Attempts to provide as short answers as possible can also be seen in the way in which the parliamentary ordinance of October 1645 and the Worcestershire Association's 'profession' of faith of 1653 were turned into catechisms. Whereas the original statements in both cases consisted of pages of continuous prose, the relevant catechetical versions consisted of a series of short questions and terse answers.[73] The Westminster Shorter Catechism may have been intended for those of 'weaker capacity', but, as we have seen, it could not slough off its origins as a cut-down version of a Larger Catechism which had been designed for those who had 'made some proficiency in the knowledge of the grounds of religion', such as adults and divinity students.[74] As a result a number of versions were soon produced which tried to prepare the young learner for the experience of learning the Shorter Catechism by making children learn first a simplified or condensed version of it, such as Thomas Lye's *Abridgement of the late reverend assemblies catechism*, Nathaniel Vincent's *The principles of the doctrine of Christ*, the anonymous *Beginner's catechism*, and the first form in John Willison's *The mother's catechism*.[75]

We are looking here mainly at abridged versions of shorter or established forms, but it may be pointed out that the question-and-answer expositions of the church catechism which were produced in the seventeenth century and mentioned in previous

and explaining (1646), *passim*; anon., *The maine grounds of religion* [1624?], and cf. S. Egerton, *A briefe methode of catechising* (1615), 1–20.

[72] Langley, *A catechisme shorter than the short catechisme*, sigs. A2ʳ⁻ᵛ, and pp. 5–6.

[73] See above, pp. 79–80 and 222–3.

[74] The phrases in quotation marks appeared on the title-pages of later editions of the Westminster Shorter and Larger Catechisms.

[75] T. Lye, *An abridgement of the late reverend Assemblies shorter catechism* [1662?]; N. Vincent, *The principles of the doctrine of Christ* (1691); anon., *The beginner's catechism* (1707); and J. Willison, *The mother's catechism* (1735), 7–24.

chapters seem collectively to have undergone a similar slimming process. William Hill rightly thought he was the first to produce a complete set of extra questions and answers to weave round those of the Prayer Book catechism; but his answers, over a hundred in all, were quite long, over forty words on average. If we compare this with the length of two equally popular expositions from the later seventeenth century, there is an interesting contrast. Marshall's exposition had nearly twice as many questions, but the answers were only twenty-five words long. Lewis's had more than three times the number of questions, but his answers were only thirty words long, and those thirty words often included a scripture text cited in full; without these the average would have been lower than Marshall's.[76] Lewis's form was designed for use in Charity Schools which had daily catechizing, but as one minister of the time who saw his catechumens only on a Sunday and was publishing a much shorter form explained, the schoolmaster 'makes it a great part of his work to cause them to learn [a catechism], which the parish ministers cannot do'.[77] These expositions come more into our second category—works to increase comprehension—rather than our first—works to help memorizing; but the length of the answers in Marshall and Lewis suggest that brevity was not being sacrificed to clarity. It is also instructive of the more realistic standards expected in some early eighteenth-century churches that the author who pointed out that Charity School teachers had more time than parish clergy had himself cut down the forty-two-page form which he admired to a mere eighteen pages, on the grounds that the children of his parish had found difficulty committing the larger work to memory.[78]

An alternative to trying to make an official or established form easier to commit to memory was to compose a brand new form without some of the problems associated with the old one. Some authors saw the need for simpler language. Touched by the willingness of his congregation to learn, especially those of the 'simple sort', William Wood had thought of trying to provide them with a précis of Nowell's catechism without the 'over scholastical' language he had used; but finding this difficult he decided to write his own form in 'familiar' 'country-like speech', 'mere, natural English'. Like Elnathan Parr later, he said that he had written his form not for the learned, but 'plain Englishmen'.[79] Other authors showed awareness of the need to be brief, either in the overall length of their catechism or in the length of individual answers. The *Breefe catechisme so necessarie and easie to be learned* of 1576 was only a few pages long, so that even 'the simple sort' could learn it; it contained the very minimum necessary knowledge, and anyone who 'can not or will not attain to the same is

[76] W. Hill, *The first principles of a Christian* (1629); [T. Marshall], *The catechism set forth* (1683); J. Lewis, *The church catechism explain'd* (1712); and Appendix 1 for repeat editions.

[77] ['A country parson'], *A short and plain exposition of the church catechism* (1715), p. v.

[78] Ibid., pp. v–vi and *passim*.

[79] W. Wood, *A fourme of catechising in true religion* (1581), sigs. *2ᵛ–3ᵛ; E. Parr, *The grounds of divinitie* (1619), sigs. A4ᵛ, *viiʳ.

not to be counted a good Christian'.[80] The *Short catechisme for little children* published in 1589 was six pages long, consisted of only forty-two questions, the answers to which were mostly no more than one line long, and was said to have been learnt by a 3-year-old; while the author of the five-page *Short catechisme containing the principles of Christian religion* of 1656 had merely 'extracted ... out of other catechisms ... what I thought most plain and short' and then added a little of what he thought his 'very loving neighbours' should believe and practice.[81] Other authors also indicated that their forms were tailor-made for their own set of catechumens. In his *Points of instruction for the ignorant* (1613) Robert Horne said he could have made the work bigger, but the vessels he had to fill could not receive more, and he had stopped pouring when he saw them filling; and William Lyford framed his short catechism of 1640 after he had observed his charges' state of knowledge first: 'You first directed and taught me, how to teach you; I learned from you, not from my books, what questions to instruct you in.'[82] John Brinsley claimed in his *Breviate of saving knowledge* (1643) that he had aimed above all at 'brevity and perspicuity' and that it was for 'such as have good desires but weak memories'.[83] If being 'plain' and 'familiar' and shorter rather than longer meant avoiding 'curious and hard questions', authors like Thomas Settle and George Webbe were prepared to do this; for example, on the 'busy' question of whether faith preceded repentance or the other way round Settle made the unusual comment that the two views were 'very nigh adjoined'.[84]

In the process of keeping a new catechism as short as possible, a number of early Stuart authors cultivated the art of snappy one-liners. To the examples of Bernard and Ball already cited, we can add the author of *The mother and the child* of 1611 and William Gouge's *Short catechisme* of 1615. Here, for example, is Gouge's version of the last five Commandments: 'What is required in the sixth commandment? Mercy. What in the seventh? Chastity. What in the eighth? Justice. What in the ninth? Truth. What in the tenth? Inward contentedness'.[85] In a later form by Gouge, *Briefe answers to the chiefe articles of religion*, the majority of the answers also consisted of a single word.[86] Indeed, by the 1640s there is a suggestion that some authors felt that the trend to short answers was in danger of going too far. In the early 1640s Herbert

---

[80] Anon., *A breefe catechism so necessarie and easie to be earned* (1576), title-page and *passim*.

[81] Anon., *A short catechisme for little children* (1589), title-page and *passim*; anon., *A short catechisme containing the principles of Christian religion* (1656), sig. A2^v.

[82] R. Horne, *Points of instruction for the ignorant* (1617), sig. A3^v; W. Lyford, *An helpe for young people* (1640), sig. A3^r.

[83] Brinsley, *Breviate of saving knowledge*, 1.

[84] T. Settle, *A catechisme briefly opening the misterie* [1587], sigs. A2^r, B8^{r-v}; G[eorge] W[ebbe], *A brief exposition of the principles* (1617), sig. A3^v; one minister cut down an existing form to suit his 'little ones' by leaving out the original 'dilations' which they had found tedious to memorize: ['A country parson'], *A short and plain exposition of the church catechism* (1715), q.v.

[85] [John Cragge/Craig], *The mother and the child* (1611), *passim*; W. Gouge, *A short catechisme* (1621), sig. B1^r.

[86] W. Gouge, *Briefe answers to the chiefe articles of religion* (1642), *passim*.

Palmer anticipated Langley's strictures on Ball's best-selling form by suggesting that at least some of the answers in a catechism should consist of complete sentences and not be dependent on the sense of the question, since these fuller answers could form a stock of divine knowledge even if the questions were forgotten.[87] The authors of the Westminster catechisms were also at pains to point out that in both of their forms:

so much of every question ... is repeated in the answer as maketh every answer an entire proposition or sentence in itself; to the end the learner may further improve it upon all occasions, for his increase in knowledge and piety, even out of the course of catechizing, as well as in it.[88]

There was a difference of philosophy here, between those who sought brevity at all costs in their answers to help the catechumen memorize it, and those who sought intelligibility to help them understand it; but as so often the gulf could be bridged, and in the later Stuart period we find a number of authors who managed to offer both succinctness and 'entire propositions'.[89]

In fact, another way round this problem that was already being grasped was to publish alongside the original full-length version an abridged version in which the content was reduced to its essence. William Wood included at the end of his form an abridgement of fifty of the longer answers (reduced from about six lines down to two), because experience had taught him, he said, that many of the answers in the original form were too long for those of 'weak capacities'.[90] William Gouge decided to include an 'abstract' of his first catechism in later editions of that work, as did his son Thomas in later editions of his own catechism after the Restoration; many other examples could be given from the 1590s to the 1690s.[91] A few authors went even further. John Davidson produced a work in which the basic twenty-four-page catechism was reduced first to four pages ('for the help of short memories'), then to four questions and answers ('for young ones' and little children), and finally to one scripture text.[92] Stephen Egerton did something very similar by boiling down his

---

[87] Palmer, *Endeavour*, sigs. A2^{r-v}; cf. Baxter above, n. 48.

[88] [Westminster Assembly of Divines], *The humble advice of the assemblie of divines at Westminster; concerning a shorter catechisme* (1658), 43.

[89] e.g. T. Gouge, *The heads of the foregoing catechism* (1679), and [Marshall], *Catechism set forth* (1683); and see above, n. 48.

[90] Wood, *Fourme of catechising*, sigs. *vi^v, and pp. 114–16.

[91] W. Gouge, *A short catechisme* (1635), the seventh edition; T. Gouge, *Heads of the foregoing catechism* (1679): see Appendix 1 for the evolution of this catechism; and for others providing summaries at much the same time as the main catechism, R. Linaker, *A short and plaine instruction* (1591), sigs. E1^r–2^r; Aldem, *Short, plaine and profitable catechise*, 49–62; S. Crooke, *A brief direction to true happinesse*, published as part 2 of *The guide unto true blessednesse* in 1613, and separately in 1614; C. Blackwood, *A soul-searching catechism* (1658), 88–92; C. Drélincourt, *A catechism: or, familiar instructions* (1698), 100–10; for some who published abridgements shortly after the full form, see the works of Nowell in Appendix 1; E. Elton, *An extract or short view*, published in editions of *A forme of catechizing* from 1624 to 1634; and J. Mayer, *Mayers catechisme abridged* (1623).

[92] Davidson, *Short Christian instruction*, sigs. B8^r–C3^r.

twenty-page catechism first to forty questions, and then to four, and Thomas Vicars followed his short form of only twenty-seven questions and answers, with a sum of that form, and then a sum of the sum.[93] Another ploy was to summarize some of the ground covered in a catechism in a concluding prayer or prayers, which could be read out by the catechist or even memorized by catechumens as a reinforcement of what had been learnt in the catechizing class; and at least one author inserted revision tests at strategic points of his text, to see how students had 'profited' by what they had just been learning.[94]

Another help to memorizing was to ensure that the amount to be learnt on a regular basis was not excessive. In his exhortation to catechists in 1623, Thomas Downing argued that the best method of training the memory was 'little by little': children and servants should not be burdened with too much plenty, but offered wisdom in small pieces suited to 'the smallest and weakest digestions'; 'vessels that have narrow mouths receive not the liquor hastily poured' into them but only fill drop by drop.[95] A fairly common pattern, especially for rather longer catechisms than we have been discussing so far, was to divide a work into short sections for weekly learning. The text of Calvin's catechism was later divided into over fifty parts, leaving only a couple of pages to be learned each week; the form based on the Heidelberg Catechism published by R.B. in 1601 was also divided into fifty-two parts and had only one or two answers to be learnt each Sunday, though the answers were quite long; John Ball was the first of a number of expositors of the Prayer Book catechism who divided his exposition the same way, in his case to ensure that between three and six relatively short answers were memorized each week; while in the late 1670s Thomas Gouge suggested that one or two answers of his form needed to be learnt each week.[96] In some cases about one-half to three-quarters of an hour was thought to be adequate to

---

[93] S. Egerton, *A briefe methode of catechising* (1615), 20–8; T[homas] V[icars], *The grounds of that doctrine which is according to godlinesse* (1631), 24–7.

[94] Prayers: [Dering and More], *Briefe and necessarie catechisme*, sigs. C1ʳ–3ʳ, and cf. C3ʳ–D1ʳ; B.A., *A treatise of the way to life* [1580?], sigs. C1ʳ–2ʳ; R. Bernard, *A large catechisme following the order of the common authorized catechisme* (1602), 53–61; E. Coote, *The English schoolmaster* (1624), 41–3; N[icholas] A[llsopp], *Certaine briefe questions and answers* [*c.*1620], sigs. A6ʳ–7ʳ; W. Gouge, *Short catechisme* (1635), sigs. C2ᵛ–4ᵛ; J. Clifford, *Sound words: The catechism of the Westminster Assembly* (1699), 176–81; J. Lewis, *Church-catechism explain'd* (1712), 79–80; J. Talbot, *The church-catechism explained by a paraphrase* (1705), 162–4; and cf. anon., *Private devotions for children, or the church catechism turn'd into a form of prayer* (12 editions *c.*1703–1709: see Appendix 1). R. Abbot, *Milk for babes; or, a mother's catechism for her children* (1646) had revision exercises at the end of each of eight sections of the main form.

[95] T. Downing, *The catechisers holy encouragement* (1623), sig. [2]ᵛ, pp. 9–11, 14. A similar metaphor can be found in works by Horne (see above, p. 250 n. 82) and Blackwood, *Soul-searching catechism*, sig. A2ᵛ.

[96] See the texts of J. Calvin, *The catechisme* (Geneva, 1556); R.B., *A breife catechisme* (1601); J. Ball, *Short questions and answers* (1639); T. Gouge, *The principles of Christian religion* (1684), sig. A3ʳ. For other examples of division into fifty-two, see anon., *Eniautos: or a course of catechizing* (1664), S. Ford, *A plain and profitable exposition* (1684), and Talbot, *Church-catechism explained*. Also divided into weekly lessons, though not for the whole year, were Z. Isham, *The catechism of the church with proofs* (1695), Thomas Bray, *The church catechism* (1704), and the two works of Joseph Harrison discussed later in this chapter.

master the weekly assignment (this did not include the testing),[97] though where the form was longer or the answers larger this was probably on the low side.

Other authors divided their forms into sections to be studied on a daily basis. Eusebius Paget used his question-and-answer form on the Bible every day in his own household for twenty-six years, with a chapter on the Old Testament being read at dinner, and a chapter on the New at supper; and James Leech said that he had found by long experience (again perhaps in his own family) that his form could be repeated every seven days.[98] Thomas Wilson had done his sums carefully: if four of his two hundred and eighty questions were tackled every day, his form could be gone through at least four times a year; two questions a day meant twice a year; twice a week with three questions at a time meant once a year—a scheme which, if carefully followed, would have assisted not only initial memorization but also retention as well. To be on the safe side, Wilson also provided a 'very little sum' of forty short questions and answers for 'the weak, as well in years as knowledge', so that thereafter they could proceed to the larger work.[99] John Lewis's catechism for Charity Schools was divided into thirteen parts of about twenty-five answers each: on the basis of each school week having six days, this is again about four answers a day to learn, with the possibility of the whole being repeated every quarter.[100]

Another method of helping memorization and retention, especially among those not used to formal learning methods, was to provide what might today be called support systems. The most obvious such system was for catechizing in one location such as the church to be supported by catechizing in another such as the school or home, though as we saw in the previous chapter this could not be guaranteed. Alternatively, there were visual aids, such as the Commandment boards in church,[101] broadsheet versions of one or more of the standard three formulae or of a simple catechism to be tacked up in the home,[102] and the embroidering onto a sampler of one of the usual formulae or some other improving text which could then be displayed on a wall.[103]

---

[97] Anon., *A catechisme, or short kind of instruction* (1588), sigs. A3ᵛ–4ʳ; Lyford, *Principles of faith*, sig. A3ᵛ; anon., *Some forms of catecheticall doctrines*, sig. A6ᵛ; see also above p. 239, and for the interval of half an hour for teaching, testing, and exposition in church, see above, pp. 112–13.

[98] E. Paget, *The history of the Bible* (1613), sigs. [¶]2ʳ⁻ᵛ; J. Leech, *A plaine and profitable catechisme* (1605), sig. A3ᵛ.

[99] T[homas] W[ilson], *An exposition of the two first verses* (1609), sig. gg1ʳ.

[100] Lewis, *Church catechism explain'd*, *passim*; as we saw above (p. 157 n. 270) Isham divided his form into twelve and expected it to be gone through four times a year.

[101] Aston, *England's Iconoclasts*, 317, 332–3, 361–8.

[102] See Appendix 1, s.v. C. Watson (1578–81); *A briefe catechisme conteining the most principall groundes* [*c*.1615?]; *A short catechisme to prepare young ignorant people* (1657); T. Doolittle ('Scheme'); and *Rules for self-examination* (1685); and Watt, *Cheap Print*, ch. 6.

[103] A. Colby, *Samplers Yesterday and Today* (1964); A. Sebba, *Samplers: Five Centuries of a Gentle Craft* (1979); and my forthcoming *Religious Instruction*. Protestants did not, however, use woodcuts in catechisms, though Catholics did: [L. Vaux], *A catechisme, or a christian doctrine* (1584); and R. Bellarmino, *A short catechisme of Cardinall Bellarmine illustrated* (1614); and cf. the comment of Fleury, in his *Historical catechism*, p. xxvii, that woodcuts were 'the scripture of the ignorant'.

A parallel move adopted by a number of catechetical authors was to turn the same formulae or indeed part or all of a catechism into verse, which could be learnt as a mnemonic.[104] In the seventeenth century the Prayer Book catechism and the start of the Westminster Shorter were turned into verse for this reason.[105] But long before that, in 1583, Thomas Roberts had published his *Catechisme in meter* 'for the easier learning and better remembering' of the principles of the Christian faith. The preface suggested that our dull natures are slow to learn heavenly things and quickly become bored, but tackling them in verse, which could also be sung to the same tunes as in Sternhold and Hopkins's metrical version of the psalms, was easier for 'the simple'. Perhaps with one eye on the 'godly' critics of poesy, he insisted that this was 'no idle or vain poetry, but a needful and Christian policy'. Readers of the last few paragraphs will not be surprised to hear that he also provided two verse summaries of his verse catechism, one in only twelve lines.[106] The summary of the long catechism which Robert Sherard composed was in the same metre as Roberts's, and was also said to be not in a lofty style or to have used hard words but to be especially suitable for 'poor, simple country-people'.[107] In the late 1620s Thomas Vicars provided a series of 'psalms' to reflect the main themes of his catechism, and also provided versions of the Decalogue and Creed in verse; the fact that some of the prayers that then followed were used in the local school may indicate that the verses had been designed partly with children in mind.[108] Rather more polished was the first of two translations into English of Hugo Grotius's catechism, which together with Latin and Greek versions of the same was published several times between the 1640s and the 1680s.[109] With the *Practical catechism: or, instructions for children, in verse*, published three times in Anne's reign by Thomas Gills, the blind poet of Bury St Edmunds, we are back to the English vernacular tradition.[110] The advantages of the mimetic over the didactic were readily reinforced by the use of forms in verse.

One can also point to different ways in which the skills of the printer were used to help catchumens with some reading skills to master a work. The most obvious of these was in providing large numbers of copies, which was a double boon to busy clergy: it saved them the chore of writing out extra copies, and, since parishioners were thought to have had greater difficulty reading handwriting than type-face, it

---

[104] For verse forms of the Ten Commandments attached to catechisms, see Horne, *Points of instruction*, sig. E8ᵛ; W. Barton, *Six centuries of select hymns … Together with a catechism* (1688), 315–22; and cf. J. Bartlett, *Hymns and songs of praise* (1710), 37–41; and for moralistic or improving verse attached to catechisms, see anon., *The maine grounds of religion* [1624?], sigs. A6ʳ–7ᵛ; Ellis, *Catechism wherein the learner*, 109–110; and J. Mason, *A little catechism, with little verses* (1692), 10–14.

[105] J. Fowler, *The catechism of the Church of England, poetically paraphrased* (1678); T.D., *Zion's song for young children* (1650).

[106] T. R[oberts], *The catechisme in meter* (1583), title-page and sigs. Aiiʳ–iiiᵛ, Biᵛ–iiiᵛ, and *passim*.

[107] R[obert] S[herard], *The countryman with his houshold* (1620), 236–54.

[108] Vicars, *Grounds of that doctrine*, 21–34.   [109] See Appendix 1, s.v. Grotius.

[110] T. Gill(s), *A practical catechism: or, instructions for children, in verse* [1710?]; and for a near contemporary Catholic example, anon., *The childes catechisme* (1678), 39–42.

meant that 'they which cannot read after the pen may take profit by the print'.[111] Print not only reinforced what the minister had told his flock, and many ministers claimed that parishioners were soliciting copies, but also held out the prospect of a work coming to the attention of someone who had not heard it used in a particular church at a particular time.[112] In the early modern period print-runs were periodically enlarged, but since it is exceptional to know the price of printed catechisms before the 1670s, we cannot be sure if the prices of catechisms actually fell. Certainly, from that decade we find a number of short catechisms being offered for as little as a penny, tuppence, or threepence, and substantial works for eightpence or a shilling.[113] And we also find authors or publishers increasingly making appeals to the generosity of the rich and to 'all charitable and well disposed Christians' to buy copies to give to the poor, and offering special rates of ten (or twelve) shillings a hundred for a work normally retailing at tuppence, or twenty shillings per hundred for threepenny works.[114]

While most books printed in England by the end of the sixteenth century were printed in the roman type with which we are familiar today, catechisms were one of a limited range of works in which the old black-letter type was often retained. This was quite deliberate in that for much of the early modern period it was thought that slow readers found it easier to read the type-face they had encountered in *The ABC with the catechisme* or *The primer and catechisme* or in cheap pamphlets and early versions of the 'penny godlies'. We have already encountered examples of authors like Mayer and Williams asking printers to use different type-faces within the same work and even on the same page, to convey a black-letter message to 'children in years and understanding', and a roman one to more advanced catechumens, and sometimes even an italic one giving scripture proofs to be learnt last of all.[115] In the early Stuart period, it is noticeable that black letter was preserved for the answers in not only

[111] *Hist. MSS. Comm. Gawdy MSS.* (1885), 23; Aldem, *Short, plaine and profitable catechisme*, sigs. A2[r–v]; Horne, *Points of instruction*, sig. A3[r]; Webbe, *Briefe exposition of the principles* (1617), sig. A3[r]; Crompton, *Explication*, sigs. ¶6[v], 9[v]; J[ohn] S[talham], *A catechisme for children* (1644), sig. A2[r]; S. Austin, *A practical catechisme* (1647), sig. A5[v].

[112] J. Tomkys, *A briefe exposition of the lordes prayer* [1585], sig. 3[v]; T[homas] W[ilson], *An exposition of the two first verses* (1609), sig. A3[v]; W. Hinde, *A path to pietie* (1626), sigs. A6[r–v]; J. Syme, *The sweet milke of Christian doctrine* (1617), sig. A4[r]; R[ichard] S[edgwick], *A short summe of the principal things* (1624), sig. A2[v]; J. Phillips, *The Christians A. B. C.* (1629), sig. A6[r]; W. Jones, *An exposition of the whole catechisme* (1633), 3.

[113] See Appendix 1 for the prices of the following publications: anon., *A word to the poor* (1692); A. Palmer, *Children's bread* (c.1700); R.W., *A sacramental catechism* (1701); anon., *The church catechism broke into short questions* (1709); [W. Bunbury], *The church catechism: with single proofs* (1711); anon., *The church catechism, with explanations* (1705); N. Clark, *A brief exposition of the catechism* (1725); E. Boughen, *A short exposition of the catechism* (1663); C. Ellis, *A catechism wherein the learner* (1674); S. Lowth, *Catechetical questions very necessary* (1673); T. Doolittle, *A plain method of catechizing* (1698). On larger print-runs, see C. J. Sommerville, *Popular Religion in Restoration England* (Gainesville, Fla., 1977), 9–11.

[114] Bunbury, *Church catechism*; R.W., *Sacramental catechism*; anon., *Church catechism broke into short questions*; anon., *The church catechism, with explanations*—as previous note; see also anon., *A new sacramental catechism* (1701), title-page.

[115] See above, pp. 153, 157.

short catechisms of twenty-four pages or less, but also a number of much longer works such as editions of the 'middle' Nowell catechism in the 1630s.[116] Of the two editions of Fotherby's very long *Covenant between God and man*, the first in 1596 was printed with italic questions and roman answers in the academic style, but the second in 1616 was printed with roman questions and black-letter answers; and while the dialogue part of Robert Sherard's *The countryman with his household* (1620) was in roman, the answers of the short catechisms he inserted periodically into the story-line were printed in black letter. In the later Stuart period, black letter was still used regularly in expositions of the Prayer Book catechism to depict the original text, even if the commentary was in roman.[117] But by then patterns were beginning to change, with *ABC*s, large folio bibles, and cheap print increasingly being printed in roman type, so that in 1699 we find one author making a point of having his catechism printed in roman on the grounds that ordinary people now found the 'old English print' hard to read.[118]

Authors were also quick to use other opportunities provided by the printer's ability to alter the layout of a page. The early practice of printing the first word of the answer immediately after the last word of the question, wherever on a line that question finished,[119] soon gave way to the practice of starting every answer on a new line, which used more paper but made it much easier for catechumens to pick out the answer. Identifying answers was also greatly helped when printers stopped using the same type-face for both questions and answers, and started using different type-face for the two: at first, usually roman for the questions and black letter for the answers, then increasingly italic for the questions and roman for the answers.[120] The anonymous author of a work published in 1708 had the Westminster Shorter and his own propositions and proofs printed in standard sized type, but the extracts from the Westminster Larger which he interspersed among these in smaller type.[121] Other printers' ploys taken advantage of were the use of square brackets and asterisks or other devices to link words in the text of an answer with an explanation or scripture proof in the margin or placed elsewhere in the work. An example of the former is William Lyford's *Principles of faith* (1642), in which he assured 'his people' in Sher-

---

[116] As examples of works of different sizes, see R. Linaker, *A short catechisme* (1610); W. Attersoll, *The principles of Christian religion* (1635); [W. Twisse], *A brief catecheticall exposition of Christian doctrine* (1633); A[lexander] N[owell], *A catechism, or institution of Christian religion* (1633).

[117] e.g. in the forms of Edward Boughen, Richard Sherlock, Thomas Comber, Thomas Marshall, John Williams, Benjamin Farrow, and Roger Davies listed in Appendix 1; an occasional exposition of the Westminster Shorter Catechism also used black letter for the original, e.g. J. Flavell, *An exposition of the Assemblies catechism* (1692).

[118] T. Salmon, *The catechism of the Church of England* (1699), sig. A2^r.

[119] e.g. [E. Allen], *A catechisme, that is to say a familiar introduction* (1548); [J. Ponet], *A short catechisme* (1553); and T. Becon, *A new catechisme sette forth dialogue wise* (1564).

[120] Different type-face for questions and answers was the norm by the 1580s, and italic and roman had replaced roman and black letter in many but by no means all catechisms by the 1610s.

[121] See Appendix 1, s.v. *Doctrines of the Christian religion*.

borne, Dorset, that the 'weighty and perspicuous answers' he had provided them were really relatively short when it was remembered that the sections which he had had placed in square brackets were 'for explication, and not to load the memory'.[122] An example of the latter is James Talbot's *The church-catechism explained by a paraphrase* (1705) which used a full range of typographical options: black letter for the original church catechism text, roman for additions to it, and italic for scripture proofs, square brackets to insert explanatory comments into the middle of the answers of the church catechism, marginal references to relevant scripture passages which were later printed in full in the text, line numbers in the margin and bracketed letters—(a), (b), (c), etc.—placed against key words or phrases in the text to assist cross-referencing between the questions he asked subsequently and the approved answer in the text, and daggers placed against some of those questions to indicate to the catechist that they could be omitted if it was thought that the age or capacity of the persons examined did not yet warrant their use.[123] Perhaps following the ideas of Ramus, a number of authors or editors used tables to provide in a visual, quick-reference form the relationship between the different points being made in a catechism and perhaps to assist their being remembered too.[124] The author of *Some forms of catecheticall doctrines* defended his use of tables to represent a series of propositions on faith and duty as a means of helping those of riper judgement and capacity to remember them, and to help produce a uniform approach among neighbouring ministers, which (in 1647) he felt was much to be desired.[125]

The full scope of catechists' inventiveness is revealed if we turn now to concentrate on techniques designed to further catechumens' *comprehension* of what they were being taught. As we saw in Chapter 3 when looking at the second level of catechizing in church, as early as the 1604 canon on catechizing there was an apparent increase in official awareness of the need for catechists to explain the meaning of the church catechism to those who were learning it, and this led to major efforts and the adoption of a variety of techniques to achieve this.[126] Comments made by catechists in the parishes also indicate, on the one hand, a growing awareness of the need to teach understanding at the same time as knowledge rather than as a supplement to it (as

[122] W. Lyford, *Principles of faith and good conscience* (1642), sigs. A3ᵛ–4ʳ.

[123] Talbot, *Church-catechism explained, passim.*

[124] See G. Babington, *A very fruitfull exposition of the commaundements* (1590); J. Sprint, *The summe of the Christian religion* (1613); W. Dyke, *A treasure of knowledge* (1620) (layout of the Decalogue); N. Byfield, *The principall grounds of Christian religion* (1625) (table added by the editor, W.C.); J. Cateline, *The rules and directions of the ordinance of parliament* (1646); and see Watt, *Cheap Print and Popular Piety*, 242, 244, though cf. F. Yates, *The Art of Memory* (1966), 233–4.

[125] Anon., *Some forms of catecheticall doctrines* (1647), sigs. A8ʳ⁻ᵛ, C4ᵛ–5ʳ, C7ᵛ; and cf. [Nicholas Gibbon], *A summe or bodie of divinitie real* (1651) for a diagrammatic representation of the Trinity, Creation, Fall, covenant of grace, etc.

[126] See above, pp. 142–66.

Luther and Bernard had done), and, on the other, a clearer insight into the alterations of technique and the variety of approaches which might help catechists achieve that end. 'They are mistaken who think … catechizing is but an examining of the memory; it is an informing of the understanding', wrote an anonymous presbyterian in 1655.[127] In 1683, in *The catechizing of families*, Baxter showed that the problem of memorization without full comprehension had not gone away when he complained that too many were deceived by a 'counterfeit of knowledge': 'millions take the knowledge of the bare words, with the grammatical and logical sense, instead of the knowledge of the things themselves by which these are signified, as if the glass would nourish without the wine'. But at least he was aware of the problem and seeking ways to overcome it.[128]

This brings us to another shift in attitude: towards a more self-critical view of catechetical technique, and a more generous view of catechumens than the naked contempt shown by some Elizabethans (mainly well-educated 'godly') for 'the veriest dullards and dunces', the 'sottish and ignorant' and 'brutish' people, whom they were called on to teach, the 'blind multitude' who gloried in their faith and wished to take the sacrament, but who upon examination by the clergy proved to have no more religion than a horse.[129] By the early seventeenth century what we find are signs of a growing awareness of the varying ability of catechumens and of elements of lay good will, albeit still hampered (in the clergy's eyes) by a lack of familiarity with scholarly methods of memorizing and expression, or with the technical vocabulary and abstract concepts which were used by churchmen without a second thought. In the 1630s, for example, Herbert Palmer came to appreciate that parishioners who could not remember or understand all that was thrust at them were not necessarily stupid or obstinate. In his Hertfordshire parish, he observed that many who had difficulty remembering 'did yet understand the matter, and were therefore not to be despised or discouraged', while many who could remember understood little or nothing of what they had learnt. As a result of confronting the difficulty of helping 'those that are not book learned (as the phrase is)' to a deeper understanding in matters of religion, he designed his innovative method to test the understanding of those 'who though they have attained some measure of saving knowledge, yet through the weakness of their abilities cannot express even that which they do conceive'.[130] In a few

[127] Anon., *An exhortation to catechising* (1655), 7.

[128] Baxter, *Catechizing of families*, sig. A2ʳ. For a Catholic author aware of the problems and actively seeking ways round them, see the 'Discourse concerning the design and use of this catechism' with which Fleury prefaced his *Historical catechism*.

[129] A. Dent, *The plaine mans path-way to heaven* (1601), 357; Cawdrey, *Short and fruitfull treatise* (1604), sig. A1ʳ; T. Ratcliffe, *A short summe of the whole catechisme* (1620), sig. A4ʳ; W. Hopkinson, *A preparation unto the waye of lyfe* (1583), sig. D8ᵛ; and cf. Thaxter's comment on the apparently limited intelligence of those 'wholly bent to the toil of manual affairs and the tilth of the ground': *Historical Manuscripts Commission: Gawdy MSS.* (1885), 23.

[130] Clarke, *Lives of two and twenty divines*, 225; Palmer, *Endeavour*, title-page and sig. A3ᵛ.

pages of *The reformed pastor* (1656), Baxter showed that he too had realized that a lot of apparent incomprehension in his flock was due not to resistance or stupidity but to poorly worded questions put by the minister, or the people's lack of a suitable vocabulary to express their meaning. He found some of his parishioners partly understood concepts like repentance and forgiveness, but could not express their meaning in words other than those they were used to, what he called a 'country answer'.

> Many men have that in their minds which is not ripe for utterance, and through want of education and practice, they are strangers to the expressions of those things which they have some conceptions of ... Many even aged, godly persons, cannot speak their minds in tolerable capacities.[131]

As we have seen in the last chapter, Baxter's experience of catechizing showed him just how many different types of parishioner there were, each requiring different treatment. Writing a few years later Philip Nye also argued strongly for the differing capacities and conditions found in different flocks, and for allowing the minister the freedom to choose what was most suitable and edifying for his particular congregation.[132] In *The reformed school*, published in English a few years earlier, John Dury had also argued for catechizing in the classroom to be arranged as the teacher thought best for 'the different ages and degrees of proficiency' of the scholars.[133] The need for more selective and sophisticated techniques of instruction to ensure greater comprehension had become evident.

Three points about the attempts to achieve this may be made briefly at the outset. First, a number of the moves made to help memorizing which have just been described, such as subdividing longer answers, using simpler language and shorter answers, designing new forms with a particular set of catechumens in mind, providing a shorter text at the same time as a fuller one, and using the tricks of the printer's trade, almost certainly helped to assist understanding as well. Secondly, most of the effort that was put into increasing students' comprehension was not put into finding radically new methods, but into fine-tuning the existing question-and-answer mechanism inherited from the sixteenth century. Thirdly, we are not talking of one group of catechists acting as the spearhead of change: both 'godly' and conformist writers tried out new ideas, and if the former on balance perhaps introduced more, the latter may in some cases have taken the ideas further or combined them in novel ways. As we have seen, about a third of the expositions of the Prayer Book catechism were notable for the readiness with which their authors used more than one technique and sometimes a whole cluster of devices to try to get the message across.[134]

Since we have already looked at a number of these, we may begin by putting them

---

[131] Baxter, *Reformed pastor*, 450, and cf. ch. 7, *passim*.
[132] [Nye], *Beames of former light*, 10–11, 81–3, 100.
[133] J. Dury, *The reformed school* (1651), 25, 27. For another author of the time evidently conscious of the need for flexible approaches to teaching and testing, see J. Brooksbank, *Vitis salutaris* (1650).
[134] See above, pp. 149, 152–4.

in context and noting that in many cases there had been previous ventures of a similar kind. In 1581 William Wood thought—perhaps rightly—that he was the first author to provide not only questions and answers to be learnt, but also 'observations' to be read out by the catechist; if there was a better method of curing ignorance, he wrote in the preface, he would like to know it.[135] In the reign of James I, John Ball did much the same thing, issuing a second version of his popular catechism with long expositions after each answer for those who lacked the time or ability 'to furnish themselves out of larger and more learned treatises'. These expositions were requested by his fellow-clergy, but were also said to be intended for 'all men' and especially householders to read to their children and servants as a means of helping them to understand what they heard in church.[136] When John Mayer produced his first form in the early 1620s, which he described as both a catechism and a commentary, he was not breaking fresh ground so much as applying an existing technique to the Prayer Book form catechism for the first time.[137] The process of refining this technique continued, for example in the combination of notes or paraphrase on the Prayer Book catechism with extra questions and answers that we find in the forms of Richard Sherlock in 1656 and Thomas Marshall in 1679.[138] The idea of using marginal notes to explain words in the text had also been tried on a small scale by Robert Linaker and Samuel Hieron long before conformists like Edward Wetenhall took it much further; in Wetenhall's case, the marginal notes were so full that they swamped the text.[139]

Another device which was perhaps developed by an interchange of ideas between 'godly' and conformists was the 'Yes'/'No' technique, though in some respects the latter took it a stage further than its first developers: Herbert Palmer and John Wallis. Palmer's aim, as we have seen, was to make the principles of Christian religion contained in the three standard formulae and the doctrine of the sacraments 'plain and familiar even to very weak capacities, and easy to be remembered even by very weak memories'. To this end he offered 'a double sort of answers and a double sort of questions' because experience had taught him that both sorts were needed 'to drop knowledge into narrow mouthed vessels'. Of the two types of answers, one was as short as it could be, merely the word 'Yes' or 'No', the other as short as it could be given that it had to comprise an entire sentence. However, the two were integrally related in that the larger answer was the sum of a series of shorter ones; the full-length answers made a general point, while the shorter ones were designed to test comprehension by making

[135] Wood, *Fourme of catechising*, sigs. *3ʳ–5ʳ.

[136] J. Ball, *A short treatise contayning all the principall grounds* (1650), sigs. A3ʳ–5ᵛ; Mitchell, *Catechisms of the Second Reformation*, p. lxxv.

[137] Mayer, *English catechisme*, title-page and sig. A3ᵛ.

[138] [R. Sherlock], *The principles of holy Christian religion*; [Marshall], *Catechism set forth*.

[139] R. Linaker, *A short and plaine instruction* (1591), sigs. A2ᵛ–3ʳ and *passim*; S. Hieron, *The doctrine of the beginning of Christ* (1613), *passim*; [E. Wetenhall], *The catechism of the Church of England with marginal notes* (1678), *passim*.

the catechumen choose between an affirmative and a negative answer. Here as an example is the seventy-seventh question, on an aspect of the ninth article of the Creed ('the holy catholic church'), laid out in the two columns as they appeared in Palmer's text, omitting only the scripture references attached to the full answers:

77Q. Why is the church called catholic, that is, universal or general?

A. The church is called catholic, because in all ages Christ hath had a church, and he gathereth it out of all countries and ranks of people.

Is it because in all ages God hath had a church?   Yes.

And because he gathers it out of all countries and ranks of people?   Yes.

Or was there never no time ... when there was no church at all?   No.

Or are there some nations or conditions of men out of which God never takes any to be of his church?   No.

Palmer encouraged the catechist using his form to read over all the questions in one group, and then see if the catechumens could answer the general question, or failing that the under-questions. If even this was beyond them, the catechist was to teach them the brief answers in order, and then the larger answer. In the fourth edition of 1644, Palmer added a further instruction: when the catechist was later examining catechumens who had learnt all the answers in a group, he or she should both start and finish with the head-question, in order to keep the larger answer, which was a statement in itself, clearly in their minds.[140]

When the Westminster Shorter Catechism appeared a few years later, Palmer wished to apply his method to it. He died before he could do this, but John Wallis took over the task, loyally noting that Palmer's method had been 'entertained with great approbation'.[141] Wallis kept the original questions but added short sub-questions demanding 'Yes' or 'No' to help those with 'weak capacities' to notice or understand things which might pass them by if they had simply learnt the original form by rote. Wallis's position was slightly different from Palmer's in that whereas Palmer had had the freedom to design the two sets of questions as an integrated whole, Wallis was converting an existing catechism to the 'Yes'/'No' method. Also Wallis seems to have assumed that catechumens had already learnt the Shorter Catechism before being exposed to his version, whereas Palmer was teaching two sets of answers simultaneously. However, as Wallis pointed out in the preface, using his version of the Shorter Catechism would not interfere with the memories of those who had already learnt that form, since 'to answer these short questions is not so much an exercise of the memory, as of the judgement'; indeed, it should help catechumens' memories.

---

[140] H. Palmer, *An endeavour of making the principles* (1644), title-page, sigs. A2ʳ–3ᵛ, and pp. 20–1.

[141] The *Endeavour* had certainly sold well, but not all the Westminster divines had been convinced of the merits of Palmer's method: see Appendix 1 and Carruthers, *Three Centuries*, 3–4.

Like Palmer, Wallis urged instructors to rehearse the main question first without expecting an answer, then go to the shorter questions, and when these were answered go back to the main question; but the catechist should be flexible. As in Palmer's form, the two sets of questions and answers were printed in two columns on one page, with the leading question and the subsidiary 'Yes'/'No' questions and answers in the left-hand column, and the summary answer in the right. Wallis's form passed through several editions in just over a decade, and its value was still appreciated over fifty years later by Matthew Henry and Isaac Watts.[142] The Palmer–Wallis method was also adopted by other presbyterians such as Joseph Alleine, Thomas Doolittle, Samuel Angier, and Matthew Henry, to test understanding of the Westminster Shorter, to press its message home to individual catechumens, and to graft selected scripture proofs onto their knowledge of the form itself.[143]

In the catechism he published in the early 1680s, Thomas Comber applied the Palmer–Wallis method to the church catechism. He was probably familiar with both men's work, since in the preface he echoed Palmer's comments about filling narrow-mouthed vessels and Wallis's about this method exercising the judgement rather than memory (like Wallis he assumed catechumens had already learnt the basic approved form). Other prefatory remarks were more his own, for example the comment that this method was particularly useful for 'those who cannot read, or cannot get long answers by heart' who needed instruction the most. However, Comber's use of the method was slightly different in that in his sub-questions and answers he did not demand an exact replication of the wording in the original question and answer, and also in that he tended to add material to the sub-questions and answers that was not in the original. Here is an example, which in Comber's case was printed not in two columns on the same page but on opposite pages, the left-hand ones being headed 'The church catechism', the right-hand ones 'The explanation of the catechism':

Question 22.	Qu. 22 Of the outward part of the Lord's Supper.
What is the outward part or sign of the Lord's Supper?	Are not both bread and wine the outward matter of the Lord's Supper? Yes.
Answer.	Is the substance of the bread and wine by consecration changed into the substance of the body and blood of Christ? No.
Bread and wine which the Lord hath commanded to be received.	Will it suffice to look only on the bread and wine in the Lord's Supper, unless we also take, eat, and drink of them? No.

---

[142] J. Wallis, *A brief and easie explanation of the shorter catechism* (1662), sigs. A2^r-v^, and pp. 11–12; M. Henry, *A scripture catechism* (1703), sigs. A2^r-v^; Watts, *Catechisms*, 64, though for his reservations, see below.

[143] J. Alleine, *A most familiar explanation of the Assemblies shorter catechism* (1672); T. Doolittle, *The young man's instructer and the old man's remembrancer* (1673); [S. Angier], *A short explication of the shorter catechism* (1695); Henry, *Scripture catechism*; also cf. anon., *A plain and easy way of catechising* (1680).

Here an anti-Catholic point has been made in the second supplementary question and an anti-Catholic slant added to the third. The reason for these additions may have been that the originals were so pared to the bone that some kind of extra instruction was thought necessary to make the exercise worthwhile, or that Comber felt that the answers to the original question would make more sense if some kind of context or indication of their wider significance was offered; in other words there was an attempt to instruct as well as to test understanding. Whichever it was, Comber claimed that the system worked well with children and adults in country congregations, and many copies of it were sold.[144]

The author of the equally popular *Art of catechizing* (1691) included a 'Yes'/'No' form among the three catechisms in that work (the others added scripture references to the church catechism, and turned *The duty of man* into questions and answers). Like Comber, he did not seek to mirror the words of the church catechism exactly in the sub-questions. However, most of the extra questions were, if not rhetorical, at least leading: 'Was it not a great happiness and favour to be baptized? Yes. Should we ever forget the mercy of God towards us? No'. The most that can be said of this form is that a few more of the students' grey cells may have been engaged than in rote repetition of the church catechism, and that, taken together with the form which linked the answers of the church catechism to scripture texts, a basis for wider knowledge as well as deeper understanding was made available.[145] R.M.'s *The church-catechism enlarg'd and explain'd* (1697) may also be accused of asking questions that are almost rhetorical: to be asked 'Was not your name given you at your baptism ... ?' does not require too much nous to come up with a 'Yes', though to be fair the author was also anxious that the affirmatives or negatives should be reinforced by scripture texts as soon as the catechumen could learn them.[146]

When we move into the next reign, however, we find a clutch of forms which are a hybrid between what might be called the Bernard method (simply dividing existing questions and answers into a series of shorter ones), the Wood–Ball–Mayer method (providing a commentary as well as a catechism), and the Palmer method (trying to make the catechumen think before he or she replied). In five works first published between 1704 and 1715, though in three cases republished quite often thereafter, we find catechists who by a combination of exposition and open-ended questions tried to overcome the problems caused by rote repetition and to test how much catechumens really understood the principles embodied in the church catechism. (It was probably no coincidence that the Charity School regulations of 1701 stressed the need for understanding as well as memorizing of the church catechism.)[147] In the

---

[144] T[homas] C[omber], *The church-catechism with a brief and easie explanation* (1686), sigs. A2^{r-v}, and pp. 28–9.

[145] Anon., *The art of catechizing* (1691), 2, and Appendix 1 for repeat editions.

[146] R.M., *The church-catechism enlarg'd and explain'd* (1697), 5.

[147] Anon., *An account of Charity-Schools lately erected* (6th edn., 1707), 4–5.

preface to his *The church-catechism explained*, Beveridge expressed his concern that a simple subdivision of the existing questions and answers in the church catechism could simply lead to more rote learning rather than greater understanding. His solution was to offer a few pages of exposition of a particular question, and then set a comprehension test by asking a series of questions, such as (in the case of the first answer) 'Why doth [the catechism] begin with this question?', 'What is a Christian?', 'What doth this name put you in mind of?', the answers to which lay in the passage of commentary that had just been read out by the catechist. If catechumens had failed to understand or remember, the catechist was to explain again, using different words, both then and when the catechumens were next examined.[148]

Beveridge realized that this approach would not be easy to implement, and others who were moving in a similar direction tried to ensure success by reducing the amount of commentary before asking the questions. In 1705 James Talbot published *The church-catechism explained by a paraphrase*, in which he explained that he had tried several methods of explaining the church catechism before landing on this one. To ensure that catechumens did not merely repeat the words of the church catechism 'without consideration, and hear them expounded without attention', and to test their understanding of what they learnt and heard, he produced a work in two parts: the first consisted of the church catechism with his own remarks interpolated to produce an explanatory paraphrase of each answer; the second was a table of questions, but no answers. For the sake of the nervous catechist or literate catechumen with a copy, he indicated where an answer could be found in part one, or even repeated parts of that text in part two with typographical clues as to where the answer might be. Today we might think these clues had made life too easy for the literate catechumen, but the student still had to identify the pertinent words of the passage, understand their relevance to the question and phrase an answer to it, which might be described as a form of discovery learning.[149] Talbot's text was much shorter than Beveridge's, but in the other three cases, all published anonymously, they were shorter still. *The church catechism broke into short questions* was the shortest of the lot, adding little new material but concentrating hard on the aims given at the outset: 'to try whether children repeat their catechism by rote, to engage their attention, and to imprint a sense of it in their minds'. Like Talbot, the author used superscript letters to give catechists a clue where an answer, in this case mostly in 'the very words of the church catechism', could be found.[150]

A new method of catechizing (1712) and *An easy method of instructing youth* (1715) provide more sophisticated examples of this emerging genre. The first of these did

---

[148] [Beveridge], *Church-catechism explained*, pp. xii–xiv, 6–7, 219–25, and *passim*.

[149] Talbot, *Church-catechism explained*, sigs. A2ᵛ–4ʳ and *passim*; for an earlier attempt, see the two parts of S. Ford, *A plain and profitable exposition* (1684): the questions from the second part were copied into a 1687 copy of *The ABC with the catechism* now in Cambridge University Library (my thanks to Helen Weinstein for this reference).

[150] Anon., *The church catechism broke into short questions* (1730), sig. A1ᵛ.

place rather a strain upon the talents and energy of the catechist, being in places more of a blueprint on how to ask probing questions and where to provide supporting information than a complete package of the material needed to perform these tasks. Nevertheless, the questions were genuinely searching, a fair amount of explanatory material was provided, more difficult notions were approached from different angles and in different ways, and the catechist was urged to be flexible and extemporize. Altogether this was the most imaginative of this group of works.[151] The most successful of the group in terms of repeat editions, however, was the *Easy method* which sold twelve editions in almost as many years in the reign of George I. The approach was nearer Beveridge's—an explanatory passage on a question of the church catechism, followed by a series of questions but no answers—but the technique of presentation was closer to that of Talbot and the author of the *The church catechism broke into short questions*—superscript numbers and letters linking parts of the exposition to relevant scripture texts and additional questions. The material added was less closely tied to the material in the Prayer Book catechism than in other forms in this group, though the author seems to have been a conformist to judge from the assertion in the subtitle of his work that it was designed to help young people to a 'better understanding of the church catechism, and to prepare them for confirmation'. The author had also thought hard about the deployment of his work: first, the whole work was to be read through (or those who could not read should hear it read) on three separate occasions, without the scripture texts; then it was to be taken one section at a time, and the scripture references checked against the explanatory passage, and then the questions were to be attempted.[152] With these two forms we have reached a new level of insight into the teaching process.

There were, however, limits to such innovations as comprehension tests and open-ended questions: as a body, catechists were prisoners of their own theories which viewed religious instruction as a combination of discipline and indoctrination. On the whole, we find relatively few examples in the surviving literature of catechists being encouraged to be flexible in their methods, of role reversal, or of students being encouraged to answer in their own words, to speak out when they did not understand something they had been told, or to find things out for themselves outside the material presented to them.[153] Authors seem to have preferred such development as there was in the individual or group to be controlled rather than spontaneous, and this

---

[151] Anon., *A new method of catechizing* (1712), pp. iii–iv and *passim*.

[152] Anon., *An easy method of instructing youth* (1728), title-page, sigs. A2^{r-v} and *passim*.

[153] For some examples of catechists being urged to be flexible, see previous note and above, pp. 239–40; J. Nichols, *An order of household instruction* (1596), sig. C6^r; I. Bourne, *A light from Christ ... or, the rich jewel* (1646), title-page and sigs. ¶¶3^v–4^r. For examples of the catechumen asking and the catechist replying, see W. Cotes, *A dialogue of diverse quections [sic]* [1585]; J. Carpenter, *Contemplations for the institution of children* (1601); [W. Bridges], *A catechisme for communicants* (1645); and R. Stookes, *A champion catechism* (1651); for children being encouraged to ask teachers questions when they were in doubt, see Dury, *Reformed school*, 27.

brings us to our last example of innovation in this chapter: the provision of graded learning.

In an earlier paragraph we looked at authors who, to help those with poor memories or limited capacity, provided a summary of their larger form at much the same time as they produced their full-length form; here we are looking not at simplification but at the reverse process—planned movement from an easier to a more advanced form or forms, to help individuals grow in their understanding of the faith. To build up the faith of 'children of riper age', Richard Mather pointed out in the 1650s, Luther had had his major as well as his minor catechismus, and Beza his larger confession of faith as well as his shorter; Alexander Nowell had made a similar point when commending his 'middle' form as a bridge between the Prayer Book form and his own original large form: diversity of catechisms both in length and difficulty for different catechumens was both allowed by godly men and practised in many reformed countries, and 'not without good reason, grounded upon the diversities of ages and capacities of wit'.[154] After half a century of catechizing in the Netherlands, some of the clergy there had also decided they needed a not totally dissimilar three-tier system of catechizing: beginners were to learn the Lord's Prayer, Creed, Commandments, the doctrine of the sacraments, and church discipline; the middle sort were to learn an abridged version of the Heidelberg Catechism; and youth were to learn the full-length version.[155]

The advisability of having a succession of forms available was appreciated in England at a relatively early date, but it did not become a reality until the late sixteenth and early seventeenth centuries.[156] In *The entrie to Christianitie* which he published in 1589, Thomas Watts provided a list of useful works in English that was 'set down by order of their easiness, beginning with the briefest and plainest, and so proceeding to the larger and most profound'. The list began with 'The little catechism with additions', presumably the Prayer Book catechism with Nowell's additions of *c*.1571.[157] Then came 'Master Some's catechism', presumably Robert Some's *Godly and short treatise* of 1583; and 'The summe of Christian religion', which was probably an early anonymous edition of Paget's *Short questions and answeares* which had the subtitle and running head 'The sum of Christian religion'.[158] Next came 'Master Dering's catechism', that is the Dering–More form, and 'Master Nowell's little catechism' which is confusing, since this was the same as the first title on his list.[159] Next came 'Master Gifford's catechism', first published in 1583; 'Master Wood's form of cate-

---

[154] [R. Mather], *A catechisme or, the grounds and principles of Christian religion* (1650), sigs. A2ᵛ–3ʳ; and see Strauss, *Luther's House of Learning*, 160–1; A. Nowell, *A catechisme, or institution* (1572), sig. A1ᵛ.

[155] Hales, *Golden Remains*, 386.   [156] See above, pp. 142–3, 188–90.

[157] T. Watts, *The entrie to Christianitie* (1589), sig. B4ᵛ; and see above, pp. 175, 190; but for the confusion caused by Watts's (other) references to the tribe of Nowell, see following notes.

[158] See Appendix 1; for other possible candidates for the 'Summe', see s.v. *Summe* and s.v. Sprint.

[159] See above, pp. 66, 190; from the position of the second item on the list, Watts may have meant to refer to Nowell's 'middle' form.

chizing', which we have already encountered in this chapter; and Nowell's 'middle catechism'.[160] The next items were Ursinus's catechism, which was probably the Heidelberg Catechism of which Ursinus was co-author, and 'Mr Beacon's catechism', probably Thomas Becon's *The demaundes of holy scripture*.[161] Thereafter, the list is largely of more general works of the type normally recommended for undergraduates and less educated clergy.[162] Watts's list is of value to us for showing how many different forms a minister in Somerset had seen and read, and how a contemporary assessed their difficulty as well as length; but his comments also indicate that he fully expected other catechists to want a list of works graded from 'easy' to 'profound' for catechumens at different stages of development.[163]

Richard Bernard's *Double catechisme* of 1607 was one of his earlier ventures into catechizing, and consisted of a shorter form 'for the weaker sort' and a larger following the order of the Prayer Book catechism but expounding the material at much greater length.[164] In his *Spirituall food, and physicke*, first published in the early 1620s, John Mico provided a trio of catechisms for catechumens at successive stages of development. In all three, he wrote in the preface, he had aimed at 'order, brevity, and plainness', which thirty years' of experience in the ministry had taught him was the best way to ensure they were remembered. The three were closely related, in that as Mico pointed out the second form incorporated the first, and the third the second. The first, 'A catechism for little children' aged from 4- to 7-years-old, was only six pages long with answers of no more than a line on average. The second, 'Milk for the younger', was for those aged from 6 or 7 to 10 to 12, and was fifteen pages long, but by dividing Creed, Decalogue, and Lord's Prayer into their constituent parts, Mico managed to keep the answers short. Finally there was 'Meat for the stronger. Or, a catechism for the elder sort', which was over forty pages long. Here Mico was concentrating on the meaning of what had been learned previously, and so the material was technically more advanced, but Mico still managed to keep the answers down to two or three lines long by breaking up potentially long answers into shorter sections by the regular insertion of the question 'What else?'.[165]

In the mid-1640s three comparable works appeared in print. In 1644 James Ussher

[160] See Appendix 1; again from the position, and the absence of a reference to Nowell's 'larger' form, by 'middle' Watts may have meant 'larger': it is all rather odd.

[161] See Appendix 1.

[162] e.g. Bullinger's *Decades*, Musculus's *Commonplaces*, Calvin's *Institutes*, Peter Martyr's *Commonplaces*, and Jewel's *Reply* and *Defence* of his *Apology*; for recommended undergraduate reading, see above, pp. 197, 200–1.

[163] Another early exponent of carefully graded learning with no less than five 'orders' of instruction—J. Nichols, *Order of household instruction* (1595), *passim*—is a marginal case, since all but one of his 'catechisms' were really mini-sermons rather than question-and-answer forms.

[164] R. Bernard, *A double catechisme* (1607), title-page and *passim*; there is a discrepancy here in that the subtitle—by the publisher?—lists the larger form first, while in the text the shorter is placed first.

[165] He also found space for a series of scripture texts on different subjects, and an anti-Catholic polemic—'A pill to purge out popery': J. Mico, *Spirituall food, and physicke* (1631), sigs. A2ᵛ–3ʳ and *passim*.

published two catechisms which he had prepared many years before when he had been appointed catechist at Trinity College, Dublin: a first form containing the 'more necessary and plainer truths', the second a 'methodical and more full declaration of the same chief points thereof' for those who had 'made a further progress in the knowledge of those heavenly truths'.[166] A year later, another intellectual giant, John Owen, published a pair of catechisms, of which the first was very short for the young to learn, and the second was much longer, containing a chapter for each of the answers indicated in the first. This second form, said Owen, was to remind parents of what they had heard in his sermons, and to enable them to explain to their families the fuller meaning of each of the answers they were learning.[167] Then in 1646 Robert Abbot published *Milk for babes* which began with a very short 'Catechism for children', moved on to a 'Briefer catechism' consisting of a series of very short 'sums' of religion and marked 'to be opened at first' (which suggests it should have been placed first rather than second), and then broadened out again into the 'Mother's catechism' which contained the same questions as the first form, but provided much more in the way of exposition of the answers.[168]

Richard Baxter produced a number of catechisms at different times, often reworking them between one publication and another, but in two of his works, *The poor man's family book* which was popular from the 1670s to the 1690s, and *The catechizing of families* (1683), he spoke of the need for catechisms to be sorted into three degrees, to suit children, youths, and Christians of a more mature age. In the first work were two catechisms: 'the shortest catechism' which contained only three questions but moderately long answers, and 'a short catechism for those that have learned the first', which contained ten questions, some rather long answers and some even longer expositions. The large form in the second publication was an exposition of the first two for those who had learned them; it was 'not to be learnt without book', but consulted for a fuller understanding of the shorter ones.[169] The Baptist Benjamin Keach probably published his *Instructions for children* as early as 1664, but owing to his difficulties with the authorities this work did not begin to sell well until the 1670s; by 1723 it had reached its fifteenth edition. The work contained successively longer and harder forms for little children (aged 3 to 4), children (aged about 10) and youth (of 'a mature age'), as well as religious verse, and a short verse dialogue between the devil, an ungodly youth, and Christ.[170] In 1698 the presbyterian Thomas Doolittle drew on decades of experience of catechizing to produce a set of three catechisms for older catechumens, at least two of which had appeared before in separate and rather

---

[166] J. Ussher, *The principles of Christian religion; with a brief method* (1678), sig. A2^r.

[167] J. Owen, *The principles of the doctrine of Christ* (1645), sigs. A2^v–3^r.

[168] R. Abbot, *Milk for babes; or, a mother's catechism* (1646), *passim*.

[169] R. Baxter, *The poor man's family book* (1674), 60–2, 65–92; id., *The poor man's family book*, sigs. A2^v–3^r and *passim*.

[170] B. Keach, *Instructions for children: or the child's and youth's delight* [1710?]; for the chequered history of this and a similarly entitled work, see Appendix 1.

different guises. The three were called a 'prefatory catechism' (on the need to be cat-echized) which from internal evidence seems to have been aimed at teenagers and servants, the 'prefatory catechism enlarged' (containing more of the same), and finally 'A plain method of catechizing with observations on the first principles of Christian doctrine', which consisted of the Westminster Shorter with extra ques-tions and answers, many in the Palmer method, together with observations.[171]

Catechists using the Prayer Book form as the basis of their teaching had a wide variety of forms at different levels of difficulty from which to choose, but those who wanted to be supplied with a series of forms within one set of covers found what they needed in Thomas Bray's *Whole course of catechetical instruction*. Published in 1704, this was a compilation of five works that Bray had published over a period of years. Like Mico and Keach before him and Watts later, Bray divided catechumens into three classes: the first up to 9 years, who were to learn by heart the words of the church catechism and a morning and evening prayer framed out of that catechism; the sec-ond aged from 9 to 13, who were at first to read over but eventually to memorize the answers of a form he had prepared for these second-level students; and thirdly the 14-to 20-year-olds who were the hardest group to persuade to attend and learn, but for whom suitable material was also prepared.[172] Three points may be made about Bray's scheme. First, that he had thought parts of it through very carefully. In the case of the second-level catechism, for example, he specified that 9- to 10-year-olds should spend their first year at this level simply reading it; that 10- to 11-year-olds should be able to recite each answer (though the catechist was not to expect great precision); that 11- to 12-year-olds should be able to repeat them perfectly; and that with 12- to 13-year-olds the catechist should break the questions and answers up to make them use their judgements in the replies. Secondly, during his career Bray tried various means of getting the church catechism across—long lectures, shortened lectures, paraphrases in the form of prayers, extra questions and answers to handle more advanced doctrines—as well as issuing exhortations to be catechized.[173] Thirdly, Bray clearly felt that the church should be providing a continuum of catechizing from early childhood through to early adulthood, a feeling echoed by other churchmen, such as William Beveridge who asked why, if a craft apprenticeship lasted seven years, children should be expected to learn the mysteries of religion in less.[174] Others spoke of the need for catechumens to be provided with suitable reading-matter after they had mastered the Prayer Book catechism, or the need for a minimum of two to three years' preparation for confirmation.[175] Yet others offered question-and-answer

---

[171] T. Doolittle, *A plain method of catechizing* (1698), *passim*.

[172] T. Bray, *The whole course of catechetical instruction through three classes of catechumens* (1704), but see also id., *A short discourse upon the doctrine* (1697), sigs. A1ᵛ–2ʳ, and id., *A preliminary essay* (1704), sig. Aa3ʳ.

[173] For the full range of Bray's publications, see Appendix 1.

[174] Beveridge, *Church-catechism explained*, p. xviii.

[175] Creffeild, *Great duty of catechising*, 80–1, and id., *A catechistical explanation of the dayly and Sunday offices* (1713), prefaces and text; Cradock, *Discourse*, 12.

works or prose expositions to be mastered—in practice, this sometimes meant to be read frequently rather than memorized—by those who had been confirmed but not yet taken communion, or for adults of all ages who felt the need to increase their understanding of the official church's teaching.[176] In this way catechetical material was made available for all age-groups.

In the case of another episcopalian minister, Joseph Harrison, we can see how he catechized the 'town-bred children' of his parish in Cirencester over a number of years by comparing the two versions of the catechism which he published. In *An exposition of the church-catechism, after a new method* (1708), he indicated that cate-chizing was already well established—apparently outside service time. After casting round for some time for an exposition of the church catechism which suited his own approach to catechizing, he had found a method that was useful enough to make him decide to convert the notes he had been used to hand out on a Monday—presumably to be learnt during the week—into a printed form. This was divided into two parts, the first consisted of extra questions and answers on the church catechism, and was divided into eighteen so that it could be gone through in the summer half of the year; while the second consisted of scripture proofs divided into fifty-four sections to be gone through over the next three summers. (During the winters, parents were urged to read a chapter of Harrison's work over every Sunday night in the family.) The the-ory was that children would first learn the Prayer Book catechism, then master the first part of Harrison's form (as in Bray's case they were to read it over first, then memorize it and be publicly tested on it), and then at about the age of 11 or 12 they would move on to part two, which would take them three years to master. By the age of 14 or 15, therefore, they would be fit both for confirmation and admission to the Lord's Supper.[177]

By the time of the second edition of his work, now entitled *A scriptural exposition of the church-catechism* and published in 1718, Harrison had decided to amalgamate the two parts of the original into a single scheme of fifty-two chapters, each chapter consisting of a segment of the church catechism paired with Harrison's explanatory questions and answers and scripture proofs in full. Harrison still catechized in the summer months only, and described his method of taking a catechism class as fol-lows. After opening with prayers, he tested first the younger children in their know-ledge of the church catechism, then moved on to examine the older or abler children who were expected to learn chapters 1–17 of his form in the first year, 18–34 in the second, and 35–52 in the third. After a short break for an anthem or psalm chosen by the children, Harrison addressed all those present including any adults for about half

---

[176]   e.g. J. Lambe, *A dialogue between a minister and his parishioner* (1690); [W. Fleetwood], *The reason-able communicant* (1704); anon., *An instruction for those that never yet receiv'd the holy sacrament* (1705); R. Roberts, *A sacrament catechism* (Chester? 1720); T. Greene, *The sacrament of the lord's supper explained* (1744).

[177]   J. Harrison, *An exposition of the church-catechism after a new method* (1708), 1–9 and *passim*.

an hour, expanding and reinforcing the points covered in the chapter of the exposition handled that week. Finally, the catechumens, led by the Charity School children, were called to repeat once again the answers to the questions in the chapter of the day and to give the scripture proofs listed there, before the class ended with more prayers.[178]

Harrison's concerns mirrored those of a number of other authors surveyed in this chapter, but his long tenure of the same living and the existence of a local Charity School which helped to create a pool of literate catechumens seem to have helped him to put his ideas into practice.[179] In his parish, not only were older children encouraged to develop some understanding of the meaning and scriptural basis of the catechism they had learnt as young children, but also they and any adults then present were treated to a catechetical exposition on a theme which the older catechumens had just been tackling. The ability to handle catechumens at different stages of development, the painstakingly planned progress over a number of years, and the carefully spaced reinforcement by oral repetition, are all remarkable testimony to what could be achieved by imagination and hard work. Harrison certainly acquired one great supporter, Mrs Rebecca Powell, the elderly widow of a local gentleman, who in her will left £10 a year to Harrison and his successors as ministers of Cirencester to catechize and expound the church catechism 'in the method practised by the said Joseph Harrison, every Sunday, at five of the clock in the evening, between the feasts of St Luke and St Matthias, for the better propagation of Christian knowledge and the breeding up of the children of the town in the principles and doctrine of the present established Church of England', of which Mrs Powell hoped to die a sincere though unworthy member.[180]

As a last example, we may cite the work of Isaac Watts, who in his 'Discourse' on catechizing argued forcefully for different catechisms for 'different ages and capacities'. Once again we are back to a three-stage plan of development, though a more complex one than any suggested before, in that in addition to the three principal catechisms there were two others to be learnt in tandem with these, and a sixth to be read over regularly rather than memorized. Children as young as 3 or 4 were to begin with the 'young child's catechism', a four-page form containing twenty-four questions and answers, and to learn an answer a week over six months, orally if necessary, but by reading it if they could. Between the age of 5 and 6 or 7, they should read over but not yet try to learn the second form, the 'child's catechism', which had seventy-eight questions and answers which were 'generally shorter and the words much easier to be understood and remembered' than those in the Westminster Shorter Catechism.

---

[178] J. Harrison, *A scriptural exposition of the church-catechism* (1735), 230–2.

[179] To gauge the full flavour of his methods, we still need to know whether his catechizing class took place before or after evening prayer, and how many adults attended; and why Charity School children were catechized after the second lesson at evening prayer but not the other children: ibid. 230.

[180] Ibid. 228–9.

Memorizing of these answers should take place between the ages of 7 and 10, though catechumens should continue to repeat the first catechism once a month until they had learnt the second, and could say them both perfectly by heart. Between about the ages of 10 and 12, abler students should memorize the scripture texts in the second form and start to read through but not learn the Westminster Shorter with Watts's annotations; memorizing this should take place from about the age of 12 to 14. The other two forms to be learnt were designed to ensure that knowledge of the Bible was acquired at the same time as that of the principles of religion, and comprised a 'catechism of scripture-names' for little children to learn alongside the first catechism listed above, and a 'historical catechism' of useful stories, significant incidents, and insights into doctrine in the Bible, to be learnt by children and youth alongside the second and third forms.[181]

What is also different about Watts's scheme are the psychological insights that underpinned it and the consequences of this for its doctrinal content. Catechizing, wrote Watts, was an ideal medium of instruction for the young for various reasons: it broke material into short segments, the questioning stimulated curiosity and a reply, and this to-and-fro was 'familiar', like a conversation. It also enabled children to be taught gradually, as in other subjects such as learning to read where the child moved from learning the letters to syllables to words and so to sentences. Children, he firmly believed, had to be taught by a mixture of reason, as far as they were capable of appreciating rational thought, and of authority. Children below the age of 8 should not be exposed to anything which was not necessary and practical, could not be plainly expressed and understood, and conveyed in such a way as to make each child feel he or she was personally involved; in other words, the material should be concrete and affective. Thus young children should be told about God—that he had made them to serve him and be happy, but that they had not done their duty to him—but not about the covenant of grace, election, regeneration, or justification by faith. They should be told about Christ being God's son and coming to earth to save them, but the details of his life and work should be reserved for the second level of catechizing. They should be encouraged to know that the Bible was God's word, and introduced to some of the leading characters therein such as Adam, but not expected to learn large chunks of it, since it was full of metaphors and 'Eastern idioms of speech'. Watts's own first form had no scripture references because he was convinced young children did not have enough powers of abstract thought to be able to compare an answer in the catechism and a verse of the Bible and see the relation of the one to the other. From the age of about 8, children could take in more of the truths of Christianity, and so be exposed to much more detail in the way of doctrine and duty; and by the age of 10 they should be able to judge the conformity between a statement in a catechism and a scripture text. It was possible and even advisable that pupils aged 10 and above

---

[181] I. Watts, *Catechisms: or, instructions in the principles of Christian religion* (1730), 38, 67–71, 74, 77–8, 80, 84–7, 117–19, 192–3, 203–4.

should be exposed to more 'speculative' concepts such as justification and adoption, though at this as at all stages all the harder words and phrases should be explained according to the capacity of the age-group. From the age of 12 to 14 catechumens could be exposed to a variety of methods to show the same truths that they had already learned in a different light. He remained convinced that the Westminster Shorter, while 'comprehensive' and 'valuable' in itself, was too deep and theoretical for young children; only when they had been well grounded by learning shorter and easier forms of instruction should they be exposed to that form. Even then help was needed, hence his annotations on the Shorter Catechism. As justification for these, he told two stories he had heard, one of a child who when asked the opening question, 'What is the chief end of man?', had replied 'His head', and another who when asked the same question had answered 'Death'. He praised those expositors who had broken the long answers of the Shorter Catechism into pieces as 'of the greatest use to young persons', but suspected that the 'Yes'/'No' method might encourage children to guess rather than lead to an increase in understanding.[182]

Watts's scheme was demanding and idealistic. It demanded much of catechists to be able to choose the most suitable words, apposite examples, and appropriate explanations for each of the age-groups they were teaching. It was idealistic in that it assumed literacy from the age of about 4 or 5, and strong motivation and plenty of time for study in subsequent years—conditions which might have prevailed in some dissenting families, but not in all of them and not in many episcopalian communities. Only occasionally did he make concessions for those with weaker memories or who had 'less leisure and advantage for learning'.[183] But Watts was also unusually clear-sighted about the problems of teaching children, and fertile in offering suggestions how they could be overcome; and as indicated at the start of this chapter, his ideas anticipated a number of findings of a later age when science rather than philosophy or theology was applied to education. Moreover, at least a dozen editions of his six catechisms together were published within forty years of their first appearance, and there were many more editions of different combinations of those forms.[184]

A good deal of space has been devoted to the work of men like Palmer, Comber, Bray, Harrison, and Watts not because they necessarily represent the most significant developments in catechetical technique. Only when historians of education and educational psychologists have looked at a sample of the works listed in Appendix 1 will we be able to pass that kind of judgement. However, these men were certainly not untypical of the changes that occurred in the techniques of catechizing, especially in the second of the two centuries under scrutiny in this monograph: a growing awareness of the different stages of development through which young catechumens

---

[182] Ibid. 5, 7, 15–16, 19–23, 38, 40–6, 50–67, 72–3, 118.   [183] Ibid. 85, 204.
[184] See Appendix 1 for the repeat editions of different combinations of his catechisms, and for another question-and-answer form: *A short view of the whole scripture history* (1732).

passed and of the need to select material as well as method of presentation to suit the needs of different age- and ability-groups, and a concern with understanding which ranked alongside the earlier concern with memory. What is also instructive from our point of view is that most of these men seem to have come to the conclusions they did as a result of their own practical experience of catechizing, and that a number of their works sold sufficiently well to give a strong impression that copies were in demand and disseminated fairly widely.

The impact of the different solutions to the problems associated with memorizing and comprehension that we have examined in this chapter must often have depended on factors beyond the control of the zealous minority who pioneered new methods: the willingness of other catechists to teach, and of catechumens to learn, one of the alternative forms or new methods on offer; the degree of catechumens' contact with the different support systems available, not least literacy; the readiness of the authorities to support new enterprises; and the willingness of the well-to-do to pay for the distribution of copies of simpler forms among the poor. For every gleam of light such as the publications of John Mico, Thomas Lye, Thomas Bray, or Isaac Watts, we can point to a complaint such as Peter Hewit's in 1704, that some parishes seldom had catechizing, and even where it was more frequent 'there are rarely any other questions' put to the children than those in the church catechism.[185] For every inventor of an even briefer catechism or new way of encouraging understanding, we have authors like Towerson, Ollyffe, and Shaw who in the late seventeenth and early eighteenth centuries were still producing multi-volume commentaries on an original catechism only ten pages long.[186] It may also be suggested that in purely technical terms the Westminster Shorter Catechism was a step backwards: young presbyterians would have been better served by a form designed specially for beginners rather than an artificially shrunk hand-me-down from their older siblings. In short, the improvements in technique that we have examined in this chapter may have anticipated the greater stress on rationality in the eighteenth century and the developments in educational psychology in the twentieth, but were not sufficiently prevalent to have made a huge impact on catechizing in the early modern period itself.

Some of the material examined in this and previous chapters may, however, support the conclusion that what some of the first generation or two of Protestant enthusiasts had condemned as outright ignorance was by modern standards either only relative ignorance or a case of partial understanding, for which the clergy were themselves in part responsible. What Perkins, Mico, Crompton, and other members of the educated élite on whom we have to rely for much of our information,

---

[185] P. Hewit, *A brief and plain explication of the catechism* (1704), sig. A3ʳ.
[186] See above, pp. 150–2, and Appendix 1 for their works.

were faced with was not total ignorance: by their own account their parishioners did know the Creed and Ten Commandments, even if they parroted them or thought they were a prayer.[187] (How many readers of this book can declaim both Creed and Decalogue in full?) By some of those same accounts, early modern parishioners also understood the need for good works, even if they saw them as a means to salvation, rather than, as they should have done, as the fruits of faith.[188] From other comments, we can see that many had some sense of the sacredness of the sacraments, even if from the better informed point of view popular opinion had an exaggerated estimate of the soteriological value of baptism, or a distorted view of the conditions attached to taking communion that made some people fearful of taking the risk.[189] In fact, if there was a degree of misconception, at least part of that may have been due to the urgency with which the clergy urged their charges to learn the Creed and Ten Commandments and partake of the sacraments, and the clergy's failure until fairly late in the early modern period to appreciate how to convey the essential meaning of those formulae and rites. When in 1579 a clergyman like John Gibson told catechumens that the religion of a true Christian consisted of the understanding and profitable use of the Ten Commandments, Apostles' Creed, sacraments, and Lord's Prayer, he was trying to distil much teaching down to its simplest form, and to encourage catechumens to learn them.[190] But given the teaching techniques of the day it would not be surprising if those catechumens grasped only part of what he was trying to convey, and combined some older ideas about merit along with his new ones about faith.

Indeed, if we widen the approach and consider not just the material discussed in this chapter but that raised in the entire first part of this study—the rapid development of catechizing, the huge number of copies of different forms produced, the levels of catechizing apparently achieved by the early eighteenth century, and the fact that catechetical techniques had continued to develop rather than stagnate—all this may suggest that we might consider looking for the origins of the Charity School movement, the Evangelical Revival, or the Sunday School movement not in a church—or chapel—which was sliding downhill or had hit rock bottom, but in one where levels of knowledge and understanding had actually improved since the days of Elizabeth. There are parallel cases of increased efforts in the late seventeenth and early eighteenth centuries in Wales, Ireland, Sweden, and Germany, leading to better results in some

---

[187] See above, p. 131 nn. 171–2 and p. 245 n. 60; and cf. Webbe, *Briefe exposition*, sig. A3ᵛ; Ratcliffe, *Short summe*, sig. A4ʳ; and Attersoll, *Principles of Christian religion*, sig. A2ᵛ.

[188] e.g. Perkins, *Foundation*, sig. A2ᵛ ('that ye can keep the Commandments as well as God will give you leave').

[189] e.g. Crompton, *Explication*, sig. ¶7ʳ (old people who hoped to be saved 'only in the grace of regeneration by baptism'); and on fear of taking communion, A. Warne, *Church and Society in Eighteenth-Century Devon* (New York, 1969), 46; and F. C. Mather, 'Georgian Churchmanship Reconsidered', *JEH* 36 (1985), 272–3.

[190] Gibson, *Easie entrance*, sig. A2ʳ.

cases.[191] The Sunday School movement in particular was one logical outcome of the awareness of the continued problems posed by the clergy having to conduct both parish worship and elementary religious instruction at the same time on Sundays, and facing resistance from ignorant adolescents and adults unwilling to be catechized; it was also a logical outcome of the clergy's growing preference for dealing with literate catechumens.[192]

At the least what the last few chapters should have shown is two things. First, many clergy and schoolteachers and some parents put a high priority on trying to provide the young and ignorant with some form of basic religious instruction, even if that ideal was achieved only in part. 'The vast variety which the divines of our church have given us of short expositions on the church catechism by way of question and answer ... does sufficiently speak the universal sense of the necessity of instilling into the minds of our youth the principles of our most holy religion.' When he wrote this in the 1690s, Thomas Bray was thinking of the efforts of churchmen, but the same attitude could be found among the 'godly' like Daniel Rogers who said he had spent one-third of his 'poor labour' on catechizing, and Thomas Doolittle, of whom it was said that 'catechizing was his special excellency and delight'.[193] Secondly, the last three chapters in particular should also have shown that what catechists were trying to communicate was often put across in different ways at different levels according to the perceived capacity of catechumens. In the second part of this study, on the doctrinal content of early modern catechisms, we will encounter both of these points again, but especially the second.

[191]   G. H. Jenkins, *Literature, Religion and Society in Wales 1660–1730* (Cardiff, 1978); I. Green, ' "The Necessary Knowledge of the Principles of Religion": Catechisms and Catechizing in Ireland *c*.1560–1800', in A. Ford, J. McGuire, and K. Milne (eds.), *As by Law Established: The Church of Ireland since the Reformation* (Dublin, 1995), 69–88 (and other essays in this volume); E. Johansson, 'The History of Literacy in Sweden', in *Literacy and Social Development in the West: A Reader*, ed. H. J. Graff (Cambridge, 1981), 156–82; R. Gawthrop and G. Strauss, 'Protestantism and Literacy in Early Modern Germany', *Past and Present*, 104 (1984), 43–55.

[192]   See above, pp. 112–13, 118, 140, 158–9, 183–4, 241–2; and T. W. Laqueur, *Religion and Respectability: Sunday Schools and Working Class Culture 1780–1850* (New Haven/London, 1976), chs. 1–3.

[193]   T[homas] B[ray], *A preliminary essay* (1704), sig. Aa2^r; D[aniel] R[ogers], *A practicall catechisme* (1640), sig. A7^r; T. Doolittle, *A complete body of practical divinity* (1723), page opposite title-page.

PART II

The Message

6

Catechetical Structures

WHEN designing a form, a catechist was soon faced by two important decisions: what material should go in, and in what sequence should it be presented? A quick glance at the contents of the beginners' catechisms written by Luther, Calvin, the leaders of the Edwardian church, the Heidelberg theologians, and the Westminster divines shows a good deal of overlap but also a number of differences;[1] and in the next few chapters we shall be looking at the decisions on content taken by the authors of the best-selling forms in early modern England. But before we do that, it might be helpful to look at the kinds of structures into which that material was placed. In many cases there was a close correlation between the framework within which an author handled his material and the theological standpoint he wished to convey. Thus in the Brandenburg–Nuremberg order of baptism of 1533, godparents were told to teach a child 'first the Ten Commandments, in order that thereby it may learn to know God's will, and its sins; then the Creed, whereby we receive grace ... lastly, also the Lord's Prayer, in order that it may call upon God, and pray to him for aid'.[2] On the other hand, a particular structure was not indissolubly wedded to a specific theology. The Prayer Book catechism of 1549 had the same sequence as Calvin's catechism of 1541, but no one has seriously suggested that its content is distinctively Calvinist; Nowell's catechism, on the other hand, followed that of Luther's short catechism, but the sequence of ideas and theological emphasis clearly owed more to Calvin than anyone else; and English authors who adopted a Heidelberg-type sequence of 'guilt, grace, and gratitude' were still able within that framework to promote certain insular preoccupations.[3] As we shall also see shortly, the agile minds of contemporary catechists were capable of inserting almost any doctrine into almost any point of the four staple items of contemporary catechizing, so that very similar structures could be used to communicate the different emphases that co-existed within early modern Protestantism.

---

[1] The easiest place in which to compare Luther's short catechism, the English Prayer Book catechism, the Heidelberg Catechism, and the Westminster Shorter Catechism is Schaff, *Creeds*; modern editions of Calvin's catechism are available in Torrance, *School of Faith*, and in a facsimile edition of the 1556 Geneva edition in English (Amsterdam/New York, 1968).

[2] Cited in Aston, *England's Iconoclasts*, 346–7.

[3] See following paragraphs, and L. D. Durbin, 'Education by Catechism: The Development of the Sixteenth-Century English Catechism', Ph.D. thesis (Northwestern, 1987), 132–3.

In considering structure, there are three chief considerations: what were the main units used in the construction, in what relationship to each other did the author place them, and how much space was allocated to each? Catholic catechisms continued to have a much larger number of units than Protestant ones. In addition to the Creed, Pater Noster, Decalogue, and an account of the seven sacraments, a work like Bellarmine's shorter catechism (which was widely used among English-speaking Catholics in the seventeenth century) included the Ave Maria, the commandments of the church, theological and cardinal virtues, gifts of the Holy Ghost, works of mercy both corporal and spiritual, capital sins and sins against the Holy Ghost, and the four last things. Reflecting their origin as primers and as means to prepare for confession, Catholic catechisms were also inclined to include a higher proportion of prayers than Protestant ones, and an account of how to prepare for confession and penance; some also had a section for boys on how to serve a priest at mass.[4] In the case of Protestant forms, however, it should be clear from preceding chapters that the prefabricated units likely to have been in most common use were the Apostles' Creed, the Ten Commandments, the Lord's Prayer, and the doctrine of the sacraments. These four staples had comprised almost the entire content of Luther's *Short Catechism* (there were a few prayers and a list of duties placed at the end), a large proportion of Calvin's 1541 catechism, most of the second and third parts of the Heidelberg Catechism of 1563, and a similar proportion of the many translations, expositions, or variants of these catechisms to be found in a number of Protestant churches of the sixteenth century. The Creed, Decalogue, and Lord's Prayer comprised the lion's share of the English Prayer Book catechism of 1549, to which a section on the sacraments was added unofficially in the early 1570s and officially in 1604; and the same four elements constituted over four-fifths of the larger official catechism, that of Alexander Nowell. The great majority of sixteenth-century English catechisms and a significant proportion of seventeenth-century ones used the same building-blocks, on the principle that they were, as Richard Bernard put it in 1613, 'the ABC of our religion'.[5] It is true that from the 1580s a number of authors decided to use either different combinations of blocks or totally new units of construction, and that by the 1640s a significant minority of authors were undertaking their own designs and even devising their own materials, for reasons that will emerge. But

---

[4] See Appendix 1 for editions of Bellarmine's *Short catechisme / Short Christian doctrine*; and for contents, see [Petrus Canisius], *A summe of Christian doctrine* [*c*.1592–6 and 1622]; [L. Vaux], *A catechisme or Christian doctrine* (1568); [Diego de Ledesma], *The Christian doctrine* (1597); James Miles, *Brevis catechismus* (1635); anon., *An abstract of the scripture-catechism* (1675); [Jean Roucourt], *A catechism of penance* (1685); anon., *A summary of Christian duties* (1687); anon., *An abstract of the Douay catechism* (Douai 1697); C[hristoper] A[nderdon], *A catechism for ... the Prince of Wales* (1692); anon., *The catechism or, Christian doctrine* [*c*.1700]; anon., *Select manuel of godly prayers* (1716) (I am very grateful to Bernard Keane for sending me details of this work); [A. Hacket], *A catechism or abridgement of Christian doctrine* (1725).

[5] R. Bernard, *Two twinnes* (1613), 12; and see R. Sherlock, *The principles of holy Christian religion* (1663), sigs. A5r–6r.

thereafter most catechisms would again consist of an explanation of three or four of the usual staples.

The sequence in which these were deployed did, however, vary considerably, not only between Protestant authors but also between Protestant and Catholic. Exact comparison with the catechetical instruction of the Middle Ages and the Counter-Reformation is complicated by the fact that Catholic teaching usually incorporated additional units such as those described in the last paragraph. As a point of departure, we may take those late medieval and early modern manuals of instruction which tackled all four of what would become the Protestant staples, and see in what order these staples were put. One suggested sequence for late medieval forms is as follows: faith (as expressed in the Apostles' Creed) made possible the appropriation of grace (through prayer, including the Lord's Prayer, and the sacraments), and grace was a means of helping the individual to live according to the Law (the Decalogue).[6] This may have been the norm, but it was a modified version of this, with the sacraments after the Commandments, that was adopted by the German Jesuit, Peter Canisius, in his much admired form of 1557, and popularized by Bellarmine in both his larger form for catechists and his smaller for catechumens. The 'catechism' ordered by the Council of Trent (in fact a manual for helping parish clergy to prepare catechetical sermons) also modified the sequence by transferring prayer from before the sacraments to after the Decalogue.[7]

There is, however, a potential contrast between catechisms which began with a description of faith, as did Canisius's, and those which began with a statement of why there was a need for faith. For Luther, for example, the Commandments had to be treated first as the best means of making fallen man aware of his sinfulness. Conscious of having broken the Law and of the penalty of sin, he was driven to Christ his saviour (who formed the subject of the central two-thirds of the Apostles' Creed), and to the means by which sinful man could appropriate the remedies offered (through petition, including the Lord's Prayer, and participation in the sacraments).[8] In his first attempt at a catechism, Calvin followed Luther's sequence, but in his second and better known one he changed his mind. For Calvin it was the need to live in the knowledge of God and to honour him that took precedence, so that he began with an exposition of the opening articles of the Creed before proceeding to the mission of Christ and the creation of a church of believers (the rest of the Creed), the law laid down for fallen man (the Commandments), and the means provided for calling upon God and acknowledging him as the fountain of all goodness (through prayer, study

---

[6] Janz, *Reformation Catechisms*, 18–19; not all would agree that there was a late medieval norm in primers, handbooks, and other vernacular literature: M. T. Brady, 'The Pore Caitif: An Introductory Study', *Traditio*, 10 (1954), 535–6; Durbin, 'Education by Catechism', 60–5; E. Germain, *Langages de la foi à travers l'histoire* (Paris, 1972), ch. 1.

[7] See Appendix 1, s.v. Canisius, Bellarmino, and anon., *The catechism for the curats*.

[8] Janz, *Reformation Catechisms*, 18, 181–215.

of the word of God, and the sacraments).[9] It might appear that Calvin had returned to Catholic practice by putting the Creed first, but he was also close to Luther: the need for faith had to be discussed before the substance of it, and before the means of obtaining and strengthening it. It is also indicative of a different view on the value of the sacraments that both Luther and Calvin placed them later in their sequences than did the catechisms of Canisius and Trent. The theologians of Heidelberg adopted a much looser structure, dividing their catechism into three sections: the greatness of man's sin and misery, attested by scripture but not involving an extended discussion of any of the four staple items; how man was redeemed, through faith in Christ—the Creed—which was confirmed by taking part in the visible seals of the Gospel promise—the sacraments; and how man was to be thankful partly by doing good works as the fruit of faith—the good works being the direct opposite of the sins forbidden in the Decalogue—and partly by thanking the Lord through prayer, including the Lord's Prayer.[10] Although close to Luther and Calvin on the essentials of the Protestant doctrine of salvation, the authors of the Heidelberg Catechism are noteworthy for their decision to place the four staples in a framework of other material—on the Fall, true faith, providence, and regeneration—which in effect made those staples less prominent than before.

At first the majority of the catechisms published in England adopted a sequence which was identical to one of the three just described. The catechism of Edmund Allen of 1548, the catechetical sermons approved by Cranmer in the same year, and the various forms of Nowell's catechism in the 1570s followed the same track as Luther had done.[11] The sequence followed by the authors of the Prayer Book catechism was the same as that of Calvin, whether consciously or not is unclear.[12] Owing to the scores of works that would be subsequently built around the Prayer Book catechism in the seventeenth century, this sequence of Creed, Commandments, prayer, and sacraments would be extremely common. In the 1570s, however, the first of a number of translations and expositions of the Heidelberg Catechism appeared, and this work may also, it has been suggested, have influenced a number of home-produced forms, such as the main form in Stephen Egerton's *Briefe methode of catechising*.[13]

An early variant on these three pathways, which merely reversed the last two items of Luther's sequence, can be found in three works published in Edward VI's reign. Two were of Continental origin, the more popular of which was the Lutheran *Sum of divinitie* by Johann Spangenberg, and the other was a native English product—the

---

[9] See n. 1 above; P. Y. De Jong, 'Calvin's Contributions to Christian Education', *Calvin Theological Journal*, 2 (1967), 176–7.

[10] Schaff, *Creeds*, 306–55.   [11] See Appendix 1.

[12] The first published English edition of Calvin's catechism dates from 1550: ibid. For indigenous or idiosyncratic elements in the 1549 Prayer Book form, see above, pp. 20–1.

[13] See Appendix 1, s.v. Heidelberg and Egerton; Durbin, 'Education by Catechism', 132–3. I have some difficulty with Dr Durbin's argument here since in assessing alternative frameworks she excludes treatment of the sacraments.

officially approved form by John Ponet.[14] From the late 1570s, however, this structure—Decalogue, Creed, sacraments, Lord's Prayer—became increasingly common in the work of English authors, such as the best-selling Dering–More and Paget catechisms, the intermediate form prepared by Richard Jones in 1583, and the 'summary of the principles delivered in the church-catechism' prepared by the eminent Cambridge theologian, William Whitaker, in the reign of Elizabeth but not published until 1630.[15] By the early seventeenth century this framework was about as common as that adopted by Calvin's form and the 1549 catechism.

What is perfectly clear, however, is that from as early as the 1580s a growing number of authors were seeking to dispense with a framework which restricted them to a sequential treatment of the four staple elements. By the reign of James I this trend was quite marked, and in the 1640s and 1650s reached a peak, and then declined.[16] There were a number of alternative paths which could be followed. The first of these was to focus on just one of the four staples. From the 1570s to the early 1640s, over a score of authors felt there was a need for a catechism or catechetical treatise devoted largely or almost entirely to Decalogue or Creed or Lord's Prayer, or to a combination of one of these with a treatment of the sacraments.[17] However, as can be anticipated from what was said in the first two chapters of this study, the single element which acted as the greatest stimulus to authors, in about three dozen cases, was the doctrine of the sacraments, and in particular the Lord's Supper. A number of the works which focused largely on the sacraments were published before 1604—the year in which a section on the sacraments was officially added to the Prayer Book form of 1549. The catechism entitled 'Certaine questions and answers' which was printed in a number of Elizabethan editions of the Geneva Bible can be taken in part as an example of a catechism designed to supplement the beginners' form of 1549 on the subject of the sacraments.[18] Others were written after 1604, however, either as full catechisms or short forms to be used shortly before communion with older children or ignorant adults. Many of these date from the 1640s when concern at unworthy candidates receiving communion became acute.[19] Of the works which focused on

---

[14] See Appendix 1, s.v. Spangenberg, Micron, and Ponet.   [15] Full details in Appendix 1.

[16] The adoption of alternative frameworks was probably never a majority tactic: see below, p. 289.

[17] See the works by the following authors listed in Appendix 1: (Decalogue) Babington, *Commaundements*; W. Burton, *Certaine questions*; R. Allen, *Treasurie*; J. Paget; Ames; Bunny; L. Andrewes (3 versions); (Creed) Dent, *Articles*; Babington, *Catholike faith*; R. Allen, *Doctrine*; (Lord's Prayer) Babington, *Lords prayer*; H. Burton, *Lordes prayer*; Tomkys; R. Hill, *Christs prayer*; T. Hooker, *Heavens treasury*. A further six works concentrated on two of the four staples: F. Davis (Creed and Lord's Prayer); Elton, *God's holy mind* (Decalogue and Lord's Prayer); Robertson (Decalogue and sacraments); and Hinde, R. Austin, and Hammond, *Practical catechisme* (Creed and sacraments).

[18] See the works by the following authors listed in Appendix 1: Rouspeau; Chub; Hopkinson; Wilcox; Whiting; Egerton (short form before communion); and next note for works published after 1604). 'Certaine questions and answers' also contained a section on the scriptures, and on predestination.

[19] Appendix 1, s.v. Bradshaw; Draxe, 'An appendix' in *Lambes spouse*; Hill, *Communicant prepared*;

the sacraments, quite a few did mention one or more of the other staples in passing: those forms which attempted to turn the parliamentary ordinance of 1645 into questions and answers, for example, dealt with a few of the articles of the Apostles' Creed before turning to the sacraments. But in other cases virtually all the questions and answers were devoted to imparting or testing an awareness of what the sacrament meant, how the worthy communicant should prepare himself for it, and how it was to be received.[20] These forms can, therefore, be regarded as having either a specialist function—to deal with one of the four staples in greater depth than a normal four-part catechism would permit—or a different emphasis from the usual catechism—a concern to ensure that potential communicants were properly prepared for worthy reception of the communion.

Another path favoured by many authors was to concentrate on three staples, and the element that was omitted by a significant proportion of these authors was the Creed. Two of the best-selling catechisms of the seventeenth century were of this kind: John Ball's *Short catechisme* and the Westminster Shorter Catechism both lacked an explicit, phrase by phrase treatment of the Creed. One estimate suggests that about half the 'puritan' catechisms of the seventeenth century omitted the Creed.[21] It may be countered that the authors of many of these three-element catechisms did at some point in their text handle much of the same material as a conventional four-element catechism did in its section on the Creed: a definition of God and a list of his properties; the identity and offices of Christ; the role of the Holy Ghost; the outward means of receiving and strengthening faith; and life after death. But against that there is the fact that the authors of such works were deliberately departing from the known practice of the first generations of Protestant catechists. Even the authors of the Heidelberg Catechism who had been one of the first to break away from a rigid four-part structure had treated the Creed in full.[22]

One reason for this departure may have been that the Apostles' Creed was not in the Bible, any more than the Nicene or Athanasian Creeds were. Certainly there were those who were worried about non-scriptural statements being accorded the same status as scriptural ones. Another suggestion is that some zealots thought the Creed had been polluted by Catholic usage, or perverted into a meaningless incantation.[23] Against this, however, is the fact that the authors of many tripartite works did not

Tye; Dod and Cleaver, *Brief dialogue*; anon., *Motives*; Littleton; Robertson; Fist; Geree; N. Hunt; Jenison; anon., *An instruction* (1634); and in the 1640s: S. Austin; S. Baker; Bourne (3 versions); J.F. (1645); Goode; Lyford, *Helpe*; Sanderson; O. Sedgwick; anon., *A short catechisme for the instruction* (1645). See also Crashaw, *Meate for men*, and works cited above, pp. 79–80.

[20] See above, pp. 79–80, and previous notes.
[21] For editions of Ball's *Short catechisme* and the Westminster Shorter Catechism, see Appendix 1; Grant, 'Cure of Souls', 72.
[22] See above, p. 282.
[23] See above, p. 166; and Grant, 'Cure of Souls', 72–3; H. Davies, *The Worship of the English Puritans* (1948), 273–7; and above, p. 275 n. 187.

deny the authenticity or the value of the Apostles' Creed, and that some of them either assumed that the Creed was already known, or, like the Westminster divines, ensured that the Creed was printed separately at the beginning or end of their form.[24] A more common reason for omission perhaps was a desire to escape from the potential strait-jacket that a close, article by article exposition of the Creed could present, at whatever point in a sequence of four staples that it was treated. In fact, there were two advantages to the omission of the Apostles' Creed, or the relegation of it to a supporting role. Authors were able to adopt a much more flexible structure than in the traditional four-part works. By dividing up the different doctrinal statements in the Creed into separate sections, and introducing different elements of that teaching at different points in their exposition, they could design a totally new sequence of statements. Secondly, it was easier to add material on subjects which were not raised explicitly in the Apostles' Creed, for example, the decree of election and reprobation, the Fall and the nature of sin, the covenants of works and grace, the nature of faith and the Calvinist *ordo salutis*, and aspects of 'experimental predestinarianism' such as introspection and preparation for grace—topics to which we shall return in more detail in Chapters 8 and 9. The sort of sequence that could result from the omission or splitting up of the Creed was as follows. First, authors could discuss the scriptural basis of the Christian religion, then treat the material raised in the first section of the Creed (on God the Father Almighty) and perhaps the double decree; then they could turn to the Fall and the covenant of works, before raising the topics covered by the second section of the Creed (on Christ as saviour); then they could discuss faith and perhaps part of the *ordo* of effective calling, justification, and sanctification, before turning to a discussion of the duties implicit in the Decalogue (if not already discussed), and to a treatment of prayer and the sacraments, under which the nature and function of the church (article nine of the Creed) might be discussed; finally they could turn to the last things mentioned in the final phrases of the Creed: 'the resurrection of the body and the life everlasting'. This sequence corresponds approximately to that of John Ball's short catechism and to the Westminster Shorter Catechism, though the latter treated the church after the Decalogue.

It should be said at once that many catechists who did devote a section of their work specifically to the Creed did not feel inhibited about introducing some of these extra topics into their account. One catechist, the moderate episcopalian John Prideaux, stated this quite specifically when answering the objection: how can the Creed be 'a perfect symbol of our faith which leaves out the chief of all, that faith only justifieth; and hath nothing concerning predestination, or man's liberty of will'? These points *were* dealt with in the Creed, said Prideaux, in the words 'I believe' and 'almighty'. Another episcopalian replied to similar criticisms by saying that the doctrines said to

---

[24] On the Westminster Catechisms, see below, p. 301 n. 4; also the works in Appendix 1, s.v. Wallis; Angier; and anon., *Explicatory catechism*; and below n. 28.

be missing from the Creed were there; they were just stated very briefly.[25] Conversely, not all those authors who omitted the Creed took the opportunity to discuss all of the extra topics mentioned above. John Ball's treatment of predestination, the covenants, and the *ordo* was selective and relatively restrained compared to that in the Westminster Shorter Catechism which in turn said less about them than the Westminster Larger.[26] However, the almost inevitable consequence of the avoidance of an article-by-article exposition of the Creed was a change in the proportions of the edifice. The authors of four-part catechisms did not devote mathematically equal space to the four staples: in some cases the ground floor was bigger, in others the first floor, and so on. On the other hand, it is noticeable that some of those authors who adopted a three-part structure did use a lot of additional material, either as pedestal, extra courses of brickwork between floors, or pediments, which had the effect of diminishing the space devoted to the three staples and could make the finished building look very different on the outside. In Ball's catechism, less than two-fifths of the space was devoted to expounding the Lord's Prayer, sacraments, and Decalogue, and in the Westminster Shorter Catechism only about one-half; and in both cases only a portion of the rest was devoted to credal material.[27]

A much more dramatic departure from the norm was to reduce the four staple elements to a supporting role, or to leave them out altogether but, as with the Creed in the cases just discussed, to incorporate much of their content into a totally new structure. In some cases, such a policy was less drastic than it sounds. Some of the authors of these catechisms mentioned the staples in passing, or devoted a few lines to them; others were designing forms for very young children who, it was assumed, would learn the four items later; yet others were intermediate forms which were quite explicitly said to be for catechumens who had already learnt the staples through an elementary catechism.[28] But in other cases authors seem to have made a deliberate attempt to bypass or short-circuit the conventional sequence in an effort to convey what they saw as the essentials. A classic case of this, both in the sense that the original form was widely used for nearly a century and that it was imitated by other authors, was William Perkins's *The foundation of Christian religion gathered into six principles*, first published in 1590. This work, aimed at 'ignorant people that desire to be instructed', was built around six points: there was one God, in three persons, who was creator and governor of all things; through Adam's fall, all men were wholly corrupted by sin and deserved eternal damnation; Christ was made man and through his sacrifice on the cross accomplished all things needed to save mankind; the ordinary

---

[25] J. Prideaux, *Suneidesilogia or the doctrine of conscience* (1656), 59–60; Sherlock, *Principles*, 52.

[26] See below, Ch. 8, and for the original forms, Appendix 1.   [27] As last note.

[28] See the following forms in Appendix 1: anon., *Maner to examine*; S. Egerton, *A briefe methode of catechizing* (1615), the first three forms; T. Ratcliffe, *Short summe*; H. Jessey, *Catechisme for babes*; B. Keach, *Instructions for children*; M. Henry, *A plain catechism for children*; I. Watts, *Catechisms*; and for intermediate forms by conformists see many of the expositions of the Prayer Book form discussed in Chs. 3–5 above.

means of obtaining faith were the preaching of the word, sacraments, and prayer; and after death, all will rise again and the godly shall go to heaven while the reprobate shall be in hell.[29] As we shall see later, much of this was conventional: Perkins does not seem to have broken with the fourfold structure used by most previous catechists (including Calvin) simply in order to stress certain distinctive Calvinist ideas. He did, after all, write and publish an extended treatise on the Creed as well as one on the Lord's Prayer. Some Calvinists doubted the wisdom of teaching certain doctrines at full strength at the elementary level. Perkins's own treatment of double predestination in his catechism was, as we shall see, restrained, and even ambiguous: he did not talk of immutable decrees, but of the 'godly' going to heaven and 'unbelievers and reprobates' to hell.[30] What seems to have worried Perkins was that his older parishioners evidently knew the basic formulae but showed little or no comprehension of what they represented for the conscientious Christian. Among the many mistakes he listed in the preface to his catechism are the following:

That God is served by the rehearsing of the Ten Commandments, the Lord's Prayer and the Creed. ... That a man prayeth when he saith the Ten Commandments. ... That if a man remembers to say his prayers every morning ... he hath blessed himself for all the day following.[31]

He seems to have felt that rather than trying to explain to such people what the Creed, Decalogue, and Lord's Prayer really represented and how they should be used (as many other catechists did), it was better to start afresh by extracting the essentials out of these staple items, and trying to ensure that these were grasped thoroughly and then used as the basis for a properly self-critical mode of behaviour.

There was nothing magical about Perkins's total of six principles, though it is noteworthy that a handful of catechists used the opening verses of chapter six of the Epistle to the Hebrews as the basis for a sixfold presentation.[32] Nor was Perkins the first or the last to try to isolate the main 'heads', 'principles', 'grounds', or 'questions' as the basis for a new catechism. The main catechism in Stephen Egerton's very popular composite work avoided direct exposition of Creed, Decalogue, and Lord's Prayer, and was based on four points: how miserable all men are by nature; God's remedy for deliverance; how to live in order to be saved; and the helps available to that end.[33] Other examples could be given of catechetical works built around five particular doctrines, or seven principles, or eight positions, or nine points, or ten

---

[29] W. Perkins, *The foundation of Christian religion* (1612), sig. A2ʳ, and pp. 1–3.

[30] See below, pp. 364–5.

[31] Perkins, *Foundation*, sig. A2ʳ; for others' concern, see above, pp. 131, 245, 274–5.

[32] See Appendix 1, s.v. A. Gerardus, *Foundation*; T[homas] W[ilson], *Exposition of the two first verses*; J. Foorthe, *Apostles catechisme*; C. Blackwood, *Soul-searching catechism*; and T. Grantham, *St. Paul's catechism*; for other forms built around six principles, see anon., *The summe of Christian religion* (1607); E. Elton, *Forme*; anon., *Short catechisme* (1646); T. Wolfall, *Childrens bread*; and W. Burkitt, *Poor mans help*; and the two revisions of Perkins's original form by Broxolme and Bacon.

[33] Egerton, *Briefe methode*, title-page and 1–19.

questions and answers, up to Thomas Greaves's forty propositions or aphorisms of 1656.[34] There was a predictable amount of overlap between the content of most of these forms and that of Perkins, and we may guess that their authors' motivation was much the same as that of the great Elizabethan divine: presenting the familiar in a manner that was both fresh and easily remembered by those with little or no formal education.

Other alternatives to the typical four-part catechism were perhaps more matters of style or emphasis. Thomas Cartwright chose to build his form round the kingdom of God: after describing God's properties, he moved on to God's decree and the execution thereof, including Christ's government in this world in 'things' and in 'persons'—a structure which gave him the maximum opportunity to develop his particular concerns. By contrast, the non-Calvinist Henry Hammond chose the Sermon on the Mount as the basis for the central portion of his catechism, which allowed him to dwell at length on the differences between the law in the Old Testament and that in the New, and the importance of obedience to the latter.[35] Edmund Littleton and John Paget adopted totally different frameworks to catch the attention and increase the understanding of their charges: in the former case by using the Gospel story of the life of Christ, and in the latter by using the marvels in the heavens, on earth, and underneath the surface of the earth.[36] There was also, as we have already seen, a growing interest in scriptural catechisms in which the answers were taken direct from the Bible: the most popular of these, Samuel Hieron's *The doctrine of the beginning of Christ ... delivered almost in the express words of the text*, was prepared in 1604 and published over twenty times in the next five decades. Some of these scriptural forms covered similar ground to earlier catechisms, especially in the case of material such as the Ten Commandments and the Lord's Prayer, while others adopted a thematic or a historical, chronological approach to the Christian story.[37] From the mid-seventeenth century, there was also a growing number of works which may be considered as responses to specific challenges or as assertions of their own particular views: the presbyterian view of church government,[38] the Baptist emphasis on believers' baptism, and the Quakers' stress on the inner light.[39]

If we look at the various frameworks described in the last few paragraphs—a focus on one, two, or three of the four staple elements or an avoidance of extended treatment

[34] See Appendix 1, s.v. H. Hammond (5); T. Bedford (7); J. Rogers, and L. Fogg (8); J. Woodward (9); J. Jackson (10); anon., *The summe of Christian religion* (1649), (14); J. Hoffman (30); and T. Greaves (40).

[35] See Appendix 1, for further details of Cartwright's *Methodicall short catechisme* and Hammond's *Practical catechisme*.

[36] See Appendix 1, s.v. Littleton and J. Paget.

[37] On scriptural forms in general, see above, pp. 32–3, 92; see also in Appendix 1, s.v. *Itinerarium Iesu Christi*, and Richard Baxter's *The mother's catechism*, and Isaac Watts's *A short view of the whole scripture history*.

[38] J. Robinson, *A briefe catechisme* (1642); J. Cotton, *The doctrine of the church* (1643); C. Love, *The main points of church-government* (1649); and see anon., *The Presbiterian catechisme* (1647).

[39] See above, pp. 83–5.

of all or most of the staples—we can seen how far by the 1650s authors were prepared to be much more adventurous about not only the units of construction but also the design of the building. Some of these experimental forms proved popular, for example Perkins's *Six principles*, Hieron's *Doctrine*, and Ball's *Short catechisme*. But others in practice proved too hard for absolute beginners, for example the Westminster Shorter Catechism,[40] or like Cartwright's form were usually published as an annexe to a much larger work which makes it harder for us to gauge how much they were used.[41] There is not much point in trying to produce exact figures on how many authors adopted one kind of framework rather than another, partly because of the enormous variations of length and manner of treatment of individual staples or topics, which make comparisons very hard and probably of limited value, and partly because, as was pointed out at the start of this chapter, the use of a particular structure did not mean that an author was inseparably committed to a particular brand of theology. However, it is probably fair to say that if we consider the number of repeat editions of works listed in Appendix 1 in which the catechism was the main item, and if we consider the evidence in previous chapters of which forms were used most by clergy and teachers, we will find that it was the catechisms which were based on the four-part structure of the sixteenth century which sold in the largest numbers and were used most widely, at least until the advent of the Westminster Shorter Catechism in the 1640s.[42] In the 1640s and 1650s the trend towards greater variety of design that had begun in the 1580s reached its zenith, but thereafter it declined as the presbyterians, easily the largest of the nonconformist bodies, tended to use the Westminster Shorter Catechism or one of the many works written to help teach it, while most episcopalians used the Prayer Book catechism or one of the dozens of variants or expositions of it. By this means, instruction in a form using a threefold or fourfold structure became standard for most later Stuart catechumens.

What will be attempted in the final six chapters of this book is an analysis of the doctrinal content of a sample of catechisms first published between the 1540s and the 1730s; and in the remainder of this chapter the nature of this sample, including the typical units and structures deployed, will be described. The sample numbers fifty-nine different forms, or just under one-tenth of the total number of Protestant forms in English then printed. These were chosen on the basis of two criteria: popularity and potential influence. In the great majority of cases, fifty-one in all, the forms selected are

---

[40] Perkins's principles took up only three pages but the exposition thirty in an octavo format; for attempts to abbreviate this and Ball's short catechism, see above, pp. 247–8; and on the perceived need for explanations of the WSC, see above, pp. 81–3, 244.

[41] See below, n. 48.

[42] See the number of repeat editions of the following works listed in Appendix 1 under: Book of Common Prayer; Nowell; Calvin; Dering and More; Paget and Openshaw; W. Hill; Mayer; Bernard; and Nicholes.

those which were sufficiently popular in England to have prompted the printing of at least five editions in the space of ten years.[43] Some of these works may have made their mark for a limited period of time, for example the works of Edward Elton in the 1620s, Richard Bernard in the 1630s, and Herbert Palmer in the 1640s, but several others were consistent sellers for two, three, or more decades. The official shorter catechism, the Prayer Book catechism of 1549, sold well throughout our period, and the official larger catechisms based on the work of Alexander Nowell sold well in different versions in the Elizabethan and early Stuart periods. Other consistent best-sellers were the alternative catechisms of 'godly' authors such as Edward Dering and John More, Eusebius Paget and Robert Openshaw, Stephen Egerton, and John Ball in the first half of our period, and of stalwart episcopalians like Richard Sherlock, John Williams, and John Lewis in the second. The works of the last two, among the last to be published in our sample, were still selling in the nineteenth century: the twenty-eighth edition of Williams's form was printed in 1804, the fifty-eighth of Lewis's in 1820.[44]

The remaining eight were selected because of their intrinsic interest and possible impact. They include English translations of four foreign works—Calvin's 1541 catechism, the Heidelberg Catechism of 1563, and a dialogue-treatise by Matthieu Virel that proved very popular in England from the mid-1590s to the mid-1630s. None of these three could be described as short works, and so to provide a basis for wider comparison with the best-selling English forms I have included a short form for children about to take communion that was apparently approved by Calvin for use in Geneva and regularly published as an appendix to English translations of Calvin's catechism.[45] The other four were home-produced works: two were by future bishops, William Nicholson and William Wake, and remained popular for some time after they were first produced, in 1655 and 1699, respectively; the third is Edward Boughen's 1646 form, which in a twin Latin and English version may well have replaced Alexander Nowell's form as the standard one used in some grammar schools and colleges in the 1660s and 1670s; and the last is Thomas Vincent's 1673

---

[43] This total excludes the full-length and the condensed versions of Nowell's catechism in Latin and the larger version of Dering and More's catechism with the scriptural citations in full, all of which were printed as separate items five times in ten years. The fact that relatively few catechumens outside a grammar school or university understood Latin and that the texts of the versions of the Dering–More catechism with and without full citations were in essence the same is the reason for this. Another work that could have been included on the five-in-ten principle is a work attributed to James Ussher—*A body of divinitie*; but Ussher disowned the work which was in fact a composite by an unknown hand of extracts from other catechisms (see Appendix 1). It has been excluded here, since it is hard to compare the motives and views of the author of such a work with original forms which were designed as an integral unit and acknowledged by their authors.

[44] The fifty-one forms, together with the eight described in the next paragraph, are described briefly in Appendix 2: for fuller bibliographical details of these forms, see Appendix 1. Please note that all short-title references to catechisms in the sample in the footnotes of the rest of this and the next six chapters will be to the editions specified in Appendix 2.

[45] See Appendix 1 under Calvin, Heidelberg, Virel, and 'Maner to examine children'; on the last of these see also Torrance, *School of Faith*, pp. xv, 237.

exposition of the Westminster Shorter Catechism, later editions of which not only carried an approving epistle signed by three dozen nonconformist clergy (and a couple of leading episcopalians), but also sold well in Scotland and Northern Ireland, thus forming a link between English presbyterianism and the wider presbyterian community.[46] A number of these eight works sold well. In two different versions (a fresh translation and a new exposition), the Heidelberg Catechism may have been published five times between 1588 and 1595, while Boughen's work (also in two versions) sold five editions in eleven years and would probably have sold more but for the troubles of the late 1640s and 1650s. Vincent's work would certainly be included on the five-in-ten rule if we were to count editions produced in Scotland and Ulster, since these were much more common than those published in England.[47] The rest sold well for a short while or sold steadily, though none was reprinted quite often enough to fulfil the criterion used in selecting the rest of the sample.

While we are defining the nature of the sample, it should also be pointed out that at least two of the works in the sample were annexes to already existing larger works, and two more were usually published as one element in a composite work. 'Certaine questions and answers' was regularly reprinted not as a separate title but on a loose sheet for insertion into selected editions of the Geneva Bible from 1579 to 1615; and Thomas Cartwright's catechism was usually published as an appendix to later editions of Dod and Cleaver's popular treatise on the Decalogue. Similarly, the 'short catechism' of Jeremy Taylor, having been printed first by itself, was thereafter published regularly only as the opening section of the very popular *The golden grove*, which also contained prose expositions of catechetical material and prayers. These catechetical forms almost certainly had some influence, but from the historian's point of view it is clearly harder to gauge compared to that of works which were published and bought as separate titles.[48] Another work in our sample, the official shorter catechism, is in one sense in a similar case, having been printed as an integral part of three works—the Book of Common Prayer, *The ABC with the catechisme*, and *The primer and catechisme*—rather than by itself. However, its key role in primary schooling as well as in parish catechizing, both of which have been described above, mean that the use of this form is much more easily demonstrated.[49] In the following chapters, however, each title in the sample will normally be treated on an equal basis whether it was reprinted five, fifty, or five hundred times.

[46] See Appendix 1. The commendatory epistle appeared in the 1673, 1693, 1701, and 1708 editions. For the use of Vincent's form in Scottish schools, see Carruthers, *Three Centuries*, 119. Editions were also published in Boston, Mass., in 1711 and 1729.

[47] Ibid. Isaac Watts's notes on *The Assembly's catechism* may have been published only four times by 1740, but have been added in to facilitate a complete picture of the aims embodied in his *Catechisms* (1730).

[48] See Appendix 1. The same point also applies, of course, though to a lesser degree to the relative impact of the different forms published by the same author in a publication containing more than one form, such as those of Egerton, Keach, and Watts.

[49] See above, Chs. 3–4, and Appendix 1.

Although the sample was chosen primarily with the likely impact of the individual works in mind, it does have a number of other advantages from our point of view. Its authors range from such stalwarts of the Continental Reformed tradition as Calvin in Geneva and Ursinus and Olevianus (the probable authors of the Heidelberg Catechism) in the Palatinate, to an English Baptist, Benjamin Keach, and a renowned Independent, Isaac Watts.[50] But in between, at least chronologically, the sample also includes a number of pillars of the established church, such as Alexander Nowell, James Ussher, Jeremy Taylor, Thomas Marshall, Thomas Comber, Zacheus Isham, John Williams, and William Wake, all of whom became deans or bishops. The author of another work in the sample, Henry Hammond, would almost certainly have become a bishop if he had not died prematurely in April 1660, but on the basis of his other writings could certainly be described as a pillar of the episcopalian church.[51] The authors of works in the sample also include a number who on the basis of their careers or other writings could be called 'puritan', 'godly', 'Calvinist', 'presbyterian', or 'dissenter', for example Edward Dering, John More, Eusebius Paget, Thomas Cartwright, William Perkins, Stephen Egerton, Samuel Hieron, John Ball, Alexander Grosse, and Thomas Gouge.[52]

The two categories just used—established and 'godly'—do not, however, represent monolithic alternatives. In their catechisms, Dering and More, Perkins, and Ball, for example, did not attack those features of the established church's structure, discipline, or liturgy of which they disapproved; nor did Ball, Gouge, and Watts state their predestinarian views nearly as strongly in their catechetical forms as did, say, Cartwright and Grosse in theirs. On the other hand, Dean Nowell and Archbishop Ussher might well be termed 'godly' or 'Calvinist' as well as conformist or episcopalian.[53] Indeed, there are some lesser known authors who defy simple categorization. Richard Bernard is often described as a puritan for his brushes with authority, but was a strong supporter and devoted exponent of the Prayer Book catechism for many years, while Martin Nicholes expounded parts of that same catechism in a predestinarian way in 1631. Conversely, John Mayer expounded the Prayer Book form twice in the 1620s, and then the parliamentary ordinance of October 1645 on admission to

---

[50] F. Wendel, *Calvin: The Origins and Development of his Religious Thought*, trans. P. Mairet (1965), 78–81; E. Cameron, *The European Reformation* (Oxford, 1991), 370–1. For Keach and Watts, see *DNB*.

[51] On Hammond, see J. W. Packer, *The Transformation of Anglicanism 1643–1660 (with special reference to Henry Hammond)* (Manchester, 1969); on the others, *DNB*.

[52] Ibid. for the label 'puritan', 'presbyterian', or 'nonconformist' divine being applied to Egerton, Hieron, Ball, Grosse, and Gouge. Also, on More, see P. Collinson, *A Mirror of Elizabethan Puritanism* (Friends of Dr Williams's Library Lecture, London, 1963), 8–10 and *passim*; on Paget, Collinson, *The Religion of Protestants* (Oxford, 1982), 233–4; on Cartwright, Lake, *Moderate Puritans*, ch. 5, and *Anglicans and Puritans?*, ch. 1; on Perkins, *The Work of William Perkins*, ed. I. Breward (Abingdon, 1970), 1–113. Copies of Edward Elton's full-length exposition of the Decalogue were burnt in 1625, but otherwise his career was 'innocuously conformist': Aston, *England's Iconoclasts*, 388.

[53] On Ball, Gouge, and Watts compared to Cartwright and Grosse, see below, Ch. 8; on Nowell and Ussher, *DNB*.

communion, in 1646, while two post-Restoration episcopalians—Thomas Marshall and Thomas Comber—made some irenic gestures towards presbyterian feelings.[54] To balance this individualism there is the fact that four of the more influential catechisms in the sample were, as far as we know, the product of more than one author or of a team of workers: the official English short catechism of 1549, the Heidelberg Catechism, and the Westminster Assembly's larger and shorter forms as published in 1648. In these cases, and in the case of Nowell's original Latin catechism which was scrutinized by Convocation, we can be reasonably confident that the final product was acceptable to a range of contemporary theologians.[55]

The sample also has the advantage of including forms which range from elementary to advanced, though the great majority are short or middling in length.[56] A number were explicitly or implicitly designed to be memorized in full: the 1549 Prayer Book catechism, and the original Dering–More, Paget, Egerton, and Ball forms were all less than thirty octavo pages in length, as were the Genevan pre-communion form and the catechisms of Perkins, Hieron, Cartwright, Taylor, and others.[57] Calvin's own form was longer, but it was probably still meant to be memorized: ostensibly aimed at schoolchildren aged from 10 to 15, it contained answers that were mostly of middling length, and was soon divided into fifty-five short sections to facilitate regular weekly learning.[58] Similarly William Wake's form was quite long and in some ways advanced, but it too was divided into fifty-two sections of a few pages each.[59] A few of the authors of works in the sample either included a summary of their form at the end of their larger catechism, for example Edward Elton and Thomas Gouge, or, like Egerton, Ussher, Keach, and Watts, they included within the covers of the same publication forms of different lengths for different purposes or for different age-groups, in the case of both Egerton and Watts no less than six different forms being offered as we saw in the previous chapter.[60] John Mayer's second catechism—the one in our sample—was itself an abridgement of his first, much longer work, but by the use of different type-faces managed to provide in this shortened form 'both milk for babes, and stronger meat for such as have attained more growth in knowledge'.[61] Three other authors—Palmer in 1640, Wallis in 1648, and Comber by 1681, as we also saw in Chapter 5—designed forms which were tests not only of memory but also of comprehension to help those of 'meanest capacities and weakest memories' and 'ignorant country people'.[62]

---

[54] See the relevant entries in Appendix 1; and also above, pp. 73, 79–80, 153, 262, and below, pp. 539, 549.

[55] On Nowell's form, see W. P. Haugaard, *Elizabeth and the English Reformation* (Cambridge, 1970), 68, 277–9.

[56] For an explanation of these terms, see the Introduction to Appendix 1.

[57] The number of pages in Cartwright's form, usually published in a quarto volume, has here been converted into an approximate octavo equivalent. The Hieron form is here cited from a folio edition, but was regularly nineteen pages long in octavo editions.

[58] Torrance, *School of Faith*, 3–4.   [59] For Wake's form, see Appendix 1.

[60] Ibid., and above, pp. 196, 211, 251–2, 267–8, 271–3.   [61] Mayer, *Catechisme*, sig. A2ʳ.

[62] Palmer, *Endeavour*, title-page and 1; Comber, *Church-catechism*, sigs. A2ʳ⁻ᵛ; and above, pp. 260–3.

All of this suggests, as one might expect from their popularity, that the majority of the forms in our sample were aimed either at a fairly young, theologically unsophisticated audience or adults with little formal education. Beyond these, however, there are a few works in the sample which were almost certainly meant to be read and studied at some length, rather than committed to memory intact, by older students, ordinands, and the better-educated laity. Six of the forms in the sample actually consist of three originals each published in two different versions, those by Alexander Nowell (the full-length and condensed versions in English), John Ball (one with and one without expositions of each answer), and the Westminster divines' Larger and Shorter Catechisms; and in each case the larger work was clearly aimed at older or more advanced catechumens.[63] Similar works include Elton's opening form for adults, the lengthy dialogue-catechisms of Virel and Hammond, and Nicholson's rather specialist account, which had probably begun life as a series of sermons on the Creed, then been boiled down to catechetical proportions, simplified somewhat in style and language, and supplemented by new sections on the other three staples.[64]

Despite variations in size and target group, a number of these works were closely related. It follows from what has been said in the first half of this chapter that the typical content of these catechisms comprised an exposition of the Creed, Decalogue, Lord's Prayer, and sacraments, usually with some prefatory or linking material.[65] Twenty-three of the fifty-nine forms in the sample contained a treatment of all four staples: these were mainly published before the 1590s or subsequently but based on the revised official shorter catechism with its sequence of Creed, Decalogue, Lord's Prayer, and sacraments.[66] A further nine, consisting of Ball's two forms, the two Westminster catechisms and those closely based on the Westminster Shorter Catechism, dealt specifically with three staples: the Ten Commandments, sacraments, and Lord's Prayer (often in that order).[67] But even those authors who did not handle all four staples in most cases either handled one or two in some detail, or referred to the missing one(s), paraphrased them, or handled them in an abbreviated form, for example William Perkins, Stephen Egerton, James Ussher, and Jeremy Taylor.[68] In only

[63]   See Appendix 2 and for further details Appendix 1; the differences, sometimes marked, between the texts of these pairs of works, and the fact that from the outset they were published separately, means that they are best regarded as discrete albeit closely related works, with different targets and functions.

[64]   See relevant entries in Appendix 1, and Nicholson, *Exposition*, 199; and cf. W. Nicholson, *Ekthesis pisteos or an exposition of the Apostles Creed* (1661), sigs. A3^r–4^r and *passim*. Wake's exposition of the church catechism was also in some cases read rather than memorized: see above, pp. 159–62.

[65]   See above, pp. 280–3.

[66]   The Prayer Book catechism and the forms of Calvin, Heidelberg, Nowell (larger and condensed), More, Paget, Virel, Hill, Mayer, Bernard, Nicholes, Palmer, Hammond, Boughen, Nicholson, Sherlock, Comber, Marshall, Williams, Isham, Wake, and Lewis: further details in Appendices 1 and 2.

[67]   Ibid.: Ball, *Catechisme* and *Treatise*; Westminster Larger and Smaller (for the inclusion of the Creed at the end of a combined form, see below, p. 301 n. 4); Wallis, *Explanation*; Vincent, *Catechism*; Gouge, *Principles* and 'Heads'; and Watts, *Assembly's catechism*.

[68]   Ibid.: Perkins, *Foundation*; Egerton, 'Familiar manner'; Ussher, 'Principles' and 'Method'; and Taylor, 'Catechism'; see also Elton, 'Forme'.

two categories of work was there no explicit exposition of at least one or two of the staples. First, there were those which were very specialized: 'Certaine questions and answers' was designed to cover three areas left out of many early short catechisms—predestination, the scriptures, and the sacraments; Bradshaw's and Hildersham's forms were intended to help people prepare for the Lord's Supper; and Grosse's was again designed to help catechumens understand predestination.[69] Secondly, there were those forms aimed at a very young or naïve set of learners, such as some of the forms prepared by Egerton, Keach, and Watts.[70] Though less typical of the catechetical mainstream in some respects, these two kinds of forms are representative of the great diversity of contemporary catechetics, and since they were published in best-selling works deserve equal consideration to those already described.

The forms in the sample are further related in that a number of their authors had borrowed material and ideas from fellow-catechists: Nowell from Calvin; Dering and More from Calvin and Nowell; Paget from Nowell and Dering–More; Egerton, Ball, and Elton from Perkins and Cartwright; Hill from Egerton; Nicholes from Ball; the authors of the Westminster catechisms from Ball, Nicholes, and Palmer; Gouge and Keach from the Westminster Shorter Catechism; Lewis from Comber, Isham, and Williams; and so on.[71] Similarly, the forms which were based on the Prayer Book catechism—those of Hill, Mayer, Nicholes, and Bernard in the period prior to 1640; Boughen, Nicholson, and Sherlock in the 1640s and 1650s; and Marshall, Comber, Williams, Isham, Lewis, and Wake in the later Stuart period—obviously had much in common, though their authors seem to have felt free to introduce different emphases, as we shall see. The same was true of authors like Wallis, Vincent, and Watts who all wrote expositions of the Westminster Shorter Catechism, and Gouge and Keach who used parts of this same form in their own catechetical works.[72] The translator of Virel's dialogues was the same Stephen Egerton who produced six forms of his own, though since there is only a limited amount in common between those forms and that of Virel the translation may have been done later.[73] There is also an isolated example of demonstrable consultation between two authors in the sample in the note in the early Restoration editions of Richard Sherlock's form, that it had been seen and approved by Henry Hammond before the latter's untimely death.[74]

---

[69] Ibid.: 'Certaine questions and answers'; Bradshaw, 'Brief forme'; Hildersham, 'Doctrine'; Grosse, *Fiery pillar*.

[70] The first five of Egerton's forms, all three of Keach's, and the first four of Watts's and see also 'Maner to examine' and Elton, 'Extract'. Hieron's insistence on a purely scriptural text made his form a special case.

[71] Most of these borrowings will be illustrated in the following chapters; the rest can easily be confirmed by comparing the forms mentioned side by side. According to the 7th edition of Ball's larger form, Martin Nicholes had helped in its revision. On the Westminster catechisms, see Mitchell, *Catechisms of the Second Reformation*, xvii–xxiv, xxvii, xxxii–xxxiii, lxix–lxxi. The work by Ussher there mentioned was probably the bogus one referred to in n. 43 above.

[72] See Appendix 1, and next few chapters.   [73] See Appendix 2 for the respective titles.

[74] Sherlock, *Principles*, 12.

In what follows, we shall attempt to isolate and describe the doctrinal norms of the catechisms in the sample, and we shall also look at those doctrines which were the subject of potentially sharp differences, in particular double predestination, covenant theology, the value of the sacraments, and the role of works. In view of the amount of space that has been devoted by theologians and historians to the divisions between English Protestants in the early modern period, it might be thought more than a little perverse to devote a lot of space to pointing out what the authors of the most popular catechisms of the period appear to have had in common. Nevertheless, if one examines works which were pitched not at the educated élite with which most recent scholars have been concerned but at a less informed, even illiterate audience, and especially perhaps at rural catechumens rather than those in the capital or larger towns—the kind of audience with which Thomas Comber claimed to have had success with his 'Yes' or 'No' technique—one does find a wide amount of shared opinion.[75] The amount of agreement was partly due to the overlaps in the materials used—the staples discussed earlier in this chapter—and partly to the considerable amount of borrowing from other authors' forms that went on in works both inside and outside our sample. As one author commented in 1617, his form had the same substance as other catechisms—it was merely differently phrased; or, as Richard Baxter put it half century later, the church abounds with catechisms which may differ in detail of content or in method or order, but are the same in substance.[76] These men were either being ingenuous, or believed that there was a good deal of common ground between catechists, especially those operating at elementary level.

Two of the conclusions thrown up by the work of the last twenty-five years are germane here. First, although there were major differences between conformists and puritans, Calvinists and non-Calvinists, and presbyterians and separatists in the reigns of Elizabeth and James, and some differences of substance between 'Latitudinarians' and 'High-Churchmen' in the later Stuart period, in some cases these should be seen as matters of degree rather than differences of kind; and, secondly, what was said depended on to whom one was speaking or in what context one said it. The first point needs little elaboration. As a result of the work of Collinson, Lake, Brachlow, White, and Milton, it is possible to view many of the differences of opinion over matters of church organization and doctrine in Elizabethan and Jacobean times as representing differing positions on a spectrum, or more realistically on a number of spectra, one for each source of disagreement. Moderate puritans and even closet presbyterians have been shown holding some of the highest offices in Elizabethan Cambridge, and, together with those of the 'godly' who were prepared to act as bishops, deans, and archdeacons, exerting much influence on many aspects of the

---

[75] P. Lake, 'Calvinism and the English Church 1570–1635', *Past and Present* 114 (1987), 33–4; Comber, *Church-catechism*, sigs. A2^{r-v}.

[76] R. Horne, *Points of instruction* (1617), sigs. A2^{r-v}; R. Baxter, *The catechizing of families* (1683), sig. A2^v; and see below, n. 87.

life of the English church. In the reign of James, it is true, many Calvinist conformists began to reduce their contacts with and protection of the puritans; but this simply left men like Ussher, Hall, Davenant, and Prideaux in a new intermediate position, being prepared to go part of the way with the Laudians on the one side, while trying not to sever all contact with those fellow-Calvinists on the other who were less flexible or less prepared to compromise than they were. Many separatists, too, are now revealed as having been very close to the presbyterians on various issues, and often very reluctant to separate.[77] In the later Stuart and early Hanoverian periods too, historians have been debating whether there really was a coherent movement called Latitudinarianism, or merely a state of mind shared, at first, by a few friends and colleagues, and then by a rather larger group of moderate churchmen; and they also have been questioning how deep and long-lived were the tensions between Whig and Tory churchmen.[78] Of course, in both early and later Stuart periods there remained substantial differences on matters of doctrine, discipline, ecclesiology, and forms of worship, or—what was as important—there were thought to be divisions on these issues, and the liberal use of pejorative labels and conscious or unconscious misrepresentation of the opponent's viewpoint served to raise the temperature. But the impression of pervasive conflict, often cultivated by some of the contemporaries who came off second best, and accepted by later historians who for different reasons were predisposed to believe them,[79] should not blind us to the possibility that these warring churchmen agreed on a number of issues, like the authority of scripture, the nature of God, the offices of Christ, the role of the Holy Ghost, the marks of a true church, and the iniquities of Rome and the Anabaptists. And if one accepts that many sincere critics of the established English church managed to find a *modus vivendi* within it, or that churchmen of differing standpoints could co-operate regularly on matters of pastoral or charitable interest, then it should be possible to approach the

[77] See the bibliography in P. Collinson, *English Puritanism* (Historical Association General Series, 106; London, 1983), 43–7, and Collinson's own studies of *Archbishop Grindal* (1979) and *The Religion of Protestants* (Oxford, 1982), and his 'Towards a Broader Understanding of the Early Dissenting Tradition', in *The Dissenting Tradition: Essays for Leland H. Carlson*, ed. C. R. Cole and M. E. Moody (Athens, Oh., 1975), 3–38; Lake, *Moderate Puritans*, chs. 1, 12, and *Anglicans and Puritans?*, 4–10, 14–28; Milton, *Catholic and Reformed*, introduction, conclusion, and *passim*; Brachlow, *Communion of Saints*; White, *Predestination*; J. S. Coolidge, *The Pauline Renaissance in England: Puritanism and the Bible* (Oxford, 1970), *passim*; and J. Sears McGee, *The Godly Man in Stuart England: Anglicans, Puritans, and the Two Tables, 1620–1670* (New Haven/London, 1976), chs. 1–2. For differences between 'Calvinists' and 'Arminians', see below, start of Ch. 8.

[78] J. Walsh, C. Haydon, and S. Taylor (eds.), *The Church of England c.1689–c.1833: From Toleration to Tractarianism* (Cambridge, 1993), 32–43, 45–7, 51–4.

[79] For those writing on the Elizabethan and early Stuart period from within a denominational or Pilgrim Fathers tradition, see C. Burrage, *The Early English Dissenters* (2 vols.; Cambridge, 1912); M. M. Knappen, *Tudor Puritanism* (Chicago, 1939); W. Haller, *The Rise of Puritanism* (New York, 1938), and id., *Liberty and Reformation in the Puritan Revolution* (New York, 1963); for those writing with social change in mind, M. Walzer, *The Revolution of the Saints (1966)*; C. Hill, *Society and Puritanism in Pre-Revolutionary England* (1964).

catechetical authors of this period without preconceived categories of 'puritan' and 'Anglican' or 'Latitudinarian' or 'High-Church' in mind, or expecting to find our authors grinding party axes or pursuing factional ends. Instead, one can at least pose the question 'What can these catechisms tell us about what a number of energetic and articulate divines found acceptable—and accepted—in the English church?'

The second point noted above was that authors were capable of adjusting their language and position according to the target they had in mind or the situation in which they found themselves. What Whitaker wrote in a polemic against Rome was not necessarily what he argued in a debate with a fellow-Protestant; and what Cartwright said in a published exchange with Whitgift was not quite the same as what he wrote in private to the separatists.[80] What Professor Lake has described as the 'ideological logic' practised in the formal debates of the period did not always find expression in ecclesiastical practice outside public controversy, as he himself has pointed out. The elements of conservatism, minimalism, and occasional ambiguity in the final versions of the English liturgy, Homilies, and Thirty-nine Articles, the final drafts of the Lambeth Articles, and even the canons of the Synod of Dort are all in their different ways examples of this. So also are the elements of caution and balance in some works of practical divinity written by leading controversialists or theologians when they were wearing a different hat.[81] The relevance of this for us here is that such authors were also likely to be quite capable of adjusting their language and arguments again when faced with an audience of uneducated catechumens. Whereas the scholastic framework in which polemics were conducted, especially against 'popery', tended to sharpen, harden, and exaggerate divisions, and to suggest that one step off the straight and narrow would lead down the slippery slope to heresy, the didactic impulse behind catechizing tried to build up knowledge and commitment, to simplify, and if necessary to gloss over or even omit disputed points. Elitist and meritocratic as most learned divines of the Elizabethan and Jacobean period were, they were still able to see the need to adopt vocabulary and techniques that would put the basics of the faith across in a way that most children or ignorant adults could grasp,[82] as will be seen in the chapters which follow.

The result of all this—shared materials, borrowing from other authors' work, similar opinions on many matters, and tempering the wind to the shorn lambs—was that until the early 1640s nearly all English catechists followed the example set by Luther

[80] Lake, *Moderate Puritans*, chs. 4, 6; Brachlow, *Communion of Saints*, 25–7, 46–8, 70.

[81] Haugaard, *Elizabeth and the English Reformation*, chs. 3, 6; S. Sykes and J. Booty (eds.), *The Study of Anglicanism* (1988), 122–30, 134–40; G. W. Bernard, 'The Church of England *c*.1529–*c*.1642', *History*, 75 (1990), 185–8; H. C. Porter, *Reformation and Reaction in Tudor Cambridge* (Cambridge, 1958), 367–71; Lake, *Moderate Puritans*, 134–5, 148, 150–3, 167–8, 285, and *Anglicans and Puritans?*, 244; White, *Predestination*, 101–10, and ch. 9.

[82] I. Green, ' "Reformed Pastors" and *Bons Curés*', in W. Sheils and D. Wood (eds.), *The Ministry: Clerical and Lay* (Studies in Church History, 26; 1989), 260; Lake, *Moderate Puritans*, 94, and id., *Anglicans and Puritans?*, 14–15.

and Calvin of avoiding contentious issues in their catechisms, or at least of eschewing the techniques of controversy that they might have used to defend their views in a different format, such as a public debate, a sermon on a prestigious occasion, or a polemical treatise. Of the catechisms in our sample, none of those published before the 1640s was overtly polemical in character. The most that one finds is occasional sniping at Catholicism, such as the explicit criticism of the papacy in Virel's treatise, or the attack on the Mass inserted into Heidelberg Catechism at the insistence of the Elector Frederick III as a response to the anathemas of the Council of Trent.[83] This is not to say that from the outset there was not material that was presented in a distinctively Protestant way, or that from the 1580s or 1590s there were not some catechisms that contained material that was implicitly controversial. But as we shall see the way in which this was done was a pale reflection of the passion engendered by most polemical debates.[84] It is also true that from the 1640s, authors in the sample (and outside it) were more likely to exhibit some aggression, but it was still limited in scale, and as likely to be directed against Catholic as against fellow-Protestants' errors.[85] It is noteworthy, for example, that when Richard Sherlock chose to defend the Prayer Book catechism against its critics, he did so not in the text of his own exposition of that form, but in a separate appendix in continuous prose.[86] Catechetical authors could and usually did continue to adopt a moderate or irenic attitude on a number of disputed areas, such as the precise meaning of the passage in the fourth article of the Creed where it is stated that Christ 'descended into Hell'. As John Mayer put it when he was preparing his third catechism, this time based on the parliamentary ordinance of October 1645, members of the reformed churches might differ in some matters, but all agreed on their foundation in Christ.[87]

---

[83] Heidelberg Catechism, 335–6.

[84] See above, pp. 39–40, 69–70, 78, and below Chs. 8–9, 12. For an example of a Catholic work which eschewed controversy, see [L. Vaux], *A catechisme or Christian doctrine* (1568), and the comments of T. G. Law in his edition of this work in *Chetham Society*, NS, 4 (1885), pp. xciii–xciv.

[85] See above, pp. 83–6, 90–2; Vincent, *Catechism*, title-page (to 'obviate the growing errors of Popery'); Williams, *Exposition*, 11, 30, 54; and Wake, *Principles*, 43, 48, 65, 171–5.

[86] Sherlock, *Principles*, 51–61.

[87] J. Mayer, *A short catechisme* (1646), 21–2. On the descent into hell, see below, pp. 316–19.

7

The Apostles' Creed

As we saw in the previous chapter, one of the most common sequences in which the staple items of catechizing were handled, if not the most common of all, was that of Creed, Decalogue, Lord's Prayer, and sacraments. Even the tripartite catechisms which eschewed an article-by-article exposition of the Creed mostly began with credal material such as the nature of God, the role of Christ, and the function of the Holy Ghost. Let us therefore begin our survey of the doctrinal norms in our sample of catechisms with the Creed, and keep in mind two questions: how far there was agreement or disagreement between authors who were on what have been thought of as an ecclesiastical 'left' and 'right'; and how far there was any difference between catechisms designed for the simplest catechumens as opposed to those destined for the more advanced.

In the simpler forms in the sample the word 'creed' was explained as meaning 'belief'; more advanced forms spoke of a Creed as 'a compendious and brief gathering of the articles' of the Christian faith, or as the 'symbol' of a Christian—a badge, mark, watchword, or token such as soldiers used in battle.[1] The Creed used in the sample works was always the Apostles' rather than the Nicene or Athanasian.[2] In many of the forms in which the Creed was taught, it was presented to catechumens as an *ex cathedra* summary of the faith; but in a few instances authors, aware of the grounds for thinking that the Creed might not have been the work of the apostles themselves, made a point of discussing its authenticity. Calvin, for example, in his catechism asserted that the Creed was 'taken out of the pure doctrine of the apostles', and Nowell stated that 'it was first received from the apostles' own mouth, or most faithfully gathered out of their writings', while Boughen in his 1646 exposition of the Prayer Book catechism went even further in saying that although not written down until the fourth century the Apostles' Creed had definitely been composed by the apostles.[3] Others struck a more cautious note. Martin Nicholes in his 1631 exposition of the Prayer Book catechism, the authors of the Westminster catechisms, and a number of

---

[1] Prayer Book catechism, 780–1; Sherlock, *Principles*, 17; Wake, *Principles*, 24; Lewis, *Catechism*, 15; Calvin, *Catechisme*, 6; Nowell, *Catechisme*, 141–2; Nicholson, *Exposition*, 22–3.

[2] Some authors who used the Apostles' Creed referred briefly to other creeds, e.g. Boughen, *Exposition*, 73, and Nicholson, *Exposition*, 20.

[3] Calvin, *Catechisme*, 6; Nowell, *Catechisme*, 142, 155–6; Boughen, *Exposition*, 5–6: Boughen cited Calvin as support for the idea that this creed had been in use before the Epistle to the Hebrews was written.

later episcopalians all indicated that the Creed might not have been composed by the apostles themselves, or at least not in the form in which we have it, but were all agreed (with Calvin and Nowell) that as a summary of the faith it was 'agreeable to the word of God and anciently received in the churches of Christ' (as the Westminster divines put it).[4] The scriptural warrant for statements based on the Creed was demonstrated to the mind and the eye by the widespread habit of festooning every single answer in a catechism with scriptural texts or references, a habit which was as pronounced in the works of conformists like Nowell, Williams, Isham, Wake, and Lewis as in the works of partial conformists like More, Paget, and Ball or full-blown nonconformists like Vincent and Watts.[5] Inclusion or exclusion of the text of the Creed was more a matter of pedagogical judgement than a statement of party loyalty. As noted in the last chapter, the decision not to treat the Creed article by article allowed authors greater flexibility of design and an opportunity to introduce new themes or to concentrate more on themes of their own choosing than those implicit in the Creed.[6] For example, some of the authors in our sample who omitted the Creed began their forms instead with a few questions and answers about the importance and credibility of the scriptures,[7] though one might add that the authors of some larger works, like Nowell, Virel, and Wake, found space for discussion of both scriptures and Creed.[8] Any difficulties that there might have been between, on the one hand, those like Calvin, the authors of the Prayer Book catechism (and its derivatives), and the authors of the Heidelberg Catechism, who all cited the full text of the Creed in their forms, and, on the other hand, those like Perkins, Ball, and the authors of the Westminster catechisms and its expositions, who did not, were minimized (as in the case of those with stronger or more cautious views on the apostles' authorship of the Creed) by the fact that both groups were prepared to admit that its content was consonant with the scriptures and that it had been 'anciently received in the churches of Christ'.[9]

To aid comprehension and memorization, authors of intermediate or longer works often divided the Creed up into twelve articles,[10] and like Calvin, Virel, and Nowell

---

[4] Nicholes, *Catechisme*, 3–4; [Westminster Assembly of Divines], *The humble advice of the Assembly of Divines … concerning a shorter catechism* (1658), 43. (There was some debate as to whether the Creed should be published or not, apparently focusing on the article 'He descended into hell': for the resolution of this, see Carruthers, *Three Centuries*, 5; the Decalogue, Lord's Prayer, and Creed were not printed at the end of all editions of the Shorter Catechism: it was more likely to be printed in expanded versions in which the supporting texts were printed in full, or in combined editions of Confession and both catechisms.) Sherlock, *Principles*, 18; Lewis, *Catechism*, 15; Williams, *Exposition*, 19; Wake, *Principles*, 24.

[5] See the texts or margins of the works of these authors cited in Appendix 2.

[6] See above, pp. 284–6.

[7] e.g. Ball, *Catechisme*, 67–8; Ussher, 'Principles', 1 and 'Method', 13; Westminster Larger, 1–3 (answers 2–5). By no means all did, however, e.g. Perkins, *Foundation*, 1–3, and see the forms by Egerton and Hierom.

[8] Nowell, *Catechisme*, 114–18; Virel, *Treatise*, 3–4; Wake, *Principles*, 20–4.

[9] See previous notes.

[10] Paget, *Questions*, sig. C5ᵛ; Hill, *Principles*, sig. A7ʳ; Boughen, *Exposition*, 8; Sherlock, *Principles*, 18; Comber, *Church-catechism*, 8–13; Isham, *Catechism*, 9–10; Williams, *Exposition*, 9.

grouped these together under four headings: God, Christ, the Holy Ghost, and the church.[11] However, the authors of some simpler forms, like the 1549 catechism, and some middling-length forms, like those of the conformist episcopalians Sherlock, Williams, and Lewis, might use a threefold division in which the church was sub-sumed under the Holy Ghost. The difference between a threefold and fourfold divi-sion was not great, wrote Nicholson: both were '*docendi causa*, for the ease of the teacher and the scholar'.[12]

The first article of the Creed expresses belief in 'God the father almighty, maker of heaven and earth'. The minimum that a catechumen was expected to know about God could be reduced to a single line, as in the Prayer Book catechism: God is 'the father who hath made me, and all the world'. The maximum, in works for more advanced students such as Hammond's *Practical catechisme* or the Westminster Larger Catechism was a complex definition of God's essence, and a list of his quali-ties or properties or of his marvellous works. The larger the work, the longer the list of attributes, as we shall see shortly.[13] In the great majority of forms, however, the two essential ideas that authors were apparently most anxious to communicate were of God as father, and God as creator and preserver. In the simpler or shorter forms the first of these concepts was put very briefly: God is my father, and I am his child;[14] in more advanced ones it might be put in a more complicated way—that God was the father of Christ, and since Christ is our saviour, so God is our father too, or that Christ was the natural son of God, but we are the sons of God by adoption.[15]

On most of the occasions on which God's fatherhood was under discussion, no lim-itations were indicated: God was father of all. But just occasionally a distinction was drawn, as in the statement in Stephen Egerton's 'Familiar forme' that God has chosen me before all beginnings in Jesus Christ to be his child, so I am bold to call him father; or Martin Nicholes's assertion (in an exposition of the Prayer Book catechism in 1631) that God is father to all that believe in him 'among whom I account myself to be one'.[16] The use of the first-person singular in both these instances, and the assertiveness of the 'bold' and 'account myself', may have softened the potentially exclusive tone of

[11] Calvin, *Catechisme*, 7; Nowell, *Catechisme*, 142; Virel, *Treatise*, 29.

[12] Sherlock, *Principles*, 19; Williams, *Exposition*, 10; Lewis, *Catechism*, 16; Nicholson, *Exposition*, 26 (Nicholson himself preferred a twofold division: God and his church).

[13] Prayer Book catechism, 780–1; Hammond, *Practical catechisme*, 308–10; Westminster Larger Cat-echism, answer 7.

[14] e.g. Paget, *Questions*, sig. C6ʳ; Hill, *Principles*, sig. A7ᵛ.

[15] Calvin, *Catechisme*, 8–9, 17–18; Nowell, *Catechisme*, 145 and cf. 154; Heidelberg Catechism, 315; Dering–More, *Catechisme*, sig. B2ᵛ; Virel, *Treatise*, 32; J. Taylor, 'An exposition of the Apostles' Creed', in *Symbolon ... or a collection of polemical and moral discourses* (1657), 6. Sometimes the idea of being sons by adoption was made under the later section of the Creed dealing with Christ's conception and birth.

[16] Prayer Book catechism, 780–1 (s.v. Creed: 'God the father' who has 'made me and all the world'; and cf. 786–7, s.v. Lord's Prayer); Egerton, 'Familiar forme', 33; Nicholes, *Catechisme*, 7.

these statements. But in any case it would probably be wrong to imagine that such authors were more cautious about stressing the concept of God as Father. 'Throughout Puritanism God's fatherhood is a favourite and insistent theme', Geoffrey Nuttall has written;[17] and what was true of puritans was true of nearly all the many English Protestants who wrote devotional works, or who tackled the preface of the Lord's Prayer in a catechism or other genre.[18]

Closely linked to God's position as father were his roles as creator and preserver. These were not easy to put across at the simplest level. 'God made me' is a phrase that can be found in elementary catechisms written at various times and places, such as the Prayer Book catechism of 1549, Paget's opening exchange in 1579, and two of Watts's forms in the 1730s.[19] The same point was sometimes made more generally: God is the 'beginning and principal cause of all things'.[20] Trying to reduce God's care for his creation to its essence was no easier: 'He being almighty ... and I his child shall lack nothing', was Paget's attempt; William Hill's wording (in a Prayer Book catechism exposition of 1616) was similar but added that God will preserve me from all dangers unto salvation; 'God preserves us, and does us good' was how Watts continued in the more advanced of the two forms just cited.[21] In longer or more advanced works, authors had to resist the temptation to write more, or to use longer words or technical terms. God is almighty in that all creatures are under his hand and government, and he disposes all things by his unsearchable wisdom and providence, was the line taken by Calvin, Nowell, and Dering and More.[22] There is one God, creator and governor of all things, Perkins told his catechumens, and his works are the creation of the world and all therein, and the preservation of this by his special providence, he added.[23]

The word 'providence' in this context did not necessarily have the predestinarian or prophetic overtones that it could acquire in other circumstances.[24] It meant simply God's unlimited capacity and merciful willingness to send the means of keeping his creation alive and to intervene in the lives of his creatures when he saw fit. The authors of the Heidelberg Catechism put it in simple, comprehensible terms:

What dost thou understand by the providence of God?
The almighty and everywhere present power of God, whereby, as it were by his hand, he still upholds heaven and earth, with all creatures, and so governs them that herbs and grass, rain

---

[17] G. F. Nuttall, *The Holy Spirit in Puritan Faith and Experience* (Oxford, 1946), 62–3.

[18] See below, Ch. 12. For examples of authors who did not use the Creed, but stressed God's fatherhood under the opening of the Lord's Prayer, see Ball, *Catechisme*, 77, Westminster Larger Catechism, 146–7 (answer 189), and Westminster Shorter Catechism, 37 (answer 100).

[19] Prayer Book catechism, 780–1; Paget, *Questions*, sig. A5^r; Watts, 'First catechism', 7, and 'Children's catechism', 2.

[20] 'Maner to examine children', 152; and cf. Gouge, *Principles*, 1.

[21] Paget, *Questions*, sig. C6^r; Hill, *Principles*, sigs. A7^{r-v}; Watts, 'Children's catechism', 4.

[22] Calvin, *Catechisme*, 8; Nowell, *Catechisme*, 145–6; Dering–More, *Catechisme*, sig. B2^r.

[23] Perkins, *Foundation*, 1, 3.

[24] B. Worden, 'Providence and Politics in Cromwellian England', *Past and Present*, 109 (1985), 55–99.

and drought, fruitful and barren years, meat and drink, health and sickness, riches and poverty, yea, all things, come not by chance, but by his fatherly hand.[25]

This use of the term 'providence' is to be found in the English liturgy, and in catechetical works by conformist clergy such as Hill, Comber, and Hammond as much as 'godly' authors like Perkins and Ball.[26] A close equivalent—God *preserves* his creation—can be found in works by the French minister Virel, the predestinarian Ussher, and the dissenters Keach and Watts, as well as in expositions of the official short catechism, for example by Marshall, Williams, Isham, and Lewis.[27]

The idea of creation and preservation was often, though not invariably at this stage of a catechism, linked to a notion of the divine purpose for man. In the simpler forms, this was stated in elementary terms which cut across all party lines and periods: God made me so that I might honour and serve him, and he will guide me to his glory.[28] As we move into slightly more advanced forms, we sometimes encounter authors raising the divine decrees here, or writing that God foreordained some men to salvation and others to damnation. But as we shall see in Chapter 8, the double predestinarian approach was by no means the typical way of looking at God's purpose in creating and preserving mankind; nor was it necessarily expressed in a divisive 'sheep and goats' manner. As in the average catechist's explanation of the second and third petitions of the Lord's Prayer ('Thy kingdom come, thy will be done'), our authors' emphasis when looking at the opening of the Creed was on God's purpose to reign in the hearts of those he had created and of the necessity of their obeying God to that end, rather than on the details of in whose hearts it was that God would reign.[29] The world was made for man's use and profit, wrote Dean Nowell in the 1560s, and man was made for God's glory; the use I should make of this first article of the Creed, said Sherlock's catechumen in the 1650s is 'that I am therefore bound to serve and worship him, and obey his laws, as being the great lord and father of all, from whom I have received all that I am, and all that I have in the world'.[30]

A more striking development in the catechetical treatment of God in the later sixteenth and early seventeenth centuries compared to that in Edwardian and early Elizabethan forms was the attempt to define and describe God. First in a number of middling forms and later in most advanced and some elementary ones as well, authors struggled to define the essence and nature of God. It was not easy, as students of Hieron's scriptural catechism may have found: 'What is God? The Almighty, which

---

[25] Heidelberg Catechism, 316; this is in part a close echo of Calvin, *Catechisme*, 11.

[26] For example in the sentence added in 1661 to the collect for the second Sunday after Trinity: Brightman, *English Rite*, ii. 467; Hill, *Principles*, sigs. A7[r–v]; Comber, *Church-catechism*, 10; Hammond, *Practical catechisme*, 308–11; Perkins, *Foundation*, 3; Ball, *Catechisme*, 69–70.

[27] Virel, *Treatise*, 8–9; Ussher, 'Principles', 6; Keach, 'Youth', 75; Watts, 'Children's catechism', 4; Marshall, *Catechism*, 9; Williams, *Exposition*, 10–11; Isham, *Catechism*, 11; Lewis, *Catechism*, 19–20, 62.

[28] Paget, *Questions*, sigs. A6[r–v]; Egerton, 'Familiar forme', 33; Taylor, 'Catechism', 2; Keach, 'Little child', 15; Watts, 'Children's catechism', 2.

[29] See below, Chs. 8, 12.   [30] Nowell, *Catechisme*, 147; Sherlock, *Principles*, 19–20.

is, which was, and which is to come. Rev. 1. 8'.[31] The most popular appellation was that of 'a spirit' or 'spiritual essence': Perkins's formulation—God is a 'spiritual essence that hath his being of himself' provoked a number of conscious or unconscious imitators from a wide range of authors.[32] The meaning of the term 'spirit' when used in this context was sometimes explained: as a spirit, God has no shape or figure and is invisible, but he is present in all places, sees and knows all things, and is all-powerful, so that nothing happens without his leave.[33] Perkins, however, was characteristically caustic about popular images of God:

How do you conceive this ... God in your mind?
Not by framing an image of him in my mind (as ignorant folks do, that think him to be an old man sitting in heaven) but I conceive him by his properties and works.[34]

(Catechists faced similar problems with the later article of the Creed, that Christ after his ascension 'sitteth at the right hand of God': this, catechumens were told, was a metaphor to help men comprehend Christ's closeness to his father, and should not be taken literally to mean that God had a right and a left hand like us.)[35]

Perkins's last comment indicates the route more commonly taken: increasingly catechumens were urged to conceive of God through his attributes—his wisdom, power, omniscience, righteousness, justice, and mercy—and through his works of creation and providence.[36] Some authors divided God's properties or attributes into categories, such as communicable and incommunicable, but there is no clear pattern that I can detect between the attributes stressed by those with strong views for or against double predestination.[37] On the other hand, there was a clear tendency for the number of divine qualities to increase with the size of the catechism, so that by the mid-1640s both Henry Hammond in his *Practical catechisme* of 1645, and the authors of the Westminster Larger Catechism of 1647 were ready to list well over a dozen, very similar attributes or qualities.[38] This rather cerebral way of teaching the concept of the deity—by a series or groups of abstract nouns or qualities such as 'eternal, unchangeable, incomprehensible'—was given more concrete form in the other half of Perkins's formula: God can also be understood through his works of creation and

[31] Hierom, *Doctrine*, 577.

[32] Perkins, *Foundation*, 3; Virel, *Treatise*, 6; Egerton, 'Briefe method', 2; Cartwright, 'Catechisme', sig. Aa3ᵛ; Ball, *Catechisme*, 68; Nicholes, *Catechisme*, 6; Palmer, *Endeavour*, 2; Marshall, *Catechism*, 9, 55; Williams, *Exposition*, 10; Keach, 'Little child', 15; id., 'Child', 20; and id., 'Youth', 74; Isham, *Catechism*, 11.

[33] Palmer, *Endeavour*, 3; Taylor, 'Catechism', 1; Watts, 'First catechism', 7; and cf. Ussher, 'Principles', 5; and Comber, *Church-catechism*, 10.

[34] Perkins, *Foundation*, 3. For the wider insistence that God should be judged by his works, not by mental images of him, see Aston, *England's Iconoclasts*, 436–7, 452–66.

[35] e.g. Nowell, *Catechisme*, 163; and Boughen, *Exposition*, 20.

[36] Perkins, *Foundation*, 3; Egerton, 'Briefe method', 2; Virel, *Treatise*, 8–9; Williams, *Exposition*, 10; Keach, 'Youth', 74; Isham, *Catechism*, 11; Wake, *Principles*, 27; Lewis, *Catechism*, 17–18.

[37] Pace Lake, *Anglicans and Puritans?*, 188.

[38] Hammond, *Practical catechisme*, 308; Westminster Larger Catechism, 4 (answer 7).

providence. Calvin had created a precedent here by arguing that God was aware of our feeble understandings and so had made himself known to us through his works, and in particular 'he hath made the world as a mirror or glass, wherein we may behold his divine majesty, in such sort as it is expedient for us to know him'.[39] Later catechumens were urged more specifically to consider the wonders of God's creation, how 'God made all things of nothing in six days ... in an excellent order, and exceeding good', and the marvels by which God preserved his creation, of the kind described in the Heidelberg Catechism quoted above.[40]

It will be appreciated, however, that the contemplation of God's works as a sign of his nature, or as a proof of his identity,[41] also tended towards a more intellectual approach than that found in the simplest forms (God made me and preserves me). Although it used to be thought that, compared to 'Anglicans' like Hooker and later the Latitudinarians, 'puritans' distrusted reason, in this case the initial thrust came from 'puritans' like William Perkins and John Ball, and in view of recent work on the rational, even scholastic strain in puritanism and Reformed Protestantism generally this may come as no surprise.[42] The mixture of cognition, deduction, and self-analysis in John Ball's form is representative of this:

How may it be proved that there is a God?
By the works and wonders which are seen, the testimony of conscience, the powers of the soul, and the practices of Satan.
How else?
By the consent of nations, defence of the church, support and comfort of the godly, but principally by the Scriptures.[43]

Another Calvinist Edward Elton suggested a similar combination in his form for adults: we are persuaded of God's existence by scripture, creation, providence, the common consent of all nations, and the accusations of conscience, and we should conceive of God as revealed by his Word, properties, and works.[44] The stress in the second question and answer of the Westminster Larger Catechism on what is revealed to man about God by 'the very light of nature, and the works of God' as well as by his

---

[39] Calvin, *Catechisme*, 10; Nowell, *Catechisme*, 146.

[40] Ball, *Catechisme*, 69 (and cf. 68 and Cartwright, 'Catechisme', sig. Aa4ʳ); and e.g. Marshall, *Catechism*, 9; Comber, *Church-catechism*, 10; Gouge, *Principles*, 25–7; Keach, 'Youth', 64, 74; and Heidelberg Catechism, 316.

[41] Palmer, *Endeavour*, 6; Gouge, *Principles*, 27; Keach, 'Youth', 64.

[42] For the older view, J. H. New, *Anglican and Puritan: The Basis of their Opposition 1558–1640* (1964), ch. 1; H. Davies, *Worship and Theology in England*, ii. *From Andrewes to Baxter* (Princeton, 1975), 180–4, and iii. *From Watts and Wesley to Maurice* (Princeton/London, 1961), 56–9. For the newer stress on 'reason', see D. Morgan, 'Puritanism and Science: A Reinterpretation', *Historical Journal*, 22 (1979), 549–53; M. Todd, *Christian Humanism and the Puritan Social Order* (Cambridge, 1987), ch. 3; Kendall, *English Calvinism*, chs. 2, 4, 5; McGrath, *Iustitia Dei*, ii. 40; Lake, *Anglicans and Puritans?*, 14–15; Clifford, *Atonement and Justification*, ch. 6. For Perkins, see above, p. 292 n. 52, and for Ball, next note; and for a rational defence of the authenticity of the Bible, see also 'Certaine questions and answers', sig. *iiiᵛ; Ball, *Catechisme*, 67–8; Westminster Larger, 2–3 (answer 4).

[43] Ball, *Catechisme*, 68.   [44] Elton, *Forme*, sig. A4ʳ.

Word and Spirit is also noteworthy (as, given the difficulty of the exercise of proving God's existence, is the fact that this question and answer was omitted from the Shorter Catechism).[45] All this is not very different from the position adopted by William Wake in his exposition of the Prayer Book catechism in 1699:

How do you profess to *believe* all this of God?
Because though some part of it might have been discovered by natural reason, and accordingly was found out by the wiser heathens; yet the full, and perfect knowledge of all this, is due to revelation: and by the accounts we have of these things in the holy scriptures, we both more clearly understand them, and are more firmly persuaded of the truth of them.[46]

It was, in fact, quite widely agreed that in trying to conceive and comprehend God, man should not only heed his conscience but also use his powers of reasoning to consider what he saw about him, read in the Bible, and heard about 'the consent of nations' on this matter. It was also agreed, however, that the driving force behind the transmission or revelation of saving knowledge remains in God's hands; and two of the key channels through which that knowledge was transmitted were Christ—the subject of articles two to seven of the Creed—and the Holy Ghost—article eight.

At this point, most catechists who were explaining the Creed article by article moved on to the second heading: 'I believe ... in Jesus Christ his only son our lord'. But a few, such as Nowell, Palmer, and Comber, did what many of those authors who eschewed a blow-by-blow account of the Creed did: they inserted a brief account of the Garden of Eden, the Fall, and the nature of sin—a move which led naturally on to a discussion of Christ's role as redeemer.[47] Others did not dwell on Eden, but did point out that man had been created out of the dust (or the slime as one author put it), and had been made in the image of God, 'in righteousness and true holiness', 'pure and innocent'.[48] But first some of the angels and then man had fallen (angels were usually mentioned only in the more demanding or advanced catechisms, such as Cartwright's and the Westminster Larger Catechism, but not the Smaller).[49] Adam became sinful by listening to the whispers of 'the devil', 'a tempting spirit'; in most of the works in our sample Eve did not incur the proportion of blame she later did.

[45] Westminster Larger, 1–2 (answer 2). [46] Wake, *Principles*, 30.

[47] Nowell, *Catechisme*, 147–50; Palmer, *Endeavour*, 8–12; Comber, *Church-catechism*, 10; and as examples of forms whose authors avoided an article-by-article exposition of the Creed, Ball, *Catechisme*, 70–2; Westminster Larger, 10–14 (answers 20–30); Gouge, *Principles*, 31–53.

[48] Nowell, *Catechisme*, 148; Heidelberg Catechism, 309; Egerton, 'Briefe method', 3–4; Virel, *Treatise*, 13; Hieron, *Doctrine*, 577; Palmer, *Endeavour*, 8; Ussher, 'Principles', 6; Westminster Larger, 8–9 (answer 17); Taylor, 'Catechism', 2; Gouge, *Principles*, 31–2; Keach, 'Child', 20–1; Comber, *Church-catechism*, 10; Heidelberg Catechism, 309. A number of authors did not mention the Creation or Fall, including the 1549 form and most of its derivatives, and the forms of Dering and More, Paget, Bradshaw, Hildersham, Grosse, and Hammond.

[49] Cartwright, 'Catechisme', sigs. Aa4^{r-v}; Westminster Larger, 8–9 (answers 16, 19), and cf. Westminster Shorter, 7–8 (answers 9–10).

Adam broke 'an easy commandment, which God gave him as the first trial of his obedience'.[50] Where an author had the space or the inclination, an explanation of the difference between original (inborn) sin and actual sin might follow,[51] but in most instances the author was content to drive home the existence and nature of the former, as in the following cases, one presbyterian, one episcopalian:

The sinfulness of that estate whereinto man fell, consists in the guilt of Adam's sin, the want of original righteousness, and the corruption of his whole nature, which is commonly called original sin ...

Adam did eat the forbidden fruit, and so sinned: and we, being in his loins, sinned with him. 'By one man's disobedience many were made sinners'. [Rom. 5: 19] Now this sin is ordinarily by divines called original sin.[52]

At this point, the opportunity was also taken, by authors of differing standpoints, to raise the question of a covenant of life or 'works' having been made between God and Adam. This covenant was usually presented in a conditional form: if Adam obeyed God, he would have eternal life; but if not, not.[53]

The effects of the Fall were depicted by some authors, such as Perkins, in stark terms: bodily diseases, aches and pains, material losses, and 'bondage under Satan the prince of darkness'.[54] However, in rather more of the forms in our sample in which the Fall and its consequences were mentioned the effects were described in a severe but less wide-ranging way, as in Ussher's first form: blindness of understanding, forgetfulness of memory, rebellion of the will, disorder of the affections, fear and confusion in the conscience, and the readiness of the body to serve sin.[55] There is no discernible difference between the views of Calvinists and non–Calvinists on the extent of the corruption of the human will, since this was apparently not a matter on which catechists wished to dwell.[56] In fact, most authors soon moved on to the next key question: if man was in such a dreadful position, how was he able to escape? The answer, of course was that since no ordinary man could satisfy God's justice, he had to rely on a mediator and redeemer who was pure and sinless to do it for him, namely Christ.[57]

---

[50] Heidelberg Catechism, 310; Taylor, 'Catechism', 2 (though cf. Nowell, *Catechisme*, 148–9); R. B. Bottigheimer, 'Religion for the Young in Bible Story Collections', *Fabula*, 32 (1991), 22–5.

[51] Marshall, *Catechism*, 17–18; Gouge, *Principles*, 42–7; Comber, *Church-catechism*, 11.

[52] Westminster Shorter, 10 (answer 18); Nicholson, *Exposition*, 12; and cf. Nowell, *Catechisme*, 150, and Virel, *Treatise*, 13.

[53] Cartwright, 'Catechisme', sigs. Aa4ᵛ–5ʳ; Ussher, 'Principles', 6–7; Westminster Larger, 10–11 (answer 20); Westminster Shorter, 8 (answer 12); Gouge, *Principles*, 32; Gouge, 'Heads', 2. But see also below, Ch. 9.

[54] Perkins, *Foundation*, 3–4; and cf. Vincent, *Catechism*, 49–52, and Gouge, *Principles*, 49–52.

[55] Ussher, 'Principles', 7; and cf. Heidelberg Catechism, 310–11; Cartwright, 'Catechisme', sig. Aa4ᵛ; Ball, *Catechisme*, 71; Palmer, *Endeavour*, 8; Westminster Larger, 13 (answer 27); Westminster Shorter, 10 (answer 19); Wake, *Principles*, 76–7.

[56] See below, pp. 371–4, and for a general view of the Protestant position, see E. Cameron, *The European Reformation* (Oxford, 1991), 112–13.

[57] Heidelberg Catechism, 311–12, and other sources as in the following paragraphs.

Whether they were expounding the second article of the Creed or merely turning to the redeemer of fallen man as the next step in their account, the majority of catechists in our sample tended to focus on the same three points: the fact that Christ was the son of God, the second person of the Trinity; the meaning of the words 'Jesus' and 'Christ'; and the nature of Christ's offices as prophet, priest, and king. The amount of time devoted to each of these points varied from work to work, partly according to the space available and the target group the author had in mind, and partly to his own particular theological interests. There were some potentially large differences of opinion,[58] but these do not need to delay us here.

The authors of most of the elementary forms in the sample found the space to make the point that Christ was the son of God (which was mentioned in the Creed), but did not necessarily devote much time to the fact that he was the second person in the Trinity (which was not).[59] In the first three of Stephen Egerton's forms—a twenty-page catechism, a forty-question summary of it and then a four-question summary of that—Christ's ancestry was handled in three different ways. In the first Egerton referred to 'the eternal son of God and second person in the Trinity, both God and man', in the middling one to Christ as 'the only begotten son of God', and in the briefest he refers simply to Jesus Christ. In his three other short forms, in which he handled slightly different material from the first ones, Egerton in two cases omitted all reference to the relationship between Christ and God, while in the third—his most detailed exposition of the Creed—he made the catechumen say that 'there is one God, and three persons, the father, the son and the Holy Ghost'.[60] Similarly, in the three forms in Keach's *Instructions for children*, the relationship between God, Christ, and the Holy Spirit was not tackled until the last and most advanced, the 'Youth's catechism', and then only briefly; and Isaac Watts moved from a brief mention of Christ's sonship in his opening form, through a reference in his intermediate catechism to father, son, and Holy Ghost being the appointer, procurer, and enabler of our salvation, respectively, to the concept of 'three persons in the Godhead' in his most advanced form.[61]

The more advanced the catechumen he had in mind, the more an author struggled to express the mystery of Christ's relationship to God and the Holy Ghost. Some tried to keep it simple by stating that there was one God but in three persons.[62] However,

---

[58]   e.g. over whether Christ died for 'me and all mankind' or for 'his people': cf. Prayer Book catechism, 780–1; Westminster Larger, 21–2 (answer 44); Marshall, *Catechism*, 55–6, Williams, *Exposition*, 12–13, and Lewis, *Catechism*, 20; Egerton, 'Familiar forme', 33; Ball, *Catechisme*, 72–3; Westminster Shorter, 12–14 (answers 25, 29); for further discussion, see below, Ch. 8.

[59]   e.g. Prayer Book catechism, 780–1.

[60]   Egerton, 'Briefe method', 6; 'Four points', 22; 'Briefe summe', 27; 'Familiar forme', 32.

[61]   Keach, 'Youth', 73, 81; Watts, 'First catechism', 8; id., 'Children's catechism', 25–6; id., 'Assembly's Catechism', 9.

[62]   'Maner to examine children', 152; Ball, *Catechisme*, 69; Elton, *Forme*, sigs. A7ᵛ–8ʳ; Taylor, 'Catechism', 1.

attempts to clarify this could soon become complex or metaphysical: a person in the Trinity is a distinct substance, having the whole godhead in it, wrote Cartwright; one essence, power, and eternity but three persons, was Mayer's version; 'a distinction of persons … a unity of essence or sameness of nature' but 'a difference of offices or operations', was Williams's attempt.[63] Virel spent nearly three pages of one dialogue trying to explain the Trinity, but in the end admitted that at the heart of the matter was a mystery beyond human understanding, which should be taken on faith rather than examined out of curiosity.[64] Yet others, from a wide variety of backgrounds, tried to solve the problem by quoting or paraphrasing the scriptures: What are the personal properties of the three persons in the Godhead?

It is proper to the father to beget the son, and to the son to be begotten of the father, and to the Holy Ghost to proceed from the father and the son from all eternity. (Westminster Larger Catechism)[65]

However, even in some longer catechisms, such as Wake's, a few authors were content at this point merely to stress that Christ was the son of God, and to defer a discussion of the Trinity until one of the later references in the Creed to the Holy Ghost.[66]

At the simplest level, the words 'Jesus' and 'Christ' were often explained by translations or synonyms: saviour, and anointed.[67] Occasionally others were offered, such as 'Emmanuel' and 'Messiah', which though scriptural may have presented as many problems as they solved for the less informed catechumen.[68] In the shorter catechisms, the fact that 'Jesus' meant saviour was stated baldly; only an author like Nowell, writing for older schoolboys and less educated clergy in the 1560s, bothered to explain that 'Jesus in Hebrew signifieth none other than in Greek, SOTER, in Latin, SERVATOR, and in English, a SAVIOUR'.[69] Similarly, the term 'Christ' might occasionally be explained in a technical way, as by Wake: 'He is called "Christ"; which is the same in Greek that MESSIAS is in Hebrew, or Syriac and as much as to say, the "anointed".' He then cited John 1: 41 and 4: 25 in full.[70]

---

[63] Cartwright, 'Catechisme', sig. Aa3ᵛ; Mayer, *Catechisme*, sig. A5ᵛ; and cf. Comber, *Church-catechism*, 9; and Williams, *Exposition*, 10.

[64] Virel, *Treatise*, 6–8, 22.

[65] Westminster Larger Catechism, 5 (answer 10); and cf. Paget, *Questions*, sigs. A5ᵛ–6ʳ; Perkins, *Foundation*, 3; Hieron, *Doctrine*, 577; Ussher, 'Method', 15; and Boughen, *Exposition*, 8–10; Isham, *Catechism*, 11–12.

[66] Wake, *Principles*, 36–9, 56–61.

[67] See following notes, and Westminster Larger, 20–1 (answers 41–2); Marshall, *Catechism*, 55–6; Williams, *Exposition*, 12–13; Lewis, *Catechism*, 20–1. Even where 'Jesus' and 'Christ' were not explicitly equated with 'saviour' and 'anointed' they were often implicitly so, e.g. Elton, *Forme*, sigs. B7ʳ and C1ʳ⁻ᵛ; Palmer, *Endeavour*, 14; Watts, *Assembly's catechism*, 50.

[68] Virel, *Treatise*, 19; Nicholson, *Exposition*, 36; Marshall, *Catechism*, 10; Isham, *Catechism*, 14.

[69] Nowell, *Catechisme*, 151–2; in the original Latin edition, the Greek equivalent was printed in Greek letters, and the English equivalent omitted; also cf. Virel, *Treatise*, 19.

[70] Wake, *Principles*, 31.

It was much more common, however, to state that the term 'Christ' should be understood as referring to his office or offices as saviour, or his being anointed to be a prophet, priest, and king: a majority of the forms in our sample adopted and developed such a threefold account. To cite an early example from an intermediate length catechism, the Heidelberg:

Why is he called Christ, that is, anointed?
Because he is ordained of God the father, and anointed with the Holy Ghost, to be our chief prophet and teacher ... our only high priest ... and our eternal king.[71]

There is an intriguing contrast in the sequence in which the three offices were handled. Calvin, Hammond, and a number of later Stuart episcopalians used a king-priest-prophet sequence,[72] while prophet, priest, and king was preferred by the Heidelberg theologians, a number of early Stuart authors (including Calvinists like Ball, Elton, and the Westminster authors), and a number of non-Calvinist episcopalians like Jeremy Taylor, Richard Sherlock, Thomas Comber, and William Wake.[73] There were other variants too: in Perkins's and Ussher's case, priest-prophet-king; in Cartwright's, priest and king only; in Virel's, king-prophet-priest; and in Keach's, priest, king, and prophet.[74] The presence of both Calvinists and non–Calvinists in the two largest groups suggests that doctrinal controversy was not at the root of this contrast, and since the second sequence was numerically the most common in our sample, we will follow it here.

As a prophet, it was suggested by a variety of thinkers, Christ brought us God's joyful message: he fulfilled all the old prophecies, made known further the will of God, revealed the way to everlasting life, and preached the gospel of the kingdom—faith and repentance.[75] The means used by Christ were held to be both outward—his teaching and preaching—and inward—by the inspiration of his Holy Spirit.[76] Some catechists, like Calvin, Ussher, and the authors of the Westminster Shorter Catechism, said that Christ taught 'us',[77] but a number of authors in the sample preferred to put it that Christ's teaching and instruction were conveyed to 'his church' or 'the

---

[71] Heidelberg Catechism, 317. The originator of the three offices motif may have been Bucer, but it was developed further by Calvin: F. Wendel, *Calvin: The Origins and Development of his Thought*, trans. P. Mairet (1965), 225.

[72] Calvin, *Catechisme*, 15; Hammond, *Practical catechisme*, 5; Sherlock, *Principles*, 10; Williams, *Exposition*, 13; Lewis, *Catechism*, 21.

[73] Ball, *Catechisme*, 73; Elton, *Forme*, sigs. C1ᵛ–3ʳ; Westminster Larger, 20–1 (answer 42); Westminster Shorter, 11 (answer 23); Gouge, *Principles*, 57; id., 'Heads', 3; Taylor, 'Catechism', 3; Sherlock, *Principles*, 10; Comber, *Church-catechism*, 10; Marshall, *Catechism*, 56; Wake, *Principles*, 32.

[74] Perkins, *Foundation*, 4; Ussher, 'Method', 18–19; Cartwright, 'Catechisme', sig. Aa6ʳ; Virel, *Treatise*, 19; Keach, 'Youth', 84–9.

[75] Calvin, *Catechisme*, 15; Virel, *Treatise*, 19–20; Ball, *Catechisme*, 73; Hammond, *Practical catechisme*, 28; Ussher, 'Method', 20; Taylor, 'Catechism', 3.

[76] Virel, *Treatise*, 20; Perkins, *Foundation*, 5; Ball, *Catechisme*, 75; Hammond, *Practical catechisme*, 23, 28.

[77] Calvin, *Catechisme*, 14; Cartwright, 'Catechisme', sig. Aa6ᵛ; Ussher, 'Method', 18–19; Westminster Shorter, 12 (answer 24); Isham, *Catechism*, 14.

church in all ages': the former term was used by both Calvinists like Perkins and Elton, and episcopalians like Hammond, Marshall, Williams, and Lewis, and the latter can be found in the Westminster Larger Catechism.[78] The obvious advantage of specifying the church as the channel of information was that it enabled the clergy to play a crucial role in interpreting Christ's teaching through 'the ministry of the Word'.[79]

As a priest, it was stated, Christ obtained grace and favour for us and reconciles us to God, he works the means of our salvation or redemption.[80] Two other ideas about Christ's priestly office were commonly stated here: that it consisted of offering himself as a sacrifice to satisfy God's anger against man; and his interceding with God on our behalf.[81] The idea of Christ sacrificing himself is mentioned by those in the moderate and orthodox Calvinist tradition and non-Calvinist episcopalians.[82] Protestants found no difficulty in accepting the idea of Christ's sacrifice: it was when it came to a discussion of the sacrament of communion that they found it necessary to stress that Christ had sacrificed himself only once, and that whatever the 'papists' said that sacrifice could not and would not be repeated.[83] The idea of sinful man offering himself as a living sacrifice can also be found in some of these catechisms.[84] Similarly, the idea of Christ as priest interceding with God for man, or in some cases for his elect, occurs in a variety of forms.[85]

In the case of Christ's kingly office, there is more variation in the treatment offered in the sample works. For authors like Calvin, Virel, and Hammond, Christ's kingdom is a spiritual one set up in our hearts, which gives us strength and grace to overcome the devil, sin, flesh, and the world.[86] For others, like Palmer, Gouge, Marshall, Williams, Isham, and Lewis, the kingdom Christ was governing was his church, though whether this was the invisible church (of saints, on earth and in heaven) or the visible church here on earth is not always clear from the context; this was sometimes

---

[78] Perkins, *Foundation*, 5; Elton, *Forme*, sig. C1ᵛ; Westminster Larger, 21 (answer 43); Hammond, *Practical catechisme*, 28; Marshall, *Catechism*, 10; Gouge, *Principles*, 57–8; Gouge, 'Heads', 3; Williams, *Exposition*, 14; Lewis, *Catechism*, 21.

[79] Virel, *Treatise*, 20.

[80] For the first of these formulations, see Calvin, *Catechisme*, 15, and Nowell, *Catechisme*, 153; for the second, Perkins, *Foundation*, 4, Cartwright, 'Catechisme', sig. Aa6ᵛ, Ball, *Catechisme*, 73, Gouge, *Principles*, 59, and id., 'Heads', 3.

[81] As last two notes, and e.g. Hammond, *Practical catechisme*, 20–1.

[82] As previous notes and Westminster Larger, 21–2 (answer 44); Westminster Shorter, 12–13 (answer 25); Keach, 'Youth', 84; Prayer Book Catechism, 789; Taylor, 'Catechism', 3; Isham, *Catechism*, 14; Lewis, *Catechism*, 73; Brightman, *English Rite*, ii. 692–3.

[83] e.g. Perkins, *Foundation*, 4–5; and see below, pp. 546–8.

[84] e.g. Calvin, *Catechisme*, 30; Nowell, *Catechisme*, 157; Heidelberg Catechism, 318; Virel, *Treatise*, 20–1; Hammond, *Practical catechisme*, 314.

[85] Egerton, 'Briefe method', 7, and id., 'Familiar forme', 33; Elton, *Forme*, sig. C2ʳ; Ussher, 'Method', 18; Hammond, *Practical catechisme*, 23. For other references to Christ acting on behalf of his people or the elect, see following notes and below, pp. 368–70.

[86] Calvin, *Catechisme*, 14; Virel, *Treatise*, 20; Hammond, *Practical catechisme*, 15.

clarified later under article nine of the Creed ('the holy catholic church').[87] For yet others, a small group including Ball, Elton, and the authors of the Westminster Larger Catechism, Christ as king gathers and governs his elect,[88] though another Calvinist, James Ussher, drew a distinction between Christ-the-king making redemption effectual for those of his subjects who were elect and Christ-the-king governing *all* those to whom as a prophet he had taught the outward ordinances of the visible church.[89] However, since Jeremy Taylor, a well-known non-Calvinist, could also talk of Christ as king, sitting at God's (metaphorical) right hand and 'comforting and defending his elect', and of God making a new covenant with believers through Christ, it may be seen that what was at issue here was not necessarily the question of whom God has chosen for salvation, but the belief that through his office as king Christ governs those whom he has redeemed and who have faith in him.[90]

The last words of article two of the Creed were 'our lord', but to a large extent this had been tackled under the previous subdivisions of that article: Christ is our lord in that by his filial obedience and sacrifice of himself he has enabled others to become the adopted sons of God; and he is our lord also in that as king, priest, and prophet he has the authority to act as God's representative on our behalf. It has been suggested that in a number of publications by orthodox Calvinists in the late sixteenth and early seventeenth centuries—mainly polemical works, or sermons and handbooks aimed at the better informed laity—there was a trend towards subordinating the centrality of Christ's role to other concerns, such as the divine decrees and whether one was elect or not.[91] However, as far as the catechetical teaching of our sample is concerned, this trend—if it was ever as strong as that—was kept within limits by the fact that most authors felt it necessary to explain who Christ was and why he had come to earth, through a discussion of his sonship and three offices.

The next few articles of the Creed—numbers three to seven—describe Christ's conception, birth, sufferings and death, resurrection, and ascent into heaven. These articles required less by way of definition and more in the way of teasing out the significance of each historical event described. The authors in our sample spent as little

---

[87] Cartwright, 'Catechisme', sig. Aa7ᵛ; Palmer, *Endeavour*, 14; Taylor, 'Catechism', 3; Gouge, *Principles*, 60, and id., 'Heads', 3; Marshall, *Catechism*, 10; Williams, *Exposition*, 14; Isham, *Catechism*, 14; Lewis, *Catechism*, 21; and see below, pp. 326–34.

[88] Ball, *Catechisme*, 74; Elton, *Forme*, sig. C3ʳ; Westminster Larger, 22–3 (answer 45).

[89] Ussher, 'Method', 19.

[90] Taylor, 'Catechism', 3 (two references to elect) and see 4 also, and 16; and cf. Westminster Larger, 14–15 (answers 30–1); Westminster Shorter, 10 (answer 20); and see below, Ch. 9.

[91] Kendall, *English Calvinism*, 8–9 and *passim*. This topic will be raised again more than once in this chapter and the next; see also Cameron, *European Reformation*, 119, and Torrance, *School of Faith*, pp. xvi–xix, xlviii–xlix, liv–lv, lxiv–lxv; and cf. J. B. Torrance, 'Strengths and Weaknesses of the Westminster Theology', in A. I. C. Heron (ed.), *The Westminster Confession in the Church Today* (Edinburgh, 1982), 45.

or as much time developing them as they wished. In the short form appended to Calvin's catechism, this section of the Creed was paraphrased very briefly:

Christ ... came down into this world, and accomplished all things which were necessary for our salvation. And ascended into heaven, where he sitteth at the right hand of the father, that is, that he hath all power in heaven and in earth.[92]

But in his own full-length catechism, Calvin spent an unusually large amount of space on Christ's trial and sufferings, and most expositors of the Prayer Book catechism devoted a few pages to articles three to seven.[93] Three other authors in our sample kept the details of Christ's sacrifice brief in their normal catechisms, but used another opportunity—an exposition in continuous prose in the first two cases and a separate historical catechism in the third—to develop articles three to seven.[94] However, with the exception of the descent into hell, there was virtually no disagreement between Protestant catechists on these articles. We shall therefore pass over them fairly quickly, drawing attention only to a few of the salient features that can be found in more than one catechism.

'Conceived of the Holy Ghost' provided an opportunity, if it had not already been taken, to say who and what the third person of the Trinity is.[95] 'Born of the Virgin Mary' provoked a predictable Protestant balancing act: as the virgin birth was a miracle and as there was scriptural warrant for saying that Mary was the mother of Christ, these facts deserved inclusion in a summary of Christian belief, but under no circumstances should Mary be seen as warranting adoration or be the object of prayer. Why was Christ born of a virgin? asked the actively anti-Catholic episcopalian John Williams in 1689; because this was a sacred birth, it had been prophesied, and it showed God's great power, was the reply.[96] It was also fairly common to stress here, if it had not already been done so under the second article of the Creed, that Christ had had to be both God, in so far as no human could be without sin, and man, in order to satisfy God's anger against the children of Adam.[97] Perhaps to aid students' memories, the different stages of Christ's life were sometimes grouped together as the degrees of Christ's humiliation and exaltation. The former embraced his becoming man, dying, and descent into hell, the latter his rising again, ascent into heaven, and sitting at the (notional) right hand of God. This division had been anticipated in Perkins's treatise on the Creed of 1595, but can be found both in expositions

[92] 'Maner to examine children', 152.

[93] Mayer, *Catechisme*, sigs. A5ᵛ–7ᵛ; Boughen, *Exposition*, 9–21; Marshall, *Catechism*, 11–15, 57–60; Wake, *Principles*, 40–56; Isham, *Catechism*, 17–24.

[94] W. Perkins, *An exposition of the symbole or creed of the apostles* (Cambridge, 1595), 148–397; Taylor, 'An exposition of the Apostles' Creed', in *Symbolon*, 6–14; Watts, 'Historical catechism', 50–7.

[95] See above, pp. 309–10 and below, pp. 324–6.   [96] Williams, *Exposition*, 15–16.

[97] Heidelberg Catechism, 312; Virel, *Treatise*, 15–16, 18; Ball, *Catechisme*, 72–3; Boughen, *Exposition*, 8–12; Ussher, 'Principles', 8; Gouge, *Principles*, 53–5; Marshall, *Catechism*, 10–11, 56–7; Comber, *Church-catechism*, 10; Keach, 'Youth', 81.

of the Prayer Book catechism and in the Westminster catechisms and derivatives of the Shorter form.[98]

What was also very common among the sample catechisms at this stage was to introduce a set of questions asking what 'profit', 'benefit', or 'fruits' the catechumen would receive from Christ's sufferings and death, or what practical lessons or duties he or she could learn from, or what uses make of, Christ's resurrection, ascension, etc. Again this was a ploy that can be found in works by Calvin himself and by a number of his followers as well as by non-Calvinists.[99] These questions were nearly always phrased in the first or second person—'What fruit or profit cometh to *us* by the death of Jesus Christ?', or 'What profit hast *thou* by the rising again of Christ?' and so on, rather than the less personal 'What benefit does mankind derive from this?'[100] The answers were in the appropriate person, and in content they also had much in common: we profit from Christ's passion by our souls' deliverance, for only Christ's blood can deliver us; we benefit from Christ's death by his appeasing of God's anger; we profit from Christ's resurrection by his overcoming death for us and assuring us that we will overcome death too; we benefit from his ascension by his mediating for us, and from his coming again by our salvation.[101]

The lessons or duties that catechumens were told to learn from a consideration of articles three to seven were to mortify the flesh, rise from sin, persevere in good works, and wait for the Lord's coming to judgement.[102] Although this listing of lessons or duties is something we perhaps associate with the 'godly', we find that the future Bishop Nicholson went into great detail in this section, listing five duties to be learnt from Christ's birth (joy, praise, humility, the justice and the necessity of our new birth), nine uses to make of Christ's passion (such as submission, compassion, confession, and mortification of the flesh), four uses of his resurrection, and eight influences on our lives of his ascension and sitting at God's right hand.[103] This elaboration was at the opposite extreme from the simple statement in Isaac Watts's easiest

[98] Perkins, *Exposition of the creed*, '172' [*recte* 173]–174; but see also Mayer, *Catechisme*, sigs. A5ᵛ, A7ʳ; Marshall, *Catechism*, 13, 56–7; Williams, *Exposition*, 12; Lewis, *Catechism*, 22–30; Westminster Larger, 23–9 (answers 46–56); Westminster Shorter, 13–14 (answers 27–8).

[99] Calvin, *Catechisme*, 29–32, 35; Nowell, *Catechisme*, 153–67; Dering–More, *Catechisme*, sigs. B3ʳ⁻ᵛ; Heidelberg Catechism, 317–24; Paget, *Questions*, sigs. C6ʳ–D1ʳ; Perkins, *Foundation*, 5; Ball, *Catechisme*, 73–4; and among the conformists, Hill, *Principles*, sigs. A8ʳ–B1ᵛ; Hammond, *Practical catechisme*, 314–15, 323–5; Nicholson: see next paragraph below; and Wake, *Principles*, 40–51.

[100] Calvin, *Catechisme*, 29; Dering–More, *Catechisme*, sig. B3ᵛ; Nowell in his *Catechisme* used the first-person plural for much of this section, 154–70, but occasionally used 'faithful' or 'godly' instead of 'us', e.g. 160, 169.

[101] Paget, *Questions*, sigs. C7ʳ–8ᵛ; Mayer, *Catechisme*, sig. A6ʳ; Calvin, *Catechisme*, 19; Dering–More, *Catechisme*, sigs. B3ʳ⁻ᵛ; and cf. Westminster Larger, 28–9 (answers 54–5, 57), and Marshall, *Catechism*, 12–15.

[102] Dering–More, *Catechisme*, sigs. B3ʳ–4ʳ; Paget, *Questions*, sigs. C7ᵛ–8ʳ; Hammond, *Practical catechisme*, 313–14, 323–5; Sherlock, *Principles*, 22.

[103] Nicholson, *Exposition*, 41, 43–4, 46–7, 49–50. For Nicholson, these duties and uses were of value not as a means of proving election, but as the products of contemplating Christ's sacrifice for us.

catechism, that Christ came down from heaven to obey God's law and to teach us to obey it also, and that he then ascended into heaven to provide a place for all that serve God and love his son.[104] But Nicholson's form was dedicated to his adult parishioners, whereas Watts's was designed for absolute beginners.

———————

The one article of this section of the Creed that did reveal some open differences of opinion was the doctrine of Christ's descent into hell, which was a problem not just for the English church but for Continental Protestants as well. Indeed, this subject had been problematic since the early days of the Christian church: not only did the phrase 'descended into hell' not appear in most early creeds, it also had not appeared in early forms of the Apostles' Creed itself. This was known in England in the later Middle Ages and repeated by a number of English Protestants in the sixteenth century, though the logical but extreme step of omitting it altogether was considered by very few of them;[105] most authors inside and outside the sample accepted the use of the clause either as hallowed by tradition or warranted by certain passages of scripture, even if it was far from clear what the latter actually meant.[106] As Professor Wallace has shown, the general pattern of doctrinal discussion of this topic in England was of an initial diversity of views, followed by a loose grouping into different camps, some acrimonious confrontations and a measure of polarization in the 1590s and 1600s, before a settling down into a more limited range of views and a generally more tolerant attitude towards those who held different opinions.[107] This pattern also largely fits the views of the authors whose works appear in our sample, though the polemical edge was largely absent.

The two poles between which most of our authors stood were a literal view and a figurative or metaphorical view. The former said that Christ's soul literally descended into hell before his resurrection. However, since Christ had been perfect and did not merit the pains normally associated with hell, there was no good reason for him to have descended there unless it was to fulfil the prophecies, to preach to those who had died before he came to earth, or 'to triumph over Satan in his own quarters'—the harrowing of hell beloved of medieval artists.[108] The figurative view, current in Reformed circles by *c.*1600, denied that Christ's soul had made a spatial

[104] Watts, 'First catechism', 8–9 and id., 'Children's catechism', 16–19.

[105] E. C. S. Gibson, *The Thirty-Nine Articles of the Church of England* (London, 1898), 159–78; D. D. Wallace, 'Puritan and Anglican: The Interpretation of Christ's Descent into Hell in Elizabethan Theology', *Archiv für Reformationgeschichte*, 69 (1978), 251–5, 258, 260, 265, 268–9.

[106] e.g. Luke 23: 43, Acts 2: 24–31, Eph. 4: 9, and 1 Pet. 3: 18, 4: 6.

[107] Wallace, 'Christ's Descent', 255–86.

[108] See the discussion of the accounts of Mayer, Boughen, Hammond, Nicholson, and Sherlock below, and Wallace, 'Christ's Descent', esp. 249–51, 265, 268–9, 273, 279, 284. The quotation is from Hammond, *Practical catechisme*, 316. The risk of triumphalism in the literal view, deriving from the idea of Christ triumphing over Satan in hell, left it open to the charge of supporting Catholic teaching on limbo and purgatory.

descent into a locality called hell but insisted instead that he had experienced the pains of hell while he was still alive, in the garden of Gethsemane and on the cross, as a means of atonement for the sin of man; this view saw Christ's experience of hell as part of his humiliation rather than as a triumph. An obvious objection to this was that in the Apostles' Creed Christ is said to have been 'crucified, dead, and buried' *before* he descended into hell and rose again. One way round this was to say nothing about what happened to Christ between his death and resurrection; another was to separate the pains of hell endured on the cross from the descent by explaining the latter as Christ's coming temporarily under the power of death or to the place of the dead—a form of words that did not necessarily have the connotation of suffering.[109]

Of the works in our sample which tackled the meaning of the phrase, those of Calvin and Nowell are for once at variance. Nowell's catechism, both in the full-length and the condensed version, reflected the literal, triumphal view of Cranmer and other Edwardian or early Elizabethan authors like Ponet, Becon, and Parker: Christ 'in his soul' descended into 'very hell itself', vanquished Satan's power, made the unbelievers there feel their damnation, and comforted the believers with the teaching 'that the work of their redemption was now finished'.[110] Calvin, on the other hand, had stressed that Christ not only suffered 'a natural death' in which body and soul were sundered, but had also endured 'grievous torments, as it were hell-like pains'; by contrast he said little about the location of 'hell'.[111] Dering and More followed Calvin in equating hell with Christ's suffering in the garden and on the cross, and said nothing at all about what happened between Christ's death and resurrection.[112] Similar views have been traced in catechisms outside our sample, especially among some of the 'godly'.[113]

However, other members of the 'godly', including the learned Cambridge academics cited by Wallace were not so sure. Perkins, for example, did not handle the Creed specifically in his catechism, though when he touched on Christ's death in that form, he did sound rather like Calvin.[114] However, from the separate and very long exposition that Perkins later published on the Creed, we can tell that he had doubts about Calvin's view that Christ's hell-like sufferings were on the cross, which contradicted the order in the Creed. His preferred solution was that Christ 'was held captive in the grave, and lay in bondage under death for the space of three days'[115]— a focus on the place of death or the power of death which anticipated the seventeenth-century philological interest in exactly what was meant by the term 'hell', or more

---

[109] See the following accounts by Calvin, More, Westminster Larger Catechism, and Wallace, 'Descent', 252–61, 276, 283.

[110] Nowell, *Catechisme*, 160–1; Nowell, *Institution*, sigs. Dv^v–vi^r.   [111] Calvin, *Catechisme*, 26–30.

[112] Dering–More, *Catechisme*, sig. B3^v.

[113] Wallace, 'Christ's Descent', 262–4; Wallace cites 'Openshaw' on p. 262 and a Latin work by 'Paget' on p. 264, but these are essentially the same work: see Appendix 1.

[114] Wallace, 'Christ's Descent', 267–8; Perkins, *Foundation*, 5.

[115] Perkins, *Exposition*, 302, and cf. 296–303.

specifically the Hebrew 'sheol' and the Greek 'hades': the grave, the state of the dead, or the place of the damned?[116]

There is no sign in our sample of best-selling catechisms of the sharp polemical exchanges of the 1590s and 1600s noted by Professor Wallace, though one of the participants in those debates justified his interventions on the ground that the doctrine was being erroneously handled in catechizing and catechisms.[117] Instead what we find is a move towards tolerating diversity of opinion—a return to the position of Erasmus, and in England of Hooper and the members of the convocation of 1563 who had either warned against speculation on the matter or refused to be too precise.[118] In England the shift is clearly visible in Thomas Rogers's conversion from a Calvin-type view of the descent in the first edition of his exposition of the Thirty-nine Articles in 1585 to a toleration of different views in the second edition in 1607,[119] but the case of John Mayer is also noteworthy. In his full-length catechism (which is not in the sample), he outlined five different interpretations of the clause, including the literal one at first favoured by the Protestant Church of England and taught in Nowell's form, and the figurative one which he himself favoured. But he made it clear that he did not want to press this view on his readers, and in the shortened version of this catechism—which *is* in our sample—he omitted the matter altogether. Mayer's decision in the shorter form to place the descent as the third degree of humiliation does, however, confirm that he was not at the 'triumphal' end of the spectrum.[120]

Henry Hammond devoted eight pages of his dialogue-catechism to a scholarly account of the respective merits of two theories: that Christ made a specific local descent into hell, not to suffer but to triumph over Satan; and that 'for the space of three days he was ... deprived of his natural life' (the latter is largely an examination of the meaning of the words 'hell' and 'hades'). But both at the start and the end of this section he warned against attacking those of a different persuasion: the matter 'may piously be believed on either side', and meekness and charity should be used in handling the point.[121] William Nicholson also listed two views and suggested that 'every man be persuaded, as the arguments produced by either side will persuade him', but he then slightly spoilt the effect of his disclaimer that 'I will not be the arbitrator' by coming down nearer the more literal end of the scale.[122]

A colleague of Hammond and Nicholson, Edward Boughen, took a stronger line. Citing the early councils, the Fathers, the Athanasian Creed, the Edwardian and Elizabethan articles, Calvin's *Institutes*, and Nowell's catechism, he gave five reasons

---

[116] Wallace, 'Christ's Descent', 280–6.
[117] Ibid. 273, 276; Bilson was perhaps thinking of Calvin's form (see p. 317 n. 111 above) and the Heidelberg Catechism (at p. 321), or possibly Nowell's.
[118] Wallace, 'Christ's Descent', 252–3, 256–60; and cf. Schaff, *Creeds*, 159–60.
[119] Wallace, 'Christ's Descent', 264, 279.
[120] J. Mayer, *The English catechisme* (1623), 58–61; id., *Catechisme*, sig. A7ʳ.
[121] Hammond, *Practical catechisme*, 315–23.   [122] Nicholson, *Exposition*, 44.

for preferring a literal, triumphal interpretation to a metaphorical view of the descent.[123] Another episcopalian, Richard Sherlock, who published his exposition of the Prayer Book catechism in 1656, also sided with a local descent and a triumphalist view, though less belligerently than Boughen.[124] Conversely the authors of the Westminster Larger Catechism seemed to side with Calvin's view by stating in one answer that Christ fought 'the powers of darkness' before his death, and then in the next that he continued 'in the state of the dead and under the power of death till the third day', which, they added, 'hath been otherwise expressed in these words, "He descended into hell" '.[125] The authors of the Shorter Catechism, however, avoided the controversy by referring neither to the powers of darkness nor to hell: Christ underwent 'the miseries of this life, the wrath of God, and the cursed death of the cross', then was buried and continued under the power of death for a time.[126] Expositors of this Shorter Catechism, such as Wallis, Gouge, and Vincent also forbore to enlarge on the matter. Gouge's version is distinctly bland: 'Christ humbled himself in his birth, life, death, burial, and lying in the grave'; not a word was said about hell.[127]

In the later seventeenth-century episcopalian catechisms in our sample, the tendency was to favour the view that hell meant death or the place where the dead stayed, though this was stated with varying degrees of authority or confidence. Wake, for example, mentioned three alternative views of the descent before coming down, in a less than categoric fashion, for the second of them: 'I suppose that it must refer to the place whither Christ's soul went in its state of separation.'[128] In short, although the differences between Boughen and the authors of the Westminster Larger Catechism demonstrate that a divide did exist, the philological approach that seems to have triumphed in the seventeenth century meant that many authors stood between these poles. Others, especially in shorter or simplified forms, solved the problem—at least as far as their catechumens were concerned—by simply avoiding the matter altogether.

The word 'faith' does not appear in the Creed (or the other staple formulae of Protestant catechetics), but in many of the works in our sample it was round about this stage

[123] Boughen, *Exposition*, 13–19.   [124] Sherlock, *Principles*, 21.

[125] Westminster Larger, 24–5 (answers 49–50).

[126] Westminster Shorter, 13 (answer 27). It should be noted, however, that after some debate on this point (see Carruthers, *Three Centuries*, 5), a marginal phrase culled from the Larger Catechism to the effect that Christ 'continued in the state of the dead, and under the power of death until the third day', was inserted alongside the text of the Creed in those editions of the Shorter Catechism which had the Creed printed at the end: see above, n. 4.

[127] Wallis, *Explanation*, 12; Vincent, *Catechism*, 68–70; Gouge, *Principles*, 63–7, and id., 'Heads', 3.

[128] Wake, *Principles*, 46–7; and cf. Comber, *Church-catechism*, 11; Marshall, *Catechism*, 13, 58; Williams, *Exposition*, 18; Isham, *Catechism*, 20; Lewis, *Catechism*, 28.

in their exposition—a discussion of Christ's mission—that authors introduced it.[129] The term 'faith' had a number of possible meanings for contemporaries. It could refer to a set of doctrines which a catechumen was supposed to learn—the Christian faith as opposed to the Muslim—as in the reference to 'all the articles of the Christian faith' at the start of the Prayer Book catechism. It could refer to an individual's intellectual and/or emotional acceptance of the truth of those ideas, a mixture of assent and trust, as when Christ urged his disciples to 'have faith in God' (Mark 11: 22). Or it could be used to indicate something much more active, as in fighting the good fight of faith (1 Tim. 4: 12), or the faith that overcomes the world (1 John 5: 4).[130] Faith was usually a mixture of all of these, even if stress was often placed on the idea of faith as confidence or assurance.[131]

The meaning deployed at the most elementary level, and occasionally at more advanced ones too, was that of straightforward belief. In the pre-communion form used in Geneva, the child's 'faith' is summarized in one sentence: 'I believe in God the father, and in Jesus Christ his son, and in the Holy Ghost: and look to be saved by none other means'; in the Prayer Book catechism, there is also a trio of statements of belief paraphrasing the Creed: 'I believe in God the father, who hath made me ... God the son, who hath redeemed me ... [and] God the Holy Ghost, who sanctifieth me'; and in the little child's catechism prepared by the Baptist Benjamin Keach, the catechumen says that if he would be saved by Christ he must believe in him.[132] Only in the first of these three forms was the word 'faith' actually used, and then only after a statement of belief had been elicited. The authors of some longer forms also seem to have preferred 'belief' or to have been quite prepared to use that term for this straightforward type of faith.[133]

Other authors, even of some relatively short forms, however, did expect their charges to grapple with the term 'faith' from a relatively early stage, and to see faith as more than just a bare act of cognition.[134] Rather it was a sure persuasion, an emotional

---

[129] e.g. Perkins, *Foundation*, 1, 5; Virel, *Treatise*, 22; Egerton, 'Forme of examining', 29; Ball, *Catechisme*, 75; Ussher, 'Principles', 8, and id., 'Method', 20; Westminster Larger, 37–9 (answers 71–2). Other favoured points were: at the end of the Creed—Calvin, *Catechisme*, 44, and Heidelberg Catechism, 326–7; after the Decalogue where that had been handled first—Nowell, *Catechisme*, 142–4, Dering–More, *Catechisme*, sig. B1ʳ, and Paget, *Questions*, sigs. C4ᵛ–5ʳ; or at the outset where the Prayer Book catechism mentioned 'the articles of the Christian faith'—Hill, *Principles*, sig. A6ᵛ, Nicholson, *Exposition*, 17–18; and Marshall, *Catechism*, 5–6. Williams and Wake discussed faith at the start of the Creed.

[130] Nowell, *Catechisme*, 142–4, and id., *Institution*, sigs. Ciiᵛ–iiiʳ; Hammond, *Practical catechisme*, 29–30, 306–7; Nicholson, *Exposition*, 17–18.

[131] Cameron, *European Reformation*, 118; and cf. Virel, *Treatise*, 26–7.

[132] 'Maner to examine children', 151–2, but cf. bottom of p. 155; Prayer Book catechism, 780; Keach, 'Little child', 16. See also Ussher, 'Principles', 8; Taylor, 'Catechism', 1, 4–5; Marshall, *Catechism*, 52; and Watts, 'First catechism', 6.

[133] e.g. Nowell, *Catechisme*, 141–2, and id., *Institution*, sig. Ciiʳ; Hammond, *Practical catechisme*, 306–13, but cf. 29–45; Wake, *Principles*, 24–5.

[134] Paget, *Questions*, sig. C4ᵛ; Egerton, 'Briefe method', 8–9, and id., 'Forme of examining', 29; Keach, 'Youth', 83; and Watts, 'Children's catechism', 20–1; and see following notes.

or spiritual conviction as well as an intellectual acknowledgement that God's promises in Christ are absolutely and unfailingly true, and that God *will* be our father and Christ our saviour. For Calvin, faith was 'a sure persuasion and steadfast knowledge of God's tender love towards us … as he hath plainly uttered in his gospel'; for the Heidelberg theologians, true faith was 'not only a certain knowledge' of the truth of God's revelation 'but also a hearty trust' in God's promise of salvation; faith in Christ, wrote Paget, is a full persuasion and steadfast assurance in my heart that all the benefits of Christ's passion are as surely mine as if I had wrought them myself.[135] Comparing the faith of someone living in the light of the Gospel with the faith of Abraham, Hammond wrote that:

The faith which is now required of you, and which God will thus accept to your justification, is a cordial sincere giving up yourself unto God, particularly to Christ, firmly to rely on all his promises, and faithfully to obey all his commands delivered in the Gospel.[136]

This faith was something which was received, not sought: it was often described as a gift of God, or a saving grace 'wrought' in man by the Holy Ghost. Faith, wrote the moderate conformist Mayer in the early 1620s, is a certain persuasion of the heart wrought by the Spirit of God, grounded upon God's promises that all my sins are forgiven in Christ Jesus.[137] 'Faith is a gracious work of the Holy Spirit whereby the heart of man is enabled to assent unto, and rely upon, the word of God's truth, and gospel of man's salvation', said the irenic episcopalian Marshall in the 1670s.[138] What one notices here and elsewhere is that the role of the recipient was described in passive or quiescent terms: faith, according to Ball, is a 'resting' on Christ alone for salvation, or, in Hammond's words, a 'giving up' of the self to God and a 'relying' on his promises.[139] The nonconformist Thomas Gouge summarized these elements when he wrote that faith is a saving grace whereby we receive Christ in all his offices and rest on him for salvation.[140]

There was, however, a more active way of describing justifying faith, as a means by which we 'apprehend' and 'apply' or 'take hold of' Christ and all his benefits. The tendency in this case was to locate faith in the regenerated will as well as, or instead of, in the mind; faith is an act of appropriation of an already known guarantee as well

---

[135] Calvin, *Catechisme*, 44; Heidelberg Catechism, 313; Paget, *Questions*, sig. C4ᵛ; and cf. Egerton, 'Briefe method', 8–9, and id., 'Forme of examining', 29; Nowell, *Catechisme*, 144; Dering–More, *Catechisme*, sig. B1ᵛ; Virel, *Treatise*, 26; Ball, *Catechisme*, 75; Hammond, *Practical catechisme*, 29–37, 39–45, 306–13; Marshall, *Catechism*, 6; Wake, *Principles*, 24–5.

[136] Hammond, *Practical catechisme*, 34; and cf. Wake's 'certain assurance' and 'absolute security': *Principles*, 25.

[137] Mayer, *Catechisme*, sig. D4ᵛ; and cf. Egerton, 'Briefe method', 9; Ball, *Catechisme*, 75, 83–4; Hildersham, 'Doctrine', 80; Elton, *Forme*, sig. C5ʳ; Ussher, 'Method', 21; Westminster Larger, 15, 38–9 (answers 32, 72); Nicholson, *Exposition*, 17.

[138] Marshall, *Catechism*, 6.

[139] As n. 137 above; Ussher, 'Principles', 8 ('receive'); and Hammond, *practical catechisme*, 34.

[140] Gouge, *Principles*, 82.

as, or rather than, a passive acceptance of a free gift.[141] In our sample of catechisms this formulation is found clearly in the forms of Perkins, Cartwright, and Elton, and to a lesser extent in those of John Ball, James Ussher, and the Westminster Assembly.[142] The development of this more active way of describing faith has been associated with changes in the doctrine of assurance to which we will return in the next two chapters: pastors, finding their flocks seeking assurance that they were elect urged their charges to find it by gauging their success and joy in 'apprehending' and 'applying' Christ's benefits to themselves.[143] But for the moment it may be sufficient to note that it is doubtful if this new definition of faith became the predominant one, even during its heyday from the 1580s to the 1610s.[144] Moreover, a variety of authors, both orthodox Calvinists like John Ball and the authors of the Westminster catechisms, as well as more moderate figures like Herbert Palmer, James Ussher, and Thomas Marshall seem to have been ready to adopt both the more passive definition of 'assenting to', 'resting on' or receiving Christ, and the more active 'taking hold of Christ' formulation of faith in their catechisms.[145] A certain amount depended on whether the author was trying to define what true faith was or trying to describe what true faith did. Thus the authors of the Westminster catechisms used the idea of 'assenting' and 'resting' for the former, and then a combination of receiving and applying for the latter.[146] The non-Calvinist Henry Hammond also stressed that the essence of the theological grace of faith was the 'assenting to, or believing the whole word of God', but he later added that belief had two parts: a speculative in the brain, and a practical in the heart (a position close to that of Calvin in his more advanced work). To believe truly, Hammond argued, meant both to assent to the truth of the Creed and to live and behave in a godly manner by 'applying [Christ's] commands to myself'.[147] In short, there may have been a shift towards an active definition of faith in some catechisms, but it was neither a total break with what had gone before nor was it universally adopted.

One final point may be made about the treatment of faith in our sample of catechisms, and that is the development of the doctrine of temporary faith. Faced by the apparent defection of some who had appeared to be good Christians, a number of orthodox Calvinists like Perkins from the 1580s took the idea of different kinds of

---

[141] Kendall, *English Calvinism*, 34, 61–2; Torrance, *School of Faith*, p. xviii; see also A. N. S. Lane, 'Calvin's Doctrine of Assurance', *Vox Evangelica*, 11 (1979), 41–5.

[142] Perkins, *Foundation*, 2, 5; Cartwright, 'Catechisme', sig. Aa7^v; Elton, *Forme*, sig. C5^r; Ball, *Catechisme*, 83–4, 88; Ussher, 'Principles', 8, and id., 'Method', 20; Westminster Larger, 38–9 (answer 73, but cf. 72).

[143] See below, pp. 388–92.

[144] This conclusion is based on the discussion on pp. 387–94 below.

[145] Ball, *Catechisme*, 75, 88–90; Westminster Larger, 15, 34–5, 38–9 (answers 32, 67, and 72, though cf. 73); Westminster Shorter, 14–15, 32 (answers 30–31, 86); Palmer, *Endeavour*, 18; Ussher, 'Principles', 8, and 'Method', 20; Marshall, *Catechism*, 6.

[146] Westminster Larger, 38–9 (answer 72); Kendall, *English Calvinists*, 159, 198, 200–1.

[147] Hammond, *Practical catechisme*, 30, 36, 39, 42, 306–7; Calvin, *Institutes*, III. xvi. 1.

faith to be found in Calvin's writings a stage further than he had done.[148] The authors of the canons of Dort applied the parable of the sower to this problem: those who receive the Word but 'suffer it not to make a lasting impression on their heart' have only 'a temporary faith' which 'soon vanishes', and they then fall away. Others, they said, had a merely historic faith based on the testimony of Scripture, that there was a man called Christ who was the son of God and had been sacrificed for the faithful; but even Satan and the fallen angels could also have this faith, and it too was not of the saving variety.[149] As far as our sample catechisms are concerned, we may note that hardly any authors touched upon the ideas of temporary or historic faith, and that of those who did two, Nicholson and Marshall, were pillars of the Restoration church. The doctrine was not raised in Elizabethan or Jacobean catechisms in our sample, even in those in which one might have expected it to appear, such as those of Calvin, Nowell, Dering and More, Paget, Perkins, Virel, Cartwright, and Elton.[150] Indeed, even in Grosse's predestinarian treatise of 1641, there was mention only of saving faith, though Grosse did point out that the reprobate could be so worked upon by the Law that they could take fourteen steps towards this faith—be troubled in conscience, confess their sins, pray, profess their faith, enjoy part of God's Word, and so on—but that they would never take the further twelve steps which the child of God would take towards true saving faith.[151]

In practice, the idea of different kinds of faith was not too hard for a non-Calvinist to swallow. The contrast between a dead and a lively faith had been drawn in the Edwardian Homily of Faith, and nearly a century later Hammond gave a typically learned disquisition on different kinds of faith. William Nicholson in a work prepared in enforced retirement in 1655 also distinguished between a historical faith ('a bare persuasion of the truth' such as devils have) and justifying faith.[152] Thomas Marshall, in an exposition of the Prayer Book catechism first published in 1679, pointed out that the faith promised in baptism was not historical faith (which the Devil and wicked men may have), nor the faith induced by miracles (which Judas and other 'wicked professors' had), nor temporary faith (which hypocrites had), but the true faith by which the 'gracious work of the Holy Spirit' enabled man to accept and believe the 'gospel of man's salvation'.[153] By faith the authors in our sample always

---

[148] Kendall, *English Calvinism*, 21–4, 67–75.

[149] Schaff, *Creeds*, 589 (third and fourth heads, art. 9).

[150] In his original form, Nowell raised general and dead faith (*Catechisme*, 142–4) but not temporary faith, and in the shortened version of this form, even this reference was omitted; Perkins referred only to different 'measures' of 'true faith': *Foundation*, 6; and Elton to differing degrees of faith among believers, but not to different kinds of faith between elect and non-elect: *Forme*, sigs. C8ʳ–D1ʳ.

[151] Grosse, *Fiery pillar*, 49–50: fourteen was many more than the five steps suggested by Perkins in *Whether a man* (Kendall, *English Calvinism*, 68).

[152] Homily on Faith, part 1: *The Two Books of Homilies Appointed to be Read in Churches*, ed. J. Griffiths (Oxford, 1859), 36–9; Hammond, *Practical catechisme*, 29–40; Nicholson, *Exposition*, 17–18.

[153] Marshall, *Catechism*, 5.

meant saving faith, and the relative silence about other types of faith in our sample of forms suggests that the average catechumen was not expected to worry about them.

In early modern catechisms one finds mention of the Holy Ghost in a number of contexts: as the third person of the Trinity and the conceiver of Christ;[154] as the inspirer of the scriptures on which the Christian faith was based, and the enlightener of those who heard the word preached or read;[155] as the means by which a number of other gifts and graces were communicated to the faithful;[156] and as an active force in the prayers of the faithful and in the strengthening of their faith in the sacraments (and in some authors' view in confirmation as well).[157] The episcopalian William Nicholson listed no fewer than fifteen gifts and graces bestowed by the Holy Ghost on the clergy and the laity at different points of their spiritual lives; while William Wake managed to find seventeen different purposes for which the Holy Ghost was given.[158] If we were to try to classify all the references to the Holy Ghost in all early modern catechisms at whatever stage of the exposition, we would probably find that the role of the Holy Ghost as inspirer of the scriptures and the means by which preaching of the Word was made effective would be among the largest categories.[159] However, in the treatment of article eight of the Creed, the highest common denominator in our sample of works was the enabling and sanctifying role of the Holy Ghost.

Sanctification was another of those words which acquired different meanings; we shall look at some of the more common uses of the term in the next two chapters. At bottom, however, most of these meanings conveyed the idea of the process of inner renewal or purification—of being made more like a saint—experienced by those with saving faith: the old Adam in us is gradually killed, and the new man gradually becomes more like Christ. Man was supposed to play his part in this process, but for him to succeed, even partially, he needed help, and this was where for many authors the Holy Ghost came into his own. The term 'sanctify' was used in this context in the 1549 catechism and its derivatives: 'God the Holy Ghost, who sanctifieth me, and all

---

[154] See above, pp. 309–10, 314; Hill, *Principles*, sigs. A8ʳ, B1ᵛ–2ʳ; Boughen, *Exposition*, 21–4; Comber, *Church-catechism*, 11 and '13' (*recte* 12); Gouge, *Principles*, 15–16, 56–7; Isham, *Catechism*, 24.

[155] Nowell, *Catechisme*, 114; Westminster Larger, 1–3 (answers 2, 4); Cameron, *European Reformation*, 138; Dering–More, *Catechisme*, sig. B5ʳ; Ball, *Catechisme*, 68, 75; Nicholes, *Catechisme*, 4–5; Ussher, 'Method', 21; Westminster Larger, 2–3 (answer 4); Westminster Shorter, 33 (answer 89); Comber, *Church-catechism*, '13' (*recte* 12); Isham, *Catechism*, 24–6; Keach, 'Youth', 97–8.

[156] See pp. 325–6 and 516, 518 below. Calvin, *Catechisme*, 36; Dering–More, *Catechisme*, sig. B4ʳ; Egerton, 'Familiar forme', 33–4; Hammond, *Practical catechisme*, 325–6; Boughen, *Exposition*, 23; Comber, *Church-catechism*, '13' (*recte* 12); Gouge, *Principles*, 53; Marshall, *Catechism*, 16, 61.

[157] Hammond, *Practical catechisme*, 326–9; Keach, 'Youth', 118–19; Watts, 'Children's catechism', 22; (see also Ch. 11 below); Ussher, 'Method', 21; Taylor, 'An exposition of the Apostles' Creed', in *Symbolon*, 10–11; Brightman, *English Rite*, ii. 794–5; Boughen, *Exposition*, 81–3; Nicholson, *Exposition*, 56; Wake, *Principles*, 184; and the section on confirmation added to some editions of Lewis's *Catechism*.

[158] Nicholson, *Exposition*, 56; Wake, *Principles*, 59–61; and cf. Ball, *Catechisme*, 75.

[159] For some examples, see above n. 155.

the elect people of God'.[160] It was also used in Nowell's catechism: 'by him the elect of God and the members of Christ are made holy. For which cause the holy scriptures have called him "the Spirit of sanctification" '. Nowell went on to describe a number of ways in which 'we' are made holy through the Holy Ghost, before concluding that 'whatsoever benefits are given us in Christ, all these we understand, feel, and receive by the work of the Holy Ghost'.[161] The term 'sanctify' was used in a similar way by many other catechists with differing theological opinions,[162] and the idea of the Holy Ghost working specifically on the elect was reflected in the work both of exponents of the Prayer Book catechism like Boughen and Marshall and of a Baptist like Keach.[163]

Although Calvin, Dering and More, and the authors of the Heidelberg and Westminster catechisms did not necessarily use the word 'sanctify', their accounts of the work of the Holy Ghost are very similar to those described in the last paragraph. Through the Holy Ghost, wrote Calvin in his catechism, we are made partakers of God's graces and benefits, our consciences are cleansed, we are made to feel Christ's goodness and see God's benefits; by him, God's grace is sealed in our hearts and we are regenerated and made new creatures. The authors of the Heidelberg Catechism also used the verb 'make': the Holy Ghost 'makes me by a true faith partaker of Christ and all his benefits, comforts me, and shall abide with me forever'.[164] Other authors used verbs like 'seal', 'work', 'imprint', and 'apply' as well as 'make'.[165] Except perhaps in the degree of stress put on the testimony of the Spirit being 'felt',[166] there is for the most part no great difference between those whose views are mentioned in this paragraph and those in the last one: the Holy Ghost makes people holy; he communicates to believers the benefits of Christ's sacrifice for them. There was, however, a potential difference within the circle of 'Calvinist' authors mentioned at the start of this paragraph. In the case of Calvin's catechism and to a lesser extent the Heidelberg Catechism, the stress on the role of the Holy Ghost in working faith was not exceptional in that various other aspects of the Holy Ghost's nature and work were also discussed: as a channel of grace, an illuminator, and a regenerator.[167] But in some other cases, such as the forms of Cartwright, Elton, and some of those based on

---

[160] Prayer Book catechism, 780; for forms deriving from this catechism, see Appendix 2.

[161] Nowell, *Catechisme*, 170–1; and id., *Institution*, sigs. Ei^v–iii^r.

[162] Paget, *Questions*, sigs. A5^r, C5^r, and D1^v; Virel, *Treatise*, 53–4, 62; Egerton, 'Briefe method', 8; Hill, *Principles*, sig. B2^r; Hammond, *Practical catechisme*, 325, 328; Boughen, *Exposition*, 23–4; Sherlock, *Principles*, 22–3; Marshall, *Catechism*, 16, 61; Comber, *Church-catechism*, '13' (*recte* 12) and 15.

[163] Nowell, *Catechisme*, 170; Prayer Book catechism, 780; Boughen, *Exposition*, 23–4; Marshall, *Catechism*, 20, 65–6; Keach, 'Youth', 120.

[164] Calvin, *Catechisme*, 36; Heidelberg Catechism, 324.

[165] Dering–More, *Catechisme*, sig. B4^r; 'Maner to examine children', 152 and cf. 155; Egerton, 'Familiar forme', 33; Westminster Shorter, 15 (answer 31); and cf. Westminster Larger, 30, 38–43, 45 (answers 58–9, 72, 74–7, 80).

[166] e.g. Ball, *Catechisme*, 75; Ussher, 'Method', 21.

[167] Calvin, *Catechisme*, 8, 36–7, 44–5; Heidelberg Catechism, 324–5; and cf. Virel, *Treatise*, 60, 62.

the Westminster catechisms, such as those of Wallis and Gouge, relatively little was said about the Holy Ghost *except* for his role of working faith in the elect. This was presumably because these authors were approaching the subject of the Holy Ghost in the context not of the eighth article of the Creed, but of their account of the effectual calling of the elect as part of God's sovereign plan for the world. For those orthodox Calvinists of the late sixteenth and early seventeenth centuries who built their doctrine of salvation around a fixed *ordo salutis* (pathway to salvation) of effectual calling, justification, sanctification, and glorification, the role of the Holy Ghost was crucial at that point where the elect were called, saving faith was worked in their hearts, and the process of sanctification began.[168] Professor Torrance has suggested that it is a weakness of the the Westminster Confession that it dealt with the Holy Ghost as a rather impersonal agent delivering the blessings of the Gospel. There is, he says, 'a wealth of biblical teaching' on the Holy Ghost which is missing from the Confession, an omission that would have been avoided if the Westminster divines had adopted a Trinitarian pattern for the Confession.[169] The difference was perhaps one of degree rather than substance, certainly if we take the Larger Catechism rather than the Confession into account. But there was a potentially important difference of emphasis between 'Calvinists' here, and as we shall see in the next two chapters it was not the only one.

   The ninth article of the Creed expressed belief in 'the holy catholic church, [and] the communion of saints'. The subject of the church was one that few well-educated and highly motivated Protestant divines were likely to pass by, given their concept of the church and its ministry was in many ways very different from that of their medieval predecessors, and given also that most catechizing probably took place in a church. But a minority of authors in the sample did pass it by. The authors of the Prayer Book catechism and some derivative forms summarized the last section of the Creed as a belief in the sanctifying role of the Holy Ghost among the elect, thus subsuming the operation of the church under that of the Spirit.[170] Others, like Perkins and Elton (who did not use the Creed as part of their structure), raised the subject under one of Christ's offices: Christ as prophet reveals God's will to his church by outward and inward means, or Christ as king exercises spiritual government over his church.[171] Yet others, like Hierom, Ball (in both forms), and the authors of the Westminster Shorter Catechism, all of whom also eschewed the Creed, said virtually nothing about the church or only by implication, for example when making the point

---

[168] Examples of such a stress are Westminster Larger, 30, 34–5, 38–40, 42–3 (answers 58–9, 67, 72, 74, 77); Westminster Shorter, 14–15, 33 (answers 29–31, 89); and Vincent, *Catechism*, 73–6.

[169] J. B. Torrance, 'Strengths and Weaknesses', 53; and cf. Torrance, *School of Faith*, pp. xlii, cxi.

[170] Prayer Book catechism, 780; Sherlock, *Principles*, 19; see above, pp. 301–2.

[171] Perkins, *Foundation*, 5; Elton, *Forme*, sigs. B8ʳ, D6ʳ.

that baptism was the sacrament of admission into the church or that the Word should be heard publicly by one who is 'sent'.[172]

The omission of a discussion of the concept of a 'holy catholic church' was probably due to lack of space in shorter forms, such as Keach and Watts's more elementary forms, and to lack of perceived need among those catechists who did not tackle the Creed line by line, rather than to a hostility to the idea. The very acts of preparing and publishing a catechism, and of catechizing the young and ignorant for a fuller role in the life of the spiritual community, presupposed a commitment to the existence and survival of an organized body of believers, whether it was the national church of 1549 or a gathered congregation such as the ones to which Keach and Watts ministered. In Keach's second catechism, for example, the child refers to what he has heard 'our minister' say; and in his most advanced form Keach offered a definition that contained a number of the features that we shall be examining shortly: the church was a company of believers, incorporated in a holy fellowship, among whom the Word is preached and Christ's ordinances (the sacraments) rightly administered.[173] Of course there were serious differences of opinion between contemporaries over the nature of the church, but before we look at such signs of that debate as there are in our sample, let us look first at the centre of the spectrum where a large number of authors of intermediate or advanced forms appear to have stood.

The church was sometimes defined as the body of Christ,[174] but more commonly as a fellowship or society of believers, a company of faithful Christians.[175] By 'believers' or 'faithful' was meant true believers, those who really feared and trusted God and genuinely hoped for salvation, those who, in the Pauline term favoured by Cartwright, are 'in Christ'.[176] It was commonly stressed that those believers who formed the 'holy catholic church' had been called by God: they were 'chosen', 'ordained', 'incorporated', 'called out from the rest of the world', 'appointed to salvation'.[177] The terms 'elect', 'predestinate', or 'saints' were also used in this context, both by admirers of Calvin and by expositors of the Prayer Book catechism.[178] It was also accepted, however, that among those claiming membership at a given time and place there were

---

[172] Hieron, *Doctrine*, 578–9; Ball, *Catechisme*, 80, and id., *Treatise*, 144, though cf. 162–4; Westminster Shorter, 24, 35 (answers 60, 95), and cf. Torrance, *School of Faith*, 262.

[173] Keach, 'Child', 25; id., 'Youth', 107; E. G. Rupp, *Religion in England 1688–1791* (Oxford, 1986), 132, 152–3; Keach, 'Child', 25.

[174] Nowell, *Catechisme*, 172; Isham, *Catechism*, 26; Lewis, *Catechism*, 2–3.

[175] Calvin, *Catechisme*, 37; Nowell, *Institution*, sig. Dv'; Dering–More, *Catechisme*, sig. B4'; Mayer, *Catechisme*, sig. A7'; Hammond, *Practical catechisme*, 329–30; Boughen, *Exposition*, 25; Comber, *Church-catechism*, '13' (*recte* 12); Keach, 'Youth', 107; Williams, *Exposition*, 22.

[176] Palmer, *Endeavour*, 19; Marshall, *Catechisme*, 16; Isham, *Catechism*, 26; Nowell, *Catechisme*, 171; Cartwright, 'Catechisme', sig. Bb1'.

[177] Calvin, *Catechisme*, 37; Nowell, *Catechisme*, 171, 174; Egerton, 'Familiar forme', 34; Mayer, *Catechisme*, sig. A7'; Isham, *Catechism*, 26; Lewis, *Catechism*, 31.

[178] Nowell and Egerton, as last note; Ussher, 'Method', 19; Hill, *Principles*, sig. B2'; Nicholes, *Catechisme*, 19; Sherlock, *Principles*, 22.

always going to be some hypocrites or half-hearted members; not all of those who said they were Christians would be saved.[179] There was, said Calvin in his catechism, an outward church and an inner church, or to use the labels often used in anti-Catholic polemics but only infrequently in Elizabethan and early Stuart catechisms, there was a visible and an invisible church.[180] In each case, the former—the outer, visible, physical church—embraced not only the truly faithful but also the counterfeiters, whereas the latter—the inner, invisible, spiritual church—constituted the true company of those chosen unto life everlasting, and, to quote Cartwright again, acted as the leaven in the lump.[181] The outer church, said Calvin, can be told by its tokens and sacraments, but the inner is known only to God and cannot be properly discerned by outward signs; Nowell reversed the order but made the same point.[182]

The potentially divisive or exclusive concept of an inner circle of 'chosen' ones was sometimes softened in practice by the way in which it was presented, as in the final clauses of the appropriate section of the Heidelberg Catechism:

What dost thou believe concerning the 'holy catholic church'? That out of the whole human race, from the beginning to the end of the world, the son of God, by his Spirit and Word, gathers, defends, and preserves for himself unto everlasting life, a chosen communion in the unity of the true faith; and that I am, and forever shall remain, a living member of the same.[183]

A similar formula—of which number I am persuaded / I believe that I am one—can be found in the widely-used English catechisms of Nowell, Dering and More, and Paget. Nowell compared the *ecclesia* or congregation of which the apostles wrote to a 'commonweal' or city-state to which all who 'truly fear, honour, and call upon God' belong; he then added: 'By the instinct of [the] divine spirit, I do also most surely persuade myself that I am also, by God's good gift through Christ, freely made one of this blessed city.'[184]

In other cases, authors like Calvin and Hammond avoided possible problems of telling invisible from visible simply by directing their catechumens' attention to what *could* be seen by the human eye, that is the visible church: they urged their catechumens to take full advantage of its privileges, and, like Nowell explicitly and Ussher implicitly, warned them that salvation outside the church was not possible.[185] Those who stayed away from the visible church (and its sacraments) obviously excluded themselves from its privileges, which, as presented in a number of forms such as the

---

[179] Nowell, *Catechisme*, 175–6; Westminster Larger, 31 (answer 61).

[180] Calvin, *Catechisme*, 38; Nowell, *Catechisme*, 173–4; Westminster Larger, 31–4, 46, 48 (answers 61–5, 82, 86). In general, see Cameron, *European Reformation*, 145–7, and on England, Lake, *Moderate Puritans*, 104–5, 115, and id., *Anglicans and Puritans?*, 28, 32–3, 35–6, 161.

[181] As last note: Cartwright's statement is cited by Lake, *Moderate Puritans*, 86, and cf. 80–6.

[182] Calvin, *Catechisme*, 38; Nowell, *Catechisme*, 174.   [183] Heidelberg Catechism, 324–5.

[184] Nowell, *Catechisme*, 171, 174; Dering–More, *Catechisme*, sig. B4ᵛ; Paget, *Questions*, sig. D1ᵛ; and cf. Hill, *Principles*, sig. B2ʳ. In his catechism, Calvin used the first-person plural throughout his section on the church (*Catechisme*, 37–8).

[185] Ibid. 38; Hammond, *Practical catechisme*, 329–30; Nowell, *Catechisme*, 173–4; Ussher, 'Principles', 10, and id., 'Method', 21.

Westminster Larger Catechism, were not inconsiderable. On the other hand, those who attended church but were notorious sinners or heretics not only received no benefits but had to be censured or expelled.[186] As for the rest, a judgement of charity was encouraged: all those who lived in the visible church and gave no contrary proof were to be accepted as members (and as we shall see later had to be admitted to the sacraments).[187] Authors of simpler or simplified forms simply omitted the distinction between the outer and inner facets of the church. Thus, in the pre-communion form used in Calvin's Geneva, articles nine and ten of the Creed were compressed into the assertion that 'the church is sanctified' and its members 'delivered from their sins through the mercies of God'.[188] While the Westminster Larger Catechism treated the subject of the visible and invisible church in a number of questions, the Shorter Catechism did not treat it at all.[189]

The definitive marks of this visible church were usually listed—among those in the sample who tackled this matter—as 'the pure Word of God ... preached, and the sacraments duly ministered according to Christ's ordinance', the norm laid down in the nineteenth article of the Thirty-nine. This was the position of authors as varied as Nowell, Ussher, Boughen, Marshall, Isham, and Keach.[190] There were occasional variations from this: Nowell at two points added prayer to the list, as did the West-minster catechisms implicitly.[191] Nowell also said that order and discipline were, if not essential, highly desirable, though discipline had decayed sadly 'since long time past'. The presbyterian Cartwright and the episcopalian Hammond both added 'censures' to the basic two prerequisites, though the former clearly wanted discipline to be under elders ('governors' who were to see good order kept, manners reformed, and goodness increased in the church) while the other saw it as being by 'bishops and pastors'.[192]

In dealing with the outer forms of church government we are approaching two major sources of polemical disagreement. Did the scriptures provide the basis for a definitive form of church organization (as Beza, Cartwright, and the presbyterians argued), or was the evidence of the scriptures, especially the New Testament, not suf-ficiently full or clear to provide a norm for all ages (as Calvin and Perkins conceded,

---

[186] Calvin, *Catechisme*, 41–2, and cf. T. H. L. Parker, *John Calvin* (1975), 62–3; Nowell, *Catechisme*, 176; Westminster Larger, 31–2, 135 (answers 62–3, 173).

[187] Nicholes, *Catechisme*, 20; Hammond, *Practical catechisme*, 312–13, and cf. 89–92; for Calvin's 'char-itable judgement', see *Institutes*, IV. i. 7–8, and cf. Parker, *Calvin*, 40–1, and on admission to the sacraments below, pp. 549–55.

[188] 'Maner to examine children', 152.

[189] Westminster Larger, 31–4, 46–7 (answers 61–5, 82–3); cf. Westminster Shorter, 16–18 (answers 36–8).

[190] Nowell, *Catechisme*, 174; Ussher, 'Principles', 10–11, and id., 'Method', 21; Boughen, *Exposition*, 25 (where he cites the first paragraph of article nineteen in full); Marshall, *Catechism*, 16; Isham, *Cate-chism*, 26; Keach, 'Youth', 107.

[191] Nowell, *Catechisme*, 174–5; Westminster Larger, 16–17, '110–111' (*recte* 119–20) (answers 35, 153–4); Westminster Shorter, 33 (answer 88).

[192] Nowell, *Catechisme*, 175, 218; Cartwright, 'Catechisme', sig. Bb1ᵛ; Hammond, *Practical catechisme*, 329.

and Whitgift and many English conformists argued)?[193] Secondly, should forms of government emerge from the communal life of the church as a means of edification, or should the church at the outset lay down forms of worship and government within which that life should operate, always allowing for the fact that in the English case those forms had already been fixed under the close supervision of the monarchy, and could perhaps fairly be described as conservative and hierarchical?[194]

However, it must be said that in the case of our sample catechisms, there is hardly any trace of these debates. There is an isolated example of support for a system of elders in Nowell's catechism, but this is placed at the very end during a discussion of how to keep the unworthy from the sacrament rather than during his discussion of the nature of the church; there are the passing references to different forms of discipline by Cartwright and Hammond already mentioned; and there are also occasional references to the importance of tradition or the powers of forgiveness deputed to the clergy, for example by Nowell in the 1560s, Mayer in the 1620s, and Boughen in the 1640s.[195] From the 1640s there was also the occasional defence of aspects of episcopal liturgical practice, or sniping at puritan practice, though not necessarily under the ninth article of the Creed.[196] Two authors, Hammond and Boughen—both writing in the 1640s when the situation of the established church was approaching the desperate—chose to stress what they saw as the apostolic origins of episcopacy and the church established by law. They quoted the statement of belief in the 'catholic and apostolic church' in the Nicene Creed, which was used in the communion service in the Book of Common Prayer. In addition, Hammond called bishops the 'successors of the apostles', while Boughen not only defended as apostolic the power to ordain invested in the English bishops but also attacked the practice of ordination by 'presbyters'. However, he did go on shortly afterwards to state that remission of sins was 'without question' found in all churches in which the word was properly preached and the sacraments duly ministered.[197] The hostile remarks listed here represent almost the sum total of implicitly or even explicitly controversial material under this article of the Creed in our sample of best-selling forms.

What is more, they have to be balanced against a large measure of agreement: on rejecting the claims of the church of Rome to be the one, true church with sole control of the means of communication between God and man; on the marks of the visible church; and (except perhaps in the minds of Keach and Watts) on the importance

---

[193] J. S. Coolidge, *The Pauline Renaissance in England: Puritanism and the Bible* (Oxford, 1970), ch. 1 and pp. 58–60; Lake, *Anglicans and Puritans?*, pp. 3–4 and ch. 1; Parker, *Calvin*, 49, 59; Hammond, *Practical catechisme*, 90–1; Boughen, *Exposition*, 29.

[194] Coolidge, *Pauline Renaissance*, ch. 2; Lake, *Anglicans and Puritans?*, ch. 1.

[195] Nowell, *Catechisme*, 218, 176; Mayer, *Catechisme*, sigs. A8ʳ⁻ᵛ; Boughen, *Exposition*, 25–7, and cf. n. 192 above.

[196] Isham, *Catechism*, 26 added 'by pastors lawfully ordained' to the ministration of the Word and sacraments; and see below, p. 438 n. 94.

[197] Boughen, *Exposition*, 26–7, 29; Hammond, *Practical catechisme*, 90–3, 329–30, 332.

of that church having a regular, full-time ministry, to preach the Word and administer the sacraments, a body of men which was separated from the laity and called by some legally approved method.[198] The relationship of the Protestant church in England to the medieval one and to contemporary churches abroad, the warrant for the Elizabethan and Stuart church polity, the role of Convocation or synods, the extent and distribution of clerical power, and the different responsibilities of church and state were simply not regarded as suitable cases for treatment at the elementary or even the intermediate catechetical levels. Just as the standard catechisms of the established church (the Prayer Book and Nowell forms) and their derivatives did not press episcopacy or the Book of Common Prayer by those names, so the standard presbyterian forms and their derivatives did not press a Genevan polity or the Directory on their catechumens. Even the authors of two of the more cerebral catechisms in our sample—Thomas Cartwright and Henry Hammond—when wearing their catechist's hat largely forebore to score party points about church government and forms of worship, though an examination of their controversial works on these subjects show just how much they could have said and how strongly they felt on these subjects.[199]

The labels 'holy' and 'catholic' applied to the church in the Apostles' Creed were sometimes handled together with the term 'church', sometimes separately. In both cases, however, it was to the core of true believers in the invisible church that the label was applied. Some authors put the focus on these true members of the church as individuals: the church was holy because all true members are sanctified, though in some of these forms it was stressed that these members were not fully sanctified in this world.[200] Others put the focus on the church as a collective unit: the church was called 'holy', wrote Nowell, 'that by this mark it may be discerned from the wicked company of the ungodly'; it was holy in the same way that the Jewish church had been, by being in covenant with God, said the episcopalian Williams.[201] As we shall see in a later chapter, episcopalian catechists seem to have been prepared to adopt both the apostolic succession and the covenanting motif as the historic bases of their church, rather than to have experienced a tension between the two or a change of attitude.[202] The only description which might be described as provocative in the context of 1644 was Hammond's assertion that the church was called 'holy' because its powers and offices,

---

[198] Ussher, 'Method', 21; Hammond, *Practical catechisme*, 325–6, 328–30; Boughen, *Exposition*, 25–6; Comber, *Church-catechism*, '13' (*recte* 12); Marshall, *Catechism*, 16; Isham, *Catechism*, 26; Wake, *Principles*, 61–5.

[199] Lake, *Anglicans and Puritans?*, 13–66; J. W. Packer, *The Tranformation of Anglicanism 1643–1660 (with special reference to Henry Hammond)* (Manchester, 1969), *passim*; J. Spurr, *The Restoration Church of England 1646–1689* (New Haven/London 1991), 138–40, 143.

[200] Hill, *Principles*, sig. B2ʳ; Palmer, *Endeavour*, 19; and cf. Hammond, *Practical catechisme*, 329; and Wake, *Principles*, 65.

[201] Nowell, *Catechisme*, 172; Williams, *Exposition*, 22. Isham adopted both the individual and collective emphases: Isham, *Catechism*, 26–7.

[202] Mayer, *Catechisme*, sig. A7ᵛ; Coolidge, *Pauline Renaissance*, 83; and see below, Ch. 9.

derived from the Holy Ghost, were holy; but the rest of this sentence—on the sanctity of life and increase in holiness that ought to be in all Christian professors in the church—was in line with other authors' comments.[203]

Protestant authors coped with the term 'catholic' easily enough by paraphrasing it as 'universal' or 'in all times and places'. This was the line taken by Calvin and English 'godly' authors,[204] and by expositors of the Prayer Book catechism.[205] Let us take Nowell as an example:

To what purpose dost thou call this church catholic?
It is as much as if I called it universal. For this company, or assembly, of the godly, is not pent up in any certain place or time, but it containeth and compriseth the universal number of the faithful that have lived, and shall live in all places and ages, since the beginning of the world, that there may be one body of the church, as there is one Christ, the only head of the body.[206]

Nowell also took the opportunity, as did others, to contrast the universality of the Christian church with the narrow, racial basis of the Jewish church.[207] Nowell and Wake used a similar argument to condemn the Roman church's claims: by denying that anyone was in the church of Christ unless he 'esteemeth for holy all the decrees and ordinances of the bishop of Rome', and 'by adding afterward the name of one nation', the papists 'abridge and draw into narrow room the universal extent of the church', and were 'herein far madder than the Jews', wrote Nowell.[208] Wake agreed, but went a step further in denouncing the pretensions of 'particular' churches to be *the* Catholic church:

we profess not our faith of any one particular church, which may cease, and fail (such as the Church of England, or Church of Rome); but of the catholic, or universal church of Christ, as that which shall never fail, and to which, alone, the promises of God belong.

The Church of England, he went on, was *a* catholic church, and it was a true part of *the* universal catholic church, whereas 'that of Rome, I doubt will hardly be able to make a good pretension to this title any more than to the other'. As others had said before him, there might be several particular churches but only one catholic one.[209]

There was another potential source of disagreement here. Was everything connected with the church of Rome so infected by its false teaching and antichristian

---

[203] Hammond, *Practical catechisme*, 329.

[204] Calvin, *Catechisme*, 38; Nowell, *Catechisme*, 172; Dering–More, *Catechisme*, sig. B4ᵛ; Paget, *Questions*, sig. D1ᵛ; Palmer, *Endeavour*, 20.

[205] Hill, *Principles*, sig. B2ʳ; Mayer, *Catechisme*, sig. A7ᵛ; Nicholes, *Catechisme*, 19; Hammond, *Practical catechisme*, 329–30; Boughen, *Exposition*, 24, 27–8; Sherlock, *Principles*, 22; Comber, *Church-catechism*, '13' (*recte* 12); Williams, *Exposition*, 22.

[206] Nowell, *Catechisme*, 172–3.

[207] Ibid. 173; and cf. Hammond, *Practical catechisme*, 329; Williams, *Exposition*, 22; and Wake, *Principles*, 64.

[208] Nowell, *Catechisme*, 173; Mayer, *Catechisme*, sigs. A8ʳ⁻ᵛ.

[209] Wake, *Principles*, 63–5, 68–9; and cf. Boughen, *Exposition*, 28; Comber, *Church-catechism*, '13' (*recte* 12); Williams, *Exposition*, 23.

ambition that it had to be discarded, or had that church, though seriously flawed, retained some claim to be a part of the universal church? Of the authors just cited, Nowell's hostility suggests that he was probably well to the left of centre on the spectrum of English opinion on this matter, while Wake's liberal caution put him near the middle, with Hammond and Boughen perhaps a little to his right. If there *were* any authors who believed that the church of Rome as a whole was a part of the universal church, or who thought that the pope might not be the Antichrist after all, they did not say it in any of the catechisms in this sample. Indeed, no one in our sample of best-sellers ever said that the pope *was* the Antichrist! And if there were any who thought that some chosen individuals within the medieval church might have been part of the universal church, they did not say so explicitly.[210]

The depiction of Christ as the head of the church and the metaphor of believers being the body of Christ were very common in the middling and longer catechisms throughout the early modern period. A number of these statements tried not only to stress the closeness but also the union or communion between Christ, as head, and the faithful, as members. Right believers were knit together in one body under Christ, whose blood had been shed to purchase the creation of the universal church; there was no life if a member became separated from the body of Christ.[211] In the church all true members had union and communion with Christ, through the 'secret impressions' of the Holy Ghost, wrote Sherlock in his exposition of the Prayer Book form in 1656.[212] There was a risk in the use of these images of conflating the invisible church of true believers with a visible church of outward professors, a trap into which Cartwright and the puritans were often accused of falling during the polemical debates of the Elizabethan and Jacobean periods.[213] Perhaps the nearest one of the authors in our sample came to this was in the more advanced of the two forms that Ussher wrote as a young man but did not publish until 1644. Ussher devoted half a page to the idea of the elect 'being ingrafted' by grace into the church—the 'body and spouse of Christ'—and of their growing up into 'one mystical body, whereof he is the head'. But he also made it clear that there was a distinction between the participation in the grace of Christ communicated by the Holy Ghost to 'the catholic church'—the invisible, inner church of the chosen—and the outward means given to 'the visible churches' to offer and effect the same.[214] Most authors, in fact, seem to have been able

---

[210] Any comments about Rome were uniformly hostile: Dering–More, *Catechisme*; sig. B4ᵛ; Mayer, *Catechisme*, sig. A7ᵛ; Hammond, *Practical catechisme*, 90–2; Williams, *Exposition*, 22; and see below, pp. 425–6, 431–3, 437.

[211] Calvin, *Catechisme*, 38; Elton, *Forme*, sig. B8ʳ; Boughen, *Exposition*, 28–9; Williams, *Exposition*, 3, 22. The simile of the faithful being, as the branches of the vine, fruitful only when they 'abide in the vine' (John 15: 1–8) was rarely used, perhaps because the vine was a less familiar sight in England.

[212] Sherlock, *Principles*, 22–3; and cf. Nowell, *Catechisme*, 170–1, 174; Ussher, 'Method', 19; and Hammond, *Practical catechisme*, 328–30.

[213] Lake, *Anglicans and Puritans?*, 28–37, 40–2, 48–53, 61–2, 126–7, 160–2.

[214] Ussher, 'Method', 19; at this stage of his catechism, the outer church interested Ussher less than the inner.

to keep in mind and present to their pupils a clear distinction between the particular 'church' in which professors met to hear sermons, worship, and communicate, and the universal 'church' in which the whole company of true believers in all ages and places were united into one body under Christ their head.[215]

The second half of article nine was 'the communion of saints'. For Roman Catholics this was a potent phrase: a reference to the links which they believed their church had with the saints in heaven, and of the benefits which sinners here below could derive from intercession with the saints and the Virgin Mary.[216] For Protestants, the phrase was also powerful, and to judge from our sample there was a broad measure of agreement as to what catechumens should understand by it. The words most commonly used to paraphrase 'communion' were 'fellowship' or 'society'; while the term 'saint' was equated with 'faithful persons', 'faithful people', and 'believers', or in Jeremy Taylor's case with those 'predestinated by God to be made conformable to the image of his son'.[217] 'Saints is a word of that large extent, that it takes in them that are glorified in heaven, and those who are in some degree sanctified on earth,' wrote Nicholson in 1655; in the New Testament, all Christians are called 'saints', wrote Wake in 1699 (like Taylor, citing several texts to support his case), but by saints 'we are most properly to understand such as answer the end of their calling, by a lively faith, and a holy conversation, in which two, the gospel saintship does consist'.[218]

On the 'communion' of the saints, the position of Nowell was that it referred to 'a community of spirit, of faith, of sacraments, of prayers ... and, finally all the benefits that God giveth his church through Christ'. This communion was experienced both between the godly and God and among the godly themselves; but since 'this communion of saints cannot be perceived by our senses ... as other civil communities and fellowships of men may be', it was a matter of belief rather than demonstration.[219] Nowell's account shows him to have been in a mild dilemma: the communion is between the 'saints', that is the elect or true believers who are invisible, since only God knows for certain who they are; but some of the mechanisms through which this fellowship operated were the outer forms adopted by the visible church, such as sacraments and public prayer, channels which might have to be shared with the non-elect. One can find in our sample catechisms a slight difference of emphasis between

---

[215] Comber, *Church-catechism*, '13' (*recte* 12); Wake, *Principles*, 63–5.

[216] J. A. Bossy, *Christianity and the West 1400–1700* (Oxford, 1985), 8–13, 17–18, 22–3; E. Duffy, *The Stripping of the Altars: Traditional Religion in England c.1400–c.1580* (New Haven/London, 1992), ch. 5.

[217] Calvin, *Catechisme*, 37; Dering–More, *Catechisme*, sig. B4ᵛ; Paget, *Questions*, sig. D1ᵛ; and Mayer, *Catechisme*, sig. B1ʳ; Heidelberg Catechism, 325; Taylor, 'Exposition', in *Symbolon*, 12.

[218] Nicholson, *Exposition*, 61; Wake, *Principles*, 66; and cf. Palmer, *Endeavour*, 19; Williams, *Exposition*, 23 (saints are 'in a large sense' visible members of Christ's church); and Lewis, *Catechisme*, 32; but contrast Boughen, *Exposition*, 24–5 (saints are sanctified in baptism).

[219] Nowell, *Catechisme*, 174.

those who wished to stress the invisible, almost mystical fellowship of the saints with one another, and those who also emphasized the outward forms that this might take—sorrowing, praying and praising God, spiritual love to other Christians, charity, liberality, and other forms of piety. However, this difference was not always along predictable lines.

It is perhaps not surprising to find the 'godly' Dering and More and Paget among the former group, stressing the spiritual fellowship of the elect with God or Christ and with each other,[220] or to find various conformists among those stressing—in most cases in addition—the intercommunion of believers through the 'offices of piety and charity' and the 'ordinances of the gospel'.[221] To quote Wake again:

all the true members of Christ's church have a right of fellowship ... with God the father, and our lord Jesus Christ; as they are received into covenant by the one, through the death and passion of the other ... they have a fellowship with the Holy Ghost ... and ... the holy angels ... they all have a fellowship with one another, as members of the same mystical body of Christ ... they ought, as living members, to have a fellowship of love and charity also towards each other. And lastly ... they have a right of communicating in all the ordinances of the gospel: in the prayers of the church; in the ministry of the word and sacraments.[222]

The belated mention of the sacraments is not untypical: virtually no authors gave them particular prominence in this context.[223]

While it was relatively predictable that leading conformist churchmen should adopt the view of intercommunion through the church, it is at first sight more surprising to find that the former group—those stressing that the communion of the elect was spiritual—also included expositors of the Prayer Book catechism like Hill and Nicholes,[224] while the latter group—those who mentioned both inward spirituality and outward actions—included the authors of the Westminster Larger Catechism and, at least implicitly, the Baptist Keach whose definition of the church was cited earlier.[225] There is in fact a curious inversion between Nicholes and the Westminster theologians. In the exposition of the Prayer Book form which he published in 1631, Martin Nicholes placed 'the communion of saints' along with the 'forgiveness of sins' among the privileges of true members of the church, that is, of the hidden inner company of the elect; but a few years later, the authors of the Westminster Larger Catechism placed the 'communion of saints' quite firmly among the benefits enjoyed by those in the visible church, and from the context it seems clear that this

---

[220] Dering–More, *Catechisme*, sig. B4ᵛ; Paget, *Questions*, sig. D2ʳ.

[221] Mayer, *Catechisme*, sig. B1ʳ; Hammond, *Practical catechisme*, 329–32; Taylor, 'An exposition of the Apostles' Creed', in *Symbolon*, 12; Nicholson, *Exposition*, 61–3; Comber, *Church-catechism*, '12' (*recte* 13), and cf. 31–2; Isham, *Catechism*, 26; Wake, *Principles*, 66–9.

[222] Ibid. 66–7.

[223] Not even Bradshaw, 'Brief forme', or Hildersham, 'Doctrine', though cf. the latter at 12–13, 41.

[224] Nowell, *Catechisme*, 173–5; Hammond, *Practical catechisme*, 328–32; Wake, *Principles*, 67; Hill, *Principles*, sig. B2ʳ; Nicholes, *Catechisme*, 20.

[225] Westminster Larger, 32–4 (answers 62, 65); Keach, 'Youth', 92–7, 107–8, 111–12.

fellowship was envisaged as being among all those who professed Christianity, even though some might be unregenerate.[226]

This inversion is perhaps symptomatic of the difficulties that pastors may have found in coping with the distinction between visible and invisible. But despite the occasional difference of emphasis or difficulty of expression, most catechists seem to have had a genuine basis of agreement in the teaching that those with a living faith were in fellowship with one another as members of Christ's church.[227] Most, perhaps all, could have accepted the formulation of the authors of the Heidelberg Catechism:

What dost thou understand by the 'communion of saints'?
First, that believers, all and every one, as members of Christ, have part in him and in all his treasures and gifts. Secondly, that each one must feel himself bound to use his gifts, readily and cheerfully, for the advantage and welfare of other members.[228]

The tenth article—'the forgiveness of sins'—was in itself not controversial; once again such differences as there were were mainly of emphasis or context. God's 'forgiveness' was generally explained as being his merciful decision to refrain from exacting the full punishment that men's sins deserved; the word 'remission'—used in English translations of the Athanasian Creed—was often deployed to explain forgiveness or even substituted for it, for example by Calvin, Hammond, and various Prayer Book catechism expositors.[229] The concept of 'sin' as any transgression against God's law had usually been explained before this stage, under the Fall or Christ's mission, or in the case of the 1549 form the baptismal vows; but some authors reminded catechumens of both the nature of sin and the dreadful consequences it merited.[230]

As to the meaning of the phrase as a whole, there were four areas of consensus. It was commonly stated throughout our period that 'forgiveness of sins' meant that since I am a believer my sins will not be laid to my charge.[231] Occasionally the technical term 'imputed' was used—for Christ's sake, my sins are not imputed to me;[232] but more commonly a number of legalistic terms were used to describe the process of

---

[226] Nicholes, *Catechisme*, 19–22; Westminster Larger, 32–3 (answer 63).

[227] Nowell, *Catechisme*, 171–5; Dering–More, *Catechisme*, sig. B4ᵛ; Mayer, *Catechisme*, sigs. A7ᵛ–8ʳ, A8ᵛ–B1ʳ; Nicholes, *Catechisme*, 20 (at this point Nicholes conceded that all in the visible church who had not shown they were not sanctified should be reputed members); Comber, *Church-catechism*, '13' and '12' (= 12–13); Sherlock, *Principles*, 22–3; and Isham, *Catechism*, 26–7.

[228] Heidelberg Catechism, 325.

[229] Calvin, *Catechisme*, 40; Hill, *Principles*, sig. C7ᵛ; Ussher, 'Method', 19; Hammond, *Practical catechisme*, 333; Nicholson, *Exposition*, 63; Sherlock, *Principles*, 23; Comber, *Church-catechism* '12' (recte 13).

[230] Marshall, *Catechism*, 17–18, 62–3; Williams, *Exposition*, 24; Keach, 'Child', 24; Wake, *Principles*, 69; Lewis, *Catechism*, 33.

[231] Dering–More, *Catechisme*, sig. B4ᵛ; Paget, *Questions*, sig. D2ᵛ; Hill, *Principles*, sig. B2ʳ; Lewis, *Catechism*, 34.

[232] e.g. Nowell, *Catechisme*, 143; Bernard, *Common catechisme*, sig. C2ᵛ; Williams, *Exposition*, 24; Lewis, *Catechism*, 34. For the idea of Christ's righteousness being imputed to sinners, see below, pp. 398–400.

forgiveness: the faithful are discharged, pardoned, delivered from judgement, given remission, acquitted, freely forgiven, their transgressions and the appropriate penalties are overlooked.[233] Nicholson stressed the punishment that every transgression of God's law merited, but in a magnificent extended simile, lasting several paragraphs, of a prisoner before the bar, he wrote of the guilty prisoner being released, acquitted, and discharged 'in respect of that relation in which we stand unto Christ (he and all his elect being taken for one body)', and of the divine judge being

pleased to remove out of his court of justice, and sit down in his seat of mercy, and there pronounce a sentence of absolution, instead of a condemnation, acknowledging the plea to be just, which the faithful and penitent sinner puts in: viz that his only son 'blotted out the handwriting or ordinances that was against us' [Col. 2: 14].[234]

The second area of agreement was that the reason for this was all to do with Christ, and nothing to do with man. Nothing that man had done, or could do, would merit an easing of God's sentence on sinners; it was only because Christ, as man, had suffered the full penalty of the sins of mankind that God would remit other men's punishments 'through the merits, and mediation of Jesus Christ our saviour'.[235] Our sins are 'fully remitted by the blood of Christ', wrote Taylor; we 'are not justified by the righteousness of works, but by the righteousness of faith'.[236] The teaching that we are forgiven for Christ's sake only, not our own, was usually reinforced by the same catechists' treatment of the fifth petition of the Lord's Prayer—'forgive us our trespasses'.[237]

Thirdly, there was a broad element of agreement that only those in the church would have their sins forgiven. This was stated baldly by some: no man can receive forgiveness of sins unless he is incorporated into the fellowship of God's church, wrote Calvin; outside it there was nothing but 'hell, death, and damnation', he warned trouble-makers and sectaries. Nowell agreed, and went on to define a true member: 'such a one as does ... earnestly, godlily, holily, yea and continuingly and to the end embrace and maintain the common fellowship of the church'.[238] Others, like Sherlock,

---

[233] Calvin, *Catechisme*, 40; Nowell, *Catechisme*, 176; Nowell, *Institution*, sigs. Evi^r–viii^r; Dering–More, *Catechisme*, sig. B4^v; Ball, *Catechisme*, 74; Hill, *Principles*, sig. B2^r; Mayer, *Catechisme*, sig. B1^r; Ussher, 'Principles', 8, and id., 'Method', 19; Taylor, 'An exposition of the Apostles', Creed', in *Symbolon*, 12.

[234] Nicholson, *Exposition*, 63–7. Wake wrote of God washing away the stain of sin by 'his sanctifying grace', *Principles*, 69; on the role of grace, see also Mayer, *Catechisme*, sig. B1^r; Westminster Larger, 69–70 (answer 70); and Taylor, 'An exposition of the Apostles' Creed', in *Symbolon*, 12.

[235] Calvin, *Catechisme*, 40, 49–50; Nowell, *Catechisme*, 176–7; Westminster Larger, 69–70 (answer 70); Sherlock, *Principles*, 25; Wake, *Principles*, 69; Lewis, *Catechism*, 34.

[236] Taylor, 'An exposition of the Apostles' Creed', in *Symbolon*, 12; cf. Heidelberg Catechism, 326–7.

[237] Calvin, *Catechisme*, 113–17; Nowell, *Catechisme*, 199–200; Dering–More, *Catechisme*, sig. B7^r; Paget, *Questions*, sig. E3^r; Ball, *Catechisme*, 78; Hill, *Principles*, sig. C7^v; Nicholes, *Catechisme*, 57–8; Hammond, *Practical catechisme*, 237, 333; Westminster Larger, 153–4 (answer 194); Westminster Shorter, 38–9 (answer 105); Comber, *Church-catechism*, 24–5; Vincent, *Catechism*, 253–4.

[238] Calvin, *Catechisme*, 41; Nowell, *Catechisme*, 176, and id., *Institution*, sig. Evi^v; and cf. Boughen, *Exposition*, 28–9, Nicholson, *Exposition*, 63, and next note below.

described 'forgiveness of sins' as one of the means by which sanctification was 'wrought by the Holy Ghost upon the church or people of Christ' in this life (the other means in this life was the 'communion of saints', and in the next 'the resurrection of the body' and 'the life everlasting'). He was followed by various other episcopalians who also described 'forgiveness' as one of the four benefits or privileges of being in the church (the other three again corresponded to articles nine, eleven, and twelve of the Creed).[239] Yet other authors, such as the authors of the Westminster Larger Catechism, treated forgiveness of sins under justification which itself was described as being part of the union and communion which the members of the invisible church enjoyed with Christ.[240] In some cases the connection between forgiveness and church membership was not stated explicitly, for example in the Heidelberg Catechism, the Westminster Shorter Catechism, and Watts's first two forms, though in the first two cases at least the context was collective or the use of the first-person plural in the catechumen's answers tended to make the same point.[241] There was a potential difference of emphasis here, but as long as most catechumens operated through organized churches, its consequences were probably in practice not serious.

The fourth area of general agreement was that not everyone's sins were forgiven: God forgives the sins of believers, the faithful, the elect.[242] There was, however, a difference of emphasis and context. For Calvin, Nowell, and a number of later Stuart episcopalians who handled forgiveness mainly under the tenth article of the Creed, the equation between forgiveness and belief was stated in the form of God forgiving the sins of those who believe in him. The faithful obtain discharge for their sins for Christ's sake; forgiveness was for all those who truly repent and unfeignedly believe his holy gospel, for the penitent believer.[243] On the other hand, those authors who did not tackle the Creed article by article but treated forgiveness either under their doctrine of Christ or faith in Christ, as Perkins and Ball did, or under justification in a high Calvinist *ordo salutis*, as the Westminster theologians did, were likely to place a greater stress on Christ's merits as the basis of men escaping the penalty of their sins, and say less about the faith of those whose sins were forgiven.[244] This contrast was

---

[239] Sherlock, *Principles*, 23; Marshall, *Catechism*, 17, 62; Comber, *Church-catechism*, '12' (*recte* 13); Williams, *Exposition*, 23–4; Wake, *Principles*, 69–70; Lewis, *Catechism*, 31. Marshall and Isham said that forgiveness was sealed in baptism: see below, Ch. 12.

[240] Westminster Larger, 36–7, 33–4 (answers 70, 65).

[241] Heidelberg Catechism, 325; Westminster Shorter, 14–16 (answers 29, 33); Vincent, *Catechism*, 93–5.

[242] Calvin, *Catechisme*, 40; Nowell, *Catechisme*, 176; Egerton, 'Briefe method', 7; Elton, *Forme*, sigs. C8r–v; Palmer, *Endeavour*, 21; Westminster Larger, 36–7 (answer 70); Comber, *Church-catechism*, '12' (*recte* 13).

[243] Calvin, *Catechisme*, 40; Nowell, *Catechisme*, 176–7; Boughen, *Exposition*, 29–30, citing the absolution used in Morning and Evening Prayer: Brightman, *English Rite*, i. 133, 157; Wallis, *Explanation*, 17; Sherlock, *Principles*, 23; and Isham, *Catechism*, 28.

[244] Perkins, *Foundation*, 4–6; Egerton, 'Briefe method', 7–8; Ball, *Catechisme*, 72–5; Ussher, 'Principles', 7–8, and id., 'Method', 18–19; Westminster Larger, 36–7 (answer 70); Westminster Shorter, 15–16 (answer 33).

partly a matter of different contexts: in article ten of the Creed the individual was articulating belief in the remission of sins as part of a wider statement of faith in God's promises; on the other hand, a Christological or soteriological context naturally led to an emphasis on the merits of Christ as the source of salvation. But behind this lay a more serious disagreement about the wider issue of salvation: on the one side, there was the view that only those who, enabled by grace, respond to the divine offer of salvation by repentance and faith would have their sins forgiven; on the other, there was the view that only those predestined to be saved would have their sins forgiven. Those who held to the former, mainly non-Calvinist episcopalians like Hammond, Comber, Williams, and Wake, but also nonconformists like Gouge, Keach, and Watts, tended to stress that the promise of forgiveness on God's part was a free one but had to be matched by faith and repentance on man's side.[245] Those who held to the latter, mainly orthodox Calvinists, argued that those who by a divine decree had been foreordained to salvation would necessarily obtain pardon of sins, faith, and repentance.[246]

There was a potentially serious division of opinion here, which we shall examine at greater length in Chapter 9. But at this point it is worth pointing out that the way in which forgiveness was presented in our sample catechisms did not highlight this rift. The translation of Calvin's explanation of the tenth article of the Creed in his 1541 catechism states that 'God doth freely forgive all the sins of them which believe in him', a formulation which can be taken either in a conditional sense—you have to be a believer to be pardoned—or an unconditional one—true believers, being predestined to salvation, are forgiven. In the section immediately following the Creed, Calvin made another remark that would have been quite acceptable to non-Calvinists: 'even as God doth present and offer this righteousness freely unto us in his gospel, even so the only mean or way to receive that excellent gift of God, is faith'.[247] Nowell, another double predestinarian, put it in the form that by forgiveness 'the faithful do obtain at God's hand discharge of their fault and pardon of their offence'. (It may be noted that though he sometimes used the characteristic double predestinarian term—the 'elect'—he relied here instead on 'faithful'.) Having stressed that this was entirely due to Christ and not to the merit of any 'godly, dutiful doings' of our own, Nowell then asked the rhetorical question: 'Is there nothing at all to be done on our behalf, that we may obtain forgiveness of sins?' His answer included confession of sins,[248] repentance, and amendment. Nowell seems to have been trying to balance the unconditional side of forgiveness—for Christ's sake alone, the faithful are pardoned—with

---

[245] Hammond, *Practical catechisme*, 333–4; Comber, *Church-catechism*, '12' (*recte* 13); Williams, *Exposition*, 24; Wake, *Principles*, 69–70; Gouge, *Principles*, 72–4; Vincent, *Catechism*, 94; Keach, 'Little child', 16; id., 'Child', 25–6; id., 'Youth', 83; Watts, 'First catechism', 8–9, and id., 'Children's catechism', 18–23.

[246] Ball, *Treatise*, 75, 92–3; Grosse, *Fiery pillar*, chs. 4, 5; Westminster Larger, 34–42 (answers 67–76).

[247] Calvin, *Catechisme*, 40, 48.

[248] Though it was not specified that this had to be to a priest; on this see Boughen, *Exposition*, 65; Isham, *Catechism*, 28; and Wake, *Principles*, 70–1, though cf. 15.

a conditional or consequential element—only the faithful are pardoned, but rather than lie back supine when they have sinned (again), there are certain things that they must do.[249]

Other authors of a similar persuasion to Calvin and Nowell, such as Dering and More, Paget, and Bernard, or of a rather different persuasion, such as Mayer and Hill, side-stepped the issue by using the first-person singular or plural in their expositions of this article: I/we believe that all my/our sins are freely forgiven in Christ. In these cases, the faith of the individual catechumens was implicit in the form in which they were manœuvred into stating their belief in the forgiveness of sins.[250] A conservative like Nicholson in his exposition of article ten can be found citing a text that was also used by double predestinarians—Jesus 'shall save his people from their sins' (Matt. 1: 21); while another non-Calvinist, Hammond, who argued that man could not bring about justification but that there were certain necessary concomitants of it, such as faith and repentance, did so in the context of a conditional covenant of grace, under which God in and through Christ promised salvation to those with a lively faith and true repentance.[251] This conditional covenant was a framework which, as we shall see later, was adopted by a wide range of authors including a number of predestinarian as well as non-predestinarian thinkers in their practical writings.[252] The message that was being put across in the different ways described in the last few paragraphs was that faith does not bring about forgiveness—only Christ can do that—but there is no forgiveness without faith.[253]

The subject of justification has now cropped up twice in this chapter—when looking at saving faith, and at forgiveness—and will recur in the next two chapters. However, despite the importance of the doctrine of justification by faith in mainstream Protestant teaching, not least for its practical consequences in cutting the ground from under many of the old popular religious attitudes and practices, it did not receive a disproportionate amount of space at catechetical level. 'Justification' was another term, like faith, which did not occur in the staple formulae that formed the backbone of most catechisms, and as a result was not discussed in a number of those forms, or at least not under that name. Indeed, in a slight majority of forms in our sample, justification was either not treated at all by that name or accorded only a single question and answer. In other cases it was mentioned, but different authors had different views on it or raised it at different points of their exposition. The term was not used at all in a number of the shortest or more elementary forms, such as the Prayer Book and Heidelberg Catechisms, or in expositions based on them; instead

---

[249] Nowell, *Catechisme*, 176–7, and cf. 120, 143–4, 179, 182, 199–200, and id., *Institution*, sigs. Evi[r]–Fiv[r].

[250] Dering–More, *Catechisme*, sig. B4[v]; Paget, *Questions*, sigs. D2[r–v]; Bernard, *Common catechisme*, sig. C2[v]; Mayer, *Catechisme*, sig. B1[r]; Hill, *Principles*, sig. B2[r].

[251] Nicholson, *Exposition*, 63; Hammond, *Practical catechisme*, 333—a cross-reference to ibid. 4–7, 9–10.

[252] See below, Ch. 9.   [253] Heidelberg Catechism, 326–7.

Christ was said to be our redemption, salvation, or righteousness.[254] The use of but one question and answer on justification was the case in works by Paget and Egerton and in the Westminster Shorter Catechism and some of its derivatives.[255] We will defer further consideration of the differences of opinion on justification until a later chapter,[256] but may briefly speculate here as to why most authors either did not use the term explicitly or used it only occasionally in their forms.

The simplest explanation would be a collective shift of theological emphasis—towards experimental predestinarianism, or federalism, or 'moralism'—any of which might have turned our authors' attentions away from the totally gratuitous nature of God's accounting us righteous through Christ and towards efforts by man to test or prove that his faith was a justifying one. As an explanation, this does not fit very happily with what most of them wrote most at the time, as we have already seen and will see again in the following chapters. An alternative is to consider the problems faced and limitations imposed by trying to compose a catechism at that date. One such problem may have been that justification was regarded as a difficult concept for beginners to grasp. It was perhaps thought easier to stress the simpler message that we have encountered in the Prayer Book catechism and Paget's form—God created me, Christ redeemed me, and the Holy Ghost sanctifies me—or in the pre-communion form published with Calvin's catechism, and the shortest forms of Keach and Watts—Christ came to redeem me, and if I believe in him my sins will be pardoned and I will be saved. Redeemer, saviour, our righteousness—these were relatively simple terms compared to those used in the scholastic debates on justification.[257] Another, partly overlapping, reason was that many, if not all, of the basic ingredients of justification were handled elsewhere in the average catechism. Certainly in the case of those authors who dealt with the Creed article by article, and even of some who did not, like John Ball, most of the constituent elements were handled under such headings as the 'I believe' of the first article, Christ's offices or sacrifice, the nature of saving faith, and the role of the Holy Ghost, as well as under the forgiveness of sins.[258] As we shall see in the chapter on the Decalogue, the doctrine of justification by faith was also driven

---

[254] In addition to the authors of the Prayer Book catechism and the Heidelberg Catechism, the following also did not use the term 'justification': Dering–More, Egerton (in 'Four points', 'Briefe summe', 'Familiar forme', and 'Familiar manner'), Hieron, Ball (in his shorter catechism), Keach (in his two more elementary forms), and Watts (in his first- and second-level forms). The following expositors of the Prayer Book catechism also did not use the term: Boughen, Sherlock, Comber, Marshall, Williams, Isham, Wake, and Lewis.

[255] Paget, *Questions*, sig. C7ᵛ; Egerton, 'Briefe method', 8, and (in effect) in id., 'Forme of examining', 30; Westminster Shorter, 15–16 (answer 33); Wallis, *Explanation*, 17; Gouge, 'Heads', 4; Watts, *Assembly's catechism*, 18.

[256] See below, pp. 398–402.

[257] Prayer Book catechism, 780; Paget, *Questions*, sigs. A5ʳ–6ᵛ; 'Maner to examine children', 151–5; Keach, 'Little child', 16, and id., 'Child', 25–6; Watts, 'First catechism', 8–10, and id., 'Children's catechism', 18–23; and see the other forms cited in nn. 67–70 above for the use of alternative terms.

[258] See previous sections of this chapter, and Ball, *Catechisme*, 73–5.

home by implication in the passages in which our authors went to great pains to reject any notion of what they saw as the heretical doctrine of justification (in part) by works, or works-righteousness.[259] Another reason, though no easier to prove, was that authors became aware of a growing debate on the nature of justification within the Protestant camp, and—as usual with contentious matters—took steps to avoid it in their catechisms. There was a precedent for this in the later Middle Ages, when academics took pains to shield their technical disagreements on justification from the public.[260] In early modern England there were at least two areas of debate: did justification include the imputation of Christ's obedience; and what was the relationship between justification and sanctification? There are some signs of these debates in our sample, which we will examine below.[261]

Of the reasons offered here, the ones which stressed the inadvisability or superfluity of teaching justification to the average catechumen were probably the more important ones. The statements which authors made by way of exposition of the central articles of the Creed, to the effect that God forgives the faithful, for Christ's sake, and that the Holy Ghost sanctifies believers, may have seemed to them to have provided sufficient knowledge and insight for the sort of catechumen for whom they were writing.

If the sins of the faithful are forgiven, asked Herbert Palmer in his catechism, why do they as well as the ungodly suffer death? The correct answer to this was that death was 'at the worst' a temporal chastisement for the faithful, and 'withal a passage to a better condition'.[262] We should pass through this transitory world as through a strange country, and wait patiently for Christ (wrote Calvin in his catechism); we gladly run to death as a release from our bodily bonds (wrote his faithful echo, Alexander Nowell), and should not encumber ourselves with transitory things—another statement with a medieval ring to it.[263] At death, it was believed that the bodies of the faithful would be laid into the grave, while their souls joined Christ in heaven; but at the appointed time their bodies would be raised by Christ, united with their souls and made like his glorious body. At the Last Judgement, the faithful would obtain bliss 'such as eye hath not seen, nor ear heard, neither hath entered into the heart of man', and they would then live with Christ for ever in his everlasting kingdom of glory and praise God forever.[264]

In their exposition of the last two articles of the Apostles' Creed—'the resurrection of the dead, and the life everlasting'—our authors' teaching on eschatology (death,

---

[259] See below, Ch. 10.   [260] Cameron, *European Reformation*, 83, 87.

[261] See below, Ch. 9.   [262] Palmer, *Endeavour*, 22; and cf. Hill, *Principles*, sig. A8ᵛ.

[263] Calvin, *Catechisme*, 42; Nowell, *Catechisme*, 178.

[264] Heidelberg Catechism, 326; Nowell, *Catechisme*, 178; Dering–More, *Catechisme*, sig. B4ᵛ; Paget, *Questions*, sigs. D2ᵛ–3ʳ; Ussher, 'Principles', 11–12; Comber, *Church-catechism*, '12' (*recte* 13).

judgement, heaven and hell) was generally uniform, perhaps not least because the same scriptural texts were cited over and over again or printed in full in the text in order to explain them.[265] As a result, differences of opinion were kept to a minimum. Both Calvinists and non-Calvinists saw the blessings of salvation as being only for the faithful members of the church, the 'saints', Christ's chosen people.[266] All authors found it possible to reconcile a position which said that man's works could do nothing to earn him salvation with the scriptural statements that at the Last Judgement men would be divided up according to their works, the righteous being sent to unspeakable happiness and the wicked to eternal torment.[267] And authors of different persuasions drew similar lessons from these articles: men should contemplate the shortness of life and the bliss of heaven, and act accordingly.[268]

The only differences of any substance were of two kinds: the relative amount of space devoted to eschatology, and whether the fate of the wicked was treated prominently. In terms of space, our authors can be divided into three groups. In a few forms the last things were not mentioned at all, perhaps due to pressure of space or because it was not thought to be pertinent for the matter in hand, for example in a form for the young or one designed to prepare communicants for the Lord's Supper.[269] Jeremy Taylor left the last things out of his question-and-answer form but handled them in a prose form on the Creed which followed; conversely, James Ussher handled them in his first, more elementary form, but then devoted only six lines to them in his more advanced form.[270] In a much larger number of cases, authors devoted relatively few questions and answers to eschatology, either in relation to the amount of space they devoted to most of the first ten articles of the Creed, or, if they did not tackle the Creed explicitly, relative to other basic doctrines. The briefness of the accounts in some of these cases may again be put down to self-imposed limits on the number of words used, for example in the Westminster Shorter Catechism and Watts's first form for very young children. Otherwise the authors of the forms in this group are fairly mixed, suggesting again that no clear doctrinal standpoint was involved.

---

[265] The usual texts were much of 1 Cor. 15, Phil. 3: 21, 1 Thess. 4: 13–17, Luke 23: 42–3, Matt. 25: 33–4, 41, 46, and John 5: 24–5, 28–9. See Calvin, Nowell, Dering–More, and Paget, loc. cit.; Perkins, *Foundation*, 8; Ball, *Catechisme*, 90–1; Hill, *Principles*, sig. B2^v; Palmer, *Endeavour*, 22–3; Westminster Larger, 48–9 (answer 87); Nicholson, *Exposition*, 51–2; Gouge, *Principles*, 110–11; Sherlock, *Principles*, 24; Williams, *Exposition*, 24–5.

[266] Nowell, *Catechisme*, 172–6, 179, 181; Egerton, 'Briefe method', 7, 20; Wake, *Principles*, 71, 73; and other authors cited in n. 85 above.

[267] Elton, *Forme*, sigs. F3^v–6^v; Hammond, *Practical catechisme*, 335–8; Comber, *Church-catechism*, '12' (*recte* 13); Isham, *Catechism*, 30–1; and see below, pp. 400–3, 468–70.

[268] Calvin, *Catechisme*, 42–3; Nowell, *Catechisme*, 178–9; Hammond, *Practical catechisme*, 335–6; Nicholson, *Exposition*, 72–3.

[269] e.g. Prayer Book catechism; 'Maner to examine children'; Egerton, 'Four points', 'Briefe summe', and 'Familiar manner'; Keach, 'Little child' (and only a brief reference to the damned in id., 'Child', 25).

[270] Taylor, 'An exposition of the Apostles' Creed', in *Symbolon*, 12–13, as against his 'Catechism'; Ussher, 'Principles', 11–12, as against 'Method', 22.

This group includes a high proportion of the first two generations of foreign and native catechists (up to the 1590s), and almost half of the expositors of the Prayer Book catechism in the seventeenth century.[271] A third group of authors—those who devoted rather *more* than average space to eschatology—included quite a few of those authors of the 1590s to 1620s who chose not to include a detailed exposition of the Creed, but also thereafter a mixed bag of some of the episcopalians who did tackle it and some non-episcopalians who did not.[272] In a few cases, this extra length can be attributed to the amount of space an author devoted to describing the signs that would herald the day of judgement, which was the nearest that catechisms in the sample (or outside it with very few exceptions) came to reflecting the growing tide of interest in the millennium and the apocalypse that swept across England in the century that separated the Spanish Armada from the fall of James II.[273] In other cases, the extra length presumably reflected the author's pastoral priorities or personal interests.[274]

There is also no clear pattern, other than personal taste, in the matter of whether the fate of the unrighteous was mentioned as well as that of the righteous. Again there are three categories: a few authors who did not mention the fate of the wicked at all;[275] a larger number, including men as varied as Calvin and Jeremy Taylor who gave them only brief treatment;[276] and the remainder who, even if they devoted little space to eschatology, gave the fate of the damned as much space as, if not more than, that of the godly.[277] Omission may sometimes have been due to an effort to be concise, as in

[271] Westminster Shorter, 17–18 (answers 37–8); Watts, 'First catechism', 9–10; Calvin, *Catechisme*, 42–3; Heidelberg Catechism, 325–6; Virel, *Treatise*, 77; Nowell, *Catechisme*, 178–9, and id., *Institution*, sigs. Eviii^r–v; Dering–More, *Catechisme*, sig. B4^v; Paget, *Questions*, sigs. D2^v–3^r; Egerton, 'Briefe method', 20, and id., 'Familiar forme', 34; Bradshaw, 'Brief forme', 136; Hill, *Principles*, sig. B2^v; Ussher, 'Method', 22; Wallis, *Explanation*, 19–20; Sherlock, *Principles*, 24–5; Comber, *Church-catechism*, '12' (*recte* 13); Marshall, *Catechism*, 18–19; Isham, *Catechism*, 29–31; Keach, 'Youth', 113–14; Williams, *Exposition*, 24–5; Lewis, *Catechism*, 34–6.

[272] Of the first group, Perkins, *Foundation*, 8; Hieron, *Doctrine*, 581; Elton, *Forme*, sigs. F1^r–8^v; Ball, *Catechisme*, 90–1, and id., *Treatise*, 236–42; of the second, Boughen, *Exposition*, 31–4; Nicholson, *Exposition*, 68–73; and Wake, *Principles*, 71–5; and of the third, Grosse, *Fiery pillar*, 99–105; Watts, 'Children's catechism', 29–35.

[273] Perkins, *Foundation*, 8; Cartwright, 'Catechisme', sig. Bb2^r; Ball, *Catechisme*, 90–1; Elton, *Forme*, sigs. F1^v–2^r (but not in id., 'Extract', sigs. G6^r–7^v). Some authors described a terrible Last Judgement under article seven of the Creed, e.g. Nowell, *Catechisme*, 169–70; Wake, *Principles*, 54–6. For the growing concern with the apocalypse and millenarianism, see K. R. Firth, *The Apocalyptic Tradition in Reformation Britain* (Oxford, 1979); W. Lamont, *Godly Rule* (1969); C. Hill, *Antichrist in Seventeenth-Century England* (1971); and P. Christianson, *Reformers and Babylon* (Toronto, 1978); W. R. Owens, ' "Antichrist must be Pulled Down": Bunyan and the Millennium', in A. Laurence, W. R. Owens, and S. Sim (eds.), *John Bunyan and his England 1628–88* (1990), 77–94.

[274] e.g. Ussher, 'Principles', 12; Vincent, *Catechism*, 85–92.

[275] e.g. Dering–More, *Catechisme*, sig. B4^v; Taylor, 'An exposition of the Apostles' Creed', in *Symbolon*, 12–13; and Gouge, *Principles*, 103–11, and id., 'Heads'; and cf. below, nn. 278, 281.

[276] Calvin, *Catechisme*, 42–3; Cartwright, 'Catechisme', sig. Bb2^r; Palmer, *Endeavour*, 22–3; Nicholson, *Exposition*, 72; and cf. n. 280 below.

[277] Ussher, 'Principles', 12; Vincent, *Catechism*, 90–2; and see below, nn. 282–3.

the pre-communion form approved by Calvin and the Westminster Shorter Catechism and some of its derivatives,[278] but it was not simply a factor of space. Isaac Watts managed to find space in his very elementary form to explain that if a child was wicked, he would be sent down to everlasting fire and hell among wicked and miserable creatures, whereas if he was a child of God he would go to heaven and dwell there with God and Christ for ever.[279] Nor was length a guarantee of equal treatment: some fairly brief accounts of articles eleven and twelve still managed to cover both sides of the question,[280] while one of the longest accounts in the sample, Nowell's full-length form, said nothing at all about hell. The reason for this omission in Nowell's case, and probably in some comparable cases such as the Heidelberg Catechism and the forms by Hill and Williams, was a very literal reading of the Creed, which, as Calvin and Nowell had pointed out, simply did not mention the fate of the wicked.[281]

What we are left with is a substantial minority of authors in the sample who devoted at least as much space to the fires of hell as to the joys of heaven—a group which included a number of double predestinarians as well as non-predestinarians.[282] From the catechist's perspective, there were clear evangelical and pastoral advantages to pressing home the message we find in Hammond's *Practical catechisme*, that God had given all men the choice (through a will enabled by grace) 'either to return and live, or to go on and perish everlastingly'; in Watts's historical catechism, the catechumen was told that heaven was for those who repent and believe, and hell for wilful and obstinate sinners, especially hypocrites and unbelievers.[283] But the majority of authors in our sample seem to have preferred to focus the minds of their catechumens on the good news of the gospel, the 'comfortable words' in the communion service which even irregular church attenders would have heard: 'So God loved the world, that he gave his only begotten son, that whosoever believeth in him should not perish, but have everlasting life.'[284]

Throughout the early modern period, therefore, the Creed provided catechumens with a summary within a summary: an encapsulation of the Christian faith, equivalent to the belief of the apostles, within the 'sum' of knowledge that a catechism was

---

[278] 'Maner to examine children', 151–5; Westminster Shorter, 17–18 (answers 37–8); Wallis, *Explanation*, 19–20.

[279] Watts, 'First catechism', 7–8.

[280] e.g. Lewis, *Catechism*, 35–6, but see n. 276 above and nn. 282–3 below.

[281] Calvin, *Catechisme*, 43–4; Nowell, *Catechisme*, 179; Dering–More, *Catechisme*, sig. B4ᵛ; Paget, *Questions*, sigs. D2ᵛ–3ʳ; Heidelberg Catechism, 325–6; Egerton, 'Briefe method', 24; Hill, *Principles*, sig. B2ᵛ; Williams, *Exposition*, 24–5.

[282] Perkins, *Foundation*, 8; Ball, *Catechisme*, 91; Westminster Larger, 50–1 (answers 89–90); Hammond, *Practical catechisme*, 335–7; Wake, *Principles*, 73–5.

[283] Hammond, *Practical catechisme*, 336; Watts, 'Historical catechism', 55–6.

[284] John 3: 17, and the 'comfortable words' after the absolution in the Prayer Book communion service: Brightman, *English Rite*, ii. 683.

designed to impart. Measured quantitatively or viewed from the standpoint of the average catechumen, there were considerable overlaps in the credal doctrine taught in our sample forms, or at least in the ways in which our authors projected their understanding of the Creed to their charges. There is no sign in our sample of best-selling forms of those rival interpretations of the Elizabethan settlement or rival claims to orthodoxy that Professor Russell has recently outlined, and no sign of any weakening of the English church's hostility to that of Rome, which some early Stuart churchmen thought they could see in the actions of Charles I and Laud.[285] Differences were as likely to be over what was suitable for different levels of catechumen to be taught as over ecclesiology or soteriology, and of the reasons for producing new forms the need for greater clarity on certain topics was perhaps a significant one.

As a footnote to this chapter on the Creed, however, we may draw the reader's attention to a couple of points of potentially wider significance. The first is to underline the difference between what was taught at elementary level and at more advanced levels, and suggest one possible consequence of this. The beginner (and as we have seen in Part I, most catechumens *were* beginners) was told that God was his father, creator, and preserver; Christ was the son of God and his saviour; the Holy Ghost would sanctify him; faith was a matter of belief in Christ, but it was important to be a member of the church, because of the spiritual fellowship and other benefits that conferred, including forgiveness of sins, and the prospect of attaining the joys of heaven for those who at the Last Judgement could show that they had had faith and tried to walk in God's ways. No divine attributes and works; no three offices of Christ, or degrees of humiliation and exaltation; nothing about apprehending faith, or different types of faith; little or nothing about justification by faith, or the difference between the visible and invisible church, or a true and an untrue church. By itself this simple paraphrase of the Creed cannot have done much to weaken the semi-Pelagianism that many clergy thought they detected among their parishioners: the view that faith could be acquired when it suited them, and that God would look favourably on their attempts to lead a good life. Indeed, a plain or unimaginative rendering of the Creed, and especially the last two articles, together with a hefty stress on the Decalogue by the same catechist, might actually and unwittingly have encouraged people to think that the Last Judgement was more about good works than about lively faith. When Perkins and others, including conformist clergy, protested that their parishioners recited the Creed or Decalogue like a prayer,[286] they were acknowledging that their flock had learnt these formulae in English and that they regarded them as something holy. But it would need a forceful rendering of the doctrine of

---

[285] C. Russell, *The Causes of the English Civil War* (Oxford, 1990), 84–105; and A. Milton's review of Tyacke, *Anti-Calvinists*, in *JEH* 39 (1988), 615–16; but see also Milton, 'The Church of England, Rome, and the True Church: The Demise of a Jacobean Consensus', in K. Fincham (ed.), *The Early Stuart Church, 1603–1642* (1993), 187–210, and id., *Catholic and Reformed*, pt. 1.

[286] See above, pp. 131, 245, 274–5, 287.

prevenient grace and justification by faith alone (or the use of an exposition or a more advanced catechism) to counter such views, and too many clergy either had not been trained for such a rendering, or were perhaps better attuned to detecting signs of more colourful heresies, such as a drift away from commitment to the wider Protestant cause, than a humble semi-Pelagianism of which the holders were themselves unaware.

The second point is the suggestion that the careful article-by-article approach to the Creed found in many catechisms, especially those of intermediate or advanced level, tended to produce parallels between authors not normally associated with one another. On the one hand, there were authors in what we might call Group A. This comprised the authors of the 1549 Prayer Book catechism and the later supporters or expositors of that form, such as Hammond, Nicholson, Wake, and several others in our sample, together with Calvin and such first-generation English Calvinists as Nowell, and Dering and More. In a separate group—let us call them Group B—there were the second-, third-, and fourth-generation Calvinists from Perkins and Cartwright to the theologians of the Westminster Assembly who did not handle the Creed line by line. Groups A and B could agree with each other on the nature of God as father, creator, and protector, but a few of those in B also stated the doctrine of election and reprobation as part of their description of divine sovereignty. Both groups stated that Christ was the son of God, the second person of the Trinity, the anointed saviour, prophet, priest, and king to fallen man. But whereas those in Group A treated *both* the historic Christ, whose life and works were described in great detail in the Gospels and reflected in articles three to seven of the Creed, *and* the significance of Christ, asserted by the Gospels and Paul and reflected in article two of the Creed, those in Group B tended to say less about the historic Christ and therefore relatively more about his mission. Both were Christological, but in rather different ways. Also some of those in Group B tended to stress more than those in A that Christ died for *his* people. For both groups, faith was a resting on the gospel promises in Christ, though some in Group B put special stress on 'applying' this faith to the inner man. Justification was a believer being forgiven or made righteous for Christ's sake, though for some authors, usually in Group B, it was also (as we shall see in Chapter 9) having Christ's righteousness imputed to the faithful. Where those in Group A stressed the sanctifying role of the Holy Ghost in broad terms, some of those in B tended to describe the special role of the Spirit as being to work faith in the elect. Those in A realized the difficulty of separating the visible from the invisible church and the need for charity in welcoming all professing Christians into the visible church. They also stressed the impossibility of attaining salvation outside the church, and the potential privileges of members of that church: fellowship, forgiveness, resurrection, and everlasting life. Those in B tended to use the orthodox Calvinist *ordo salutis* as a framework within which to chart the spiritual progress of the faithful from the cradle to the grave. The church, if mentioned at all, was likely to be raised during a discussion of the sacraments or of sanctification rather than justification. Further differences will emerge in Chapters 8 and 9.

It would not be true to say that Calvin had more in common with Hammond and Wake than with Perkins, Cartwright, or the Westminster divines: on certain key issues relating to predestination, some of which we will examine in the next two chapters, the reverse was clearly true. It would also be simplistic to suggest that a credal approach produced uniformity of approach or unanimity of doctrine: as pointed out in the chapter on structures, some who expounded the Creed incorporated double predestinarian teaching into it, while not all of those who avoided the Creed necessarily taught double predestination, or at least taught it at full strength.[287] Nevertheless, what this chapter does suggest is that a conscientious pursuit of the twelve articles in the Creed, one by one, did lead to a number of shared norms or common emphases, including a broader view of divine power, a fuller pic-ture view of Christ's life and significance, a more rounded view of the work of the Holy Ghost, and a stress on the church as the forum in which Christ's sacrifice for the salvation of the faithful was outwardly visible and in which salvation was secured. As a leading modern presbyterian theologian, Professor Tom Torrance, has written, a focus on the Creed can lead to a 'more universal' teaching, and one that keeps us 'close to the mighty acts of God in Christ'.[288] This convergence between men like Calvin and Hammond needs to be borne in mind alongside the well publicized differences of opinion between 'conformists' and 'puritans' or 'Calvinists' and 'Arminians' when we try to assess the doctrinal teaching heard in the parishes and schools of early modern England. In their debates with the critics of the established church's structure and doctrine, men like Whitgift, Bancroft, Laud, Boughen, and Nicholson were not being facetious when they said in public that they agreed with much of what Calvin had said;[289] and if by the 1620s there was a cooling of relations between, on the one hand, 'credal' or 'conformist Calvinists' such as Archbishop Abbot and, on the other, puritans or hard-line Calvinists like the successors of Cartwright and Perkins, in part at least because the conformists had decided that the visible church needed defending, then continuing official sup-port for credal-based catechisms such as the Prayer Book and Nowell forms, rather than a switch to an alternative, more strongly 'Calvinist' form, is easier to explain.[290]

---

[287] See above, pp. 285–6, and below, Ch. 9.

[288] Torrance, *School of Faith*, pp. xvii, xxi, and cf. J. B. Torrance, 'Strengths and Weaknesses', 45.

[289] For example, Coolidge, *Pauline Renaissance*, 29–30 (and cf. ibid. chs. 3–6 for Coolidge's view that whereas the first generations of the puritans adopted a church-centred approach, some in the second and third generations moved away from that to a grace-centred approach which had the potential for exclu-sivity within or separation from the official church); Lake, *Moderate Puritans*, 220–1, and id., *Anglicans and Puritans?*, 26; P. Collinson, 'England and International Calvinism, 1558–1640', in M. Prestwich (ed.), *International Calvinism 1541–1715* (Oxford, 1986), 213–14; Milton, *Catholic and Reformed*, 425–7, 433–4, 540; Boughen, *Exposition*, 15, 17, 75–6, 83; Nicholson, *Exposition*, 5–6, 20 n.

[290] Milton, *Catholic and Reformed*, introduction, conclusion, and *passim*.

The result was that at the humbler level of instruction in parish churches and petty schools, and at the intermediate level where a form by Nowell or Calvin or an exposition of the Prayer Book form was being studied, it was the credal-based, church-focused approach which catechumens continued to be much more likely to encounter.

8

Predestination

THE subject of double predestination provoked some of the sharpest disagreements in sixteenth-century Europe, not only between Protestant and Catholic but also between Lutheran and Calvinist, and between different shades of Calvinist opinion.[1] On the Protestant side, some of the best minds of the day were drawn to the subject, their capacity for argumentativeness enhanced by the revival of Aristotelianism and the rise of Ramism.[2] That England was not immune from these divisions is demonstrated by the debates on free will in the mid-Tudor period, the number of treatises and university theses on predestinarian topics written in the Elizabethan and early Stuart periods, and the periodic attempts to change the church's official position on predestination.[3] Opponents of Calvinism were dismissed by their rivals as 'Lutherans' or—worse—'Arminians' (after Jacobus Arminius, the leading spokesman of the more liberal Reformed element in the United Provinces), even though many had not read Arminius's work, while by the 1620s Calvinists were being dubbed 'puritans' by their opponents, even though many were fully conformable to the established church.[4] This name-calling and stereotyping was in no small degree the result of an

[1] McGrath, *Iustitia Dei*, i. 137–43, ii. 15–16, 30, 40, 48–51, 114–20; Schaff, *Creeds*, 185, 199; A. W. Harrison, *The Beginnings of Arminianism to the Synod of Dort* (1926); C. Bangs, *Arminius* (Nashville, 1971); B. G. Armstrong, *Calvinism and the Amyraut Heresy* (Madison, 1969); Weir, *Federal Theology*, ch. 2.

[2] Armstrong, *Calvinism*, 38–42; Clifford, *Atonement and Justification*, ch. 6; Weir, *Federal Theology*, 69–74, 103, 111; White, *Predestination*: 17–18, 25; and see above, p. 306 n. 42, and below, pp. 428–30.

[3] D. A. Penny, *Freewill or Predestination: The Battle over Saving Grace in Mid-Tudor England* (Woodbridge, 1990), chs. 1, 8, and *passim*; D. D. Wallace, *Puritans and Predestination: Grace in English Protestant Theology 1525–1695* (Chapel Hill, NC, 1982), chs. 1–2; works cited in Weir, *Federal Theology*, 95 n. 72; H. C. Porter, *Reformation and Reaction in Tudor Cambridge* (Cambridge, 1958), pt. 3; Lake, *Moderate Puritans*, ch. 9; N. Tyacke, *Anti-Calvinists: The Rise of English Arminianism c.1590–1640* (Oxford, 1987), pp. 23–5, chs. 2–3, pp. 135–6, 267–8; but see also P. White, 'The Rise of Arminianism Reconsidered', *Past and Present*, 101 (1983), 36–9, and id., *Predestination, passim*.

[4] For the perception and the reality, see N. Tyacke, 'Puritanism, Arminianism and Counter-Revolution', in C. Russell (ed.), *The Origins of the English Civil War* (1973), 133–4, and Tyacke, *Anti-Calvinists*, 7–10, 137–9, 166–8, 185–6; C. R. Trueman, *Luther's Legacy: Salvation and English Reformers 1525–56* (Oxford, 1994); Penny, *Freewill or Predestination*; B. Hall, 'The Early Rise and Gradual Decline of Lutheranism in England', in D. Baker (ed.), *Reform and Reformation: England and the Continent (1520–1660)* (Studies in Church History, Subsidia 2; Oxford, 1979), 103–31; Porter, *Reformation*, 282–3; Wallace, *Puritans and Predestination*, 73–5; D. D. Wallace, 'The Anglican Appeal to Lutheran Sources', *Historical Magazine of the Protestant Episcopal Church*, 52 (1983), 355–67; Tyacke, *Anti-Calvinists*, 20, 33; and cf. Patrick Collinson's remarks on Lutheran works in Cambridge booklists, in *JEH* 39 (1988), 279–81; H. R. Trevor-Roper, 'Laudianism and Political Power', in his *Catholics, Anglicans and Puritans* (1987),

already complex set of theological issues becoming entangled with both academic politics in the universities and (as in Holland) with the wider ecclesiastical and political disputes of the day.[5] All of this makes it hard for historians when they try to see if there was a clear and consistently held set of Calvinist principles[6] or of non-Calvinist principles[7] in England, or whether what was more important was what members of one group *thought* they had in common with each other and in distinction from their opponents, whether those assessments were accurate or not.

The current historiography on the contemporary debate over predestination is approaching a climax. Nicholas Tyacke set the ball rolling by arguing for a long-standing dominance of 'Calvinist' influence in the universities and the Elizabethan and Jacobean churches, and suggesting that there was a marked heightening of

41–50; T. M. Parker, 'Arminianism and Laudianism in Seventeenth-Century England', in C. W. Dugmore and C. Duggan (eds.), *Studies in Church History*, 1 (1964), 29–30; White, *Predestination*, 51, and id., 'Rise of Arminianism', 34–54, but for Baro's distancing himself from Luther, see White, *Predestination*, 112–14; Milton, *Catholic and Reformed*, 384–95, 439–46.

[5] Porter, *Reformation*, pts. 2 and 3; C. M. Dent, *Protestant Reformers in Elizabethan Oxford* (Oxford, 1983); White, *Predestination*, ch. 6, and pp. 303–7, 309–10; Parker, 'Arminianism', 21–5; A. Milton, 'The Church of England, Rome, and the True Church', in K. Fincham (ed.) *The early Stuart Church* (1993), 187–210; Trevor-Roper, 'Laudianism', 51–7, 92–105; White, 'Rise of Arminianism', 45–54, and id., *Predestination, passim*; J. den Tex, *Oldenbarnevelt* (Cambridge, 1973), chs. 10, 12; P. Collinson, 'England and International Calvinism, 1558–1640', in M. Prestwich (ed.), *International Calvinism 1541–1715* (Oxford, 1986), 213–23; J. P. Sommerville, *Politics and Ideology in England 1603–1640* (1986), 44–6, 207–8; I. M. Green, ' "England's Wars of Religion?" Religious Conflict and the English Civil Wars', in J. van den Berg and P. G. Hoftijzer (eds.) *Church, Change and Revolution* (Publications of the Sir Thomas Browne Institute, Leiden, NS, 12; Leiden, 1991), 103–6.

[6] For shades of difference between the attitudes of 'Calvinists' such as Nowell, Whitgift, Hutton, Fenner, Cartwright, Chaderton, Perkins, Bradshaw, Abbot, Ames, and Preston, and others, see W. P. Haugaard, 'John Calvin and the Catechism of Alexander Nowell', *Archiv für Reformationgeschichte*, 61 (1970), 50–3, 56–65; Porter, *Reformation*, 350–1; P. Lake, 'Calvinism and the English Church 1570–1635', *Past and Present*, 114 (1987), 38–41, 56–9; White, *Predestination*, 117–22; Lake, *Moderate Puritans*, chs. 3, 5, 7, 9, 11; Lake, *Anglicans and Puritans?*, ch. 1; Weir, *Federal Theology*, 137–47; on Perkins, Kendall, *English Calvinism*, pts. 1–3; *The Work of William Perkins*, ed. I. Breward (Abingdon, 1970), 80–99; Wallace, *Puritans and Predestination*, ch. 2; and Porter, *Reformation*, ch. 12; on Abbot, K. Fincham, 'Prelacy and Politics: Archbishop Abbot's Defence of Protestant Orthodoxy', *Bulletin of the Institute of Historical Research*, 61 (1988), 36–64; on Ames and Preston, Kendall, *English Calvinism*, chs. 8, 11. For differences between delegates at Dort and in the Westminster Assembly and subsequently, see Harrison, *Arminianism*, 336–7, 342; Tyacke, *Anti-Calvinists*, 94–100; Lake, 'Calvinism', 51–60; White, *Predestination*, ch. 9; A. P. F. Sell, *The Great Debate* (Worthing, 1982); Wallace, *Puritans and Predestination*, chs. 3–5; Clifford, *Atonement and Justification*, 26–7 and *passim*.

[7] For the attitudes of Hooker, Andrewes, Overall, and Hales, see Lake, *Anglicans and Puritans?*, ch. 4; Porter, *Reformation*, 281–6, 318, 331, 385, 391–413; White, *Predestination*, 124–39, 107–10, 146–7, 165–7, 190–2; Trevor-Roper, 'Laudianism', 59–60; and for the laity, B. Donagan, 'The York House Conference Revisited: Laymen, Calvinism and Arminianism', *Bulletin of the Institute of Historical Research*, 64 (1991), 312–29; and in general, White, *Predestination, passim*, and id., 'The *Via Media* in the Early Stuart Church', in Fincham, *Early Stuart Church*, 211–30. It is even harder to pin down a clear set of Calvinist or non-Calvinist ideas if one moves from the centre of the predestinarian debate into its consequences for piety, federal theology, ecclesiology, and church–state relations: J. S. Coolidge, *The Pauline Renaissance in England* (Oxford, 1970), chs. 2, 3; Lake, *Moderate Puritans*, ch. 7, and id., 'Calvinism', 39–40, 58; P. F. Jensen, 'The Life of Faith in the Teaching of Elizabethan Protestants', D.Phil. thesis (Oxford, 1979), ch. 5; Weir, *Federal Theology*, chs. 2–6; and Brachlow, *Communion of Saints*.

religious and political tensions when this dominance was first challenged and then under Charles I eclipsed by the rise of English 'Arminianism', whose members were intent on overthrowing 'Calvinist' views on predestinarian grace and (he suggests) promoting the role of the sacraments and the grace they conferred.[8] Peter Lake (in reply to an early challenge to the Tyacke thesis from Peter White) argued that there may have been shades of Calvinism, with 'credal' or 'doctrinal Calvinists' like Whitgift accepting the characteristic double predestinarian teaching of Calvin but holding back from the consequences of that teaching, either in terms of a distinctive style of piety and techniques of gaining assurance (dubbed 'experimental predestinarianism' by R. T. Kendall) or a particular view of the godly community which led some, though by no means all, Calvinists towards presbyterianism or semi-separatism. Nevertheless, he believed, the ideological cement which bound 'credal Calvinists' and 'experimental predestinarians' together—resistance to attacks on double predestinarian teaching and hostility to what they saw as the emergence of a dangerously conservative view of the visible church and Christian community in the writings of Hooker, Andrewes, and Montagu—was much stronger than the centrifugal forces forcing them apart.[9] Next, in a full-length monograph, Peter White cast doubt on the starkness of the dichotomy between 'Calvinists' and 'anti-Calvinists' or 'Arminians' by arguing that 'perhaps there was a middle ground' between these extremes—an indigenous latitudinarianism of opinion from which these polarities developed, partly in response to the new harder line taken by a 'Calvinist' element within that spectrum.[10] In reply Tyacke and Lake have accused White, first, of trying to create a doctrinal *via media* where none existed, and, secondly, of exaggerating the impact on English thought of the ideas of Calvin's successor, Beza, and so setting up a false yardstick of extreme Calvinism against which many English Calvinists appear to occupy a middling position. Lake has recently conceded that the 'nature of Reformed orthodoxy was never fixed' and that as categories both 'Calvinist' and 'Arminian' are difficult to use, since they represent loose and unstable coalitions of individuals with strong views on a number of issues, not just predestination alone. Like Tyacke, however, he clearly feels that both labels are still useful and reflect the existence of two strongly opposed schools of thought.[11] Most recently of all, Anthony Milton has suggested that historians of the early Stuart period should look beyond single-issue doctrinal divisions or a simple division between two groupings. Even before the advent of Laud, he argues, the early Stuart church was subject to increasing strains, partly on doctrine such as the predestinarianism espoused by the majority at Dort, but increasingly on the question of how the Church of England should be seen in relation

---

[8] Tyacke, 'Puritanism, Arminianism and Counter–Revolution', and *Anti-Calvinists, passim*.

[9] White, 'Rise of Arminianism', and Lake, 'Calvinism', *passim*.

[10] White, *Predestination, passim*, and cf. id., 'The *Via Media* in the Early Stuart Church'.

[11] Tyacke's review of White, *Predestination* in *English Historical Review*, 110 (1995), 468–9, and P. Lake, 'Predestinarian Propositions', *JEH*, 46 (1995), 110–23.

to the Catholic church and Protestant churches abroad. Many 'Calvinist conformists', including several bishops, were sufficiently concerned about recent developments in Calvinist theology and convinced of the need to defend the institutional church that they began to distance themselves from some aspects of the high Elizabethan position, and were prepared to work with Laud in the 1630s, even though they did not want to go as far as the remodelling of that church on sacramentalist, sacerdotalist lines as he did. The Laudians themselves, we are told, 'were not strongly Arminian', and rejected Calvinism less for its doctrine than for the status it had achieved as a symbol of orthodoxy that rivalled the official formularies of the church, and because it was deemed potentially subversive. At heart, it was the bluntness with which the Laudians rejected the symbols of high Elizabethan Protestantism, the contrast between the Laudian style of discourse and the Calvinist, that did most damage, rather than the disagreements on doctrine.[12]

This is not the place to try to resolve this debate, but since it has coloured so much writing on the religious history of the period it cannot be avoided in a study such as this; indeed, catechisms provide a good opportunity to test the different hypotheses. It is also necessary to explain some of the terms that have crept into the text of the last two chapters, such as 'Calvinist' or 'non-Calvinist'. Two points need to be made by way of preliminary. First, one's definition of 'Calvinism' depends to some extent on one's view of the separate debate on how far the second generation of Calvinists— Beza and the Heidelberg theologians on the Continent, and men like Cartwright and Perkins in England—deviated from the views of the master. The view that was once widespread was that many Calvinists, and Beza in particular, had moved away from Calvin's position on a number of points, sometimes quite sharply; but in recent years a rival view has increasingly gained ground: that such developments as there were after Calvin's death were limited, and were either logical developments from his thought or attempts to resolve problems which had not arisen or not been conceived in the same way in his day, so that Calvin would have accepted and welcomed these changes.[13] Steering a course between these rival views, we may conclude that what was at the heart of what both Calvin and the Calvinists believed was an absolute and unchangeable divine decree of double predestination by which God had elected some to salvation and others to damnation. (These and other technical terms used here will be explained later in this chapter or in the next.) In the case of the elect, Calvin and his followers all argued that this predestination was unconditional, not dependent on any faith that God foresaw they would have or good works they would do; in the case of the reprobate, there was a tension, with Beza arguing for an equally

---

[12] Milton, *Catholic and Reformed*, introduction, conclusion, and *passim*.

[13] B. Hall, 'Calvin against the Calvinists', in G. E. Duffield (ed.), *John Calvin* (Abingdon, 1966), 26–36; T. H. L. Parker, *Calvin's New Testament Commentaries* (1971), 26–88; J. S. Bray, *Theodore Beza's Doctrine of Predestination* (Nieuwkoop, 1975); Weir, *Federal Theology, passim*; and J. R. Beeke, *Assurance of Faith: Calvin, English Puritanism and the Dutch Second Reformation* (New York, 1991).

unconditional decree, but many Calvinists, including many English ones, persisting with the view that the reprobate were condemned on account of their sins.[14] It is hard to be sure whether Calvin thought that the divine decree was made prior to the decision to permit the Fall or that God already conceived of man as created and fallen when he decreed to save some and pass by the rest, since the matter was not clearly formulated in the 'supralapsarian' or 'sublapsarian' (or 'infralapsarian') terms that were subsequently used. But pressure was exerted to adopt supralapsarianism as the norm by Beza and by some of the speakers at the Synod of Dort in Holland and the Westminster Assembly in London, though it was usually resisted by a sublapsarian majority; thus the Westminster Confession of 1647 reflected the supralapsarianism of Ussher's Irish articles of 1615 in some clauses, but was perhaps sublapsarian as a whole.[15] Similarly on the subject of the atonement, we cannot be sure what Calvin would have made of subsequent distinctions. It has often been suggested that he leant to the view of a limited atonement, by which Christ had died to atone for the sins of the elect alone, but he did not speak of it in those terms; nor did he use Peter Lombard's distinction between Christ's atonement being 'sufficient' for everybody but 'efficient' (effective) for the elect alone which became popular in some Calvinist circles in the half century after his death, for example with the Heidelberg theologians, Perkins, and Ussher. Beza, however, disliked this distinction, and others such as William Ames and Robert Abbot (Archbishop George's brother) and later John Owen stressed the equivalence of the divine intention and its application to the elect; there was a strong current in favour of a statement of a limited atonement at Dort and in the Westminster Assembly, whose members stated in their Confession that none were redeemed by Christ 'but the elect only'.[16] Other subtle or more important changes were made by Calvin's followers in England after his death: a greater stress on preparation for faith and introspection, and a narrower view of the role of the Holy Spirit; a clearer or more forceful statement of imputation in justification; a refinement of Calvin's preliminary attempt to map out the stages along the pathway to salvation, or *ordo salutis* as this later version is often known; and a replacement of Calvin's view of a single covenant (albeit in different dispensations) by a twin covenant (of works and grace), though this 'federal' teaching soon spawned further differences of opinion on the precise nature and terms of the covenant of grace.[17]

In terms of early modern England, therefore, it seems fair to use the term 'Calvinist'

[14] L. Berkhof, *Systematic Theology* (1971), 100–5, 114–17; and White, *Predestination*, 104, 184–6.

[15] Berkhof, *Systematic Theology*, 118–25; and see below, pp. 358–60, 367–8, and E. D. Morris, *Theology of the Westminster Symbols* (Columbus, Oh., 1900), 187–9.

[16] W. R. Godfrey, 'Reformed Thought on the Extent of the Atonement to 1618', *Westminster Theological Journal*, 37 (1974–5), 133–71; F. H. Klooster, 'The Doctrinal Deliverances of Dort', in P. Y. De Jong (ed.), *Crisis in the Reformed Churches: Essays in Commemoration of the Great Synod of Dort, 1618–19* (Grand Rapids, Mich., 1968), 73–8; Morris, *Westminster Symbols*, 337; Clifford, *Atonement and Justification*, pt. II; and below, pp. 367–71.

[17] These are all discussed below, in this chapter or the next.

to refer to those who believed in double predestination, unconditional election, and irresistible and indefectible grace; to use 'orthodox' for what came to be widely held refinements of Calvin's views, such as introspective assurance, the *ordo salutis*, and the twin covenant; and to keep in reserve 'strict' or 'moderate' for those who adopted a hard line or a more liberal position on the spectra of opinion that developed on subjects such as irrespective reprobation, supralapsarianism, and the atonement. Lake's distinction between 'credal Calvinists' and 'experimental predestinarians' will also be used where applicable. 'Non-Calvinists' by contrast is used of those English authors who expressed caution at or hostility to some aspects of double predestinarian teaching, and in particular to its teaching on the irresistibility and indefectibility of grace. (Its use is not, however, meant to indicate a commitment to the new type of 'Anglicanism' that Lake has suggested, for reasons that will become clear in Chapter 12.) Thus, of the four official and unofficial yardsticks on these matters to which reference will be made in this chapter, the Thirty-nine Articles of 1571 reflect a very early stage of the debate and a perhaps naïve or cautious assessment of the issues, but are arguably as near a non-Calvinist as a Calvinist position in that the statement of predestination in article seventeen refers to election alone, not reprobation, there are clear assertions in various articles of the universality of Christ's redeeming work, and there is a statement in article sixteen that those who have received the Holy Ghost may fall from grace.[18] The shortcomings of the Thirty-nine Articles in Calvinist eyes are also evident in the attempt made by a number of Cambridge academics to move them in a clearly double predestinarian direction by the Lambeth Articles of 1595,[19] and in the hope that King James would accept the canons of the Synod of Dort of 1619 which represented the new Calvinist orthodoxy, and included a balancing act between strict and moderate views on the atonement.[20] With its federal framework, elements of support for supralapsarianism, and assertion of a limited atonement, the Westminster Confession of 1647 represented a further refinement of the Calvinist position, with some strict elements built into it.[21]

---

[18] Schaff, *Creeds*, 486–517; W. P. Haugaard, *Elizabeth and the English Reformation: The Struggle for a Stable Settlement of Religion* (Cambridge, 1970), 247–72; B. M. G. Reardon, *Religious Thought in the Reformation* (1981), 260–1, 270–5; White, *Predestination*, 52–9, 66–7. The Book of Common Prayer and the two official volumes of homilies could have been used here as well, but since they contain virtually no predestinarian teaching it would have been otiose to raise them. The Irish Articles of 1615 could also have been used, but these were applicable only to Ireland; for English interest in Dort by comparison, see below.

[19] The Lambeth Articles were not published until 1651; they are translated into English in Porter, *Reformation*, 371. I follow Porter, *Reformation*, 364–75, and White, *Predestination*, 115–17, 122–3, on the Lambeth Articles rather than Lake, *Moderate Puritans*, 218–26; on royal reluctance to adopt them, see White, *Predestination*, chs. 6, 8, 10–12, 15.

[20] Schaff, *Creeds*, 550–97; for an English translation of the *rejectio errorum* as well, see Harrison, *Arminianism*, 352–75; and in general White, *Predestination*, ch. 9. On attempts to get the Canons of Dort ratified by the Church of England, see Tyacke, *Anti-Calvinists*, 75–6, 105, 152, 170, 176–7, 179.

[21] Schaff, *Creeds*, 608–24; and on the Westminster Assembly in general, R. S. Paul, *The Assembly of the Lord* (Edinburgh, 1985). For the view that the conclusions of Dort and Westminster were essentially the same, see J. Murray, 'Calvin, Dort and Westminster on Predestination', in De Jong, *Essays in Commemoration*

The second general point to make at the outset is that although there undoubtedly were differences on double predestinarian teaching, we must not necessarily imagine that the tensions these produced were as great away from the universities and the capital. The debate between Tyacke, Lake, White, and Milton has been conducted mainly on the relatively narrow basis of the new 'war of the schoolmen' which itself was conducted in the university schools and the polemical treatises of the period from the 1570s to the 1630s (and even these have their drawbacks as sources: as historians more than most should know, the subject of university theses often bears little relation to undergraduate studies and is wide open to the dictates of fashion and the influence of a few powerful teachers; and, if viewed statistically in terms of which works sold most copies, the published religious literature of the period shows a strong preponderance of non-controversial works without overt Calvinist, 'Arminian', or Laudian content).[22] Moreover, only one of the participants—White—has tried to examine the relationship between, on the one hand, formularies like the Thirty-nine and Lambeth Articles and the canons of Dort, and, on the other, the much more widely used formularies of the Elizabethan and early Stuart period—the Book of Common Prayer (including its catechism), the two volumes of Homilies, and Nowell's catechism.[23] If one asks how these predestinarian issues were presented at different levels, not just at the academic level and in the ecclesiastical and political debates in London, but in the churches and grammar schools of the day and in the non-controversial religious literature prepared for non-specialists, one finds either a loud silence—we simply do not know what most clergymen thought or preached on these matters—or a different emphasis emerging: a stress on faith and repentance, good works as the fruit of faith, and use of the means provided to help the faithful, such as Word, prayer, and sacraments, all of which represented common ground between Calvinists and non-Calvinists, and even between puritans and Laudians.[24]

Official formularies of the day both in England and abroad spoke of the need for 'discretion' or 'special prudence' when handling the subject of predestination in public, and other leading figures in church and state doubted the wisdom of airing the finer points of the predestinarian debate outside the university schools.[25] It is

---

of the Great Synod of Dort, 150–60; for the view that Westminster differed from earlier statements in some respects, see the essays by S. B. Ferguson and J. B. Torrance in A. I. C. Heron (ed.), *The Westminster Confession in the Church Today* (Edinburgh, 1982). It is, of course, dangerous to read 1647 back into the 1620s, but assertions that Bezan influence was waning in England under James should perhaps be checked against what was said by the older members of the Westminster Assembly.

[22] The latter point will be developed in my *Print and Protestantism* (forthcoming). The description of the new 'war of the schoolmen' is in S. Lambert, 'Richard Montagu, Arminianism and Censorship', *Past and Present*, 124 (1989), 36.

[23] See the index of White, *Predestination*, s.v. Book of Common Prayer, catechisms, Homilies, and Nowell.

[24] Green, ' "England's Wars of Religion"?', 103–4; my *Print and Protestantism*.

[25] e.g. in the Thirty-nine Articles and Westminster Confession in England, the Lutheran Formula of Concord in Germany, and the canons of Dort in Holland: Schaff, *Creeds*, 498, 584, 601–11, and cf. 169–70;

instructive that Luther did not tackle predestination in his small catechism, and that Calvin who had treated it in his original catechism of 1537 seems to have changed his mind when composing that of 1541, which turned out to be the one more widely used;[26] the authors of the Heidelberg Catechism also avoided the subject.[27] To gauge the extent to which predestinarian teaching *was* inserted into English catechisms in the early modern period, we may isolate a few aspects of the debate when it was nearing its peak in the early seventeenth century, and see how often and in what ways these issues were handled by the catechists in our sample. As in the previous chapter, however, the possibility of horizontal variation between the ways a subject was explained at elementary as opposed to intermediate or advanced levels has to be borne in mind alongside the vertical variation between the teaching of authors of differing doctrinal views.

Scholars of all persuasions could agree that in the scriptures God is said to have 'predestined' some to eternal life (Rom. 8: 29–30) or to have adopted some as his sons 'according to the good pleasure of his will', who 'worketh all things after the counsel of his own will' (Eph. 1: 5, 11). Those predestinated were equated with the 'elect', those 'chosen in Christ before the foundation of the world' (Eph. 1: 4), in contradistinction to the 'reprobate' who were given or gave themselves over to sin and would be rejected by God at the last day (Rom. 1: 28, 2 Cor. 13: 5, 2 Tim. 3: 8, Titus 1: 16). However, from an early stage of the Reformation (as in the Middle Ages), there was disagreement as to whether there was a single decree—of election—or a double decree or two decrees—of election and reprobation.[28] Luther and Calvin spoke of God both predestinating some to life and reprobating others to death, as did Bucer and Bullinger on some occasions; and from Beza onwards the orthodox Calvinists accorded the double decree a high priority in their theology, stressing what election

---

Porter, *Reformation*, 360–1, 400, 405–6; G. W. Bernard, 'The Church of England *c*.1529–*c*.1642', *History*, 75 (1990), 188–90, 193–4, 197–8; J. P. Kenyon, *The Stuart Constitution*, 2nd edn. (Cambridge, 1986), 129.

[26] Schaff, *Creeds*, 74–92; F. Wendel, *Calvin: The Origins and Development of his Religious Thought*, trans. P. Mairet (1965), 266–7; P. Y. De Jong, 'Calvin's Contributions to Christian Education', *Calvin Theological Journal*, 2 (1967), 174–82. Unlike some other reformers, Calvin thought predestination should be taught in sermons and treatises, but he also urged caution on readers who were not specialists: E. Cameron, *The European Reformation* (Oxford, 1991), 131–2; Calvin, *Institutes*, III. xxi. 1; III. xxiii. 7. Even Beza rarely preached on the double decree and related matters—Bray, *Beza's Doctrine*, 69–85— and did not tackle them frontally in the catechetical works listed in Appendix 1.

[27] But for the differences between the 'Major Catechism' for theology students which did tackle double predestination but was never translated out of the original Latin, and the 'Heidelberg Catechism' which did not tackle it and was translated into many vernacular languages, see Weir, *Federal Theology*, 102–3, 108.

[28] The term 'decree' or 'decrees' was not used in the scriptures but was commonly adopted by theologians needing a term to describe the divine choice. Those who did not use the term included the authors of the Formula of Concord (Schaff, *Creeds*, 93–180) and the Saxon Visitation Articles of 1592 (ibid. 180–9), and the authors of the Lambeth Articles (Porter, *Reformation*, 365–6).

showed about God's power and mercy and reprobation about his justice.[29] On the other hand, Zwingli, Oecalampadius, Capito, Bullinger (on other occasions), Peter Martyr, the authors of the Thirty-nine Articles, and from the mid-sixteenth century the later Lutherans, either rejected or had reservations about the idea that God had actively foreordained the non-elect to hell, as opposed merely to knowing in advance that they would damn themselves by their sins and permitting this to happen.[30]

Other points of difference emerged or were exacerbated as a result. Beza made a distinction between the prime causes of the decree, which he thought were hidden, and the secondary, which he said were revealed in the scriptures.[31] Against this the Lutherans insisted that God's purpose *was* revealed in the scriptures, while other authors combined a reference to the inscrutability of God's purpose in general with a reference to what God had said about his reasons for leaving the non-elect to their deserts.[32] Beza also insisted that election and reprobation were irrespective of faith and sin foreseen: faith might be a secondary cause of election, and sin of reprobation, but these were part of the execution rather than the original design of the decree.[33] The Lutherans, on the other hand, rejected the idea of an irrespective decree in the case of the non-elect, and drew a strong connection between election and responding to Christ's offer in the Gospel; in this sense, election *was* for the faith that God could foresee in the elect. Equally, many Calvinists or non–Calvinists drew a strong causal connection between a lack of faith and reprobation.[34] Beza also believed that logically the decree to elect some and reprobate others 'goes before all the things that follow upon it', that is, it even goes before the decision to create man or to send Christ as a redeemer after Adam fell. Even within the Calvinist camp, however, this 'supralapsarian' view—that the decree was prior to the decision to permit the Fall—remained a minority view; as late as the Synod of Dort the majority adopted a 'sublapsarian' (or 'infralapsarian') view—that God had already conceived of man as created and fallen when he decreed to save some and pass by the rest.[35] Some liberal Calvinists adopted different views, for example Arminius who argued that the decree to send Christ was logically prior to the decree to save and damn particular persons,[36] while the Lutherans

    [29] McGrath, *Iustitia Dei*, ii. 15–16; Kendall, *English Calvinism*, 29–30 n. 3; Cameron, *European Reformation*, 129–31; but see also Weir, *Federal Theology*, 80–1, and White, *Predestination*, 45–8, 74–80; and on Scotland, J. B. Torrance, 'Strengths and Weaknesses of the Westminster Theology', in Heron, *The Westminster Confession*, 46. For the position of an English orthodox Calvinist, William Perkins, see his *Workes* i (1612), 15–16, 24, 105, and cf. 108–9.
    [30] Cameron, *European Reformation*, 130–1; White, *Predestination*, 29–30, 49–52; Schaff, *Creeds*, 165–72, 185, 189; McGrath, *Iustitia Dei*, ii. 30, 48.
    [31] White, *Predestination*, 16–20.
    [32] Schaff, *Creeds*, 166; Hemmingsen, whose works were popular in England, followed the line of the Formula of Concord in his *Enchiridion theologicum*: White, *Predestination*, 89–90.
    [33] White, *Predestination*, 17–19.
    [34] Schaff, *Creeds*, 166–70, 185; White, *Predestination*, 26–8, 40, 42, 72, 104, 137, 184–6.
    [35] Armstrong, *Calvinism*, 41–2; Kendall, *English Calvinism*, 30–1; Harrison, *Arminianism*, 342, 353; White, *Predestination*, 184–6.
    [36] Ibid. 31–2, and cf. Overall's view, ibid. 165–6.

not only condemned speculation on such matters, but also reacted with horror at a schema which made it seem that God had 'created the greater part of mankind for eternal damnation'; this would make God the author of sin in that he could be said to have created a race of people who were predestined to sin.[37] While the authors of the Lambeth Articles, canons of Dort, and Westminster Confession all clearly leant more towards Calvin than the later Lutherans on the twin decree, they were far from being completely Bezan in the stress they put on the elect being chosen 'in Christ' or the connection they drew between the sins of the non-elect and their dreadful fate.[38]

When we turn to our sample of best-selling English catechisms, it is obvious that most authors either chose not to discuss the aspects of predestinarian doctrine just considered or treated them as briefly or generally as possible. Of the fifty-nine catechisms in our sample, for example, only five or perhaps six contain explicit questions and answers on the divine decree as the basis of double predestination. The authors of the five may be described as orthodox or strict Calvinist in doctrinal matters, and the sixth, James Ussher, was a moderate rather than a strict Calvinist on some issues.[39] In nearly every case too, the works in which these questions occur were among the more specialized or intellectually demanding in our sample. Thus in Thomas Cartwright's uncompromising form, perhaps written in the 1590s and tucked in at the end of a number of editions of Dod and Cleaver's exposition of the Decalogue in the reign of James I, it was stated that there were two parts of God's kingdom: his decree and the execution thereof (the Bezan distinction already noted).[40] There were also, wrote Cartwright, two parts of the decree itself: election, which was the eternal predestination of 'certain men and angels' to life, to the praise of God's glorious grace; and reprobation, which was the eternal predestination of 'certain men and angels' to destruction, to the praise of God's glorious justice.[41] Our second statement was similar, and was made in the larger and less popular of the two versions of John Ball's catechism in the sample. There were two parts to the decree, the election of 'some' to faith was for the praise of God's glorious mercy and for his own will and pleasure, and the reprobation of 'some' to punishment for the praise of God's unspeakable and great justice.[42] These are the most explicit statements in our sample before the 1640s,

---

[37] Schaff, *Creeds*, 165–7, 169, 189. The allegation that orthodox Calvinists made God the author of sin proved hard to shake off: ibid. 584 (first head, art. 15); Weir, *Federal Theology*, ch. 2; White, *Predestination*, 19, 21, 49, 76, 185–6.

[38] Porter, *Reformation*, 365–6, 371, for the connection between sin and reprobation (and for the views of Parker and Andrewes on election being 'in Christ', ibid., 369, 371, and cf. Whitgift's view: White, *Predestination*, 104); Schaff, *Creeds*, 581–5, and cf. White, *Predestination*, 184–6; the Westminster divines also said the elect were 'chosen in Christ' and seemed to combine divine permission and prescription in the fate of the non-elect—God passed them by and ordained them to wrath for their sins: Schaff, *Creeds*, 608–10.

[39] On the one hand, Ussher backed the Irish Articles, but, on the other, was a strong episcopalian: R. B. Knox, *James Ussher Archbishop of Armagh* (1967); and see below, pp. 360, 369–70, 381, etc.

[40] Cartwright, 'Catechisme', sig. Aa4ʳ; White, *Predestination*, 18; Perkins, *Workes* i (1612), 24.

[41] Cartwright, loc. cit. The form of words was similar to that found in Beza and Perkins (see n. 29 above), but may have a common scriptural base in texts like Eph. 1: 6.

[42] Ball, *Treatise*, 55–6.

though it may be noted that in both cases it was implied rather than stated specifically that elect and reprobate had been chosen without regard to their faith or lack of it. Also, despite the explicit statements in the third Lambeth article to the effect that the number of the elect was immutable, no indication or impression was given of this fact, and no assessment was offered of whether the proportion of the human race who were elect were a majority or a small minority or what.

The third statement was made in a work which was really a treatise on the doctrine of salvation but has been included in our sample because it was 'composed by way of catechism' in question and answer form 'for the direction of all sorts of people to life eternal': Alexander Grosse's *A fiery pillar of heavenly truth*, which was published ten times between 1641 and 1663. Grosse was able to devote a dozen pages— one-eighth of the whole work—to the decree, and he described both the 'eternal decree' of election whereby God appointed 'some men' to everlasting life, and an 'eternal and unchangeable decree' of rejection by which he decided not to bestow grace on 'some men'. He also gave seven reasons why God could not be considered the author of sin, offered a number of infallible signs by which election and reprobation could be identified, and offered fourteen rules for consideration of the decree, for example that it was grounded on nothing in man, only on God's free will and good pleasure, and that although the decree was eternal and was made before sin was committed, its execution was temporal. Grosse did stress that the decree of rejection was unchangeable, but did not say the same of that of election; and as in the Cartwright and Ball forms, one notes that the formula 'certain men' or 'some men' formula did not indicate whether the elect or the reprobate were in a majority.[43]

The fourth statement may be found in the more advanced of the two forms prepared and used by James Ussher as a young man but not published by him until the mid-1640s. In this he referred to the decree made from all eternity, before man was created, whereby God, for his own good pleasure and before they had done good or evil, chose a 'certain number' to whom he would in time show the riches of his mercy, and determined to withhold the same from others (more an absence of action than an active reprobating) to show them the severity of his justice. Again there was no indication that the division was made irrespective of faith or sin foreseen, and no suggestion of the size of the different groups . Ussher also chose to treat the decree only in his second and larger form, 'framed to the capacity of such as had made a further progress in the knowledge of these heavenly truths'. He omitted all mention of it in the first, shorter form 'containing the more necessary and plainer principles ... fit to be known of all'. In that form he distinguished merely between the fate of the 'righteous' or 'God's children' and that of the 'wicked'.[44]

The fifth statement was made in the Westminster Larger Catechism of 1647,

---

[43] Grosse, *Fiery pillar*, 7–19. Few concessions were offered to those readers not used to the terms used in contemporary exercises in logical thinking.

[44] Ussher, 'Method', 15, and cf. sig. A2ʳ, and id., 'Principles', 12.

where God's decrees (plural) are described as 'the wise, free, and holy acts of the counsel of his will, whereby, from all eternity, he hath, for his own glory, unchangeably foreordained whatsoever comes to pass in time'. By 'an eternal and immutable decree' God elected 'some men' to eternal life 'for the praise of his glorious grace', and also 'according to his sovereign power, and the unsearchable counsel of his own will ... passed by and foreordained the rest to dishonour and wrath ... to the praise of the glory of his justice'. There were separate questions on the decree and its execution, and this distinction was later reinforced by questions on sin and salvation in which it was asserted that Adam had condemned all mankind by breaking the covenant of works—a move which stressed man's responsibility for his fall rather than God's foreknowledge of it.[45] Though one of the most specific accounts of the decree in a conventional catechism, this account differs in one interesting respect from the Westminster Confession on which it was based: the assertion that election was 'without any foresight of faith' in the elect, which can be found in chapter three of the Confession, was not included in the Larger Catechism. It is also noteworthy, as in the case of Ball's and Ussher's more elementary forms, that the equivalent question and answer on the decrees in the Westminster Shorter Catechism omitted all reference to elect and reprobate, merely saying that by his decrees God 'foreordained whatsoever comes to pass'. It was only later in the Shorter Catechism, in the section on the covenant of grace (the second covenant made by God, with Christ, to save the elect), that the idea that 'some' had been elected to eternal salvation was introduced; and even then nothing was said about the fate of those who had not been chosen.[46]

A number of the authors who wrote expositions of the Westminster Shorter Catechism also avoided discussion of the decrees, including four in our sample as we shall see shortly. But the author of one such exposition did tackle the doctrine, and this comprises the sixth explicit statement in our sample. In 1673 Thomas Vincent drew a distinction between God's 'general decrees' by which he had foreordained whatever comes to pass and his 'special decrees ... of predestination of angels and men, especially his decrees of election and reprobation of men', the latter being described in phrases borrowed from the Westminster Larger Catechism.[47] The distinction between general and special decrees was, however, not in the Larger Catechism; indeed, it was similar to one that had been condemned at the Synod of Dort. Perhaps Vincent was allowing himself room to expound a sublapsarian view.[48] In other respects, however, Vincent's line was uncompromisingly orthodox, a fact that may help to explain why his exposition was more popular in Scotland and Ulster than England.[49]

As for the remaining catechisms in the sample, one treated the subject in some detail without actually using the word 'decree': the form known as 'Certaine questions

---

[45] Westminster Larger, 6–7, 11–12, 14 (answers 12–13, 21–4, 30); and see above n. 38.
[46] Westminster Shorter, 7, 10 (answers 7, 20).   [47] Vincent, *Catechism*, 29–31.
[48] Harrison, *Arminianism*, 353.   [49] See Appendix 1, s.v. Thomas Vincent.

and answers touching the doctrine of predestination, the use of God's word and sacraments' inserted into some editions of the Geneva Bible. This, like Beza in his interpretation of Romans 9: 21, spoke of some people as 'vessels of mercy' 'ordained' to
everlasting life, while others, 'vessels of wrath', were 'ordained' to destruction. Since
this form was apparently designed to plug the gaps left by most catechetical authors,
it is not surprising that it was also one of the few in our sample to confront such questions as 'How does it stand with God's justice that some are appointed to damnation?'
and 'Why should a reprobate man bother to be good if he is already damned?'[50] The
great majority of authors of works in our sample, however, adopted one of a number
of other strategies: either they avoided the subject of the decree altogether; or they
mentioned it only briefly or tangentially; or they discussed its implications only in
general terms.

Those forms which did not mention a decree at all include some whose authors we
know from their other writings to have been committed to the doctrine of double predestination, such as Calvin, the authors of the Heidelberg Catechism, and Perkins. It
also includes the authors of the 1549 Prayer Book catechism and most of the later
expositors of that form who either may have had doubts about or positively opposed
a doctrine of double predestination, and Nowell who did not raise the subject in the
shorter and more popular of his works in the sample.[51] Similarly, the authors of those
forms which contained only an oblique reference to the decree, such as the longer of
the two Nowell forms in the sample and Hammond's *Practical catechisme*, may have
adopted this tactic for different reasons: in Nowell's case a sense that the doctrine was
not appropriate to catechetics, even for the advanced students and ordinands for
whom he had designed this form; and in Hammond's case that the teaching of the
Bible had been seriously distorted by some Calvinist interpreters. As Hammond put
it, in an unusually pointed remark in his catechism: 'if I do repent, and lay hold on
Christ for pardon, no power of heaven or earth, no malice of Satan, no secret unre-
vealed decree shall ever be able to deprive me of my part in the promise' made in the
Gospel.[52]

A less stark form of words than that found in the first six forms discussed above
was that adopted by Stephen Egerton in the first of his short forms. By his decree
God had appointed some men, the elect or chosen, to eternal glory and others to eternal fire; but Egerton did not refer to these 'others' as reprobates or make it clear that

[50] 'Certaine questions and answers', sigs. *iii^r; Kendall, *English Calvinism*, 30.

[51] Wendel, *Calvin*, 263–84; Weir, *Federal Theology*, 101–15, 120–5; Cranmer's position was presumably that of the Forty-two Articles which had included a cautious predestinarian statement (Haugaard,
Elizabeth and the English Reformation, 250, 261–2). For Nowell (in his shorter form) and later Stuart
expositors of the Prayer Book form, see below.

[52] In his *Catechisme*, Nowell referred to the decree by which we are condemned for sin (p. 160), to those
that are 'appointed, and (as we term it) predestinated' to be faithful (p. 171), to 'the elect' (p. 170) and
God's 'secret election' of those he has adopted in Christ (p. 174), but nowhere does he enlarge on the
meaning of these terms; nor did he use them in his shortened form, the *Institution*, at the relevant points;
Hammond, *Practical catechisme*, 40 (and cf. 337).

their individual identity had been fixed before all time. Indeed, in the two condensed forms of this catechism which he then provided, he omitted all mention of the decree and of the fate of the elect and the non-elect.[53] Another approach, quite often found in the sample, was that adopted by John Ball in his shorter and more popular form, Martin Nicholes in his exposition of the Prayer Book catechism in the 1630s, and the authors of the Westminster Shorter Catechism, namely, to make the less specific and so perhaps less disturbing statement that by his decree God 'from eternity set down with himself whatsoever shall come to pass'.[54] This approach tended to focus less on the origins or causes of election and reprobation than on the execution of the decree, usually with particular reference to God's works, such as the creation of the world and the providence by which he governs it.[55] However, as we saw in Chapter 7, the idea of God's 'decreeing and fore-appointing of all things' and of his providential preservation of his creation was not necessarily tied to double predestinarian thinking and can be found in many non-Calvinist works.[56]

The fact that so few of the authors of works in our sample chose to talk of a decree does not mean that the majority of the forms in the sample did not contain a reference to the elect, or did not draw a distinction between elect and non-elect. A minority of authors, it is true, did not use the term 'elect' at all, such as the authors of the short pre-communion examination for children attached to Calvin's catechism, and dissenters like Keach and Watts in their very elementary forms.[57] This small minority also includes, perhaps surprisingly, the authors of the Heidelberg Catechism who referred only to believers and unbelievers and to the righteous and hypocrites. Indeed, their assertion that 'only such as by true faith are ingrafted into him, and receive all his benefits' would be saved, was later cited by Arminius with the comment: 'From this sentence I infer that God has not absolutely predestinated any men to salvation, but that he has in his decree considered (or looked upon) them as believers.'[58]

In fact, most of the authors of works in our sample did write of the 'elect', but in most cases the use of the term was either not linked to a Calvinist double decree, or was part of a more cautiously worded statement of predestination than that found in the more advanced or polemical statements of the orthodox Calvinist position. The authors of those forms which were written before the full flowering of Calvinism or who wrote thereafter but were not committed to that viewpoint had no difficulty in using the term 'elect', any more than they had with using the term 'saint' in their

[53] Egerton, 'Briefe method', 3, as compared to id., 'Four points' and 'Briefe summe'; but see also the reference to the elect in id., 'Forme of examining' for would-be communicants, 30.
[54] Ball, *Catechisme*, 69; Nicholes, *Catechisme*, 8; Westminster Shorter, 7 (answer 7).
[55] For the relationship between 'the decrees of God' and his 'works of creation and providence' in Westminster theology, see Westminster Larger, 6–7 (answers 12, 14), and Westminster Shorter, 7 (answers 7–8).
[56] See above, pp. 303–4.
[57] 'Maner to examine children', 153–4; Keach, 'Youth', 113; Watts, 'Children's catechism', 33–5, but cf. id., 'First catechism', 7–8, 9–10, and below nn. 77–8.
[58] Heidelberg Catechism, 325–6, 332, 337; 312–13; Bangs, *Arminius*, 309–10.

exposition of 'the communion of saints' which we looked at in the last chapter.[59] Most interpreted the references to the elect or election in the New Testament as signifying that God had chosen to save those who, through grace, responded to the message of the Gospel and became faithful members of the church of Christ, as he knew they would. Thus the authors of the Prayer Book catechism of 1549, shortly after making their catechumens say that they and all mankind had been called by Christ to a state of salvation, stated specifically that the catechumen and 'all the elect people of God' would be sanctified by the Holy Ghost.[60] They thus avoided using the term 'decree', and also avoided awkward questions such as why God had chosen to proceed this way, how many were elect, and how (if at all) they could be distinguished. Also, following in the footsteps of the authors of the Apostles' Creed (article twelve) and anticipating article seventeen of the Thirty-nine Articles, the authors of the Prayer Book catechism chose not to refer to the fate of those who did not believe.[61] Those forms which were built around the 1549 catechism, including a number in the sample under examination here, tended to follow in its wake, equating the elect with believers, the faithful, those sanctified by the Holy Ghost, or the invisible church.[62] Equally, where an author of one of these forms referred to the fate of unbelievers, he was likely to place the onus for their punishment squarely on their own persistent disobedience or lack of repentance and faith rather than the inscrutable decisions of the divine will.[63]

In his 1541 catechism, Calvin treated neither the decree nor election and reprobation explicitly, and in the hundred and fifty pages of the 1556 translation of this catechism into English, the terms 'elect' and 'reprobate' are used only once each (in connection with the second and sixth petitions of the Lord's Prayer, respectively).[64] It is true that on the latter occasion Calvin referred to God's withdrawing his grace 'from such as his pleasure is to punish', but earlier, under a discussion of article nine of the Creed, he had stated that the church was a fellowship of 'them that believe, whom God hath ordained and chosen unto life everlasting'—a statement which later Lutherans and other non-Calvinists could have accepted. Otherwise Calvin was apparently content to draw a distinction between, on the one hand, 'the faithful' or 'them which believe in [God]' and, on the other, 'impenitent sinners' or 'infidels and wicked'.[65] In his elementary catechism Perkins drew a more specific distinction between on the one hand 'the godly', 'the faithful', 'the elect', and 'the good', and on

---

[59]   See above, pp. 334–6.

[60]   Prayer Book catechism, 780; the later reference to the 'children of wrath' (p. 789) is to the inheritance of original sin at birth.

[61]   There was a reference in art. 17 to vessels of honour, but not to vessels of wrath as there was in Beza (White, *Predestination*, 15–17) and 'Certaine questions and answers', sig. *3ʳ.

[62]   Boughen, *Exposition*, 24; Nicholson, *Exposition*, 27, 137; Marshall, *Catechism*, 20, 66; Williams, *Exposition*; 3; Wake, *Principles*, 59–61.

[63]   Mayer, *Catechisme*, sigs. A6ᵛ–7ʳ; Boughen, *Exposition*, 13; Sherlock, *Principles*, 58.

[64]   Calvin, *Catechisme*, 108, 119.   [65]   Ibid. 37 and cf. 38, 26, 29, 128.

the other 'unbelievers and reprobates', 'the bad', and 'the wicked'.[66] As in Calvin's catechism, however, in the absence of a specific account of the twin decree or a statement of unconditional election, it was possible to conclude from a term like 'godly' or 'faithful', or an unadorned phrase like 'unbelievers and reprobates', that the fate of such people was attributable to the fact that the former had faith while the latter had rejected belief and persisted in sin. The same point can be made of other authors' work. In his scriptural catechism Hieron distinguished between the sheep, who heard the shepherd's voice, and the goats, who did not, either living in open disbelief or making 'a show of godliness, but deny[ing] the power thereof'.[67] Others did begin to draw a distinction between unconditional election and conditional reprobation. Two authors who did mention the divine decree briefly in the text of their catechisms, though not in connection with double predestination specifically, were Egerton (in his first form) and Ball (in the shorter of his catechisms). Egerton drew a distinction between the elect—those believers chosen by God to eternal life in Christ—and 'others', the 'obstinate' who would not repent; while Ball, in a different section from that in which he referred to the decree, distinguished between, on the one side, the elect and chosen and, on the other, 'evil' angels and 'wicked' men.[68]

What also stands out in a number of the forms in our sample is that the point at which the elect or election were first mentioned was often not at the start, during a discussion of God's nature or power or his decree—the position which Beza had pioneered in his polemical works and in which it was tackled in English orthodox Calvinist treatises—but at some other stage.[69] In the forms which were built around the Prayer Book catechism, the 'elect' were first mentioned either during the opening questions on the baptismal vow or under the third part of the Creed.[70] In John Ball's shorter catechism, the elect were first discussed under Christ's mission, in Alexander Nowell's longer form under the eighth article of the Creed (on the role of the Holy Spirit in sanctification), and in Calvin's catechism during an exposition of the next article of the Creed (the 'holy catholic church and the communion of saints') though the word Calvin's translator used at this point was 'chosen' rather than 'the elect'.[71] In one of Stephen Egerton's forms, election was raised after a treatment of the sacraments as the seal of God's promises to the faithful; in the Westminster Shorter Catechism, it was first mentioned under the covenant of grace.[72] In a few catechisms, such as those by Perkins, Virel, and Elton, the first clear distinction between

---

[66] Perkins, *Foundation*, 3, 5, 8. For the use of 'godly' and 'ungodly', 'righteous', and 'wicked' by English predestinarians in non-catechetical works, see Lake, *Moderate Puritans*, 151–2.

[67] Hieron, *Doctrine*, 581; earlier he had stated that Christ's benefits appertained to 'believers', 578.

[68] Egerton, 'Briefe method', 3, 17; Ball, *Catechisme*, 91.

[69] See above, nn. 6, 29.

[70] e.g. Marshall, *Catechism*, 8, 54 (and 20, 66); Williams, *Exposition*, 3; Boughen, *Exposition*, 24; Wake, *Principles*, 59–61.

[71] Ball, *Catechisme*, 74; Nowell, *Catechisme*, 170, 174; Calvin, *Catechisme*, 37.

[72] Egerton, 'Forme of examining', 30; Westminster Shorter, 10–11 (answers 20–1).

elect and non-elect was not raised until a very late stage. Perkins raised it under his sixth and last principle, in an eschatological context: at the Last Judgement the godly elect will possess the kingdom of heaven while ungodly unbelievers will be sent to hell.[73] Virel raised the topic of election in a 'sum' tacked on as a sort of revision exercise after nearly three hundred pages of text. Even then, he devoted only a short and rather general section to it, not mentioning decrees or reprobation, and he did so with the caveat that this was 'a doctrine which to some seemeth difficult and hard' and that the more men searched into it, 'the darker it becomes'.[74] Elton likewise did not offer a definition of the decree or of election and reprobation until the very last lines of his ninety-page catechism for adults.[75]

In many if not all of these cases, the apparent harshness (to human eyes) of the Calvinist view of an all-powerful God deciding for his own unfathomable reasons to send some men to bliss irrespective of faith while condemning others to perdition for their sins was softened by placing the discussion of election either in a hopeful context such as Christ's mission, the benefits thereby made available to the faithful, the covenant of grace, or membership of the church, or in a less comforting but readily comprehensible context such as the penalty meted out to the wicked. The measure of reassurance offered by manœuvring catechumens into using the first person in their replies about salvation was also perhaps considerable—a point to which we shall return below and again in the next chapter. In other cases, the fate of the elect and the non-elect was raised so late, as in the cases of Virel and Elton, that it appears almost as an afterthought or as a precaution by their authors against being accused of having omitted such a focal doctrine. One is left with really very few cases in which election was first raised or treated at length in the context of the divine will alone: such an early statement was made only by Cartwright and Grosse, and by Ball and the Westminster theologians in their longer forms.

One final comment may be made about the treatment of the basic tenets of predestinarianism, whether single or double, in our sample: that with the single exception of Thomas Vincent's expansion of the Westminster Shorter Catechism, described above, treatment of it is largely absent from works first published after 1650. This is partly because many of the later seventeenth-century works in our sample are expositions of the Prayer Book catechism of 1549 which had not referred to the decree or to reprobation, and conversely because most of the expositions of the Westminster Catechisms published after 1650 were not reprinted often enough to qualify for our sample. However, of the authors whose forms did qualify for this sample and who did rely heavily on the Shorter Catechism (which as we have seen contained only a general reference to decrees), none except Vincent chose to highlight the decrees. Thomas Gouge, the son of another renowned catechetical author (William), was expelled from his London living in 1662, and in his

---

[73] Perkins, *Foundation*, 8.   [74] Virel, *Treatise*, 276.
[75] Elton, *Forme*, sig. F8ᵛ; and cf. sigs. F3ʳ–8ʳ, and see also id., 'Extract', sig. G7ᵛ, and cf. sigs. G6ᵛ–7ᵛ.

enforced retirement made extraordinary efforts to spread the word, especially in Wales. In his own catechism he used material from the start and end of the Westminster Shorter Catechism in a simplified form, but among the material he chose to omit were the rather general definition of the divine decrees and the brief reference to election.[76] Isaac Watts, the noted hymnologist and author of childrens' works, in all published six catechisms, the most advanced of which was the fifth— a supplement to the Westminster Shorter Catechism. This contained a reference to the decree of the general kind mentioned above—by it God foreordained whatever comes to pass—and occasional references to the elect being chosen by God, but Watts, a moderate Calvinist, did not stress these points, and in his other forms simply contrasted the conduct of the obedient with those of the wicked or drew attention to the contrasting fates of the 'righteous', who were the children of God, and the 'wicked', who were the children of Satan.[77] Our sample also includes the catechetical forms in a popular elementary schoolbook by a later seventeenth-century Baptist, Benjamin Keach, but in these he too distinguished only between those who believed with a true and living faith, who would go to heaven, and the wicked and impenitent who did not truly believe, and would go to hell.[78] While there were references to double predestination in some catechetical works outside the sample, in works based on the Westminster Shorter Catechism and lectures on the Larger Catechism, these were in a small minority among the works published after 1650.[79] In fact, both before and after 1650, the authors of the great majority of works inside our sample seem to have drawn a discreet veil over the deeper questions relating to the nature and causes of the decree and its position in the divine plan.

If we turn to the doctrine of the atonement, we find a not dissimilar pattern: growing tension among the experts, but little said about it in catechisms. Those who agreed with Beza that the double decree took logical precedence over other divine decisions naturally argued that Christ died only for those who had already been predestined to salvation, as in effect did those sublapsarians who placed the double decree after the permitting of the Fall but before the decision to provide a redeemer. Only those like Arminius who put the decision to send Christ prior to that to elect some and not

[76] Gouge, *Principles*, and 'Heads', *passim*.

[77] Watts, *Assembly's catechism*, 9, 13–14; and see n. 57 above; Clifford, *Atonement and Justification*, 76, 88; E. G. Rupp, *Religion in England 1688–1791* (Oxford, 1986), 156, 160.

[78] Keach, 'Little child', 16; id., 'Child', 25; and id., 'Youth', 83, 97, 113.

[79] e.g. H. Binning, *The common principles of Christian religion* (1659), sermons 14–16; and T. Ridgley, *A body of divinity* (2 vols.; 1731), i. 203–6, 243–9 (and in general 203–68). The following by contrast added little to what the Shorter Catechism had said about predestination: J. Alleine, *A most familiar explanation* (1672); T. Lye, *The Assemblies shorter catechism* (1674) (the decrees were omitted altogether from Lye's *Abridgement of the Assemblies shorter catechism*); J. Flavell, *An exposition of the Assemblies catechism* (1692); and T. Watson, *A body of practical divinity* (1692).

others could logically argue that Christ had died for all, even though he knew that many would not take the offer of salvation.[80] The Lutherans and many others also argued that the scriptures spoke clearly of Christ dying for the sins of all mankind, and God wanting all men to be saved. On the other hand, Bucer and some Calvinists followed Augustine in saying that 'all' meant all sorts of men or some of all sorts of men, and the whole world meant all over the world. They also pointed out that other scriptural passages spoke of Christ interceding with God only for the faithful or his chosen.[81] From the 1550s to the 1610s the rift was in practice not complete, since many Calvinists adopted either the distinction made popular by Peter Lombard and Aquinas that Christ's death was 'sufficient' to redeem all mankind but 'efficient' only for the elect, or a variant such as hypothetical universalism.[82] No sixteenth-century Protestant confession contained a clear statement of limited atonement, and even at the Synod of Dort, where a majority favoured a strongly worded statement in support of a limited atonement, the final wording was more cautious, due it has been argued to pressure from the British delegation which pressed a more cautious stance which would not offend the Lutherans by 'too particular and curious a restraint' of redemptive grace.[83] It is only when we reach the Westminster Confession that we find an explicit statement that none are redeemed by Christ 'but the elect only'.[84]

In our sample of catechisms, moreover, there are only two explicit and carefully documented statements of a particular view of the atonement. In 1641, as part of his chapter on redemption in his *Fiery pillar*, Alexander Grosse wrote that 'the father did not choose all, therefore neither did the son die for, and redeem all'; similarly Christ does not pray for all, the Holy Spirit does not sanctify all, and so on.[85] Contrariwise, in 1646, Edward Boughen reinforced the idea of a universal atonement by lavish use of capitals for his citation of scriptural texts to the effect that Christ had died for the sins of the 'WHOLE WORLD', and that 'ALL THAT BELIEVE IN HIM' should not perish. He also added citations from the Book of Common Prayer communion service and the Thirty-nine Articles to support his case.[86] In other catechisms in our sample, however, the norm was either a bald but explicit statement of universal atonement or an implicit equation of the beneficiaries of Christ's redeeming work with those who truly believed, the faithful, or with the group being catechized; only occasionally do we

---

[80] See above, pp. 354–5.

[81] Schaff, *Creeds*, 167–8, 185, and White, *Predestination*, 46, 49–50 (but cf. 72, 151).

[82] W. R. Godfrey, 'Reformed Thought on the Extent of the Atonement to 1618', *Westminster Theological Journal*, 37 (1974–5), 133–71 (for Beza's reservations about this dualism, see ibid. 142–4) and for English examples, see ibid. 147–8, 167–70; Tyacke, *Anti-Calvinists*, 94, 97–9; Clifford, *Atonement and Justification*, 79; and Porter, *Reformation*, 408.

[83] For statements of universal atonement or the use of the first-person plural to the effect that Christ died for 'our' sins, see Schaff, *Creeds*, 167–8, 195, 216–17, 254, 256–7, 507; and cf. White, *Predestination*, 40–1, 72, 76, 89–90, 113, 151, 190–1, 269–70; and Clifford, *Atonement and Justification*, 78–80. On Dort, cf. Schaff, *Creeds*, 586–7; Klooster, 'Doctrinal Deliverances', 73–8; White, *Predestination*, 187–92.

[84] Schaff, *Creeds*, 610, and cf. 621–2.   [85] Grosse, *Fiery pillar*, 30–1.

[86] Boughen, *Exposition*, 12–13; and cf. Brightman, *English Rite*, ii. 692–3.

find a form that contained a statement of atonement in the dual, sufficient/efficient form. And with the exception of Grosse and Boughen, all of these statements were cautiously worded or were combined with the use of the first person in subsequent questions and answers.

The view that Christ had made a universal atonement was stated briefly but quite explicitly and without reservation in the Prayer Book catechism of 1549: 'Christ hath redeemed me, and all mankind'. Predictably, authors of the dozen best-selling expositions of the 1549 form in our sample also adopted this position, beginning with John Mayer in 1623 and Richard Bernard in 1630.[87] Henry Hammond tackled the subject indirectly in his advanced catechism of 1644, designed to take catechumens much further than the Prayer Book catechism, when he argued that since the Bible made it clear that Christ had died to save us all, it could be said with confidence that all who believed in Christ and turned to him would be saved.[88] One of the heresies that fifty-two Presbyterian ministers in the London province alleged that they had found in Hammond's *Practical catechisme* was that he was preaching universal salvation. In reply, Hammond pointed out that all he had referred to was universal *redemption*: Christ had died 'for all the sins of all mankind'; he had no trouble in asserting that 'the whole number of the impenitent, unbelieving, reprobate world shall never be saved'.[89] Richard Sherlock defended the same view in his exposition of the Prayer Book form in 1656, though he chose to do so not in the text of his catechism but in a separate appendix. Christ, he said there, had died for all sufficiently and intentionally, though not effectually since the greater part of mankind would not accept the offer or keep the condition of redemption.[90] It should be noted, however, that most of the statements recorded in this and the last paragraph were made in the 1640s or 1650s, and that the normal method of stating the case for a general atonement in episcopalian catechizing was much more low-key, as in the original 1549 form, as can be seen in the expositions of that form by Comber, Williams, Isham, Wake, and Lewis.[91]

If we look at those catechisms which were not based on the Prayer Book form, we find that authors like Calvin, Nowell, Dering and More, and Ussher spoke of Christ dying for 'sinners', or for the sins of 'man' or 'mankind' or the 'world', without linking

---

[87] Prayer Book catechism, 780; Mayer, *Catechisme*, sigs. A6v–7r; Bernard, *Common catechisme*, sigs. B2r–v; and cf. below, nn. 90–1.

[88] Hammond, *Practical catechisme*, 311–12, but see also 5–7, 11–12, 23–4, 34, 40–2, 48–9, 85–7, 97–8, and 337.

[89] J. W. Packer, *The Transformation of Anglicanism 1643–1660 (with special reference to Henry Hammond)* (Manchester, 1969), 53–5, 59–60; for a similar incident *c*.1653 when the Prayer Book catechism was used to show that universal redemption was 'the doctrine of the Church of England before Arminius was born', see ibid. 56; cf. McGrath, *Iustitia Dei* ii. 106–7; and Clifford, *Atonement and Justification*, 78–80.

[90] Sherlock, *Principles*, 58–60.

[91] Comber, *Church-catechism*, 10, 14–15; Williams, *Exposition*, 16; Isham, *Catechism*, 13–15, 20; Wake, *Principles*, 46, 59–61; Lewis, *Catechism*, 24–5; and cf. Hill, *Principles*, sigs. A8v and B2v; Nicholson, *Exposition*, 27, 33; Marshall, *Catechism*, 19–20, 65; and Williams, *Exposition*, 21.

this to a statement that this meant the elect.[92] Virel cited texts which some 'universal-
ists' like Boughen and Sherlock would later highlight, such as John 1: 12 and 3: 16.[93] In
answer to the question whether the fact that Christ had died for man's sins meant that
all were discharged thereby, Dering and More replied that only those who 'took hold'
of Christ and his merits with true faith, were discharged—a reply which does not in
itself imply that their action was foreordained.[94] Similarly, the authors of the Heidelberg Catechism, having stated that Christ is 'freely given unto us for complete redemption and righteousness' went on to say that only those with true faith would receive
Christ's benefits.[95] At various points in his catechism, William Perkins also made
expansive statements: Christ had accomplished all things needful for the salvation of
'mankind'; Christ offered the means of salvation to many and this was sufficient to save
all mankind. But we know from Perkins's other writings that he believed in the suffi-
cient/efficient distinction, so it is no surprise that on the latter occasion we find him
adding that not all would be saved by these means because not all would receive them
by faith.[96] Perkins's catechism was first published in 1590, and from the late 1590s one
finds a limited number of more restrictive statements, like Stephen Egerton's to the
effect that Christ had pacified God's anger against the sins of the elect.[97] A belief in
Christ's redemptive work being for the elect alone was hinted at in the twenty-first
answer of the Westminster Shorter Catechism, and this was stated more strongly (if
not altogether categorically) in answer fifty-nine of the Larger Catechism. But the
more explicit denial of universal atonement in the Westminster Confession—none are
redeemed by Christ but the elect—was not used in either catechism.[98]

Indeed, in one important respect the impact of any attempts to teach limited
atonement, and double predestination as well, was probably softened in the minds of
catechumens by the way in which the doctrine of redemption was presented in many
catechisms. Those authors who believed in a fixed decree of election and an effectively limited atonement also believed that the names of the chosen were known only
to God, so, like those who believed without reservation in a universal atonement,
they were prepared to argue that the good news of Christ's atonement for sin must be
made known to everybody on earth.[99] As a result catechists of all hues tended not to

---

[92] Calvin, *Catechisme*, 27; Nowell, *Catechisme*, 156; and id., *Institution*, sigs. Diii^r–iv^r; Dering–More,
Catechisme, sigs. B1^v, B3^r; Ussher, 'Principles', 8, and id., 'Method', 19.

[93] Virel, *Treatise*, 22; Boughen, *Exposition*, 12–13; Sherlock, *Principles*, 58.

[94] Dering–More, *Catechisme*, sig. B1^v; and cf. Bradshaw, 'Brief forme', 135.

[95] Heidelberg Catechism, 312–13.

[96] Perkins, *Foundation*, 4–5; Godfrey, 'Reformed Thought', 147–8. On one occasion (p. 5) Perkins
said that Christ interceded for 'the faithful'.

[97] Egerton, 'Briefe method', 7.

[98] Schaff, *Creeds*, 586, 622; Clifford, *Atonement and Justification*, 26–7, 75. Some answers in the Westminster Larger seem to imply a larger constituency than others, for example, 32 (sinners) and 35 (all
nations), as against 30–1 (elect) 38 and 44 (a peculiar people or Christ's people): 14–18, 22.

[99] Porter, *Reformation*, 310; White, *Predestination*, 22, 46; Clifford, *Atonement and Justification*, 76–7,
82–3, 88–9. For the ideas of a general calling for all and a particular calling for the elect, or a common grace

stress the exclusion clauses in the divine plan, but to treat all their catechumens as potential saints. This is exemplified by the fact that most catechists were prepared to use the first- or second-person singular and plural in the soteriological sections of their works, forming there a ready match for the use of 'we' and 'you' in the sections on the Decalogue and Lord's Prayer (what are *you* commanded to do in the second Commandment? what do *we* pray for in the third petition?).[100] The opening exchange in the Heidelberg Catechism was as follows:

What is thy only comfort in life and in death?
That I ... am not my own, but belong to my faithful Saviour Jesus Christ who ... has ... satisfied for all my sins, and redeemed me ... and so preserves me ... that all things must work together for my salvation.[101]

Similar first-person expressions of being among those for whom Christ had died can also be found in the Prayer Book form of 1549, as cited above, and in the opening exchanges of Paget's short form.[102] In short, there is only the occasional hint in our sample of catechisms that Christ's atonement might not have been universal, and the regular use of the first person for catechumens' answers about redemption encouraged them to see themselves as among those for whom he had died.

Another aspect of the predestinarian debate was the extent of the freedom of the human will and the related question of whether grace was resistible or not. Views of the extent of the corruption of the human will after the Fall might vary, but no mainstream Protestant seriously suggested that man had an independent capacity to turn to God or to achieve something good. Later Lutherans, orthodox Calvinists, and Arminians could all agree that without divine help, in the form of prevenient grace communicated through the Word and Spirit, the will of fallen man was perfectly incapable of responding to the divine call, and that even after the will was regenerated it could do nothing good except through the assistance of further grace to which any merit of such acts was ascribed.[103] Grace, it was almost universally accepted, was

---

offered to all and a special grace offered only to the elect, see Schaff, *Creeds*, 624–5 (Westminster Confession, ch. 10, paras. 2, 4); Clifford, *Atonement and Justification*, 102–5, 109–10; and White, *Predestination*, 33, 47–8.

[100]   See below, Chs. 10, 11.   [101]   Heidelberg Catechism, 307–8.

[102]   Prayer Book Catechism, 780; Paget, *Questions*, sig. A5ʳ; and see below, pp. 394–7. It was probably only a relatively small number of thinkers of the later seventeenth and the eighteenth centuries, like the hyper-Calvinists, who denied the 'free offer', who might have had serious qualms about using 'you' to a mixed congregation of saints and sinners in specifying for whom Christ had died. But their ideas were not sufficiently popular to be represented by a catechism in our sample: cf. Clifford, *Atonement and Justification*, 104–5, 110, 112–13. For the high Calvinist John Owen's mixture of 'elect' and first-person plural, see his two forms in *The principles of the doctrine of Christ* (1645).

[103]   McGrath, *Iustitia Dei*, ii. 15–16, 28–30; Cameron, *European Reformation*, 112–14; Kendall, *English Calvinism*, 20, 55–6; White, *Predestination*, 53–5, 66, 72, 192–4; and see Schaff, *Creeds*, 493–4, 497; 106–14; 546–7; 623–5; and cf. 587–92.

the key, and there was even a measure of agreement that the operation of grace did not force the will to turn to God, but powerfully persuaded it, and at the very moment of success transformed it into a regenerate will capable, through further grace, of taking positive steps of its own. This idea of a simultaneous persuasion and regeneration of the will avoided the twin pitfalls of saying, on the one hand, that grace acted on men as if they were 'a block of wood or ... a lump of stone', and, on the other, that conversion was the result of unaided human will.[104]

There were, however, further problems, and it was in trying to solve these that the name-calling began. Was the process of conversion or calling (the terms are not synonymous but were often used interchangeably) a sudden once-and-for-all event, or a process that took some time? Double predestinarians thought that effectual calling was an event, non-Calvinists that it was a process.[105] And how far was the human will (including the regenerate will which it was generally agreed retained some of its old corruption) capable of resisting grace? Orthodox Calvinists at Dort made very clear their belief that grace was irresistible in the elect—otherwise God's foreordained will would not be accomplished; anyone who argued otherwise was opening the door to the Pelagian or semi-Pelagian heresy.[106] But Lutherans and Arminians clearly regarded grace as resistible, and backed their case by scripture passages showing people resisting the Holy Ghost.[107] However, the technical problems of explaining on the one side why irresistibility should not be equated with compulsion, and on the other why resistibility did not mean free will, meant that the authors of catechisms in our sample barely touched on these questions.

One of the few to tackle free will frontally was Henry Hammond in his dialogue-catechism for advanced catechumens. Man's will, he wrote, is a free faculty, but since the Fall it has been diseased and therefore strongly inclined to ill. But Christ has sent the Spirit to cure the disease, and 'the will being by the grace of God recovered to some tolerable health ... may, being thus set at liberty, by the strength of that grace,

---

[104] Schaff, *Creeds*, 109–10, 113, 590–1, 625; and cf. Bangs, *Arminius*, 343; White, *Predestination*, 41, 47, 54, 220, 274; Porter, *Reformation*, 371; L. B. Tipson, 'The Development of a Puritan Understanding of Conversion', Ph.D. thesis (Yale, 1972), 16–19, 112. For the problems Beza and Perkins seem to have had in trying to describe the exact point at which the unregenerate will was sufficiently renewed by grace to be capable of acting in a regenerate manner, see T. Beza, *A booke of Christian questions and answers* (1578), fos. 30ᵛ–31ᵛ, and Kendall, *English Calvinism*, 64–5.

[105] In Elizabethan and early Stuart times it was rare for conversion to be described as a dramatic, road-to-Damascus event: Coolidge, *Pauline Renaissance*, 64–6, 147; Tipson, 'Puritan Understanding of Conversion', 40–1 and chs. 3–5. The only reference to calling or conversion in the Book of Common Prayer was in the 'Collect for the festival of the conversion of St Paul': Brightman, *English Rite*, ii. 560–1.

[106] That all men had a free choice to do good or evil and that anyone could become regenerate through choosing to do good; for the position of those at Dort, see Schaff, *Creeds*, 589–90 (third and fourth heads, paras. 8, 10).

[107] Ibid. 110 (Formula of Concord, second art., negative, clauses 2–3); and p. 547 (fourth Arminian art. of 1610); Bangs, *Arminius*, 215–16 (where the Pelagians attributed the faculty to achieve grace wholly to nature or only partly to grace, Arminius attributed it entirely to grace); and for use of the simile of the beggar stretching out his hand to receive divine alms, see Kendall, *English Calvinism*, 143; and White, *Predestination*, 121, 220.

choose that good which the Spirit inclines it to'.[108] This limited capacity to choose good had to be viewed in the context of divine initiative and divine help rather than of man enjoying complete freedom of action.[109] At one point Hammond wrote of the preventing, exciting, and illuminating grace sent by God to educate our souls, and at another of the 'preventing, sanctifying, and assisting' grace which the Holy Ghost works in us ' "both to will and to do of his good pleasure" ' (Phil. 2: 13).[110] Elsewhere in the sample, the idea of freedom of the will was mentioned but rarely and then only in general terms or by implication. It was also always condemned, as in Perkins's denunciation of those 'ignorant people' who thought that they could repent when they felt like it and still be guaranteed salvation.[111]

Nor was the question of resistibility discussed at length in our sample, not even in Cartwright's form, Grosse's catechetical treatise on salvation, or the Westminster Larger Catechism. Grosse pointed out that the ministry of the Word outwardly called both good and bad people, but that the Spirit inwardly called only the chosen.[112] In other words, for the elect, resistance was out of the question, but for those not elect there was no inward call and so, in effect, no resistance to it. The authors of the Westminster Larger Catechism came near to the matter when they referred to the 'neglect' and 'contempt' of grace shown by the non-elect, which implies a capacity for resistance among the reprobate.[113] The authors of the Shorter Catechism did not even consider the possibility of resistance, even though they described the call to faith by the Holy Ghost in terms which were far from implying a mechanical or automatic act: we are convinced, enlightened, persuaded, and enabled to embrace Christ.[114] Indeed, one of the exponents of the Shorter Catechism, the high Calvinist Thomas Vincent, seems to suggest that there were two acts in the Spirit's application of redemption to the elect, and that the second represented an act of human will: we are united into Christ by the Spirit and by faith on our part, he wrote; this faith is 'our act', though it is God's gift and the work of his spirit.[115] The Baptist Keach in his catechism for a little child went further: if I would be saved, I must believe in Christ and be converted (the child is led to say), and to obtain the special grace which I need in order to believe, I must pray to God for Christ's sake to give me that grace.[116]

In general, resistibility was not a subject on which predestinarian catechists, or indeed non-predestinarian ones, wished to dwell: only reprobates or hardened sinners

---

[108] Hammond, *Practical catechisme*, 338–9.

[109] This statement is virtually the same as that in paragraphs 4 and 9 of the third and fourth heads of the Canons of Dort: Schaff, *Creeds*, 588–9.

[110] Hammond, *Practical catechisme*, 232, 325. [111] Perkins, *Foundation*, sig. A2ʳ.

[112] Grosse, *Fiery pillar*, 35–6, and cf. 45–50.

[113] Westminster Larger, 30, 34–6 (answers 59, 67–8). The Canons of Dort also imply a capacity for resistance: Schaff, *Creeds*, 589, 591 (third and fourth heads, paras. 9 and 14). Note also that the 'special grace' which the Westminster Confession mentions as being communicated to the elect is not raised in either of the Assembly's catechisms.

[114] Westminster Shorter, 15 (answer 31). [115] Vincent, *Catechism*, 74.

[116] Keach, 'Little child', 16 and cf. id., 'Child', 25–6, and n. 78 above.

would resist, and for all practical purposes catechumens were assumed to be neither. In fact, through a common stress on the regenerating role of grace and the Holy Ghost, there was probably less difference than might have been imagined between the Calvinist author seeking to avoid the charge of making the elect look like robots at the moment of their effectual calling and the non-Calvinist catechist endeavouring to make sure that the catechumen remembered that his response to the Gospel promise was not possible without the grace communicated by the Holy Spirit.

Two further points about the way in which the access of faith was handled by pre-destinarian authors in our sample of catechisms may be mentioned briefly. One concerns the idea of preparation for faith, the other the use of active or voluntaristic verbs such as 'obtaining', 'applying', and 'taking' in the context of faith. The idea that the elect might be prepared for faith was one on which the 'Calvinists' did not march in step. Calvin himself was positively hostile to the idea that the elect could in any sense prepare themselves for faith: any awareness of his own disobedience in unregenerate man or any attempt by him to pray for a clean heart was itself a motion from God rather than from man.[117] However, a number of his followers, while in agreement that the initiative came solely from God, chose to present effectual calling in a way which suggested that faith did not come to the elect totally without warning. They stressed that the normal way in which faith was outwardly engendered, or 'attained' as Paget put it, was through the preaching of the Word; it was necessary therefore for the as yet unregenerate to attend and listen closely to sermons—a sort of preparation for faith.[118] The text that preachers often chose to open was the Law, as a result of which even the reprobate who heard it might come to see their own sinfulness, and certainly the unregenerate elect might see it and feel accordingly guilty.[119] Perkins is a good example of an author who adopted this approach, both in the diagram in *A golden chaine* in which 'effectual hearing and preaching' and 'mollifying of the heart' precede faith, and in his catechism. In the latter he had just turned from treating Christ's sacrifice to the means by which 'a man' could apply Christ and all his benefits to himself, when he asked:

How doth God bring men truly to believe in Christ?
First, he prepareth their hearts, that they might be capable of faith: and then he worketh faith in them.
How doth God prepare men's hearts?
By bruising them, as if one would break an hard stone to powder; and this is done by humbling them. Ezek. 11. 19; Hos. 6. 1–2.
How doth God humble a man?

---

[117] Calvin, *Institutes*, II. ii. 27, and id., *Catechisme*, 88–9.   [118] Paget, *Questions*, sigs. D3ʳ.

[119] Dering–More, *Catechisme*, sig. B5ʳ; Paget, *Questions*, sig. D3ʳ; Heidelberg Catechism, 328; Perkins, *Foundation*, 1, 7; Egerton, 'Briefe method', 14; Elton, *Forme*, sig. D4ʳ; Ball, *Catechisme*, 75; Ussher, 'Method', 21; Grosse, *Fiery pillar*, 45; Westminster Larger, 16–17, 53–5, 119–21 (answers 35, 95–7, 155); Westminster Shorter, 33 (answer 89); and see below, Ch. 10, and von Rohr, *Covenant of Grace*, 59–63 for a puritan stress on the preaching of the Law as preparation for grace.

By working in him a sight of his sins, and a sorrow for them.
How is this sight of sin wrought?
By the moral law; the sum whereof is the Ten Commandments.[120]

In his catechisms Edward Elton echoed and amplified Perkins on this point,[121] and in his shorter form John Ball put in a similar but slightly different way. In the section before that in which he discussed effectual calling, Ball implied that the bare knowledge of Christ's redemptive work could 'work' on the heart of the elect by bringing the individual to 'a serious consideration of his own estate, to grieve for sin and the fear of God's displeasure whereby the heart is broken and humbled', and 'to confess his sin, highly to prize Christ and hunger after him until he obtain his desire'.[122] The authors of the Westminster Larger Catechism did not use the term 'preparation', but under a question placed later, after the Decalogue, they warned their catechumens that to escape God's wrath and curse for breaking his Law, he required of them repentance, faith, and the diligent use of 'the outward means whereby Christ communicates to us the benefits of his mediation', namely the Word, prayer, and sacraments. Whether those catechumens who were to repent, believe, and use the outward means were already regenerate or not was not made clear—presumably they were.[123]

It is probably going too far to say, as Dr Kendall has done, that in talking of the bruising of the heart (and in other ways) Perkins and his admirers regularly put repentance before faith, and that in so doing they not only reversed the order laid down by Calvin but also became barely distinguishable from the 'Arminians'.[124] In his 'ocular catechism' on the *ordo salutis*, Perkins might have put the preaching and hearing of the Word and the mollifying of the heart before the advent of faith, but faith was still considered as part of the first stage of the pathway to salvation, while *true* repentance was part of the third stage.[125] Moreover, the statements made by Calvinists to the effect that the Law acts as a schoolmaster to bring us to Christ were made in the context of those already regenerate and in process of sanctification, rather than those yet to be called.[126] Leading on from this, it was quite possible for those authors who from the 1590s grafted a double covenant framework onto their soteriological thought, to stress that all people (both elect and non-elect) were still

---

[120] Perkins, *Foundation*, 5, and the chart in id., *A golden chaine* in *Workes* i (1612), opposite p. 11.

[121] Elton, *Forme*, sigs. C5^(r–v), and id., 'Extract', sigs. G3^v–4^r.

[122] Ball, *Catechisme*, 74–5; cf. Gouge, *Principles*, 7–8.

[123] Westminster Larger, 118–19 (answer 153); Westminster Shorter, 31–2 (answer 85).

[124] Kendall, *English Calvinism*, chs. 4, 5, 10.

[125] See the chart in *A golden chaine* referred to in the previous paragraph; Elton, *Forme*, sigs. C5^r, D1^r–2^v. Authors who wrote of preparation probably drew a distinction between the quality of the sorrow for sin felt before effectual calling and that of the true repentance experienced afterwards, e.g. Elton, *Forme*, sigs. C7^v, D3^r.

[126] e.g. Westminster Larger, 38–9, 41–2, '110–11' (*recte* 118–19) (answers 72, 76, 153), but cf. 53–6 (answers 95–7); also Nowell, *Catechisme*, 140–1; Paget, *Questions*, sig. D3^r; Cartwright, 'Catechisme', sig. Aa5^r; Ussher, 'Principles', 8, and id., 'Method', 20; Vincent, *Catechism*, 94–5.

under the covenant of works and bound by the Mosaic law. Not only were the reprobate to be shown why they merited punishment, but also the elect (even though they were in the covenant of grace) had to have their hearts bruised and to feel fear and sorrow for their sins, whether they were yet regenerate or not.[127]

It remains the case, however, as Dr Kendall's work suggests, that some predestinarian authors, including a few in our sample of catechists like Perkins, Elton, and Ball, did seem to imply in some of their statements that the elect should experience a sense of sin or shame or sorrow for sin either before or at the moment of their coming to faith. The result was to leave their catechumens in a position not far removed from those of an author like Hammond, who argued that the regenerate had to respond consciously to the Holy Ghost's attempts to convince them of their sin and the grace offered to enable them to triumph over sin: a choice had to be made between good and evil in which a sense of guilt at having broken the Law would play a part.[128] The practical consequence of teaching that the hearts of the elect were being prepared was thus to reduce the gap between the rival tendencies on the calling to faith.

A similar conclusion can be reached about the number of active verbs or 'voluntaristic' expressions used in many catechisms by authors more or less committed to a double predestinarian stance. As we have seen in a previous chapter, it was not uncommon practice for authors writing about the nature or the life of faith to combine verbs like 'wrought' or 'made' to describe the work of the Holy Ghost, with verbs of motion or action such as 'take hold', 'apprehend and apply', and 'obtain' to describe man's response or part in the process.[129] 'Are all discharged by Christ from the guilt of their sin?', asked Dering and More; 'No', was the reply, 'only those that take hold upon Christ and his merits with a true and lively faith' which is 'wrought in me by the Holy Ghost'.[130] Similarly, Edward Elton wrote of faith being 'bestowed' on God's chosen and 'wrought' in their hearts, by which means they 'apprehend and apply' Christ and all his benefits to themselves.[131] To make Christ ours, wrote the nonconformist Thomas Gouge, two things are needed: God's giving (which is already done) and our taking. ''Tis the latter that lieth to us', he added; 'labour to get Christ', he urged his catechumens.[132]

We are here close to the more 'active' definition of faith—as an act of appropriating—that we encountered briefly in Chapter 7 and will meet again in the next chapter when looking at introspective techniques of assurance.[133] Again it must be stressed

---

[127] See below, p. 405 n. 78.   [128] Hammond, *Practical catechisme*, 23, 57, 79, 82–3, 337–8.

[129] See above, pp. 321–2, and below, following notes. For the use of another verb with connotations of human initiative—'escape'—see Heidelberg Catechism, 311; Ball, *Catechisme*, 72; Watts, 'Children's catechism', 16.

[130] Dering–More, *Catechisme*, sig. B1ᵛ; and cf. Paget, *Questions*, sigs. C4ᵛ–5ʳ, D3ʳ; Perkins, *Foundation*, 1; in the case of the full-length exposition of these articles the idea of being 'made' a partaker is less clearly stated: 5–7.

[131] Elton, *Forme*, sig. C5ʳ; and cf. Cartwright, 'Catechisme', sig. Aa7ᵛ; and Egerton, 'Briefe method', 8–9.

[132] Gouge, *Principles*, 53, 69; and cf. Vincent, *Catechism*, 74.

[133] See above, pp. 321–2, and below, pp. 389–94.

that the authors who used such terms were not saying that men exercised some form
of free will in 'taking hold of Christ': that was the work of the Holy Ghost and grace.
But in seeking to rebut the notion that the grace of regeneration treated the elect as
'senseless stocks and blocks' who supinely endured a compulsory call to faith, double
predestinarians often found themselves devoting as much space to the human will in
its 'apprehending', 'applying', and 'taking hold of' Christ and all his benefits as to the
divine will which 'wrought' faith in the elect through the Holy Ghost. And in so doing
they also ran the risk of reducing the differences between themselves and the non-
Calvinists, for whom man's exercise of his will, through grace at the moment of calling, and subsequently through further grace, posed no problems.[134] Like the idea of
preparation for faith, the teaching of an active taking hold of Christ may have contributed to a blurring of the edges of the idea of irresistible grace, and as such may have
made the contrast with non-Calvinist ideas seem less sharp to the theologically unsophisticated catechumen.

The logical corollary of saying that God had decreed the salvation of his chosen ones
was that they could not fall from grace: in the elect, said the Calvinists, grace was
indefectible, that is, it would not decay.[135] Faced by the apparent defection of some
who for a time had appeared to be good Christians, double predestinarians developed
theories of temporary faith or general vocation, according to which the reprobate
were held to have some measure of understanding and commitment to God's teaching before they fell away.[136] But as far as the elect, with their true faith and true
amendment of life, were concerned, they were destined to persevere in the faith.
However, the authors of the Thirty-nine Articles (responding to an Anabaptist
claim) stated that 'after we have received the Holy Ghost, we may depart from grace
given, and fall into sin, and by the grace of God we may arise again, and amend our
lives'. In other words, this fall from grace could be temporary; on the other hand, it
might prove to be permanent.[137] This was also the later Lutherans' view, while the
authors of the Arminian articles of 1610 preferred an agnostic position—not denying
indefectible grace flatly, but arguing that some passages in the scriptures did seem to
suggest that 'believers' could fall totally.[138] What particularly worried many moderate Calvinists and non-Calvinists was the construction that could be put on too

---

[134] See above, pp. 371–4.   [135] Porter, *Reformation*, 366, 371; Schaff, *Creeds*, 592–5; 636–7.
[136] See above, pp. 322–3.
[137] Schaff, *Creeds*, 496–7; the sense of loss or rupture in 'depart' is arguably stronger than anything in
the later statements of Lambeth, Dort, and Westminster, implying not just a reversion to sin, but a complete loss of divine favour. For similar views held by Latimer, Hooker, and Arminius, see White, *Predestination*, 36, 43, 137, 145; and Kendall, *English Calvinism*, 143–4.
[138] Schaff, *Creeds*, 189 (Saxon Visitation Articles, 'False and erroneous doctrines of the Calvinists',
para. 3), and 548–9; and for the perception of the British delegation at Dort that 'many learned and saintly
men' insisted that believers could fall totally from favour, see White, *Predestination*, 198.

strong an assertion of the doctrine of perseverance: that since the elect were inevitably going to be saved there was no incentive for them to try to be good.[139] And in England, especially after the rapid growth in the mid-seventeenth century of fears of a tidal wave of antinomianism (the idea that the elect were absolved from the Law), many more churchmen came out strongly against the orthodox Calvinist position on indefectible grace.[140]

In our sample of catechisms, the few references to perseverance of the saints that there are predictably occur in forms that have already been identified as containing an explicit statement of double predestinarian doctrine. In 'Certaine questions and answers' it was made clear that such as had felt the motions of the Holy Spirit would not perish—God's purpose was not changeable, and he would not cast off those he had once received; and in the Westminster catechisms it was made clear that true believers could not fall from grace, but would persevere in a state of grace to the end.[141] The authors of a few other catechisms who taught double predestinarianism in an open or qualified manner tackled the related question of whether the elect could sin once they had been called, and what happened to them if they did. The consensus among Ball, Elton, Grosse, and Vincent was that believers could commit grievous sins while they were in the process of sanctification, but though they might lose some degrees of sanctification they would never lose it altogether, and through repentance, reformation of life, and laying hold on the promise of mercy, they could rise again.[142]

Once again, if rephrased somewhat—the regenerate could commit serious sins but could also recover God's favour—this teaching would have been acceptable to the great majority of our authors who did not discuss indefectible grace, including the non-Calvinists who taught that the believer who sinned had to rise again if he or she was to be saved. Similarly, most of those authors of catechisms in our sample who expounded the Decalogue and the fifth petition of the Lord's Prayer in some detail raised the subject of the continuing sinfulness of the faithful and the need to petition daily for sins to be forgiven through Christ's satisfaction for the same.[143] Also those authors who put considerable emphasis on repentance in their catechisms, including Calvin and Watts, on the one side, and episcopalians like Hammond and Marshall,

[139] Schaff, *Creeds*, 167 (Formula of Concord, art. 11, para. 10), 189 (Saxon Visitation Articles, para. 3); White, *Predestination*, 146–7.

[140] The wave of antinomianism may have been 'principally in the eye of the beholder': J. Spurr, *The Restoration Church of England, 1646–1689* (New Haven/London, 1991), 304, 319–21, and chs. 4–5; see also Clifford, *Atonement and Justification*, 194–5, 207–9, 212, 215, 234–5, 243.

[141] 'Certaine questions and answers', sigs. *iii^{r-v}; Westminster Larger, 44–5 (answers 79–80); Westminster Shorter, 16–17 (answer 36).

[142] Ball, *Catechisme*, 88–90; and id., *Treatise*, 214, 234–5; Elton, *Forme*, sig. D3^v; Grosse, *Fiery pillar*, 78–9; Vincent, *Catechism*, 84–5.

[143] All men daily break the commandments in thought, word, and deed, stated the Westminster catechisms: Westminster Larger, 111 (answer 149); Westminster Shorter, 30–1 (answer 82); and cf. Heidelberg Catechism, 308–9, 349; and see also below, Chs. 10–11.

on the other, were anxious to explain not only what true repentance was but also how necessary it was and what benefits it brought.[144] It was more in the theory than the practice that the differences emerged: a member of the Calvinist elect, if assured of his election, could be certain of salvation even if he had sinned grievously just before his death; a member of the non–Calvinist faithful could not be so assured, though he was encouraged to look to God's promises in Christ, and to be optimistic that, if he had begged sincerely for pardon for his previously committed sins and made a genuine (if unsuccessful) attempt not to sin again, his last sin would be forgiven for Christ's sake and he would be united with him in heaven.[145]

This brings us to the closely related problem of assurance which was raised at various points of predestinarian teaching. If God has foreordained some to salvation, irrespective of faith foreseen, and reprobated or passed by the rest, how can I determine whether I am one of the elect? If Christ sacrificed himself to atone effectively for the sins of only part of mankind, how can I be sure he died for me? Do the sins I have continued to commit suggest that my faith may prove to be merely temporary? These questions were pressing and required a convincing answer. From the scholars' standpoint, there were two aspects to the doctrine of assurance: the extent to which man could achieve it; and the means by which it could be achieved. Calvinists tended to the view that the elect could be 'secure' or have 'full assurance' or 'certain persuasion' that their sins would be forgiven and they would be saved. It was conceded that the assurance might not be continual or always strong, but the possibility of such assurance was stated as a fact.[146] Calvin himself had been less categoric: he implied a distinction between the kind of absolute assurance I can have that God is God and the kind of relative assurance I may have that Christ is *my* saviour.[147] Some moderate Calvinists and many non–Calvinists also doubted the orthodox Calvinists' certainty, either arguing that in this life no-one could be absolutely positive that they were saved, or, more cautiously, suggesting that it was given to very few people on earth to have complete assurance.[148]

The methods to be adopted in seeking assurance were usually either outward-looking—look to Christ and the promises of the Gospel—or introspective—look into oneself to see if there are signs of election there—or a mixture of the two.[149] The method

---

[144] Calvin, *Catechisme*, 51–2 (and see below, p. 380 n. 151); Watts, 'Children's catechism', 20–22; Hammond, *Practical catechisme*, 56–70 (and see below, pp. 400–2); Marshall, *Catechism*, 44, 90–1.

[145] For Coleridge's conclusion that the 'Arminian' position would drive men to despair, while 'Calvinism' was a much more 'soothing and consoling system', see C. F. Allison, *The Rise of Moralism: The Proclamation of the Gospel from Hooker to Baxter* (1966), 94. But see also below, pp. 419–20, 472–6.

[146] Porter, *Reformation*, 371; Schaff, *Creeds*, 594–5, 637–40; and cf. White, *Predestination*, 102, 186, 196–7.

[147] Clifford, *Atonement and Justification*, 203.

[148] Article 17 of the Thirty-nine did not mention assurance, though it did point out the risk of desperation among those who had the sentence of God's predestination constantly before their eyes and were led to think that they were reprobate: Schaff, *Creeds*, 498; for others who doubted or were worried by the possible consequences of the idea of absolute assurance, see White, *Predestination*, 103, 106, 116, 121, 147, 197, 219–21, 261, 281–2.

[149] For examples of the last of these, see Hemmingius: ibid. 90; and below, pp. 393–4.

that would probably have been pressed by catechists at the start of our period, including Calvin and the authors of the Heidelberg Catechism, and by a number of authors at the end of it as well, was the first of these. But in the period from the 1570s or 1580s to the 1640s some authors pressed the value of introspective techniques—a point which will be developed in greater detail in the next chapter. But this trend was never universal, even in its heyday, and by the 1620s some of its supporters were becoming more cautious about these techniques. Meanwhile, the majority of authors were more inclined to stress the importance of resting on faith in Christ and the truth of the Gospel promises as a means of assurance, while many later authors raised the matter in the context of baptism and/or membership of the covenant of grace. Some of these authors were not averse to introducing a measure of introspective assurance into their forms, but in general the line taken was that assurance was not of election but of the truth of the objective promises of the Gospel which were given outward expression in the teaching of the church and confirmed in the sacraments of the New Testament.[150]

The subjects of perseverance and assurance lead us to a consideration of one last aspect of predestinarianism: the *ordo salutis*, or pathway to salvation. The authors or translators of catechisms used in England before the 1590s tended to eschew a rigid or detailed *ordo*. Calvin's pastoral emphasis on the dualism of faith and repentance, reflecting the age-old battle between good and evil, was reflected both in the structure of his *Institutes* and in his catechism, where at the end of the section on the Creed he stated that the doctrine of the gospel consists of two points: faith and repentance.[151] In their threefold formula of guilt, grace, and gratitude, the authors of the Heidelberg Catechism under the second heading (redemption) raised faith and the benefits of Christ's mediation (adoption as the son of God, forgiveness of sin, being accounted righteous, and the promise of everlasting life), and under the third heading (gratitude) expounded 'true repentance or conversion' (subdivided into 'the dying of the old man, and the quickening of the new'). But there was no formal or rigid *ordo*.[152] In his dialogues Pierre Virel chose to highlight faith, by which we are made one with Christ and justified, and sanctification or regeneration, under which he discussed repentance, which again was subdivided into the mortification of the old and the resurrection of the new; but again no rigid system was laid down.[153] Of the forms written in England, the Prayer Book form began with a rehearsal of the threefold baptismal vow to renounce sin, believe the faith, and obey God's Law, while in Nowell's form the stress was put on the obedience required by the Law and the faith required by the Gospel.[154]

It was not until Perkins's catechism of 1590 that we find an early example of the orthodox Calvinist *ordo* in our sample of best-selling catechisms. In the famous table

---

[150] See below, pp. 387–94.   [151] Calvin, *Institutes*, Books I–III; and *Catechisme*, 51.
[152] Heidelberg Catechism, 308 and *passim*.   [153] Virel, *Treatise*, 22–5, 53–7.
[154] Prayer Book catechism, 778; Nowell, *Catechisme*, 118 (though cf. 119).

which he had published with *A golden chaine* as 'an ocular catechism to them which cannot read' so that by tracing with their finger 'they may sensibly perceive the chief points of religion, and the order of them', Perkins (relying heavily on an earlier table by Beza) had started at the top with the Trinity, the decrees, creation, and Fall, and then split the flow chart into two routes—the left-hand taking the elect, with Christ's mediation, through the various stages of effectual calling, justification, and sanctification to glorification, while the right-hand route took the reprobate through a partial response to God's calling (including temporary faith) but anticipating their relapse into hardness of heart and inevitable damnation.[155] Similarly in Perkins's catechism, God prepares men's hearts through preaching ('effectual hearing') and by working in them sorrow for sin (the 'mollifying of the heart'); he then works faith in them, they are justified (cleared of sin by the imputation of Christ's righteousness), and are sanctified (they put off the old man, and put on the new, one of the signs of which is repentance).[156] Other authors of catechisms in our sample who described or implied an *ordo*, such as Egerton and Elton, used slightly different terms to Perkins or seem to have tried to combine the emphases of earlier Continental authors with those of Perkins.[157] But by the 1640s, there was a relative consensus among those who raised the subject. Grosse opted for a Perkins-style sequence of decree, vocation (calling), justification, sanctification, and glorification (though he added the interesting rider that justification might be before sanctification in the order of nature, but not in time).[158] Ussher in his shorter form said that the two main benefits of receiving Christ were justification and sanctification (the latter being seen in repentance and new obedience), but in his longer one he inserted adoption between those two.[159] The authors of the Westminster catechisms followed the Confession in opting for an *ordo* of effectual calling, justification, adoption, and sanctification, with extra questions not on glorification but on repentance unto life and assurance of God's love in this world and the next.[160] After the 1640s, treatment of the pathway in works in our sample was either confined to forms derived from the Westminster catechisms, such as those by Wallis, Vincent, and Keach (in one part of his most advanced form), or reduced to fairly general remarks like that of Thomas Comber in his 1681 exposition of the Prayer Book form: by the ministry of the word, the Holy Ghost enlightens, converts, sanctifies, and comforts us.[161]

---

[155] Beza's table is reproduced and discussed in Weir, *Federal Theology*, 71–3, and White, *Predestination*, 13–15; for a comparison with Perkins's table, see R. A. Muller, 'Perkins' *A Golden Chaine*: Predestinarian System or Schematized *Ordo Salutis*?', *Sixteenth-Century Journal*, 9 (1978), 70–7; and in general, Wallace, *Puritans and Predestination*, chs. 1–2; Kendall, *English Calvinism*, chs. 2, 4–5.

[156] Perkins, *Foundation*, 5–7.

[157] Egerton, 'Briefe method', 7–8, 9–10, and id., 'Forme of examining', 30–1; Elton, *Forme*, sigs. C5ᵛ, C8ᵛ–D2ᵛ; and id., 'Extract', sigs. G3ᵛ–4ᵛ.

[158] Grosse, *Fiery pillar*, chs. 1–7.   [159] Ussher, 'Principles', 8–9 and id., 'Method', 19.

[160] Westminster Larger, 34–46 (answers 67–81); Westminster Shorter, 15–17 (answers 31–6).

[161] Wallis, *Explanation*, 16–18; Vincent, *Catechism*, 73–85; Keach, 'Youth', 90–2; Watts, *Assembly's catechism*, 17–20; Comber, *Church-catechism*, '13' (*recte* 12). For use of the *ordo* outside the sample, see Wallace, *Puritans*, 139, 150–1, 177.

The *ordo* taught by Perkins and the Westminster Assembly raised both pedagogical and theological issues at catechetical level. Its great advantage was that it offered catechumens a framework for their spiritual development—a sequence which was almost certainly a source of comfort for those believers who understood it and could see how far they had travelled. However, for those who did not understand terms like 'imputation of righteousness', 'mortification', or 'vivification', or had difficulty assessing how far they had reached, it was probably not. A strict *ordo* also raised theological debates, for example over the relative positions and natures of justification and sanctification, as we shall see in Chapter 9. The fact is that only a minority of authors in our sample did offer a detailed *ordo*, and among those who did not were prominent double predestinarians like the authors of the Heidelberg Catechism, Cartwright, and Ball as well as some who disputed orthodox Calvinist views, like Mayer and Boughen.[162] (The same is true of many catechisms outside the sample too, for example, the minimum knowledge required of communicants by Parliament in 1645, and the several catechisms based on it, did not include any of Perkins's steps.[163]) It would seem, then, that most catechists were either not persuaded of the theological necessity or the practical wisdom of taking up time and space in their forms with a detailed treatment of an extended *ordo*, or they were prepared to adopt an alternative framework to that of the Calvinists.[164]

As indicated earlier, there were various alternatives to the orthodox Calvinist *ordo salutis*, many of them simpler or more flexible, and not without their own internal dynamic. In one based on faith and repentance or obedience, for example, the faith had to be nurtured, the repentance renewed, and the obedience persisted in by the true believer.[165] There was, however, one other alternative which is worth examining here, partly because in terms of its impact it rivalled that of the Calvinist *ordo*, and partly because, although it was first enunciated before the *ordo* became popular, it reached its peak in the second half of our period when the Calvinist star was on the wane. This was a sequence based on the outer, visible life of the Church of England as represented in the sacraments and other ceremonies with which most members of the official church came into physical contact at certain stages of their lives.

Within the Edwardian Prayer Book and its associated catechetical form there was the basis of a liturgical-cum-spiritual odyssey, from baptism in infancy, through catechizing as a child and confirmation in late childhood or early adolescence, to full participation as an adult in the life of the church through the Lord's Supper and other church rites, until the church carried out the final obsequies for the dear departed. In

---

[162] The views of these authors are explained elsewhere in this chapter, the last two under limited atonement.

[163] See above, pp. 79–80.

[164] In a handful of more advanced forms, there was a sharp division, occasionally explicit, over the nature of justification and the relationship between justification and sanctification; these will be considered in Ch. 9 below.

[165] See the forms cited above, in nn. 151–4.

baptism, as we shall see in Chapter 12, the infant was received into the church and held to be 'regenerate and born anew of water and of the Holy Ghost'; according to the 1549 catechism, the infant was also made a member of Christ, the child of God, and an inheritor of the heavenly kingdom. Godparents were ordered to ensure that the baptized child was taught a basic knowledge of the Christian faith, and how to perform the baptismal vow to renounce sin and walk in God's ways. Later when he or she came to the appropriate age, these vows were consciously and voluntarily reaffirmed at confirmation; there God was asked that those being confirmed might 'receive strength and defence against all temptations to sin'.[166] While attending morning and evening prayer or the Lord's Supper, mature members of the church were repeatedly urged to repent their sins, and through prayer to ask God to send his grace (what the catechism called his 'special grace') to strengthen their faith and help them obey his Commandments. Faithful Christians were told that they were justified (made righteous) for Christ's sake, would grow in grace with the help of the Holy Ghost (part of the process of sanctification), but despite trying hard would fall again, and so would need to repent and sue for forgiveness again. Along the bumpy road of life they stumbled, trying to fulfil their baptismal vow, but frequently falling and needing a helping hand, and making use of the means of grace such as the Word, prayer, and sacraments. They were urged to participate in the sacraments as a means by which (according to the section added to the short catechism in 1604) they could receive grace and in the case of the Lord's Supper strengthen and refresh their souls. Hoping that they were still heading in the right direction—were justified and pursuing new obedience—they reached the end of the earthly part of their odyssey, and at their burial the minister would read over their coffin the words 'I am the resurrection and the life, saith the Lord: he that believeth in me, though he were dead, yet shall he live' (John 11: 15–16).[167] Subsequent revisions of the formularies of 1549 and differing emphases in later official statements (such as the homilies, articles, and canons) did not lead to any major adjustments of the route recommended in 1549. Through the regular use of the Prayer Book itself and the many expositions of the Prayer Book catechism from the 1610s to the 1730s, this map was widely disseminated, and details added of how and why the forsaking of sin, belief in God and obedience to his will should be pursued by all those in the church.[168]

The verdict suggested by the catechisms in our sample of best-selling and influential forms in terms of the debate between Tyacke, Lake, and White is that there is some

---

[166] Brightman, *English Rite*, ii. 724–47.

[167] Ibid. i. 129–67; ii. 638–721, 787–91, 848–78. The relationship of a regularly recurring justification and a slow and painful journey to sanctification is explored more fully below, pp. 400–3.

[168] I hope on a later occasion to move on to a wider examination of all these expositions rather than just the dozen in the sample.

support for both sides. As Tyacke and Lake have suggested, there are relatively few signs of Bezan influence before 1640, at least in terms of unconditional reprobation, an effectively limited atonement, or support for supralapsarianism. On the other hand, as Kendall and White have intimated, there was clearly some movement between the position of Calvin and that of his English followers, for example over preparation for faith, and the deployment of the *ordo salutis*; moreover, after 1640 there is the somewhat stronger line on the atonement taken in the Westminster catechisms.

However, much more striking than the relative weight given to some of the points raised in academic debate at the time is the general dearth of predestinarian teaching in the great majority of these forms, and this at a time when we are assured that Calvinism was the dominant doctrine. The main conclusion from our survey must be that the insertion of double predestinarian teaching into both elementary and intermediate catechisms before the 1640s was limited in scale and often cautious or ambiguous in its wording. Certainly until the 1640s, most of the forms that we can be moderately sure from bibliographical and other evidence were in common use—the Prayer Book catechism, those of Calvin, Nowell, Dering–More, Paget, and Ball's shorter catechism—either did not touch on double predestination at all or did not accord the twin decrees, an effectively limited atonement, effectual calling, perseverance, or the *ordo salutis* a central place. Perkins, Egerton (in two of his six forms), and Elton gave some of these teachings a slightly higher priority, as did the authors of 'Certaine questions and answers' and Cartwright, though in the last two cases it is hard to know how often these forms were used because of their unusual publishing history. At an elementary level it was probably only Perkins's and Egerton's forms that had much impact, but numerically their sales were heavily outnumbered by the distribution of the Prayer Book form throughout the country and perhaps by Paget's form too. At an intermediate level, Ball's larger form and Elton's form for adults may have disseminated more explicit double predestinarian ideas quite widely in the 1620s and 1630s, but again these were probably overshadowed by the works of Calvin and Nowell, which we can be reasonably confident were used in many schools and at university, and possibly by works like those of Mayer, Hill, and Bernard.[169]

The 'excesses' of the Laudian period may have exacerbated the growing divisions within the early Stuart church, and, when interrupted at a point when the church was but 'half-Laudianized', provoked even sharper divisions in the 1640s and 1650s and for the rest of the century.[170] But at a lower level than church politics, there was perhaps less change than this suggests: relatively little Calvinism had been taught in catechisms before 1640, and not much more was taught thereafter, especially after the return of the old church in 1660. It is true that from the 1640s, and especially in the

---

[169] For the sales of these works, see above, Ch. 2 and Appendix 1.
[170] Milton, *Catholic and Reformed*, 26, 546.

works by Grosse and the Westminster catechisms, there was less ambiguity in the teaching of some features of orthodox or strict Calvinism; and in parts of Hammond's advanced catechism and Boughen's form for older students there was an implicit or explicit criticism of some of those features. But even later Stuart catechisms should not be approached in terms of a sharp dualism on this area of doctrine. As we have seen above and will see again shortly, the predestinarian teaching in the Westminster Shorter Catechism was presented in a much more circumspect manner than that in the Larger, and it was the Shorter which was reprinted much more often and spawned a variety of expositions, many of whose authors exhibited a similar caution over matters like the atonement or reprobation. There was also thought to be sufficient common ground between the shorter official episcopalian form and the shorter presbyterian catechism for some children to be taught first the one and then the other, and for some irenically minded authors to make efforts to reconcile the two forms in the 1670s and 1680s.[171] In cases such as these, the different forms were clearly not seen as being at opposite ends of a spectrum, and the measure of overlap made it easier to ensure that divisions at the top of the church did not necessarily produce comparable disruption at the bottom.

There remains the possibility that some zealous catechists used the questions and answers included in the works in our sample as the basis for a much more overtly predestinarian exposition culled from a full-length treatise, such as Perkins's *Golden chaine* or Ursinus's commentary on the Heidelberg Catechism.[172] In some cases, for example where an undergraduate had been taught an advanced catechism or read Ursinus at university[173] and wished to elaborate on the text to an intelligent group of catechumens on the mysteries of the effectual calling, this almost certainly happened. However, we cannot be certain how often it happened since the evidence for such extempore exposition is limited, and there are two a priori reasons for thinking it did not happen very often. In the first place, many of those catechists who used someone else's form as the basis of their catechizing may have done so because of a lack of time or a lack of confidence in their ability to devise their own; and such catechists were perhaps likely to stick close to the text rather than indulge in extra study of catechetical material or extended impromptu exposition on contested points. Secondly, it would have run contrary to the general pattern of catechetical teaching suggested in this chapter and the last: that the younger or less educated the target group, the simpler the message should be.[174] In this situation, it would seem more likely that a catechist using one of the less advanced forms in our sample and confronted by

[171] I. Watts, 'A Discourse on the Way of Instruction by Catechisms', in *Catechisms* (1730), 39; and see above, pp. 91–2.

[172] See above, pp. 199–200, 380–1 and below, Appendix 1, s.v. Ursinus.

[173] As last note, and Dent, *Protestant Reformers in Elizabethan Oxford*, 91–2, 186; White, *Predestination*, 87–9.

[174] For authors who selected and simplified in order to get their message across, and the popularity of their works, see above, Chs. 1–2 and 5.

catechumens of average ability would have found himself in a similar situation and kept to the basic ABC of Christianity that they contained.

Indeed, if double predestinarianism was less prominent in the catechisms and catechizing of Elizabethan and early Stuart times than in many of the university theses and some types of books produced in this period, this situation may have owed something to those monarchs, statesmen, and church leaders who were concerned at the possibly unsettling effect of exposing the average parishioner to the full force of the predestinarian debate; but it perhaps also owed much to other considerations. One of these was the built-in tension within Calvinism between, on the one hand, the duty to teach that only some were chosen, and, on the other, the principle that the Gospel should be preached to all. The practical experience and common sense of the parish clergy of the day in trying to get the basics of the faith across to their mainly unlettered charges may have convinced them of the advantages of stressing the positive side of this—preaching the good news of the Gospel to all—rather than the negative—that many had been destined to hellfire from eternity. It is also conceivable that a significant proportion of catechists, including those who had not attended university, were not committed Calvinists, but closer (consciously or unconsciously) to the Edwardian reformers who had composed the church's formularies. Whatever the reason, when attempting to assess the doctrinal teaching of English Protestantism in early modern times, perhaps we should imitate those women of Israel who compared the achievements of Saul and David (1 Sam. 18: 7), and take into account not only the polemical works of the new schoolmen which sold in their thousands, but also the humbler fruits of the catechetical authors of the period which sold in their tens or hundreds of thousands, and through a combination of oral delivery and literacy reached a far larger audience.

9

Assurance, Justification, and the Covenant of Grace

SOME of the topics raised in the last two chapters could not be dealt with fully within the frameworks dictated by a discussion of the twelve articles of the Creed and the main issues of the predestinarian debate, in particular the relationship of faith and assurance, the nature of justification, and its relationship to sanctification. These are not matters which dominated the texts of the works in our sample, but they are important in themselves and have been the subject of much recent debate, so that it may be wise to clarify our authors' positions on these issues before we proceed to discussion of the remaining three staples of catechetical instruction. The opportunity will also be taken to discuss at length a subject only mentioned in passing so far—the covenants of works and grace which, like justification, sanctification, and assurance, had an obvious soteriological dimension of which a growing number of both Calvinists and non-Calvinists took advantage in the seventeenth century. Again not all of the authors in our sample of forms did so, but a sufficient number did to make the exercise worthwhile. The covenants of works and grace can also be usefully raised here since they will form a distinctive part of the background to our examination in the closing chapters of our authors' expositions of the Decalogue and the sacraments.

For Augustine and Luther, assurance of salvation was through faith in Christ, though both doubted whether absolute assurance was possible, since the process of being drawn by grace was not a once-in-a-lifetime conversion but a continually recurring situation. Calvin and his followers thought that assurance *was* possible on this earth because of the fixed nature of the divine decree, but the greater stress placed on double predestination by Calvin and especially by Beza and his successors served to highlight the question of what God's purpose was for each individual: how could they be sure if their name was written in the Book of Life? Calvin restrained any tendency to concentrate on the fate of the individual by stressing that the effectual calling of the elect normally took place in church through preaching, and that this calling was to membership of the church. But in Beza, the Heidelberg theologians, and Perkins, there was a tendency to focus on how individuals could tell whether they had been called genuinely or not, and in particular whether they had saving faith or merely historic or temporary faith (which we have seen were developed as explanations of why some of those who appeared to be called subsequently fell away). Moreover, where Calvin had said that assurance would be obtained through faith in Christ and only very much as a secondary means by looking at the effects of faith on the individual, Beza and his followers encouraged men to look equally or even primarily within themselves for evidence of the fruits of faith: a piercing sense of sin, a desperate longing to do God's will, and so on. It has often been suggested in recent decades that this move towards a concern with the individual's subjective experience of saving grace and with the best means of identifying the marks of grace as a source of assurance of election, represented a shift away from not only Augustine and Luther but also the Christocentricity of Calvin.[1] A reaction against this last point has begun: Joel Beeke has recently made a case for the later Calvinists in England and Holland having advanced and clarified Calvin's view on assurance rather than deviated from it.[2] But in the case of England, the state of play still seems to favour the older opinion.

Dr L. B. Tipson has suggested that many of those writing from the 1550s to the 1580s (including a Scotsman whose catechism was published in England, John Craig) would probably have agreed with Calvin that assurance of election was a matter of faith, and that effectual calling was to membership of the church. However, he also detected in the writing of a number of them (including three authors or co-authors of catechisms—Edward Dering, Thomas Cartwright, and Richard Greenham) a growing interest in 'the intensity of the psychological warfare that took place in the Christian', which was the result of preachers' continual application of the Law (which damned) and the Gospel (which saved). Need for personal assurance of election led to a greater stress on personal preparation rather than corporate religion and an unusual degree of introspection among those who took predestinarian teaching seriously. And with the teaching of Perkins we find the argument that assurance of election should be sought not in heaven, but by the signs and testimonies of the Holy Ghost within ourselves, and in the continual struggle between the old and the new which a genuine calling produced.[3]

Working independently of Dr Tipson and each other, A. N. S. Lane and R. T. Kendall also came to the conclusion that there was a difference between Calvin and what came to be orthodox Calvinism on assurance, which may be summarized as follows. For Calvin faith included assurance, whereas for the high Calvinists faith and assurance were separable in that assurance was obtained by examining the fruits

---

[1] For surveys of the theological background and the historiography, see L. B. Tipson, 'The Development of a Puritan Understanding of Conversion', Ph.D. thesis (Yale, 1972), introduction and chs. 1–2; and J. R. Beeke, *Assurance of Faith: Calvin, English Puritanism and the Dutch Second Reformation* (New York, 1991), 1–5 (I am grateful to Mr A. N. S. Lane for bringing this book to my attention). See also works cited above, pp. 379–80 nn. 148–50; and J. B. Torrance, 'Strengths and Weaknesses of Westminster Theology', in A. I. C. Heron (ed.), *The Westminster Confession in the Church Today* (Edinburgh, 1982), 44–53.

[2] Beeke, *Assurance of Faith*, 369–70 and *passim*.

[3] Tipson, 'Puritan Understanding of Conversion', chs. 3–4.

of faith. These two authors disagree somewhat on the reasons for this change, and Lane tends to give a nuanced approach where Kendall favours a categoric; but on the basic difference between Calvin, on the one hand, and later Calvinists such as Beza, the Heidelberg theologians, Perkins, or the Westminster divines, on the other, they are in agreement. For Calvin (wrote Kendall), faith was in the mind, but for his followers it was also or exclusively in the will. Faith thus came to be viewed less as a passive receiving of a free gift than an active appropriation by the regenerated will of the benefits which Christ had secured for believers. The consequences were what Kendall sees as the characteristic concerns of men like Perkins: urging people to make their calling and election sure (2 Pet. 1: 10); an introspective searching for faith or the fruits of faith; the use of 'active' or 'voluntaristic' terms such as 'taking hold of' Christ; preparationism; and the use of a doctrine of temporary faith to explain the defaulting of erstwhile 'saints'. Kendall dubbed Perkins and his followers 'experimental predestinarians' to convey the way in which they experimented in self-analysis in order to establish that they were elect, and came to treat assurance as a matter more of technique than of belief and trusting in the promises God made in Christ.[4] Lane reached a not dissimilar conclusion by a different route. He casts doubt on the sharpness of the distinction between mind and will: Calvin (he says) believed faith was not only in the mind but also in the heart. He also points out that although Calvin insisted that the ground of assurance was objective and outside man, he also believed self-examination had a part to play, as long as that self-analysis was not of one's own works or the type or strength of one's faith but of the object of faith, that is, Christ. The essence of Calvin's doctrine of assurance, writes Lane, is not 'am I *trusting* in Christ?' but 'am I trusting in *Christ?*' The authors of the Westminster Confession, on the other hand, saw faith 'primarily in active rather than passive terms', in terms of what it does to the elect, thus shifting some attention away from the objective promises to the subjective evidence of perceived inner feelings.[5]

At this point we may turn to Dr P. F. Jensen who, in his thesis on the life of faith in the teaching of English Protestantism had also reached similar conclusions, albeit on the basis of a different corpus of material—over three dozen unofficial catechisms published *c.*1570–1620. His is the most sophisticated analysis of the doctrinal content of English catechisms in the late Elizabethan and Jacobean period yet undertaken, and in it he devotes much more space than Kendall or Lane to the actual techniques of introspection adopted by English Calvinists at that time. Dr Jensen

---

[4] Kendall, *English Calvinism*, 8, 71, chs. 4–5, and *passim*; Kendall also argues for a gulf between Calvin and the 'Calvinists' on atonement, but Lane doubts whether there was a sharp difference.

[5] A. N. S. Lane, 'Calvin's Doctrine of Assurance', *Vox Evangelica*, 11 (1979), 33–8, 41–8; and Lane's review of Kendall, *English Calvinism*, in *Themelios*, 6 (1980), 29–31. Beeke also notes that the English double predestinarians put more stress on faith as an act where their Dutch counterparts talked of the 'habit' of faith: *Assurance of Faith*, 369–70.

concluded that there were broad overlaps between the various forms he examined, and between these unofficial ones and the official forms of the period—the Prayer Book one and Nowell's catechism. But he also made a case for believing that due to tensions over faith and assurance building up inside Protestantism, there were a number of significant changes in the nature of English catechetics. The result, he argues, was a threefold divide among the alternative catechisms of the period. Using the names of the authors of some of the more frequently reprinted catechisms of the period, he divides his sample of catechisms into a conservative More–Paget 'family' of about twenty catechisms dating mostly from the 1570s and the 1580s, a more innovatory Perkins–Hieron 'family' of a dozen works dating from the late 1580s to the 1600s, and another set of innovators, the Egerton–Cartwright 'family' of half a dozen catechisms published between the late 1570s and the 1610s.[6]

The teaching in the first group of catechisms was very close to that in Nowell's catechism (and official formularies such as the Book of Common Prayer and the Homilies) in defining faith as a confident belief in God and his promises in Christ, and arguing that faith came through the preaching of the Word and the work of the Holy Ghost, and assurance came through hearing more sermons and through showing love for God in everyday actions. Faith included assurance, and the latter was not dependent on introspection. The authors in the Perkins–Hieron group, however, began to separate faith and assurance. Finding (argues Jensen) that their flocks were anxious for a measure of assurance that their faith was genuine, these authors encouraged their pupils to become more introspective, by asking themselves if, for example, they felt joy in good works; they also tried to help them become more adept at methods of proving their faith, such as keeping careful note of the daily duties they had performed, increasingly long lists of which were made available to catechumens. The authors in the third family began with a similar concern, but gave a higher priority to the decree of predestination and the idea of a covenant with God as a means of overcoming doubts and fears. This was the only group, says Jensen, to consider teaching predestination at an elementary level (though how explicit this teaching was in the case of Egerton and how elementary the level aimed at in Cartwright's form is open to debate). The consequences, he believes, were not only modifications to or even abandonment of the conventional sequence of exposition of the four staples, but also important doctrinal shifts to a less Christocentric and more introspective and legalistic way of thinking about the life of faith.[7]

Jensen's conclusions help to provide a theological and pastoral rationale for the composition of a number of these alternative catechisms, and his comments also tie in with those made in a previous chapter of this study on how catechists who adopted a more flexible structure could introduce new material into their forms.[8] There are,

[6] P. F. Jensen, 'The Life of Faith in the Teaching of Elizabethan Protestants', D.Phil. thesis (Oxford, 1979), 186–227.

[7] Ibid.   [8] See above, pp. 285–8.

however, some reasons for caution before we take his line of argument too far. In the first place, we may make an informed guess that the authors studied by Jensen were alive to a crisis provoked by a lack of assurance in their flocks, but we can rarely prove it. A recent survey has pointed to the apparent spread of religious despair in the late sixteenth and early seventeenth centuries, but the sources are often hard to evaluate and for the most part not part of the catechetical tradition.[9] Also we may strongly suspect that the men in Dr Jensen's sample had read other authors' catechisms and perhaps been influenced by them, but only in a few cases can we be moderately sure that they had.[10] Moreover, where authors added a preface to their works, they tended to say more about the intended function of their catechism (to help the very young or ignorant) or its innovations in technique (shorter answers, fewer technical terms, or whatever) than about its doctrine. Indeed, predictably enough, any comments about the latter were usually on the lines that they were not teaching anything new: Thomas Ratcliffe, one of the authors in Dr Jensen's second 'family', stated, apparently without guile, that the substance of his catechism was the same as that in the 'common catechism'; his was merely a fuller treatment.[11] In short, to imply that there were 'families' of catechisms which were the product of like-minded men facing the same doctrinal dilemmas may be both more than we can prove and less than the whole picture. It might be ungenerous but perhaps not inaccurate to suggest also that Dr Jensen's sample is not without its problems. As Appendix 1 below shows, there were a number of other forms published between the 1570s and the 1610s in addition to those he discusses, and some of these perhaps do not fit neatly into any of his 'families', for example the works of Matthieu Virel, Richard Bernard, and William Hill. Furthermore, his families are rather mixed bags in terms of types and levels of catechism, including dialogues and relatively advanced works alongside very simple ones; and some of the works he has analysed were regularly reprinted less in their own right than through being inserted into editions of other works.[12] Moreover, some of the authors he discusses seem to me to have been more cautious than he implies about the way in which they handled, or the prominence they gave to, concepts such as the double decree, as was suggested in Chapter 8.

This having been said, it remains the case that the introspective nature of assurance outlined by Tipson, Kendall, Lane, and Jensen and the stress on rules of behaviour in

---

[9] J. Stachniewski, *The Persecutory Imagination: English Puritanism and the Literature of Religious Despair* (Oxford, 1991), 27–61.

[10] See above, p. 295, for some examples of catechetical authors influencing each other that can be demonstrated moderately well.

[11] T. Ratcliffe, *A short summe* (1620), sigs. A3^v–4^r; from the length of Ratcliffe's form, the 'common' catechism must be the 1549 form. On attempts at being simple, see B. Andrewes, *A very short and pithie catechisme* (1586), sig. A2^r, and T. Settle, *A catechisme* (1587), sigs. A2^r, A4^v.

[12] e.g. 'Certaine questions and answers', and Cartwright's 'Catechisme'; it is also not clear how often Greenham's 'short form' and Hieron's *Doctrine* were published separately as opposed to as part of a larger volume of collected works: for all these works, see Appendix 1.

Jensen's second and third 'families' of catechisms did constitute an emphasis that was different from the earlier and to a lesser extent the later equation of faith with a sure persuasion in God's promises in Christ. This emphasis does also emerge in the sample of steady-selling catechisms used in Part II of this study. Thus Perkins frequently urged his catechumens to use self-analysis to assess their position. Among the questions he posed were 'How may a man know whether Satan be his God or not?', 'how shall a man perceive this obedience?', and 'How do you know that ... a man hath faith?', and the answers referred to 'evil motions' in the heart and to the Holy Ghost stirring up 'a longing and a lusting after heavenly things'. The following exchanges are also revealing:

Q. When shall a Christian heart come to ... full assurance?
A. ... when he hath been well practised in repentance, and hath had divers experiences of God's love unto him in Christ: then ... will appear in his heart the fullness of persuasion: which is the ripeness and strength of faith ...
Q. How may a man know that he is justified before God?
A. He need not ascend into heaven to search the secret counsel of God; but rather descend into his own heart to search whether he be sanctified or not.[13]

Samuel Hieron may be cited as an example of an author in our sample who put particular stress on duties. His scriptural catechism dealt with catechetical topics of a fairly conventional nature, except for a long section on how God's children dealt with afflictions, which included a good deal of introspective material. But after nineteen pages of ordinary catechism, he then embarked on a further seventeen pages of questions and answers on the duties of an ordinary man, a magistrate, a subject, a pastor, a member of his congregation, a householder, his neighbour, and a young man. These duties were similar to those found in many of the 'godly living' manuals of this period, but were not normally dealt with at length in shorter or intermediate level catechisms. Hieron used them to show the elect how they could see their faith being shown in their deeds, and gauge their emotional response to these deeds.[14]

Two additional comments may be made from a wider angle of approach than that found in Kendall and Jensen. The first is that their suggestion that catechumens were increasingly urged to examine their actions and feelings as a measure of their spiritual state and therefore their election, may not be as valid for the period after the 1610s or 1620s. This may have been due to other shifts in doctrine, or perhaps to a discovery that a reliance on introspection raised new pastoral problems. Like Arminius in Holland,[15] 'godly' ministers in England like Sibbes and Baxter also came to worry about the possible psychological damage being done to their flocks by the stress on the need for 'evidences of grace'.[16] As an example of the relative decline of

[13] Perkins, *Foundation*, 4, 6.
[14] Hieron, *Doctrine*, 577–81, 581–4 (a folio edition: the numbers of pages given in the text above are taken from a typical octavo edition).
[15] C. Bangs, *Arminius* (Nashville, 1971), 174.   [16] Stachniewski, *Persecutory Imagination*, 53–61.

introspection, we may take John Ball's best-selling shorter catechism. In this, he regularly stressed the inner emotions of the faithful: how knowledge of Christ's work would bring man 'to a serious consideration of his own estate, to grieve for sin and the fear of God's displeasure whereby the heart is broken and humbled', and how we must confess our sins in prayer 'with grief, hatred, and shame, freely accusing and condemning ourselves before God with broken and contrite hearts'. But Ball was also cautious about using these emotions as a litmus-test of salvation:

We must judge ourselves not by our own present feelings, or by our own discerning the fruits of grace, but by that we have felt [in the past], and the fruits of grace which appear to others.[17]

In the Westminster Larger Catechism, it was the double basis of assurance stated in the Westminster Confession that was taught: students were told that they could be assured that they were in a state of grace 'by faith grounded upon the truth of God's promises, and by the Spirit enabling them to discern in themselves those graces to which the promises of life are made'. The Westminster theologians were arguably nearer to Calvin than to Perkins on the relatively greater weight to be given to the former than the latter, and the next answer in the Larger Catechism suggests that they too may have been distancing themselves from too high an estimate of introspection: assurance was not 'of the essence of faith', and even for true believers it might be long in coming and sometimes weakened.[18] Indeed, in the Shorter Catechism these references to assurance were omitted: apart from a brief reference to 'assurance of God's love' as one of the benefits of believers in this life in answer thirty-six, there is no discussion of the matter.[19] It is also interesting to observe how the orthodox Calvinist, Thomas Vincent, handled answer thirty-six of the Shorter Catechism in 1674. Vincent asked how a child of God might get a sure evidence of his justification and adoption, to which the reply was sanctification. What is a sure evidence of sanctification? he then asked, to which the reply was 'increase of grace'. This was nearer the second ground of assurance in the Larger Catechism, but this statement was not accompanied by a detailed description of a particular programme of behaviour or introspection of the type that characterized some forms of the 1590s and 1600s such as those of Perkins and Hieron.[20]

There are signs of a measure of introspective assurance in the works of some of those authors who espoused the Prayer Book catechism. It can be found in Martin Nicholes's exposition of that form in the early 1630s, though it was not expressed in such direct terms as in Perkins's form or supported by as many new duties as in Hieron's.[21] In Hammond's and Nicholson's case, catechumens were told that a

---

[17] Ball, *Catechisme*, 74, 89.   [18] Westminster Larger, 44–6 (answers 80–1).
[19] Though cf. the regular use of the first-person plural in Westminster Shorter, 16–17, 11–16 (answers 36, 23–35).
[20] Vincent, *Catechism*, 84.   [21] Nicholes, *Catechisme*, 22–3.

thirsting after righteousness and a desire for reconciliation with God together with the influence these had on one's life were signs of a true faith and assurances of future blessings.[22] But in general, the treatment of assurance in the later catechisms in our sample seems either to have returned to something closer to that of the early cate-chists in our sample, such as Calvin and Nowell—assurance was not dependent on self-analysis but on using the means available for increasing faith and showing one's love for God—or to have been placed in the context of baptism and the covenant of grace. Thus, for William Wake's catechumen, assurance came through knowing 'that by my baptism I was put into a state of salvation'; later it was asserted that assur-ance was of forgiveness of sins for those in the covenant of grace which was 'founded upon the promise ... that if we believe that Christ died for our sins, we must also believe that God, for Christ's sake, will forgive all those, who truly repent of their sins'.[23] Non-Calvinist authors were not blind to the value of duties, just as they were capable of using highly charged language to drive home the need for repentance and obedience in their charges. But for most churchmen, assurance was not of election but of the truth of the objective promises of the Gospel which were given outward expression in the teaching of the church and confirmed in the sacraments of the New Testament; and if one fell into sin, one used the means made available by God to rem-edy that situation, by praying for forgiveness and new repentance.[24] Thus a state-ment of the introspective, self-validating type of faith which the elect were said to be able to experience was not typical of non-Calvinist works in our sample, and even in predestinarian works it can be found at its peak only in the period from the 1580s to the 1610s.

The second point that may be made from a wider angle of approach is that a mea-sure of assurance of a practical as much as a theoretical kind was given by the way in which many authors in our sample consistently used the first-person singular or plural for the answers in their section on salvation—a point to which we have referred more than once in previous chapters. The pattern of using the first person for cate-chetical treatment of salvation was set by Luther, Calvin, the official shorter cate-chism of 1549, the Belgic confession of 1561 and the Heidelberg Catechism of 1563. Luther's short catechism instructed catechumens to say that 'I believe that Jesus Christ ... has redeemed me ... secured and delivered me from all sins, from death, and from the power of the devil', while Calvin's students were expected to refer at regular intervals to 'our saviour Christ', to say that Christ 'hath redeemed us from death, and purchased life unto us', that it was necessary that 'every one of us be fully assured in his conscience, that he is beloved of God', and to state that 'this is life ever-lasting, to know the very living God, and him whom he has sent, our saviour Christ'.[25] A similarly direct, personal approach can be found in various English catechisms too.

[22] Hammond, *Practical catechisme*, 49, 84–5, 97–8; Nicholson, *Exposition*, 18–19.
[23] Wake, *Principles*, 10–11, 69–70.   [24] See above, pp. 311–12, 320–1, and below, Chs. 10–12.
[25] Schaff, *Creeds*, 79; Calvin, *Catechisme*, 13 (2), 19, 40; 5, 122; and cf. Schaff, *Creeds*, 405–7 (both

In the answer to a question on the Creed in the English catechism of 1549, the catechumen says that through these articles 'I learn to believe in God the Father, who hath made me and all the world. Secondly, in God the Son, who hath redeemed me, and all mankind. Thirdly, in God the Holy Ghost, who sanctifieth me, and all the elect people of God'.[26] Paget's short form also began with three pithy questions and answers in the first person, and in the answer to a later question about the 'communion of saints', Paget's catechumens were told to say 'of which number I believe I am one'—a practice anticipated in the Heidelberg Catechism and followed by a number of other English catechists.[27]

Some later authors with strong predestinarian views appear to have had doubts about using the first person all the time, and so we find them alternating between the use of the first and third persons. Perkins wrote of Christ being 'our saviour' and of his bestowing upon 'us' the means of salvation, but at other times he used 'a man' or 'the faithful' to describe those who would be saved.[28] Matthieu Virel spoke one moment of God giving Christ for 'the elect', then equated these with 'the faithful' and then 'us': God has taken us for his children. Similarly, Virel's translator into English, Stephen Egerton, in one of his own forms also spoke one moment of Christ pacifying God's anger against the sins of the elect, but finished the same sentence by saying that by this means 'Christ is made our redemption', adding for good measure in the next answer that Christ was also made 'our righteousness'. In his case, however, it is interesting that when Egerton compressed this form into even shorter forms, he avoided the third person and used the first person throughout.[29]

One of the best examples of alternating between first and third persons comes from a few pages of John Ball's best-selling shorter catechism. By what means may 'we' escape the penalty of the Fall, he asks? By Christ, comes the answer, who died for 'his elect'; Christ as the son of God repaired God's image in 'us' and conquered the enemies of 'our' salvation; Christ became man to suffer death for 'us', sanctify 'our' nature, and give 'us' access to the throne of grace. Next he says that Christ became mediator between God and 'man'. Christ as prophet revealed to 'us' the way to everlasting life; Christ as priest 'purchased for us righteousness and life eternal'; but Christ as king gathered and governed 'his elect and chosen'. He then asks what benefits 'we' receive by Christ's death and resurrection, ascension and sitting at the right hand of God, intercession and so on, and the answers vary

Remonstrants and Counter-Remonstrants appealed to the Belgic confession of 1561: Bangs, *Arminius*, 309–10, 314–15, 354); and Heidelberg Catechism, 307–8.

[26] Prayer Book catechism, 780–1.

[27] Paget, *Questions*, sigs. A5^{r-v}, D1^v–2^r; and see above, p. 328.

[28] Perkins, *Foundation*, 4–5.

[29] Virel, *Treatise*, 32; Egerton, 'Briefe method', 7; id., 'Four points', 22, and id., 'Briefe summe', 27; in both his forms, James Ussher also soon moved from a third-person account of those for whom Christ had paid the price to the first person to describe those for whom he would intercede or who would receive him: 'Method', 18–19, and id., 'Principles', 8.

between the first–person plural and 'his people' or 'the faithful'. Ball was evidently trying to balance a concern for theological precision with his sense of evangelical mission.[30]

Some authors like Cartwright and Elton tended to be more consistent in their use of what for double predestinarian thinkers was probably the theologically safer third person—Christ died for his people and they will benefit thereby.[31] Elton, for example, expected his more advanced catechumens to learn that as a prophet Christ was the 'only teacher of his Church', as a priest Christ reconciled God to 'his elect', and as a king he disposed all things for the good of God's chosen. Elton changed briefly into the first person for the next three questions and answers—on how Christ and his benefits were made available to us, and we are united with Christ, but then he reverted to and stayed with the safer designation of 'his chosen' and 'a man' for the rest of his treatment of salvation. Indeed, Elton was untypical in using the third person for his sections on the Creed and the sacraments as well, and especially unusual in not using the first person in most of the shorter form 'for the younger sort' that he prepared from his full-length catechism.[32]

But the clearest example of all is provided by the two Westminster catechisms of 1647. The authors of the Larger Catechism, designed for more advanced catechumens, followed the lines of the Westminster Confession in their fairly consistent use of the third person (though the authors of this catechism did use the first person a number of times); but the authors of the Shorter Catechism, for beginners, used the first person regularly if not unfailingly. It is known that the Shorter Catechism was a hastily prepared contraction of the Larger, though this contraction was not as straightforward as the one made of Nowell's catechism in similar circumstances at the start of Elizabeth's reign: in 1647 not only were some questions and answers omitted and others shortened, but there were also occasional changes in the sequence and as a result some new material was needed to provide linkages.[33] Moreover, given the shortage of time in which it had to be prepared, one must assume that the decision to change a large number of questions and answers from third to first person was taken quite deliberately, since it would have been much quicker to retain the third person or impersonal forms of the original form. The resulting differences between the two forms are sometimes intriguing. Both versions stated that Christ was the redeemer of God's elect, and that in the covenant of grace he acted as 'our mediator' (Larger, answers 30–2) or 'our redeemer' (Shorter, answers 20–1). Thereafter the differences can perhaps best be seen in a tabular form, with the respective numbers of the questions and answers in brackets.

---

[30] Ball, *Catechisme*, 72–5.   [31] Cartwright, 'Catechisme', sig. Aa4ʳ and *passim*.

[32] Elton, *Forme*, sigs. C1ᵛ–3ᵛ, though cf. C4ʳ⁻ᵛ; and id., 'Extract', *passim* (though cf. sigs. G2ʳ–3ʳ).

[33] R. S. Paul, *The Assembly of the Lord* (Edinburgh, 1985), 519; Westminster Shorter, answers 42, 86–7 (pp. 18–19, 32–3), for example, are not in the same position as relevant material in the Westminster Larger.

Westminster Larger Catechism	Westminster Shorter Catechism
(43) How doth Christ execute the office of a prophet?	(24) [Same question]
... in his revealing to the church ... the whole will of God in all things concerning their edification and salvation.	... in revealing to us ... the will of God for our salvation
(44) How doth Christ execute the office of a priest?	(25) [Same question]
... in ... offering himself ... to be a reconciliation for the sins of his people; and in making continual intercession for them.	... in his once offering ... to ... reconcile us to God, and in making continual intercession for us.
(45) How doth Christ execute the office of a king?	(26) [Same question]
... in calling out of the world a people to himself ... in bestowing saving grace upon his ... elect and restraining and overcoming all their enemies.	... in subduing us to himself, in ruling and defending us, and in restraining and conquering all his and our enemies
(59) Who are made partakers of redemption through Christ?	(30) How doth the Spirit apply to us the redemption purchased by Christ?
... all those for whom Christ hath purchased it.	The Spirit applieth to us the redemption purchased by Christ by working faith in us and thereby uniting us to Christ in our effectual calling.

The same pattern is also visible in all the questions on the *ordo salutis*—Larger Catechism answers 67–75, Shorter 31–5—and elsewhere, namely that in the Larger, God acts on behalf of 'his elect', but in the Shorter on behalf of 'us'.[34] This shielding of the beginner from the harder facts of life which the more advanced catechumen was expected to confront was followed by most subsequent expositors of the Shorter form in the later seventeenth century,[35] just as those expounding the church catechism adopted the first person used in that form.[36]

In the great majority of the catechisms in our sample, then, it was the first-person singular or plural that was used in the section on faith and salvation. In practical terms and especially at elementary level, theologians of different persuasions were working on the assumption that all catechumens were actually or potentially of the elect; and a potentially large measure of assurance was offered those catechumens through the weight given to the objective grounds of assurance—Christ's sacrifice—and the certainty with which they were made to say that the benefits of that sacrifice would be applied to them.

---

[34] Westminster Larger, 14–15, 21–3, 30, 34–41; Westminster Shorter, 10–16.

[35] e.g. Wallis, *Explanation*, 12–18; Gouge, *Principles*, 57–60, 63, 69; but there was the odd exception: Thomas Vincent substituted 'elect people' for 'us' in explaining Westminster Shorter art. 26, but not 24 or 25: Vincent, *Catechism*, 61–7.

[36] See the forms listed above on p. 295.

In the course of the last few pages we have inevitably strayed from a discussion of faith into the closely related areas of justification and sanctification: let us now take a closer look at these.[37] While the theologians of Trent reaffirmed the older view that a faithful man, through the merits of Christ and an infusion of grace, was able to justify himself to some extent through his devotions and good works which God treated as if they were of value,[38] Protestants insisted that the only way sinful man could be made righteous in God's sight was through Christ's sufferings. Even with the help of grace, man's own works remained irremediably tainted with sin and of no merit whatsoever in securing salvation. Justification was through faith in Christ's merits alone; faith might be a necessary condition of salvation, but it was only the instrumental cause or the non–meritorious condition of justification; the meritorious cause remained Christ's sufferings alone.[39] However, despite the importance of this doctrine at the levels of official statements of faith and academic debates on doctrine, it received a surprisingly small amount of space at catechetical level. The nature of justification and a definition of justifying faith were certainly accorded a few questions and answers in a number of catechisms in the sample, notably in those whose authors were pressing a Calvinist *ordo salutis*, but justification was not handled at any great length in the majority of our sample, as we saw in an earlier chapter.[40] The longest connected accounts are to be found in the highly specialized treatise on salvation by Grosse and in one of the longest works in the sample, Hammond's advanced catechism. And that length was partly due to the fact that both these authors felt obliged to engage with the technical language of moving, formal, and instrumental causes in which debates on justification were then conducted.[41] Here let us focus on two of the trouble spots, and see what the authors in our sample said about them.

The first area of controversy concerned the nature of justification. Whereas some early Continental and English reformers, such as Calvin (most of the time) and Cranmer, had a simple view of justification—one that equated it with pardon or forgiveness of sins and so being accepted by God as righteous—Calvinist thinkers from Beza and Perkins through to John Owen and beyond thought it was more than that: in justification Christ's obedience (both passive and active) was 'imputed' to the believer, that is a quality of one person was ascribed to another.[42] There is a hint of this in Calvin's catechism: at first he equated justification with righteousness, adding that through faith we 'enter into possession of this righteousness'; but later when discussing the worthlessness of human works he wrote of God 'accounting' Christ's righteousness to be ours, which is part way towards a notion of imputation.[43] A simi-

---

[37] For earlier discussion see above, pp. 324–6, 340–2.   [38] McGrath, *Iustitia Dei*, ch. 7.

[39] E. Cameron, *The European Reformation* (Oxford, 1991), ch. 8; Clifford, *Atonement and Justification*, 176–7, and pt. 3, *passim*.

[40] See above, pp. 340–1.

[41] Grosse, *Fiery pillar*, ch. 5; Hammond, *Practical catechisme*, 78–82; McGrath, *Iustitia Dei*, and C. F. Allison, *The Rise of Moralism: The Proclamation of the Gospel from Hooker to Baxter* (1966), *passim*.

[42] Clifford, *Atonement and Justification*, pt. 3.   [43] Calvin, *Catechisme*, 40, 47–8.

lar usage can be found in Nowell's catechism: being 'accounted in the number and state of the righteous ... even as if they themselves had fulfilled the law ... is the justification which the holy scriptures do declare that we obtain by faith'.[44] A more explicit statement can be found in the Heidelberg Catechism where righteousness is one of three qualities of Christ which God 'grants and imputes' to those with true faith.[45]

Perkins's position was made clear both in the 'Table declaring the order of the causes of salvation and damnation' inserted into his *Golden Chaine*, and in his catechism. In the former, opposite 'justification' in this diagram were two separate items, bracketed together: 'remission of sin' and 'imputation of righteousness'.[46] Similarly in his catechism, Perkins wrote that for a man to be justified 'comprehendeth two things': to be cleared from the guilt and punishment of sin through Christ's sufferings and death on the cross, and 'to be accepted as perfectly righteous before God ... by the righteousness of Christ imputed to him'.[47] Imputation was also raised explicitly in the definition of justification offered by other English Calvinists. Cartwright, Elton, and the Westminster divines adopted a clear twofold definition of justification: pardon of sins, and being accepted as righteous through Christ's righteousness imputed to us.[48] Grosse, on the other hand, put the spotlight on the second element; indeed, he actually put imputation first and remission second. Grosse and Vincent were also two of only four authors in our sample who referred to the idea that Christ's active and passive obedience were both required for our justification.[49]

This incipient divide, between those with the new stress on imputation and those without it, was never total: a double predestinarian like Ball did not use the concept of imputation in his shorter form, while non-Calvinists like Hammond and Nicholson occasionally seem to have done.[50] However, by the latter half of the seventeenth century, perhaps prompted by fear that a stress on imputation might reinforce the spread of antinomianism, writers like Baxter and Tillotson had begun to challenge this new orthodoxy, and by the end of the century there was a strong move back towards the position of Calvin and Cranmer, not only among conformists but also moderate Calvinists like Watts.[51] The word 'justification', said Tillotson, has different uses in the New Testament, but 'when it is applied to a sinner, it signifies nothing else but the pardon of his sin'.[52] If we examine the late-seventeenth-century catechisms in our sample, we find that, as in the Prayer Book form of 1549, there is no mention of the concept of imputation. We obtain 'forgiveness or justification', wrote Jeremy Taylor in his exposition of the tenth article of the Creed, by the righteousness

---

[44] Nowell, *Catechisme*, 180, and id., *Institution*, sig. Fiᵛ.   [45] Heidelberg Catechism, 326–7.

[46] W. Perkins, *A golden chaine*, in *Workes* i (1612), opposite p. 11.   [47] Perkins, *Foundation*, 6.

[48] Cartwright, 'Catechisme', sig. Aa7ʳ; Elton, *Forme*, sigs. D1ʳ⁻ᵛ; Westminster Larger, 36–7 (answer 70); Westminster Shorter, 15–16 (answer 33); and cf. Egerton, 'Forme of examining', 30.

[49] Grosse, *Fiery pillar*, 39; Vincent, *Catechism*, 77; the other two were Hammond, *Practical catechisme*, 25, and cf. Nicholson, *Exposition*, 64.

[50] Hammond, *Practical catechisme*, 25, 96, 327; Nicholson, *Exposition*, 64, 67.

[51] Clifford, *Atonement and Justification*, chs. 10–13.   [52] Ibid. 195.

of faith in Christ who has fully remitted our sins.[53] Either to avoid confusing their catechumens or raising matters under debate, or because of personal doubts about its legitimacy, most later Stuart authors avoided the doctrine of imputation.

A second area of debate was over the relationship between justification and sanctification—the process of inner renewal or purification—of being made literally more like a saint—experienced by those with saving faith. Man was supposed to play his part in this process, but for him to succeed, even partially, it was agreed, he needed help, through the grace brought by the Holy Ghost. It was also generally agreed that there was a close link between sanctification and repentance: Perkins, the Westminster divines, Hammond, and Boughen could all write of repentance as a grace or part of the sanctifying grace sent by God to the faithful. Also it was agreed that the process of sanctification begun in this life would not be finished until the next.[54] As far as the relationship between justification and sanctification was concerned, there were also some areas of apparent agreement, for example that the two were intimately connected. In their larger catechism, the Westminster divines asserted that in texts like 1 Cor. 6: 11 'sanctification be inseparably joined with justification', and in his own advanced catechism Henry Hammond described the two as interacting processes.[55] The orthodox Calvinist Grosse also made the interesting caveat that justification is before sanctification in the order of nature but not in time.[56] But here we are moving closer to two areas of disagreement. Was justification a once-only event followed by a slow process of sanctification, as the Calvinist *ordo* implied; or was justification activated every time a believer sinned and repented, so that justification and sanctification proceeded in harness as it were? Moreover, if justification preceded sanctification, did this not mean that a man might be justified before he was repentant? The differences here were potentially serious, though the signs of them in works in our sample are relatively few.

Among the authors of those works, Calvin clearly put faith before repentance, just as he put the Creed before the Decalogue in his catechism; and by talking of God 'once' receiving us into favour seemed to imply that justification was a single event. Shortly afterwards, however, he quoted Psalm 143: 2 to warn his catechumens that in God's sight no man living will be justified, and urging them to pray not be called to account. In his commentaries, moreover, Calvin argued that justification in the form of forgiveness was a daily happening: 'by a daily forgiveness God receives us into his favour' and 'This alone keeps us in God's family'.[57] The orthodox Calvinist consensus by the 1590s was that justification preceded sanctification, with the occasional

[53] J. Taylor, 'An exposition of the Apostles' Creed', in *Symbolon* (1657), 11.

[54] Perkins, *Foundation*, 6–7; Westminster Larger, 41–2 (answer 76); Westminster Shorter, 32–3 (answer 87); Hammond, *Practical catechisme*, 70; Boughen, *Exposition*, 80–1.

[55] Westminster Larger, 42 (answer 77); cf. von Rohr, *Covenant of Grace*, 104; and for Hammond, see below, pp. 401–2.

[56] Grosse, *Fiery pillar*, 80.

[57] Calvin, *Catechisme*, 48, 50; and Clifford, *Atonement and Justification*, 173.

rider such as Grosse's noted above.[58] Though earlier reformers like Calvin and Cranmer might have demurred, justification had also generally come to be regarded by Calvinists as a single event, at which sins were forgiven and Christ's righteousness imputed, while sanctification was seen as a process by which the old Adam in us was gradually destroyed and the new Christ put on. The concept of indefectible grace or perseverance also meant that once one was called and justified, one would never fall from God's favour. At the end of their section on the *ordo*, the authors of the Westminster Larger Catechism asked the question 'Wherein do justification and sanctification differ?' The answer, in part, was:

God in justification imputeth the righteousness of Christ, in sanctification his spirit infuseth grace, and enableth to the exercise thereof; in the former, sin is pardoned, in the other, it is subdued; the one doth equally free all believers from the revenging wrath of God, and that perfectly in this life, that they never fall into condemnation; the other is neither equal in all, nor in this life perfect in any, but growing up to perfection.[59]

What the phrase 'perfectly in this life' seems to mean is that at the moment of justification the imputation of Christ's righteousness made to the believer frees him or her once and for all from God's wrath; it was a perfect act, whereas sanctification was an imperfect process, begun but not completed in this life.

Hammond's position in his catechism for older students was very different: a measure of sanctification had to precede justification, and both were ongoing, interacting processes, so that if one failed to maintain the effort to stay on track, one would not necessarily reach the desired destination. Hammond's position was that 'I must first believe, repent, and return' to the ways of God before he will pardon me. God is sufficiently reconciled to give us grace at first, to enable us to believe in the conditional promises of salvation, but he will not pardon or justify us at the same time. Those whom God justifies, he will glorify (Rom. 8: 30), but he will not glorify anyone who has not been sanctified (Heb. 12: 14). If God were to justify (forgive) an unsanctified man who then died on the instant, 'it must follow, either that the unsanctified man is glorified, or the justified man not glorified', either of which would be contrary to scripture.[60]

Hammond's alternative 'order' of salvation was as follows: first, God gave his son to die for sinners on condition that if they lead a new life they will be saved; secondly, he strikes with Christ a new covenant, of mercy and grace; thirdly, through this covenant the Spirit and the Word call the sinner powerfully to repentance, and

if he answer to that call, and awake, and arise, and make his sincere faithful resolutions of new life; God then (4.) justifies, accepts his person, and pardons his sins past: then (5.) gives him more grace, assists him to do, as before he enabled him to will, i.e. to perform his good resolutions: then (6.) upon continuance in that state ... he gives to him ... a crown of life.[61]

---

[58] On the *ordo*, see above, pp. 380–2; and also above, n. 56.
[59] Westminster Larger, 42–3 (answer 77).   [60] Hammond, *Practical catechisme*, 79–82.
[61] Ibid. 82–3.

At a later stage of his catechism, Hammond also interpreted the last three petitions of the Lord's Prayer ('Give us this day ... Forgive us our trespasses ... Deliver us from evil') as follows:

God (1.) gives grace to sanctify ... that 'bread of life' without which we are not able to live to God. (2.) He pardons sins to them that are thus fitly qualified to receive his pardon. (3.) He assisteth and upholds from falling into sin, i.e. he first sanctifieth, secondly, justifieth, thirdly, gives grace to preserve. And in this order we must desire and pray for these several degrees of grace.[62]

The fact that these degrees of grace were to be prayed for daily underlines the point that justification was not a single act, but a recurring decimal—a view advanced much earlier by Luther, and by Calvin in his commentaries and Cranmer in his homily on justification.[63] As a result, a believer who sinned afresh but did not take steps to repent and seek forgiveness again, would die unjustified. Hammond did hold out an olive branch of sorts to the Calvinists: if they would take justification as God's pardoning of those who, through grace, have promised amendment but have yet to fulfil those vows, then he and they would be in agreement.[64] Of course, they did not: from their standpoint, for a man's promise to be a precondition of justification was to elevate man's role in his salvation and to limit God's task to that of forgiving those who had decided to turn to him. Strict predestinarians also believed that the call given to the predestined elect was bound to be answered positively, rather than being a matter of human choice; and that salvation was not tied to God's foreknowledge of man's faith, perseverance, or good works, but 'only the will of the good pleasure of God' (in the words of the second Lambeth article).[65]

At academic level and the level of advanced catechisms such as Hammond's and the Larger Westminster form, the divide remained, and at that level both sides were prepared to dismiss the other's views as heretical or dangerous. But at lower levels it may have been less important to the average catechetical author and less obvious to the average catechumen. Where 'justification' was tackled in our sample it was usually presented as meaning 'made righteous' or 'forgiven', without an indication of whether this was done once and for all or more than once. It was also often attached to faith which was a living organism rather than an event. Similarly, 'sanctification' was usually presented as being a long drawn out process of inner renewal, rather than the intermediate stage between justification and glorification. Moreover, the concept of a covenant of grace (which as we shall see shortly came to be quite widely adopted) had the potential to smooth over some of the sharper edges: whichever came first— justification or sanctification—those already in the covenant of grace, through birth and baptism, who turned to God and were forgiven, would receive the benefits

---

[62] Hammond, *Practical catechisme*, 239.

[63] Tipson, 'Puritan Understanding of Conversion', 40–1; Clifford, *Atonement and Justification*, 173; Baxter also saw justification as a continuous process: von Rohr, *Covenant of Grace*, 99.

[64] Hammond, *Practical catechisme*, 81.   [65] Porter, *Reformation*, 371.

Christ had earned them. And it was only through divine grace at the outset, and then further 'saving graces' later, that a member of the covenant would be saved.[66]

The idea of a covenant between God and man, or the identification of the members of the Christian church with the members of the covenant of grace, is a subject which we have encountered more than once in the last two chapters, and will do so again in the next three.[67] What the growing number of references to covenants in our sample of catechisms tells us is that the covenants of works and grace came to be used in a variety of ways at catechetical level: as an important element in some authors' doctrines of salvation and assurance, as an inducement to piety, as a way of explaining the historic continuity of the church and the relationship of its members to each other as well as to God, and as a justification for infant baptism and regular participation in the Lord's Supper. Two questions may be posed here: how far did this catechetical teaching of the covenant correspond to the federal theology of the sermons or treatises of the period; and how common was covenantal teaching in our sample? In order to answer these questions, we need to take a brief look at the emergence of federal theology (the term comes from the Latin *foedum*—a pact or covenant—though in practice the term is usually applied to a particular type of covenant theology which evolved in Reformed circles in the late sixteenth and seventeenth centuries).[68]

The idea of a covenant had solid scriptural foundations in the history of the Jews in the Old Testament, for example in Genesis chapters 15 and 17, Exodus 19 and 24, and Jeremiah 31, though as we shall see distinctions were drawn later between the covenant God made with Abraham (which did not stipulate conditions of performance in advance) and that made with Moses (which did).[69] There are also a few references in the New Testament to God's covenant or covenants with his people, though some of these refer back to the Jewish covenant with God rather than to a new covenant in Christ. Even the assertion in Hebrews 8: 6 that Christ in heaven was 'the mediator

[66] See below, pp. 412–21.

[67] See above, pp. 308, 331, and below, pp. 431, 459, 469, 471, 474, 520, 523, 525–7.

[68] For some landmarks on this subject, on the whole stressing the importance of the covenant concept, see P. Miller, 'The Marrow of Divinity', in *Errand into the Wilderness* (New York, 1964), 48–98; W. W. McKee, 'The Idea of Covenant in Early English Puritanism (1580–1643)', Ph.D. thesis (Yale, 1948), *passim*; J. Coolidge, *The Pauline Renaissance in England: Puritanism and the Bible* (Oxford, 1970), 150 and ch. 5, *passim*; J. von Rohr, *The Covenant of Grace in Puritan Thought* (Atlanta, 1986), 17–33; Weir, *Federal Theology*, 5–7 and conclusion. For somewhat different views, see J. G. Moller, 'The Beginnings of Puritan Covenant Theology', *JEH* 14 (1963), 46 ff; M. McGiffert, 'American Puritan Studies in the 1960's', *William and Mary Quarterly*, 3rd ser., 27 (1970), 47–50; J. F. H. New, *Anglican and Puritan: The Basis of their Opposition* (1964), 94–5; D. D. Wallace, *Puritans and Predestination: Grace in English Protestant Theology 1525–1695* (Chapel Hill, NC, 1982), 10–11, 197–8.

[69] Compare Gen. 15: 18, 17: 2, 7, with Exod. 19: 5; Coolidge, *Pauline Renaissance*, 101–7; Brachlow, *Communion of Saints*, 33–4, 72; and Weir, *Federal Theology*, 51–5, on different translations of 'berith' in sixteenth-century lexicons.

of a better covenant' (later referred to as 'the new covenant'—Hebrews 12: 24) was based on the statement in Jeremiah 31: 31 that God would make a new covenant with the house of Israel and with the house of Judah. Paul had to explain on other occasions, such as Romans chapter 9, that the covenants, along with the Law and other benefits given by God, pertained not to the 'children of the flesh', that is Israelites by birth, but to the 'children of the promise', who included the faithful among the gentiles.[70] In the case of the New Testament references, it was also not uncommon to translate the Greek 'diatheke' as 'testament' in the sense of last will and testament. The words attributed to Christ in Matthew 26: 28, Mark 14: 24, Luke 22: 20, and 1 Corinthians 11: 25—'this is my blood of the new testament' or 'the new testament in my blood'—echo Moses's reference to 'the blood of the covenant' in Exodus 24: 8; and the references in Hebrews 7: 22 and 9: 15–17 to Christ as surety and mediator of a new testament can be treated as synonymous with the new covenant in Hebrews 12: 24. Although some today would see a testament as a unilateral statement and a covenant as a bilateral agreement, contemporaries seem to have equated the two.[71]

Such ideas were not altogether new. In the later Middle Ages, some theologians had talked of a single *pactum* having been made between God and man, by which God's obligations to man and the people's to God had been defined,[72] and the young Luther was clearly influenced by the teaching of the *via moderna* on this matter, though later he would reject it as exaggerating man's role in initiating forgiveness.[73] Other early reformers in Germany, Switzerland, and England wrote of the covenant in relation to the sacraments,[74] though it was perhaps theologians associated with Zurich, such as Zwingli and Bullinger, who first gave the idea of a single covenant between God and man greater prominence. The idea probably reached England through William Tyndale's prefaces and notes to his translation of the Bible, many of which were transferred to the officially approved Matthew Bible, and through Bullinger's *Decades*, which were highly regarded in England. There is, however, a noticeable lack of covenanting language in the English liturgy and official formularies of 1547–71.[75]

---

[70] Moller, 'Beginnings', 49–50; J. A. Ziesler, *Pauline Christianity* (Oxford, 1991), 9, 11, 51, 66–8, 78, 103–8. According to Coolidge, *Pauline Renaissance*, loc. cit., Paul saw two ways of understanding the Old Testament which came together in Christ; but by subordinating the Sinai covenant (with its clear, legal requirements to the Jews) to the earlier one with Abraham (which relied on a pre-Law, natural understanding of God's views on good and evil) he could argue that the gentiles were included in the earlier covenant.

[71] e.g. *The Bible* (Geneva, 1560), sig. CCciiii'; Schaff, *Creeds*, 617 (Westminster Confession, ch. 7, para. 4); Hammond, *Practical catechisme*, 385, 389; Williams, *Exposition*, 55 (though 'testament' was retained at the appropriate points of the liturgy and other official formularies); see also von Rohr, *Covenant of Grace*, 25–6, 32–3, and on the different translations of 'diatheke' in the sixteenth century, Weir, *Federal Theology*, 51, 56–8.

[72] McGrath, *Iustitia Dei*, i. 170–2.   [73] Ibid. i. 127, ii. 4–7.

[74] McKee, 'Idea of Covenant', 7, 9–11, 20, 41–5; Moller, 'Beginnings', 47–9, 62–3.

[75] Ibid. 50–4; L. J. Trinterud, 'The Origins of Puritanism', *Church History*, 20 (1951), 37–57; von Rohr, *Covenant of Grace*, 25–6, 193; McGrath, *Iustitia Dei*, ii. 40–1, 112–13; Moller, 'Beginnings', 54; D. J. Keep, 'Henry Bullinger and the Elizabethan Church', Ph.D. thesis (Sheffield, 1970); von Rohr,

Through the writings of Heidelberg theologians like Ursinus and Olevianus, and later the work of Cartwright, Fenner, and Junius, the concept found more commonly in Reformed circles from the 1580s and 1590s was that of a *double* covenant, and this was the version which strongly affected a number of English authors such as Perkins, Preston, and Sibbes. Where earlier thinkers such as Calvin and Bullinger had noted differences between Old and New Testament dispensations of the covenant but argued essentially for one covenant,[76] the new view put much greater stress on the differences than the continuity; and where other thinkers stuck with the scriptural references to Abraham and Moses, the new view placed the first covenant clearly in the Garden of Eden. For Ursinus, there was a prelapsarian covenant between God and Adam, which was conditional and mutual—if Adam obeyed, God would guarantee eternal life; then there was a postlapsarian covenant which was unilateral, unconditional, and so not mutual: for the sake of Christ's sufferings, God would redeem his chosen people by a covenant 'because there is no apter form or meeter way of doing it'.[77] As it evolved in the orthodox Reformed way of thought, the first covenant was referred to as a covenant of 'nature' or 'works', the terms of which were implanted in man's nature and offered eternal life on condition of absolute obedience to God's will; the second was a covenant of 'grace', made known to man by revelation and guaranteeing salvation to the elect.

Different theories have been proposed for this shift to a double covenant: to separate the grace promised in the Gospel from possible contamination by the legalism that could result from paying excessive attention to keeping the Law;[78] to circumvent the problems of theodicy (vindicating God's providence in the face of the existence of evil) which beset double predestinarians in the 1550s; or to provide 'an instrument for assurance' for those worried whether they were elect.[79] Whatever the reason, the effect of the stress on two covenants was to reinforce the high Calvinist position on the twin decrees. Thus, Perkins, in his full-length treatise, *The golden chaine*, specifically combined the double-covenant teaching of Heidelberg with the *ordo salutis* of Bucer and Beza to suggest that God's covenant with his elect was the 'outward

Covenant of Grace, 24–7; White, *Predestination*, 78–81; and the two volumes of official homilies, Prayer Books, and official catechisms of the years 1547–71.

[76] Moller, 'Beginnings', 47–9; Calvin, *Institutes*, II. x. 1–5; von Rohr, *Covenant of Grace*, 194; Weir, *Federal Theology*, 9–11.

[77] Kendall, *English Calvinism*, 38–40; M. McGiffert, 'Grace and Works: The Rise of the Covenant Divinity in Elizabethan Puritanism', *Harvard Theological Review*, 75 (1982), 463–502; Weir, *Federal Theology*, pp. vii–viii, 1–22.

[78] McGrath, *Iustitia Dei*, ii. 41–2; McGiffert, 'Grace and Works', art. cit., and id., 'God's Controversy with Jacobean England', *American Historical Review*, 88 (1983), 1163–4; cf. also von Rohr, *Covenant of Grace*, 103–5. According to this view, the covenant of works binds all men at all times to obey the Law, but as far as salvation is concerned only those in the covenant of grace will be saved.

[79] Weir, *Federal Theology*, *passim*; von Rohr, *Covenant of Grace*, pp. 12–15, ch. 3, p. 114 and ch. 7; and cf. E. B. Holifield, *The Covenant Sealed: The Development of Puritan Sacramental Theology in Old and New England, 1570–1720* (New Haven/London, 1974), 40–4.

means' by which the decree of election was executed.[80] This equation of the covenant of grace with the decree of election was arguably part of that shift away from Calvin's Christological standpoint—salvation through Christ—to the more theocentric one associated with Beza and much later Reformed theology—salvation through the divine decree and its 'outward means', the covenant of grace. The fact that Christ was the mediator of the second covenant meant that Calvin's idea had not been abandoned, but there was, it has been suggested in recent years, a change of substance or at least of emphasis here.[81] However, not all double predestinarians deployed the new equation, or used it in the same way. John Preston, John Ball, and Richard Sibbes tended to pass over reprobation when discussing the covenants,[82] while others, such as Paul Baynes, William Whitaker, Richard Rogers, Samuel Ward, and William Twisse apparently decided to forgo a federal framework. On the other hand, even non-predestinarians like Andrewes and Hammond felt able to adopt the idea of a twin covenant and a covenant of grace or faith, though they regarded the membership and operation of the latter in a different light from double predestinarians in some respects.[83] It also seems clear that the closer one came to associating the covenant of works with the situation of Adam in Eden, and the covenant of grace with the effecting of the decree of election, the more problems of exegesis were created: which covenant was made first?[84] what evidence was there for the covenant with Adam?[85] and what was the status of the covenant with Abraham compared to those made with Adam and Christ?[86]

Other questions arose, such as how far the covenant was unconditional or conditional, and if the latter how men could be sure that they were keeping those conditions properly. A covenant would be unconditional if it was a legal compact like a marriage contract promising mutual love with no conditions attached; alternatively it could be conditional in the sense of 'if you do this, I will do that'.[87] Calvin had tended towards an unconditional covenant, albeit between totally unequal partners,

---

[80]   Kendall, *English Calvinism*, 58; McGiffert, 'Grace and Works', 496–7.

[81]   See above, pp. 313, 358–9; and McGrath, *Iustitia Dei*, ii. 40–2, 112–14; Coolidge, *Pauline Renaissance*, 128–31; Brachlow, *Communion of Saints*, 31–3; and cf. Moller, 'Beginnings', 64–7; J. B. Torrance, 'The Covenant Concept in Scottish Theology and Politics and its Legacy', *Scottish Journal of Theology*, 34 (1981), 234–5, 239–40.

[82]   McKee, 'Idea of the Covenant', 144–5.

[83]   Ibid. 82; Wallace, *Puritans and Predestination*, 197–8; Andrewes, *Works*, vi. 62; for Hammond and others, see C. H. Lettinga, 'Covenant Theology and the Transformation of Anglicanism', Ph.D. thesis (Johns Hopkins, 1987), ch. 4, and below, pp. 414–16, 419.

[84]   R. L. Greaves, 'Introduction' to *Miscellaneous Works of John Bunyan* (general editor R. Sharrock), ii (Oxford, 1976), pp. xxiv–xxvi.

[85]   Cf. Calvin, *Institutes* II. i. 4; von Rohr, *Covenant of Grace*, 37. For an interesting statement on this and other issues in the early eighteenth century, together with comments on how confused his congregation were, see W. Notcutt, *A compendium of the covenants* (1733), 3–4 and *passim*.

[86]   Cf. Calvin, *Institutes*, II. ix–xi; Cartwright, 'Catechisme', sig. Aa4ᵛ–5ʳ; Schaff, *Creeds*, 617–18 (Westminster Confession, ch. 7, paras. 5–6); cf. also von Rohr, *Covenant of Grace*, 50–1.

[87]   Moller, 'Beginnings', 64–7; Torrance, 'Covenant Concept', 228–31.

since puny man could not possibly satisfy conditions set by God in such a way as to trigger a divine response; God made the covenant, and man's obligation was met by Christ not by his own efforts, though man was still under the command to believe and obey.[88] Others may have agreed, at least in theory, that the covenant was unconditional, but often found it necessary to adopt the language of mutual promises. It was in such terms that Ursinus in practice described the covenant: God promises to be gracious and favourable to men, and men bind themselves to faith and repentance; there is no 'if' about it, but the covenant has two sides to it.[89] Perkins also seems to adopt a conditional stance when he describes the single, essential covenant in *The golden chaine*: God's 'contract with men concerning the obtaining life eternal' was 'upon a certain condition': God would be their God, and they would vow allegiance and obey—again a mutual promise rather than a pair of stipulations. However, when he went on to state that there were two kinds of covenant and turned specifically to the covenant of grace, he described it in one-sided terms: 'God freely promising Christ, and his benefit', and 'exact[ing]' from man faith and repentance. 'In this covenant we do not so much offer, or promise any great matter to God, as in a manner only receive'.[90] Similarly, the authors of the Westminster Confession adopted a conditional stance with regard to the covenant of works, in which eternal life was promised to Adam 'upon condition of perfect and personal obedience', but in the case of the covenant of grace they used the verb 'require': God offers sinners life and salvation by Christ, 'requiring of them faith in him, that they may be saved'.[91]

There was, however, a possibility that the theologians' reluctance to accept a conditional element in the covenant of grace would undermine its value as a pastoral tool: if the initiative in making the covenant was God's, and Christ had met the conditions for man, and if all the elect had to do was to receive the divine grace which enabled them to believe and repent, was there not a risk that members of the covenant would become complacent about their duties or promises, or, worse, veer towards antinomianism? These risks seem to have persuaded some authors to use voluntaristic language: man should seek to be in covenant with God, said Ames and Preston; though God performs both parts of the covenant, man must consent and will to take part in it, wrote Sibbes.[92] Despite the fresh risks they ran of appearing to make man to some

---

[88] Moller, 'Beginnings', 49; Greaves, 'Introduction', p. xxiv.

[89] Kendall, *English Calvinism*, 39: Ursinus was talking here of a covenant that was 'one in substance and matter'.

[90] Ibid. 58; and cf. the view of Sibbes and Ball that God engaged to perform both parts of the covenant: McKee, 'Idea of Covenant', 104–5.

[91] Schaff, *Creeds*, 617 (ch. 7, para. 3). The Confession retained an element of conditionality in that God did not love the elect in it regardless, but because, of the faith which he knew they would have; on the other hand, those 'ordained unto life', the elect, would be made willing and able to believe by the Holy Spirit, which takes us back to irresistible grace, as in Ch. 8 above.

[92] McKee, 'Idea of the Covenant', 102–5, and cf. 121, 138–9, 154–9, 161–5; for Baxter's concern about

extent the arbiter of his fate, authors in situations such as preaching, catechizing, counselling, and writing godly handbooks may have leant towards a more explicitly conditional or reciprocal position. Thus John Preston told the 'weak saints' who found they could not fulfil some condition of the covenant, to 'go to Christ' for help, and 'urge him with this, it is a part of his covenant, that he hath confirmed by oath, and *must do it*'.[93] This trend was perhaps also encouraged by questions from worried members of the flock, such as 'how can I be sure that I am in the covenant of grace?' The result may have been to accelerate that trend towards the internalizing of assurance and 'preparationism' that we have encountered in this chapter and the last.[94] Those who were unsure if they were in the covenant could find 'evidence' that they were in it by assessing their performance of the terms of the covenant, and in this way obtain psychological validation of their election as well as a sense of membership of a wider community.[95] The potential was also there for what some authors have called moralism: a preoccupation with doing one's best to keep God's commandments, or even a belief that pardon would come from the fulfilling of the conditions of the covenant, which (if this was what some authors were urging on their flocks) came close to the justification by works denounced by Protestant critics of 'works righteousness'.[96] But perhaps we should not be too ready to divide authors into 'conditional' and 'unconditional' camps. Von Rohr argues that the mainstream (puritan) federal theologians saw the covenant of grace as 'both conditional and absolute', while Brachlow has suggested that many authors adopted a differential approach: stressing the gracious, unmerited nature of the covenant in their doctrinal statements or in dealing with diffident believers, but putting more emphasis on its conditional or ethical nature when dealing with hardened sinners.[97] Alternatively, or in addition, we should perhaps adopt a spectrum of opinion like that suggested by Professor Greaves: at one extreme an antinomian view which downgraded the role of the Law; next a 'strict Calvinist' position (derived from Calvin) of a promissory covenant between God and the elect with the contractual element subordinated but not quite

antinomians and the covenant, see von Rohr, *Covenant of Grace*, 99–100; and for Bunyan's repeatedly urging the saints to obey the Law even though they were exempt from its 'ministration', see Greaves, 'Introduction', pp. xxxi–xxxii.

[93] Coolidge, *Pauline Renaissance*, 124 (my italics), and cf. 121–5; see also Moller, 'Beginnings', 64–7; McKee, 'Idea of the Covenant', 130–3, 155–61, 164; Greaves, 'Introduction', pp. xxv, xxvii; Wallace, *Puritans and Predestination*, 136–7, 181; McGrath, *Iustitia Dei*, ii. 116; Brachlow, *Communion of Saints*, 151–6.

[94] McKee, 'Idea of the Covenant', 134–8, 154–5, 167; Coolidge, *Pauline Renaissance*, 125–6; von Rohr, *Covenant of Grace*, 58–63; and see above, nn. 1, 4, 6, for the works by Tipson, Torrance, Kendall, and Jensen.

[95] Von Rohr, *Covenant of Grace*, pp. 12–15, chs. 3, 7; and Coolidge, *Pauline Renaissance*, 127, 132 ff.

[96] Allison, *Rise of Moralism*, 63–5, 68–72, and *passim*; but for the parallel stress on obeying the moral law in puritanism, and the creeping in of a language of 'reward' in puritan works, see the authors cited by Wallace, *Puritans and Predestination*, 10–11; McKee, 'Idea of the Covenant', 143–4; and von Rohr, *Covenant of Grace*, 77–80, 102–5.

[97] Ibid. 17, 32–3, and *passim*; Brachlow, *Communion of Saints*, 34–5.

obliterated; next a 'moderate Calvinist' view of a reciprocal, conditional covenant between God and his elect based on vows taken in baptism; and finally, on the other wing, the 'Arminian' view, for whom grace was made available to all in the covenant, so that (their opponents alleged) responsibility for salvation fell on the individual's will and efforts to believe and obey.[98]

There were other developments in federal theology both in Europe and America during the seventeenth and early eighteenth centuries. There was, for example, the Scots' interweaving of a number of existing strands of covenanting thought in the later 1630s to produce a new brand of it with explosive political overtones.[99] Then, in New England, there was the 'half-way covenant' by which baptized members of moral character were treated as church members in some but not all respects.[100] Perhaps the best-known, however, was the separatists' use of a conditional covenant for their ecclesiology, a move which raised in an acute form the question of who was and was not in the covenant of grace.[101] Especially among those who sought assurance of election through a study of the godliness of their actions, the correct observance of the scriptural polity as part of the wider range of divine commands could be vital, and those like Richard Harrison, Robert Browne, and Henry Barrow who were prepared to act on their conviction that even partial conformity to a corrupt church was an idolatrous violation of Christ's commands, decided to break away and set up their own church in which individual members could fulfil the demands of God's covenant and gain assurance of their salvation.[102] Thus in his catechism of 1605, Henry Jacob asked 'How is a visible church constituted and gathered?', and replied 'By a free mutual consent of believers joining and covenanting to live as members of a holy society together in all religious and virtuous duties as Christ and his apostles did institute and practise in the Gospel.' The idea of church covenants like this one spread rapidly among separatists in England and elsewhere during the seventeenth century.[103] The only exception to their insistence on a recognizable faith as precondition of entry, at least in the separatist mainstream, was in the case of children, who

---

[98] Greaves, 'Introduction', pp. xxiv–xxvii; von Rohr, *Covenant of Grace*, 190–1 and *passim*. On the evidence to be cited below, however, the differences between 'moderate Calvinists' and non-Calvinist theologians were less than Greaves might imply: both allowed a conditional element, but both saw the covenant as an unparalleled act of divine grace which its members neither had deserved nor could deserve.

[99] See below, pp. 459–60. See also McKee, 'Idea of the Covenant', ch. 6; and McGiffert, 'God's Controversy', 1151–74, and id., 'Covenant, Crown and Commons in Elizabethan Puritanism', *Journal of British Studies*, 20 (1980), 32–52.

[100] McGrath, *Iustitia Dei*, ii. 119, and references there.

[101] McKee, 'Idea of the Covenant', ch. 5; Brachlow, *Communion of Saints*, 35 and *passim*.

[102] Still valuable are the older account by C. Burrage, *The Early English Dissenters* (2 vols.; Cambridge, 1912) and editions of the separatists' works by A. Peel and L. H. Carlson. Of the more recent accounts, see McKee, 'Idea of the Covenant', 45–6, 50–6, 63, 263–4; B. R. White, *The English Separatist Tradition* (Oxford, 1971); and Brachlow, *Communion of Saints*, chs. 1, 3, 5–7.

[103] Ibid., p. 138, and ch. 3, *passim*; and the older account of C. Burrage, *The Church Covenant Idea* (Philadelphia, 1904).

were allowed in on the ground that the covenant was 'made with the faithful and their seed'.[104]

The question of who was in the covenant, and, beyond that, of to whom the covenant of grace was offered, was the occasion of some polemical debate, for example between John Cotton and William Twisse, and between John Owen and Richard Baxter.[105] For Owen, the covenant of grace was 'not made universally with all, but particularly only with some', and so it was not conditional but promised benefits 'absolutely' to the elect alone. For Richard Baxter, as for Preston and moderate Calvinists abroad such as the Amyraldians, grace was intended for all conditionally, but for the elect absolutely.[106] Non-Calvinists or 'Arminians' in Europe and America also adopted a universalist stance: grace was understood to be made available to all men, and those who believed and obeyed would be saved.[107] The distinction was often less sharp in practice. In the first place, whatever their theoretical position, most predestinarians accepted that in terms of outward appearance it was impossible to know for certain who was in the covenant of grace and who was not. In effect, therefore, membership of the covenant was coterminous with that of the visible church except in the case of blatant and persistent sinners.[108] Secondly, there was the practice of infant baptism. From an early stage of the Reformation, authors like Zwingli, Bullinger, and Knox had expressed the opinion that the covenant covered the children of believers as well as the believers themselves, and that baptism was a sacramental entry into that covenant.[109] As the authors of the Heidelberg Catechism put it, since infants

> as well as their parents, belong to the covenant and people of God, and both redemption from sin and the Holy Ghost, who works faith, are through the blood of Christ promised to them no less than to their parents, they are also by baptism, as a sign of the covenant, to be ingrafted into the Christian church, and distinguished from the children of unbelievers, as was done in the Old Testament by circumcision, in place of which in the New Testament baptism is appointed.[110]

Here we have the main elements of the thinking of a large number of Protestant churchmen on the place of baptism in a federal framework. The covenant is seen as being organic, expanding and contracting from generation to generation; membership

---

[104] Infants had to exhibit faith when they came of age, so that their admission was of a temporarily conditional kind; the Baptist insistence on visible obedience before admission was more consistent: Brachlow, *Communion of Saints*, pp. 144–5, and chs. 3–4, *passim*; and cf. McKee, 'Idea of the Covenant', 109–10.

[105] Coolidge, *Pauline Renaissance*, 116–18; McGrath, *Iustitia Dei*, ii. 116–17, and cf. 119–20.

[106] McKee, 'Idea of the Covenant', 165; Clifford, *Atonement and Justification*, 117, 153–4, 192–3.

[107] Greaves, 'Introduction', p. xxvii (on Goodwin); Clifford, *Atonement and Justification*, 154; McGrath, *Iustitia Dei*, ii. 120–1; and see below, pp. 415–19.

[108] McKee, 'Idea of the Covenant', 139–40 (though cf. 117–18); Brachlow, *Communion of Saints*, 114–15, 128, 146.

[109] See above, nn. 74–5, and R. L. Greaves, 'John Knox and the Covenant Tradition', *JEH* 24 (1973), 26–7.

[110] Heidelberg Catechism, 331.

is equated with the people of God, and in effect with the visible Christian church; and the baptism of infants before they have faith or can obey is defended on the basis of the Old Testament practice of circumcision, which was itself based on the order by God to Abraham (Genesis 17: 10) that as part of keeping the covenant all male infants should be circumcised.[111]

We are now in a position to return to our questions as to the nature and extent of covenantal teaching in our sample of catechisms. It soon becomes clear that there are virtually no references to the covenant in the first generation of popular catechisms: Calvin's 1541 form, the Prayer Book form of 1549, and the forms of Dering–More and Paget. Nowell made only a brief historical reference to the fact that God entered into covenant by circumcision with Abraham and his seed, and that he confirmed the promise, first to Abraham, then to Isaac and Jacob, and continued the assurance through Moses and other prophets.[112] Brief references to the covenant appear in the translations into English of the Heidelberg Catechism and Virel's dialogues, and in the forms of native authors such as Perkins and Cartwright from the 1590s (and Henry Jacob in the 1600s, as we have seen, though his work is not in our sample).[113] From that point, however, the frequency increased, and thereafter covenant vocabulary was used in at least half of the forms in our sample, mainly those of intermediate or larger size, rather than the smaller ones like those of Egerton, Keach, and Watts. If we break down these references into groups, we find that covenantal teaching was used to a limited extent as an organizing principle of soteriology, slightly more often as an inducement to piety or a means of assurance, but most frequently of all in relation to the sacraments.

Only a handful of authors gave prominence to the covenant at an early stage of their catechism or in whatever section they tackled salvation. Despite their influence in spreading the idea of a double covenant through their more advanced works, the authors of the Heidelberg Catechism did not use it as part of their teaching on salvation; their only reference to a covenant was under the sacraments where they referred to baptism being for the 'people and covenant of God', and to the 'covenant of God' being profaned by unworthy receivers at communion.[114] Again, though he probably more than anyone else helped to spread federal thinking in England, William Perkins also did not mention the covenants under the first four of the six principles in his

---

[111] There were other uses to which covenant thinking was put, including God being a third party to marriage and the family: McKee, 'Idea of the Covenant', ch. 6; but the main uses were those indicated in previous pages of this chapter.

[112] Nowell, *Catechisme*, 151 (though cf. 183).

[113] Virel, *Treatise*, 251, 259 (raised under baptism and the Lord's Supper), and following notes.

[114] Heidelberg Catechism, 331. The covenant was also mentioned only in a sacramental connection in the Belgic, Gallican, and Second Helvetic Confessions: McKee, 'Idea of the Covenant', 20.

catechism (those on God, the Fall, and salvation); and under the fifth he raised only the covenant of grace, in his short section on the sacraments as outward means to obtain God's blessings through faith.[115] Thomas Cartwright, on the other hand, did introduce the idea early in his form, as a subdivision of his section on the execution of the divine decree, but did not develop it much thereafter. He had reached the point at which he was discussing what the Word said about the 'repair' of man after the Fall when he stated that the Word could be subdivided into the Law, 'otherwise called the covenant of works', and the gracious promise, the covenant of grace, which from the time of Christ was called the Gospel. He did not tie the covenant of grace explicitly to the decree of election; nor did he talk of conditions or promises, but of the commands of the Law under the covenant of works and of the means of applying Christ's bene-fits to ourselves under the covenant of grace. In the remainder of his form, he barely alluded to the covenant, not even under the sacraments.[116]

In the early seventeenth century, predestinarian authors like Ball and Elton fol-lowed Perkins's practice rather than Cartwright's, though we know from his other writings that Ball had well-developed views on the covenant.[117] Apart from James Ussher, who wrote his forms as a young man but did not publish them until later, there was no extended discussion of the covenants in a soteriological context until the publication of Hammond's catechism in 1644 and the Westminster catechisms in 1648. In his first, more elementary form, Ussher had raised the covenant in almost the same sentence as he introduced Adam: 'How did God deal with man after he made him? He made a covenant with Adam, and in him with all mankind.' From the following exchanges it is clear that Ussher, like many other authors of the time, saw this first covenant as being conditional: if man kept God's commandments, he would live; if he broke them, he would die. In connection with the second covenant, Ussher did not refer to any conditions or promises on man's part, but he did ask 'What is required of man for obtaining the benefits of the Gospel?' and expected the answer that he receives Christ, whom God freely offers him, by faith.[118] In his more advanced form, however, Ussher used conditional language for both covenants. In the first covenant, 'God promiseth everlasting life unto man, upon condition that he perform entire and perfect obedience unto his law ... and in like sort threateneth death unto him, if he did not perform the same'; and in the second, 'God promiseth everlasting life unto man, upon condition that he be reconciled unto him in Christ ... the condi-tion of the second is the obtaining of that righteousness which is without himself,

---

[115] Perkins, *Foundation*, 7–8. The covenant was also raised only in connection with the sacraments in two specialist forms in our sample, those of Bradshaw, 'Brief forme', 139, and Hildersham, 'Doctrine', 21.

[116] Cartwright, 'Catechisme', sigs. Aa4ᵛ–5ʳ, Aa6ʳ. On Cartwright's role in disseminating the idea of a twin covenant, see Weir, *Federal Theology*, 144–7, but on Cartwright's limited use of the idea in other works, see McKee, 'Idea of the Covenant', 45–6.

[117] Ibid. 68; Ball, *Catechisme*, 79–80, though see also id., *Treatise*, 140–1, 143–4 (and von Rohr, *Covenant of Grace, passim*); Elton, *Forme*, sigs. D6ʳ⁻ᵛ, D8ᵛ–E1ʳ, though see also id., 'Extract', sig. G5ᵛ.

[118] Ussher, 'Principles', 6–8.

even the righteousness of God which is by faith in the mediator Jesus Christ'.[119] It is also of interest that Ussher, though a double predestinarian, like Cartwright equated the members of the second covenant not specifically with the elect, but with 'man' or 'mankind'. The one occasion on which he equated the covenant of grace with the elect was in the context of the invisible church: those who hold by Christ, the mediator of the new covenant, participate in his grace, 'effectually communicated to the elect, of whom the catholic church doth consist'.[120] This equation of the covenant with the church would have echoes, albeit in the context of a more visible church, in other forms in our sample such as those of episcopalians like Williams, Isham, and Lewis who wrote of the Christian church being in covenant with God just as the old Jewish church had been.[121] Some puritans might have used the covenant of grace to replace the apostolic succession as the basis of the church's continuity through the ages, but episcopalians probably had no difficulty in using the covenant as a supplement to the apostolic succession to explain the historic continuity of their church.[122]

The clearest equation of covenant and election in our sample is to be found in the Westminster catechisms which followed the line laid down in the Westminster Confession. The authors of these two catechisms tackled the covenant about midway between the decrees and the role of Christ as mediator or redeemer.[123] In both forms, the covenant of life or works was presented as a special act of providence by which God promised life 'upon condition of personal, perfect, and perpetual obedience'.[124] In both, the covenant of grace is stated quite specifically to have been made (or to be effective) with the elect alone:

God ... of his mere love and mercy delivereth his elect out of [the covenant of works], and bringeth them into an estate of salvation by the second covenant, commonly called the covenant of grace.[125]

Where the authors of the Westminster Confession had avoided the use of conditional language on the terms of the covenant of grace, the authors of the Larger Catechism did let it slip in (though the end-result is the same as in the Confession): God offers sinners a mediator, and life and salvation by him, and 'requires' faith 'as the condition to interest them in him'. But this faith is a 'condition' only in a limited, evidential sense—to provide an interest or stake for the elect in Christ; in them, the faith that God 'requires' will be worked irresistibly by the Holy Ghost.[126] The authors of the

---

[119] Ussher, 'Method', 16–18.   [120] Ibid. and 19.

[121] Williams, *Exposition*, 23; Isham, *Catechism*, 31; Lewis, *Catechism*, 31. In his longest form, the Baptist Benjamin Keach also spoke of a 'visible covenant' into which believers entered in baptism: 'Youth', 102 (though cf. 107).

[122] Coolidge, *Pauline Renaissance*, 13; and previous note above.

[123] Westminster Larger, 5–6 (answers 10–12), 17–29 (answers 36–57); Westminster Shorter, 7 (answers 7–8), 11–14 (answers 21–8).

[124] Westminster Larger, 10–11 (answer 20); Westminster Shorter, 8 (answer 12).

[125] Westminster Larger, 14 (answer 30); and cf. Westminster Shorter, 10 (answer 20).

[126] Westminster Larger, 15 (answer 31).

Shorter Catechism did *not* refer to a condition, but again used verbs like 'deliver' and 'bring' to describe the way in which God arranges the redemption of the elect in the covenant of grace, and as was usually the case, where the Larger Catechism used the third person, the Shorter used the first. Having been told that Christ redeemed God's elect through the covenant of grace, the catechumen was asked 'How are we made partakers of the redemption purchased by Christ?', and replied 'by the effectual application of it to us by the Holy Spirit'.[127] The Larger Catechism thus remained the most uncompromising statement of a predestinarian covenant of grace, though the simpler and more personal expression of the same point in the Shorter Catechism was mirrored by some of the authors who expounded that form or borrowed from it.[128]

The line taken in the Westminster catechisms was in some respects middle-of-the-road. It is interesting to observe, for example, that in 1681 in the preface to his exposition of the Prayer Book catechism, the episcopalian Thomas Comber used almost exactly the same description of the two covenants as had appeared in the Westminster Larger Catechism. The sole difference was at the point in the description of the covenant of grace where the Larger Catechism referred to the covenant as being for the elect; here Comber substituted the statement that the covenant was offered to all who repent and believe.[129] This was one of the three areas where the Westminster catechisms may be said to have been less typical of those works in our sample which used covenanting terms. The first was that the Larger Catechism gave fuller treatment of the two covenants than most other forms,[130] and certainly than any form written by the 1630s (which may cast some doubt on the claim of Miller and Coolidge that the covenant had become a central organizing principle of the puritan understanding of the theology of grace by the early seventeenth century).[131] The second was its explicit equation of the membership of the covenant of grace with the elect: even Perkins had not done this in his catechism, and Cartwright and Ussher did it only by implication or context, and further softened the edge by sometimes using the first person to describe its impact. Thirdly, in their leaning towards the unconditional end of the spectrum the Westminster forms were typical neither of those predestinarians who were occasionally tempted into using contractual ideas or speaking of mutual duties, nor of those non-Calvinists, like Andrewes, Hammond, and others, who also spoke of reciprocal responsibilities or the conditions of the covenant of grace.[132]

Hammond was the one author in our sample who introduced the covenants at the very outset of his catechism, though arguably this was as much as an inducement to piety as a principle of soteriology. Hammond's work was designed as a 'practical'

[127] Westminster Shorter, 10–11, 14 (answers 20–1, 29).
[128] Wallis, *Explanation*, 7, 10–11, 41; Gouge, *Principles*, 32–3, 96, 99–100, and id., 'Heads', 2, 6; Keach, 'Youth', 77–9, 102; Watts, *Assembly's catechism*, 8, 13.
[129] Comber, *Church-catechism*, 5.
[130] With the possible exceptions of Hammond (see below) and Vincent, *Catechism*, 54–7.
[131] See above, n. 68.   [132] See above, pp. 411–13 and below, nn. 134, 150.

catechism for those who had already mastered the basics through the 1549 catechism, and at the outset the scholar beseeches the master to tell him 'what kind of
doctrines, and what parts of scripture, will be likely to have the most present influence on my heart, or contribute most to Christian practice'. The catechist chooses
five, of which the first is 'the doctrine of the first and second covenant', and he then
spends ten pages defining and explaining these covenants. His conditional approach
is evident from the opening definition: 'A covenant is a mutual compact, as we now
consider it, betwixt God and man, consisting of mercies on God's part made over to
man, and of conditions on man's part required by God.' The first covenant, was 'that
which is supposed to be made with Adam' before his first sin, 'and with all mankind
in him'; in it God gave some things absolutely—a law written in man's heart to teach
him his duty and the ability to perform all that was required of him—and some conditionally—continuation of the same and eternal felicity, on condition of using that
ability to obey God.[133] The second covenant was made with Adam after his fall, and
promised Christ would be the second Adam to break the serpent's head, to perform
perfect obedience as a satisfaction for Adam's sin, and 'to taste death for every man,
to die for all those which were dead in Adam' (Hammond added a historical note that
'it was the custom of the eastern nations to seal all covenants with blood', and Christ
was no exception). Of the five promises or mercies made over to us in Christ in the
second covenant, the first three were similar to those in the first: a law of faith
according to which Christians ought to live, pardon of our sins, and grace or strength
sufficient to perform what is necessary under the second covenant. The other two—
more grace, and a crown of glory—were conditional, on using 'those weaker degrees
of grace given us', and on being 'such a man as Christ now under the second
covenant requires him to be', that is not perfect and free from sin, but seeking faithfully to obey the Gospel, and performing what God enables us to perform.

In a word the condition required of us, is a constellation or conjuncture of all those gospel
graces, faith, hope, charity, self-denial, repentance, and the rest, every one of them truly and
sincerely rooted in the Christian heart.[134]

What one makes of this depends on what one thinks of Hammond. If one is disposed to see him as an arch-'Arminian' and a leading apologist for a largely indefens-
ible Caroline church, one is likely to depict this as a simple 'moralism': Hammond
is telling men that if they are as good as they can be, they will wear the victor's
crown.[135] If, on the other hand, one sees him as a defender of the principles of a system
under threat from what he saw as new and erroneous doctrines and root-and-branch

---

[133] Hammond, *Practical catechisme*, 2–4.
[134] Ibid. 4–9; Hammond gave a slightly different version of the new covenant at pp. 82–3, but the difference was perhaps only between the promise before Christ—with the fallen Adam—and the actuality—
after Christ's death.
[135] Allison, *Rise of Moralism*, 96–106, 132, 137; Wallace, *Puritans and Predestination*, 121–2, 125–7,
145–6, 160, 162, 187.

reformers, one might be tempted to point out that elsewhere he regularly denounced the idea of justification by works, and to suggest that in this section of his catechism he was trying to use the weapons of the church's enemies against them.[136] Hammond was perhaps as far towards one end of the spectrum in our sample as the Westminster theologians were to the other. But much of what Hammond wrote was compatible with the Westminster theologians' views: two covenants, one with Adam before the fall, and one with Christ the second Adam; the Law written in men's hearts and to be obeyed even by the faithful; faith as a condition of interest in the covenant; and grace given to men to enable them to obey. The main difference, as we saw in the chapter on predestination, was that Hammond thought the grace was resistible, and the double predestinarians did not, so that where they leant towards an equation of covenant and election, he leant towards a conditional universalist position: all might be members, if they were to use the grace given, and if they did, more grace would be given. Also, where the Westminster theologians leant towards an unconditional covenant whose members (being certain to be saved) performed duties rather than observed conditions, Hammond was one of the many who, while accepting the absoluteness of the divine promise, also saw the need to remind those in the covenant of grace who hoped to be saved that they had to do their best to believe and obey, on the score that faith without works is dead.[137]

William Nicholson borrowed heavily from Hammond in his account of the two covenants at the start of his *Plain and full exposition of the catechism of the Church of England* (1655), though Nicholson made greater use of Biblical texts to bolster his case. Another difference was that Nicholson raised the covenants under the second answer of the Prayer Book catechism, where the catechumen says that he was given his name in baptism, wherein he was made a member of Christ, the child of God, and an inheritor of the kingdom of heaven. As a result Nicholson was able to move smoothly on from the two covenants to describing baptism as 'the seal of those promises made over unto man by this second covenant', and to the 'promise and vow' the godparents then made on the infant's behalf, that he would renounce evil, believe in the Christian faith and keep God's commandments. This promise and vow of repentance, faith, and obedience is thus man's part of the covenant with God, though at this point Nicholson did not use the word 'condition', and shortly afterwards the catechumen acknowledges that he feels 'bound' to believe, and to do as his godparents had promised for him. At the same time he thanks God for having called him to this state of salvation, and prays for grace to continue in the same throughout his

---

[136] J. W. Packer, *The Transformation of Anglicanism 1643–1660 (with special reference to Henry Hammond)* (Manchester, 1969), *passim*; J. Spurr, *The Restoration Church of England, 1646–1689* (New Haven/London, 1991), 10–13, 138–40; Hammond, *Practical catechisme*, 78–9, 311 ff; his use of 'supposed' and the reference to Eastern religions perhaps suggests a degree more detachment about federal theology than the Westminster divines showed.

[137] See above pp. 372–3 and p. 413 n. 126; and cf. von Rohr, *Covenant of Grace*, 102–4.

life.[138] In a later section, on the Decalogue, and in the closing section of his form, on the sacraments, Nicholson did briefly use the language of conditions. In the first case he said that a regenerate man, informed by God's special grace 'may, nay must walk in the commandments of God'; 'This is the condition of the second covenant; and God's grace, shed in a good man's heart, enables to perform it.'[139] On the second occasion, he stated that in the covenant, as in 'an indenture, we have the conditions agreed upon betwixt both parties set forth and represented, after sealed and delivered'. But he did not explain what they are, and he soon reverted to the idea of what is 'required': what is required for participation in the sacraments—which are the seals of the covenant—is true repentance, a lively faith, and charity. This faith was not a condition of the covenant, he wrote, but 'the instrument by which we receive the seal of the covenant' and 'a gift of the Spirit'.[140] Thus by grafting the covenant concept onto the opening and closing sections of the Prayer Book form, Nicholson was reinforcing the idea of baptism as an entry into a 'state of salvation', and reaffirming the need for those who had been baptized to believe and obey and to take part in the sacraments; and by stressing that the promises in the covenant are unchangeable, he offered assurance as well.[141]

Nicholson was neither the first nor the last to do this. William Hill had anticipated this grafting of the covenant onto the Prayer Book catechism in his own exposition of that form, published fourteen times between 1616 and c.1640. To the question of whether the catechumen was bound to perform the promises made for him by his godparents in baptism, Hill offered an amended reply: I am bound to do so 'because of the covenant which I have made with God (Hosea 2: 23)'. Later on, at the end of the section on the Decalogue, Hill's catechumen says that we must obey the Commandments as we have made a covenant with God to do so (Ezekiel 11: 20).[142] In 1631 Martin Nicholes, a predestinarian expositor of the Prayer Book form, made the catechumen say that without the covenant ratified between God and the infant in baptism he or she would continue to be by nature a 'child of wrath, a member of the devil, an heir of hell and damnation'. But having been made a member of Christ, the child of God, and an inheritor of heaven through the covenant in baptism, I must renew that covenant if I should fall into sin.[143]

A few decades later, Thomas Comber followed up his borrowings from the Westminster Larger Catechism on the origins and nature of the covenants by praising the wisdom of the authors of the compilers of the Prayer Book form for beginning with a

---

[138] Nicholson, *Exposition*, 11–13.   [139] Ibid. 127.
[140] Ibid. 156. The penultimate phrase may suggest that faith precedes the sealing of the covenant, which the Westminster divines probably would not have accepted; but elsewhere Nicholson had said very firmly that admission into the covenant occurs at baptism.
[141] As last notes, and op. cit., 163–6, 193.
[142] Hill, *Principles*, sigs. A5ᵛ, B5ʳ, and cf. C3ʳ; and cf. Taylor, *Catechism*, 4.
[143] Nicholes, *Catechisme*, 1–2, 70; and cf. Nicholson, *Exposition*, 163.

reminder of our obligations and privileges in the covenant of grace. He then stated that in our infancy we solemnly enter the covenant of grace by baptism; that when we come to years of understanding the Christian name given us in baptism should remind us of our duties and privileges in the covenant; that we should be heartily grateful to God for entry into 'this covenant of faith and repentance, and so into a capacity of salvation'; and that we should pray daily for grace to continue steadfast in this covenant. Comber's version of the covenant is implicitly conditional: those who perform the 'conditions' of their baptismal vow will not fail to reap the blessings of their baptism; those who wilfully break those conditions will not escape God's wrath and curse. However, the word 'conditions' is actually applied to the baptismal vow rather than the privileges of the covenant.[144] William Wake was another to introduce the covenant at the start of his exposition of the Prayer Book form, though he forbore to mention the covenant of works and concentrated instead on the covenant made through Christ. In an introductory section, he suggested that the proper subject of a catechism was what was generally necessary to be known of all Christians, 'in order to their due serving of God here, and to their being saved hereafter', and this could be reduced to two heads:

> The knowledge of the Gospel covenant; that is to say, of the promises made by God to mankind through our Lord Jesus Christ, and of the conditions upon which we may become partakers of them. And secondly, the knowledge of the means which God has appointed whereby to convey his grace to us; and thereby both to assist and confirm us, in the discharge of our duty to him.[145]

The promises made to mankind in Christ were pardon of sins, grace to fulfil our duty in this life, and 'upon our sincere performance thereof' everlasting salvation in the world to come. The conditions required of us by God are hearty repentance for sins past, sincere endeavour to live according to God's commands in future, and 'a lively faith in God's mercies towards us, through Jesus Christ'. The church catechism instructed people satisfactorily in both the promises and conditions, and in the means whereby God conveyed grace to us—Word, prayer, and sacraments.[146] He then moved on in section two to show how in baptism the catechumen was 'federally admitted into the communion of Christ's church', and later referred to the need for those who had been baptized to ratify their baptismal covenant at confirmation, and to discharge their duty under their 'baptismal vow and covenant'.[147] As we shall see later, in the chapter on sacraments, other episcopalian authors in the sample,[148] and a number outside as well,[149] also spoke of the 'condition' of keeping the covenant or of

---

[144] Comber, *Church-catechism*, 5, 7, 9.   [145] Wake, *Principles*, 2.   [146] Ibid. 2–3.

[147] Ibid. 4, 158–9, 185–9. The phrase 'baptismal vow and covenant' had been previously used by the nonconformist Thomas Gouge in his best-selling form: *Principles*, 99.

[148] e.g. Marshall, *Catechism*, 7, 53; Lewis, *Catechism*, 71.

[149] e.g. G. Towerson, *Of the sacrament of baptism* (1687), 185–7; and cf. anon., *The catechism of the Church of England* (1688), 9; B. Farrow, *A practical exposition of the catechism* (1708), 16–26; G. Burnet, *An*

the connection between the baptismal vow and what was required of those in the covenant.

Comber's reference to a 'covenant of faith and repentance' may have been influenced by the reference in the printed version of Lancelot Andrewes's catechetical lectures to a 'covenant of faith',[150] or by Jeremy Taylor's discussion of the subject in his form. Writing his own original form in the 1650s, Taylor had raised the subject of the covenant during a discussion of the three offices of Christ. In all of these, he said, Christ had acted as a mediator, and 'made a covenant between God and us of an everlasting interest'. The covenant was described as follows: 'God will write his laws in our hearts, and will pardon us, and defend us, and raise us again at the last day, and give us an inheritance in his kingdom', and the conditions to which God 'bound us on our part' are faith and repentance. Like Hill before him and Comber and others later, Taylor argued that we enter this covenant 'in our baptism' but to this he added '*and* at our ripe years, when we understand the secrets of the kingdom of Christ, and undertake willingly what in our names was undertaken for us in our infancy'.[151] Taylor also drew an unusual distinction between a covenant of faith and a covenant of repentance. The former is a promise of belief in Christ, the latter a promise to leave our sins and to endeavour 'to give up our will and affections to Christ'. We may through infirmity break this promise and commit sin, but still we are within the covenant of repentance, that is, within the

promise of pardon, and possibility of returning from dead works, and mortifying our lusts; and though this be done after the manner of men, that is, in weakness, and with some failings, yet our endeavour must be hearty, and constant, and diligent.

Christ has appointed the Word and sacraments to help us in this duty, and he will accompany these with his grace and Spirit.[152] Taylor was clearly among those who thought that the covenant had value as a means both of explaining salvation through faith in Christ and as an inducement to piety.

Taylor's position has been spelt out for a reason other than his possible influence on Comber, Wake, and others, in that Taylor is a leading figure among those accused by C. F. Allison of having perpetrated the 'rise of moralism' in Caroline thought. According to Allison (whose ideas we will examine in more detail at the end of the chapter on the Decalogue), Jeremy Taylor was so upset by what he saw as the distorted, predestinarian soteriology of the mid-seventeenth century that he decided to

---

exposition of the church catechism (1710), pt. 1; E. Creffeild, *The great duty of catechising* (1713), 13–15; L. Fogg, *An entrance into the doctrine of Christianity* (1714), 8, 17–20, and cf. id., *A general view of the Christian religion* (c.1712), 7–11, 20–3, 31–41; R. Newton, *A practical exposition of the church catechism* (1727), 11–13, and cf. 379, 385. Most of these stressed the positive side of the covenant relationship, but for a stronger stress on the conditionality of the covenant comparable to Comber's, see 'A divine of the Church of England', *Catechumenorum ductor* (1714), 10, and S. Adams, *A plain and full instruction* (1718), 7–8, 10.

[150] Andrewes, *Works*, vi. 62.
[151] Taylor, 'Catechism', 4 (my italics); Hill, *Principles*, sig. A5ᵛ; Comber, *Church-catechism*, 5.
[152] Taylor, 'Catechism', 4–5.

put much greater stress on repentance and holy living, and ended up with what Allison calls a 'new and strange doctrine of … the new covenant' according to which God acts only when and after man has by works of repentance fulfilled his part of the new covenant. Taylor, he says, was preoccupied with the steps that had been taken 'for *admission* to the covenant and eternal life', and thought that only on the fulfilment of these conditions were the rewards of heaven given. At the same time, the conditions of this new covenant are twice described as being 'lenient', on the basis that 'our hearty endeavour is accepted'.[153] However, it seems clear from the section of his catechism cited above that Taylor regarded those who had been baptized as already *in* the covenant, though they had later to understand and undertake the terms promised before by proxy; and both in the catechism and, as Allison concedes, at other times, Taylor spoke of the grace which was necessary to empower the works upon which the conditions of the new covenant are based.[154] As for the greater leniency of Taylor's covenant, this is perhaps more in the eye of the beholder than in Taylor's text. As we will see when we look at our authors' comments on the keeping of the Law, no one was pretending that it was easy, but there was a fairly widespread agreement that Christ's law, freed from the burden of the Jewish ceremonies and supported by greater grace, was relatively easier to keep than the Law of Moses, and in this sense not more grievous than the faithful could bear.[155] Taylor's evangelical concern for greater piety may have led him to ignore some of the theological distinctions made by earlier writers on the covenant, but much of what he said in his catechism seems to put faith before works, and grace before holy living. If there was a risk of 'moralism' in Taylor's stress on the conditions of keeping the covenant, it was comparable to the risk of 'moralism' in the experimental predestinarians and federal theologians of the late sixteenth or early seventeenth century who had said that the elect could tell by introspective analysis of their good works if they were in the covenant, and that if they did not find joy in those works they must redouble their prayers and efforts until they did.[156]

Indeed, in general terms it may be suggested that the introduction of covenantal teaching into catechizing did not precipitate major divisions between catechists. The authors of a number of the intermediate or larger works in our sample and a few shorter forms did reflect the rise of federal thinking in their work, though by no means all authors adopted it.[157] Moreover, of those catechists who did introduce the

---

[153] Allison, *Rise of Moralism*, 63–5, 68, 71, 73 (my italics).

[154] Ibid. 64; Taylor, 'Catechism', 4; and cf. Hammond, *Practical catechisme*, 5–6, 10–11.

[155] See below, pp. 472–5; also McKee, 'Idea of the Covenant', 96.

[156] As pointed out by von Rohr, *Covenant of Grace*, 105, and by Wallace, *Puritans and Predestination*, 197–8, though the latter still feels that the 'Arminians' were more moralist than the experimental predestinarians (pp. 127–8); cf. also above n. 96.

[157] Among those who did not were staunch episcopalians like Boughen and Isham and confirmed dissenters like Keach and Watts; the simpler forms of the last two show how it was still possible in the late seventeenth and early eighteenth centuries, as in the period before the 1590s, to teach Christ's saving work at catechetical level without recourse to federal concepts.

covenant, most used the concept sparingly, in many cases grafting it onto existing teaching such as the baptismal vow in the Prayer Book catechism of 1549, the Calvinist *ordo salutis*, or the value of the sacraments. As for the small number of authors in our sample who did make more detailed and conflicting statements on the covenants, such as Hammond and the Westminster divines, they too would probably have been able to agree that all were bound by the Law in the covenant of works, and that for those in the covenant of grace faith without works was dead, so that catechumens must make their election sure and work out their salvation by the means God had made available.[158] With this in mind, we may turn in the remaining chapters to consider our catechists' treatment of the Ten Commandments, prayer, and the correct use of the sacraments.

[158] See above, pp. 413–16.

10

The Ten Commandments

'No civilization has ever attached as much importance to guilt and shame as did the Western world from the thirteenth to the eighteenth centuries.' So wrote Jean Delumeau in the second of two studies in which he attempted 'a cultural history of sin' and an account of the 'evangelism of fear'. This was practised first by Catholic and then by Protestant clergy as well, and stressed not only the pains of hell awaiting unrepentant sinners but also the punishments in this world sent by a God who was angered by the continued sinfulness of man. These teachings helped to create and then heighten (he said) a 'Western guilt culture' and a siege mentality that was fed by fears of enemies without (Turks, Jews, witches, and heretics) and within (Satan trying to steal men's souls).[1] At the heart of the Catholic evangelism of fear was the depiction of the Seven Deadly Sins, both in word and image, the latter reaching a climax in the early and middle sixteenth century, whereas at the forefront of the Protestant equivalent were the Ten Commandments of the Old Testament. Even if we were to accept Delumeau's thesis of an overpowering collective guilt complex in the West, we must remember that the picture is not that simple, since as John Bossy has clearly demonstrated Catholic reluctance to use the Ten Commandments was already declining in the fifteenth century, and from the mid-sixteenth century, with the increase of catechizing associated with the Counter-Reformation as well as the Reformation, Catholic teaching would give more space to the Decalogue than the Seven Deadly Sins.[2] Professor Bossy has also pointed out some of the consequences of this shift. Not only did the Decalogue have unimpeachable scriptural origins, it was more precise (albeit requiring some interpretation in places), more penetrating, and as a Law more binding. It also gave much more space to obligations to and offences against God rather than just the more social or communal aspects associated with avoiding envy, lust, usury, and so on. Above all, he argues, 'the rationale of the Decalogue was the prohibition of idolatry'. It was a ritual as well as a moral code, designed to keep the people of Israel in the fear of the Lord as well as in holiness, and may have led to an increased fear of the Devil-worship associated with witchcraft.

---

[1] J. Delumeau, *La Peur en Occident: Une cité assiégée* (Paris, 1978); id., *Sin and Fear: The Emergence of a Western Guilt Culture 13th–18th Centuries*, tr. E. Nicholson (New York, 1990), 3 and *passim*.

[2] Before Trent, the priest was expected to have precise knowledge of the Decalogue, but the laity only a general familiarity: Aston, *England's Iconoclasts*, 344–54.

On a more positive note, the stress on honouring one's parents in the fifth Commandment may have helped 'to fix the notion of childhood in the European mind'.[3]

The Ten Commandments was a staple of Reformation teaching from the very outset, but the manner in which it was treated by catechists was not completely uniform. Their main problems when setting out to write a section on the Decalogue were tactical. Did they have space to expound all ten equally and at length, or should the treatment be compressed in some way? And should the Law be deployed at the outset, as Luther and many others had done, as a means to convince us of our sinfulness and so bring us to Christ for mercy; or should it be used later in the catechism as a means of showing the committed, regenerate Christian how to obey God's will, as Calvin (in his 1541 catechism) and many others did?[4] This last difference was not crucial in that catechists who treated the Commandments later as a guide to serving God might also embrace the idea of the Law as a means of bringing home man's sinfulness to him, and vice versa.[5] In the English case, it is interesting that despite the popularity of starting with the Decalogue noted in Chapter 6, inside our sample of best-selling or influential catechisms the Decalogue was put first only in the two Nowell forms and in Dering and More's and Paget's catechisms.[6] On the other hand, Calvin and the authors of the Prayer Book form and over a dozen expositors of the latter put it second, after the Creed, as did Virel in his dialogues and Palmer in his form of 1640.[7] Among those authors in the sample who did not handle the Creed but treated the other three staples, the Ten Commandments tended to be discussed first, as in the case of the Westminster divines and some of their followers.[8] But such expositions of the Decalogue always came after an extended treatment of credal material on God, Christ, and faith of the kind described in a previous chapter;[9] and their authors were as likely as other authors to refer to the Decalogue as the moral law or as a summary of the moral law.[10] In this sense they too fall into the category of authors

---

[3] J. Bossy, 'Moral Arithmetic: Seven Sins into Ten Commandments', *Conscience and Casuistry in Early Modern Europe*, ed. E. Leites (Cambridge, 1988), 215–34 (the quotation is at p. 216); and cf. Aston, *England's Iconoclasts*, ch. 7. For a rather different point about the possible connection between catechizing and belief in witchcraft, see J. Delumeau, *Catholicism between Luther and Voltaire* (1977), 174.

[4] See above, Ch. 5; Schaff, *Creeds*, 74–80; Calvin, *Catechisme*, 6–91; and below n. 7.

[5] The authors of the Heidelberg Catechism raised the Law both at the start, to show the misery of man's condition after the Fall, and much later, after Creed and sacraments, to show man how to thank God for his salvation: 308–9, 338–42, and cf. e.g. Calvin, *Catechisme*, 53–4, 86–9; Cartwright, 'Catechisme', sig. Aa5ʳ; Keach, 'Youth', 78–9; and cf. Andrewes, *Works*, vi. 71–2.

[6] See above, Ch. 6, and Appendix 2, s.v. Nowell, Dering–More, and Paget.

[7] See Appendix 2, s.v. Calvin, Prayer Book catechism, Hill, Mayer, Bernard, Nicholes, Boughen, Nicholson, Sherlock, Comber, Marshall, Williams, Isham, Wake, and Lewis; Virel, and Palmer.

[8] See Appendix 2, s.v. Westminster Larger, Westminster Shorter, Wallis, Vincent, and Watts, *Assembly's catechism*: in these cases a definition of the covenant of works was provided at an early stage, even if detailed discussion of the Law came much later. Thomas Gouge in his forms put the Decalogue between the sacraments and the Lord's Prayer: ibid.

[9] See above, pp. 302–7, 309–13, 319–24.

[10] Perkins, *Foundation*, 5; Virel, *Treatise*, 81; Elton, *Forme*, sigs. C5ᵛ–6ʳ; Hill, *Principles*, sig. B4ʳ; Palmer, *Endeavour*, 24; Ussher, 'Principles', 9; Westminster Larger, 52–6 (answer 98 and cf. answers

who treated the Decalogue as a guide to godly living as much as, or more than, a means of convincing men of the need for faith.[11] It is also noteworthy that although the majority of authors in our sample did tackle all Ten Commandments in turn, the large minority who did not—either because they were aiming at a very short and simple level of instruction or because their priorities lay elsewhere[12]—nevertheless provided some account of the Decalogue or some kind of moral guidance based on it. This might take the form of rules for holy living,[13] a short, accompanying treatise on the 'sins, vices, and frailties' of the young,[14] a loose paraphrase or versified form of the Decalogue,[15] or a reference to Christ's summary of the Ten Commandments in the Old Testament by his two commandments in the New in Matthew 22: 37, 39, or the 'commandments and laws of Jesus Christ' which he set down in his sermons, especially in the Sermon on the Mount.[16]

Among the majority of authors who tackled the Decalogue in full, there was some variation in the way in which the text of Exodus 20: 1–17 was cited. Most authors quoted the text in full, but this could be done in two ways: either all at once, or one Commandment at a time as each new one was broached. It is perhaps indicative of authors' concern for improving the techniques of catechizing, which we examined in Chapter 5 above, that the initial practice of citing the seventeen verses together at the outset, as in the Prayer Book catechism and the Dering–More form of 1572, gave way to the quoting and explanation of each Commandment in turn.[17] In the case of a number of expositions of the Prayer Book catechism, the old practice was not so

---

92–7); Westminster Shorter, 18 (answers 40–1); Nicholson, *Exposition*, 75; Comber, *Church-catechism*, 15; Gouge, *Principles*, 112; Isham, *Catechism*, 31; Watts, *Assembly's catechism*, 21.

[11] The double predestinarian John Ball placed the Decalogue last of all in his two forms: Ball, *Catechisme*, 84–8, and id., *Treatise*, 175–214.

[12] A score of works in our sample can be put in one of these categories: see Appendix 2, s.v. 'Maner to examine children'; 'Certaine questions and answers'; Perkins; Egerton (the first five forms, but not the sixth); Bradshaw; Hildersham; Hieron; Elton (both forms); Grosse; Keach (all three forms); Watts (first four forms).

[13] S. Egerton, *A briefe method* (1615), 42–7 ('Certaine rules for the direction of a Christian life') and 47–50 (the same in verse); S. Hieron, *The doctrine of the beginning of Christ* (1626), sigs. B7ᵛ–C7ᵛ.

[14] I. Watts, *Catechisms: or instructions in the principles of Christian religion* (1730), 152–88; and cf. Jeremy Taylor's 'agenda' following his 'credenda' in his *Symbolon ... or a collection of moral and political discourses* (1657), 15 ff. and Edward Elton's catechetical lectures on the first six and then all ten Commandments: *A plaine and easie exposition of sixe of the commandements* (1619) and *Gods holy mind* (1625). For the 1623 version, see S. B. Lewkowicz, 'Elton's *An exposition of the ten commandements of God* (1623): A Burnt Book?', *Papers of the Bibliographical Society of America*, 71 (1977), 201–8.

[15] Perkins, *Foundation*, 5; B. Keach, *Instructions for children* [1710?], 49–50 (and cf. 17–18).

[16] Cartwright, 'Catechisme', sig. Aa5ʳ; and cf. Westminster Shorter, 18–19 (answer 42), and Gouge, *Principles*, 112 (though these authors also cited the Commandments in full subsequently); Taylor, 'Catechism', 5; and cf. Hammond, *Practical catechisme*, lib. ii. Another variation was a bare citation of the text of the Decalogue with no exposition, e.g. Egerton, 'Familiar manner', 37–9; Gouge, 'Heads', 7–8; Watts, 'Historical catechism', 44–5.

[17] Prayer Book catechism, 781–3; Dering–More, *Catechisme*, sig. A6ᵛ; for separate citation of each Commandment at the relevant stage of catechesis, see the Westminster catechisms; Williams, *Exposition*, 27–43; Wake, *Principles*, 85–127; and Lewis, *Catechism*, 37–58.

much replaced as supplemented by the new: Exodus 20: 1–17 was first given in full, then repeated in stages.[18] Equally, although some authors clearly expected catechumens to tackle the longer Commandments such as numbers two and four whole, at a sitting as it were, other authors split such Commandments into sections, presumably to facilitate memorization and comprehension.[19] Yet others cited the Commandments in an abbreviated form, usually the first few words, followed by an 'etc.', for example 'Honour thy father and thy mother, etc.', but sometimes in a highly condensed form which did not even convey the basic meaning of the individual command, as in Paget's and Ball's forms: 'Thou shalt not make to thy etc.' (for number two), or 'Thou shalt not take the name, etc.' (for the third).[20] This must have been done on the assumption either that the catechumen had already learnt the complete text in an elementary catechism or by some other means, or that the full text was available elsewhere in the book or booklet of which the catechism formed only a part.[21] The fullness of citation was not necessarily dictated by the length of the form. Though among the shorter forms in the sample, the Prayer Book and Dering–More catechisms did, as already noted, print the Decalogue in full; conversely, the forms in which the text was omitted altogether or presented in a shortened form were of all sizes and destined for different kinds of catechumens.[22]

The translation used in the sixteenth century by those English authors who cited the text of Exodus at any length was the Great Bible; and even after the appearance of the Authorized Version, this was still largely the case, for example in the many expositions of the Prayer Book catechism.[23] Those authors in the sample who adopted the wording of the King James Bible for their citation of the Commandments included the presbyterians who sat in the Westminster Assembly and the later expositors of their Shorter Catechism.[24] The numbering of the Commandments was always the Reformed one, in which the condemnation of idolatry in Exodus 20: 4–6 was treated as a separate second Commandment (where Catholics treated it as the tail-end of the

[18] Hill, *Principles*, sigs. B4^{r-v}; Mayer, *Catechisme*, sigs. B3^v–C1^r; Boughen, *Exposition*, sigs. +B3^r–4^r and pp. 35–58; Sherlock, *Principles*, 3–5, 28–38; Comber, *Church-catechism*, 16–21; and Marshall, *Catechism*, sigs. A3^v–4^v, and pp. 21–30, 67–78.

[19] See below under the relevant Commandments. The later portions of Commandments two to five were omitted from the 1549 version of the Prayer Book catechism, but inserted in 1552 and kept in 1604 and 1661: Brightman, *English Rite*, ii. 781–3.

[20] Paget, *Questions*, sigs. B2^{r-v}; Ball, *Catechisme*, 84–5; and cf. Palmer, *Endeavour*, 24–30; Ussher, 'Principles', 9–10; and Nicholson, *Exposition*, 86, 96, 101.

[21] e.g. Cartwright's form was appended to Dod and Cleaver's long treatise on the Decalogue, though the Commandments were cited only in stages.

[22] See previous notes.

[23] See Appendix 2, s.v. Prayer Book catechism, Hill, Mayer, Boughen, Nicholson, Sherlock, Comber, Marshall, Williams, Wake, and Lewis. The Great Bible version was also used by Nowell (in both forms), Dering and More, Paget, and Egerton (in 'Familiar manner'). Dod and Cleaver worked mainly from the Great Bible translation, but cf. 'before my face' in Commandment one, and 'I am Jehovah' in number two: *Plaine and familiar exposition of the ten commandments* (1622), 27, 79.

[24] Appendix 2, s.v. Westminster Larger and Smaller, Wallis, Vincent, and Gouge (both forms); but see also Ussher, 'Principles', 9–10.

first), and all the coveting in verse 17 was subsumed into Commandment number ten (whereas the Catholics split that verse into commands nine and ten).[25] The reason for these differences was sometimes explained by scholars, as in Lancelot Andrewes's catechetical lectures at Cambridge, but it was rare for authors in our sample to do so. Only in the 1690s, at a time of renewed worry about Catholicism, did a couple take the time to suggest that the Roman practice of conflating verses 3–6 was done in order to play down the prohibition against idolatry.[26] A few authors, such as Calvin, Nowell, and the Heidelberg theologians put Exodus 20 verse 2—'I am the lord which hath brought thee out of the land of Egypt, out of the house of bondage'—as the first sentence of the first Commandment; but the usual practice in the forms in our sample was to treat this as a preface, so that verse three—'Thou shalt have no other gods but me'—became the first Commandment proper.[27] These and other small variations in the citing of the text do not seem to have had much impact on the content of catechetical teaching, but suggest that in terms of technique a number of authors were thinking hard and independently about how best to present the raw material of this section of their form.

It was not uncommon for the authors of more specialized works on the Decalogue to suggest certain rules of interpretation to help the reader understand Exodus 20: Andrewes, Perkins, and Dod and Cleaver all offered sets of rules to this end in their larger works.[28] Few authors in our sample of catechisms (or indeed outside it) found the space for such rules, though a few did, nearly all in larger than average works. Thus in his treatise Virel offered three rules, while in his full-length form John Ball offered seven rules, some of them so similar to Dod and Cleaver's that plagiarism seems very likely. The authors of the Westminster Larger Catechism offered eight rules 'for the right understanding' of the Commandments, which again seem to have leant heavily on Dod and Cleaver, either directly or through Ball,[29] while in the 1650s and 1690s three conformist clergy also offered a number of rules which in places are very similar in content though different in wording from these.[30] Since a number of

[25] Aston, *England's Iconoclasts*, 372–92, 426–45, 458–62.

[26] Andrewes, *Works*, vi. 74; Williams, *Exposition*, 30; Wake, *Principles*, 79–80 (Wake alleged that in some Catholic books of devotion the prohibition against idolatry was omitted altogether); and cf. Aston, *England's Iconoclasts*, 385–7.

[27] Calvin, *Catechisme*, 54; Nowell, *Catechisme*, 121; Heidelberg Catechism, 340; and *The Decades of Henry Bullinger*, ed. T. Harding (Parker Society, vols. 35, 39, 42, 47; Cambridge, 1849–52), i. 215; but cf. e.g. Hill, *Principles*, sig. B5ʳ; Westminster Larger, 60–1 (answers 101, 103); and Wake, *Principles*, 85–6.

[28] Andrewes, *Works*, vi. 73–81; Perkins, *A golden chaine*, in *Works*, i (1612), 32; Dod and Cleaver, *Exposition*, 26 (and for other editions, STC² 6967–79); and cf. also the work attributed to James Ussher, *A body of divinitie* (Wing² U 151–8) and Mitchell, *Catechisms of the Second Reformation*, p. lxx.

[29] Virel, *Treatise*, 84–6; Ball, *Treatise*, 176–7 (Ball's form was one of those examined by Westminster divines as possible models for their form—Mitchell, *Catechisms of the Second Reformation*, pp. xvii–xx, lxxi—and there are certainly many parallels between Ball's account and that in the Larger Catechism). For examples of catechisms outside the sample with rules of interpretation, see W. Attersoll, *The principles of Christian religion* (1635), sigs. A4ᵛ–5ʳ, and W. Fenner, *The spiritual mans directory*, in *Works* (1650–1), 20.

[30] Nicholson, *Exposition*, 77–9; Sherlock, *Principles*, 28; Wake, *Principles*, 83–5. Of the three, Nicholson's was the most idiosyncratic.

contemporary churchmen who did not state such rules explicitly often followed them implicitly, it may be worthwhile to look briefly at three of the more common principles of interpretation adopted.

The first rule followed by those authors who tackled the Decalogue at any length in their forms was to divide the Ten Commandments into two tables, of four and six, respectively. In language which is remarkably uniform across the gamut of forms in the sample, these tables were said to have contrasting functions—the first listed the duties owed to God, while the second listed duties to our neighbours or to man.[31] Exodus 20 itself gives no indication of such a division: elsewhere in Exodus and in Deuteronomy, there are certainly references to two tables,[32] but the division of the resulting Ten Commandments into groups of four and six was a matter of interpretation, resting heavily on Christ's reduction of the ten to two commandments in Matthew 22: 37–40, which was almost certainly the source of the similarity of language noted above.[33] This division into two tables with different emphases was not a matter of controversy among English catechists. However, an influential study by Professor J. Sears McGee has argued that from the 1620s to the 1660s attitudes towards the two tables acted as a litmus-test by which 'puritans' could tell fellow-puritans from 'Anglicans'. Although both groups urged their followers to obey all Ten Commandments to the best of their ability, the puritans (says McGee) tended to emphasize the duties of the first table, such as avoiding idolatry and the profanation of the sabbath, while 'Anglicans' tended to emphasize those of the second, such as obedience and charity. For the puritans, he suggests, the first table was a touchstone for the second; for the 'Anglicans' the duties of the second were a touchstone for the first.[34] At polemical level and especially from a 'puritan' point of view, there is a case to be made for different imperatives or priorities at least partly along the lines indicated: the 'godly' clearly did have more sensitive noses when it came to detecting a whiff of idolatry, and in many cases they adopted a harder line on sabbath observance. Furthermore, they were prepared to be disruptive and suffer for their beliefs, as McGee argues.[35] However, some aspects of this thesis are perhaps open to question as far as it is applied to the cut and thrust of controversy inside the educated

---

[31] Calvin, *Catechisme*, 53; Nowell, *Catechisme*, 120; Paget, *Questions*, sig. A7ᵛ; Cartwright, 'Catechisme', sig. Aa5ʳ; Ball, *Catechisme*, 84; Hill, *Principles*, sigs. B5ʳ⁻ᵛ; Ussher, 'Principles', 9; Westminster Larger, 56, 83 (answers 98, 122); Comber, *Church-catechism*, 18, 20; Wake, *Principles*, 79; Lewis, *Catechism*, 57–8. Nicholes, *Catechisme*, 24, 30, followed Calvin's *Catechisme* in adding to the duties of the second table our duty to *ourselves* and other men.

[32] Exod. 31: 18, 32: 9, 34: 1, 4, 28, and Deut. 5: 22, 10: 1–2; as was pointed out in Ball, *Catechisme*, 84, and Wake, *Principles*, 79–80.

[33] Cf. n. 16 above; Bullinger, *Decades*, i. 212–15; Andrewes, *Works*, vi. 75; Calvin, *Catechisme*, 84; Prayer Book catechism, 784–5; Nowell, *Catechisme*, 136–7; Ussher, 'Principles', 9; Williams, *Exposition*, 26; and Lewis, *Catechism*, 57–8. There are also of course the Old Testament roots of Matt. 22, such as Lev. 11: 13, and Deut. 4: 5.

[34] J. Sears McGee, *The Godly Man in Stuart England: Anglicans, Puritans and the Two Tables, 1620–1670* (New Haven/London, 1976), 93–4.

[35] Ibid., chs. 3–4.

élite;[36] and at catechetical level it is hard to find pronounced disagreements along the lines he suggests, either between 'godly' and conformist authors of the Elizabethan and early Stuart forms in our sample, or even between presbyterians and episcopalians in the mid-seventeenth century—a point to which we shall return below.

The second principle of interpretation was that the specifics raised in a Commandment should be understood as having a broad application. This was adopted to some extent by sixteenth-century authors, but it was not systematically applied until the early seventeenth. To quote Ball, a vice expressly forbidden or a duty specifically enjoined embraces all similar ones; or as the Westminster Larger Catechism put it, 'under one sin or duty, all of the same kind are forbidden or commanded'.[37] There were three or four routes by which this conclusion could have been reached. One was that the Commandments, as we have seen, were often described as a summary of the moral law, and so it was permissible and indeed incumbent on the catechist to expand this brief summary of what men should do, just as he had enlarged on the main headings of what they were to believe in the Apostles' Creed. A second route was through viewing some of the Commandments as 'figures' or 'types'—a common device in contemporary exposition.[38] Calvin told his catechumens that the bondage in Egypt referred to in Exodus 20: 2 was a 'figure' for man's spiritual slavery to the devil, while the 'sabbath' referred to in verses 10 and 11 was a 'figure' of the duty man owed to God on all the days of the week, and the keeping of the sabbath was a 'type' of our regeneration.[39] A third route to broader application was that taken by Hammond, and probably by others before him, but he is the clearest and earliest example in our sample: Christ had annexed new details to those given in the Mosaic law. Hammond did not deny that the moral law of the Old Testament was still applicable in the days of the Gospel, but built the central section of his 'practical' catechism around the Sermon on the Mount and the contrasts that Christ there drew between old and new, contrasts which in many cases meant that Christ was demanding more than the Mosaic law had done.[40] Other authors in the sample made a similar point when they stated that Christ came not to destroy the Law, but to fulfil it.[41] A fourth route may

[36] e.g. McGee's selection of authors, the uneven chronological distribution of the works cited, the quality of the evidence for the assertion that for 'Anglicans' the second table was the touchstone for the first, and the stress on certain matters not specified in the Commandments, such as preaching, charity, and the example of Christ.

[37] Ball, *Treatise*, 176–7; Westminster Larger, 56–7 (answer 99); for Andrewes's six rules for the application of the principle of extension, see *Works*, vi. 75–8.

[38] B. K. Lewalski, *Protestant Poetics and the Seventeenth-Century Religious Lyric* (Princeton, 1979), pts. 1, 2; and cf. S. Hardman, 'Puritan Asceticism and the Type of Sacrifice', in *Monks, Hermits and the Ascetic Tradition*, ed. W. J. Sheils (Studies in Church History, 22; Oxford, 1985), 285–97.

[39] Calvin, *Catechisme*, 55, 68, 71–2; Nicholson used 'type' to make the same point about the Egyptian captivity: *Exposition*, 80; and see Virel, *Treatise*, 134; Ussher, 'Method', 22; and Boughen's use of 'shadows and figures' in *Exposition*, 45.

[40] Hammond, *Practical catechisme*, 83–108, and esp. 108–14.

[41] Nicholson, *Exposition*, 75–6; Isham, *Catechism*, 31 and Lewis, *Catechism*, 37, cited Matt. 19: 17 and 22: 37–40; also cf. Sherlock, *Principles*, 27–8, and Wake, *Principles*, 119.

have been through the application of Ramist logic, especially its focus on relationships such as subject and adjunct and on resemblances in quality.[42] It has been suggested that Thomas Cartwright, for example, applied Ramist logic to his analysis of the Commandments in his *Treatise of Christian religion*, and we know of at least two catechetical forms—not in our sample—in which a Ramist approach was consciously adopted.[43] But the application of the language of formal logic to biblical exegesis at catechetical level was on the whole a rarity.[44] Whatever the route or routes by which authors reached their decision, the effect was dramatic. Catechumens were regularly told that the 'father' and 'mother' who were to be honoured in the fifth Commandment should be taken as including all superiors—masters, magistrates, teachers, ministers, and those of greater age or gifts; the adultery mentioned in the seventh was widely taken to refer to all forms of intemperate desire, such as gluttony and drunkenness, excessive display in apparel or bad language; and the prohibition on stealing in the eighth was generally taken to cover all forms of cheating or pressurizing that might fall well short of the legal definition of theft. The larger the catechism, the longer the list of supplements to the specifics.[45]

The third principle of interpretation concerned the twin concepts of command and prohibition. Of the Ten Commandments, two—numbers four and five on observing the sabbath and honouring parents—were positive, the rest were all negative; and at first most authors tended to take each Commandment literally, by stressing the sinfulness of breaking Commandments one to three and six to ten, and the necessity of observing the duties enjoined in four and five. Some authors occasionally pointed out that a prohibition could have a positive side to it,[46] but again this was not done systematically until the early seventeenth century. By that date scholars like Andrewes and Dod and Cleaver had been arguing for some time that all Commandments included both a sin forbidden and a duty enjoined, and this principle was being taken up by catechists.[47] John Ball, in his shorter form of *c*.1615, and William Hill, in his Prayer Book catechism exposition of 1616, were the first authors in our sample to apply this rule thoroughly to their treatment of the Commandments in their catechism, but thereafter it was as common in expositions of the official short catechism as in alternatives such as the Westminster catechisms and their derivatives.[48] The acceptance of this principle may have been a natural development from the limited

---

[42] The extent of Ramist influence has been debated. For a recent assessment, see M. Todd, *Christian Humanists and the Puritan Social Order* (Cambridge, 1987), 54–6, 63, 67–73; see also L. Howard, *Essays on Puritans and Puritanism*, ed. J. Barbour and T. Quirk (Albuquerque, N. Mex., 1986), 119–20, 138–40.

[43] Ibid. 140–55; J. Yates, *A Short and briefe summe* (1621) and id., *A modell of divinitie* (1622).

[44] For an isolated example, see Wake's comment in *Principles*, 83.

[45] See below under the relevant Commandments.

[46] Calvin, *Catechisme*, 54; Dering–More, *Catechisme*, sigs. A7ʳ, A8ʳ; Paget, *Questions*, sig. B6ʳ.

[47] Andrewes, *Works*, vi. 75, 81; Dod and Cleaver, *Exposition*, 26; Ball, *Treatise*, 176; Nicholson, *Exposition*, 77.

[48] Ball, *Catechisme*, 84–8; Hill, *Principles*, sigs. B5ᵛ–C1ʳ; and e.g. Bernard, *Common catechisme*, sigs. B3ʳ–6ʳ; Nicholes, *Catechisme*, 24–44; Nicholson, *Exposition*, 77–121; and Sherlock, *Principles*, 29–38; also

practice of this idea in the sixteenth century, or a matter of changing patterns of exegesis of one of the kinds just described for the second principle. But it was something which may again have appealed to those authors who had been exposed to Ramist logic and were thereby encouraged to split every Commandment into a negative and a positive command; certainly the coincidence of timing between the consolidation of Ramism in England and the wider application of this third principle is quite close.[49] Once again, however, whatever the origin of this principle, its effect was to give catechetical authors considerable latitude in their instruction. The corollary of the ban on idolatry and profanation of the sabbath was the need to worship God aright on Sundays and other days; the other side of the prohibition on adultery was a catalogue of ways in which the speech, conduct, and inner feelings of the faithful were to be supervised rigorously in order to preserve their bodies in temperance, soberness, and chastity; the orders not to steal or covet were also interpreted as positive orders to be content with one's lot and be just and charitable to others.[50] Again the longer the catechism form the greater the number of antonyms or contraries that was likely to be given, especially in the case of the fifth Commandment, where authors who adopted both the second and third principles of interpretation provided long lists not only of subordinates to superiors, but also of superiors to subordinates, and even of equals to each other.[51] All this appears to a mind not versed in early modern theology or logic to be quite a long way removed from the simple exhortation and inducement in Exodus 20: 12, but was standard catechetical practice in the seventeenth century.[52]

The opening verses of Exodus 20 are: 'And God spake all these words, saying "I am the Lord thy God which have brought thee out of the land of Egypt, out of the house of bondage".' These were used by some authors to stress that God was the author of the Commandments, to drive home the lesson also made at the start of the Creed that God was eternal, immutable, and almighty, and to add the point that he would deliver those that seek to obey his Law, hence the necessity of obedience to his will.[53]

Westminster Larger, 61–110 (answers 104–48); Westminster Shorter, 19–30 (answers 46–80); Wallis, *Explanation*, 22–35; and Vincent, *Catechism*, 98–118.

[49] It is possible Aristotelian predicates were being used here. For an argument that Ramism affected some of Perkins's and Cartwright's treatises and the latter's short catechism, see Howard, *Essays on Puritans*, 138–55.

[50] See below under the relevant Commandments, and specifically on the second Commandment, Aston, *England's Iconoclasts*, 387–8, 444–5.

[51] Ball, *Catechisme*, 86; Ussher, 'Principles', 9–10; Westminster Larger, 83–91 (answers 124–33); and see below, s.v. fifth Commandment.

[52] Other principles of interpretation were stated occasionally, for example that the Law is perfect and spiritual: Andrewes, *Works*, vi. 75; Dod and Cleaver, *Exposition*, 26; and Mitchell, *Catechisms of the Second Reformation*, p. lxxi; cf. also Fenner, *Spiritual mans directory*, 20. Andrewes's additional point, that in the first table the commandments contain both a precept and a reason, can be found in a number of later catechisms in our sample, e.g. Mayer, *Catechisme*, sig. B3ᵛ; and Bernard, *Common catechisme*, sigs. B3ᵛ–4ʳ.

[53] Calvin, *Catechisme*, 54; Nowell, *Catechisme*, 121; Paget, *Questions*, sig. A8ᵛ; Hill, *Principles*, sig. B5ᵛ;

A few also took the pains to explain that while God was clearly referring here to the Jewish people, the deliverance of souls applied to all those redeemed by Christ.[54] Some of these did so by using the covenant motif that we examined in the previous chapter: the preface meant 'he is a God in covenant, as with Israel of old, so with all his people'.[55]

The main thrust of the first Commandment, 'Thou shalt have none other gods before me', was widely taken as a positive order to worship God alone. A few authors reinforced and expanded the negative side of the command: it prohibited not only 'the giving of that worship and glory to any other, which is due to him alone', but also by extension idolatry, atheism, and ignorance.[56] Indeed, the authors of the Westminster Larger Catechism managed to gather over forty sins forbidden by the first Commandment, from idolatry and ignorance through distrust and carnal delights to discontent and impatience at God's dispensations—and all this compared to a mere twenty duties that they could find to be required by the same Commandment.[57] But in many other forms the positive aspects tended to come to the fore, or at least to balance the negative, as in the Prayer Book catechism with its series of positive duties to God, to believe, fear, love, and worship God, and the Westminster Shorter Catechism with its four duties and four prohibitions.[58] In fact, as in the Prayer Book catechism, the command to 'worship' was often supplemented by other authors in our sample by instructions to 'trust', 'love', 'fear', 'call upon' or 'pray to', 'acknowledge', or 'know' and 'glorify' God.[59] Conscious of a possible overlap between first and second Commandments, some authors also drew a distinction between the correct forms of inward worship required by the first and of outward worship demanded by the second.[60]

This brings us to the second Commandment, and the ban on the making of 'any graven image' or 'the likeness of anything that is in heaven above, or in the earth beneath, nor in the water under the earth' and of bowing down to or worshipping such images, which Professor Bossy sees as central to the whole Decalogue. As recent research on the Continental and English Reformations has amply demonstrated, the use of images was a particularly sensitive subject, even by the standards of those

---

Westminster Larger, 60 (answer 101); Westminster Shorter, 19 (answer 44); Nicholson, *Exposition*, 79–80; Gouge, *Principles*, 113.

[54] Calvin, *Catechisme*, 54–5; Nowell, *Catechisme*, 121.

[55] Westminster Larger, 60 (answer 101); and see Cartwright, 'Catechisme', sig. Aa4ᵛ–5ʳ; Nicholson, *Exposition*, 80; Gouge, *Principles*, 113; Wake, *Principles*, 86; and cf. Ussher, 'Principles', 6–7.

[56] Westminster Shorter, 20 (answer 47); and see Nowell, *Catechisme*, 121–2; Mayer, *Catechisme*, sigs. B3ᵛ–4ʳ; Nicholes, *Catechisme*, 24–5; Gouge, *Principles*, 114; Marshall, *Catechism*, 22.

[57] Westminster Larger, 61–5 (answers 104–5).

[58] Prayer Book catechism, 784–5; Westminster Shorter, 19–20 (answers 46–7).

[59] Calvin, *Catechisme*, 55; Dering–More, *Catechisme*, sig. A7ʳ; Paget, *Questions*, sigs. B1ʳ⁻ᵛ; Westminster Shorter, 19 (answer 45); Sherlock, *Principles*, 29; Marshall, *Catechism*, 22–3; Isham, *Catechism*, 35–6; and Lewis, *Catechism*, 38–9.

[60] Cartwright, 'Catechisme', sig. Aa5ʳ; Hill, *Principles*, sig. B5ᵛ; Ussher, 'Principles', 9.

touchy times. Professor Eire has suggested that the reformers' concern for scrip-
turally correct worship and their fear of 'idols' were central tenets of the Protestant
Reformation in mainland Europe.[61] Dr Aston has shown how the opponents of images
in England drew inspiration not only from Lollard hostility to the worshipping of
golden 'idols' but also from Erasmus and Luther and the theologians of Strasburg and
Zurich, and in the second quarter of the sixteenth century gradually extended their
definition of 'image' from three-dimensional representations to paintings, stained
glass, mass books and vestments, tombs and inscriptions, and even mental images.[62]
Professor Collinson has also charted the shift from the relatively straightforward
desire of the first iconoclasts to destroy images to the more insidious iconophobia and
'creeping ascetic totalitarianism' of the later sixteenth century which outlawed the
depiction of God and Christ in religious drama and bought about a considerable
reduction of pictorial representations of 'religious' material in books.[63] Monarchs and
archbishops and a number of other senior members of the civil and ecclesiastical
authorities felt the need to step in to prevent iconoclasm from going too far, and in the
canons of 1604 and under Charles I and Laud, attempts were made not simply to hold
the line but to push it back a little, although this led to a fresh outburst of accusations
of 'popery' and iconophobia in some quarters.[64]

In the catechisms in our sample, these tides of perception and action are reflected
to some extent, as we shall see shortly. In the simplest forms of all, however, the
subjects of false gods and images were barely touched upon: authors were perhaps
too concerned to drive home the existence and qualities of the one true God to
spend much time on possible rivals. In the brief exposition of the first table in the
Prayer Book catechism, for example, the stress was as already noted entirely positive: the ideas of loving God with 'all' one's heart, mind, soul, and strength and
putting one's 'whole' trust in him had an exclusive edge which precluded the
giving of any love or trust towards other gods or forms of deity, but this latter was
not spelt out.[65] In the majority of forms, idolatry was certainly tackled, but at a
fairly basic level: the main aim of many catechists was apparently not to define
what an idol was, or seek to explain how far such a definition should be pushed, but
to drive home the two simple points that any representation of God was not permitted, and that the use of any such idol or image as a means of worshipping God

[61]   C. M. N. Eire, *War against the Idols: The Reformation of Worship from Erasmus to Calvin* (Cambridge, 1986), *passim*.
[62]   Aston, *England's Iconoclasts, passim*.
[63]   P. Collinson, *From Iconoclasm to Iconophobia: The Cultural Impact of the Second Reformation* (Sten-
ton Lecture 1985; University of Reading, 1986). But Professor Collinson would concede that his case
needs modifying in the case of popular print in the light of the findings of Tessa Watt, in *Cheap Print and
Popular Piety, 1550–1640* (Cambridge, 1991).
[64]   Aston, *England's Iconoclasts*, 295–342; Tyacke, *Anti-Calvinists*, 71, 192–4, 198–9, 219–220; G.
Parry, *The Golden Age Restor'd: The Culture of the Stuart Court* (Manchester, 1981), ch. 10.
[65]   Prayer Book catechism, 784–5.

was forbidden.[66] On the positive side, it was also generally agreed that this Commandment laid down the duty of engaging in true worship as opposed to false, and a number of authors took the opportunity to lay down what they saw as the public and private practices approved by scripture. Others did this under the fourth Commandment—the correct way of spending the sabbath—and we shall defer consideration of this aspect until then.[67]

The proscription of idols was defended on two grounds: the impossibility of puny man being able to conceive, let alone replicate in some physical shape, the spiritual form of the almighty; and God's jealousy lest his sovereignty be impugned and his worship profaned.[68] But in practice in Protestant England the ban was employed primarily as an anti-Catholic device and a means of persuading the common people to give up the veneration of saints and carrying mental pictures of a corporeal God. Whether we look at Andrewes's lectures or Dod and Cleaver's treatise, or at the sample catechisms from early ones like those of Calvin and Nowell to late ones like those of Williams and Wake, it is the praying to images and the kneeling or bowing before them as if they were living, potent creatures that is being condemned above all. It was wrong to make any image 'whereby the simple may take occasion to abuse it unto any kind of superstition or idolatry', wrote Calvin, which sad experience showed they were all too likely to do, added Nowell. Representations of angels and saints were as bad as those of God, said Dering and More.[69] The defence offered in former times that images are 'unlearned men's books' or 'books for the laity' was dismissed out of hand: 'dumb idols' can teach us 'nothing but errors', said Nowell and the authors of the Heidelberg Catechism; God wishes us to be taught not by images, which teach only vanity and lying, wrote Virel, but by the lively preaching of the Word.[70] Over a century later John Williams compared the worship in Catholic churches to that of Baal and Moloch, while William Wake condemned the 'scandalous and intolerable' practice of image worship still being practised and encouraged by the church of Rome.[71]

There was only limited disagreement in our sample about whether all images were forbidden or only some. Calvin set the pace on this matter: God did not 'utterly forbid' the making of any carved or painted image, but he did expressly command us not to make 'any image ... to represent or figure God: [or] to make any image to

---

[66] Nowell, *Catechisme*, 123; Hill, *Principles*, sig. B6ʳ; Ussher, 'Principles', 9; Westminster Shorter, 21 (answer 51); Wake, *Principles*, 90.

[67] e.g. Ball, *Catechisme*, 84; Westminster Larger, 66–8 (answer 108); and see below.

[68] Calvin, *Catechisme*, 57; Nowell, *Catechisme*, 123; Heidelberg Catechism, 343; Westminster Shorter, 21 (answer 52); Vincent, *Catechism*, 105–7, 109–10; Williams, *Exposition*, 29.

[69] Andrewes, *Works*, vi. 123–4, 128–32; Dod and Cleaver, *Exposition*, 59–79; Calvin, *Catechisme*, 57–8; Nowell, *Catechisme*, 123–4; Dering–More, *Catechisme*, sig. A7ʳ; Virel, *Treatise*, 100–9; Perkins, *Foundation*, 1.

[70] Nowell, *Catechisme*, 123; Heidelberg Catechism, 343; Virel, *Treatise*, 95; and cf. Vincent, *Catechism*, 108.

[71] Williams, *Exposition*, 30; Wake, *Principles*, 91–2; and see above, n. 26.

worship it'.[72] Nowell conceded 'the lawful use of making portraitures and of painting' as long as they were not of God, or set up in church, and the authors of the Heidelberg Catechism said that 'creatures ... may indeed be imaged' as long as the likenesses were not used for worship.[73] 'Godly' Elizabethans, the authors of the Westminster Larger Catechism, and nonconformists as well as episcopalian conformists in our sample would all repeat the point that the use of any kind of image for worship was wrong; in the case of catechisms written later in our period, it was not so much the case that the limited approval given to secular sculpture or portraits in the mid-sixteenth century forms was rescinded, as that the subject was just not raised.[74] The details of how this ban on representational art was to be applied were, however, often left unclear. Among the authors in our sample, it is far from clear how many of the following they would have approved: the finely carved monuments to pious individuals, often 'godly' gentlemen and women, of the kind erected in many Elizabethan and Stuart churches; the magnificently engraved title-pages of the Great, Bishops' and King James Bibles, and indeed the illustrations in some English editions of the Geneva Bible; the portraits of Elizabeth and staunchly Protestant ministers like Burghley and Leicester inserted between the sheets of the Bishops' Bible; and the episcopal portraits and monuments which became quite a vogue in the later sixteenth and early seventeenth centuries.[75] James Ussher, when a young catechist, urged his charges to think of God as an incorporeal spirit, and condemned even the least degree of outward worship of 'any image or representation, either of God, or of any thing else whatsoever'. But as a conformist cleric he was presumably prepared to tolerate the use of some symbolic vestments and ritual gestures, the continued presence of older forms of church furniture and decoration such as pulpits, fonts, communion cups and pattens, and stained glass, and later in life he had his portrait painted a couple of times as a senior figure in the church.[76]

A limited defence of the deployment of ecclesiastical images was offered by some seventeenth-century authors in our sample. Boughen and Nicholson, for example, pointed out that God had not forbidden the 'carved cherubims, and palm-trees' on the walls and doors of the Temple, nor the other carvings, ornaments, and utensils in that complex. But the bottom line was again no representations of God, and no

[72] Calvin, *Catechisme*, 56–8.

[73] Nowell, *Catechisme*, 123–4; id., *Institution*, sigs. Avi^r–v; Heidelberg Catechism, 343.

[74] Dering–More, *Catechisme*, sig. A7^r; Paget, *Questions*, sig. B2^v; Westminster Larger, 68–9 (answer 109); Gouge, 'Principles', 115; Vincent, *Catechism*, 105–6; Ussher, 'Principles', 9; Marshall, *Catechism*, 23; Lewis, *Catechism*, 40. There was the occasional exception, such as Herbert Palmer in his *Endeavour* of 1640, who said that pictures of 'one's friends, and the like' were not unlawful, but all representations of God were abominable (p. 25).

[75] I propose to examine these ecclesiastical images in my *Religious Instruction in Early Modern England* (forthcoming).

[76] Ussher, 'Principles', 9; at least two portraits of Ussher as bishop are extant, in Trinity College, Dublin and the National Portrait Gallery, London.

images of Christ, angels, saints, or crosses for purposes of worship.[77] The nearest that we come in our sample to a direct confrontation, as opposed to differences of degree or simple ambiguity, was over the representation of Christ. In so far as Christ was man as well as God, Wake thought that he could be represented, 'provided that no use were made of any such image, in any part of our religious worship'. The presbyterian Thomas Vincent, on the other hand, argued that Christ cannot be represented, because his divine nature cannot be pictured, nor can his body which is now glorified. To this he added a pair of reasons which constituted an updated version of Morton's fork: if a picture of Christ does not stir up devotion, it is in vain; and if it does, it is a worshipping by image and so a palpable breach of the second Commandment![78] In other words, Wake seems to have felt that pictures could be used for purposes other than worship; Vincent reiterated the hard-line view that any representation capable of being worshipped was banned by the second Commandment.

Differences of opinion were also possible when authors widened their definition of an image to try to include what they adjudged to be false worship in general: a wider definition of idolatry could become the basis for criticism of fellow-Protestants as well as Catholics. In the catechisms of the 'godly' Dering–More and Paget in the 1570s, we find the idea of worshipping God according to men's 'fantasies' being condemned alongside that of worshipping images;[79] and the formula used in the Westminster Shorter Catechism was that the second Commandment 'forbiddeth the worshipping of God by images, *or any other way not appointed in his word*'.[80] In the Larger Catechism of 1648 we find a much tougher statement of the illegality of any form of worship 'not instituted by God himself' and 'all superstitious devices' that corrupted his worship; and in a couple of expositions of the Shorter Catechism, one by a moderate Calvinist and one by a committed presbyterian, we find a strong denunciation both of the 'will-worship' of 'adding human inventions unto God's institutions' and the superstitious idolatry of crucifixes and pictures and of kneeling for communion in the Catholic church.[81] Even these forms, however, did not specify by name what had been roundly condemned in the early 1640s as the 'innovations' of Laudians, though it would have been quite easy to do so. On the episcopalian side, there were occasional barbed remarks about those who were 'little better than atheists' in that they would not bow down to God in church or rejected all ceremonies of order, decency, and edification, though the authors in question were writing in the 1640s and 1650s and may have been thinking of sectaries as much as presbyterians.[82] But these comments were

---

[77] Boughen, *Exposition*, 36; Nicholson, *Exposition*, 90 (he also referred readers to his pamphlet on idolatry).

[78] Wake, *Principles*, 91; Vincent, *Catechism*, 106–7.

[79] Dering–More, *Catechisme*, sig. A7^r; Paget, *Questions*, sig. B2^r; and cf. Mayer, *Catechisme*, sigs. B4^v–5^r.

[80] Westminster Shorter, 21 (answer 51): my italics.

[81] Westminster Larger, 68–9 (answer 109); Gouge, 'Principles', 115; Vincent, *Catechism*, 106–9.

[82] Boughen, *Exposition*, 37; Nicholson, *Exposition*, 90.

exceptional, and as we shall see under the fourth Commandment, both moderate puritans or presbyterians and episcopalians accepted the need for set forms of worship and for the people to behave with reverence at them.

Relatively few authors devoted much space to the interpretation of the second sentence in the second Commandment:

For I the Lord thy God am a jealous God, and visit the sins of the fathers upon the children unto the third and fourth generation of them that hate me, and shew mercy unto thousands of them that love me, and keep my commandments.

A wide variety of authors stressed the divine power as well as zeal for his own worship that this sentence revealed, but, perhaps worried that they might seem to be condoning the idea of gaining righteousness through good works, did not draw attention to the apparent connection between the correct worshipping of God and the prospect of mercy. Calvin gave quite a wide interpretation to the nature of the divine mercy on offer here: it embraced both prosperity in worldly matters and the gifts of the spirit; Wake confined it to temporal blessings alone; while authors in between, such as the Westminster divines in their larger catechism and Nicholson, did little more than repeat or paraphrase the idea of mercy, without specifying what form it might take.[83] The authors of a number of shorter or middling forms, such as the Prayer Book catechism, the Heidelberg Catechism, Ball's shorter form, the Westminster Shorter Catechism, and the forms of Keach and Watts, saved themselves the problem of sorting out the mysteries of what form the mercy took, and why it should be three or four generations of the one who were punished and thousands of the other who were not, by simply omitting to discuss this part of the Commandment.

Compared to the difference of opinion between Karlstadt, on the one hand, and Luther, on the other,[84] there was relatively little disagreement in our sample of best-selling English catechisms. The silence of many authors in our sample on exactly what an idol was and the limited number of clashes over pictures and acceptable forms of worship indicate the relatively narrow band within which most authors in our sample seem to have been prepared to operate on this matter. Again we are faced with the conclusion either that most catechetical authors were anxious to avoid controversy, even on a highly sensitive and emotive matter like this, or that when they were catechizing they may have been more outspoken and made oral additions to what was stated in the written text—a suggestion that can neither be proved nor disproved. There was a limited polarization over this Commandment in that some authors like Calvin and the Prayer Book form's authors appear to have been as interested in the positive aspects of the Commandment—what it taught about God's power and the need to worship him alone—as in the negative aspect of the danger of

---

[83] Calvin, *Catechisme*, 58–62; Wake, *Principles*, 92–4; and cf. Nowell, *Catechisme*, 124–6; Westminster Larger, 70 (answer 110); Nicholson, *Exposition*, 88–9; and Vincent, *Catechism*, 110–11.

[84] Eire, *War against the Idols*, 55–73.

'outward idolatry'; whereas others like the authors of the Westminster Larger Catechism spent rather more time on their search for spiritual 'whoredom'.[85] But as so often, the difference is in many ways one of degree or temperature. Moreover, it should be set in a context of a large measure of agreement on the reasons for the ban on images and the falseness of Catholic worship, and a not insubstantial measure of agreement on what constituted true worship, a point to which we shall return shortly.

The third Commandment was both shorter and less contentious than the second, though as the authors of the Heidelberg Catechism pointed out, no sin was greater or more provoking to God than the profaning of his name, 'wherefore he even commanded it to be punished with death'.[86] It was generally agreed that on the negative side this Commandment condemned any blasphemous use of God's name, while on the positive it encouraged people to use the name of God reverently.[87] At its simplest, this could be reduced to one line, as in the Prayer Book catechism—'to honour his holy name and his word', or to a few lines of verse, as in Keach's work: '... God's name in vain / I never more will use; / For guiltless he can never be / That does God's name abuse'.[88] However, other authors, using the lines of interpretation outlined above, readily extended both positive and negative teachings as far as teaching time and publication space permitted. Thus 'the name of the Lord' was held by Cartwright and the authors of the Westminster Shorter Catechism and by Boughen and Nicholson to include all his names, titles, attributes, ordinances, Word, and works, or any means by which he made himself known.[89] The idea of equating the Word with God was one found in conformist works, such as the 1549 catechism and some expositions of that form, as well as in alternatives such as the Westminster catechisms.[90] In a few forms, mainly Elizabethan, the taking of God's name in vain was held to include sorcery, conjuring, witchcraft, charming or enchantments, and cursing—some of the relatively few references to witchcraft in early modern catechisms.[91] It was also applied to 'popish' oaths, such as by the 'saints, angels, rood, book, cross, mass', and to perjury or false swearing, profane jests, and idle oaths as

---

[85] See previous notes. [86] Heidelberg Catechism, 344.

[87] Calvin, *Catechisme*, 63; Ball, *Catechisme*, 85; Nicholes, *Catechisme*, 27–8; Sherlock, *Principles*, 31–2; Marshall, *Catechism*, 24–5.

[88] Prayer Book catechism, 784–5; B. Keach, *Instructions for children* [1710?], 49.

[89] Cartwright, 'Catechisme', sig. Aa5ᵛ; Westminster Shorter, 22 (answer 54); Boughen, *Exposition*, 40; Nicholson, *Exposition*, 91.

[90] Prayer Book catechism, 784–5; Lewis, *Catechism*, 42; Westminster Larger, 72–3 (answer 112); Westminster Shorter, 22 (answer 54).

[91] Nowell, *Catechisme*, 126; Dering–More, *Catechisme*, sig. A7ᵛ; Paget, *Questions*, sig. B2ᵛ; Hill, *Principles*, sig. B6ᵛ; and cf. Bullinger, *Decades*, i. 221; and Sherlock, *Principles*, 31 (though 'cursing' did not necessarily imply witchcraft); and cf. Bossy, 'Moral Arithmetic', 231, for mention of witchcraft in a work that became Cranmer's *Catechismus*.

well as straightforward misuse of God's own name.[92] Two Interregnum sufferers, a senior Restoration academic, and a Williamite bishop all extended the prohibition until it embraced meddling with God's word, sacraments, or any other part of his holy worship; and it was argued by a few authors that being involved in or conniving at the blasphemy of others was as serious a sin as committing the blasphemy oneself.[93]

According to one's standpoint, the palm for godly concern or the award for sheer persistence was again won by the authors of the Westminster Larger Catechism who listed over three dozen sins under this Commandment. Episcopalians were not necessarily far behind, as we can see from Nicholson's sixteen offences against this Commandment—from speaking of God without due reverence to 'tavern oaths' and 'street-oaths'—and the list in Marshall's much shorter work of the five sins forbidden and five duties enjoined by it.[94] Catechists also agreed that there were some occasions on which God's name could be used lawfully, in seeking his glory, praying, or efforts to 'save our brethren'.[95] It was also generally agreed among the authors in the sample, which does not include any works by Quakers, that it was lawful to use the name of God before a magistrate or on 'any other matter of great importance' or on a 'just and necessary occasion'.[96]

The injunction in the fourth Commandment to remember to 'keep holy the sabbath day' was another which, like the second, caused a good deal of contemporary dispute, the traces of which have been closely scrutinized recently by Patrick Collinson and Kenneth Parker.[97] Parker's thesis is that the version of the dispute presented by some Laudians in the 1630s, and in particular by Peter Heylyn, was misleading: Heylyn's anxiety to defend or bolster episcopal authority in the matter of sabbath observance led him to misrepresent the views not only of puritans but also of a number of bishops and other leading lights of the church from the 1560s to the 1620s. The latter, says Parker, had consistently argued along the scholastic line of the high Middle Ages that the fourth Commandment contained a ceremonial and a moral imperative, and that although the ceremonial had been abrogated by the mission of Christ, the

---

[92] Dering–More, *Catechisme*, sig. A7ᵛ; Heidelberg Catechism, 343; Hill, *Principles*, sig. B6ʳ; Mayer, *Catechisme*, sig. B5ʳ⁻ᵛ; Westminster Larger, 73 (answer 113).

[93] Sherlock, *Principles*, 32; Nicholson, *Exposition*, 91; Marshall, *Catechism*, 24; Wake, *Principles*, 98–9; Heidelberg Catechism, 343–4; Boughen, *Exposition*, 40.

[94] Westminster Larger, 73–6 (answer 113 and references); Nicholson, *Exposition*, 95–6 (though his account also took some side-swipes at the 'godly'); Marshall, *Catechism*, 24–5.

[95] Dering–More, *Catechisme*, sig. A7ᵛ; Paget, *Questions*, sig. B2ᵛ; Hill, *Principles*, sig. B6ʳ.

[96] Paget, *Questions*, sigs. B3ᵛ–4ʳ; Nowell, *Catechisme*, 127; Heidelberg Catechism, 344; Mayer, *Catechisme*, sig. B6ʳ; Boughen, *Exposition*, 39–40; Nicholson, *Exposition*, 92–5; Isham, *Catechism*, 39–40.

[97] P. Collinson, 'The Beginnings of English Sabbatarianism', in *Studies in Church History 1*, ed. C. W. Dugmore and C. Duggan (1964), 207–21; K. Parker, *The English Sabbath: A Study of Doctrine and Discipline from the Reformation to the Civil War* (Cambridge, 1988); but see Collinson's review of Parker's book in *Times Literary Supplement*, 17–23 Feb. 1989, 155–6.

moral element constituted a perpetually binding imperative to observe one day in seven. However, as Parker points out, Heylyn and some other (but by no means all) strong supporters of the Church of England in the 1630s 'argued against the moral and perpetual nature of the Saturday or Sunday Sabbath', and 'claimed that Sunday observance was a human convention, and that its use was defined and regulated by the church authorities'.[98]

It must be said, however, that Parker's readiness to posit the existence of a Jacobean consensus followed by a Caroline controversy on this matter rests heavily on his unilateral decision that this one strand—the moral imperative to rest one day in seven—was crucial, while the other strands in a complex web of issues were what he terms 'peripheral'.[99] This overstates the case. In the first place it is clear from Parker's own evidence that some Laudians did not totally deny the moral validity of the fourth Commandment as the basis for setting aside some time for worship, but used either a figurative or analogical interpretation as Calvin and others had done in the mid-sixteenth century.[100] Secondly, it is open to question whether the strand he regards as crucial was quite as distinct from the rest as he suggests, and from one other strand in particular—the question of authority for the move of that day from the Jewish Saturday to the Christian Sunday: was this the work of the apostles or the Early Church (as was suggested in the late Elizabethan period and again in the 1630s) or a matter of divine institution (as was suggested in the period in between)?[101] And beyond these there were other debates: on exactly how the Lord's Day was to be spent and the extent to which 'moderate' or 'harmless' recreations should be permitted (as was suggested at the start and end of the period 1560–1640) or not (as was more commonly stated in the middle); on the penalties to be inflicted on sabbath-breakers; and on related matters such as whether the church had the authority to impose the observance of holy days such as Christmas when these did not fall on a Sunday.[102] It may be doubted whether contemporaries were able or willing to isolate these strands from the two already mentioned, partly because in practice they often had to cope with a number of entangled threads at the same time, and partly because of the impact on an essentially doctrinal debate of a number of political, legal, and social tensions long before the 1630s. On the one side, the crown and some bishops were reluctant to let Parliament and lay magistrates take too much of the initiative in trying to 'purify' the sabbath, and James, Charles, and Laud in particular were apt to react to resistance to their own initiatives on the matter as if it had much deeper or more sinister motives. On the other side, those who had broad views on what qualified as profanation of

---

[98] Parker, *English Sabbath*, 200, 6.   [99] Ibid. 48–9, 137.

[100] Ibid. 200, 203, 205, 17–18, 25–7; and see below, p. 442.

[101] Parker, *English Sabbath*, 22–3, 27–8, 33–4, 49–50, 57–9, 96–106, 166–9, and ch. 7, *passim*.

[102] Ibid. 50–6, 60–2, 106–14, 117–22, 128–35, 137, chs. 5 and 7, and 218–19; I. M. Green, 'The Persecution of "Scandalous" and "Malignant" Parish Clergy during the English Civil Wars', *English Historical Review*, 94 (1979), 521–2.

the sabbath, who wished to exercise a measure of social control over the populace, especially on Sundays, and who felt that the failure of the church leadership to take a tougher line or to enforce existing laws on sabbath observance was due to a lack of desire rather than of effective machinery, were also disposed to take a stand on principle.[103]

Although there were evidently marked differences of opinion here, among the authors of works in our sample who handled this Commandment at any length there was a large measure of agreement on most of these matters, and not only were differences of interpretation marginal, but also what we know from other sources to have been contentious subjects such as the 'Book of Sports' were not mentioned by name or even by implication in the forms in our sample. The clearest difference of opinion was in a handful of forms on the related subject of 'popish' saints' days and holidays such as Christmas.

Since the works we are examining were dealing here with the meaning of the fourth Commandment, we are unlikely to find in many of them a clear exposition of the view that the warrant for religious observance of one day in seven could or should be derived from any *other* source. In fact the authors of most shorter forms did not deem it necessary to highlight the fourth Commandment among the general run of divine precepts,[104] while authors of middling sized works lacked the space to devote more than a sentence or two to sabbath observance and so did not comment on the precise authority for this duty.[105] Even in more advanced forms, such as that of Cartwright and the Westminster catechisms, there was a tacit assumption that the moral imperative in the Decalogue was enough to warrant setting aside one day in seven, though in none of these cases was it stated that the ceremonial aspect of the Decalogue had been abrogated. In the case of the Westminster forms this omission is mildly surprising, since the debate on the basis for worship one day in seven had according to Parker become heated by the 1640s, and the abrogation of the ceremonial aspects of the law had been clearly stated in the Westminster Confession on which these forms were based.[106]

---

[103] Parker, *English Sabbath*, 50–5, 57–9, 63–71, 77–83, 87–90, 112–21, 124–6, 129–31, 133–7, 139–53, 161–6, 168, 170, 172, 174–7, 180–94, 197–200, 203–15, 220–1.

[104] Prayer Book catechism, 782–5; 'Maner to examine children', 153; Egerton, 'Familiar forme', 34–5 (a very brief summary of the Decalogue); id., 'Familiar manner', 37–9 (a citation of the text of the Commandments without any comment); Keach's forms did not cover the Decalogue, but for an accompanying verse-summary, see above n. 88; Elton, 'Extract', sigs. G3ᵛ–4ʳ; Gouge, 'Heads', 8; Watts's first two forms did not cover the Decalogue.

[105] Dering–More, *Catechisme*, sig. A7ᵛ; Paget, *Questions*, sigs. B4ʳ⁻ᵛ; Perkins, *Foundation*, 5; Bernard, *Common catechisme*, sigs. B4ʳ–5ʳ; Palmer, *Endeavour*, 16; Comber, *Church-catechism*, 19. Even in the larger version of his catechism, Ball contented himself with giving references to support the duty required and sin forbidden in the fourth Commandment, and adding a comment on the shift from Saturday to Sunday: Ball, *Catechisme*, 85; id., *Treatise*, 188–90.

[106] Cartwright, 'Catechisme', sigs. Aa5ʳ⁻ᵛ; Westminster Larger, 52–6, 78–9 (answers 92–8, 115–16); Westminster Shorter, 18, 23 (answers 39–41, 57–8); but see below on the change from the sabbath to the Lord's Day; Schaff, *Creeds*, 640–1 (Westminster Confession, ch. 19, para. 3).

What we do find in some early forms in our sample is a combination of arguments for setting one day in seven apart, rather than a straightforward reliance on a moral imperative deduced from the fourth Commandment. Calvin told his catechumens that the ceremonial part of the command applied only to the Jews and to the time of the Old Testament: 'the use of all ceremonies ceased at the coming of Christ, who was the end and substance of them'. The fourth Commandment was, he said, given us for three considerations: as a figure to represent spiritual rest in which 'it is our bounden duty to continue', for 'a comely order to be used in the church' which we are 'bound to observe', and for the refreshing of servants (to which we shall return shortly). The seventh day was chosen because the number seven signified 'a certain perfection in the holy scripture' and because of God's own example of resting after six days' labour. Calvin's emphasis here then was on the symbolic importance of the Commandment rather than on any precise instruction: 'the figure or shadow' did not have to correspond 'in all points' to 'the thing it is ordained to represent', only in the majority. The editor of the English edition of Calvin's catechism used marginal headings to insert an antithesis not found explicitly in the text: the ceremonial sabbath is ended, but the spiritual sabbath is continual—a line of thought also found in Bullinger's *Decades* which was widely recommended for use by the less well educated Elizabethan clergy.[107] Nowell's section on the fourth Commandment is mostly a reworking of Calvin's, though on balance he seems much less concerned about the warrant for the observance of one day in seven than the nature of that observance, which may explain why in the more widely used condensed version of this form the reference in the full-length original to the abrogation of the ceremonial aspect was omitted.[108] The authors of the Heidelberg Catechism side-stepped the issue of the exact origin of the imperative by stating that what God required in the fourth Commandment was in the first place that the ministry of the Gospel and religious education and observance be maintained on that day, and secondly that 'all the days of my life I rest from my evil works'. The reference to allowing the Lord to work in me through his Spirit 'and thus begin in this life the everlasting Sabbath' is linked to the spiritual aspect of the original Commandment, but not in a specifically one-in-seven way.[109] Matthieu Virel was working along similar lines when he wrote that the sabbath was sanctified to the performance of holy and religious works, and that the sabbath was 'a type or shadow of our regeneration'.[110] In short, in these works an allegorical or analogical interpretation tended to co-exist with, or even dominate, the scholastic idea of a moral and perpetually binding kernel within a ceremonial husk.[111]

[107] Calvin, *Catechisme*, 66–72; Bullinger, *Decades*, i. 259; D. J. Keep, 'Henry Bullinger and the Elizabethan Church', Ph.D. thesis (Sheffield, 1970), ch. 3.

[108] Nowell, *Catechisme*, 128–30; the parallel section in the *Institution* was sig. Bi^r–ii^v.

[109] Heidelberg Catechism, 345.

[110] Virel, *Treatise*, 134; again see below on the switch from seventh to first day.

[111] For an explanation of these terms, see Parker, *English Sabbath*, ch. 2.

Among later forms in our sample, the precise nature of the imperative was rarely confronted. The nearest we get to a Laudian position in our sample is in the advanced catechism by Henry Hammond of 1644, though this is not a perfect example of the extreme Laudian view. He had already pointed out that the ceremonial aspect of the 'natural or moral law' of the Old Testament had been abrogated when Christ came to perfect the Law, and when he turned to the fourth Commandment he began by saying it had something 'typical' in it (that is of a 'type'). He then followed the less extreme Laudian position by saying that while the Commandment was meant for the Jews and so not 'in every particular obligatory to us Christians' it had in equity 'many things of use unto us'. Among these was that while God had decreed the sabbath to the Jews, so Christ had transmitted his power to 'the apostles and succeeding church of God' who may 'direct all its members into some uniform way'—a remark which is as applicable to the switch from sabbath to Lord's Day as from one form of imperative to another.[112] In an exposition of the Prayer Book catechism published a few years later, William Nicholson combined a variety of ideas: the 'moral part' of the Commandment is 'perpetual and eternal'; the ceremonial is 'as St Paul saith ... "a shadow of good things to come" (Col. 2: 17)'; and equity requires that men should set aside one day a week to spiritual and religious duties.[113] Two other episcopalians sounded an even more cautious note: the fourth Commandment commands us to devote one day in seven to the public and solemn worship of God, wrote Sherlock in 1656; God sanctified the seventh day, and commanded his people to sanctify it, said Marshall in 1679; (both stated that after Christ's resurrection the day had been switched from seventh to first).[114] William Wake also stressed that the original command had been delivered to the Jews, and went on to say that although 'this command obliges us now ... as much as ever it did the Jews' it was 'not exactly after the same manner', since Christ had ended the Jewish dispensation.[115] Once again there was no statement of ecclesiastical warrant for observing one day in seven beyond that contained in the Commandment itself.

This brings us more specifically to the switch of the sabbath from Saturday to Sunday. In general it was only in a few intermediate or longer catechisms, for the most part aimed at more advanced catechumens, undergraduates, or ordinands, that this was examined in any detail,[116] though the matter was referred to briefly in some shorter forms.[117] The reasons for the change to Sunday were broadly speaking not at

[112] Hammond, *Practical catechisme*, 108–17, 179–80, 183–5; and cf. Parker, *English Sabbath*, 200, 203–4. Boughen was another royalist to state that the fourth Commandment was still binding in the sense of one day in seven, but that it did not have to be the Jewish Saturday: *Exposition*, 41–6.

[113] Nicholson, *Exposition*, 97.

[114] Sherlock, *Principles*, 33; Marshall, *Catechism*, 25.   [115] Wake, *Principles*, 102–4.

[116] Ball, *Treatise*, 190–1; for the works of Hammond, Boughen, Nicholson, and Wake, see previous notes; also Virel, *Treatise*, 135; and Westminster Larger, 78 (answer 116).

[117] e.g. Ball, *Catechisme*, 85; Westminster Shorter, 23–4 (answer 59); Marshall, *Catechism*, 25; Isham, *Catechism*, 37.

issue: the ceremonies of the Old Testament had been abrogated by the mission of Christ, and the choice of Sunday was a commemoration of the day on which Christ rose from the dead and completed his work of redemption of fallen man.[118] What was at issue was the specific command for this change: here there was a difference of opinion or emphasis in the wider sabbatarian debate. Some of the authors involved in that debate claimed that there was scriptural evidence that God had planned and wanted the change, and sought authority in references to the 'first day' of the week and to the 'Lord's Day' in the New Testament, though these texts are ambiguous on God's part in this initiative.[119] An alternative was to stress that the fourth Commandment was a figure for the Christian sabbath, since, as Calvin had said, the figure did not have to correspond in every detail to what it foretold. This still left unresolved, however, who had decided that the new day should be Sunday (rather than, say, Friday as a commemoration of Christ's sacrifice for man), and how, when, and on what authority the change was effected.[120] Others came out strongly in favour of the apostles as the architects of change, guided either by Christ himself, perhaps orally, or by the Holy Ghost: in holding their assemblies on the Lord's Day, wrote Beza, the apostles were doubtless acting under some kind of divine prompting. As the 'doubtless' suggests, there were evidential problems here, for even after one had accepted the references to first day and Lord's Day one found, as Bullinger pointed out, that there were no references in the apostles' writings to the *keeping* of this day as a separate day. 'They of the primitive church, therefore, did change the sabbath-day', he concluded, though what made this binding on Christians was the perpetual as opposed to the ceremonial element in the fourth command.[121]

In the works in our sample, a majority of authors either avoided the question, or chose a form of words that avoided commitment to a particular standpoint. John Ball, for example, in his original short form used the verb 'ordained' of the move to Sunday, but did not say who had ordained it; and in his larger version he said that since Christ rose again on the first day, it was 'as divines agree' meet that the sabbath should be changed to Sunday, again not specifying exactly who first thought that it was meet and acted accordingly.[122] In other works in our sample, produced mainly in the 1640s or later, we find more specific statements of the different views. Some authors, like those of the Westminster catechisms gave a strong impression that God was the initiator of the change. The Westminster Shorter Catechism stated the case briefly in 1648 as follows:

From the beginning of the world to the resurrection of Christ, God appointed the seventh day of the week to be the weekly sabbath; and the first day of the week ever since, to continue to the end of the world, which is the Christian sabbath;

---

[118] e.g. Ball, *Treatise*, 191; Hammond, *Practical catechisme*, 184–5; Sherlock, *Principles*, 33; and see preceding and following notes.

[119] See above, n. 114 and below, nn. 123–5.   [120] See above, n. 107.

[121] Beza is cited in Parker, *English Sabbath*, 28; Bullinger, *Decades*, i. 259–60.

[122] Ball, *Catechisme*, 85; id., *Treatise*, 191.

in the New Testament, added the Larger, this was called 'the Lord's Day'; the syntax in both cases seems to suggest that it was God who had 'appointed' the transfer from seventh to first days.[123] Thomas Vincent, a hard-line presbyterian expositor of the Shorter Catechism scornfully dismissed 'popish holidays' as 'not appointed in the Word', but then had to work hard to justify the change from seventh to first day when, as he admitted, 'we do not read expressly of any repeal in the Scripture' of the seventh-day observance. His justification is a mixture of deduction, inference, and finely tuned exegesis of the usual texts.[124] A reliance upon such sources was not confined to the presbyterians: episcopalians like Marshall, Isham, and Lewis, for example, relied on John 20: 19, 26, Acts 20: 7, and other texts, albeit in rather different ways. Marshall stated that they proved that the observance of the first day was 'the practice of *Christ and* his disciples'; Williams used them to show the basis of observance was a commemoration of Christ's resurrection on that day; and Isham cited them as demonstrating the apostolic practice on which the Christian church based its own custom, though he also adhered to the view that Sunday was a day of remembrance.[125] Another who combined the idea of remembrance with that of apostolic practice was the dissenter, Thomas Gouge, though he went further than Isham in saying that just as God had sanctified the seventh day, so Christ had sanctified the day of his resurrection which had been kept ever since.[126]

Other authors in our sample, such as the Continental reformer Matthieu Virel,[127] but mainly strong supporters of episcopacy like Hammond, Boughen, Nicholson, and Wake, had no hesitation in placing the main responsibility for the switch to Sunday at the apostles' door. Boughen's is the most interesting of these in that he devoted no less than three questions and answers to the change from seventh to first day in order to prove that the change was agreeable to the meaning if not the letter of the fourth Commandment, that after Christ's coming had made such 'shadows' as the sabbath vanish, the apostles had made the change, and that although they did not command us to keep that day, we should adopt the rule of St Paul in 1 Cor. 11: 1—'Be ye followers of me, even as I also am of Christ'—and imitate the apostles. 'The practice of the apostles is a sufficient warrant,' he concluded.[128] Hammond argued on the basis of the testimony of the scriptures and the Fathers that Christ had transmitted his power to the apostles 'and succeeding church of God' who could reasonably arrange matters such as the day of the week on which God should be worshipped.[129] According to Nicholson, 'the primitive church' on the basis of what 'is commonly

---

[123] Westminster Shorter, 23–4 (answer 59); Westminster Larger, 78 (answer 116): seven scriptural texts were cited by the Larger, three by the Shorter: Gen. 2: 2–3, 1 Cor. 16: 1–2, Matt. 5: 17–18.

[124] Vincent, *Catechism*, 118, 121–4.

[125] Marshall, *Catechism*, 25 (my italics); Isham, *Catechism*, 37; Lewis, *Catechism*, 45; and Williams, *Exposition*, 33.

[126] Gouge, *Principles*, 117–18.		[127] Virel, *Treatise*, 135.

[128] Boughen, *Exposition*, 44–5.		[129] Hammond, *Practical catechisme*, 185.

reputed to be an apostolical tradition' chose the day of Christ's resurrection as 'a day of gladness and exaltation', while Wake stated categorically that it was the apostles' doing, at the direction of the Holy Ghost 'no doubt'—a phrase found both in Beza and Vincent.[130] We have here a difference of emphasis or of exegetical method between presbyterians and episcopalians, but not totally opposed conclusions. The 'godly' might be more anxious to assert divine warrant but conceded that the apostles were the means by which the change was introduced; the conformists said that the apostles effected the change by transferring the imperative in the fourth Commandment from the sabbath to the Lord's Day, but did so perhaps as a result of a charge from Christ or direction from the Holy Ghost. Indeed, looking back over the two issues together—the imperative for setting aside one day in seven, and the authority for that day being Sunday—we find that most authors either avoided the contentious aspects of these subjects or found a form of words that skirted them; and, while differences of opinion or emphasis did exist among those who did tackle these matters, their statements did not correspond neatly with any ecclesiastical grouping. The Heylyn view of a purely ecclesiastical warrant for worship one day in seven had not taken root among the authors in our sample, and even in the case of the move to Sunday (which aroused more interest among our authors) we find both leading establishment figures and some strict Calvinists positing a divine message to the apostles to make the switch.

The reasons for God wishing that all men—whether the Jews of the Old Testament or the Christians of the New—should rest on one day in seven—were, it was generally agreed, twofold: that it should be a day sanctified to his use, and that men, like God during the Creation, should have a break from their labours.[131] To take the second point first, since it comprises most of the fourth Commandment, we may point out that a number of authors explained that the word 'sabbath' meant 'rest', partly in the sense of physical rest though it was sometimes described more broadly as a 'spiritual rest' or 'holy resting'.[132] According to the original Commandment, everybody—even cattle and strangers within the gates—had to rest, though it is interesting to note that Calvin and Nowell picked up the references to man- and maid-servants in the original text and made the egalitarian suggestion that it was servants in particular who needed 'some relief of their travail' on that day. Both, however, also made the remark that it was better for the 'commonwealth' and 'masters' for servants to rest from their labour one day of the week in order that 'they may return more fresh and lusty to it again' thereafter.[133] Most other authors returned to

---

[130] Nicholson, *Exposition*, 97; Wake, *Principles*, 104; for Beza, see above, n. 121; Vincent, *Catechism*, 123.

[131] See following notes; Calvin and Nowell added a third reason: see above, nn. 107–8.

[132] Calvin, *Catechisme*, 67; Nowell, *Catechisme*, 128–9; id., *Institution*, sigs. Bi^r, Bii^r; Dering–More, *Catechisme*, sig. A7^v; Hill, *Principles*, sig. B6^v; Westminster Larger, 79 (answer 117); Westminster Shorter, 24 (answer 60); Williams, *Exposition*, 32; Lewis, *Catechism*, 44.

[133] Calvin, *Catechisme*, 70; Nowell, *Catechisme*, 129.

the broader focus of the Commandment by saying that it was a rest 'from labour in *our* callings' or that '*all* God's creatures' should have a time for rest.[134] Emergency work in one's calling and work for the good of others, what were often referred to as works of necessity and charity or mercy, were widely permitted on the sabbath, but nothing else.[135]

All authors made it clear, however, that while the sabbath might be a day of physical release it was not meant to be a day of pleasure or idleness. The sabbath was to be set apart from the common uses of the weekday, and that included the sort of behaviour condemned in the official homily on the place and time of prayer: 'prancing in their pride, pranking and pricking … gluttony and drunkenness … brawling and railing', 'wantonness', 'toyish talking', and 'filthy fleshliness'.[136] Most authors who enlarged on the fourth Commandment picked up this theme. All sinful actions and exercises 'tending to sin, as drunkenness, dancing, dalliance, and the like' were forbidden, Hill told his catechumens in his exposition of the Prayer Book catechism in 1616. They sin against the Commandment 'that spend the day in idle and vain sports, forbidden recreations, or actions of sin and folly; eat, drink, discourse, or sleep it away', the future Bishop Nicholson told his readers in the 1650s.[137] Nicholson's formulation of 'forbidden recreations' left the door open to approved ones, the subject of much anger among the 'godly' in the wake of the Book of Sports of 1618 and 1633, though Nicholson did not say which pursuits might or should be allowed. Indeed, the authors of the Westminster catechisms of 1647 were similarly restrained: the reply to the question 'what sins are forbidden in the fourth Commandment?' contains no long list of forbidden sports, merely a condemnation of 'idleness', 'that which is in itself sinful', and 'all needless works, words, and thoughts about our worldly employments and recreations'.[138] Even an enthusiastic expositor of that form, Thomas Vincent, did not add much to this except to explain that the things in themselves sinful included drunkenness, wantonness, or going to 'a base house'.[139] The nearest we get to what might be expected is Thomas Gouge's statement that the fourth Commandment orders us to abstain from 'all worldly recreations; as shooting,

---

[134] Dering–More, *Catechisme*, sig. A7ᵛ (my italics); Paget, *Questions*, sigs. B4ʳ⁻ᵛ (my italics); Boughen, *Exposition*, 43–4; Westminster Shorter, 24 (answer 60).

[135] Paget, *Questions*, sig. B4ᵛ; Hill, *Principles*, sig. B6ᵛ; Boughen, *Exposition*, 45–6; Westminster Larger, 79 (answer 117); Westminster Shorter, 24 (answer 60); Wallis, *Explanation*, 28; Sherlock, *Principles*, 33; Marshall, *Catechism*, 25–6, 71; Comber, *Church-catechism*, 19; Gouge, *Principles*, 119; Williams, *Exposition*, 33–4; Watts, *Assembly's catechism*, 28. This confirms Parker's observation (*English Sabbath*, 108, 130) that there was a broad consensus on the justification of necessary works on the sabbath. For works of charity in particular, see below, nn. 157, 161.

[136] The official homily on the place and time of prayer is cited in Parker, *English Sabbath*, 56; and for similar condemnations of gaming, merry company, and stage plays, see Bullinger, *Decades*, i. 262–3; and Andrewes, *Works*, vi. 160.

[137] Hill, *Principles*, sig. B6ᵛ; Nicholson, *Exposition*, 98–9; and cf. Comber, *Church-catechism*, 19.

[138] Westminster Larger, 80–1 (answer 119); Westminster Shorter, 24–5 (answer 61).

[139] Vincent, *Catechism*, 131–2.

bowling, wrestling, ringing, dancing; as also from too liberal eating and drinking, especially wine or strong drink', or at least a quantity of alcohol that would make us 'drowsy or unapt to serve God' at church and at home.[140] Apart from this, nothing was said in our sample either for or against the use of Sunday 'sports' approved by James and Charles.

For authors of all persuasions, the greater offence seems to have been not so much 'the works of our own lusts and will' or the 'carnal pleasures' in themselves as the fact that they took men's time away from the proper performance of the special duties of the sabbath.[141] The first part of the relevant answer in the Westminster catechisms (of which the second part has already been summarized) reads as follows: 'the sins forbidden in the fourth Commandment are all omissions of the duties required, all careless, negligent, and unprofitable performing of them, and being weary of them'.[142] The sabbath had to be devoted entirely to 'sanctified work', wrote William Hill in his Prayer Book form exposition, and both paterfamilias and magistrates should see that every Sunday all under their care 'do sanctify it unto the Lord'.[143] The idea that the sabbath must be 'sanctified' was derived naturally from the terms 'keep holy' and 'hallowed' used in the Commandment, and was taught both by presbyterians and conformist episcopalians.[144]

Of what did this sanctification of the sabbath consist? The main ingredients of the answer provided in the Heidelberg Catechism were typical of a majority of forms in the sample: the ministry of the Gospel maintained, diligent attendance at church, use of the sacraments, public calling on the Lord, and giving Christian alms.[145] There was, for example, general agreement in the first place that attendance at church was necessary. The fourth Commandment was given that a 'comely' or 'politic order', 'an ecclesiastical discipline, and a certain order of the Christian commonweal' be established 'by public order', said Calvin and Nowell; the sabbath should be spent in 'diligent frequenting the public assemblies of the Church', said Hill; we should devote the day to 'public and solemn worship of God, with the rest of his Church and people', was Sherlock's formulation; 'public duties … in the public congregation' was Gouge's.[146] Those authors who did not specify the church by name nevertheless made it clear that there were public 'means' and public 'duties' or 'exercises' to be

---

[140] Gouge, *Principles*, 118.

[141] Calvin, *Catechisme*, 67, 72; Vincent, *Catechism*, 131; and cf. Perkins, *Foundation*, 5 on the weakness of the flesh.

[142] Westminster Larger, 80–1 (answer 119); Westminster Shorter, 24 (answer 61—a slightly abbreviated version of the Larger answer).

[143] Hill, *Principles*, sig. B6ᵛ.

[144] Cartwright, 'Catechisme', sig. Aa5ᵛ; Westminster Larger, 78–9 (answers 116–17); Westminster Shorter, 24 (answer 60); Hill, *Principles*, sigs. B6ᵛ–7ʳ; Nicholson, *Exposition*, 97–8; Marshall, *Catechism*, 25; Comber, *Church-catechism*, 19; and cf. Williams, *Exposition*, 32–3.

[145] Heidelberg Catechism, 345.

[146] Calvin, *Catechisme*, 67, and cf. 70–1; Nowell, *Catechisme*, 129, 139; and cf. Dering–More, *Catechisme*, sig. A7ᵛ; also Hill, *Principles*, sig. B6ᵛ; Sherlock, *Principles*, 33; Gouge, *Principles*, 119.

performed.[147] There was a broad band of agreement also that the church had the right to appoint ceremonies for public worship. The convinced presbyterian Thomas Vincent, during his exposition of the second Commandment, argued that 1 Cor. 14: 40 permitted the church to ensure that 'things appointed by God be done decently and in order'; the equally convinced episcopalian, Thomas Comber, author of various books on liturgical practice, argued (under the fourth Commandment) that the church had the right to appoint 'decent ceremonies'.[148]

What this public worship should consist of was seen as comprising a number of elements. The three elements mentioned most often in the sample catechisms under the fourth (or sometimes the second) Commandment were hearing the Word read and expounded, public prayer, and the use of the sacraments. These were mentioned by a wide range of authors, but relatively little can be gleaned from the sequence in which they presented these elements. The informed reader might guess correctly that Calvin and a number of the 'godly' such as Nowell, Dering and More, Paget, and Vincent put the preaching of the word first, but so did exponents of the Prayer Book catechism such as Hill, Nicholes, and Williams.[149] It might be expected that most episcopalian conformists might put prayer or 'divine service' first; but so too did the authors of the Westminster Larger Catechism, as for that matter did Stephen Egerton in one of his catechisms and Dod and Cleaver in their treatise on the Decalogue.[150] The sequence in the Larger Catechism was:

all such religious worship and ordinances as God hath instituted in his Word; particularly prayer and thanksgiving in the name of Christ; the reading, preaching, and hearing of the Word; the administration and receiving of the sacraments.[151]

Partaking of the sacraments never came higher than third in a list of Sunday duties, except for the Heidelberg Catechism in which it was placed second.[152]

The three duties most commonly mentioned tended to subsume others, such as worship and thanksgiving, but apart from these a number of other sabbath duties were listed by different authors: making a profession of faith;[153] singing

---

[147] Egerton, 'Briefe method', 13–18; Ball, *Catechisme*, 85; Ussher, 'Principles', 9; Westminster Larger, 79 (answer 117); Westminster Shorter, 24 (answer 60); Vincent, *Catechism*, 128–9.

[148] Vincent, *Catechism*, 108; Comber, *Church-catechism*, 18.

[149] Calvin, *Catechisme*, 70; Nowell, *Catechisme*, 129; Dering–More, *Catechisme*, sig. A7ᵛ; Paget, *Questions*, sig. B4ʳ; Vincent, *Catechism*, 128; Hill, *Principles*, sig. B6ᵛ; Nicholes, *Catechisme*, 25 (under the second Commandment); Williams, *Exposition*, 33.

[150] Hammond, *Practical catechisme*, 185; Nicholson, *Exposition*, 97–8; Comber, *Church-catechism*, 18; Marshall, *Catechism*, 25; Wake, *Principles*, 104; Lewis, *Catechism*, 44; Westminster Larger, 66–7 (answer 108); and cf. Egerton, 'Briefe method', 13, and Dod and Cleaver, *Exposition*, 144.

[151] Westminster Larger, loc. cit. As we shall see in the chapter on the Lord's Prayer, there was also much common ground between presbyterian and episcopalian catechists on forms of worship.

[152] Heidelberg Catechism, 345.

[153] Calvin, *Catechisme*, 70; Nowell, *Catechisme*, 129 (perhaps Nowell was thinking of the congregation's participation in the Apostles' Creed at morning and evening prayer, and in the Nicene Creed in the communion service).

psalms;[154] catechizing or instruction of youth;[155] and fasting (though Comber's insistence on the 'fasts and festivals of the church' probably differed in kind from the more spontaneous or irregular ones envisaged by John Ball and the authors of the Westminster Larger Catechism).[156] One duty quite widely prescribed—that of charity— could be performed either in church, by giving alms to the poor ('relieving [God's] saints', as the episcopalian Marshall put it), or outside church, by works of mercy.[157] With the occasional exception, the principle that works of charity should be performed on Sundays is found more in the seventeenth-century works in the sample than in sixteenth-century ones, but it is then found in expositions of both the Prayer Book form and the Westminster Shorter Catechism.[158] Such works 'may and ought to be done', wrote the Bartholomew sufferer, Thomas Gouge; while the royalists Henry Hammond and Edward Boughen reminded their catechumens that 'The sabbath was made for man, and not man for the sabbath' (Mark 2: 27), Boughen adding the example of Christ's healing the sick on the sabbath as a justification for acts of mercy on that day.[159]

A variety of seventeenth-century authors also specified that there were private as well as public duties to be performed on the sabbath.[160] There was clearly some overlap between the two kinds of duty, as in the case of prayer, praise, reading the Bible, and acts of charity. Other duties could be performed more conveniently in private, such as the reading of improving works, mentioned by Hammond and Vincent, and the meditation on God's works of creation and redemption enjoined by Paget, Egerton, Nicholson, Marshall, and Williams.[161] The private duties mentioned most commonly were praying and reading good books, but Gouge and Vincent added some which, though not surprising in themselves, were not usually mentioned in our sample as *domestic* Sunday duties: 'catechizing, repeating the sermons heard that day, singing psalms, holy conference, and the like'. In fact, these two authors were unusual in having a third category beyond public and private, the latter for them

---

[154] Mayer, *Catechisme*, sig. B7ᵛ; Vincent, *Catechism*, 128.

[155] Heidelberg Catechism, 345, and Ball, *Catechisme*, 75, implicitly; Hammond, *Practical catechisme*, 185, and Nicholson, *Exposition*, 98, explicitly.

[156] Ball, *Catechisme*, 83 (followed by Nicholes, *Catechisme*, 25–6); Westminster Larger, 66–8 (answer 108, under the second Commandment); Comber, *Church-catechism*, 19.

[157] Hill, *Principles*, sig. B6ᵛ; Comber, *Church-catechism*, 19; Marshall, *Catechism*, 25.

[158] Westminster Shorter, 24 (answer 60); Wallis, *Explanation*, 28; Sherlock, *Principles*, 33; Wake, *Principles*, 104; Hill, Comber, and Marshall—as in previous notes, and Hammond, Boughen, and Williams as in succeeding. For an exception, see Heidelberg Catechism, 345.

[159] Gouge, *Principles*, 119; Hammond, *Practical catechisme*, 185–6; Boughen, *Exposition*, 46.

[160] Egerton, 'Briefe method', 13, 17–18; Hill, *Principles*, sig. B6ᵛ; Nicholes, *Catechisme*, 28–9; Westminster Larger, 66–8, 79 (answers 108, 117); Westminster Shorter, 21, 24 (answers 50, 60); Sherlock, *Principles*, 33; Comber, *Church-catechism*, 19; Gouge, *Principles*, 119; Williams, *Exposition*, 33; Lewis, *Catechism*, 44.

[161] As previous notes, and Hammond, *Practical catechisme*, 185; Vincent, *Catechism*, 122; Paget, *Questions*, sig. B4ʳ; Nicholson, *Exposition*, 98; Marshall, *Catechism*, 25, 71.

apparently meaning domestic: there were also 'secret' duties in which the individual Christian came face to face with God on his or her own.[162]

It was also stressed by many of our authors, throughout our period, that the duties of the sabbath did not cease to be necessary at midnight on Sunday. A wide range of authors said that, although God had laid aside one day for nothing but such duties, they should also be performed as far as possible on weekdays as well, or as the Prayer Book catechism put it 'all the days of my life'.[163] One or two also pointed out that some mental and spiritual preparation for the Sabbath observances was also highly desirable. In the 1620s, the conformist Mayer urged preparation for the sabbath by prayer and meditation, and in the late 1640s the authors of the Larger Catechism urged the faithful to prepare their hearts so that they would be 'the more ... fit for the duties of that day'.[164] Enforcement of the sabbath was raised only by a few authors in our sample, but it was the opinion of a cross-section of them that fathers and other governors or superiors such as magistrates should ensure that duties were performed by those under their care.[165] A very occasional dissenting note was struck, as in 1646 when Hammond defended the celebration of Christmas and other festivities at some length against the charge that they were based on 'will-worship'. In 1681 Thomas Comber did the same but much more briefly, while on the other side in 1673 Thomas Vincent briefly attacked all 'popish holidays' as unscriptural.[166] There is also the interesting observation by Richard Sherlock, in the appendix to his form, that sabbath observance, as opposed to profanation, should really be handled under the fifth Commandment and the obedience owed to our mother the church.[167] But such sparring was really very rare, and with the sole exception of Hammond's advanced form phrased in very general terms too.

Looking back over the way that the first table was taught to catechumens, we find very few ways in which 'puritans' adopted different attitudes to 'Anglicans'. On a number of key areas like the sinfulness of idolatry, keeping the sabbath holy, and the necessity of attending church and hearing the word preached, the works in our sample are remarkably similar. Presbyterian and episcopalian authors might have had a different view of what forms of church decoration or church festivals were permitted, or what forms of worship the Word permitted, but both agreed that what catechumens needed to be taught was that they should conform to the practice of the

---

[162] Gouge, *Principles*, 119; Vincent, *Catechism*, 130.

[163] Calvin, *Catechisme*, 67–70; Nowell, *Catechisme*, 130; Dering–More, *Catechisme*, sig. A7ᵛ; Heidelberg Catechism, 345; Mayer, *Catechisme*, sigs. B8ʳ⁻ᵛ; Sherlock, *Principles*, 33, 39; Comber, *Church-catechism*, 19; Isham, *Catechism*, 40.

[164] Mayer, *Catechisme*, sig. B7ʳ; Westminster Larger, 79 (answer 117); not in the Shorter, but cf. Vincent, *Catechism*, 129.

[165] Hill, *Principles*, sig. B7ʳ; Westminster Larger, 80 (answer 118); Nicholson, *Exposition*, 99; Comber, *Church-catechism*, 19; Marshall, *Catechism*, 26.

[166] Hammond, *Practical catechisme*, 186–97; Comber, *Church-catechism*, 19; Vincent, *Catechism*, 118.

[167] Sherlock, *Principles*, 60.

church. This was spelt out clearly by Calvin and Nowell, and by exponents of the Prayer Book catechism. It was spelt out in somewhat different terms by 'godly' authors like Egerton, Ball, and the Westminster theologians who spoke of preaching, prayer, discipline, or public duties rather than 'comely order' or 'divine service'. But it is there none the less in that on neither side did those in authority seem to want their catechumens to decide what should be done and when.[168]

What all these authors focused on was what they saw as the essence of the first table as a whole: that God was determined that he should be worshipped properly. The way in which he was to be worshipped was expressed in general, typically non-controversial terms by the nonconformist Gouge: the first Commandment shows us the object of divine worship, the second the means, the third the manner, and the fourth the time.[169] 'What is the sum of what is required in these first four command-ments?', asked John Lewis, in the form used in many Charity Schools in the eighteenth century. 'To serve God truly all the days of my life', was the correct reply.[170] The simpler the form, the briefer the message and the less space there was for even a whiff of disagreement. The shorter the form, the more likely also that that essence was to be interpreted in a positive way: rather than a set of 'Thou shalt nots', the cate-chumen was encouraged to believe, worship, thank, trust, honour, and serve God, in short to 'love the Lord thy God with all thy heart, and with all thy soul, and with all thy mind'. Authors had it on no less an authority than Christ that 'This is the first and great commandment'.

'And the second is like unto it, thou shalt love thy neighbour as thyself.' The Com-mandments of the second table were treated as a group conveying man's duty to his neighbour. The authors of the Prayer Book catechism in the 1540s, the presbyterian leader Thomas Cartwright round about the 1590s, Henry Hammond and the authors of the Westminster Larger Catechism in the 1640s, and fifty years later the episco-palians Zacheus Isham and William Wake were just a few of those who suggested that the second table was based on the principle of 'do as you would be done by'.[171] How-ever, although Commandments six to ten can be treated as common-sense bans on hostility towards a neighbour or depredations against his property, lest he in turn should be aggressive towards you, the exhortation to honour one's parents in the fifth Commandment is at first sight rather different, and had received relatively little attention in expositions of the Seven Deadly Sins. Authors of longer works on the Decalogue often devoted a great deal of space to this Commandment: treatment of it occupied one-sixth of the printed text of Andrewes's catechetical lectures, and over

---

[168] See above, nn. 145–52. [169] Gouge, *Principles*, 117. [170] Lewis, *Catechism*, 45.
[171] Prayer Book catechism, 784–5; Cartwright, 'Catechisme', sig. Aa5ᵛ; Hammond, *Practical cate-chisme*, 283; Westminster Larger, 83 (answer 122); Isham, *Catechism*, 42; Wake, *Principles*, 106.

one-fifth of Dod and Cleaver's treatise.[172] One reason for this was the extent to which its application was stretched, another that it had important political implications, which is why we too will devote more space to this Commandment than the others in table two.

The first point to make is the way in which the command to 'honour thy father and thy mother' was generally interpreted. Calvin treated it as referring primarily to natural parents, but at the end of his exposition of this Commandment he pointed out that it also applied to magistrates and others in positions of authority or pre-eminence; Luther in his short catechism and the authors of the Heidelberg Catechism, on the other hand, bracketed parents and those in authority at the outset of their exposition.[173] In England too, from as early as the Prayer Book form and Nowell's catechism, the fifth Commandment was seen as an occasion to enjoin obedience not only to one's natural parents, but also to those in authority, be they schoolteachers, employers, clergymen, magistrates, or above them the monarch.[174] Other categories quite often used were those of superior age, the 'grey-haired', or those of superior gifts.[175] It was also a matter of common accord that since God had placed parents and superiors there, they must be obeyed. The 'one fountain' out of which the authority of both parents and superiors came was 'the holy decree of the laws of God', wrote Nowell in the early 1560s; 'it has pleased God to rule and govern the world' by 'parents, princes, magistrates, or other superiors', and so they must be loved, feared, revered, and given all due obedience.[176] We must obey all superiors, 'especially such as by God's ordinance are over us in places of authority, whether in family, church, or state', said the ejected minister, Thomas Gouge, in 1668.[177] The necessity of obedience was driven home by the second half of Exodus 20: 12: 'that thy days may be long upon the land which the Lord thy God giveth thee', though in a typically cautious Protestant exegesis on the matter of merit, this promise of reward was either hedged around with caveats (only on earth, as far as suits God's glory), or interpreted

---

[172] Andrewes, *Works*, vi. 174–213; Dod and Cleaver, *Exposition*, 178–247; for other examples of extensive treatment, see J. Mayer, *The English catechisme* (1622), 308–36; and Wake, *Principles*, 109–14 (though Wake wrote more about the third Commandment). On the Seven Deadly Sins, see Bossy, 'Moral Arithmetic', 232.

[173] Calvin, *Catechisme*, 72, 75–6; Schaff, *Creeds*, 75; Heidelberg Catechism, 345; and cf. Virel, *Treatise*, 140.

[174] Prayer Book catechism, 784–5; Nowell, *Catechisme*, 130; id., *Institution*, sig. Biii[r]; and e.g. Mayer, *Catechisme*, sigs. C2[r–v]; Palmer, *Endeavour*, 26–7; Lewis, *Catechism*, 46–9; and see following notes. There was an occasional exception: Bernard, in his *Common catechisme*, sig. B5[r], referred to natural parents only.

[175] Nowell, *Catechisme*, 130; Dering–More, *Catechisme*, sig. A8[r]; Paget, *Questions*, sig. B5[v]; Ball, *Catechisme*, 86; Nicholes, *Catechisme*, 31; Westminster Larger, 84 (answer 124); Westminster Shorter, 26 (answer 64); Sherlock, *Principles*, 33–4; Gouge, *Principles*, 121; Wake, *Principles*, 108, 113–14. For occasional references to obeying those of superior wealth or condition, or one's 'betters', see Prayer Book catechism, 784–5; Nowell, *Catechisme*, 130; Boughen, *Exposition*, 47, 55; Westminster Larger, 84 (answer 124); Nicholson, *Exposition*, 105–6; Sherlock, *Principles*, 34; Williams, *Exposition*, 35–6.

[176] Nowell, *Catechisme*, 130–1.

[177] Dering–More, *Catechisme*, sigs. A7[v]–8[r]; Ball, *Catechisme*, 86; Gouge, *Principles*, 121.

less as 'obey this command, and you will be rewarded' than 'disobey this command, and God is certain to punish you'.[178] The extent of the obedience demanded was almost unlimited, as we shall see, though the shorter the form, the less detail was given. Thus the Westminster Shorter Catechism simply recommended 'preserving the honour, and performing the duties belonging to every one in their several places and relations' and condemned the neglect of the same, while the Larger used nearly a dozen different nouns and gerunds to describe the duties and honour inferiors owed their superiors: reverence, prayer and thanksgiving, willing obedience, defence of their persons and authority, covering them in love, and so on.[179]

This stress on obedience to authority has prompted a number of suggestions from historians. One account of the political thought of the period, by Professor Schochet, has cited catechists who treated the fifth Commandment in this way as exemplars and disseminators of a patriarchal view of society in which the head of state was thought to have as much power and influence over his people as a father (in contemporary eyes) was supposed to have over his family.[180] There is a good deal of truth in this. It would be hard if not impossible to find a catechist in a settled church of the early modern period who did not see society in terms of a divinely ordained chain of command, or wish the power of princes and parents (which as Nowell said 'come out of one fountain') to be defended and fully exercised. When Dr Durbin examined the treatment of the fifth Commandment in a number of sixteenth-century catechisms, she came to the conclusion that in general English catechists put a stronger emphasis on obeying the authority of the state than Continental ones.[181] This does not, however, mean that the preservation of the political and social *status quo* was the prime aim in catechizing: catechists' treatment of the fifth Commandment has to be set in the context of their stated motives for catechizing, which as we saw in the first chapter of this study was to lay a groundwork of Christian knowledge that would lead to a fuller understanding and a fuller role in the life of the church. Catechists' support for hierarchy should also be viewed in the light of the fact that many authors stressed the duties of fathers and princes to their families and subjects. From the early seventeenth century, if not before,[182] catechetical authors appear to have tried hard to be even-handed by listing not only the duties and obligations of inferiors, but also the corresponding duties and obligations of superiors. A clear statement of the reciprocity of duties between

---

[178] Calvin, *Catechisme*, 73–5; Nowell, *Catechisme*, 131–3; Westminster Larger, 91 (answer 133); Nicholson, *Exposition*, 108–9; Vincent, *Catechism*, 149–50; Williams, *Exposition*, 356 ('ordinarily').

[179] Westminster Shorter, 26 (answers 64–5); Westminster Larger, 85–6 (answer 127).

[180] G. J. Schochet, *Patriarchalism in Political Thought: The Authoritarian Family and Political Speculation and Attitudes Especially in Seventeenth-Century England* (Oxford, 1975), 46, 75–80.

[181] L. D. Durbin, 'Education by Catechism: The Development of the Sixteenth-Century English Catechism', Ph.D. thesis (Northwestern, 1987), 191–8. For some comments on how the fifth Commandment was handled in Germany, see Strauss, *Luther's House of Learning*, 239–41.

[182] To some extent this was anticipated in Nowell, *Catechisme*, 131, 139, and Dering–More, *Catechisme*, sig. A8ʳ.

superior and inferior, and detailed examples of the duties of 'superiors' such as
princes, fathers, and husbands to 'inferiors' such as subjects, children, and wives can
be found in a wide variety of middling and longer forms, both by 'godly' and conformists. The duties of masters to their servants, wrote Vincent in 1673, was to be
wise and gentle in governing them, provide sufficient food, pay their wages in full and
on time, reprove their sins, and instruct them in the ways of God; the husband's duty
to his wife, said Wake in 1699, was to be 'true to her bed, kind and loving to her person', share his wealth with her, and to 'protect her ... and to cherish her ... as his own
flesh'; and similar comments were made about the duties of kings and magistrates, as
by William Nicholson in 1656: the king should see that 'truth be maintained, justice
executed', God honoured, the church protected as by a 'nursing father', the bad punished, the good encouraged and rewarded, and the peace maintained, unless war had
to be waged 'upon a just ground'.[183] A few authors like Ball, Nicholes, Ussher, and the
Westminster divines took this reciprocity a step further by deploying a third category
as well: the duties of equals to each other.[184] Patriarchalism was undoubtedly there,
but it was presented in a rounded and humane light.

Another historian to look at contemporary treatment of the Decalogue, Professor
McGee in the study already mentioned, would readily agree that both 'Anglicans'
and 'puritans' pressed the necessity of obedience to authority, but in his case he
believes that within this consensus there was a divergence of emphasis, especially in
the period 1620–60. Anglican imperatives, he says, were obedience to the higher
powers, maintaining the unity of the church, and preserving the public peace and the
natural order, while puritan ones were defence of preaching and the avoidance of
idolatry and profanation (as enjoined in Commandments one to four); puritans also
believed that the obedience enjoined in the fifth Commandment could be demanded
only in so far as the Word of God allowed.[185] A similar distinction is hinted at in Professor Greaves's survey of catechizing in the age of Bunyan when he suggests that the
Anglican catechisms of the later seventeenth century exhibited a broader concern
than the 'more narrowly religious concerns' of their nonconformist counterparts:
Anglican catechisms were about more than religion alone.[186] Again there is some
mileage in these claims: those who were on the whole content with the established
church and state naturally had more cause to preach submission to the authorities
than those who were not content or had broken with them. But it would perhaps be

[183] Vincent, *Catechism*, 138 (and cf. 134–41); Wake, *Principles*, 112–13 (and cf. 109–14); Nicholson,
Exposition, 107 (and cf. 106–8); for other examples of reciprocity, see Mayer, *Catechisme*, sigs. C2^{r-v}; Nicholes, *Catechisme*, 31–2; Marshall, *Catechism*, 26–7, 72; and following notes.

[184] Ball, *Catechisme*, 86; Nicholes, *Catechisme*, 31–2; Ussher, 'Principles', 10; Westminster Larger,
85–91 (answers 127–32); Westminster Shorter, 26 (answers 64–5). The authors of the last of these were so
busy stating the duties of all to all that they barely mentioned duties to natural parents specifically.

[185] McGee, *Godly Man*, ch. 4.

[186] R. L. Greaves, 'Introduction' to *Miscellaneous Works of John Bunyan* (general editor R. Sharrock),
viii (1979), pp. xxi–xxiv.

unwise to take these claims much further than this, and three points may be made quickly about the period 1540–1740 as a whole on the basis of the best-selling catechisms in our sample.

First, virtually all authors, whatever their background, placed duty to natural parents before that to other superiors, as in the Prayer Book catechism where the catechumen is told to say that his duty is 'To love, honour, and succour my father, and mother. To honour and obey the king, and all that are put in authority under him.'[187] Only Nowell, a Calvinist but also dean of St Pauls's, when enlarging on the meaning of the fifth Commandment, apparently argued that offending the king was worse than offending one's natural parents.[188] Secondly, as we have already noted, it was common for authors of all standpoints to list not only the duties of inferiors but those of superiors too; and as we shall see shortly one can find examples of conformists as well as critics indicating the limits of what rulers could legitimately demand of their subjects.[189] Thirdly, it would be very hard to demonstrate convincingly on a quantitative basis that conformist episcopalians as a group said significantly more about obedience to the higher powers than 'godly', presbyterian, or nonconformist ones. On the contrary, one can probably find as many stern exhortations to 'inferiors' to obey their 'superiors' in forms written by 'godly' authors, such as Dering and More, Ball, Palmer, the Westminster divines, and the nonconformist Gouge, as in forms written by conformists; and a readiness to contribute to national defence and pay required dues to the state was specified by both presbyterians like the Westminster divines and Thomas Vincent and episcopalians like Nicholson and Wake.[190] Some 'godly' authors, it is true, used 'magistrate' or 'superiors in office' rather than 'king',[191] while expounders of the Prayer Book form not unnaturally used 'king', since it was in the original form upon which they were enlarging. But this was not an unbreakable rule: Calvin and the 'godly' Dering and More specified princes, rulers, and magistrates, while Nowell and more conservative authors such as Mayer, Marshall, and Wake referred at first only to 'magistrates' or the 'civil power'.[192] In their minds, some authors may have drawn a distinction between a 'godly' JP and a less than 'godly' prince, but if so, it was not spelt out in their forms. If we look at the Westminster Larger Catechism, for example, we find a reference to 'all superiors … especially such as, by God's ordinance, are over us in place of authority, whether in

---

[187] Prayer Book catechism, 784–5.

[188] Nowell, *Catechisme*, 132–3 (last answer on the fifth Commandment, but cf. 130–2); Durbin, 'Education by Catechism', 191–4.

[189] See above, nn. 183–4, and below, nn. 204–7.

[190] Dering–More, *Catechisme*, sigs. A7ᵛ–8ʳ; Ball, *Catechisme*, 86; Palmer, *Endeavour*, 27; Westminster Larger, 85–6 (answers 127–8, but cf. answers 129–30); Gouge, *Principles*, 121; and on defence and taxes, Westminster Larger, 85–6 (answer 127); Vincent, *Catechisme*, 140; Nicholson, *Exposition*, 108; Wake, *Principles*, 110. For more precise comparisons on attitudes to royal power, see following paragraphs.

[191] Paget, *Questions*, sig. B5ʳ; Ball, *Catechisme*, 86.

[192] Calvin, *Catechisme*, 75–6; Dering–More, *Catechisme*, sigs. A7ᵛ–8ʳ; Nowell, *Catechisme*, 130; Mayer, *Catechisme*, sigs. C2ʳ⁻ᵛ; Marshall, *Catechism*, 26; Wake, *Principles*, 110–11.

family, church or commonwealth' which did not draw any distinction between higher and lower officials. (It may also be noted that this is one of the few cases where English—or in this case British—authors placed ecclesiastical power before secular)[193]. In short, the common ground between 'Anglican' and 'puritan' on the meaning of the fifth Commandment may have been much greater than that which divided them for the greater portion of the early modern period.

This does, however, leave the period that is McGee's special area of interest and has received intense scrutiny in recent years—the 1620s to the 1650s—and the changes in political thinking that have been associated with that period. The great majority of churchmen and lawyers who spoke or wrote on the subject of royal power in early modern Europe argued that the prince derived his power from God, and that any restraints on that power were imposed only by divine or natural law, not by the will of the people or purely human laws. The relatively few statements in favour of the legality of resistance in sixteenth-century Europe were the products of specific circumstances and had a large element of special pleading, and even in the countries which provoked and first heard them they tended to have a very mixed reception.[194] In England too, at least until the 1620s, as Dr Sommerville has recently argued, there was a broadly-based consensus that royal power was of divine origin and was limited only by divine and natural law. There had been occasional sources of friction between crown and people, but nothing to endanger the general agreement that what the kingdom needed was a firm, effective ruler capable of protecting it against foreign threat, rebellion, and faction. From the 1620s, however, this consensus began to dissolve, leaving Charles, Laud, and their followers defending the original theory of royal power, reinforced in places, while other clergy and laymen began to drift away from it. One reason for this drift seems to have been that when James and Charles met resistance to some policies, they responded with statements that asserted royal power much more specifically than had been done before; and what had been acceptable to their subjects when left in general terms was much more worrying when tied down to a specific case, such as the forced loan of 1626.[195] Other reasons were apprehension at the growing strength of Catholic forces in Europe and fear of a resurgence of 'popery' in the English church, fears which fused with constitutional disquiet to reinforce the view that popery meant tyranny, and vice versa.[196] By the late 1640s, however, those who had felt that they had to resist what they saw as a revival of 'popery' had fallen out among themselves, and after the Restoration the theory that the subject

[193] Westminster Larger, 83–4 (answer 124). For English authors, including puritans, putting secular before ecclesiastical authority, see Durbin, 'Education by Catechism', 195–8.

[194] J. W. Allen, *A History of Political Thought in the Sixteenth Century* (1964), 125–33, 302–42; see also Q. Skinner, *The Foundations of Modern Political Thought* (2 vols.; Cambridge, 1978), pt. 3.

[195] J. P. Sommerville, *Politics and Ideology in England 1603–1640* (1986); and cf. C. Russell, *Parliaments and English Politics 1621–1629* (Oxford, 1979), and R. Cust, *The Forced Loan and English Politics 1626–1628* (Oxford, 1987), esp. ch. 3.

[196] Sommerville, *Politics and Ideology*, 44–6, 138–9, and ch. 6.

owed absolute obedience to the prince was adopted again. Indeed, despite the accession of a truly Catholic king in 1685, the theory of passive obedience was pressed even harder than before, and the revolutions of 1688 and 1714–15 were treated, by the Whigs at least, as providential exceptions to the general rule rather than heroic acts of resistance.[197]

How far did the authors of works in our sample reflect this pattern of events? Calvin's statement of princely power was not fulsome, but he saw no need to qualify his statement of obedience, unless the word 'due' in the last clause is meant to convey a caveat:

As God hath given unto them all [magistrates, rulers, and superiors], their authorities and preeminence: and because there is no prerogative of superiority, neither of father nor mother, neither of prince, or ruler, magistrate, or master, neither any other office or title of pre-eminence, but such as God hath ordained: therefore they require all by one manner of reason their due obedience.[198]

Nowell's attitude to rebellion was one of open horror almost as great as that conveyed by the official homily on rebellion of 1571. He wrote:

if it be for every private man a heinous offence to offend his private parents, and parricide to kill them; what shall we say of them that have conspired and borne wicked armour against the commonweal ... the most ancient, sacred, and common mother of us all ... and against the prince, the father of the country itself, and parent of the commonweal ...? So outrageous a thing can in no wise be expressed with a fit name.[199]

A few decades later, John Ball, though egalitarian in terms of insisting on the reciprocity of duties between those of different degrees, was not the subversive his namesake of 1381 had been: inferiors 'must be subject, reverent, and thankful to their superiors, bearing with their wants and covering them in love'; the main duty outlined in the fifth Commandment was that 'we carefully observe that order which God hath appointed amongst men, and do the duties which we owe unto them in respect of their places and degrees'.[200] In his exposition of the Prayer Book catechism in 1616, William Hill not only repeated the phrases in the original form about being commanded to love, honour, and obey the king, but also said that we were forbidden to hate or disobey our superiors in thought, word, or deed.[201]

By the mid-1640s greater praise was being lavished on the crown in some quarters. When Edward Boughen wrote in 1646 that the king was 'the father of his country', or Nicholson in the 1650s quoted Isaiah to the effect that kings and queens were our 'nursing-fathers' and 'nursing-mothers', they were saying no more than Nowell had

---

[197] J. N. Figgis, *The Divine Right of Kings* (Cambridge, 1914), 143; J. P. Kenyon, *Revolution Principles: The Politics of Party 1689–1720* (Cambridge, 1977), 64–5, 88–9, 129, 136, 201; J. C. D. Clark, *English Society 1688–1832* (Cambridge, 1985), ch. 3.

[198] Calvin, *Catechisme*, 75–6.

[199] Nowell, *Catechisme*, 32–3; Allen, *History of Political Thought*, 131–2. [200] Ball, *Catechisme*, 86.

[201] Hill, *Principles*, sig. B7^r; though cf. Hammond, *Practical catechisme*, 173.

done in the 1560s. But in arguing that 'the king is worth ten thousand of the best of us' and calling the king the 'fountain of all civil power' and God's substitute and immediate vice-gerent, Boughen was arguably going further than Nowell; and when, ten years later, Nicholson claimed that monarchy came 'from nature itself' and was as old as man, he was probably revealing intellectual as well as political conservatism.[202] But such statements cannot be found before 1646, and can be found only occasionally thereafter. Moreover, such assertions of support for the monarchy did not descend to the personal level or reflect the martyrological excesses of works like *Eikon Basilike*.

In 1647 the authors of the Westminster Shorter Catechism said little more than Ball had done: the fifth Commandment requires us to preserve the honour of, and perform the duties belonging to, every one in their several places and relations. But the authors of the Larger Catechism were more explicit and more fulsome in their support for the powers that be, as in their account of the list of duties and honours that inferiors owe to their superiors that was mentioned a few pages back. The sins of inferiors against superiors, they went on in the next answer, included

contempt of, and rebellion against, their persons and places, in their lawful counsels, commands, and corrections ... and all such refractory and scandalous carriage, as proves a shame and dishonour to them and their government.[203]

There were hints of limitations in this catechism: inferiors should obey the 'lawful commands and counsels' of superiors (answer 127, and see also 'lawful counsels' in 128); superiors are forbidden to command 'things unlawful, or not in the power of inferiors to perform' (answer 129). But one has to look to an exposition of the Shorter Catechism, by a theological hard-liner, Thomas Vincent, in the 1670s to find the assertion that illegal acts by a ruler might be the grounds of disobedience; and even this is slipped in as a qualification to the second in a list of five duties owed by subjects to their magistrates:

(1.) High estimation and honour of them. 'Fear God; honour the king'—1 Peter 2: 17. (2.) Subjection to them, and obedience unto their laws, so far as they are not contrary to the laws of Christ. 'Let every soul be subject unto the higher powers'—Rom. 13: 1. (3.) Ready payment of their dues ... (4.) Defence of them in danger ... (5.) Prayer and thanksgiving for them.[204]

The caveat 'as far as the law of God allows' might seem to mark a move towards a warning against ungodly actions by rulers of the type that Professor McGee has indicated,[205] but if so it was not necessarily a dividing line between parliamentarians and monarchists. The homily on obedience of 1547 (which was still official doctrine in

---

[202] Boughen, *Exposition*, 47, 49–50, 52 (citing 2 Chr. 9: 8, *inter alia*); Nicholson, *Exposition*, 106 (Isa. 49: 23, *inter alia*); and cf. Williams, *Exposition*, 35.

[203] Westminster Shorter, 26 (answer 64); Westminster Larger, 67 (answer 128), though neither stressed the penalties of disobedience (answers 66 and 133, respectively).

[204] Vincent, *Catechism*, 139.   [205] See above, n. 185.

the early 1640s) taught that 'we may not obey kings, magistrates, or any other ... if they would command us to do anything contrary to God's commandments'; and in Boughen's catechism of 1646, we find the statement that the king should be obeyed as far as he commands nothing contrary to the law of nature or the law of God: if the king orders something 'evil' or 'unlawful' in his actions towards the 'commonwealth' he must be obeyed, but if he orders anything against God's law, he may be disobeyed.[206] In 1689 John Williams told his catechumens that the king and his ministers should be honoured and obeyed 'in all lawful and honest things', and in 1699 William Wake urged his pupils to obey God rather than man if the civil power commanded something contrary to their duty to God.[207]

The dividing line lay elsewhere. One assumption behind the position adopted by authors like Hammond, Boughen, Williams, and Wake was that a distinction could be drawn between man's business and God's business or between man's law and God's law: as Hammond put it in his catechism, Christ did not meddle with dominion among men.[208] Kings who kept within their terms of reference should be obeyed. The drawing of this particular line of demarcation, bolstered by texts like Romans 13: 1–7 and 1 Peter 2: 13–18,[209] was not an action that would prove acceptable to critics of Charles I, passionately concerned as they were about the apparent growth of 'popery' within areas of state policy normally regarded as in the king's prerogative: foreign policy, appointments to high office, and ecclesiastical matters. The English critics were slow to develop a rival theory that would justify resistance, but in Scotland, where Charles and Laud were also trying to impose political control and religious uniformity, at least three different lines of precedent or argument were gathered together to produce the National Covenant of 1638 as the basis of resistance to Charles: the historical line based on bands for mutual defence against an intruder; the theoretical one of a contract between government and people which Charles was held to have broken; and the theological argument of a partnership between God and his people in the form of the covenant of grace. Aided by a wave of millenarian feeling in the 1630s, this coming together of different elements led to the unique concept of a covenanted nation fighting against the forces of darkness among which—in the eyes of the Scots—were Charles and Laud.[210]

---

[206] Allen, *History of Political Thought*, 127–8; Boughen, *Exposition*, 48–50.

[207] Williams, *Exposition*, 35; Wake, *Principles*, 110–11. Wake added that if the rules of religion were silent on a matter, the laws of the state should be obeyed.

[208] Hammond, *Practical catechisme*, 173, and cf. 177–8.

[209] Boughen, *Exposition*, 47, 49; Williams, *Exposition*, 35; Isham, *Catechism*, 43–4; Wake, *Principles*, 110; Lewis, *Catechism*, 46–7.

[210] S. A. Burrell, 'The Covenant Idea as a Revolutionary Symbol: Scotland, 1596–1637', *Church History*, 27 (1958), 338–50; J. B. Torrance, 'The Covenant Concept in Scottish Theology and Politics and its Legacy', *Scottish Journal of Theology*, 34 (1981), 225–43; and M. Steele, 'The "Politick Christian": The Theological Background to the National Covenant', in *The Scottish National Covenant in its British Context*, ed. J. S. Morrill (Edinburgh, 1990), 31–55; R. Mitchison, *Lordship to Patronage: Scotland 1603–1745* (1983), 39–40.

Even if there had been agreement that many of Charles I's actions lay within the field of divine law, there were, for loyalists, other sticking points further down the line. Who was to decide if the king was breaking the law of God—the individual or the official church? And if it was generally agreed that the king's demands were unlawful, should they be resisted or simply endured? In his catechism Henry Hammond, already the author of a standard royalist pamphlet on obedience, took the line that it was unlawful for private men to act without a commission from the supreme power. Others like the Scottish minister, Alexander Henderson, had made the case for the existence of 'inferior magistrates' who were not necessarily holding state office but were capable of deciding whether the king had broken God's law and so could be resisted.[211] The second problem—active or passive resistance—was there both in the 1640s and again the late 1680s. The view of men like Boughen was that if a king broke God's law, he should not be obeyed, but nor should he be resisted either;[212] the Covenanters and the English parliamentarians decided otherwise. With very few exceptions, however, catechetical authors were not anxious to encourage catechumens to take the initiative in deciding on the legality or illegality of their superiors' actions or whether such actions should be resisted or not.

The traumas of civil war did leave a mark on some of the catechisms in the sample, but considering how deep those traumas were, and how divided the educated élite was at the time, the marks are remarkably few and slight. There is no substantial evidence in our sample of different lines of obedience being pushed by the official church and by puritans in the late sixteenth century, and relatively few signs of a different one being pushed in the middle or late seventeenth century; and there are certainly no signs of our authors being prepared to denounce and lambast the sins of ungodly rulers under the fifth Commandment or anywhere else in their forms. In the 1640s there were some more outspoken comments in catechisms outside the sample, and as noted in an earlier chapter there were isolated works, such as the two catechisms written for the rival armies in the 1640s, which were overtly political.[213] But these were the products of unusual political circumstances rather than a regular feature of English catechetics. For most of the century, and in the most commonly used catechisms, the possibility of royal misdeeds and of popular resistance were barely mentioned. As far as the authors of the forms in our sample were concerned, generalities about obedience to the powers that be, bolstered by scriptural examples and citations, were the order of the day; politics were best avoided.

———————

Readers who remember the rules of interpretation listed at the start of this chapter will probably be able to write the next few paragraphs for themselves. The prohibition on

[211] Hammond, *Practical catechisme*, 178–9; D. Stevenson, *The Scottish Revolution 1637–44: The Triumph of the Covenanters* (Newton Abbot, 1973), 133–7.
[212] Boughen, *Exposition*, 48.   [213] See above, p. 86.

killing in the sixth Commandment was regularly extended to include fighting, mocking, and quarrelling, and hostile thoughts such as anger, revenge, and intent to kill as well as murder. The positive command was taken to be that we should not only try to preserve the lives of our neighbours, but also seek to love them from the bottom of our hearts, be reconciled should any differences arise, and succour them when in need.[214] Some forms extended the meaning of the Commandment to cover the life of the catechumen as well as that of his neighbour by including suicide or the risking of one's own life unnecessarily, and a few authors took it to include what today would pass for healthy living by encouraging careful diet, sober use of drink, and a cheerful demeanour towards others.[215] A minority of authors in the sample took on the difficult task of separating different kinds of killing. Mayer said there were six different forms of unlawful killing; Williams contented himself with two, while suggesting that in scriptural terms manslaughter 'in heat of blood' was just as culpable as wilful murder.[216] (Despite the apparent popularity of duelling in some circles at this time, there are only a few specific condemnations of it in our sample.[217]) The legitimate use of force was taken to include 'public justice' (that is, executing legally condemned criminals), 'lawful war', and 'necessary defence' (the last two of these appearing more frequently from the later 1640s).[218] Compared to the suggestion in Dod and Cleaver's treatise that it was one's duty to procure a neighbouring Christian's welfare in soul as well as body, the authors of catechisms in our sample did not stray beyond the physical and social dictates of goodneighbourliness.[219]

The seventh Commandment was 'Thou shalt not commit adultery'. Predictably this was extended to include fornication and all forms of physical or mental uncleanness and lust. Once again the Westminster Larger Catechism takes the palm for the longest and most imaginative list: from the most serious of sexual crimes, such as rape, incest, and sodomy, through the merely heinous, such as 'keeping of stews' and bigamy, to what another age would perhaps see as unbecoming rather than illegal: wanton looks, impudent behaviour, immodest apparel, undue delay of marriage, and

---

[214] For example, Calvin, *Catechisme*, 76–7; Nowell, *Catechisme*, 133; id., *Institution*, sigs. Biiiᵛ–ivʳ; Dering–More, *Catechisme*, sig. A8ʳ; Paget, *Questions*, sigs. B6ʳ⁻ᵛ; Ball, *Catechisme*, 86; Hill, *Principles*, sigs. B7ʳ⁻ᵛ; Westminster Larger, 191–5 (answers 135–6); Westminster Shorter, 27 (answers 68–9); Nicholson, *Exposition*, 110–12; Comber, *Church-catechism*, 20; Vincent, *Catechism*, 150–2; Marshall, *Catechisme*, 27; Williams, *Exposition*, 36–8; Wake, *Principles*, 118.

[215] Nicholes, *Catechisme*, 33 (and cf. 36 under the seventh Commandment); Westminster Larger, 191–4 (answer 135); Hammond, *Practical catechisme*, 118–19; Vincent, *Catechism*, 150–5; Wake, *Principles*, 116–17.

[216] Mayer, *Catechisme*, sig. C3ʳ; Williams, *Exposition*, 36–7; and see following notes.

[217] Hammond, *Practical catechisme*, 120–2, 364; Nicholson, *Exposition*, 112; Vincent, *Catechism*, 154; Wake, *Principles*, 117; V. G. Kiernan, *The Duel in European History* (Oxford, 1988).

[218] Westminster Larger, 94 (answer 136); Hammond, *Practical catechisme*, 118; Nicholson, *Exposition*, 111; Vincent, *Catechism*, 154; Gouge, *Principles*, 122 (though he omitted 'lawful war'); Wake, *Principles*, 115.

[219] Dod and Cleaver, *Exposition*, 273, 270; but cf. below, n. 235 for Vincent's quotation of their phrase 'household of faith' in a similar context.

so on.[220] This was not the only form to condemn lascivious looks and provocative attire or to include drunkenness and gluttony as incitements to lust—both 'godly' and conformists did that[221]—but it was one of the relatively few forms to include 'lascivious songs, books, pictures, dancings, [and] stage plays' in its list of unclean acts.[222] On the positive side, the catechumen was taught the duty to keep his or her body in 'temperance, soberness, and chastity': we must keep our bodies and souls undefiled as temples of the Holy Ghost, wrote Nowell, followed by Dering and More and Paget.[223] The virtues of marriage and the sinfulness of adultery and separation were mentioned only rarely in the sample at this point,[224] since the need for mutual love and respect between husbands and wives had usually been dealt with under the fifth Commandment by those authors who wished to do so. We should also perhaps consider that most catechumens were either children or young adolescents, and that in general the shorter the catechism, the shorter the list of positive virtues taught by the seventh Commandment tended to be.[225] If young people did imbibe the church's attitude towards adult sexuality, it was perhaps less through the sparing treatment of these subjects in the more popular catechisms of the day than through hearing the wedding service or a marriage sermon or hearing about the proceedings of the church courts.[226]

The eighth Commandment—against theft—gave authors almost as good a stage for their creative talents as moral teachers as did the fifth. In various expositions of the Prayer Book catechism in the seventeenth century, 'theft' was taken to include covetousness, all 'unlawful getting' from a neighbour by false weights and measures, any oppression of the poor by the rich, unlawful trades such as fortune-telling, secret theft, theft under colour of the law, not returning things found, usury, bribery, and any form of force or fraud which breached 'the rule of righteousness or charity'.[227]

---

[220] Westminster Larger, 96–8 (answers 138–9); serious sexual misdemeanours were also specified and condemned in Mayer, *Catechisme*, sig. C3ᵛ; Nicholes, *Catechisme*, 36; Nicholson, *Exposition*, 113; and Wake, *Principles*, 120.

[221] e.g. Dering–More, *Catechisme*, sig. A8ʳ; Paget, *Questions*, sig. B7ʳ; Vincent, *Catechism*, 159–60; Nicholson, *Exposition*, 113–14; Sherlock, *Principles*, 35–6; Marshall, *Catechism*, 28; Williams, *Exposition*, 39.

[222] Though the 'godly' Dering and More and Paget warned against 'filthy' songs (*Catechisme*, sig. 8ʳ, and *Questions*, sig. B7ʳ), and the conformist Mayer against 'filthy' stage-plays, 'cross-dressing', and 'mixed lascivious dancing' (*Catechisme*, sig. C3ᵛ); also cf. Virel, *Treatise*, 152, and Gouge, *Principles*, 122.

[223] Prayer Book catechism, 784–5; Nowell, *Catechisme*, 133; id., *Institution*, sigs. Bivʳ⁻ᵛ; Dering–More, *Catechisme*, sig. A8ᵛ; Paget, *Questions*, sig. B7ᵛ; and cf. Hill, *Principles*, sigs. B7ᵛ–8ʳ; Williams, *Exposition*, 39.

[224] Nicholes, *Catechisme*, 36 (and cf. Ussher, 'Principles', 10); Hammond, *Practical catechisme*, 136–44 (and cf. Nicholson, *Exposition*, 113); Williams, *Exposition*, 38; see also Virel, *Treatise*, 153–4.

[225] In his first, more elementary form, Ussher listed just the one duty—the preservation of chastity: 'Principles', 10.

[226] On the last of these in particular, see M. J. Ingram, *Church Courts, Sex and Marriage in England, 1570–1640* (Cambridge, 1987), *passim*.

[227] Hill, *Principles*, sig. B8ʳ; Mayer, *Catechisme*, sig. C4ʳ; Nicholes, *Catechisme*, 39–41; Sherlock, *Principles*, 36.

Thomas Comber clearly had an impoverished set of catechumens in mind when he told them that it was wrong to steal small things 'because we are poor'.[228] ' "Cursed is he, that removeth away the mark of his neighbour's lands" either by merestones, evidences, records, or the like', Boughen warned his catechumens, 'for this is cozenage at the least'.[229] The list did not end there: gaining by another's loss or weakness, taking excessive profits or selling too low to undercut rivals unfairly, concealing faults in a commodity, engrossing commodities to enhance the price, not paying just debts or proper wages to employees, imposing upon ignorance or credulity, vexatious lawsuits, 'unjust enclosures', and depopulation were added by other authors.[230] As the seventeenth century wore on, the list of potential economic crimes grew ever longer and the reminders to seek honest employments more frequent, a situation which may have reflected the increasing complexity of economic life as well as catechists' attempts to cope with what they saw as the persistent greed of their flocks.[231]

On the positive side, what Sherlock had called 'the rule of righteousness and charity' dictated that we should not only be honest in all our dealings and apply ourselves to a legitimate calling, but also give to the poor and further the wealth and outward estate of our neighbours as well as ourselves.[232] The idea of helping one's neighbours might have been the occasion to stress the need to help any fellow 'godly' who had fallen on hard times, and thus combine edification with charity,[233] but there do not seem to have been any restrictions of this kind at catechetical level. 'Who is my neighbour', asked Nowell in the 1560s and Boughen in the 1640s, and either of their replies would probably have been acceptable to the other authors in our sample. Nowell, following Calvin, said that our neighbour is anyone we knew, and even those we did not know and our enemies; Boughen said it was any one in the country or even of another nation or religion (the attitude of the Good Samaritan).[234] The sort of terms used to describe suitable recipients of charity were the obvious ones like 'the poor' and one's 'neighbour'; the only references to helping the devout or the 'saints' were in a couple of expositions of the Prayer Book form in 1616 and 1679, and in an exposition of the Westminster Shorter Catechism by Thomas Vincent, where he told his catechumens that it was their duty to help all who were poor or in want, 'especially if they be of the household of faith'.[235] On the other

---

[228] Comber, *Church-catechism*, 21.   [229] Boughen, *Exposition*, 57 (citing Deut. 27: 17).

[230] Hammond, *Practical catechisme*, 283–9; Westminster Larger, 101–2 (answer 142); Palmer, *Endeavour*, 28; Williams, *Exposition*, 39–40.

[231] In addition to those cited in previous notes, see Ball, *Treatise*, 204–9; Nicholson, *Exposition*, 115; Vincent, *Catechism*, 186–98; and Wake, *Principles*, 121–3.

[232] Dering–More, *Catechisme*, sig. A8ᵛ; Paget, *Questions*, sigs. B7ᵛ–C1ʳ; Virel, *Treatise*, 155–61; Ussher, 'Principles', 10; Westminster Larger, 99–101 (answer 141); Westminster Shorter, 28 (answer 74); Nicholson, *Exposition*, 114–15; Marshall, *Catechism*, 29; Williams, *Exposition*, 40–1; Wake, *Principles*, 123–4 (and cf. 118 under the sixth Commandment); Lewis, *Catechism*, 49–50.

[233] McGee, *Godly Man*, ch. 5.

[234] Nowell, *Catechisme*, 138 (and cf. Calvin, *Catechisme*, 85–6); Boughen, *Exposition*, 57–8; Marshall combined the two: *Catechism*, 31.

[235] See previous notes, and Hill, *Principles*, sig. B8ʳ; Marshall, *Catechism*, 25; and Vincent, *Catechism*, 164.

hand, the duty of being content with one's station and portion of goods in this life was stated both in the Prayer Book form and some expositions of it, and in works by a number of 'godly' authors.[236] It was the authors of the Westminster Larger Catechism who urged their students to moderate their desire for worldly wealth, and to study to use those things 'which are necessary and convenient for the sustenation of our nature and suitable to our condition'.[237] A similar warning against covetousness was also, of course, implicit in the tenth Commandment as we shall see shortly.

The prohibition against bearing false witness—Commandment number nine—was, said Calvin, against not just open perjury, but also reproaches, backbiting, and telling lies that would cause a neighbour loss.[238] Nowell, working on the principle that 'one example containeth a general doctrine', added to Calvin's list a ban on all lies, slander, and 'evil speakings', while Dering and More added to Nowell's list the sins of flattering, dissembling, telling false tales, and believing evil spoken behind a person's back.[239] Various Elizabethan and Jacobean authors made the point that what was reprehensible was speaking falsely as a witness, though whether this was in a court of law or at the parish pump was not specified.[240] The legal ramifications of this command did become clearer later: the authors of the Westminster Larger Catechism and conformist divines like Nicholson and Williams included in their catalogue of sins to be avoided under this Commandment the giving of false evidence, 'especially in public judicature', the suborning of witnesses, the passing of unjust sentences by judges, and the making of false records by registrars and notaries.[241] In some of these instances the spotlight had also moved from the honesty of the witness to that of officials and powerful litigants.

The authors of the Larger Catechism mentioned over fifty sins against this Commandment. These included the completely illegal such as forgery, the unexpected such as whispering or speaking the truth unseasonably, and specialized faults such as 'unnecessary discovering of infirmities' and 'denying the gifts and graces of God'.[242] Against this, the authors of shorter forms concentrated on a few simple sins, such as lying, slandering, malice, and wrongful suspicion.[243] On the positive side (and compared to the twenty-five ways of being nice to one's neighbour given in the Larger Catechism), authors of shorter forms again kept it simple: think well of your neighbours,

---

[236] Prayer Book catechism, 784–5; Nicholson, *Exposition*, 114; Marshall, *Catechism*, 29; Lewis, *Catechism*, 56; Dering–More, *Catechisme*, sig. A8ᵛ; Paget, *Questions*, sig. B8ᵛ; Ussher, 'Principles', 10; Vincent, *Catechism*, 162 (and cf. 156 under the seventh Commandment).

[237] Westminster Larger, 100 (answer 141).   [238] Calvin, *Catechisme*, 80–1.

[239] Nowell, *Catechisme*, 134–5; Dering–More, *Catechisme*, sig. A8ᵛ.

[240] Ibid.; and Paget, *Questions*, sig. C1ʳ; Hill, *Principles*, sig. B8ᵛ.

[241] Westminster Larger, 105 (answer 145): Nicholson, *Exposition*, 117; Williams, *Exposition*, 41; and cf. Boughen, *Exposition*, 57, and Gouge, *Principles*, 123.

[242] Westminster Larger, 105–9 (answer 145).

[243] For example, Prayer Book catechism, 784–5; Calvin, *Catechisme*, 80–1; Hill, *Principles*, sig. B8ᵛ; Marshall, *Catechism*, 29–30.

defend their reputation, promote truth between man and man, and judge charitably.[244] The emphasis had slipped here from an absence of perjury or malice to a positive effort to promote social harmony. Occasional efforts were also made on this side of the equation to stress that one should be concerned for the preservation of one's own good name as well as that of one's neighbour.[245]

The prospect of an 8-year-old catechumen in seventeenth-century Warwickshire coveting his neighbour's house, wife, maid, ox, or ass—the subject of the tenth Commandment—may have been remote. Moreover, the subject of covetousness had also been raised by a number of authors under the eighth Commandment. These considerations, together in some cases perhaps with a sense that time or space was running short, may help to explain the fact that most authors, even the indefatigable divines of the Westminster Assembly, said much less about the tenth than the other Commandments. Indeed, Calvin and Nowell even had their catechumens ask the question whether the tenth Commandment added anything to the other nine. The answer was 'Yes': number ten forbade all evil thoughts, desires, or actions against our neighbour not covered by the previous Commandments, even those thoughts or actions 'we never fully purpose … neither endeavour … or consent willingly to do'.[246] The same considerations, together with the support of texts from the New Testament such as Matt. 6: 25–34, Phil. 4: 11, and 1 Thess. 4: 11–12, may also help to explain why much of what was said was on the positive side rather than the negative, as in the words of John Ball: we are here commanded 'that we be truly contented with our own outward condition, and heartily desire our neighbour's good in all things belonging unto him great and small'.[247] The same point was made in the Westminster catechisms, whose authors urged 'full contentment with our own condition, with a right and charitable frame of spirit toward our neighbour, and all that is his', and in half a dozen expositions of the Prayer Book catechism, which itself had urged on generations of children their duty 'to labour truly to get mine own living, and to do my duty in that state of life, unto which it shall please God to call me'.[248]

The discussions of the last six or seven of the Ten Commandments in early modern English catechisms constitute a rich and largely untapped vein of clerical thought

[244] As last note; and Ball, *Catechisme*, 87; Ussher, 'Principles', 10; Westminster Shorter, 29 (answer 77); Williams, *Exposition*, 41–2.

[245] Ball, and Westminster Shorter, as last note; Vincent, *Catechism*, 173–6; but note also the warning against boastfulness in Westminster Larger, 107 (answer 145), and Comber, *Church-catechism*, 21.

[246] Calvin, *Catechisme*, 82; Nowell, *Catechisme*, 131; id., *Institution*, sig. Bvi[r]; and cf. Cartwright, 'Catechisme', sig. Aa6[r]; Boughen, *Exposition*, 58; and Nicholson, *Exposition*, 117.

[247] Ball, *Catechisme*, 87–8; and cf. Nicholes, *Catechisme*, 44; Nicholson, *Exposition*, 120; Sherlock, *Principles*, 38; Comber, *Church-catechism*, 21; Gouge, *Principles*, 123–4; Marshall, *Catechism*, 30–1; Williams, *Exposition*, 42–3; Isham, *Catechism*, 49–50; Wake, *Principles*, 127; Lewis, *Catechism*, 56.

[248] Westminster Larger, 109–11 (answers 147–8); Westminster Shorter, 29–30 (answers 80–1); and cf. Wallis, *Explanation*, 34–5; Vincent, *Exposition*, 181–3; for Prayer Book catechism expositions, see previous note.

on a wide variety of contemporary social and moral as well as religious issues. If scholars are prepared to allow for the idiosyncracies of authors, for the different targets at which different forms were aimed, and the much greater distribution of some forms than others, and if they are prepared to view these discussions in the broader context of the Prayer Book liturgy and other common forms of formal and informal instruction conveyed by the literate minority to the less educated majority, then they might extract much of value. On the other hand, if they ignore the fact that most authors were not consciously aiming at social control, or if they approach catechisms expecting contrasts between 'Anglican' or 'puritan' views, or major changes between one period and another, they may be disappointed. As we have seen, there were some differences of emphasis, but there was also a large measure of agreement among authors, even after 1640, on the virtues of honesty and charity towards one's neighbour and of abstaining from any form of violent or antisocial behaviour. The great majority of the authors in our sample (and probably the great majority of those outside it as well) seem to have tried to avoid controversy on those aspects of social or economic life, such as enclosure, engrossing, high prices, and rackrenting where active debate was being conducted in other fora. It was no more the task of the catechist to engender debate on such matters than it was to encourage controversy on matters of doctrine or worship or on politics. Wearing their other hats, as authors of sermons and treatises, and as advisers to the lay power, catechists might feel free, even duty-bound, to deliver trenchant criticism of those greedy cormorants battening onto those less prosperous than themselves; but as catechists their main enemies were ignorance and sin, not social problems.[249]

At the end of the last Commandment, some of those authors who had not already cited Christ's summary of the Decalogue, did so here.[250] Christ had referred to the first of his two commands—love God—as 'the first and great commandment'; and nothing that has been suggested in this chapter would suggest that catechists saw it otherwise. Nor has there been any sign that they felt there was any tension or competition between the two tables of the old Law, which lay down duties to God and man, respectively. Catechists saw the two tables as complementary but with God featuring prominently in both: as the episcopalian Marshall put it in 1679:

The two branches of love to God and man complete a Christian's duty, and are not to be separated. God must be loved above all things, and that for his own sake. A man's neighbour must be loved as himself, and that for God's sake.[251]

---

[249] This view may be overthrown or modified by further study, but it is one shared by Dr Durbin as a result of her survey of sixteenth-century English catechisms: 'Education by Catechism', 191.

[250] e.g. Calvin, *Catechisme*, 84; Nowell, *Catechisme*, 136–7; Lewis, *Catechism*, 56–8.

[251] Marshall, *Catechism*, 31; cf. also Nicholson's assertion that one of the king's duties to his subjects was to keep 'both tables': *Exposition*, 107.

Certainly catechists of all standpoints had a lot to say about Commandments five to ten, which affected the everyday lives of their charges more obviously than the first four. But, with a few exceptions such as Calvin, Nowell, and Wake who wrote more about the first table, most authors either devoted equal space to the two or slightly more overall to the six Commandments in the second table than the four in the first, for example the authors of the Westminster Larger Catechism devoted twenty-two pages to the first table, twenty-eight to the second, and Thomas Vincent, thirty-three to the first and fifty-five to the second.[252] The idea that for 'Anglicans' the second table was a touchstone for the first and for 'puritans' the other way round[253] thus receives little support from the run of catechisms in our sample.[254] In their catechetical writings, the 'godly' and the presbyterians certainly stressed that all worship must be dictated by God, not man, but they were no more anxious than episcopalians to encourage individuals to decide for themselves which forms of worship were divinely appointed and which were merely human 'will-worship'. Nor did they present a clear or strong view on the limits of political and ecclesiastical obedience to rulers like Charles I and Laud—another of McGee's criteria of puritan attitudes to the two tables; and the suggestion that puritans showed an exclusive concern for the welfare of their 'godly' neighbours—another of his criteria—is also not reflected in our sample. The zeal with which the 'godly' attacked idolatry, profaning the sabbath, and lewd behaviour and pastimes is sometimes evident in the works discussed above, but the extent to which that zeal was different from conformists' zeal is perhaps more a matter of temperature than a difference of kind.[255]

McGee's view that it was the Anglicans who thought that the essentials of religion were few and easy to master also does not tally with the catechetical evidence: simplicity was a factor of size and target group, not sectional opinion.[256] We have seen this in the way that the Creed was handled, and we can see the same in the case of the Decalogue. The point is made by the way in which the Ten Commandments were tackled by the 'godly' Elizabethan minister and the two later Stuart nonconformists in our sample who all composed a sequence of forms. Stephen Egerton did not include the Decalogue in the first four of his six forms; in the fifth he summarized it by using scriptural texts as a substitute; and in the sixth he had the text of Exodus 20

---

[252] These calculations are based on the total number of pages used to expound the Commandments rather than the number of questions asked; they can easily be checked by looking at the relevant sections of the catechisms cited here and over the last few paragraphs.

[253] McGee, *Godly Man*, 70, 91, 93–4, 244.

[254] Sherlock's comment (*Principles*, 60) that, while profanation of the sabbath must be tackled under the first table, the way in which the sabbath was spent was a matter of obedience under the fifth Commandment might appear to support McGee's thesis; but it was not very different from the point made in the Westminster Larger, 80 (answer 118).

[255] For the use of this distinction in general terms, see P. Collinson, *The Elizabethan Puritan Movement* (1967), 26–7.

[256] McGee, *Godly Man*, 103–4, 154. On the subject of relative 'easiness', see also below, pp. 472–5.

printed in full but without a single word of exposition. In his set of forms Benjamin Keach did not quote the Decalogue or expound it at length, though he did provide a little more information about its significance each time he moved to another, more advanced form, and intercalated these forms with verses on good behaviour, including ten four-line verses which paralleled the Ten Commandments. Isaac Watts expected a little more than this. He taught his first set of catechumens (aged 4 to 7 years in theory) that they had a duty to God and a duty to man. In the child's catechism (for those aged 8 to 12), the catechumen was taught that he must serve God by keeping all his Commandments, and the Decalogue was cited in an abbreviated form and in Christ's summary of it in the New Testament; a little later there was an account of the different types of sins to be avoided in a loose paraphrase of most of the Ten Commandments. Only when a student advanced to the age of 12 and was tackling the Westminster Shorter Catechism, with notes by Watts to explain the harder terms used in it, would he or she come up against a number of the features discussed in the last few pages: the full text of Exodus 20 divided into two tables, one vice representing many, each Commandment having a duty and a sin attached, and so on.[257] In short, at the elementary level, these three authors kept the meaning of the Commandments as simple as they could, at about the same level as that in the Prayer Book catechism. Perhaps the only difference between these authors' work and that of others in our sample was the willingness of Keach and Watts to try a variety of techniques to get the message across.[258]

As we saw at the start of this chapter, the Law was often regarded both as a means of showing sinful men their perilous position and as a guide to living a better life. The Law, said Nowell, was like a schoolmaster—a synonym in those days for a disciplinarian—who by regular indoctrination would certainly 'lead us the right way to Christ, by knowing of ourselves, and by repentance and faith'.[259] Catechists, however, had to make apparently contradictory statements: on the one hand, they had to insist that every one must try to keep the Law to the full; on the other, they had to point out that this was impossible. In our sample of catechisms a large number of authors closed their section on the Decalogue with remarks such as these: 'My good child, know this, that thou art not able to do these things of thy self, nor to walk in the commandments of God, and to serve him' (the Prayer Book catechism); since the Fall, 'no mere man … is able in this life perfectly to keep the commandments of God, but doth daily break them in thought, word, and deed' (the

---

[257] For the forms of Egerton, Keach, and Watts discussed here, see Appendix 2.

[258] Innovation in techniques of religious instruction was in general much more common by this date: see my *Religious Instruction in Early Modern England* (forthcoming).

[259] Nowell, *Catechisme*, 141; and id., *Institution*, sigs. Ci^{r-v}; and cf. Calvin, *Catechisme*, 89 (and 85–9); and Cartwright, 'Catechisme', sig. Aa5^r; and cf. above, n. 5.

Westminster catechisms).[260] Since the penalty for even one sin was death, the thinking catechumen might well have echoed Calvin's question at this point: 'Why doth God therefore require of us such an exquisite perfection as we be not able to reach unto?' Calvin here captured the same mood of pained incredulity that he had done at an earlier point of his catechism when discussing whether good works had a role to play in justification: 'Thou meanest not hereby that the good deeds of faithful men are to no purpose and unprofitable?'—'I mean nothing less', was the perplexing reply.[261] The combined effect of the doctrines of original sin and justification by faith might well have inclined catechumens to think that there was little point in even trying to obey the Commandments. How did Protestant catechists reconcile their insistence on trying to keep the Law with their view that it was not possible and that in any case good deeds were 'unprofitable'?

In their scholarly treatises and more advanced sermons, the theologians of the period had a number of answers to this problem, but at catechetical level the answers basically came down to two complementary ones: justification is by faith, though faith without works is dead; and although complete obedience to the Law is not possible, God does not demand more than man can achieve and provides help to the faithful. As we saw in the last chapter, a number of our seventeenth-century authors set their teachings in a framework of the covenant of grace, the great advantage of which from a pastoral standpoint was that the faithful in the new covenant were still bound by the Law, but the successful keeping of that Law was no longer a condition of the covenant of grace as it had been of the covenant of works. Christ, the second Adam, had paid the price for the breaking of the first covenant, and the task of the faithful in the second which he had mediated with God was to believe and obey as far, with the help of further grace, as they could.[262] Let us look in more detail at the way in which these two doctrines were presented in the works in our sample.

The position of our authors on the first point was as follows: works did not justify, but they were the inevitable product of a saving faith. Good deeds were the fruits of faith, it was regularly stated; and just as a healthy tree brings forth healthy fruit, so a lively faith brings forth good works; a dead faith cannot produce good fruit.[263] We must do good works, said a variety of authors, not to deserve salvation by them, but to glorify God and show our love to him, to make our election sure, and to win others

---

[260] Prayer Book catechism, 784–5 (in 1549 the word used was 'son', from 1552 'child'); Westminster Larger, 111 (answer 149); and Westminster Shorter, 30–1 (answer 82); and cf. Nicholson, *Exposition*, 125–6; Sherlock, *Principles*, 41; Comber, *Church-catechism*, 22–3 (some exponents of the Prayer Book form developed this point during their account of the opening question and answer on keeping God's Commandments, e.g. Wake, *Principles*, 76–7). Also cf. Calvin, *Catechisme*, 86–7; Heidelberg Catechism, 349; Dering–More, *Catechisme*, sig. B1ʳ; Egerton, 'Familiar manner', 39; and Ball, *Catechisme*, 88.

[261] Calvin, *Catechisme*, 87, 45–6.   [262] See above, pp. 401–4, 407–9, 414–19.

[263] Calvin, *Catechisme*, 46–7, 51; Nowell, *Catechisme*, 143–4; Egerton, 'Briefe method', 9; Elton, *Forme*, sig. D1ʳ; Nicholes, *Catechisme*, 22; Westminster Larger, 39 (answer 73).

to Christ.[264] It may be added that those in our sample who urged the value of examining one's works as a means of testing if one was elect did not give this undue prominence: in the cases of Dering and More, Paget, Egerton, and Elton this was only one of three or four reasons, and took second or third place to other motives such as the glorifying of God's name and winning others to God; and in Hill's exposition of the Prayer Book catechism, making our election sure was almost swallowed up by the variety of reasons for doing good works which he offered under each of four headings: doing good works for God, for ourselves (to make our election sure, because they are the way to glory, and for the reward thereof), for God's children, and for the enemies of our faith.[265]

In the catechisms in our sample, faith was linked to justification in that the sincere believer is for Christ's sake made righteous in God's eyes; but it also leads to sanctification in that, with the help of grace, it persuades the faithful to try to kill the old Adam in them and be more like the saints in heaven.[266] Our justification is not by our good works, Calvin told his catechumens, but good works spring from faith as water from a fountain; although there can be no merit in our 'godly, dutiful doings', justification cannot be severed from good works, echoed Nowell.[267] Works done by those received into favour by God which are performed through grace, in faith, and by virtue of the Holy Spirit are acceptable unto God, Calvin continued, but such works are accepted only because of God's goodness, not any worthiness that makes them estimable in his eyes.[268] Calvin's lead was followed by some of our Elizabethan authors, and a century later, in effect, by Marshall when he wrote that just as faith without works is dead, so works without faith cannot please God.[269] At the Last Judgement, catechumens were told, true believers would be told from hypocrites and unbelievers by their actions; their fate, in Protestant eyes, did not depend directly or indirectly on those actions, but they were a means by which God could distinguish those who had glorified his name, repented of their sins, and tried to obey his laws from those who had not.[270]

The only substantial exceptions to the general pattern of trying to explain the link between faith and works were the Westminster catechisms whose authors chose not to devote space to the role of works or to the assertion that faith without works was dead. This omission must have been deliberate, since in the Westminster Confession (which in general was followed quite closely at this stage of the Larger Catechism on the *ordo salutis*) there was a whole chapter on 'good works', in which they were

---

[264] Dering–More, *Catechisme*, sig. B6[r]; Paget, *Questions*, sigs. C3[v]–4[r]; Egerton, 'Briefe method', 10–11; Elton, *Forme*, sig. D1[v]; Hill, *Principles*, sigs. B3[r]–4[r]; and cf. Nowell, *Catechisme*, 143–4, 179–82; Marshall, *Catechism*, 7.

[265] As last note.   [266] See above, pp. 324–6, 340–2, 398–402.

[267] Calvin, *Catechisme*, 45–6, 51; Nowell, *Catechisme*, 176, 180.   [268] Calvin, *Catechisme*, 48–9.

[269] Nowell, *Catechisme*, 181–2; Dering–More, *Catechisme*, sig. B6[r]; Paget, *Questions*, sig. C3[v]; Egerton, 'Brief method', 9–10; Hieron, *Doctrine*, 578; Marshall, *Catechism*, 7.

[270] Elton, *Forme*, sigs. F3[v]–4[r]; and see above, pp. 342–5.

described as 'the fruits and evidences of a true and lively faith'.[271] The authors of the Westminster catechisms decided to put their stress instead on the idea of man's 'duty' to obey the moral law: the Law shows those in the covenant of grace how much they are bound to Christ, and provokes them to express their gratitude by conforming to the divine rule of obedience.[272] At the end of their treatment of the Decalogue, the same authors said that to escape the curse due for our breach of the Law, God requires of us repentance, faith, and the diligent use of the outward means provided (Word, sacraments, and prayer).[273] It was not that the authors of the Westminster catechisms were against the idea of men doing their best to keep the Law: as we have seen in previous sections of this chapter, the authors of the Westminster Larger Catechism were among the most inventive in teasing out the number of different sins to be avoided and duties to be performed that might be found in each Commandment. But at no stage were these duties described as 'good' works; nor was much space devoted to the 'active' vocabulary of applying Christ's benefits to ourselves (which we have encountered in previous chapters), or to the idea of using one's emotional reactions to the performance of duties as a litmus-test of one's election; the faithful were urged to try to 'discern in themselves' not emotions but 'those graces to which the promises of life are made'.[274] This avoidance of linking faith and works was probably due in part to the fact that the Westminster divines were using a federal framework which treated the faithful as already saved, and to the fact that these authors were nearer the 'unconditional' end of the spectrum of those who adopted covenantal teaching, the end which stressed the role of God and Christ rather than man.[275] But one might also speculate that they may have been worried at the connotations of merit or possible reward in the use of the term 'good' applied to works, and perhaps worried also at the excess of zeal among those using 'active' vocabulary or urging their charges to look inside themselves to see if their sorrow for sin was piercing and their joy in good works transforming.[276]

Certainly it may be suggested that some of the authors in our sample were occasionally at risk of being carried away by their enthusiasm for works. At the end of both the full-length and condensed version of Nowell's catechism, the schoolmaster tells the student to bend all his care and thought to following the 'rule and prescribed form of godly life' which he had been taught in the catechism; the student promises to do his utmost, with God's help, to 'bring forth plentiful fruits of godliness to be bestowed and laid up in the barn and granary of the kingdom of heaven'; and the master concludes by saying:

---

[271] Schaff, *Creeds*, 633–6 (Westminster Confession, ch. 16).

[272] Westminster Larger, 52–6 (answers 91–7); Westminster Shorter, 18 (answer 39). For an isolated reference to good works, see the former, 39 (answer 73).

[273] Westminster Larger, '110–11' [*recte* 118–19] (answer 153); Westminster Shorter, 31–2 (answer 85).

[274] Westminster Larger, 45 (answer 80).   [275] See above, pp. 406–9, 413–14.

[276] See above, pp. 321–2, 390–3; and following paragraphs.

Do so, my child; and doubt not, but as thou hast by God's guiding, conceived this mind and will, so thou shalt find and have the issue and end of this thy godly study and endeavour, such as thou desirest and lookest for, that is, most good and happy.[277]

Similarly at the end of his catechism and the accompanying list of duties, the 'godly' Samuel Hieron offered this 'sum of all':

What is the brief sum of the whole duty of man?
To fear God and keep his commandments. Eccles. 12: 13.
What is the reward of all?
He that doeth these things shall never be moved. Ps. 15: 5.[278]

In a long section (in a relatively short form) on inducements to good works, Stephen Egerton told his catechumens that there were very great rewards for such works, especially in the life to come, though this was not from merit, but from God's free grace alone; and the term 'reward' was also used by William Hill as a motive for doing good works, as we saw above.[279] In other catechisms in our sample, by Ball and Gouge, there are examples of that 'active' vocabulary we looked at in previous chapters—the faithful Christian must labour to grow in grace, he must labour to get Christ—which made it sound as if effort alone might achieve that end.[280] Of course, in all these cases, the author was giving the credit for any achievement or good work of man to God without whose intervention such action would not have been possible; but in all these cases there was also an implied connection between effort and reward.

This point is worth making in that it is not the 'godly' activists or experimental predestinarians but the later seventeenth-century 'Anglicans' who have been accused of straying towards saying that God would reward a man's efforts, and specifically that man could justify himself by his efforts to keep the Law. In *The Rise of Moralism* C. F. Allison has argued that authors like Henry Hammond, Herbert Thorndike, Jeremy Taylor, and George Bull became so concerned with the rise of antinomianism, which they attributed to the erroneous theories of justification then prevailing, that they were led to place less stress on the gratuitous nature of grace and more on holy living, which for Taylor, says Allison, became 'the only hope of justification'.[281] Despite Allison's obviously deep antipathy to what he sees as a new teaching—the doctrine of 'the lowered market' as he calls it—he has often been followed. Professor McGee, for example, has suggested that puritan critics might be pardoned for thinking that 'Anglicans' taught that works could justify.[282] Allison's book has a number of useful

---

[277] Nowell, *Catechisme*, 219–20, and id., *Institution*, sigs. Hiv^v–v^r.

[278] S. Hieron, *The doctrine of the beginning of Christ* (1626), sig. C7^v.

[279] Egerton, 'Briefe method', 12; Hill, *Principles*, sig. B3^v.

[280] Ball, *Catechisme*, 88; Gouge, *Principles*, 68–9, 71–2, 74–8.

[281] C. F. Allison, *The Rise of Moralism: The Proclamation of the Gospel from Hooker to Baxter* (1966), *passim*, but esp. 184–6.

[282] McGee, *Godly Man*, 208–9; and cf. H. Davies, *Worship and Theology in England*, ii. *From Andrewes to Baxter* (Princeton, 1975), 127, 179–80, 183–4; and iii. *From Watts and Wesley to Maurice* (Princeton/London, 1961), 67, 72–3; D. D. Wallace, *Puritans and Predestination: Grace in English Protestant Theology*

insights on the contemporary debate on the technical matter of the formal cause of justification, and on variations within Taylor's writings. But he also seems at times to have relied heavily on certain genres of writing rather than a full range of contemporary religious writing; and he also relies on the 'slippery slope' method of argument (popular in the early modern period, but less so today), that if A disagrees with B he must inevitably slide rapidly downhill into some blatant heresy—in the case of the later Stuart 'Anglicans' a return to justification by works. Allison chooses not to consider the genuine worries which some contemporaries had about the orthodox Calvinist *ordo* which put justification before any form of sorrow or repentance, or about an interpretation of justification which put such a stress on Christ's righteousness as the source of man's forgiveness that it seemed to make any attempt at human righteousness superfluous. Instead he focuses on the counter-charges made by double predestinarians that in putting repentance and faith before justification 'moralists' were giving man's response to grace precedence over God's will and power.[283] An interpretation such as Allison's which plays down the emphasis in pre-1640 publications on men's need to try to keep the Law, and then suggests that for post-1640 'Anglicans' works were 'the only hope of justification' is clearly swinging from one extreme to another.

A more measured response is that of Alan Clifford who has suggested recently that the later Caroline divines, by reacting against the orthodox Calvinist position of the early seventeenth century, restored the teaching of the first generation of reformers in several respects. 'If some of their "antisolifidian" expressions were excessive', he writes, 'many of their insights were anticipated by … reformers' like Calvin and Cranmer who 'were anxious to maintain that "faith is pregnant with good works" '. An author like John Tillotson, Clifford feels, was able to produce a middle way between Calvinist orthodoxy, on the one hand, and Roman and Socinian heterodoxy, on the other. On the one hand, Tillotson stressed the conditional nature of justification, that man must believe and that this faith must contain obedience to God's will (through regenerating grace and union with Christ), but, on the other hand, he did not detract from 'the exclusive, meritorious mediation of Christ'.[284] If we were to attempt a modified form of the Allison thesis, to the effect that many early Stuart authors stressed the totally gratuitous nature of grace, while some later Stuart ones *in addition* put a greater stress on holy living as an antidote to antinomianism, that might fit the broader base of evidence better.

Certainly in our sample of catechisms there is no evidence to support the original Allison thesis, partly because catechisms were not considered the proper place to discuss technical issues such as the formal cause of justification, and partly because it

---

1525–1695 (Chapel Hill, NC, 1982), 99, 127, 162, 197–8, 228–9; and McGrath, *Iustitia Dei*, ii. 105–9, 229–30; and see below, n. 291.

[283] See above, pp. 400–2.
[284] Clifford, *Atonement and Justification*, 174–9, 184–5, 212–15, 231–5.

is far from clear that most later Stuart episcopalians would have accepted the belief in the justifying value of works which Allison claims to have detected. From what we have in the sample by later Stuart authors, we may deduce that, like Calvin and Nowell, they thought that good works were the inevitable fruit of a lively faith, but they either carefully avoided any statement that might imply that works contributed to salvation or actively refuted the idea. We may cite the comments made by Thomas Marshall as an example of the former, and William Wake's as an example of the latter. Marshall incorporated the covenants of works and grace into his exposition of the Prayer Book form, but stressed that while the condition of the former (the covenant with Adam and through him all men) was perfect obedience, which was impossible for man, that of the latter (through Christ with all believers) was faith, which with divine help was possible. But works are also 'necessarily required' in the covenant of grace, not only to glorify God and edify my neighbour but also to prove my faith, since faith without works is dead, and works without faith cannot please God.[285] Enlarging on the answer in the Prayer Book form about the catechumen's commitment in baptism to keep God's Commandments all the days of his life, Wake asks: 'Do you then expect to be saved by virtue of your own good works?'. The reply is: 'God forbid: on the contrary I am persuaded that when I shall have done all that I can, I shall be but "an unprofitable servant" (Luke 17: 10)'. Wake did believe that obedience was essential to salvation in the sense that it was part of the true faith by which men were justified; but he was adamant that men could not be saved 'by virtue of' their good works. God, says his catechumen, will reward me when I try to keep his Commandments 'not according to my deserts, but according to his own mercy and promises to us in Jesus Christ'.[286]

It is true that in his short catechism Jeremy Taylor wrote that the commandments of Christ 'are many, but easy',[287] but this statement should be viewed not in the light of a 'lowered market' but of the difference between the commands in the two Testaments. In the New Testament, wrote Hammond in his catechism, Christ was demanding more than in the Old: love your enemies as well as your friends, avoid adulterous thoughts as well as adultery, and so on; but, he argued, the burden is made lighter, because the weight of the 'unprofitable' Jewish ceremonies is lifted, and because of 'the greater revelations, and effusion of grace ... under Christ'.[288] Sherlock echoed this in his catechism: the Gospel is clearer, greater, and communicates more grace than the Law of Moses.[289] Salvation was not being made a soft option, and the required level of human effort was not being scaled down: it was merely that a clearer law backed by more grace is relatively easier for man to follow than the old one. As indicated at the end of the last chapter, some later Stuart episcopalians were nearer the 'conditional' end of the spectrum of those authors who adopted the covenant of

---

[285] Marshall, *Catechism*, 7, 53.   [286] Wake, *Principles*, 76.   [287] Taylor, 'Catechism', 5.
[288] Hammond, *Practical catechisme*, 115–16.   [289] Sherlock, *Principles*, 27.

grace as a framework for catechetical teaching: men and women in the covenant had to do their best, since faith without works was dead. But it would be a close race between authors like Nicholson and Wake and those like Egerton and Hieron or the authors of the Westminster Larger Catechism as to who included the longest lists of suitable works or duties for the faithful to perform.[290]

Jeremy Taylor has also often been held up (with Richard Allestree, probable author of the later Stuart best-seller, *The Whole duty of man*) as an example of the 'holy living' approach to religious life, partly because of his own best-selling treatise with that title, and partly because of another work called *The great exemplar* in which he described the life of Christ not in the conventional soteriological terms but in terms of the moral example he set for others to follow.[291] However, it was the 'godly' Samuel Hieron in his scriptural catechism of *c*.1604 who several decades earlier had raised the idea of the 'whole duty of man' being to 'fear God and keep his Commandments', and said that the 'reward' for this was that 'he that doeth these things shall never be moved'.[292] Moreover, the one author in our sample of catechisms who regularly held up the life of Christ as a model of conduct was not an episcopalian, but the Independent Isaac Watts. In his simplest form, Watts wrote of Christ coming down from heaven to save us and to teach us how to obey God's law; in the third one, he said that Christ set men a pattern of holiness by his own practice; in his historical catechism Watts told his students that Christ gave us a perfect example of piety; and in a note following the questions on the three offices of Christ in the Westminster Shorter Catechism, he added 'I wish there had been something added here concerning Christ's office as an example or pattern of holiness'.[293] Watts's concern may have been based on educational rather than theological priority: the realization that children responded better to stories of Christ's life and to identification with 'Gentle Jesus, meek and mild' than to abstract doctrines—a point which was certainly made in aids to Bible study prepared for children at that time.[294] But Watts's forms also make the point that an emphasis on behaving like Christ was not an 'Anglican' monopoly.

Keeping God's commands was, therefore, an important element in the catechetical teaching of authors of all shades. The reasons given at catechetical level for doing those works might vary: at the outset of our period and at the end in episcopalian forms, the reason tended to be that works were part of a lively faith; for some in the predestinarian camp, works were (also) a means of applying Christ's benefits to ourselves and proving our election; and for the authors of the Westminster catechisms,

---

[290] See above, pp. 211, 390–2, 416–18, 431, 461–2, 464.

[291] Allison, *Rise of Moralism*, chs. 3–4; and cf. C. J. Sommerville, *Popular Religion in Restoration England* (Gainesville, Fla., 1977), 38–9.

[292] Hieron, *Doctrine*, sig. C7ᵛ.

[293] Watts, 'First catechism', 8–9; id., 'Children's catechism', 18; id., 'Historical catechism', 54–5; id., *Assembly's catechism*, 15.

[294] See above, pp. 232–3, 271–3, and my *Print and Protestantism* (forthcoming).

good deeds were the duties of those in the covenant of grace. But what of the warnings to catechumens that they would never be able to keep the Law properly? Here we turn to the second of the two doctrinal points commonly used by our authors: God did not ask more than could be achieved, and to those who asked for it he provided help.

What was needed in keeping the Law, catechumens were told, was not perfection but sincerity and diligence. My duty to God, according to the Prayer Book catechism, is to fear and love God with all my heart, with all my mind, with all my soul, and with all my strength.[295] According to Calvin, God requires nothing but what we know we must do, and if we try diligently to frame our lives according to his Law, 'then albeit we be far from being able to attain unto the perfection thereof, yet the Lord will not lay to our charge that default or lack of doing the same as our duty requireth'.[296] The authors of the Heidelberg Catechism spoke of the need for an 'earnest purpose' to live according to the Law, and Nowell of men making an 'earnest endeavour' to 'travel toward the highest uprightness'; on other occasions, Nowell wrote that God will save all who put their trust in him and try to do his works, and that the godly must try to live free of faults 'so much as they are able to do'.[297] 'The child of God ought, may, and usually doth walk according to the Law sincerely', wrote the Calvinist Ball; although he cannot keep the Law to the extent God requires, he should strive 'with diligence and singleness of heart' to resist sin, and 'look for the assistance of God's Spirit, and labour to grow in grace'.[298] 'The law of God expects from us in this life, not absolute perfection, but such a perfection as is to be had in this life', Nicholson told his parishioners in the 1650s, and at the tail end of the same century, Wake echoed previous authors in urging sincere, hearty endeavour and a zealous and honest heart in trying to keep all God's commands.[299] The fact that Calvin and 'godly' authors like Nowell and Ball tried to reassure the nervous or faint-hearted among their charges by telling them that God would not lay to their charge the failure to do their duty completely is another riposte to the charge that later Stuart 'Anglicans' were deviating from the norm by adopting an approach to salvation along the lines of 'do your best, and God will be merciful'.[300] Calvin and episcopalians like Hammond, Marshall, and Wake were not arguing that obedience to the Law would save a person—only Christ could do that—but that an inevitable failure to keep the Law to the letter was not an excuse for not trying; God would not demand more than his faithful could perform.[301]

Further reassurance was provided by statements to the effect that God would send his grace to help the faithful try to keep the Law. If we return to the section in

---

[295] Prayer Book catechism, 784–5.   [296] Calvin, *Catechisme*, 87.

[297] Heidelberg Catechism, 349; Nowell, *Catechisme*, 118, 121, 140, 143–4, 171, 219–20.

[298] Ball, *Catechisme*, 88. On the importance to the godly of sincerity in trying to keep the Law, see also von Rohr, *Covenant of Grace*, 182–5.

[299] Nicholson, *Exposition*, 125; Wake, *Principles*, 76, 78.

[300] See previous notes.   [301] See above, nn. 285–8, 296.

the Prayer Book form, we find that catechumens are told that they could not keep God's Commandments 'without his special grace, which thou must learn at all times to call for by diligent prayer', a point picked up by various expositors of that form.[302] Calvin had described the Law as a target set up by God 'to the end, that we every one, according to the grace wherewith God hath endued us, might continually ... walk towards it'.[303] A century later Boughen would encourage his catechumens by citing Phil. 4: 13: 'I can do all things in God that strengtheneth me';[304] and Nicholson would quote the same text and also Paul's experience (in 2 Cor. 12: 7–9) that 'after he had received "sufficient grace", he confesseth that Christ's "yoke was easy, and his burden light" '. Without grace, men in their natural condition could only go so far in keeping the Law, but with Christ 'they may go far, they may walk uprightly and sincerely in this way', said Nicholson. Like a cart-wheel 'that creaks, and complains all the way it goes, under the smallest burden', but with just a drop of oil 'runs on merrily, and without any noise', so a sinner groaning under the burden of God's law, 'being supplied with this holy oil, runs on with comfort, and murmurs not'.[305] Wake taught his catechumens to say that 'It is the grace of God which must work in me, "both to will and to do according to his good pleasure". (Phil. 2: 13)'. When it was established that, even when assisted by the Holy Spirit, the catechumen could not keep God's Commandments fully, he was asked a trick question:

Will not this undervalue the grace of the Holy Spirit by which we are sanctified?
Not at all: forasmuch as I ascribe to that the glory of all the good I do; and take to myself the shame of whatsoever is evil, or defective in me.[306]

At the end of the day, there was a large measure of agreement that it was not possible for fallen man to keep the Law by his own unaided efforts, but that he must nevertheless make the attempt as part and parcel of his faith, and could expect God's help. It is this concern to keep a balance between the stress on human sinfulness and the prospect of divine assistance, together with the teaching on assurance and the last things that we have examined in previous chapters, which makes it hard to fit this sample of catechisms neatly into Delumeau's 'evangelism of fear' and 'Western guilt culture'.[307] While our authors were adamant about the evils of sin and the need to try to overcome temptation, they were also anxious to reassure their charges that all was not lost and that they were not alone. Divine help was available through the use of the means which God had made available—Word, prayer, and sacraments,

---

[302] Prayer Book catechism, 784–5; Hill, *Principles*, sigs. A5ᵛ–6ʳ; Nicholes, *Catechisme*, 45; Marshall, *Catechism*, 8; Comber, *Church-catechism*, 22–3.

[303] Calvin, *Catechisme*, 89; cf. Hieron: 'our sufficiency' to do good comes only from God: *Doctrine*, 578.

[304] Boughen also explained why, when the Decalogue was read out in Prayer Book services, the congregation prayed God to 'incline our hearts to keep this law': *Exposition*, 58–9 and 80–3.

[305] Nicholson, *Exposition*, 125–8.   [306] Wake, *Principles*, 76–7.

[307] For Delumeau's own thoughts on the limitations of the 'evangelism of fear', see his 'Prescription and Reality', in *Conscience and Casuistry in Early Modern Europe*, ed. E. Leites (Cambridge, 1988), 134–58.

and it is to the last two of these that, like many early modern catechists before us, we now turn. The linking question and answer between the sections on the Decalogue and the Lord's Prayer in the Heidelberg Catechism may serve as a conclusion to this chapter:

Why, then, doth God so strictly enjoin upon us the Ten Commandments, since in this life no one can keep them?
First, that all our life long we may learn more and more to know our sinful nature, and so the more earnestly seek forgiveness of sins and righteousness in Christ; secondly, that we may continually strive and beg from God the grace of the Holy Ghost, so as to become more and more changed into the image of God, till we attain finally to full perfection after this life.[308]

[308] Heidelberg Catechism, 349.

11

The Lord's Prayer

THE Lord's Prayer was not only the shortest but also probably the most frequently reproduced of the staple formulae of early modern English catechizing. It was short enough, and deemed sufficiently important, to be inscribed or printed on hornbooks, abecedaries, and battledores; used as an exercise in handwriting, and embroidered on samplers; and, together with the Apostles' Creed and the Ten Commandments, painted on boards or directly onto the walls of many, perhaps most, early modern churches.[1] As a prayer, it was also repeated in the regular morning and evening services of the church and in holy communion, and in the rites of passage and the churching of women; and it was almost certainly used regularly in school prayers and in those households which held domestic worship.[2] It would be surprising therefore if a high proportion of children and adults in Elizabethan and Stuart times had not at some stage been taught the English version of the Lord's Prayer or grown familiar with it through some other means, just as many of their predecessors in England or peer groups in contemporary Catholic states had learnt the Paternoster. Many authors of short or medium-length catechisms, including a few in our sample, did not even bother to include the full text of the Lord's Prayer. The great majority of catechists were, however, very anxious that their charges should understand what this prayer meant and how it should be used, and so most forms contain a few questions and answers or a few pages (according to size) on the purpose of prayer in general and the Lord's Prayer in particular.

To pray was to call on God, said a wide variety of the authors in our sample,[3] though a few used more evocative terms in their initial definitions: 'a familiar speech with God', 'a pouring out of the soul before the Lord', a 'humble, hearty and holy

---

[1] A. W. Tuer, *The History of the Horn Book* (2 vols.; 1896); V. E. Neuberg, *Popular Education in Eighteenth Century England* (1971), 58–9; A. Colby, *Samplers Yesterday and Today* (1964), 106, 112, 170; A. Sebba, *Samplers: Five Centuries of a Gentle Craft* (1979), 52–5; and on ABCs and Commandment boards, see above, pp. 172–8, 253. I propose to return to this subject in more detail in *Religious Instruction in Early Modern England*.

[2] Brightman, *English Rite*, i. 132–3, 146–7, 156–7, 162–3; ii. 705–7, 743–5, 872–3, 882–3. Relatively little is known about the content as opposed to the existence of school and domestic devotions, but on the use of the Prayer Book catechism (which included the Lord's Prayer) in both locations, see Ch. 4 above.

[3] Calvin, *Catechisme*, 92; Egerton, 'Briefe method', 13; Cartwright, 'Catechisme', sig. Aa8ʳ; Ball, *Catechisme*, 76; Nicholes, *Catechisme*, 45; Marshall, *Catechism*, 32; Wake, *Principles*, 128–9.

request', and 'the elevation of the mind to God'.[4] Some catechists distinguished between two, three, or four aspects of prayer, such as the confession of sins, petition or supplication, intercession, and thanksgiving.[5] The authors of the Westminster catechisms, for example, offered a tripartite definition of prayer: an offering up of our desires, with a confession of sins, and thankful acknowledgement of God's mercies.[6] But most authors, like Calvin and the authors of the Prayer Book and Heidelberg catechisms, chose to spend less time on defining prayer than on describing its role in the life of the faithful and the correct way to set about it.

Like careful attention to the Word and the correct use of the sacraments with which it was frequently teamed, regular prayer was presented not only as a duty (commanded in the first table of the Law and elsewhere in the scriptures),[7] but also as a means to strengthen faith[8] and to advance the process of sanctification. In a variety of catechetical forms, usually those in which the subject of prayer was tackled immediately after the section on the Decalogue, the function of prayer was stated as being the means by which individual catechumens actively sought divine grace to enable them to keep the Law.[9] Most exponents of the Prayer Book catechism, for example, picked up the point that catechumens 'must learn at all times to call' for God's 'special grace' to help them to walk in the Commandments of God, and to desire God 'to send his grace unto me, and to all people, that we may worship him, serve him, and obey him, as we ought to do'.[10] We must be 'especially concerned' to seek God's help through prayer, wrote Wake, since it was 'by the special grace of the Holy Spirit; which he never denies to any Christian who heartily prays for it, and duly improves that portion of it, which God had before bestowed upon him' that we are enabled to live according to the Law.[11] A stress on seeking grace through prayer was completely in line with that in the services and especially the collects in the Book of Common Prayer, such as for the first, eleventh, and seventeenth Sundays after Trinity, and in keeping also with the thrust of article ten of the Thirty-nine Articles.[12]

The authors of some catechisms did not have the time or did not feel it necessary to provide a list of the dos and don'ts of praying correctly, but among those who

---

[4] Perkins, *Foundation*, 8; Hieron, *Doctrine*, 579 (citing 1 Sam. 1: 15, and Ps. 62: 8); Elton, *Forme*, sig. E5^r; Wake, *Principles*, 129.

[5] Perkins, *Foundation*, 8; Egerton, 'Briefe method', 13; Ball, *Catechisme*, 76; Nicholes, *Catechisme*, 45; Hammond, *Practical catechisme*, 222–3; Marshall, *Catechism*, 40; Vincent, *Catechism*, 241.

[6] Westminster Larger, 142 (answer 178); Westminster Shorter, 36 (answer 98).

[7] e.g. Nowell, *Catechisme*, 183–4; Elton, *Forme*, sigs. E5^{r-v}; Mayer, *Catechisme*, sigs. C6^{r-v}; Isham, *Catechism*, 51.

[8] Dering–More, *Catechisme*, sig. B6^v; Perkins, *Foundation*, 7–8; Hieron, *Doctrine*, 579; Elton, *Forme*, sig. E5^v; Ball, *Catechisme*, 75–7, 79; Hill, *Principles*, sigs. C1^{r-v}, C5^r; Nicholes, *Catechisme*, 64–5.

[9] Prayer Book catechism, 784–7; Heidelberg Catechism, 349–50; and see the end of Ch. 10 above.

[10] Comber, *Church-catechism*, 23; Sherlock, *Principles*, 41; Williams, *Exposition*, 44.

[11] Wake, *Principles*, 129–30.

[12] e.g. Brightman, *English Rite*, ii. 462–3, 498–9, 520–1, 664–5; J. A. Devereux, 'Reformed Doctrine in the Collects of the First "Book of Common Prayer" ', *Harvard Theological Review*, 58 (1965), 49–54; Schaff, *Creeds*, 493–4.

did, including a substantial number in our sample, there was almost universal agreement on what these were. On the negative side, prayer was not to be directed to saints or angels, the dead, or 'holy men' in heaven, or the Virgin Mary; nor was it to be performed in an unfamiliar tongue, as the old Paternoster had been; nor was it to be based on our own 'fancies' or 'fantasies'.[13] On the positive side, prayer had to be made in faith and in a mood of contrition; it had to be heartfelt and persistent; it had to be directed to God, through Christ, and based on what God wanted or what the Holy Spirit indicated to us.[14] Given the anti-Catholic context in which much English catechizing took place, it is not surprising to find the condemnation of praying to the saints and of rote repetition of prayers, especially in a 'foreign' language, and the corresponding insistence on praying only to God, through Christ: this was in line with the fear of idolatry and concern for correct forms of address and worship exhibited by catechists when discussing the first table of the Commandments.[15] Perhaps more interesting are the prerequisites for prayer and the approved content specified by these authors. Faith was one obvious prerequisite, but one of which a variety of authors saw fit to remind their pupils: catechumens should pray with assurance, through faith, that though they were unworthy of it, their prayers would be heard and their sins pardoned.[16] They also needed to pray with an awareness of their miserable condition and their need of divine assistance, and with an earnest desire for help; and they must forbear praying if they were not in love and charity with their neighbours or already endeavouring to live according to God's will.[17]

A number of authors also stressed that prayer must come from the heart, and that mental concentration was needed rather than just reliance on memory.[18] 'The petition of the lips, without the desire of the heart, may be accounted prayer by men,' wrote Vincent, 'but it is not acceptable prayer unto God.'[19] Few went as far as

[13] e.g. Calvin, *Catechisme*, 92, 101; Nowell, *Catechisme*, 184–5; Dering–More, *Catechisme*, sig. B6ᵛ; Wallis, *Explanation*, 44.

[14] Calvin, *Catechisme*, 92–102; Nowell, *Catechisme*, 184–90 (the section on prayer in Nowell's *Institution* is much shorter); Dering–More, *Catechisme*, sig. B6ᵛ; Paget, *Questions*, sigs. D6ᵛ–7ᵛ; Heidelberg Catechism, 350; Egerton, 'Briefe method', 13–14; Elton, *Forme*, sigs. E6ʳ–7ᵛ; Palmer, *Endeavour*, 33; Gouge, *Principles*, 107–9; Westminster Larger, 142–6 (answers 179–85); Hill, *Principles*, sigs. C5ʳ⁻ᵛ; Mayer, *Catechisme*, sigs. C6ᵛ–7ʳ; Comber, *Church-catechism*, 23; Marshall, *Catechism*, 32; Wake, *Principles*, 130–1.

[15] Devereux, 'Reformed Doctrine in the Collects', 55–6; Calvin, *Catechisme*, 92–4, 98, 100; Virel, *Treatise*, 89–93; Elton, *Forme*, sigs. E5ᵛ–6ʳ; Vincent, *Catechism*, 242–4; Marshall, *Catechism*, 32; Wake, *Principles*, 128, 133; and see above, pp. 431–8.

[16] Calvin, *Catechisme*, 98–9; Heidelberg Catechism, 350; Hill, *Principles*, sig. C5ʳ; Elton, *Forme*, sigs. E5ᵛ; Mayer, *Catechisme*, sig. C5ᵛ–6ʳ; Hammond, *Practical catechisme*, 228, 239; Vincent, *Catechism*, 244; Marshall, *Catechism*, 32; Williams, *Exposition*, 44; Isham, *Catechism*, 55–6; Wake, *Principles*, 130; and see below for catechists' treatment of 'Amen'.

[17] Heidelberg Catechism, 350; Nowell, *Catechisme*, 187–8; Ball, *Catechisme*, 76; Hill, *Principles*, sig. C5ᵛ; Palmer, *Endeavour*, 34; Hammond, *Practical catechisme*, 227–8; Marshall, *Catechism*, 32; Keach, 'Youth', 114.

[18] Calvin, *Catechisme*, 95; Virel, *Treatise*, 188; Hammond, *Practical catechisme*, 228.

[19] Vincent, *Catechism*, 241; and cf. Marshall, *Catechism*, 32; and Comber, *Church-catechism*, 23.

Nowell, in the original version of his catechism, when he spoke of the need for hearts to be 'sore grieved with feeling of our need and poverty' and 'burn with great desire of deliverance from that grief, and of God's help', or as far as Ball, who wrote of confessing sins in prayer with 'grief, hatred, and shame' of our sin and with 'broken and contrite hearts'.[20] But we find nearly a dozen different authors in our sample who stressed the need for fervency in prayer, or talked of 'craving', 'earnest desire', and 'zeal'.[21]

Perseverance was another quality often stressed by authors in our sample: God would give his grace only to those who 'earnestly and without ceasing' seek it; we must persist, be constant and continual in our prayers, faint not, but persevere.[22] Persistence naturally led some authors to discuss how often their charges should pray. The priority given to participating in public worship by conformist episcopalians in our sample was arguably stronger than in the form of a 'godly' author like Elton, but the divide was not sharp. Mayer suggested six special times for prayer: now (not later); at appointed times of public worship; every morning and evening; mealtimes; in times of trouble; and every day, at some hour other than those already indicated; and Hammond distinguished between prayer of the heart, public prayer (in the church or family), and private prayer (by husband and wife together, or individually).[23] If a Christian had the opportunity and the leisure to do so, said Wake, he should come 'every day to the public prayers of the church';

> but if this cannot be done, he must at least, every day, without fail, pray to God in private, morning and evening; and, if he has a family, he should every day, at some convenient time, pray with that also, in order to the better keeping up a sense of religion in it.[24]

But although a number of 'godly', presbyterian, or nonconformist authors said little or nothing about congregational prayer at the outset, at the point where they were defining the nature of prayer, a number at a later stage indicated that prayer 'more especially belongeth to the members of the church militant', that men should not be content to pray in private only but 'must use both public and private prayer', and 'diligently attend to the seasons allotted to public prayer in the public congregation'.[25] The appropriate gestures and physical position to be adopted during such prayers were raised by very few authors in the sample, but the orthodox Calvinist

[20] Nowell, *Catechisme*, 187; Ball, *Catechisme*, 26.

[21] Calvin, *Catechisme*, 95; Nowell, *Catechisme*, 188; Ball, *Catechisme*, 76, 79; Westminster Larger, 145–6 (answer 185); Hill, *Principles*, sig. C5ᵛ; Nicholes, *Catechisme*, 45; Hammond, *Practical catechisme*, 228; Marshall, *Catechism*, 32; Wake, *Principles*, 130; and see also Egerton, 'Briefe method', 13; Perkins, *Foundation*, 8; Vincent, *Catechism*, 266 (and cf. Hieron, *Doctrine*, 579).

[22] Hammond, loc. cit.; Westminster Larger, loc. cit.; and following notes below.

[23] Mayer, *Catechisme*, sigs. C6ʳ⁻ᵛ; Hammond, *Practical catechisme*, 222–3; Wake, *Principles*, 131–2; and cf. Prayer Book catechism, 784–5; Marshall, *Catechism*, 32; Williams, *Exposition*, 44; Comber, *Church-catechism*, 23; also Elton, *Forme*, sigs. E5ʳ⁻ᵛ; and e.g. Egerton, 'Briefe method', 18.

[24] Wake, loc. cit.

[25] Ball, *Catechisme*, 76, 79; Westminster Larger, 144–5 (answers 183–4); Gouge, *Principles*, 108.

Edward Elton was one of them and the royalist episcopalian, Edward Boughen, was another.[26] There is no sign in our sample of a new attitude to prayer and liturgy of the kind associated with Laudianism and later the High-Church movement.

A much more common concern of catechists was proper content. Here there was a clear difference of opinion between conformists like Mayer, Hammond, and Wake who defended the use of set forms, and an outright nonconformist like Keach who in the 1690s spoke of praying in the spirit.[27] In 1699 Wake wrote that

> to pray to God by a set form, is so far from being a thing either in itself unlawful, or injurious to the Holy Spirit, that we see our saviour himself has here given us an example for it; as under the Law God was pleased in several cases to direct the very words in which he would be addressed to by the Jews.[28]

Keach, on the other hand, conceived of prayer as being in the spirit (by the help of the Holy Ghost), in truth, and in faith.[29] As so often in this situation, however, the gulf was not unbridgeable, and in the case of episcopalians and presbyterians the gap between them was much smaller. On the conformist side, Hammond warned against vain repetition of set forms, and Marshall encouraged 'occasional expressions' as well as set forms; and one might mention here a work outside our sample by Bishop Ken, in which he tried to teach his flocks how to construct their own prayers using phrases culled from the services and catechism in the Book of Common Prayer.[30] On the presbyterian side, the authors of the Westminster Larger Catechism made it clear that there was a 'rule' for prayer laid down by God in the scriptures, and especially in the Lord's Prayer, a sentiment with which Keach—and Watts—actively agreed.[31] Moreover, all types of author insisted that the help of the Holy Spirit was essential to fruitful prayer, even if the nonconformist emphasis was perhaps on the Spirit helping and quickening the individual rather than shaping the exact phrases of prayer.[32] Though dissenters were outraged at the thought of being coerced into using certain set forms of prayer which they thought were popish or sterile, the clear majority of authors in the sample who discussed the correct content of prayer either avoided this contentious issue or found a common platform in certain general guidelines.

Authors were also anxious to make the point that if prayers were to be answered they must not be made for selfish or petty wants, but for what God wanted, and what

---

[26] Elton, *Forme*, sigs. E7ᵛ–8ʳ; Boughen, *Exposition*, 69–70; and cf. Hammond, *Practical catechisme*, 228.

[27] Mayer, *Catechisme*, sig. C7ᵛ; Hammond, *Practical catechisme*, 225–7; Wake, *Principles*, 133; Keach, 'Youth', 118–19.

[28] Wake, loc. cit.   [29] Keach, loc. cit.

[30] Hammond, *Practical catechisme*, 229–30; Marshall, *Catechism*, 32; [T. Ken], *The church-catechism, with directions for prayer* (1685).

[31] Westminster Larger, 146 (answer 186); Keach, 'Youth', 114 (Keach also said children should pray under their parents' guidance); Watts, *Assembly's catechism*, 41 (though see below, n. 40).

[32] Keach, loc. cit.; Westminster Larger, 144 (answer 182).

would redound to his glory.[33] How one found out what that approved content was was also made clear to catechumens: the Holy Spirit and the scriptures provided a guide to what God wanted us to pray for.[34] The two most commonly deployed guidelines to correct content in our sample were that prayer should thank God for what he had already done for us, and it should ask God for more of those things which are 'needful both for our souls, and bodies'.[35] But whereas the authors of a number of earlier forms in our sample tended to move from thanksgiving or worship for gifts already received to petition for more of the same, John Ball moved from petition to thanksgiving, a sequence which, as on so many other matters, was reflected in the Westminster Larger Catechism.[36] The difference was perhaps one of logic or presentation rather than dogma.[37]

What nearly all authors could agree on was that 'the form of prayer which Christ taught his disciples (commonly called the Lord's Prayer)' was the perfect 'rule' of prayer, both in the technical sense of how to pray, and in terms of content in that it indicated what we should ask for.[38] Calvin was quite emphatic on this:

> Albeit we are not forbidden to use other words and to frame them also after another sort, yet there can no prayer be acceptable unto God, unless it be in effect and sense framed after this [the Lord's Prayer], which is unto us (as it were) a perfect rule whereby to pray as we ought to do.[39]

A number of others in our sample spoke of the Lord's Prayer as a perfect 'pattern' of prayer; for example Egerton who wrote that the Lord's Prayer was 'a perfect pattern and full direction' of prayer'.[40] The Lord's Prayer was seen as not only a model for prayer in general, but also a form that could be used in its own right, though it is possible that some conformists commended the use of this prayer more warmly than others, on the grounds that it had been recommended by Christ and 'used in all the churches of the saints', and that it excelled all other prayers in that in a few sentences

[33] Calvin, *Catechisme*, 98–9; Heidelberg Catechism, 350–1; Isham, *Catechism*, 55–6; Wake, *Principles*, 130.

[34] Calvin, *Catechisme*, 102; Westminster Larger, 146 (answer 186); and Westminster Shorter, 36–7 (answers 98–9).

[35] Prayer Book catechism, 786–7; Elton, *Forme*, sig. E7ʳ; and cf. Heidelberg Catechism, 350–1; Perkins, *Foundation*, 8; Cartwright, 'Catechisme', sig. Aa8ʳ; Ball, *Catechisme*, 76–7.

[36] Ball, loc. cit.; Westminster Larger, 142 (answer 178).

[37] Cf. ibid. 144–5 (answers 183–4) against 142 (answer 178). Putting worship first had the advantage of corresponding to the way in which the Lord's Prayer was usually divided, into three petitions on God's glory, and three on man's needs; but as we shall see shortly the Ball–Westminster connection did not make much of this division.

[38] Wallis, *Explanation*, 45; Calvin, *Catechisme*, 102, 120; Nowell, *Catechisme*, 190; Dering–More, *Catechisme*, sig. B6ᵛ; Paget, *Questions*, sig. D7ᵛ; Egerton, 'Familiar forme', 36–7; Cartwright, 'Catechisme', sig. Aa8ᵛ; Ball, *Catechisme*, 77; Palmer, *Endeavour*, 34; Boughen, *Exposition*, 59–60; Westminster Larger, 146 (answers 186–7); Westminster Shorter, 37 (answer 99); Williams, *Exposition*, 44; Keach, 'Youth', 114.

[39] Calvin, *Catechisme*, 120.

[40] Egerton, 'Familiar forme', 36–7; and cf. Sherlock, *Principles*, 44; Comber, *Church-catechism*, 23; Williams, *Exposition*, 44; Wake, *Principles*, 132. A mild note of dissent was struck by Watts in his comments on the Westminster divines' description of the Lord's Prayer: Watts, *Assembly's catechism*, 41.

it comprehended 'a whole sea of matter', a 'breviary or epitome of the whole Book of God' and of our duties to God, ourselves, and others.[41] A slightly more cautious note was struck by some of the 'godly'. Stephen Egerton's catechumens were told that when praying they needed to use more than the Lord's Prayer, though they could 'fruitfully shut up [their] particular prayers' in that prayer, since it contained 'whatsoever concerneth the glory of God, the good of his church, comfort of my body, and salvation of my soul'. As well as being a pattern for our other prayers, said the Westminster divines, the Lord's Prayer 'may also be used as a prayer, so that it be done with understanding, faith, reverence, and other graces necessary to the right performance of the duty of prayer'.[42] Perhaps here we are back to the early puritans' distaste for the rote repetition of the Paternoster, and their later worry about its being misused, even after it had been mastered in English. However, both sides believed that a careful use of the prayer that Christ had taught his disciples was legal and advisable, and in a catechetical context both also felt the need to dissect and expound the Lord's Prayer to their pupils rather than teach them how to pray extempore.

The minister. For the more easy understanding hereof, tell me how many articles or particular requests be contained herein?

The child. Six, of which the three first do concern the glory of God, without any respect or consideration of ourselves: the other three touch us properly, and concern our wealth and profit.

Calvin's opening salvo on the Lord's Prayer is typical of the great majority of forms that examined it at any length. Just as the Creed was divided up into twelve articles and the Decalogue into two tables of four and six Commandments, so the Lord's Prayer 'for the more easy understanding' was generally divided into six petitions.[43] Only Edward Boughen and Thomas Comber deviated from this norm by splitting the sixth petition into two to make seven, as Luther and some English authors in the 1530s had done, though this was frowned on by Calvin in the *Institutes*.[44] The inclusion of the doxology—'for thine is the kingdom, the power and the glory, for ever and ever'—was also a mildly controversial move, since it appeared only in the version of the Lord's Prayer in Matthew 6: 13, not that in Luke 11: 4. Luther and the authors of the original Prayer Book catechism of 1549 decided to omit the doxology from their

---

[41] Boughen, *Exposition*, 59–60; Nicholson, *Exposition*, 130; Comber, *Church-catechism*, 23; Sherlock, *Principles*, 44; Isham, *Catechism*, 51; and cf. Lewis, *Catechism*, 59, and Wake, *Principles*, 132–3.

[42] Egerton, 'Familiar forme', 36–7; Westminster Larger, 146 (answer 187).

[43] Calvin, *Catechisme*, 103.

[44] Boughen, *Exposition*, 66; Comber, *Church-catechism*, 22–3; Schaff, *Creeds*, 80–4; for Marshall's *A godly prymer in Englysshe* (1535) and Hilsey's *Manual of prayers* (1539), see E. Burton (ed.), *Three Primers Put Forth in the Reign of Henry VIII* (Oxford, 1834), 55, 64–6, 329. Calvin disapproved of the sevenfold division: *Institutes*, III. xx. 35; curiously, Nowell referred to the possibility of a sevenfold division of the Lord's Prayer in the shorter *Institution*, sig. Fvii', but not in the full-length *Catechisme*, 191.

forms, and in the English services of morning and evening prayer and holy communion the Lord's Prayer was from 1662 recited once with and once without it.[45] Calvin knew there was an element of doubt about the provenance of the doxology, but it was included in the catechetical forms of Geneva and Heidelberg, and in England too it became standard catechetical practice both in forms based on the original 1549 catechism and in alternatives.[46] Of the authors in the sample of works being studied here, however, only Hammond pointed out that the doxology was possibly not in the original but might have been added 'out of the liturgies of the ancient Greek church': the silence of the other authors on the matter is an interesting example of how reticent catechetical authors could be on matters of scriptural exegesis which might carry a risk of confusing their students.[47] The word 'Amen' is also to be found only in Matthew, not Luke; in fact, in the English translation of Calvin's catechism, the Lord's Prayer ended with the words 'So be it'. But Luther had used 'Amen', and this was the norm in both official and unofficial forms in England.[48] The only minor changes in catechetical handling of the Lord's Prayer dated from the late sixteenth century and early seventeenth century, and consisted of referring to the opening of the prayer—'Our father, which art in heaven'—as a preface, and the ending—'for thine … Amen'—as a conclusion, thanksgiving, or doxology, thus making eight units in all as opposed to the six mentioned by Calvin.[49] Calvin's subdivision of the six central units into three on God and three on man was, however, widely adopted,[50] though not by the Ball–Westminster connection, perhaps because they saw the first three as involving man as much as the last. Also the phrasing of the description given to petitions four to six shifted from Calvin's 'wealth and profit' and Nowell's 'commodity', to 'our own souls' and bodies' needs', 'our necessities', 'wants' or 'good', or simply 'ourselves',[51] perhaps to avoid a possible misconception that the end of prayer was wealth.

[45]   Schaff, *Creeds*, 84; Prayer Book catechism, 786–7; Brightman, *English Rite*, i. 132–3, 146–7, 157, 163, 640–1, 696, 707.

[46]   Calvin, *Catechisme*, 103; Heidelberg Catechism, 351.

[47]   Hammond, *Practical catechisme*, 231; Boughen, *Exposition*, 68–9 cited Matt. 6: 13 as warrant for its inclusion.

[48]   Calvin, *Catechisme*, 102; Schaff, *Creeds*, 84; Prayer Book catechism, 786–7. Some authors explained 'Amen' at the end of the Creed rather than the Lord's Prayer: see below, p. 505. For other variations of text, such as 'debt' for 'trespass', see also below, pp. 497–8.

[49]   Virel, *Treatise*, 194, 215; Cartwright, 'Catechisme', sigs. Aa8^v–Bb1^r; Ball, *Catechisme*, 77; Hill, *Principles*, sig. C6^r; Bernard, *Common catechisme*, sig. B8^v; Westminster Larger, 146 (answer 188); Sherlock, *Principles*, 41–2; Gouge, *Principles*, 124; Marshall, *Catechism*, 32–3. Mid-sixteenth-century authors had discussed these flanking units as a form of address and closure of the prayer rather than as discrete items: Calvin, *Catechisme*, 106, 119; Paget, *Questions*, sig. D7^r; Heidelberg Catechism, 351, 354.

[50]   Nowell, *Catechisme*, 190; Egerton, 'Familiar manner', 42; Cartwright, 'Catechisme', sig. Aa8^v; Hill, *Principles*, sigs. C6^{r-v}; Mayer, *Catechisme*, sigs. C8^r, D1^r; Marshall, *Catechism*, 32–3; Williams, *Exposition*, 45–7; Lewis, *Catechism*, 60–1; Hammond's account of petitions 4–6 was idiosyncratic: *Practical catechisme*, 238–9. Authors of some shorter or more elementary forms did not subdivide or even cite the text, merely mentioned or paraphrased it: Perkins, *Foundation*, 8; Egerton, 'Familiar manner', 36; Keach's first two forms, and Watts's first four.

[51]   As previous note.

In expounding the preface, authors usually adopted the tried and trusted method of explaining the significance of individual words such as 'Our', 'father', and 'heaven', as well as that of the whole. Treatment of the words 'father' and 'heaven' often reinforced the points made in the first article of the Creed and to a lesser extent the first table of the Decalogue: because God is our father, by grace and by adoption (through Christ), we may come boldly to him, as a child to a parent; he will 'preserve what he has begotten', and like the father of the prodigal son will pardon and welcome us; he will hear us when we call his name and give us whatever we ask or need.[52] (This idea of receiving what we ask for was supported by various texts, and viewed in terms of what God wanted us to ask for.[53]) We say 'our' rather than 'my' father because we are taught to pray with and for others, it was commonly asserted.[54] God is the father of every one of us in particular as well as all of us in general, wrote William Wake; and to use the word 'our' corrects pride and increases our charity to our brothers. 'There is no man so mean, but what he has the right to call God his father, as the greatest among us', continued the future archbishop. 'As there is a communion of saints, so the saints ought to communicate in each other's prayers', wrote another future bishop, William Nicholson.[55] The mention of 'heaven' in the preface reminds us that although we may come boldly to God, we must also come 'with reverence of his majesty that filleth the heaven', who is infinite and lord and master of all, and being all-sufficient and the giver of all goodness can furnish us with all the things we need.[56] 'Heaven' also reminds us of where we originally came from and 'the inheritance we hope for', and that God has promised through Christ to help us achieve that end.[57] We learn from the preface as a whole, it was concluded, that our prayers must be directed to God alone, and that we must ask only for what our heavenly father wants.[58]

Explanation of the first petition focused on the words 'hallowed' and 'name'. The most sophisticated account was provided by Hammond in his form for advanced

---

[52] Calvin, *Catechisme*, 105; Nowell, *Catechisme*, 191–2; Cartwright, 'Catechisme', sig. Aa8ᵛ; Ball, *Catechisme*, 77; Hill, *Principles*, sig. C6ʳ; Hammond, *Practical catechisme*, 231; Boughen, *Exposition*, 60–1; Westminster Shorter, 37 (answer 100); Nicholson, *Exposition*, 132; Sherlock, *Principles*, 42; Gouge, *Principles*, 124–5; Comber, *Church-catechism*, 23; Vincent, *Catechism*, 246; Marshall, *Catechism*, 33.

[53] e.g. Luke 11: 11, Col. 3: 17, and Eph. 2: 18; Heidelberg Catechism, 351; Hill, loc. cit.; Mayer, *Catechisme*, sig. C8ʳ (and cf. sig. C6ʳ); Williams, *Exposition*, 46–7; Wake, *Principles*, 134.

[54] Calvin, *Catechisme*, 104–6; Nowell, *Catechisme*, 192–3; Boughen, *Exposition*, 59; Westminster Larger, 147 (answer 189); Westminster Shorter, 37 (answer 100); Vincent, *Catechism*, 247; Comber, *Church-catechism*, 23; Marshall, *Catechism*, 33; Lewis, *Catechism*, 60.

[55] Wake, *Principles*, 135; Nicholson, *Exposition*, 132.

[56] Cartwright, 'Catechisme', sigs. Aa8ʳ⁻ᵛ; and cf. Calvin, *Catechisme*, 106–7; Nowell, *Catechisme*, 193; Heidelberg Catechism, 352; Hill, *Principles*, sig. C6ʳ; Boughen, *Exposition*, 61–2; Westminster Larger, 147 (answer 189); Nicholson, *Exposition*, 133; Gouge, *Principles*, 124–5; Marshall, *Catechism*, 33; Vincent, *Catechism*, 247; Williams, *Exposition*, 46–7; Wake, *Principles*, 135; Lewis, *Catechism*, 60.

[57] Boughen, *Exposition*, 62; Ball, *Catechisme*, 77.

[58] Nowell, *Catechisme*, 193–4; Marshall, *Catechism*, 33; Williams, *Exposition*, 46–7; Wake, *Principles*, 134; and cf. Nicholes, *Catechisme*, 47.

catechumens where he explained that 'hallowing', according to 'the Hebrew word, or Syriac dialect' in which Christ delivered it, signifies 'to separate from vulgar common use', 'to use in a separate manner', 'with that reverence and respect that is not allowed to anything else', and that the 'name' of God meant God himself, in his essence and attributes, 'it being an ordinary Hebraism that "thing" and "word" ... "name" and "essence" ... should be taken promiscuously the one for the other'.[59] Most authors, however, were content to make the same points in simpler terms: catechumens were told to equate God's name with his attributes and works, which should have been familiar to them through the exposition of the opening of the Creed and the Decalogue, and to see 'hallowing' as a separating out for special reverence and glorification.[60]

It was also generally agreed that the thrust of this petition as a whole was a request to God to enable us by his grace to know him better, and to esteem, worship, and glorify him.[61] Earlier forms, such as Calvin's and the Prayer Book catechism, stressed the role of praise in magnifying God's glory; but beginning with the Heidelberg Catechism and Nowell's form there was a tendency to supplement this straightforward recognition and praise of God's greatness with a stress on the individual catechumen leading a godly life as a means of glorifying God's name.[62] Thereafter this twofold stress on acknowledging God's name and on godly behaviour and conversation can be found in many forms by both 'godly' authors and expositors of the Prayer Book catechism.[63] Among authors who added this stress on a godly life, it was always placed second to praise or reverence, and sometimes third or lower if authors found space for other ideas, as happened in a few forms such as Nowell's original form, the Westminster Larger Catechism, and Nicholson's exposition of the Prayer Book catechism, where the first petition was also held to contain the desire that the names of all rivals to God be utterly destroyed, and all sacrilege, atheism, and profanity removed.[64] In the Westminster Larger Catechism there is the additional request that God 'by his over-ruling providence, direct and dispose of all things to his own

---

[59] Hammond, *Practical catechisme*, 232–3.

[60] Calvin, *Catechisme*, 107; Nowell, *Catechisme*, 194; Dering–More, *Catechisme*, sig. B6ᵛ; Hill, *Principles*, sig. C6ᵛ; Westminster Larger, 147–8 (answer 190); Nicholson, *Exposition*, 134; Marshall, *Catechism*, 34; Vincent, *Catechism*, 248; Williams, *Exposition*, 47; Wake, *Principles*, 137; Watts, *Assembly's catechism*, 42.

[61] Nowell, *Catechisme*, 194–5; Perkins, *Foundation*, 8; Hammond, *Practical catechisme*, 233–4; Boughen, *Exposition*, 63; Nicholson, *Exposition*, 134; Westminster Shorter, 36 (answer 101); Wallis, *Explanation*, 46; Sherlock, *Principles*, 42; Gouge, *Principles*, 125, and id., 'Heads', 9; Comber, *Church-catechism*, 23; Isham, *Catechism*, 52; Lewis, *Catechism*, 61; and see following notes.

[62] Calvin, *Catechisme*, 107; Prayer Book catechism, 786–7; Heidelberg Catechism, 352; Nowell, *Catechisme*, 194–5.

[63] Paget, *Questions*, sig. D8ʳ; Ball, *Catechisme*, 77; Gouge, *Principles*, 125; Westminster Larger, 148 (answer 190); and cf. Vincent, *Catechism*, 248; and of Prayer Book form expositions, Nicholes, *Catechisme*, 48–9; Nicholson, *Exposition*, 134–5; Marshall, *Catechism*, 34; Williams, *Exposition*, 48; and cf. Hill, *Principles*, sig. C6ᵛ; Boughen, *Exposition*, 63; and Isham, *Catechism*, 52.

[64] Nowell, *Catechisme*, 195; Westminster Larger, 148 (answer 190); Nicholson, *Exposition*, 135.

glory';[65] on the episcopalian side, however, this petition was extended in some longer works by senior churchmen to cover those things associated with God: 'his Word ... his house ... his priests ... the revenues of the church ... the first day of the week', 'his service and religion', and 'his sacraments'.[66] However, these additions did not dominate or change the balance of the explanations of this petition; as in the case of the interpretation of a number of the Commandments, these additions were more a matter of accumulation than major reinterpretation.[67]

In the case of the second petition—'thy kingdom come'—there is in our sample forms a certain amount of overlap with the treatment of the first, over God's glory being increased, and a rather greater overlap with the third, over the need for obedience to God's will in order that those ends be attained. There were a number of regularly recurring elements in the explanation of 'kingdom' and of its 'coming' offered by our authors; and for the first half of our period at least, most of these elements are captured in the relevant answer in the Heidelberg Catechism:

'Thy kingdom come'. That is: So govern us by thy Word and Spirit that we may submit ourselves unto thee always more and more; preserve and increase thy church; destroy the works of the devil, every power that exalteth itself against thee, and all wicked devices formed against thy holy Word, until the full coming of thy kingdom, wherein thou shalt be all in all.[68]

Let us first take a brief look at the idea of God's kingdom 'coming', in so far as it may help us to explain the nature of the 'kingdom' being expounded here. God's kingdom was said to 'come' through the number of the faithful being daily increased, so that his kingdom (or his kingdom of grace as it was often later termed) was enlarged. Through outward means, such as 'the sceptre of his word', and inward means, in particular the governing of the soul by the Holy Spirit, men's sinful desires were overturned and their minds made anew, or as Ball put it they were converted from being under the power of Satan to having Christ rule in their hearts.[69] There were other dynamic features of this kingdom. Not only were more and more believers to be brought under God's command in a particular area, but also the individual believers therein were to come more and more under God's sway.[70] From the 1640s the coming of the kingdom was also increasingly held to include its spreading from

---

[65] Westminster Larger, 148 (answer 190); in the Westminster Shorter, 37 (answer 101), this was abbreviated to the last eight words; and see also below n. 67.

[66] Hammond, *Practical catechisme*, 233; Wake, *Principles*, 136; Nicholson, *Exposition*, 135; and cf. Williams, *Exposition*, 48.

[67] All the authors cited here stressed the need to revere God's attributes and works, including (in Hammond's case) his works of grace and (in Williams's) his providence: Hammond, *Practical catechisme*, 232–4; Nicholson, *Exposition*, 134–5; Williams, *Exposition*, 47–8; Wake, *Principles*, 136–7.

[68] Heidelberg Catechism, 352–3.

[69] Calvin, *Catechisme*, 108–9; Dering–More, *Catechisme*, sig. B7ʳ; Paget, *Questions*, sigs. D8ᵛ–E1ʳ; Ball, *Catechisme*, 77; Nicholes, *Catechisme*, 50.

[70] Calvin, *Catechisme*, 108–9; Heidelberg Catechism, 352; Hill, *Principles*, sigs. C6ᵛ–7ʳ; Mayer, *Catechisme*, sig. D1ʳ; Vincent, *Catechism*, 249–50.

those areas where it was established to those where it was not: a variety of seven-teenth-century authors spoke of the gospel being 'propagated' and believed 'over the face of the whole earth' in all nations.[71] There was a further element of change in that this process of enlargement of the kingdom was seen as culminating at Judgement Day, when the faithful would be received into glory and the wicked destroyed. Many catechumens were thus urged to see the second petition as calling for the hastening of the coming of the kingdom of glory,[72] though references of an explicitly millennial kind were noticeably absent in our sample of forms. The nearest we get is in the exposition of the second petition in the Westminster Larger Catechism (but not the Shorter) where, among a multitude of other petitions for the destruction of sin and for Christ to rule in our hearts here, it is said that we also pray for the conversion of the Jews and that Christ would 'hasten the time of his second coming, and our reign-ing with him for ever'.[73]

We are now in a better position to view the ways in which the idea of 'kingdom' was handled. The first and most obvious way, though this is found less often in the seven-teenth than in the sixteenth century, was that God was a king ruling his subjects: the verbs used to convey this sense of power on the monarch's side were 'guide', 'govern', 'reign', and 'rule',[74] and on the subjects' 'obey', 'serve', or 'submit'. We serve God, wrote Sherlock, as all faithful subjects serve their king.[75] There was also (especially in the seventeenth rather than the sixteenth) said to be a rival kingdom or kingdoms—of Satan, sin, and death: the kingdom of the devil ('and his instrument, the Turk and the Pope', added Nicholes in an unusually explicit aside) was one of darkness facing God's kingdom of light.[76] The result was that whereas Calvin saw the second petition as a request to God to bring to confusion 'the wicked which will not become subjects to his kingdom', and Ball spoke of Christ converting 'such as be under the power of Satan', the Westminster theologians said that *all* men, being in the kingdom of sin, should pray that Satan's kingdom be destroyed and that 'Christ rule in our hearts here'. The conservative episcopalian Thomas Comber adopted a similar sequence.[77] This development did not make a substantial difference to interpretation of the

---

[71] Palmer, *Endeavour*, 35; Boughen, *Exposition*, 63; Westminster Larger, 149 (answer 191); Nicholson, *Exposition*, 136; Williams, *Exposition*, 48–9; Wake, *Principles*, 137.

[72] Calvin, *Catechisme*, 109; Paget, *Questions*, sig. E1^r; Hill, *Principles*, sig. C7^r; Westminster Shorter, 37–8 (answer 102); Marshall, *Catechism*, 35; Wake, *Principles*, 137–8.

[73] Westminster Larger, 149 (answer 191).

[74] Calvin, *Catechisme*, 108; Heidelberg Catechism, 352; Nowell, *Catechisme*, 195–6; Dering–More, *Catechisme*, sig. B7^r; Paget, *Questions*, sig. D8^v; Perkins, *Foundation*, 8; Hill, *Principles*, sig. C6^v; Palmer, *Endeavour*, 35; Isham, *Catechism*, 52–3; Lewis, *Catechism*, 62.

[75] Prayer Book catechism, 786–7; Heidelberg Catechism, 352; Sherlock, *Principles*, 43.

[76] As previous notes, and Virel, *Treatise*, 199–201; Nicholes, *Catechisme*, 50–1: for bare references to the existence of a rival to the heavenly kingdom in the mid-sixteenth century, see Calvin, *Catechisme*, 108–9, and Heidelberg Catechism, 352.

[77] Calvin, loc. cit.; Ball, *Catechisme*, 77; Westminster Larger, 148–9 (answer 191); Comber, *Church-catechism*, 24.

petition and was perhaps related to the spread of covenant teaching: those in the covenant of grace were still subject to the Law which had governed the covenant of works, because while they were on earth they still contained something of the old Adam in them.[78] Most authors, however, seem to have been content either to avoid this particular issue, or simply state the existence of two rival kings vying for the same subjects.

Related to the idea of a divine monarchy is the idea that those whom God governed were his chosen people. The terms used for this varied. Calvin talked of God guiding and governing 'his elect' (the only reference to the elect in his catechism) or his 'faithful flock', while the theologians of Heidelberg spoke of God preserving his church, and Nowell wrote of 'his number and holy company, that is to say, his church'.[79] Dering and More used the phrase 'the number of his faithful', while John Ball preferred 'his chosen', and Martin Nicholes (in a Prayer Book exposition) the 'elect'. Moderate or more conservative episcopalians such as Mayer, Hammond, and Nicholson, wrote of 'the number of true believers', 'all his [Christ's] saints', or of 'the number of the elect' being accomplished.[80] Throughout our period, authors of all persuasions normally used the first-person singular or plural in explaining the second petition: in the Westminster Shorter Catechism, catechumens were told to pray that 'the kingdom of grace may be advanced, ourselves and others brought into it, and kept in it'.[81] But a few authors like Cartwright and Ball used an impersonal form such as 'Christ's kingdom' or 'his chosen' and the third-person plural.[82]

Another way of explaining the 'kingdom' to come is first found in our sample in the condensed catechism of John Mayer in the early 1620s but quite widely thereafter, namely to distinguish between God's kingdom of grace and his kingdom of glory. The former was an imperfect form of rule, begun on earth in the faithful members of the Christian church, whereas the latter, in the next world, would be perfection.[83] This pair of terms can also be found in the forms of royalist episcopalians, the Westminster Shorter Catechism (but not the Larger) and its derivatives, and in that of Isaac Watts.[84] Some later Stuart episcopalians preferred a slightly different, threefold

---

[78] See above, pp. 405–21; and e.g. W. W. McKee, 'The Idea of Covenant in Early English Puritanism (1580–1643)', Ph.D. thesis (Yale, 1948), 102–3; and M. McGiffert, 'Grace and Works: The Rise of the Covenant Divinity in Elizabethan Puritanism', *Harvard Theological Review*, 75 (1982), 496–502.

[79] Calvin, *Catechisme*, 108; Heidelberg Catechism, 352; Nowell, *Catechisme*, 195.

[80] Dering–More, *Catechisme*, sig. B7r; Ball, *Catechisme*, 77; Nicholes, *Catechisme*, 49; Mayer, *Catechisme*, sig. D1r; Hammond, *Practical catechisme*, 234; Nicholson, *Exposition*, 137.

[81] Westminster Shorter, 37 (answer 102); and cf. previous notes, and Prayer Book catechism, 786–7; Paget, *Questions*, sigs. D8v–E1r; Elton, *Forme*, sig. E7r; Westminster Larger, 148–9 (answer 191).

[82] Cartwright, 'Catechisme', sigs. Aa8v–Bb1r; Ball, *Catechisme*, 77; and cf. Gouge, *Principles*, 125.

[83] Mayer, *Catechisme*, sig. D1r. The epistle of Mayer's original *English catechisme* shows his familiarity with Ursinus's work, and there may be some debt here to the Heidelberg theologian's work.

[84] Boughen, *Exposition*, 63–4; Hammond, *Practical catechisme*, 234; Westminster Shorter, 37 (answer 102); Wallis, *Explanation*, 46–7; Gouge, *Principles*, 125, and id., 'Heads', 9; Vincent, *Catechism*, 249–50; Comber, *Church-catechism*, 24; Williams, *Exposition*, 48; Isham, *Catechism*, 52–3; Watts, *Assembly's catechism*, 42; and cf. Nicholes, *Catechisme*, 49.

concept of the divine monarchy: of power over all creatures in this world, of grace given to God's children in the church, and of glory in heaven.[85] But rather more typical of later Stuart forms was the idea of God's twofold kingdom facing that of Satan, as in Williams's widely used catechism: the 'kingdom of God' is 'begun by grace in this world, and perfected by glory in the world to come'; and we pray that this kingdom may so ' "come with power" ' that 'the kingdom of Sin and Satan may be utterly destroyed, and "all the kingdoms of this world may become the kingdoms of our Lord, and of his Christ", when "he shall reign for ever and ever" '.[86]

The third petition was normally handled in two halves: 'thy will be done', 'on earth as it is in heaven'. Because of the structure of the Prayer Book catechism in which prayer followed the moral law, a connection was implied between keeping God's Commandments and obeying him 'as we ought to do'.[87] Other early forms in the sample, such as Calvin's, the Heidelberg Catechism, and Nowell's, seemed to take God's will as read: there was little or no attempt to define it, merely a contrast drawn between God's will 'which alone is good' and man's which is repugnant to him, or an exhortation to renounce our own will and follow God's without murmuring or grudging.[88] It is true that in explaining the petition that God's will be done, Calvin wrote of God bringing all things to pass that are 'appointed by his unsearchable counsel and providence', and Nowell spoke of praying that what God has decreed may come to pass, but the nature of this counsel or decree was not spelt out. Ball and Hammond explained that God's will was spelt out in his Word,[89] but it was Nicholson in 1655 who went a little deeper by drawing a clear distinction at this point between God's revealed will, in Old and New Testaments, and his secret will, 'that whereby he determines of all events, good or bad; for there is nothing comes to pass without his will'.[90] This was taken up (or developed independently) by three other authors in our sample: a presbyterian dissenter and two episcopalians; but while Nicholson had warned against using God's secret will as the rule of our actions because it was 'hid from us', Vincent and Marshall urged their catechumens to pray for submission to the secret will but for knowledge and ability to perform the revealed one. Wake said that we should study both expressions of the divine will, and 'discern what it is that he would have us either do, or suffer, in obedience thereunto'.[91]

---

[85] Nicholson, *Exposition*, 135–7; Marshall, *Catechism*, 34–5; Lewis, *Catechism*, 62.

[86] Williams, *Exposition*, 48–9; the stress on the role of grace in all varieties of catechism reinforces points made in Chs. 7–9 above.

[87] Prayer Book catechism, 784–7; and cf. Comber, *Church-catechism*, 24; Lewis, *Catechism*, 62.

[88] Calvin, *Catechisme*, 110; Heidelberg Catechism, 353; Dering–More, *Catechisme*, sig. B7ʳ; Paget, *Questions*, sig. E1ʳ. For later brief treatments of 'will', see e.g. Comber, *Church-catechism*, 24, and Lewis, *Catechism*, 62.

[89] Calvin, loc. cit.; Nowell, *Catechisme*, 196–7; Ball, *Catechisme*, 78; Hammond, *Practical catechisme*, 235, and cf. Westminster Larger, 150 (answer 192).

[90] Nicholson, *Exposition*, 137–8.

[91] Vincent, *Catechism*, 251–2; Marshall, *Catechism*, 36; Wake, *Principles*, 138.

The keynote to this will being 'done' was seen as man's obedience. In shorter catechisms and in some shorter expositions of the Lord's Prayer, the focus was on simple obedience, usually of a positive kind, but sometimes in a more passive fashion, as in resigning oneself to God's will.[92] In others, obedience was presented both in an active sense of doing cheerfully what was agreeable to that will, and a passive one of patiently submitting and resigning ourselves when it ran contrary to our sinful wishes. This could be stated quite briefly,[93] but there was a clear tendency towards increasing the number of adjectives used to describe man's disposition when obeying God's will. Whereas in the sixteenth century a couple of adjectives or phrases sufficed, such as 'willingly and truly' or without 'gainsaying', 'murmuring', or 'grudging',[94] in the early seventeenth the total was rising: what God wills should be obeyed 'cheerfully, speedily, faithfully, and constantly', ran Ball's paraphrase, and by the 1640s, admittedly in two longer works, by Hammond and the Westminster divines, the number had doubled again.[95] The authors of a number of subsequent forms, though much shorter than these two, used at least three but often four or more of the same adjectives, or new ones such as 'wholly ... harmoniously, peaceably' or 'with alacrity, affection, fervency'.[96]

The occasion for listing these qualities was often in the exposition of the second half of the petition. 'As it is in heaven' was generally taken to refer to the perfect obedience shown by the angels to God's wishes (though in one case the obedience of the sun, moon, and stars, and in another three cases the obedience of the saints was cited as well).[97] The angels, Calvin told his catechumens, studied nothing but how to please God, and men should do the same.[98] A small minority of forms in the sample omitted all mention of angels at this point,[99] but equally very few of those who did mention angels bothered to describe these 'heavenly spirits' or 'ministering spirits' in any detail, or to give scriptural warrant for their statements. Psalm 103: 20–21— 'Bless the Lord, ye his angels ... that do his commandments'—was the text cited by the Westminster divines and some of their followers, and by William Wake.[100] Either

---

[92] Prayer Book catechism, 786–7; Hill, *Principles*, sig. C7^r; Perkins, *Foundation*, 8; Ball, *Catechisme*, 78; Dering–More, *Catechisme*, sig. B7^r; Paget, *Questions*, sigs. E1^{r-v}; Cartwright, 'Catechisme', sig. Bb1^r; Gouge, *Principles*, 125–6; id., 'Heads', 9.

[93] Heidelberg Catechism, 353; Westminster Shorter, 38 (answer 103); Comber, *Church-catechism*, 24; Williams, *Exposition*, 49; and Isham, *Catechism*, 53.

[94] Heidelberg Catechism, 353; Dering–More, *Catechisme*, sig. B7^r; Paget, *Questions*, sig. E1^r.

[95] Ball, *Catechisme*, 78; and cf. Hill, *Principles*, sig. C7^r; Hammond, *Practical catechisme*, 235; Westminster Larger, 150–1 (answer 192).

[96] Sherlock, *Principles*, 43; Wake, *Principles*, 139; Nicholson, *Exposition*, 138; Gouge, *Principles*, 125.

[97] Nowell, *Catechisme*, 197; Gouge, *Principles*, 125; id., 'Heads', 9; Isham, *Catechism*, 53; Lewis, *Catechism*, 62.

[98] Calvin, *Catechisme*, 110–11; and cf. Heidelberg Catechism, 353.

[99] Dering–More, *Catechisme*, sig. B7^r; Paget, *Questions*, sig. E1^r; Williams, *Exposition*, 49.

[100] Nowell, *Catechisme*, 197; Hammond, *Practical catechisme*, 235; Westminster Larger, 151 (answer 192); Westminster Shorter, 38 (answer 103); Wallis, *Explanation*, 47–8; Vincent, *Catechism*, 252; Wake, *Principles*, 139.

our authors did not want to dwell on angels too long, or they thought that most cate-chumens would know who the angels were. Certainly from the pedagogical point of view, one imagines that angels must have been very useful in setting standards of per-fection in doing God's will which students could be urged to emulate.

It can be seen from the last few pages that while the first three petitions were thought to redound to God's glory, man was very much involved in all three. Nichol-son provided a summary of the first half of the Lord's Prayer in the following terms:

In the first [petition], the soul puts on the affections of a child, that regards the father's inter-est, honour, and glory. In the second, the duty of a subject to his legitimate prince, seeking the promotion of his regal power. In the third, the affection of a spouse, that submits and conforms to her husband's will, loving what he loves, and choosing what he makes choice of.[101]

His attitude could be dismissed as patriarchal, royalist, and male chauvinist; but his summary does capture the familiar similes of the day which were used to convey the relationships between man and God implied in the first three petitions of the Lord's Prayer.

Nicholson's exposition continued:

Those petitions now follow that concern ourselves and our profit. God's three stand first, as in reason they ought: For 'seek ye first the kingdom of God and His righteousness' (Matt. 6: 33); and now our three follow, which also declare our dependence upon him.[102]

A few pages later he summarized the last three also:

In the first of which the soul puts on the affection of a poor indigent beggar. In the second, of a delinquent but penitent servant. In the third, of a person in affliction or danger.[103]

The last three petitions, as we have seen, were generally held to concern man's needs, the most obvious of these being survival in a hard and often harsh environment, which is reflected in the way that the first of this second group of petitions was explained: 'Give us this day our daily bread'.

In his short catechism, Luther gave a very full answer to the question 'What is, then, our daily bread?':

All that pertains to the nourishment and needs of the body, as drink, food and clothing, shoes, house, home, land, cattle, money, property, pious husband or wife, pious children, pious ser-vants, pious and faithful rulers, good government, good seasons, peace, health, education, honour, good friends, trusty neighbours, and the like.[104]

The authors of English forms or English translations of foreign catechisms did not go as far. A few said that 'bread' was meant to refer also to meat, drink, and clothes:

---

[101] Nicholson, *Exposition*, 138.
[103] Nicholson, *Exposition*, 144.
[102] Ibid.; cf. Nowell's bridge passage: *Catechisme*, 197.
[104] Schaff, *Creeds*, 82–3.

William Hill was clearly a carnivore since he told his students to thank God for sanctifying his creatures for their use;[105] and a couple of longer forms provided a longer list of 'blessings', including 'health', 'physic, sleep, peace, [and] seasonable weather'.[106] But the most commonly used paraphrase of this petition as a whole was a request to God for 'all things needful' to sustain this present life. The idea of praying for 'all our daily needs' or 'necessities' can be found at the start and end of our period, and in a wide range of forms.[107] But from the mid-seventeenth century, some authors preferred to use the phrase 'portion'—as in 'a competent portion of the good things of his life'—for example in the Westminster catechisms and the forms of some episcopalians.[108]

What 'needful', 'necessary', and 'competent portion' were all intended to convey was that the petitioner was not to ask for plenty, but simply enough on which to survive: not what is 'superfluous, and desired rather to gratify our lusts, than to preserve our life', but 'such as God seeth necessary and most convenient for us'.[109] Indeed, a fair amount of time was spent in a number of catechisms in our sample driving home points already made under the second table of the Commandments: men must work at a lawful calling, seek God's blessing on their labours, and be content with the portion or means which God has provided for them.[110] Thus Nicholes urged his catechumens to pray that God would enable them to labour in their callings and give them grace to be content therein. Making a virtue of necessity perhaps, Nowell urged his catechumens to 'seek not ... curiously dainty things for banqueting, or precious apparel, or sumptuous household stuff, for pleasure', but to be satisfied with 'temperate and healthful diet, and with mean and necessary apparel'; although much was omitted when Nowell's original form was condensed, this sentence was left in.[111] Some later authors may have thought this too ascetic: Cartwright and Ball (in his larger form) thought the petition meant we should ask God to provide for our necessities and for 'sober' or 'fitting delights', while the authors of the Westminster catechisms and Dean Comber spoke of praying for a competent portion 'of the good

---

[105] Hill, *Principles*, sig. C7^r; Calvin, *Catechisme*, 111; Nowell, *Catechisme*, 197–8; Hammond, *Practical catechisme*, 235–6; Wake, *Principles*, 140.

[106] Nicholson, *Exposition*, 139; Ball, *Treatise*, 123–4.

[107] Prayer Book catechism, 786–7; Calvin, *Catechisme*, 111; Heidelberg Catechism, 353; Dering–More, *Catechisme*, sig. B7^r; Paget, *Questions*, sig. E1^v; Cartwright, 'Catechisme', sig. Bb1^r; Hill, *Principles*, sig. C7^r; Ball, *Catechisme*, 78; Sherlock, *Principles*, 43; Marshall, *Catechism*, 36–7; Isham, *Catechism*, 53; Wake, *Principles*, 140.

[108] Westminster Larger, 152 (answer 193); Westminster Shorter, 38 (answer 104); Nicholes, *Catechisme*, 54–5; Comber, *Church-catechism*, 24; Williams, *Exposition*, 50; Nicholson combined 'competent' and 'necessity': *Exposition*, 139.

[109] Wake, *Principles*, 140; Vincent, *Catechism*, 252.

[110] Calvin, *Catechisme*, 111–12; Nowell, *Catechisme*, 198; Dering–More, *Catechisme*, sig. B7^r; Paget, *Questions*, sig. E1^v; Ball, *Treatise*, 123; Nicholes, *Catechisme*, 55; Williams, *Exposition*, 50; Isham, *Catechism*, 53; Wake, *Principles*, 140 (his remarks about a man's 'property' being in the products of his labour have a modern ring).

[111] Nicholes, *Catechisme*, 54–5; Nowell, *Catechisme*, 197–8, and cf. id., *Institution*, sigs. Giii^v–iv^r.

things of this life', and to enjoy God's blessings in their use.[112] The basic point remained the same: the Christian was asking for a modicum, not an excess; but the manner in which it was described was less austere, and rather closer to the petition for pious relations, trusty friends, and good weather that had been suggested by Luther.

The fact remained that many men were rich enough to afford dainty food and expensive clothes, and a few catechists felt it necessary to ask why rich men had to pray for bread, when they 'have flowing plenty and store of all things'. The answer was that all men had to pray, because all must realize that it was God who gave them the use and enjoyment of their goods: 'It is the same providence of God which sustains both' rich and poor (wrote Wake), 'and gives an abundance to the one, as well as a competency to the other.'[113] The rich in particular had to realize that worldly goods 'can nothing profit them', said Calvin, and Nowell drove the point home: 'In vain shall we heap together and lay up plenty ... unless God of his grace do make the use of them healthful to us for our life.' It is no good cramming food into our stomachs 'unless God's power, by which we are rather fed and sustained ... do give both to the meat power to nourish, and to the stomach ability to digest it'. Paget added that the rich had a duty to pray for the poor as well as themselves.[114] A similarly cautious defence of moderate wealth was made by a couple of seventeenth-century authors in our sample, Hammond and Wake, who pointed out that the Christian did not have to frame his existence on the basis of a twenty-four hour cycle. The word 'daily' (in the phrase 'daily bread') had an element of futurity in it, they suggested; it meant what is sufficient for the next day, or in the original Greek (and the Hebrew sense) for the rest of our lives. Thus as Christians we are praying for our needs to be met 'day by day for the remainder of our lives'. This encouraged Wake to argue that it was lawful for any man 'to take care of, or provide for ... more than the next day'; it was an 'immoderate concern for the future' that Christ condemned, not 'a prudent foresight', he said.[115] Hammond was also encouraged to try another meaning of daily needs, which was not limited to 'the lowest proportion with which a man can subsist or live', but the lowest proportion 'agreeable to his condition' in life.[116] In both authors' cases, however, these were merely additional points, rather than their main thrust.

Thus far, there was general agreement on the meaning of this petition. But there was one respect in which a different conclusion was reached: did 'bread' refer to phys-

---

[112] Cartwright, 'Catechisme', sig. Bb1ʳ; Ball, *Treatise*, 123; and see n. 108 above.

[113] Calvin, *Catechisme*, 113; Nowell, *Catechisme*, 198–9; Paget, *Questions*, sig. E1ᵛ; Nicholes, *Catechisme*, 55; Wake, *Principles*, 141.

[114] Calvin, loc. cit.; Nowell, *Catechisme*, 198–9; id., *Institution*, sig. Givᵛ; Paget, *Questions*, E1ᵛ; and cf. Virel, *Treatise*, 207.

[115] Hammond, *Practical catechisme*, 235–6; Wake, *Principles*, 140–2.

[116] Hammond, *Practical catechisme*, 236.

ical nourishment only, or to spiritual as well? On the one hand, the Prayer Book form spoke of asking God to 'send us all things that be needful both for our souls, and bodies', and from the 1640s Hammond and half a dozen other episcopalians followed this lead in suggesting that the necessities of life were spiritual—the need for continual grace—as well as physical. Boughen even went back to the Greek to prove that bread was a spiritual as well as a physical food.[117] On the other side, Cartwright drew a distinction between the fourth petition, which he said was asking for necessities for this life, and the fifth and sixth petitions, which were about the life to come; and Perkins, Ball, and the Westminster divines under the fourth petition spoke only of 'the means of this temporal life' or 'our temporal support and comfort'.[118] Cartwright's position was not diametrically opposed to that of the conformists, but his successors were certainly adopting a different line on the fourth petition in particular, if not on the fourth to sixth petitions as a group. Other authors adopted a position which was nearer to that of Cartwright but not divorced from that in the Prayer Book catechism. Calvin and Nowell, for example, had suggested that the petition referred to 'all manner of things that God knoweth to be expedient for us in this world, whereby we may have the fruition of his benefits in quietness'; and while they were probably thinking primarily of physical expedients, such as work and good health, they indicated that there was a spiritual side to all this in their insistence that the sustaining of life had a divine purpose, and that goods could be enjoyed only if God gave them.[119] Beyond that, one has to put this contrast down either to the authors cited here having been drawn into different networks of influence or to a readiness to adopt a metaphorical as well as a literal interpretation. Hammond, for example, stressed that the 'prime sense' in which 'bread' should be understood was 'the most obvious and natural sense' of the word: 'the bodily necessaries of this life, food and raiment'; bread as 'the food of the soul, the grace of God' was 'a secondary sense', though from his point of view it was 'a more weighty considerable sense'.[120] The difference was there, but it was not total: 'godly' and conformists could agree that the petition meant that Christians should wait upon the divine providence for their physical needs.[121]

The form in which the fifth petition is cited in modern translations of Luther's small catechism, Calvin's 1541 catechism (and the corresponding section of the

---

[117] Prayer Book catechism, 786–7; Hammond, *Practical catechisme*, 236–7; Boughen, *Exposition*, 65; and cf. Nicholson, *Exposition*, 140–1; Sherlock, *Principles*, 43; Marshall, *Catechism*, 37; Williams, *Exposition*, 49; Isham, *Catechism*, 53; Wake, *Principles*, 139–40; Lewis, *Catechism*, 63.

[118] Cartwright, 'Catechisme', sig. Bb1ʳ; Perkins, *Foundation*, 8; Ball, *Catechisme*, 78; Westminster Larger, 151–3 (answer 193); Westminster Shorter, 38 (answer 104); and cf. Wallis, *Explanation*, 48; Gouge, *Principles*, 120; id., 'Heads', 9; Vincent, *Catechism*, 252–3.

[119] Calvin, *Catechisme*, 112; Nowell, *Catechisme*, 197–9. The Westminster divines said petitioners should ask for God's blessing for a 'holy and comfortable use' of the portion they had received: Westminster Larger, 152 (answer 193); Westminster Shorter, 38 (answer 104); and cf. Comber, *Church-catechism*, 24.

[120] Hammond, *Practical catechisme*, 236.

[121] Perkins, *Foundation*, 8; Virel, *Treatise*, 207; Westminster Larger, 152 (answer 193); Nicholson, *Exposition*, 138; Wake, *Principles*, 141.

Institutes), and the Heidelberg Catechism is: 'And forgive us our debts, as we forgive our debtors'. In most translations of the Bible into English the word or concept of debt was also used: in the Great Bible of 1539, the Geneva Bible of 1560, the Bishops' Bible of 1568, and the Authorized Version of 1611 the words used in Matthew 6: 12 are 'debts' and 'debtors' (though see the parallel references to 'trespasses' in verse 15). The corresponding point in Luke 11: 4 was translated as 'our sins' and 'every man that trespasseth us' in the Great and Bishops' Bible versions, while in the Geneva and Authorized Version it was 'sins' and every one 'indebted to us'.[122] However, in the Book of Common Prayer, the Prayer Book catechism of 1559, and in the translation into English of Calvin's catechism, the version was that pioneered by Marshall's *Godly prymer in Englysshe* of 1535, Hilsey's *Manual of prayers* of 1539, and the official primer of 1545, namely, 'And forgive us our trespasses, as we forgive them that trespass against us'.[123] Having come under both English and Genevan influences, Nowell cited both versions at different points of his exposition of the fifth petition.[124] Presumably catechists did not wish to confuse their students, who by definition were the less informed members of the church, with rival versions of the petition, so 'trespasses' remained the standard form of text for both liturgical and catechetical purposes until the 1640s, even in the works of 'godly' authors like Dering and More, Paget, and Ball.[125] In 1647, however, the authors of the Westminster catechisms came into line with Reformed tradition abroad and in Scotland by using 'debt' and 'debtors', and were followed by most but not all of those authors who built on those forms.[126] The majority of later Stuart authors in our sample, however, continued to use 'trespasses' and 'trespass'.[127]

The fifth petition was, like the third, often handled in two parts. In the earlier forms in our sample, there was little attempt to define the terms 'forgive' or 'trespasses' used in the first half of the petition. Instead straightforward alternatives were used, such as 'pardon' and 'sins'.[128] Some authors adopted harder or more technical terms, such as 'our manifold transgressions' not being 'imputed to us' or 'the remission of sins',[129] but most additional synonyms were fairly self-explanatory,

---

[122] Schaff, *Creeds*, 83; Janz, *Three Reformation Catechisms*, 198; Torrance, *School of Faith*, 44; Calvin, *Institutes*, III. xx. 45; Heidelberg Catechism, 353; and the appropriate verses of the different translations cited.

[123] Prayer Book catechism, 784–7; Calvin, *Catechisme*, 113; Burton, *Three Primers*, 62, 211, 459.

[124] Nowell, *Catechisme*, 199–200.

[125] Dering–More, *Catechisme*, sig. B6ᵛ; Paget, *Questions*, sig. E2ᵛ; Ball, *Catechisme*, 78.

[126] Westminster Larger, 153 (answer 194); Westminster Shorter, 38 (answer 105); Wallis, *Explanation*, 48; Vincent, *Catechism*, 253; Watts, *Assembly's catechism*, 43; but cf. Gouge, *Principles*, 126; id., 'Heads', 9; and Keach, 'Youth', 114, for the use of 'trespasses'.

[127] Nicholson, *Exposition*, 141; Sherlock, *Principles*, 7; Comber, *Church-catechism*, 25; Marshall, *Catechism*, 37; Williams, *Exposition*, 50; Isham, *Catechism*, 53; Wake, *Principles*, 142; Lewis, *Catechism*, 63; and see Gouge's forms in the previous note.

[128] Prayer Book catechism, 786–7; Calvin, *Catechisme*, 114; Ball, *Catechisme*, 78.

[129] Heidelberg Catechism, 353; Hill, *Principles*, sig. C7ᵛ.

for example, being 'acquitted' or 'released from the guilt and penalty of sin', or forgiving the 'wrongs and injuries' we receive from others.[130] The authors of the Westminster catechisms and their derivatives also used familiar language when they wrote of the debt owed by sinful man, and urged catechumens to beg God to 'acquit us both from the guilt and punishment of sin'.[131] From the 1640s, however, some episcopalian authors decided to offer specific definitions of the key words. In Hammond's form for advanced catechumens which first appeared in 1645, we read that 'to forgive' is 'to absolve', 'pardon', 'free from punishment'; and the 'trespasses' signifies all manner of offences against God: the word in Greek is 'debts', which is a Syriac expression to signify 'sins'.[132] Similar or slightly shorter definitions can be found in the forms by other later Stuart episcopalians;[133] and the similarity of these to the phrases and synonyms used by those following current Reformed practice suggests that there was no substantial disagreement as a result of the different forms of text being used.

What the first half of the petition as a whole meant was also not the subject of any disagreement: all men are sinners, and all must seek forgiveness, just as the apostles, to whom Christ gave this prayer, had to do.[134] We must beg daily for pardon, just as we ask daily for food in the previous petition, wrote Marshall; not to do so is to exclude oneself from the fellowship of the faithful, from Christ's flock.[135] A wide variety of authors told catechumens that we obtain forgiveness not through our own efforts, which can never be sufficient to satisfy God's justice; it is only through God's free mercy that our sins are not laid to our charge. God accepts Christ's death and passion as full satisfaction for our sins, and it is for this which we must pray.[136]

In their explanations of the second half of the petition, authors tried to balance two elements. On the one hand, there was the need to press home that our forgiving others was a virtue and a duty, which if not performed would mean that we ourselves would not be pardoned; and on the other, there was a concern that the performance of this duty did not appear meritorious in the sense that our forgiving others would

---

[130] Comber, *Church-catechism*, 25; Isham, *Catechism*, 53–4; Ball, *Catechisme*, 78.

[131] Westminster Larger, 153 (answer 194) (the reference here to 'original and actual sin' tested the catechumen's memory, since it had been explained as far back as answer 25); Westminster Shorter, 38 (answer 105); Gouge, *Principles*, 126; id., 'Heads', 9; Vincent, *Catechism*, 253–4.

[132] Hammond, *Practical catechisme*, 237.

[133] Nicholson, *Exposition*, 141; Marshall, *Catechism*, 37–8; Williams, *Exposition*, 50–1; Lewis, *Catechism*, 63–4.

[134] Calvin, *Catechisme*, 113–14; Nowell, *Catechisme*, 199; Paget, *Questions*, sig. E2ᵛ; Hill, *Principles*, C7ᵛ; Vincent, *Catechism*, 253.

[135] Marshall, *Catechism*, 37; Calvin, *Catechisme*, 113–14; Nowell, *Catechisme*, 199.

[136] Calvin, *Catechisme*, 114–15; Prayer Book catechism, 786–7; Nowell, *Catechisme*, 200; Dering–More, *Catechisme*, sig. B7ᵣ; Paget, *Questions*, sigs. E3ʳ⁻ᵛ; Heidelberg Catechism, 353–4; Ball, *Catechisme*, 78; Hill, *Principles*, sig. C7ᵛ; Bernard, *Common catechisme*, sig. C2ᵛ; Nicholes, *Catechisme*, 57; Hammond, *Practical catechisme*, 237; Boughen, *Exposition*, 65–6 (though note Boughen's rider about the powers of forgiveness delegated to priests); Westminster Larger, 153–4 (answer 194); Westminster Shorter, 38–9 (answer 105); Comber, *Church-catechism*, 25; Vincent, *Catechism*, 253–4; Marshall, *Catechism*, 37–8.

force God to forgive us. To forgive others was to follow Christ's example, and show that we are his children; it was a pledge of our confidence in God's mercy; it was to teach us charity and warn us against pride.[137] To wish heartily to forgive the wrongs that others have done us was a product and a sign of God's grace in us.[138] Not to forgive others, on the other hand, meant that we would not be counted as one of God's children. The litigious, the vengeful, and the envious should beware that they would not be forgiven by God. This did not take away our common law rights, argued Nowell, but taught us to 'follow the rule of Christian lenity and love', and not return evil for evil.[139]

The conjunction between the two halves of the petition was ambiguous: did 'as' mean that the two processes mentioned were parallel and simultaneous, or that the first was a consequence of the second? Some authors managed to convey the former either by sticking closely to the original wording of the petition, or by a careful choice of verbs and tenses, as in the case of the Westminster Shorter Catechism: we are 'encouraged to ask' God to pardon all our sins 'because by his grace we are enabled from the heart to forgive others'.[140] But a number of other authors, in straining to get across the point made at various points in the New Testament (Matt. 6: 14–15, 18: 35, Mark 11: 25, and Luke 6: 37) came close to saying that our forgiving others was a condition of our own salvation: there is 'no place of forgiveness with God' for those who would not forgive others, warned Nowell.[141] However, even this latter group of authors were of the opinion that we do not 'merit, or deserve to have our sins forgiven in that … we forgive other men their faults'.[142] The two processes of forgiveness though related were distinct, and in neither case could man take the credit: God forgives the penitent faithful for Christ's sake; we forgive others through the grace God gives us.

The reference to forgiving in this petition might be thought to have provided catechetical authors with a good opportunity to enlarge on the subject of forgiveness generally, and in particular on justification.[143] However, in our sample of catechisms

---

[137] Calvin, *Catechisme*, 115–16; Nowell, *Catechisme*, 200; Nicholson, *Exposition*, 142; Wake, *Principles*, 143.

[138] Heidelberg Catechism, 354; Westminster Larger, 154 (answer 194); Vincent, *Catechism*, 254; Hammond, *Practical catechisme*, 237; Gouge, *Principles*, 126; id., 'Heads', 9; Marshall, *Catechism*, 38; Williams, *Exposition*, 50.

[139] Nowell, *Catechisme*, 200–1; Hammond, *Practical catechisme*, 143–4; and cf. Paget, *Questions*, sigs. E3ʳ⁻ᵛ; and Wake, *Principles*, 143–4.

[140] Ball, *Practical catechisme*, 78; Hill, *Principles*, sig. C7ᵛ; Westminster Shorter, 38–9 (answer 105); and cf. Nicholson, *Exposition*, 141–2.

[141] Nowell, *Catechisme*, 200; Boughen, *Exposition*, 66–7; Westminster Larger, 153–4 (answer 194); Nicholson, *Exposition*, 142; Gouge, *Principles*, 126–7; Vincent, *Catechism*, 254; Isham, *Catechism*, 54; Wake, *Principles*, 142–3; Lewis, *Catechism*, 63–4.

[142] Calvin, *Catechisme*, 115.

[143] On the non-Calvinist view that justification was a recurring event, to be reinforced by daily petitioning, see above, p. 402.

this opportunity was rarely taken (at least not in the printed version of the catechizing process). Perkins paraphrased the fifth petition as saying that we 'may be justified and at peace with God', and Cartwright expressed the view that in the first half of the petition we pray for justification, and in the second for sanctification.[144] Hammond in a rather different way also equated part of this petition with justification as we shall see shortly, while Boughen and Wake pointed out that there was a connection not only between man's being forgiven and his forgiving others, but also between forgiveness, faith, and repentance. Wake put it as follows: 'that I may be forgiven by God, I must not only forgive others, but must myself repent of my sins and ask pardon for them in the name and through the merits and mediation of Jesus Christ our Saviour'.[145] The majority of our authors, however, stuck closely to the wording of the fifth petition, perhaps because they had said nearly all they wanted to say on this subject already at an earlier part of their exposition. It may be added that most of the authors who had a section on the Lord's Prayer presented forgiveness in a very positive way, stressing the assurance, confident hope, or trust of forgiveness available to their pupils in the fifth petition, and giving catechumens every incentive to pray regularly and fervently.[146]

In a sense it was rather odd to move from this discussion of forgiveness for sin in the fifth petition, to a request to be delivered from temptation to sin in the sixth. Some authors endeavoured to explain this by saying that the former dealt with sins already committed, and the latter with possible future sins, or by arguing that the one dealt with the guilt of sin and the other with the power of sin being negated.[147] There were also potential problems of interpretation within the sixth petition. Did the first half—'lead us not into temptation'—imply that it was God who was tempting us? And did the second half—'but deliver us from evil'—follow naturally from the first, or constitute a separate request, perhaps logically prior to the first: please release us from the evils that already oppress us, and do not allow us to enter new temptations in the future. These difficulties were reflected in the way that this petition was handled at the start of our period, though later authors, perhaps as a result of their experience of putting across this petition in their own catechizing, may be said to have made more effort or shown more skill in resolving the problems posed.

At the start there was a tendency to conflate the two halves of the petition, as in the hope expressed in the Prayer Book form that 'it will please him to save and defend us

---

[144] Perkins, *Foundation*, 8; Cartwright, 'Catechisme', sig. Bb1ʳ.

[145] Boughen, *Exposition*, 66 (and for the absolution he cites there, Brightman, *English Rite*, i. 132–3, 157); Wake, *Principles*, 143; like Nicholson—*Exposition*, 142—Wake added a cross-reference to his account of the tenth art. of the Creed, on 'the forgiveness of sins'.

[146] Calvin, *Catechisme*, 115; Nowell, *Catechisme*, 199; Dering–More, *Catechisme*, sig. B7ʳ; Hammond, *Practical catechisme*, 237; Westminster Larger, 153–4 (answer 194); Wake, *Principles*, 142; Vincent, *Catechism*, 253.

[147] e.g. Nowell, *Catechisme*, 201; Westminster Larger Catechism, 153–6 (answers 194–5); Nicholson, *Exposition*, 142; Marshall, *Catechism*, 38; and see following notes.

in all dangers ghostly and bodily: and that he will keep us from all sin and wickedness, and from our ghostly enemy, and from everlasting death'.[148] In his catechism Calvin suggested that the second part of the petition expounded the first, and that the 'pith and substance' of the petition as a whole was that we desired God to keep us from falling into wickedness, being overcome by the devil, or led by the 'naughty lusts of our flesh'; it was also to give us power through the Holy Spirit to withstand all these, and to 'be our protector and guide'.[149] Nowell's summary of the petition—we seek God's *protection* against temptation, and that he will help us overcome the devil— might also be termed an impressionistic rather than a literal paraphrase.[150] A possible cause of this was the equation of both the 'temptation' and the 'evil' in petition six with the devil and all his works: the 'wily guiles and subtle assaults' of our 'ghostly' enemy the devil, together with the world and our own flesh, were ready to wage constant spiritual war against us to tempt us into evil.[151]

A growing number of authors, however, tried to make a clearer distinction between the two halves of the petition, without going as far as those who, like Luther, divided it into two separate petitions. This was attempted in various ways. Dering and More and Paget described a two-stage process: God brings us into a controlled spiritual battle with our enemies, limited in the sense that the conflict is no sharper than we, with the help of the Holy Spirit, can endure; then God gives us the power, again through the Holy Spirit, to overcome our spiritual enemies.[152] John Ball distinguished between asking God to be freed from trials, as far as was consonant with his good pleasure, and seeking to be delivered from 'the evil thereof', presumably of the trials.[153] This was similar to the attempt of Thomas Marshall to produce a conditional/ absolute distinction: deliver us, if it pleases you, from temptation, but please deliver us absolutely from evil.[154] Hammond had a similar approach through a negative/positive contrast: the first part of the petition asks for us not to be brought into a hazardous position, the second to be delivered from temptation through grace.[155] This in turn is close to the position of the authors of the Westminster Larger Catechism— who asked for catechumens 'to be kept from being tempted to sin, or, *if tempted* to be supported and enabled to withstand it—and the authors of the Shorter who asked either to be kept from temptation or for support '*when* we are tempted'.[156] In the second half of the seventeenth century, Sherlock drew a distinction between asking God to preserve us from the evil of sin by his grace, and delivering us from the evil of punishment by his mercy;[157] while Nicholson and Wake offered multiple but separate

---

[148] Prayer Book catechism, 786–7.   [149] Calvin, *Catechisme*, 117–18.

[150] Nowell, *Catechisme*, 201–2.

[151] As previous notes; Heidelberg Catechism, 354; and Prayer Book catechism, 778–9.

[152] Dering–More, *Catechisme*, sig. B7ᵛ; Paget, *Questions*, sig. E3ᵛ.

[153] Ball, *Catechisme*, 78; it is possible that Ball means the evils consequent on failing the trials.

[154] Marshall, *Catechism*, 38–9.   [155] Hammond, *Practical catechisme*, 238.

[156] Westminster Larger, 155 (answer 195), and Westminster Shorter, 39 (answer 106), (my italics).

[157] Sherlock, *Principles*, 43; though cf. Isham, *Catechism*, 54–5, and Lewis, *Catechism*, 64.

definitions of temptation and evil, and suggested that the former was a trial from God and the latter a seduction into evil by the devil.[158]

A considerable part of the problem lay exactly here, with the question of whether 'leading into temptation' meant leading into 'sin' or whether it referred to a test of faith. A number of authors, from differing periods and backgrounds, denounced the idea that God could or would deliberately lead men into sin: any leading must therefore be done by Satan or by man's corrupt desires. And what God did in this situation was not so much lead good men into evil as withdraw his grace from 'such as his pleasure is to punish' (Calvin's description) or 'the wicked' (Nowell's alternative), and so leave them to the less than tender mercies of Satan.[159] But if 'temptation' meant trial, as some other authors suggested,[160] then God could reasonably and accurately be said to be leading men towards it. If God so ordered it by his providence, even his 'best children', 'the most godly men', could be tempted, in the sense of having their faith tested by God 'in mercy and love'.[161] And if it was a test, then faithful Christians could pray either to be allowed not to have to sit this particular exam, or, if they had to, to be helped through it by the Holy Spirit,[162] or, as it was more commonly put in the seventeenth century, by grace.[163]

The difference between the two approaches, and even between that of a Calvinist like Nowell and that of a non-Calvinist like Hammond, was perhaps not great. The one put a much greater emphasis on the role of the devil than the other did; the earlier view was that God would withdraw his grace from those who were led into wickedness by the devil, while the later view urged the faithful to pray that God would not withdraw his grace from them while he was testing them, and so abandon them to the clutches of Satan.[164] Both sides could agree that the only tempter to evil was Satan, and that with God's help the faithful would not be tested beyond their capacity and their victory over sin would in the end be total.[165] Although there was a difference of substance between those who thought the identity of the wicked reprobates was fixed and those who did not, this did not correspond exactly with the two groups just described, since in some respects Hammond was on this occasion much closer to the authors of the Westminster catechisms than to Calvin. As we

---

[158] Nicholson, *Exposition*, 142–4; Wake, *Principles*, 144–5.

[159] Calvin, *Catechisme*, 118–19; Nowell, *Catechisme*, 202; Boughen, *Exposition*, 67; Marshall, *Catechism*, 39; Isham, *Catechism*, 55.

[160] Ball, *Catechisme*, 78; Nicholson, *Exposition*, 142–3; Wake, *Principles*, 144.

[161] The phrases cited come respectively from Nicholes, *Catechisme*, 60; Hammond, *Practical catechisme*, 238; and Nicholson, *Exposition*, 142.

[162] Dering–More, *Catechisme*, sig. B7ᵛ; Westminster Larger, 155–6 (answer 195).

[163] Hill, *Principles*, sigs. C7ᵛ–8ʳ; Hammond, *Practical catechisme*, 238–9; Nicholson, *Exposition*, 144; Sherlock, *Principles*, 43; Vincent, *Catechism*, 255; Wake, *Principles*, 145.

[164] Nowell, *Catechisme*, 202, though cf. Calvin, *Catechisme*, 119; Hammond, *Practical catechisme*, 238; Nicholson, *Exposition*, 143–4; Marshall, *Catechism*, 39.

[165] Heidelberg Catechism, 354; Hammond, loc. cit.; Westminster Larger, 156 (answer 195); Sherlock, *Principles*, 43; Wake, *Principles*, 145.

have already seen in a previous chapter, however, Hammond also used the occasion of the second half of the Lord's Prayer to press for an alternative *ordo salutis* to that of the orthodox Calvinists, and in effect to reply to Cartwright's case for justification and sanctification being sought in the fifth petition. In the last three petitions, wrote Hammond, are set out sanctification, in the form of the spiritual 'bread of life' asked for in petition four, then justification, in the form of the forgiveness sought in petition five, and finally further grace to preserve men from sin, in petition six.[166] But Cartwright and Hammond were almost unique in taking this opportunity: for most catechists the second half of the Lord's Prayer was about men's physical and spiritual needs here on earth rather than the wider ramifications of the divine plan.

The remaining stages of the Lord's Prayer can be handled briefly. Not all sixteenth-century authors included the doxology, but it was regularly discussed, then and later. Although the 1549 Prayer Book form omitted it, it was given in Nowell's official forms and in later expositions of the official short form, where it was often referred to by its technical name; the Westminster divines also included it, but referred to it as 'the conclusion of the Lord's Prayer'.[167] Although there were persistent doubts about its provenance, it was widely conceded that it represented, as Hammond put it, 'a very fit form of acknowledgement to God to enforce the granting of the petitions'.[168] The line generally taken at the start of our period was that this conclusion had two functions. 'Thine' acted as a reminder that all our prayers and our hopes should be grounded on God, who alone was capable of answering them; while the references to 'kingdom', 'power', and 'glory' taught us that we should end our prayers by praising God.[169] A number of authors treated the two aspects in this order, and gave roughly equal weight to both. Thus Cartwright wrote that we ground our assurance of obtaining our desires in God, from whom comes all the things for which we ask, and to whom therefore all glory must be returned; and the Westminster divines stated that the conclusion 'teacheth us to take our encouragement in prayer from God only; and in our prayers to praise him, ascribing kingdom, power, and glory to him'.[170] Others, such as Nowell and some later Stuart conformists, devoted more space to the

---

[166] Hammond, *Practical catechisme*, 239.

[167] Prayer Book catechism, 786–7; Nowell, *Catechisme*, 190, 202; id., *Institution*, sigs. Gvi^v–vii^v; Heidelberg Catechism, 354; Hill, *Principles*, sig. C8^r; Hammond, loc. cit.; Nicholson, *Exposition*, 144–8; Isham, *Catechism*, 55; Wake, *Principles*, 145–6.

[168] See above, nn. 45–7; Hammond, *Practical catechisme*, 239; Calvin, *Institutes*, III. xx. 47; and Nowell, *Catechisme*, 202–5; Wake, *Principles*, 146; Westminster Larger, 156 (answer 196); Westminster Shorter, 39 (answer 107); Vincent, *Exposition*, 255.

[169] Calvin, *Catechisme*, 119–20; Nicholes, *Catechisme*, 61–3; Westminster Shorter, 39 (answer 107); Wake, *Principles*, 145–6; and see following notes.

[170] Calvin, loc. cit.; Dering–More, *Catechisme*, sig. B7^v; Cartwright, 'Catechisme', sig. Bb1^r; Hill, *Principles*, sig. C8^r; Heidelberg Catechism, 354; Westminster Larger, 156–7 (answer 196).

second aspect of the doxology, on the grounds that it was (in Williams's words) the 'perpetual office of the church militant and triumphant to ascribe' to God all his 'perfections'.[171] This stress was perhaps partly the result of later Stuart interest in, or defensiveness about, liturgical forms, but partly also, as in the case of Nowell and some early Stuart authors, the consequence of giving due weight to the main elements of the doxology—'kingdom', 'power', 'glory', and 'for ever'—all of which had potential for a renewed paean of praise to God's authority and greatness, of the kind found elsewhere in catechisms under the first article of the Creed, the first table of the Law, or indeed the preface and first three petitions of the Lord's Prayer itself.[172] We acknowledge God's excellencies 'in a super-eminent manner' said Wake near the end of his explanation of the doxology:

Others may have authority; but as derived from him, who only is the supreme king, over all the earth. Others may have power, but God only is almighty. Others may have glory, a majesty suitable to their station and character in the world: but to God only belongs the excellency of divine honour, and worship.[173]

Such accounts did not ignore the first function of the doxology mentioned above, that of teaching men to see God alone as the ground of their prayers, but their tactic was to stress the divine powers before the advisability of man appealing to them.

The possibility of human confidence in God's capacity to help them was reinforced by those authors who took the opportunity to expand on the meaning of 'Amen'. (A few authors did not, such as Calvin, or had already done so at the end of the Creed, for example Sherlock, Comber and Lewis.[174]) The simplest way of explaining this word was to substitute a phrase for it, such as 'so be it',[175] 'so it is',[176] 'so it shall be',[177] or in some cases two or all three of these.[178] Other phrases used were 'so shall the Lord bring to pass', and 'may all this be so'.[179] A longer way was to explain that it was a declaration and confirmation of faith, a 'note of confidence', or a 'word of wish and approbation',[180] or, if the author was so inclined, that it was a Hebrew word taken over by the Christian church as a means of bringing to an end and reinforcing the petitions of

---

[171] Nowell, *Catechisme*, 202–4; Nicholson, *Exposition*, 144–8; Williams, *Exposition*, 52–3; Lewis, *Catechism*, 65; and cf. Isham, *Catechism*, 55.

[172] See previous notes, and above, Chs. 7, 10; and cf. Hammond, *Practical catechisme*, 239.

[173] Wake, *Principles*, 146–7.

[174] Calvin, *Catechisme*, 119–20; Sherlock, *Principles*, 25 (though see 44); Comber, *Church-catechism*, '12' [*recte* 13] (though see also 25); Lewis, *Catechism*, 36 (though see 66).

[175] Prayer Book catechism, 786–7; Bernard, *Common catechisme*, sig. C4ʳ; Hammond, *Practical catechisme*, 240; Nicholson, *Exposition*, 148; Sherlock, *Principles*, 44; Marshall, *Catechism*, 40; Williams, *Exposition*, 53; Lewis, *Catechism*, 66.

[176] Cartwright, 'Catechisme', sig. Bb1ᵛ; Ball, *Catechisme*, 78; Nicholson, *Exposition*, 148.

[177] Heidelberg Catechism, 355; Hill, *Principles*, sig. C8ʳ; Bernard, *Common catechisme*, sig. C4ʳ.

[178] Hill and Bernard, loc. cit.; Nicholes, *Catechisme*, 63; Nicholson, *Exposition*, 148–9; Gouge, *Principles*, 128.

[179] Paget, *Questions*, sig. E5ʳ; Boughen, *Exposition*, 69.

[180] Nowell, *Catechisme*, 202; Cartwright, 'Catechisme', sig. Bb1ᵛ; Wake, *Principles*, 147.

the Lord's Prayer.[181] Whatever the phrase they adopted, our authors tended to draw certain lessons from it.

Three motifs occur regularly. The use of 'Amen' signifies a wish or desire—either 'a fervent desire', a 'desire of the heart', or 'earnest desire' to obtain the things we have asked of God in the Lord's Prayer,[182] or just a simple 'desire' or 'wish' that God will grant our requests.[183] Secondly, it betokens faith or belief: to use it is to testify to our conviction that God is capable of granting our requests.[184] Thirdly, it indicates that we are hopeful that God will hear our petitions and accept our praise.[185] Again various synonyms were used, such as 'trust', 'assurance', and 'confidence'.[186] Authors occasionally tried to draw fine distinctions between these different motifs, such as Richard Bernard, William Nicholson, and Thomas Gouge, who argued that 'so be it' represents our desires, whereas 'so it shall be' is spoken with the voice of faith.[187] But this was rare: some combination of two or three of the usages indicated was easily the most common tactic adopted, and by those of differing persuasions on other matters. There are elements of at least two usages, trust and faith, and a touch of desire also, in the Prayer Book catechism's exposition of 'Amen': 'And this I trust he will do of his mercy and goodness, through our Lord Jesu Christ. And therefore I say. Amen. So be it.'[188] Similarly, Nicholes wrote of praying with the assurance of faith, which conflated the second and third meanings.[189] The answer in the Westminster Shorter Catechism betokens a wish and a confidence, and in the context faith too: 'in testimony of our desire and assurance to be heard, we say "Amen" '. The Larger has all three: 'so we by faith are emboldened to plead with him that he would, and quietly to rely upon him, that he will fulfil our requests. And to testify this our desire and assurance, we say, Amen.'[190]

Will God hear our prayers? Most authors were confident that he would. Indeed,

---

[181] Hammond, *Practical catechisme*, 239–40; Boughen, *Exposition*, 69; Nicholson, *Exposition*, 148.

[182] Dering–More, *Catechisme*, sig. B7ᵛ; Paget, *Questions*, sig. E5ʳ; Hill, *Principles*, sig. C8ʳ; Nicholes, *Catechisme*, 63; Gouge, *Principles*, 128; Wake, *Principles*, 147.

[183] Heidelberg Catechism, 355; Ball, *Catechisme*, 78; Bernard, *Common catechisme*, sig. C4ʳ; Westminster Larger, 157 (answer 196); Westminster Shorter, 39 (answer 107); Nicholson, *Exposition*, 148; Comber, *Church-catechism*, 25; Marshall, *Catechism*, 40; Williams, *Exposition*, 53.

[184] Ball, *Catechisme*, 78; Bernard, loc. cit.; Hammond, *Practical catechisme*, 240; Nicholson, *Exposition*, 148–9; Comber, loc. cit.

[185] Ibid.; and Dering–More, *Catechisme*, sig. B7ᵛ.

[186] Prayer Book catechism, 786–7; Paget, *Questions*, sig. E5ʳ; Cartwright, 'Catechisme', sig. Bb1ᵛ; Hammond, *Practical catechisme*, 240; Westminster Larger, 157 (answer 196); Westminster Shorter, 39 (answer 107); Marshall, *Catechism*, 40; Williams, *Exposition*, 53; Isham, *Catechism*, 55; Wake, *Principles*, 147; Lewis, *Catechism*, 66.

[187] Bernard, *Common catechisme*, sig. C4ʳ; Nicholson, *Exposition*, 148–9; Gouge, *Principles*, 128; and cf. Nicholes, *Catechisme*, 63.

[188] Prayer Book catechism, 786–7.

[189] Nicholes, *Catechisme*, 63–4; and cf. Nowell, *Catechisme*, 202 ('assured faith' applied to the doxology as a whole).

[190] Westminster Shorter, 39 (answer 107); Westminster Larger, 157 (answer 196).

only John Ball tackled the subject of apparently unanswered prayer, and that only briefly: 'What must we do if God answer us not at the first or second time? Examine how we pray, and continue fervent therein, waiting upon the Lord until we speed.'[191] The rest of the authors in our sample who tackled the Lord's Prayer at any length were apparently content to leave the matter in the general terms indicated at the start of their sections on prayer or in the way just described when looking at the doxology: if we pray aright and for the things that God wants us to pray for, as indicated in the Lord's Prayer and elsewhere in the scriptures, we may be assured that he will hear our requests and grant such of them as seems good to him or will promote our salvation.[192]

The Lord's Prayer, as indicated at the start of this chapter, was probably the most ubiquitous and possibly the best known of the staple formulae used in catechizing. It also reinforced what had been said in earlier sections of most catechisms, under the Creed and the Commandments, about the nature of God as creator, father, and preserver, the sinfulness of man and the need for forgiveness, and the role of the Holy Ghost and of grace in bringing the faithful closer to God. If catechumens knew and understood little more than the Lord's Prayer, as explained in the simpler works in our sample of catechisms, they had mastered a goodly proportion of the elements of Christian teaching of the day. The prime function of the Lord's Prayer, however, was seen by our authors as being a way of calling upon God. For catechists, the Lord's Prayer was a perfect model of prayer. It was directed to God alone, through Christ; those who used it had to do so sincerely and in faith; used daily, it encouraged perseverance; it provided thanks for what had already been done for man, and petitions for more of the same for the needs of his body and soul. The Lord's Prayer was also the cause of very few disagreements of substance between catechists, and, though it was perhaps praised most highly by conformists, it is noteworthy that hardly any of the authors of works in our sample spoke of the Lord's Prayer itself with anything less than considerable warmth. All catechumens were told that they could and should use it, and those who did so with the necessary faith, sincerity, and persistence were told that they could be assured that they would be heard, even if God's response was not quite what they expected. One other general point may be made about catechetical treatment of the Lord's Prayer that perhaps also worked in its favour with catechumens. Compared to the traumas of the Last Judgement with which many catechetical accounts of the Creed ended, and the attempt to balance pessimism and optimism at the end of the Decalogue, the tone at the end of the typical exposition of the Lord's Prayer was almost always optimistic. The same was also largely true of catechists' treatment of the sacraments, to which we now turn.

---

[191] Ball, *Catechisme*, 79.

[192] Calvin, *Catechisme*, 98–9, 120; Nowell, *Catechisme*, 202; Nicholson, *Exposition*, 148; Isham, *Catechism*, 55–6; and Wake, *Principles*, 130–1, 146.

12

Sacraments

IT was not easy to explain sacraments to catechumens. Although ministers performing the sacraments used commonplace materials, such as water, bread, and wine, and although they used everyday terms like 'signs' and 'seals' to describe their meaning, the fact remained that at the heart of baptism and the Lord's Supper lay deep spiritual mysteries. Further problems were posed by the fact that the theology of sacraments was particularly difficult—it even caused headaches for a master like Calvin—and that in England doctrine did not remain static, but shifted subtly from one generation to the next. Another tension arose because catechists, especially in the sixteenth century, wished to wean their charges away from the old attachment to the mass and 'popish' sacraments such as confession and extreme unction and from any mistaken views that sacraments automatically produced benefits for the participant; but at the same time they did not wish their flocks to undervalue the two ordinances which Protestant leaders judged to have been instituted by God for the spiritual benefit of the faithful. It is true that some authors, such as Keach and Watts, seem to have thought that young children were either not capable of understanding such mysteries, or that, since they were too young to receive communion, it was not necessary to teach them about the sacraments until they were older. In addition some authors who were seeking to break away from accepted catechetical structures in order to get the essential message across, such as Cartwright and Hieron, decided that it was not necessary to devote more than a few lines to the sacraments.[1] But such men were in a very small minority: as we saw in an earlier chapter, many authors were at least in part prompted to write a catechism by concern for what they saw as the inadequate knowledge of potential communicants about their faith in general and the sacraments in particular. In practice, the typical catechism of early modern England had a substantial section—rarely less than a couple of pages, even in the shortest forms, and often more—on the purpose and function of the sacraments and how they should be approached by the faithful. In the Westminster Larger Catechism, for example, seventeen of the hundred and ninety-six questions were devoted to the sacraments; as a comparison, the Lord's Prayer merited only eleven

---

[1] Cartwright, 'Catechisme', sig. Aa7ᵛ; Hieron, *Doctrine*, 579. Keach did not tackle the sacraments in 'Little child', and 'Child', only in 'Youth', 98–112; there is a two-line reference to the sacraments in Watts, 'Children's catechism', but none in 'First catechism'.

questions.[2] In most forms the section on the sacraments was placed either last, after discussion of Creed, Decalogue, and Lord's Prayer, or in the penultimate position, with the Lord's Prayer at the end.[3] The typical author of such a section first offered a definition of a sacrament and indicated what baptism and the Lord's Supper had in common, then he dealt separately and at greater length with what was distinctive about each of them—a sequence which will be followed in this chapter also.

It is also worth noting at this stage that despite well publicized disagreements amongst Protestants on the Continent over both baptism and the Lord's Supper in the second and third quarters of the sixteenth century, the spectrum of differing views in England on the nature and significance of the sacraments was much smaller, especially at catechetical level. On the Continent there was a deep rift over baptism between 'magisterial' reformers such as Luther, Zwingli, and Calvin and 'radicals' such as the Anabaptists, and there were also persisting divisions between the Lutheran and Reformed churches over the nature of the Lord's Supper, at least at the level of official confessions of faith and some advanced theological discussion.[4] In England, however, to judge from the works in our sample, catechetical authors experienced little difficulty in agreeing with their colleagues on a number of issues related to the sacraments. Such differences as emerged were mainly on the subject of baptism, and even these (with the single exception of Keach's support for believer's baptism) were often not clear-cut, but related to how much was conveyed to the baptized child in actuality as opposed to potentiality. Nor does our sample of catechisms lend much support to the idea that a new concept of holy communion was established in England from the 1590s, and especially in the reign of Charles I. On the sacraments as a pair, there was even a limited convergence in the seventeenth century through the shared concern of conformist and more conservative nonconformists at the apparent threat to sacraments posed by some radicals, and through the widespread adoption by both 'godly' or presbyterian and conformist or episcopalian of the view that the sacraments were seals of the covenant of grace. This is not to deny that there were disputes over the mode of administration of sacraments—over whether they must always be accompanied by a sermon, the use of godparents and the sign of the cross in baptism, kneeling and the use of wafers in communion, who should be admitted, and so on.[5] But as was so often the case with

---

[2] Westminster Larger, 126–42 (answers 161–77), 146–57 (answers 186–96); there were also eight questions on prayer in general.

[3] The Heidelberg Catechism was unusual in placing the sacraments second: see above, p. 282.

[4] For general accounts, see B. M. G. Reardon, *Religious Thought in the Reformation* (London, 1981), 77–8, 104–7, 111, 141, 153–4, 200–1, 208–9, 214–16, 220–2, 227–9, 235; E. Cameron, *The European Reformation* (Oxford, 1991), ch. 11; E. B. Holifield, *The Covenant Sealed: The Development of Puritan Sacramental Theology in Old and New England, 1570–1720* (New Haven/London, 1974), ch. 1; B. A. Gerrish, *Grace and Gratitude: The Eucharistic Theology of John Calvin* (Edinburgh, 1993), chs. 4–5.

[5] J. F. H. New, *Anglican and Puritan: The Basis of their Opposition, 1558–1640* (London, 1964), 70–1; Holifield, *Covenant Sealed*, 33–4.

such differences of practice, these were not usually debated in catechisms; and what concerns us here is doctrine rather than discipline.

If we look first at the definition of a sacrament offered by our authors, we immediately find several areas of agreement. First of all, there was a widespread adoption of the Augustinian dichotomy between visible and invisible in the sacraments, derived either directly from Augustine or through Luther and Calvin.[6] Among English catechists, therefore, it was widely agreed that a sacrament was an outward representation, a 'token', a 'visible' or 'sensible' 'sign', of something which could not be seen or touched by ordinary means: the gospel promise of salvation through Christ.[7] According to Calvin (in his catechism of 1541), a sacrament was an outward token of God's favour which by a visible sign represented spiritual things to us; it was an aid or instrument devised by God to help the feeble intelligence of man grasp the significance of the gospel promise.[8] 'Sign' was also used in another sense as an outward indicator of the faith of the individual: to participate in the sacraments was a 'mark', 'token', 'witness', or 'badge' of our open profession of the Christian religion.[9] This usage had its origins in the Zwinglian view of sacraments as tokens of Christian profession and fellowship; but the view generally adopted in England (as the following paragraphs will demonstrate) was that while sacraments may have been badges by which Christians could be distinguished from non-Christians, they were also more than corporate recollections of past events or man-centred acknowledgements of divine goodness.

Sacraments were also regularly described as 'seals'. In some cases, this was meant to convey the affixing or imprinting of the Gospel promise on our heart, so that it could become better established there. For Egerton, for example, a sacrament was a seal in that it 'effectually applies' Christ and his benefits to the faithful receiver.[10] 'Seal' was also used in the legal sense of confirming the authenticity of a statement in a document.[11] Similar terms such as 'pledge' or 'assurance' were used by a variety of authors to make a similar point. Sacraments, said Dering and More, were 'sure pledges of those benefits of our salvation which we receive in Christ to be ours'.[12]

---

[6] Gerrish, *Grace and Gratitude*, 103–4, 107–8, 164–5.

[7] Calvin, *Catechisme*, 125, 147; Heidelberg Catechism, 328; Nowell, *Catechisme*, 205–6; Dering–More, *Catechisme*, sig. B5ʳ; Paget, *Questions*, sig. D3ᵛ; Perkins, *Foundation*, 7; Ball, *Catechisme*, 80; Hill, *Principles*, sig. C2ʳ; Ussher, 'Principles', 11; Hammond, *Practical catechisme*, 347–8; Boughen, *Exposition*, 71; Westminster Larger, 127 (answer 162); Taylor, 'Catechism', 5; Comber, *Church-catechism*, 27; Marshall, *Catechism*, 42, 89.

[8] Calvin, *Catechisme*, 125, 127, 141; and cf. Cartwright, 'Catechisme', sig. Aa7ᵛ; Watts, 'Children's catechism', 24.

[9] Calvin, *Catechisme*, 125, 147; Nowell, *Catechisme*, 206; Dering–More, *Catechisme*, sig. B5ʳ; Hill, *Principles*, sig. C2ʳ; and cf. Cardwell, *Synodalia*, i. 66.

[10] Egerton, 'Briefe method', 14–15; and cf. Calvin, *Catechisme*, 130; Nowell, *Catechisme*, 205; Nicholson, *Exposition*, 151; Marshall, *Catechism*, 42, 89.

[11] Egerton, 'Forme of examining', 30; Hieron, *Doctrine*, 579; Hill, *Principles*, sig. C2ʳ; Ussher, 'Principles', 11.

[12] Dering–More, *Catechisme*, sig. B5ʳ; and cf. Perkins, *Foundation*, 7; Boughen, *Exposition*, 71;

From the early seventeenth century, a growing number of authors also used the term 'seal' in this second sense, of a legal confirmation of a promise, in the context of the covenant of grace. William Bradshaw in his popular pre-communion form and John Ball in his best-selling short catechism both defined sacraments as a 'seal' (singular) of the covenant of grace,[13] while the authors of the Westminster Larger Catechism said that what baptism and the Lord's Supper had in common was that 'both are seals of the same covenant'; episcopalians would also happily refer to sacraments as seals of the covenant.[14] There was no problem in combining the idea of a seal with that of a sign, as we can see from the definitions of a sacrament offered by the authors of the Heidelberg Catechism and others in our sample, and in the section on sacraments added provisionally to the Prayer Book catechism in the early 1570s and in its final form in 1604.[15]

It will already be clear that in England sacraments were widely seen as means of not simply providing a guarantee of the divine promise of salvation that was comprehensible to the intellect, but also transmitting positive spiritual benefits. Sacraments were described as 'effectual', faith was said to be nourished, and 'benefits' or 'graces' were said to be conveyed or applied to or received by those who, in the sixteenth century, were usually called the 'faithful' or 'faithful receivers', but in the seventeenth were often termed 'believers'.[16] The subject of exactly what was conveyed, when, and how is one to which we will have to return more than once in this chapter, but here it is perhaps worth dwelling on to try to help us understand how terms like 'benefits' and 'graces' were being used in a general sense at this definition stage. Of the two terms, the first is easier to explain. The benefits of Christ's sacrifice and mediation on behalf of fallen man were those which have been described in a previous chapter, on the Creed: as a result of his fulfilling the three offices of prophet, priest, and king, and of his humiliation and exaltation, Christ saves and protects his people. In the seventeenth century, this was often put in covenanting terms, as in the Westminster Larger Catechism: Christ was the mediator of the covenant of grace, and through his

---

Sherlock, *Principles*, 46; Comber, *Church-catechism*, 27; and cf. Hammond's use of 'pawn' as well as 'pledge' in *Practical catechisme*, 347, 352.

[13] Bradshaw, 'Brief forme', 139; Ball, *Catechisme*, 79.

[14] Westminster Larger, 141 (answer 176); Hammond, *Practical catechisme*, 389–90 (and cf. 378, 385); Nicholson, *Exposition*, 166; Taylor, 'Catechism', 4; Williams, *Exposition*, 2, 55–6. Many examples could be given from works outside the sample.

[15] Heidelberg Catechism, 66; Prayer Book catechism, 787; and cf. Dering–More, *Catechisme*, sig. B5ʳ; Egerton, 'Briefe method', 14–15. Egerton was perhaps what Gerrish (*Grace and Gratitude*, 166–8) calls a symbolic parallelist in thinking that the signs were for all, but the seals only for the truly faithful (the elect). But most authors in the sample seem to have treated signs and seals as two facets of the same stone, or (especially in the case of the Lord's Supper) said the sign was the visible representation of what was sealed invisibly.

[16] Calvin, *Catechisme*, 128–30; Nowell, *Catechisme*, 205–6; 'Certaine questions and answers', sig. *iiiᵛ; Egerton, 'Briefe method', 14–15; Cartwright, 'Catechisme', sig. Aa7ᵛ; Elton, *Forme*, sig. D5ʳ; Hill, *Principles*, sig. C2ʳ; Westminster Larger, 127 (answer 162); Westminster Shorter, 34 (answers 91–2); Nicholson, *Exposition*, 152; Marshall, *Catechism*, 42.

offices and sufferings its members have 'communion in grace' with Christ by 'partaking of the virtue of his mediation, in their justification, adoption, sanctification, and whatever else, in this life, manifests their union with him'.[17] Many episcopalian catechists also used the covenant of grace in their sacramental teaching, though they did not necessarily use the same labels as predestinarians to describe its benefits.[18]

'Grace' was a term often used but rarely explained in the catechisms of this period. When used in the singular it sometimes seems to have had the connotation of a single, all-powerful form of saving grace, as in the covenant of grace which God made with Christ to save his people, or in Nicholson's reference to 'the vital or saving grace of Christ'.[19] On other occasions, it seems to have meant any act of divine mercy or unmerited divine assistance, as in the Heidelberg divines' statement that the sacraments are signs and seals of God's promise by which 'he grants us, out of free grace, the forgiveness of sins and everlasting life', or in Paget's assertion that a sacrament is an outward sign that may be seen of 'grace that cannot be seen for the better assurance and strengthening of our faith'.[20] When used in the plural or of different types of grace, it seems to have had the sense of a number of undeserved gifts which assisted the faithful towards salvation, such as regeneration or inspiration by the Holy Ghost, faith, hope, and charity, or the strengthening of faith.[21] Some authors switched between plural and singular, so that in answer 162 of the Westminster Larger Catechism the authors referred to participants being strengthened and increased in 'faith, and all other graces', but in answer 168 faithful communicants are said to feed on Christ 'to their spiritual nourishment and growth in grace'.[22] It has been suggested that since double predestinarians put such a strong emphasis on prevenient grace in the calling of the elect, they expected less of the grace received through the sacraments; non-Calvinists, on the other hand, are said to have had a much higher expectation of grace in the sacraments.[23] This may or may not have been so, but both presbyterians and episcopalians appear to have had a fairly dynamic view of the power of sacraments by the mid-seventeenth century, though as we will see there was sometimes a difference of opinion over whether the benefits were guaranteed for the future or actually conveyed in the present.

How these concepts of 'grace' and 'benefits' were deployed may become a little clearer if we look more closely at the work of a few of the authors in our sample, starting with one—Alexander Nowell—who may have played the largest part in spreading

---

[17] Westminster Larger, 15–36 (answers 32–69), and cf. 127 (answer 162).

[18] See above, pp. 417–19.

[19] Westminster Larger, 14–15 (answers 30–2); Nicholson, *Exposition*, 151.

[20] Heidelberg Catechism, 328; Paget, *Questions*, sig. D3ᵛ.

[21] Hammond, *Practical catechisme*, 29, 232, 325; Westminster Larger, 15 (answer 32), 39–41 (answers 72–6); Wake, *Principles*, 149.

[22] Westminster Larger, 127, 129 (answers 162, 168).

[23] New, *Anglican and Puritan*, 64–8; Tyacke, *Anti-Calvinists*, 10, 52, 55, 84, 165, 175–6, 202; Lake, *Anglicans and Puritans?*, 173–7.

the association of sacraments with grace, both in his own work and in the section on sacraments added to the Prayer Book form which was in part based on his form. In his original form, Nowell suggested that the outward elements in a sacrament represented 'invisible grace', or 'secret and spiritual grace' as he later termed it (in the 1604 supplement to the Prayer Book catechism this became 'an outward and visible sign of an inward and spiritual grace'). By the means God has provided to help our defective eyesight, he added, we can behold the 'heavenly graces which otherwise we are not able to see' (note the switch from singular to plural).[24] At the stage of defining a sacrament, then, Nowell still talked of grace or graces as something which the faithful behold or understand as having been promised to them. Later on in his form, however, 'grace' seems to be something which is actually received: in baptism, 'we certainly receive' grace of two sorts: forgiveness and regeneration; in the Lord's Supper, it is 'Christ himself, with whom our souls, as with their proper food, are inwardly nourished'.[25]

This second stress—on a delivery of grace rather than just a promissory note—may have been derived from what Calvin had written at various points in his catechism where he talked of the 'gracious benefits' conferred by Christ in the sacraments, and of the receipt of grace in baptism and communion, apparently in a present sense.[26] It may also have derived from Nowell's reading of the *Institutes* and other works by Calvin. According to an excellent recent study of Calvin's sacramental theology by Professor Gerrish, diplomacy may have prevented Calvin from coming out too openly against Zwingli, and his predestinarian views may have hampered his affirmation of sacramental efficacy, but (Gerrish suggests) his scriptural literalism meant that he was always leaning towards Luther's view of sacraments which not only mean something but also do something. If a sign is given, then the reality is also, or God is deceiving us, Calvin believed. God can and does work through instruments or means such as the sacraments, and if in the case of the Lord's Supper the signs were not efficacious means of grace, then we are not spiritually eating Christ's life-giving body as the New Testament tells us we are.[27] Alternatively or in addition, in suggesting delivery of benefits Nowell may have been thinking of the definitions of sacraments in articles twenty-five and twenty-six of the Thirty-nine Articles, or possibly the first official homily on the Lord's Supper. The first paragraph of article twenty-five asserted that sacraments are 'sure witnesses' and 'signs' of grace, but they are also effectual and through them, and God's good will, our faith is increased; while in successive sentences of the homily, probably the work of Jewel, were stated a cognitive act of understanding that a sacrament was a seal of God's mercy, and a spiritual or emotional act of feeling an increase of faith 'and many other sundry graces of God'.[28]

---

[24] Nowell, *Catechisme*, 205–7.   [25] Ibid. 207–8, 212.

[26] Calvin, *Catechisme*, 133, 140–1; id., *Institutes*, IV. xiv. 7.

[27] Gerrish, *Grace and Gratitude*, 105–8, 137–40, 162–7, and *passim*.

[28] Cardwell, *Synodalia*, i. 66; *The Two Books of Homilies Appointed to be Read in Churches*, ed. J. Griffiths (Oxford, 1859), pp. xxxiii, 443.

Both these statements can be taken to refer either to a state of assurance being achieved in the future, or to a further state of salvation being attained in the present; but the idea of 'sundry graces of God' being felt is again a step beyond a mere beholding of God's gospel promise.

The two tendencies within Nowell's view of the sacraments can be found in most other authors inside and outside our sample. Some of the 'godly' may have tended to stress the idea of sacraments as signs or seals rather than as actual deliveries of grace, at least in their general definitions of a sacrament.[29] On the other hand, the section on sacraments added to the Prayer Book catechism in 1604, based partly on Nowell's catechism but perhaps in its final wording the work of Bishop Overall, incorporated both tendencies but arguably leant towards delivery: a sacrament is 'an outward and visible sign of an inward and spiritual grace, given unto us, ordained by Christ himself, as a means whereby we receive the same'.[30] This was followed by most (though not all) of the authors who later expounded this form, as we shall see. However, the temptation to see in the sacraments something more than a sign or seal of some future benefit was felt by many authors who, perhaps concerned that their catechumens might undervalue these divine ordinances, also gave space to the benefits to be derived from the sacraments by the faithful. In both of their catechisms, the Westminster theologians, for example, refer to sacraments as 'effectual means of salvation', which are administered 'by the working of the Holy Ghost, and the blessing of Christ'; and at an earlier point of both forms they say that 'the Word, sacraments, and prayer' are the outward means by which the benefits of Christ's meditation 'are made effectual to the elect for their salvation'.[31] At an even earlier point of the Larger Catechism, on Christ as the mediator of the covenant of grace, the authors say that in the New Testament the sacraments of baptism and the Lord's Supper hold forth 'grace and salvation ... in more fulness, evidence and efficacy, to all nations' than had the sacraments of the Old; and at a later point, catechumens are told that by sharing in the Lord's Supper communicants will 'have their union and communion with Christ confirmed'.[32] If one takes the whole of answer 162 in the Larger Catechism, and assumes that the later infinitives all depend on 'instituted by Christ', then it is clear that a number of actual changes were expected in the faithful receiver:

A sacrament is an holy ordinance instituted by Christ in his church, to signify, seal, and exhibit unto those that are within the covenant of grace, the benefits of his mediation; to strengthen and increase their faith, and all other graces; to oblige them to obedience; to testify and cherish their love and communion one with another; and to distinguish them from those that are without.[33]

It has recently been suggested that in the work of Hooker, Andrewes, and the English 'Arminians' the leaders of the English church took a decisive turn towards a

[29] Ball, *Catechisme*, 80; Westminster Larger, 127 (answer 163).
[30] Prayer Book catechism, 787.   [31] Westminster Larger, 119–20, 126–7 (answers 154–5, 161–2).
[32] Westminster Shorter, 16–17, 131 (answers 35, 168).
[33] Westminster Larger, 127 (answer 162).

theology of grace which focused on the sacraments; and there were some contemporary allegations that the Laudians adopted Catholic notions of propitiatory sacrifice and corporeal presence in the Lord's Supper and stressed the sacerdotal powers of the clergy.[34] In view of these charges, we might expect that staunch episcopalians in our sample like Hammond, Boughen, and Nicholson would have devoted a good deal of space to the subject of grace or the value of the sacraments in their longer than average forms; but this was not the case. Boughen said virtually nothing at the outset, though under baptism he would later state (in a phrase reminiscent of Calvin and Cartwright) that the Word added to the element of water delivered grace.[35] Hammond stated that the term 'grace' in the context of the sacraments meant 'some special favour and gift of God bestowed upon us'. Later he amplified this by suggesting that the 'graces' referred to were, in this world, 'pardon of sins past, and acceptance of sincere performance, and also grace or strength so to perform', and, in the next, final pardon of sin and 'a pure and happy condition'.[36] This is not very different from the way in which in the *Institutes* Calvin said he was wont 'familiarly to explain' the effect of the Lord's Supper on the faithful receiver: 'By the effect, I understand redemption, justification, sanctification, eternal life, and all other benefits which Christ bestows upon us.'[37] Nicholson reiterated both of the points made by Hammond just noted, though in a slightly modified form. In his case, he stated that the 'grace' referred to in the Prayer Book form is 'the whole obedience, merit, death, and passion, of our saviour; and the benefits that flow from thence, justification, wisdom, sanctification, [and] redemption' (which is even closer to Calvin's 'familiar' explanation). At one point Nicholson quoted Hooker's statement that in sacraments 'that saving grace which Christ originally is, or hath for the general good of his whole church' is instilled individually into every member thereof. But at the outset he also described the value of sacraments in terms very similar to the answer in the Westminster Larger Catechism cited above, though in a different order.[38] Nicholson was also quite happy like Hammond to place sacraments in a federal context:

A covenant God hath made with man for salvation and for grace, without which salvation cannot be had; and by the sacrament it hath pleased him, as in a fair deed to represent it, to convey and make it over, to seal and deliver it to us.[39]

The two sides found in Nowell—representing and conveying—are reflected here, as also is the idea of grace being 'made over' to man. But for Nicholson and Hammond, as for Nowell and indeed Calvin, the delivery was only part of the story: there was

---

[34] See above, n. 23; but cf. Holifield, *Covenant Sealed*, 110.

[35] Boughen, *Exposition*, 71–2; and cf. Gerrish, *Grace and Gratitude*, 107–8; and Cartwright, 'Catechisme', sig. Aa7ᵛ.

[36] Hammond, *Practical catechisme*, 347; for a later work by Hammond that touched on the sacraments, see his *On fundamentals*, discussed in C. H. Lettinga, 'Covenant Theology and the Transformation of Anglicanism', Ph.D. thesis (Johns Hopkins, 1987), 192–6.

[37] Calvin, *Institutes*, IV. xvii. 11.   [38] Nicholson, *Exposition*, 155, 151–2.   [39] Ibid. 156.

also the receiving, which depended not on membership of the visible church or bare participation in the sacrament but on the operation of the Holy Ghost. The instrument by which we receive the seal of the covenant, wrote Nicholson, is faith, and that is a gift of the Spirit.[40]

In at least some ways, rather than drifting further apart predestinarians and non-predestinarians were perhaps getting closer in the 1640s and 1650s. It has been suggested that at that time mainstream 'puritans', in part in response to challenges from Baptists and Quakers, were developing a sacramental theology in which they reaffirmed the importance of baptism in the scheme of salvation, reasserted an efficacious doctrine of the Lord's Supper of the type espoused by Calvin, and encouraged pious practices which centred round the Lord's Supper.[41] This is outside our terms of reference here, but it should be clear from Chapter 9 and the last few paragraphs that in our sample of catechisms both episcopalians and presbyterians believed that the sacraments were seals of the covenant, but were more than a bare sign or seal so that, in reality or in prospect, benefits were received by the faithful. There remained differences of opinion: where the Westminster theologians saw sacraments as being effectual only in those predestined and already called to 'grace and salvation',[42] non-Calvinists like Hammond and Nicholson saw them as means by which those with faith and so capable of salvation could receive saving grace (in the case of children in baptism the faith was that of their parents or the congregation). The former saw the elect, having already been called to faith, proceeding inevitably towards glory, so that sacraments were necessary, in that they were commanded by Christ, and effective, in that they strengthened faith, but in the larger setting of the divine plan they were not crucial. The latter did not see the faithful as proceeding inexorably towards heaven, and so naturally gave a higher priority to those means ordained by Christ to help the faithful on their way to salvation.

Authors like Hammond and Nicholson did not go on from that to say that participation in the sacraments was essential to salvation, or that salvation should be pursued through sacraments rather than the Word. For them, sacraments were not *the* means, but *a* means by which grace was conveyed, though they would certainly have agreed with Calvin and Cartwright that the sacraments were 'a more lively, effectual and sensible instrument' than the Word alone for offering and conveying Christ and his benefits to the faithful.[43] Other conformist episcopalians in our sample who offered a definition of the sacraments between the 1610s and the 1690s did little more than paraphrase the wording of the Prayer Book form on this matter—sacraments are outward signs ordained by Christ whereby we receive an inward and spiritual grace—or supplement it by using some of the terms listed above: sacraments are 'signs', 'means', 'pledges', and 'seals' by which graces (plural) are assured and conveyed to

---

[40] Nicholson, *Exposition*, 156.   [41] Holifield, *Covenant Sealed*, pp. ix–x, and chs. 3–4.
[42] Westminster Larger, 15–17 (answers 31–5).   [43] See above, n. 35.

those believers who receive the sacraments in faith.[44] It is true that the Prayer Book form does state that the two sacraments were 'generally necessary to salvation'. However, the interpretation placed on this by authors inside the sample like Hammond, Nicholson, Williams, Wake, and Lewis, and by some outside such as Hooker, Bancroft, and Laud, was that all good Christians are obliged to participate in the sacraments of baptism and communion if they have the opportunity, and that they should not neglect them wilfully.[45] Nicholson put it this way:

'Generally necessary to salvation'. That is, which all men ought to receive who desire to attain salvation; which is not to be understood, as if God could not save without them; but that they are the means instrumental, and ordinary seals by which God hath promised to convey and assure Christ's merits unto us.

'Wilfully to neglect them ... when they may be had, is to cast aside God's ordinance,' he added.[46] Exactly the same point had been made by Calvin and Nowell a century earlier, though again neither man believed that God was tied to the sacraments: not to use the sacraments is to dishonour Christ and refuse his gracious benefits; those who refuse the sacraments are not worthy to be accounted Christians, and (added Nowell) it was wicked to refuse God's grace.[47] Occasionally stronger statements can be found in episcopalian catechisms, but should be treated in their entirety and context. Writing of baptism alone, John Williams said that it was necessary to salvation since it comprised admission into the church, and outside the church no salvation was possible; but, he went on, baptism was not sufficient for salvation without the new birth signified therein.[48]

The allegations of sacerdotalism against the Laudians are also weakened by the existence of a shared belief among mainstream English Protestants that sacraments were for those in the church and should be administered by a regular, ordained clergy. This was more implicit than explicit in the definitions offered by the authors of some Edwardian and Elizabethan forms,[49] but Stephen Egerton remarked that God set his seal on his promise of salvation by 'the ministry of the sacraments', and Thomas Cartwright said quite specifically that sacraments were instruments by which Christ and his benefits were offered to all in the church.[50] There were also clear

---

[44] e.g. Hill, *Principles*, sigs. C2^{r-v}; Boughen, *Exposition*, 71; Marshall, *Catechism*, 42, 89; Williams, *Exposition*, 55.

[45] Hammond, *Practical catechisme*, 346; Nicholson, *Exposition*, 1–2; Williams, *Exposition*, 53; Lewis, *Catechism*, 67. For the position of Whitgift and Bancroft, see also G. W. Bromiley, *Baptism and the Anglican Reformers* (London, 1953), 61–4. For the view that 'generally' meant for all men, the whole 'genus' of man, see H. E. Symonds, *The Council of Trent and Anglican Formularies* (1933), 33.

[46] Nicholson, *Exposition*, 151.

[47] Calvin, *Catechisme*, 128; Nowell, *Catechisme*, 206; Gerrish, *Grace and Gratitude*, 172.

[48] Williams, *Exposition*, 54, 57; Isham, *Catechism*, 60–1; Lewis, *Catechism*, 69, 71.

[49] Nowell, *Catechisme*, 205–19 (though cf. 207, 217–19); the 'godly' Dering and More, Paget, Perkins, and Ball also refrained from mentioning the church at first.

[50] Egerton, 'Forme of examining', 30; Cartwright, 'Catechisme', sig. Aa7^{v}.

statements in Elton's form and in the Westminster Larger Catechism that a sacrament was 'an holy ordinance' 'instituted by Christ in his church', a formulation which was very close to the 'holy rite, a sacred ceremony used in the service of God' of Henry Hammond, or the 'outward ceremony ordained by Christ' of Jeremy Taylor.[51] Sacraments 'are to be dispensed by ministers of the gospel, and by none other; and to be continued in the church of Christ until his second coming': this statement may be found in the Westminster Larger Catechism, but would probably have satisfied most episcopalian catechists.[52] It was also agreed by a number of authors, as the authors of the Westminster Larger Catechism put it, that 'The sacraments become effectual means of salvation, not by any power in themselves, or any virtue derived from the piety or intention of him by whom they are administered, but only by the working of the Holy Ghost and the blessing of Christ, by whom they are instituted'.[53] 'The union of the things with the signs', wrote Nicholson, 'is altogether mystical and spiritual, and depends merely upon Christ the ordainer's will and counsel.'[54]

Of the various definitions offered by our authors that we have examined in the last few pages, none was paramount. The usual practice, as we have seen, was to combine two or more of the metaphors or labels on offer, sometimes more. In his popular exposition of the Prayer Book form, first published in 1616, William Hill defined a sacrament as a visible sign of invisible grace; the sacraments of the New Testament were outward signs to assure us that Christ and all his benefits have been made ours. He also indicated five different functions of sacraments: as badges of our Christian profession, signs to our senses of God's promise, seals to confirm the truth thereof, means to convey inward and spiritual graces where there is faith to apprehend them, and effectual means of the increase of faith and piety in our hearts.[55] In 1699 William Wake listed five characteristics of the two true sacraments, compared to those called sacraments by the Church of Rome. They have an outward and visible sign; an inward and spiritual grace; and a divine institution; they are ordained as a means to convey 'their several graces' to us and a pledge to assure us of them; and 'all Christians have a right to them: nor may any, without hazard of missing of these graces, refuse to use them'. Wake then went on to examine rites such as confirmation, penance, extreme unction, matrimony, and ordination to point out how many of the five characteristics they did or did not possess.[56] Like Hammond before him,[57] Wake may have been defensive about some of these rites, but the authors in our sample

---

[51] Elton, *Forme*, sig. D5ʳ; Westminster Larger, 127 (answer 162); Hammond, *Practical catechisme*, 345; Taylor, 'Catechism', 5; and cf. Nicholson, *Exposition*, 151.

[52] Westminster Larger, 141 (answer 176); and for an episcopalian's stress on the ecclesiastical character of the sacraments, Williams, *Exposition*, 54.

[53] Westminster Larger, 126 (answer 161).

[54] Nicholson, *Exposition*, 155 and cf. 152. We shall return to the exact nature of the elements in the separate sections on the two sacraments which follow.

[55] Hill, *Principles*, sig. C2ʳ.   [56] Wake, *Principles*, 148–51.

[57] Hammond, *Practical catechisme*, 345–6.

were in complete agreement that only two sacraments were instituted by Christ in the New Testament, as replacements to circumcision and the passover in the Old.[58] It is to the first of these that we can now turn.

In their treatment of baptism, the catechists in our sample had at least two tactical problems. One was that at the start of their section on the sacraments, most of them felt obliged, as we have just seen, to offer a definition of the New Testament sacraments as a pair, though it was not easy to find a form of words that described with equal felicity both baptism—a sacrament received but once and by the great majority of the church-going population in their infancy—and holy communion—supposedly received frequently but only by mature, professing Christians.[59] The temptation was to describe baptism as if it were being received by one of the tiny minority not baptized at birth—an adult raised in a non-Christian environment or who had converted to Christianity—in which case authors could insist on preconditions such as repentance and faith being met that were comparable to those for admission to the Lord's Supper. They could also describe the effects of baptism on a mature baptized person in similar terms to communion, for example, assurance of a heavenly inheritance and the strengthening of faith. This was a temptation to which many authors succumbed, including Calvin, and the composers of the Prayer Book, Heidelberg, and Westminster catechisms and their respective followers; but it did tend to produce a lopsided exposition or to run the risk of conflating the effects of baptism on a mature believer with those on a baby. The second difficulty stemmed from this, in that those catechists who had defined baptism in terms of adult baptism then had to explain why infants who were too young to have faith or be repentant were baptized. This problem was pressing because the children and adolescents who formed the great bulk of their catechumens had to be given a clear picture of what their baptism had entailed, and also because, though the supporters of believer's baptism in England were never very large, infant baptism remained a sensitive issue between mainstream reformers and radicals.[60] Catechists had to find an explanation which neither exaggerated the value of baptism to the point where those already baptized might think they were already saved (or parents whose children had died prematurely might fear that their unbaptized child was doomed to hell-fire), nor downgraded it to the point where charges of error or heresy could be levelled against them.

---

[58] Hill, *Principles*, sig. C2ᵛ; Ussher, 'Principles', 11; Hammond, *Practical catechisme*, 347, 378–9; Westminster Larger, 16–17, 127 (answers 35, 162); Nicholson, *Exposition*, 150–1.

[59] Though in practice many did not receive as often as they could: S. J. Wright (ed.), *Parish, Church and People: Local Studies in Lay Religion 1350–1750* (1988), 127–39, 215–17.

[60] Bromiley, *Baptism*, pp. xiv–xv; Brachlow, *Communion of Saints*, 54–5, 150–6; though see also D. A. Penny, *Freewill or Predestination: The Battle over Saving Grace in Mid-Tudor England* (Woodbridge, 1990).

For those authors in our sample expounding the Prayer Book catechism of 1549, there was an additional, though minor problem. The original form had been designed for those adolescents about to be confirmed, so that it began with a summary of the significance of baptism and of the vows made on their behalf by their godparents, vows which they were about to confirm for themselves on the basis of their understanding of the Creed, Decalogue, and Lord's Prayer as taught in the rest of the form. At a later stage, however, apparently in response to a perceived need, a new section was added at the end of the original form, offering a definition of both sacraments, and then an examination of each one in turn. The result was that after 1604 there were two separate sections on baptism in the official short catechism, one at the start and one near the end, and an organizational problem for those expounding this text: should they treat the two together, to reduce the risk of repetition, or separately, since that was how catechumens, at least initially, would confront them? The great majority opted for the latter, but in what follows here the two sections will be kaleidoscoped in order to facilitate comparison with the single section in other authors' catechisms.

In many of the initiation rites studied by anthropologists, the initiate has to be prepared by undergoing certain set rituals and a token separation from the society of which he is about to become a full member. In the medieval English rite of baptism and even in the 1549 revision of that rite, there are examples of such preparation and symbolic separation. By 1552, however, under the influence of Bucer, all remaining traces of these practices had disappeared, and baptism was reduced to the brief ceremony at the font.[61] The only separation was asserted verbally: the children of believing parents are 'distinguished from the children of unbelievers, as was done in the Old Testament by circumcision, in place of which in the New Testament baptism is appointed', wrote the Heidelberg divines in their catechism; those who are born 'children of wrath' become 'children of grace', said the author of the supplementary section of the 1549 Prayer Book form.[62] The only symbol left was the water, which had unimpeachable scriptural credentials. The fact that baptism was usually carried out when an infant was only a few days or weeks old also militated against anything too rigorous by way of initiation.[63]

The line taken by our authors on who should be baptized and when was simple. Baptism was for two categories of persons: adults who were born in another faith or outside the church but had converted to Christianity; and the children of Christian parents.[64] The only dissenting voice in our sample was that of the Baptist, Benjamin Keach, who in his third-level catechism made a polite but determined defence of

---

[61] S. A. Sykes, ' "Baptisme doth represente unto us oure profession" ', in M. Johnson (ed.), *Thomas Cranmer* (Durham, 1990), 136–9.

[62] Heidelberg Catechism, 331; Prayer Book catechism, 789.

[63] See Williams, *Exposition*, 57–8; Wake, *Principles*, 158–9; these authors specified eight days as the age for infants to be baptized.

[64] Ball, *Catechisme*, 80; Westminster Smaller, 35 (answer 95); Westminster Larger, 129 (answer 166).

adult baptism. Dropping his role of simple guide, he suddenly became quite technical in defence of total immersion and believer's baptism: only such who believe, are repentant, and are capable of entering into a visible covenant with Christ, should be baptized.[65] All other accounts of baptism in our sample, however, adopted the twofold classification of eligibility, which in practice meant infant baptism.

The most common rationale for infant baptism was that God's blessings were promised, to 'the lineage of the faithful', those whose parents 'belong to the covenant and people of God'.[66] From the 1580s to the end of our period, and in the works of the supporters of both the official and the Westminster Shorter catechisms, we regularly find the assertion that children of believers could be baptized because through their parents they were in the covenant.[67] A less theoretical and more historical rationale was provided by some authors in the mid-sixteenth century and some episcopalians in the later seventeenth century. Calvin and Nowell cited the testimony of 'Moses and the prophets' to prove that Jewish children though 'not yet capable of faith and repentance, were nevertheless circumcised', and argued that what was good for the chosen people of the Old Testament was good for all nations under the New; in the late 1690s a similarly jingoistic note was struck by Wake: 'our infants are as capable of covenanting as theirs' (the Jews').[68] Perhaps borrowing from the *Institutes*, Nowell actually suggested that 'it were a great indignity' to imagine that what applied in the Old Testament was not even more true of the New, in which 'the grace of God is both more plentifully poured and more clearly declared in the Gospel of Christ'.[69] A number of later Stuart authors also tried to find a defence of infant baptism either in the practice of the Old Testament or in Christ's command in the New.[70] The line that the children of Christian parents were 'capable' of covenanting with God found in some of these forms[71] was more contentious, since it raised the question of what exactly happened in baptism, which we shall come to later. Here it may be enough to point out that infant baptism was widely regarded as an entry into, or confirmation of membership of, the covenant of grace; and that the generation-to-generation continuum of the Jewish people in the Old Testament covenant provided a welcome and standard defence for the practice of baptizing the children of those already in the church, a practice which it would perhaps have been hard to defend on New Testament grounds alone.

---

[65] Keach, 'Youth', 98–104.   [66] Calvin, *Catechisme*, 138; Heidelberg Catechism, 331.

[67] Egerton, 'Briefe method', 16; Hill, *Principles*, sig. C3ʳ; Palmer, *Endeavour*, 41–2; Westminster Larger, 129 (answer 166); and cf. Nicholes, *Catechisme*, 66, for membership of the covenant being 'judged by authority'; Nicholson, *Exposition*, 166, 170, 172; Sherlock, *Principles*, 55; Comber, *Church-catechism*, 5; Marshall, *Catechism*, 45; Williams, *Exposition*, 2; Wake, *Principles*, 158; Lewis, *Catechism*, 60; Wallis, *Explanation*, 42; Gouge, *Principles*, 97; Vincent, *Catechism*, 225.

[68] Calvin, *Catechisme*, 136–8 (and cf. Gerrish, *Grace and Gratitude*, 121); Nowell, *Catechisme*, 209; Wake, *Principles*, 158–9.

[69] Nowell, loc. cit.

[70] Marshall, *Catechism*, 45; Williams, *Exposition*, 57–8; Wake, *Principles*, 158–9; and Nicholson, *Exposition*, 168–71; Sherlock, *Principles*, 55; and cf. Lewis, *Catechism*, 3–4.

[71] Wake, loc. cit.; and see also Marshall, *Catechism*, 45; and Lewis, *Catechism*, 71.

In baptism, the faithful or, more commonly, the children of the faithful were symbolically washed with water. Authors were aware of the ritual ablutions of the Jews,
and aware also that the practice of sprinkling a handful of water on a baby was not the
way that baptism had always been performed. In the hot climates of the East
Mediterranean, explained the authors of some longer forms, it was possible for adults
being baptized to be immersed totally in water, 'but when the Gospel was spread into
colder regions, sprinkling instead of dipping was thought sufficient', since children
'for the great part of the year cannot be dipped in water without the hazard of their
lives'.[72] In the Church of England the choice was at first 'left to discretion': the 1604
addition to the Prayer Book catechism refers to the person about to be baptized being
'dipped or sprinkled' (this was changed to the more general 'baptized' in 1661).[73] But
although one finds the occasional reference to dipping or to the baptized being under
the water,[74] the terms more commonly used were 'wash',[75] 'sprinkle',[76] or 'cleanse'.[77]
It was also widely asserted that this sprinkling must be accompanied by the words 'in
the name of the father, and of the son, and of the Holy Ghost', as stated in Matthew
28: 19.[78] As Watts put it, we are baptized in the name of the father, who appointed
this salvation, and the son, who procured it, and the Holy Ghost, who reveals it and
enables us to benefit from it.[79] The invocation was also said to remind the baptized,
either a mature convert or a child growing up in the faith, to acknowledge 'these three
persons, and consequently his whole Creed'.[80]

In line with the distinction they drew when they were defining a sacrament (and
the baptismal office in the Book of Common Prayer), most authors explained that the
water had both an outer and an inner significance. As water physically washes away
the filthiness of the body, so Christ's blood washes away the sins and the guilt and
punishment due for them.[81] Water was a 'figure' or 'sign': outward washing did not
itself wash away sins; 'only the blood of Jesus Christ and the Holy Spirit cleanse us
from all sin'.[82] Remission or forgiveness of sin was regularly paired with regeneration

---

[72] Hammond, *Practical catechisme*, 346; Nicholson, *Exposition*, 158; and cf. Gouge, *Principles*, 95;
Wake, *Principles*, 153; and Vincent, *Catechism*, 221–2.

[73] Nicholson, *Exposition*, 158; Prayer Book catechism, 789.

[74] Perkins, *Foundation*, 7; Ball, *Catechisme*, 80; Ussher, 'Principles', 11; Keach, 'Youth', 99–102.

[75] Calvin, *Catechisme*, 132; Heidelberg Catechism, 329; Dering–More, *Catechisme*, sig. B5ʳ; Paget,
Questions, sig. D4ʳ; Egerton, 'Familiar manner', 42; Hill, *Principles*, sig. C2ᵛ; Westminster Larger, 128
(answer 164); Westminster Shorter, 35 (answer 94); Taylor, 'Catechism', 5.

[76] Perkins, *Foundation*, 7; Egerton, 'Briefe method', 15; Ball, *Catechisme*, 80; Nicholson, *Exposition*,
158; Williams, *Exposition*, 55.

[77] e.g. Ussher, 'Principles', 11.

[78] Heidelberg Catechism, 330; Prayer Book catechism, 789; Egerton, 'Briefe method', 15; Ball, *Catechisme*, 80; Westminster Larger, 128 (answer 165); Taylor, 'Catechism', 5.

[79] Watts, 'Children's catechism', 25–6.

[80] Nicholson, *Exposition*, 159–60; and cf. Boughen, *Exposition*, 61.

[81] Heidelberg Catechism, 329–30; Dering–More, *Catechisme*, sig. B5ʳ; Egerton, 'Familiar manner',
42; Prayer Book catechism, 789.

[82] Calvin, *Catechisme*, 133; Nowell, *Catechisme*, 208; Hieron, *Doctrine*, 579; Prayer Book catechism,

or newness of life.[83] Luther had led the way in regarding baptism as both a washing away of guilt, a drowning of the old man and his sinful works, and a rising again into a new life, a rebirth in spirit which means that we must try not to be defiled again with sin. At its simplest level, as in the non-technical vocabulary used by Isaac Watts, this could be stated very simply: baptism signifies our being cleansed of sin and being made new creatures and the disciples of Christ.[84] But in longer or more advanced forms the simple dichotomies of dirt and cleanliness, death and rebirth, gave way to more authentic but from a catechumen's standpoint more difficult phrases such as being 'reborn of water and the Holy Ghost' or the 'washing of regeneration'.[85] Ussher for once was also quite technical: in baptism the cleansing of the body represents 'the cleansing of the soul by the forgiveness of sins and imputation of righteousness'. As the basis of another question and answer, Ussher also, like Jeremy Taylor, used the passage in Romans 6: 3–6 about those baptized in Christ being baptized into his death, which might be thought to have been rather hard for the average catechumen to grasp.[86]

Including remission and regeneration, there were half a dozen 'inward graces' or 'benefits', which water was commonly supposed to represent or convey to those baptized, though the authors of more elementary forms might restrict themselves to two or three of these.[87] There was relative agreement on what these blessings were, but there were differences of opinion over whether such blessings were merely signified and ratified in baptism, or whether they were actually conveyed, and if so how and when (to which we shall return later). While remission of sins and regeneration were regularly mentioned as benefits at the outset, and both had an essentially personal significance as far as the individual person baptized was concerned, there were other aspects of baptism which had a strong communal dimension as well, as is the case with many initiation rites. These included entry into the fold of the church, being engrafted into or becoming a member of Christ along with all the others of God's children, entry into the covenant of grace with the rest of the faithful, and making an undertaking to be the Lord's, an engagement which godparents or the rest of the congregation were supposed to check was kept.

At a purely human level, baptism was an initiation into the visible church, with all the privileges and responsibilities which that entailed; but at a higher, spiritual level

---

787; Hammond, *Practical catechisme*, 348; Heidelberg Catechism, 329, 331; and cf. Perkins, *Foundation*, 7; and Ussher, 'Method', 22 ('types and figures').

[83] e.g. Nowell, *Catechisme*, 208; Heidelberg Catechism, 329–30; Dering–More, *Catechisme*, sig. B5ʳ; Egerton, 'Briefe method', 15; Prayer Book catechism, 789; Hill, *Principles*, sig. C2ᵛ; Westminster Larger, 128 (answer 165); Isham, *Catechism*, 57–8; and cf. the idea of being sanctified in baptism: Heidelberg Catechism, 329–30; Egerton, 'Briefe method', 15.

[84] Watts, 'Children's catechism', 24.

[85] Boughen, *Exposition*, 1–2 (a modification of John 3: 6); Sherlock, *Principles*, 14; Marshall, *Catechism*, 43 (citing Titus 3: 5).

[86] Ussher, 'Principles', 11; Taylor, 'Catechism', 5.

[87] See preceding paragraphs and following notes, and Egerton, 'Briefe method', 15; Prayer Book catechism, 789; Ball, *Catechisme*, 80; Watts, 'Children's catechism', 24.

it was also initiation into the family of God, or the body of Christ. The manner in which this was expressed varied somewhat. In his catechism Calvin wrote of baptism as a certain witness of our entry into the fellowship or congregation of God; in his, Nowell spoke of an entry or reception into the church, and into the number of the children of God. Perkins was probably thinking of the invisible church when he wrote that in baptism 'we have our admission into the true church of God', but according to the authors of the Westminster Larger Catechism 'the parties baptized are solemnly admitted into the visible church'.[88] Some authors, such as the predestinarians Ball, Elton, and Ussher and the occasional later Stuart episcopalian like Lewis spoke of baptism as the sacrament of entry or admission into *the* church; others, like the 'godly' Hildersham, and a string of conformists like Nicholes, Sherlock, and Marshall, wrote of admission into Christ's church.[89] Virtually all the authors cited here spoke of the admission as a fact, as something which definitely occurred in baptism, rather than something promised or 'sealed' for some future date;[90] and since baptism as a mark of initiation into the church, for infants as well as adults, was something which even Zwinglians accepted, this consensus is not surprising.

Closely related to this idea of admission into the church, though more problematic in the sense of how far it was conveyed to an infant being baptized, was the idea of being 'engrafted into Christ', which can be found stated explicitly in the forms of Nowell and Ball, and in a more guarded way in the works of Elton and the Westminster divines, where the engrafting was said to be represented or signified and sealed.[91] The Heidelberg divines combined the idea of engrafting with that of membership of the church: in baptism the children of believing parents 'be engrafted into the Christian church', while in later Stuart episcopalian forms, the wording sometimes found is that baptism represents our engrafting into Christ, whose mystical body was the church.[92] Another way of creating the impression of some kind of physical union between Christ and the baptized was to use the metaphor of becoming a member (in the sense of a limb) of Christ,[93] or of having communion with Christ through baptism.[94] Other authors preferred to use the idea of adoption to make the point to their catechumens: through baptism, I am adopted as a child of God, and so become a joint heir with Christ of the kingdom of heaven.[95]

[88] Calvin, *Catechisme*, 131; Nowell, *Catechisme*, 207; Perkins, *Foundation*, 7; Westminster Larger, 128 (answer 165).

[89] Ball, *Catechisme*, 80; Elton, *Forme*, sig. D5ᵛ; Ussher, 'Principles', 11; Hildersham, 'Doctrine', 21; Lewis, *Catechism*, 3–4; Nicholes, *Catechisme*, 65; Sherlock, *Principles*, 45; Marshall, *Catechism*, 42.

[90] Nicholes, loc. cit.

[91] Nowell, *Catechisme*, 207; Ball, *Catechisme*, 80; Elton, *Forme*, sig. D6ᵛ; Westminster Larger, 128 (answer 165); and Westminster Shorter, 35 (answer 94).

[92] Heidelberg Catechism, 74; Sherlock, *Principles*, 14; Marshall, *Catechism*, 2; Isham, *Catechism*, 2; and cf. Nowell, *Catechisme*, 207; Ball, *Catechisme*, 80; Nicholes, *Catechisme*, 65.

[93] Mayer, *Catechisme*, sigs. A3ᵛ–4ʳ; Nicholson, *Exposition*, 13–14.

[94] Egerton, 'Briefe method', 15; Ball, *Catechisme*, 80; Ussher, 'Principles', 11.

[95] Prayer Book catechism, 778–9; Nicholson, *Exposition*, 9, 14–15; Sherlock, *Principles*, 14; Marshall,

Another way of making a similar point to those raised in the last two paragraphs, and often adopted from the 1590s, was to describe baptism as an entry into, or confirmation of membership of, the covenant of grace, of which Christ was the mediator. We have already looked at this as a justification for infant baptism, but are now considering it as a potential benefit and consequence of baptism for all baptized persons, old as well as young. One of the first to use a covenant framework for baptism in an English catechism was William Perkins. As we saw in Chapter 9, Perkins passed by the opportunity to discuss the covenants in a soteriological or a pietistic context, and his only references to the covenant of grace are in relation to the sacraments.

What is done in baptism?
In the assembly of the church the covenant of grace between God and the party baptized is
    solemnly confirmed and sealed.
In this covenant what doth God promise to the party baptized?
Christ with all blessings that come by him.
To what condition is the party baptized bound?
To receive Christ and to repent his sin.[96]

Here then we have a mutual arrangement: God promises, and the party is bound by a condition. Perkins states that the benefit of baptism is that 'it seals unto us remission of sins and sanctification', and apparently equates this with the condition of keeping the covenant, since the next question is:

How cometh it to pass that many after their baptism for a long time feel not the effect and fruit
    of it, and some never?
The fault is not in God, who keepeth his covenants, but the fault is in themselves in that they
    do not keep the condition of the covenant, to receive Christ by faith and to repent of all their
    sins.

He goes on to argue that a man will see 'the effect of his baptism' as soon as he receives Christ by faith; then he will 'feel the power of God to regenerate him' and to work in him all the things 'offered in baptism'. But if a man never keeps 'the condition to which he bound himself in baptism', his damnation will be the greater for having broken his vow to God. In fact, in Perkins's brief account of baptism almost half of the space was devoted to concerns about assurance and the damnation of the wicked.[97]

The position of John Ball, author of larger works on the covenant as well as of the best-selling unofficial catechism of the early Stuart period, was similar, though perhaps less fringed with reservations than in Perkins's form. Ball also deferred discussion of the covenant until his section on the sacraments, and his answer to the question of what a sacrament is, was 'a seal of the covenant of grace' which he then defines in reciprocal but relatively unconditional terms by citing Jeremiah 31: 33: ' "I will be

Catechism, 2; Williams, *Exposition*, 1, 56; Isham, *Catechism*, 3; Lewis, *Catechism*, 3. Mayer combined physical and legal metaphors: Mayer, *Catechisme*, sigs. A3ᵛ–4ʳ.

[96] Perkins, *Foundation*, 7.   [97] Ibid. 7–8.

thy God, and thou shalt be my people" '. However, once he had established that the author of the covenant had instituted two sacraments, and what the outward sign and the inward grace signified in baptism are, Ball asked 'To what conditions doth the party baptized bind himself?', and expected the reply 'To believe in Christ and forsake his sin', which was very close to Perkins's conditions.[98] That Ball did believe in mutual promises being made in the covenant of grace is evident from the larger catechism he produced, which is also in our sample. In the covenant of grace, he there wrote,

God doth promise to be our saviour, king, and father, to pardon our sin, sanctify our nature, bestow all good things upon us, and protect us from evil. We promise to choose God to be our God, trust in him, love and fear him, and walk in obedience before him.[99]

Other early Stuart Calvinists, such as Edward Elton and Martin Nicholes, also said that the washing in baptism represents and seals entry into the covenant of grace, and stated that the party baptized promises to believe and obey.[100] But, unlike Perkins, none of these authors tackled the problem of why many of those baptized did not feel the benefits for some time, or indeed ever.

The authors of the Westminster Larger Catechism adopted a very similar position to Perkins: baptism was a seal of the benefits promised to believers, and an admission into the visible church and into 'an open and professed engagement to be wholly and only the Lord's'.[101] But they adopted a different strategy on the relationship between baptism and the covenant of grace. By introducing the covenant at a much earlier stage of their form, when discussing the framework of salvation, they had firmly equated membership of the covenant with the predestined elect long before Perkins did, and much more explicitly. Also by leaning towards an unconditional covenant at the outset, insisting on what God 'required' of those in the covenant', and handling the *ordo salutis* and assurance before they reached the sacraments, they were in a position to avoid the kind of awkward question that Perkins felt he had to handle about the relationship between non-performance of certain 'conditions' and delayed 'feelings' of regeneration of those in the covenant.[102] In fact, when they eventually came to their discussion of baptism they did not actually mention the benefits of the covenant of grace by name. It was in the Shorter Catechism that there was a specific indication of 'the benefits of the covenant of grace' that were sealed in baptism. Moreover, by using the first person ('our ingrafting into Christ' and 'our engagement') in answer 94, it is arguable that the authors of the shorter form made the relationship between baptism and what was required in the covenant seem closer than in the larger form.[103] Non-predestinarian authors were not hampered by problems of

---

[98] Ball, *Catechisme*, 80.　　[99] Ball, *Treatise*, 141.

[100] Elton, *Forme*, sigs. D6ʳ–7ᵛ; Nicholes, *Catechisme*, 65–7.

[101] Westminster Larger, 128 (answer 165), and Westminster Confession, ch. 28, para. 1.

[102] See above, pp. 413–14; and Perkins, *Foundation*, 7.

[103] Westminster Shorter, 35 (answer 92).

having to explain why all had to be baptized even though not all would be called. Equally they had no difficulty with the idea that baptism had an ethical dimension: it carried with it certain duties, which were laid down both at the start of the original Prayer Book form (to renounce the devil and all his works, believe all the articles of the Creed, and keep God's will) and in the section added later (where it was pointed out that when they came of age children were bound to perform the promises made on their behalf at baptism).[104] It did not require much imagination to graft the idea of a conditional covenant of grace onto this basis, and as we saw in Chapter 9 this was done by increasing numbers of episcopalian authors in the seventeenth century.

The weight of interpretation placed on the simple act of sprinkling water on a child's head was a heavy one. A few authors in our sample were prepared to boil it down to a minimum, as in the short pre-communion form appended to Calvin's catechism: 'First it signifieth that we have forgiveness of our sins by the blood of Christ. Secondly it setteth before our eyes our regeneration or new spiritual birth.'[105] But many authors (too many, one might guess from a catechumen's point of view) felt the duty to be more precise, or to reflect recent doctrinal thinking, or to cover their backs against charges of encouraging a return to popery or veering towards radicalism. And as a result their accounts lost the simplicity that can be found in other catechisms, or indeed in their own forms when handling the Ten Commandments or the Lord's Prayer. It is to some of the problem areas associated with baptism that we now turn.

In addition to the areas of broad agreement outlined in the previous section, there were others in which agreement was either less than wholehearted or positively lacking. How far were the different benefits or effects of baptism merely 'signified' or 'sealed' (in the sense of ratified or promised), and how far or at what point were they conveyed or received? How far was a week-old baby capable of receiving benefits from baptism, beyond admission into the church or covenant, and perhaps the making of a commitment by proxy? How far was there an antipathy between official teaching on the baptism of infants, spelt out in the baptism service of the Book of Common Prayer, and the double predestinarian teaching that the spiritual progress of the elect began at the moment of effectual calling, usually in adulthood as a result of hearing the Word preached? There were clearly tensions here, and from the later sixteenth century there was a tendency to pull apart. The official statements on baptism, in the Book of Common Prayer, Homilies, Thirty-nine Articles and official catechisms, were capable of both a Lutheran reading, that infants who were baptized were regenerate according to their infant state, and a Calvinist or Reformed reading, that infants were regenerate only in a sacramental sense, and that the enjoyment of grace was dependent

---

[104] Prayer Book catechism, 778–9, 789; and cf. Hill, *Principles*, sig. A5ᵛ; Comber, *Church-catechism*, 5, 7; Williams, *Exposition*, 2; Lewis, *Catechism*, 71.

[105] 'Maner to examine children', 154–5.

on their prior election and the operation of the Holy Ghost at their effectual calling. On one wing, some of the godly pulled back from the former interpretation of baptism and moved towards an emphasis on 'signs' and 'seals', though relatively few went as far as the Zwinglian position of baptism as a mere sign of Christian profession, at least not until the 1640s. On the other side, some conformists and some of the more conservative puritans, in reaction against what they saw as a downgrading of the value of baptism, emphasized a more Lutheran or efficacious view of baptism; and, although aiming at a middle ground between seeing baptism as inevitably efficacious and seeing it as a bare sign of membership, came out with a strong emphasis on the benefits conveyed at once, in some cases perhaps stronger than the first English reformers would have favoured.[106] The result was that by the later seventeenth century we are faced either with a sharper difference than had existed a century earlier, or with much the same difference but more sharply expressed.

If we are to understand that difference, we must again briefly step outside our sample of catechisms for a while to look at the views of the leading reformers in the mid-sixteenth century, and then try to relate this wider range of views to our sample forms. In doing so, it may help if a modern simile is offered at this stage. Infant baptism was like a modern Grand Prix race: the minister/race official checks that the infants are the children of Christian parents and so are qualified to enter the spiritual race of life, and in baptism the standard rules of the race are made clear, the contestants are put under starter's orders, and lined up for the start. In earlier Grand Prix races, the contest began at once, without any preliminary circuit to warm engines and tyres properly; but in more recent times, contestants proceed round the track once on a slow, warming-up lap, halt, rev up, and when the lights change, the race starts in earnest. Now some early modern authors seem to have regarded baptism as the former kind of race: through baptism the child was placed in a new relationship with God, and the rules and mutual responsibilities of race organizer and contestants had to be followed as soon as the contestant crossed the starting-line, even if, spiritually speaking, the infant had to warm up his engine and tyres as he or she sped rapidly through childhood and adolescence into the full-speed contest of faith. Other authors saw baptism as the latter kind of race, in which the period from baptism to the moment of effectual calling was merely a warming-up lap. The infant was registered as participating in the race and following the rules, but in the preliminary lap this was done at less than full throttle, a going through the motions without a full understanding of what was to come; the race proper could not and did not start until that moment in their adolescent or adult lives when at the moment of effectual calling the Holy Ghost waved the real starting-flag. The former view was that of Luther towards which the Edwardian reformers, and their later supporters, leant; the latter was that towards

---

[106] On the puritans, including more conservative ones such as Samuel Ward and Cornelius Burges, see Holifield, *Covenant Sealed*, chs. 2–3; on the conformists, see below.

which Calvin (with some reservations) leant in the *Institutes*, and which was adopted (with fewer reservations) by English Calvinists from Perkins to the Westminster divines. However, when it came to expressing these views in a catechism the difference between the two kinds of race was not always that clear, partly because of the common ground described in the previous section, and partly because of the way in which technicalities were either avoided or simplified.

In his short catechism, Luther told his catechumens that baptism 'effects forgiveness of sins, delivers from death and the devil, and grants eternal salvation to all who believe, as the Word and promise of God declare', and that the water in baptism signified 'that the old Adam in us … is to be drowned by daily sorrows and repentance … and that the new man is to come forth daily and rise up, cleansed and righteous, to live forever in God's presence'. In another answer Luther talked about 'our faith', which might suggest that he was describing baptism in terms of adult baptism.[107] But if we look at the third answer on baptism in his short catechism and at a more advanced work of his on the subject, we find that Luther was of the opinion that faith is unconsciously present in the child at baptism, by virtue of the proclamation of the Word there made and the conscious faith of the sponsors. The baptized child is set in a new relationship to God, even if a full comprehension of what that entailed must develop as he matures, through God's promise and prevenient grace.[108]

The authors of 'The ministration of the public baptism of infants' in the English Prayer Book of 1549 would appear to have been close to Luther's view of baptism in that the sacrament was said to bring about changes in the relationship between God and the child at once, though there was perhaps just sufficient ambiguity to permit a non-Lutheran reading as well later on, along the lines that the changes were promised rather than delivered at once, in other words that they took the form of a seed rather than a flower. In the service for infant baptism, the minister begins by stating that 'none can enter into the kingdom of God (except he be regenerate and born anew of water and the holy Ghost)', and urging those present to call on God to grant that 'these children' will be made 'lively members' of Christ's holy church. Using the future tense, he then prays that God will

mercifully look upon these children, sanctify them and wash them with thy Holy Ghost, that they … may be received into the ark of Christ's church, and being steadfast in faith … may so pass the waves of this troublesome world, that finally they may come to the land of everlasting life, there to reign with thee, world without end.

The future tense is still employed when he prays that the children 'may receive remission of their sins by spiritual regeneration', and when he expounds Mark 10: 13–16 by

---

[107] Schaff, *Creeds*, 86–7; an alternative translation to 'is to' is 'should': Janz, *Reformation Catechisms*, 201.

[108] The statements in Luther's larger catechism and the fourth answer of his smaller that in baptism a Christian was given enough to practise all his life, and from the day of his baptism must die unto sin, can be taken as referring to infant as much as adult baptism: Reardon, *Religious Thought*, 77.

telling the adults present to 'earnestly believe' that Christ 'will most surely keep and perform' the promise he made in the Gospel to receive these children, release them from their sins, sanctify them with the Holy Ghost, and give them the kingdom of heaven and everlasting life.[109] At the moment of christening, however, the tense changes, as the minister says: 'We receive this child into the congregation of Christ's flock, and do sign him with the sign of the cross, in token that hereafter he shall ... continue Christ's faithful soldier and servant unto his life's end.' He then immediately adds that these children 'be regenerate, and grafted into the body of Christ's congregation', and urges all present to give thanks and to pray that they 'may lead the rest of their life according to this beginning'. The next prayer offers thanks that it has pleased God 'to regenerate this infant with thy Holy Spirit, to receive him for thy own child by adoption, and to incorporate him into thy holy congregation'; and the minister begs God to grant that the child 'being dead unto sin, and living unto righteousness ... may crucify the old man, and utterly abolish the whole body of sin', and that he may partake of Christ's resurrection, so that 'finally, with the residue of thy holy congregation, he may be an inheritor of thine everlasting kingdom'.[110] Here and elsewhere in the latter part of the service, for example in the closing call to adults to remember their 'profession' of faith in baptism, we have many of the same motifs as in the opening section of the service, but now most of them are treated as accomplished facts.

The stress on church membership and on baptism being a token of faith may be more Zwinglian than Lutheran, but for the rest it is evident that many of the ideas found in Luther's teaching can also be found in the English rite: forgiveness of sins, regeneration, a lifetime's pattern of behaviour laid out, and the assurance of deliverance from death for all who believe. Quite how the repeated statements in the English service that the child had been regenerated were to be understood in the context of infant baptism is not altogether clear: perhaps as a fresh start, by being incorporated into Christ through his church, or more specific blessings having been conveyed, and new possibilities and powers being placed in the baptized infant's grasp. Alternatively, it could be taken to mean that these blessings were confirmed to the baptized, in the sacramental sense of a divine promise, even if the moment of their full realization still lay some years away. Either way, the use of the term 'regeneration' was not meant to suggest that baptized children were saved, but that they had the possibility of salvation which they had not had before their fresh start in baptism.

Ironically, the most positive statement of the effects of infant baptism occurs not in the text of the baptism service but in the rubric at the start of the confirmation service which followed:

And that no man shall think that any detriment shall come to children by deferring of their

---

[109] See also the prayer before the marking of a cross on the child's forehead: Brightman, *English Rite*, ii. 726–40.

[110] Ibid. 740–7; the word 'congregation' was later changed to 'church' throughout this section.

confirmation, he shall know for truth, that it is certain by God's word that children being baptized have all things necessary for their salvation, and be undoubtedly saved.[111]

This may have been designed to comfort the parents of children who died after baptism but before confirmation, and since the rate of infant and child mortality in early modern England was extremely high their numbers were considerable. This rubric does, however, tend to reinforce the impression that the correct interpretation of the service as far as the leaders of the Edwardian church were concerned was that a new relationship to God had begun, even for infants, one that was free from the taint of original sin and could be described as a state of salvation. This impression is reinforced if we turn back for a moment to the opening section of the short catechism of 1549 prepared at the same time, whose authors employed many of the same terms and concepts as those in the Prayer Book baptism service. There are two points at which the authors of the catechism may have gone a shade further than the position adopted in the liturgy. The first is where the catechumen says that in his baptism he 'was made a member of Christ, the child of God, and an inheritor of the kingdom of heaven', whereas the minister in the service had prayed that God might make him an inheritor. (The difference here is perhaps marginal: those who in their baptism had been engrafted into the body of Christ's church and become children of God through adoption could be regarded as co-heirs with Christ.) The second is where the catechumen thanks God for having called him in baptism 'to this state of salvation' and prays for grace 'that I may continue in the same unto my life's end'.[112] The confidence with which the catechumen asserts he has reached a state of salvation again may go beyond the position stated in the Prayer Book service, though perhaps not that asserted in the rubric of the confirmation ceremony. Certainly catechumens were not expected to think that they had reached the end of their spiritual journey: in an answer to a question on the Creed, they refer to Christ 'who hath redeemed me', in the past tense, and the Holy Ghost 'who sanctifieth me, and all the elect people of God', in the present continuous tense. Later too, they are told by the catechist that without God's 'special grace', for which they 'must learn at all times to call', they are not able to walk in the Commandments of God (one of the baptismal promises); in reply, the catechumen duly desires God to 'send his grace unto me, and to all people; that we may worship him, serve him, and obey him, as we ought to do', and expresses his trust that God will deliver him from everlasting death.[113] The fact that a catechumen was able to memorize and to some extent understand the Creed also meant that he had passed from the passive state of infancy (or of unconscious faith, according to Luther) into a condition of active belief and of being aware of his 'profession'—to follow the example of Christ by dying unto sin and growing daily in godliness of living. In short, the catechumen had left the starting-point of the race well behind

---

[111] Ibid. 778–9.   [112] Prayer Book catechism, 780–1, and cf. 778–9, and 789.
[113] Ibid. 780–1, 784–5.

and was passing the pits at the end of the first of many laps round the circuit. But it was at the original start of the race that he had been given the opportunity and the directions as to how to proceed round the track, and a guarantee of continued help in competing in the race and perhaps even completing it, subject to pit stops for reinfusions of divine grace.

The concept of baptized infants being regenerate and having 'all things necessary for their salvation' was one that caused some dispute in Elizabeth's reign, and was later picked up by some later Stuart episcopalians in order to defend their views on the significance of this sacrament. For Thomas Cartwright, baptism was of secondary importance to election: it was prevenient grace that enabled the elect to be saved. If the elect died without being baptized, God would ensure in his own way that they were saved; if children died after baptism, the fact that they had received the sign and seal of forgiveness and salvation made no difference to their fate unless they were among those already chosen by God.[114] Whitgift complained that this view encouraged the people to see sacraments as 'base ceremonies and in no sense necessary to salvation'; the bishop was worried that the absence of baptism, which he referred to as 'the sacrament of regeneration', might make it 'seem' to parents that their child was reprobate.[115] Hooker went further, partly by suggesting that 'predestination bringeth not to life, without the grace of external vocation', and partly by arguing that we are not Christians until we are new born 'according to the manifest ordinary course of divine dispensation' in baptism; therein we receive 'that grace which is the first and most effectual cause out of which our belief groweth'.[116] Both sides misunderstood or misrepresented the other. Puritans tried to foist onto the official formularies the idea that baptism was absolutely necessary or that it functioned *ex opere operato*, while churchmen accused the puritans of treating sacraments as mere signs or memorials. Mutual accusations rumbled on to the 1630s and beyond, as conformable churchmen defended what they saw as a divinely instituted sacrament with efficacious powers, whose value was confirmed by their own pastoral experience, while predestinarian critics chafed at the bold claims made in the baptism service and official catechism.[117] But it was the Prayer Book service, supported by the Prayer Book catechism, that was deployed in the great majority of English parishes, and it was the more positive, immediate interpretation of the benefits of baptism that would surface again in the later Stuart period.

How one judges the relationship between the views of Calvin and those expressed in the English formularies to some extent depends on where one looks: at Calvin's earlier writings or his last thoughts, and at the *Institutes* or the catechism. On the

---

[114] Cartwright's views are cited in New, *Anglican and Puritan*, 64–6; and Lake, *Anglicans and Puritans?*, 35–6.

[115] Ibid. 36, 38; and New, *Anglican and Puritan*, 65–6.

[116] Ibid.; and Lake, *Anglicans and Puritans?*, 173–6.

[117] As previous notes, and Bromiley, *Baptism*, 60–2, and Holifield, *Covenant Sealed*, 33–4, 111.

one side, Calvin rejected Zwingli's minimalist views. Baptism for Calvin was much more than just a badge of Christian faith: it effectually performed what it symbolized; it was a divine gift to symbolize incorporation into the church, strengthen faith, and aid sanctification. On the other hand, at least in the *Institutes*, Calvin tended to stress the future benefits and promissory nature of infant baptism. Being spiritually blind and unbelievers, infants do not receive baptism in faith, and their baptism profits them nothing, since they neglect the promise of favour there made by the Lord. For several years after baptism, this state of affairs continues, though the promise remains fixed, firm, and true. However, when by the grace of God they begin to repent, they believe the promises of remission of sins and other benefits of which believers had been assured at their baptism. Calvin also stresses that although all children of Christian parents must be baptized, baptism is effectual only in the elect, those who apprehend by faith the offer of mercy and pledge of grace in baptism. For the elect what is represented in baptism are pledges or seals of what already belongs to them, through their being predestined to salvation, and will one day be theirs. Hence the term 'obsignatory' which has been applied to his position: baptism is like the placing of a seal on a document which testifies to what the named party already has a claim to and will some day inherit when he reaches his spiritual majority.[118]

There are some potentially ambiguous remarks in Calvin's full-length, scholarly treatment of the sacraments in general and baptism in particular, for example a reference to first regeneration at baptism, as if there might be more than one rebirth. Some of these comments may represent his views on adult baptism, others perhaps show him trying to fend off Anabaptist attacks on infant baptism and in the process admitting that not all children have to wait for maturity before they are spiritually reborn. Elect infants, who have been adopted by God even before they are born, may be regenerated in the womb (like John the Baptist) or in early infancy (like Christ). None of the elect is called out of this world without being previously sanctified and regenerated in some way expedient to God; otherwise he or she would carry the corruption of original sin into heaven. Faith normally comes by hearing the Word preached, but may come internally through the Holy Spirit without preaching. Where is the danger, he added, if infants thus receive some part of that grace of which they are to have a full measure shortly afterwards?[119] This aside (which anticipates the remark of Hooker cited above) was the product of Calvin's problems with the present tense in baptism. He had no problems with the past (God had already adopted the elect before they were born and baptized), or the future (the promise sealed in baptism would eventually yield faith), but what about the present? Here Calvin turned to the scriptural precedent provided by circumcision, and to the

---

[118] Gerrish, *Grace and Gratitude*, 104–6, 115–23; Calvin, *Institutes*, IV. xv–xvi.

[119] Ibid., IV. xv. 4; F. Wendel, *Calvin: The Origins and Development of his Religious Thought*, trans. P. Mairet (1965), 321–8; Gerrish, *Grace and Gratitude*, 110–14, 117–18.

benefits of the young and impressionable being engrafted into the Christian community and symbolically adopted by God.[120] None of this undermined Calvin's basic position on baptism, but it may be said to reflect the practical difficulties faced by mainstream Protestant theologians in handling the practice of infant baptism, and in Calvin's case a hankering after stressing that many of the benefits of baptism were immediate.

In his treatment of baptism in his catechism for children, moreover, Calvin does seem to use language which is closer to that of Luther or the authors of the English formularies of 1549. At the start and the end he is cautious: baptism is 'as it were' an entry into God's family and household; it represents the remission of our sins and our regeneration or new birth in spirit; only the faithful feel its comfort—others 'through their perverse mind and unbelief, do refuse this free offer'. Later he says that for infants baptism is a 'token and witness that they are inheritors of the blessing of God, which is promised to the lineage of the faithful', and that 'when they come to age' they must learn how to profit from the substance and meaning of baptism.[121] But in between it often sounds as though the benefits of baptism are not something that will one day be apprehended but have already been received. His 10 to 15 year-old catechumens are encouraged to use the present tense to say that 'regeneration is wrought in us' and 'our old Adam is crucified', and that 'it is certain that remission of sins, and newness of life is offered unto us in baptism, and that we receive the same there'. To the question 'How is it that we obtain this grace [newness of life] in baptism?', the reply is 'It is given unto us in that Christ doth there garnish and deck our souls with the garment of his Holy Spirit if so be that we make not ourselves unworthy of his promises which be there given unto us'. To the question 'What is the right using or receiving of baptism?', the child replies:

faith and repentance … in that we be sure that we have our consciences cleansed in the blood of Christ. And in that we both feel in ourselves, and make it known to others by our works, that his Spirit abideth in us, to mortify our affections and desires, and so to make us ready to do the will of God.

Calvin then asks why, if all this is required in the use of baptism, little children are baptized, and offers the reply that in their case it is enough that they 'show forth the fruits of baptism when they are come to sufficient age to know it'.[122]

Calvin's view remained in essence obsignatory and promissory: as he put it in the *Institutes*, 'children are baptized for future repentance and faith'.[123] But his simplified expression of those views in the catechism is not free of ambiguity. His catechumens seem to be being treated as if they had reached the state of faith and repentance, that is had been effectually called; it is implied that they are of sufficient age to profit from their baptism, and that they had already received some benefits, some 'fruits' from it,

[120] Gerrish, *Grace and Gratitude*, 117–18; Holifield, *Covenant Sealed*, 16–17.
[121] Calvin, *Catechisme*, 131–4, 138.   [122] Ibid. 134–5.   [123] Calvin, *Institutes*, IV. xvi. 20.

and must not make themselves unworthy of them. Such statements are not dissimilar to those of the authors of the two sections of the Prayer Book catechism of 1549 and 1604. All seem to be saying that infants should be baptized, that there are certain fruits of that baptism, but that some of these are not felt until years of discretion are reached and/or an effectual calling occurs. Of course, Calvin believed that only the elect would benefit; but since he also argues that all children of adults in the church should be baptized as if they were elect, and since he uses the first-person plural for many of his catechumens' replies, the sharpness of this distinction is blurred. Calvin's position meant that he had to defend the practice of baptizing all young people even though 'divers through their perverse mind and unbelief' would render themselves unworthy of the gifts promised in baptism; the sacrament, he insisted, does not lose its 'property' (or as Nowell later put it, its 'force and nature') because these gifts are promised to unbelievers as well as believers.[124] This was less of a problem for the authors of the Prayer Book form, who argued that all those baptized were given the potential for salvation, but that they must have faith and must try to observe their vows, with the help of grace, if they were to hope for salvation.

Another catechism in common use in schools and colleges in the 1570s and 1580s was that of Alexander Nowell—the larger official catechism. In this, as in many other sections of his form, Nowell followed Calvin's catechism closely, but arguably Nowell's statements on the nature and effects of baptism had even fewer qualifications than the original:

baptism is, as it were, a certain entry, by which we are received into the church, whereof we also receive a most substantial testimony that we are now in the number of the household, and also of the children of God; yea, and that we are joined and [en]grafted into the body of Christ, and become his members, and do grow into one body with him.

The caution implied by 'as it were' (borrowed from Calvin) and 'testimony' is countered by the 'now', 'are joined', and 'do grow', which convey an immediacy which is much closer to both the baptism service of the English Prayer Book (a rite that Nowell must have administered many times) and the English short catechism.[125]

Other best-selling English catechisms of the 1580s to the 1620s, including a few whose authors incorporated a cautious statement of predestination of the kind indicated in a previous chapter, treated baptism in a similar way. The authors of the Heidelberg Catechism and English catechists like Dering and More, Paget, Egerton, and Hieron all used the present tense to describe remission and regeneration. Through outward washing with water, 'I am washed with [Christ's] blood and spirit from the pollution of my soul', wrote the Heidelberg divines; to be washed thus is to have forgiveness of sins and to be renewed by the Holy Ghost; as water washes my filth away, so Christ's blood sprinkled by the Holy Ghost washes away my guilt and

---

[124] Calvin, *Catechisme*, 134; Nowell, *Catechisme*, 208.
[125] For a later section, with a more obsignatory tone, see ibid. 209–10.

the punishment due, and I am raised again in newness of life, said Dering and More's catechumens.[126] Did these authors have a different view of the effect of infant baptism from that of the authors of the Prayer Book sacrament of baptism and of the original 1549 catechism? In some ways, they did: by avoiding the opening exchanges of the 1549 catechism, they avoided making their young catechumens claim to have been made an inheritor of the kingdom of heaven, and to have been called to a 'state of salvation' through Christ. In other ways, they did not: they made positive statements about immediate benefits in the present tense. They sometimes used the language of signs and seals or pledges to indicate promises of future benefits,[127] but not much more than the official formularies did, and usually in similar circumstances, such as pledges of future salvation. All of the authors cited in this paragraph may have made some mental reservations to the effect that the blessings of baptism they were describing were really for adults with faith or repentance, or as far as infants were concerned were merely symbolic promises until (in the case of the elect) they came to faith. But this is not what they *said* in the space of the half page or so in which they had to describe the essence of baptism to a predominantly young body of catechumens.

More cautious statements came, perhaps not surprisingly, from authors like Perkins, Cartwright, Ball, and Elton. As we have seen, Perkins began by using the present tense to say that in baptism we 'have our admission into the true church of God', but he then adopted an obsignatory standpoint on other benefits. For Perkins, baptism appears to have been two slightly different things combined: it is a seal to confirm that some things will happen to the elect, such as remission and sanctification; it is also an entry into a covenant, the terms of which we must keep from the moment that we enter it properly. What is remarkable about Perkins's section on baptism compared to most other Edwardian and Elizabethan forms is not just the higher proportion of sealing and promising, but also the use of the third person, as in 'the party baptized' and 'they that do not keep the condition of the covenant'. Indeed, there is nothing explicitly about infant baptism, and the question about when 'a man' shall see the benefit of his baptism gives the section a distinctly adult tone.[128] In his catechism, Cartwright confined himself to the brief observation that baptism is a seal of our entrance into Christianity, which leant towards the Zwinglian end of the spectrum,[129] while John Ball avoided awkward questions about the effects of baptism on infants by saying very little about it. For part of his section on baptism, Ball talked of present benefits, such as 'ingrafting into Christ, communion with him, and entrance into the church', but like Perkins he also soon reverted to the third person ('the party

---

[126] Heidelberg Catechism, 329; Dering–More, *Catechisme*, sig. B5ʳ; and cf. Paget, *Questions*, sigs. D4ʳ⁻ᵛ; 'Certaine questions and answers', sig. *iiiᵛ; Egerton, 'Briefe method', 15; id., 'Familiar manner', 42; Hieron, *Doctrine*, 579: Hieron seems to assume faith already existed, so presumably was thinking of adults being baptized.

[127] e.g. Heidelberg Catechism, 329; Elton, *Forme*, sig. D6ᵛ.   [128] Perkins, *Foundation*, 7–8.

[129] Cartwright, 'Catechisme', sig. Aa7ᵛ.

baptized', 'a man'), and generally treated the sacrament as something undergone by adults. Only as a tailpiece did he add that the children of one or both Christian parents should also be baptized.[130] In his catechism for adults, Elton adopted the same strategy, but was even more careful in his choice of words: baptism seals to 'the right receiver' his ingrafting into Christ, new birth, and entry into the covenant of grace; the party baptized promises to believe and obey, but only the elect will have the inward washing of their sins.[131]

The authors of the Westminster Larger Catechism tended to follow in these authors' footsteps. 'The parties baptized' are admitted into the church and make an engagement to be the Lord's in the present tense; like Luther and other sixteenth-century authors, they also stated that 'all our life long' we must 'improve' our baptism, that is, fulfil all the duties we then undertook but have tended to neglect before we came to faith and repentance.But for the rest, baptism simply signifies and seals a large number of 'privileges and benefits' to the elect; and baptism is treated in a framework of calling, justification, and sanctification which alone would make that baptism effective and shape the individual saints' progress in 'improving' their baptism.[132] The spiritual status and development of infants who were baptized is simply ignored: even the authors of the Larger Catechism who, in the chapter on the Decalogue we saw taking the prize for endlessly detailed coverage, remained almost totally silent on this. When it is mentioned, it is almost as an afterthought: baptism is to be administered 'even to infants', because their parents were in the covenant rather than because of the benefits that might accrue to them. At best for presbyterian infants the period from baptism to effectual calling was a warming-up lap before the real race began.[133]

Such authors were, however, only a relatively small minority among those who composed the catechisms in our sample. Moreover, even during the potential peak of their influence in the first half of the seventeenth century, there were always other popular forms expressing views reflecting the more positive, immediate interpretation of the 1549 formularies, for example the work of Mayer, Bernard, Hammond, and Boughen, and to some extent in that of William Hill;[134] and from the 1650s to the 1700s much more catechetical space would be given to this more positive view in the works in our sample than to the alternatives.[135] Thus in the abridgement of his larger commentary on the Prayer Book catechism, first published in 1623, John Mayer told

[130] Ball, *Catechisme*, 80.   [131] Elton, *Forme*, sigs. D6ᵛ–8ʳ.

[132] Westminster Larger, 128–30 (answers 165, 167), and see above, Ch. 9.

[133] Westminster Larger, 141 (answer 177). On the other hand, the Westminster divines did not use their catechisms to attack either episcopalians or radicals with different views of baptism from theirs.

[134] Mayer, *Catechisme*, sigs. A3ʳ⁻ᵛ; Bernard, *Common catechisme*, sig. C6ʳ; Hammond, *Practical catechisme*, 348–74; Boughen, *Exposition*, 1–2, 61, 71–3; Hill, *Principles*, sigs. C2ʳ⁻ᵛ.

[135] Nicholson, *Exposition*, 157–74; Sherlock, *Principles*, 14–16, 45–7, 54–5; Comber, *Church-catechism*, 5, 7, 27, 29; Marshall, *Catechism*, 1–2, 17, 42–5, 62; Williams, *Exposition*, 1, 4, 6–8, 54–6; Wake, *Principles*, 148–55; Lewis, *Catechism*, 68–72.

his catechumens that baptism was the sacrament of regeneration, by which they were sacramentally made members of Christ and the children of God.[136] In his catechism for older catechumens, first published in 1644 and later read by many episcopalian teachers and ordinands, Henry Hammond adopted the not uncommon tactic of describing baptism as an undertaking for adult converts, but he did then apply the same arguments to infants as well. The inward and spiritual grace in baptism is, says Hammond's catechist,

Christ's giving me strength to walk righteously, and means to obtain God's favour, the begetting me to that double righteousness that the young tender Christian hungers and thirsts after, the righteousness of sanctification … and the righteousness of justification.[137]

(In arguing that sacraments were both channels of grace and pledges to assure us of the same, he was not breaking new ground but walking in step with the official formularies of the mid-sixteenth century that we examined above.) Hammond also reinforced the assertion in the Prayer Book catechism that those baptized when young were 'bound to perform' the vow made on their behalf by godparents, by saying that when these infants were 'fitted by age and abilities of understanding and instruction', they would be 'enabled and strengthened by Christ'.[138]

As often before in Part II of this study, there are ways in which the position of Hammond and other Stuart conformists was much closer to that of Calvin than to that of English orthodox Calvinists. Like Calvin, Hammond clearly wished to distance himself from those who in his eyes were downgrading the value of baptism, and like Calvin but unlike Perkins, Ball, and the authors of the Westminster catechisms (who were stronger supporters of the sacraments than many radicals, but had doubts about the effects of baptism on young children), Hammond was also prepared to tackle what baptism should mean to children and adolescents. The two saw immediate benefits for the baptized infant in their admission into the church, as well as the promise of more benefits which would only be fully appreciated or received when the child was 'fitted' and 'enabled' by Christ. Calvin had even been tempted to talk like Luther and Hammond of infant regeneration, though for most people he expected the benefits to come later.[139] On the other hand, Calvin's belief in predestination hampered if it did not altogether negate his views on sacramental efficacy, and Hammond's suggestion that anyone with repentance and faith could benefit from the grace offered in baptism would obviously not have been acceptable to Calvin.

In the second half of the seventeenth century and the early eighteenth century, the legacy of the gulf between Hammond and the Westminster divines on the impact of baptism is very evident in the positive, even optimistic tone adopted by episcopalian authors compared to the continuing caution shown by presbyterian ones. As children of grace through baptism, wrote Wake, young children are not only taken into

---

[136] Mayer, *Catechisme*, sigs. A3[r–v].   [137] Hammond, *Practical catechisme*, 348–51, 355–7, 370–4.
[138] Ibid. 355.   [139] See above, n. 119.

covenant with God, regenerated, sanctified, cleansed, and made heirs of heaven, but also 'should they die before they commit any actual sin, we are assured by God's word, that they shall certainly be saved'—a comment which shows that he accepted the assertion made in the rubric in the confirmation service noted above.[140] On the other hand, it should not be thought that expositors of the Prayer Book form were making larger claims than their predecessors. Every time we find a positive assertion, we find a qualification added. Thus when Williams and Lewis made their charges say that in baptism 'I have ... all the means necessary to salvation', they hastened to add that to continue in the state of salvation into which they had been called in baptism they would 'depend upon the grace of God to prevent, assist, and confirm me in it', which they should seek through prayer.[141] There was the occasional concession to puritan sensibility, as when Sherlock, Comber, and Wake substituted the less categoric 'heir' for the unconditional and possibly misleading 'inheritor' when explaining the phrase (in the second answer of the original Prayer Book catechism) about the baptized being made inheritors of the kingdom of heaven.[142] Most of the later Stuart expositors of the Prayer Book form in our sample (and many outside too) treated baptism as a rite of entry into the covenant of grace, and, although as far as the operation of that covenant was concerned they leant much more firmly towards the conditional end of the scale than the presbyterians, they can also be found telling catechumens that those taken into the covenant by baptism had a title to the grace and blessings of that covenant, just like a Westminster divine might have done.[143] Indeed, Thomas Marshall, as so often, tried to bridge the position between episcopalian and moderate presbyterian by combining the terms of the Prayer Book form with the language of 'signs' and 'seals' and of 'privileges' being assured to the baptized that was found in the Westminster catechisms.[144] Isaac Watts's comment that many had been taught first the Prayer Book catechism and then the Westminster Shorter Catechism is significant not only in an irenic sense, but also in that, if he is right, these children had been given a strong dose of the episcopalian view of infant baptism before they moved on to a form which said virtually nothing on the subject.[145]

The second sacrament which Protestants agreed had been ordained by Christ was

[140] These statements may be found not in the first editions but in section 2 of later editions of Wake's *Principles*.

[141] Williams, *Exposition*, 8; Lewis, *Catechism*, 11–13.

[142] Sherlock, *Principles*, 14, 54 (he defended the use of both 'heir' and 'inheritor'); Comber, *Church-catechism*, 7; Wake, *Principles*, 156, though cf. 5; see also Marshall, *Catechism*, 2.

[143] See above, pp. 406–9, 411–21; one of the few not to describe baptism in terms of the covenant was Isham, *Catechism*, 1–4, 57–61; on titles under the covenant, see Williams, *Exposition*, 56, and Lewis, *Catechism*, 69.

[144] Marshall, *Catechism*, 42–5; and cf. the relatively mild tone of Wake's rebuff of the supporters of believer's baptism in his *Principles*, 158–9.

[145] I. Watts, *Catechisms: or instructions in the principles of Christian religion* (1730), 39.

referred to by Luther in his short catechism as the sacrament of the altar, but the name used in England for both official and unofficial catechisms was the Lord's Supper, 'because it was both instituted by our lord at supper, and was designed to succeed into place of the paschal supper among the Jews'.[146] Terms such as 'eucharist' and 'holy communion' are rare in our sample.[147] In forms designed for younger catechumens, information on this sacrament, in which only full, professing members of the church were expected to participate, was often given a lower priority than Creed or Decalogue. But most intermediate and advanced forms and an increasing number of simpler forms (including the Prayer Book catechism from 1604) devoted a few answers to the Lord's Supper, and the longer the form, the more was likely to be said on its origins, the manner in which Christ was present in the sacrament, and on what preparation was needed by the faithful who wished to participate in it.[148] Indeed, one publication which contains two of the titles in our sample, William Bradshaw's *A direction for the weaker sort of Christians*, was devoted largely to explaining the full significance of the Lord's Supper, and what to do before, during, and after communion. This work had three sections—the first two were by Bradshaw himself—a prose work on preparation (not included in our sample), and an eight-page 'brief form of trial whether one be in any measure to receive the sacrament of the Lord's Supper'; the third work was by 'a godly and faithful pastor', probably Arthur Hildersham this time, and consisted of a long question-and-answer treatise on 'The doctrine of communicating worthily' which Bradshaw said had come to hand just as his own work was being sent to the press.[149] This combination of works is an early example of an increasingly popular genre of pre-communion handbooks written in late Elizabethan and Stuart times, the majority, like Bradshaw's first item, being in prose; I hope to say more about these on another occasion.

The difference between official and 'godly' or presbyterian forms in our sample was limited, at least compared to the potential or actual differences of opinion on baptism, mainly because in the case of the Lord's Supper all those who received were supposed to have reached years of discretion and an awareness of their spiritual standing. So, although many authors spoke of the Lord's Supper as a sign, or seal, or representation, there was general agreement that most of the benefits of participation for the faithful, such as a strengthening of faith and union with Christ, were immediate, rather than prefigured as some authors thought was the case in baptism. There was also widespread agreement that the Lord's Supper had been instituted as a means of remembering Christ's sacrifice and of partaking in the benefits he had thus earned for mankind. Indeed, it was the 'godly' Hildersham who asserted that in the Lord's

---

[146] Schaff, *Creeds*, 90; Wendel, *Calvin*, 102–3, 329–55; Heidelberg Catechism, 332; Wake, *Principles*, 159; and cf. art. 25 of the Thirty-nine, and Westminster Confession, ch. xxix, and the catechisms cited in the following pages.

[147] e.g. Nicholson, *Exposition*, 177–8.

[148] See above, Chs. 1 and 2, for growing concern about ignorant communicants.

[149] Appendix 2, s.v. Bradshaw and Hildersham.

Supper the benefits of Christ's passion are particularly offered to us, more than by other means.[150] There was also a unanimous rejection of the doctrine of a real physical presence (though the way in which this was done did vary somewhat), and a broad consensus on what was needed for correct participation (though the advice given to those who were not sure if they met all the conditions required again varied slightly).[151] It is not being suggested that there were no differences of opinion: as over baptism, there were charges and counter-charges in the period from the 1580s to the 1630s, and from the 1640s there was a broader spectrum of views on the function and administration of the sacrament. But for the most part, these are not reflected in the best-selling catechisms in our sample.[152]

Catechetical authors had a much clearer case to put about the origins of the Lord's Supper than those of infant baptism. Catechumens who could read and had an annotated catechism were directed towards the appropriate passages in Matthew 26, Mark 14, Luke 22, and 1 Corinthians 11; those who could not read or did not have a Bible were encouraged by some authors to memorize at least part of one of these texts, or related ones such as John 6: 35 and 1 Corinthians 10: 16–17, either in the original or a close paraphrase.[153] As in the case of baptism, a distinction was drawn between the outer elements—the bread and wine, which was seen and tasted—and their inner meaning or significance, which was perceived only spiritually. While the basic premiss was that the bread represented Christ's body and the wine his blood, most authors made the significance of these elements clearer by saying that they represented Christ's sacrifice for man—his body broken and blood shed on the cross to satisfy God for their sins. How much further authors went depended on their individual views and target audience, but some general patterns can be traced.

The view that the sacrament was ordained as a way of commemorating Christ's death was made by a number of authors in our sample.[154] Despite Zwingli's preference for viewing sacraments as bare signs of allegiance or profession and of the eucharist as a thanksgiving and commemorative testimony of faith, the idea of the sacrament as a form of remembrance did not secure much attention in the catechisms of Calvin, the Heidelberg divines, or orthodox Calvinists like Cartwright and Perkins.[155] It is in the

---

[150] Hildersham, 'Doctrine', 33–4; on the overlaps between different elements in English Protestantism, the limited extent of controversy on this sacrament for much of the early modern period, and the importance attached to it by separatists, see S. Mayor, *The Lord's Supper in Early English Dissent* (1972), pp. xix, 32, 91–3, 158–9.

[151] See below, pp. 546–53.

[152] See above, pp. 509–10; and Holifield, *Covenant Sealed*, ch. 3.

[153] Paget, *Questions*, sigs. D5ʳ⁻ᵛ; Perkins, *Foundation*, 8; Ball, *Catechisme*, 81; Boughen, *Exposition*, 75; Sherlock, *Principles*, 48–9; Gouge, *Principles*, 101–6; Isham, *Catechism*, 61–4; Williams, *Exposition*, 58–62; Lewis, *Catechism*, 72–8.

[154] The command that this be done 'in remembrance of me' occurs only in Luke 22: 19 and 1 Cor. 11: 24–5, and in the former in connection only with the breaking of bread.

[155] Reardon, *Religious Thought*, 107–8; there is a brief scriptural reference to commemoration in the Heidelberg Catechism, 333–4.

official forms—Nowell's catechisms and the section added to the Prayer Book catechism and its derivatives—that the idea that the sacrament was ordained 'for the continual remembrance of the sacrifice of the death of Christ, and of the benefits which
we receive thereby' was stated most clearly, as it had been earlier in the communion
service in the Book of Common Prayer.[156] Some 'godly' authors like Bradshaw, Ball,
and Watts included remembrance as one of the functions of the sacrament, but only
in conjunction with others; in Ball's case it was placed fourth of the five ends for which
the sacrament was instituted.[157] But it is commonly found in the work of mainstream
episcopalians; Williams and Wake, for example, stressed that the sacrament was a
means of remembering Christ's sacrifice, but hastened to add that it was not a re-
enactment of it—a disclaimer which may help to explain the apparent caution of the
English 'godly' about a stress on commemoration.[158]

What rather more authors felt happy to teach was that the bread and wine 'represented', 'showed forth', or 'set forth' Christ's sacrifice, or that the visible, tangible
elements were a 'sign', 'image', 'figure', or 'representation' of Christ's death and passion, and that our reception of them signified our receiving and feeding on Christ by
faith.[159] Calvin used a variety of verbs and nouns to make the point: the bread and
wine 'represent' Christ's sacrifice; Christ and his benefits are more obviously 'set
forth' to our senses in the sacrament, which was ordained as a 'witness' and to 'assure'
us that our souls will be nourished; in it we receive not only the 'tokens' but Christ's
very substance.[160] Many other authors used similar terms: in the Lord's Supper
Christ's death is 'showed forth', stated the authors of the Westminster Catechisms;
the sacrament was ordained, said the future bishop, John Williams, as a sign and representation of Christ's death and as a means to convey and a pledge to assure us of the
benefits we receive thereby.[161] The term 'seal' was also used, in two ways. The first
was as a guarantee of present or future blessings. I am taught in this sacrament that all
Christ's benefits and righteousness are 'as surely sealed to be mine as if I myself had
wrought them', wrote Paget.[162] Combinations such as 'signify and seal' or 'exhibit and

---

[156] Nowell, *Catechisme*, 212; Prayer Book catechism, 789; Brightman, *English Rite*, ii. 692–3, 701; for
Luther's use of 1 Cor. 11: 23–5, see Schaff, *Creeds*, 91.

[157] Bradshaw, 'Briefe forme', 137–8; Ball, *Catechisme*, 81; Watts, 'Children's catechism', 27–8.

[158] Williams, *Exposition*, 58–9; Wake, *Principles*, 160; and cf. Hammond, *Practical catechisme*, 346, 388;
Nicholson, *Exposition*, 175–80, 194–5; Taylor, 'Catechism', 5; Comber, *Church-catechism*, 29; Isham,
Catechism, 63; and Lewis, *Catechism*, 73–4.

[159] Calvin, *Catechisme*, 139–42, 144; Nowell, *Catechisme*, 213–14; Heidelberg Catechism, 332, 335;
Hieron, *Doctrine*, 579; Bradshaw, 'Brief forme', 137–8; Ball, *Catechisme*, 81; Marshall, *Catechism*, 92–3;
Williams, *Exposition*, 58; Nicholson, *Exposition*, 176–80, 184–6; Keach, 'Youth', 108.

[160] Calvin, *Catechisme*, 139, 144; and cf. the 'signified and sealed' and 'certain tokens' in Heidelberg
Catechism, 332.

[161] Westminster Larger, 131 (answer 168); Westminster Shorter, 35 (answer 96); Williams, *Exposition*,
58.

[162] Paget, *Questions*, sig. D5r (I have substituted 'surely' from the 1580 edition for the 'freely' in 1617
which I think is a misprint in copying); and cf. Egerton, 'Forme of examining', 29–30; and cf. Hieron, *Doctrine*, 579 for use of the same text; Ussher, 'Principles', 11, and id., 'Method', 22; Taylor, 'Catechism', 5.

seal' were also not uncommon, for example, in the Heidelberg Catechism, and in Nicholson's assertion that the elements of bread and wine 'represent, exhibit, and seal' Christ's passion and the benefits thereof to a worthy communicant.[163] The second meaning of seal was as a means of confirming that we belong to Christ now and for ever, which was often presented in the context of the covenant of grace. The Lord's Supper, said Perkins in his catechism, was the second seal of the covenant; the covenant made in baptism was renewed in the Lord's Supper.[164] Similar language was used by a variety of authors including the semi-separatist Bradshaw, the 'godly' Hildersham and Elton, conformist episcopalians, and presbyterians.[165] What was also 'sealed' now, though in this case its implementation was still in the future, was an assurance of future salvation through Christ for all who truly believed.[166]

Among the other reasons for which the Lord's Supper was instituted, according to our authors, were the increasing of our faith, the nourishing of our souls, securing a closer union with Christ, and as an expression of mutual love among Christians, all of which we will come to in a moment. What was not made clear by many authors as being among the benefits of participation in the Lord's Supper was 'remission of sins' (Matthew 26: 28). This had been stressed by Luther in his short catechism, and may have been regarded as implicit in other authors' references to the 'benefits' or 'merits' of Christ's death for fallen man, or to the sacraments being seals of the covenant of grace.[167] But it is interesting that forgiveness of sins was stated explicitly only rarely in works in our sample, for example by Palmer, Hammond, Nicholson, and Taylor.[168] Of the reasons which were mentioned more often, the first was a strengthening of faith. As we shall see shortly, faith was regarded as a prerequisite for taking part in communion, and a number of 'godly' authors in our sample specified the strengthening of that faith as one of the functions of the sacrament. Here is the Dering–More statement of the case:

The Supper of the Lord, through the Holy Ghost, doth strengthen my faith, that I should not doubt, but as surely as I receive the bread and wine into my body, to become wholly mine, so my soul receiveth withal Christ, with his passion and righteousness to be wholly mine.[169]

---

[163] Heidelberg Catechism, 332; Nicholson, *Exposition*, 178; and cf. Egerton, 'Foure points', 25; Elton, *Forme*, sigs. D8ᵛ–E1ʳ; Marshall, *Catechism*, 42, 89; Sherlock, *Principles*, 48.

[164] Perkins, *Foundation*, 8.

[165] Bradshaw, 'Brief forme', 139; Hildersham, 'Doctrine', 21; Elton, *Forme*, sig. D6ʳ; Mayer, *Catechisme*, sig. D5ᵛ; and cf. Hammond, *Practical catechisme*, 391; Westminster Larger, 140–1 (answer 176); Gouge, *Principles*, 94, 103; and Vincent, *Catechism*, 229. Cartwright made a similar point to these authors without actually using the word 'covenant': 'Catechisme', sig. Aa7ᵛ. For later Stuart episcopalians one way for children to renew their covenant was in confirmation.

[166] Heidelberg Catechism, 334–5; Egerton, 'Forme of examining', 29–30; Bradshaw, 'Brief forme', 139; Taylor, 'Catechism', 5.

[167] Janz, *Three Reformation Catechisms*, 205–6; and see above, pp. 511–16.

[168] Palmer, *Endeavour*, 42; Hammond, *Practical catechisme*, 395, 398; Nicholson, *Exposition*, 183; Taylor, 'Catechism', 5. Perhaps we are in part back here to the conflicting views on the nature of justification discussed in Ch. 9 above.

[169] Dering–More, *Catechisme*, sig. B5ᵛ; and cf. Paget, *Questions*, sig. D5ʳ; Egerton, 'Forme of examining', 28; Hieron, *Doctrine*, 579; Ball, *Catechisme*, 81; Elton, *Forme*, sig. D6ʳ; and Keach, 'Youth', 110.

Closely allied to this was a sense of assurance that Christ was ours and would strengthen our hearts, which we have already encountered as a 'seal' but was also stated in other contexts by authors in the Elizabethan and early Stuart periods.[170]

Much the most common reason for or benefit of participation in the Lord's Supper, stated throughout the early modern period and by all shades of opinion, was the nourishing, refreshing, feeding, or strengthening of the soul. As the bread and wine sustain and strengthen the body of man in this transitory life, Calvin told his catechumens, so Christ's body and blood nourish and refresh our souls spiritually. Nowell followed this, but added that as in baptism we are born again, so in the Lord's Supper we are fed and sustained to spiritual nourishment and everlasting life.[171] Perkins also followed Calvin, though he put it in the third person (the faithful 'receiver' will be nourished 'both body and soul to everlasting life'), while the supplement to the Prayer Book catechism used the more usual first person.[172] 'The true and lively food of our souls, sacramentally apprehended by faith', 'spiritual food' by which our souls are 'strengthened and refreshed', 'nourished', or 'fed' were the phrases used in forms by episcopalians like Hill, Hammond, Boughen (citing Calvin's commentary on 1 Corinthians 11: 24), Ussher, Taylor, and several others.[173] But the same concepts of spiritual nourishment or refreshment can also be found in the forms of Herbert Palmer and other members of the Westminster Assembly and their supporters such as Thomas Gouge, and in the Baptist Benjamin Keach's most advanced form.[174]

The idea of grace or graces being confirmed in us or given to us in the Lord's Supper was again widespread, though as in the case of baptism the meaning of the term was elastic. Egerton counted sacraments as one of the public means by which God has appointed 'to continue and increase his graces in us', while Arthur Hildersham said that grace is promised us in the Lord's Supper, and the grace of perseverance we receive thereby will help us persist in faith and obedience.[175] Similarly the orthodox Calvinist John Ball said that one of the ends of the Lord's Supper was to confirm all saving graces in us, and the Westminster theologians talked of exercising graces already possessed before communion, growing in grace by regular participation in

[170] Calvin, *Catechisme*, 131, 142; 'Certaine questions and answers', sig. *iii^v; Egerton, 'Briefe method', 25–6; id., 'Familiar manner', 42; Bradshaw, 'Brief forme', 139; Hildersham, 'Doctrine', 21–2; Hammond, *Practical catechisme*, 396–7.

[171] Calvin, *Catechisme*, 138; Nowell, *Catechisme*, 213; and cf. Heidelberg Catechism, 332; Egerton, 'Familiar manner', 41; id., 'Brief forme', 16; Gouge, *Principles*, 100–2.

[172] Perkins, *Foundation*, 8; Prayer Book catechism, 789–91.

[173] Hill, *Principles*, sig. C3^v; Hammond, *Practical catechisme*, 395; Boughen, *Exposition*, 76; Ussher, 'Principles', 11; Taylor, 'Catechism', 5; and cf. Sherlock, *Principles*, 49; Marshall, *Catechism*, 42; and cf. Comber, *Church-catechism*, 31; Williams, *Exposition*, 62; Isham, *Catechism*, 31; Wake, *Principles*, 169; and Lewis, *Catechism*, 74–5.

[174] Palmer, *Endeavour*, 42; Westminster Larger, 131 (answer 168); Westminster Shorter, 35–6 (answer 96); Gouge, *Principles*, 100–2; Keach, 'Youth', 110.

[175] Egerton, 'Briefe method', 13; Hildersham, 'Doctrine', 21–3; on the six graces that he said were needed in communicants, see below, n. 214.

the sacrament, and thanking God for his grace at the moment of reception.[176] On the conformist episcopalian side, William Hill pointed out that the body and blood of Christ was 'the invisible grace' mentioned in the Prayer Book form's definition of a sacrament; Henry Hammond described the sacrament as a means of grace, and the benefits of the sacrament as being grace and pardon; while Jeremy Taylor described the benefits as the nourishing of our souls and the increasing of our graces.[177]

The account of John Mayer in the early 1620s also brought in two of the other benefits listed above—union with Christ and communion with other Christians. There were, he said, three inward graces conferred by outward signs in this sacrament: the giving of Christ for us (symbolized by the minister taking the bread and wine), our 'near union' with Christ (by digesting the bread and wine), and our 'near union' with the faithful (symbolized by the fact that the bread is of many grains, and the wine made of many grapes).[178] Other authors also talked of the Lord's Supper as a means of being united more and more to Christ's body, or of full spiritual union or communion with Christ;[179] and of the corollary of this, the sacrament as an opportunity for the faithful to show 'mutual love and fellowship each with other, as members of the same mystical body', to quote the Westminster Larger Catechism, or as a sacrament of thanksgiving and a feast of love, to quote the conformist Isham.[180]

As in the case of baptism, authors of intermediate or longer works and even some shorter ones in our sample were likely to combine a number of concepts or metaphors of the type listed above.[181] One of the longest definitions of the sacrament, that in the Westminster Larger Catechism, is also one of the fullest in terms of the number of ideas mentioned in the last few paragraphs which it embraced.[182] By comparison, there are much shorter answers in the Prayer Book catechism, and the two sentences in the pre-communion form appended to some editions of Calvin's catechism. In the latter it was stated that the Lord's Supper signifies 'that by the spiritual eating and drinking of the body and blood of our lord Jesus Christ, our souls are nourished unto life everlasting … with the virtue of Christ's body and blood'.[183] At heart this is what all the authors in the sample wished to ensure was understood: the symbolism of the

---

[176] Ball, *Catechisme*, 81; Westminster Larger, 131, 133–4, 136, 139 (answers 168, 171, 174); and cf. Palmer, *Endeavour*, 42; Vincent, *Catechism*, 237.

[177] Hill, *Principles*, sig. C3ʳ; Hammond, *Practical catechisme*, 347, 397–8; Taylor, 'Catechism', 5; and cf. Sherlock, *Principles*, 49.

[178] Mayer, *Catechisme*, sigs. D5ʳ⁻ᵛ.

[179] Heidelberg Catechism, 333; Hill, *Principles*, sig. C3ᵛ; Ball, *Catechisme*, 81; Westminster Larger, 131 (answer 168); Isham, *Catechism*, 63.

[180] Westminster Larger, loc. cit.; Isham, *Catechism*, 64; and cf. also Ball, *Catechisme*, 81; and Lewis, *Catechism*, 77–8.

[181] Calvin, *Catechisme*, 138–44; Perkins, *Foundation*, 7–8; Egerton, 'Briefe method', 16; id., 'Foure points', 25; id., 'Forme of examining', 30; Ball, *Catechisme*, 81; Hill, *Principles*, sigs. C3ʳ⁻ᵛ; Hammond, *Practical catechisme*, 346–7, 388–97; Nicholson, *Exposition*, 176; Williams, *Exposition*, 58–61.

[182] Westminster Larger, 131 (answer 168).

[183] Prayer Book catechism, 789; and 'Maner to examine children', 155.

bread and wine, and the promise of spiritual as well as physical nourishment for those who received in faith.

In tackling the subject of the real presence, Protestant catechists were in a cleft stick. They wished to persuade their charges that the bread and wine did not become the actual body and blood of Christ as the Catholics argued took place in the mass, but they also wanted to adhere as closely as possible to the scriptural statements of Christ that 'This is my body' and 'this is my blood' upon which their own version of the sacrament was based. Their job was not made any easier by the necessity of forgoing the armoury of logical methodology and scholastic distinctions with which such debates were conducted on formal occasions,[184] and the self-denying ordinance which prevented catechists from resorting to the tricks of the polemical trade. Some of the authors in our sample did not confront the problem of the real presence at all, for example Perkins, Ball, and Watts, probably from lack of space or different priorities. Other authors, both conformist and nonconformist, did tackle it frontally but did not mention the mass by name, while yet others, who did name it in order to explain where its authors and supporters were mistaken, used language which was usually restrained.[185] It may be remembered that the specific question on the difference between the Lord's Supper and the 'accursed idolatry' of 'the popish mass' in the Heidelberg catechism was not in the original form but was added on the express orders of the Elector Frederick III as a riposte to the anathemas of Trent.[186]

An early example of the narrow path being trodden by the authors in our sample is provided by the writing of Calvin. On the one hand, Calvin had a strongly subjective and deeply spiritual view of the Lord's Supper. He expressed a powerful belief in a sacramental presence of the body of Christ in the Lord's Supper, a presence which bridged the gap between heaven and earth, but which he had to admit was at heart a mystery, a miracle, which he experienced rather than understood. He also retained some of the language of sacrifice: the Lord's Supper was a sacrifice of praise and thanksgiving for the fact that Christ through his office as priest had sacrificed himself for us and intercedes for us still. On the other hand, Calvin abhorred the notion that the sacrifice of Christ had to be renewed, or that Christ's body and blood were physically present in the eucharist.[187] Some of this is evident in Calvin's catechism.

---

[184] For an exception, see Nicholson's use of 'relatum', 'correlatum', 'fundamentum', 'terminus', etc., in *Exposition*, 178–9, and Vincent's use of 'substance' and 'accidents' in *Catechism*, 231–2.

[185] Hill provided three reasons not to believe in transubstantiation: *Principles*, sigs. C3ʳ–4ᵛ; Vincent devoted four pages to the same purpose: *Catechism*, 231–5; and cf. Nicholson, *Exposition*, 175–6; Comber, *Church-catechism*, 29; Gouge, *Principles*, 101; and Wake, *Principles*, 161–2, 166–7, 171–5.

[186] Heidelberg Catechism, 335–6 and n.

[187] Gerrish, *Grace and Gratitude*, 152–6, 174, 180–1, 186–9. For the importance of the sacraments to Calvin, and his proximity to Luther and Cranmer, see Mayor, *Lord's Supper in Early English Dissent*, pp. xii, xv–xvi, xviii.

The minister asks the child whether in his previous reply, on the signification of the bread and wine, he is saying that 'we must be indeed partakers of the body and blood of the Lord' and the child replies 'Yea verily, I mean so', for since our assurance of salvation consists only in Christ's obedience, we must needs 'possess' Christ and receive him by faith 'in such sort as we may feel in our consciences the fruit and efficacy of his death and passion'. Later the minister asks if we receive only the tokens of Christ's death, and the child replies that we cannot doubt that what Christ promised at the last supper is 'indeed accomplished, and that which is figured by the signs is truly performed'. Accordingly 'there is no doubt, but he maketh us partakers of his very substance, to make us also one with him, and in one life with him'. But how can this be, says the minister, if Christ's body is in heaven, and 'we are here as pilgrims on the earth?' 'By the wondrous and unsearchable working of his Spirit who joineth easily together there things being far asunder in place'. But then just when Calvin seems to be close to talking of a physical presence, clarification is offered. Your opinion, then, is that the body is not present in the bread or the blood in the cup, says the minister. 'No not a whit: but clean contrary wise', replies the confident child, but if we will have the substance of the sacrament, we must at the moment of reception lift our hearts to heaven where Christ sits in glory, and not search for him in the corruptible elements of the bread and wine. The conclusion was that while the faithful partake of Christ's 'very substance', they must maintain a clear distinction between the outer substances, which our senses can recognize, and 'our saviour Christ by whom our souls are inwardly nourished' in a spiritual manner.[188]

Nowell for the most part trod in his master's footsteps at this point. If Christ had said the bread was his body and the wine his blood, shed for the remission of sins, then 'the thing which he testifieth in words, and representeth in signs, he performeth also in deed, and delivereth it unto us'. Like Calvin, Nowell believed in a mysterious, non-physical change taking place in the sacrament, but Nowell perhaps put rather more emphasis on the idea of a mystical union with Christ than on spiritual communion as Calvin had done. When we believe that Christ died and rose again to deliver us from death and procure us life, 'he coupleth us to himself by secret and marvellous virtue of his Spirit, even so that we be members of his body, and be of his flesh and bones, and do grow into one body with him'; but this is accomplished not by any physical change in the bread and wine, but as we receive the elements 'by faith, as the mouth of our soul'. He later stated that this union is 'not any gross joining' but a 'secret and marvellous communicating of Christ's body' which is 'most near and strait, most assured, most true, and altogether most high and perfect'.[189]

The line taken by nearly all of the other authors in our sample who broached the subject of the real presence was not very different from those already cited: Christ

---

[188] Calvin, *Catechisme*, 139–40, 143–5.
[189] Nowell, *Catechisme*, 213–14; like Calvin, Nowell said that Christ's sacrifice was eternal and therefore not repeatable; cf. Heidelberg Catechism, 334.

was present in the sacrament in a real but spiritual sense, but not physically, and those who received these elements in faith received Christ and his benefits. Some contemporaries, such as Keach in our sample, tended towards a position that minimized the change that occurred in the bread and wine and stressed the symbolism involved,[190] while other authors bypassed this problem to some extent by focusing on the idea of a spiritual feeding or spiritual union. It was, however, quite possible to blend the two elements. Dering and More told their catechumens that the nature and substance of the bread and wine were not changed into the body and blood of Christ, but in so far as they were used in a sacrament they differed from common bread and wine in that they were appointed by God to serve as seals and pledges of Christ's benefits for us.[191] A number of the Stuart episcopalians in our sample agreed that there was no change in the nature or substance of the outer symbols in the sacrament, only in their use as consecrated signs to represent something inner and spiritual. Hammond followed 'the ancient fathers of the church' in suggesting that the bread and wine were changed, but not into the body and blood of Christ, or in such a way as 'to cease to be bread and wine by that change'.[192] There is no sign of anything resembling a belief in a real physical presence in our sample.

Authors were anxious to make it clear, however, that, although the elements might not change physically, the reality of the spiritual nourishment received was not diminished. The relevant answers in the section added to the Prayer Book form come after the questions about the sacrament as commemoraton and its outward parts or signs, and include the statement that 'The body and blood of Christ ... are verily, and indeed taken and received by the faithful in the Lord's Supper' to 'the strengthening and refreshing of our souls'. The crucial phrase 'verily, and indeed taken' is a literal translation of one in Nowell's 'middle' Latin form—'vere tamen atque reipsa'—though as one of the expositors of this form was quick to point out, what was 'verily, and indeed taken' was the 'thing signified', and that only by true believers who receive Christ by faith.[193] The body and blood of Christ 'are not corporally or carnally present in, with, or under the bread and wine in the Lord's Supper', said the Westminster divines, but the body and blood 'are spiritually present to the faith of the receiver, no less truly and really than the elements themselves are to their outward senses';

so they that worthily communicate ... do therein feed upon the body and blood of Christ, not after a corporal and carnal, but in a spiritual manner, yet truly and really, while by faith they receive and apply unto themselves Christ crucified, and all the benefits of his death.[194]

---

[190] Keach, 'Youth', 108–9.

[191] Dering–More, *Catechisme*, sig. B5ᵛ; and cf. Paget, *Questions*, sig. D5ᵛ.

[192] Hammond, *Practical catechisme*, 384–5; and cf. Hill, *Principles*, sig. C4ᵛ; Boughen, *Exposition*, 76; Comber, *Church-catechism*, 29, 31; Marshall, *Catechism*, 92; Williams, *Exposition*, 59.

[193] Prayer Book catechism, 788–9; Williams, *Exposition*, 60.

[194] Westminster Larger, 132 (answer 170).

Indeed, in some of the expositions of the Prayer Book form, it is hard to tell whether the inspiration was the line of thought that ran through Calvin and Nowell to the supplementary section on sacraments to the form of 1549, or the Westminster Larger Catechism, for example Sherlock's reference to the body and blood being 'truly taken and received corporally', Marshall's 'really and spiritually', and Isham's 'truly and spiritually received'.[195] In at least one case, it was clearly the Westminster form: Thomas Comber paraphrased the last passage cited above in his explanation of 'verily, and indeed taken' in the Prayer Book form.[196]

At the core of the sacrament was, as Calvin and other authors in our sample admitted, a mystery which had to be taken on trust. The faithful receive Christ 'mystically, and after an ineffable manner', said Hammond in 1645, but the manner in which this was achieved was unclear and was left to faith.[197] Christ's body is received after a spiritual, not a corporal manner, wrote Boughen in 1646, but it is a mystery how: the bread is bread before consecration, at the time of consecration, and after consecration, but after consecration it is also the body and blood of Christ.[198] Nicholson also regarded the heart of the sacrament as a mystery; Christ imparts himself to believers, and 'though mystically, yet it is truly; though invisibly, yet it is really done'.[199] The crux, whether one was in the broad majority who favoured spiritual presence or in the small minority (like Keach) who preferred a bare symbolism, was the faith of the receiver. Christ is 'sacramentally apprehended by faith, whereby our spiritual life is supported', wrote Hill in 1616.[200] Without the faith of the people and the help of the Holy Ghost, there was no change in the outward elements, a point of departure from the Catholic position where the priest worked the miracle before offering it to the people. Through faith, and with the help of the Holy Ghost, there was a sacramental partaking of Christ.

Faith was, however, only one of the prerequisites laid down by our authors for participation in the Lord's Supper. Those who handled the subject of preparation—and a majority in the sample did—made their catechumens learn the identity of three or four 'marks and tokens' which they had to be able to recognize in themselves before they took communion. Of these, faith, repentance, and love for one's neighbour were the three most commonly listed.[201] Others added by a number of authors

---

[195] Sherlock, *Principles*, 49; Marshall, *Catechism*, 93; Isham, *Catechism*, 63.

[196] Comber, *Church-catechism*, 31.   [197] Hammond, *Practical catechisme*, 385.

[198] Boughen, *Exposition*, 75–6 (and p. 77 for a reference to 'dreadful mystery'); and cf. Nicholson, *Exposition*, 179.

[199] Ibid. 183.

[200] Hill, *Principles*, sig. C3ᵛ; and cf. Boughen *Exposition*, 76; Gouge, *Principles*, 93, 102; Marshall, *Catechism*, 93, and Williams, *Exposition*, 60.

[201] See the works cited in the last few pages and below. Of the larger forms in the sample, a few did not mention preparation. e.g. Cartwright, 'Catechisme', and Ussher's two forms.

were knowledge of the grounds of religion, an intention to lead a new life, and thankfulness for Christ's death or his institution of the sacrament.[202] There were other prerequisites, such as the consideration of whether communicants were baptized, and of sufficient age and sound judgement to be able to examine themselves for some or all of the above qualities, but these were deployed less often.[203] A substantial minority of our authors warned of the dangers of receiving unworthily, and some of these offered advice as to what a catechumen should do if he or she was not sure if they were suitably qualified for partaking in the sacrament, or if, having received, they did not feel the expected benefits.[204] Hardly any authors tackled controversial matters such as kneeling at communion, excommunication, or the issue of the legality of a 'mixed' communion of saints and hardened sinners which vexed so many ministers in the 1640s and 1650s.[205]

Calvin's instruction to his adolescent catechumens was to examine themselves to see whether they were 'a true member of Christ our saviour'. The sure signs of this were 'a faith or right confidence in God's promises', being inwardly sorry for sins, and love of one's neighbour with 'an unfeigned charity, not keeping in his heart any rancour, hatred, or debate'.[206] This particular combination of faith, repentance, and charity can be found in other forms in the sample, such as those of Dering and More and Paget, and in conjunction with one or more other qualities in many other forms.[207] What Nowell did was to change the order slightly by putting repentance first, and insert a new element; the result was adopted by a number of other authors subsequently. Like the bidding prayer in the communion service in the Prayer Book which put earnest repentance first, and the Heidelberg Catechism which started with displeasure for sin and trust of forgiveness, Nowell began with hearty repentance for sins already committed, and then moved on to a sure hope of God's mercy through Christ. His third 'mark' was a purpose to lead a godly life hereafter, comparable to the Heidelbergers' desire to amend one's life, and his fourth was brotherly love to one's neighbours, which was in Calvin's form but not the German one.[208] This sequence was adopted (with a slight alteration) in the section on the sacraments added to the Prayer Book form, and so by the large number of expositors of that form in subsequent reigns. Stephen Egerton inserted a new element into the equation by stating that communicants must prove to themselves 'that they know the grounds of religion', as well

[202] e.g. Egerton, 'Briefe method', 16; 'Certaine questions and answers', sig. *iii'; Prayer Book catechism, 791; Marshall, *Catechism*, 93–4.

[203] Bradshaw, 'Brief forme', 137–8; Elton, *Forme*, sig. E3'; Nicholes, *Catechisme*, 68; Taylor, 'Catechism', 5; Sherlock, *Principles*, 45.

[204] See below, nn. 222–30, and more generally for the early period, J. E. Booty, 'Preparation for the Lord's Supper in Elizabethan England', *Anglican Theological Review*, 49 (1967), 131–48.

[205] Cartwright, 'Catechisme', sig. Aa8'; Boughen, *Exposition*, 78–80; Hammond, *Practical catechisme*, 376–7; Keach, 'Youth', 111; and see below, nn. 231–8.

[206] Calvin, *Catechisme*, '144' [recte 146].

[207] Dering–More, *Catechisme*, sigs. B5'–6'; Paget, *Questions*, sig. D4'; and see above, nn. 201–2.

[208] Nowell, *Catechisme*, 216; and Heidelberg Catechism, 336.

as believing in Christ, hating their sin, and loving their brethren.[209] This addition provides an interesting insight into the attitudes and priorities of an innovative teacher, and it was picked up by other 'godly' authors such as Ball and the Westminster divines, and by conformist episcopalians, though a number of the latter put it in the more precise form of understanding the doctrine of the sacraments.[210] 'Can they partake worthily that are ignorant and cannot discern the Lord's Body?' asked Wallis; 'No' was the firm reply.[211]

A few authors in our sample preferred a simpler approach: Perkins mentioned only two marks: true belief and heartfelt repentance; and in his scriptural catechism Hieron simply urged self-examination but did not say for what, perhaps because he could not find a single text to suit his purpose.[212] Others gave way to the temptation to elaborate that was noted in previous chapters of this study. This can be seen in a mild form in the section tacked onto the Prayer Book form, which added a thankful remembrance of Christ's death to the 'tokens' listed by Nowell,[213] and in a slightly more pronounced way in the works of Arthur Hildersham, John Ball, and the Westminster divines. Hildersham devoted the great bulk of his work, which admittedly was a specialist work on the subject, to the six 'graces' we must find in ourselves by examination: a desire to receive the sacrament; knowledge of the Law, the Gospel, and the sacrament; faith; repentance;newness of life; and charity. Each of these was defined, and its uses explained.[214] Ball devoted what were for him two quite long answers to the subject of self-examination, where many authors of comparable forms devoted only one; and the Westminster Larger Catechism listed ten prerequisites (cut down to five in the Shorter).[215] Indeed, the Larger Catechism's treatment of what to do before, during, and after reception rivalled the extended treatments of conservative episcopalians like Nicholson, Comber, and Wake, which may confirm the point made by Professor Holifield that during the seventeenth century puritans were developing 'a widespread sacramental piety'.[216]

Other traits noted in Chapters 8 and 9 above were an exhortation to catechumens to be introspective, and the use of a vocabulary of 'feeling' as a means of determining the spiritual state of the individual. To some extent this can be found also in the treatment of preparation for communion. All authors who tackled this were anxious that

---

[209] Egerton, 'Briefe method', 16.
[210] Ball, *Catechisme*, 82; Westminster Larger, 136 (answer 174); Westminster Shorter, 36 (answer 97); and cf. Elton, *Forme*, sigs. E3ᵛ–4ʳ; Wallis, *Explanation*, 43; Gouge, *Principles*, 103; Hill, *Principles*, sig. C5ᵛ; Nicholson, *Exposition*, 194; Comber, *Church-catechism*, 32; Marshall, *Catechism*, 48; and Isham, *Catechism*, 63.
[211] Wallis, *Explanation*, 44.　　[212] Perkins, *Foundation*, 8; Hieron, *Doctrine*, 579.
[213] Prayer Book catechism, 791.　　[214] Hildersham, 'Doctrine', 16–110.
[215] Ball, *Catechisme*, 82; Westminster Larger, 133 (answer 171); Westminster Shorter, 36 (answer 97); and cf. Gouge, *Principles*, 103, and id., 'Heads', 6.
[216] Nicholson, *Exposition*, 191–8; Comber, *Church-catechism*, 31–2; Wake, *Principles*, 175–80; and cf. Holifield, *Covenant Sealed*, pp. x, 126–33.

communicants should have proved to themselves that they were true members of Christ, were genuinely sorry for their sins, and were in a state of unfeigned charity with their neighbours. Nowell referred to 'hearty' repentance and 'sure' hope of God's mercy; Bradshaw to 'unfeigned' hatred of sins and purpose to lead a new life; and the Prayer Book additional section to 'true' repentance', 'steadfast' purpose of amendment, a 'lively' faith, and a 'thankful' remembrance of Christ's death.[217] This was raised to a slightly higher level of intensity in some early Stuart works, as in Ball's references to 'utter' forsaking of sin and 'longing desire' for our brethren's good.[218] But the tone of the Westminster catechisms on preparation tended towards the clinical rather than the ardent, unless one counts the reference in the Larger form to the need for 'fervent prayer'.[219] In these forms, even the accounts of what feelings should be experienced during and after reception of the elements rarely rose above the level of 'earnest hungering and thirsting after Christ' or a tangible 'increase of faith, love, and all saving graces'.[220] Catechumens, it would appear, were encouraged to be honest with themselves and to seek some emotional commitment, but not to expect heightened emotions of the kind felt by well-educated and highly articulate poets or Catholic mystics. Indeed, it has been suggested that the tendency to subjective and psychological explanations of sacramental efficacy found in some late Elizabethan and early Stuart puritan accounts of the Lord's Supper tended to undermine the element of mystery which Calvin saw at its heart.[221]

A problem raised by catechists' insistence on self-examination in general, and of intensity of emotion in particular, was what a catechumen should do if he could not find within him what he had been told should be there. Relatively few of our authors tackled this, and the slight variation in their answers was kept within narrow bounds. The moderate position was laid down by Calvin and Nowell: a would-be communicant's faith, charity, and other marks of readiness could never be perfect, but if they were 'sincere and unfeigned' he or she should not hold back from participating, but rather come to it 'as an help and succour, against our infirmity'.[222] This was also the line taken by other authors in our sample, mostly drawn from the ranks of the 'godly': if one was weak in faith or in the other qualities needed, one should bewail one's unbelief, pray for faith, and seek God's help and favour, but one should nevertheless receive the sacrament, since it was intended as a means of strengthening what was weak.[223] The more rigorous position, which can be found in the work of Egerton and a couple of expositors of the Prayer Book catechism, was reserved for

---

[217] Nowell, *Catechisme*, 216; Bradshaw, 'Brief forme', 140; Prayer Book catechism, 791; and cf. Comber, *Church-catechism*, 31–2.

[218] Ball, *Catechisme*, 82; and cf. Mayer, *Catechisme*, sigs. D4ᵛ–5ʳ; and Palmer, *Endeavour*, 44–5.

[219] Westminster Larger, 133 (answer 171).

[220] Ibid. 134 (answer 174); and Ball, *Catechisme*, 82.   [221] Holifield, *Covenant Sealed*, 58–61.

[222] Calvin, *Catechisme*, '144–141' [*recte* 146–7]; Nowell, *Catechisme*, 216–17.

[223] Ball, *Foundation*, 82; Mayer, *Catechisme*, sigs. D3ʳ–4ᵛ; Westminster Larger, 134–5 (answer 172); and cf. Egerton, 'Briefe method', 17.

those with a total lack of the requisite marks. If one cannot find knowledge, belief, hatred of sin, and love of one's brethren, wrote Egerton, one must forbear until God has wrought them, though the potential communicant should use 'all other helps appointed for that purpose'.[224] But even here the gap was not large. Nicholes said that as soon as a sincere desire for these qualities was felt, this was 'the beginning of them', which was close to the view expressed in the Westminster Larger Catechism; and Wake urged anyone who, upon self-examination and after consultation with a minister, still felt unworthy to attend communion to 'make all the haste he can to remove the impediment, and reconcile himself to God', so that he could partake of the graces communicated therein to all faithful receivers.[225] A somewhat different case was that of the communicant who did receive but then did not feel the expected benefits afterwards. This lack of result was viewed as proof that the receiver had been in some way unworthy, or had failed to make careful or honest preparation beforehand; he or she was told to use all means available to come to sound faith and repentance.[226]

It was not those who had communicated in what they thought was good faith, but the irreverent or dishonest who were the object of the often repeated fulminations against unworthy receivers—that they provoked the wrath of God and would eat and drink their own damnation. We find this in the Heidelberg Catechism and in English forms by 'godly' authors as well as by expositors of the Prayer Book form.[227] In the 1640s both Hammond and the authors of the Westminster Shorter Catechism spelt out the doom awaiting those who communicated unworthily.[228] There was even a risk that the clergy might be too successful in putting this point across. The sacrament is called by some a dreadful mystery, wrote Boughen, 'because he that rightly considers of it will not approach to this table without dread and trembling', though he went on to try to reassure genuine believers that if they humbled themselves before God they would not be judged unworthy.[229] Would it not be the safest way to abstain altogether from the holy table rather than run the risk of coming unworthily to it, asked Wake? To avoid it would be not only to break Christ's command, was the reply, but also to 'deprive ourselves of the grace of God, which this sacrament was designed to convey to us'.[230] Fear of damnation remained a problem which a number

[224] Ibid., 'Briefe method', 16; Nicholes, *Catechisme*, 68; Wake, *Principles*, 180–1.

[225] As previous note.

[226] Perkins, *Foundation*, 8; Nicholes, *Catechisme*, 68–9; Westminster Larger, 139–40 (answer 175); Vincent, *Catechism*, 240.

[227] Heidelberg Catechism, 336; Paget, *Questions*, sigs. D5ᵛ–6ʳ; Wallis, *Explanation*, 44; Gouge, *Principles*, 105–6; id., 'Heads', 6; Vincent, *Catechism*, 238–40; Hill, *Principles*, sigs. C4ᵛ–5ʳ; Bernard, *Common catechisme*, sig. C8ʳ; Nicholes, *Catechisme*, 68–9; Comber, *Church-catechism*, 31–2; Marshall, *Catechism*, 94.

[228] Hammond, *Practical catechisme*, 389–90; Westminster Shorter, 36 (answer 97); there was no such reference in the Westminster Larger, perhaps because it was hoped that there would be no unworthy receivers among those who had progressed to that form.

[229] Boughen, *Exposition*, 77–8.   [230] Wake, *Principles*, 177–8.

of authors of pre-communion forms in the later Stuart period felt they had to tackle, as I hope to show on another occasion. It is perhaps significant of the pastoral sensitivity of the authors in our sample that many did not mention the risk at all, but left the matter in the positive light that only the faithful should participate and only they would benefit thereby.

The subject of unworthy receivers was one that provoked a few authors to tackle the question of whether any should be turned away from the sacrament. Authors took a hard line against those who showed themselves to be 'unbelieving and ungodly'; they should be excluded 'by the office of the keys' until they amended their lives.[231] But as for the rest, pastors should 'receive all indifferently, without choice', as Nowell put it; even hypocrites should not be turned away 'so long as their wickedness is secret', which is why Judas was not turned away from the Last Supper. By his own account, Nowell was treading a fine line here. Those 'openly known to be unworthy' could be excluded, but if only the pastor knew or he was only 'privily informed' of someone's unworthiness, he could not debar them; he could preach at them in public, and threaten them in private, 'but put them back from the communion he may not, unless the lawful examination of the church be first had'. If this meant the ungodly took the sacrament alongside the godly, it did not detract from the efficacy of the sacrament for the faithful: the ungodly 'do not receive the gifts', but the godly are never disappointed of 'a most good conscience of mind, and most sweet comfort'.[232] Predictably Hammond agreed: the governors of the church should withdraw the sacrament from those who 'go on wilfully, scandalously, and impenitently in any sin', but those not under the church's censures should not be barred. The sacrament was a confederation of all professing Christians, and if some recipients proved to be unworthy, then the only damage they did was to themselves.[233]

A 'godly' author like Hildersham felt that the minister on the spot should decide, and urged his readers to submit to examination by their minister who was their superior in all matters relating to God's worship, but such a position was rarely stated in our sample.[234] Others from a similar background acknowledged the role of the wider church, though the exact mechanisms of detection and correction were not usually specified. John Ball was of the opinion that 'the unruly' should be admonished and 'the obstinate' excommunicated, while in the Westminster Larger Catechism it was stated that 'such as are found to be ignorant or scandalous', even if they say they believe and have a desire to attend, 'may and ought to be kept from that sacrament, by the power which Christ hath left in his church', until they are instructed and show a reformation of their ways.[235] Only one author in our sample adopted a much harder line. Believers and unworthy receivers should not communicate together,

---

[231] Heidelberg Catechism, 336–7.   [232] Nowell, *Catechisme*, 217–18.
[233] Hammond, *Practical catechisme*, 375–7, 389–90.   [234] Hildersham, 'Doctrine', 10.
[235] Ball, *Catechisme*, 82; Westminster Larger, 135 (answer 173).

said Benjamin Keach; only godly men and women or such as are truly converted should come to the Lord's Table.[236] As a statement of an ideal, most other authors in our sample would probably not have demurred; but as the basis for a programme of intrusive enquiry at congregational level or for a restriction of communion to a small number of the saints, some would certainly have objected.

These were important and emotive issues, but also complex and controversial ones, and most of our authors seem to have decided that a catechism was not the proper place in which to pursue them. The norm was to leave the testing for worthiness to the individual; hence the crucial value of catechizing as a means of informing would-be communicants what to look for in themselves. If catechumens then made a sincere effort at preparation and found some of the 'marks and tokens' specified, they should be admitted to the Lord's Supper; and if they were worthy receivers, they would benefit thereby, and if not, not. No indication is given in the forms examined here of how long this self-examination should take, or if any steps were taken to check that it had been performed satisfactorily and honestly. But one may suspect that the onus on the clergy was to work on the mustard-seed principle, that even the smallest amount of faith was acceptable as a starting-point, and to give those who said they wanted to take the sacrament the benefit of the doubt. Ministers might be genuinely worried about unworthy receivers, but they were also anxious for their flocks to attend and participate in the Lord's Supper, which was, as we have seen, regularly portrayed by catechists as a means of demonstrating and strengthening faith. It was an act of personal faith but performed—ideally—in a supportive rather than a hyper-critical community. The Lord's Supper was a means of testifying and renewing 'mutual love and fellowship each with other, as members of the same mystical body', said the Westminster divines. It was 'a feast of love, and a communion of Christians one with another; and signifies their conjunction in one spiritual body', wrote Isham, and was echoed by John Lewis in the form widely used in charity schools in the eighteenth century.[237] It was also generally agreed, from Calvin and Nowell to the Westminster divines and Comber, that the sacrament must be taken as often as it was offered, both to reinforce the individual's commitment and to increase the Christian community's strength.[238]

And it is with that community that we may end this chapter. As baptism was the rite of initiation into the church, so the Lord's Supper was the rite of communion not only with Christ but also his ecclesial body. In his catechism, Calvin wrote that the one effect of the work of Christ is that there should be a church, and in his commentary on 1 Corinthians 10: 16 he argued that 'the sacrificial death of Christ establishes a community, which is the body symbolized by the one eucharistic bread'. In the

---

[236] Keach, 'Youth', 111–12.

[237] Westminster Larger, 131 (answer 168); Isham, *Catechism*, 64; Lewis, *Catechism*, 77–8.

[238] Calvin, *Catechisme*, 148; Nowell, *Catechisme*, 212; Westminster Larger, 141–2 (answer 177); Comber, *Church-catechism*, 29; and cf. Marshall, *Catechism*, 42.

Lord's Supper, Christ makes us not simply one body, but his body.[239] The sacraments thus represent a coming together of all the teaching considered in the last few chapters: what Christians should believe, what they should do, how they should pray, and how in the sacraments they should take the opportunity to thank God for all he had done for them, and confirm and strengthen their faith by the means he had provided.

[239] Gerrish, *Grace and Gratitude*, 186, 189.

Conclusion

SOME years ago Jean Delumeau drew attention to the parallels between the strenuous efforts made by Protestant and Catholic authorities in the sixteenth and seventeenth centuries to raise the level of religious knowledge and spiritual awareness among their respective charges, and there can hardly be a better example of this than the campaigns that both sides undertook to teach an officially approved version of the faith to their flocks.[1] Not all historians would agree with Delumeau that these campaigns represented an attempt to 'Christianize' a hitherto pagan or semi-pagan society, but few would probably deny the energy put into preaching, teaching, and catechizing which followed close on the heels of the German and Swiss reformations and, rather more slowly, after the deliberations at Trent,[2] and in many ways this study of catechizing in early modern England tends to support his argument. However, some contemporaries' conviction of the need to catechize and the demonstrable existence of many attempts to catechize do not mean that they necessarily had the impact that Delumeau seems to have thought, or hoped, was the case; and in this Conclusion we may return first of all to the impact of catechizing in early modern England, in part by comparing it with that of a catechetical campaign in another part of Protestant Europe at the time. The second part of this monograph has surveyed the teaching contained in English catechisms, and suggested that although there was a great deal of continuity and consensus, catechetical teaching was not a straightforward mirror image of the approved official teaching of the established church, as Delumeau implied. There were not only some differences between the theology of different groups within English Protestantism (though less sharply stated than might have been expected), but also variations between the kind of message delivered to the very young or totally ignorant and that given to the older, more knowledgeable, or more literate catechumen. In the second part of this Conclusion, we will examine some of the broader implications of these suggestions.

Gerald Strauss's study of religious instruction in sixteenth-century Germany is one of the most detailed accounts of early modern catechizing that is currently available, and it will be obvious from what has been said in the first part of this study that there are many parallels between what happened in Luther's Germany and early modern England. Catechists' motives were very similar: catechizing would lay the

---

[1] J. Delumeau, *Catholicism between Luther and Voltaire* (1977), 161, 171, 173, 199; and cf. the works by Delumeau cited at the start of Ch. 10 above.

[2] See e.g. John Bossy's Introduction to Delumeau, *Catholicism*; Bossy, 'The Counter-Reformation and the People of Catholic Europe', *Past and Present*, 47 (1970), 64–8; and id., *Christianity in the West*, 118–22 and *passim*.

necessary foundations of religious knowledge, enable the faithful to understand more of the scriptures and sermons they heard and the meaning of the sacraments and other ceremonies that took place in church, and it would both encourage virtue and discourage vice. The methods too had much in common: rote memorizing of short forms leading on (in theory) to mastery of a larger form or greater understanding of what had already been learnt, though it seems that explanation of these staples on a regular basis began at a later date in England than in Germany. The content of German and English forms was very similar—the four basic staples of Creed, Decalogue, Lord's Prayer, and sacraments; and the targets were much the same—children and adolescents, especially children, although in some Elizabethan and early Stuart parishes perhaps greater efforts were made than in Germany to get adult communicants to learn a catechism too. The locations in which basic catechizing took place were also predictably the same: church, school, and home. Germany had a head start in so far as state and church co-operated in setting up a large number of schools in which religious instruction would be an integral and important part of the curriculum. But in Germany the reality did not always match the ideal as far as such school instruction was concerned, and in some areas ministers and sextons apparently had to step in and provide basic instruction in the catechism.[3] In England, as we saw in Chapters 3 and 4, the main catechetical thrust from the beginning was made in church, but support did come from the large number of schools which were set up privately, in which the use of the official *ABC* or *Primer* meant that the acquisition of literacy and mastery of the approved short catechism often went hand in hand. In both countries there was probably a limited amount of catechizing in the home, but this is now particularly difficult to trace.

The results of these efforts to catechize are harder to compare. Strauss's conclusions, derived from careful analysis of the detailed reports made by visitors sent to check up on catechetical knowledge and other matters, were that little real impression was made, due to the reluctance of children to learn and parents' slowness to make them learn. While the adoption of rigid techniques of catechizing led to some short-term success in getting the children who did attend to parrot answers, it brought about only a limited amount of comprehension or long-term retention.[4] A few points may be made about these findings in relation to the English experience. First of all, conditions for effective catechizing were in some ways much less favourable in Germany than in England. In the former the continued existence of powerful Catholic states nearby posed a constant threat to the survival of Protestantism until the 1550s and beyond; and many states which did remain Protestant either faced serious internal opposition, for example from the nobility, or switched back and forth between different types of Protestantism. In England, by contrast, there was from the 1560s relative stability of political and ecclesiastical conditions and homogeneity of language, a fairly rapid

---

[3] Strauss, *Luther's House of Learning*, Introduction and pts. 1–2.   [4] Ibid., pt. 3.

increase in the number of educated, committed parish clergy and schoolteachers, and persistent attempts to improve new techniques of religious instruction to compensate for the loss of older techniques such as the use of visual aids and confession. With dissenting voices from both Catholic and radical puritan wings, and the existence of divisions within the Protestant establishment, conditions in England were never ideal, but apart from the middle decades of the seventeenth century there was sufficient unity of outlook and approach between church and state to ease the sting of most of these forces for much of the time.

Secondly, there have been criticisms of Strauss's interpretation of and reliance upon visitation returns: perhaps the well-educated clergy who conducted these visitations were demanding unreasonably high standards of learning and insight from their flocks, and their reports of gross ignorance and superstition should be viewed in a more cautious light. Strauss has rebutted these criticisms vigorously and adduced new evidence to support his case, and his thesis has received support from a wide-ranging survey of Protestant achievement by Geoffrey Parker. But it would appear that in some areas of Germany—and elsewhere in early modern Europe—results were more positive than Strauss originally suggested.[5] For England we do not have the detailed visitors' reports on catechizing that survive for Germany and later for Sweden, at least not until the early eighteenth century, and even then the replies to the episcopal questionnaires tended to focus on the existence and type of catechizing rather than the level of success. But if one looks down column six in Appendix 1, it is noticeable how many supplementary catechisms dating from the period 1560–1640 were drawn up in the south-eastern quarter of England, whereas in the period 1640–1740 a growing number were drawn up in the Midlands or further North and West. If one looks at the replies to the episcopal questionnaires of the early eighteenth century one notes other patterns. Some catechists seem to have secured more co-operation in medium-sized towns and villages than in either very large or very small communities; others did well in parishes where the social or educated élite supported catechizing actively.[6] It was also generally the case, as Strauss pointed out in his original study of Germany, that throughout the early modern period there was probably more catechizing in towns than in the country, since the greater concentration of population, schools, and book suppliers, and the more limited and regular hours of urban labour compared to the burdensome and seasonally erratic hours worked in the countryside, made it easier for a catechist to get children together to

---

[5] J. M. Kittelson, 'Successes and Failures in the German Reformation: The Report from Strasbourg', *Archiv für Reformationgeschichte*, 73 (1982), 153–75; id., 'Visitations and Popular Religious Culture: Further Reports from Strasbourg', in K. C. Sessions and P. N. Bebb (eds.), *Pietas et Societas: New Trends in Reformation Social History* (Kirkville, Mo., 1988), 89–101; for further criticisms and Strauss's reply, see G. Strauss, 'The Reformation and its Public in an Age of Orthodoxy', in R. P. Hsia (ed.), *The German People and the Reformation* (Ithaca, NY, 1988), 194–214; see also G. Parker, 'Success and Failure during the First Century of the Reformation', *Past and Present*, 136 (1992), 43–82, esp. 43–51.

[6] See above, pp. 135, 139, 270–1.

learn a catechism, whether in church, school, or household unit. It was also suggested above that the longer a young person stayed at school or university, the greater his exposure to catechetical teaching. What we may have in England was a parting of the ways between, on the one hand, an elusive majority who were exposed to a limited amount of catechizing in church and who for the most part probably did little more than master the staple formulae and a few basic answers built around them, and, on the other, a captive minority in schools who were exposed to more regular bouts of catechizing and who were expected to learn more, retain it for longer, and achieve greater understanding as well.[7] It was from a minority within this minority—those who spent several years in secondary or higher education and were exposed to a growing number of forms designed largely for them—that the next generation of ministers, teachers, and magistrates would for the most part be drawn, and would in their turn be strong supporters of catechizing for the majority. Further work on these and other variables may yield greater insight into patterns of performance and 'success' or 'failure' in early modern English catechizing.

Thirdly, Strauss for perfectly good reasons stopped his survey in the closing decades of the sixteenth century or the very start of the seventeenth: by then the strong upward curve of early pressure for results seemed to be declining in the face of apathy or resistance. The German experience may, however, have been characterized by two fairly distinct curves. The first upward sweep started in the second quarter of the sixteenth century, and was backed by Luther's great energy and the speedy creation of many new schools, while the second began in the late seventeenth and early eighteenth centuries, with the onset of pietism and a new drive to literacy and godliness (as Strauss has himself pointed out on another occasion).[8] In other countries, and one could perhaps include not only England but also some Catholic states here,[9] the curve may have been different, rising much more slowly at the outset due to the limited organization, drive, and skilled manpower available for the task, but despite occasional setbacks achieving modest heights of success over a longer time-scale of a century or a century and a half. If we take the longer perspective in England, there are a number of possible pointers to such a conclusion. There is the large number of new forms written, published, and in many cases republished time and time again, as we saw in Chapter 2. Above all, the scale of reprints, not just in the first or second generation of Protestantism but through to the third and fourth generations and beyond, especially in the case of the *ABC* and the *Primer*, would seem to suggest that not just the printers and publishers who produced millions of copies of these forms, but also the many people who bought and distributed them continued to think that catechizing was of some value well into the eighteenth century. (The production

---

[7] See above, Chs. 3–4.

[8] R. Gawthrop and G. Strauss, 'Protestantism and Literacy in Early Modern Germany', *Past and Present*, 104 (1984), 47–55.

[9] Delumeau, *Catholicism*, 199–201; Bossy, 'Counter-Reformation and People', 65–7.

of new forms did reach two peaks in the period from the 1580s to the 1620s and in the 1690s and 1700s, as can be seen from Table 1, p. 51 above, but the effect of adding reprints of old stand-bys and of newly popular forms into the equation is to smooth out these bumps.) Then there are the figures for various dioceses in the period from the 1710s to the 1740s which suggest that by then, despite the onset of a limited toleration in 1689, catechizing took place in a clear majority of parishes for at least part of the year, and that in a number of parish churches and elementary schools there was also some second-level catechizing in the form of exposition of what had been taught already. There is also the admittedly more general point that there seems to have been in England a shift away from stating that the laity did not *know* the basics to saying that they did not *understand* them fully; hence the much greater efforts at improving techniques of instruction and at explaining catechetical material in the second century after the Reformation. This greater stress on comprehension and exposition did presuppose a modicum of knowledge among those being catechized at that time, albeit from a clerical point of view a still insufficient level of understanding or application.[10]

Fourthly, Strauss appears to treat catechizing in Germany as a predominantly oral exercise. Also many of the German forms that survive from that period apparently do so in manuscript rather than print,[11] which may indicate both very localized use, in a particular parish by an individual minister, and again predominantly oral use, with the catechist declaiming the answers to catechumens from his own single copy, rather than going to the bother of having multiple copies made. In England, by contrast, most catechisms that survive are in print, and the large numbers of new and repeat editions of a wide variety of forms suggest consistent sales and wide distribution for much of the period 1570–1740. This prompts the question whether catechizing in England was more reliant on a mixture of orality and literacy than in Germany, and, if so, whether the element of literacy involved helped to disseminate and fix the content of the forms in those being catechized. This is not the place to go into the debate about how many people in England acquired reading skills, though at the moment the balance seems to be tilting towards those optimists who believe that by the seventeenth century the numbers of people with at least some basic skills were quite high.[12] However, in the specific case of catechizing, the prevalence of the use of the *ABC* and *Primer* in a wide variety of schools, and in unofficial learning situations as well, may suggest that throughout our period, but perhaps especially in the later Stuart and early Hanoverian periods, a high proportion of English scholars learnt the church catechism through a mixture of listening, speaking, and reading. Moreover, as Helen Weinstein has recently argued, the fact that the same catechetical forms were probably being used right across England and for such a long period may well have contributed to the eroding of regional dialects and the standardizing of the

---

[10] See above, pp. 65–8, 81–3, 88–9, 140–2, 165–6, 257–9.

[11] Strauss, *Luther's House of Learning*, ch. 8.   [12] See above, p. 241 n. 40.

English language, and even to the centralizing of a state which actively supported the use of these forms.[13]

If the conclusion of this comparison is that catechizing may have had a marginally and cumulatively more positive impact on the population at large in early modern England than in sixteenth-century Germany, not only in getting a large number of young people to the point of being able to repeat a catechism in rote fashion, but also in getting a sizeable minority to progress beyond that point to both greater understanding and greater knowledge, this is not to argue that catechizing was performed as often or as effectively as English idealists wanted. The preliminary conclusions reached in Chapters 3, 4, and 5 above were cautious,[14] and what is needed now is further work to determine whether those conclusions were too optimistic or not optimistic enough. Further research on visitation returns, school records, records of the printing trade, and personal papers and memoirs may help us determine how much catechizing there was, and in what combinations of circumstances it secured co-operation or did not. Carefully worded questions put to materials such as wills and depositions in court cases might also elicit fuller answers about the extent of knowledge or understanding of the staples of catechetical instruction.

Two considerations may be offered to those tempted to pursue such enquiries. First, allowance should be made for the variables encountered above: different levels of catechizing and types of catechumen; the differences between teaching an elusive body of catechumens in church and a captive audience in school or home; changes in technique (on the whole perhaps for the better) from the rather clumsy first efforts to the shorter or more sophisticated forms of the second century after the Reformation; the fact that in some cases memorization and comprehension went hand in hand, but in others there was more of the one than the other; and so on. Catechizing, it has been argued here, was not one but a series of activities and was not set in tablets of stone but forever adjusting to new situations and ideas; and as a result historians may need a clearer or more subtle definition of what is meant by 'success' or 'failure' in catechizing in the early modern context before they can apply either label persuasively.

Secondly, to be judged correctly, catechizing needs to be set in some kind of context, especially the most common kind of catechizing, which took place in church. One element of this context was the regular repetition of formulae such as the Lord's Prayer, Creed, and Decalogue in the morning and evening services of the Book of Common Prayer and the communion service. Another was the doctrinal content of the prayers and collects in these and other services such as baptism, matrimony, churching of women, and funerals—services which were attended by most parishioners at some time or another, and which articulated many of the points made in the answers of even the most basic catechisms of the day. Yet another was the regular use

[13] Ms Weinstein made these comments at a conference on Education and the State held at St Peter's College, Oxford, in March 1994.

[14] See above, pp. 136–42, 165–6, 168–9, 184, 203–4, 229, 274–6.

of religious verse, especially in school and home, and, accompanied by music, in church and school in the form of metrical psalms, canticles, and 'hymns', or metrical versions of the standard catechetical formulae—a genre which intentionally or not probably helped people to memorize officially accepted teaching and perhaps raised their spirits as well. Also in or near the church there were the many symbols and fittings which survived from the past or were added, despite the disapproval of iconophobes: gestures such as bowing and kneeling, priestly vestments, sacred utensils, the font and pulpit, communion table and lectern for the Bible, Commandment boards and scripture texts painted on the wall or on separate boards, improving texts and comments or symbols carved on gravestones—all of which could reinforce the points made in catechisms about the need to worship God aright and to do his will as laid down in the scriptures. The possibility of words being reinforced by images is also raised in other ways: the newly erected monuments of the rich or powerful which showed them kneeling in prayer and surrounded by emblems with religious significance such as memento mori; those representations of the Law (on Bible title-pages, church walls, and samplers) which depicted the two tablets brought down by Moses, and indeed often had partial or full–length portraits of Moses and Aaron as well; and the illustrations added to some of the shorter catechisms and to a larger number of the popular religious broadsheets and tracts of the day.[15] Last but not least there was preaching. As we saw in Chapter 1, many catechists drew a close connection between success in catechizing and success in ensuring that congregations understood the sermons they heard. The two activities intersected at various points: they had the same element of orality, the same didactic intention, and often covered the same doctrines; a minister was commonly both catechist and preacher in a parish; and a catechumen might have both to memorize the answers of a catechism and to prepare a summary, orally or in writing, of a sermon he had just heard. Some clergy even seem to have felt that catechizing was more use to the average parishioner than preaching. In 1585 John Thaxter reported that the public catechizing he had undertaken 'both at Cambridge and in the country' for a period of more than six years had proved more profitable than 'other preachings'. Even so, like many other clergy he clearly regarded the two exercises as cognate.[16] Only when we have a fuller understanding of the impact of catechizing in relation to that of the many other stimuli described in this paragraph will we be in a proper position to pass judgement on the efforts of all those catechists in early modern England.

The second part of this survey has said much more about doctrine and spent much more time on close textual comparison of catechetical texts than might have been expected from someone who is a historian by training. However, there seemed to be

[15] I hope to develop these points in *Religious Instruction in Early Modern England.*
[16] *Historical Manuscripts Commission: Gawdy MSS.* (1885), 23.

good reasons for attempting this. In the first place, many of the authors of the catechisms we are dealing with said that their prime aim was to convey the basics of their
faith to the less educated members of their church. Although we cannot discount the
existence of some conscious or unconscious attempts to exert social control or conduct political indoctrination through catechizing, as Strauss thought was the case in
Germany,[17] there seemed to be no strong a priori reasons for thinking that English
authors did not mean what they said. Moreover, the fact that their intention was (on
the whole) to instruct and exhort also means that less allowance needs to be made today
for distortion of an opponent's view (as was regularly the case in polemical works by
clerical authors), for how a statement was designed to appear to other trained theologians (as in the case of official or unofficial statements such as the Thirty-nine Articles or the Lambeth Articles), or for the fact that many religious best-sellers were
aimed at the already strongly committed or reasonably literate and leisured sections
of society (for example Bayly's *Practise of pietie* or Allestree's *Whole duty of man*). In
the catechisms of the day, we can see accomplished theologians trying to cover all
angles, not just the particular set of doctrines with which, from their other writings,
they are often associated today, but the complete gamut of Christian teaching which
they thought the faithful ought to know and understand. This leads us to a second
point. Elementary and intermediate catechisms provide a unique opportunity for
historians to try to gauge the type of doctrinal teaching that was put across at that
intermediate level between official doctrine and popular belief about which we know
much less than we do about, on the one hand, the Thirty-nine Articles or Hooker's
Lawes of ecclesiasticall politie, and, on the other, the mixture of old and new, pagan
and Christian beliefs which characterized a number of popular attitudes and practices.[18] One of the conclusions often reached in Chapter 5 and Part II of this study was
that in shorter or more elementary catechisms technicalities were avoided, difficult
points simplified, and harder messages deferred until a later date, since catechists did
not wish to confuse their charges or deter them from taking further part in the life of
the church. At the same time authors of shorter forms were still aiming at greater
breadth and depth than was to be found in most of those 'godly' broadsheets or little
pamphlets such as *The school of grace* or *The school of piety* produced by publishers for
beginners or less informed readers. In this sense, as McLuhan might have said, the
medium *was* the message: the characteristically short, pithy sum of Christian belief
in a catechism was both simpler, and, through the use of oral question-and-answer
teaching or testing, was communicated more directly, than the message delivered by

---

[17] Strauss, *Luther's House of Learning*, 7–14, 36, 43–5, 108–31, 163–4, 169, 239–43.

[18] e.g. J. F. H. New, *Anglican and Puritan: The Basis of their Opposition, 1558–1640* (1964); W. P. Hau-
gaard, *Elizabeth and the English Reformation* (Cambridge, 1968); Lake, *Anglicans and Puritans?*; E. Duffy,
The Stripping of the Altars (New Haven/London, 1992); K. Thomas, *Religion and the Decline of Magic*
(1971); T. Watt, *Cheap Print and Popular Piety* (Cambridge, 1991); M. J. Ingram, 'From Reformation to
Toleration: Popular Religious Cultures in England, 1530–1690', in T. Harris (ed.), *Popular Culture in
England, 1500–1850* (1995), pp. 95–123.

most other means.[19] Thirdly, since a number of historians and scholars interested in other aspects of contemporary life, such as language and literature,[20] education,[21] science,[22] cultural differentiation and social tension,[23] and in particular the political tensions that led to civil war in 1642, have recently become more involved in the realm of theology than used to be the case, it seemed that catechisms might provide an excellent means of testing a number of their theories, especially those which concerned the essential nature of mainstream Protestantism in early modern England. Catechisms are not without their drawbacks as a source for this purpose, as was indicated in the Introduction and Part I of this study; but against that they do constitute not only a relatively coherent and consistent genre, but also one which survives in roughly equal quantities from the 1570s to the 1730s and beyond; and in terms of the numbers of copies printed of a best-selling catechism and a best-selling treatise or sermon there is simply no comparison.

If we review the conclusions reached in Chapters 7 to 12, we find in the first place that at the level of elementary and most intermediate catechisms there was a large measure of continuity from the 1540s to the 1730s. The reliance on the same staple formulae and topics—Creed, Decalogue, Lord's Prayer, and sacraments—and the fact that in ten, twenty, or fifty pages only a limited amount can be said about each, meant that there was only limited scope for innovation. Such innovation as there was was probably due as much to new techniques of presentation as to new ideas of doctrine being introduced. Secondly, there was a large element of common ground in the content of these catechisms: on God's fatherly roles as creator and preserver; on Christ's offices as prophet, priest, and king; on the importance of the Holy Spirit in delivering help; on the difference between the two tables of the Law, and the broad interpretation of each Commandment; on the importance of trying to keep the Law, even though total success was impossible; on the nature and value of prayer in general,

---

[19] M. McLuhan, *Understanding Media* (1964), pt. 1, ch. 1; and cf. id., *The Gutenberg Galaxy: The Making of Typographic Man* (1967).

[20] e.g. N. Smith, *Perfection Proclaimed: Language and Literature in English Radical Religion 1640–1660* (Oxford, 1989); G. Reedy, *The Bible and Reason: Anglicans and Scripture in Late Seventeenth-Century England* (Philadelphia, 1985); id., *Robert South (1634–1716): An Introduction to His Life and Sermons* (Cambridge, 1992); I. Rivers, *Reason, Grace, and Sentiment: A Study of the Language of Religion and Ethics in England, 1660–1780*, i. *Whichcote to Wesley* (Cambridge, 1991).

[21] J. Morgan, *Godly Learning: Puritan Attitudes towards Reason, Learning, and Education, 1560–1640* (Cambridge, 1986).

[22] I am thinking here of the work of James and Margaret Jacob in America and Charles Webster in England, but see also J. Gascoine, *Cambridge in the Age of the Enlightenment: Science, Religion and Politics from the Restoration to the French Revolution* (Cambridge, 1989).

[23] K. Wrightson and D. Levine, *Poverty and Piety in an English Village: Terling 1525–1700* (London, 1979); K. Wrightson, *English Society 1580–1680* (1982), ch. 7; M. J. Ingram, 'Religion, Communities and Moral Discipline in Late Sixteenth- and Early Seventeenth-Century England: Case Studies', in K. von Grayerz (ed.), *Religion and Society in Early Modern Europe 1500–1800* (London, 1984), 177–93; P. Collinson, *The Religion of Protestants* (Oxford, 1982), esp. chs. 5–6; and id., *The Birthpangs of Protestant England* (1988).

and the meaning of the six petitions of the Lord's Prayer in particular; on the existence of two covenants, one with Adam before the Fall, and the other with Christ thereafter; on the sacraments having been instituted by Christ as seals of the covenant of grace; on baptism being a rite of initiation into the church and a symbolic cleansing from sin; and the Lord's Supper being a rite of communion with Christ and his ecclesial body. Where there were marked differences of opinion, these were usually treated briefly or cautiously, or concealed by omission or the use of an all-embracing first person rather than a theologically more precise third person or an impersonal label such as 'the faithful'. Other differences were due less to the adoption of diametrically opposed standpoints than to a second element being added by one party, as in the double definition of faith and the twofold method of seeking assurance taught by the orthodox Calvinists. In Chapters 7 to 9, it is true, we did note a potential or actual parting of the ways between those conformists who in their catechisms focused on the visible church as the forum in which Christians received most help in working out their salvation, and those 'godly' authors who not only tended to see spiritual development as taking place within a theoretical *ordo salutis* rather than the physical church, but also focused increasingly on introspection as a means of securing assurance that one was among the elect. But this divergence was often kept in check at the simpler levels of catechizing, and where it was more overt it was often not along the lines that we have been led to believe. Even great admirers of Calvin, such as Nowell and Ussher, chose to side on a number of issues with the more traditional church-centred approach rather than the potentially centrifugal attitude of the orthodox Calvinists. Moreover, as we saw in Chapters 7 to 9 and 12, there were many respects in which 'Arminians', 'Laudians', and later Stuart 'moralists' were much nearer Cranmer and Calvin than their Calvinist critics, all of which may help to explain why so many clergy felt able to serve under both Abbot and Laud, and later under both Parliament and Charles II. It may also help explain the speed and thoroughness of the restoration of much of the old church in the early 1660s.

These elements of continuity and common ground in a number of widely disseminated catechisms need to be weighed in the balance against ideas of large-scale change or deep divisions in doctrine in the early modern church, such as Professor Russell's thesis of two competing views of Protestantism evolving under Elizabeth and the early Stuarts and eventually tearing the English church apart in the 1640s, Dr Tyacke's view that there was a strong preponderance of predestinarianism in the teaching of the Elizabethan and Jacobean church, Professor Lake's idea of a new brand of 'Anglicanism' (including a new doctrine of the sacraments) emerging through the efforts of men like Hooker and Andrewes, Dr Milton's view of the importance of symbols and modes of discourse in the gradual disintegration of the compromise settlement of the late Elizabethan period, Dr Spurr's thesis of a new 'Anglicanism' arising from the ashes of the old in the mid-seventeenth century, and the oft-repeated notion of a large gulf between 'Latitudinarian' and 'High-Church' ideologies by the late seventeenth century.[24] All of these ideas receive a little support from the best-selling catechisms whose doctrine has been analysed in the second part of this study, but surprisingly little, especially the idea of a sharp divide between 'Calvinism' and 'Arminianism', or the recent, qualified version of this which concedes that there were different brands of Calvinism but argues that what was important was the perception that fellow-Calvinists could be trusted even if they were unsound on some matters, whereas 'Arminians' or Laudians could not.[25] If anything the evidence from Part II suggests that in the Elizabethan or Jacobean period what credal Calvinists like Nowell, Whitgift, Abbot, and Hall had in common with non-Calvinists such as Hooker, Andrewes, Overall, and Laud—a concern to defend the church as the main forum of spiritual life, and a suspicion of some of the directions being taken by orthodox Calvinist soteriology and introspection—was just as important as what divided them. By the 1620s the situation was changing, with political tensions rising at home and abroad and being both fed by and feeding anti-Catholic prejudice, which in turn fed on any scrap of evidence of 'Romishness' or 'Arminianism' in Charles's circle of allies, while Laud and his supporters responded to what they genuinely saw as signs of 'puritan' insubordination or levelling tactics by restating the power of the church in more forceful terms than before. The more advanced catechisms of the day, Ball's larger form, Mayer's original commentary, and later the works of Reeve, Boughen, and Hammond and the Westminster Larger Catechism, reflected these new tensions, but these were untypical in both their length and their greater readiness to confront the doctrinal disputes of the day. It would have taken more than exposure to a basic catechism like Perkins's, John Ball's shorter form, William Hill's exposition of the Prayer Book catechism, or John Mayer's abridged form[26] to turn the average catechumen into a militant: either pressure from parents, encouragement from a famous preacher or teacher, or a recommendation to a promising student to read a more advanced catechism or an aggressively worded treatise; and only a minority within a minority of catechumens were likely to be exposed to such conditions—those living in a very pious, informed household, or who

---

[24] C. Russell, *The Causes of the English Civil War* (Oxford, 1990); N. Tyacke, 'Puritanism, Arminianism and Counter-Revolution', in C. Russell (ed.), *The Origins of the English Civil War* (1973), 119–43; Lake, *Anglicans and Puritans?*; A. Milton, *Catholic and Reformed* (Cambridge, 1995); J. Spurr, *The Restoration Church of England 1646–1689* (New Haven/London, 1991), esp. ch. 5–6; W. M. Spellman, *The Latitudinarians and the Church of England 1660–1700* (University of Georgia Press, Athens/London, 1993); R. Cornwall, *Visible and Apostolic: The Constitution of the Church in High Church Anglican and Non-Juror Thought* (Newark, Del., 1993).

[25] P. Lake, 'Calvinism and the English Church 1570–1635', *Past and Present*, 114 (1987), *passim*; J. Sears McGee's review of White, *Predestination*, in *Albion*, 26: 1 (1994), 130–1; but now cf. Milton, *Catholic and Reformed passim*. There are some of us who still feel that in the English context 'Arminianism' was much more a term of abuse directed at an ill-defined set of bogymen than a term with specific soteriological, sacramental, or ecclesiological connotations.

[26] The works cited in this paragraph are all listed in Appendix 1, and most are discussed in Part II above.

stayed on longer at school or university, or had the skills and leisure to read larger works.

It is of course possible that when the average Elizabethan or early Stuart catechist was operating, using a fairly simple or middling-sized form, he added more steel or spice to the bare summary of doctrine in the catechism he was using, through an extempore or more contentious exposition of the answers it contained. However, until we find some hard evidence for the use of controversial expositions, at least for the Elizabethan and Jacobean periods, it will tend to remain speculation, and, as was indicated in an earlier chapter, the balance of probability may lie against it.[27] It is also possible that, while catechisms were widely accepted as providing milk for babes, the printed sermons and treatises and the university theses of the day represent the red meat that was more typical of what was offered to adults. Again, this may well be true, but until more work is done on the sermons given in obscure parishes by even more obscure preachers, on the general character of the religious best-sellers of the day, and on the probable readership of works like Perkins's *Golden chaine*, we cannot be sure what was the norm.[28] Was what went on in the parishes and households of zealous clergy and laity, whether 'godly' or conformist, the norm, or was it a goal towards which many aspired but never came very close, while others actually turned their backs on it?

It is, in fact, equally possible that what bothered clergy most was not the current state of doctrinal debate or the use and misuse of symbols of orthodoxy in the fevered atmosphere of London and the universities or the pulpits of high-profile clergy, whether 'godly' or conformist, High-Church or 'Latitudinarian', but the semi-Pelagian tendencies of many of their flocks. Archbishops and assemblies might come and go, but the poor, and those who clung on to what was seen as a misguided 'country' religion, they always had with them. It is also possible that the relatively calm, uncontentious nature of catechetical teaching which most authors adopted was actually more typical of what happened in a great many parishes which were situated some distance from the capital and the universities—in other words a lower-key and perhaps less well informed but not necessarily insincere commitment to conveying the basics, combined with a due performance of the annual round of ceremonies and the rites of passage which parishioners expected and demanded. Certainly what most catechumens absorbed through the Prayer Book catechism would have been reinforced rather than challenged by what they heard and saw around them and what they did when they attended divine service, no matter how rarely: the reiterated formulae, the symbolic fittings and gestures, and the other features mentioned a few paragraphs ago. From the 1620s to the 1730s and beyond, the basic elements of doctrine in the church catechism would also have been reinforced by the increasingly common practice adopted

---

[27] See above, pp. 385–6.

[28] The work of Arnold Hunt of Trinity College, Cambridge, should greatly help our understanding of sermons; on religious best-sellers see my *Print and Protestantism* (forthcoming).

by conformist ministers of giving short homilies or even full sermons on points raised in that catechism, or encouraging children and parents to read an exposition of that form at home. The growing attachment shown by ordinary parishioners to the Book of Common Prayer, the perplexity but not necessarily hostility they showed to non-conformists, the resistance offered to puritan iconoclasts by ordinary parishioners in the 1640s, even elements of the 'King and Church' hysteria of the early eighteenth century—all may reflect an attachment to the established church which may have owed something to the solid grounding in its teaching provided by the Prayer Book catechism.[29]

There was a positive and a negative side to all this. The positive was that, in trying to ensure that the majority of its charges had grasped some of its basic tenets, the church had adopted an approach designed to meet the needs of the less well-educated, and to judge from some of the indicators just mentioned may have achieved a moderate degree of success. The negative, as hinted at the end of the chapter on the Creed, though it would also apply to very elementary instruction on the Decalogue, Lord's Prayer, and sacraments too, was that in those parishes, schools, or homes where these basics were taught with little imagination or additional explanation, there was a risk that relatively little was done to undermine the existing popular trust in the value of works or an outward show of faith that was not necessarily matched by a strong sense of commitment or repentance. In successfully simplifying much of the basic message in order to make it easily mastered, and through seeking to balance warnings with reassurance, the instructors of the day ran the risk of making it harder to convey a more difficult doctrine such as the worthlessness of good works in God's eyes but man's inescapable duty to perform them. Much of the emphasis in Part II of this work has been on the way in which elementary catechetical instruction may have appeared to catechumens, compared to the more advanced teaching with which churchmen were then, and historians have since become, much more familiar. The next and crucial step for historians is to try to work out how far there was a connection or osmosis between what people in the parishes were told to believe in these catechisms (and other elementary material) and what they actually believed, and it is hoped that the material offered in Part II of this study will facilitate such a step.

One final comment may be made. Recent work on the early modern period has stressed the importance not just of trying to see things as contemporaries did, but

---

[29] J. Maltby, ' "By this Book": Parishioners, the Prayer Book and the Established Church', in K. Fincham (ed.), *The Early Stuart Church, 1603–42* (1993), 115–37; I. M. Green, 'The Persecution of "Scandalous" and "Malignant" Parish Clergy during the English Civil War', *English Historical Review*, 94 (1979), 522; John Morrill, 'The Church in England, 1642–9', in Morrill (ed.), *Reactions to the English Civil War 1642–49* (1982), 103–14; C. Marsh, *The Family of Love in English Society, 1550–1630* (1994), 188–95; D. A. Spaeth, 'Parsons and Parishioners: Lay-Clerical Conflict and Popular Piety in Wiltshire Villages, 1660–1740', Ph.D. thesis (Brown University, 1985), 235–7; G. Holmes, *The Trial of Doctor Sacheverell* (1973), 177–8; id., 'The Sacheverell Riots: The Crowd and the Church in Early Eighteenth-Century London', *Past and Present*, 72 (1976), 55–85.

also of recognizing the different types of language and modes of discourse which were commonly adopted to describe and discuss different aspects of such vital matters as the the best form of government and the respective roles of rulers and ruled.[30] In the realm of ecclesiastical debate, the opponents of Laud—'evangelical episcopalians and moderate puritans'—were 'held together by a common style of discourse', an agreed use of the symbols of orthodoxy, whereas the Laudians refused to use the same codes and symbols and adopted a different style of discourse—a move which, it has been suggested, was much more damaging than any actual disagreement on the details of doctrine or ecclesiology.[31] Now in the language of the most widely used catechisms of the day, especially the elementary and many intermediate ones, we have another way of defining and discoursing, in this case about what lay beyond the visible and mundane, whether life had a meaning, and if so what that meaning was. Like the rhetorics adopted in political and cultural matters and in ecclesiastical polemics, the language of catechisms was not completely distinct from other ways of talking about religion, such as the liturgical and the moralistic. On the other hand, it did have its own conventions of content and method and its own characteristic symbols and codes. The language of the simpler catechisms of the day was neither that of official pronouncements (in the normal sense) nor that of the popular press; it was a monopoly of neither the 'godly' nor the ultra-conformist; it was somewhere in the middle, maybe even a bridge between them all. Perhaps the language of catechisms should be added to the growing list of modes of discourse in use in the early modern period, and its relationship to those other modes examined more closely. From the material presented in this study, it can be argued that catechisms created a pattern of words that we can be moderately sure was heard regularly in a great many parishes and schools of the early modern period, which is more than can be said of many other modes of discourse upon which historians have tended to rely.

[30] For an excellent survey, see the Introduction of K. Sharpe and P. Lake (eds.), *Culture and Politics in Early Stuart England* (1994); for new literary genres in the 1640s and 1650s, see N. Smith, *Literature and Revolution in England, 1640–1660* (New Haven/London, 1994).

[31] Milton, *Catholic and Reformed*, 26, 542–3.

PART III

A Finding List of English Catechisms

APPENDIX 1

Catechisms and Catechetical Material Produced, Used, or Recommended for Use in England, *c.*1530–1740

Introduction

THIS Appendix was designed with two purposes in mind. First of all, it was hoped to provide for the first time a list of all the works written or published in England between *c.*1530 and 1740 which have been or might be called catechisms, arranged alphabetically by author or where a form was anonymous the first word of the title. Such a list would provide its own justification, as a quick-reference guide to the catechetical writings of a particular author or to the short title, date, number of editions, or short-title reference number of a particular form or group of forms that a scholar had encountered or wished to pursue. It might also help librarians to track down the authors of anonymous works in their care. It is surprising, for example, how many libraries have a copy of a very popular form published anonymously by Thomas Marshall—*The catechism set forth in the Book of Common Prayer briefly explained*—but file it under C (it can quickly be recognized by not only the title but also the illustration of the Sheldonian Theatre on the cover and the imprimatur of 20 March 1678 by the vice-chancellor of Oxford on the reverse of the title-page). However, it was also hoped that such a list would facilitate research into various aspects of early modern history: ecclesiastical, theological, devotional, educational, social, political, or literary. In my own case it was a broad analysis of the quantity, quality, and chronological distribution of such works, and a general comparison of the products of one era with those of another that attracted me. But the information given here should enable those who are interested in finding out what catechetical works are known to have been used in a specific decade or area, or were of a particular size, or related to a particular aspect such as treatment of the Ten Commandments or the sacraments, to track these down by a few minutes' careful scanning of the appropriate columns. The following notes are designed both to explain the methods and terms used in describing the works listed, and to describe the types of information contained in the different columns.

Before describing what has been included in this Appendix, it may be helpful to draw readers' attention again to the method used here to track down catechisms (see above, pp. 48, 50–8), since other scholars may find alternative means of tracking down catechisms. Beyond what I have said at the start of Chapter 2, I have relied on a process of serendipity: looking at all the items in a volume that was called up from a library stack for one particular item, but proved to contain a number of related titles bound together; or checking under 'catechism' in the catalogues of libraries visited in Britain, Ireland, and America. Fellow-historians have also kindly sent me titles, for which I am very grateful. Secondly, I should make it clear what has been excluded from the following list. It does not include all the works listed in the Stationers' registers or term catalogues which may or may not have been catechetical but in the titles of which the word 'catechism' did not appear. The following list would be much longer and also have a much higher ratio of queries if it included all such items as the anonymous *Groundes of godlyness* of *c.*1602 (*TSR* iii. 186) which was, as far as one can see, never published. In the absence of a published text to compare with such descriptions and to enable us to fit such works into the analyses of size and content attempted in this study, it was decided reluctantly not to pursue or list them here systematically. A few much stronger candidates have been listed, especially where the word 'catechism' occurs in the title. The list also does not include all works described, either in contemporary records or recent short-title catalogues, as dialogues, since, as has been explained above (pp. 17–19, 54–6), I do not regard these as being synonymous with catechisms. I have included here only those dialogues which seem to me to have been aimed at basic instruction or improvement of some kind, to teach a beginner some simple ideas, or have been described at some date as catechisms. For the reason indicated in the text (p. 50), I have listed all the printed Catholic forms which I have encountered, but have not tried to trace all such works. Similarly, I have not tried to trace all Scottish, Welsh, Irish, or American catechisms, and include here only those which were first or also published in England. For Scottish ones, see H. S. Aldis, *A List of Books Printed in Scotland before 1700* (Edinburgh, 1970), as well as Carruthers, *Three Centuries*, and Torrance, *School of Faith*. For Wales, see the index of G. H. Jenkins, *Literature, Religion and Society in Wales, 1660–1730* (Cardiff, 1978), s.v. catechising, and catechisms. For Irish ones, see Ian Green, ' "The Necessary Knowledge of the Principles of Religion": Catechisms and Catechizing in Ireland *c.*1560–1800', in A. Ford, J. McGuire, and K. Milne (eds.), *As by Law Established: The Church of Ireland since the Reformation* (Dublin, 1995), 69–88. For American ones, see G. E. Brown, 'Catechists and Catechisms of Early New England', D. R. E. (Boston University, 1934); W. Eames, *Early New England Catechisms* (Detroit, 1969); and M. E. R. Wall, 'Puritanism in Education', Ph.D. thesis (Washington University, 1979).

The first column [**Author**] gives the author's name where known. In some cases authors identified on the title-page by their initials alone can be identified from the full name at the end of a preface or epistle dedicatory; in others they have been identified by hand-written notes in a contemporary hand or by the bibliographers who have prepared the short-title catalogues (see column 5). To save space, cross-references have been kept to a minimum. Where they were deemed essential, they have been included: in the case of forms published anonymously but where the author is now known, as in the case of Marshall's *Catechism set forth*; and in the case of a mistaken attribution, e.g. Edmond Allen and Leo Jud. But where a cross-reference was only a matter of convenience, they have not been included, e.g. from 'I.B.' to John Batchiler. In the latter case, someone coming across a catechism by I.B. should look at all the entries under B, using title and date as additional guides. Readers should also note that occasionally a catalogue heading has been used in this column, e.g. Heidelberg Catechism, or Westminster Assembly of Divines, where the work was the product of a number of authors, and the title of the published form was not completely standard.

The second column [**Title**] gives a shortened form of the title, always the first few words, and sometimes some later ones as well where these are helpful in distinguishing it from a similarly entitled work or in revealing the contents or purpose of the work. Greek letters have been transliterated, but not Hebrew or Arabic. Where more than one work by an author is listed, this has been done not alphabetically but chronologically by dates of first publication. Where there are slight variations in the title, or different titles were used in different editions but the text was substantially the same, the differences are indicated (by a slash or square brackets), but the work is treated here as a single form. Conversely, in some cases a later edition with the same title had a much revised version of the text; where this is known, this is indicated in column 6, but only if a significant proportion of the text is different have the two versions been listed separately (see s.v. Thomas Gouge for an example). The publishing histories of specific works can be more complex than at first sight appears: thus of the three works whose titles begin *A light from Christ* published by Immanuel Bourne between 1645 and 1647, that of 1647 has a much modified but recognizably similar version of the text of 1645, while that of 1646 has not only a different subtitle but also a largely different text from both the others.

The third column [**Date**] gives the date or dates of publication of known editions; the place of publication is London unless otherwise stated. Where a hyphen precedes the first date, as in the case of John Ball's *A short catechisme*, it is because there is a strong possibility that there was an earlier edition (for reasons given in column 5 or 6) but no copy of that edition has survived. Where a hyphen follows the last date, this indicates that there were later editions after the year 1740 which is the terminal date used in this Appendix. The use of a question mark indicates that there is some doubt about the date of the particular edition being cited: the year may have been left off by the printer, or the title-page of the only surviving copy may be incomplete. In such cases the years have been taken from the short-title catalogues (see column 5), whose compilers have used a variety of methods to produce a likely date, or some other source such as a preface or the term catalogues.

The fourth column [**Editions**] indicates the number of separate editions of a particular form that is known to have been published in England by December 1740. These should not be added up willy-nilly, since there must always be an element of doubt about the numbers of contemporary editions, especially of shorter catechisms which were so flimsy that whole editions have been destroyed without trace. It has not proved possible, for example, to check whether each supposedly new edition of a work is a predominantly new publication rather than a reissue of old sheets with a new title-page claiming it to be a fresh edition. However, where there are multiple editions I have attempted to examine a sample of different editions to see whether this practice did occur. Where the title-page of a work claims it to be the fifth edition, but we do not have a copy of each of all four previous editions, it has been entered here as '5?'. Alternatively, where there were some pirate editions, inside or outside England, or editions published legally outside England, as in the case of John Ball's *A short treatise*, this has been indicated as 16+ (i.e. probably at least sixteen separate editions printed in England, and probably more, either 'pirate' editions inside England or separate editions outside England). The plus symbol has also been used to indicate reissues, as opposed to largely new editions, within our period, for example, when a collection of separate titles was bound together to form a combined volume of the author's works. It has also been used to indicate fresh editions published after 1740. An isolated question mark indicates that there is no proof a particular work was printed, though from the reference in *TSR* or wherever we may assume that such a work existed in manuscript.

Two additional points should be noted. First, where the catechetical form was published only as part of a much larger work, such as a volume of collected works (e.g. Babington's exposition of the Creed) or a treatise (e.g. most editions of Cartwright's catechism), this is indicated in column 5 or 6. Secondly, to distinguish between works that are (by the criteria discussed in the opening chapters of this work) fairly typical catechisms and works which are not, the number of editions of the latter have been surrounded by angled, round, or square brackets. **Angled brackets** have been used for a few dialogue-catechisms which seem to me to contain almost as many features of a typical catechism as of that closely related genre: the dialogue. **Round brackets** have been used for categories of works which were fairly closely related to the typical catechism of the day but in some respect distinct: instructive or improving dialogues, in which the elements of the dialogue genre are prominent and the material was not the usual catechetical staples; treatises with only a limited number of questions and answers on catechetical material; catechetical works which were not in question-and-answer form, for example, long expositions of catechetical staples in continuous prose; sermons on catechizing, or other exhortations to catechize or be catechized, and other sermons delivered to classes of catechumens; works described as catechisms of which the content, though mainly concerned with doctrine or ecclesiology, was predominantly controversial or handled in a polemic fashion; and/or works in which the bulk of the text is not in English. **Square brackets** have been inserted round the numbers of editions of works in the following categories which seem to me to be further removed from the mainstream of English catechizing: those catechisms which were in English but published on the Continent; those whose authors were not Protestant; and works referred to as 'catechisms' on the title-page but which prove to have been of a distinctly political or satirical nature (see above, pp. 56–7).

The fifth column [**Source/Location**] indicates where I have obtained information about or seen a copy of a particular work. In the great majority of cases, the source is one of the two short-title catalogues referred to throughout this study as **STC**^{2} and **Wing**^{2} (see list of abbreviations), and unless there is any indication to the contrary it may be assumed that all references in this column for the period up to 1640 are to STC^2, and all references to works from 1641 to 1700 are to Wing^2. STC^2 identifies works by a single number, though where later editions or new works have emerged this is often indicated by the addition of a number after a decimal point (e.g. *The ABC … set forthe* is 19.6). Wing^2 uses a letter (the first letter of the author's surname or of the title where no author is known) and a number (again sometimes supplemented, this time by a letter or letters, e.g. under Lancelot Andrewes A3146A). It is generally agreed that as a bibliographical guide Wing^2 is not as reliable as STC^2, hence the occasional demurrers in columns 5 and 6, details of which were sent to the Wing STC Revision Office (though no reply has yet been received). Occasionally in the period prior to 1700 and regularly thereafter, I have listed the British location in which I have seen a copy, though a quick check in **Wing**^{2}, the National Union Catalogue (**NUC**), or the Eighteenth-Century Short-Title Catalogue (**ESTC**) will often reveal a copy in an American collection. The locations most often mentioned in this column are the British Library (**BL**), Dr Williams's Library (**DWL**), United Reformed Church Library, **Lambeth** Palace Library and Sion College, all in London, the **Bodleian** Library, Oxford, the John Rylands University Library (**JRUL**) in Manchester, and some of the college libraries at Oxford and Cambridge, and that of Trinity College Dublin (**TCD**).

The sixth and last column [**Description**] contains a mixture of information and opinion on such matters as size and content, and the possible origins and geographical use of different works. The number of pages indicated by the categories 'short', 'mid', and 'long' were arrived at by combining common-sense publishing factors (such as the numbers of pages commonly printed in a short octavo or duodecimo work) with rule-of-thumb mathematical ones: the total number of pages of text of the different catechisms in the list were plotted to see where these totals bunched, and the lines drawn where there was least bunching. It was also thought helpful to subdivide two of these categories. Thus '**short**' is 25 pages or less, but '**very short**' is 10 pages or less; '**mid**' is between 26 and 60 pages; '**long**' is 61–250 pages; and '**very long**' is over 250 pages. Sometimes the term '**advanced**' has been used as an alternative to 'very long', specifically of works which were partly or all in 'q + a' (question and answer) form, but which seemed to me from the concepts, vocabulary, and syntax used to be aimed at a more advanced kind of catechumen or indeed at catechists rather than the children and ignorant adults who constituted the majority of catechumens. '**Exposition**' refers to the expounding of catechetical material by continuous prose rather than by question and answer (e.g. by Lancelot Andrewes in his catechetical lectures). However, the two were, in practice, often combined ('q + a with expositions') as many authors inserted a paragraph of explanation before or after each answer; the main difference between John Ball's two most popular forms was that the shorter had no expositions, but the longer did. '**Form**' is used as shorthand for a question-and-answer catechism; '**dialogue**' has been reserved for works, sometimes of an improving but often of a controversial nature, in which the speakers have been assigned names or descriptive labels and where a certain amount of plot or other material designed to ease the flow of discussion has been inserted (see above, pp. 54–6, 60–1, 63–4).

Partly due to pressure on space and partly to problems of evidence, it has not proved possible to provide a precise description of the content or intended function of every work in this list, but some broad categories have been attempted. An explanation of one or more of the four staples described above in Chapter 6 has been regarded as the norm, and so '**unusual content**' is likely to refer to a form which did not expound at any length the Apostles' Creed, the Ten Commandments, the Lord's Prayer, or the sacraments of baptism and the Lord's Supper (failure to do so might simply be due to lack of space, as in 'very short' forms). Conversely where there is some sustained development of one or more of these staples (rather than a mere reference to them) they have been listed here in the sequence in which they appear in the text, using the abbreviations **Cr** (for Creed), **Dec** (for Decalogue), **Pr** (for Lord's Prayer), and **Ss** (for sacraments). Many authors built their forms around one of three models: the Prayer Book catechism (**PBC**), the Heidelberg Catechism (**Heidelberg**), and the Westminster Shorter Catechism (**WSC**), which had a very similar structure to its big brother the Westminster Larger Catechism (**WLC**). Rather than repeat the sequence of staples in those three models (discussed in the text above) every time they are mentioned as providing the basis or model for a later form, it should be noted that the sequences are as follows: Prayer Book catechism—Cr, Dec, Pr, Ss; Heidelberg Catechism—Cr, Ss, Dec, Pr; Westminster Larger and Shorter Catechisms—credal material, Dec, Ss, Pr. As explained in Chapter 6, the absence of 'Cr' in such a case does not mean a total lack of treatment of credal material (e.g. God, the Creation, Christ, the Holy Ghost, last things), but rather a selective and flexible use of such material as opposed to the strictly sequential and complete handling of such material in forms marked 'Cr'. The term '**pre-comm.**' stands for pre-communion, i.e. a work designed to test a potential communicant's knowledge or to prepare a catechumen for receiving the Lord's Supper. The authors of most of the works so described tended to focus on the meaning and value of the Lord's Supper, but a number contained some credal material and/or some treatment of the moral law. For the **par-liamentary ordinance of 20.10.1645**, see above pp. 79–80. Where a work is stated on the title-page or in the preface to have been aimed at a specific group or type of catechumens, this is mentioned, space permitting.

Placenames and **counties** have been taken from the title-pages, epistles dedicatory, or prefaces where there is some indication that the form in question was produced by a minister working there or used on a congregation or other set of catechumens in that area. Thus Samuel Adams dedicated his *Plain and full instruction* to the inhabitants of Alvescot in Oxfordshire whom, he tells us, he had catechized for some years. However, a simple indication that an author was incumbent of a particular parish at the time of publication has to be used with caution as evidence of use in that parish, since in some cases, such as that of James Ussher, forms were written and tested at one stage of an author's career but published only at a later stage when he had moved on or was about to move on to other responsibilities. The addition of a question mark after a place or county is meant to indicate that the form may have been used there but we cannot be certain. Prices have usually been taken from the title-pages or the term catalogues.

Finally, it must be stressed that a list such as this one has to be provisional. For the reasons indicated in Chapter 2 above, no historian, even with a little help from his friends, is going to discover all the catechetical forms lurking at the back of or in the middle of non-catechetical publications, or under titles such as *A handfull of goateshaire*. In addition, copies of a work mentioned in the **TSR** that was thought not to be extant may turn up in manuscript or prove to have been printed after all, though not as a separate item; new titles may be added in the final revision of Wing, or be thrown up in the final stages of constructing the ESTC data base. A methodical search through the advertisements printed at the end of many late seventeenth- and early eighteenth-century publications might well yield many more catechisms. I would be very grateful if any titles that have escaped my notice, either of catechetical works that were published or of ones that were only registered, were brought to my attention. Both these and any corrections to the details or opinions given below could then be incorporated into a list of revisions, perhaps to be made available on IBM-compatible software.

Catechisms and Catechetical Material Produced, Used, or

1	2	3
A., B.	A treatise of the way to life	[1580?]
A., H.	The tenets and principles of the Church of Rome	1732
A., T.	A catechisme for young children	1619
Abbot, Robert	Milk for babes; or, a mother's catechism for her children	1646
anon.	The ABC with the Pater noster, Ave, Credo and X commaundements … set forthe by the kynges maiestie	[1545]
anon.	The/An ABC with the/a catechisme, that is to say an instruction to be [taught and] learned by every childe/person, before he be brought to be confirmed by the bishop	1551–1725–
anon.	A, B, C, des Chrétiens	[1705?–10?]
anon.	The ABC with the shorter catechism	–[1740?]
Abraham, Chanania Jagel	Catechismus Judaeorum	1679
——	The Jews catechism	1680–
anon.	An abridgement of the … assemblies shorter catechism	1675
anon.	An abstract of the catechism	1681 (Basel)
anon.	An abstract of the Douay catechism	1682 (Douai) –1716 (Douai)
anon.	An abstract of the scripture-catechism	1675 (n.p.)
anon.	An account of the methods whereby/ of charity-schools lately erected	1705–19
[Acryse, Lewis]	The church catechism explained	1702

Recommended for Use in England, *c*.1530–1740

4	5	6
1	[STC²] 2	Mid; Dec, Cr, Ss, Pr; has concluding prayer summarizing contents of catechism
[1]	Liverpool Univ. Lib.	Satirical, anti-Catholic piece in the form of a short catechism; preface signed by H.A.
—	*TSR* iii. 645	See below, s.v. *Elements*
2	A69–69aA	3 forms, 2 very short, 1 long (qs + as with expositions); Dec, Ss, Pr; Hants., Kent; still on sale in 1658: W. London, *Catalogue*, sig. K1ᵛ
1	19.6	Contains Pr, Cr, + Dec in English, + a modified version of the form in the Gough primer (1536), q.v., s.v. *Primer*
See col. 6	20.2–21.3 + A36 + + A36A–38B + BL	PBC, preceded by the means of teaching children their letters (+ later their numbers as well) + followed by prayers ('graces'); reprinted in huge numbers throughout the period: see above pp. 65–6, 175–6. For an Irish version, see STC² 22.3 (*Aibidil gaoidheilge & caiticiosma*, Dublin, 1571) and for a Welsh, *Y'r ABC. neu catechisme* (1633), see 22.5
(2)	BL	After an ABC come the anonymous *Maner to examine chyldren* (q.v.), Beza's *Little catechisme* (q.v.), + the PBC, with the Nicene and Athanasian Creeds, all in French
1	BL	WSC published with an ABC (+ unsuitable woodcuts + adverts); more suitable edns. had been published in Scotland + Ireland from the late 17th century: Carruthers, 39–41
—	—	See below, s.v. A. Jagel
—	—	Ditto
—	—	See below, s.v. T. Lye
[1]	A126A	Catholic
[6]	A131A–32 + BL	Catholic; 1703, 1713, + 1715 edns. published in Paris; cf. below, s.v. H. Turberville
[1]	A142B	Catholic; long; q + a; Cr, Pr, Dec, Ss, *et al.*
(17?)	BL + Bodleian	Description of origins + purpose of the Charity School movement, stressing the importance of catechizing and learning the PBC; also gives details of public examinations of catechumens; see also below, s.v. *Order* and *Orders*
—	Bodleian	Bodleian catalogue attributes this work to Acryse, but it is by John Lewis (q.v.), curate of Acrise in Kent

1	2	3
Adams, Samuel	A plain and full instruction	1718 (Oxford)
Adams, Thomas	The main principles of Christian religion	1675–7
Addison, Lancelot	The primitive institution	1674–90
——	The catechumen	1690
——	The Christian's manual	1691–1719
anon./ R. Tutchin *et al.*	The address of some ministers of Christ in the Isle of Wight	1658
anon.	The agreement of the associated ministers in … Norfolk … concerning publick cate-chizing	1659
[Alcock, John]	Plain truths of divinity	1647
A[ldem], M[ordechai]	A short, plaine, and profitable catechisme	1592
Alleine, Joseph	A most familiar explanation of the Assemblies shorter catechism	1658?–1702–
Alleine, Richard	A breife explanation of the common catechisme	1630–1
[Allen, Edmond]	A catechisme, that is to say a familiar intro-duction/ christen instruccion	1548–62
——	A shorte catechisme	1550
A[llen], R[obert]	A treasurie of catechisme … The first part	1600
——	The doctrine of the gospel	1606
Allen, William	Certain select discourses	
[Allestree, Richard?]	A clear and short catechism	[1696?]–1717–
A[llsopp], N[icholas]	Certaine briefe questions and answers	[*c*.1620]

4	5	6
1	BL	Long; course of lectures on PBC turned into q + a; Oxon
2	A493–4	Long; WSC qs + as with expositions; adopts an irenic approach; Cheshire?
(3?)	A530–1	A 'discourse' in praise of catechizing; price bound 1*s*. 6*d*.
(2)	A511A–11B	Prose paraphrase of and commentary on PBC
(7?+)	A513–15 + BL	3 expositions including the previous 2 + a pre-comm. form, none in q + a; Dublin edn. 1724
(1)	A545	Exhortation to parents to catechize their children + servants, by clergy in Hants + Isle of Wight
(1)	A778	Attempt by Norfolk clergy to 'revive' catechizing, using the WSC; contains articles of agreement, reasons for these, and exhortations to parishioners to co-operate
1	A887	Long; unusual; mostly composed in 1620s; still on sale in 1658: London, *Catalogue*, sig. K2^r
1	287.5	3 forms: a mid (unusual in stress on prayer + partly scriptural answers), a short summary of the same, + a very short pre-comm. form; prayers at end; Herts.?
5+?	Grant, 353, A973A–75A, *TC* iii. 30, + Carruthers, 95	Long; WSC with extra qs + as; first used in Somerset; other edns. published in Belfast + Glasgow; extra qs + as, directions, exhortation to godliness + a prayer at the end
2	357.5–58	Mid; PBC; aimed at youth; prayers at end; Somerset
<5>	358.5–60.7	Long; has some dialogue features + many long answers, + catechumen is labelled 'scholar', but title-pages say the form is for 'simple', 'youth', + others that are willing to learn; Dec, Cr, Pr, Ss; section on daily devotions at end; according to title-page this work was 'collected' + translated by Allen
—	—	See below, s.v. Leo Jud
1	366	Advanced; Dec only; preface is addressed to 'reverend and learned examiners + readers'
1	364	Advanced; Cr only; preface addressed to 'reverend and learned ministers' + all true-hearted Christians
—	—	See below, s.v. T. Bray
5+	A1195B + ESTC	Very short; pre-comm.; published in *The whole duty of receiving worthily*, said to be by the author of *The whole duty of man*
1	382.5	Very short + simple; several prayers at end, including one summarizing the catechism; for the young in a London parish, but 'may serve generally for all places'

1	2	3
A[lport], E[dward]	David's catechisme	1623
[Altham, Michael]	A dialogue between a pastor and parishioner	1684–5
[Ames, William]	The chiefe heads of divinitie	1612 (Dordrecht)
——	The substance of Christian religion	1659
anon.	The anabaptists catechisme	1645
anon.	The ancient church catechism ... printed in the time of the church'es dissettlement	[1680?]
A[nderdon], C[hristopher]	A catechism for ... the Prince of Wales	1692 (Paris)
Andrewes, Bartimaeus	A very short and pithie catechisme	1586–91?
Andrewes, Lancelot	A patterne of catechistical doctrine	1630–41
——	The morall law expounded	1641–2
——	The patterne of catechistical doctrine	1650–75
[Angier, Samuel]	A short explanation/ An explanation of the [Assembly's] shorter catechism	1689–95
[Annesley, Samuel]	A supplement to The morning-exercise at Cripplegate	1674–6
Arrowsmith, John	Armilla catechetica. A chain of principles	1659 (Cambridge)

4	5	6
(1)	537	Defence of catechizing, + exhortation to be catechized; based on exposition of Ps. 34: 11
<2>	A2932A–33	An instructive dialogue in which a pastor explains to a parishioner the nature of and the need to take part in the Lord's Supper. (Altham also wrote a series of pamphlets containing questions + counter-questions, e.g. *Some queries to Protestants answered* (1686–7))
[1]	551.7	Mid; not the usual material except for Dec; used by Ames with sons of his former patroness, Lady Vere
(1)	A3003	A series of very short sermons on a variety of scripture texts, through which credal material, Ss, Dec, + Pr are explored; not in q + a; published posthumously
[1]	A3039	Satirical
1	A3067A	Very short; PBC; very similar to the anonymous *A cate-chisme to be learned* (1653), q.v.; prayers at end
[1?]	A3077	Catholic; for the son of James II, in exile
2?	586 + Maunsell, 28	Short; designed for family instruction prior to commu-nion; followed by confession + prayers; Great Yarmouth; Maunsell lists a 1591 edn.
(6)	603–603.5, + A3145–46A	Long exposition; Dec only
(2)	A3139A–40	As last
(4?)	A3147–8A	As last

[These 3 titles have essentially the same text, but the 2nd + 3rd are said to be nearer the original catechetical lectures given at Cambridge in the late 1570s and early 1580s. For the differences between the three, see P. A. Welsby, *Lancelot Andrewes 1555–1626* (1958), 22–3. London, *Catalogue*, sig. K1^r, listed duodecimo and octavo edns. in 1658]

2	A3165aA–65A	Long; WSC with propositions added, + extra qs + as in Palmer method (q.v.), taken from Lye (1672) and Wallis (q.v.); attribution to Angier in DWL's 1695 copy (which is identical to E3884 except for title-page); Carruthers mentions this work twice: 95, 128; price (1695) 6*d*. stitched
(2)	A3239–40	The second of four volumes of sermons on a variety of matters of practice + conscience, delivered by various preachers in a London church (see Wing^2 A3231–5, A3228, + A3225, and T. Case below); the 11th ser-mon in this volume, by T. Lye (q.v.), asked what scriptural rules should be applied to make catechizing universally profitable
(1)	A3772	Catechetical lectures given at St John's Coll., Cam-bridge, probably in the late 1640s

1	2	3
anon.	The art of catechizing	1691–1718
anon.	The assemblies catechism illustrated	1708
[Assheton, William]	A short exposition of the preliminary questions and answers of the church-catechism	1694
——	An exposition of the church-catechism	1701
Attersoll, William	The principles of religion	1606
——	The principles of Christian religion	1623–35
Austin, Robert	The parliaments rules and directions	1647
Austin, Samuel	A practical catechisme	1647
B., D.	The protestant guide	[1715?]
B., E.	A catechisme, or briefe instruction	1617
B., I.	The catechism of the Church of England	1669
B., I.	A short catechisme	—
B., P., gent.	The church catechism explained by way of paraphrase	1724
B., R.	A breife catechisme	1601
B., R.	A most briefe and learned catechisme	[*c*.1608]
B., R.	The dissenters catechism	1703
B., S.	A book of knowledge ... in a scriptural catechism	1722
Babington, Gervase	A very fruitfull exposition of the commaundements	1583–1637

4	5	6
5	A3786–8 + BL	3 mid forms: 1 based on PBC, using the Palmer method (q.v.); 1 providing scripture references for PBC; and 1 applying Palmer's method to *The whole duty of man*; also a long discourse on the PBC. Said to be aimed at the simplest learners + plainest teachers; cost, 1691, 18*d*.; 1692, 1*s*.
1?	Carruthers, 125	Cannot be traced, either at Magee College or Union Theological College, Belfast; the illustrations are more likely to have been scriptural than pictorial
1	A4044	Mid; based on opening questions of PBC only; divided into 12 parts; partly controversial: anti-Baptist; Kent
1	Bodleian + *TC* iii. 252	Long; modified version of last: has compressed section on opening qs + as, + added new section on Creed; also has two types of extra qs + as, in different type-face, with different function; divided into 18 weekly sections; Kent
1	889, pt. 2	Short; Dec, Cr, Pr, Ss; pre-comm.; tucked in at the end of the same author's *The badges of Christianity* (1606)
2	898.5–99	Mid: a much enlarged version of the last, published separately; an edn. was planned by Jaggard + Bourne *c*.1619 (sig. A3ʳ)
1	A4254	Very short; based on parliamentary ordinance of 20.10.1645; drawn up for his own congregation
1	A4258	Mid; pre-comm. (Ss + Dec); Bucks., Beds., + London
1	BL	Fenton's 1582 form, q.v., placed in a set of pro-Hanoverian devotions
1	1024 (ex 4802)	Mid; a version of Heidelberg, similar to 1601 work by R.B. (q.v.), but preface in this form has a long exhortation to parents, masters and teachers to catechize those in their charge
1	B82A	Short; PBC with extra qs + as; Devon?
—	—	See below, s.v. J. Ball
—	—	See below, s.v. P. Bedingfield
1	1055	Long; based on Heidelberg; divided into 52 sections, one for each Sunday; see E.B. above
?	*TSR* iii. 373	Unless this is the same as the last, no copy survives: ever published?
[1]	BL	Satirical
1	DWL	Long and quite difficult; unusual content: predestinarian, + partly controversial; Congregational
7	1095–8 + 1077–80 (*Works*)	Advanced; Dec only

1	2	3
——	A profitable exposition of the Lords prayer	1588–1637
——	An exposition of the catholike faith	1615–37
Bacon, James	A plaine and profitable catechisme	1660 (Oxford)
Bacon, Robert	Christ mighty in himself and members	1646
Baillie, Robert	Catechesis elenctica errorum	1654
B[aker], I[ohn]	Lectures ... upon the XII articles	1581–1613
Baker, John	A short preparation to the worthy receiving of the Lords Supper	1645
Bale, John	A dialoge ... betwene two chyldren	1549
Ball, John	A short treatise/ catechisme containing all the principles	–1628–88
——	A short treatise contayning the principles/ all the principall grounds, together with an exposition	1615–70
——	Short questions and answers, explaining the catechisme in the book of common prayer	1639–90/1
——	A short catechisme composed according to the rules and directions	1646
[Balmford, James]/M. Th. I. B.	A short catechisme, verie necessarie to be learned/ summarily comprizing	1597–1610
Bankes, Lawrence	The safeguard of the soule	1619
anon./[Keach, B.]	The Baptist-catechism	—
B[arclay], R[obert]	A catechism and confession of faith	1673–1740–

4	5	6
5	1090–1 + 1077–80 (*Works*)	Advanced; Pr
3	1077–80 (*Works*)	Advanced; Cr
1	B344	Two forms, 1 short, 1 long; the latter + an appendix were based on the 6 principles in Perkins' *Foundation*, q.v.; published by Bacon's son-in-law H.W.; London? Suffolk?
1	B368	Long form, but consists of very short, sometimes contentious qs + as; covers Dec + Ss, but has unusual amount of material on Christ + the Holy Ghost
(1)	B455	In Latin; controversial: denounces a wide variety of erroneous views through q + a
(4)	1219–22	Catechetical lectures, delivered before Sir Francis Walsingham, but later printed for the 'simple + ignorant' to read at home; also has at end a translation of Garnier's *Confession* (q.v.) by J. Hooper
1	B497	Short; pre-comm. (Ss); Kent
(1)	1290	Very short but not simple dialogue; unusual content: on whether the young can partake of the Gospel message (they can)
58?	1313.2–13.7 + B563–69A	Mid; credal material, Pr, Ss, Dec; 'very profitable for all sorts of people'; the best-selling unofficial form; first surviving edn. is the 12th—first edn. probably published pre-1615: see next; Somerset
16+	1314.2–18.5 + B570B–74	Long; same qs + as the last but with exposition added after each answer, possibly with the help of Martin Nicholes, q.v.; 'very profitable for all men, but especially for householders', though published at request of fellow-clergy; B575 is an edn. in Arabic; 1670 edn. cost 1*s*. 6*d*.
4	1314, B570A–70AC, + *TC* ii. 353	Mid; PBC; divided into 52 short sections; adds material on covenants but not predestination; 1691 reprint cost 3*d*.
2	B562–2A	Very short; based on the parliamentary ordinance of 20.10.1645; for the help of 'ignorant people'
6?	1336.5–37.5	Short; simple; prayers at end; 1607 edn. corrected + augmented by Balmford
(1)	1363	A treatise in the holy dying genre, but has qs + as on catechetical material; Derbyshire, Glous.?
—	—	See below, s.v. *Brief instruction*
9?+	B725–9 + BL	Long; mixture of usual and unusual material; largely scriptural answers; 15 chapters of catechism followed

1	2	3
——	Catechismus, et fidei confessio	–1727
Barksdale, Clement	[A short practical catechism out of Dr Hammond]	1649–50
Bartlett, Jeffrey	Hymns and songs of praise, with a dialogue	1710
B[artlet], J[ohn]	Directions for the right receiving	1679
Barton, William	Six centuries of select hymns … Together with a catechism	–1688?–90
Basset, John	A scripture catechism in two parts. Part the first	1733
Bassett, William	A discourse on my lord archbishop of Canterbury's … letters … touching catechising	1684
Bastingius, Jeremias	An exposition or commentarie	1589 (London) –1614 (Cambridge)
Bastwick, John	The Independents catechisme	1645
B[atchiler], J[ohn]	A tast of a catechetical-preaching-exercise	1667/8
Bate, Thomas	An explication of the church catechism	–1736
[Bates, William]	The upright Christian discovered	1693
Baxter, Richard	The Quakers catechism	1655–7
[——]	The agreement of divers ministers … for catechising	1656
——	Universal concord … The Christian religion	1660

4	5	6
		by 3 of confession; Quaker; Dublin edns. 1711, 1741; price bound 9*d*.
(2?)	DWL	Latin version of last
2?	Harvard	Mid; a reworking of Hammond's form, q.v. below; missing title-page supplied from A. Wood, *Athenae Oxonienses* (1813–20), iv. 222
(1)	BL	A volume of religious verse, which includes a dialogue between Christ + a penitent sinner, + Lord's Prayer, Cr, + Dec all in verse form
1	B100	Long; pre-comm. (Ss); by a nonconformist minister; Devon
(2+?)	B1004 + *TC* ii. 210, 316	Barton wrote + published hundreds of hymns + metrical psalms; this volume also contains 'A brief summary of Christian religion' (in verse, but not in q + a), covering credal material, Pr, + Dec; in *TC* ii. 210 this work is listed as being reprinted in Nov. 1687
2	BL + Bodleian	Mid; in 43 sections; to teach the ignorant true knowledge and 'revealed religion'; irenic intentions; largely scriptural answers; credal material, Ss, Pr + much else; price stitched 4*d*.; a pt. 2, on duties, was promised but has not been traced; 'printed + sold by the book-sellers in town and country'; Warks.?
(1)	B1052	Sermon defending the use + contents of PBC
5?	1564–7	Long; Heidelberg qs + as with expositions 'gathered out of Calvins Institutions'; see also below, s.v. *Catechisme of Christian religion*, and Scottish edns. of Bastingius's translation + exposition of Heidelberg, STC² 1562, 13023–5, + Wing² C 1466, 1468
—	—	See J. Bernard
1	B1075A	Combines preaching + catechizing through exegesis + questions; aimed at families; contains one complete short form; attribution to Batchiler by Calamy
5?	Bodleian	Mid; PBC with extra qs + as; Derbyshire
1	B1129A	Short form, with very long answers, on how to avoid sin; 'gathered' from Bates's treatises
(4)	B1362–5	Controversial: anti-Quaker
2	A773–4	Very short form, composed by Baxter + others in the Worcs. Voluntary Association as a means of agreement on basics, + a basis for catechizing the 'ignorant' (see preface of next); WSC parallels?
1	B1444	Very short; revised + enlarged version of the last, this time mainly in the form of statements with the option of prefixing them by questions

1	2	3
——	The poor man's family book	1674–97
——	Compassionate counsell/ warning	1681–1720
——	The catechizing of families	1683
——	The grand question resolved	1692–1726
——	[The mother's catechism, or] A familiar way of catechising of children	1701 + 1717 (Nottm.)
Baynes, Paul	A helpe to true happinesse	1618–35
anon.	The beaus catechism	1703
Becon, Thomas	[Catechism]	[pre-1543]
——	The principles of Christian religion	[*c*.1550]–[*c*.1580]
——	A new catechisme sette forth dialogue wise	1564
——	The demaundes of holy scripture	1577
B[edingfield], P[hilip]	The church catechism explained by way of paraphrase	1724
anon.	The beginner's catechism: to prepare the ignorant to learn … the [WSC]	–1707

4	5	6
8+?	B1352–7 + *TC* ii. 226	2 forms, 1 very short, 1 mid (q + a with expositions) to help 'the poor man' in his family; both forms focus on usual catechetical topics but with a stress on the covenant; price of 1684 edn. was 2*s.* bound
(5)	B1228–30 + BL	Advice to young men, not in q + a, but includes some rhetorical questions
1	B1205	Very long, + fairly advanced; designed as a successor to *Poor man's ... book*, for householders, teachers, + tutors to use; Cr, Pr, Dec, Ss
5?	B1279–79C + BL	2 short forms; modified versions of those in the 1674 work listed above
<2>	*TC* iii. 253, JRUL Manch., Nottm Univ. Library + Nottm Public Library	Long dialogue-catechism, designed to be read rather than memorized; published posthumously by M. Sylvester; mother asks, child replies, mainly on aspects of Old Testament history; Sylvester said the work was unfinished but a continuation 'by another hand' could be published
3	1642–43.5	Very long exposition of 40 qs + as, slightly modified versions of those in S. Egerton's 'Foure principall points' in his *Briefe method* (q.v.); published posthumously by E. C. (Ezekiel Culverwell?), and 3rd edn. enlarged by Egerton; for householders; some unusual content
[1]	Bodleian	Satirical, though not a parody of a well-known catechism; by the author of *The ladies catechism*, q.v.
1?	See col. 6	[An early catechism by Becon was ordered to be destroyed in 1543: P. Tudor, *JEH* 35 (1984), 407]
(5)	1751–13.5	Long exposition of catechetical material for the 'faithful' who can read; not in q + a
<1>	1710 (*Works*)	Very long dialogue-catechism, written for Becon to use with his children; covers repentance, faith (Cr), the Law (Dec), Pr, Ss, and duties
1	1718	Long; commended for school use in Sandwich, Kent; most unusual content (drawn from his larger works): almost a religious commonplace book in q + a
1	Bodleian	Mid; BCP in left-hand column with paraphrase in right-hand; by a gentleman (title-page); for those of 'ordinary capacities'; price 4*d.* or 25*s.* per 100
2?	Christ Church Oxford, *TC* iii. 585 + Carruthers, 125	Short; designed to help the 'ignorant' prepare to learn the WSC: a greatly simplified + very selective version of WSC; also has 2 pp. of explanations of hard words in WSC, + a q + a form including a confession for more advanced catechumens (very like episcopal confirmation); to be sold at 8*s.* per 100 copies

1	2	3
B[elke], T[homas]	A scripture inquirie	1642
Bellamy, Daniel	The Christian schoolmaster or an abstract of scripture history	1737
Bellarmino, Roberto	An ample declaration of the Christian doctrine	[1604]–35 (mainly English secret press)
——	A short catechisme of Cardinall Bellarmine/A short Christian doctrine/Christian doctrine	1614 (Augsburg)/ 1633 (St Omer)/ 1676 (n.p.), 1677 (n.p.), 1686 (London) + 1688
Bernard, Saint	Querela sive dialogus ... (Dialogue betwixt the soule and the body)	1613–32
Bernard, John	The Independents catechisme	1645
Bernard, Richard	A large catechisme following the order of the common authorized catechisme	1602
——	The faithfull shepheard	1607–21
——	A double catechisme	1607–9
——	Joshuas [godly] resolution ... A twofold catechisme	1612–29
——	Two twinnes ... I. Is of catechising	1613
——	The common catechisme	1630–40
——	Good Christian, looke to thy creede	1630
[Beveridge, William]	The church-catechism explained: for the use of the diocese of St Asaph	1704–36–

4	5	6
(1)	B1793	Referred to as a catechism by Mitchell (p. lxxxvi), but consists of advice in continuous prose on 'the duty of piety'
1	BL	30 lessons (in prose) on aspects of Old + New Testament history, each followed by a page of qs + as; a modified version of P. H., *Historical catechism* (q.v.)
[7?]	1834–37.7	Catholic; translation by R. Hadock of Bellarmine's larger catechism: a very long dialogue designed to instruct catechists
[6]	1843–4, B1822, Lambeth + Bodleian	Catholic; a translation by R. Gibbons of Bellarmine's shorter catechism, in q + a, to be learned by heart; covers Cr, Pr, Dec, Ss + much else; 1614 edn. has large number of woodcuts; 1633 has omissions + additions
(4)	1908.5–9.7	Dialogue between the soul, the body, + other 'characters' on the need to prepare for death; a supposititious work, reproduced in Latin (*Visio Sancti Bernardi*) + in English metre, the latter by W. Crashaw, q.v. There was another translation *c.*1640: *Saint Bernards vision* (STC² 1910)
(1)	'B1064' + BL E1186(5)	Controversial: anti-Independent; mainly on the nature and conditions of church government; 'gathered' out of J. Bastwick, *Independency not Gods ordinance* (1645) with which Wing² has conflated it; for a similarly entitled work see below, s.v. *Independent*
1	1955.5	Mid; based on PBC but heavily supplemented; published for the inhabitants of 1 Notts. + 2 Lincs. parishes
(3)	1939–41	Pastoral handbook, but contains advice on catechizing; 2nd + 3rd edns. revised
2	1936–7	2 forms: a very short 'for the weaker sort', + a mid—a modified version of the 1602 above
2	1953–54.5	2 forms: short + mid; modified versions of last, preceded by dialogue on how to run a good household, printed separately at first (1609) (STC² 1952.5)
(1)	1964	Sermon in 2 parts, the 1st containing an exhortation to catechize + advice thereon
11?	1929–33	Mid; PBC; probably the best-selling supplementary form of the 1630s; Somerset
1	1941.5	Mid; mainly Creed, but some other staples + some controversial material covered too
7+	BL	Long; BCP qs + as with expositions, + additional qs + as on the latter; also has exhortation + advice; epistle to clergy of St Asaph diocese; price 1s.; edition in Welsh 1708 (at Lambeth)

1	2	3
[Beverley, Thomas] (of Lilley)	A catholick catechism	1683
Beverley, Thomas	The catechism of the kingdom of Jesus Christ/ The prophets catechism	1690–1704
Beza/ de Bèze, Théodore	A brief and piththie summe	1563–89
——	Quaestionum et responsum chistianarum libellus	1571–7
——	A booke of Christian questions and answers	1572–86
——	Quaestionum et responsum … libellus. Pars altera.	1577
——	The other part of Christian questions and answeares	1580
——	A little catechisme	1578–9
Biddle, John	A twofold catechism	1654
——	Duae catecheses	1664/5
Binning, Hugh	The common principles of Christian religion … or a practical catechism	1659–1718–(Edinburgh + Glasgow)
Bird, Benjamin	The catechism of the Church of England with the proofs thereof	1674
——	The Jacobites catechism	1691–2
——	The Williamites catechism	1691
Bird, R.	'his catechisme, intituled A communication dialogue wise to bee learned of the ignorant'	1595
'Birdales'/ 'Byrdall'	'Birdales' or 'Byrdalls catachisme'	1626/38

4	5	6
1	B2188aA	Long; unusual content: partly polemic, partly instruction ('catholic' = apostolic); Herts?
5?	B2126–7, P3686 + *TC* iii. 313–14, 405	Mid; designed to supplement usual catechetical material by discussion of prophecy and the coming kingdom of Christ; 2nd edn. (B2127) enlarged with extra computations; only the title-pages + prefaces of B2127 + P3686 differ; 1702 and 1704 reprints cost 6*d*.
(7)	2006.7–13	Long exposition; not the usual staples, + partly polemical (anti-Catholic); Swiss origin
(2)	2036–36.5	Long; relatively advanced; not the usual staples; partly controversial; Latin; Swiss origin
5	2037–40.5	Translation (by A. Golding) of last; see below, s.v. *Booke* for a much shorter work with a similar title published 1578–81
(1)	2044	Long; 250 qs + as on Ss only; Latin; Swiss origin
1	2045	Translation of last
3	2022–23.5	Short—72 qs + as in 10 sections; only touches briefly on Cr, Dec, + Pr; printed at end is prayer to be said by children 'before the lesson'; Swiss origin
(1)	B2882	A long contentious form, + a mid condensed version for children in years or understanding, both heavily scriptural; a Unitarian, Biddle was probably translator of the Socinian *Racovian catechism* of 1652 (q.v.); this 1654 work provoked a reply by John Owen (q.v.)
(1)	B2875	Latin version of the last by a 15-year-old disciple of Biddle: Nathaniel Stuckey
[8+]	B2924–9 + Carruthers, 96–7	Sermons on the opening qs + as of the WSC; Scottish origin, + several Scottish edns., but it is possible that a 1660 edn. in DWL was published in London, and a 1672 edn. may have been published there too
1	B2947	Mid; PBC with scripture 'proofs' to encourage dissenters to use this form; for youth in general + those in his Dorset parish in particular
[1+]	B2949–50	Williamite propaganda; Scottish + American edns. as well
[1+]	B2950A–51	As last; also a Scottish edn.
1?	Maunsell, 31	No copy survives
?	*TSR* iv. 158, 407	Not traced; ever published?

1	2	3
'Birket'		—
Bishop, Thomas	A plain and practical exposition	1736
Blackwood, Christopher	The storming of Antichrist	1644
——	A soul-searching catechism	–1653–8
Blake, William	The farmers catechize, or a religious parly between the father and the son	1657
Blithe, Nathaniel	A plain and brief explanation upon the [PBC]	1672–4
Bonner, Edmund (Bp. of London)	A profitable and necessary doctrine	1555
——	An honest godlye instruction	1556
anon.	A booke of Christian questions and answers	1578–92?
Book of Common Prayer	A catechisme, that is to say, an instruction to be learned of every childe before he be brought to be confirmed of the bishop	1549–1740–
Boreman, Robert	The country-mans catechisme: or, the churches plea for tythes	1652
Boughen, Edward	[Principles of religion or] A short exposition of the catechism of the Church	1646–1707
B[oughton], I[ohn]	God and man. Or a treatise catechisticall	1623
Bourn, Samuel (II)	An address to Protestant dissenters	1736

4	5	6
—	—	[The catechism by 'Birket' referred to by C. Hoole in his influential work on teaching, *New discovery* (1660) is probably one of the versions of Calvin's *Catechisme* in Greek (q.v.) in the production of which Toussaint Berchet played a part]
1 (1)	BL B3103	Very long; PCB with extra qs + as; Suffolk? A two-part polemical work, against religious intolerance + infant baptism, with some q + a elements; also contains 'A brief catechisme' against infant baptism, drawn from the latter; author a Baptist + former American colonist
3 (1)	B3101–2 B3151B	2 forms: 1 long, 1 very short; not the usual content Long dialogue; lay author, an anticlerical; unusual, heavily scriptural content, with some touches of humour + rural imagery
2	*TC* i. 110 + B3197	Long; PBC with extra qs + as; 'gross error' in 1st edn. may explain lack of copies of that edn.; tract on confirmation at end; Lincs.?; price bound 1s. 4d.
[5]	3282–5	Catholic; expositions + homilies on catechetical material; not in q + a; for London diocese
[1]	3281	Catholic; Marian replacement for PBC; not in q + a
(3+?)	3294.3–94.7 + Maunsell, 31	Mid; controversial; anti-Catholic; with verses at end; Maunsell lists what is probably a 1592 edn.; this work is different from the work of the same title by Beza, q.v.
See col. 6	16267–422, Wing B3612–703 + BL Catalogue, s.v. Liturgies	[PBC]; the most commonly used short form; printed regularly in the Book of Common Prayer, but also in the *ABC with the catechisme*, + the *Primer and catechisme* qq.v.; for an edn. in Welsh (with prayers + Bible texts), see STC² 4804; for scale of production of Prayer Book, see STC², Wing² + BL Catalogue
(1)	B3757	Controversial: a defence of a separate ministry + the payment of tithes by the laity; not in q + a
10	B3816–22A + *TC* iii. 550	Long; PBC; the 1663, 1671, 1679, 1700, + 1707 edns. were published in Latin as well as English; edn. *c*.1683 'much revised' according to *TC* ii. 53; preface included confirmation service; prayers at end; English only price 8d. stitched, 1s. bound; English + Latin bound 1s.
(1)	3410	Long, wide-ranging dialogue, to help the 'ignorant'
(1)	Bodleian	Challenges the 6th answer in the WSC (on the Trinity) + defends attempts to amend + correct that form; author was minister of a Presbyterian congregation in Birmingham

1	2	3
——	An address to the congregation of Protestant dissenters	1738
——	Lectures to children and young people in a catechetical method	1738 (London) –1739 (Birmingham)
Bourne, Immanuel	The true way of a Christian, to the New Ierusalem	1622
——	A light from Christ ... or, a divine directory	1645–7
——	A light from Christ ... or, the rich jewel	1646
[Bowles, Edward]	A plain and short catechism	–1647–76
Boyes, John	'Mr. Boyes principles wherin he catechized the poore people at Hallifax'	[1610s?]
——	'The Christians horne booke or ABC'	[1610s?]
Bradshaw, William	A briefe forme of triall	1609
——	A briefe forme of examination	1614–43
B[randon], J[ohn]	A form of sound words, or a brief family-catechisme	1682
B[ray], T[homas]	A course of lectures upon the church catechism ... Vol. I / Catechetical discourses	1696–1703
——	A short discourse	1697–1704
—— (ed.)	Certain select discourses	1699/1703
——	An introductory discourse	1704
——	The church catechism, to which are	1704–29

4	5	6
(1)	DWL + Birming- ham Publ. Lib.	A reply to an attack on the last
3+	BL + Carruthers, 97	3 forms: 2 short, 1 long, none covering the usual staples; also reprints Strong's revision of the WSC, q.v.
(1)	3419	Includes an exhortation to catechize or be catechized
2	B3854, 3856	Long; pre-comm. but wide-ranging; 2nd edn. much modified; Derbyshire and London
1	B3856A	Very long; much enlarged + modified version of 1st edn. of last; fairly advanced, though said to be 'profitable' for parents to use in families
8?	B3877B–77C	Very short + simple; 8th edn., 1676, was reprinted by Edmund Calamy in *Continuation of the Account* (1727), ii. 935–9; Yorkshire
MS	BL Addit. MS 4928, fos. 1ʳ–2ʳ	6 principles on which the following was based; Boyes was preacher at Halifax 1613–20
MS	BL Addit. MS 4928, fos. 2ᵛ–34ᵛ	40 qs + as, some subdivided; Dec, Cr, Pr, Ss
1	3510	Very short pre-comm. form derived from the treatise, also by Bradshaw, with which it was printed: *A direction for the weaker sort*; to these 2 items was added a pre-comm. q + a form by Hildersham, *The doctrine of communicating worthily*
8?	3511–15.4 + B4159	An enlarged but still short version of the *Briefe forme of triall*; Bradshaw's treatise was also revised + renamed *A preparation to the receiving of the sacrament*; when this was done is not clear; 2nd + 3rd edns. not extant
1	B4249B	Mid; the 'chief heads' for those of weakest capacities; unusual content, with an early concern (at this level) about atheism; followed by 'Proofs that there is a God', + prayers
(4+)	B4292–92AA + ESTC	32 lectures on the opening qs + as of PBC, to be read; 3 further vols. promised. Also published as part of *Certain select discourses*: see below
(5+?)	B4297–99A + BL	Shortened version of the last, to be read by the young
(1)	DWL	A composite volume including reprints of two discourses by William Allen (originally published in 1673), Bray's own catechetical lectures on the start of PBC + on faith + justification, + Kettlewell's *Practical believer*, q.v.
(1+)	BL	An exhortation to the clergy of Maryland (whose commissary Bray had become) to catechize
2+	BL	Mid; PBC (divided into 4 lessons), 3 lessons on duties

1	2	3
	subjoin'd, some of the most apposite texts of scripture	
——	A preliminary essay towards rendring the various expositions	1704–10
——	A pastoral discourse to young persons	1704
——	The whole course of catechetical institution	1704–7
anon.	A breefe catechisme so necessarie and easie to be learned	1576–82
anon.	A breife catechisme and dialogue betwene the husbande and his wyfe	1545 (Antwerp)
B[reton], F[rancis]	Crossing of proverbs. The second part	1616–*c*.1670
B[ridges], F[rancis]	Gods treasurie displayed	1630
[Bridges, Walter]	A catechism for communicants	1645
anon.	A brief and plain exposition of the church catechism	–1698
anon.	A briefe catechisme conteining the most principall groundes	[*c*.1615?]
anon.	A brief instruction in the principles of the Christian religion	[1695]–*c*.1700–
Briggs, Joseph	Catechetical exercises	1696 (Cambridge)
——	The church–catechism explain'd	1722

4	5	6
		(quotations, not q + a), 5 lessons consisting of PBC 'paraphrased by way of prayer', + morning + evening prayers for children
2+	BL + Harvard	Short; for 2nd level students, mainly on aspects of doctrine raised in PBC
(1+)	BL	Mid treatise reminding the young of 'the necessity + advantage of an early religion', + giving reasons why they should be catechized
2?	BL	Reprints the 4 previous works; the combined whole was designed to meet the needs of 3 levels of catechumens; for 1707 edn. see H. P. Thompson, *Thomas Bray* (1954), 84
3?	4798–9 + Maunsell, 31	Very short; so easy that even 'the simple sort' can learn it; also contains pre-comm. instructions, + prayers at end; similar form appears in work by R. Cawdrey, q.v.; also similar to a work by E. Chapman, q.v.; perhaps the same as the *Briefe catechisme which standeth on three partes* printed by H. Singleton in 1579 (Maunsell)
[1]	4797.3	1st dialogue (husband–wife) is on Cr, Dec, + Pr; 2nd (translated by Robert Legate) is between Truth + an unlearned man, + covers various catechetical topics, the answers taking the form of scripture texts
[3?]	3644–5	Has a section of 'Certain briefe questions and answeres' that includes questions on the Bible, but on balance aimed at entertainment more than edification
1	3733	Very long form with short qs + as on a selection of scriptural + other themes
1	B4483C	Long; pre-comm.; for children + servants; drawn from sermon notes; London
3?	*TC* iii. 86	Composed for the use of a private school, supported by charity, in Westminster parish; no copy survives
1	4797.5	Very short: broadsheet; tabular layout; does not cover the staples at length
10+?	See col. 6	A work with a complex history, known by the 1760s as *The Baptist catechism* + attributed by then to Benjamin Keach (q.v.); 1st surviving edn. the 5th (B4602); 10th edn. *c.*1703; price 6*d.* bound : see advert at end of J. Saltmarsh, *Free grace* (1700); and W. T. Whitley, *A Baptist Bibliography* (1916–22), i. 39; text mid, + largely the same as WSC as an irenic gesture
1	B4662	Long (formerly sermons); PBC; extra qs + as, + expositions too; for youth; Yorkshire
1	BL	Long; revision of last; for the 'meanest capacity'; Yorkshire

1	2	3
B[rinsley], I[ohn] (the younger)	A breviate of saving knowledge	1643
Bristow, John	An exposition of the Creede [etc.]	1627
'British Protestant Divine': see below, s.v. F. Shaw		
Bromley, John	Catechism of the council	1687
'Brontius, Adolphus': see below, s.v. E. Cary		
Brook[e]s, Thomas	Apples of gold for young men and women	1657–1717–
Brooksbank, Joseph	Vitis salutaris, or the vine of catechetical divinity	1650–6
[Brough, William]	Sacred principles, services, and soliloquies	1650–79
Brown, John	A plain and distinct account of our Christian religion	1724
Browne, John	The truth of Christianity	1734
Browne, Samuel	The summe of Christian religion	1630
Brox[h]olme, Charles	The good old way: or, Perkins improved	1653–7
Bucanus, Gulielmus	Institutions of Christian religion / A body of divinity	1606–59
Bugg, Francis	A Quaker catechism. To which is added, The shortest way with Daniel De-Foe	[1706]
Bullinger, Heinrich	A most necessary and frutefull dialogue	1551 (Worcester)
——	Catechesis pro adultioribus	1559 (Zurich)–
——	Fiftie godlie and learned sermons	1577–87

4	5	6
1	B4708	Short; for those with 'good desires but weak memories'; credal material, Dec, Ss, Pr
1	3798	Mid, but followed by long exposition; Cr, Pr, Dec, Ss; for adults as well as children; Surrey
[1?]	—	Wing[2] has a cross-reference under 'catechism', but nothing s.v. Bromley or J.B.; cf. *Catechism for the curats* + *Catechismus ad parochos* below
(21?)	B4922A–28D + NUC + ESTC	Near the end of this series of 'doctrines' is a section in which the young person's objections are answered
2	B4980–1	Mid; derivative; divided into sections on faith, hope, + charity; primary + secondary answers printed in different typefaces; to be learnt in 34 weeks
8?	B4991–5	A long 'manual of devotions' which contains near the start a very short form which mentions Cr, Dec, Pr, + Ss
1	Bodleian	Long; to instruct children in the knowledge of religion + in particular their duties; in three parts; echoes of PBC in pt. 1 + to a lesser extent later
1	DWL	Mid; for use in schools; to be learnt after PBC; covers the authority of the Bible, confirmation, Lord's Supper, and Bible reading; Leics.?
1	3911	Mid; Dec, Cr, Pr, Ss; Shropshire? extant in 1622 (*TSR* iv. 86), and still on sale in 1658: London, *Catalogue*, sig. K3[r]
(3)	B5217–18	Long and detailed exposition of the 6 principles in Perkins's *Foundation* (q.v.); originally sermons; Derbyshire
2	3961 + B5269	Advanced: 1,570 qs + as on 49 religious 'common places'; not the usual staples; Swiss origin; translated into English by Robert Hill, q.v.
(1)	Wm. Andrews Clark Memorial Lib., Calif., + Friends' Library, London	Controversial, by a rabid anti-Quaker polemicist; provoked a reply by Defoe: *D'foe's answer* (1706)
(1)	4068	Dialogue on the legitimacy of obeying the magistrate in a Christian commonweal
[1+]	BL	Catechism for older catechumens recommended to Oxford undergraduates in 1579; no editions in English or published in England; for copies at Cambridge, see E. L. Leedham-Green, *Books in Cambridge Inventories* (1986), ii, 160
(3)	4056–8	In the list of catechetical works provided by T. Watts, *The entrie to Christianitie* q.v.; there was also an edn. in Latin in 1586: STC[2] 4076

1	2	3
[Bunbury, William]	The church catechism: with single proofs	1710–11–
Bundy, Richard	Sermons on several occasions	1740–
Bunny, Francis	An exposition of the Lordes prayer	1602
——	A guide unto godlinesse	1617–18
Bunyan, John	Instruction for the ignorant	1675
——	The pilgrim's progress	1678–1738–
Burch, Dorothy	A catechisme of the severall heads	1646
Burkitt, William	The poor man's help	–1694–1736–
——	Family instruction: or principles of religion	1715
Burnet, D.	The no-church catechism	1710
Burnet, Gilbert	An exposition of the church catechism	1710
Burridge, Richard	The Dutch catechism	[pre-1703]
B[urton], H[enry]	Grounds of christian religion	1631–6
Burton, William	Certaine questions and answeres	1591–1602
——	An exposition of the Lords prayer	1594–1602
Bury, Edward	A short catechism	1660
Butterfield, Swithune	The principles of the true Christian religion	1582?–90
Byfield, Adoniram	The summe of [all] the principles	1630–65
Byfield, Nicholas	[The principles, or] the paterne of wholesome words	1618–65
——	The principall grounds of Christian religion	1625

4	5	6
2+	BL + *TC* iii. 658	Short; PBC with scripture proofs in an innovative lay-out; price 2*d*. or 10*s*. per 100; 8th edn. 1743
(1+)	BL	Includes 7 catechetical lectures on the PBC
(1)	4098a	Long exposition of Lord's Prayer
1	4100–4100.5	Long; Dec only; for 'simple + ignorant people'; Durham
1	B5544	Mid; for 'public and common benefit' but dedicated to his church in Bedford; not the usual content, + not his most sparkling work
(25+?)	B5557–75 + BL	Some catechetical exchanges, e.g. between Christian + Ignorance; cf. D. Danielson, 'Catechism, *The Pilgrim's Progress*, and the Pilgrim's Progress', *JEGP* forthcoming
1	B5612	Short; lay author, originally designed for private use (Kent); not the usual staples
22+	B5738–38A + BL + ESTC	Godly living manual which contains a mid pre-comm. form; 19th edn. cost 1*s*. (ex inf. 1730 edn. of Stinton, q.v.)
1	BL	The last published separately
(1)	BL	Satirical and polemical: anti-dissenter; begins with a parody of PBC
2	BL	Very long; PBC with extra qs + as and expositions; for use in his diocese (Sarum)
?	—	Not traced; referred to in the same author's *The recantation*; political?
4	4143–45.5	Mid; summary of his teaching in a London parish, printed for parents to use in their families; stresses covenants in relation to Ss; prayer at end
2	4167, 4165a (*Sermons + treatises*)	2 forms, 1 long, 1 short, neither handling the staples; Bristol
2	4174, 4165A, (*Sermons + treatises*)	Lectures turned into q + a; Lords's Prayer only; for 'the simpler sort'; Reading?
1	B6210	Short; pre-comm.; based on the parliamentary ordinance of 20.10.1645, but quite wide-ranging
(2?)	Maunsell, 33 + STC² 4206	Long exposition; Cr, Dec, Pr, Ss
(4?)	See col. 6	London, *Catalogue* sig. K2ᵛ lists this as a separate work; it is a short summary of the next below, with which it was published from 1630, with separate title-page + signatures; not in q + a
(7)	4226–31 + B6389	The bulk of this is a long exposition, stressing the need to use the principles learnt through catechizing; not in q + a; see also last above
1	4232	Short; for the 'younger sort'; not the usual staples; edited by W.C. after author's death

1	2	3
C., B.	A brief and perspicuous manuduction to practical divinity	1670–92
C., E.	An ABC or holy alphabet	1626
anon./ C., E.	The/A new catechisme according to the form of the kirk of Scotland	1644–5
C., J.	A briefe examination of the Christian faith	1623
C., J.	The Independants catechism	1654
C., J. (Mrs)	The mother's catechism	1734
C., R.	A briefe and necessarie catechisme	1602
C., T. (D.D.): see Thomas Comber		
C., W.	[no title]	1584
Calamy, Edmund	Sobermindedness recommended	1717
Calvin, John	Instruction	1537
——	The forme of common praiers used in … Geneva	1550
——	Le catéchisme de Genève	1552
——	The catechisme or manner to teache children	1556 (Geneva) + 1560–98 (London)
——	Catechismus ecclesiae Geneuensis	1562–[1590?]
——	Three propositions or speeches	1580
——	Katechesis tes Christianikes pisteos	–1648–55

4	5	6
2	C13A + *TC* ii. 430	Mid; not the usual staples; finished by B.C. from a draft by 'a learned, reverend man now with God'; 2nd edn. also has 'An help to prayer for the catechized youth' of the C. of E.
2	4264.5	Described as a catechism in *TSR*; has 24 'lessons for young beginners in the school of Christ' and 'poor ignorant people' numbered A–Z; 2 lessons have short q + a forms on preparation for Lord's Supper, and fasting
2	G1095 + N592A	Short; preceded by ABC, vowels, + king's crest, + followed by prayers; Scottish origin; Cr, Dec, Pr, Ss; for children and youth; formerly erroneously attributed to William Goode, q.v.
?	*TSR* iv. 101	Described as a catechism, but not traced; perhaps the work by J. Craig, q.v.
(1)	C58	Revision of 1647 work of same title: see below, s.v. *Independent*; J.C. described on title-page as 'gent'
1	BL	Long; explanation by extra qs + as of the 1st 40 (+ a selection of later) qs + as of WSC; for the use of children + servants
—	—	See s.v. R. Greenham
1?	Maunsell, 31	Maunsell refers to a form by W.C. in his list of catechisms; not traced
(1)	BL	A sermon preached to 'a society of catechumens in London', + printed at their request
—	—	[For a translation and adaptation of Calvin's 1537 form, see below, s.v. R. Taverner]
1	16560	Contains English translation of the 1541 form, placed after the prayers, which were translated by W. Huycke; Swiss origin
(1)	4391	French version of last, published in England; see also below, s.v. *Psaumes*
[1] + 12	4380–87a.5 + Maunsell, 31	English translation of the 1541 catechism; long; Cr, Dec, Pr, Ss; for children aged 10 to 15; divided into 55 parts; very influential; Maunsell lists a 1592 edn.; for other edns., published in Geneva and Scotland, see STC² 2106, 16561; 16577–91, 1564–5, 4382, 4383, 4389–90.7, + Wing² C328
(6)	4375–9	Latin version of last
(1)	4464	At the end is Calvin's exposition of the qs + as set for the 43rd week of Calvin's 1541 form
(3?)	C1463–63A + BL Voyn 69	Greek version of 1541 form, in the translation of Estienne revised by Toussaint Berchet; previous edns. had been published abroad in the later 16th century

1	2	3
——	Stoicheiosis tes Christianon	1648
——	The institution of Christian religion	1561–1634
Camfield, Benjamin	A serious examination of the Independent's catechism	1668–9
[Canisius, Petrus]	Certayne necessarie principles	1579? ('Douai' / London?)
——	Ane catechisme or schort instruction	1588 (Paris)
——	A summe of Christian doctrine	*c*.1592–6 (secret press in London) + 1622 (St Omer)
——	Petri Canisii ... parvus catechismus	1687
[Capito, W.]	A lytle treatous or dialogue very necessary	1527 (Strasburg)
——	The true beliefe in Christ + his sacraments	1550
Carpenter, John	Contemplations for the institution of children	1601
Carter, John	Winter evenings communication with young novices in religion	1628
[Cartwright, Thomas]	Christian religion: substantially ... treatised	1611
——	A treatise of Christian religion	1616
——	A methodicall short catechisme: containing briefly all the principall grounds	1623
[Cary, Edward]/ 'Adolphus Brontius'	The catechist catechiz'd	1681

4	5	6
(1)	C329aA	As last, but with Berchet's copious notes; was used as a textbook for students of Greek
(9)	4415–25	Treated as a catechetical work at Oxford in 1579 (see above, p. 197), and also in a list of catechetical works given by T. Watts, *Entrie to Christianitie*, q.v.; there was also an edn. in Latin (STC² 4414) + abridgements, in English (4426.8) + Latin (4426.4–6.6, 4427–8)
(1)	C383–4	A detailed rebuttal of J. Owen's *Brief instruction* (1667), q.v. below, + a defence of the established church's beliefs + government
[1]	4568.5	Catholic; long; q + a; translation (by T.I.) and condensation of Canisius's *Parvus catechismus*; for another translation, see *Introduction* below
[1]	4568	Another translation of the last, but this time aimed specifically at the Scots
[3+]	4751.5–52.5	Another translation, in part by H. Garnet; very long; there was another issue of the 1622 edn. in 1639 (St Omer again)
[1]	C436B	An edition of the same, printed by Henry Hills, James II's printer
[1]	24223.3	Translation by Wm. Roye of Capito's dialogue *De pueris instituendis*; Cr, Ss; banned in England
(1)	24223.5	Another issue of last with cancelled dedication + new title-page
<1>	4662	Long dialogue-catechism: son asks, father replies at length; for children; credal material, Dec, Ss, Pr; prayers at end
1	4696	Mid; scriptural answers; unusual content; for children; Suffolk?
1	4707.5	Advanced; apart from Dec, unusual content: predestinarian, federal; unauthorized, according to Bradshaw's preface
1	4707.7	Modified version of last; followed by the 'Methodicall short catechisme' (see next)
1	4803	Last mentioned form published separately but also published as part of Cartwright's *Treatise* + at the end of Dod + Cleaver's *Exposition*, q.v.; manuscript versions exist at Huntington (Ellesmere MS 6166) + TCD (MS 295); unusual content apart from Decalogue
(1)	C722	Polemical: why Catholics should take the oath of allegiance; also attacks a 'Jesuit' catechism

1	2	3
Case, Thomas	The morning exercise methodized ... in a monthly course ... at St. Giles in the Fields. May 1659	1660–76
Castalio	see below, s.v. Châteillon	
anon.	Catechesis ecclesiae anglicanae, una cum precibus	1673 (Cambridge)–1702 (London)
anon.	Catechesis ecclesiae anglicanae, una cum precibus ... in usum scholae ... Gippovicensi	1722 (Ipswich)
anon.	Catechesis ecclesiarum quae in regno Poloniae	[after 1635] + 1651
anon./ [Heidelberg Catechism]	Catechesis religionis Christianae	1623 (London), + 1629 (Oxford)
anon.	Catechesis religionis Christianae brevior	1689

See also below, s.v. 'Katechesis' for catechisms in Greek

anon.	Catecheticae versiones variae	1638
anon.	A catechetical instruction	1728–*c*.1730–
anon.	Of catechisinge	1620s
anon.	A catechism containing the substance	1676–93
anon.	A catechisme for children	1657
anon.	A catechisme for children in yeeres + ... understanding	1644
anon.	A catechism for souldiers	1659
anon.	The catechism for the curats	1687
anon.	A catechism for the times	1645
anon./ 'Philander'	A catechism for the use of deists	1739
anon.	A catechisme in brief questions and answeres	1629

4	5	6
(3)	C835–6	The successor to an earlier set of sermons (see C834), but this time devoted to the 'essentials' to provide in printed form 'a stock of divinity' to be kept with a Bible + communicated to children + servants
(3)	C1464A, Whitgift School Croydon + U. of Illinois at Urbana	PBC in Greek + Latin, morning prayers in Latin + evening in Greek; for the use of King Edward VI School, Bury St Edmunds, and Whitgift School; information on latter's copy from Mr F. H. G. Percy
(1)	Ipswich School	PBC + prayers in Latin only (ex inf. Dr J. M. Blatchly); for comparable forms see last above + *Catechismus ... Katechesis* below
(2+)	20083.3 + C1465	Racovian Catechism in Latin; earliest edns. published in Cracow (1609); for other edns. with an English connection see STC² Addenda, + an edn. *c.*1659 published at 'Irenopolis' (Antwerp?); the work was condemned by Parliament in 1652: (see *Votes of Parliament* below); for an edition in English + the outcry it caused, see below, s.v. *Racovian*
(2?)	13025.4, 13026	Heidelberg form in Latin, published in England; divided into 52 sections; for Scottish editions, see STC² 13023–5; edns. in Greek and Latin were published abroad from 1597
(1)	C1464 (= S2178)	WSC translated into Hebrew by W. Seaman
(1)	4806	PBC in English, Latin, Greek, + Hebrew; plus graces; preface signed by G.S., possibly George Sandys (note in Guildhall Library copy)
2+	BL	Short; not the usual staples; for those of 'meanest capacity'; later an SPCK title
MS	Emmanuel Coll. Cambridge MS III. 1. 13.[8]	Exhortation to catechize or be catechized
—	—	See below, s.v. E. Fowler
—	—	See below, s.v. G. Fox
—	—	See below, s.v. J. Stalham
[1]	C1471	Defence of soldiering by q + a; cf. R. Ram below
[1]	C1472	Tridentine catechism; not in q + a; published by James II's printer
—	—	See below, s.v. I.K.
(1)	BL + DWL	Controversial; a short form by a C. of E. cleric to show deists they are bound by morality
—	—	See below, s.v. J. Geree

1	2	3
anon.	Catechism made practical	1688
anon.	The catechism of the Book of Common-Prayer explained	–1672
anon.	A catechisme of Christian doctrine	1637–
anon.	A catechisme of Christian religion	1617
anon.	A catechisme of the Christian religion	1721
anon.	The catechism of the Church of England briefly paraphrased	1688
anon.	[The catechism of the Church of England translated into Arabic]	1671
anon.	The catechism of the Church of England with marginal notes	1678–
anon.	The catechism of the Church of England with some questions	1669
anon.	The catechism of the Church resolved	1699
anon.	The catechism of the Church: with proofs	1694–
anon.	The catechism of the kingdom of … Christ	1690–
anon.	A catechism of penance	1685
anon.	A catechism or abridgement of Christian doctrine	1725
anon.	A catechisme, or brief instruction	1617
anon.	The catechism or brief instruction	1702
anon.	A catechism: or an instruction … in three parts	1733
anon.	The catechism or, Christian doctrine	[*c*.1700]
anon.	The catechisme, or maner [how] to teach/instruct … children and others	1570?–8
anon.	A catechisme, or short kind of instruction	1588
anon.	The catechism set forth	1679–
anon.	A catechisme: so short for little children	1639

4	5	6
1	C1474	Contains the irenic *Short catechism according to the doctrine*, q.v.; a long exposition on faith and godliness; + another on duties; has been attributed to T. Doolittle (MS note in Cong. Lib. copy), but not listed in 1723 list of his works: *Complete Body*, sig. c2^v
3?	C1475AB	Mid; PBC with extra qs + as
—	—	See below, s.v. T. White
1+	13031.5 (ex 1563)	Translation of Heidelberg; by Bastingius, q.v. For editions published abroad, see 13031.2 + 13031.7, 13031.8, C1475 + BLC (Utrecht, *c*.1701); for Scottish edns. 13031.3, 13031.4
1	BL	Revised translation of Heidelberg, by C. Coorne
1	C1475B	Mid; derivative; PBC with extra qs + as; for children + servants who cannot learn 'the larger expositions'; + prayers for children
1	C1476	PBC in Arabic; translation by Edward Pocock, according to F. Madan, *Oxford Books*, iii. 254
—	—	See below, s.v. E. Wetenhall
—	—	See above, s.v. I.B.
—	—	See below, s.v. B. Love
—	—	See below, s.v. Z. Isham
—	—	See above, s.v. T. Beverley
—	—	See below, s.v. J. Roucourt
—	—	See below, s.v. A. Hacket
—	—	See above, s.v. E.B.
—	—	See below, s.v. J. Jacob
1	BL	Mid; for adults; Cr, Dec, Pr, Ss; quasi-'rational'?
[1]	C1478	Catholic; similar in places to but not the same as *Abstract of Douay catechism*, q.v.; date taken from Yale catalogue
3?	Maunsell, 31 + STC^2 13028–9	Translation of Heidelberg Catechism, by W. Turner; Maunsell has a 1570 edn. of the Heidelberg Catechism, also printed for J. Harrison; 1578 edn. adds marginal refs. to the relevant passages of scripture
2	13030–1	Heidelberg translated + supplied with proofs by J. Seddon; prefaced by long treatise of exhortation to ministers and parents to catechize by T. Sparke; also has prayers at end
—	—	See below, s.v. T. Marshall
1	4802.5	Only the title-page survives; capable of being learnt by

1	2	3
anon.	A catechisme, that is to say, an instruction regarding the priesthood	[1720?]
anon.	A catechisme, that is to say an instruction to be learned ... To which are prefixed briefe and plain rules for reading the Irish language	[1710?]
anon.	A catechisme to be learned ... of all those professors	*c*.1589
anon.	A catechisme to be learned for the training up of youth and others	1653
anon./'A Protestant of the Church of England'	A catechisme truly representing	1686
anon.	[A catechism] whereas all men desire to be blessed	*c*.1602
anon.	A catechism wherein the learner	1674
anon.	A catechisme with a prayer annexed	1583
anon.	Le catéchisme de Heidelberg	1720
anon.	Le catéchisme pour l'examen de la jeunesse ... en l'église Walonn de Canterbury	1664
anon.	Catechismus ad parochos ex decreto Concilii Tridentini editus	1687
anon.	Catechismus catechizandus, or a catechism to be catechiz'd	1674
anon.	Catechismus cum ordine/Katechesis kai taxis	1683–1732
anon.	Catechismus pro parvulis	1660
anon.	The catechist catechiz'd	1681
anon.	Catechistical discourses	1654
anon./ [Norton, J.?]	A catechistical guide to sinners	1680

4	5	6
		2–3-year-olds; same as the *Short catechisme for little children* of 1589 (q.v.)? Prayers + graces at end
(1)	Regent's Park College, Oxford	Controversial; short form (44 qs + as) defending the maintenance of clergy by tithes
(1)	BL	PBC in English and Irish, published with an Irish grammar; for use in Ireland. Date of publication sometimes given as late as [1740?]
1?	*TSR* ii. 524	Not traced; ever published?
1	C1479	Short; PBC with minor alterations (e.g. stronger defence of infant baptism) + scripture refs. added; for 'youth and others'
—	—	See below, s.v. J. Williams
1?	*TSR* iii. 220	Not traced: ever published?
—	—	See below, s.v. C. Ellis
—	—	See below, s.v. E. Chapman
(1)	Christ Church, Oxford	Heidelberg Catechism in French, but published in London with a new dedication, to George I, + an interesting account of why it was being republished at that particular date
(1)	C1479BA	For Walloon church in Canterbury
[1]	C1479BB	The 'Roman catechism', first issued in 1564, for priests: in Latin + not in q + a; printed by the Catholic publisher Nathaniel Thompson
1?	*TC* i. 162	Not traced; mid? (price 6*d*.)
(7)	C1465A, K28A–B, BL *et al.*	PBC + order for confirmation in Greek + Latin, + Latin prayers (varying from school to school); for use at Merchant Taylors' School, Eton College, + Ipswich School; see *Catechesis* above
—	—	See below, s.v. G. Fox
—	—	See above, s.v. E. Cary
—	—	See below, s.v. A. Errington
1	C1480	Long; qs + as plus expositions; for use by adults who are sinners or babes in Christ, + by children; author seeks to shun controversies; heavily scriptural; not the usual content; attribution to Norton in Wing, *Early English Books*

1	2	3
anon.	The catechizing of families	*c.*1692
anon.	The catechumen, or an account given	1690
anon./'A divine of the Church of England'	Catechumenorum ductor: or an instruction to young people	1714
Cateline, Jeremy	The rules and directions of the ordinance	1646–8
anon./'British Protestant divine'	A catholic catechism	–1717–24
Caussé, Barthélemy	The very true shield, and buckler of faith	1569
anon.	The cavaliers catechisme	1643
anon.	The cavaliers catechisme and confession of his faith	1647
C[awdrey], D[aniel]	Family reformation promoted. In a sermon … and by short catechismes	1656
Cawdrey, Robert	A short and fruitefull treatise, of the profite [and necessitie] of catechising	1580–1604
[Cawdrey, Zachary]	A brief and methodical catechism	1662–4
[Cena]	De coena Domini dialogus	[*c.*1575]
anon./ [Theodore Beza?]	Certaine questions and answers touching the doctrine of predestination, and the use of God's word and sacraments	1579–1615
anon.	Certayn short questions and answeres	1580–4
C[halloner], R[ichard]	A short history of the … beginning … of the Protestant religion	1735
——	The catholic Christian instructed in the sacraments	1737
C[hapelin], G.	A familiar and Christian instruction	1582

4	5	6
?	Carruthers, 125–6	Advert in [Day], *Communicant's instructor* (1692); the work is by R. Baxter, q.v.
—	—	Part 1 of L. Addison's *The Christian's manual* (q.v.)
1	Lambeth	Long; derivative; PBC with extra qs + as + scripture proofs; for all people, and children in general, especially those in Charity Schools
3	C1482–3	Short; based on the parliamentary ordinance of 20.10.1645
—	—	See below, s.v. F. Shaw
(1)	4870	23 dialogues, some on conventional topics such as faith + Decalogue, others controversial (anti-Catholic); French origin
[1]	C1567	Satirical: anti-Royalist; parodies PBC in places
(1)	C1568	Not the same as last: pro-Royalist; partly religious, partly political
(1)	C1627	Mainly an exposition of duties (parents/children, masters/servants) but some qs + as; material borrowed from father, Robert's, *Godly form of household government*, but method was his own
3?	4882–3 + Maunsell, 31	1604 edn. contains a short pre-comm. form (cf. *Breefe catechisme* of 1576); but bulk of 1580 + 1604 edns. is exhortation + advice, much enlarged in the 1604 edn.; 1580 also has work by Charke at end, q.v.; Maunsell lists a 1592 edn.
2	C1642A–4	Short; qs + as (to be learnt by children) + expositions (to be learnt by adults); credal material, Ss, Pr, Dec; much indebted to WSC
(1)	4911.3	Short, pre-comm. dialogue in Latin? (cannot be found at location given by STC)
25+?	[2126–2241]	Short; on the topics indicated in the title; not published separately but bound into many quarto Geneva Bibles printed in black letter from 1579 to 1615. Has been attributed to Beza, but can also be viewed as supplement to 1549 version of PBC
3	20558–60	2 very short forms, 2nd a condensation of 1st; for young children; not usual content
[1]	BL	Catholic; a hostile account of the evolution of Protestantism, in q + a
[1]	BL	Explanation of Catholic sacraments, ceremonies, + observances, by q + a
—	—	See below, s.v. *Familiar*

1	2	3
C[hapman], E[dmund]	A catechisme with a prayer annexed	1583
anon.	The Charity-School, or reading and spelling made easy	1704
Charke, William	Of the use of catechising	pre-1580
Châteillon, Sébastien	Dialogorum sacrorum libri quatuor	1560–1739
Chauncy, Isaac	The doctrine which is according to godliness	1694?–1737
Cheynell, Francis	Chillingworthi novissima	1644
anon.	The chiefe heads of divinitie	1612
anon./ T. Vincent/ Vincent Sadler	The childes catechisme	1678 (Paris, possibly London)
Chitwin	?	?
anon.	The Christian directorie, or, rules of Christian pietie	1635
anon.	The Christian doctrine	1678
anon.	Christian knowledge and practice	1737 (Hamburg)
anon./'A well-wisher of the cause of Christ'	The Christian souldiers magazine	1644
Chub, William	A Christian exercise for private housholders	[1585?]
anon.	The church catechism, analysed, explained and improved. The first part	1683–1703 (Norwich)

4	5	6
1	4962	Short; a different version or translation of the *Breefe catechisme* of 1576; 'meet' for all Christian families (but designed for and approved by Dedham classis, Essex); prayers at end
1?	*TC* iii. 428	Includes PBC, psalms, prayers, + aids to Bible study; 'for bringing up children in the Protestant religion'; no copy survives
(1)	4882	Written as a preface to Charke's translation into Latin of Robert Le Maçon's French form, q.v., this was translated into English by J. Stockwood, + inserted by him at end of 1580 edn. of R. Cawdrey's *Short ... treatise*, q.v.
[23+]	4770–76.7, C3732–34cA + BL + NUC	Dialogues in Latin based on Bible; Swiss origin; widely used in schools
3	C3749 + Carruthers, 101	Very long; 1st 38 qs + as of WSC with extra qs + as, though author also cites the 39 Articles; for the ignorant, weak, + less educated; London?
(1)	C3810	The 'brief' 'profane' catechism in this work consists of selected quotations from Chillingworth's works, preceded by loaded or slanted questions by Cheynell to make it appear Chillingworth was popishly inclined
—	—	See above, s.v. W. Ames
[1]	C3875	Catholic; father asks, child replies
?	?	A catechism by Chitwin is mentioned by P. Nye in *Beames of former light* (1660), 85; not traced
1	5157.5	A very short form entitled 'Short points of Christian religion' is appended to this improving treatise, published posthumously + dedicated to the governess of the Prince of Wales
—	—	See below, s.v. J.S.
[1]	BL	'Catechetical lectures' on PBC, consisting of extra qs + as plus meditations + thanksgivings, + discussion of disputed points; to explain the Church of England to the Hanoverians?
[1]	C3949	To arm parliamentarian soldiers with zeal + courage; only partly in q + a, + only marginally catechetical in the conventional sense
1	5211	Short but quite difficult form, to be read rather than learnt? Focuses on works, prayer, + Ss; pt. 2 of *The true travaile*
2?	C3993A + BL	Mid; PBC with additional qs + as, + some explanations; 1703 edn. for use in Norwich School, but also recommended for the rich to give to the poor

1	2	3
anon.	The church catechism broke into short questions	1709–34–
anon.	The church-catechism enlarg'd and explain'd	1697
anon.	The church catechism explained and proved	1708
anon.	The church catechism explained by way of question and answer	1701–
anon.	The church-catechism explained, for the ease … of instruction	1666
anon.	The church-catechism resolved into scripture proofs	1681
anon.	The church-catechism resolved into short questions and answers	1681
anon.	The church catechism: to which are subjoin'd	1729
anon.	The church catechism, with explanations and scripture-proofs	1705–20
anon.	The church-catechism with scripture proofs	1685–1701
anon.	The church catechism: with single proofs	(1711)
Clark, Nicholas	A brief exposition of the catechism	1725
Clarke, Samuel D.D.	An exposition of the church catechism	1729–31–
Clifford, James	A catechism containing the principles	1694–1701

4	5	6
3+	Bodleian + BL	PBC broken into shorter qs (but without answers) to test comprehension; also explains some words used in PBC, + has prayers for the use of charity schools; copies of 1709 edn. sold at 2*d*. or 12*s*. per 100; Dublin edn. published in 1718
—	—	See below, s.v. R.M.
1+	*TC* iii. 598	Usually published in Dublin, e.g. 1699 (C3994) + 1719; but this '4th' edn. was sold in London; Wing attributes the work to Narcissus Marsh, but in the preface he only recommends it
—	—	See below, s.v. J. Lewis
1	C3993B	Mid; PBC with extra qs + as; answers set in separate columns from questions; for use both publicly and privately
1	C3994aA	An earlier version of *The church catechism with scripture proofs* (1685); slightly modified PBC, divided up into short phrases, + supported by scripture texts printed in full
1?	C3994bA	PBC broken up into shorter qs + as? designed so that PBC might be better understood and remembered by children; not traced unless it is the same as *Church catechism analysed* (1683), q.v.
—	—	See above, s.v. T. Bray
5?	*TC* iii. 434 + Queens', Cambridge	Mid; PBC with extra qs + as + scripture proofs; for use in a 'private parish'; 5th edn. (1720) corrected; price 3*d*. or 20*s*. per 100
3	C3994cA, Trinity Cambr. + Duke Univ. N. Carolina	PBC (in black letter) with scripture proofs added (in roman); printed for the Stationers Company, which was also responsible for *ABCs* + *Primers*, q.v.; for earlier version see above, s.v. *Church catechism resolved* (1682); price in 1685 2*d*.
—	—	See above, s.v. W. Bunbury
(1)	Liverpool Univ. Lib.	Mid; exposition of PBC in 'an easy + familiar method' for 'those of tender years'; price 3*d*. or 20*s*. a 100; Dorset
3+	BL	PBC with exposition of each answer; edited by brother John (Dean of Sarum) from notes of Thursday lectures given in London; 2 edns. also published in Dublin, with added essays; owing to Clarke's alleged Arianism, the work was the object of some controversy: see below, s.v. T. Emlyn, A. A. Sykes + D. Waterland
3?	C4702–2A + *TC* iii. 262	Long; mainly on Creed; commends PBC, but has some WSC parallels; published with pre-comm. sermon

1	2	3
Clifford, John	Sound words: the catechism of the Westminster Assembly	1699
Clutterbuck, John (gent.)	A plain and rational vindication and explanation of the liturgy of the Church of England	1694–1727
Cobhead, Thomas	A briefe instruction	[1579]
Cockburn, Patrick	In secundae partis catechismi enarrationem	1561
Cole, E.	The young schollar's best companion	1689–1704
Cole, Nathanael	A short catechisme collected out of the whole work	[1615]–33
Collins, Hercules	An orthodox catechism	1680
Colyer/Collier Thomas	Certaine queries: or, points now in controvercy	1645
anon./Colman, Henry	An essay by way of catechism on confirmation	1709–16
C., T. (D.D.) /Thomas Comber	The church-catechism: with [a brief and] easie explanation thereof	1681–1700
——	A companion to the altar	1675–1721
[——]/'An English Protestant'	The plausible arguments of a Romish priest ... answered	1686–1735
anon.	A commentary by way of question and answer upon that part of the church-catechism	1702
anon.	The common Christian instructed in some necessary points	1722

4	5	6
1	C4705	Long; WSC with scripture proofs in full; volume also contains advice on singing, 100 psalms + hymns, a confession + prayer both using the words of the WSC, + rules for godly living
7+	C4742–3 + BL + ESTC	A long explanation + defence of the official liturgy (culled from approved authors) in q + a; for use in schools + by those of riper years; for similar works see below, s.v. *An explanation of the terms*, and E. Creffeild (1713)
1	5455	Mid; Dec, Cr, Pr, Ss; 'collected for the exercise of youth, + simple sort of people'
(1)	5459	Continuation of *In dominicam orationem pia meditatio* (St Andrews, 1555); covers Cr only; in Latin, and not in q + a
3	C5021 + *TC* iii. 429	To teach reading + grammar, but contains a short form, influenced by WSC, + staple formulae published separately beforehand; work also contains improving sentences + proverbs, meditations, prayers, *et al.*
4?	5536–7	Short form on assurance of salvation summarizing the larger work by Cole of which it forms part: *The godly mans assurance*; Essex?
1	C5364	Long; by a Baptist with a London church; Cr, Ss, Dec, Pr; heavily indebted to Heidelberg except on adult baptism; has appendix on church music
(1)	C5273	Mid; handles controversial matters relating to church government + discipline in q + a; Baptist
2	Lambeth + BL	Lectures on confirmation turned into q + a as a follow-up to PBC; Norfolk
6?	C5444A–46A + *TC* ii. 529	Mid; PBC; uses Palmer's method (q.v.); for those of 'meanest capacities + weakest memories'; advert in 1686 edn. refers to its success with young children + ignorant country people; Yorkshire; price of 1681 edn. (2 sheets) 2*d.*; in 1694 cost 3*d.*
(5?)	C5450–1 + BL	From 2nd edn. this devotional, pre-comm. work also has an essay on the 'office' of catechism; the same essay probably also appeared in *A treatise on the sacrament* (1699), *TC* iii. 115, which cannot be traced
(8?)	C5481–3 + ESTC	A dialogue between a 'popish priest' and a Protestant on the usual matters in dispute; said to be 'seasonable for all Protestant families'
1	University of Illinois at Urbana	Covers section of PBC on Lord's Supper only; also has a form of examination, + suitable prayers
(1)	BL	Dialogue between a clergyman + a layman over the liturgy; in answer to S.D.'s *Abridgement of the controversy*

1	2	3
anon.	The communicant's catechism	1680
anon.	The communicant's instructor or a sacramental catechism	1692–1726
anon.	The compleat English tutor ... with a short catechism	1703
anon.	The conditions of obtaining salvation	1717–39
anon.	Confessio fidei ... cum catechismo	1656
anon.	The confession of faith together with the larger and lesser/shorter catechisms	1649–
Cooke, Thomas	A brief but plain explication of the church-catechism	1706
Coote, Edmund	The English schoolmaster	1596–1700
Cordier, Mathurin	Colloquiorum scholasticorum libri quatuor	1584–1725–
Cotes, William	A dialogue of diverse quections [*sic*]	[1585]
Cotton, Clement	The converts catechisme	1616
——	The sicke mans ABC	1629–55
Cotton, John	The doctrine of the church	1642–4
——	[Spiritual] Milk for babes drawn out of the breasts of both Testaments	1646–72
Cotton, W., B. D.	A new catechisme drawn out of the breasts	1648
anon.	The country-gentlewoman's catechism	[1710?]

4	5	6
1?	*TC* i. 392	Pre-comm.? (no copy survives); for the full information of all true believers; price 6*d*.; perhaps T. Warmestry, *The communicants guide* (W881A–B)
—	—	See below, s.v. G. Day
1?	*TC* iii. 349	How to teach reading + writing, but includes prayers + a 'short' catechism; price 1*s*.; not traced
3?	BL	Short; not the usual staples; simple vocabulary; echoes of WSC but conditional on salvation; prayers at end; suitable for Charity Schools
—	—	See below, s.v. Westminster Assembly
—	—	Ditto
1	Bodleian	Mid; PBC with extra qs + as, + scripture proofs; designed for use in 2 London grammar schools by a minister who had been educated at the one + was examiner of the catechumens at the other; copies priced 3*d*. or 20*s*. per 100
49+?	5711–16.5 + C6067–78A	Best-selling textbook: contains a very short catechism (Dec, Cr, Ss, Pr), a prayer framed round that form, other prayers, improving verses, religious texts to copy, etc.
[20+]	5759.1–61, C6285A–90C + BL	Improving dialogues for use in school; Swiss origin; also sold moderately well in English translations by J. Brinsley (1614) + C. Hoole (1657)
<1>	5829	Long dialogue-catechism: son asks + father replies at length; covers Dec, Cr, Pr, Ss
1	5847	Advanced account (through short questions + very long answers) of 7 divine graces (faith, hope, love, etc.); for converts being tempted by the devil
7?	5852–3 + C6405A–B	Short form for the sick; added to last 7 edns. of Cotton's *None but Christ*
3	C6428–30	Very short: on the nature of a visible church; American origin
3+	C6443, 6462–3	Short form; credal material, Dec, Pr, Ss; for children in New England and elsewhere; American origin, and American edns. under the title *Spiritual milk for Boston babes* (e.g. C6460–1)
1	C6507	Short; has clear parallels with last, but is a discrete work
[1]	National Library of Scotland	Satirical, though less broad than other works in this genre; an answer to *The town-ladies catechism* (not traced, but see below, s.v. *The town-misses catechism*)

1	2	3
anon./ 'The country parson'	The country-parson to the country-people	1712
anon.	The covenanters catechisme	1644–7
Coverdale, Miles	[a catechism on the Creed]	[pre-1540]
Cox, Richard	A short catechisme. Very necessary	1591?–1620
C[radock], S[amuel]	The chief principles of the Christian faith	1665–8
Cradock, William	A discourse of due catechising, and confirming of youth	1718
Craig, John	A short summe of the whole catechism	–1583– [1608?]
[Cragge/Craig, John]	The mother and the child: A short catechisme	1611
[Cranmer, Thomas]	Catechismus, that is to say a shorte instruction	1548
Crashaw, William	Milke for babes. Or, a north-countrie catechisme	–1618–33
——	Meate for men. Or, a principall service	1629
Crathorne, William	A practical catechism	1711–
——	A catholick's resolution	1717
——	An historical catechism	1726
Creffeild, Edward	The great duty of catechising	1712–13
——	A catechistical explanation of the … common-prayer	1713
anon.	The cristall of Christianitie	1617
Crofton, Zachary	Catechizing Gods ordinance	1656–7

4	5	6
1	Mass. Hist. Soc.	Mid; PBC with extra qs + as; an abbreviated version was prepared by another 'country parson': see below, s.v. *A short and plain exposition* (1715)
[2]	C6622–3	Polemical: defence of Solemn League + Covenant in q + a
1?	—	This was ordered to be burnt in 1546: Tudor, 'Religious Instruction', 407
2?	Maunsell, 31 + 5948	Mid; Dec, Cr, Ss, Pr; pre-comm.; for 'all Christians'; Maunsell lists a 1591 edn.
2	Emmanuel College Cambridge + C6746	Mid; some qs + as but bulk is texts under headings such as God, Christ, Trinity; for all who desire to save their souls; followed by 20 practical directions to the same effect
(1)	BL	A sermon (+ interesting comments) on catechizing and confirmation; delivered in Gloucestershire in 1718
7+?	5963–66.5 + Maunsell, 31	Long; for 'common people + children'; not the usual content; Scottish origin, and includes Scottish confession of 1580 at end; Maunsell lists a 1591 edn.
1	5961.5	Mid; said to be 'gathered' out of the last, but often very different: personae are mother + child, and contents include Cr, Ss, Dec, Pr; also has meditations at end; STC² says possibly related to 21496.3: cf. H.S. below
(3)	5992.5–93	Series of little 'sermons' for children + young people, by Osiander, turned into Latin by Justus Jonas the younger; English translation commissioned by Cranmer; variant editions: see *A catechism set forth by ... Cranmer*, ed. D. G. Selwyn (Appleford, 1978), 25–31, 56–65, 78–100
6?	6020–2	Mid; Dec, Cr, Ss, Pr; for country people (1618)/the simplest (1622); prayers at end; Yorks.
1	6019.5	Mid; Ss, but includes defence of infant baptism + kneeling at communion, in q + a for the 'simple'
[1+]	Texas Univ.	Catholic; on the Sundays, feasts, + fasts of the church; 2nd edn. 1749
[1]	National Lib. of Scotland	Controversial: defence of being a Catholic, in the 'plain method' of q + a, for those of ordinary capacity
—	—	See below, s.v. C. Fleury
(2)	Liverpool Univ. + BL	Two sermons, exhorting to the use of the PBC; Suff.
1	BL	A simplified (but still long) version of Clutterbuck (q.v.), for his Suffolk parishioners
—	—	See below, s.v. R.P.
(2)	C6990–1	Treatise, based on sermons given in his London parish, on the importance of catechizing

1	2	3
Crompton, William	An explication of those principles	1633
Crook[e], Samuel	The guide unto true blessedness	1613–50
——	A briefe direction to true happinesse	1613–43
Culverwell, Ezekiel	Questions and answers upon … the way	–1623–48
D., J.	A church-catechism: or brief instruction	1701
D., J. (M.A.)	Feed my lambs. Or, a small systeme of divinity minced into a catechism	1686
D., T. (M.A.)	Zions song for young children	1650
D., T.	The Quakers catechism	1703
anon.	Daniel Ben Alexander the converted Jew of Prague	1621
Davenport, John + Hooke, William	A catechisme containing the chief heads	1659
D[avidson], I[ohn]	A short christian instruction	[1588]
Davies, Roger	An explanation of the principles	1726
[Davis, Francis]	A catechisme, wherin is contained	1612
[Day, George]	The communicant's instructor. Or a sacramental catechism	1692–1700–
——	A persuasive to full communion … in all Gospel-ordinances	1698
Day, John	Day's dyall, or … twelve severall lectures by way of catechisme	1614

4	5	6
1	6057	Very long and fairly advanced; PBC; for householders; based on his own notes; Devon; still on sale in 1658: London, *Catalogue*, sig. L4^v
7	6066–8 + C7228	Long; credal material, Ss, Dec, Pr; Som.
8	6063.2–64 + C7226A	Mid; abridgement of last, 'for the more convenient use of private families'; the 2 works were often bound together
8?	6113.5–18 + 6118.8 + C7567	Very short form, on faith, summarizing the very long *Treatise of faith* for 'the weakest Christians' of which it forms part; the form was published separately once, in 1633; the *Treatise* was still on sale in 1658: London, *Catalogue*, sig. M1^r
—	—	See below, s.v. G. Doughty
1	D34	Short; borrows from other catechisms, especially PBC; Pr, Ss, Cr, Dec; for 'children and young beginners in Christianity'; to be sold in Nottingham + London
1	D94	Parts of the WSC (excluding Dec + Pr) turned into verse
[1]	BL	Satirical: anti-Quaker (and anti-Presbyterian)
1	6266	Gives a translation of Daniel's letters to other Jews, an account of his conversion (+ rejection of Catholicism) in France, and then the very short catechism he learnt
1	D357	Mid; modified WSC (no Pr); American origin
1	6173	Short form (Dec, Cr, Ss, Pr) with 2 very short summaries; first used in a private family, now offered to other flocks + families; Scottish origin? A much longer version was published in Edinburgh in 1602 as *Some helpes for young schollers* (STC^2 6324.5)
(1)	BL	26 short 'discourses' on successive portions of PBC; then more discourses on confirmation + other topics, and prayers; Pembrokeshire?
(1)	6368	20 'sabbath exercises' for children to learn: partly controversial dialogues between 'Protestant' and 'Papist' on Cr + Pr
2+	D459D–60	Long; pre-comm., but also tackles baptism as the other seal of the covenant of grace; Scottish edn. in 1726
1	D461	Includes 2 very short forms, one (incorporating parts of WSC) aimed at persuading unbaptized adults to be baptized, the other at persuading baptized ones to communicate regularly; published posthumously by W. Bates + G. Hammond
(1)	6425	12 catechetical lectures given in Oriel College Oxford in 1612–13 by Day acting as 'catechism reader' for a

1	2	3
Deacon, J.	Compendious catechisme	*c*.1600
Defoe, Daniel	D'foe's answer to the Quakers catechism	1706
[——]	A new catechisme	1710
——	The family instructor	1715–34–
——	A new family instructor; in familiar discourses	1727
[Dekker, Thomas]	Satan turned moralist/A new political catechism	1740
[Denhoff, Jan Kazimierz]	The poor mans library/A short historical catechism	1730–2
Denison, Stephen	A compendious catechisme	[*c*.1618]–1632
Denne, Henry	A conference between a sick man and a minister	1642–3
Dent, Arthur	A plain/short exposition of the articles	1589–1616
——	The plaine mans pathway to heaven [part 1]	1601–82
——	The plaine-mans pathway to heaven. The second part	1609–12
——	A pastime for parents/ A recreation	1606–37
——	The opening of heaven gates	1610–24

4	5	6
		year; each lecture was based on a scripture text, only 2 of which covered staples (Pr, Dec); advanced standard
(1?)	*TSR* iii. 157	Probably the *Dialogicall discourses* (1601) by Deacon + J. Walker: dialogues on the nature of 'spirits + devils' and how to cope with them
(1)	Bodleian	A reply to the work by F. Bugg (q.v.)
—	—	See below, s.v. M. Tindal
(11+)	BL	A series of moralistic dialogues, built round a story-line + supplemented by author's comments, which highlight the gap between religious profession + practice at the time; a 2nd vol., (on family relations) appeared in 1718; 4th edn. (of original vol.) was published in Glasgow in 1717; 19th edn. 1809
(1)	BL	10 dialogues between a father + his children: 6 anti-Catholic, 4 against deists, atheists, Jews, etc.; also a poem in blank verse on Christ's divinity
[2]	BL	A purely political work by the Elizabethan dramatist, given a new title in this reprint
[2]	BL + Bodleian	Catholic: pt. 1 consists of 29 'historical' lessons, + 27 doctrinal lessons (faith, hope, charity, Cr, Pr, Dec, Ss) each prose paragraph being followed by short qs + as to test understanding; pt. 2 has controversial material, but not in q + a, and pts. 3–4 consist of prayers, meditations, hymns + psalms
7?	6599–600	Mid; 1st surviving edn. (1621) is 3rd, enlarged; work entered 1618; for children + servants to learn pre-comm.; Ss, Cr, Dec, Pr; London?
(2)	D1015A–16	Dialogue on assurance, for the sick; Herts.; part 2 of 2nd + 3rd edns. of *The doctrine + conversation of John Baptist* (D1017–9)
6?	6625.3–25.8	Mid; 'gathered' by Dent for 'the simple'; some conversational features; covers Creed only; Essex
(33?)	6626–37 + D1052B–56A	Very long dialogue for 'the ignorant + vulgar sort'; on salvation, + how to see if one is saved or damned. A Welsh edition, *Llwybr hyffordd yn cyfarwyddo*, appeared in 1630: 6639
<2>	6637.5–38	Long dialogue, for the 'ignorant', but covers Dec, Cr, Ss, Pr; published posthumously by W.S.
(5)	6622–5	Long dialogue for parents to use with their children for recreation; apart from Ss, not the usual content; answers often long + quite hard
(5)	6619–21	Long dialogue between 'Reason' + 'Religion' on predestination + free will; for those of 'weakest capacity' as well as the stronger; published posthumously

1	2	3
——	A learned and fruitfull exposition upon the Lords prayer	1612–24
Dent, Joseph	A short catechism for the instruction of persons	–1731 (Lincoln)
D[ering], E[dward] + More, John	A brief and necessary [catechisme or] instruction	1572–1614
Dering–More, + Stockwood, John	A short catechisme for housholders with praiers/[and] the prooves of the scripture	1580–1634
anon.	Desiderius, or the original pilgrim: a divine dialogue	1717–25–
De Witte, Petrus	Catechizing upon the Heidelberg catechism	[1664]–[after 1683] (all Amsterdam)
anon.	A dialogue between a young divine, and an old beggar	1683
anon.	A dialogue between riches, poverty, godliness	1659
anon.	A dialogue between Satan and a young man	1700
anon.	A dialogue betwixt two Protestants	1685–
anon.	A dialogue or communication	1554 (Rouen)
D[ickenson], W[illiam]	Milke for babes. The English catechisme ... briefly explained	1628
anon.	A discourse concerning the lawfulness ... of keeping	1708
Dochant, George	A new catechism short and plain	1654

4	5	6
(3+)	6617–18.5	Long exposition of Lord's Prayer, word by word; only the occasional question or objection
2?	Trinity Coll. Cambridge	Short; unusual content; for children especially; followed by religious verses; Baptist? Lincs.
13+	6679–82.3	Original form largely by More, but published in collaboration with Dering (P. Collinson, *A Mirror of Elizabethan Puritanism* (1964), 9–10) who signed the first preface; by 1573 the form had been extensively revised (by whom is not clear), and this was the version used thereafter. Short; Dec, Cr, Ss, Pr; said to be for householders, but see next; prayer at end summarizing catechism; Dutch edn. in 1590
27?	6710.5–24.5	The form is the 1573 version of last, but with full scripture proofs added by Stockwood (after the 3rd edn. these were abridged); ABC printed on reverse of title–page in pre-1606 edns., but then banned; prayers at end; still on sale in 1658: London, *Catalogue*, sig. M3ʳ
(3+?)	BL	Pious narrative in which characters occasionally speak; Spanish origin
[3?]	W3224–24A	Very long; Heidelberg with extra qs + as, translated for the English Reformed congregation in Amsterdam; there is some doubt over the date of the 1664 edn. in BL
(1)	D1300aA	An uplifting dialogue between a beggar who has achieved spiritual contentment + a young divine who wishes to attain it
(1)	D1322	Allegorical tale, told in the 3rd person, with some dialogue between characters like Godliness, Labour, + Content
—	—	See below, s.v. J. J.
—	—	See below, s.v. J. Rawlet
[1]	10383	Very short, simple form for 2 children or 'unlettered folks'; printed at the end of *A dialogue or familiar talk between two neighbours*—a long, polemical, anti-Catholic dialogue
1	6822	Mid; PBC with extra qs + as, notes, reasons, explanations, + texts; for the 'younger and more unlearned sort' of his Berkshire parishioners
<1>	BL	Dialogue-catechism, perhaps used orally (see p. 24), on the legality + necessity of keeping Christmas + other holy days; 'intended for the use of a charity-school'
1	D1757	Very short pre-comm. form, for the younger sort (+ especially those at 'Shaffham School', Norf.)

1	2	3
anon.	Dr. Sacheverels catechism	1710
anon.	The doctrine of the Bible … by way of questions and answers	1602–1726–
anon.	The doctrines of the Christian religion	1708
Dod, John + Cleaver, Robert	A plaine and familiar exposition of the ten commandements	1603–62
——	A brief dialogue concerning preparation	1609–61
Doolittle, Thomas	A treatise concerning the Lords Supper	1667–1726
——	The young man's instructer, and the old man's remembrancer	1673
[——]	Catechism made practical	1688
——	Catechizing necessary for the ignorant young and old	–1692
——	Scheme of the Assemblys catechism printed in a single sheet	pre-1693
——	A plain method of catechizing	1698–1700/1
——	A complete body of practical divinity	1723

4	5	6
[1]	Lilly Lib. Indiana Univ.	Most unusual: polemical in intent?
34+	3022.7–32.5, D1771A–73B, + BL	A cross between a catechism + a teaching aid for Bible study: mainly a digest of the Bible, chapter by chapter, but some doctrines, lessons + duties are stressed; 31st edn. (1698) cost 18*d*. (*TC* iii. 103); for a parallel series entitled *The way to true happinesse* (1610–[50?]), see below
1	Bodleian + Union Theological College Belfast	Long; WSC with propositions and proofs (in standard type-face) and extracts from WLC (in smaller type-face) interspersed; for 'beginners' + families, but the WLC extracts to be tackled only by those 'well versed' in the WSC
(21?)	6967–79 + D1786A	Very long exposition of Dec; from 1604 a version of Cartwright's 'Methodicall short catechisme' (q.v.) was printed at the end
10+?	6935.5–7, 6944.7–49, + D1788	Mid; pre-comm. form 'taken for the most part' out of Dod + Cleaver's *Ten sermons*, and often printed at the end of that work as well as separately; section on Dec is largely exposition
<27+>	D1899–1905A + BL	A pre-comm. treatise, with some rhetorical qs + as 'to excite us to greater diligence'; also has 3 dialogues, 1st of which is designed to inform the weak more fully in the nature + use of the sacrament (similar to other catechisms in style + content); other 2 are more specialized; price in 1670 1*s*. bound
1	D1906	Very long; modified WSC; uses various methods including Palmer's (q.v.); based on a 'catechetical exercise' in London in which he explained the WSC; for masters, etc., to use with children + 'the more ignorant sort of people'; also attacks various erroneous doctrines + offers 'practical applications'
—	—	Attribution dubious; see above under *Catechism*
(3?)	D1882	A short defence of catechizing, and exhortation to be catechized, in q + a, plus further exhortation in prose
1?	—	Referred to in anon., *Earnest call* (1693) (q.v.), 4; not traced; presumably a diagramatic summary of WSC for displaying on a wall
4	D1889–91 + *TC* iii. 237, 265, 280	3 forms: 1st similar to that in *Catechizing necessary*, 2nd an enlargement of it, + 3rd a very long form similar to that of 1673 (modified WSC, various methods used); price in 1698 1*s*.
1	BL	Very long; originally lectures on WSC, turned into hybrid work: partly devotional, partly catechetical

1	2	3
anon./ 'Cordiall well-wisher'	A door opening into Christian religion	1662
'Doresh, Nee-man'/A lover of truth	An impartial catechism	1733
Doughty, G. / 'J.D.'	A church-catechism: or brief instruction in the faith	1701
'Doulye, George'	A briefe instruction	1604–37
Downame, John/[Sir Henry Finch]	The summe of sacred divinitie	1599–[1620?]
Downame, John	A treatise tending to direct a weak Christian	1645
Downe, John	A short catechisme	1635
——	Instructions for preparation unto the holy communion	1635
Downing, Thomas	The catechisers holy encouragement	1623
Draxe, Thomas	An appendix … touching the doctrine, nature and use of the sacraments	1608
——	The sicke-mans catechisme	1609
——	The Christian armorie	1611
Drélincourt, Charles	Catéchisme ou instruction familière	1697–1708
——	A catechism: or, familiar instructions	1698
[Dudgeon, William]	A catechism founded upon experience and reason	–1739

4	5	6
1	D1909	Extremely long 'directory' 'in the manner of a catechism', for more advanced, adolescent catechumens; credal material, Pr, Dec, + Ss; perhaps by J. Goodwin, q.v.
(1)	TCD	Partly controversial; by a rationalist, non-Calvinist dissenter?
1	Bodleian	Mid; the attribution to Doughty is in a MS note on the Bodleian copy; covers scriptures, Dec, credal material, + church ordinances in a mixture of short qs, long as, reasons, + uses; Congregational
—	—	See below, s.v. William Warford
(3?)	7148, 10872.5–72.7	Very long exposition, trying to provide a touchstone for faith; Downame was only the editor; not in q + a but this was possibly the 'catechism' referred to by I. Bourne in 1646 (see also next)
(1)	D2077	Very long, pre-comm. form but not in q + a, though perhaps cited in 1646 by I. Bourne, q.v., as an example of English catechizing; prayers + 'ejaculations' at the end; still for sale in 1658: London, *Catalogue*, sig. M2^r
1	7153–53.3	Published posthumously in Downe's collected works; very short; Dec, Cr, Ss, Pr
1	7153–53.3	Published as last; very short; pre-comm.
(1)	7158.5	Mid dialogue: an exhortation to 'the profitable exercise of catechizing in the Church of England'
1	7185	Short; Ss; an appendix to an exposition of Matt. 25: 10 entitled *The lambes spouse*; Coventry + Lichfield diocese?
1	7186	Long; in q + a but part of the 'godly dying' genre; partly derived from L'Espine + Perkins
1	7182	2 books, both long; qs + as mainly on Christians finding comfort in affliction
(2)	D2159A + BL	3 forms in French, written for use in his own family: a long (Cr, Dec, Pr, Ss); a short (an epitome of the long for little children); + a very short with additional material for older catechumens
1	D2159	Translation of the last, by a French woman, who claimed it was broader than English forms; said to be useful for older as well as younger catechumens; printed for the author; see also, s.v. T. Wise below
2?	BL	Short; 'collected' by a father for his children; based on 'natural' religion + morality

1	2	3
Dudley, Lady Jane	An epistle of the ladye Jane/ The life, death and actions of ... lady Jane Gray	[1554?]–1636
anon.	The Duke of M catechism	1709
anon.	The Dutchess of M. catechism	1709
Du Ploiche, Pierre	A treatise in Englishe and Frenche	[1551]–78
Dyke, Jeremiah	A worthy communicant	1635–96
——	The grounds of religion by way of catechism	pre-1658
Dyke, William	A treasure of knowledge	1620
E., A.	The watch-mans lanthorn	1655
E., G.	The Christian schoole-maister	1613
[E., R.]	A scriptural catechism	1676–1729
anon.	An earnest call to family-catechising	1693
anon.	An easy method of instructing youth	1715 (Oxford)–1728 (London?)
Eaton, Samuel	A catechism book	—
Egerton, Stephen	A briefe methode of catechising	1594?–1671

4	5	6
[5]	7279–79.5, 7281–2	Contains what is called a catechism (on 1615 title-page) but is really an account of a public debate between Lady Jane Dudley + a Catholic priest in the Tower on the usual points of debate between Protestant + Catholic
[1]	BL	Political
[1]	Bodleian	Political; 'written by a lady of St. James's'
(3)	7363–4	Very short; PBC in English + French on opposite pages followed by prayers + more secular material; a means of learning French quickly?
<1>	7429–31, D2961–66 + *TC* ii. 606	To the 17th edn. was added an instructive, reassuring dialogue between minister + parishioner on the Lord's Supper; see also next
?	—	London lists this separately from the last in his *Catalogue*, (sig. M2ᵛ), but it has not been traced, either separately or in Dyke's *Works* (1635)
1	7431.5	Long; credal material, Dec, Ss, Pr; derivative?
<1>	E2	Long dialogue-catechism, originally intended for use in author's family; covers the scriptures, Dec, Cr, + Pr
1	7433	Mid; slightly modified version of Bastingius's translation of Heidelberg (see STC² 1562–); prayers + graces at end
7?	E32–4 + 36, *TC* ii. 582, iii. 43–4, 86, + BL	Mid; pt. 1 contains credal material, pt. 2 consists of R. Allestree's *The whole duty of man* condensed + turned into q + a; also has prayers at end; R.E. signs epistle dedicatory of 1678 + 1682 edns.; attribution to Fowler by Wing² (F1714B) perhaps based on Fowler's recommendation of some edns. e.g. 1696, 1729 (though cf. G. Burnet, *Exposition*, 1); price of 1678 + 1696 edns. 6*d.*; 10,000 copies said to have been sold by 1698
(1)	E95	Mid; exhortation to catechize, but of interest on practice too
12?	Univ. of Illinois at Urbana	Long; mixture of exposition of + extra qs + as on PBC, comprising a carefully designed course of study, in 40 sections, to help develop understanding of the PBC; prayers at end
—	—	Mentioned in E[dw.] B[urrough], *Some false principles* (1659); not traced
45?	Maunsell, 31–2, 7527.9–36.4 + E252–52A	Maunsell lists a 1594 edn.; original edns. later abridged + simplified; in its best-selling version (from 1610s to 1630s) this work consisted of 6 forms: 1 short, 5 very short, of varying kinds (see Appendix 2); prose rules + verses at end

1	2	3
anon.	The elements of the beginning of the oracles	1619
Ellesby, James	A short essay of catechism upon the holy sacrament	−1695?−1705
Ellis, Clement	A catechism wherein the learner	1674
——	Christianity in short	1682–99 (London + Nottingham)
——	The communicant's guide	1685
——	The lambs of Christ fed with the sincere milk of the word	1692–1700
——	The summe of Christianity	1696–9
——	The scripture catechist	1738
Ellis, Tobias	The English school	−1680
Elton, Edward	A forme of catechising	1616–34
——	An extract or short view	1624–34
——	A plaine and easie exposition of sixe of the commandments	1619–23
——	Gods holy mind touching matters morall ... Also Christs holy mind touching prayer	1625–48

4	5	6
1	7569	2 forms: a very short for young children, and a mid (Cr, Ss, Dec, Pr); instructions + prayers at end. By T.A. (*TSR* iii. 645)?
3?	Advert (see col. 6) + *TC* iii. 368, 456	Pre-comm., for 'the ignorant + younger sort of people'; first mentioned in advert at end of Seller's *Exposition of the church-catechism* (q.v.); presumably the same as *An essay by way of catechism* (1695), *TC* ii. 555, price bound 6*d.*; no copies survive
2?	E550–50A	Long; for use after PBC, by those who have been reading the Bible for some years; content partly unusual, + heavily scriptural answers; published with a short treatise on faith, + the chief heads of faith in verse; to be sold in London + Nottingham; price bound 8*d.*
(4)	E552aA–53	Exposition of catechetical material on faith and a godly life, handled in a variety of ways (but not q + a); for his Notts. neighbours who lack the 'time or capacity to read longer + learneder discourses'
(1)	E554	Pre-comm. treatise, but includes a number of qs for the 'poorer + weaker sort of Christians' to use in self-examination before communicating
2	E564–4A +	Long; as in 1674 form, answers are scripture texts, but this is a very different form, with some WSC parallels; 1692 copies to be sold in both London + Mansfield, Notts., price 6*d.*
(2)	E573A–73B	Short exposition of catechetical material, plus form of engagement to keep baptismal covenant, + prayers; same target as 1682 work; price (1699) 3*d.*
1	BL	Very long; PBC with extra qs + as + explanations; for families; published posthumously
(5+)	E607–7A	Reading primer which tries to take children from their ABC to the 'first principles' of religion, but not in q + a
10?	7615–18	Long; based on 6 principles, which cover credal material, Dec, Ss, Pr; prayers at end of later edns.; London
5?	7616–18	Short summary of above, printed in later editions of that work
(1)	7620–20.5	Catechetical lectures on the 1st 6 commandments; for the fate of the expanded text, see S. B. Lewkowicz, 'Elton's *An exposition of the ten commandements*', *Papers of the Bibliographical Soc. of America*, 71 (1977), 201–8
3	7619 + E650cA–50A	2 forms in 1 work printed with continuous signatures: 1st a very long + fairly advanced form on all 10 commandments; 2nd a long form on Pr; a preface by

	1	2	3

Emlyn, Thomas   Letter to Dr Waterland   1730

Emmanuel College Cambridge Library MS III. 1. 13[8]

Emmanuel College MS III. 1. 14

[England, Church of]	Articuli, de quibus in synodo Londiniensi/Liber quorundam canonum disciplinae	1563–1636
anon.	The English teacher. Or the ABC enlarged	1623
anon.	Eniautos: or a course of catechizing	1664–85?

| Erasmus, Desiderius | Christiani hominis institum/Institutum Christiani hominis | 1520–56 |
| ——— | A playne and godly exposytion | 1534, 1726 + [1733?] |

E[rrington], A[nthony]	Catechistical discourses	1654 (Paris)
anon.	An essay by way of catechism on confirmation	1709
anon.	An essay by way of catechism	1695
Evance, Daniel	A baptismal catechisme	1655
anon.	An exercise against lying	1715–
anon.	An exhortation to catechising	1655
anon.	An explanation of the Assembly of Divines shorter catechism	1689–95

4	5	6
		Thomas Gataker praised Elton's skill in resolving cases of conscience; in 1658 London seems to have had copies with a catechism added: *Catalogue*, sig. M3^v
(1)	BL	Controversial: part of the controversy over Samuel Clarke's *Exposition* (q.v.)
		Dating from late 1620s or later, this contains some anonymous catechetical works, on predestination, the Lord's Prayer, the Law, and the Gospel of a broadly catechetical nature (though not in q + a), as well as those mentioned in this list by name, where this was stipulated in the manuscript: see Hopkins, Mayden, Richerson, + Tuckney, and also 'Of catechisinge'
		This also handles catechetical material, especially the Decalogue, but again not in q + a; author had access to a copy of Lancelot Andrewes's catechetical lectures, q.v. above
(5+)	10035–8	Among the works recommended for catechumens at Oxford to read, in 1579 (see above, p. 197); an English edition was reprinted much more frequently: STC^2 10038.3–61
—	—	See below, s.v. J. Mayer
4?	E3125–26A + *TC* ii. 131	Very long; PBC with extra qs + as, scripture proofs, + occasional interjections by the minister to explain, exhort, pray, or recommend further reading; divided into 52 sections, the last 5 of which defend church discipline + worship; derived from 'orthodox + practical expositions' of the PBC; 1674 edns. also contain 84 engravings, first used in other works; price bound 4*s*.
(4)	10450.2–50.5	Colet's catechism (see above, p. 16) paraphrased in verse for students to learn at St Paul's School + elsewhere
<3>	10504–504a, Huntington Lib. San Marino, Calif. + BL	English translation of his *Dilucida et pia explanatio symboli*; very long dialogue on Cr + Dec, with a brief treatment of Pr; in early 18th century there were 2 reprints
[1]	E3246	Polemical: anti-Protestant; not q + a
—	—	See above, s.v. H. Colman
—	—	See above, s.v. J. Ellesby
1	E3441	Short, partly controversial work on infant baptism
1+	BL	A very short q + a form for use in Charity Schools on the sinfulness of lying + the dreadful fate of liars
(1)	E3867	Exhortation to catechize + to use the Westminster Catechisms; issued by the Provincial Assembly at London in August 1655
—	—	See above, s.v. S. Angier

1	2	3
anon.	An explanation of the terms, order and usefulness of the liturgy	1692–1717
anon.	An explicatory catechism	1673–
anon.	An explicatory catechism: or, an explanation of the assemblies shorter catechism. Wherein those principles are enlarged	1675
anon.	An exposition of the church-catechism	1695–
anon.	An exposition of the preliminary questions and answers	[1730?]
anon.	An exposition on the church-catechism	1685–
anon.	An exposition on the church catechism by way of question and answer	1688
F., I.	The necessitie and antiquitie of catechising	1617
F., J.	A compendious chatechisme	1645
F., J.	A most breefe manner of instruction	[*c*.1585]
anon.	The faith and practice of the Church of England	–1719
anon.	A familiar and Christian instruction	1582
anon.	Familiar instructions about predestination and grace. By way of question and answer	1714
Farquhar, George	Love's catechism	1707
Farrow, Benjamin	A practical exposition of the catechism	1708
anon.	A farther instruction for those who have learnt the church catechism	–1708
Featley, Daniel	The hand-maid to private devotion: the second part/The summe of saving knowledge	1625–6
Fenner, Dudley	The groundes of religion	[1590?] (Middelburg)

4	5	6
3+	E3886–86A + DWL	Short; explanation + defence, in q + a, of the official liturgy, 'to be learned after the church catechism'; Scottish edn. 1710
—	—	See below, s.v. T. Vincent
1	Bodleian + St. John's College, Cambridge	Different prefaces, text + publisher from the similarly titled work by T. Vincent, q.v.; MS note in Cambridge copy suggests this is perhaps the work of John Wood, fellow of St John's; very long (bound 1*s*. 6*d*.); WSC with extra qs + as
—	—	See below, s.v. A. Seller
1	BL	Mid; PBC with extra qs + as, but to be read out loud or listened to rather than memorized; has a strong stress on the covenant of grace; not the same as similarly entitled work by Assheton (q.v.)
—	—	See below, s.v. T. Ken
1	*TC* ii. 237 + Trinity Coll., Cambr.	Mid; PBC with extra qs + as (which contain 'the substance of larger expositions') + scripture proofs; for the use of a 'private parish'
(1)	10641	Exhortation to catechize, in q + a
1	F29	Very short; pre-comm.
1	11238	Short; for the 'simpler sort', young + old; Dec, Cr, Pr; attribution to John Foxe probably erroneous; perhaps by John Field
2?	BL	Mid; PBC with extra qs + as; for the 'meanest capacities'; divided into 52 sections
(1?)	16814 but cf. Maunsell, 31	Not in q + a; Pr, Cr, Dec, Ss; French origin; translated by G[eorge] C[hapelin], gent. Maunsell states there was a 1581 edn.
[1]	BL	Catholic; French origin, possibly Jesuit (see BL copy), since author attacks both Jansenists + Protestants; layperson asks, divine answers
[1]	BL + Bodleian	Satirical: witty, but not a parody of a well-known catechism
(1)	BL	Very long exposition of PBC in 30 'lectures'; Lincs.?
1	Lambeth	Short; a follow-up to PBC, on the church's festivals + fasts, built around the Cr; for use in Charity Schools; published by Joseph Downing (see *Account* and *Order*); price 1*d*. or 6*s*. a 100
3?	10725–6, 10739	Mid; not the usual content: strong stress on duties; in 52 sections; printed in 1625 + 1626 as part 2 of *Handmaid* and in 1626 separately
[1]	10768.5	Very short; pre-comm.; part of a larger work: *A brief treatise upon the first table*

1	2	3
Fenner, William	The spirituall mans directory	1648–58
Fenton, Edward	So shorte a catechisme, that whosoever cannot	[*c*.1582]–1662
[Field, John]	An answer to a catechism against Quakerism	1693
anon.	The first book for children: or, the compleat school-mistress	[1705?]
anon.	First catechisme touching the sacraments	1632–45
anon.	First principles of the oracles of God	1712 (Norwich)
F[isher], E[dward]	A touch-stone for a communicant	1647
F[ist], M[artin]	A briefe catechisme of Christian religion	[1624]
Flavell, John	The seaman's catechism	1677–1733
——	An exposition of the Assemblies catechism	1692/3–1702
[Fleetwood, William]	The reasonable communicant	1704–*c*.1730–
Fleury, Claude	An historical catechism	1726
[Fleury, Claude]/'A clergyman'	An historical catechism	1740
Fogg, Lawrence	Two treatises. I. A general view ... II. An entrance into the doctrine ... by catechetical institution	1712–14 (Chester)
John Fountein/de la Fontaine		—

4	5	6
4?	F702–4 + republished in *Works* (1657)	Mid; 185 qs + as, with heavy reliance on scriptural texts in the answers; Cr, Dec, Pr; some echoes of PBC at the start, some anti-Catholic points later
12?	10787.2–89.5 + F718–18B	Best-selling of the very short forms; pre-comm.; see also D.B. above
(1)	F860A	Reply to a work by N.N. (not traced); to remove misunderstandings about Quakerism
1	Lilly Lib., Indiana Univ.	Designed to teach spelling + reading, but also to instruct children in 'the grounds of the Christian religion', in a catechism; see also below, s.v. *Second book*
—	—	First of the forms in W. Twisse, *Exposition*, q.v.
1	Bodleian	Mid; PBC with extra questions, to test understanding, linked to PBC text by a system of superscript numbers; also has scripture proofs; for those of 'meanest capacities' in 'a country parish in the diocese of Norwich'; also has 2 long prayers at end using phrases from PBC + the Book of Common Prayer
(1)	F1002	Long dialogue (3 personae: a minister, a worthy and an unworthy communicant) to test readiness for reception of the Lord's Supper
1	10921	Mid; mainly on Ss
7	F1171A–73A + BL	Short form urging sailors to be prepared for death; ends with a long exhortation-cum-prayer; published only as part of a larger work: *Navigation spiritualiz'd*; American edn. in 1726
4+	F1160–1 + *TC* ii. 451, + iii. 328	Long; WSC with extra qs + as; finished by 'a ruder hand' (perhaps Increase Mather's) after Flavell's death; long rather than advanced; for Scottish edns. in 1695 + 1714 see Wing + BL
<2+>	BL	Long dialogue between a minister + a parishioner, to be read frequently; explains the nature of the Lord's Supper, + how to prepare for it correctly; 24th edn. published in 1807
[1]	BL	Catholic; French origin; contains 2 forms, only 1 partly in q + a; see next
1	BL	This is an expurgated + revised version of the shorter form in the last + now deemed 'necessary for all families' in the Church of England
3?	BL	Pt. 1 is a general view of Christianity in 8 positions, adapted to the 'vulgar capacity' of those in his Cheshire curacy; pt. 2 is PBC with extra qs + as + explanations, and was also published separately *c*.1712
—	—	See below, s.v. Robert Le Maçon

1	2	3
Food	\<F\>oode for fami\<lies.\> Or, an wholsome houshold discourse	[*c*.1623]
Foord/Foorthe, John	The apostles catechisme	1623
Ford, Simon (of Reading)	A sermon of catechizing	1655
——	A short catechism declaring the practical use	1657
Ford, Simon (of Old Swinford)	A plain and profitable exposition	1684–6
——	The catechism of the Church of England	1694
F[otherby], I.	The covenant between God and man	1596–1616
anon./ [Fowler, Edward]	A catechism containing the substance	1676–93
Fowler, Edward	Scriptural catechism	1696
Fowler, James	The catechism of the Church of England	1678
F[ox], G[eorge]	A catechisme for children	1657–60
——	Catechismus pro parvulis	1660
——	Priests and professors catechisme	1657
—— and H[ookes], E[llis]	A primmer and catechism for children/ Instructions for right spelling	1670–1700
[Foxwell, Nathaniel]	A plain and short catechism	1719
Franke, Walter	The epitome of divinity poetically compos'd by way of dialogue	1655

4	5	6
(1)	11126.5	Only a damaged title-page survives; a dialogue between father + son, presumably about the spiritual food needed in a godly household
1	11128.3	Long; unusual structure: based on 6 'articles' in Heb. 6: 1–2; profitable for all, but especially for the unlearned + those that desire more knowledge; Coventry + Lichfield diocese
(1)	F1481	A sermon on the historical background + necessity of catechizing, giving reasons 'for superiors to teach + inferiors to be' taught, and answers to the most common objections to being catechized; published at the end of Ford's *Dialogue concerning … infant baptisme* (1654–7); Berks.
1	F1502	Mid; defence of infant baptism; 'extracted' out of 2 dialogues by the same author (F1481–2 + 1499)
3?	F1493–4	2 forms: a mid (PBC with extra qs + as and expositions, in 12 parts); and a short (qs based on PBC, but no answers, these to be provided by catechumens from PBC text); for 'the more adult children, + other elderly persons that need it'; F1493A to be sold in Worcester; F1494 a '2nd' edition said to be 'more correct'
1	F1478A	Mid; PBC divided into shorter qs + as; for the 'younger', 'children + servants', especially in his own Worcs. parish
2	10638.5–39.3	Advanced; covers covenant, Cr, Ss, Dec; attribution to Fotherby in BL Catalogue
4	C1468B–70	Mid; not the usual staples; scriptural; prayers at end; attribution to Fowler is in DWL Catalogue
—	—	See above, s.v. R.E.
1	F1729A	Paraphrase of PBC in verse; for youth + children, not critics
4	F1756–56C	Long; for children; unusual content: Quaker
(1)	F1757	Extended version of 1657 form, in Latin; the added portion is partly controversial
(1)	F1882	Polemical: aimed at priests + false Christians
8?	F1883B + F1849–52A	Mid form (not the same as 1657) in a larger work, revised by 1673, designed to teach literacy + religious knowledge to children
1	Congregational Lib. London	Short; for children + youth; not the usual staples; Baptist; London; attribution in Cong. Lib. copy
1	F2075	Mid; qs + as in verse on credal material, Dec, Pr, Ss, in 24 sections; to be read + memorized; author probably a sequestered episcopalian

1	2	3
anon.	The freeholder's political catechism	1733
[Freeman, Samuel]	A plain and familiar discourse	1687–1738
[Freke, William]	A dialogue by way of question	1693
French, Nicholas	Polititians catechisme	1658
anon.	The French king's catechism	1709
anon.	The French prophets new catechism	1708
Frewen, John	Certain choise grounds	1621
anon.	A fruitfull dialogue touching the doctrine of Gods providence and mans freewill	[*c*.1580]
anon.	A fruteful and a very Christen instruction	1547
G., I.	The Christians profession, or a treatise of the grounds and principles	1630
Galloway, Patrick	A cathechisme: conteyning summarely the chief points of Christian religion	1588
Garnier, Jean	A brief and plain confession	[1562]
——/ 'Gardiner, John'	A briefe and cleare confession	1577–83
Gataker, Thomas	A short catechisme for the simpler sort	1624
Gawton, Richard	A short instruction	1612
Gay, William	XI choice sermons ... With a catechisme	1655
G[aynam], J[ohn]	The use and excellency of the church catechism	1709
Gee, Alexander	The ground of Christianitie	1581–1613

4	5	6
[1+]	ESTC	Political; by Henry St John, Viscount Bolingbroke
(2)	F2142 + BL	A dialogue between a minister + a parishioner; designed to provide answers for the people to 'Romish' allegations against the English church
(1)	F2163	A dialogue tackling controversial questions about God + the Trinity, but unusual in that all the replies are taken verbatim out of the Bible
—	—	See below, s.v. Peter Talbot
[1]	Bodleian	Political + satirical; subtitled 'Madam Maintenon's last advice'
[1]	Newberry Lib. Chicago	Controversial + partly satirical; against false prophets in general + 'French prophets' in particular
1	11379	Very long; qs + as with expositions; based on 26 heads of doctrine; for the people of his Sussex parish
(1)	6805.6	Dialogue on providence + free will 'briefly + plainly set forth, as the simplest may easily understand it' (+ epistle by A. Gilby); unfortunately only the title-page survives
1	14106	Contains a modified form of Joye's 1530 'dialogue' (q.v.); short; for children
1	11498	Long; predestinarian + federal; credal material, Dec, Ss, Pr; designed for his own family's use, but now made available to others: for those of 'meanest capacity' to read; many parallels with T. Cartwright's form (q.v.)
1	11542.5	Short; Cr, Dec, Pr, Ss; used by author in the family of a Scottish nobleman then resident in Newcastle
(1)	11621	100 'I believe' statements based on Creed: not in q + a; foreign origin; translated by N. Malbie
(2?)	11620.7 + Maunsell, 32	A different translation of last, by J. Brooke; in his list of catechisms Maunsell notes a 1583 edn. [A third translation, by Bishop John Hooper, was included in J. Baker, *Lectures*, q.v.]
1	11654	Very short form; 40 qs + as, for the younger or simpler sort; pre-comm.; published after a sermon entitled *The christian mans care*; Kent?
1	11697	Short, pre-comm. form revised to include Dec, Cr + Pr; Herts.
1	G397	Long form, in 42 sections; faith and helps to faith (Ss, Cr, Pr, Dec), published with 14 sermons; Herts.
(1)	BL + Bodleian	Exhortation to catechize, with the PBC; dedicated to governors of religious societies; prayers at end
<5>	11696.4–99	A long dialogue-catechism between Paul + Titus, which covers Dec, Cr, SS, + Pr, then more advanced material

1	2	3
Gerardus, Andreas/ 'Hyperius'	Elementa Christianae religionis	1563 (Basle)
——	The foundation of Christian religion	1583
[Geree, John]	A catechisme in briefe questions and answeres	1629–47
Gibbs, Philip	A letter to the congregation ... at Hackney	1737
G[ibson], I[ohn]	An easie entrance into the principall points	1579–81
G[ifford], G[eorge]	A brief discourse	1581–1612
——	A cathechisme conteining the summe	1583–6
Gilbert, Eleazer	The prelatical cavalier catechiz'd	1645
Gill(s), Thomas	[A practical catechism: or,] Instructions for children in verse	1707–[1710?]
Good(e), William	A new catechisme, commanded to be set forth	1645
Goodman, John	A winter–evenings conference between neighbours	1684–1720
Goodwin, John	Philadelphia: or XL queries	1653
——	Thirty queries modestly propounded	1653
——	A catechism, or principal heads of the Christian religion	1665
Goodwin, Thomas	The government and discipline of the churches of Christ	1722
Gordon, Thomas	A new catechism for the fine ladies	1733–40
[Gother, John]	Instructions for children	1698–1704
——	A practical catechism in fifty-two lessons	1701–35

4	5	6
[1+]	BL	Recommended for undergraduates at Oxford in 1579 (see above, p. 197); no edns. in English or published in England are known
1	11756	Only fragments remain: minister-child; derived from Heb. 6: 1–2; German origin; translated by I.H.
2	4800	Short; pre-comm.; Gloucestershire + London? 1st edn. published anonymously, 2nd slightly revised
(3?)	BL	Controversial: Gibbs criticizes explicitly + implicitly a number of answers in WSC; there was a reply by David Millar, q.v., + further *Explications* by Gibbs in 1740
2	11832–3	Short; Dec, Cr, Ss, Pr; for the 'simpler sort'; very short qs + as
(7?)	11845–47.5	Uses dialogue form to attack 'country' (i.e. simplistic, erroneous) 'divinity'
2	11848–48.3	Long + quite difficult; Cr, Dec, Ss, Pr; Essex?
[1]	G706	Polemical: anti-royalist; not really in q + a; designed to encourage parliamentarian troops
3	BL + National Lib. of Scotland	Short or very short (according to format); a verse-catechism, mainly on prayer + Dec, for children; content said to be derived from an existing catechism, but the verse was the work of Gills, the 'blind man' of Bury St Edmunds
2	G1096–7	Short, pre-comm. form, with directions for examining all potential communicants; Norf.
(11?)	G1129–37 + BL	2 dialogues to show the advantages of religious discourses over secular domestic diversions
(1)	G1189	40 rhetorical questions about mixed communion
(1)	G1208	30 rhetorical questions, on the power of the civil magistrate in religious matters
1?	Calamy, *Account*, 53	Not traced; any link to last two, or to *Door*, q.v.?
(1)	BL	A long form, by a leading Independent of the 1640s, on church government + discipline: perhaps part of Goodwin's much larger work on the subject (see *Works* (1861–6), xi. 1–484) turned into q + a; 1722 edn. destined for Notts.
—	—	See below, s.v. U. Price
[2]	G1329fA + BL	Mid; moralistic; part of a series by a Catholic author for different social groups
[3]	BL	A Catholic treatise on Christian behaviour turned into 52 q + a lessons; with a further 19 chapters on the obligations of different social groups

1	2	3
Gouge, Thomas	The principles of Christian religion	1668–75
——	The principles of Christian religion	1679–84
——	The heads of the foregoing catechism	1679–84
[Gouge, William]/ G., W.	A short catechisme/ A briefe method of catechizing	1615–39
——	A briefe abstract of the former catechisme	1635–9
——	Briefe answers to the chiefe articles of religion	–1642
Graie, Henry	A short and easie introduction	1588
Granger, Thomas	The tree of good and evil	1616
Grantham, Thomas	St Paul's catechism	1687–93
Grave, Jean de	The pathway to the gate of tongues	1633 (Oxford)
Greaves, Thomas	A brief summe of Christian religion	1656
anon./[Thomas Greene?]	The principles of religion explain'd	1726–
Greene, Thomas	The sacrament of the lord's supper explained	–1744
Greenham, Richard/C., R. [*recte* G. R.?]	A short forme of catechising/ A brief and necessarie catechisme	1599–1612
——	Godly instructions	1599–1611
Grosse, Alexander	A fiery pillar of heavenly truth	1641–63
Grosvenor, Benjamin	The preservative of virtuous youth	1714

4	5	6
5+	G1371–3	First edns. short; influenced by WSC, but no Cr, Dec, Pr; extended to mid length by 1675; for an edn. in Welsh (1676), see G1369A
4	G1373A–76	Much longer, largely rewritten version of last, heavily influenced in parts by WSC
4	G1373A–76	Very short summary of the last, published at the end of it, but with separate pagination + signatures; for sale at 6*d*. per dozen copies
8+	12126–30.5 + 12110.5 (*Works*)	Mid; pre-comm. but covers Dec + Pr as well; later edns. have a prayer drawn from the form, + most edns. have prayers before + after the catechism
3	12130–30.5 + 12110.5	Very short summary of last, published near end of 1635 + later edns. of it; for 'the younger + ignoranter sort'
4?	G1389	Very short: majority of answers consist of a single word, yet manages to refer to Dec, Cr, Ss, Pr; not the same as the last above
1	12170	Mid; pre-comm., but covers Dec, Pr, Cr, + Ss
(1)	12185	Treatise on Dec; listed as a catechism by Grant, 349, but the work is not in q + a
2	G1545–45A	Mid; based on the 6 'principles' in Heb. 6: 1–2 (cf. Gerardus + Foord above); written for 'growing Christians, children + servants' in all families; author was a General Baptist
(1)	12198	Designed to teach languages to young children: PBC in Latin, English, + French
1	G1805	Short; cross between exposition + catechism, showing the reader how to turn propositions into qs + as; for the 'plain, + unlearned people' in his Lincs. parish
—	—	See below, s.v. *Principles* (1726)
<7?>	BL	A 'familiar dialogue' between a minister + a parishioner, explaining the sacrament to those of 'meanest capacity'; also has prayers at end; first surviving edn. is 7th edn. of 1744, which suggests 1st edn. may have been pre-1740
6	4296, 12312–18 (*Works*)	Mid, but unfinished; Dec, Cr, Pr; for all who seek consolation in Christ; only 1 edn. printed separately in 1602, under the second title; Cambridgeshire
(5)	12312–18 (*Works*)	Ch. 21 provides an account of + exhortation to the 'catechizing + instruction of youth'
10+	G2070–5	Long; mainly on the *ordo salutis* (see Appendix 2); for the direction of 'all sorts of people' to life eternal; Scottish edn. 1735
(1)	BL	Sermon delivered to a society of catechumens in London

1	2	3
Grotius/de Groot Hugo	Hugonis Grotii baptizatorum puerorum institutio	1647–1706
——	The English version of Hugo Grotius his catechisme	1668–82
——	The whole duty of a Christian	1711
anon.	Groundes of godlynes; or sentences of holye scripture	*c.*1601?
anon.	The grounds and principles of religion	1648–
anon.	A guide to young communicants	1691?–*c.*1695
Guild(e), William	A young mans inquisition or triall	1608
Guyse, John	Remarks on a catechism	1735
H., A.	The Jesuites catechism	1679–85
H., J.	The principles of Christian religion	1645
H., P. / 'A reverend divine'	The historical catechism	1706
H., W.	The comunicants examinacion	1634
[Hacket, Andrew]	A catechism or abridgement of Christian doctrine	1725 (London?)
H[acon], J[oseph]	A review of Mr. Horn's catechisme	1660 (Cambridge)
Hall, Eben[ezer]	A guide to the Christian religion	1721 (Boston, Lincs.)

4	5	6
(11?)	G2086–92A + Bodleian	Greek + Latin versions of Grotius's work; early edns. also had translation of it into English, in verse, by Francis Goldsmith; short; credal material, Pr, Dec, Ss
2	G2110–11	Separate publication of Goldsmith's translation
1	BL	Another translation of the original Grotius form; again in verse as well as in q + a
1?	*TSR* iii. 186	Scripture sentences 'set down after the manner of catechism'; not traced: ever published?
—	—	See below, s.v. Westminster Assembly
4?	*TC* ii. 366 + G2187B	Very short pre-comm. form of 12 qs + as, drawn up by Dr J [King?] Bishop of London, but now published to prepare those who wished to be worthy receivers of the Lord's Supper; with prayers for communion days, directions for holy living + dying, a dialogue between a beggar + a divine, + some fillers; said to have been distributed among the poor; price 2*d.* in 1695
(1)	12494	Despite the title, not in q + a; a guide to godly life, based on Ps. 119: 9
(1)	BL + DWL	Detailed rebuttal of the proposed revisions made to the WSC by J. Strong (q.v.); Guyse also printed the original WSC as an appendix
—	—	See below, s.v. E. Pasquier
1	H77A	Short; not the usual staples; intended for use by householders, but described as profitable for all, useful for the young, + plain for those of meanest capacity
1	BL	Mid; short qs + as on the main events + characters in the scriptures and early church; for children to learn before they read the Bible by themselves; published in a modified version by David Bellamy, q.v.
?	*TSR* iv. 325	Not identified; ever published?
[1]	Congregational Lib. London + National Lib. of Scotland	Long; Catholic; place of publication unclear; translated from the French; much larger than the *Short abridgement* of 1728 (q.v.); attributed to Hacket by Nat. Lib. of Scotland
(1)	H177	Long attack on some of the views in J. Horne's *Briefe instruction*; there were two follow-up pieces: *A vindication of the review* (1662) + *A review of a late heterodox catechism* (1668) (Wing² H178, 176); cf. also H2807A
1	New College Library, Edinburgh	Short form + very short abridgement; for all to believe and teach their children; General Baptist; partly controversial; London + Lincs.

1	2	3
Hall, Joseph	A brief summe of the principles of religion	1624–48
[Hamilton], John (archbishop of St Andrews)	A catechisme ... set furthe	1552
[Hammond, Henry]	A practical catechisme	1645–1715
——	Large additions to the practical catechisme	1646
——	A brief vindication of three passages	1648–51
anon.	Handsome F–ng's catechism	1706
Harrington, Sir James	Horae consecratae ... Also, A scripture catechism	1682
Harris, John	The child's catechism fitted for the easier learning the Assemblies	*c.*1700
Harris, Robert	Peters enlargement upon the prayers of the church	–1624–40
Harris, Samuel	Scripture-knowledge promot'd by catechizing	1712
Harris, William	The nature and reasonableness of consideration	1717
Harrison, Joseph	An exposition of the church-catechism after a new method	1708
——	A scriptural exposition of the church-catechism	1718–35–
H[arrison], R[obert]	Three forms of catechismes	1583 (Middelburg)

4	5	6
8?	12635–40, 12706–8 + H361B–62A	Short, but quite full; pre-comm.; regularly published in Hall's collected *Works*, but also on occasion separately: cf. *TSR* iii. 345 *et al.*
[1]	22056	Catholic; not q + a; Scottish origin; covers Dec, Cr, 7 sacraments, + prayer
<21?>	H581–96 + H506–9 + BL	Advanced; dialogue-catechism, based in part on the covenant of grace + the Sermon on the Mount; see next also; although criticized, Hammond's work was still on sale in 1658: London, *Catalogue*, sig. N4^v
<1+>	H544 + as last	Short sections added to above; first published separately, then in all edns. from 1646; combined work covered Dec, Pr, Cr, Ss
(2)	H518–18A	A reply to the attack on his *Practical catechisme* in *A testimony to the truth of Jesus Christ* (by William Jenkyn?)
[1]	Leeds Univ. Brotherton Collection	Satirical; 'written by a club of bullies + misses'
2?	H803E–F	Mainly meditations, but also a scriptural form sent in a letter to the author's wife + children; has no questions, only scripture quotations with marginal headings; unusual content; 1 edn. printed for the author; said to be useful for families + 'as an appendix to catechizing'
?	—	Mentioned in advert at end of 1700 (10th) edn. of John Saltmarsh's *Free grace*; preface by Dr Williams; price 6*d.*; no copy traced, but see above, s.v. *Beginner's catechism*
5?	12840–6	From 5th edn. this sermon on prayer contains a short q + a form on prayer
(1)	BL	Sermon including an exhortation to catechize or be catechized; praises WSC
(1)	BL	Sermon given to a society of catechumens in London
1	BL	Long; PBC with extra qs + as + scripture texts; divided into 18 parts; also prayers at end; for use in Cirencester, Glos.; see next also
2?+	Bodleian + BL	Modified version of last (the 2nd edn. was 'improved'); it was now divided into 52 sections; materials at end (on methods, psalm-singing, etc.) also different; Glos. again; Dublin edn. in 1738 is referred to as 4th edn. improved
[1]	12862.5	Mid, + 2 very short forms (for those who cannot memorize the larger); credal material, Dec, Ss, Pr; the work was banned for asserting that ungodly rulers could be disobeyed

1	2	3
Hart, John	The school of grace	–1675–[88]
[Heasse, Robert]	A chrysten exhortation verye profitable [for those] in agony of death	1566

HEIDELBERG CATECHISM
See above s.v.

E. B.	A catechisme or briefe instruction (1617)	
R. B.	A breife catechisme (1601)	
J. Bastingius	An exposition or commentarie (1589–1614)	
———	A catechisme of Christian religion (1591)	
anon.	Catechesis religionis Christianae (1623–60?)	
anon.	A catechisme of Christian religion (1617–39)	
anon.	The catechisme, or maner to teach (1570?–78)	
anon.	A catechisme, or short kind of instruction (1588)	
anon.	Le catéchisme de Heidelberg (1720)	
De Witte, Petrus	Catechizing upon the Heidelbergh catechism (1664–)	

and below s.v.

anon.	The Heidelberg catechism (1720)	
Ursinus, Z.	Doctrinae Christianae compendium (1585)	
———	The summe of Christian religion (1587)	

anon.	The Heidelberg catechism	1720
Henry, Matthew	A [plain] catechism for children. To which is added another	1700/01?–25–
———	A scripture catechism in the method of the Assemblies	1703–20
———	The communicant's companion	–1706–37–
———	A sermon concerning the catechizing of youth	1713–26–
Herbert, William	Herberts careful father and pious child	1648
Hewit, Peter	A brief and plain explication of the catechism	1704

4	5	6
19?	H959D–95E	Very short form, for children, in a larger work on godly living; Dec, Cr; see also below, s.v. *School*
1	13017	Treatise for the dying, translated by Heasse, but contains short form (minister/sick man) on Creed to be recited by the sick person, followed by prayers by the minister

1	BL	Reprint of Heidelberg, with a title-page and dedication (to George I) making some polemical anti-Catholic points
5+	BL	2 forms: a short to prepare children for learning the WSC, + a very short pre-comm.; edns. also published in Welsh (1708 + 1727), + in America + Scotland, where a '15th' edn. was printed in 1747; 5th edn. cost 2*d.* (ex inf. Stinton, q.v.)
4+	BL	Long; WSC with additional qs + as in the Palmer method (q.v.) + full scriptural citations; Welsh translation (1717)
(12+)	BL	Pre-comm. form, but not in q + a; 18th edn. 1806
(2+)	Huntington Lib., San Marino, Calif. + BL	A sermon in praise of catechizing given to a group of catechumens in London in April 1713; also published in his collected sermons (1726–)
<1>	H1539	Very long (1,200 qs + as); called a catechism, but in many ways nearer a dialogue; composed for author's own infant daughter to learn
1	Bodleian	Mid; PBC with extra qs + as, + proofs; intended to show parents how to teach children to understand rather than just memorize PBC; also has an exhortation to pray + prayers at end

1	2	3
Hewlett, Ebenezer	Mr. Whitefield's chatechise	1739
——	A catechism for Mr. Whitefield and his followers	1740
[Heyden, Cornelis van der]	The ordinarye for all faythfull Chrystians ... A right goodly rule	1548
——	A bryefe summe of the whole Byble	[1549?]–[1550?]
Heydon, John	Some gospel truths catechistically laid down/ Mans badness and Gods goodness	–1647
Heylyn, Peter	The rebells catechisme	1643–4
Hicks, Thomas	A continuation of the dialogue	1673
Hieron, Samuel	The preachers plea	1604–13
——	The doctrine of the beginning of Christ	1604?–58
——	A brief direction for the commers to the Lords table	[1620?]
Hildersham, Arthur	The doctrine of communicating worthily	—
Hill, Robert	Christs prayer expounded/ The pathway to prayer/pietie	1606–41
Hill, William	The first principles of a Christian	1616–[39?]
Hinde, William	A path to pietie	1613 (Oxford)–1626 (London)
'Hinde, William'	A briefe and plaine catechisme	1620
'A reverend divine'	The historical catechism	1706

4	5	6
(1)	BL	Open letter on Methodism; not q + a
(1)	Cambridge Univ. Lib.	Controversial: on various matters. Linked to the last?
(2)	5199.7–5200	Contains a form (not in q + a) on the mutual duties of different social groups, based on scripture texts (+ Luther's catechism); illustrated by woodcuts; also has series of prayers for all occasions; translated by A. Scoloker from the Dutch *Corte instruccye*
(2)	3017–17.5	Contains the form mentioned in the last above
4?	H1679–79A	Long; unusual content; fairly advanced; only 3rd edn. + '3rd edition revised + amended' survive
[3?]	H1731–1B	Political: on the illegality of rebellion
(1)	H1919	Hicks wrote a number of dialogues between a Christian + a Quaker (see H1921–3, 1926–7); but in this one he summarized the dialogue in a 'catechism' to help the memories of those of weaker capacities; the content was still largely controversial
(3)	13419–21	Long dialogue on the value of preaching
17?	Grant, 348, 13399.5–405.5 + in *Works* (13378–) + H1924A	Short; heavily scriptural; unusual content; 'short for memory, plain for capacity'; long list of duties for various social groups at the end; Devon?
1	*Works* (13377.5)	Very short pre-comm. form (13 qs + as)
—	—	Long, pre-comm. form, regularly published with Wm. Bradshaw's *Direction/Preparation*, q.v.
9	13472–77.5 + H2005A	1st 2 edns. have 3 items: a long dialogue (on Pr) a mid (on holy living) + a catechism (short, pre-comm.); in later edns. last of these is enlarged (to mid), + an extra dialogue (on godly dying) added; London?
14?	13503–5.5	Mid; PBC with extra qs + as (making 105 in all); 3 epistles: to fellow-clergy, parents, + children, urging on all the importance of catechizing; work aimed at own charges (in Somerset?: Venn, *Alumni Cantabrigienses*); prayers at end
2	13515–15.5	Mid; mainly Cr, Ss; for his own flock + family in Cheshire
1	13512	Mid; Dec, Cr, Pr, Ss; 197 qs + as, divided into 52 weeks; not the same as last: a pirated edn. (see 1626 edn. of *Path*), or did John Barnes turn over the wrong copy in assignment of rights?
—	—	See P.H. above

1	2	3
Hobson, Paul	A garden inclosed	1647
Hodges, Thomas	A scripture-catechisme	1658 (Oxford)
Hoffman, John	The principles of Christian religion	1653–75
Hole, Matthew	A practical exposition of the first part	–1707
——	A practical exposition of the church catechism	1707/8–31/2
Holland, Henry	The historie of Adam	1606
Hollingworth, Richard (the elder)	The catechist catechized	1653
anon.	Honeymoon. To which are added ... The catechising puritan	1726
Hooker, Thomas	Heavens treasury opened, or a fruitfull exposition/ A briefe exposition of the Lordes prayer	1645
——	An exposition of the principles of religion	1645
'Hopkins, Mr.'	A catechisme by Mr. Hopkins	[1620s or earlier?]
Hopkins, Ezekiel	An exposition on the Lords Prayer ... by way of question and answer	1692–1710
Hopkinson, William	A preparation unto the waye of life	1581–3
Horne, John	Brief instructions for children	1654–6
Horne, Robert	Points of instruction for the ignorant	1613–17

4	5	6
(1)	H2274	Exposition of God's love to the saints; contains a number of qs + as, but mainly rhetorical
1	H2322	Very long; to confute the errors of the past (e.g. Catholic) + the present (e.g. Quaker), but covers conventional material as well; Oxon.?
2	H2348–9	2 forms: 1 short (30 qs + as); 1 mid (on the Bible); Oxon.
(1?)	BL	Discourses on first part of PBC; Somerset; Hole implies an earlier edn. had been published
(3)	BL	Two vol. series of discourses on PBC; derivative; 'useful for all families'
1	13587	Advanced; Dec, Cr; unfinished? Published posthumously by E. Topsell
(1+?)	H2487–87A	Two polemical attacks: on an 'Anabaptistical' catechism published in Lancashire which supported believers' baptism; + on a convert to popery; one edn./impression to be sold in Manchester
[1]	Bodleian	Various salacious verses, including a satirical one about a Puritan + a 'holy sister' who 'a catechising sate' until 'the spirit moved him' to make a trial of her virtue
2	H2650 + 2642	Long (+ with exceptionally long answers); Pr only; the 2 works are essentially the same, despite the different titles, but see next; still on sale in 1658: London, *Catalogue*, sig. O1ᵛ
1	H2647	Mid; pt. 2 of *Heavens treasury*; again unusually long answers; based on 6 principles
MS	Emman. Coll. Lib. MS. III. 1. 13[8]	Credal material, Dec, Ss, Pr; identity of author unclear
4	H2730–1, + NUC (*Works* 1701, 1710)	Mid; covers Pr only, + follows a long exposition of the same, probably first delivered as sermons; said to have been used to examine youth every Sunday that Hopkins was preaching on the Lord's Prayer, perhaps in Exeter, possibly in Ireland to which he moved in 1669
2	13774–5	Long; pre-comm., but has unusual + partly controversial (anti-Catholic) material; epistle seeks the protection of the Lord President of the Council of Wales for the work
2	Emman. Coll. Cambridge + H2795A	Long; credal material, Dec, Ss, Pr; also interesting remarks on technique; attacked by Joseph Hacon (q.v.) for its Arminianism + other errors
2	13822.5 + 13824	1613 edn. was pt. 2 of his *Life and death*, + had 3 short or very short forms, + Dec in 2 different verse versions; 2nd edn. much enlarged by a mid form on Dec + short form on Pr

1	2	3
Horne, William	A Christian exercise	[1585?]–1610
Horneck, Anthony	Questions and answers concerning the two religions	1688–1731
Hoskins, John	A short catechism upon the Lords Prayer [etc.]	1678
Hughes, Lewis	A plaine and true relation of the goodnes	1621
———	The covenant of grace and seales thereof	1640
———	The errors of the common catechisme	1645
anon.	The humble inquiry, by way of catechism	1657
Hunt, Nicholas	The devout christian communicant instructed	1628
Hunt, Richard	A catechisme for christians	'1549'/1649
Hutchins, Robert	A short catechisme	c.1619
Hyperius	See above, s.v. A. Gerardus	
anon.	An impartial catechism	1733
anon.	The Independent catechisme	1647
Inman, Francis	A light unto the unlearned	1622
anon.	An instruction for all those that intend to goe to the ... Lords Supper	1634–46
anon.	The instruction of questions for children of the Lordes supper	c.1558/9
anon.	Instructions for those that never yet receiv'd the holy sacrament	1705
anon.	Instructions for children	1698–1704
anon./ tr. Dorothy Martin	Instructions for Christians	1581
anon.	An introduction to the Catholick faith	1633 (Rouen)
I[saacson], H[enry]	The summe and substance of Christian religion	1646–7
[Isham, Zacheus]	The catechism of the church: with proofs	1694–1735

4	5	6
3?	13826–6.5 + Maunsell, 32	2 forms: 1 very short, 1 mid (Dec, Cr, Ss, Pr); no copy of 1590 edn. by Thomas Woodcock extant
(4?+)	H2848 (+ 2831) + BL	Polemical: anti-Catholic; on the churches of England + Rome; for the use of the younger sort of people; 6th edn. 1760; Dublin edn. 1732, + edn. in French + English 1723
1?	*TC* i. 329	No copy survives, but from description covered Pr, Dec, + Cr; profitable for children + others
1	13920	Mid; on sabbath, worship + Ss; written for the people of the 'Summer Islands' (Bermuda)
1	13918	Long; covers covenant of grace + Ss; also for the Bermudas
(1)	H3316	An attack on PBC in a dialogue between a gentleman + a minister
1	H3418	Mid; Pr only
1	13987	Long; pre-comm., but covers baptism as well as Lord's Supper
2	H3742–3	Short; unusual content; to teach Christians how to live up to their baptismal obligations
?	*TSR* iii. 654	Not traced: ever published?
—	—	See above, s.v. 'Doresh'
1+?	I146	Short; odd; cf. J.C. above; not the same as work by J. Bernard, q.v.
(1)	14090	Catechetical material: 'principles' to be learned, pre-comm.; treated as a catechism by P. Collinson, *Religion of Protestants* (Oxford, 1982), 233, but not in q + a
2	16824 + I234	Single sheet folio; pre-comm.
?	*TSR* i. 97	Not traced; ever published?
1	DWL	Short; extra qs + as on the last 5 qs + as of PBC; pre-comm.
—	—	See above, s.v. J. Gother
1?	Maunsell, 32	Not traced; listed as a catechism by Maunsell; said to contain a 'fruitful + godly exercise'
[1]	14123.5 + Addenda	Includes a different translation of Canisius' *Parvus catechismus* from that in 4568.5 (q.v.)
2	I1059A–60	Long; credal material, Dec, Pr, Ss; been used in private families, but many learned divines + others wish it to be published for public use
13?	I1066–7B, *TC* iii. 327, 485, 516, BL + ESTC	Mid; PBC with scripture proofs + extra qs + as; divided into 12 weekly parts; for use in a London parish; price (1703) 4*d.*

1	2	3
anon.	Itinerarium Iesu Christi: Or, our blessed saviour his journall on earth	1639
J., J.	A dialogue between Satan and a young man	1700
Jackson, John	Epitome … or a taste of truth	1648
Jacob, Henry	Principles and foundations of Christian religion	*c.*1604–5
Jacob, Joseph	The covenant and catechism of the church of Christ meeting at Horsly-Down	1700–2
——	The catechism, or, brief instruction	1702
——	The scripture instructor	1701
Jacombe, Samuel	A short and plaine catechisme	–1657–94
Jagel/Jaghel, Abraham	Catechismus Judaeorum	1679
——	The Jews catechism	1680–1721
Jekyll, Thomas	A brief and plain exposition of the church-catechism	1690–1700
Jenison, Robert	Directions for the worthy receiving	1624
Jenney, George (gent.)	A catholike conference, between a protestant and a papist	1626
Jessey, Henry	A catechisme for babes or little ones	1652
[Jewel, John]	Apologia ecclesiae anglicanae	1562–1639
——	A replie unto M. Hardinges answeare	1565–6
——	A defence of the Apologie	1567–71
anon.	The Jews catechism	1680–

4	5	6
1	14552.3	Long; detailed chronological account of Christ's life, from the Gospels, in q + a; had a specially commissioned engraved title-page
(1)	D1323A	An improving verse-dialogue, published on a broadsheet; by 'a pious young divine', to persuade 'young persons' to resist Satan's temptations to delay repentance
1	J77	Very short form (10 qs + as only, unusual content), followed by mid form (same qs + as with long expositions), then answers to objections; Essex
MS	See col. 6	Printed in C. Burrage, *Early English Dissenters* (1912) ii. 153–61; credal material, Dec, Ss, Pr; Congregational on church composition + control
1+	J99A	The catechism is mid; not the usual staples; divided into 7 lessons; for use in Southwark, London
1	Bodleian + BL	As last, but published separately; a new edn. perhaps planned in 1732 (see BL 1018.f.20)
1?	*TC* iii. 276	Designed to teach literacy, but includes a catechism (possibly related to last, but no copy survives); for children
7?	J109–10	Short; not the usual staples; some later edns. were published anonymously e.g. 4th
(2)	J122A–B	In Latin + Hebrew; controversial; foreign origin
(2)	J122C + Bodleian	Translation into English of the last; 1721 edn. also had a discourse against atheism
5?	J531A–32 + *TC* ii. 407	Long; PBC with extra qs + as; for a 'private' school lately built in London; some anti-Catholic content; prayers at end; price 6*d.* in 1692
1	14490	Mainly pre-comm. 'directions', but has very short pre-comm. form (12 qs + as); Newcastle-on-Tyne?
(1)	14497	Called a catechism in *TSR* iv. 155, but this is a an anti-Catholic dialogue between George (a Protestant) + Philip (a 'papist') on the visible + invisible church
1+?	J686A	Three forms: 1 mid (unusual content) + 2 very short; all aimed at the very young; Baptist; possibly a 2nd edn. in 1673: B. Ritter Dailey, in *Harvard Lib. Bull.* 30 (1982), 54
(7)	14581–9	Recommended to Oxford catechumens in 1579 (see above, p. 197); there was also an edn., in English: STC² 14590–3
2+	14606–7	This + the next were on a list of catechetical works recommended by T. Watts, *Entrie to Christianitie*, q.v.
4	14600–602	See last
—	—	See above, s.v. A. Jagel

1	2	3
Jones, Richard	A briefe and necessarie catechisme	1583–[*c*.1630]–
Jones, William	An exposition of the whole catechisme	1633
Joye, George (tr. + ed.)	[H]ortulus anime. The garden of the soule	1530
anon./Jud, Leo	A shorte catechisme	1550 (Zurich)
K[irby], I./ J[oshua]	A catechisme for the times/A scripture catechism very usefull	1645–6
——	Scripture security for conscience … with a scripture catechism very usefull in these times	1646
anon.	Katechesis kai taxis … Catechismus cum ordine	1685–1732
anon.	Katechesis tes Christianikes pisteos	–1648–55
anon./Harmar, J.	Katechesis tes Christianikes threskeias	1659–98
Kaye, William	The reformed protestant's catechism	1658
Keach, Benjamin	Instructions for children: or the child's and youth's delight	[1664?]–1723–
——	War with the devil	1673–1737–
[——?]	A brief instruction in the principles	[1695]–
——	The child's delight: or instructions for children	–1703–7

4	5	6
5+?	14729–31 + Maunsell, 32	Mid; Paget's form (q.v.) with different expansions of the scriptural proofs to Openshaw's; Jones also has a short pre-comm. form; for householders + families; Cardiff? Maunsell lists a 1589 edn.; 19th edn. 1823
1	14744.5	Long; extra qs + as on PBC drawn from 'many catechisms + learned expositors'; for his flock on Isle of Wight, where he had used it for years; still available in 1658: London, *Catalogue*, sig. 02ᵛ
—	—	See below, s.v. *Primer*
[1]	361	Long dialogue-catechism between teacher + child on covenant, Dec, faith, prayer, + Ss; also a short version of same for younger children; sometimes attributed to Edmond Allen (q.v.) who perhaps translated the German original, *Der kurtzer catechismus* (Zurich, 1541), into English
(2)	K11–12	Controversial: anti-sects; answers are scriptural texts; the 2nd edn. was published as part 2 of next item below; for Kirby, see Calamy, *Account*, 794
(1)	K13	Part 1 covers two 'ranks' of doctrines in 40 qs + as, answers are scripture texts; largely on controversial matters; part 2 is last above
—	—	See above, s.v. *Catechismus cum ordine*
—	—	See above, s.v. J. Calvin
—	—	See below, s.v. Westminster Assembly
1	K40	Mid; qs + as with expositions; Baptist
15+	K72A + BL	A reading primer by a leading Baptist, but also contains three forms (see Appendix 2), for little child, child, + youth, as well as ABC, syllables, precepts + much else; perhaps the same as *The child's instructor*, 1st edn. of which was destroyed by Council order in 1664; 5th edn. published in 1679; 7th edn. recommended to parents + schoolmasters by Hanserd Knollys; some variation of content between edns.; price bound (1704) 6*d.*
(20+)	K103–7 + BL	Contains an instructive uplifting dialogue in verse between a youth and his conscience (other verse dialogues by Keach, in *War with the devil + Grand impostor*, are more controversial)
—	—	See above, s.v. *Brief instruction*
3+	Regent's Park College, Oxford + *TC* iii. 446–561	Like the [1664?] work, this is in essence a reading primer, but contains 1 (mid) form which is a modified version of the most advanced of the 3 in his *Instructions*, q.v.; price 6*d.*

1	2	3
Keith, George	The fundamental truths of Christianity ... by way of question and answer	1688–
——	A Christian catechisme for the instruction of youth and others	1698
——	A short Christian catechisme for the instruction of children	[1698/9]
[Ken, Thomas]	An exposition on the church-catechism; or, the practice of divine love	1685–1718–
——	The church-catechism, with directions for prayer	1685–6
Kettlewell, John	The practical believer	1688–1713
anon.	A key to catechisms	1682
anon./'Philo-delphus'	A key to the church-catechism	1719
Kidder, Richard	An help to the smallest children's more easie understanding	1709
King, Manasseth	A new and useful catechism	–1693–9
anon.	Die kirchen-catechismus	1709
L., H.	A divine hornbook: or, the first form in a true Theosophick school	1688
anon.	The ladies catechism	1703

4	5	6
1+	K168–9	Short; unusual content; the accompanying 'treatise' on prayer is less a catechism (as is implied) than a controversial work with some leading questions + objections answered; 2nd edn. Philadelphia
1	K150	Long; not the usual staples; Quaker; this work was used against Keith after his change of stance in [Keith], *The divinity … of the light within* (1701)
1+	K212 + *TC* iii. 105	Mid; a simplified version of the last; an earlier edn. had been published in Philadelphia in 1690 as *A plain short catechism*; price 3*d*.
6+	K261–4 + BL	Long; PBC qs + as with comments + pious ejaculations; also has directions for using PBC as a basis for prayer; later editions revised; 1st edns. for Bath + Wells diocese; Welsh + American edns.; price 6*d*. though 1686 edn. 'in a larger character' cost 18*d*. bound
(2+)	Lambeth + K260A	How to pray using the PBC as a basis; part 2 of last published separately—price 1*d*.; further edns. 1769, 1773
3+	K380–80A + BL	Very long; based on Creed, though devotes an unusual amount of space to proving Christ was the messiah; to form a true Christian heart + practice in those without leisure to read or the capacity to retain a larger volume; also reprinted in the composite volume edited by Bray in 1699 (q.v.)
1	K385	Short; mainly credal material; questions designed to elicit answers 'Yes' or 'No', partly from Wallis (q.v.); for those of meanest capacities + weakest memories
1	Bodleian + Cambridge Univ. Lib.	Very long; PBC with expositions, extra qs + as some requiring 'Yes' or 'No' answers (see Palmer) + scripture proofs; apparently designed for use in N. America, possibly by someone called Smith (ink note on Bodleian title-page)
1	DWL	Short; PBC simplified by breaking up the larger answers into shorter qs + as; for young children; for a London parish
4	K512AB–12B	Mid; not the usual staples, apart from Ss; for children + young Christians; also has lists of duties for children + servants; Baptist; Coventry?
(1)	BL	PBC in German + English, with scripture proofs; also paraphrase of PBC in the form of prayer; for incoming Hanoverians?
(1)	L21B	Very short; most unusual 'theosophic' content
[1]	BL + Bodleian	Satirical; less of a direct parody of PBC than similarly entitled work by U. Price (q.v.)

1	2	3
Lambe, John	A dialogue between a minister and his parishioner	1690
Lamplugh, Thomas	[A pastoral letter to the clergy ... about catechisms]	[167?]
L[angley], S[amuel]	A catechisme shorter than the short catechisme	1649
anon.	A large summary of the doctrines contained	1675
anon.	The larger and shorter catechisms	1649–
Joannes a Lasco	Brevis et dilucida ... tractatio	1552
——	De catechismus	1551–3
——	De[n] cleyne catechismus	1552–66
Laud, William	A summarie of the devotions/ The daily office of a Christian	1667–1705/6
[Laythes, Thomas]	Some questions and answers	[1691]
[Ledesma, Diego de]	The Christian doctrine in manner of a dialogue	1597 (secret London press)
Leech, James	A plaine and profitable catechisme	1605
Legate, Robert	A breife catechisme and dialogue	1545
Leighton, Robert	An exposition of the Creed ... To which is annext a short catechism	–1701–8
Le Maçon, Robert/ 'De La Fontaine'	A catechisme and playne instruction for children	1578?–1580?
——	Catéchisme et instruction familière	1602
[L'Estrange, Roger]	Toleration discuss'd in two dialogues	1663–81

4	5	6
(1)	L217	Mid dialogue on the Lord's Supper, and the need to participate; also prayers + 3 'discourses'; Herts.?
(1)	L304B	Episcopal letter urging the clergy of the diocese of Exeter to catechize
1	L58	A short 'epitome + contraction' of John Ball's best-selling form (q.v.); also contains 'hymns'
[1]	L439	Catholic; English translation of a very long summary of the doctrine in the Tridentine form; not in q + a; foreign origin
—	—	See below, s.v. Westminster Assembly
(1)	15259	Latin; not q + a; Ss only; advanced + in places controversial; originally used in Emden
(2)	15260–60.5	Translation of last into Dutch by J. Utenhove for use by Dutch reformed congregation in London
(6+)	15260.7–62a, 2739.5, 2740, 2740.3	Adaptation + abridgement of last by Marten Micron (q.v.): see A. Pettegree, *Foreign Protestant Communities* (1986), 50; in Dutch
(6+)	L600–600A, + L583–4 + Bodleian	Primarily devotional, despite claims on the title-page to contain 'several catechetical paraphrases'
(2)	L753–3A	A broadsheet, with 7 qs + as on Quaker ideas; partly instructive, partly controversial
[1]	15353	Catholic; foreign origin; translated into English for 'children, + other unlearned Catholics'
1	15363.3	Mid; for parents + householders to teach their children + servants; a much modified version of the Dering–More catechism, q.v.; Dec, Cr, Ss, Pr
—	—	See above, s.v. *Breife catechisme*
2+	Wm. Andrews Memorial Lib., Calif., BL + DWL	The exposition of Cr, Pr + Dec of 1701 was followed by 2 discourses on scripture texts and a very short but wide-ranging catechism which was a slightly modified version of *Bishop Lighton's catechism for children* (Edinburgh, [1695]); this version was also reprinted in *Three posthumous tracts* (1708)
1+	Maunsell, 32 + 15450	Mid; Cr, Dec, Pr, Ss; French origin; there is a clear debt to Calvin's form (q.v.), but the alterations consist of much more than the abridgement indicated in the epistle by the translator T. W[ilcox]; there was also a translation into Latin: STC[2] 4882; see s.v. W. Charke above
(1)	15499	Somewhat different version of last in French
(4?)	L1315–18	Controversial dialogue between a conformist + a nonconformist on the merits + demerits of toleration

1	2	3
Lewis, John	The church catechism explain'd by way of question and answer	1701–32–
—— and John Richardson	The church catechism explain'd ... and render'd into Irish	1712–
anon.	Liber precum ecclesiae cathedralis Christi Oxon.	1726 (Oxford)
anon.	Liber precum publicarum	[1560]–1604
Lily, William	Institutio/ Brevissima institutio/ An intro-duction/ A short introduction	1540/1542– 1735–
Linaker, Robert	A short and plaine instruction	1591
——	A short catechisme	1610
'Bishop of Lincoln'	Exposition of the church catechism	18th century
anon.	A little catechism	1692
Littleton, Edmund	A briefe catechisme, containing the summe	1616–31
anon.	La liturgie ou formulaire des prières	1717
Love, Barry	The catechism of the church/church catechism resolved into short and easy questions	–1699–1706 (Norwich)
[Love, Christo-pher (ed.)]	The main points of church-government and discipline	1649
——	The sum of practical divinity	1654
Lowth, Simon	Catechetical/Catechistical questions very necessary	1673–4
anon.	The loyal catechism	1710
anon.	The loyal catechism	1713

4	5	6
15+	*TC* iii. 240, Christ Church, Oxford + BL	Long; PBC with extra qs + as + scripture proofs; collected from other authors' works; divided into 5 parts, + 12 sections; prayer at end contains catechetical material; recommended for Charity Schools; 58th edn. 1820; Welsh edn. 1713; price 4*d.* or 25*s.* for 100
3+	BL Catalogue, s.v. Liturgies	Same as last in English + Irish, with 'elements' of the Irish language, + prayers; 13 edns. by 1825
(1)	Christ Church, Oxford	Sections of the Book of Common Prayer in Latin, including the PBC in post-1604 version; Oxford
(4+)	16424–9	As last, but the catechism is the pre-1604 form
(150– 200 +?)	15610.5–633.8, L2274F–304B + BL	The standard approved 'grammar' of the period, in two parts; contains Cr, Pr, Dec, improving verses + prayers, all in Latin verse; not in q + a
1	15644	Two forms: a mid (Dec, Cr, Ss, Pr), + a very short pre-comm. summary of the same; author says this is a modified version of an earlier catechism, to ensure that those of 'very simple understanding' benefit fully from the sacrament; a prayer at the end summarizes the catechism
1	15643.5	Two very short forms to preserve little children from the 'infection of popery + atheism'; to be taught by parents in private families; prayers at end
?	—	Listed as a work recommended for Charity Schools in M. G. Jones, *Charity School Movement* (1938), 374; almost certainly the work by William Wake (q.v.), who recommended it for use in his Lincoln diocese in 1708 (*TC* iii. 597); price 2*s.*
—	—	See below, s.v. J. Mason
2	15717.5–18	Short; qs + as based on the Gospel story; with prayers for before + after communion; Kent?
(1)	BL	Book of Common Prayer, including PBC, in French
3	L3142A + BL	Long; PBC with comments, extra qs + as, + scripture proofs; for children; divided into 12 sections; 2nd edn. corrected + enlarged; Great Yarmouth
1	L3167	23 qs + as pressing the case for Presbyterian church government
1?	Carruthers, 111	The 'grounds of religion in a catechetical way'; no copy survives
2	L3324–5	Long; PBC with extra qs + as; for his own children + those of his native Leics. parish; price bound 1*s.*
[1]	BL	Political: dialogue between Dr Sacheverell + a pupil on non-resistance
[1]	Bodleian	Political: qs + as on non-resistance

1	2	3
Lye, Thomas	A plain and familiar method of instructing	1662–76–
——	An abridgement of the late reverend assemblies shorter catechism	1662?–75
——	The assemblies shorter catechism drawn out into distinct propositions	1672–4–
——	An explanation of the shorter catechism	1675–1702
	[For a sermon on catechizing by Lye, see above, s.v. S. Annesley.]	
[Lyford, William]	An helpe for young people	1640–9 (Oxford)
——	Lyford's legacie	1656–8
——	Principles of faith and good conscience	1642–58
Lyster, John	A rule how to bring up children. A treatise	1588
M., R.	The church–catechism enlarg'd and explain'd	1697
Mackworth, Sir Humphrey	A discourse by way of dialogue	–1705
anon.	The maine grounds of religion	[1624?]–30
Manby, Peter	A reformed catechism in two dialogues	1687
anon.	The maner and forme of examination	1581

4	5	6
(5+)	L3540–41A + Car-ruthers, 111	Advice to householders on how to catechize the younger sort, sometimes published or bound with one of the next 3 works; extended by the 1670s (compare BL 3505.aa.48(1) + BL 1551/77); Dublin edn. 1683
3	BL, DWL, A107A + Carruthers, 111	Short; WSC condensed into 33 qs + as, but order changed, + little on Dec + Pr; for those of 'weakest capacities + memories'; the DWL copy also has an alphabetical table explaining the 'difficult words and phrases' in the WSC
2+	L3527B–28	Long; WSC with expositions + proofs; divided into 30 sections for daily use; published with 'rules' similar to those of *Plain + familiar method*; Dublin edn. 1703
6?+	L3532–6 + Car-ruthers, 111	Long; WSC with extra qs + as; for 'poor, ignorant, + unbelieving persons + families'; Somerset; edns. in Edinburgh + Dublin
2+	15114 + L3546B	Short; pre-comm.; for the young; Dorset; see next also
2	L3547–8	Reprints last together with a controversial work on 4 'perplexed questions' on admission to communion
5	L3552–6	Very long, explaining Cr, Dec, Pr, + Ss in a 'catechetical form'; also has an appendix of theological terms; Dorset
<1>	17122	Very long but by no means elementary dialogue (father/son) on credal material, Dec, *et al.*; often anti-Catholic; Yorks.?
1	M70A	Mid; PBC with extra questions to test understanding requiring 'Yes'/'No' answers (cf. works by Palmer, Wallis, and Comber), + scripture proofs
(2)	BL	Dialogue between two lords, a divine, a merchant, a physician, lawyers, *et al.*, on such topics as provi-dence, the happiness of a religious life, the divinity of Christ; written to instruct rather than to score points? Book III was published separately as *A treatise concerning the divine authority* (1704)
2	12402a.4–a.6	Very short; pre-comm.; a modified version of the first form in Egerton's best-selling *Briefe method*; for those without the money to buy or the time or memory to master a larger form; + rules for a godly life, in metre to help the memory; prayers at end
[1+]	M388	Controversial work on the English reformation of the 1530s + 1540s, by a convert to Catholicism; 1st 2 edns. published in Dublin
1	11183.5	Mid; pre-comm.; Cr, Dec, Pr, Ss; for householders to use with their families; Scottish origin (see STC^2 11183)

1	2	3
anon.	The maner to examine children	–1563–94
[Marsh, Narcissus]	The church catechism explain'd	1708
Marshal, Richard	Fifteen considerations stirring us up/XXIX directions	1645–6
[Marshall, Thomas]	The catechism set forth in the Book of Common Prayer briefly explained	1679 (Oxford)–1731–
Marshall, William	A prymer in englyshe	[1534]
——	A goodly prymer in englyshe	1535
Martyr, Petrus/Vermigli, Pietro Martire	The common places of ... Peter Martyr	1582
[John Mason]	A little catechism, with little verses, and little sayings	1692–[c.1730]
Mason, William	A little starre, giving some light	1653
Masterson, George	Milk for babes: or a catechistical exercise	1654
[Mather, Richard]	A catechisme or, the grounds + principles	1650
M[athew], N. [A.]	A catechism: being an enlargement of the church-catechism	1677–9
'Mayden, Mr'	'Mr Mayden his catechisme concerninge ye Lords Supper'	[1620s?]
Mayer, John	The English catechisme Or a commentarie	1621–35
——	The English teacher/ Mayers catechisme abridged. Or the A.B.C. inlarged	1623–39
——	A short catechisme necessary to be learned	1646

4	5	6
5+?	4381, 4383, 4385–7	A very short pre-comm. form for children, printed at the end of some editions of Calvin's *Catechisme*, beginning with the Geneva edn. of 1556
—	—	See above, s.v. *Church catechism*
2	M723–4	Very short form, based on Perkins's (q.v.), plus an exposition; also considerations on sin, + directions on duties; partly political in aim
15+	M800–807, BL + NUC	Early edns. consist of prose notes on PBC, but from 1683 also included a q + a form using the same material; scripture references in margin; for 'young Christians'; prayers at end; edn. in Welsh 1682
—	—	See below, s.v. *Primer*
—	—	Ditto
(1)	24669	One of the catechetical works recommended by T. Watts, *Entrie to Christianitie*, q.v.; also 2 edns. in Latin: STC² 24667–8
6?	M916B + see col. 6	Very short + simple; also has improving verses + sayings; for 'little children'; price of 6th edn. 1*d.* (ex inf. advert at end of 1730 edn. of Stinton's catechism, q.v.)
1	M948	Long; credal material, Dec, Pr, Ss; Baptist; for 'all the saints scattered through' Oxon., Warks., Northants, + England generally
1	M1072A	Long; modified WSC; for 'little ones' who 'lisped it' before the congregation of St Clement Danes, London
1	M1268	Long: a 'larger catechism' for 'children of riper age'; predestinarian emphasis; New England origin
2	M1288B–C + *TC* i. 327	Short; modified PBC; written for those not baptized in infancy, but now published for their + others' benefit; scripture texts on duties, + prayers at end; price 2*d.*
MS	Emmanuel Coll., Cambridge III. 1. 13⁸	Pre-comm., but not in q + a (my foliation 28ᵛ); Mr Mayden has not been traced
5+	17732–8	Very long; PBC with extra qs + as + expositions; for ministers, schoolmasters, + householders; later editions revised + corrected; prayers at end; still for sale in 1658: London, *Catalogue*, sig. P2ᵛ; see next also
7?	17739–40.5	Mid; abridgement of last, but within the one text there is a simpler form, for 'babes', in black letter, + a more advanced one, in roman type; for title of 1st edn. see his *Short catechisme*, sig. B7ᵛ
1	Queens' Coll., Cambridge	Short; pre-comm.; based on parliamentary ordinance of 20.10.1645, but adds extra material including Dec + Pr

1	2	3
Mayo, Daniel	The intercession for the fruitless fig-tree	1726
Mears, John	A catechism: or, an instruction in the Christian religion	1731–2–
anon.	A methodicall short catechisme	1623
Michelthwait, Thomas	His catechisme for howsholders	1589
M[ico], J[ohn]	Spirituall food, and physicke	1623–31
anon./[John Mico]	A pill to purge out popery: Or a catechisme for Romish Catholikes	1623–4
Micron, Marten	A short and faythful instruction	[1556?] (Emden)–[1560?] (London)
Milbourne, Luke	The catechisme of the Church of England explain'd, by short questions and answers	1700 (Rott.)–1704 (Lond.)
Miles, James	Brevis catechismus pro hereticis Anglicis, Scotis & aliis	1635 [Naples]
Millar, David	The Assembly's short catechism rescu'd from the late reviser	1738
Miller, Benjamin	A Christian catechism	1703
Mingzeis, Alexander	A confutation of the new Presbyterian error	1648
Mockett, Thomas	A new catechisme	1647
Moore	The grounds of Christian religion by way of catechising	pre-1658
[Moore, John]/Phi-lalethes Christophilus	A dialogue betixt an awakened sinner and a merciful saviour	1723

4	5	6
(1)	BL	Sermon given to a society of catechumens in London
2+	BL	Mid; in three parts: on reasons for belief; Cr; + Dec, Pr, + Ss; 1732 edn. has 'for the use of adult persons' added to the title-page, + is much modified in pt. 3; Irish + Scottish edns. have an additional short catechism for children
—	—	See above, s.v. Thomas Cartwright
1?	Maunsell, 32	Not traced
3+	17861–3.3 + Addenda	Three forms: 1 very short, 1 short, 1 mid, for little children, the younger, and the older sorts, respectively; some edns. also contain supporting texts, + anti-Catholic works (see next); Exeter; still for sale in 1658: London, *Catalogue*, sig. P3ʳ
(4)	17858–61	Series of dialogues (minister/'weak Christian') attacking Catholic position, + defending English church; in 1623 it was reprinted with last (17861)
1+	17864–64.5 + Addenda	Short; pre-comm.; translated by T. C[ranmer? or Cottesford?] from a Dutch original for the Dutch congregation in London, dated 1553; Dec, Cr, Ss, + Pr; an edn. in Dutch was published in London in 1561 (STC² 18812)
4?	M2029B + BL	Mid; PBC text slightly modified + extra qs + as added; 1st edn. for the English church in Rotterdam of which Milbourne was then pastor; 4th edn. corrected and enlarged
[1]	17920.5	Catholic form, in Latin + English; covers the usual 4 staples + standard extra Catholic items but not in q + a
(1)	BL	Controversial: an attack on the recent revision of WSC by Strong (q.v.); + defence of the original version
1?	*TC* iii. 354	For children; 'very useful for all families'; price 2*d.*, or 18*d.* a dozen, suggests form was short; by a Baptist; no copy survives
(1)	M2191	Controversial; not in the usual q + a form
1	M2308	Short; Dec, Cr, Ss, Pr; an existing form modified to fit the parliamentary ordinance of 20.10.1645; for those of 'meanest capacity + shortest memory'
1?	See col. 6	London, *Catalogue* sig. P2ᵛ; not traced; perhaps a copy of a later edn. of Dering–More (q.v.) though London lists the latter separately
(1)	Congregational Lib., London	A verse dialogue between an anxious sinner + a merciful saviour; there is also a poem on Christ; attribution to Moore (a Baptist minister in Northampton) in the Cong. Lib. copy

1	2	3
'The Moral Society'	The plan of the Moral Society ... To which is added the moral catechism	1729
More, John	Brief and necessary instruction/Short catechism for housholders	1572–
More, William	A short and plain tractate of the Lords Supper	1645
Morecroft, Jo.	Abridgement of Ursinus' catechism	1586
Morehouse, John	'Mr Morehouse catechisme'	1590s?
[Morrice, John]	A defence of lecturers	–1733
Mosse, Miles	A short catechisme	1590
anon.	A most excellent and profitable dialogue	1610
anon.	The mother and the child	1611
anon./A reverend divine	The mothers catechism	1717 (Nottingham)
anon.	Motives to godly knowledge	1613
Mulcaster, Richard	Catechismus Paulinus	1599?–1601
Musculus, Wolfgang	Common places of Christian religion	1563–78
N., N.	The polititians catechisme	1658
[Nab, Ralph]	An address to the right worshipful the batchelors	[1735?]–7
anon.	A national catechism	1687
[Nayler, James]	An answer to a book called the Quakers catechisme	1655–6
——	Milk for babes; and meat for strong men	1661–8

4	5	6
1	BL	Members of the established church + Protestant dissenters aiming at preaching morality issued a very short catechism arguing man was 'a moral agent', who could repent of sin + believe
—	—	See above, s.v. E. Dering
1	M2694	Long, pre-comm. form; 'grounded upon 1 Cor. 11. 23', etc.
1?	Maunsell, 32	Not traced; other versions of Ursinus's catechetical works were published about this date: see below
MS	BL Egerton MS 2877, fo. 83	The date is suggested by J. Freeman, 'Parish Ministry in the Diocese of Durham', Ph.D. thesis (Durham, 1979), 295; covers Ss, Pr, + other material
(3?)	BL	A letter defending London lecturers against the charge of interfering with catechizing raised in W. Wake's *Principles*, q.v.; stresses the close link between preaching + catechizing
1?	Maunsell, 32	No copy survives, but sections of the preface are quoted in the intemperate attack on it by Thomas Rogers in *Miles Christianus* (1590); possibly the same as *A short catechisme. Brieflie contayning* (published without a preface at Middelburg in 1590), q.v.
(1)	6809.5	A dialogue between Lewis + Frederick, on the obstacles to a true + justifying faith; translated from the Latin original by A. Golding
—	—	See above, s.v. J. Cragge/Craig
—	—	See above, s.v. R. Baxter
1	18213	Short; pre-comm.; published without the author's knowledge, according to preface
(2?)	18249 + Addenda	Mid form in Latin blank verse; built around PBC, but much longer + more detailed; for use in St Paul's School, London, of which author was then High Master
(2)	18308–9	One of a range of works recommended to catechists by T. Watts, *Entrie to Christianitie*, q.v.; covers a number of catechetical topics
—	—	See below, s.v. P. Talbot
[2?]	BL	Includes 'The [Pretty] Miss's catchism': a short, satirical, misogynist piece
—	—	See below, s.v. W. Popple
(2)	N258–9	Controversial: a reply, point by point, to the work by Baxter, q.v.
(3)	N299–301	The title is a favourite for catechists, but this is not in q + a; it offers comfort in affliction, + urges the faithful to put off the old man

1	2	3
anon.	A necessarie doctrine and erudition	1543–5
anon.	The necessity of coming to church	–1709
anon./[Nelson, Robert]	The Whole Duty of a Christian by way of question and answer	–1705–27–
———	Instructions for them that come to be confirmed	1714–
———	Mr Nelson's Companion for the festivals and fasts ... abridged	1739–
Nesse, Christopher	A New Year's gift for children	1684
anon.	A/The new catechisme	1644–5
anon./'A reverend divine'	A new catechisme commanded to be set forthe	1647
anon.	A new catechism for the fine ladies	1733–40
anon.	A new catechism with Dr. Hickes's thirty-nine articles	1710
anon.	A new method of catechizing	1712
anon.	A new political catechism	1740
anon.	A [new] sacramental catechism	1701–3
anon.	The new school of education for the behaviour of children	[*c*.1680]
Newcome, Peter	A catechetical course of sermons	1700–12
Newton, Robert	A practical exposition of the church catechism	1727
N[icholes], M[artin]	A catechisme, composed according to the order	1631–42

4	5	6
(13)	5168–77	This is listed as a catechism by Maunsell, 32, but is not in q + a; better known as 'The King's Book'
(4)	Lambeth	A dialogue to persuade absentees to attend church; of interest on perceived attitudes of non-attenders
9+	Bodleian	Mid; Allestree's best-seller turned into q + a; prayers at end
1+	BL	Short; a work in q + a to explain confirmation, + prepare confirmands; with suitable prayers for the occasion; 22nd edn. 1758
1+	BL	Twelve 'catechetical exercises' for St Bride's Charity School; unusual content: based on Nelson's own best-seller; to teach children + the poor to know their duty during church festivals
1?	*TC* ii. 68	Does not survive, but appears to combine moral instruction, improving stories, religious poems, + a 'plain + easy catechism' for those of 'meanest capacity'; author Congregational
—	—	See above, s.v. E.C.
(1)	LT	Partly controversial: for 'those who still affect a reading ministry' (for an earlier work with similar title, see above, s.v. E.C.)
—	—	See below, s.v. U. Price
—	—	See below, s.v. M. Tindal
1	BL	Mid; BCP with extra questions (+ advice to catechists) but no answers; interesting on technique + parallel works recommended
—	—	See above, s.v. T. Dekker
2+?	*TC* iii. 240, 284, 325, 331	Pre-comm.? (no copies found); for the use of poor servants, + at 2*d*. or 12*s*. per 100 designed to be bought + given away by 'charitable ... Christians'
1	N748A	After a series of prayers comes a very short form, including Pr, Cr, + Dec, + more prayers; to instruct children in the Protestant religion practised by Elizabeth I
(3)	N901, BL + *TC* iii. 148, 180, 192, 224, 314	Very long: 52 sermons on PBC 'for the whole year'; designed for clergy + recommended to families; printed by subscription (suggesting demand for such a work); 2 vols. 12*s*., but an abridgement in q + a planned; Herts., London?
(1)	BL	Very long: 24 lectures on PBC, delivered in a London parish, + published by author's son
6?	18531–31.7 + N1083	Long; PBC with extra qs + as, some owing a debt to Ball's best-seller, q.v.; 1642 edn. corrected + much augmented; still on sale in 1658: London, *Catalogue*, sig. P3ᵛ

1	2	3
Nichols, Josias	An order of household instruction	1595–6
Nicholson, William	A plain but full exposition of the catechisme	1655–89
N[ixon], A[nthony]	The dignitie of man	1612–16
anon./A minister of the Gospel	No popery, or a catechism against popery	1682–
Norton, John	A brief and excellent treatise	1648
N[otcutt], W[illiam]	A short explanation of the Assembly's shorter catechism	1726
N[owell], A[lexander]	Catechismus, sive prima institutio	1570–95–
anon./ [Nowell, Alexander]	A catechisme, or first instruction of Christian religion	1570–7
anon./[Nowell, Alexander]	Katechismos ... Catechismus	1573
[Nowell, Alexander]	Christianae pietatis prima institutio	–1574–1664
N[owell], A[lexander]	A catechisme, or institution of Christian religion	1572–1663
[Nowell, Alexander]	Christianismou ... Christianae pietatis	1575–1687
N[owell], A[lexander]	Catechismus parvus pueris primus Latine	1573–1687

4	5	6
(2)	18539.5–40	A long, original work with lessons of graded difficulty, but mostly not in q + a; for householders, including those of the 'meaner sort', to use with children + servants for 2 hours a week
(9)	N1113–20A	Long exposition of PBC (not in q + a) 'collected out of the best catechists'; author claimed it was a summary of his catechizing in Wales; although he + the PBC were then out of favour, Nicholson's work was listed in London's 1658 *Catalogue*, sig. P3^r; used in some schools; MS version in Magdalen College, Oxford, Archives MS 546
(1+)	18584–5	Long; most unusual content dealing more with the welfare of the body than the soul, by a poet
(1+)	N1187	Largely controversial (anti-Catholic) though some sections simply state Protestant position; 3 edns. published in Scotland in 1683
1	N1315	Long; credal material, Pr, Ss, Dec; New England origin; from the subtitle this is probably a longer version of the *Brief catechisme* the author published in Cambridge, Mass., in 1660
1	BL	Long; WSC with extra qs + as; for those who have mastered the WSC; catechumens encouraged to amplify the answers in their own words; Congregational; Ipswich
<9+>	18701–706a	Nowell's original catechism in Latin; referred to in the 1572 abridged form (see below) as the 'larger', a usage followed by STC^2; Dec, Cr, Pr, Ss
<5>	18708–710a.5	The 'larger' catechism translated into English by Thomas Norton, who arranged for this version to match the original page for page to help those learning Latin
<1>	18707	The 'larger' catechism in Greek + Latin; translation into Greek by William Whitaker
<22+>	18712–25.5, 17991–2 + N1436D	A form 'of a middle sort' abridged from Nowell's 'larger' one; 1st edn. probably pre-1574 (see above p. 189 n. 111); psalms + prayers in Latin at the end
<18?>	18730–8 + N1436–36A	English version of last by T. Norton, for those who had mastered the 'little' catechism (see below) but still needed instruction; prayers at end
<8>	18726–9 + N1437–9	The 'middle' in Greek + Latin, the Greek again being the work of W. Whitaker
(4)	18711–11.5 + N1436B–C	STC^2 refers to this as Nowell's 'shorter' catechism, but the great bulk of it is actually the PBC translated into Latin, by Nowell, with extra qs + as on duties + Ss at

1	2	3
N[owell], A[lexander]	Catechismus parvus ... Latine et Graece	1574–1633
Nowell, Alexander/Stone, William	Nowell's catachisme grammatically translated	*c.*1617–18
Nye, Philip	Beames of former light	1660
anon.	The observator's catechism	1690
Olevian, Caspar	An exposition of the symbole of the Apostles	1581–2
———	[on the Creede, Commandementes, Lords Praier, and sacramentes]	1589
Ollyffe, John	A practical exposition of the church catechism	1710
anon.	The one necessary thing to be sought	1724 (Nottingham)
Openshaw, Robert	Short questions and answers	1582?–
anon.	The order and rules of the charity-school for boys in the parish of—	[1701?]
anon.	The order and rules ... for girls	[1701?]
anon.	Orders read and given to the parents	1708
Osterwald, J. F.	Catéchisme ou instruction	1704
———	Grounds and principles of the Christian religion	1704–34–
Owen, John	The principles of the doctrine of Christ/ Dr John Owen's two short catechismes	1645–1700

4	5	6
		the end (these derive from Nowell's earlier forms, + anticipate the additions to the end of PBC in 1604); prayers at end
(4)	18711a–c	Last work above in Latin + Greek, latter translated by W. Whitaker; prayers at end; for a similar work used at Eton + Merchant Taylors' schools, see above, s.v. *Catechismus cum ordine*
?	*TSR* iii. 1619	Not traced; ever published?
(1)	N1484	Defence by a leading Independent of the minister's right to be flexible in catechizing rather than being forced to use WSC or PBC; he shows a great deal of knowledge of contemporary catechetical forms
[1]	O123KB	Political
(2)	18807–7.3	Long exposition (not in q + a) of Cr, based on catechetical lectures; translated from the original Latin by John Field
1?	See col. 6	Maunsell, 33 lists this as a catechism, translated by Richard Saintbarb; this may be a translation of a larger work by Olevian, but Maunsell also lists an identical work by Saintbarb himself: 33 (2), 94–5, + see below, s.v. Saintbarb
1	BL	Very long (2 vols.); PBC with extra qs + as, short qs but often long answers, to be read; Bucks.?
(1)	BL	Four dialogues, covering very diverse material, but generally of a moralistic or improving kind
—	—	See below, s.v. E. Paget
(1)	Bodleian	Stresses the importance of learning the PBC (see above *Account of the method*) + of those who have mastered it being sent to be examined in church
(1)	Bodleian	As last but for girls
(1)	Bodleian	Single sheet for parents of children admitted into Charity School to set up at home; reminds parents to call on children frequently to repeat their catechism at home
(1+)	BL	Very long form in French; Cr, Dec, Pr, Ss; Swiss origin
6+	BL	Translation of last (by H. Wanley), revised by G. Stanhope, + dedicated to S.P.C.K.; the form is preceded by an abridgement of Bible history; Edinburgh edn. 1732
3	O796–7, 819	A short + a mid form, based on his preaching + the parliamentary ordinance of 20.10.1645; short form for

1	2	3
——	The primer: or, an easie way to teach children	1652
——	Vindiciae evangelicae	1655 (Oxford)
[——]	A brief instruction in the worship of God	1667–76
P., C.	Two briefe treatises	1616
P., R. (ed.)	The cristall of Christianitie	1617
P., T.	A short catechisme for householders	1624
[Paget, Eusebius]	Short questions and answeares, conteyning the summe of Christian religion	1579–1639
Paget, Eusebius + Openshaw, Robert	Short questions and answeres … newly enlarged with testimonies of scripture	[1586?]–1633
Paget, Eusebius ——	Eusebii Pagetti catechismus Latine aeditus The history of the Bible	1585 1603–82
P[aget], I[ohn]	A primer of Christian religion	1601
Painter	?	?
anon.	The palace miscellany containing … The young lady's catechism	1733
anon.	The Palatines catechism	1709

4	5	6
		younger sort, mid for adults; avoids staples which he intends to tackle separately; for use in an Essex parish
1	O795A	Designed to teach reading, but includes a short 'necessary catechism' to teach youth the grounds of Christian religion (different from the short form of 1645), suitable scriptural readings, + prayers
(1)	O823	Controversial: an attack on Racovian Catechism + Biddle's form, qq.v.; see also his *Diatriba* (1653) against the former
(3?)	O721–2 + DWL	53 relatively short qs + as with long 'explications' defending the Congregational view of church-government; attacked by B. Camfield, q.v.
(1)	19059	First treatise is on the laity's need to be catechized; has revealing comments on lay attitudes
<1>	6099.7	Mid; completed by R.P.; in 3 parts—on Dec + Cr, + 2 Ss—each followed by a prayer; 'by way of disputation', but nearer a catechism than a dialogue; suitable for schools + families; prayers at end; Denbighshire; (cf. 'Painter')
1	19079	Very short; unusual content (e.g. covenant of grace at start), but the section on Ss is taken from the PBC
19?	18816–30.2	This work was by Paget (see STC² Addenda s.n. 18816), but in part is indebted to the Dering–More form (q.v.) + is often associated also with Openshaw (see next); short; Dec, Cr, Ss, Pr; interesting preface; prayers for before + after catechizing; Maunsell lists a 1591 edn.; Northants.?
9+	Maunsell, 33 + 18830.2A–30.9	Paget's form with the scripture references he cited now printed in full (Openshaw's idea), + many answers subdivided; long; different prefaces from original work
(1)	19101	Paget's original form in a Latin version; mid
15?	19105.9–109.4D + P185–6	Contents of the Bible converted into q + a form; (for a similar work see above, s.v. *Doctrine*)
1	19100	Very long; unusual content (contemplating God's work in nature); Cheshire
?	?	Said to have devised three catechisms (P. Nye, *Beames of former light* (1660), 82, but cannot now be traced (though cf. R.P. (1617))
[1]	BL	Satirical: the 'catechism' contains parodies of several lines in the PBC + WSC
[1]	BL	Political; attacks the Palatine refugees encamped at Blackheath + Camberwell; one speaker—an 'English tradesman'—says charity begins at home

1	2	3
Palmer, Anthony	Childrens bread: or, the first principles	1671–*c*.1700
[Palmer, Herbert]	An endeavour of making the principles of religion	1640–5
anon.	A paraphrase with annotations	1674
anon.	Paraphrasis cum annotatis	1674
P[arker], H[enry]	A political catechisme	1643–1710
Parker, John	A true patterne of pietie	1592?–99
anon.	The parliaments new and perfect catechisme	1647
Parr, Elnathan	The grounds of divinitie	1614–51
anon.	'Pasreus catachisme in Greek and Latin'	1629
Pasquier, Eti-enne/ A. H.	The Jesuites catechisme	1602–85
'Philo Probaton'/ S., B. ?	The pastors pasport	–1646
anon.	The pater noster, [the Ave], ye crede, and the commaundements in englysh	1537–9?
Patrick, Simon	A brief exposition of the ten commandments and the lords prayer	1665–88
Pearston, Thomas	A short instruction	1590
Peck, Francis	The kernell of Christianity	1644–6
anon./[Peirce, James]	A scripture-catechism or the principles	1722
——	Fifteen sermons on special occasions	1728
Penington, Isaac (junior)	Some queries concerning the work of God in the world	1660
——	Some questions and answers for the opening	1661

4	5	6
2?	P215A	Short; not the usual content, apart from Dec; author an Independent minister in London; advert for edn. *c*.1700 (price 1*d*.) at end of J. Saltmarsh, *Free grace* (1700)
6	19154.5, P230aA–32	Long; Cr, Dec, Pr, Ss; innovative technique to test comprehension in which a series of questions are posed on one particular topic to which the catechumen has to reply 'Yes' or 'No'; Herts.
—	—	See below, s.v. W. White
—	—	Ditto
[4?]	P416–17 + DWL	Political: on royal government; 'for the more complete settling of consciences'
2?	Maunsell, 33 + 19217	Mostly prayers + guide to godly living, but also contains a short form (Dec, Cr, Ss, Pr), + a very short, pre-comm. 'Card for communicants'; Cheshire
[1]	P518	Satirical: hostile to parliament + the army
9?	19314–18 + P543 (*Works*)	Very long; qs + as (not on usual content) with long 'explications' and 'uses', much of it derived from other authors; written for the unlearned in 'familiar', 'plain' style; 2nd edn. enlarged; Suff.?
?	*TSR* iv. 217	Not traced; perhaps a link through David Paré to Ursinus (q.v.) + the Heidelberg Catechism
(4+)	19449 + H3A–D	Polemical: anti-Jesuit; French origin; 1602 translation by W. Watson
2?	P680	Mid; Cr, Dec, Pr, Ss; to help 'young Christian readers' from the font to the communion table; has meditations at end; 2nd edn. corrected; B.S. signs preface
(7?)	16820–21.7	Explains Pr, Cr, + Dec line by line, but not by q + a; designed to meet the requirements of the 1536 injunctions
5?	P757A–59	Mid: Dec + Pr only; to help his parishioners in a central London parish examine themselves for sin + pray to God for help to lead a better life
1	19520	Mid; built around original PBC form, but contains some original touches; short prayer at end; London diocese
2	P1032–3	Short; not the usual staples apart from Ss; Herts.
1	Eton College	Mid; scripture texts (including Pr + Dec) with leading qs, + Cr in full at the end; for authorship, see preface of next
1+	BL + DWL	After the sermons is added the scripture catechism of 1722
(1)	P1200	8 long, rhetorical questions answered by scripture references only
(1)	P1201	2 forms, a mid (on the history of the Jews) + a long (on more typically Quaker concerns)

1	2	3
——	Some questions and answers shewing	1662
——	Some sensible, weighty queries	1677
Pennington, Robert	A catechisme common place booke	1619
Perkins, William	The foundation of Christian religion	1590–1723
——	An exposition of the lords prayer	1592–7
——	An exposition of the symbole or crede	1595–1631
——	The first part/ The whole treatise of the cases of conscience	1604–52
——/Hill, Robert	A golden chaine … now drawne into familiar questions and answers	1612–21
P[eters], H[ugh]	Milk for babes, and meat for men	1630 (Amsterdam)–1641 (London)
Petrus, Joannes (Luccensis)	A dialogue of dying well	1603 (Amsterdam)
P[etto], S[amuel]	A short scriptural catechisme	1672
——	A large scriptural catechisme	1672
'Philalethes'	See above, s.v. J. Moore	
'Philander'	A catechism for the use of deists	1739
Phillips, John	The Christians A.B.C.	1629
'Philo-delphus'	A key to the church-catechism	1719
'Philotheos'	See below, s.v. *Threefold dialogue*	
anon.	A pill to purge out popery	1623–4

4	5	6
1	P1202	2 forms, both short, one on fearing God + keeping his commands, the other on the true church + the covenant of faith
(1)	P1203	20 queries on the state of the soul or heart, some answered by scripture references. Penington often used rhetorical qs to make more polemical points in defence of the Quaker position: e.g. P 1183, 1194, 1199, 1171 + 1206
1	19601	Mid; cross between catechism + scriptural commonplace book, to be read; unusual content, including how to lead a godly life; for young + old who desire salvation; Essex?
34+	19709–21, STC² Addenda, P1563–70 + BL	Mid; unusual approach, based on 6 principles; edns. in Welsh (1649), Irish (1652), *et al.*, + published in America (1682); P1560A not traced
(6+)	19699.5–702a.5	Long exposition of Pr; said to be 'in the way of catechizing', but for the most part not in q + a; Scottish edn. 1593
(6)	19703–706	Very long exposition of Cr only; not q + a
(11+)	19668–76 + P1574–5	Very long treatise of 'case-divinity' answering queries about what to do or think in specified situations
<2>	19664–64.5	Perkins's famous treatise turned (by Hill, q.v.) into a dialogue-catechism, between Theophilus + Theologus, to help readers understand the original work
2	19798.5, P1712	Short; predestinarian; possible debt to Cartwright; followed by q + a section on how to defeat the arguments of Romanists, Pelagians, + Arminians
[1]	19815	Catholic treatise, of Italian origin, on making a good end; has elements of dialogue in it
1	P1901A	Very short; for little children, as soon as they can speak; scriptural answers; not the usual content, apart from Dec; preface implies this work contains 2 catechisms, but this form + the next were published with separate title-pages + signatures; Congregational
1	P1899A	Mid; for 'children + others'; scriptural answers, + not the usual content: staples treated very briefly at end; see last
—	—	See above, s.v. *Catechism*
1	19877.5	Long; unusual alphabetical form, combining doctrines, expositions, + scripture references, with qs + as to help explain the proofs; Kent
—	—	See above, s.v. *Key*
—	—	See above, s.v. J. Mico

1	2	3
Piscator, Johann	Expositio capitum catecheseos religionis	1603
anon.	A plain and easie way of catechising	1680–1705
anon.	A plain and profitable scheme of the catechism	1711
anon.	A plain and short catechism	1719
anon.	Plain instructions for the young and ignorant	–1703–1706–
anon.	A plain practical exposition of the Apostles Creed	1716
'An English Protestant'	The plausible arguments of a Romish priest answered	1686–8
anon.	The polititians catechisme	1658
Pomfret, Samuel	The evening exercise for catechising	[1715?]
[Po(y)net, John]	Catechismus brevis	1553
——	A short catechisme, or playne instruction	1553
Poole, Matthew	A dialogue between a popish priest and an English protestant	1667–87–
anon.	A popish political catechism	[168–?]
Popple, Sir William	A rational catechism	1687–92–
Pouget, François Aimé	General instructions by way of catechism	–1723
Powell, Vavasor	The scriptures concord; or, A catechisme	1646–73
——	Saving faith set forth	1651
[——]	The sufferers–catechism	1664
anon./A divine of the Church of England	A practical exposition of the first part of the church catechism	1700
anon.	Praecipuorum theologiae capitum	1665–1700

4	5	6
(1)	19960	Latin exposition, point by point of Cr, Dec, Ss, Pr, + the church; not in q + a
2	P2340A + *TC* iii. 436	Mid; for those with weakest memories + of meanest capacities; Cr, Dec, Pr, Ss; questions designed to elicit answer 'Yes' or 'No' (cf. Palmer); price in 1705 6*d*.
1	BL	Mid; PBC with extra qs + as, to help younger catechumens; prayers at end
—	—	See above, s.v. N. Foxwell
—	—	See below, s.v. E. Synge
1	Bodleian	Long; Cr only; extracted from the 'best authors' for the use of 'ordinary persons'
—	—	See above, s.v. T. Comber
—	—	See below, s.v. P. Talbot
(1)	Congregational Lib., London	Sermon given after catechizing a London congregation; on the importance of the young holding fast to what they had learnt
(4?)	4807–11	A long + quite difficult form in Latin, approved for use in schools; credal material, Dec, Ss, Pr; there was also a version in Italian (4813)
1	4812	English version of last; to be mastered after PBC; followed by articles agreed in Convocation
(11+?)	P2828–35	Dialogue: mainly controversial, but with some attempt to instruct + reassure Protestants; Scottish edns. also
[1?]	P2957	Political + polemical: anti-Catholic
(2+)	P2966, *TC* ii. 443 + BL	Instructive dialogue, father-son, on how to live a Christian life; Amsterdam edns. 1712, 1722
[2]	BL	Catholic; very long, partly historical, partly thematic account of the church, in q + a; French origin; 2nd edn. corrected + amended by S[ylvester] Ll[oyd]
5?	P3093–4 + W. T. Whitley, *Baptist Bibliography* (1916–22), i. 26	Mid; scriptural answers; predestinarian; for the use of 'little ones' in Dartford, Kent, + Wales
(1)	P3092	3 dialogues between Christ + a publican, a pharisee + a doubting believer, the answers being as far as possible in the words of scripture
1	S6153	Mid; to encourage the persecuted; attribution to Powell is in [E. Bagshaw], *Life of ... Powell* (1671)
1?	*TC* iii. 210	Not found; different publisher from similarly entitled works by Assheton + Towerson (q.v.)
—	—	See below, s.v. T. Tully

1	2	3
anon.	Preces, catechismus, et hymni	1705–18
anon.	Preces privatae, in studiosorum	1564–74
'Presbyter of the Church of England'	A primitive catechism	1718
anon.	The Presbiterian catechisme	1647
Preston, Richard	Short questions and answers	1621
anon./Price, Uvedale	A new catechism for the fine ladies	1733–40
Prideaux, John	Suneidesilogia, or the doctrine of conscience	1656
PRIMERS [Joye, George (tr.)]	[H]ortulus anime. The garden of the soule; or the englisshe primers	1530
[Wyer, Robert]	This prymer of Salysbury use	[1533?]
[Marshall, William]	A prymer in englyshe	[1534?]
[——]	A goodly prymer in englyshe, newly corrected	1535–[8?]
[Godfray, Thomas]	A prymer in Englysshe	[1535?]
[Gough, John]	This prymer of Salysbery use	1536
anon.	The primer set furth/primer and catechisme	1551–75
anon.	A primmer/prymmer or boke of private prayer	1553–68

4	5	6
(2)	Univ. of Illinois + National Lib. of Scotland	Greek + Latin version of PBC with prayers + hymns for use in St Paul's School, London; Lord's Prayer, Cr, + Dec printed in English also at the end; also see next
(3+)	20378–81	Latin version of PBC, + prayers from official primers of 1546 + 1560
—	—	See below, s.v. D. Whiston
1	P3224	Short; apart from Ss, not the usual staples; nor related to WSC at all; for parallel works by the same publisher in 1647, see above, s.v. *Cavaliers + Independent*; prayers at end
1	20286	Short; on Ss only, for those who want to know more about them; Northants?
[3]	BL	Satirical; parodies PBC; published with *Trial of William Whyston* by Thomas Gordon in 1739–40; for an earlier work of a similar kind, see above, s.v. *Ladies*
(1)	P3436	An advanced work, for his wife; 'framed' on points in PBC; mainly in continuous prose but with some q + a
1	13828.4	An early Protestant version of a Catholic primer translated into English; contains a 'dialogue' between father + son which was used in the same or a modified form by the editors of other primers in the 1530s + 1540s (see following entries + *Fruteful instruction* above); banned by proclamation 22.6.1530
[1]	15983	Latin primer, but contains 'A lesson for children', not in q + a but in English + including Lord's Prayer, Cr, + Dec in English at the start; still more Catholic than Protestant (there are a series of qs + as on penitence + confession at the end)
1	15986	Contains the 'dialogue' found in Joye, q.v.
2	15988 + 15998	Has the same form as last, but with a new title + the roles reversed: son asks, father replies
1	15988a	Contains the same form as Joye
1	15992	Contains a modified version of the form in Godfray, q.v.; but also borrows from the Wyer 'Lesson'
6	16053–4, 16057, 16090–2	Edwardian revision of the Henrician primer; contains the 1549 version of the PBC
5?	20373–73.5, 20375–7	The prayers in this work are based on the Book of Common Prayer; also contains the PBC

1	2	3
anon.	A/The primer and … catechisme	[*c.*1570]–1724–
anon.	A primitive catechism	1718–
anon.	Prince Eugene's catechism concerning a general peace	1709
anon.	Principles made practical	1674
anon.	The principles of the Christian religion in English-and-Latine	[1670?]
anon.	The principles of the doctrine of Christ	1701
anon./Green, Thomas, Bp. of Ely	The principles of religion explained	1726
anon.	Private devotions for children	–1703–9
anon.	A profession of Catholick faith … by way of question and answer	–1734
anon.	The prophets catechism	1696
anon.	A Protestant catechisme for little children	1673–87
anon.	A Protestant catechism: or a dialogue	1681
anon.	The Protestant prayer-book … to which is added a Protestant catechism	1683
anon.	The Protestant tutor	1679–[1720?]
Provincial Assembly at London	An exhortation to catechising	1655
[Prynne, William]	Diotrephes catechized	1646
anon.	Les psaumes de David … avec … le catéchisme	1701–10–

4	5	6
See col. 6	20377.3–77.7, P3463 + ESTC	Abridged version of last; the partner of *The ABC with the catechisme* (q.v. above); reprinted in huge numbers throughout the period: see above, pp. 65–6, 176–7; BL has copies dated as late as 1775 + 1785
—	—	See below, s.v. D. Whiston
[1]	Houghton Lib., Harvard	Political
1	P3494	How to pray, + prepare for Lord's Supper by the use of the WSC; price 8*d.* bound; possibly by Hercules Collins or John Collinges: see M. Henry, *Life of Philip Henry* (1825), 79
(1)	P3497A	Not q + a; tackles Cr, Dec, Ss, faith, + repentance, + Pr in parallel pages of English + Latin text for beginners in Latin
1	DWL	Long; WSC with extra qs + as; for babes in knowledge; not the same as work by N. Vincent with similar title, q.v.
1	Bodleian	Long; not the usual content; originally designed for use in Charity Schools, but parents, + all 'weak + igno-rant' could benefit from it too; attribution to Green in ink note on Bod. copy
(12?)	*TC* iii. 330, 419, 585, 631	PBC turned into prayers, for use twice daily; enlarged in 1708, but still only 1*d.* or 6*s.* a 100 (so probably short); no copies survive
[4?]	BL	Catholic; confession of faith in q + a, extracted from Tridentine decrees; for use with converts to Catholicism
—	—	See above, s.v. T. Beverley
(2)	P3824, 3826	Short; largely controversial: anti-Catholic
(1)	P3825	Mid; mainly controversial: anti-Catholic
(1?)	*TC* ii. 26	Not found: the 'prayer-book' would appear to be contro-versial, so the catechism added may well be one of the previous two forms listed.
(5)	P3843–3C + BL	A reading primer with much anti-Catholic material, including dialogues + verses, but also contains a short 'catechism' of 43 qs + as similar to the *Protestant cate-chisme for little children* (1673), q.v.
—	—	See above, s.v. *Exhortation*
(3)	P3944–6	Controversial: Prynne offers queries through which he attacks 'over rigid Protestants' over the church settle-ment
(2+)	BL	Metrical psalms as used by Huguenots, with Genevan liturgy + confession, + Calvin's catechism, all in French; Dublin edns. in 1731

1	2	3
anon.	Questions and answers for youth to learn	1685 (York)
R., I./J.	A free school for Gods children	1593
R., O.	An easie entraunce	[*c.*1585]
R., R.	The house-holders helpe, for domesticall discipline	1615
anon.	The Racovian catechisme	1652 (Amsterdam)
Ram, Robert	The souldiers catechisme	1644
——	The countrymans catechisme	1655
Randall, John	Three and twentie sermons	1630
Randolph, J.	A short catechisme	1553
Ratcliffe, Thomas	A short summe of the whole catechisme	1594?–1620
Rawlet, John	An explication of the creed	1672–9
——	A dialogue betwixt two protestants	1685–1738
Raymond, George	An exposition on the church catechism	–1695
——	A short and plain account of religion	1700
anon.	The redcoats catechisme	1659/60–1660
Rees, David	A free and sober enquiry	1736
Reeve, Edmund	The communion book catechisme expanded	1635–6

4	5	6
1	Q182B	Mid; PBC with extra qs + as, some raising the covenants of works + grace; to help 'youth' understand the PBC; Yorks.?
1?	See col. 6	Maunsell, 32 lists this as a catechism; not traced
1	20585.3	Very short; designed as a New Year's gift by a minister to those in his charge; not the same as similarly entitled work by Gibson, q.v.
(1)	20586	3 short dialogues in which father exhorts grown-up son to catechize in his own household; long prayer at end; possibly by Richard Rogers, q.v.
[1]	R121	Long; Polish origin; see above, s.v. *Catechesis ecclesiarum*; source of controversy: see Biddle, Owen, + Wren, + *Papers of the Bibliographical Society of America*, 32 (1958), 196
[1]	R196	Political: justifies parliamentarian cause fighting to save the king from a 'popish malignant company'
1	R193	Long; based on author's catechizing in Lincs.; now printed for householders to use with their families; credal material, Ss, Dec, Pr; some unusual features
(1+)	20682–82A	Catechetical sermons given the week before monthly celebrations of communion in London parish
—	—	Mistaken by BL Catalogue for work by Ponet, q.v.
3?	Maunsell, 33 + 20746–7	Mid; for the ignorant, children, + common people; form has 'the same substance' as PBC; London
2	R356–7	Mid; Cr, Dec, Pr (built on PBC); drawn up for private use, but now with bishop's encouragement being published for his parishioners in Lancs.; prayers at end
(6)	R352–5 + BL	Partly controversial, anti-Catholic dialogue, in reply to a Catholic one (see *A short catechism against all sectaries*), but partly instructive too; reprinted in 1738 as part of E. Gibson's *Preservative against popery*
2?	R411B	Mid; PBC; unusual in that author does not quote PBC qs + as in full, but either paraphrases or supplements them; the substance of his expositions of the PBC to his Ipswich flock; followed by a 'Short system' which anticipates the next
(1)	R414	Series of points on the Christian religion, not in q + a; a summary of his teaching to his flock
[2]	R656–7	Satirical: anti-parliamentarian; parodies PBC
(1)	BL	Controversial: criticism (from a Baptist) of Strong's revision of WSC, q.v.
1+	20830–1	Long + often contentious explanation of PBC; officially

1	2	3
anon.	The reformed dissenter in conference	1684
anon.	Religious principles in verse	1658
[Reynolds, Edward]	Questions extracted out of the ordinance of parliament	1648
Reynolds, John	[An essay towards] A confirming catechism	1708–34
R[ichardson], A[lexander]	A short and briefe summe of saving knowledge	1621
Richardson, Charles	The doctrine of the Lords supper	1616
Richardson, Thomas	A true catechisme concerning the word of God	1664
Richerson, Mr	'Mr Richerson his catechisme'	?
Ridgley, Thomas	A body of divinity	1731–4
Ridpath, George	An appeal to the word of God	–1719
Rigge, Ambrose	A scripture-catechisme for children	1672–1702–
Roberts, Robert	A sacrament catechism	1720 (Chester?)
R[oberts], T.	The catechisme in meter	1583–91?
Robertson, Bartholomew	The heavenly advocate	1617

4	5	6
		approved in 1630s, but still on sale in 1658: London, *Catalogue*, sig. Q4^r; for a reply on communion table's position see STC 20474
(1)	R744	An instructive 'conference' between a conformist minister + a separatist parishioner on the lawfulness + duty of holding communion with the established church; price 6*d*.
(1)	R909	First verse lists Christian principles; others are more devotional in character
1	R1273	Broadsheet: 20 questions based on the parliamentary ordinance of 20.10.1645; the answers are bare scripture references, which 'may be easily gathered' out of the Bible by those wishing admission to the Lord's Supper; Northants.?
5	BL	Mid to long: unusual in that it was designed for the use of more adult catechumens
—	—	See below, s.v. J. Yates
1	21014	Mid; pre-comm. (Lord's Supper only); 'gathered out of' 1 Cor.xi.23–33, + based on sermons; London
1	R1415	Mid; composed in Wisbech jail by a Quaker; published with a vision of the author, + an attack on the local clergy
MS	Emman. Coll. Lib. MS. III. 1. 13[8]	A very methodical but quite demanding form on credal material, Dec, Pr, + Ss; in broad terms this may be the model from which A. Richardson or J. Yates produced his *Short and brief summe*, q.v., but it is not the same as DWL Modern MSS Folio no. 2
(1+)	BL	2 vols. of lectures on the WLC by a conservative Presbyterian; vol. 1 reprinted in 1734
(2?)	National Lib. of Scotland	Part of a larger debate on the Trinity + Christ's divinity, but this author appeals to the 5th + 6th answers of the WSC to make his point
2+	R1489 + BL	Long; Bible turned into qs + as; to help fathers + schoolteachers train the young in the knowledge of God; Quaker
1	BL	Mid, pre-comm. form in Welsh + English for use in Denbighshire
(2?)	4800.3 + Maunsell, 33	Short; handles Dec, Cr, Ss, + Pr in metrical verse, for easier learning + better remembering; could be sung to same tunes as metrical psalms
1	21098	A composite work: a help to understanding the New Testament, a very short pre-comm. catechism (Cr, Dec, Ss, Pr; for Christian families), a dialogue between Frailty + Faith, prayers, + a poem

1	2	3
Robinson, John	An appendix to Mr Perkins his six principles/A briefe catechisme concerning church-government	−1635 [Amst.]−1656
Roe, Richard	A short catachisme taken out of a larger treatise	1640
R[ogers], D[aniel]	A practical catechisme	1632–40
Rogers, Ezekiel	The chief grounds of Christian religion	1642–8
Rogers, John	The summe of Christianitie	[1578?]–85?
[Rogers, Richard]	The practise of Christianitie	1618–35
Rogers, R.	The plaine mans catachisme	1625
Ross, Alexander	The first booke of questions and answers upon Genesis	1620–6
——	The second book of questions and answers	1622–6
[Roucourt, Jean]	A catechism of penance	1685
anon.	The round-heads catechisme	1643
Rouspeau, Yves	A treatise of the preparation to the holy supper	[1570?]–9
Rowlandson, John	A briefe and plain catechisme	1644
anon.	The rules and directions of the ordinance	1646–8
anon.	Rules for self-examination	1685
anon./Feofan, Archbishop of Novgorod	Russkaia pravoslavnia tserkov. The Russian catechism	[1723]–5

4	5	6
3+	21107.5–7.7 + R1691–3	A short work, 'fit' to be an appendix to William Perkins's catechism (q.v.); on church government; London edns. perhaps 1641, 1642, 1656; Dutch ones perhaps 1624 (according to *DNB*: not traced) or 1625 (as part of STC² 21108?), 1635, 1636, + 1644 (DWL)
1?	*TSR* iv. 498	Not traced; ever published?
3+	21166–8 + 21173	Very long; based on catechetical sermons on 2 N.T. texts; focuses on 3 themes: sin, grace, + obedience; both 2nd + 3rd edns. enlarged; also issued as pt. 1 of his *Two treatises* in 1640; still on sale in 1658: London, *Catalogue*, sig. Q2ᵛ
2	R1800–01	Short; credal material, Dec, Ss, Pr; 'gathered long since' for the use of an 'honourable family'; Yorkshire?
(4?)	21183–4.5 + Maun-sell, 33	Expositions of 8 propositions covering the usual catechetical materials
5+	21221–23.7	7 of Rogers's popular treatises abridged + turned into q + a by S. Egerton (q.v.), first for private use, then for public benefit; London
1?	*TSR* iv. 138	Not traced (unless it is the last by a different name)
1+	21325, 21326, 21324	A long aid to Bible study; consists of qs + as on the 1st 6 chapters of Genesis; reissued with next in 1622 + 1626
1+	21325.5–26, 21324	Long; qs + as on chaps. 7–14 of Genesis
[1]	R2005C	Catholic; covers penance only; translated from French by W.B.
[1]	R2008	Political, + satirical; perhaps by J. Nutt
3	21351.5–53	Pt. 1 expounds the meaning of the sacrament, pt. 2 how to prepare for it; only pt. 3 is in q + a, a short catechism (called a 'dialogue') summarizing the above; translated from the French by R.B.; another translation of this work was published in Rouspeau + Jean de L'Espine, *Two treatises* (Cambridge, 1584), STC² 21354
1	R2090B	Short; Dec, Ss, Pr; prayers at end; 'very necessary for every housekeeper'; prayer at end; Sussex
—	—	See above, s.v. J. Cateline
(1)	R2256	Broadsheet; lists sins against the Dec for faithful to search for in themselves when preparing for Lord's Supper; not in q + a; 'extracted' from the writings of an eminent divine
2	BL	Official Russian catechism, together with an account of Russian church government + ceremonies, + wood-cuts; translated into English by J. T. Phillips; presumably of curiosity value

1	2	3
S., H.	The mother and the child	1628
S., I./J.	A Christian exhortation	1579
[S., J.]	The Christian doctrine: or, a short catechism showing how to become [+] continue a Christian	1678
S., S.	A brief instruction for all families	1583
anon.	A sacramental catechism	1702
anon.	Sacred principles, services, and soliloquies	1650
Saintbarb, Richard	Certaine points of Christian religion	1589
Saint George, Arthur	The blessings of Christian philosophy	−1738
[Saller/Salter, William]	Sundry queries tendred/formerly tendred ... for clearing the doctrine of the fourth commandement	[1653?]−[c. 1660]
S[aller], W[illiam]	Christian instruction: directed to a more perfect and saving knowledge	[1670?]
Salmon, Thomas	The catechism of the church ... divided into five parts	1699/1700
[Saltmarsh, John]	The fountaine of free grace opened	1645–8
Sanderson, Thomas	A brief summe of Christian religion	1640
anon.	A satyrical catechisme betwixt a neuter and a roundhead	1648
Scandrett, Stephen	Doctrine and instructions: or a catechism	1674
Scarbrough, Gervase	The summe of all godly and profitable catechismes	1623
anon.	The school of holiness ... together with a short catechism	−1686

4	5	6
1?	21496.3	A 'little catechism to teach little children the principles of religion'; untraced since 1939; since it was assigned by the Mans this is perhaps the same as the form gathered from Craig in 1611, q.v.
1	21500	A treatise in the 'holy dying' genre, translated from the French, but contains a short form on the knowledge of God's goodness + salvation
1?	S49aA	Short + relatively simple form; not the usual content, though there are echoes of PBC + other forms; divided into 10, for ease of memory; General Baptist? J. S. (perhaps John Spittlehouse) signs the preface
1	21518	Short; Dec, Cr, Ss; Norfolk
—	—	See above, s.v. *A new sacramental catechism*
—	—	See above, s.v. W. Brough
1	21556	Long + relatively advanced; designed to supplement other forms; Cr, Dec, Ss, Pr; predestinarian; possibly related to a work by Olevian, q.v.
(1+)	BL	A treatise on the Beatitudes in a dialogue between 'doctor' + parishioner; 1st edn. Dublin 1737
(1)	S400aA, S400	Controversial: 13 questions on the Sabbath, then a reply; preface signed by W. 'Salter' whom Wing equates with Saller, a General Baptist
1	S398C	Short; some unusual, relatively advanced material + some controversial; by a General Baptist; work signed by W. 'Sellers', but W. T. Whitley *Baptist Bibliography* (1916–22), i. 96 identifies author as Saller
1	S416B + *TC* iii. 168	PBC printed in roman rather than the usual black letter, + divided into five sections; then a short exposition of each section, not in q + a, though the author says his material can easily be turned into such; Beds.; price 3*d*.
(2)	S482–3	Controversial, but in q + a
1	21710.7	Short, pre-comm. form, for the 'simpler sort' of people in a London parish; a prayer at end; this form was apparently in existence in 1626
[1]	S724	Political, + satirical
1	S818	Mid; quite difficult (on 'weighty' points of divinity); Suffolk
1	21806.5	Mid; for children + 'poor ignorant souls', + especially his own family + London parishioners; Dec, Cr, Pr, Ss
14?	S883A	A very short form (some unusual content at the start, then Dec, Pr, Cr) in a larger work consisting mainly of prayers, but with some 'holy sayings' at the end

1	2	3
anon.	The school of learning	−1668–87
anon.	The school of piety, or, the devout Christian's duty	−1687
Scoffin, William	A help to true spelling	1690?–1705
Scot	?	1647?
[Scott, John]	Certain cases of conscience resolved	−1683–6
'Scottes catechisme'		
anon.	A scriptural catechism in opposition to the Popish catechism	1686
anon./R. E.	A scriptural catechism: or the [whole] duty of man	1676–1729
anon.	A scripture catechism	17th century?
anon.	A scripture catechism or the principles	1722
[Seaman, William]	Catechesis religionis Christianae brevior	1689
anon.	The second book for children, or the compleat schoolmaster	1704
Sedgwick, Obadiah	A short catechisme, being a briefe instruction	1647
S[edgwick], R[ichard]	A short summe of the principall things	1624
anon.	A select manuel of godly prayers with a short … introduction	1716

4	5	6
57?	S883B–4A	Very short form (Dec, Cr, Ss, Pr) in a larger work consisting almost entirely of prayers; 1668 edn. (in BL) said to be 15th, 1687 (in Bodleian) the 57th
4?	Magdalene Coll., Cambr. [PL365(16)]	Consists mainly of duties (man's to God, parents' to children, etc.), but ends with a very short form (100 qs + as on Bible knowledge) + verses from the psalms to memorize. The short form is not the same as that in J. Williams's *School of godliness*, q.v.
2	*TC* iii. 303 + Toronto Public Lib.	Reading primer + guide to Bible study, but adds a 'scriptural catechism'; mid; credal material, Dec, Ss, Pr; uses scripture texts for many answers; also has improving verses
1?	?	A scriptural catechism by Mr Scot was published in 1647, according to P. Nye, *Beames of former light* (1660), 76, but not traced
(3+)	S2039–40A	Some questions, but mainly an exposition of the lawfulness of set forms of prayer; attribution to Scott is in an ink note on BL copy; there was also a Part II (S2041–2)
		Copyright changed hands in London in 1591: *TSR* iii. 275: a Scottish form? e.g. by J. Craig, q.v
1	E35	Mid; scripturally-based catechism on the principles + duties of Christianity; especially for the younger sort
—	—	See above, s.v. R.E.
MS	BL Huth 81 (1)	Written in an interleaved copy of the Heidelberg Catechism; strong scriptural emphasis; origin not yet established
—	—	See above, s.v. J. Peirce
—	—	See below, s.v. Westminster Assembly
1?	*TC* iii. 414	How to read + write, but includes the 'grounds + principles of religion … in a shorter catechism, according to the advice of the Assembly of Divines', prayers, + woodcuts; no copy traced, but possibly related to *The first book*, q.v.
1	S2380A	Short, pre-comm. form, to instruct the 'most ignorant'; 40 qs + as, on credal material + Ss; some parallels with parliamentary ordinance of 20.10.1645
1	22152.5	Long, + relatively advanced; Cr (including Ss), Dec, + Pr; for author's London congregation; still on sale in 1658: London, *Catalogue*, sig. R3ᵛ
[1]	St Patrick's Coll., Manly, Sydney	Catholic; a combination of prayers + catechetical material, but framed by a dialogue in which a Catholic tries to persuade a Protestant to adopt the true faith

1	2	3
[Seller, Abednigo]	An exposition of the church-catechism	1695–9
Settle, Thomas	A catechisme briefly opening the misterie of our redemption	[1587]
[Sharp, Thomas]	A table of questions for examining [young] children	1723 (London)–1734 (Newcastle)
[Shaw, Ferdinando]	A catholic catechism, in an explanation	–1717–24
Shaw, John	The fundamental doctrines of the church	1720–2
Shephard, Thomas	The first principles of the oracles of God	1649–55
Sheppard, William	A new catechism	1649
S[herard], R[obert]	The countryman with his houshold	1620
[Sherlock, Richard]	[The] principles of holy Christian religion	1656–99–
anon.	A short abridgement of Christian doctrine	1728–
anon.	A short and plaine catechism	–1668–82
anon./'A country parson'	A short and plain exposition of the church catechism	1715
anon.	A short and useful explanation of the catechism	1686
anon.	A shorte catechisme	1550
anon.	A short catechism according to the doctrine of the Church of England	1688

4	5	6
2	S2451 + *TC* iii. 164	Long; PBC; mainly explanations, comments + scripture references, but there are some extra qs + as, mainly rhetorical or repetitious; price 1*s.* 6*d.*
1	22267	Mid; not the usual staples, + heavily scriptural answers; also contains a 'fardle' of Christian duties; for author's parishioners in Suffolk
2	Lambeth + New-castle Publ. Lib.	Mid; about 350 questions (but no answers) drawn from S. Ford's 1686 work + J. Lewis's (qq.v.); to test catechumens' understanding of PBC; for children + young persons; Northumberland; attribution to Sharp is in the Lambeth copy
3	DWL + BL	Mid; (2nd edn. corrected + abridged); offers an explanation of Cr, Dec, Pr, + Ss in the express words of scripture; author had irenic aims; price (1724) 6*d.*
1	BL	Very long (3 vols.); PBC with extra qs + as; based on catechetical lectures given in Wilts; for those of 'weakest + meanest capacity' but often quite advanced, + sometimes controversial
3+?	S3144–6 + S3104	Short, but quite hard; credal material, Dec, + Ss; devised for use in New England, but published in England as supplement to some editions of his *Theses sabbaticae* + *Certain select cases*
1	S3193	Mid; credal material, Ss, Pr, Dec; written by a leading lawyer; for parents + masters to use with children + servants on Sundays; dedicated to the corporation of Gloucester
<2>	22427–27a	A long dialogue between various speakers (pastor, parent, child, etc.) on catechetical staples, interspersed with short q + a forms on the same topics; summary of the whole in metrical verse at the end
18	S3246–53	Mid; PBC with comments + extra qs + as; also a separate reply to objections to PBC, + prayers; edn. in Welsh, + published in America in 1704
[1+]	BL	Catholic; short; used in America in 18th + 19th centuries
—	—	See above, s.v. S. Jacombe
1	National Lib. of Scotland	Short; PBC with extra qs + as; a shortened version of *The country parson to the country people* (1712), q.v. above
1	S3558A	Short; PBC with exposition after each answer or group of answers; also has an abecedarie on reverse of title-page
—	—	See above, s.v. Leo Jud
1	S3567	A long, modified version of WSC, with the irenic intent of reconciling episcopalian + Presbyterian standpoints; pt. 1 of *Catechism made practical*, q.v.

1	2	3
anon.	A short catechism against all sectaries	1662
anon.	A short catachisme. Brieflie contayning the whole summe	1590 'London' [= Middelburg?]
anon.	[A short catechisme, by law authorized] (in Hebrew)	1633
anon.	A short catechism by way of question and answer	1686
anon.	A short catechism collected by a Christian	[1575?]
anon.	A short catechism composed	1646
anon.	A short catechisme containing the principles	1656
anon.	A short catechism containing the principles	1718
anon.	A short catechisme for all the kings ... subjects	1660
anon.	A short catechism for instructing	1738
anon.	A short catechisme for the instruction of the inhabitants of S.M.	1645
anon.	A short catechisme for little children	1589
anon.	A short catechisme for their help	–1676 (Dort)
anon.	A short catechisme: holding forth	1646
anon.	A short catechisme opening the principles	1650
anon.	A short catechism: or an abridgement of Christian doctrine	1687
anon.	A short catechisme or the examination of communicants	1646–7
anon.	A short catechism. Section 1	1659
anon.	A short catechisme. The seventh edition	1632

4	5	6
[1]	S3568	Catholic; controversial dialogue, translated by C.M.; replies by F[rancis] H[owgill], *Rock of ages* (1662), + J. Rawlet, *Dialogue* (q.v.)
[1]	4803.3	Very short; Dec, Cr, Pr, Ss; related to the Dering–More version (q.v.), but not just an abridgement of it; possibly by M. Mosse, q.v.
(1)	16461	PBC translated into Hebrew by T. Ingmethorpe
[1]	S3568A	Catholic; controversial (on the apostolic succession + Ss); author abandons q + a format after the first few pages
1	4803.4	A very short form of only 6 qs + as, learned by 20 poor men, 20 poor women, and 10 poor children in a London parish in 1575, for which they were given money + clothes; prayers at end
—	—	See above, s.v. J. Ball
1	Emmanuel Coll., Cambr.	Very short form 'extracted for the most part out of other catechisms'
1	BL + Carruthers, 22	Mid; WSC with q + a 95 omitted + scripture references in full; approved for use in a London charity school
(1)	S3569	Uses q + a form + scriptural precepts + examples to urge obedience to Charles II; for families; ends with prayers for the king + the churches in the 3 kingdoms
1	BL + DWL	Short; not the usual content; for 'such as are disposed to enter into the great end + design of the Christian religion'
1	S3571	Short; pre-comm.: 'the first part'; there is no indication where S.M. is
1	4803.8	Very short: 42 qs + as (some unusual) between a father + child, said to have been learned by a 3-year-old; Dec, Cr, + Lord's Pr printed in full at end, + advice on duties; cf. *A catechisme so short* (1639) above
[2?]	S3571A	[not yet seen: copy at Canterbury Cathedral]
1	S3572	Short form; based on 6 principles, + at outset follows + abridges Perkins's form (q.v.), but deviates thereafter
1?	S3573A	Not found in BL catalogue
1?	S3573B	Not traced at location given by Wing[2]; a version of the 'Douay catechism'?
3?	S3574–5	Very short; pre-comm.; based on parliamentary ordinance of 20.10.1645; 3rd edn. enlarged by extra qs + as on the doctrine of sacraments
1	S3576	Very short form with some unusual phrases; credal material, Pr, Ss, Dec; presumably unfinished
—	—	See below, s.v. J. White

1	2	3
anon.	[Short catechisme to bee learned before the admision to the lordes supper]	pre-1595
anon.	A short catechisme to prepare young ignorant people for the sacrament	1657
anon.	A short catechisme, with exposition of the same	1637
anon.	A short essay of catechism	[pre-1695]
anon.	A short explanation of the shorter catechism	1689
anon.	A short exposition of the church–catechism	[17—] (Norwich)
anon.	A short exposition of the catechism of the church	1683
anon.	A short historical catechism	1730–2
anon.	Short instructions for them … preparing for confirmation	1736–40
anon.	Short principles of religion	1644
anon.	Short questions and answers	1590
anon.	Short questions and answers	1690/1
anon.	A short scripture catechism	1699
anon.	A short summe of the trueth	1592
anon.	A short treatise containing	1615–
anon.	A short view of the Assemblies catechism	1699
S[hutte], C[hristopher]	The testimonie of a true fayth / A compendious forme and summe	1577–1637
Simson, John	A catachisme	1631

4	5	6
1?	See col. 6	Maunsell, 33, lists this as published by Christopher Barker; not identified or traced
1	B570	Pre-comm. form in broadsheet format; 30 qs + as on Cr, Dec, Ss, + Pr; attibuted by Madan, *Oxford Books*, iii. 63–4 to J. Ball, but seems to be nearer to PBC than Ball's forms
1?	See col. 6	Copy offered for sale in Thos. Kerslake's *Catalogue of Books* [186–?], 6, but not listed in STC[2]
1?	See col. 6	Advert in Seller's *Exposition*, q.v.; see above, s.v. J. Ellesby
—	—	See above, s.v. S. Angier
1	Bodleian	Mid; based on Williams's + Wake's explanations of PBC (q.v.); designed for children, + learnt by 10-year-olds; recommended for use by parents + Charity Schools; Norwich
—	—	From the description in *TC* ii. 53 this is almost certainly an edn. of the work by E. Boughen, q.v.
—	—	See above, s.v. J. K. Denhoff
2	Liverpool Univ. Lib. + BL	Mid; some overlaps with work by Nelson, q.v., but this is a discrete work; prayers + advice to the newly confirmed at the end; 1740 edn. also has a supplement explaining regeneration; apparently designed for godparents to give to their godchildren before confirmation; price 6*d.* or £2 2*s.* a 100
1	S3612	Short; credal material, Dec, Ss; at the end are rules for a godly life
1?	Maunsell, 33	Not traced; not the same publisher as similarly entitled works by Paget-Openshaw, + Whiting, qq.v., unless latter was transferred to a new publisher by 1593
—	—	See above, s.v. J. Ball
1?	*TC* iii. 121	Not traced; same publisher (T. Parkhurst) as a similarly entitled 1672 work by S. Petto, q.v., but that is said to be for little children, whereas this one is 'necessary for all sorts of persons'
(1)	23432	Broadsheet; in tabular form; not q + a
—	—	See above, s.v. J. Ball
(1)	S3638AB + *TC* iii. 134	Not traced at location given in Wing[2]; defence of PBC in relation to WSC, to judge from the title
5	22467–69.7	A mid form (Dec, Cr, Ss, Pr; meet for all well disposed families), a prayer, + a very short pre-comm. form for simple people, a sermon on true religion, + a form of confession for household or individual use
1?	*TSR* iv. 250	Not traced; ever published? Simson was said to have been minister at Maldon, Essex

1	2	3
anon.	Six awakening questions	1694
Slater, Samuel	The two covenants from Sinai	1644
Smith, John	Essex dove, presenting the world with a few of her olive branches	1629–37
Smith, Samuel	The Christian's guide or the Holy Bible	1738
Smith, William	A catechism for bishops	1661–2
——	A new primmer	1663–8
——	A new catechism	1665–7
Some, Robert	A godly and short treatise upon the lordes prayer	1583
——	A godly and shorte treatise of the sacraments	1582
anon.	Some forms of catecheticall doctrines	1647
anon.	Some gospel truths catechistically laid downe	1647
anon.	The souls magazine of scripture truths	1722
Spangenberg, Johann	The sum of divinitie	1548–67
——	Margarita theologia	1566–73
Sparke, Thomas	A short treatise … for all troubled in theyr consciences	1580

4	5	6
1	S3911	Very short; unusual content: aimed at unconverted sinners
1	S3978	Short; focuses on covenants of works + grace; for an Essex parish; on sale in 1658: London, *Catalogue*, sig. R2ᵛ
3+	22798–800.5	Long; original structure + touches, but also tackles Cr, Pr, + Ss; same work contains the sum of a series of sermons on Pr; work ed. by John Hart; Essex?
1	BL	The Bible turned into qs + as; cf. *Doctrine of the Bible* above
(2)	S4290A–91	Largely controversial; Quaker attack on restored Church of England
<3>	S4321–3	Partly instructive, partly controversial dialogue between son + father; written in Nottingham jail in 1663; mid
2	S4318–19	As last partly instructive, partly controversial; mid; followed by history of Quakers in q + a; written in the same jail, 1664
(1)	22906.5	Not in q + a, though author called it a catechism, + Maunsell (p. 33) + Watts (*Entrie to Christianitie*) list it as one; mid; covers Pr, Cr, + Dec
(1)	22906	Referred to as a follow-up to last, but published first (perhaps by Lady Hynde: see preface to the above); not in q + a; long; Ss only; Some also published *A godlie treatise of the church* (1582) + *A godly treatise … deciding certaine questions* (1588), but neither was in q + a
1	S4506A	A short historical catechism on God's dealings with man, + 2 sets of catechetical propositions, on faith + obedience; designed for those of all degrees + capacities, young + old; preface of interest for attitudes to catechizing
—	—	See above, s.v. J. Heydon
(1)	BL + Bodleian	A very long 'historical dialogue' in which the Body asks + the Soul replies at great length on key aspects of Old + New Testaments; published in London, but to be sold also in Cambridge + Norwich
5	23004–7	Very long, with very long answers too; covers wide range of topics; Lutheran origin, tr. by R. Hutten; said to be very useful for curates + divinity students, + all Christian men + women
(3)	23001–3	Last item in Latin; 1566 edn. possibly printed in Antwerp
2	23025–25.5	Pt. 2 of this work contains 'A brief and short catechisme'—a mid form (Dec, Cr, Ss, Pr) used publicly

1	2	3
anon.	Spelling-book for children, with a short catechism	1707
Sprint, John	The summe of the Christian religion	1613
S[talham], J[ohn]	A catechisme for children in years and children in understanding	1644–50
Standfast, Richard	A caveat against seducers	1711–13–
anon.	The state catechise	1707
Stebbing, Henry	Polemical tracts ... to which are added a short exposition / The young Christian instructed	1727 (Cambridge)–1728–
Sterry, Peter	The appearance of God ... Together with ... a short catechism	1710
Stinton, Benjamin	A short catechism, wherin the principles	–1730
Stock, Richard	A stock of divine knowledge	1641
Stockton, Owen	A treatise of family instruction	1672
——	A scriptural catechism	1672–6
Stockwood, John	A sermon preached at Paules Crosse [24.8.1578]	1578
Stookes, Richard	A champion catechism	1651

4	5	6
		in his flock (in Bucks.), + a short pre-comm. form used privately 'even to the simplest', + a long prayer; see also above, s.v. *A catechisme, or short kind*
1	BL	A reading primer, with exercises based on the Bible, + a short catechism in which the longer words are subdivided into syllables; content is quite technical in places, + may be a Congregational alternative to the *ABC with the catechisme*, q.v.
1+?	23111 + Jaggard, sig. A2^r	Mid; not the usual staples, apart from Ss; Gloucestershire; a 2nd edn. perhaps planned in 1618; not the same content as *The summe* of 1607–17, q.v.
2	S5182–3	Short (with short summary at end); credal material, Ss, Pr, + Dec very briefly; been used with 'little children + most ignorant servants'; author became Congregational; Essex
(2+)	Bodleian	Contains a sermon + a series of improving verses, including a short verse dialogue between a blind man + death
[1]	National Lib. of Wales	Political: satirical
2+	Bodleian	The 9th of the 10 items is 'The young Christian instructed': a 2-part exposition of the PBC, to further + test understanding of its doctrine, by discourses followed by questions but no answers, + scripture proofs; 1727 edn., to be sold in London as well as Cambridge; 1728 edn. of *Young Christian* described as 5th corrected; BL has 9th + 10th edns. dated 1756 + 1763
1	BL	A series of discourses, with a short catechism for the young at the end; a longer version of the same, apparently unfinished, was also included
2	BL	Short; scriptural answers (with staple formulae printed at the end); by a Baptist
1	S5693	Very long; short questions but very long + relatively advanced answers, not on the usual staples; London?
(1)	S5701	Dialogue on duty of masters + parents to instruct children + servants in Bible knowledge; incorporated next; price 3*s*. 6*d*. bound; Essex
3+	S5700–700A + *TC* i. 248	Long, difficult; scriptural answers; useful for all sorts of persons, both teachers + learners; first published as part of last; Essex
(1)	23284	Exhortation to catechize, claiming England was weary of sermons; see also, s.v. Dering + More
1	S5740A (part 2)	Short; quirky in places; a trailer for 2 larger works by the same author; Baptist

1	2	3
[Strong, James]	The Assembly's shorter catechism revised	1735–9
[——]	A vindication of the [WSC] revised	1736–8
anon.	The sufferers-catechism	1664
anon.	A summary of Christian duties	1687
anon.	A summe of Christian doctrine	1686
anon.	The summe of Christian religion	1607–17
anon.	The summe of Christian religion, breifly comprised	1649
anon.	The summe of Christianitie containing eight propositions	1585
anon.	The summe of Christianitie, set down in familiar questions and answers	[*c.*1600]
S[wadlin], T[homas]	The souldiers catechisme … for the kings armie	1645 (Oxford)
Sykes, Arthur Ashley	An answer to the remarks upon Dr Clarke's exposition	1730
Syme, John	The sweet milke of Christian doctrine	1617
Synge, Edward	Plain instructions for the young and ignorant	1701–37
T., T.	A handfull of goates-haire	1616
anon.	A table of questions	1723–34

4	5	6
3?	Liverpool Univ. Lib. + BL	A revision of the WSC to render it 'fitter for general use' by making it clearer, fuller + less controversial on matters 'not absolutely necessary to salvation'; also some scripture proofs were altered; for support, see S. Bourn + P. Gibbs above, for attacks see works cited in next entry.
(1+?)	BL + DWL	Defence of last against the attacks by J. Guyse + D. Rees, qq.v., especially over the softening of the line on predestination; for another attack see D. Millar above; for another possible edn., see Carruthers, 118
—	—	See above, s.v. V. Powell
[1]	S6127A	Catholic; long; not in q + a
[1]	S6167	Catholic; short; also covers the sacrament of confirmation; published by James II's printer
2	23432.3–32.5	Mid, but long answers; built around six 'principal questions'; for the simpler sort to use in families; also has 'precepts' + 'steps'; not the same as similarly entitled work by J. Sprint, q.v.
1	S6168	Short, with a summary at the end; divided into 14 'heads', so children could learn it in as many weeks; composed for private use in a country parish, school + family; has parallels to WSC
—	—	See above, s.v. J. Rogers
1	23432.7	Short with a summary in the last q + a; covers Cr, Dec, + Pr, but also contains some unusual features
[8?]	S6224–6	Mainly political: a royalist reply to Ram, q.v.
(2)	BL	Controversial: a reply to D. Waterland (q.v.) on Samuel Clarke's *Exposition* (q.v.); BL's T757 contains later exchanges between Waterland + Sykes
1	23585	Short; for use after PBC form by those of riper years; Cr, Dec, Ss, Pr; author requested to publish this form by his Essex parishioners; a larger work was supposed to follow
7+	BL + Bodleian	Mid; PBC with extra qs + as + preface on the value + technique of catechizing; for those of meanest capacity; probably originated in Ireland, + some copies almost certainly used there; price (1706) 3*d.*; 9th edn. 1762
1	23626.5	Short; mentions Dec, Cr, Ss, Pr only briefly, + has some unusual features; for beginners; author perhaps Twisse, Twine, or Thompson
—	—	See above, s.v. T. Sharp

1	2	3
Talbot, James	The church-catechisme explained by a paraphrase	1705
[Talbot, Peter]/N. N.	The polititians catechisme	1658 (Antwerp)
Taverner, Richard	A catechisme or institution of the Christen religion	1539
[Taylor, Jeremy]	A short catechism for the institution	1652
——	The golden grove	1655–1735
——	Symbolon … or a collection of … discourses	1657–74
Taylor, Nathaniel	A practical and short exposition	1683–5
Taylor, Thomas	Certain catechistical exercises	1653–9
anon.	The tenets and principles	1732
Thaxter, John	?	?
Thomas, Lambrocke	Milke for children	1654
'Philotheos'	A threefold dialogue	1708
Tillotson, John	Six sermons	1694–7
[Tindal, Matthew]	A new catechism, with Dr Hickes's 39 articles	1710
Tombes, John	A short catechism about baptism	1659

4	5	6
1	Bodleian	Long; PBC with expositions + proofs, divided into 52 sections; also revision questions + prayers from PBC + BCP; interesting preface on technique; Yorks.?
[1]	T117A	Controversial; authorized Catholic polemic against Protestantism; not in q + a; has also been attributed to Nicholas French, Bishop of Ferns
(1)	23709	A translation into English + adaptation of Calvin's 1537 *Instruction*; not in q + a
1	T397	Short: mainly credal material + Ss; also provided an exposition of Cr in prose rather than q + a; intended for schools in South Wales; listed by London: *Catalogue*, sig. S1^r
27?	T336–41A + BL	Reprint of last, together with a 'diary' of how to spend each day, prayers + hymns
3?	T398–9	Reprint of catechism + exposition of Creed along with a variety of discourses
3	T544B + 546–6A, *TC* ii. 25	Long; PBC with extra qs + as; mildly controversial in places, + interesting citations; for youth; price bound 1*s*.; Lincs.
3+	T562, + 560–1 *Works*	Long + fairly advanced; mainly on religion, scriptures, + credal material; for those with honest hearts but weak heads; these sermons were given in a London church on Sunday afternoons before Taylor's death in 1633: *TSR* iv. 518
—	—	See above, s.v. H.A.
?	—	Thaxter asked his patron to have some copies printed of 2 small catechisms—1 for young people, the other more advanced—which he had used in his living at Bridgham, Norfolk: *Hist. MSS. Comm. Gawdy MSS* (1885), 23; neither has been traced
1	T967A	A reading primer, but contains a short catechism, a mid dialogue expounding the same, and then expositions of Cr, Dec, + Pr in continuous prose; interesting on technique; for ministers, teachers, + parents to use with 'ruder sort' + young; also has an appendix of prayers; Sussex?
(1)	Regent's Park Coll., Oxford	Dialogue between a Scots Presbyterian + an English Baptist on 3 controversial matters, but tone mostly not polemical; author perhaps J. Maulden
(3)	T1268–68B	3rd and 4th sermons contain some interesting observations on catechisms + catechizing
[2]	BL	Polemical + satirical; also attributed to Daniel Defoe
1	T1820	Short; partly polemical; Baptist

1	2	3
Tomkys, John	A briefe exposition of the Lordes prayer	[1585]
Towerson, Gabriel	An explication/exposition of the decalogue/the catechism of the church ... Part II	1676–85
——	An explication/exposition of/to the catechism ... the preliminary questions and ... Creed/Part I	1678–85
——	An explanation/explication of the Lords Prayer/catechism of the church ... Part III	1680–5
——	Of the sacraments in general	1686
——	Of the sacrament of baptism	1687
——	An explication of the catechism ... Part IV	1688
anon.	The town-misses catechism	1703
anon.	A tried method of catachising	1698–
anon.	The trimmer catechised	1683
Trosse, George	The Revd. Mr. Trosse's arguments	1718 (Exeter)
[Trott, Thomas]	The communicant instructed, how to examine himself	1668
anon.	The true beliefe in Christ	1550
anon.	A true-protestant-catechism	1683
anon.	A true relation of some proceedings at Salters–Hall	[1719]
Tuckney, Anthony	A breife and pithy catechisme	1628
[Tully, Thomas]	Praecipuorum theologiae capitum enchiridion	1665–1700
T[urberville], H[enry]	An abridgement of Christian doctrine	1648 (Douai)–1734–
[Twisse, William]	A brief catecheticall exposition	1632–45

4	5	6
1	24109	Short; Pr only; parent asks, child replies; for the unlearned; prayer at end; Salop.
(4?)	T1970, T1967A–C + *TC* i. 215	Very long exposition of Dec section of PBC (not in q + a): published in folio, 14*s*. bound; presumably aimed at clergy, teachers + well-educated or prosperous laity; Herts.
(2)	T1966–7	Very long exposition of opening qs + as + Cr section of PBC
(3?)	T1965A, 1967D + 1968	Long exposition of Pr section of PBC
(2)	T1973–73A	Exposition of start of last part of PBC; the first section of Towerson's opus to be published in both folio + octavo
(2)	T1971A–72	Exposition of section of PBC on baptism; again published in folio + octavo
(1)	T1969	The first 2 sections of this folio volume are the 1686 + 1687 works listed above: only the final third, on the Lord's Supper, is new, though published with continuous signatures + pages from the 1687 work
[1]	Bodleian	Satirical; no obvious element of parody
—	—	See below, s.v. E. Wetenhall
[1]	T2277	Political, + anti-dissenter
(1)	BL	A controversial work, but refers to a catechism by Trosse (as does T. Emlyn's reply to this work); no copy of the catechism has been traced
1	Bodleian	Long, pre-comm. form, but consists of questions only, no answers; derived from F. Roberts's treatise *A communicant instructed* (1651–); for 'poor householders' to use it to test their worthiness to receive communion; prayers at end
—	—	See above, s.v. W. Capito
[1]	T2862	Satirical: anti-Whig + dissent
(1)	BL	Part of a controversy in which answers in the WSC were used as a test of orthodoxy against Arians.
MS	Emmanuel Coll. Cambr. MS III. 1. 13[8]	'as … delivered in Emmanuel College chapel 1628'; unusual content: 2 covenants, *ordo salutis*
(6?)	T3246A–50	Long, advanced form in Latin; credal material, Dec, Ss, + some controversial material
[14+]	T3252B–56C + BL, etc.	Catholic; long; most edns. published in Douai (hence nickname: 'the Douai catechism'), but other edns. were published in Basel + London
5	24400–41.7, + T3418	4 short forms on Ss, Pr, Dec, + Cr

1	2	3
Tye, William	A matter of moment	1608
Ursinus, Zacharias	Doctrinae Christianae compendium/ Explicationum catecheticarum	1585 (London)– 1587 (Cambridge)
——	The summe of Christian religion	1587 (Oxford)–1645 (London)
(Ursinus) + 'Pareus'/ [Paré], David	A collection of certaine learned discourses	1600–13
Ussher, James	The principles of Christian religion; with a brief method	1644–1720
——	De Romanae ecclesiae symbolo apostolico vetere … in prima catechesis … diatriba	1647–60
'Ussher, James'	A body of divinitie, or the summe and substance	1645–1702
V., D.	An enlargement of a former catechisme	1637–41
Vaughan, Edward	A plaine and perfect method, for the easie understanding of the whole Bible	1603–17
[Vaux, Laurence]	A catechisme, or [a] christian doctrine	1568–1620 (abroad)
Vesey, Henry	The scope of the scripture	1614–37
V[icars], T[homas]	The grounds of that doctrine	–1630–1

4	5	6
(1+)	24414–14.5	A dialogue between a Christian gentleman + a minister on self-examination before receiving the Lord's Supper; derived from a sermon
(3+)	24529–31	A reprint of the 1584 Geneva edn. of Ursinus's Latin lectures on the Heidelberg Catechism, q.v.; 1586 edn. pirated; in 1658 London was offering for sale what was perhaps a later edn. of this work, entitled, *Corpus doctrinae Christianae*: London, *Catalogue*, sig. Q1^r
(9+)	24532–39.7 + U142	Translation by Henry Parry of last: a monolith of scholarship with occasional objections + answers; 1st 5 edns. published in Oxford; still for sale in 1658: London, *Catalogue*, sigs. S2^{r-v}
(1+)	24527–7.5	Translation by I.H. of a Latin volume by Paré which contained a miscellany of works, including some by Ursinus on 'divers difficult points' in the Heidelberg Catechism
10?	U201–7, *TC* iii. 628–9, + BL	Two forms, a long (credal material, Dec, Ss) + a short, the 2nd developing points from the 1st; 1702 edn. entitled *A short catechism: or the principles*; 1708/9 edn. included PBC + cost 3*d*. or 20*s*. a 100; reprinted in 1720 as part of a composite work entitled *Compassionate advice* (see BL Catalogue under R. Baxter)
[2]	U167–8	Scholarly treatise, in Latin, on the creeds used in early catechesis
8+?	U151–8 + BL	A composite work with extracts from catechisms by Cartwright, Crook, + others which Ussher denied was by him: *Whole Works* ed. C. R. Elrington (1847), i. 248–9; very long; 1670 edn. cost 8*s*. bound; the same publisher had a controlling interest in this work + the *Principles* (above)
2	24563 + V2	Mid; credal material, Dec, Ss, Pr; stress on scripture proofs; for 'novices' in Christ's school; the 'former' work has not been traced
(2)	24599.5–600	Described as 'a kind of scripture catechism', but is a dialogue in which the pastor explains to a parishioner the meaning + significance of the contents of the Bible
[9?]	24625.5–27a.4	Catholic; printed at Louvain, Antwerp, Rouen + St Omer + once by the secret press in England
6	24693.5–95a	Long; Dec, Cr, Ss, Pr; for use at home, to teach ignorant the saving knowledge of God's word; Essex
3	24700–701	Short form of 27 qs + as 'gathered' out of several (named) works; Dec, Cr, Pr, Ss; followed by prayers,

1	2	3
Vincent, Nathaniel	The little childs catechisme. In which the principles	1679–1701–
——	The principles of the doctrine of Christ	1691
——	A catechism for conscience	1691
Vincent, Thomas	An explicatory catechisme: or an explanation of the Assemblies shorter catechism	1673–1721–
Virel, Matthieu	A learned + excellent treatise … set down by conference	1594–1635
Viret, Pierre	A verie familiare and fruiteful exposition of the xii articles	[1548?]
——	The firste parte of the Christian instruction	1565
——	A christian instruction	1573
——	The Christian disputations	1579
——	A faithfull and familiar exposition upon the prayer of our Lorde	1582
anon.	A voice from heaven, to the youth of Great Britain	[1690?]
anon./ [English Parliament]	Votes of Parliament touching the book commonly called … the Racovian catechism	1652
W., E.	The principles of Christian religion delivered by questions and answeres	1621
W., J.	A catechism for young scholars in the school of Christ	1683
W., R.	A sacramental catechism	1701

4	5	6
		a psalm based on the catechism, a sum of the catechism, + a sum of that sum, Dec + Cr in verse, + prayers for several occasions; Suff.
3?+	V412, *TC* i. 415, 449, + DWL	Short; for little children; WSC parallels; volume also contains examples of 'popish cruelty' + of contempt of God being punished, + godly verses; Scottish edn. 1716; London?
1	V418	Short: 17 qs + as with scripture proofs at length; similar to last; London?
1	[ex-V401]	Part 2 of the last: questions to be put to the conscience of a 'grossly ignorant sinner' + suitable replies
8+	V432–6A + BL	Very long; WSC with extra qs + as; 'useful to be read in private families, after examination in' the WSC itself; many edns. published in Scotland + one each in Belfast + Boston, Mass.; different edns. have different prefaces
<14>	24767.5–73	Long dialogue-catechism between Theophilus + Matthew, translated from the French by S. Egerton (q.v.); covers Cr, Dec, Pr, + Ss; written in a 'plain + familiar method'; to be studied regularly at home
(1)	24784	7 dialogues between Nathaniel + Philip on Cr; partly controversial (anti-Catholic)
(1)	24777	4 dialogues between Timothy + Daniel, largely controversial: anti-Catholic
1	24778	Although the title-page refers to dialogues, this is essentially a very long catechism, divided into 53 chapters, on Cr, Pr, Dec, Ss + much else; translated by J. Shute from the French
(1)	24776	6 dialogues: all anti-Catholic
(1)	24780	10 dialogues between Simon + Zacharie on Pr; preface by John Field
(1)	V675A	Contains 2 dialogues: between Christ, a Youth, + the Devil, and Dives + Lazarus; also has advice to children, + prayers
(1)	E2453	Resolution by the Rump to seize + burn all copies of the *Catechesis ecclesiarum quae in regno Poloniae* (q.v. above) because of its blasphemous and erroneous content
1?	*TSR* iv. 57	Not traced; ever published?
1?	*TC* ii. 12	No copy traced: contains 'some evangelical truths' for the use of young Christians
1	Bodleian	Contains 2 forms: a very short, pre-comm. one, for poor servants + others of short memory + plain capacity;

1	2	3
W., S.	A short and plain explication of the shorter catechism	1667
W., T.	Preparation to the Lords Supper	pre-1595
Wadsworth, Thomas	Short catechism of twelve questions	1676
Wake, William	The principles of the Christian religion	1699–1731–
Walker, George	The key of saving knowledge	1641
W[alkington], T[homas]	An exposition of the two first verses	1609
Wallis, John	A brief and easie explanation	1648–62
Ward, Richard	Theologicall questions	1640
Ward, William	Short grounds of catechisme	1627 (Cambridge)
Warford, William/'George Douley'	A briefe instruction. By way of dialogue	1604–37 (abroad)
Warren, Erasmus	The truest scripture-catechism of the Trinity	1714
Warren, John	Principles of Christian doctrine	1654–8

4	5	6
		and a short 'communicant's guide' on what to do before, during, + after reception, for young who had not yet received, + those ignorant adults who had received unworthily; further material + a prayer; price 2*d*. or 12*s*. a 100—to be given away by charitable Christians
1	W110A	Long; WSC with extra qs + as + scripture proofs, to help those of mean capacities; DWL Catalogue suggests the author may have been Sam. Willard
1?	Maunsell, 33	Not traced; ever published?
1?	Grant, 355	Not traced; it is not the same as Wadsworth's sermon *How may it appear?* (1676), though the latter is built round some rhetorical questions + objections
5+	W258–9 + BL	Long; PBC with extra qs + as; recommended for Charity Schools, but its length + price (2*s*. a copy) suggests was aimed at older or more advanced students; prayers at end; often reprinted in Ireland; edns. in French + German too; for a reply to one part of it, see Morrice, *A defence of lecturers* (1733), above
(1)	W360	Long dialogue between father + son; not the usual staples; predestinarian; London
—	—	See below, s.v. T. Wilson
9?	W559–61A	Mid; uses Palmer's 'Yes'/'No' method to explain the WSC; 9th + 10th edns. published in Ireland
(1)	25024	A very long, verse-by-verse exposition of the gospel of Matthew, with 2,650 very short questions, + as many very long answers; still on sale in 1658: London, *Catalogue*, sig. S4[r]
1	25058	Long; PBC with extra qs + as + proofs; for youth; Yorks?
[4?]	25068–70	Catholic; dialogue; published at Louvain + St Omer
(1)	Lambeth	Author calls it a catechism + says it is to help 'meaner Christians' understand the Trinity, but it is technical, being in part taken out of Warren's own anti-Arian treatise on the subject
3	W977–8	Mid; each of 19 propositions is followed by questions to which the answers are scripture proofs; some WSC influence at the start; for parents + householders; used in 'conferences' in his Essex parish

1	2	3
Waterland, Daniel	Remarks upon Dr Clarke's exposition	1730
Wats[on], Chr[istopher]	Briefe principles of religion, collected	1578–81
Watson, Thomas	A body of practical divinity	1692–8–
Watts, Isaac	Prayers composed for the use of children ... together with instructions	1728–
——	Catechisms: or, instructions in the principles of the Christian religion	1730
——	Two sets of catechisms and prayers	–1730
——	The first sett of catechisms + prayers	–1734–
——	The second sett of catechisms and prayers	–1730–8–
——	The assembly's catechism with notes	1730–6–
——	A short view of the whole scripture history	1732–
——	A preservative from the sins and follies of youth	–1734–8–
——	A discourse on the way of instruction by catechisms	–1736

4	5	6
(1)	BL + Lambeth	Part of the controversy provoked by Samuel Clarke's *Exposition* of 1729 (q.v.); Waterland also wrote *Nature … of the Christian sacraments* (1730) + *A supplement to the treatise* (1730) as part of this debate
2+?	25109.5–110 + Maunsell, 31	Very short: 1st edn. a broadsheet; covers Dec, Cr, Ss, + Pr; for youth and simpler sort of people; Maunsell's 'brief catechisme … [in] three parts' may refer to another edn. in 1579
(2+?)	W1109 + *TC* ii. 419	Very long exposition, in 176 sermons, of WSC; mainly explanation, but there are some subsidiary questions added; 3rd edn. Glasgow 1734
2+	BL + NUC	Mainly prayers for young people of different ages + in different situations, but also contains a short 'catechism to teach children to pray', covering the different parts of prayer (invocation, petition, thanksgiving, etc.)
2	BL + New College, Edinburgh	Six forms, some conventional, others less so (see Appendix 2); published with other material (see *Discourse* below); 2nd edn. cost 2*s*.
2	Ibid. + DWL	Contains 'first' and 'second set' of forms (see next 2 items)
6+	BL	A very short form for the very young, + a q + a form on biblical names (both from *Catechisms*); price 2*d*. or 1*s*. 6*d*. a dozen; 20th edn. 1788; also reprinted in Gibson's *A preservative against popery* (1738)
5+	BL	A mid form for 7- to 12-year-olds + a 'historical catechism' on episodes in the Bible (both from *Catechisms*); 12th edn. 1768
(4+)	Carruthers, 121 + BL	Separate publication of form from *Catechisms*; adds explanatory notes on the harder words in the WSC; for 3rd-level students; price 4*d*. or 3*s*. 6*d*. per dozen; later edns. published in America
2+	BL + DWL	Very long series of qs + as on the historical content of the Bible, supplemented by explanatory notes + engravings; designed to be read by those of 'younger years' + the 'common ranks of mankind' with 'fewer conveniences and advantages of knowledge'; 26th edn. 1820
3+	BL	A separate edn. of a q + a form showing the young what sins to avoid and why; each q + a is followed by a reason + a proof text; volume also contains a catalogue of scripture names; first published in *Catechisms*; 11th edn. 1792
(3+)	BL	A separate edn. of the discourse which opened *Catechisms*; 7th edn. 1786

1	2	3
Watts, Robert	The lawfulness and right manner	1710
Watts, Thomas	The entrie to Christianitie	1589
anon.	The way to true happiness	1610–[50?]
Webb, Richard	A key of knowledge for catechizing children in Christ	1622
W[ebbe], G[eorge]	A briefe exposition of the principles	1612–17
[Welchman, Edward]	A dialogue betwixt a Protestant minister and a Romish priest	1716–35
Wells, Edward	The common Christian rightly and plainly instructed	1707–12 (Oxford)
Welsthed, Robert	The cure of a hard heart	1630
Wensley, Robert	The form of sound words	1679

WESTMINSTER ASSEMBLY OF DIVINES

	2	3
——	The humble advice ... concerning a larger catechisme	1647–58–
——	The humble advice ... concerning a shorter catechisme	1647–87
——	The grounds and principles of religion ... in a shorter catechism	1648–1737–
——	The confession of faith, and/together with the larger and shorter catechisms	1649–1717–
——	The shorter catechism compos'd by the reverend assembly	1656–1737–
——	Confessio fidei ... cum catechismo duplici	1656–60–

4	5	6
(1)	BL	A 'familiar conference' between a churchman + a dissenter on the lawfulness + right way of keeping Christmas
(1)	25128	An exhortation to householders to instruct their families, with a list of suitable catechisms
11	25132–9 + W1173A–73C	A q + a analysis of the Bible with a large amount of overlap with *The doctrine of the Bible* (q.v. above)
1	25150a.5	Mid; covers Dec, Cr, Ss, Pr, but followed by long section of additional material especially on duties laid down by Dec; for all well-disposed persons; Gloucestershire
2	25158–9	Mid; Dec, Cr, Ss, Pr; 2nd edn. revised by author; for those who want to hear sermons + receive the sacraments with comfort; Wiltshire
(4?)	BL	An anti-Catholic but instructive dialogue, priced 4*d.* + aimed at those who would not buy long books
3	BL + Bodleian	Long; BCP with extra qs + as + definitions; derived from lectures already given in his Leics. parish; for the common people; published in conjunction with *Prayers on common occasions* (1707–8), which is mainly prayers but also has rules for preparation for the sacrament
(1)	25236	Treatise on conversion turned into dialogue by John Hart
(1)	W1353	A sermon turned into a short treatise in defence of PBC, proving its content + use were consonant with apostolical belief + practice
6+?	W1436–9	The WLC; mid or long according to format; Scottish edns. also published
7+?	W1440–41A + Carruthers	The WSC; from 1648 this had scripture proofs added; short or mid according to format; an edn. was also published in Rotterdam (in '1647')
13+	G2135A–8bA + Carruthers	The WSC with a more suitable title
15+	Carruthers, C5760A–76A, C5796–8 + BL	The Westminster Confession of Faith, WLC, + WSC; many Scottish edns.
10+	W1448–54B, Carruthers + see col. 6	The WSC with scripture proofs printed in full; Regent's Park College Oxford has a 1734 edn. not listed in Carruthers
(3+)	C5737–39A (+ Carruthers)	WLC + WSC translated into Latin by William Dillingham; 1st 2 edns. published in Cambridge, 3rd in London; other edns. in Scotland

1	2	3
——	E katechesis tes Christianikes threskeias … sive catechesis religionis	1659–98
——	Catechesis religionis Christianae brevior	1689
For revisions of the WSC, see also above:		
anon.	A short catechism containing the principles (1718)	
and s.v. J. Strong		
[Wetenhall, Edward]	The catechism of the Church of England with marginal notes	1678–
——/Edward Cork + Ross	A tried method of catachising	1698–
Whateley, William	A pithie, short, and methodicall opening	1622
[Whiston, Daniel]/ 'A presbyter of the Church of England'	Four sermons upon most important topics	1715
[——]	A primitive catechism	1718–
Whitaker, William	A short summe of Christianity	1630–51
White, Josias	A plain and familiar exposition	1632–7
[——?]	A short catechisme. The seventh edition	–1632
[White, Thomas gent.]	A catechism of Christian doctrine	–1637 (Paris)–1659 (Paris)
[White, William]	Paraphrasis cum annotatis	1674
[——]	A paraphrase with annotations	1674

4	5	6
(3)	K29A–30A	Translation of WSC into Greek + Latin by John Harmar
(1)	C1464/S2178	Translation of WSC into Hebrew by William Seaman
1	W1491	In a revised version of this, published in Dublin in 1696 (W4192) Wetenhall said he had 'often' printed these notes in England + Ireland; only this copy survives; mid; PBC with notes + paraphrases; for children; price stitched 6*d*.
1+	T2272A	A shortened version of his 1696 revision of the 1678 original; also published in Dublin in 1706; short; PBC with explanations + scripture proofs
(1)	25315	Very long exposition of Dec; not in q + a
(1)	BL	Four 'catechistical lectures' on matters relating to baptism; plans for others to be published
1+	BL	Long; in 2 parts, the 1st for beginners, the 2nd for 'illuminates'; some unusual emphases; qs + as repeated at end without scripture proofs
2	25369 + W1717	Published posthumously (ed. 'J. Martinus'); mid; a summary of the principles in the PBC, but in a different sequence: Dec, Cr, Ss, Pr; for those of weakest capacity + frailest memory
2	25399.5–400	Mid; Cr, Dec, Pr, Ss; in existence as early as 1623 (*TSR* iv. 93); to be learned + understood before admission to Lord's Supper; work also contains a short moral story
7?	4803.2	Short; similar to but discrete from last; an abridgement by White or someone else?
[3?]	25403.4 + W1811	Catholic; 1637 edn. is 2nd, corrected + enlarged; White's name appears on the 1659 title-page; series of dialogues on credal material, Ss, + other catechetical material
(1)	P342B	PBC with additions to explain the harder parts, all in Latin; title-page refers to next as well, but the 2 have separate signatures + appear to have been published separately
1	P342A	Short; PBC with insertions, in square brackets, to explain the 'harder passages'; attribution to White is in the Bodleian catalogue; Oxon?

1	2	3
Whiting, Giles	Short questions and answeres	1593–1629
anon.	The whole duty of a Christian	1684 (Antwerp)
anon.	The wid[ow's] catechism	1709
[Wigginton, Gyles]	An introduction to the Christian faith	–1646
[Wilcox, Daniel]	The duty of holding fast the form of sound words	1717
W[ilcox], T[homas]	A forme of preparation to the Lords Supper	1587
Wilkinson, Henry	A catechisme, contayning a short exposition	–1623–37
Willes, Thomas	Milk for babes, or a little catechisme	[pre-1708]
Willet, Andrew	An English catechism	1621
Willets, W.	A poor man's monitor, or a call to ... conversion	1699
Williams, Daniel	The vanity of childhood ... [+] a catechism for youth	1691–1729–
Williams, John (minister)	The school of godliness	[1680?]
[Williams, John]/'A Protestant of the Church of England'	A catechism truly representing the doctrines	1686–1713
——	A brief exposition of the church-catechism	1689–1731–

4	5	6
3	25433.7–35	Short; pre-comm.; Dec, Cr, Ss, Pr; for the ignorant to learn; at the end are 20 spiritual precepts; one edn. (1613) published at Cambridge
[1]	Y196	Catholic; long; q + a; French origin; not the same as Y 195 *pace* Wing
[1]	BL	Humorous/ satirical: attacks those widows who remarry too soon
1+?	W2099A	Very short (5 pp.); for the very young; also has prayers (2 pp.) + Bible texts (4 pp.); published by author's grandson; was used at 'Sadbarrow' (Sedburgh?) in the North; prayers at end 1589 edn. cited in *DNB* not traced
(1)	DWL + Bodleian	Defence of Westminster Confession + catechisms against criticisms; in doing so author adds extra qs + as to the opening qs + as of the WSC
1+	25622.5–2.7	Long; pre-comm. but covers Cr + Dec as well as Ss; some very long answers suggest this was designed to be read; Herts?
4	25644–45.5	Mid; said to be based on 'the ordinary catechisme', this form has some shared material with the PBC, but a different sequence: Dec, Cr, Ss, Pr, + a prayer at the end; Bucks.
1?	See col. 6	Advert in 1708 edn. of H. Palmer, *Memorials of godlinesse*; publisher T. Parkhurst; for little children; no copy traced
1?	Grant, 349	Not traced; one of Willet's larger works, *Synopsis papismi*, was built loosely round qs + as, though the former were basically headings under which the Catholic church could be denounced
1?	*TC* iii. 130	Contains an exhortation to a holy life, a short catechism, prayers, *et al.*; price 1*d.*; no copy traced
3+	W2657, BL + NUC	Short form (not the usual content) following sermons for youth; echoes of WSC; 1691 edn. cost 1*s.*; editions in Welsh, 1739, 1759 (BL + DWL)
1	W2746A	An amalgam of 'rules of civility', selections from the psalms, + other material, but includes a very short q + a form to test scriptural knowledge
(3)	W2693–4 + BL	Controversial: anti-Catholic; consists of selected citations from Catholic catechisms on left-hand page, with rebuttals on opposite page
23+	W2685–8 + BL	Mid; PBC with extra qs + as + scripture proofs; recommended for Charity Schools; 28th edn. 1804; price (1690) 6*d.*; also edns. in Welsh (1699) + French [1701?]

1	2	3
Willis, Thomas	The church catechism explained by way of question and answer	–1701
Willison, John	The mother's catechism for the young child	–1735
Wilson, A[a]ron	A catachisme	1629
Wilson, John	Some helpes to faith	1625–30
W[ilson], T[homas]	An exposition of the two first verses of [Hebrews 6]	1609
——	A sermon preached'd in August the 13. 1610	1610
——	A dialogue about justification by faith	1611
——	A commentarie upon ... Romanes. In forme of a dialogue	1614–27
Wilson, Thomas (bishop of Sodor and Man)	The principles and duties of Christianity	1707–38
Wise, Thomas	Knowledg and practice: or, the Christian briefly guided	1709
W[ither], D[r George]	Certaine godlye/ necessarie instructions	1579–[86?]

4	5	6
2?	*TC* iii. 237	PBC with extra qs + as? (no copy traced); 'for the use of children bred up in the working hospital' in London; price, 3*d*., suggests a mid size; similarly entitled work by J. Lewis (q.v.)
15+?	Liverpool Univ. Lib.	Two forms: a short to prepare 'children + others' for the WSC (has same framework as WSC, but is more than just a paraphrase + simplification of it); and a very short form consisting of historical questions, mainly out of the Old Testament; also has Dec in verse, a paraphrase of the Lord's Prayer, prayers, graces + a 'spiritual song for young ones'; 1735 said to be 15th edn.; for later edns. in Scotland and America + Willison's other forms, see BL Catalogue, NUC, + Carruthers, 123–4
1?	*TSR* iv. 214	Not traced; ever published?
(3)	25769–69.5	A treatise on faith, with a number of objections + replies; not a q + a form as such
1+	24966–66a + Addenda	Two forms: a mid (based on 6 principles, + apart from Ss not the usual staples; quite difficult); + a short summary of the same, for the younger sort; also has very interesting advice to users of the work; Kent
?	25797	According to title-page this work contains a catechism, but not found in extant copies: perhaps it was one of those published in 1609, or the dialogue about justification (see next)
(1)	25795	A long dialogue on justification with 6 stereotypical speakers; published with *Jacob's ladder* + various other works by Wilson in 1611
(3?)	25791–3	A very long dialogue between Timothy + Silas on the correct interpretation of the Epistle to the Romans
6	BL	Long; extra qs + as for those who had already mastered the PBC; this work was in Manx + English for the diocese of Sodor + Man; from 5th edn. also had advice on method; published in conjunction with short book of directions + prayers in Manx
1	Lambeth	Long; based on Drélincourt's original French form (q.v.); Cr, Dec, Pr, Ss; for the younger members of his Canterbury parishes (+ for his use of it there see Wake MS 284, Christ Church, Oxford, fo. 60ʳ); prayers at end
(3?)	20974, 24901–2 + Maunsell, 32	Very short set of pre-comm. instructions for the younger sort, but not in q + a; published with a set of precepts for 'students at Christ's School'; 1579 edn. tacked onto R. Rice, *An invective against vices*; date of 3rd edn. guessed from entry in Maunsell; Essex

1	2	3
Wolfall, Thomas	Childrens bread. Or, a briefe forme	1646
Wood, James	Stedfastness in religion recommended	1724
Wood, John	see s.v. Explicatory catechism	
Wood, William	A fourme of catechising in true religion	1581
Woodward, Ezekias /Hezekiah	A childes patrimony ... A/Of the childes portion	1640–9
[——]	A treatise of prayer	1656
Woodward, Josiah	A short catechism, explaining the substance	1709–20–
anon.	A word to the poor, ignorant, and careless people	1692
Worthington, John	Hupotuposis ... A form of sound words	1673–1733–
——	A systeme of Christian doctrine	1723
Wren, Matthew	Increpatio Barjesu: sive polemicae	1660
Wright, John	The most material difficulties	1713–14 (Nottingham)
[Wright, Samuel]	The great concern of human life	1729

4	5	6
1	W3248	Short; in 6 sections linked by covenant theme; for the instruction of the ignorant + the edification of those with some knowledge; Northumberland?
(1)	BL	Sermon given to a society of catechumens in London
1	25956	Long; Dec, Cr, Ss, Pr; each question (by Teacher) + answer (by Learner) is followed by a long 'Observation'; experience taught author the need to provide abridgements of the longer answers for those of weak capacities; claimed to be written in 'mere natural English speech'; Northants
(2?)	25971–71a + W3500	Pt. 1 contains advice to devout parents on their children's education; pt. 2 advice to children on sin + a godly life; neither is in q + a; 1640 edn. has complex publishing history
(1)	W3508	A series of largely rhetorical queries on prayer in general + Lord's Prayer in particular, followed by tendentious answers
2+	BL + Bodleian	Mid; designed to explain to children + those of meanest capacities the terms most commonly used in sermons + books; prayers, graces, + hymns at the end; recommended for use in Charity Schools; price 2*d*. or 12*s*. per 100; 4th edn. (Edinburgh) (1735)
1	W3572	Contains 2 forms: a very short scripture catechism for children, + a short form for adults + those that had learnt the former; these are preceded by 'A call to speedy conversion' + 'Directions to a holy life', + followed by prayers; price 1*d*.
8+?	W3625–9, BL + Carruthers	Long; some WSC influence; credal material, Dec, Pr, Ss; prayers at end; by a conformist but very popular with presbyterians; said to have been published in edns. of 10,000 copies; Scottish edn. 1683 (+ a variant in 1722?) + an edn. in Welsh (1733)
1	BL	Long; modified version of the last, prepared by the author's son, adding useful notes + observations culled from his father's papers
[1]	W3676	Controversial: attack, in Latin, on the *Racovian catechisme* (q.v.)
2	BL	Long; designed to explain some of the more difficult points in PBC, + shades into controversy as a result; Notts.?
(1)	Bodleian	Handles a number of catechetical themes, but in prose, not q + a; cited approvingly by S. Bourne in *Lectures* (1738) (q.v.), p. xxxii

1	2	3
Yates, John	A short and briefe summe of saving knowledge	1621–
——	A modell of divinitie, catechistically composed	1622–3
Zwingli, Huldrich	The rekenynge and declaracion of the faith/The accompt rekenynge and confession	1543 (Zurich), [1548?] (London) + 1555 (Emden)

4	5	6
1+	26088	Short; an introduction to a larger work (see next) of which it formed the first chapter; composed according to the method of Alexander Richardson, a Ramist logician, as a result of which this work has sometimes been attributed to him; see also above, s.v. 'Mr Richerson'
2	26085–6	Very long; extremely long answers; contains the *Summe* listed above; edited by T. Goad; 2nd edn. corrected + enlarged; Norf.?
(3)	26138–40	2 translations of a statement of faith, but not in q + a

APPENDIX 2
The Sample of Catechisms Used in Chapters 7–12

Below are listed the abbreviations used to describe the fifty-nine forms in the sample, and the bibliographical details of the copy of each work that has been used. For the earliest surviving edition of each work, see Appendix 1.

Ball, *Catechisme*	A. F. Mitchell, *Catechisms of the Second Reformation* (1886), 67–91, an accurate reprint of the 1642 edition of John Ball's *A short catechisme containing all the principles*, Wing[2] B563.
—— *Treatise*	John Ball, *A short treatise contayning all the principall grounds* (1635), STC[2] 1318. This is the larger version of Ball's catechism with expositions of each answer.
Bernard, *Common catechisme*	Richard Bernard, *The common catechisme* (1630), STC[2] 1929. For Bernard's other catechisms, see Appendix 1.
Boughen, *Exposition*	Edward Boughen, *A short exposition of the catechism of the Church of England* (1668), Wing[2] B3818, the text of which is the same as in the first edition of 1646 entitled *Principles of Religion* (B3816).
Bradshaw, 'Brief forme'	W[illiam] B[radshaw], 'A brief forme of triall', printed after his *A direction for the weaker sort of Christians* (1609), STC[2] 3510; this publication also contains Hildersham's 'Doctrine', q.v. below.
Calvin, *Catechisme*	Jean Calvin, *The catechisme or manner to teache children the christian religion* (Geneva, 1556), STC[2] 4380. This was reprinted in facsimile as part of the English Experience series, no. 46 (Amsterdam, 1968).
Cartwright, 'Catechisme'	[Thomas Cartwright], 'The catechisme', printed at the end of J. Dod and R. Cleaver, *A plaine and familar exposition of the ten commandements* (1622), STC[2] 6975. For Cartwright's authorship, see Appendix 1.

'Certaine questions and answers'	anon., 'Certaine questions and answers touching the doctrine of predestination, the use of God's word and sacraments'. This was inserted into a number of black-letter quarto editions of the Geneva Bible printed in England: Appendix 1. The edition cited here is bound in a copy of the quarto Geneva Bible published in 1588 (STC² 2148) and kept in the Bodleian Library: Bib. Eng. 1588.d.1.
Comber, *Church-catechism*	T[homas] C[omber], *The church-catechism with a brief and easie explanation thereof* (1686), Wing² C5446.
Dering–More, *Catechisme*	Edward Dering, *Workes* (1590) which contains a reprint of 'A briefe and necessarie catachisme or instruction'.
Egerton, 'Briefe method'	Stephen Egerton, *A briefe method of catechizing* (London, 1615), STC² 7530, pp. 1–20. This work also contains five other question and answer forms, namely:
—— 'Foure points'	'The foure principall points' (pp. 20–6), a summary of the last in forty questions and answers;
—— 'Briefe summe'	'A more briefe summe' (pp. 27–8), an even briefer sum of the original form, in four questions and answers;
—— 'Forme of examining'	'A forme of examining such as are to receive the Lords Supper' (pp. 28–32);
—— 'Familiar forme'	'Another familiar forme', part two of the last but presented as a distinct form (pp. 32–7);
—— 'Familiar manner'	'Another familiar manner of instruction' (pp. 37–42).
Elton, *Forme*	Edward Elton, *A forme of catechizing* (1629), STC² 7617.
—— 'Extract'	id., 'An extract or short view of the ... catechisme: a summary of Elton's *Forme* printed at the end of that work, for the 'help of the younger sort'.
Gouge, *Principles*	Thomas Gouge, *The principles of Christian religion* (1684), Wing² G 1376—a later and expanded version of the catechism first published under the same name in 1668 (G1370). See also next.

Gouge, 'Heads'   'The heads of the foregoing catechism'—a sum-
                                  mary of the last and printed at the end of it.

Grosse, *Fiery pillar*   Alexander Grosse, *A fiery pillar of heavenly truth*
                                  (1644), Wing² G2071. A specialist treatise on
                                  predestination, but in question-and-answer
                                  form.

Hammond, *Practical catechisme*   Henry Hammond, *A Practical Catechism*, ed. N.
                                  Pocock (Library of Anglo-Catholic Theology,
                                  Oxford, 1847)—a reprint of the second edition
                                  of 1646 (Wing² H 583) which contains a number
                                  of additions compared to the first edition of
                                  1645 (see Pocock's preface, p. vii, and H 581 and
                                  H 544).

Heidelberg Catechism   Schaff, *Creeds*, 307–55. This is a translation into
                                  English of the original 1563 edition of the 'Cat-
                                  echismus oder Christlicher Underricht'. For
                                  contemporary English editions from *c.*1570?,
                                  see Appendix 1.

Hieron, *Doctrine*   Samuel Hieron, *All the sermons* (1614), STC²
                                  13378, which includes a 1613 reprint of
                                  Hieron's *The doctrine of the beginning of Christ*.

Hildersham, 'Doctrine'   A[rthur] H[ildersham], 'The doctrine of com-
                                  municating worthily': a question-and-answer
                                  form printed at the end of Bradshaw's *Direction*,
                                  q.v. above.

Hill, *Principles*   William Hill, *The first principles of a Christian*
                                  (1629), STC² 13504.

Isham, *Catechism*   Zacheus Isham, *The catechism of the church*
                                  (1695), Wing² I 1067.

Keach,   Benjamin Keach, *Instructions for children*
                                  [1710?]; this work contains three catechetical
                                  forms:

—— 'Little child'   'The little child's catechism', (pp. 14–17);
—— 'Child'   the second form entitled 'Youth's catechism' (as
                                  is the third) but the personae are 'Child' and
                                  'Father' (pp. 19–26);

—— 'Youth'   another 'Youth's catechism', but clearly a more
                                  advanced form than the previous two (pp.
                                  63–120).

Lewis, *Catechism*   [John Lewis], *The church catechism explain'd by
                                  way of question and answer* (1712)

'Maner to examine children' anon., 'The maner to examine children', printed at the end of several editions of Calvin's *Catechisme*, for example STC² 4380, 4381, 4383, and 4385–7. The version cited here is that of 1556 printed at the end of the edition of Calvin's *Catechisme* cited above.

Marshall, *Catechism* [Thomas Marshall], *The catechism set forth in the Book of Common Prayer briefly explained* (1683), Wing M² 802.

Mayer, *Catechisme* John Mayer, *Mayers catechisme abridged* (1639), STC² 17740.5.

Nicholes, *Catechisme* M[artin] N[icholes], *A catechisme* (1642), Wing² N1083.

Nicholson, *Exposition* William Nicholson, *A plain but full exposition of the catechism of the Church of England* (Library of Anglo-Catholic Theology, Oxford, 1842)—a reprint of the 1686 edition which is virtually the same as the original edition of 1655 (Wing² N1113).

Nowell, *Catechisme* Alexander Nowell, *A catechisme, or first instruction and learning of Christian religion*, ed. G. E. Corrie (Parker Society, Cambridge, 1853)—a reprint of the first edition of the full-size catechism in English published in London in 1570 (STC² 18708).

—— *Institution* id., *A catechisme or institution of christian religion* (London, 1572), STC 18730—the first edition of this, the condensed form of the last.

Paget, *Questions* 'Robert Openshaw', *Short questions and answeares* (1617), STC² 18830.7. For Eusebius Paget's authorship, see Appendix 1. The edition cited here is one of those in the larger format with the scripture texts printed in full (Openshaw's contribution), but the text is otherwise very similar to that in the original.

Palmer, *Endeavour* Herbert Palmer, *An endeavour of making the principles of Christian religion plain and easie* (1644), Wing² P230A.

Perkins, *Foundation* William Perkins, 'The foundation of Christian religion', from the 1616 edition of Perkins's *Workes*, STC² 19651.

Prayer Book catechism	Brightman, *English Rite*, ii. 778–91; this collates the texts of 1549, 1552, 1604, and 1661.
Sherlock, *Principles*	Richard Sherlock, *The principles of holy Christian religion* (1663), Wing² S 3250.
Taylor, 'Catechism'	Jeremy Taylor, 'A short catechism for the institution of young persons', reprinted in *Symbolon ... or a collection of ... discourses* (1657), Wing² T398, pp. 1–5.
Ussher, 'Principles'	James Ussher, *The principles of Christian religion* (1678), Wing² U207: contains two short forms, of which the first and simpler was entitled 'Principles'.
—— 'Method'	'The method of the doctrine of Christian religion', the second and more advanced of the two forms.
Vincent, *Catechism*	Thomas Vincent, *An explicatory catechism* (1708).
Virel, *Treatise*	Matthieu Virel, *A learned and excellent treatise* (1594), STC² 24767.5; translated from French into English by Stephen Egerton, q.v.
Wake, *Principles*	William Wake, *The principles of the Christian religion in a brief commentary upon the Church-catechism* (1700), Wing² W 259.
Wallis, *Explanation*	John Wallis, *A brief and easie explanation of the [Westminster] shorter catechism* (1662), Wing² W561A.
Watts,	Isaac Watts, *The first sett of catechisms* (1734) contains:
—— 'First catechism'	a 'First catechism', pp. 6–10;
—— 'Scripture-names'	a 'catechism of scripture-names', pp. 11–18.
	Isaac Watts, *The second sett of catechisms* (1733–4) contains:
—— 'Children's catechism'	the 'Children's catechism', pp. 1–35;
—— 'Historical catechism'	a 'historical catechism', pp. 36–65.
—— *Assembly's catechism*	*The Assembly's catechism with notes* (1736).
—— 'A preservative'	'A preservative from sins and follies of childhood and youth': in Isaac Watts, *Catechisms: or instructions in the principles of the Christian religion* (1730), 154–88.
Westminster Larger	[Westminster Larger Catechism] *The humble advice of the Assembly of Divines ... at Westminster, concerning a larger catechisme* (1658), Wing² W1439.*

Westminster Shorter

[Westminster Shorter Catechism] *The humble advice of the Assemblie of Divines ... at Westminster; concerning a shorter catechisme* (1658), Wing[2] W1441.*

* To facilitate comparison with the many later editions of these catechisms in which the questions and answers are numbered, both the page numbers (from the 1658 editions) and the question-and-answer numbers (from Torrance, *School of Faith*, 185–235, 261–78) are provided.

Williams, *Exposition*

John Williams, *A brief exposition of the church catechism* (1707).

INDEX

Abbot, Abp George 106–7, 147–8, 354, 566–7
Abbot, Robert 214, 219, 268
The ABC with the catechisme 30, 53, 65–9, 88–9,
    170–6, 186–7, 255, 560–2
Addison, Lancelot 21, 116, 237
Alleine, Joseph 82, 222, 226, 262
Allen, Edmund 41, 60–2, 282
Allison, C. F. 379 n., 415 n., 419–20, 472–5
Ames, William 49, 219, 354
Andrewes, Bp Lancelot 106, 108, 153, 220,
    232 n., 236
  catechetical lectures at Cambridge 1, 147,
    201–3, 446 n., 451
  compares catechizing to erecting a building 28
  manuscript copies of his lectures circulate 1, 46
  refers to a covenant of faith 419
  rules for interpreting the Decalogue 426–30
Antichrist, not a catechetical subject 333
antinomianism, fear of 378, 399
Apostles' Creed:
  article-by-article exposition of in best-selling
    catechisms 300–49
  as a basis of a profession of faith 34, 222, 236
  in Catholic catechetics 59–60
  expounded in catechetical sermons or prose
    147–8, 151, 186, 202–3, 294
  knowledge of misused by the ignorant 131,
    245, 274–5
  knowledge of necessary in communicants 34,
    93, 123, 236
  omitted from some catechisms 80, 284–6,
    294–5, 301 n., 347–8
  in the Prayer Book catechism 16
  as a staple of Protestant catechetics 4, 9, 21, 73,
    94, 186, 243, 275, 279–83
Aristotelianism 306, 350, 430 n.
'Arminians', 'Arminianism' 40, 78, 85, 350,
    352–3, 356, 367–8, 371–2, 409, 415, 514–15,
    566–7
Arrowsmith, John 203
assurance 379–80, 387–97, 405, 408
Aston, Margaret 432
atonement 367–71

Babington, Bp Gervase 6, 53
Ball, John:
  author of various forms 7, 45, 67–8, 78–9, 156,
    260

best-selling form perhaps used as alternative or
    supplement to Prayer Book catechism
    138, 143, 196
  best-selling form revised 244, 247–8
  Calvinism of 70, 78, 359–78
  catechizes in the summer months 115
  content and structure of his best-selling forms
    Chs. 6–12 *passim*
  exposition of Prayer Book catechism 78, 156,
    252
  on knowledge required in the faithful 26, 29
  larger form used by more advanced catechu-
    mens 200, 203, 567
  work recommended by other catechists 45, 153
Bancroft, Abp Richard 122, 348, 517
baptism 519–39
  areas of agreement on 520–7
  areas of disagreement on 527–9
Baptists 41, 83–4, 166, 410 n., 520–1
  see also Keach, Benjamin
Barclay, Robert 84, 199
Baxter, Richard 126, 145, 203, 392, 399, 407 n.,
    410
  author of different forms 53, 196, 222–3, 258,
    268
  author of *Quakers catechism* 56–7, 85
  aware of many catechisms written in England
    45
  aware of problems in teaching the unlearned
    243, 248–9
  catechetical form on the Bible 52, 214
  catechizing at Kidderminster 130, 139, 222–7
  concern at decline of catechizing by 1650s 131,
    139
  strong supporter of catechizing 42, 91, 167,
    222–7
Becon, Thomas 6, 22, 47, 61, 213, 267
Bedfordshire, catechizing in 587, 713
Beeke, Joel 388
Berkshire, catechizing in 192, 206–7, 607(2),
    635, 650
Bernard, Richard 63, 280
  author of different forms 267
  author of form used in gentry household 218
  best-selling form widely used 33–4, 73, 156
  content and structure of his best-selling form
    Chs. 6–12 *passim*
  defends confirmation 33–4

defends use of Prayer Book catechism 77, 143, 246
description of his catechizing 14, 238–9
puritan background 33–4, 70, 77, 156
strong supporter of catechizing 14, 77, 91, 99
Beveridge, Bp William 113, 131–2, 154, 159–61, 163, 208, 242, 263–4, 269
Beza, Theodore 266, 443
catechetical forms by 40, 61, 64, 199
high Calvinist views of 352–4, 357–9, 365, 367, 372 n., 387–9, 398, 405–6
Biddle, John 7
Blackwood, Christopher 50, 83
Blake, William 55, 213
Book of Common Prayer 30, 65, 68, 87, 105, 122, 125, 241, 298, 356, 368, 382–3, 522, 527, 529–32, 562, 569
Bossy, John 410–11, 431, 437 n., 452 n., 557 n.
Boughen, Edward 87–8, 156, 193, Chs. 6–12 *passim*, and 567
Boughton, John 7
Brachlow, S. 296, 408
Bradshaw, William 295, 370 n., 511, 540, 542–3, 550, 552
Bray, Thomas 89, 123, 150–1, 269–70, 274, 276
Briggs, Joseph 148, 152
Brinsley, John, the elder 174, 198, 239–40
Brinsley, John, the younger 79, 250
Bucer, Martin 114, 357, 368, 405, 520
Buckinghamshire, catechizing in 587, 693, 745
Bullinger, Heinrich 31, 45, 197, 357–8, 404–5, 410, 441, 443, 446 n.
Bunyan, John 63, 407 n., 454
Burch, Dorothy 214
Burnet, Gilbert 113, 116–17, 132, 149–50, 165, 200
Burton, William 145

Calvin, John:
author of two forms 19, 32–3, 59, 281–2
avoids controversy in catechetics 39, 298–9
catechism of 1541: compared to Prayer Book catechism 20, 71, 279; content and structure of 42 and Chs. 6–12 *passim*; divided into 52 parts 252; studied in languages other than English 188–9, 196–7; widely used in England 19, 39, 65–6, 95, 97, 188–9
catechetical lectures on 1541 form 202
condemns medieval instruction 13
Institutes 45, 197–8, 485, 513, 515, 521, 529, 532–4
Nowell's debt to Calvin's 1541 form 62
supports catechizing by the minister 98

'Calvinism', 'Calvinists' 70, 78, 156, 209, 286, 292, 296–7, 306–421, 503–4, 527–9, 535–8, 566–7
see also presbyterianism, and Westminster Confession
Cambridge, catechizing in 1, 199–203, 585 (2), 605, 723
Cambridgeshire, catechizing in 102, 657
Cartwright, Thomas 13–14, 27, 46, 53, 70, 78, and Chs. 6–12 *passim*
catechism, catechisms:
Continental origins of early English forms 17–21, 48–9, 54, 58, 60–2, 64–5
controversy in minority of forms 56–7, 83–6, 90–1
dedications in 6, 76
definition of 4–5, 13–16, 62–3
different types of 4–5, 51–8
evolution of first English forms 19–21
in languages other than English 4, 48, 53–4, 97, 188–93, 196–9, 201, 211, 254
labels used to describe 26–9, 48, 74
limited controversial teaching in 39–41, 91–2
manuscript 46–7
numbers of different forms produced in England 45–6, 50–8, 76–9; *see also* catechisms, printing of
oral use of 5, 8, 52, 94–5, 241–3, 564–5; *see also* catechizing, elementary
political and satirical 56, 86–7
price 255
printing of 5–8, 47–50, 65–8, 76, 88–9, 254–7
reaction against proliferation of 76–9, 88
scriptural catechisms 52, 92, 253
scriptural origins alleged 21–5
scriptural references and citations in 32–3, 66–7, 80
sermons turned into 145–6
staple contents 9, 279–89, 565, 578; *see also* Apostles' Creed, Ten Commandments, Lords' Prayer, and sacraments
target groups 33–8, 73–6
in verse 82, 254
catechizing:
advanced 97, 196–203
an aid to understanding sermons 31–2
aims of 7, 26–43, 72–5, 129
in church 98–169
efforts to improve techniques of 35–6, 75–6, 154–8, 230–76
elementary 93–5, 98–142, 172–87, 234–57
exhortations to catechize or be catechized 3–4
frequency 102–4, 114–22
in the home 45–6, 49, 144, 204–39

impact of 1, 129–41, 168–9, 203–4, 225–6, 229, 557–70
intermediate level 95–7, 142–69, 187–96, 257–74
in Lent 115–19, 158–9, 163–4
neglect of or resistance to catechizing alleged 96–7, 129–32
official statements on 3–4, 99–100, 105–9, 110–11, 113–16, 120–3, 125, 146–8, 170, 205–6, 235–6
origins of 21–5
question-and-answer 14–16, 21
a range of interlocking activities 5, 51–3, 93–7
role of literacy in 241–3
in school 2, 16, 48, 53, 66, 68–9, 91, 97, 147, 170–98, 202, 210, 259; *see also* Charity Schools
support systems to 94–5, 234–5, 253–4, 479, 562–3
at university 197–203
catechumens:
adult 35–8, 73–5, 113, 122–3, 133–4, 144, 222–7, 244–5
children, adolescents, and youth 33–5, 38, 75, 94, 98, 122–3, 125, 142, 144, 269, 271–2
servants 122, 124–5, 142, 144
Catholic ideas and practice on catechizing 1, 14–17, 19, 24–5, 42–3, 50, 59–60, 98 n., 281–2, 479, 557, 560
Cawdrey, Robert 6, 77, 130, 139, 217, 219, 221, 239–40
censorship 6–7, 40, 47–50, 78–9
'Certaine questions and answeres' 53, 283, 291, 295, 306 n., 361–2, 378, 391 n., 424, 536 n., 544 n.
Charity Schools:
catechetical forms used in 91, 157, 160, 194–5, 253, 451, 581, 603, 619, 627, 635, 645, 647, 677, 679, 689, 693, 705, 721, 737, 745, 749
catechizing a regular feature in 121, 170–3, 177–8, 231, 249, 271
students' catechetical knowledge tested in public 104, 179, 237
parents to test students' knowledge 178–9
teachers in 181–2
teachers to ensure understanding as well as knowledge 263
Charles I 100, 108–10, 112, 147, 156, 432, 439, 447, 456, 459–60, 509, 567
Charles II 100, 110, 148
Cheshire, catechizing in 130 n., 178, 206, 220, 583, 649, 665, 695, 697

chosen, *see* elect
Christ:
catechetical treatment of 308–19
descent into hell 316–19
identity 309–10
life and death 313–15
offices of prophet, priest, and king 311–13
'profit' and lessons from his sufferings and death 315–16
as saviour 310–11
church:
as the body of Christ 327, 333–4
definition of, in catechisms 329–32
'holy, catholic' 326–34
visible and invisible 328–9
Clarke, Samuel (puritan hagiographer) 102, 144–5, 167 n., 217–22
Clarke, Samuel (episcopalian minister) 57, 85
clergy as catechists 98–169
Clifford, Alan 475
Colet, John 16, 20, 59, 188
Collinson, Patrick 209, 296–7, 432, 438
Comber, Thomas 81, 88, 116, 156, 262–3, and Chs. 6–12 *passim*
Commandments, Ten:
in Catholic instruction 59, 422
citation and division of 424–6
expositions of 1, 58 n., 59, 147–8, 151, 186, 202–3
knowledge of misused by the ignorant 131, 245, 274–5
knowledge of required in communicants 34–5, 93, 123, 235
paraphrased in verse 214, 254 n.
in the Prayer Book catechism 16, 94, 424–6
rules for interpretation of 426–30
a staple of Protestant catechizing 4, 9, 21–2, 41–2, 73, 243, 275, 279–83, 422–4
treatment of individual Commandments: first 431; second 431–7; third 437–8; fourth 438–51; fifth 451–60; sixth 460–1; seventh 461–2; eighth 462–4; ninth 464–5; tenth 465
communion, *see* Supper, Lord's
communion of saints, *see* saints
confirmation 33–5, 41–2, 62, 125–8, 134–5, 142, 195–6, 324, 543 n.
Coolidge, J. S. 348 n., 404 n., 414
Coote, Edmund 53, 185–6
Cotton, Clement 76
Cotton, John 50, 84, 410
covenant of grace 365, 402–3, 405–21, 475–6, 511–12, 538–9

see also federal theology, and sacraments, as seals
covenant of works 405–6, 412
covenant theology, *see* federal theology
Craig, John 214
Cranmer, Abp Thomas 20–1, 42, 61, 71, 78, 398, 401, 546 n., 566
Crofton, Zachary 131, 221–2
Crompton, William 6, 99–100, 131, 139, 155, 200, 217, 274
Crooke, Samuel 212
Culverwell, Ezekiel 102–3

Davies, Julian 107, 108 n.
Day family of publishers 7, 175
Day, John (Oriel College, Oxford) 201–2
Decalogue, *see* Commandments, Ten
decree, divine 357–63
Delumeau, Jean 421, 477, 557
Dent, Arthur 54, 63, 145
Derbyshire, catechizing in 49, 589, 591, 601
Dering, Edward, and More, John, co-authors of *A briefe and necessarie catechisme* 9, 30, 32, 66–8, 78, 143, 209–10, 244, 247, 266, and Chs. 6–12 *passim*
Devon, catechizing in 99, 117 n., 139, 217, 587, 591, 665, 675, 685
dialogue(s) 17–20, 54–7, 60–1, 63–4
Dod, John, and Cleaver, Robert 53, 153, 359, 426, 429–30, 433, 451–2, 461
Doolittle, Thomas 28, 82–3, 167–8, 262, 268–9, 276
Dorset, catechizing in 137, 256–7, 597, 623, 675, 681(2)
Dort, Synod of 298, 352, 354–6, 358–9, 361, 368, 372
Dugard, Thomas 199–200, 203 n.
Durbin, L. D. 282 n., 453, 466 n.
Durham, County, catechizing in 46, 607

educational theory of the period 231–5
Egerton, Stephen 45, 67–8, 78, 211, 247, 251–2, and Chs. 6–12 *passim*
elect, election 70, 363–6, 405–6, 412–14
Ellis, Clement 52, 206–7
Elton, Edward 78, and Chs. 6–12 *passim*
England, New 49–50
Eniautos: or a course of catechizing (1664) 45, 153
episcopal questionnaires 100–1, 103–5, 111–13, 116–27, 132–5, 140–1, 158–66, 180–4, 28–9
Erasmus, Desiderius 18, 64, 188, 234
Essex, catechizing in 1, 123, 145, 166, 179, 218–19, 236 n., 621, 633, 655, 671, 693, 721(2), 723, 725(3), 727, 733, 737, 747

Evelyn, John 131, 228
faith 26, 319–24, 543–4, 548–51
Fall, the 307–8
Farrow, Benjamin 151–2
federal theology 354–5, 375–6, 403–11
    in expositions of Prayer Book catechism 417–19, 420–1
Ferrar, Nicholas 126, 218
Fincham, Kenneth 137
Flavell, John 167
Ford, Simon 154 n., 246–7
Fox, George 84, 167, 187, 199
France, catechizing in 2, 21, 112, 117 n., 122 n., 136
free will 371–4, 376–7

Germany, catechizing in 2, 13, 16, 21, 46, 75, 78, 96, 98, 124, 171, 235, 237, 275, 453 n., 557–62
Gerrish, B. A. 511 n., 513
Ghost, Holy, *see* Spirit, Holy
Gibson, Bp Edmund 100–1
    see also episcopal questionnaires
Gifford, George 54, 63, 266
Gloucestershire, catechizing in 134, 178, 270–1, 589, 607, 629, 655, 661(2), 717, 725, 741
God, catechetical treatment of 302–7, 357–67, 430–8, 487–94
    as father, creator, and preserver 302–4
    essence and attributes 304–6
'godly' 96–7, 208–13, 216–28, 335, 392, 434, 455–6, 527–8, 542–3, 554, 568
Gouge, Thomas 103, 215, 251–2 and Chs. 6–12 *passim*
Gouge, William 78, 144–5, 153, 219, 250–1
grace 312, 321, 324–5, 370 n., 477, 512–17, 544–5
    indefectible 377–8
    irresistible 371–4, 416
Greaves, Richard L. 408–9, 454
Greenham, Richard 1, 13, 53, 102–3, 106, 388
Grosse, Alexander 295, 360, 378, 381, 398, 400
Grotius, Hugo 199, 254

Haigh, Christopher 69 n., 130 n., 217
Hall, Bp Joseph 53, 206–7, 567
Hammond, Henry 55, 64, 112, 115, 153, 163, 196, 200–1, 204
    content and structure of his *Practical catechisme* Chs. 6–12 *passim*
    catechetical statements compared with Calvin's 311–12, 322, 327–8, 336, 338–40, 347–8, 362, 378, 400–2, 503–4, 515–17, 538, 544
Hampshire, catechizing in 139, 219, 581, 583

Harrison, Joseph 270–1
Harrow School 171, 188, 202
Heidelberg Catechism 20, 36, 42, 46, 63, 65, 71,
    82, 197, 199–200, 219, 245, 252, 267, and
    Chs. 6–12 *passim*
Henry, Philip 168, 227
Henry, Matthew 168, 227–8, 262
Herbert, George 29, 109
Herbert, William 213
Herring, Abp Thomas 100
    see also episcopal questionnaires
Hertfordshire, catechizing in 144, 151, 186, 258,
    583, 597, 653(2), 675, 689, 697(2), 731, 745
Hewit, Peter 207–8, 228, 274
Heywood, Oliver 167, 227
Hieron, Samuel 37, 260, and Chs. 6–12 *passim*
'High-Church' 483, 567–8
Hildersham, Arthur 219, 295, 540–1, 543–4, 551,
    554
Hill, William 73, 143, 155, 249, Chs. 6–12 *passim*,
    and 567
Hoby, Lady Margaret 105, 217, 219
Hole, Matthew 14, 151, 159, 192, 197, 201
Homilies, Book of 298, 323, 355 n., 356, 457–9,
    513, 527
Hooker, Richard 106, 514, 517, 532–3, 564,
    567
Hoole, Charles 174, 185, 201
household catechisms, catechizing 8–9, 71,
    204–29
Hughes, Lewis 40–1

images, fear of 431–7
imputation of sin 398–400
Independents 84, 166–7, 169
Ingram, Martin 128–9, 137
Ireland 275, 354, 574
Isham, Zacheus 88, 112, 157, 159–60, 195, 253 n.,
    and Chs. 6–12 *passim*
Isle of Man 747
Isle of Wight 155, 583, 671

Jacob, Henry 409, 411
Jaggard, William 48
Jackson, Thomas 130, 147
James VI and I 31, 69, 100, 106–7, 109–10, 112,
    130, 147, 439, 447
Jensen, P. F. 389–92
Jessey, Henry 83
justification 323, 337, 340–2, 398–403, 469–74
Jones, Richard 185–6, 283
Jones, William 38, 155
Jud, Leo 49, 61
Juxon, Bp William 108–10

Keach, Benjamin 84, 167, 169, 196, 268, and Chs.
    6–12 *passim*
Kempe, William 174
Ken, Bp Thomas 242, 483
Kendall, R. T. 313 n., 352, 375–6, 384, 388–9,
    391–2
Kent, catechizing in 101, 105, 116–19, 121,
    124–5, 133, 135, 140–1, 158–60, 181–3,
    185–6, 192, 194, 228, 581, 583, 587(2), 589,
    593, 617, 653, 679, 699, 701, 747(2)
Kidder, Richard 247
Kidderminster 130, 139, 222–7

Lake, Peter 296, 298, 305 n., 352, 355–6, 383–4,
    512 n., 514–15, 566
Lambeth Articles 298, 355–6, 359–60, 377 n.,
    402, 564
Lamplugh, Bp Thomas 111, 148
Lancashire, catechizing in 130 n., 136, 138 n.,
    178, 206, 226, 667, 707
Lane, A. N. S. 388–9, 391
'Latitudinarianism' 297–8, 567–8
Laud, Abp William 107–10, 147, 156, 348, 432,
    439, 456, 459, 467, 567
Laudians, Laudianism 78–9, 107–10, 297, 353,
    356, 384, 435, 438–9, 442, 483, 515, 517, 566,
    570
Leicestershire, catechizing in 105, 115, 132,
    135–6, 152, 178, 185, 189, 197, 231, 679, 741
Lewis, John:
    author of widely used form 88, 157, 159,
        161–4, 184, 240
    aware of large number of catechisms published
        45, 194–5
    content and structure of his form Chs. 6–12
        passim
    designs a form for use in Charity Schools
        194–5, 249, 253
    tells Abp Wake of the problems of catechizing
        101, 116, 121, 124, 127–8
Linaker, Robert 212, 220, 260
Lincolnshire, catechizing in 101, 103, 105,
    116–25, 133, 140–1, 151–2, 158, 160–2,
    182–4, 208, 228, 595, 599, 635, 647, 657, 659,
    707
London, William 47–8 and Appendix 1 *passim*
London, catechizing in 96, 103, 112, 129, 131,
    151, 177, 179, 191, 194, 216–17, 219,
    583–747 *passim*
Lord's Prayer, *see* Prayer
Lord's Supper, *see* Supper
Love, Christopher 84–5
Luther, Martin:
    avoids controversy in catechetics 39

catechetical forms written by 17–18, 32–3, 266
catechetical method 235, 238
concern for understanding as well as memo-
    rization 17, 19, 235, 238
condemns medieval instruction 13
shorter form compared to Prayer Book cat-
    echism 20, 62, 71
structure of shorter form 279
views on: assurance 387–8, 394; idolatry 436;
    justification 402; Lords' Prayer 485–6,
    497–8, 502; obedience 452; predestina-
    tion 350, 357, 394; sacraments 509–10,
    523, 527–31, 540, 542, 546 n.
Lutherans 78, 358–9, 364, 368, 371–2, 377, 509
Lye, Thomas 82, 167–8, 215, 244, 248, 274
Lyford, William 36, 236, 250, 256
Lyster, John 213

McGee, J. Sears 427–8, 454–6, 458, 463 n.,
    467–8, 472
McLuhan, Marshall 564–5
Man, Samuel 7
'Maner to examine children' 290, 303, 309, 314,
    320, 325, 341, 343, 345, 363, 424, 440, 545,
    680–1
Marshall, Thomas 88, 154, 249, 260, and Chs.
    6–12 passim
Martindale, Adam 172, 226
Maunsell, Andrew 47–9, 63, and Appendix 1
    passim
Mayer, John 73, 79, 115, 131, 143, 153, 159, 193,
    200, 203, 255, 260, Chs. 6–12 passim, and 567
Melanchthon, Philip 23
Mico, John 131, 267, 274
millenarianism, dearth of in the sample 344,
    490–1
Milton, Anthony 296, 352–3, 356, 384, 566–7,
    570
Morgan, John 185, 209–10, 221
Morton, Bp Thomas 138–9, 206
Mulcaster, Richard 174

Nayler, James 85
Netherlands 21, 82, 98 n., 104 n., 136, 147, 245,
    266, 350–1, 392
Nicholes, Martin 70, 156, and Chs. 6–12 passim
Nichols, Josias 211–12, 216–17, 237
Nicholson, William 87, 150, 153, 156, 163, and
    Chs. 6–12 passim
Norfolk, catechizing in 136, 177, 187, 194, 210,
    583, 585, 620–1, 625, 635, 679, 713, 721, 723,
    751; see also Norwich diocese
Northamptonshire, catechizing in 210, 683, 685,
    703, 749

Northumberland, catechizing in 653, 671, 717,
    747
Norton, Thomas 39–41, 189–90, 198
Norwich diocese 115, 134, 136, 139, 206, 218,
    236 n., 649
Nottinghamshire, catechizing in 99, 136, 140,
    206–7, 592, 595, 631, 643(3), 655, 723(2),
    749
Nowell, Alexander:
    author of widely used forms for more advanced
        catechumens 39, 45, 66, 95, 97, 143,
        189–93, 203, Chs. 6–12 passim, and 567
    catechisms studied in languages other than
        English 54, 189–93, 196–7
    concern for graded instruction 189–90, 266–7
    content and structure of his forms Chs. 6–12
        passim
    debt to Calvin's 1541 form 62
    defends confirmation 33
    elements of dialogue in his catechisms 55, 64
    forms approved by authority 71–3, 249
    forms expounded by others 202
    'godly' opinions 78
    idiosyncratic elements in his forms 62
    limited Calvinist content of his catechisms 7,
        70, 362–80
    original catechism considered too long and
        hard 71–3, 75, 249
    work cited by other catechists 45, 163, 202
Nye, Philip 45, 78, 166, 259

Openshaw, Robert, see under Paget, Eusebius
ordo salutis 52, 70, 380–2
Overall, Bp John 514, 567
Owen, John 186, 219–20, 268, 354, 398, 410
Oxford, catechizing in 188, 197–202, 631, 679
Oxfordshire, catechizing in 101, 117, 119, 123–5,
    140–1, 152, 162–4, 177, 665, 683, 743

Paget, Eusebius 52, 67, 78, 143, 199, 210–11, 247,
    253, 266, and Chs. 6–12 passim
Palmer, Herbert 78, 82, 104–6, 156, 185–6,
    250–1, 258, 260–3, and Chs. 6–12 passim
Parker, Kenneth 438–43, 446 n.
parliamentary ordinance of 20.10.1645 37–8,
    79–80, 236, 248, 284, 579
Parr, Elnathan 78, 249
Patrick, Bp Simon 113, 116–17, 147–50, 200
Perkins, William:
    author of widely used form 45, 67, 185, 567–8
    Calvinist beliefs 7, 78, 351–81
    cited by other catechetical authors 84, 153
    complains of misuse of catechetical staples
        131, 274–5

content and structure of his form Chs. 6–12
   passim
expects catechumens to be literate 242
form criticized or modified 84, 244, 247–8
form possibly used in church 138, 143
insists on knowledge of basics 26, 29
perhaps catechist at Christ's, Cambridge 201
perseverance 378–9
Peters, Hugh 40, 50, 79
Ponet, John 54, 61–2, 142–3, 188, 190, 283
prayer 30–1, 479–84
Prayer, Lord's:
  element of Catholic instruction 59
  exposition of each petition in turn 479–507
  exposition of the whole in sermons or prose
    147–8, 151, 186, 202–3, 214
  knowledge of misused by the ignorant 245
  knowledge of required by communicants
    34–5, 93, 123, 235
  in Prayer Book catechism 16
  a staple of Protestant catechetics 4, 9, 21, 73,
    94, 131, 243, 275, 279–83
'Prayer Book catechism':
  attempts to improve techniques of using 73,
    132, 143, 146–66, 246–7, 252, 259–65
  compared to Calvin's 1541 form 20, 71,
    279
  compared to Luther's shorter catechism 20,
    62, 71
  compared to Westminster Shorter Catechism
    89–90
  content and structure of Chs. 6–12 *passim*
  enlarged in 1604 71–2, 175
  expositions of 88–90, 146–66, 168–9, 193–5,
    206–8, 259–65, 290–5
  genesis of 20, 33, 61–2, 71–2, 520
  in languages other than English 190, 192, 196,
    198–9
  modified by Alexander Nowell 175, 190
  objections to 69–73, 90–1, 186, 244
  recommended for use in the home 206–8
  used by Calvinists 70, 156, 252
  turned into verse 254
  widely used 39, 45, 53, 58, 65–6, 79, 87–8,
    138–9, 141, 170, 192, 203, 266; *see also*
    The ABC with the catechisme and *The*
    primer and catechisme
preaching 27, 29, 31–2
predestination 70
  debates on 350–5, 367–8, 371–2, 377–8,
    383–6
  see also decree, elect, free will, grace, *ordo*
    salutis, and perseverance
preparation for faith 374–6, 408

presbyterians, presbyterianism 2–3, 80–1, 84–5,
  166–9, 450–1
  see also Westminster Confession, and Westmin-
    ster Larger and Shorter catechisms
Preston, John 202–3, 406–8, 410
The primer and catechisme 30, 53, 65–9, 88–9,
  176–7, 186–7, 255, 560–1
providence 303–4, 363, 488–9
puritan 8–9, 454
  and see Baptists; 'godly'; Independents; presby-
    terians; Quakers

Quakers 41, 56, 83–5, 121–2, 166, 199, 438

Racovian catechism 7
Ramism 350, 428–30
Rawlet, John 55
Reeve, Edmund 6, 30, 78, 112, 143, 156, 567
resurrection of the dead 342–5
Reynolds, Edward 80, 206
Roberts, Thomas 254
Rogers, Daniel 78, 243, 276
Rogers, Ezekiel 50, 219
Rogers, Richard 42, 213, 221, 406
royal authority discussed in catechisms 452–3,
  455–60
Russell, Conrad 346, 566

sabbatarianism 438–51
sacraments 9, 243, 275, 508–56
  as seals of the covenant of grace 411–12,
    418–19, 516–7, 542–3
Saintbarb, Richard 6
saints, communion of 334–6, 363–4
St Paul's School 16, 171, 188
Sancroft, Abp William 100
sanctification 398–403
Sandys, Bp Edwin 106, 114, 120, 206
Sargeant, Richard 130, 223–4
Scandinavia, catechizing in 2, 275
schools, *see* catechizing, in school
Scotland 49–50, 574
Secker, Thomas 101
  see also episcopal questionnaires
semi-Pelagianism 346–7, 568
Shakespeare, William 170
Shaw, John 152, 274
Sheldon, Abp Gilbert 100, 110
Sherlock, Richard 30, 87–8, 153, 156, 159, 260,
  and Chs. 6–12 *passim*
Shropshire, catechizing in 605, 729
sin:
  forgiveness of, 336–42, 543
  types of, 307–8

Smith, John 77
Somerset, catechizing in 115, 137, 151, 222, 267, 583, 589, 595, 631, 665, 667, 681
Spangenberg, Johann 62, 282
Sparke, Thomas 31, 35–6, 136, 144, 216, 219
Spirit, Holy 309–10, 314, 324–6, 371–4, 388–92, 502–3, 516, 518, 528
Spurr, John 378 n., 566
Stationers' Register 47
Sterne, Laurence 105
Stock, Richard 28, 103
Stockton, Owen 227
Stockwood, John 32, 66–7, 185, 216, 219
Strasburg 120, 123 n.
Strauss, Gerald 557–61
Strong, James 57, 85
Suffolk, catechizing in 135, 178, 192, 589, 599, 611, 613, 617, 629(2), 655, 691, 707, 713, 715, 733; *see also* Norwich diocese
Sunday Schools 242, 275–6
Supper, Lord's 34–8, 58 n., 74–5, 94–5, 126, 144, 211–12, 236, 283–4, 509–15
    description and function of 539–46, 555–6
    preparation for 35–8, 549–53
    real presence discussed 546–9
    unworthy reception of 553–5
Surrey, catechizing in 102, 219, 605, 613
Sussex, catechizing in 186, 225–6, 229, 711, 729
Switzerland, catechizing in 2, 21, 78, 82

Talbot, James 208, 240–1, 257, 264–5
Taylor, Jeremy 42, 186, and Chs. 6–12 *passim*
temporary faith 322–3, 377
Ten Commandments, *see* Commandments, Ten
Term Catalogues 47–8
Thaxter, John 46–7, 563
Thirty-nine Articles 202, 298, 355–6, 358, 364, 368, 377, 379 n., 564
Tillotson, John 1, 25, 399, 473
Tipson, L. B. 388, 391
Torrance, T. F. 348
Torrance, J. B. 326, 356 n.
Towerson, Gabriel 25, 150, 201, 274
Trinity, the 309–10, 324, 326
Tuckney, Anthony 203
Tudor, Philippa 59, 68
Turner, Thomas 229
Twisse, William 78, 201, 406, 410
Tyacke, Nicholas 351–2, 356, 383–4, 512 n., 566
type-face 7, 90, 255–7

Ursinus, Zacharias 47, 65, 199–200, 204, 267, 292, 385, 405, 407, 491 n.

Ussher, James 31, 107, 130, 201, 267–8, and Chs. 6–12 *passim*

Vicars, Thomas 254
Vincent, Thomas 168, 215, 248, and Chs. 6–12 *passim*
Virel, Matthieu 64–5, and Chs. 6–12 *passim*
Von Rohr, J. 408, 420 n.

Wake, Abp William 88, 100–1, 116–20, 123–4, 126, 151, 158–62, 184, 194–5, 208, 229
    content and structure of his catechism Chs. 6–12 *passim*
Wales 574, 595, 631, 633, 655, 671, 683, 691, 695, 699, 701, 709, 717, 729, 745, 749
Wallace, D. D. 316–19, 408 n., 420 n.
Wallis, John 82, 156, 167, 261–2, and Chs. 6–12 *passim*
Ward, Samuel 199, 406
Warren, John 220
Warwickshire, catechizing in 117 n., 140, 675, 683
Watts, Isaac 52–3, 91, 167, 169, 196, 216, 232–3, 237, 244, 271–4
    content and structure of his catechisms Chs. 6–12 *passim*
Watts, Thomas 45, 73, 266–7
Weinstein, Helen 176, 561–2
Westminster Confession 80, 355, 368, 370, 396, 407, 413, 440
Westminster Larger Catechism 80–1, 196, 251, 256, Chs. 6–12 *passim*, and 567
Westminster Shorter Catechism:
    authors' concern for understanding as well as memorization 251
    compared to Prayer Book catechism 81, 89–90, 91–2, 168–9
    content and structure of Chs. 6–12 *passim*
    criticisms and defences of 57, 82, 85–6, 244, 271–2
    efforts to improve techniques of using 132, 248, 256, 261–2, 268–9, 272–3; *see also* next entry
    expositions of 81–3, 89–90, 167–9, 214–5
    genesis 80–2
    in languages other than English 192, 197–8
    partly turned into verse 82, 254
    taught catechumens after the Prayer Book catechism 91
    widely used 39, 58, 89–90, 167–9, 196, 208
Whitaker, William 78, 189–90, 283, 406
White, Peter 296, 352, 355 n., 356, 383–4
Whitgift, Abp John 42, 100, 106, 108, 146, 348, 517 n., 567

Williams, Bp John 88, 157, 159, 162, 194, 244, 255, and Chs. 6–12 *passim*
Willison, John 214
Wilson, Thomas 103, 253
Wiltshire, catechizing in 152, 225–6, 607, 717, 741
Winchester College 171, 191, 197, 202
Winchester diocese 115, 139
witchcraft 422, 437
Wood, William 31, 72, 131, 249, 251, 260, 266–7
Worcestershire, catechizing in 222–7, 236, 247, 591, 650–1

Wordsworth, William 127–8, 134
Worthington, John 81

Yates, John 77–8, 429 n.
Yorkshire, catechizing in 46, 101, 105, 111, 117–21, 123–5, 127, 129, 133–5, 140–1, 148, 152, 156, 164–5, 178, 180–5, 217, 219–20, 228–9, 240, 601(2), 603(2), 625, 629, 681, 711, 727, 737, 745

Zwingli, Huldrich 61–2, 404, 410, 509, 513, 524, 528, 530, 533, 541, 750–1